CORONAVIRUS POLITICS

CORONAVIRUS POLITICS

The Comparative Politics
and Policy of COVID-19

*Scott L. Greer,
Elizabeth J. King,
Elize Massard da Fonseca,
and André Peralta-Santos,*
Editors

UNIVERSITY OF MICHIGAN PRESS
ANN ARBOR

Copyright © 2021 by Scott L. Greer, Elizabeth J. King, Elize Massard da Fonseca, and André Peralta-Santos
Some rights reserved

This work is licensed under a Creative Commons Attribution-NonCommercial 4.0 International License. Note to users: A Creative Commons license is only valid when it is applied by the person or entity that holds rights to the licensed work. Works may contain components (e.g., photographs, illustrations, or quotations) to which the rightsholder in the work cannot apply the license. It is ultimately your responsibility to independently evaluate the copyright status of any work or component part of a work you use, in light of your intended use.
To view a copy of this license, visit http://creativecommons.org/licenses/by-nc/4.0/

For questions or permissions, please contact um.press.perms@umich.edu

Published in the United States of America by the
University of Michigan Press
Manufactured in the United States of America
Printed on acid-free paper
First published April 2021

A CIP catalog record for this book is available from the British Library.

Library of Congress Cataloging-in-Publication data has been applied for.

ISBN 978-0-472-03862-6 (paper : alk. paper)
ISBN 978-0-472-90246-0 (OA)

https://doi.org/10.3998/mpub.11927713

We would like to thank the International Institute of the University of Michigan for its generous support in making Open Access publication possible.

Contents

PART I

1. Introduction: Explaining Pandemic Response
   *Scott L. Greer, Elizabeth J. King,
   and Elize Massard da Fonseca*   3

2. Playing Politics: The World Health Organization's Response to COVID-19
   *Matthew M. Kavanagh, Renu Singh,
   and Mara Pillinger*   34

3. State Responses to the COVID-19 Pandemic: Governance, Surveillance, Coercion, and Social Policy
   Holly Jarman   51

PART II   ASIA

4. China's Leninist Response to COVID-19: From Information Repression to Total Mobilization
   Victor C. Shih   67

5. Public Policy and Learning from SARS: Explaining COVID-19 in Hong Kong
   John P. Burns   86

6. Institutions Matter in Fighting COVID-19: Public Health, Social Policies, and the Control Tower in South Korea
   June Park   105

7. Unified, Preventive, Low-cost Government Response to COVID-19 in Việt Nam
   Emma Willoughby   127

8. Fighting COVID-19 in Japan: A Success Story?
   *Takashi Nagata, Akihito Hagihara, Alan Kawarai Lefor,
   Ryozo Matsuda, and Monika Steffen*   146

9. Singapore's Response to COVID-19: An Explosion of Cases despite Being a "Gold Standard"
   Rebecca Wai   163

10 India's Response to COVID-19
Minakshi Raj   178

11 COVID-19 Response in Central Asia: A Cautionary Tale
Pauline Jones and Elizabeth J. King   196

PART III   EUROPE

12 COVID-19 in the United Kingdom: How Austerity and a Loss of State Capacity Undermined the Crisis Response
Gemma A. Williams, Selina Rajan, and Jonathan D. Cylus   215

13 The European Union Confronts COVID-19: Another European Rescue of the Nation-state?
Eleanor Brooks, Anniek de Ruijter, and Scott L. Greer   235

14 Denmark's Response to COVID-19: A Participatory Approach to Policy Innovation
Darius Ornston   249

15 France's Multidimensional COVID-19 Response: Ad Hoc Committees and the Sidelining of Public Health Agencies
Sarah D. Rozenblum   264

16 Political Resonance in Austria's Coronavirus Crisis Management
Margitta Mätzke   280

17 Three Approaches to Handling the COVID Crisis in Federal Countries: Germany, Austria, and Switzerland
Thomas Czypionka and Miriam Reiss   295

18 Italy's Response to COVID-19
Michelle Falkenbach and Manuela Caiani   320

19 Spain's Response to COVID-19
Kenneth A. Dubin   339

20 A Tale of Two Pandemics in Three Countries: Portugal, Spain, and Italy
André Peralta-Santos, Luis Saboga-Nunes, and Pedro C. Magalhães   361

21 Greece at the Time of COVID-19: Caught between Scylla and Charybdis
Elena Petelos, Dimitra Lingri, and Christos Lionis   378

22 COVID-19 in Turkey: Public Health Centralism
Saime Özçürümez   393

23 COVID-19 in Central and Eastern Europe:
Focus on Czechia, Hungary, and Bulgaria
Olga Löblová, Julia Rone, and Endre Borbáth   413

24 COVID-19 in the Russian Federation:
Government Control during the Epidemic
Elizabeth J. King and Victoria I. Dudina   436

PART IV   AMERICAS

25 The Politics and Policy of Canada's COVID-19 Response
Patrick Fafard, Adèle Cassola, Margaret MacAulay,
and Michèle Palkovits   459

26 Anatomy of a Failure: COVID-19 in the United States
Phillip M. Singer, Charley E. Willison, N'dea Moore-Petinak,
and Scott L. Greer   478

27 COVID-19 in Brazil: Presidential Denialism and the Subnational
Government's Response
Elize Massard da Fonseca, Nicoli Nattrass,
Luísa Bolaffi Arantes, and Francisco Inácio Bastos   494

28 Colombia's Response to COVID-19: Pragmatic Command,
Social Contention, and Political Challenges
Claudia Acosta, Mónica Uribe-Gómez, and
Durfari Velandia-Naranjo   511

29 The Politics of the COVID-19 Pandemic Response in Chile
Claudio A. Méndez   522

PART V   AFRICA

30 Pandemic amid Political Crisis: Malawi's Experience
with and Response to COVID-19
Kim Yi Dionne, Boniface Dulani,
and Sara E. Fischer   541

31 Adapting COVID-19 Containment in Africa:
Lessons from Tanzania
Thespina (Nina) Yamanis, Ruth Carlitz,
and Henry A. Mollel   560

32 Confronting Legacies and Charting a New Course?
The Politics of Coronavirus Response in South Africa
Joseph Harris   580

33 Comparative Analysis of COVID-19 Transmission
and Mortality in Select African Countries
Kanayo K. Ogujiuba and Uviwe Binase   600

34 Conclusion
*Scott L. Greer, Elize Massard da Fonesca,
and Elizabeth J. King*   615

Contributors   639
Index   651

Digital materials related to this title can be found on the Fulcrum platform via the following citable URL https://doi.org/10.3998/mpub.11927713

PART I

1 INTRODUCTION

Explaining Pandemic Response

*Scott L. Greer, Elizabeth J. King,
and Elize Massard da Fonseca*

The COVID-19 pandemic created unprecedented and turbulent mixtures of political, social, economic, and epidemiological forces. It has caused the world to pause and think about how and why some countries have fared worse than other countries in addressing the threat of SARS-CoV-2, and in many cases fared far worse than expected. In putting many different political systems to the test, it has caused many to ask why different countries did what they did.

A novel coronavirus was recognized as an emerging public health threat in Wuhan, China, in late 2019, but the year 2020 will be remembered for the shock that the virus administered to essentially every political system in the world. By spring 2020, COVID-19 had governments around the world scrambling to address a virus for which much remained unknown scientifically, but which was ravaging through the inequities in societies and exposing gaps in public health systems and social policy structures. Higher-income countries were not immune, and in fact many appeared to be the least prepared (or willing) to respond to the pandemic.

Many countries did take decisive and abrupt action, sometimes unsurprising and sometimes quite out of character. Governments put their entire economies into the equivalent of a medically induced coma, shutting businesses, schools, and social lives and sometimes keeping them alive with unorthodox social policy measures. The response varied worldwide. Although we may not know the long-term effects of these varying responses, a comparative analysis of the public health and social policies can tell us a lot about how and why governments respond the way that they do.

As of this writing, the pandemic is far from over. Many lessons have been drawn; some might be learned. Nonetheless, the politics of COVID-19 during the "first wave" of the pandemic warrant a multidisciplinary and multinational analysis. This knowledge can be useful as the world continues to fight COVID-19 and is equally important for thinking about other ongoing and future infectious disease pandemics.

This book is about what governments did to respond to COVID-19 and why they did it. It covers the first ten months of the pandemic, the first wave that struck the globe between December 2019 and September 2020. We conceptualized the idea for this book in February 2020, aiming to bring together regional experts to try to identify what approaches to controlling the COVID-19 pandemic were being implemented and to explain the differences among countries' responses. As the pandemic continued to expand, so did the number of experts ready to contribute to this comparative analysis of the public health and social policy response to COVID-19. The book is organized according to how COVID-19 and the responses unfolded. After an overview of the role that the World Health Organization (WHO) has played and a comparative analysis of global response there are a series of country case studies. We start with Asia and conclude with Africa, following roughly the order in which the pandemic hit.

This first year of the COVID-19 pandemic has also once again highlighted the importance of interdisciplinary analysis to understanding global health threats and their solutions. This book brings together political scientists and other social scientists, public health experts, and medical professionals to analyze critical decisions made in various countries and globally. Governments from the smallest town's mayor to the grandest national leader made important decisions, often with incomplete information. That gives us an opportunity to understand better their leadership, public health decision-making, and politics. Previously, the small number of comparative studies connecting political regimes with health mostly focused on big and slow-moving health outcomes such as infant mortality (Kavanagh & Singh, 2020). COVID-19, by contrast, presented a fast-moving, sudden shock to almost every political system in the world. As such, it presented a challenge for adapting theories that tend to ignore crises that are "neither mundane nor militarized" (Lipscy, 2020).

There is a long tradition of using exogenous shocks such as financial crises to understand politics and decision-making (Bermeo & Bartels, 2014; Gourevitch, 1986; Hall, 1989). This edited volume is a contribution to that literature as well as to our specific understanding of politics and health. It joins what will soon be a number of efforts to understand pandemic response (Capano et al., 2020; Colfer, 2020). Public health and health policy literature has only a tenuous connection with political science, to the detriment of both (de Leeuw et al., 2014; Fafard & Cassola, 2020; Gagnon et al., 2017; Greer et al., 2017, 2018). We hope that if some good comes out of the pandemic of 2020, which was disastrous for most of the world, perhaps it will be in showing not just that politics matter to health, but how, when, and why they matter.

Explaining Pandemic Response

This book is a work of comparative politics and public policy. That means we are trying to understand the policy decisions made by governments in response to COVID-19 in the first months of the pandemic. We focus on the period of December 2019 to September 2020, which covers what many have labeled the "first wave" of the pandemic. During this time, public health response was relying on non-pharmaceutical interventions (NPIs) to prevent the spread of the virus. Vaccination campaigns had yet to start in most places in the world, and there was great uncertainty about when vaccine clinical trials would be complete and the vaccines would be authorized for use.

Understanding Government Responses

We divided health policy responses into two broad categories. One is health policy, comprising public health policy and healthcare policy. In 2020 public health policy primarily meant NPIs and the construction of test-trace-isolate-support (TTIS) systems. NPIs are public health actions to slow or stop the spread of disease that do not involve vaccines or medicines (Markel et al., 2007). In 2020 prominent NPIs included hand washing, social distancing, travel restrictions, school closures, restrictions on businesses or closures of activity in places or sectors ("lockdowns"), mask mandates, and restrictions on working and socializing. NPIs could be extremely broad, effectively closing entire cities, sectors, or countries, or could be relatively limited. TTIS systems are a package of interventions (Rajan et al., 2020): testing extensively (to find people with virus), contract tracing (to find out whom they might have infected and from whom they caught it), isolation (keeping infected people away from the public and opportunities to infect others), and support (ensuring that infected people have what they need to isolate, e.g., income, food, support for dependents while their caregivers were in isolation, a secure place to live). Together, NPIs and TTIS systems were the core of the successful efforts to manage the pandemic. In successful cases as diverse as Vietnam and New Zealand, they effectively eliminated COVID-19.

Healthcare responses refer to the ways governments tried to manage the impact of the pandemic on their health systems. There were first-order problems such as procuring and distributing personal protective equipment (PPE) or creating and managing staffed hospital beds in time. (It is an axiom of health care, but not widely appreciated, that finding somebody with the right training to staff a hospital and appropriate specialist equipment is harder than finding a frame and mattress.) There were second-order problems in responding to the disruption, from protecting healthcare workers' own health and helping them with the additional demands on their time, to maintaining income flows to within the healthcare sector in the absence of elective procedures, to the backlog of untreated problems and procedures among people who could not or would not seek medical attention during a pandemic wave. The European Observatory on Health Systems and Policies' Health Systems Response Monitor provides extensive description of these complex problems and solutions. All of these problems were made more difficult by the characteristic complexity of healthcare systems, with their complicated payment structures, legal arrangements, and interest-group and territorial politics. There were, of course, a variety of other government responses, ranging from democratic backsliding to massive corruption, which individual chapters discuss as is relevant.

It is tempting to want to ask for more—for an explanation of the course of the pandemic in different countries, for an explanation of the timing, scale, and impact of different waves, and ultimately for an explanation of the sickness and death it caused. That quest will occupy many social scientists of many different fields for years to come, but it is not certain that we will ever have clear answers to these questions.

The Politics of Pandemic Data

There are two major reasons why COVID-19 deaths, or even excess mortality, cannot presently be used in comparative political analysis. The first is the politics of data. Measuring the pandemic is not as easy as it might seem. Widely used data such as infections or deaths attributable to COVID-19 are endogenous to the politics of the pandemic because governments make policy decisions that influence testing and attribution of deaths. As with many diseases, the ultimate cause of death from COVID-19 may be something else, such as pneumonia or a heart attack exacerbated by virus. Professionals or governments, in some cases, decide to register these causes of death as COVID-19, and others decide to register these as pneumonia or heart attack deaths. These decisions about official causes of death introduce discrepancies in the data, which make it difficult to compare across contexts. Belgium, for example, has very efficient death recording systems and established guidance to attribute deaths to COVID-19 when uncertain. It has also regularly topped international COVID-19 statistics as a country with a particularly severe and lethal outbreak, but it is not entirely clear how much of that is due to its reporting versus reporting systems in other countries. Moreover, in many cases around the world people have died without being tested. In short, data about COVID-19 specifically are problematic within countries and hard to compare between even countries that test extensively.

Furthermore, many observers' self-taught short courses in epidemiology during 2020 turned out to be incomplete. Some metrics that are useful for epidemiological purposes have been misused during the pandemic. Test positivity, for example, is the percentage of tests that are positive. It is not a measure of incidence (new infections) or prevalence (infections); it is a measure of the extent to which testing is giving an accurate picture of actual prevalence. If it is above 3% or at most 5%, all it tells us is that sampling bias among administered tests is severe enough to call any further results into question. Test positivity of 10%, for example, did not mean 10% prevalence; it meant that prevalence was unknown and probably underestimated. Test positivity was a perfect example of a statistic that was routinely misunderstood despite problems that social scientists should immediately understand. It is an instrument for calibration and interpretation of reporting more than a statistic about COVID-19.

The best data for political scientists are probably excess mortality. This is a statistic that simply calculates the number of deaths in a given period and compares them to the number of deaths on average in that same period in a given year. Excess deaths calculations are also based on the data that governments are most likely to collect, because core public activities including taxes, military service, and disbursements such as pensions or conditional cash transfers all work better if there is a list of births and deaths. For example, if there are an average 100 deaths on a given day over the last ten years in a specific country, then there are 120 deaths on that day in 2020, the data show 20 excess deaths in that country on that day. We would provisionally conclude that something—probably COVID-19—explains the difference (especially if NPIs mean we should expect a reduction of other causes of death, such as workplace accidents or drunk driving). Excess mortality, unlike any statistic recording COVID-19, has the immense advantage of not being endogenous to the same political process we are studying.

The drawback is that it is a slow statistic, with information filtering slowly through a web of individual doctors and local governments over weeks or sometimes months. That makes it useful for political scientists or other writers of after-action reports, rather than governments in a crisis. Also, despite their undeniable usefulness, many states do not effectively collect death data, or they collect them for just a few places. Not only is gathering this data costly, it might also be unhelpful to some. Although a pension scheme may function better as a pension scheme if deaths are recorded, better death data might undermine those whose income depends on fraudulent pensions—the very plot of Gogol's *Dead Souls*.

Health surveillance in low- and middle-income countries lacks sufficient human and other resources (Ibrahim, 2020). For instance, in Brazil, as in other developing countries, disease notification is usually handwritten to then be entered into the health information system, where it undergoes further review before it is disclosed. The process is directly influenced by the availability of qualified professionals. A delay in this process may bias the data interpretation. The number of cases and official "new" deaths disclosed daily by the Brazilian Ministry of Health represented information that was entered in the system over the previous twenty-four hours and does not necessarily represent recent infections.

All of these points come back around to what we might term, in its strongest form, "Trench's Law," after its formulator Alan Trench: data are useful or comparable but not both (Greer, 2019). Data are expensive to collect and maintain. We should therefore expect that they will be designed to serve the interests of powerful forces in politics. They may have public health in mind; they may even have international comparability in mind. But we cannot assume so. Viewed this way, much of the creativity of quantitative social science is in repurposing data to shed light on issues that did not interest its creators, and much of the political energy of social scientists and activists goes into persuading powerful people to create data of use to social science (Herrera, 2010).

Hazards of Attribution

The second reason why policy is a better dependent variable than deaths or infections is the difficulty of attributing mortality outcomes to particular factors. A vast diversity of social practices, economic structures (such as tourism or service sector dependence), travel patterns, labor protections and economic structures, family structures, pre-existing population health, and demographics influenced what happened in the pandemic (see Jarman, chapter 3, this volume). Each of these phrases contains an enormous number of issues and empirical problems, from differential ways of socializing to different ways of staffing elder care homes to different numbers of indigent day laborers. Public policy decisions are only part of the puzzle. And understanding public policy decisions is enough of a challenge, as this book shows.

In particular, the problem of compliance with NPIs and public health guidance is a tricky one. Even in relatively authoritarian societies with strong state coercive capacity, it is hard to ensure a high level of compliance with restrictions on working, socializing, traveling, and mask wearing, let alone personal hygiene. Compliance is partly an effect of policy and of the consistency and quality of public health communication, but it depends on much else, from the extent of coercion used to existing cultural norms. In China, once mobilization for containment was ordered, local officials immediately were placed under enormous pressure from higher-level authorities to put the quarantine in place both at the provincial level and at the neighborhood level (Shih, chapter 4, this volume). Japanese policy seemingly gained extremely good compliance, allowing comparative weak NPIs to work better than they would elsewhere (Nagata et al., chapter 8, this volume). Brazil, Russia, the United States, and the United Kingdom all had serious compliance issues early in the pandemic (Massard et al., chapter 27; King & Dudina, chapter 24; Singer et al., chapter 26; Williams et al., chapter 12, this volume). Was this because their governments did not inspire confidence, because they were culturally "freedom-loving people" (as a UK minister said when excusing noncompliance), because of confused government messaging, a combination, or something else? Greeks—a population with historically low trust in government—certainly complied surprisingly well early in the emergency (Petelos et al., chapter 21, this volume). Later in summer and in the autumn of 2020, when many countries found they faced compliance problems, were they attributable to policy, politics, or the sheer exhaustion that historically attends pandemics as they drag on? And how and when do governments take their estimation of likely compliance into mind when developing NPIs? It is clear that policy and compliance with policy do not have a simple relationship, which is another reason to shy away from efforts to explain overall pandemic outcomes in any simple way. We set out to answer these questions through the analysis of COVID-19 responses from around the world.

Approach and Chapters

The book begins with a chapter on the WHO by Kavanagh et al. and a chapter by Jarman, which synthesizes and presents what governments have done in the pandemic and consequences. Each country chapter in this book has the same basic structure, which was designed to explore the hypotheses published in June 2020 in concise form by the editors (Greer et al., 2020b). Each chapter introduces the specific country and salient points in its story. Then the health measures and the social policy measures are presented. A fourth section explains why the government made those decisions. Each chapter concludes by highlighting key lessons and questions about the country, the politics of the pandemic, and what the pandemic has taught us. The chapters are grouped by geographical region, loosely following the progress of the pandemic from Asia through Europe to the Americas and Africa.

Certain chapters are devoted to only one country. Comparative chapters on Southern Europe, German-speaking Europe, Central Europe, Central Asia, and three African states also explore comparative themes that arose. The European Union (EU) and WHO, as international organizations, are not strictly comparable to any country, but the pandemic has already changed them and taught us much about their politics.

Hypotheses

What hypotheses from existing literature, developed and tested before the pandemic, shed light on decision-making in the pandemic? We drew our hypotheses from the broad comparative politics literature on the assumption that, although COVID-19 is effectively unprecedented in the modern world, the political systems that are responding to it and showing themselves in its light are known entities. There is no need to reinvent the wheel. As de Waal writes, "Although the pathogen may be new, the logic of social response is not, and it is here that we can see historical continuities" (2020). Historical continuities, as well as novelties, are often political. Each section here is divided into two parts: a statement of the hypothesis and its literature and then a summary of what we, based on our reading of the chapters in this book, saw in its case studies.

Regime Type Matters: Authoritarianism Produces Distinctive Information Problems

The Hypothesis

One of the most basic issues in political science, going back to Aristotle at least, is the development and operation of different political regimes. Regimes are the rules governing a polity. They are the combination of institutions, coalitions, and political norms that govern how politics works. Regimes fall into broad and frequently debated families such as democracies, monarchies, and authoritarian states. Governments exist within regimes: monarchs change while monarchical regimes persist, and heads of government can change while leaving regimes intact. The ways in which regimes affect politics, policies, and people's life choices are the subject of much discussion in popular and scientific circles. For example, there is a lively and largely inconclusive debate about whether and how democracies could produce better health and social policies (Greer & Méndez, 2015; Haggard & Kaufman, 2008; Kavanagh & Singh, 2020; Kosack, 2012; Linos, 2013).

Defining regimes is tricky (Collier & Levitsky, 1997). Democracies are regimes that have *both* extensive participation in politics (also known as inclusion; the most important form of inclusion is the vote) and contestation (public debate about rules, rules, and policies, such as the presence of a free press and democratic opposition parties) (Dahl, 1971). Authoritarian regimes have limited contestation or participation; many have, for example, extensive participation in elections that are nonetheless not contested (Levitsky & Way, 2002). Both participation and contestation are continuous variables, which means that regimes exist in a two-dimensional space and can change position. Databases such as V-DEM at the University of Gothenburg, Freedom House, and the Polity database all create and regularly update indices of authoritarianism. The two dimensions mean that a variety of logical possibilities exist and are regularly found in the world, such as high contestation and low participation (competitive oligarchies), authoritarian regimes with elections but no real opposition or debate (inclusive hegemonies), and regimes with neither contestation nor participation (Dahl, 1971).

Many hypotheses could be derived from the differences between more and less authoritarian and democratic regimes (admittedly, these are big and contested categories). We focus on two of particular relevance to public health but revealing about policy-making and its consequences in other cases.

The first is that authoritarian regimes have problems of information flow that shape their politics. Put simply, there is a justified assumption in authoritarian regimes that people lie to each other and that the regime lies to the public (Little, 2017; Wallace, 2016).This leads to the internal information problem (Egorov & Sonin, 2011; Svolik, 2009; Wintrobe, 2000). A major threat to authoritarian leaders comes from within the regime. Therefore, incumbent leaders constantly watch for signs of disloyalty among senior officials. However, this creates incentives for senior officials to exaggerate their degree of loyalty and hide instances of policy failures, lest they are perceived by the leaders as signs of disloyalty. Another threat to regimes stems from large-scale uprising, so authoritarian regimes generally try to weaken the incentive to rise up by suppressing information about bad policy outcomes and information about the pervasiveness of popular dissatisfaction. Authoritarian leaders also often limit information sharing among state agencies to "coup-proof" their regime. They keep their bureaucracies fragmented to stop collusion and prevent any one agency from growing politically powerful enough to carry out a coup (Greitens, 2016).

These incentives work against the free flow of information in the absence of transparency demands by opposition politicians or a free press. If the regimes use coercion to enforce policies within their bureaucracies, they create incentives to lie about each and every case of underperformance (Tsai, 2008; Zhou, 2010). Misbehavior within such a system can lead to severe consequences. This leads to the internal information problem. Some scholars model authoritarian political institutions and strategies around precisely the internal information problem (Boix & Svolik, 2013; Gandhi & Przeworski, 2007; Gao, 2016): people at the top of the hierarchy are constantly trying to find out what lower-level officials and their own rivals at the top are doing, but in an environment of pervasive perverse incentives, official opacity, and limited public contestation.

Authoritarian regimes also have an external information problem, which is that in a variety of ways they will often have earned public distrust (Kuran, 1991; Little, 2017; Stockmann, 2013). Creating a climate of pervasive distrust can be a powerful political strategy from the point of view of an authoritarian leader (or would-be authoritarian). Pervasive disbelief and misinformation make collective action more difficult, reduce public confidence in the ability of government to deliver public goods, and enable a variety of political actions from theft to human rights violations that are easier to deny if all facts are seen as politicized and provisional (Stockmann & Gallagher, 2011). Appeals to nationalism, an emergency, or performance legitimacy (e.g., a good economy, a disease-free country) can increase public trust in the information governments provide. The effect, however, might be temporary because of widespread agreement that government reports and advice are not to be taken too seriously (Li, 2016). Singapore is arguably the only authoritarian country in the world that has sustained public trust and reasonable transparency over time (Greer & Trump, 2019; Perry, 2017; Wai, chapter 9, this volume). Most would-be authoritarians may not actually want to subject themselves to the disciplines that the Singapore regime imposes upon itself. Similarly, the case of Hong Kong's broad success in responding to COVID-19 comes with a political context from which it is even harder to draw lessons (Burns, chapter 5, this volume).

In short, we should expect that authoritarian regimes, with few possible exceptions, will have problems of internal and external information flow. The regimes will have difficulties gathering and diffusing accurate information because in the absence of contestation, information is primarily a pawn in internal regime politics. Some regimes will also not benefit from a reserve of public trust because the mechanisms of contestation that promote trust over time are disabled in authoritarian regimes. Thus, for example, they will have difficulty gathering data about their cases and the effectiveness of their response and will not benefit from public trust in their advice on NPIs nor implementation of TTIS systems.

The Findings

Our findings suggest that authoritarian information barriers and government inaction formed a lethal combination that plagued China in January 2020 and Russia and other authoritarian regimes for longer periods. This is a lethal combination because the authoritarian reflex of hiding disasters prevented health authorities and individual health professionals and citizens from spreading information about the pandemic, leading to accelerated spread of the disease, as occurred in Wuhan and the rest of Hubei Province. At the same time, the state did not mobilize its (at times) considerable resources to combat the spread of the disease, so it was allowed to spread in the midst of general ignorance.

China clearly demonstrated the problems of information flow within authoritarian regimes. (Ironically, there is a Sino-centric bias in research on comparative authoritarianism.) Early in the pandemic, city and provincial officials in Wuhan suppressed evidence of the outbreak, in keeping with a reluctance to be associated with problems (Shih, chapter 4, this volume; Ang, 2020). A January 14, 2020, attempt by Wuhan's city government to win the Guinness World Record for the world's largest banquet was particularly ill advised but unsurprising, again because of the lethal combination of general ignorance and inaction (Kynge et al., 2020). Once the scale of the problem came to the surface, though, the Chinese state seems to have responded effectively. (It is interesting to imagine what would have happened had the first cases been identified in early January 2020 in a democracy.) Other early hotspots, such as Iran, also saw denialism within the regime and in its external communications.

In a number of other authoritarian regimes, internal and external information flow did not seem to matter as much. Vietnam's relatively coherent authoritarian regime was able to enact and maintain strong NPIs very early; presumably the regime made it clear that failing to find or report a case would lead to very strong sanctions (Willoughby, chapter 7, this volume). Singapore's regime had problems stemming from its lack of information about conditions among migrant laborers, which in turn stemmed from the regime's general lack of interest in their welfare. However, once it established the importance of their housing in its outbreak, it moved quickly to monitor them (Wai, chapter 9, this volume). Hong Kong also moved quickly and effectively (Burns, chapter 5, this volume). As ever with Hong Kong and Singapore, their nearly unique political systems make it a challenge to replicate their successes in any simple way.

Before we give too much credit to authoritarian decisiveness and state capacity, though, we can point to other, diverse, authoritarian, and hybrid states in the book that did not show such effective public health responses. Turkey's autocratic presidentialism was important to increase decisiveness and implement authoritative policy tools such as curfews and keeping citizens at home, but at the cost of public trust; citizens were concerned that public health measures were an excuse to increase political control (Özçürümez, chapter 22, this volume). Egypt used coercion to enforce stay-at-home measures and even declared the intention to prosecute anyone spreading fake news about the pandemic. Although some Egyptians criticized the government's response in mitigating the burden of the poor, others argued that the authorities had not done enough to contain the virus (Ogujiuba and Binase, chapter 33, this volume). Russia's record was spottier: the federal government exerted control over the statistical reporting but left implementation to the regional authorities, exposing the geographical disparities rampant through the underfunded healthcare system (King and Dudina, chapter 24, this volume). Tanzania's federal government minimized the threat of the pandemic, and local health officials were left to respond amid an inadequate healthcare system and low levels of authority (Yamanis et al., chapter 31, this volume).

The opacity of authoritarian regimes also leaves us in something of a bind: if this hypothesis is correct, then it is hard to tell that from the outside. It is not likely that anybody really knows the incidence and prevalence, let alone the course, of COVID-19 in many authoritarian regimes for most of 2020. This is partly because authoritarian regimes still cluster on the lower-income range of countries, and many of them do not really govern their whole territory or provide many public goods. Any claim about COVID-19 anywhere in Central Asia, for example, is necessarily somewhat speculative given testing limitations and the lack of centralized, comprehensive healthcare data (Jones and King, chapter 11, this volume). Other factors clouding the results are the incentives to represent the truth in keeping with internal regime politics rather than the satisfaction of outside observers.

Regime Type Matters: Some Authoritarian Regimes Are Extremely Effective in Execution

The Hypothesis

Do authoritarian regimes do better than democracies in a crisis such as COVID-19 (Stasavage, 2020)? The hypothesis that they might is in line with a certain kind of common sense, captured by the old saying that Italian dictator Mussolini made the trains run on time, or that China's success in stamping out COVID-19 within its borders showed the value of authoritarianism as a key to an effective state. Authoritarian rulers need not argue nor compromise with opposition parties, legislators, or subnational governments, and in theory they can override opposition within government or society.

There are, nonetheless, two problems with this argument. The first problem lies in the conflation of authoritarian states and effective states. Authoritarian states might brook no public debate, be able to ignore slow legal procedures and rules, and be able to punish resistance or sabotage, but that impunity also creates drawbacks that can systematically undermine their administrative effectiveness. There is no guarantee that authoritarian governance leads to the choice of effective and public-spirited policies. Because authoritarian regimes are isolated from popular accountability, members of the regime may take advantage of the lack of transparency and accountability to pursue corrupt or particularist policies (Chang & Golden, 2010; Kunicova & Rose-Ackerman, 2005). In general, authoritarian regimes have narrower accountability (by definition), and that means they are under less pressure to provide public goods. The conditions under which authoritarian regimes *do* opt to provide public goods such as public health are variable, rather than anything we can assume. History is full of authoritarian regimes that did not provide public goods. That is why democratization is associated with increased provision of public goods (Deacon, 2009).

Further, a decision to provide a public good—such as public health—is not necessarily easily implemented in an authoritarian regime. In the absence of participation and contestation, fighting corruption is a serious problem. Obviously, corruption is also a serious problem in democracies, but it takes different forms. Corruption is both lower in democracies overall and more prevalent in authoritarian enclaves within democracies such as the Italian south, Brazilian north, or parts of South Africa, India, and the United States (Gibson, 2013).

Finally, authoritarian regimes are tremendously diverse and range from the poorest to some of the richest countries. Even if we rule out other undemocratic regime types such as absolute monarchies, authoritarian regimes are as diverse as Russia, Venezuela, Rwanda, Hungary, and Vietnam. There is scope to include or exclude a number of other countries in the category, from Bolivia to Turkey. We could draw a suggestive line from lack of participation and contestation to lack of trust and good information in the previous hypothesis, but there is no reason to expect that lack of contestation and participation will consistently produce administrative effectiveness.

The Findings

Overall we saw no evidence that authoritarian regimes as a group were more effective at making and implementing policy than democratic regimes, or that they clustered in any particular way. Policy implementation was extremely effective and heavy handed in Vietnam (Willoughby, chapter 7, this volume), Singapore (Wai, chapter 9, this volume), the People's Republic of China (Shih, chapter 4, this volume), and Hong Kong (Burns, chapter 5, this volume), but democratic South Korea (Park, chapter 6, this volume) as well as New Zealand, Norway, Taiwan, and even the Isle of Man (Yeh & Cheng, 2020) achieved equivalent results. A similar finding was reported in the comparative cases in Africa (Ogujiuba and Binase, chapter 33, this volume). The sustainability of NPIs likewise did not seem to vary with regime type either. Some authoritarian regimes relaxed their NPI regimes as quickly as any democracy (as with Russia), and a few, including Tanzania (Yamanis et al., chapter 31, this volume) as well as some post-Soviet personalist regimes remained in denial for too long (Jones and King, chapter 11, this volume).

In some cases, authoritarian regimes did effectively impose NPIs but could not sustain implementation or political support, producing a first wave mirage and a damaging second wave. Hungary rapidly and effectively imposed NPIs that quashed the first wave, but so did its more democratic neighbors Czechia and Austria, and in the second wave Hungarian policies were noticeably weaker and worse implemented (Löblová et al., chapter 23, this volume).

In short, some authoritarian regimes were effective in making and implementing policy, but only some. For every Vietnam there was a Tanzania. Authoritarianism is clearly no panacea, and it is hard to see why we would expect that a lack of public accountability and open debate would reliably produce better policy implementation.

Social Policy Is Crucial to the Effectiveness of Health Policy Responses

The Hypothesis

"Social policy" refers to policies that are, in Richard Titmuss's definition, "beneficent, redistributive, and concerned with economic as well as non-economic goals" (Alcock & Glennerster, 2001, p. 213). That effectively means the welfare state, including health, pension, family, educational, and similar policies as well as income replacement policies such as unemployment insurance, short-time work (*kurzarbeit*) schemes that subsidize salaries for underemployed employees, and cash payments. Our hypothesis is that social policy is crucial to the effectiveness of public health responses.

On the level of the individual, compliance with NPIs depends on resources. We can call this the "Cask of Amontillado problem," after an 1846 short story by Edgar Allen Poe. In the story, a murderer lures somebody to a basement (with the promise of Amontillado sherry) and walls them up to die. The problem that the gothic horror story lays bare is simple: locking people at home is fatal. Telling people to stay home only works if they can eat and otherwise maintain their life situations without leaving home to work. Telling businesses to stay closed without helping them meet payroll, rent, and other expenses is akin to closing them. Telling local governments dependent on tax revenue from business to enforce NPIs is asking for bad enforcement. As a result, NPIs without accompanying social policy measures have a high risk of failure as time goes on.

This naturally puts lower- and middle-income countries in a bad situation, because they did not all have the resources to pay businesses to close and workers to stay at home (as we saw in, for example, India and South Africa). It is also a problem for countries such as the United States, which clearly had the capacity to use social policy measures to stay home but chose to use them for only a short time (Singer et al., chapter 26, this volume). To a variable and unpredictable extent, civil society (Greer et al., 2017), family networks, and others can fill in the gaps, as with the Sikhs in India (Raj, chapter 10, this volume), but in most places there is no substitute for government in sustaining NPIs.

On another level, that of politics, the problem is that social policy interacts with the political preferences and actions of business owners. Without imputing any motivations to business owners, we can assume a business that must pay rent and other expenses will want to open in the absence of subsidy such as *kurzarbeit*. Businesses, to be kept alive, need revenue. If they are not paid to stay closed, they will campaign to open. If we impute further motivation to business owners (e.g., a preference for opening over being paid to be closed), then we can easily imagine how and why businesses might mobilize to be open.

The tragic irony, which will influence politics, is that individual decisions might end many of these businesses, regardless of formal NPIs. Many of the service sector businesses that seemed riskiest in the pandemic were also businesses run on thin service-sector margins, such as restaurants, bars, gyms, and hair or other salons. A business may need, for example, a 3 percent profit margin to be viable, but a call for vulnerable people to stay away might easily lead to a 20, 40, or 60 percent decline in its revenue without a single NPI enacted. NPIs taken by policy-makers may be a convenient target for business owners' ire, but if those same policy-makers' call for "vulnerable" populations to stay home is heard, that could easily lead to a drop in business sufficient to bankrupt many service sector businesses. It was clear by the time of writing in late 2020 that in countries that did not undertake and sustain strong social policies, there was an enormous business mortality rate concentrated among smaller service sector enterprises such as restaurants.

The Findings

Virtually every chapter in this book confirmed the hypothesis that social policy is directly and indirectly crucial to sustainable pandemic response, but not all countries provided extensive social protection. Even in countries that saw infections and quickly dispatched them, such as South Korea or Hong Kong, short-term social policy measures enabled NPIs, including over several waves, and softened the blow of the worldwide economic slowdown. In countries around the world that did not manage the pandemic with NPIs quite so successfully, social policy nonetheless enabled NPIs. In Brazil and the United States, over the summer, for example, federal health policies were erratic at best, but state governors were able to take relatively decisive NPIs if they chose because the social policy was highly supportive (Massard et al., chapter 27; Singer et al., chapter 26, this volume).

Meanwhile, problems arose in middle-income countries where NPIs were not supported by social policy. India and to some extent South Africa began with a national lockdown largely unaccompanied by social policy supports (Raj, chapter 10; Harris, chapter 32, this volume). In particular, the weak point this revealed was the plight of migrant laborers, who needed to work every day to survive, who were poorly connected with social policy programs (federal or state), and whose response to the sudden loss of income was often informal migration. That led to the state restarting transport, conveying six million migrant workers by rail from virus-ridden cities to the whole of rural India, and rapidly abandoning federal public health measures. In short: supportive social policy intended to replace lost income (and help businesses in many cases) was a necessary condition for the enactment, sustainability, and maybe effectiveness of NPIs.

The caveat is that some authoritarian regimes provided limited social protection but were effective enough to nonetheless impose NPIs. In China there was virtually no additional support. Vietnam's social policies meant military personnel and workers delivering food and supplies to all individuals on the street (see Willoughby, chapter 7, this volume) with no extensive cash transfer support, as in Brazil. In Singapore, "the government's approach to supporting the unemployed is focused on helping them find jobs through skills training and such" (see Wai, chapter 9, this volume). Singapore, however, did have a generous cash transfer program in place but excluded vulnerable populations such as migrant workers. If there is a limitation to the hypothesis, it is that it might be possible to impose very effective NPIs through coercion alone if a regime has already built a repressive apparatus as enormous, sophisticated, and entrenched as that of the People's Republic of China (Shih, chapter 4, this volume). Most countries have not and probably could not.

Majoritarianism Shapes Responses: Presidentialism, Populism, and Agency

The Hypothesis

Broadly democratic regimes vary in endless ways, with political institutions alone offering differences in territorial organization, federalism, bicameralism, judicial review, electoral rules, composition of the executive, and referenda. These institutional features explain outcomes in interaction with each other and with features of the society such as social cleavages and economic structures.

We focus on one key division, which is between more majoritarian and consensus democracies. Majoritarian democracies are ones that assign a great deal of agency to the government, whether through the great powers of a government with a legislative majority (as with the "Westminster" systems modeled on the United Kingdom, including Canada, India, and Australia) or through the powers of a powerful president as found in presidentialist systems such as France, the United States, or Brazil (Lijphart, 1984, 1999). Majoritarianism is a continuum, and a long-debated concept, but we found it promising as a way to explain pandemic response decisions.

Majoritarianism as a concept is one end of a continuum that clusters multiple political institutions. One of those institutions stands out in the context of the pandemic as possibly having additional explanatory power. Presidentialism, in particular, creates its own distinctive class of problems because it separates the power and electoral incentives of the head of government from the legislature (Fix-Fierro & Salazar-Ugarte, 2012). In a presidentialist system, in Linz's definition, "an executive with considerable constitutional powers—generally including full control of the composition of the cabinet and administration—is directly elected by the people for a fixed term and is independent of parliamentary votes of confidence. [The president] is not only the holder of executive power but also the symbolic head of state and can be removed between elections only by the drastic step of impeachment. In practice . . . presidential systems may be more or less dependent on the cooperation of the legislature; the balance between executive and legislative power in such systems can thus vary considerably." Linz continued that "two things about presidential government stand out. The first is the president's strong claim to democratic, even plebiscitarian, legitimacy; the second is [the president's] fixed term in office" (1990, pp. 52–53).

Linz was interested in the drawbacks of presidentialism for democratic stability, and the considerable subsequent debate about the topic has largely followed him in that interest. As the literature evolved, it increasingly downplayed the power of presidentialism alone, emphasizing its complex interactions with party systems in particular. That elaboration and debate never really undid Linz's initial insight that a president is, as another presidency scholar (Skowronek, 1992) put it, a disruptive force (Elgie, 2005; Mainwaring & Shugart, 1997; Shugart, 1999; Shugart & Carey, 1992). Our interest is in pandemic response, and more broadly the response of governments to shocks, which highlights presidentialism because of its particular characteristic: the concentration of agency in a single person at a time of crisis. Some research has indeed found that parliamentary systems are more likely to effectively provide public goods (Shugart, 1999). If we are correct, then although *some* parliamentary regimes, notably those with majoritarian electoral systems, concentrate agency in the leader, almost all presidentialist systems will give the president, in command of the executive, considerable agency to determine responses. Majoritarian and especially presidentialist systems' decisions depend especially heavily on the leader, for better or for worse.

The Findings

The countries discussed in this book span a variety of more or less majoritarian democratic regimes. For once we can use excess mortality for a first approximation because many of the strongest cases are in countries that report it in useful form. It is perhaps coincidental that of our governments, some of the most erratic and apparently ineffective (measured by excess mortality) were at the majoritarian end of the scale: Brazil, the United States, the United Kingdom, Spain, and India. In each of these the electoral system granted considerable agency to single executives. The relationship is hardly perfect: majoritarian Australia and Canada all effectively managed, or even wiped out, COVID-19, whereas relatively consensual democratic procedures in Sweden did not prevent high excess mortality.

In consideration of the policy decisions and course of pandemic politics, the effect of majoritarianism was clear: to the extent that political agency was in the hands of one leader, whether because of dominance of a ruling party in a majoritarian system (Johnson in the United Kingdom, Modi in India, Ramaphosa in South Africa) or institutions that empower a president (Bolsonaro, Trump), there was scope for politics erratic enough to rival some authoritarian regimes. Other leaders such as Macron of France (Rozenblum, chapter 15, this volume), Márquez of Colombia (Acosta et al., chapter 28, this volume), Piñera of Chile (Méndez, chapter 29, this volume), or Trudeau of Canada (Fafard et al., chapter 25, this volume) enjoyed similar agency because of their countries' institutional arrangements but chose not to deploy it in the same way as populist radical right politicians such as Bolsonaro, Johnson, Modi, or Trump. For instance, although Piñera is not as flamboyant a leader as Trump and Bolsonaro, he opted to centralize pandemic key decisions in his hands with little discussion with Congress and subnational governments. Similarly, President Mutharika of Malawi (Dionne et al., chapter 30, this volume) enacted strict, even draconian, public health policies, which might be overturned as the new president Chakwera took office with higher levels of public trust than his predecessor. On the other hand, Márquez of Colombia used his agency to delegate pandemic response to technocrats and found in the pandemic a space to regain popularity and to improve his communication with the population.

Looking at our cases also shows the interaction of institutions and populist politics. Majoritarianism, and in particular presidentialism, appear to have distinctive interactions with populism and the radical right because of the way it assigns so much agency to an individual. One of the running media debates of 2020 was precisely about the extent to which populism shaped pandemic responses. The debate specifically focused on the populist radical right affiliations of figures such as Bolsonaro in Brazil, Johnson in the United Kingdom, Modi in India, or Trump in the United States (Kavakli, 2020). The literature on the effects of populism and the populist radical right in government is relatively clear that the effects of a populist radical right party or politician do matter but are shaped by institutions and party systems (Falkenbach & Greer, 2020, 2021; Falkenbach et al., 2019; Rinaldi & Bekker, 2020). Thus the Austrian or Swiss political systems, in which populist radical right parties must be in coalition with larger parties, show less direct effect from those parties than more majoritarian political systems in which a single leader can wield a great deal of power. An anti-science or clientelistic leader in a majoritarian system can express those impulses more and do more to block others than one in a system in which other parties can temper them in coalition or parliament. Thus, anti-scientific or other problematic impulses found in a Bolsonaro, Johnson, or Trump administration are magnified in systems in which their office and command of the executive machinery are largely independent of their legislatures (as with Bolsonaro and Trump) or in which they enjoyed legislative majorities in majoritarian systems (as with Johnson and Modi). Majoritarian political institutions gave populists, some of them COVID-19 deniers, the opportunity to make, or not make, pandemic response policy. It is a politics of agency, and concentrating agency in one leader with limited accountability seems to have more obvious risks than benefits.

Federalism Shapes Pandemic Responses

Federalism is a kind of political institutional arrangement. It refers to a political system in which there are at least two separate levels of elected general-purpose government, neither of which can unilaterally abolish the other. This means that it includes countries not always understood as federal, such as Italy and Spain, and that many analytical components of comparative federalism apply to the EU.

There is a vast and confusing multidisciplinary literature on the impact of federalism on politics (Costa-i-Font & Greer, 2013; Greer, 2017b; Greer & Elliott,

2019). Some scholars agree with Hayek that its salient characteristic is the promotion of intergovernmental competition, which supposedly promotes efficiency and limited government (Qian & Weingast, 1997; von Hayek, 1992; Weingast, 2014). The basic idea operates by analogy with firms (Tiebout, 1956): just as companies compete to provide different services to customers at different prices, governments compete to provide different levels of public goods to mobile taxpayers. In both cases a very simple model suggests the result will be Pareto-efficient: it might not be fair in any normative sense, but everybody will get what they want within what they can afford. This logic undergirds a wide range of models suggesting that competition between governments will subject them to discipline, making them efficient and curing a putative habit of excessive expenditure. Scholars working in this area, who are often already normatively uninterested in fairness, often ignore resilience, prioritizing efficiency over the slack that is necessary to withstand any kind of a shock and bounce back.

A second school views federalism as a creator and multiplier of veto points, which slows and limits policy-making, entrenching opponents of change and then making coordination harder by demanding that the interests of more diverse elected governments be considered (Huber & Stephens, 2001; Swank, 2001). The empirical basis for this view as an explanation of policy is surprisingly thin, often reliant on indices of fragmentation that lump federalism together with other kinds of veto points. These authors also tend to be insensitive to the extent to which federal states' autonomy (self-rule) differs from their participation in other governments' decisions (shared-rule) (Elazar, 1987; Hooghe et al., 2016). It is very important to distinguish between self-rule and shared-rule. The most common patterns we found in a study of rich countries' federalisms (Greer & Elliott, 2019) are that self-rule operates within bounds set by federal programs (because even if the federal government is constitutionally constrained, it is usually financially stronger and more flexible) and that shared rule in which states can shape or veto federal decisions is rare and can be vitiated by the influence of political parties (Greer, 2019; Greer, 2020b). That federalism creates obstacles to coordination, though, is well established and has been seen in the pandemic (e.g., Huberfeld et al., 2020; Migone, 2020; Rocco et al., 2020).

A third school sees federalism as a contributor to the resilience of a country, even if they do not always phrase it that way. This school focuses on the advantages of policy divergence, allowing innovation, local adaptation, local accountability, learning and beneficial competition, as well as quarantining disappointments: if the federal government fails, state governments can compensate, and vice versa (Banting, 2006). This case is plausible, but the very limited systematic comparative research on it is skeptical. First of all, size matters (Stepan, 1999). A medium-sized American state such as North Carolina or Michigan has roughly the 10 million-person population of Sweden; the 41 million people of São Paulo state in Brazil rival the 46 million people of Spain, and the four biggest Indian states (Uttar Pradesh, Maharastra, Bihar, and West Bengal) have a combined population of 507 million, compared to the EU's 447 million. North Carolina and

Sweden are hardly deliberative democracies, and what kind of deliberative democracy or clear accountability is to be expected among the 200 million inhabitants of Uttar Pradesh? Instead, it seems that decentralizing public policy decisions to states produces what the simplest theory would suggest: divergence among states (Greer, 2006; Kleider, 2015). Federations produce divergence within bounds set by law, finance, and programmatic design.

There are two unpromising sets of hypotheses that the chapters in this book gave us no cause to revisit. An old school of "public choice" theory, ever on guard against public expenditure, saw it as breeding excessive government expenditure; this is clearly not the case. Another school of mostly historically oriented scholars discounts federalism, seeing it primarily as a form of adaptation to deep territorial cleavages that would exist under any regime, and perhaps as a cost of staying together at all (Erk & Koning, 2009). This latter approach has value but, for our purposes, creates imponderable counterfactuals: to draw conclusions about federalism from such an approach, we would have to imagine Canada or India as a unitary state facing COVID-19. That strains credulity.

Parsing out and weighing these different perspectives are challenging theoretical and empirical exercises (Greer & Elliott, 2019; Greer et al., 2015). Federalism's effects clearly vary with the exact design of the federal system (e.g., the nature of its taxes and intergovernmental transfers shape the extent of interstate competition) as well as interaction with other institutions and features of the economy (e.g., party systems, social cleavages, and policy legacies). For our purposes, the basic hypothesis is that federalism does matter in at least one of these three ways: by keeping governments thin (at best, efficient but perhaps not resilient); by multiplying governments, creating diversity as well as potential backups in case of failure; and by slowing policy change or coordination. Broadly, though, we would expect that federalism's impact matters most in interaction with some other institutions and political forces, but would reflect some of these dynamics.

The Findings

We found no particular evidence that federal states per se have intergovernmental competition that produces better government than more centralized systems. The obvious mediating factor is intergovernmental finance: German federal states have more consistent funding than American ones, for example, and a number of countries such as Spain and Brazil operate highly redistributive fiscal systems that direct money from richer to poorer places. The competitiveness hypothesis would suggest that more competitive federations would have better or more efficient responses, but it seems that they were just underfunded in many cases. It is hard to see the metric by which the United States, the country with the least federal equalization between states and therefore the most competitive state governments, turned in a superior performance relative to other federations. It is possible that efficiency is achieved at the price of resilience: state governments in the United States have incentive to cut costs too much in pursuit of efficiency (Greer, 2020a; Greer & Singer, 2016). That can lead to frustration in normal times but lead to serious problems in the face of compounding shocks, such as 2020's combination of pandemic, recession, and a variety of natural disasters and contentious politics. Insofar as the competitiveness hypothesis is correct—and it seems correct entirely within the margin created by systems of intergovernmental finance—it might produce efficiency, but it could equally well be producing systems that lack resilience in the face of predictable emergencies such as pandemics.

Did federalism generate veto points that slowed change? This breaks down into two questions. One is whether legislative action to address the pandemic—in health or social policy—was impeded by federal political institutions. Although a number of surprisingly influential accounts assimilate federal failure or inaction to federalism, it is important when studying legislation to divide between self-rule and shared rule. Strictly speaking, only if there is shared rule, in which state governments have a formal say over federal decisions, or substantial reliance on state cooperation to enact and implement policy, can we say that federalism is an impediment to legislation. Federalism may tend to covary with other impediments to legislation, such as bicameralism or extensive judicial review, but that does not mean we can attribute problems created by bicameralism (such as the malapportioned US Senate) or judicial review to federalism.

In fact, almost every federation saw substantial centralization, just as almost every government saw substantial initial centralization (with heads of government gathering power relative to their ministers and agencies in the spring and summer of 2020) (see Jarman, chapter 3, this volume; Greer et al., 2020a). Most of them saw emergency legislation covering health and social policy measures. Ones with substantial shared rule—a small category—saw, if anything, unusually good coordination, in part because of political elites and party systems long adapted to managing coordination challenges in systems filled with interlocking veto points. As for notable failures to legislate, in most cases they happened at the federal level and in social and economic policy—in areas in which federal states' fiscal advantages are most prominent, and failure to use them most important.

In terms of practical coordination, decentralization did lead to problems. Dubin writes about how, in Spain, long-standing "politics of who, not what," focused more on which governments would act than on the substance of their actions, produced inexcusable failings in public administration such as failure to connect data sets across the country (Dubin, chapter 19, this volume; Dubin, 2019). Regional and state coordination failures magnified by partisan disagreement plagued Italian response (Falkenbach and Caiani, chapter 18, this volume). The United Kingdom was plagued with difficulties in what should have been the relatively simple problem of coordinating policy between its four governments (Williams et al., chapter 12, this volume). Almost every federal government, even ones generally regarded as effective, such as Germany or Austria, saw coordination problems as well as a politics of blame-shifting and credit-claiming between its politicians (Czypionka and Reiss, chapter 17; Mätzke, chapter 16, this volume).

Externalities also caused problems. The US state of Minnesota adopted relatively forceful and effective NPIs. They did little good when neighboring South Dakota inexplicably hosted almost a half million motorcyclists for an August 2020 party in the town of Sturgis. It was probably the world's largest gathering at the time, unmasked and wholly unnecessary, and it led to cases around the country. Canada largely avoided the externalities of the US outbreak by closing borders, but that tool was unavailable to US states. In the EU, initial border closures proved too economically, socially, and institutionally disruptive. The member states who initially had "gone it alone" rapidly found themselves coordinating with each other on new, more federal policies to manage a level of interdependence comparable to that of many federations. By summer 2020 they were ready to relax restrictions, and by September 2020 it was clear that summer holiday movements across the continent were creating a second wave that showed the scale and public health importance of movement around the EU (see Brooks et al., chapter 13, this volume; Brooks et al., 2020). The EU and US responses and their effects were very different, but both were shaped by the fact of open borders and externalities.

We did notice that alignment of responsibility for social policy and state roles in NPIs was a problem in some federations (Adolph et al., 2012; Rocco et al., 2020). In the United States and India, states could enact NPIs but mostly lacked the resources to make compensating social policy decisions on the necessary scale. As a result, when federal government resources were unavailable (or when the federal government chose not to help), state governments faced as stark a tradeoff between NPIs and tax revenue as any bar or restaurant. Governments and businesses alike needed the revenue from business activity, even if they knew it would be immensely destructive to end NPIs.

Finally, did federalism increase resilience through fail-safes, learning, or adaptiveness? To a limited extent, we saw federations in which the federal government failed but state governments took compensating action, notably Brazil, the United States, and India as well as, to a more limited extent, the United Kingdom and Spain. In those countries, state governments did act as fail-safes, enacting NPIs and some limited social policies once the federal government had failed to act. As comparative federalism would lead us to expect, though, the states operated within a decision space set by constitutional law, intergovernmental finance, and programmatic design as well as nationalized politics in some cases and nationalized economies in all cases, which limited what they could effectively do. There was learning, but there was also a strong partisan effect in some cases, such as Spain and the United States (Singer et al., chapter 26; Dubin, chapter 19, this volume). Deliberate partisan polarization led to additional policy conflict about NPIs, social policies, healthcare priorities during surges, and masking. In sophisticated studies of the United States, it has become clear that it was partisanship rather than actual policy problems that shaped NPI decisions (Adolph et al., 2020).

Just what was learned from variation in COVID-19 responses within federations, and then usefully adopted, is not clear, and in our reading the authors of this book did not find a consistent story of policy diffusion. Where there was learning, there was also usually some well-established set of coordinating mechanisms, whether the federal-provincial-territorial conferences of Canada or Germany's numerous and normally ponderous coordinating forums (Czypionka and Reiss, chapter 17, this volume; Fafard et al., chapter 25, this volume; Migone, 2020; Wallner, 2014). These normally manage conflict and frustrate policy advocates with their slowness (Scharpf, 1988) but in an emergency turned out to be very useful for learning and coordinating. In cases where they were absent or not used, as in Southern Europe, multilevel government did often turn out to slow coherent responses (Peralta-Santos et al., chapter 20, this volume).

Public Health Capacity Contributes to Effective Response

The Hypothesis

The October 2019 Global Health Security Index (GHSI) from a consortium led by Johns Hopkins University was, in retrospect, very well timed. It has become the subject of much discussion. The GHSI ranked almost every country in the world by their pandemic preparedness and scored the United States highest. By late 2020 no serious observer, including the GHSI authors, claimed that the United States had responded well to the pandemic (Nuzzo et al., 2020). In fact, there was little evident relationship between the GHSI rankings and countries' actual decisions or performance (Abbey et al., 2020; Haider et al., 2020; Kavanagh & Singh, 2020).

The problem lay in good part not in the data of the index nor its peer rankings, which were often accurate in their assessment of countries. The problem lay in its composition. The index effectively weighted countries' adherence to a particular model of public health response and capacity that was intended to prepare them for a pandemic such as COVID-19. In other words, the GHSI scored countries against a particular concept of specialist public health bureaucracy.

Most countries have some form of specialist public health bureaucracy, but their size, ambition, breadth of ambition, and legal position have varied a great deal. The scope of "public health" is immense in theory (almost everything can be called public health if public health means organized efforts to reduce avoidable morbidity and mortality). The scope of public health bureaucracies is much more variable from country to country and often includes different kinds of bureaucratic units and tasks such as restaurant inspection, workplace safety, border health, water quality inspection, and basic health care (Greer & Jarman, 2020). It is never wise to make assumptions about what "public health" means in the politics, bureaucracy, or scholarship of another country.

Despite that high level of variation, there is something of an international model that has been promoted by the WHO, the GHSI, the US CDC itself, regional organizations, and even a specialist international organization (the International Association of National Public Health Institutes, based in Atlanta and started with Gates Foundation support) (Binder et al., 2008a, 2008b). The model is broadly that of the US CDC, a high-level central agency with extensive scientific capacities that can organize surveillance, conduct research and laboratory analyses, formulate guidance, advise government, and communicate its recommendations to the rest of government (for implementation) and the public (Greer, 2017a). Echoes of the model are found around the world, even if implementation of or desire for a copy of the US CDC is highly variable. The philanthropic and intellectual push for the model echoes earlier drives toward public health professionalization supported by the Rockefeller Foundation (Fee, 1987).

The hypothesis is that investment in this kind of autonomous science-focused agency will improve pandemic response as well as public health in general. Public health agencies with substantial executive capacity of their own are relatively rare, and that executive power is often a fairly small group of disease detectives who can bolster local field epidemiology or microbiological capacity. In most cases they rely on others, such as local governments, the police, the military (in a crisis), or the healthcare sector to actually administer vaccines, implement NPIs, or inspect restaurants. They might look like a fire department but in a crisis actually are often part of a bucket brigade (Mätzke, 2012). The CDC agency's contribution is in science and scientifically grounded advice to government and the public. If the model works, its influence on policy-making and policy should be clear in the analysis of decisions. The agency, if not organizing the bucket brigade directly, should at least have the organizers' attention.

The Findings

To our surprise, the relationship between dedicated public health capacity and government response was poor in most cases. In country after country, we found that heads of government centralized power unto themselves in the first wave and put their public health agencies, and the public health profession to the extent that they had one, in a firmly subordinate position (Jarman, chapter 3, this volume; Greer et al., 2020a). In some cases, such as the United States and England, the sidelining was particularly dramatic and humiliating given the ambition and prestige of the countries' public health establishments at the start of the year (Singer et al., chapter 26; Williams et al., chapter 12, this volume). The Trump administration silenced the CDC and subjected it to political manipulation. In England, the government abruptly decided to eliminate its public health agency, folding it into a new agency designed to be much more clearly subordinate to political decisions and tasked only with implementation and scientific resources. But in other countries such as Denmark or France we also saw ambitious agencies sidelined from a leadership role (Rozenblum, chapter 15; Ornston, chapter 14, this volume). In Japan (Nagata et al., chapter 8, this volume) the number of PCR tests was low compared with other countries due to bureaucratic silo phenomenon in governmental organization and the agencies involved in managing the pandemic.

In a few countries such as Germany and Canada the system worked as intended, but in those cases the agency had never been designed with a prominent role in policy advice (Czypionka & Reiss, chapter 17; Fafard et al., chapter 25, this volume). In lower-income countries, such as Malawi (Dionne at al., chapter 30, this volume), the healthcare system was already overburdened before COVID-19, and the lack of PPE and critical care units made it even harder to deal with any surge in coronavirus cases.

Only in two cases did we find a communicable disease control agency in the lead: South Korea and Sweden. The results in both countries were different, with Korea effectively eliminating the virus and Sweden adopting a controversial "herd immunity" strategy that led to far more deaths than its neighbors (Irwin, 2020; Pierre, 2020). Even in those cases, it is likely that the prominence and power of the communicable disease control agency could be attributed to a political decision by the head of government to step back and let the agency make decisions (Park, chapter 6, this volume; Lee et al., 2020). A highly political decision to center an agency was what happened in Colombia (Acosta et al., chapter 28, this volume). It seems that governments can find expertise to their satisfaction (though policy in Czechia was first driven by a businessman with a model and then a prominent dentist, hardly the level of expertise we might like; Löblovà et al., chapter 23, this volume), and that when they cultivate specific public health expertise and capacity, they explicitly want it to be on tap rather than on top.

This book's broad conclusion about capacity of any sort is shared with other analyses of COVID-19 (Bosancianu et al., 2020; Capano, 2020; Capano et al., 2020; Kavanagh & Singh, 2020): using it is as important as having it. Highly capable states misused or did not apply their strength. The strong agency model of public health capacity is in part a way to skew politics of pandemic response toward public health thinking by creating a putatively apolitical expert agency that can bring scientific answers to questions. It was an effort to shape decisions by shaping capacity. Not only was public health capacity only erratically applied, the capacity of public health agencies to advise governments was only erratically sought.

Conclusion

We can draw several conclusions from the findings in this book. Many countries that should have been best prepared to deal with a pandemic, based on existing global health preparedness measures, were not able to implement effective strategies to prevent infections and deaths. Countries that implemented swift responses such as robust testing and efficient contract tracing fared better in these first months of the pandemic.

Social policy is equally important to health policy during a pandemic; this is true in higher-income and lower-income countries. Without social policies to support lower-income and vulnerable populations, health policies to promote social distancing cannot be fully effective and are likely not sustainable long enough to end the epidemic in a country. However, we saw significant misalignment between social and health policies in most countries, exacerbated in some cases by federations that misaligned public health and social policy powers. Apparently, the more authoritarian countries were largely less inclined to provide broad social policies as they relied primarily on coercion and a historical pattern of compliance with government orders.

Regime type was not a particularly conclusive variable in our findings. There is little evidence that authoritarian regimes were more effective than democratic regimes in implementing health and social policies, or that the country cases in this book clustered in any meaningful way according to regime type. Information flow and trust were also critical variables in a number of countries, across the spectrum of regime types, but there was evidence that authoritarian regimes suffered distinctive problems of internal and external information flow. Broadly, we found similarities across regime type, and distinctive paths within regime type, more promising than regime types alone.

Institutional variables such as presidentialism and federalism greatly shape pandemic response. For example, a pandemic endows controversial leaders with power to push their agendas despite the magnitude of infectious disease threat and socioeconomic consequences of COVID-19 restrictions. Those most affected by the pandemic can seemingly do little to stop these controversial government leaders in majoritarian systems.

It is clear that the COVID-19 pandemic is moving forward with us in 2021, in many places even harsher than in the first months that this book focuses on. We assembled this book in the midst of uncertainty, changing evidence-based public health guidelines, testing of therapeutics and rapid development of promising vaccines, and ongoing and new political struggles around the world. Some countries learned from their own miscalculations and other governments' missteps, whereas other countries seemingly believed that they had surpassed the COVID-19 threat or did not have the capacity or will to continue providing adequate social and health policies needed to curb the epidemic.

What is clear from this "first wave" is that politics matter and there is a great need to understand government responses to the COVID-19 pandemic. Pandemic preparedness must consider "political capacity" (Kavanagh & Singh, 2020), which is to say politics. Our book is an initial effort to systematically identify what these variables are and explore how they operate in practice. We hope that the findings presented throughout this book will draw the attention of and resonate with a diverse global health audience of practitioners, researchers, policy-makers, and scholars.

Acknowledgments

We would like to thank Victor Shih and Rebecca Wai for their advice and contribution to the sections on authoritarianism.

References

Abbey, E. J., Khalifa, B. A. A., Oduwole, M. O., Ayeh, S. K., Nudotor, R. D., Salia, E. L., Lasisi, O., Bennett, S., Yusuf, H. E., Agwu, A. L., & Karakousis, P. C. (2020). The Global Health Security Index is not predictive of coronavirus pandemic responses among Organization for Economic Cooperation and Development countries. *PLOS ONE*, *15*(10), e0239398.

Adolph, C., Amano, K., Bang-Jensen, B., Fullman, N., & Wilkerson, J. (2020). Pandemic politics: Timing state-level social distancing responses to COVID-19. *Journal of Health Politics, Policy and Law*. https://doi.org/10.1215/03616878-8802162

Adolph, C., Greer, S. L., & Massard da Fonseca, E. (2012). Allocation of authority in European health policy. *Social Science & Medicine*, *75*(9), 1595–1603.

Alcock, P., & Glennerster, H. (2001). *Welfare and wellbeing: Richard Titmuss's contribution to social policy*. Policy Press.

Ang, Y. Y. (2020). When COVID-19 meets centralized, personalized power. *Nature Human Behaviour*, *4*(5), 445–447.

Banting, K. G. (2006). Social citizenship and federalism: Is the federal welfare state a contradiction in terms? In S. L. Greer (Ed.), *Territory, democracy, and justice* (pp. 44–66). Palgrave Macmillan.

Bermeo, N. G., & Bartels, L. M. (Eds.). (2014). *Mass politics in tough times: Opinions, votes and protest in the great recession*. Oxford University Press.

Binder, S., Adigun, L., Dusenbury, C., Greenspan, A., & Tanhuanpaa, P. (2008a). National public health institutes: Contributing to the public good. *Journal of Public Health Policy*, *29*, 3–21.

Binder, S., Adigun, L. E., & Greenspan, A. L. (2008b). NPHI Creation: Lessons learned and future directions. *Journal of Public Health Policy*, *29*, 459–466.

Boix, C., & Svolik, M. W. (2013). The foundations of limited authoritarian government: Institutions, commitment, and power-sharing in dictatorships. *The Journal of Politics*, *75*(2), 300–316.

Bosancianu, C. M., Dionne, K. Y., Hilbig, H., Humphreys, M., Sampada, K. C., Lieber, N., & Scacco, A. (2020). Political and social correlates of Covid-19 mortality. *SocArXiv*. https://doi.org/10.31235/osf.io/ub3zd

Brooks, E., de Ruijter, A., & Greer, S. L. (2020). COVID-19 and European Union health policy: From crisis to collective action. In B. Vanhercke, S. Spasova, & B. Fronteddu (Eds.), *Social policy in the European Union: State of play 2020*. European Social Observatory (OSE)/European Trades Union Institute: Brussels.

Capano, G. (2020). Policy design and state capacity in the COVID-19 emergency in Italy: If you are not prepared for the (un)expected, you can be only what you already are. *Policy and Society*, *39*(3), 326–244.

Capano, G., Howlett, M., Jarvis, D. S. L., Ramesh, M., & Goyal, N. (2020). Mobilizing policy (in) capacity to fight COVID-19: Understanding variations in state responses. *Policy and Society*, *39*(1), 285–308.

Chang, E., & Golden, M. A. (2010). Sources of corruption in authoritarian regimes. *Social Science Quarterly*, *91*(1), 1–20.

Colfer, B. (2020). Public policy responses to COVID-19 in Europe. *European Policy Analysis*, *6*(2), 126–137.

Collier, D., & Levitsky, S. (1997). Democracy with adjectives: Conceptual innovation in comparative research. *World Politics*, *49*(3), 430–451.

Costa-i-Font, J., & Greer, S. L. (2013). Territory and health: Perspectives from economics and political science. In J. Costa-i-Font & S. L. Greer (Eds.), *Federalism and decentralization in European health and social care* (pp. 13–44). Palgrave Macmillan.

Dahl, R. A. (1971). *Polyarchy: Participation and opposition*. Yale University Press.

de Leeuw, E., Clavier, C., & Breton, E. (2014). Health policy: Why research it and how: Health political science. *Health Research Policy and Systems*, *12*(1), 55.

de Waal, A. (2020, April 3). New pathogen, old politics. *Boston Review*. http://bostonreview.net/science-nature/alex-de-waal-new-pathogen-old-politics

Deacon, R. T. (2009). Public good provision under dictatorship and democracy. *Public Choice*, *139*(1–2), 241–262.

Dubin, K. (2019). Spain: The politics of who not what. In S. L. Greer & H. Elliott (Eds.), *Federalism and social policy: Patterns of redistribution in 11 democracies* (pp. 57–90). University of Michigan Press.

Egorov, G., & Sonin, K. (2011). Dictators and their viziers: Endogenizing the loyalty–competence trade-off. *Journal of the European Economic Association*, *9*(5), 903–930.

Elazar, D. (1987). *Exploring federalism*. University of Alabama Press.

Elgie, R. (2005). From Linz to Tsebelis: Three waves of presidential/parliamentary studies. *Democratization*, *12*(1), 106–122.

Erk, J., & Koning, E. (2009). New structuralism and institutional change: Federalism between centralization and decentralization. *Comparative Political Studies*, *42*(11), 1–23.

Fafard, P., & Cassola, A. (2020). Public health and political science: Challenges and opportunities for a productive partnership. *Public Health*, *186*, 107–109.

Falkenbach, M., Bekker, M., & Greer, S. L. (2019). Do parties make a difference? A review of partisan effects on health and the welfare state. *European Journal of Public Health*, *30*(4), 673–682.

Falkenbach, M., & Greer, S. L. (2020). Denial and distraction: How the populist radical right responds to COVID-19 Comment on "A Scoping Review of PRR Parties' Influence on Welfare Policy and its Implication for Population Health in Europe." *International Journal of Health Policy and Management*. https://doi.org/10.34172/IJHPM.2020.141

Falkenbach, M. I., & Greer, S. L. (Eds.). (2021). *The populist radical right and health: National policies and global trends*. Springer.

Fee, E. (1987). *Disease and discovery: A history of the Johns Hopkins School of Hygiene and Public Health, 1916–1939*. Johns Hopkins University Press.

Fix-Fierro, H., & Salazar-Ugarte, P. (2012). Presidentialism. In M. Rosenfeld & A. Sajó. (Eds.) *The Oxford handbook of comparative constitutional law*. Oxford University Press.

Gagnon, F., Bergeron, P., Clavier, C., Fafard, P., Martin, E., & Blouin, C. (2017). Why and how political science can contribute to public health? Proposals for collaborative research avenues. *International Journal of Health Policy and Management*, *6*(9), 495.

Gandhi, J., & Przeworski, A. (2007). Authoritarian institutions and the survival of autocrats. *Comparative Political Studies*, *40*(11), 1279–1301.

Gao, J. (2016). "Bypass the lying mouths": How does the CCP tackle information distortion at local levels? *The China Quarterly*, 950.

Gibson, E. L. (2013). *Boundary control: Subnational authoritarianism in federal democracies*. Cambridge University Press.

Global Health Security Index. (2019). Johns Hopkins Center for Health Security & Nuclear Threat Initiative.

Gourevitch, P. (1986). *Politics in hard times: Comparative responses to international economic crises*. Cornell University Press.

Greer, S. L. (2006). The politics of divergent policy. In S. L. Greer (Ed.), *Territory, democracy, and justice: Regionalism and federalism in western democracies* (pp. 157–174). Palgrave Macmillan.

Greer, S. L. (2017a). Constituting public health surveillance in twenty-first century Europe. In M. Weimer & A. de Ruijter (Eds.), *Regulating risks in the European Union: The co-production of expert and executive power* (pp. 121–141). Bloomsbury.

Greer, S. L. (2017b). Health policy and territorial politics: Disciplinary misunderstandings and directions for research. In K. Detterbeck & E. Hepburn (Eds.), *Edward Elgar handbook of territorial politics* (pp. 232–245). Edward Elgar. https://deepblue.lib.umich.edu/handle/2027.42/136224

Greer, S. L. (2019). Comparative federalism as if policy mattered. In S. L. Greer & H. Elliott (Eds.), *Federalism and social policy: Patterns of redistribution in 11 democracies* (p. 289–309). University of Michigan Press.

Greer, S. L. (2020a). Debacle: Trump's response to the COVID-19 emergency. In M. del Pero & P. Magri (Eds.), *Four years of Trump. The US and the world* (pp. 88–111). ISPI.

Greer, S. L. (2020b). Health, federalism and the European Union: Lessons from comparative federalism about the European Union. *Health Economics, Policy and Law*, 1–14.

Greer, S. L., Bekker, M., de Leeuw, E., Wismar, M., Helderman, J.-K., Ribeiro, S., & Stuckler, D. (2017). Policy, politics and public health. *European Journal of Public Health, 27*(4), 40–43.

Greer, S. L., Bekker, M. P. M., Azzopardi-Muscat, N., & McKee, M. (2018). Political analysis in public health: Middle-range concepts to make sense of the politics of health. *European Journal of Public Health*, 28(suppl_3), 3–6.

Greer, S. L., & Elliott, H. (Eds.). (2019). *Federalism and social policy: Patterns of redistribution in eleven democracies*. University of Michigan Press.

Greer, S. L., Elliott, H., & Oliver, R. (2015). Differences that matter: Overcoming methodological nationalism in comparative social policy research. *Journal of Comparative Policy Analysis: Research and Practice, 17*(4), 408–429.

Greer, S. L., & Jarman, H. (2020). What is EU public health and why? Explaining the scope and organization of public health in the European Union. *Journal of Health Politics, Policy and Law*. https://doi.org/10.1215/03616878-8706591

Greer, S. L., Jarman, H., Rozenblum, S., & Wismar, M. (2020a). Centralisation within and between governments. *Eurohealth, 26*(2).

Greer, S. L., King, E. J., da Fonseca, E. M., & Peralta-Santos, A. (2020b). The comparative politics of COVID-19: The need to understand government responses. *Global Public Health*, 1–4.

Greer, S. L., & Méndez, C. A. (2015). Universal health coverage: A political struggle and governance challenge. *American Journal of Public Health, 105*(S5), S637–S639.

Greer, S. L., & Singer, P. M. (2016). The United States confronts Ebola: Suasion, executive action, and fragmentation. *Health Economics, Policy and Law, 12*(1), 81–104.

Greer, S. L., & Trump, B. (2019). Regulation and regime: The comparative politics of adaptive regulation in synthetic biology. *Policy Sciences, 52*(4), 505–524.

Greer, S. L., Wismar, M., Pastorino, G., & Kosinska, M. (Eds.). (2017). *Civil society and health: Contributions and potential*. European Observatory on Health Systems and Policies.

Greitens, S. C. (2016). *Dictators and their secret police: Coercive institutions and state violence*. Cambridge University Press.

Haggard, S., & Kaufman, R. R. (2008). *Development, democracy, and welfare states: Latin America, East Asia, and Eastern Europe*. Princeton University Press.

Haider, N., Yavlinsky, A., Chang, Y.-M., Hasan, M. N., Benfield, C., Osman, A. Y., Uddin, M. J., Dar., O., Ntoumi, F., Zumla, A., & Kock, R. (2020). The Global Health Security index and Joint External Evaluation score for health preparedness are not correlated with countries' COVID-19 detection response time and mortality outcome. *Epidemiology and Infection, 148*, e210.

Hall, P. A. (Ed.) (1989). *The Political power of economic ideas: Keynesianism across nations*. Princeton University Press.

Herrera, Y. M. (2010). *Mirrors of the economy: National accounts and international norms in Russia and beyond*. Cornell University Press.

Hooghe, L., Marks, G., Schakel, A. H., Osterkatz, S. C., Niedzwiecki, S., & Shair-Rosenfield, S. (2016). *Measuring regional authority: A postfunctionalist theory of governance* (Vol. 1). Oxford University Press.

Huber, E., & Stephens, J. D. (2001). *Development and crisis of the welfare state: Parties and policies in global markets*. University of Chicago Press.

Huberfeld, N., Gordon, S. H., & Jones, D. K. (2020). Federalism complicates the response to the COVID-19 health and economic crisis: What can be done. *Journal of Health Politics, Policy and Law, 45*(6), 951–965.

Ibrahim, N. K. (2020). Epidemiologic surveillance for controlling Covid-19 pandemic: Types, challenges and implications. *Journal of Infections and Public Health, 13*(8), 1057–1186.

Irwin, R. E. (2020). Misinformation and de-contextualization: International media reporting on Sweden and COVID-19. *Globalization and Health, 16*(1), 62.

Kavakli, K. C. (2020). *Did populist leaders respond to the COVID-19 pandemic more slowly? Evidence from a global sample* [Working paper, Bocconi University]. https://kerimkavakli.com/research/

Kavanagh, M. M., & Singh, R. (2020). Democracy, capacity, and coercion in pandemic response—COVID 19 in comparative political perspective. *Journal of Health Politics, Policy and Law, 45*(6), 997–1012.

Kleider, H. (2015). *Decentralization and the welfare state: Territorial disparities, regional governments and political parties* [Unpublished doctoral dissertation]. University of North Carolina, Chapel Hill. https://cdr.lib.unc.edu/record/uuid:b39944d8-8e40-4e92-88de-8a867cebe2ef

Kosack, S. (2012). *The education of nations: How the political organization of the poor, not democracy, led governments to invest in mass education*. Oxford University Press.

Kunicova, J., & Rose-Ackerman, S. (2005). Electoral rules and constitutional structures as constraints on corruption. *British Journal of Political Science*, 573–606.

Kuran, T. (1991). Now out of never: The element of surprise in the East European revolution of 1989. *World Politics: A Quarterly Journal of International Relations*, 7–48.

Kynge, J., Yu, S., & Hancock, T. (2020, February 6). Coronavirus: The cost of China's public health cover-up. *Financial Times*.

Lee, S., Hwang, C., & Moon, M. J. (2020). Policy learning and crisis policy-making: Quadruple-loop learning and COVID-19 responses in South Korea. *Policy and Society, 39*(3), 363–381.

Levitsky, S., & Way, L. A. (2002). Elections without democracy: The rise of competitive authoritarianism. *Journal of Democracy*, *13*(2), 51–65.

Li, L. (2016). Reassessing trust in the central government: Evidence from five national surveys. *The China Quarterly*, 100.

Lijphart, A. (1984). *Democracies: Patterns of majoritarian and consensus government in twenty-one countries*. Yale University Press.

Lijphart, A. (1999). *Patterns of democracy: Government forms and performance in thirty-six countries*. Yale University Press.

Linos, K. (2013). *The democratic foundations of policy diffusion: How health, family and employment laws spread across countries*. Oxford University Press.

Linz, J. J. (1990). The perils of presidentialism. *Journal of Democracy*, *1*, 51–69.

Lipscy, P. Y. (2020). COVID-19 and the politics of crisis. *International Organization*, 1–30.

Little, A. T. (2017). Propaganda and credulity. *Games and Economic Behavior*, *102*, 224–232.

Mainwaring, S., & Shugart, M. S. (1997). Juan Linz, presidentialism, and democracy: A critical appraisal. *Comparative Politics*, 449–471.

Markel, H., Lipman, H. B., Navarro, J., Sloan, A., Michalsen, J. R., Stern, A. M., & Cetron, M. S. (2007). Nonpharmaceutical interventions implemented by US cities during the 1918–1919 influenza pandemic. *JAMA*, *298*(6), 644–654.

Mätzke, M. (2012). Commentary: The institutional resources for communicable disease control in Europe: Diversity across time and place. *Journal of Health Politics, Policy, and Law*, *36*(1), 967–976.

Migone, A. R. (2020). Trust, but customize: Federalism's impact on the Canadian COVID-19 response. *Policy and Society*, *39*(3), 382–402.

Nuzzo, J. B., Bell, J. A., & Cameron, E. E. (2020). Suboptimal US response to COVID-19 despite robust capabilities and resources. *JAMA*, *324*(14), 1391–1392.

Perry, J. C. (2017). *Singapore: Unlikely power*. Oxford University Press.

Pierre, J. (2020). Nudges against pandemics: Sweden's COVID-19 containment strategy in perspective. *Policy and Society*, *39*(3), 478–493.

Qian, Y., & Weingast, B. R. (1997). Federalism as a commitment to preserving market incentives. *The Journal of Economic Perspectives*, 83–92.

Rajan, S., D. Cylus, J., & Mckee, M. (2020). What do countries need to do to implement effective "find, test, trace, isolate and support" systems. *Journal of the Royal Society of Medicine*, *113*(7), 245–250.

Rinaldi, C., & Bekker, M. (2020). A scoping review of populist radical right parties' influence on welfare policy and its implications for population health in Europe. *International Journal of Health Policy and Management*. https://doi.org/10.34172/ijhpm.2020.48

Rocco, P., Béland, D., & Waddan, A. (2020). Stuck in neutral? Federalism, policy instruments, and counter-cyclical responses to COVID-19 in the United States. *Policy and Society*, 1–20.

Scharpf, F. (1988). The joint decision trap: Lessons from German federalism and European Integration. *Public Administration*, *66*, 238–278.

Shugart, M. S. (1999). Presidentialism, parliamentarism, and the provision of collective goods in less-developed countries. *Constitutional Political Economy*, *10*(1), 53–88.

Shugart, M. S., & Carey, M. (1992). *Presidents and assemblies: Constitutional design and electoral dynamics*. Cambridge University Press.

Skowronek, S. (1997). *The politics presidents make: Leadership from John Adams to Bill Clinton*. Harvard University Press.

Stasavage, D. (2020). Democracy, autocracy, and emergency threats: Lessons for COVID-19 from the last thousand years. *International Organization*, 1–17.

Stepan, A. (1999). Federalism and democracy: Beyond the U.S. model. *Journal of Democracy*, *10*(4), 19–34.

Stockmann, D. (2013). *Media commercialization and authoritarian rule in China*. Cambridge University Press.

Stockmann, D., & Gallagher, M. E. (2011). Remote control: How the media sustain authoritarian rule in China. *Comparative Political Studies*, *44*(4), 436–467.

Svolik, M. W. (2009). Power sharing and leadership dynamics in authoritarian regimes. *American Journal of Political Science*, *53*(2), 477–494.

Swank, D. (2001). Political institutions and welfare state restructuring: The impact of institutions on social policy change in developed democracies. In P. Pierson (Ed.), *The new politics of the welfare state* (pp. 197–236). Oxford University Press.

Tiebout, C. M. (1956). A pure theory of local expenditure. *Journal of Political Economy*, *64*, 416–425.

Tsai, L. L. (2008). Understanding the falsification of village income statistics. *The China Quarterly*, *196*, 805–826.

von Hayek, F. A. (1992). *Individualism and economic order*. University of Chicago Press.

Wallace, J. L. (2016). Juking the stats? Authoritarian information problems in China. *British Journal of Political Science*, *46*(1), 11–29.

Wallner, J. (2014). *Learning to school: Federalism and public schooling in Canada*. University of Toronto Press.

Weingast, B. R. (2014). Second generation fiscal federalism: Political aspects of decentralization and economic development. *World Development*, *53*, 14–25.

Wintrobe, R. (2000). *The political economy of dictatorship*. Cambridge University Press.

Yeh, M.-J., & Cheng, Y. (2020). Policies tackling the COVID-19 pandemic: A sociopolitical perspective from Taiwan. *Health Security*, *18*(6), 427–434.

Zhou, X. (2010). The institutional logic of collusion among local governments in China. *Modern China*, *36*(1), 47–78.

2 PLAYING POLITICS

The World Health Organization's Response to COVID-19

Matthew M. Kavanagh, Renu Singh, and Mara Pillinger

Understanding WHO as a Political Institution

The challenges of the World Health Organization (WHO) begin, perhaps, with its name—framed as one organization, spanning the globe, and tasked with securing, as defined by article 1 of its constitution, "the attainment by all peoples of the highest possible level of health" (WHO, 1946). Yet the gap between the expectations of WHO and how global political actors have shaped its structure and its capacities is vast—never more so than during the COVID-19 pandemic.

It is necessary to look at WHO from at least two perspectives: (1) its role as a scientific, technical, and humanitarian organization and (2) as an international organization and venue for international political negotiation, diplomacy, and policy-making. These two different, at times conflicting, missions leave WHO in a precarious position and have opened it to criticism over the years (Siddiqi, 1995). Some argue that WHO's importance stems primarily from its political and agenda-setting functions, whereas others argue the technical information-gathering, standard-setting, and cooperation-related activities are paramount and that the agency's political nature detracts from these activities (Clift, 2014; Jamison et al., 1998; Retreat, 1996; Ruger & Yach, 2009). There have even been calls over the years to split these functions (Hoffman & Røttingen, 2014).

In practice, though, WHO's mandate to "act as the directing and coordinating authority on international health work" requires both, even where they sit uneasily together (WHO, 1946). Indeed, some of the agency's most important work in recent years, such as fighting the recent Ebola outbreak in the Democratic Republic of the Congo in an active war zone, would not have been possible without combining science, politics, and diplomacy. Yet this combination has also led to perhaps the biggest threat to the organization since its founding as the United States—WHO's biggest financial contributor—declared its intention to withdraw in July 2020 over accusations that WHO is acting as a "political, not a science-based, organization" (Sabbagh & Stewart, 2020).

Founded in 1948, the WHO was established as a specialized agency of the United Nations (UN), governed by an executive board and parliamentary World

Health Assembly (WHA), both made up of member states. Its creation followed an extended negotiation over the direction of international health, culminating in the merging of functions that had previously been held across various international entities (Lee, 2009). During its first decades, WHO stood at the center of a global network of scientists and policy-makers, enjoying recognition as the international leader in issues of health and disease. The eradication of smallpox by a global program led by WHO demonstrated the power of international coordination and technical expertise (Burci, 2018). Over the years, however, WHO has repeatedly been challenged by political rivalries, expanding and competing priorities, fiscal constraints, and competition with other private and public organizations in global health (Davies, 2010; Youde, 2018). With regard to public health emergencies, the severe acute respiratory syndrome (SARS) outbreak of 2003 was a watershed when WHO, under the leadership of Director-General Gro Harlem Brundtland, took the nearly unprecedented step of directly, publicly criticizing China, a powerful member state, for its lack of transparency. Brundtland also rallied governments to respond with a set of scientifically based control measures. These actions eventually led, in 2005, to a major revision of the legally binding International Health Regulations (IHR) treaty. The revised IHR placed new obligations on states to share information about outbreaks within their borders and gave WHO new powers to gather and share data, declare "public health emergencies of international concern" (PHEICs), and issue recommendations about how countries should respond (Heymann et al., 2013). Yet WHO quickly came under scrutiny for how it exercised these powers during the 2009 swine flu (H1N1) epidemic and the 2014 Ebola outbreak in West Africa, leading to multiple inquiries and reform efforts to make WHO more effective (Gostin et al., 2016; Moon et al., 2017). During the former, the agency was criticized for acting too aggressively, and during the latter, for not acting aggressively enough (Kamradt-Scott, 2016).

In this chapter we seek to explain how political factors and history help explain WHO's actions—both where it has stumbled and where it is innovating to address problems in new ways. We begin with the challenges that existed at the outset of the pandemic, explain WHO's actions in three specific areas, and then seek to explain these actions. WHO's capacities have been shaped by member states in a set of evolving geopolitical contexts. In the current pandemic, many past strategies have proven untenable as its responsibilities, particularly vis-á-vis high-income countries, have rapidly expanded and forced WHO to innovate.

Three Sets of Challenges

Against this backdrop, the roots of WHO's COVID-19 response can be found in three sets of political and structural challenges: the decentralized structure of the organization, the competing and conflicting pressures of member states, and the finances of the organization.

First, WHO is far less of a unitary "world" "organization" than its name suggests. In practice, it is characterized by familiar geopolitical divisions and tensions between the organization's headquarters and regional offices. Advanced industrialized countries began to lose their control over the WHA by the 1970s as decolonization led to a growing number of voting members from developing nations (Chorev, 2012; Cueto et al., 2019). This brought a loss of influence and prestige for wealthy nations and a deepening of WHO's focus primarily in low- and middle-income countries (LMICs). Meanwhile, WHO's Secretariat is based in Geneva, but much of its operations function through six semiautonomous regional offices. The Director-General has remarkably weak authority over these offices, each of which is led by a regional director elected by its member states and with command over its own budget. The increasing focus on LMICs has further decreased the political heft of Geneva. With three-quarters of staff and more than half of total expenditure under the control of the regional offices, the decentralized structure creates centers of power and jockeying between member states, as well as variable capacities between regions (Clift, 2014; Lee, 2009). Although this structure can have the advantage of fostering closer relations, better coordination, and cooperation between WHO and governments, it can also cause "pathological fragmentation," creating inefficiencies, overlaps, and unaccountability resulting from a principal-agent problem between the Geneva and regional offices (Graham, 2013; Hanrieder, 2015). During the West African Ebola outbreak, for example, disjuncture and miscommunication between the country, regional, and headquarters levels contributed to the agency's failure (Kamradt-Scott, 2016; Wenham, 2017). The post-Ebola restructuring built a new Health Emergencies Program that has significantly improved the capacity of WHO headquarters to coordinate and respond, including by creating direct lines of reporting authority between Geneva and the regional offices (Ravi et al., 2019). Yet the continuing weakness of WHO Geneva (where much of the global political and media attention is focused) compared to the regional offices (where much of WHO's influence and capacity lies) is notable.

Second, WHO has also always been subject to the competing priorities of its 194 member states and especially its donors. Cold War politics kept WHO torn between focus on biomedicine and social medicine, between a focus on Eastern Europe versus Asia, Latin America, and Africa (Lee, 2009). More recently, the tensions have been multipolar and multipriority. WHO has as many priorities as it has masters. Disease-specific efforts on human immunodeficiency virus (HIV) and polio, universal health coverage, pandemic preparedness, humanitarian emergency response, innovation, access to medicines, and a host of other priorities have been tasked to WHO at annual WHAs by overlapping coalitions of member states and promoted by nonstate actors such as the Bill & Melinda Gates Foundation. The 2017 election of Dr. Tedros Adhanom Ghebreyesus as Director-General, Ethiopia's former minister of health and of foreign affairs, marked the most open and competitive WHO election in which this complex prioritization challenge was clearly articulated. Yet WHO still faces a principal-agent problem, in which "when the signals from the principals are conflicting, it can paralyse the agent" (Youde, 2016). Chorev argues that the WHO Secretariat has not been a passive agent but has engaged in strategic adaptation to external pressures—reframing demands and regimes to fit the organizational culture and building space for autonomy and action driven by the bureaucratic leaders of the organization (Chorev, 2012). That task has grown harder, though, as the principals' demands have grown, and it is particularly difficult in issue areas such as pandemic responses, which are high visibility and high priority and therefore subject to high levels of oversight from principals.

Finally, WHO is operating on a budget roughly the size of a large hospital in a wealthy nation. The budget is predominantly endowed by a handful of actors, with the United States contributing up to 20 percent of WHO's budget in recent years (WHO, 2019). The current biennial budget for 2020–2021 is set at $4.84 billion, without taking any potential additional, emergency expenditures into account. WHO's funding comes in two forms: assessed contributions from member states and voluntary contributions from member states, private organizations, and individuals. The latter are usually tied to specific uses and projects. Assessed contributions from member states based on income and population originally provided the majority of WHO's income (Lee, 2009). However, because assessed contributions were essentially frozen in the early 1990s, the scales have tipped (S. K. Reddy et al., 2018). Voluntary contributions now account for up to 80 percent of the organization's budget (Kaiser Family Foundation, 2020). Furthermore, member states often fail to pay their assessed contributions on time or at all (Daugirdas & Burci, 2019). This leaves WHO increasingly dependent on unstable voluntary contributions, subject to the whims of donors and constrained in how it can spend even the money that it has (K. Reddy & Selvaraju, 1994). In addition, half of the top ten contributors to WHO are also nonstate actors (e.g., the Bill & Melinda Gates Foundation) (WHO, 2020e). Private funders lack the same level of democratic accountability and institutional durability as states (Marion, 2020). Further, extrabudgetary funds also provide disproportionate funding in certain areas and make it difficult for WHO to make long-term plans (Davies, 2010; Lee, 2014; Youde, 2015). Member states have recognized these financial problems and taken partial steps to shift budgetary control back to the WHA and the Secretariat, yet they have consistently rejected efforts to increase assessed contributions (Daugirdas & Burci, 2019). These funding difficulties are visible in WHO's struggle to raise emergency funds for its response to COVID-19.

WHO would benefit from greater power, autonomy, and funding to fulfill its mandate. Although these benefits would apply to any number of health concerns that the agency addresses, COVID-19 provides a powerful example of both the high expectations and historically rooted institutional constraints the agency faces in its work.

WHO Response to COVID-19

COVID-19 quickly evolved from an isolated set of "viral pneumonia" cases into a full-blown pandemic that overwhelmed health systems, brought countries to a halt, and pulled the global economy into a deep recession. As the leading global health agency, WHO has played a central role in alerting the world to the threat of and coordinating efforts to fight the disease. However, it also has become a target of criticism. Although sometimes deserving of—and learning and evolving from—such criticism, the body is also an easy target because of its status as an international organization that seems to have more capacity and freedom than it actually does. We can see these dynamics play out in at least three roles WHO has played in the COVID-19 response: gathering and reporting epidemiological data; issuing scientific and technical guidelines; and promoting development of, and equitable access to, diagnostics, therapeutics, and vaccines.

Sharing Epidemiological Data

A key piece of WHO's role is overcoming individual states' incentives to suppress damaging news of outbreaks and ensuring outbreak information is rapidly shared. On December 31, 2019, a statement about "viral pneumonia" by the Wuhan Municipal Health Commission and media reports of the outbreak were picked up by WHO office in China. This information was reported through various channels in accordance with the IHR and eventually verified by Chinese authorities. Other governments, including Taiwan's, inquired with WHO about similar reports they had received. By January 5, 2020, WHO had shared news about the outbreak on Twitter and through official channels, with the update that it was caused by a novel coronavirus coming shortly thereafter. On January 11, WHO tweeted that it had received the genetic sequence, with the first protocol for a diagnostic test published by WHO on January 13 (WHO, 2020a). WHO's actions were rapid, although it would later become clear that the disease had been circulating in China for some time. That country's authoritarian power structures played a role in delaying public reports, including downplaying human-to-human transmission until after international spread had occurred (Kavanagh, 2020). WHO had to engage in a series of high-stakes negotiations with China for greater information sharing and access for expert investigative teams, including access to Wuhan in late January and an international mission to China in mid-February, which resulted in important information about the mortality and transmission dynamics of the virus (WHO, 2020f).

Here WHO's limited power was on display. Because the IHR contain no enforcement mechanism, WHO had no real recourse if the Chinese government decided to stop sharing information or refused access to international experts. The option of publicly "shaming" the government as under SARS was a risky strategy with a more powerful China of 2020 and could lead to significant delay. WHO instead sought to stay on good terms with Chinese authorities, focusing on praise and private diplomacy. But although WHO arguably had few other cards to play, it may have overplayed its hand. Dr. Tedros' press conference upon his return from China strongly praised China's response, which included harsh lockdowns many believed were problematic (Kavanagh & Singh, 2020). This strong praise would later come to be used against the Director-General by those seeking to cast doubt on WHO's independence and who claimed he was too close to China.

Similarly, the question of human-to-human transmission would become a political flash point, with critics claiming a cover-up by China and pointing to an early WHO tweet on January 14, 2020, that "Preliminary investigations conducted by the Chinese authorities have found no clear evidence of human-to-human transmission" (WHO, 2020b). But that same day in a press conference, officials at WHO Geneva suggested it was possible there *was* human-to-human transmission, a reality confirmed by WHO's regional office on January 19, 2020, and an investigative trip to Wuhan by WHO officials on January 20 to 21, 2020 (WHO, 2020b). On January 30, the Director-General declared a PHEIC, WHO's highest level of alert. Although this followed the advice of an independent expert IHR Emergency Committee, some still claimed that it should have happened sooner (Pillinger, 2020a; WHO, 2020g). On March 11, 2020, the Director-General stated that COVID-19 was a pandemic; even though declaring an outbreak a "pandemic" is a colloquial term, with no formal or legal meaning (unlike the PHEIC declared in January), the statement would later provide fodder for those critical of WHO (WHO, 2020g).

Taken as a whole, though, WHO's efforts to push countries to share data rather than hide it have been successful. An online dashboard displays daily case counts for nearly all WHO member states (WHO, 2020j). In the first six months of the pandemic, WHO conducted press briefings at least three times a week, sharing data and scientific updates. Its success is perhaps best illustrated in the breach, as only two countries, Turkmenistan and North Korea, have at the time of this writing continued to claim they have no confirmed COVID-19 cases, despite evidence to the contrary. In mid-July 2020, a health advisory team from WHO was allowed to visit Turkmenistan and did not question the government's assertion publicly but urged health authorities to act "as if COVID-19 was circulating" (Auyezov & Gurt, 2020).

Issuing Scientific Guidelines

A second important part of WHO's COVID-19 response has been gathering and aggregating scientific information and issuing guidance to governments and the public about how to respond. One of the first and highest-profile pieces of guidance advised countries not to enact travel restrictions or bans—first from China and then from other parts of the world (WHO, 2020i). This is rooted in the IHR's goal of moving away from border restrictions and quarantines that were highly disruptive to global trade. Restricting travel from countries experiencing disease outbreaks has not proved effective in stopping disease, with porous borders and significant opportunity costs (Pillinger, 2020b). They also undermine movement of goods and people needed to fight disease. WHO also seeks to avoid travel restrictions because they give countries incentive to hide outbreaks. In this case, however, many countries ignored WHO's advice, racing to close borders to China. Early reports suggest that countries that had not closed their borders had done as well or better in preventing the spread of COVID-19 than countries that had, such as the United States and Italy (Kiernan et al., 2020). This recommendation, however, has opened WHO to criticism—most pointedly by US President Donald Trump, who said WHO "actually criticized and disagreed with my travel ban at the time I did it. And they were wrong" (Hjelmgaard, 2020).

WHO has issued a vast range of other scientific pronouncements, guidance, and advice, with more than one hundred different documents on the SARS-CoV-2 virus, case identification, personal protective equipment, contact tracing, health worker protection, community response, and much more. It has published so much that it had to publish a guide to its guidance (WHO, 2020l). It is notable that most of this work was well received and quickly taken up around the world. However, a few critical issues have generated significant attention and controversy, including WHO's response on lockdowns, masks, and whether COVID-19 is "airborne."

WHO for many months advised against widespread mask mandates, worrying that masks would "create a false sense of security, with neglect of other essential measures" and "take masks away from those in health care who need them most" (WHO, 2020d). It was only on June 5, 2020, several months into the pandemic, that WHO recommended the widespread use of masks (WHO, 2020h). However, by that point, WHO was behind the curve. More than one hundred countries had already adopted some form of nationwide mask-wearing mandates before WHO updated its guidelines, and 95 percent of countries were already recommending mask usage in public in at least some cases (Community Initiatives, 2020). And WHO's initial endorsement of masks was lukewarm, noting that lack of "high-quality" scientific evidence to support their use and numerous disadvantages of wearing them, including "potential discomfort" and "difficulty with communicating clearly" (Mandavilli, 2020). Critics have said that mandating masks was long overdue as a simple, inexpensive, and effective measure, and they fault WHO delay.

Relatedly, WHO had a long and complicated public messaging challenge around whether COVID-19 was technically airborne (i.e., spread through small, aerosolized droplets that can float through the air, rather than just through larger droplets that quickly fall to the ground). The agency acknowledged the possibility of airborne spread after a group of 237 international experts and scientists published a commentary in *Clinical Infectious Diseases* urging them to do so (Lewis, 2020; Morawska & Milton, 2020). As with masks, WHO has also remained adamant in emphasizing the uncertainty of scientific evidence and in recommending mitigation strategies through other means (Mandavilli, 2020).

During COVID-19, much of the criticism has centered on WHO moving too slowly in a rapidly evolving pandemic. But it is worth remembering that in the past, such as during the H1N1 pandemic, the criticism has gone in the other direction. Governments complained of costly and disruptive efforts necessary to implement WHO recommendations. Rapid recommendations can also create backlash against the international agency if the measures are later proven to be unnecessary, as during H1N1. Regardless, during COVID-19 controversies have occurred amid a fast-moving scientific context, unfolding in real time in the glare of media headlines. WHO's position as global technical leader has taken a hit from controversies that may have gone unnoticed in other contexts.

Access to Diagnostics, Therapeutics, and Vaccines

A third major part of WHO's response has been seeking to expand access to diagnostics, therapies, and future vaccines worldwide—where WHO has innovated, building new strategies in the face of new threats and an absence of other authoritative actors. WHO launched the Access to COVID-19 Tools (ACT) Accelerator in April 2020—with words of strong commitment from heads of state, particularly from Europe, Africa, Latin America, and the Caribbean. Notably missing from this nominally global effort were the United States and Russia, who declined to participate in any form, and China, who participated only at a very low level. This initiative aims to facilitate coordination between governments, scientists, businesses, civil society, philanthropists, and global health organizations to expedite the development and production of COVID-19 tests, treatments, and vaccines, and to provide equitable access. There is a particular emphasis on developing an allocation strategy to ensure that LMICs receive an equitable and accelerated delivery of vaccine doses, treatments, and other commodities, with the logic that no one is safe in a pandemic until everyone is safe (WHO, 2020c).

The fundamental challenge, however, is that global solidarity has been hard to find, as ethical distribution would require powerful states to share access to limited supplies even as their populations clamor for greater access. Although the ACT Accelerator was launched in April 2020, with fanfare by heads of state, it initially struggled to secure funding: as of late September, it had raised only $4 billion of the needed $38 billion, and $15 billion of this shortfall was said to be urgent (WHO, 2020k). But despite WHO's efforts to coordinate procurement, action has been fragmented and duplicative. For example, the African Union is seeking its own pooled procurement. Multiple different technology pools emerged, but with little commitment from leading companies. Particularly on vaccines, WHO has struggled to prevent the development of "vaccine nationalism" (i.e., competition among countries to secure limited stocks of vaccine for their own populations, especially by high-income countries that can afford to place massive preorders for multiple vaccines, which *de facto* limits access for other countries). The Trump administration's initiative to accelerate vaccine, treatment, and diagnostics development for COVID-19, Operation Warp Speed, recently brought about the largest contract to date with Sanofi and GlaxoSmithKline at $2.1 billion (Johnson, 2020). In addition, the European Commission announced an EU vaccines strategy on June 17, 2020, that prioritizes securing the production of vaccines in the European Union and sufficient supplies for its own member states over that of others

(European Commission, 2020), even though key EU governments have already committed to supporting the COVAX facility of the ACT Accelerator. Large advance purchases by European governments raise the possibility that these governments will wind up essentially negotiating against COVAX or restricting the vaccine doses that are actually available for it to purchase, undercutting WHO's coordinated strategy (Paun, 2020; Ren, 2020).

Political Backlash during COVID-19

Within months of the COVID-19 outbreak, finger pointing began, and WHO was in for its share of criticism. As in past international challenges, this has involved a normal stream in independent evaluations—including a major review agreed upon at the WHA and headed by former heads of state Ellen Johnson Sirleaf and Helen Clark, former prime minister of New Zealand. But it has also included a highly charged irregular political stream as politicians in the United States, Brazil, Taiwan, and other nations have publicly attacked WHO and its Director-General, accusing it of failures and of too close of a relationship with China. Meanwhile African leaders rallied to the defense of the first African head of WHO (Shaban, 2020). This once-in-a-century pandemic is testing the politics of WHO in ways it has never been tested before.

Political Explanations for WHO's COVID-19 Response

Born out of a post-World War II era of internationalism and multilateralism, WHO was meant to embody the principles of solidarity and transparency in keeping with the UN's founding ideals. Concerns over how to combat infectious disease epidemics from cholera, typhus, smallpox, and others have been a driving force behind international cooperation for centuries. And yet, the COVID-19 pandemic appears to have accelerated a trend away from global cooperation, leaving WHO in a precarious position.

WHO's political history, its structure, and its leadership help explain why WHO has taken on so much, where it has succeeded, and why it has been unable to meet some of the high expectations of the organization. Chorev's (2012) assertion that WHO's Secretariat creates space and initiative through strategic adaptation remains true, but rather than broad ideological swings, we increasingly see specific and directly opposing demands that are harder to reconcile or elide.

When it comes to information sharing, WHO has succeeded where it has *because* of its political nature rather than in spite of it, and it has failed where member states have restricted its capacity. For example, internal emails from January 2020 reveal that WHO officials were deeply frustrated by China's failure to share information in a timely manner. As discussed, their generally positive and praising tone toward China was a deliberate, strategic attempt to coax the Chinese government into sharing vital epidemiological data and allow international expert investigators into the country (Associated Press, 2020). The debate will rage on over whether this was successful (China did share epidemic data and the genome sequence that enabled testing in weeks) or whether the Director-General should have been more publicly critical. (Lockdowns mimicked elsewhere have been highly problematic, and many have criticized Chinese data as incomplete and misleading.) But, regardless of position, WHO's struggle is clear—it has no coercive power at its disposal. States have, in the IHR, required WHO to consult with a member state before sharing data it gathers for that country and provided no sanction for states who do not comply with their IHR obligations to report. In that context, WHO has only diplomacy—particularly when dealing with a state such as China, a permanent security council member and the second largest economy in the world. It is notable that all the data that modelers used early in the epidemic came through WHO's access to China; indeed, even the US government relied on its participation in WHO mission to get direct access to Wuhan. WHO, given financial constraints, has only so much capacity and must rely on member states and others located within a given country for much of the reporting and surveillance work.

Looking beyond China, though, we see many governments sharing information that may surprise us: WHO was successful in receiving data from countries in Africa, Latin America, and the Middle East that have been reluctant to do so in other settings. This is at least in part because states feel ownership over the organization and particularly because the regional offices are staffed by their own nationals, fostering greater trust and communication. A Geneva-based organization of technocrats alone would be unlikely to have received this level of cooperation. In this context many criticisms are unfair but also expected. On guidance, the decline, and then sudden rise, of WHO's influence in high-income countries under COVID-19 explains many of the challenges. It is of little surprise that countries ignored WHO advice on border closures as their populations demanded it. Forty-seven countries did the same during the 2009 H1N1 pandemic, and many did at the start of the COVID-19 pandemic as well (Worsnop, 2017, 2019).

But other realities are less expected. As described in the beginning of the chapter, high-income countries pulled away from WHO as LMICs gained more power, with even more of its work focusing on LMICs. WHO has felt a strong burden to ensure its recommendations are relevant to its core LMIC audience, having experienced backlash from good ideas that are infeasible in low-resource settings. There would also be political-optical, and arguably ethical, challenges involved if WHO issued different sets of guidance for different resource contexts. Meanwhile, high-income countries tend to worry less if WHO's recommendations are geared toward establishing a globally applicable baseline, because they can supplement those recommendations with guidance from other sources. For example, the US Centers for Disease Control and Prevention (CDC) generally issues its own guidelines (often developed through close working consultation with WHO), which are looked to by other wealthy countries around the world. However, under COVID-19 the United States has floundered, and the CDC has been sidelined. This has had the effect of *increasing* the attention on WHO, including from higher-income countries.

Much of what WHO has said and shared has been used widely in higher-income countries and LMICs alike—with many countries looking to the organization's expertise to step up COVID-19 testing (WHO polymerase chain reaction [PCR] protocol is particularly valuable), set standards for health workers, and shut down transmission. But when it came to both masks and airborne transmission, WHO has been accused of lagging far behind (Tufekci, 2020). Part of what delayed WHO, though, was exactly this focus on LMICs—as officials worried over limited PPE supplies in many countries and the implications of stating the virus was airborne in contexts where investments in ventilation would come at the cost of other interventions. There have been struggles across the regionalized structure to reach consensus and strong pushback from some to moving too quickly. In other circumstances, this slower, more conservative approach is what states have demanded. However, as higher-income countries' experts looked to WHO, with its staff a fraction of the size of the US CDC's, speed and answers for high-resource settings instead were demanded.

WHO's rise reflects a century of evolution in global health governance that sought to facilitate cooperation among states on health concerns that extend beyond national borders. However, the rise of aggressively nationalist rhetoric and priorities in some countries has tipped the scale back toward Westphalian governance, a focus on state sovereignty, and a resistance to interference in domestic affairs. This shift has created significant hurdles for the pursuit of global public health, including during the COVID-19 pandemic, where it has resulted in several powerful governments refusing to cooperate with WHO or even challenging its recommendations and authority outright even as—and perhaps because—those governments have performed poorly (Eckermann, 2017; Lasco, 2020; Wilson et al., 2020; Żuk & Żuk, 2020). In this context, massive criticism of WHO—for being too slow, for offering recommendations political leaders dislike, for failing to curb the actions of China—are driven largely by domestic political considerations. But that does not diminish the existential threat to the organization as the United States announced its withdrawal and Brazil, which has long been a powerful supporter of WHO, threatened the same.

Meanwhile, work under the ACT Accelerator has been an innovative response to the crisis, even in a context in which WHO has insufficient political and convening power. It has fundamentally been tasked by member states with solving a massive problem of collective action and global trade as it seeks to rapidly advance science and equitably distribute it. Powerful countries have every incentive to push their own scientists to achieve the breakthrough and backstop that with advanced orders in the market economy for as much of a vaccine or other technology as they can afford. The gambit with the ACT Accelerator and its various pillars has been that there is enough uncertainty about which vaccines will succeed that states can be brought to the table to cooperate through fear of losing out completely if they do not, as well as by the argument vaccinating high-risk people around the world will bring a swifter end to the pandemic. But WHO's rallying calls for solidarity, rational arguments about risk distribution, and appeals to science have so far been insufficient to fully overcome the powerful pull of vaccine nationalism. WHO also lacks a sufficient pool of funding from which to work as a base: its Contingency Fund for Emergencies has been chronically depleted (most recently by the Ebola outbreak in the Democratic Republic of the Congo) and most of the rest of its funding is tied to other functions. Member states did pledge $8 billion, although the majority has not yet been delivered (Sulcas, 2020). Meanwhile an online concert, "One World: Together at Home," planned by Lady Gaga and the NGO Global Citizen raised one of the larger contributions at $128 million, although not exclusively for WHO (Global Citizen, 2020).

It is too early to fully assess which WHO efforts will work. But it is important to remember again that WHO has no stick to match its carrot. The international organizations that *do* have sticks—the UN Security Council, the World Trade Organization—have been notably avoided by member states as venues for negotiation. The international order in which WHO was established and the underlying shared values that it embodies have been waning as the forces of nationalism and populism have strengthened in recent years. In the postwar era, there was a rise in globalization and global governance as the dominance of state-centric relations shifted toward cooperation between states, international organizations, and non-state actors. In this context, WHO became a driver of global health governance, with an emphasis on sharing medical and epidemiological data and research across borders, monitoring of public health by global networks, and emphasizing collective public health interests. But in a context in which these efforts are challenged, so too will WHO's efforts to ensure equitable access.

Finally, WHO's response to COVID-19 cannot be explained without reference to the increasing size and diversity of other global health actors with which WHO must now compete—for funds, legitimacy, and the limited political attention of states. For example, the COVAX facility, the ACT arm focused on global procurement of a vaccine, is anchored by two public-private partnerships—Gavi and the Coalition for Epidemic Preparedness Innovations (CEPI). Neither of these organizations has the reach nor legitimacy of WHO, but neither do they have the baggage that comes from being governed by a parliament of more than 190 member states. As WHO frames its mission, it has at times taken on a far larger portfolio than its capacity allows in an effort to ensure its mandate and its existing funding is not further diminished in a competitive space.

Looking Forward

On July 6, 2020, the Trump administration officially notified UN Secretary-General António Guterres of its intention to withdraw from WHO membership as the political maneuvering behind the scenes of WHO broke into public. Although the move was criticized as neither legal nor advisable (Gostin et al.,

2020; Kavanagh & Pillinger, 2020), it represented an existential threat to WHO. Outside the period covered in this book, Joe Biden was elected US president and pledged to halt the withdrawal. The WHO, however, still faces an uncertain political future. As much as anything, the maelstrom around the WHO is a symptom of a geopolitical realignment toward a multipolar world. WHO has been caught up in a high-politics confrontation between the United States and China, with the EU seeking a path between and the African Union seeking to defend the first-ever African Director-General. This comes as WHO seeks to grapple with a pandemic in which its structure, its political foundations, and its split personality as both technical-scientific agency and venue of international relations have left the organization open to criticism. Amid all of this, WHO's successes can be underappreciated. As the UN Security Council all but closed up shop, WHO has forged ahead in bringing states together in negotiation. As the US CDC has been sidelined at home, WHO has managed to rapidly build a credible base of science from which policymakers can act (even if it cannot force them to do so).

The organization often leads with its identity as a scientific and humanitarian agency, yet it is also a creature of international politics, an international organization governed and financed by, and thus beholden to, member states. Its historical loss of influence in high-income countries and focus on LMICs have been upended by a global spotlight during COVID-19, as many of the countries believed most capable have stumbled badly in their response. Yet its structure provides WHO far less capacity than it would need to meet the expectations of its member states. Reversing this requires addressing the balkanized structure of regional offices, dramatically expanding assessed contributions to ensure sufficient resources, and rewriting the IHRs to give WHO new powers to uncover information that member states refuse to share and sanction states that do not meet their international obligations. As the pandemic dissipates, there will be inevitable reviews and calls for reform. Whether member states are willing to make the big-picture changes needed to give WHO what it needs is yet unclear.

References

Associated Press. (2020, June 2). *China delayed releasing coronavirus info, frustrating WHO.* AP News. https://apnews.com/3c061794970661042b18d5aeaaed9fae

Auyezov, O., & Gurt, M. (2020, July 15). *WHO urges Turkmenistan to take steps "as if COVID-19 was circulating."* Reuters. https://www.reuters.com/article/us-health-coronavirus-turkmenistan-idUSKCN24G276

Burci, G. L. (2018). Health and infectious disease. In T. G. Weiss & S. Daws (Eds.), *The Oxford handbook on the United Nations.* Oxford University Press.

Chorev, N. (2012). *The World Health Organization between north and south.* Cornell University Press.

Clift, C. (2014). *What's the World Health Organization for?* Chatham House.

Community Initiatives. (2020). *What countries require or recommend masks in public?* https://masks4all.co/what-countries-require-masks-in-public/

Cueto, M., Brown, T. M., & Fee, E. (2019). *The World Health Organization: A history.* Cambridge University Press.

Daugirdas, K., & Burci, G. L. (2019). *Financing the World Health Organization: What lessons for multilateralism?* SSRN Scholarly Paper ID 3434603. Social Science Research Network. https://papers.ssrn.com/abstract=3434603

Davies, S. (2010). *Global politics of health.* Polity.

Eckermann, E. (2017). Global health promotion in the era of "galloping populism." *Health Promotion International, 32*(3), 415–418. https://doi.org/10.1093/heapro/dax030

European Commission. (2020, June 17). *Coronavirus: Commission unveils EU vaccines strategy.* https://ec.europa.eu/commission/presscorner/detail/en/ip_20_1103

Global Citizen. (2020, April 19). *One world: Together at home' raised almost $128 million in response to the COVID-19 crisis.* https://www.globalcitizen.org/en/content/one-world-together-at-home-impact/

Gostin, L. O., Hongju Koh, H., Williams, M., Hamburg, M. A., Benjamin, G., Foege, W. G., Davidson, P., Bradley, E. H., Barry, M., Koplan, J. P., Roses Periago, M. F., El Sadr, W., Kurth, A., Vermund, S. H., & Kavanagh, M. M. (2020). US withdrawal from WHO is unlawful and threatens global and US health and security. *The Lancet, 396*(10247), 293–295.

Gostin, L. O., Tomori, O., Wibulpolprasert, S., Jha, A. K., Frenk, J., Phumaphi, J., Piot, P., Stocking, B., Dzau, V. J., & Leung, G. M. (2016). Toward a common secure future: Four global commissions in the wake of Ebola. *PLoS Medicine, 13*(5), e1002042.

Graham, E. R. (2013, May). International organizations as collective agents: Fragmentation and the limits of principal control at the World Health Organization. *European Journal of International Relations.* http://journals.sagepub.com/doi/10.1177/1354066113476116

Hanrieder, T. (2015). The path-dependent design of international organizations: Federalism in the World Health Organization. *European Journal of International Relations, 21*(1), 215–239. https://doi.org/10.1177/1354066114530011

Heymann, D. L., Mackenzie, J. S., & Peiris, M. (2013). SARS legacy: Outbreak reporting is expected and respected. *The Lancet, 381*(9869), 779–781.

Hjelmgaard, K. (2020, April 11). Fact check: President Donald Trump vs. the World Health Organization. *USA TODAY.* https://www.usatoday.com/story/news/factcheck/2020/04/11/coronavirus-fact-check-donald-trump-vs-world-health-organization/5128799002/

Hoffman, S. J., & Røttingen, J-A. (2014). Split WHO in two: Strengthening political decision-making and securing independent scientific advice. *Public Health, 128*(2), 188–194.

Jamison, D. T., Frenk, J., & Knaul, F. (1998). International collective action in health: Objectives, functions, and rationale. *The Lancet, 351*(9101), 514–517.

Johnson, C. Y. (2020, July 31). European drugmakers Sanofi and GSK strike $2.1 billion deal with U.S. for a coronavirus vaccine. *Washington Post.* https://www.washingtonpost.com/health/2020/07/31/coronavirus-vaccine-deal-sanofi-gsk/

Kaiser Family Foundation. (2020, April 16). *The U.S. Government and the World Health Organization.* https://www.kff.org/coronavirus-covid-19/fact-sheet/the-u-s-government-and-the-world-health-organization/

Kamradt-Scott, A. (2016). WHO's to blame? The World Health Organization and the 2014 Ebola outbreak in West Africa. *Third World Quarterly, 37*(3), 401–418.

Kavanagh, M. M. (2020). Authoritarianism, outbreaks, and information politics. *The Lancet Public Health*. https://www.doi.org/10/ggpxrb

Kavanagh, M. M., & Pillinger, M. (2020, July 7). Leaving the WHO will hurt Americans' health. *Foreign Policy*. https://foreignpolicy.com/2020/07/07/trump-leave-who-world-health-organization-american-health/

Kavanagh, M. M., & Singh, R. (2020). Democracy, capacity, and coercion in pandemic response—COVID 19 in comparative political perspective. *Journal of Health Politics, Policy and Law, 45*(6), 997–1012.

Kiernan, S., DeVita, M., & Bollyky, T, J. (2020, April). Tracking coronavirus in countries with and without travel bans. *Think Global Health*. https://www.thinkglobalhealth.org/article/tracking-coronavirus-countries-and-without-travel-bans

Lasco, G. (2020). Medical populism and the COVID-19 pandemic. *Global Public Health, 15*(10), 1417–1429. https://doi.org/10.1080/17441692.2020.1807581

Lee, K. (2009). *World Health Organization*. Routledge.

Lee, K. (2014). World Health Organization. In *Handbook of governance and security*. Edward Elgar Publishing.

Lewis, D. (2020). Mounting evidence suggests coronavirus is airborne—but health advice has not caught up. *Nature 583*(7817), 510–513. https://doi.org/10.1038/d41586-020-02058-1

Mandavilli, A. (2020, June 5). W.H.O. finally endorses masks to prevent coronavirus transmission. *The New York Times*. https://www.nytimes.com/2020/06/05/health/coronavirus-masks-who.html

Marion, S. (2020, May 20). Withdrawing from the WHO would hurt global security—and global respect for the U.S. *The Washington Post*. https://www.washingtonpost.com/politics/2020/05/20/withdrawing-who-would-hurt-global-security-global-respect-us/

Moon, S., Leigh, J., Woskie, L., Checchi, F., Dzau, V., Fallah, M., Fitzgerald, G., Garrett, K., Gostin, L., & Heymann, D. L. (2017). Post-Ebola reforms: Ample analysis, inadequate action. *BMJ, 356*, j280.

Morawska, L., & Milton, D, K. (2020, July). It is time to address airborne transmission of covid-19. *Clinical infectious diseases: An official publication of the Infectious Diseases Society of America*. https://doi.org/10.1093/cid/ciaa939

Paun, C. (2020, August 7). *Europe has yet to live up to its Covid-19 promises*. Politico. https://www.politico.com/news/2020/08/07/europe-has-lots-of-covid-talk-but-few-results-392493

Pillinger, M. (2020a, January 26). Analysis: The WHO held off on declaring the Wuhan coronavirus a global health emergency. Here's why. *The Washington Post*. https://www.washingtonpost.com/politics/2020/01/26/who-held-off-declaring-wuhan-coronavirus-global-health-emergency-heres-why/

Pillinger, M. (2020b, February). Virus travel restrictions don't work. *Foreign Policy*. https://foreignpolicy.com/2020/02/23/virus-travel-bans-are-inevitable-but-ineffective/

Ravi, S. J., Snyder, M. R., & Rivers, C. (2019). Review of international efforts to strengthen the global outbreak response system since the 2014–16 West Africa Ebola Epidemic. *Health Policy and Planning, 34*(1), 47–54.

Reddy, K. N., & Selvaraju, V. (1994.) *Health expenditure by government in India 1974–5 to 1992–92*. National Institute of Public Finance & Policy.

Reddy, S. K., Mazhar, S., & Lencucha, R. (2018). The financial sustainability of the world health organization and the political economy of global health governance: A review of funding proposals. *Globalization and Health, 14*(1), 119. https://doi.org/10.1186/s12992-018-0436-8

Ren, G. (2020, August 14). Scramble to preorder COVID-19 vaccines may leave poorer countries behind. *Health Policy Watch.* https://healthpolicy-watch.news/scramble-to-preorder-covid-19-vaccines-may-leave-poorer-countries-behind-threatening-global-response/

Retreat, P. (1996). *Enhancing the performance of international health institutions.* The Rockefeller Foundation. Social Science Research Council, Harvard School of Public Health.

Ruger, J. P., & Yach, D. (2009). The global role of the World Health Organization. *Global Health Governance: The Scholarly Journal for the New Health Security Paradigm, 2*(2), 1–11.

Sabbagh, D., & Stewart, H. (2020, July 21). Mike Pompeo attacks WHO in private meeting during UK visit. *The Guardian.* http://www.theguardian.com/world/2020/jul/21/mike-pompeo-attacks-who-in-private-meeting-during-uk-visit

Shaban, A. R. A. (2020, April 9). African leaders trump Trump for attack on WHO, back Ethiopia's Tedros. *Associated Press.* https://www.africanews.com/2020/04/09/african-leaders-trump-trump-for-attack-on-who-back-ethiopia-s-tedros/

Siddiqi, J. (1995). *World health and world politics: The World Health Organization and the UN system.* University of South Carolina Press.

Sulcas, A. (2020, May 7). *Solidarity, solidarity, solidarity: The ACT Accelerator, the $8 billion, and the Global Fund.* IHP. https://www.internationalhealthpolicies.org/featured-article/solidarity-solidarity-solidarity-the-act-accelerator-the-8-billion-and-the-global-fund/

Tufekci, Z. (2020, April 16). Why the World Health Organization failed. *The Atlantic.* https://www.theatlantic.com/health/archive/2020/04/why-world-health-organization-failed/610063/

Wenham, C. (2017). What we have learnt about the World Health Organization from the Ebola outbreak. *Philosophical Transactions of the Royal Society B: Biological Sciences, 372*(1721), 20160307.

Wilson, K., Halabi, S., & Gostin, L. O. (2020). The International Health Regulations (2005), the threat of populism and the COVID-19 pandemic. *Globalization and Health, 16*(1), 70. https://doi.org/10.1186/s12992-020-00600-4

World Health Organization. (1946). *WHO constitution.* https://www.who.int/governance/eb/who_constitution_en.pdf

World Health Organization. (2019). *Contributors.* http://open.who.int/2018-19/contributors/contributor

World Health Organization. [@WHO]. (2020a, January 11). BREAKING: WHO has received the genetic sequences for the novel #coronavirus (2019-NCoV) from the Chinese authorities [Tweet]. *Twitter.* https://twitter.com/WHO/status/1216108498188230657

World Health Organization. [@WHO]. (2020b, January 14). Preliminary investigations conducted by the Chinese authorities have found no clear evidence of human-to-human transmission of the novel #coronavirus [Tweet]. *Twitter.* https://twitter.com/WHO/status/1217043229427761152

World Health Organization. (2020c, June 26). *ACT-Accelerator update.* https://www.who.int/news-room/detail/26-06-2020-act-accelerator-update

World Health Organization. (2020d). *Advice on the use of masks in the context of COVID-19.* https://apps.who.int/iris/handle/10665/331693

World Health Organization. (2020e, May 29). *How WHO is funded.* https://www.who.int/about/planning-finance-and-accountability/how-who-is-funded

World Health Organization. (2020f, January 22). *Mission summary: WHO field visit to Wuhan, China 20–21 January 2020.* https://www.who.int/china/news/detail/22-01-2020-field-visit-wuhan-china-jan-2020

World Health Organization. (2020g). *Of WHO's response to COVID-19.* https://www.who.int/news-room/detail/29-06-2020-covidtimeline

World Health Organization. (2020h). *Timeline: WHO's COVID-19 response.* https://www.who.int/emergencies/diseases/novel-coronavirus-2019/interactive-timeline

World Health Organization. (2020i, January 10). *WHO advice for international travel and trade in relation to the outbreak of pneumonia caused by a new coronavirus in China.* https://www.who.int/news-room/articles-detail/who-advice-for-international-travel-and-trade-in-relation-to-the-outbreak-of-pneumonia-caused-by-a-new-coronavirus-in-china

World Health Organization. (2020j). *WHO coronavirus disease (COVID-19) dashboard.* https://covid19.who.int

World Health Organization. (2020k). *UN welcomes nearly $1 billion in recent pledges—to bolster access to lifesaving tests, treatments and vaccines to end COVID-19.* https://www.who.int/news/item/30-09-2020-un-welcomes-nearly-1-billion-in-recent-pledges-to-bolster-access-to-lifesaving-tests-treatments-and-vaccines-to-end-covid-19

World Health Organization. (2020l, July 17). *A guide to WHO's guidance on COVID-19.* https://www.who.int/news-room/feature-stories/detail/a-guide-to-who-s-guidance

Worsnop, C. Z. (2017). Domestic politics and the WHO's International Health Regulations: explaining the use of trade and travel barriers during disease outbreaks. *The Review of International Organizations, 12*(3), 365–395. https://doi.org/10.1007/s11558-016-9260-1

Worsnop, C. Z. (2019). Concealing disease: Trade and travel barriers and the timeliness of outbreak reporting. *International Studies Perspectives, 20*(4), 344–372. https://doi.org/10.1093/isp/ekz005

Youde, J. (2015). MERS and global health governance. *International Journal, 70*(1), 119–136. https://doi.org/10.1177/0020702014562594

Youde, J. (2016, December 27). The Rashomonization of the World Health Organization. *Duck of Minerva.* https://duckofminerva.com/2016/12/the-rashomon-ization-of-the-world-health-organization.html

Youde, J. (2018). *Global health governance in international society.* Oxford University Press.

Żuk, P., & Żuk, P. (2020.) Right-wing populism in Poland and anti-vaccine myths on YouTube: Political and cultural threats to public health. *Global Public Health, 15*(6), 790–804. https://doi.org/10.1080/17441692.2020.1718733

3 STATE RESPONSES TO THE COVID-19 PANDEMIC

Governance, Surveillance, Coercion, and Social Policy

Holly Jarman

Looking for an Exit

The coronavirus pandemic has systematically challenged how states govern, exposing the weaknesses in every political system. In the first months of what became the COVID-19 pandemic, there were no effective vaccinations or treatments for the virus. Medical professionals knew little about how to treat the disease and were forced to settle for methods that supported patients while hoping that their bodies would recover.

Without medical means of addressing the pandemic, states had to rely on measures designed to prevent the spread of the disease. The first reaction of many countries was to close their borders in the hope that COVID-19 would not spread to their shores. But in many cases, these restrictions were too little, too late. As they became aware of the extent to which the coronavirus was already circulating among their population, more and more countries decided to enter some form of "lockdown," essentially shutting down aspects of society deemed to be non-essential. For many states, lockdown involved significant non-pharmaceutical interventions (NPIs) in public and private life: quarantine; physical distancing requirements; bans on large gatherings; stay-at-home orders; closures of schools, businesses, and public transport; masking requirements; and other measures. When effectively implemented, these public health measures controlled the spread of the virus and so reduced its death toll. But they also came with significant economic costs and political implications (Jarman, 2020c; Jarman et al., 2020a, 2020b, 2020d, 2020e, 2020f).

In the first half of 2020, NPIs put a huge strain on states, challenging decision-making and legitimating structures, infrastructure and policy programs, government finances, workforce, communications, and more. Policy-makers found themselves having to quickly invent and implement new policies and figure out how to communicate those decisions to the public. Governments were faced with huge logistical problems, as they struggled to mobilize people and resources around testing, contact tracing, isolation, and treatment; procure specialized equipment and medicines; and support vaccine development. Almost all countries used their authority to place tough restrictions on the behavior of individuals and businesses, and some states decided to expand health and social policies to address the fallout from closing down society (Jarman, 2020b, Jarman et al., 2020c).

The success or failure of lockdown interventions in controlling the spread and impact of COVID-19 was not reliant upon resources alone, but contingent on politics. Rich countries with seemingly adequate resources to tackle the pandemic struggled to act because of high partisanship and a lack of public trust in government (see chapters 12 and 26). Societies with an unequal distribution of power and wealth saw that unequal distribution replicated in the impact of COVID-19. And international organizations designed to coordinate actions among states struggled as countries began to turn inward and compete against each other for resources.

Despite these political challenges, some countries were initially successful in what became known as "flattening the curve," controlling the spread of the virus to such an extent that predicted peaks of cases and deaths were less severe and did not overwhelm their health systems. In these countries, public health measures successfully reduced transmission to a relatively low level, such that commentators and politicians began talking about "exit strategies," ways to transition out of lockdown and back to something like normal life (Jarman et al., 2020c). It slowly became clear, however, that an easy exit from strict pandemic measures was not an option. Jurisdictions that lifted lockdown measures too soon saw a resurgence in cases and deaths. Rather than being an acute crisis, COVID-19 was a crisis with no identified end point, likely requiring months and possibly years of sustained government action to address.

This chapter looks at the political consequences of governing during a sustained global crisis, synthesizing published work from researchers who are contributors to the HMP Governance Lab at the University of Michigan. We are certainly not experts in every country nor region of the world. Furthermore, much of our research focuses on high-income countries, particularly in Europe and North America. The following analysis is therefore biased toward those countries and should be read with that in mind. Nevertheless, hopefully the discussion is useful in identifying global political trends and in understanding how countries' responses to COVID-19 may vary and how they are the same.

The following section gives an overview of the functions and capacities of the state involved in tackling the crisis: governance, surveillance, coercion, and social policy. Using country examples, I explore the major political challenges faced by governments across those four categories. The conclusions are clear. On one hand, many states have responded to the pandemic by creating and enforcing what are often very strong public health measures, relatively quickly and in some cases with limited resources. These initial lockdowns were often successful, although many states perhaps exited lockdown too soon and saw a resurgence in cases. The ways in which lockdowns were achieved, however, and the prospects of entering lockdown again, raise questions for the future of democratic governance.

Four Capacities of the State: Governance, Surveillance, Coercion, and Social Policy

Managing COVID-19 as an ongoing crisis with significant consequences for human life, the economy and society tests every aspect of a country's political system, but particularly its capacity to respond to a systemic, multivalent threat. Understanding state responses to COVID-19, therefore, can tell us something about the nature of democratic and nondemocratic political systems, as well as shed light on how they may change in the wake of a disruptive, punctuating event such as the pandemic.

In particular, state responses to managing COVID-19 in the first half of 2020 can be understood with reference to four types of state capacity: governance, surveillance, coercion, and social policy capacity. Across each of these categories, politicians have used their authority and resources to manage the pandemic, sometimes with the goal of saving lives, sometimes with the goal of saving their own political careers, and often both.

Governance

The first capacity of the state relevant to its COVID-19 response is governance. Governance is the process of making and implementing decisions that affect a whole society (Greer et al., 2015, 2019; Jarman, 2020a). It is important because of our expectations that the state should be the first line of defense in so many areas pertinent to the pandemic (Jarman & Greer, 2020). We expect that governments dealing with the pandemic should deal with (sometimes conflicting) objectives that include protecting lives, maintaining peace, borders and the rule of law, ensuring economic stability and stepping in to be the lender of last resort or the provider of welfare and health care.

Politicians in the executive branch, in particular, are expected to provide leadership for the whole state and whole of society, and the signals they send, alliances they form, and decisions they take have a huge impact on the course of the pandemic. Although some leaders attempted to unify their populations in support of lockdown measures, others played down or denied the impact of COVID-19 (Falkenbach, 2020; Falkenbach & Greer, 2020). Because of the importance of individual behavior on the spread of the disease, this likely had an impact on the severity of the outbreak in many states.

The pandemic challenges a state's ability to coordinate action both horizontally and vertically. Horizontally, lockdown measures are a test of a government's ability to coordinate activities across different functions. Putting public health measures in place often requires cross-sectoral decision-making and mobilization of resources, such as coordination between public health, education, and transportation functions in the case of closing and reopening schools. In some states, competing views from health and economic ministries were apparent in COVID-19 responses, resulting in some cases in relaxing lockdown restrictions too quickly and a subsequent increase in the number of COVID-19 cases.

Vertically, the pandemic posed challenges to federalism and devolved government structures. The coronavirus does not respect human-made political borders, making coordination across jurisdictions an important part of pandemic response. Even in countries where subnational governments normally have a lot of autonomy, subnational governments still rely on the central government for a number of vital functions essential to pandemic response, such as finance, or procuring needed equipment and medicines. In countries where subnational governments were left without significant central direction or were starved of needed resources, a patchwork of outcomes is visible. Some countries chose to centralize previously decentralized government functions, particularly in terms of public health and health systems, where they used central government authority to do things like close down large parts of the health system to make room for emergency capacity (Greer et al., 2020a; Greer et al., 2020c). It remains to be seen whether an extended period of central control over these functions will have an ongoing impact on the vertical distribution of power within certain countries.

Central control comes with risks. Many concerns around governance during the pandemic stem from the suspension of routine procedures and rules during a crisis and the fear that governments will not want to give up their "emergency" powers. Because the pandemic is a long-term crisis likely to last a significant period of time, many commentators have raised concerns that governments will permanently become less transparent or accountable. The veil of "crisis" allows the state to make decisions without adequately communicating to the public the reasons for the decisions or the evidence base (if any) that informed them. With fluid governing structures such as ad hoc advisory committees or "expert groups" (that may not be full of experts), it becomes difficult for the public to understand how a decision was made, and easier for governments to conceal decisions that were made for reasons of political expediency. In these circumstances, stakeholder consultation may be ignored or downgraded. With poor scrutiny of decision-making, politicians may find opportunities to exercise their authority to their own benefit or in other harmful ways.

State governance capacity also extends to the management of elections. Elections in the time of COVID-19 pose a couple of significant problems. They can spread the virus as people gather to cast their votes. But they can also suppress voting: people staying at home because of fears about contracting the virus or a reduction in state capacity to process votes in person, by mail, or, in some cases, through corrupt practices exacerbated by coronavirus politics. Many countries had elections during the first half of 2020 with very different outcomes. Some jurisdictions, such as South Korea, appear to have had successful elections that were orderly and resulted in very little spread of the virus. Other countries (e.g., Israel, Malawi [see chapter 30]) experienced severe problems. In Belarus, adding a corrupt election on top of existing COVID-19 disruption resulted in widespread protests against the existing authoritarian regime. Widespread waves of arrests followed ("Hundreds

Arrested at Mass Protests in Minsk," 2020). In Israel, the Knesset passed a law banning people from protesting more than a kilometer from their homes, a move that many believed was an attempt to silence criticism of Netanyahu ("Massive Demonstrations Grip Thailand," 2020). In Thailand, antigovernment, prodemocracy protesters have been calling for reforms to the Monarchy ("Israelis Protest Against Netanyahu despite Coronavirus Lockdown," 2020).

In this sense, additional pressure on political systems arising from the pandemic has the potential to destabilize states. Only time will tell whether some of these changes will be ultimately positive, but we do know that the process of destabilizing regimes is often painful.

Surveillance

The second capacity of the state relevant to its COVID-19 response is surveillance. Surveillance is the process of collecting and analyzing data relevant to public health to inform decision-making. As a government function, public health surveillance tends to be ignored, downgraded, and underfunded in times of relative calm, only to come to the fore during a public health crisis such as a disease outbreak. This happens because day-to-day surveillance is often not politically salient and can be overshadowed by debates about other aspects of health or health care (Greer et al., 2019). The tried and tested methods of public health surveillance are, however, robust and effective as controlling the spread of disease, even while raising important political and ethical questions (Greer, 2017).

In the context of the COVID-19 pandemic, government surveillance actions centered around testing people for the virus, then using the results to identify and isolate people who had been exposed (often reflecting some form of the epidemiological maxim: "test, trace, isolate" or "test, trace, isolate, protect"). States' success in these activities has been largely dependent upon the readiness of its public health system as well as the integration of surveillance functions (gathering, analyzing, and disseminating data) with the state at large (e.g., integration with health systems, ability to enforce quarantine restrictions) (Trump et al., 2020). Surveillance is a labor-intensive activity that requires specialized training and knowledge. Many states lacked enough day-to-day surveillance capacity at the start of the pandemic, having cut back on public health functions as part of decades-long welfare state retrenchment.

Yet even the most well-prepared states needed to ramp up their surveillance capacity in the face of a large-scale pandemic, and the ability to do so made the difference between success and failure in some states. It is notable that some predictions about which states would be well prepared for the pandemic, made on the basis of WHO's SPAR (State Party Self-Assessment Annual Reporting) scores or numbers from the Global Health Security (GHS) Index, published jointly by the Nuclear Threat Initiative and the Johns Hopkins Center for Health Security, were very inaccurate. The United States ranks first in the GHS Index and the United Kingdom ranks second. Both states have severely underperformed on surveillance functions during the pandemic when compared to lower-ranked countries (see chapters 12 and 26). One reason for this may be that surveillance functions are closely related to a country's governance, particularly the ability to overcome political polarization and jurisdictional fragmentation (Greer, 2020a).

Testing people for COVID-19 requires significant mobilization of resources, including workers, materials, and environments as well as the ability to rapidly collate and analyze the data from multiple testing sites. This is vital, because without rapid testing that is accurate and reaches enough people, much surveillance is useless. Ideally, public health experts agree that test results should be available within twenty-four hours, with enough tests conducted to ensure that the spread of disease is fully understood (less than 3 percent of all tests returning positive results) (Harvard Global Health Institute, 2020). With good enough testing, however, outbreaks can be controlled through effective contact tracing. Once testing data have been collected, staff trace the contacts made with infected persons, informing them of their exposure and placing them in isolation. All of this has to be done as soon as possible, ideally within forty-eight hours, if it is to be effective in controlling the outbreak (Harvard Global Health Institute, 2020).

It is not a coincidence that some of the states most successful at curbing COVID-19 have demonstrated a strong ability to conduct public health surveillance during the pandemic. States with the capacity to track progress of the disease have been able to control it, whereas those caught with holes in their public health safety nets have had to go farther to ramp up testing and contact tracing activity. A further challenge for those countries with poor permanent public health capacity is how to manage surveillance capacity at lower levels of disease prevalence. Testing and contact tracing capacity must be maintained when cases are low, because the disease can often spread much more quickly than a government can recruit and train contact tracers or obtain testing supplies. This has been a challenge in some states where funding is seen to be tight, resources have been mismanaged, and/or political pressure is strong to make the COVID-19 problem go away.

In this way, surveillance is at once a logistical and a political issue. One of the biggest political debates around surveillance has been public concern about how governments will store and use personal information. Contact tracing, for example, asks detailed behavioral questions about individuals and their families. A lack of trust in government officials, therefore, or a fear of punishment for wrongdoing, can significantly hamper contact tracing efforts. Some of these fears have been intensified with the introduction of technology such as phone applications (apps) that trace location and identify proximity via Bluetooth (Fahy, 2020; Hernández-Quevedo et al., 2020). The effectiveness of contact-tracing apps has been called into question because far fewer people than expected have downloaded apps to their phones. Some states are going farther than this by introducing wristbands that track proximity, location, and health data, in some cases notifying the police when those in quarantine leave their homes ("Coronavirus:

People-Tracking Wristbands Tested to Enforce Lockdown," 2020). Civil society groups in some countries have voiced concerns that some governments will use the pandemic as an excuse to further track their citizens, potentially with the goal of curbing their freedoms (Human Rights Watch, 2020).

Coercion

The third capacity of the state relevant to its COVID-19 response is coercion. Specifically, this refers to the use of the state's legal authority to make and enforce rules that protect society from the worst effects of the pandemic by changing the behavior of individuals and organizations. As mentioned previously, in a situation where there is no vaccine, the state's capacity to make and enforce public health protections can make a difference in the impact of the coronavirus on its population, society, and political system. We know from prior experience as well as the current pandemic that restrictions on behavior can be effective at controlling the spread of the virus and reducing its harmful effects on health. But although state coercive power has the potential to benefit society in this way, it can also be extremely damaging.

In the first half of 2020, many countries chose to put tough protective public health measures in place, including physical distancing requirements, stay-at-home orders, bans on travel, public events and gatherings, masking requirements, and forced business closures. They also introduced quarantine and isolation measures for exposed residents and for many foreign visitors, regardless of exposure. In addition, some countries used their authority to make and change rules to protect vulnerable workers from being forced to work in dangerous environments by requiring businesses to offer alternative work from home (Jarman et al., 2020c), to prevent evictions in cases of financial hardship, to protect businesses from bankruptcy resulting from lockdown policies, or to protect consumers and purchasers in the health system from dangerous or misleading products, for example, inadequate tests or fake medicines (Jarman et al., 2020g; Rozenblum & Jarman, 2020). Some states chose to use their coercive capacity to govern production and distribution of things such as personal protective equipment, ventilators, and treatments (e.g., by requiring manufacturers to produce certain needed products). The same dynamic would apply to any vaccine that becomes available.

The most significant political concerns raised about the state's use of coercive power in these instances relate to enforcement of the new rules. In many places, noncompliance with policies such as physical distancing requirements, bans on gatherings, or masking requirements carried the possibility that individuals or businesses could be fined, cautioned or, in serious cases, prosecuted for violations or detained.

In many cases, states relied on the police to enforce COVID-19-related policies. In some countries, police officers are armed; in most, they have considerable discretion around how to enforce the law, creating many potential opportunities for injustice and state-sanctioned violence. Protests against the police, beginning in the

United States in response to police brutality against Black Americans and quickly spreading to other countries, have shone a spotlight on the long-term ways in which law enforcement systems in many countries discriminate against, and pose a physical threat to, minority groups.

As well as being significant stand-alone issues, bias and use of force in policing raise overlapping concerns in terms of states' coronavirus responses. These include the potential for COVID-19-related rules to be unfairly enforced against some groups in society and not others, the possibility that enforcing COVID-19 policies could provide cover for some governments, organizations, and individuals to use force in ways that violate fundamental human rights, and the potential for the enforcement of COVID-19 policies to pose a threat to physical and mental health of individuals and communities such that it forms a public health problem in its own right.

Related questions have been raised as to the sustainability of coercive measures over time. Ultimately, coercive measures were not designed to be implemented long term; rather, they were envisioned as a tough but necessary set of policies that would allow a government to put better long-term measures in place, such as adequate testing and contact tracing. As cases rise again, many states are putting lockdown measures back in place. But populations asked to lock down once may be far more compliant than those asked to lock down a second or third time. Masking requirements and renewed lockdown measures in some European countries have been followed by mass protests (Jones, 2020; Kirka, 2020; Specia, 2020). This raises a concern that the long-term effectiveness of lockdown policies may be poor, as well as a fear that in some cases governments could sanction increasingly unjust and violent responses to noncompliant populations over time.

Social Policy

The final capacity of the state relevant to its COVID-19 response relates to social policy. Social policies are policies designed to improve the overall welfare of a society by meeting social goals such as educating children, supporting older people, providing incomes to those experiencing financial hardship, or caring for the sick.

Social policy plays into the success of state responses to the pandemic in two distinct ways. First, a state's historic track record (i.e., the extent to which its welfare state, health system, or macroeconomic policies pre-COVID-19 address overall need and address inequalities in society) has a direct impact on morbidity and mortality relating to the pandemic. The prepandemic state of social policies is important because COVID-19 is not an equal-opportunity condition. Certain groups are more vulnerable to contracting and/or experiencing the worst outcomes from COVID-19 because of combinations of factors that can include age, existing health conditions, occupation, and living conditions. Some of these factors are, in turn, determined by structural divisions within society, such as discrimination among racial, ethnic, class, or age groups that affect access to things such as work, education, health care, housing, clean water, and adequate food and contribute to higher rates of institutionalization and incarceration. Paying attention to existing state policies that impact these factors and measuring how unequal a society is after redistributive policies are applied is therefore very important.

Second, a state's immediate COVID-19-related social policy response also has an effect on health outcomes. It is likely that people whose COVID-19-related health costs are covered will more readily seek medical advice, testing, and treatment. Likewise, people whose immediate economic needs are met are more likely to be able to comply with stay-at-home orders. Businesses whose immediate economic needs are met are more likely to be able to retain workers and infrastructure. Workers who are entitled to paid sick leave are less likely to come to work sick, and so on.

By necessity, many of the NPIs that prevented people from getting the virus also diminished economic activity (in addition to people who could afford to stay at home doing so out of fears that they would catch the virus). In many countries, this left businesses in financial trouble and caused unemployment to soar. Some countries addressed this problem through existing unemployment insurance schemes, in some cases expanding their criteria for eligibility or the generosity of benefits. Other states modified or instituted income replacement programs and/or announced additional support for small businesses in financial trouble. But many of these COVID-19-specific social policy measures were not long term, even in the richest countries.

A significant proportion of the people who contracted the virus needed health care, with the most serious cases requiring extensive hospitalization. For this reason, an early goal for many states was to "flatten the curve," meaning they aimed to control the spread of COVID-19 to prevent their hospitals and health systems from being overwhelmed with cases. Many countries ultimately succeeded in avoiding this fate, although in some parts of the world, early or ongoing uncontrolled spread exceeding hospital capacity likely contributed to the death toll. Although some states made additional financing available to their healthcare systems and/or sought to reduce out-of-pocket healthcare costs for their citizens, many did not take these actions.

In addition to providing care, a state's ability to lessen the impact of COVID-19 on its population likely relates to its ability to coordinate health, social care services, and other forms of support. For those who survive a serious case of coronavirus requiring hospitalization and/or intubation, the impact on quality of life can be severe. They may suffer temporary or permanent mental or physical degradation, meaning that even if they still have employment after being hospitalized, they may not be able to work. In many cases, their ability to get back to "normal" will rely in part on the social services they can access, such as physical rehabilitation, counseling, and ongoing medical treatment, which can all be affected by eligibility and the administrative burdens of obtaining support even when eligible. Other factors include out-of-pocket costs and income, ongoing lockdown, and physical distancing requirements.

The virus had a devastating impact on older populations in many countries, shining a spotlight on systems of social care and structures of intergenerational support within each society. Care homes, in particular, often provided an optimal environment for the virus to spread, with residents in close proximity to one another and staff and receiving visitors who may be carrying the virus. Several European governments with aging populations, including Sweden, France, Spain, and the United Kingdom, were criticized for their inability to anticipate and control the spread of the virus in care homes, as well as for failing to include statistics about care home cases and deaths in national records.

All tiers of education have been disrupted by the virus. Countries with normally robust school systems have had to cope with unanticipated school closures during lockdown and the resulting disruption in students' learning. In many countries, school closures during lockdown also caused problems with childcare for those who remained at work, whereas in the poorest countries, children displaced from schools were forced to enter the workforce (Pérez-Peña, 2020). In many countries, higher education institutions were deemed a risk for spreading the virus and in-person activities were canceled, although the start of the new academic year in September 2020 brought new students and a wave of new infections in many cases.

Policies and politics affecting housing also had a huge effect on the course of the virus in many countries. With proximity to others as a key component of contagion, people housed in more cramped conditions were automatically put at greater risk of catching the virus. In terms of pandemic-specific policies, some countries chose to place moratoriums on evictions, although some of those measures have since expired. The long-term consequences of the economic crisis on homelessness remain to be seen.

In addition to these sector-specific issues, overarching concerns have been raised that reflect long-term deficiencies in the structure of social support programs in various countries as well as the additional needs imposed by the pandemic. Many states routinely rely on civil society groups and/or donor organizations to meet the basic needs of their populations, and those groups have been economically damaged by the pandemic (Greer et al., 2020a, 2020d). Where social policies do exist, they do not always provide an adequate level of support for those in need. Often, programs do not provide universal benefits that apply across the population. Rather, many countries tie access to health care, social care, unemployment benefits, pensions, education, or other social services to a person's citizenship status. In addition, social programs are often organized in ways that are biased against certain groups in society, posing administrative burdens that can have discriminatory effects.

The pandemic replicates these patterns, meaning that many people who are routinely excluded from social benefits and services continue to be excluded at a time of greater need. Many migrant workers, for example, are likely to be more at risk from the virus and its economic consequences than the general population. They are more likely to be engaged in work that is precarious, with few legal and economic protections, and/or that requires them to be indoors in close contact with others, with many migrant workers employed in the hospitality, domestic services, healthcare, agriculture, and food processing sectors. They may also be more likely to have to rely on mass transportation, which poses a higher risk of infection, and to be housed in relatively crowded conditions that make it harder to physically distance themselves from others. Yet they are also less likely to have access to health and social services and to benefit from income replacement or unemployment benefits (International Labour Organization, 2020). These patterns of inequality will likely be replicated in terms of access to any future vaccine against COVID-19.

Consequences

There are important political consequences that stem from the ways states are governing during the pandemic, their surveillance activities, the coercive measures enacted to protect public health, and governments' social policy responses. Many countries have demonstrated the capacity to put recommended public health policies in place, and enforce them, at short notice and in some cases with limited available resources. A perhaps unprecedented amount of data on the spread and consequences of the disease has been made publicly available, although many deficiencies and discrepancies in the data remain, and we still know little about some aspects of the disease. Some countries have been successful at controlling the virus and/or have seen it inflict limited damage on their populations because of strong surveillance or lockdown measures, high hospital capacity, low population density, or other population health factors.

In many cases, the pandemic is throwing existing trends and patterns into sharp relief: some leaders are governing in less-than-transparent or undemocratic ways, disregarding science and abusing their authority, while people and political parties in many countries are divided. Many are voicing their criticism of political leaders on the streets. In many places, the pandemic is highlighting clearly existing deficiencies in the welfare state, the economy, social policy, the justice system, or the electoral system.

It remains to be seen whether changes in governance and politics precipitated by the pandemic may prove to be long-term trends, with potentially severe consequences for democracy everywhere. In liberal democracies, we know that much of the functioning of the political system relies on the belief that governments are legitimate. What the COVID-19 pandemic emphasizes is just how much the compact between people and governments has been eroded in many liberal democratic systems. There is a distinct lack of trust in governments that impacts many aspects of COVID-19 response, including surveillance, compliance with protection measures, and vaccination. In patterns that political scientists are familiar with, state-sanctioned violence against protesters (including prodemocracy and antipolice protesters) justifies and strengthens this lack of trust (Diamond, 2020). The effect, if these trends continue, may well be that democracy as a model of government is further discredited in the eyes of many people around the world.

References

Coronavirus: People-tracking wristbands tested to enforce lockdown. (2020, April 24). BBC News. https://www.bbc.com/news/technology-52409893

Diamond, L. (2020). Democratic regression in comparative perspective: Scope, methods, and causes. *Democratization.* https://www.doi.10.1080/13510347.2020.1807517

Fahy, N. (2020). *How are countries using digital health tools in responding to COVID-19?* WHO Coronavirus Health Systems Response Monitor. https://www.analysis.covid19healthsystem.org/index.php/2020/04/28/how-are-countries-using-digital-health-tools-in-responding-to-covid-19/

Falkenbach, M. (2020). *Deny and distract: The populist radical right responses of Trump, Johnson and Bolsonaro to COVID-19.* HMP Governance Lab. https://www.hmpgovernancelab.org/health-politics-blog/deny-and-distract-populist-radical-right-responses-of-trump-johnson-bolsonaro-to-covid-19

Falkenbach, M., & Greer, S. L. (2020). Denial and distraction: How the populist radical right responds to COVID-19; Comment on "a scoping review of PRR parties' influence on welfare policy and its implication for population health in Europe. *International Journal of Health Policy and Management.* https://doi.org/10.34172/IJHPM.2020.141

Greer, S. L. (2017). Constituting public health surveillance in twenty-first century Europe. In M. Weimer & A. de Ruijter (Eds.), *Regulating risks in the European Union: The co-production of expert and executive power* (pp. 121–141). Bloomsbury.

Greer, S. L. (2020a). *PHE, RIP: The botched elimination of England's public health agency is just a symptom.* HMP Governance Lab. https://www.hmpgovernancelab.org/health-politics-blog/phe-rip-the-botched-elimination-of-englands-public-health-agency-is-just-a-symptom

Greer, S. L. (2020b). *The welfare state is not enough: Lessons about inequality from Chile's 2019 crisis.* HMP Governance Lab. https://www.hmpgovernancelab.org/health-politics-blog/the-welfare-state-is-not-enough-lessons-about-inequality-from-chiles-2019-crisisnbsp

Greer, S. L., Fahy, N., Rozenblum, S., Jarman, H., Palm W., Elliott, H., & Wismar, M. (2019). *Everything you always wanted to know about European Union health policies but were afraid to ask* (2nd ed.). World Health Organization/European Observatory on Health Systems and Policies.

Greer, S. L., Rozenblum, S., & Jarman, H. (2020a). *COVID-19 is making civil society more important than ever, but also more fragile.* HMP Governance Lab. https://www.hmpgovernancelab.org/health-politics-blog/covid-19-is-making-civil-society-more-important-than-ever-but-also-more-fragile

Greer, S. L., Rozenblum, S., Jarman, H., & Wismar, M. (2020b). Who's in charge and why? Centralization within and between governments. *Eurohealth, 26*(2), 99–103.

Greer, S. L., Rozenblum, S., Wismar, M., & Jarman, H. (2020c). *How have federal countries organized their COVID-19 response?* WHO Coronavirus Health Systems Response Monitor. https://analysis.covid19healthsystem.org/index.php/2020/07/16/how-have-federal-countries-organized-their-covid-19-response/

Greer, S. L., Rozenblum, S., Wismar, W., & Jarman, H. (2020d). *What is the value of civil society in the COVID-19 crisis?* HMP Governance Lab. https://analysis.covid19healthsystem.org/index.php/2020/06/05/what-is-the-value-of-civil-society-in-the-covid-19-crisis/

Greer, S. L., Vasev, N., Jarman, H., Wismar, M., & Figueras, J. (2019). *It's the governance, stupid! TAPIC: A governance framework to strengthen decisionmaking and implementation.* Policy Brief 33: WHO Europe/European Observatory on Health Systems and Policies.

Greer, S. L., Wismar, M., & Figueras, J. (Eds.). (2015). *Strengthening health systems governance: Better policies, stronger performance.* WHO Europe, European Observatory on Health Systems and Policies/OUP.

Harvard Global Health Institute. (2020). Key metrics for COVID-19 suppression: A framework for policymakers and the public. https://ethics.harvard.edu/files/center-for-ethics/files/key_metrics_and_indicators_v4.pdf

Hernández-Quevedo, C., Scarpetti, G., & Webb, E. (2020). *How do countries structure contact tracing operations and what is the role of apps?* WHO Coronavirus Health Systems Response Monitor. https://analysis.covid19healthsystem.org/index.php/2020/06/18/how-do-countries-structure-contact-tracing-operations-and-what-is-the-role-of-apps/

Human Rights Watch. (2020, May 13). *Mobile location data and COVID-19: Q and A.* https://www.hrw.org/news/2020/05/13/mobile-location-data-and-covid-19-qa

Hundreds arrested at mass protests in Minsk. (2020, September 7). BBC News. https://www.bbc.com/news/world-europe-54044750

International Labour Organization. (2020, June 23). *Social protection for migrant workers: A necessary response to the Covid-19 crisis.* https://www.ilo.org/wcmsp5/groups/public/—ed_protect/—soc_sec/documents/publication/wcms_748979.pdf

Israelis protest against Netanyahu despite coronavirus lockdown. (2020, September 27). Al Jazeera. https://www.aljazeera.com/news/2020/9/27/israelis-protest-against-netanyahu-despite-coronavirus-lockdown

Jarman, H. (2020a). *A governance explainer: What does TAPIC stand for and where did it come from?* HMP Governance Lab. https://www.hmpgovernancelab.org/health-politics-blog/what-does-tapic-stand-for-where-did-it-come-from

Jarman, H. (2020b). *What we can learn from COVID-19 transition planning in Europe?* https://www.hmpgovernancelab.org/health-politics-blog/what-can-we-learn-from-covid-transition-planning-europe

Jarman, H. (2020c). *What should governments do to tackle the COVID-19 pandemic?* HMP Governance Lab. https://www.hmpgovernancelab.org/health-politics-blog/what-should-governments-do-to-tackle-the-covid-19-pandemic

Jarman, H., & Greer, S. L. (2020). *Why is governance important for responding to COVID-19?* HMP Governance Lab. https://www.hmpgovernancelab.org/health-politics-blog/why-is-governance-important-for-covid-19

Jarman, H., Greer, S. L., Maffioli, E., Mehta, N., Klasa, K., Wai, R., Willoughby, E., Trump, B. D., Ligo, A., Raj, M., Linkov, I., Bridges, T. S., Cegan, J., Glover, G., Lafferty, B., & Rozenblum, S. (2020a). *Comparative configurational analysis of SARS-CoV-2.* White Paper, US Army Corps of Engineers.

Jarman, H., Greer, S. L., Rozenblum, S., & Wismar, M. (2020b). In and out of lockdowns, and what is a lockdown anyway? Policy issues in transitions. *Eurohealth, 26*(2), 93–98.

https://apps.who.int/iris/bitstream/handle/10665/336284/Eurohealth-26-2-93-98-eng.pdf

Jarman, H., Rozenblum, S., & Greer, S. L. (2020c, May 11). What US States can learn from COVID-19 transition planning in Europe. *The Conversation.* https://theconversation.com/what-us-states-can-learn-from-covid-19-transition-planning-in-europe-137694

Jarman, H., Rozenblum, S., Greer, S. L., & Wismar, M. (2020d). *How are countries getting out of lockdown?* WHO Coronavirus Health Systems Response Monitor. https://analysis.covid19healthsystem.org/index.php/2020/05/07/how-are-countries-getting-out-of-lockdown/

Jarman, H., Rozenblum, S., Greer, S. L., & Wismar, M. (2020e). *How will governments know when to lift and impose restrictions?* WHO Coronavirus Health Systems Response Monitor. https://analysis.covid19healthsystem.org/index.php/2020/05/07/how-will-governments-know-when-to-lift-and-impose-restrictions/

Jarman, H., Rozenblum, S., Greer, S. L., & Wismar, M. (2020f). *What do governments need to consider as they implement transition plans?* WHO Coronavirus Health Systems Response Monitor. https://analysis.covid19healthsystem.org/index.php/2020/05/07/what-do-governments-need-to-consider-as-they-implement-transition-plans/

Jarman, H., Rozenblum, S., & Huang, T. (2020g). Neither protective nor harmonized: The crossborder regulation of medical devices in the EU. *Journal of Health Economics, Politics and Law.* https://doi.org/10.1017/S1744133120000158

Jones, S. (2020, September 20). *Protests in Madrid over coronavirus lockdown measures.* https://www.theguardian.com/world/2020/sep/20/protests-madrid-coronavirus-lockdown-measures-spain

Kirka, D. (2020, September 26). *London police, protesters clash at COVID-19 demonstration.* https://apnews.com/article/virus-outbreak-london-archive-d79023478fbfd6168e03555d6fb6a7bf

Massive demonstrations grip Thailand. (2020, September 25). Al Jazeera. https://www.aljazeera.com/program/inside-story/2020/9/20/massive-demonstrations-grip-thailand/

Méndez, C. A., Greer, S. L., & McKee, M. (2020). The 2019 crisis in Chile: Fundamental change needed, not just technical fixes to the health system. *Journal of Public Health Policy.*

Pérez-Peña, R. (2020, September 27). Futures in peril: The rise of child labor in the coronavirus pandemic. *New York Times.* https://www.nytimes.com/2020/09/27/world/asia/coronavirus-education-child-labor.html

Rozenblum, S., & Jarman, H. (2020). *Antibody tests and regulatory reforms: Why delegating pre-market control to private companies is a bad idea.* HMP Governance Lab. https://www.hmpgovernancelab.org/health-politics-blog/antibody-tests-and-regulatory-reforms-why-delegating-pre-market-control-to-private-companies-is-a-bad-ideanbsp

Specia, M. (2020, September 28). *As Europe's coronavirus cases rise, so do voices crying hoax.* https://www.nytimes.com/2020/09/28/world/europe/europe-coronavirus-protests.html

Trump, B. D., Bridges, T. S., Cegan, J., Cibulsky, S. M., Greer, S. L., Jarman, H., Lafferty, B., Surette, M., & Linkov, I. (2020). An analytical perspective on pandemic recovery. *Health Security, 18*(3), 250–256.

PART II ASIA

4 CHINA'S LENINIST RESPONSE TO COVID-19
From Information Repression to Total Mobilization
Victor C. Shih

As of September 2020, China has had one of the most successful responses to COVID-19 in the world, despite being the origin of the epidemic and having the largest population and multiple dense urban centers. Yet China's response did not begin serendipitously. Despite receiving a wealth of information about COVID-19 by the end of the first week of January, the top authorities in China decided to keep vital information on the epidemic from the public for two weeks, thus allowing the disease to spread through much of Hubei province and in other major cities. This led to the unfolding of a large-scale tragedy in Wuhan, a city of ten million people, and in other cities in Hubei. The precise scale of the death toll caused by COVID-19 and by draconian government lockdown policies remains unknown.

On January 20, 2020, the ruling Chinese Communist Party (CCP) shifted gears and initiated mobilization for containment. The resulting draconian quarantine and self-quarantine, as well as the rapid construction and production of quarantine sites, personal protective equipment (PPE), and medical supplies, allowed China to quickly control the spread of COVID-19 so that by early March, untraceable community transmission had come to an end in the vast majority of regions in China. This mobilization not only stopped the epidemic in Wuhan but also prevented the large-scale spread of COVID-19 in another major urban center in China. Because the mobilization mainly focused on containing COVID-19, medical care for other diseases and many social welfare issues were largely ignored by the government.

In both the information repression phase and in the mobilization phase, the CCP's hierarchical and authoritarian structure, the party's ability to transcend state institutions, and the state's ownership over vital economic resources greatly facilitated the party achieving key objectives in these two different phases. In the first phase, through its control of the media and arbitrary detention, the party largely succeeded in preventing the spread of not only information but also panic about COVID-19, thus largely preventing urban unrests. In the second phase, the mobilization of state and societal resources toward containment allowed the government to control the trajectories of the epidemic relatively quickly, compared to other countries. Beyond the party's Leninist structure, the containment effort was greatly helped by community parastatal organizations, the neighborhood committees, which the party relied on to implement core tasks related to the quarantine. Without their frantic effort, the outcomes in China would have been much worse. The digital surveillance program, which facilitated contact tracing, likely did not play a decisive role in controlling COVID-19 in China.

Yet the mobilization of the party-state could not make up for the shortfalls in China's medical insurance and social security system. Although otherwise healthy urban residents working for state-owned entities or major private corporations continued to receive the benefits owed to them throughout the lockdown, the state chose not to devote significant resources to address challenges faced by both the urban and rural vulnerable population and migrant workers. Many of China's 290 million migrant workers, especially, found themselves unemployed and largely outside of China's patchy social welfare system, desperately fending for themselves on paltry government "minimal assistance insurance." Although the Chinese government easily could have devoted greater resources to the sick and unemployed, in the absence of a free media or democratic pressure, it chose not to do so.

Public Health and Repressive Responses

The public health responses in China can roughly be broken down into two phases: the information repression phase and the mobilization for containment phase. Clear evidence from China suggests that the information repression phase from December 2019 to January 20, 2020, allowed COVID-19 to spread widely around China, especially in Wuhan and in the rest of Hubei province. The campaign to repress information on COVID-19 likely had to do with the regime's imperative to ensure social stability in the political and economic centers along the eastern coast of China. The mobilization phase began on January 20, 2020, which was soon followed by the closing of Wuhan to the outside world and by the self-quarantine of all rural and urban households in China in the weeks following. This was associated with the rapid decline in the new caseload across China, beginning in the second half of February 2020.

According to epidemiologists interviewing the first wave of patients, human COVID-19 cases likely began to proliferate in Wuhan starting in early December 2019 (Huang et al., 2020). Among patients with contacts to the Huanan Seafood Market, the site of the first major cluster of infection, the first patients manifested symptoms starting on December 1, 2019 (Huang et al., 2020). By December 31, 2019, the Wuhan Health Commission (WHC) admitted publicly that there was an outbreak of "pneumonia of unknown origin" based around the Huanan Seafood Market, which was promptly shut down for disinfection on January 1, 2020 (Huang et al., 2020).

On January 1, 2020, the Wuhan police also announced that eight "rumor purveyors" were "dealt with according to the law," but they were all doctors who had communicated their worries about a spike of patients with pneumonia symptoms in private social media discussions with families and friends ("Xianchangpian: Wuhan

Weicheng" ["Live: The Closing of Wuhan"], 2020). Still, because of total surveillance in China, they were detained and had to sign confessions of wrongdoing. Although their posts were widely circulated online, they were ultimately scrubbed on order from the Chinese government. For workers in the medical community, this detention by the police directly prevented many of them from spreading the news of the "pneumonia of unknown origin" to friends and families and to the wider community, which helped COVID-19 spread further in Wuhan and beyond ("Xianchangpian: Wuhan Weicheng" ["Live: The Closing of Wuhan"], 2020).

On January 5, 2020, the WHC announced to the public additional cases of the "pneumonia of unknown origin," but still insisted that there was no evidence of human-to-human transmission and that no medical worker had contracted the disease (Huang, 2020). This was clearly untrue because the detained doctors and many others working in frontline hospitals had already noticed many cases of suspicious pneumonia among their colleagues ("Xianchangpian: Wuhan Weicheng" ["Live: The Closing of Wuhan"], 2020). Yet the pressure for information control persisted as the local committees of the CCP at frontline hospitals ordered all workers to "not create or convey rumors so as to avoid social panic" ("Xianchangpian: Wuhan Weicheng" ["Live: The Closing of Wuhan"], 2020). On January 10, 2020, the WHC announced, again contrary to evidence, that "no new case has been recorded after January 3rd" and that wearing masks was "required only when necessary" ("Xianchangpian: Wuhan Weicheng" ["Live: The Closing of Wuhan"], 2020). On January 15, 2020, during a question-and-answer session at a press conference, the WHC finally admitted that the possibility of human-to-human transmission "cannot be ruled out" (Zhang et al., 2020).

Despite growing worries, Wuhan still held its annual "ten thousand families banquet" on January 18, 2020, in which groups of several hundred gathered in multiple neighborhoods to share local delicacies that they had cooked for each other (Zhang et al., 2020). In fact, lower-level party officials also were not privy to the growing alarm at the highest level because the Hubei Provincial People's Congress meeting, attended by hundreds of mid-level party functionaries, was still held in Wuhan from January 11 to 17, 2020 ("Xianchangpian: Wuhan Weicheng" ["Live: The Closing of Wuhan"], 2020). Undoubtedly, many low- and mid-level government officials, as well as a much larger number of ordinary citizens, unnecessarily contracted COVID-19 because higher-level party authorities did not cancel these two major events. After the Hubei Provincial People's Congress sessions ended on January 18, 2020, the WHC finally announced an additional twenty-one cases to the public, but frontline doctors were already reporting hundreds of suspected cases to the health authorities ("Xianchangpian: Wuhan Weicheng" ["Live: The Closing of Wuhan"], 2020).

The tone of the information repression campaign finally changed on January 18 and 19, 2020, when the WHC suddenly announced an additional 136 confirmed cases of COVID-19 ("Xianchangpian: Wuhan Weicheng" ["Live: The Closing of Wuhan"], 2020). On the night of January 20, 2020, China Central Television, watched by the majority of Chinese households, broadcasted an interview with leading infectious disease specialist, Dr. Zhong Nanshan, who stated unambiguously that "there is definitely human-to-human transmission" and that "the diseases is still at its starting stage and is in a growth period" (China Central Television, 2020b). This TV interview was followed by a series of drastic government actions to combat COVID-19 and thus spelled the end of the information repression phase of the response.

Although public information about potential human-to-human transmission of COVID-19 was systematically suppressed by the authorities, government experts and frontline doctors channeled the latest information in a relatively unimpeded way to the central government in Beijing. According to the authors of the first major clinical study of COVID-19, published online in *Lancet* on January 24, 2020, a central government team, composed of the leading infectious disease specialists from around China as well as national level health officials, first arrived in Wuhan in early January and immediately reviewed clinical data on forty-one patients who had been admitted to Wuhan hospitals with pneumonia-like symptoms before January 2, 2020 (Huang et al., 2020). The fact that the government team did not review clinical data after January 2 indicates that they had begun drafting a version of the eventual *Lancet* paper during the first week of January, which strongly suggests that a version of the findings was available to the leadership soon after the first week of January. Based on a review of this clinical data in early January, the central government health team concluded, "Taken together, evidence so far indicates human transmission for 2019-nCoV" (Huang et al., 2020).

By January 3, 2020, the team had agreed on a set of protocols and criteria to identify a much larger sample of potential cases so that much more clinical data could be reviewed (Li et al., 2020b). By January 5, Shanghai health authorities had isolated and sequenced the genes of COVID-19 based on a late-December sample from Wuhan and had submitted reports to both the Shanghai Health Commission and the National Health Commission in Beijing ("Xianchangpian: Wuhan Weicheng" ["Live: The Closing of Wuhan"], 2020). RNA testing of samples also began in the first week of January 2020 in both a Wuhan-based level-2 laboratory and in a lab run by the National Institute for Viral Disease Control (Li et al., 2020b). In essence, by the end of the first week in January, the central government team had determined a high likelihood for human transmission of COVID-19 and had confirmed the presence of a large number of infections, but the Chinese government did not disclose these facts to the public until Dr. Zhong Nashan's television interview on January 20.

Meanwhile, it seems that the shocking findings of the central government team had elicited a response from the top leadership. According to remarks by Xi Jinping in early February 2020, by the January 7 Politburo Standing Committee meeting, he "raised demands on the prevention and control of the novel coronavirus" (Xi, 2020). It was also revealed in a government press release that by the January 25, 2020, Politburo Standing Committee meeting, Xi Jinping had "convened meetings and listened to reports by experts on multiple occasions" on the novel coronavirus (Xinhua, 2020). It is very likely that an earlier version of the *Lancet* findings, published just two and one-half weeks later, had made it on to the desk of Xi Jinping himself after the first week of January; yet, publicly, the Chinese government still maintained a calm demeanor. It remains unclear what the thinking of the Chinese government was between January 7 and 19, when a more concerted reaction to COVID-19 began to manifest publicly. Perhaps the leadership had hoped that COVID-19 would be a relatively controllable disease and would not require a drastic lockdown. This seems unlikely because the authors of the *Lancet* paper, all leading Chinese government experts, were clear about the "pandemic potential of 2019-nCoV" (Huang et al., 2020). After the lesson of SARS, it was unlikely that the Chinese leadership would have ignored such a consensus among its top experts. Perhaps the leadership had realized the magnitude of the problem early on but had decided to keep it a secret from the public for one and a half weeks while it prepared for total mobilization.

One possible explanation is that the period between January 7, 2020, and January 23, 2020, or so fell on the busiest traveling time for China: 290 million migrant workers working in eastern and southern China traveled to their mostly rural hometowns in central and western China for the Lunar New Year celebration, which fell on January 25, 2020 (National Bureau of Statistics, 2020). If the regime had instituted a lockdown in early January, most of the migrant workers would have been trapped in major cities along the coast, where they lived in cramped quarters. This obviously was far from ideal from an epidemiology perspective. Also, their presence in major cities would have taxed the medical resources in these urban centers and would have represented a much greater social stability risk for the regime. Given the regime's perennial worries about instability in the major cities (Wallace, 2014), it was logistically and politically much more facile to first disperse them to the countryside before instituting a lockdown. The tradition of returning home for the Lunar New Year holiday provided the regime with a perfect opportunity to do so. Whatever the reason for the delay in the regime's reaction, it very likely caused tens of thousands of additional infections in Wuhan and in the rest of Hubei. By January 20, when seven hospitals in Wuhan were designated for COVID-19 treatment, hundreds of patients with high temperature were lining up outside each of them, and scores would die in their hallways ("Xianchangpian: Wuhan Weicheng" ["Live: The Closing of Wuhan"], 2020).

In any event, on January 19, the regime began to manifest a systematic response to COVID-19. On that day, the National Health Commission announced the formation of a leading group within the agency to coordinate responses to COVID-19. Among the many tasks of this leading group, it began to coordinate the announcement of more realistic infection figures, starting with the announcement of 136 new cases on the January 20 after over a week of no new cases ("Xianchangpian: Wuhan Weicheng" ["Live: The Closing of Wuhan"], 2020). This was followed in the evening of January 20 by Dr. Zhong Nanshan's confirmation of human-to-human transmission. Also on January 20, Xi Jinping instructed the entire party to "focus a high level of attention on the infection; use all resources to prevent and control the disease" (Xi, 2020). On January 25, a Politburo Standing Committee meeting chaired by Xi announced the formation of the Central Leading Group on Confronting the Novel Coronavirus Pneumonia (CLGCNCP), a plenipotentiary body headed by Premier Li Keqiang and the regime's top propaganda official, Wang Huning (Xinhua, 2020). At the same Politburo Standing Committee meeting, Xi Jinping also issued a flurry of instructions, including the summary command of "Preserving life is the highest priority; let responses be guided by the trajectory of the epidemic; all will be held responsible for preventing and controlling the epidemic" (Xinhua, 2020). It was also at this meeting that the principles of "all infected will be concentrated in designated containment facilities; all those who had contacts (with the infected) will be placed in home quarantine" were issued (Xinhua, 2020).

With these orders from the highest authority in the party, the entire regime mobilized to contain COVID-19 while maintaining the CCP's iron grip on society. As discussed in greater details later, because key state and even commercial institutions were supervised by communist party cells, the party cells issued orders to their institutions that superseded existing laws and regulations, thus allowing resources to be mobilized quickly. As of August 2020, the Chinese government more or less had achieved its two major objectives: containment of COVID-19 and maintaining social stability.

The major challenges faced by the government by late January were threefold. First, as the number of symptomatic patients exploded, it quickly overwhelmed both testing and treatment capacity in Wuhan. The government needed to quickly mobilize resources to overcome these gaps. Second, although the vast majority of cases were in Wuhan, there was a possibility that the end of the Lunar New Year holiday would lead to a large-scale transmission of the disease to other major urban centers. Finally, if the regime is seen as dealing with the disease ineptly or if the containment caused too much collateral damage, social instability in the form of protests or riots may emerge in major urban centers, jeopardizing overall regime stability. As a vast amount of literature points out, the Chinese government devoted enormous online and physical resources to "stability maintenance" (King et al., 2013; Mattingly, 2019; Wallace, 2014).

As treatment and testing capacity were surpassed by the explosion of COVID-19 symptomatic patients in late January, the Wuhan municipal government (WMG) first designated seven hospitals for COVID-19 treatment, which made available over two thousand beds. Wuhan also began construction of two temporary treatment facilities, each with one-thousand-bed capacity, on January 23 ("Yisi Bingren Nanti" ["The Dilemma of Symptomatic Patients"], 2020). Because the construction was undertaken by state-owned enterprises each controlled by their own CCP party committees, they immediately heeded Xi Jinping's order to "use all available resources" and began construction of these hospitals. The third bureau of China Construction Corporation, tasked with building the Huoshenshan Hospital, began construction on January 23, even before any contract was signed with WMG or with the central government (He et al., 2020). Within days, over ten thousand workers working twenty-four hours a day and a thousand trucks and construction machineries were deployed, allowing the completion of the hospital in ten days (He et al., 2020). Again, in the process of this break-neck pace of construction, numerous safety and labor regulations were likely ignored. Yet, because both the regulators and the firms took orders from the CCP, construction proceeded apace. State Grid, the state-owned monopoly for electricity distribution, deployed thousands of workers to makeshift hospitals across China to lay down the electricity grids for them (He et al., 2020). Monetary concerns were set aside for the moment with the expectation that further central government policies would address these needs in the near future. Meanwhile, thousands of doctors and nurses from around the country, including a large number of medical personnel from the military, were mobilized to help with the containment effort in Wuhan (Qin, 2020b).

Eventually, the Wuhan model was replicated in multiple cities across China as authorities in several major cities around China scrambled to ensure sufficient treatment facilities for the infected. Because the caseload turned out to be smaller than expected, some of these facilities were repurposed for quarantine. This was the case with Xiaotangshan Hospital in Beijing, which was first built in 2003 during the SARS outbreak but was repurposed into a quarantine facility for international travelers when caseload in Beijing turned out to be relatively modest (Xia, 2020). The surplus in quarantine facilities eventually allowed the Chinese government to pursue the policies of "taking in all who should be taken in" (*yingshou jinshou*), which entailed placing confirmed patients, suspected patients, and those who had been in contact with confirmed patients in designated quarantine facilities (Wen et al., 2020).

As the first country faced with a COVID-19 outbreak, China initially faced a severe shortage in testing kits, even after medical firms began to develop them on January 10, 2020 ("Yisi Bingren Nanti" ["The Dilemma of Symptomatic Patients"], 2020). By January 19, however, the National Health Commission had approved testing kit production by three biotech firms, all Shanghai-based, thus enabling mass production of the nucleic acid tests. By January 26, some thirty firms around China had received approval to produce some 600,000 nucleic acid testing kits per day, more or less overcoming the initial bottleneck in testing availability ("Yisi Bingren Nanti" ["The Dilemma of Symptomatic Patients"], 2020).

While the regime mobilized resources for testing and treating COVID-19, it also simultaneously instituted the strictest quarantine the world has ever seen. This began with the January 23, 2020, lockdown of Wuhan along with fourteen other cities in Hubei, cutting off these cities and their tens of millions of residents from all forms of traffic, including air, rail, and vehicular traffic, allowing only official vehicles to go into and out of the quarantine zone ("Xianchangpian: Wuhan Weicheng" ["Live: The closing of Wuhan"], 2020). This lockdown did not end until a color-coded system designating the risk profiles of residents of all cities and counties in China allowed people from some parts of Hubei province to travel outside of the province starting in late March ("Shijianchou: Wuhan 'Fengcheng' de 76tian" ["Timeline: 76 Days of the Wuhan Lockdown"], 2020). Since the airports, the railroads, and the police all had party committees, once the highest authorities in the party ordered the lockdown, it was executed immediately by party cells and committees across China with little time lag between jurisdictions. Also, nationally, the Lunar New Year holiday was extended indefinitely so that most workers and university students remained in their hometowns instead of traveling back to their workplaces and schools in major urban centers (China Central Television, 2020a).

The key to China's success in containing COVID-19 was its draconian stay-at-home policy, which saw nearly all of its 1.3 billion population remain in their homes over the course of four to eight weeks starting in late January. This was enforced at the lowest level by neighborhood committees in the cities and by village committees in the countryside. These committees are parastatal bodies at the neighborhood or village level mostly led by party members and staffed by local activists such as demobilized soldiers and former state-owned enterprise (SOE) workers on a part-time basis (Read, 2012, p. 52). During normal times, they mainly channeled information about potential sources of unrests to the authorities and helped the local governments distribute information and propaganda about the latest policies (Read, 2012, p. 32). In times of emergency, however, they provided additional personnel for the Chinese state authorities to implement policies at the grassroots level.

In the case of COVID-19, the party soon mobilized neighborhood and village committees to implement the quarantine. As a decree issued by the Beijing municipal government (BMG) made clear, neighborhood and village committees were to "carry out the task of investigating and recording all the coming and going of residents within their jurisdictions" (BMG, 2020). The neighborhood committees carried out in-person surveillance and contact tracing, which provided much of the underlying data for China's impressive digital COVID-19 surveillance program (Lin, 2020). Neighborhood committees also regulated or even outright blocked residents from leaving their homes and required residents to check their temperatures on a periodic basis and reported results to local health authorities and to digital surveillance platforms (BMG, 2020). As more and more households were placed in strict home quarantine because of contacts with confirmed patients, residential committees also delivered food and other supplies to these households and checked their temperature on a regular basis (Zhang et al., 2020).

Throughout the pandemic, the government also ordered several waves of comprehensive testing, whereby all suspected patients or even the entire population underwent nucleic acid testing. Again, the neighborhood committees either carried out the testing or assisted health authorities to compile lists of households and to notify the neighborhoods about impending testing drives (Wen et al., 2020). As these tasks multiplied, the party also mobilized staff in local schools and government-controlled civic organizations, as well as state-owned enterprises to augment the neighborhood committees so that twenty-four-hour surveillance and lockdown could be enforced (Wen et al., 2020). For all the crucial tasks performed by these community workers during the pandemic, the government only compensated them with a modest bonus, free insurance policies, and free meals while on the job (Central Leading Group on Confronting the Novel Coronavirus Pneumonia, 2020b).

Finally, although the government began to release to the public more accurate information about the trajectory of the pandemic and government responses, it continued to deploy a concerted information manipulation campaign, including heavy censorship. First, although the WHC and the National Health Commission began to report a much higher caseload and death rate related to COVID-19 after January 20, 2020, the true infection figures remained undercounted as thousands of suspected cases were excluded from the official figures (Qin, 2020a). Even according to the official media, the COVID-19 death toll for Wuhan was vastly undercounted until the middle of April 2020, when the government suddenly increased the official COVID-19 death toll in Wuhan by 50 percent (Qin, 2020a). As China struggled with economic recovery in March and April 2020, analysts of China's economy also doubted the accuracy of China's economic numbers, including those for electricity use (Qin, 2020b). For several weeks in late January and early February 2020, the government allowed journalists, both Chinese and foreign, relatively unimpeded access to Wuhan, and they provided excellent reporting on the real situation in Wuhan (Wang, 2020). The authorities likely tolerated such reporting because they had mistrusted the flow of information from the WMG and wanted on-the-ground verification. As the number of central officials in Wuhan expanded, however, the party once again reasserted a monopoly on publicly available information on the epidemic. By the middle of February, the authorities had rounded up 350 people around China for "spreading rumors," including famous bloggers Fang Bin and Chen Qiushi (Wang, 2020). They remained in detention as of September 2020.

Social Policies

Although the mobilization for containment meant that the Chinese government quickly agreed to undertake the full medical costs of COVID-19 treatment and testing, it could not make up for the uneven nature of China's health insurance and social security regimes. Like in the United States, those covered by the most resourceful health insurance and pension schemes and were healthy could go for months without working, whereas those who were not covered or were covered by bare-bone insurance schemes had to fend for themselves during illnesses and periods of unemployment. Anecdotal evidence suggests that this was especially a major problem for China's 290 million migrant workers, who were trapped in the countryside away from their workplaces and had much less access to adequate social insurance coverage. Like more advanced countries, China had a powerful central bank, which began to subsidize government spending via a form of quantitative easing. Yet, in the absence of democratic pressure, the Chinese government devoted central bank funds to the government and to firms, rather than toward financing social spending.

Soon after the Chinese government began to acknowledge the potential of a pandemic, the issue of treatment and testing costs emerged. Even after the reform of the medical insurance system in 2009, some 17 percent of the 290 million or so migrant laborers did not have any form of public health insurance (Chen et al., 2017). Among those with health insurance, out-of-pocket costs for urban residents were still over 50 percent for inpatient care (Huang, 2013). For patients in rural areas, out-of-pocket costs were even higher. For multi-day inpatient care, the costs, even after insurance reimbursement, can surpass the annual salaries of migrant workers. Thus, in late January 2020, some hospitals in Wuhan actually turned away patients because they had insufficient cash or insurance coverage to pay for the potentially high costs of inpatient care. After receiving reports on this phenomenon, the central government on January 25 made a decision to cover the full medical costs of all patients, both confirmed and symptomatic patients, as well as for testing ("Yisi Bingren Nanti" ["The Dilemma of Symptomatic Patients"], 2020). This eliminated a major treatment bottleneck in the system.

Although the government devoted enormous resources to COVID-19 patients, the lockdown exacerbated existing inequality in the medical system, both geographically and across residency status. Geographically, Hubei province had some of the lowest capacity to treat infectious diseases before the COVID-19 outbreak. It only had 1 percent of the hospital beds for treating infectious disease in China, despite having 4 percent of China's population (Liu, 2020). Thus, when the COVID-19 surge began, nearly all the other hospitals in Hubei, especially in Wuhan, were converted to COVID-19 care. This left patients with other critical illnesses without any care. The lockdown instituted on January 23, 2020, meant that patients critically ill with other diseases could not seek help from hospitals outside of Hubei province, even though neighboring provinces all had excess capacity to care for patients (Liu, 2020). Anecdotal evidence suggests that a significant number of patients in Wuhan with critical illnesses such as cancer and HIV died because of the absence of care for one month or more during the lockdown (Qin, 2020c).

Although workers in the government or in state-owned enterprises benefited from a well-funded pension and social security systems, China's traditional social security regime provided little to no coverage to urban workers outside of the state system and especially left out migrant workers, whose household registrations were in the countryside (Frazier, 2010). Since 2010, nationwide minimal assistance insurance (*dibao*) has become available to most urban and rural residents who are unemployed or unable to work (Frazier, 2014). As the quarantine shuttered the majority of economic activities in China, the central government mainly relied on *dibao* to provide basic necessities to unemployed healthy working-age workers and disabled workers, instead of providing additional fiscal assistance. As the CLGCNCP decree on this issue states, "As for those urban residents whose livelihood faces difficulties because Covid-19 prevents them from working in other cities, operate businesses, or otherwise engage in gainful employment, they can be included in the coverage of minimal assistance insurance if they fulfill its enrollment criteria" (CLGCNCP, 2020b).

Yet this was in a sense the least the government could have done. According to a schedule published by the Ministry of Finance, the minimal assistance insurance standard for rural residents in Hubei province, for example, amounted to $67 a month, which was a paltry sum considering the 2019 average per capita rural income of $165 a month for the province and food inflation of over 13 percent in the first half of 2020 (Li et al., 2020a; Ministry of Finance, 2020). For an average Hubei household made up entirely of unemployed rural residents, monthly *dibao* payments only provided 40 percent of the income it had earned in 2019, which allowed it to buy 34 percent of the food it could have purchased with 2019 income. For urban residents in Hubei, the decline was even steeper if they only had received *dibao* payments. The Ministry of Finance–mandated payments to urbanites in Hubei amounted to $90 a month, whereas their per capita disposal monthly income in 2019 was $452, representing an 80 percent drop in income (Ministry of Finance, 2020). To be sure, the majority of urban residents likely had access to other forms of social insurance through their workplaces and thus on average were better off than their counterparts trapped in the countryside, including migrant workers normally employed in cities (Frazier, 2014).

As the quarantine continued and as more people were placed under quarantine in designated facilities, the central government also did not deploy too many additional resources to look after vulnerable populations typically cared for by the quarantined patients. Instead, the neighborhood committees, already inundated with the demands of the quarantine, were also asked to perform this task (CLGCNCP, 2020b). The central decree on this issue states vaguely that "upon notification, the neighborhood (village) personnel should visit and evaluate, and contact relevant persons or organizations to provide care and monitoring of the target population" (CLGCNCP, 2020b). The decree never made clear who the "relevant persons or organizations" would be, leaving the neighborhood committees with the unenviable task of scrambling for resources, or to do nothing. This clearly was one task too far for some of the neighborhood committees as cases of children or elderly starving while their loved ones underwent treatment soon emerged (Li, 2020). In a widely publicized case, a sixteen-year-old with cerebral palsy died of starvation because his caretaker underwent a prolonged period of COVID-19 treatment (Li, 2020). The true extent of this public health crisis remains untold because of government censorship.

At a time of widespread firm shutdown and heightened public health expenses, the Chinese government mobilized the state-controlled financial sector to finance various needs. Because the Chinese government owns the vast majority of banks and because state-owned banks were all governed by party committees (Shih, 2008), the January 20 edict by Xi Jinping and subsequent commands from him and Premier Li Keqiang also were transmitted to the financial sector. By January 31, 2020, the central bank had rolled out an earmarked lending program to provide 300 billion yuan to designated firms, mainly state-owned ones, which engaged in priority activities including the construction of makeshift hospitals, the production of vital medicines and PPE, and the procurement of essential food and necessities (People's Bank of China, 2020). As the containment and recovery effort continued, the central bank unveiled additional programs to finance major policy priorities directly or to subsidize the interest payments of firms affected by the lockdown. In total, the central bank ultimately provided 1 trillion yuan to firms via lending or re-discounting programs ("Yiwan Yi Zaidaikuan Zaitiexian Shiyong Mingque" ["The Usage of the 1 Trillion Yuan in Re-lending Became Clear"], 2020).

Yet little of this was devoted to financing additional government social security spending. Official spending on social security and unemployment for both the central and local governments rose by only 2 percent in the first half of 2020 (Euromoney Institutional Investor PLC, 2020). Given the enormous size of China's supply-side response, the Chinese government certainly could have ordered the central bank to directly or indirectly purchase government bonds to dramatically boost unemployment aid. Yet this was not done.

Explaining Outcomes: Leninist Party Structure with Grassroots Mobilization Capacity

The trajectory of outcomes in China, the rapid ascent in caseload, followed by a rapid and persistent decline in COVID-19 cases, can be explained by two major factors: the Leninist structure of the party-state and the enormous grassroots mobilization capacity of the regime stemming from the socialist legacy of party control over basic social and economic units in society. These features enabled the top leadership to repress information related to COVID-19 in the first phase. When the leadership saw fit to begin national quarantine, these institutional features also allowed for the total mobilization of state and community resources and personnel. Meanwhile, the complete lack of democratic accountability in China compelled the government to provide the minimum level of social aid to economically stressed households to prevent mass starvation. Despite having a clear capacity to provide more help, the Chinese government refrained from doing so.

Three key features of the Leninist party-state played an important role in shaping China's COVID-19 responses. First, within the CCP, lower-level officials must obey decisions made by higher-level party authorities, or else face punishment (CCP, 2017). Although the party constitution allows for debates among party members on policies, once higher-level authorities make a decision, all lower-level party members are obligated to carry out these orders. Thus, the dictates of the highest party authority, that of Xi Jinping himself, become laws for all lower-level party officials to follow, superseding most existing laws and regulations. During emergency periods, failure to obey the dictates of higher-level party authorities brought about especially harsh punishment. During the information repression phase, for example, some grassroots level officials had called for the cancellation of the "ten thousand families banquet," but district party authorities ignored such pleas, and the banquets went ahead (Zhang et al., 2020). Likewise, the party committees in frontline hospitals in Wuhan were ordered to not disclose caseload numbers to the public and only do so to higher-level public health authorities ("Xianchangpian: Wuhan Weicheng" ["Live: The closing of Wuhan"], 2020). As long as the party center did not reveal a strong preference for fighting the epidemic, local officials did not do much on their own initiative, and the epidemic proliferated without much hindrance.

Once mobilization for containment was ordered, local officials immediately were placed under enormous pressure from higher level authorities to put the quarantine in place both at the provincial level and at the neighborhood level. As Xi Jinping stated at a February 3, 2020, Politburo Standing Committee meeting, "for those who are unwilling to take responsibility, who do not take this seriously, who shirk their duties, not only will they be punished. If the consequences are dire, their party and government supervisors also will be held responsible. Dereliction of duty will be punished according to the law" (Xi, 2020). This high-level political pressure was passed down through every level of government down to the grassroots level. As the follow-up order from the BMG reveals, the BMG would "thoroughly implement regional responsibility, departmental responsibility, work unit responsibility and individual responsibility" (BMG, 2020). That is, every party committee and individual party member was held responsible for the proliferation of the disease. At the same time, because the party center hardly focused on other health challenges and economic hardship faced by ordinary people, few government resources were deployed to address these issues.

Second, the Communist Party is a hierarchical command structure embedded in all levels of the government, major firms, major social organizations, and nearly all financial institutions in China (Koss, 2018; Shih, 2008). Thus, when the highest authority in the party issued a clear order, the formal jurisdictional cleavages between these various institutions did not hinder the implementation. Again, when the party center did not reveal a high level of alarm about COVID-19, the rank-and-file party members across various state institutions, including hospitals and China's public health authorities, did very little to disclose to the public the true extent of the epidemic and at times even suppressed information. Behind the scenes, the top leadership likely was very worried starting in early January 2020, but there was only a limited mobilization effort to investigate the severity of the epidemic. Once the highest authorities publicly mobilized the party, however, decrees from the party center quickly cut through the fragmented institutions in China's party-state. Thus, during periods of emergency at least, China's perennial problem of "fragmented authoritarianism" suspended as all party cadres set aside bureaucratic interests for fear of harsh punishment to fulfill commands from the highest authorities (Lieberthal & Oksenberg, 1988).

The formation of the CLGCNCP was the modern manifestation of an old institutional trick from the revolutionary years, which centralized power in the hands of essentially one senior official, who also took full responsibility for the outcome. Even in the late 1920s, the party formed "frontline committees," which entrusted enormous powers in the hands of a senior party official on the front line, who exercised plenipotentiary power over all communist forces on the front line (Gao, 2000). In a similar vein, the party not only formed the CLGCNCP at the central level to coordinate nationwide containment effort; it also formed a Central Guidance Small Group (*Zhongyang Zhidaozu*) headed by Politburo member and Vice Premier Sun Chunlan and top Hubei officials, which directed containment efforts on the ground in Wuhan. Again, the purpose of this Guidance Group was to leverage the high political stature of Sun to cut through jurisdictional cleavages, including the military. The work of the Guidance Group was very granular, including sending leading epidemiologists to neighborhoods in Wuhan to instruct local community cadres on garbage disposal and carrying out nucleic acid testing (Cao, 2020). Despite the effectiveness of these elite bodies in addressing issues directly related to COVID-19, they did not focus on or devote too many resources on severe welfare challenges caused by the lockdown, such as the cessation of income for migrant workers and care for patients with other critical illnesses. Because these leading groups saw these issues as less urgent priorities, the entire Chinese government also neglected these issues.

Third, the mobilization of resources was sped up by the party's existing control over major assets and institutions in China. Despite decades of reform and waves of restructuring and privatization, the Chinese government, and by extension the CCP, still owned and controlled all of the major oil companies, the largest construction companies, almost all of the banks, the railroad, major electricity producers and the grid operator, as well as the largest industrial and electronics firms in the country (Naughton, 2015). During the information repression phase, the party's control over all major media allowed it to suppress information fairly successfully, although rumors of the pandemic spread through private chatrooms online. After January 20, 2020, the massive economic resources directly under the control of the party were mobilized immediately.

Moreover, because the party also controlled the police and the courts, other economic actors had no way of refusing government decrees to mobilize resources under their control. By early February 2020, China's economy was under direct state control whereby the CLGCNCP imposed production targets on designated producers for testing kits, PPE, and other essential medical supplies (China Central Television, 2020a). The leading group also ordered priority material to be channeled to Wuhan at state-mandated prices (China Central Television, 2020a). Even if producers had wanted to sell PPE to the highest bidder, for example, in Shanghai, they did not have that option, nor could they have challenged the government's decision in court. In the case of the COVID-19 pandemic, this feature in China's political system facilitated the production and distribution of PPE and testing kits to areas with the greatest needs. The government's total control over the media and the courts also prevented citizens with concerns about their welfare from suing the government or complaining to the media.

As the preceding discussion demonstrates, China's massive quarantine effort likely would not have succeeded to the same extent had it not been for the millions of neighborhood and village level committees. The neighborhood committee system was reintroduced by the communist authorities in 1949 on the basis of a much older system of local governance, the *baojia* system (Read, 2012). Although it languished through much of the Cultural Revolution and deteriorated some more in the wake of mass SOE closure through the early 1990s, by the late 1990s, the increasingly resourceful central government began to experiment with ways of reviving neighborhood committees (Read, 2012, p. 52). By 2010, the central and municipal governments had provided enough funding such that the heads of residential committees in major cities could expect monthly stipends of $100 to $200, which would have been a nice bonus on top of pension payments that many in these positions already received (Read, 2012, p. 53).

Still, in the face of the epidemic, even the neighborhood committees did not provide sufficient personnel. In a large neighborhood in Wuhan, for example, twenty-one members of the Baibuting neighborhood committee oversaw more than ten thousand residents living in dozens of residential buildings (Zhang et al., 2020). If the entrance of each apartment building needed to be staffed by six community workers, two per eight-hour shift, seventy-two people would be needed to watch over twelve buildings. Clearly, the Baibuting residential committee itself did not provide sufficient personnel. It had to be augmented by SOE workers, teachers, and staff from social organizations (Zhang et al., 2020). Because all of these organizations were loosely or tightly controlled by the party, the party deployed personnel from these organizations to needed areas. Most likely, millions of party members across China were mobilized to augment the neighborhood committees to enforce the quarantine.

Still in the face of enormous health risks and the multiplication of missions piled on to them by the central government, neighborhood committees in heavily affected regions acquitted themselves surprising well, basically ensuring that the stay-at-home order was carried out and facilitating waves of testing, as well as delivering various essential social services to some extent. They likely did not do as well on addressing other social issues confronting the millions of households in lockdown, but that was due to the government's unwillingness to devote greater resources at the community level. Future works will unravel the puzzle of their effectiveness in instituting the quarantine during the COVID-19 pandemic in China.

Discussion

In a way, the relative success with which China dealt with COVID-19 was the product of luck. Because so much power is invested in the hands of Xi Jinping alone, had he chosen to delay mobilization even longer for idiosyncratic personal reason, thousands more would have been infected, and more would have died.

The machineries under the party's control are enormously powerful and resourceful, but they only go into motion when the party center issues a clear signal for mobilization. The initial hesitation by the party center led to a horrendous spike in infection and death in Hubei province and in other parts of China, which was reversed only after the January 25, 2020, Politburo Standing Committee meeting ordered a containment mobilization. The top leadership's singular focus on the pandemic itself, however, led to a systematic neglect of other challenging social and welfare issues confronting vulnerable populations in China, especially the migrant workers.

Certain features of COVID-19 made a strong response by Xi and other senior officials more likely. First, COVID-19 mainly affected urban residents in dense major cities, where the majority of mid-level officials and SOE managers—the main constituency of the party—lived (Wallace, 2014). Potential harm to these core supporters of the party motivated the top leadership and the rank and file party members to devote their energy to fighting this pandemic. Second, COVID-19 spread so rapidly and easily that the authorities were compelled to act, or else risk losing control of it entirely. China's reaction to an epidemic with different features likely would have been less successful. For example, because the acquired immunodeficiency syndrome (AIDS) epidemic mainly affected a more marginalized population and was much slower moving than COVID-19, the Chinese government did not even begin to keep accurate statistics on AIDS patients or to have any coherent policy until ten years after cases had begun to appear in China (Huang, 2013). The dearth of public health response or even basic information campaigns on AIDS led to the rise of AIDS villages in Henan province, which saw the reusing of needles from blood sales causing thousands of infections (Huang, 2013). Future research should further specify features of diseases that would elicit an effective or delayed response from a Leninist party-state such as China.

References

Beijing Municipal Government. (2020, January 25). Guanyu jinyibu mingque zeren, jiaqiang xinxing guanzhuang bingdu ganran de feiyan yufangkongzhi gongzuo de tongzhi [Notice concerning further clarifying responsibilities and strengthening the prevention and control of novel coronaviral pneumonia]. http://www.gov.cn/xinwen/2020-01/25/content_5472169.htm

Cao, Z. (2020, February 16). Zhongyang fu Hubei zhidaozu shequ fangkong jiceng zhuanjiazu fuzeren: yong kexuefangfa, dahao Yiqing fangkong "renmin zhanzheng" [The leading expert for the community transmission prevention section of the Central Guidance Small Group to Hubei: Using scientific methods, we will triumph in the "people's war" against the epidemic]. *Jiankang Bao [Health Tribune]*.

Central Leading Group on Confronting the Novel Coronavirus Pneumonia. (2020a, March 4). Guanyu quanmian luoshi yiqing fangkong yixian chengxiang shequ gongzuozhe guanxin guan'ai cushi de tongzhi [Notice concerning measures for caring for front-line urban and rural community workers engaged in the prevention and control of the epidemic]. http://www.gov.cn/zhengce/content/2020-03/04/content_5486761.htm

Central Leading Group on Confronting the Novel Coronavirus Pneumonia. (2020b, March 7). Guanyu jinyibu zuohao yiqing fangkong qijian kunnan qunzhong doudi baozhang gongzuo de tongzhi [Notice on further improving minimum protection for groups facing difficulties during the quarantine period]. http://www.gov.cn/zhengce/content/2020-03/07/content_5488352.htm

Chen, W., Zhang, Q., Renzaho, A., Zhou, F., Zhang, H., & Ling, L. (2017). Social health insurance coverage and financial protection among rural-to-urban internal migrants in China: evidence from a nationally representative cross-sectional study. *CMJ: Global Health, 2*, 13.

China Central Television. (2020a, January 31). Li Keqiang zhuchi zhaokai zhongyang yingdui xinxing guanzhuang bingdu ganran feiyan Yiqing gongzuo lingdao xiaozu huiyi. [Li Keqiang convenes a Leading Group on Confronting the Novel Coronavirus Pneumonia meeting to arrange for post-new year travel surge and strengthening work on controlling the epidemic]. In *Xinwen Lianbo* [Unified Broadcast]. http://tv.cctv.com/2020/01/31/VIDENDPDzpRo19GityXdgtl6200131.shtml

China Central Television. (2020b, January 21). Bai Yansong bawen zhongnanshan: xinxing guanzhuang bingdu feiyan, qingkuang daodi ruhe? [Bai Leisong asks Zhong Nanshan 8 questions: What is the real situation with the novel coronavirus?]. http://m.news.cctv.com/2020/01/20/ARTIpzG9gFnLXsE7amZvU9MY200120.shtml

Chinese Communist Party. (2017). Zhongguo Gongchandang Zhangcheng—19Da Xiugai [Constitution of the Chinese Communist Party—Revision at the 19th Party Congress]. http://www.12371.cn/special/zggcdzc/zggcdzcqw/

Euromoney Institutional Investor PLC. (2020). *CEIC China Premium Data. Euromoney*. Retrieved July 10, 2020, from https://info.ceicdata.com/en-products-china-premium-database

Frazier, M. W. (2010). *Socialist insecurity: Pensions and the politics of uneven development in China*. Cornell University Press.

Frazier, M. W. (2014). State schemes or safety nets? China's push for universal coverage. *Dædalus, 143*(2), 69–82.

Gao, H. (2000). *Hong taiyang shi zeme shengqide: Yan'an zhengfeng yundong de lailong qumai* [How did the red sun rise: The origin and consequences of the Yan'an Rectification Movement]. Chinese University of Hong Kong Press.

He, G., Wang, X., Linliang, H., Cheng, Y., & Xian, G. (2020, April 21). Wanming jianshezhe 10 tian zuoyou jiancheng huoshenshan he leishenshan yiyuan [Ten thousand builders built Huoshenshan and Leishenshan Hospitals in about 10 days]. *People's Daily*.

Huang, C., Wang, Y., Li, X., Ren, L., Zhao, J., & Hu, Y. (2020). Clinical features of patients infected with 2019 novel coronavirus in Wuhan, China. *Lancet, 395*, 497–506.

Huang, Y. (2013). *Governing health in contemporary China*. Routledge.

Huang, Y. (2020). China's public health response to the COVID-19 outbreak. *China Leadership Monitor, 64*.

King, G., Pan, J., & Roberts, M. (2013). How censorship in China allows government criticism but silences collective expression. *American Political Science Review, 107*, 1–18.

Koss, D. (2018). *Where the party rules: The rank and file of China's Communist State*. Cambridge University Press.

Li, J., Luo, S., & Wu, B. (2020a, July 18). Hubeisheng jumin shouru zengfu paying quanguo pingjun shuiping [The income growth of Hubei residents beat the national average]. *Hubei Tribune*. https://www.hubei.gov.cn/zwgk/hbyw/hbywqb/201907/t20190718_1402979.shtml

Li, Q., Guan, X., Wu, P., Wang, X., & Zhou, L. (2020b). Early transmission dynamics in Wuhan, China, of novel coronavirus–infected pneumonia. *The New England Journal of Medicine, 382*(13), 1199–1208.

Li, Y. (2020, March 9). In coronavirus fight, China's vulnerable fall through the cracks. *The New York Times*, 1–3.

Lieberthal, K., & Oksenberg, M. (1988). *Policy making in China: Leaders, structures, and processes*. Princeton University Press.

Lin, L. (2020, March 10). How China slowed coronavirus: lockdowns, surveillance, enforcers. *The Wall Street Journal*, 2.

Liu, L. (2020). Sustainable COVID-19 mitigation: Wuhan lockdowns, health inequities, and patient evacuation. *International Journal of Health Policy and Management*. https://www.ijhpm.com/article_3798.html

Mattingly, D. (2019). *The art of political repression in China*. Cambridge University Press.

Ministry of Finance. (2020). 2020 nian yijidu dibao biaozhun [The payment schedule for minimum assistance insurance in the first quarter of 2020], Ministry of Finance. http://www.mca.gov.cn/article/sj/tjjb/bzbz/

National Bureau of Statistics. (2020). 2019 nian nongmingong jiance diaocha baogao [Monitoring and investigative report on rural migrant workers, 2019]. *National Bureau of Statistics Bulletins*. http://www.stats.gov.cn/tjsj/zxfb/202004/t20200430_1742724.html

Naughton, B. (2015). The transformation of the state sector: SASAC, the market economy, and the new national champions. In B. Naughton & K. S. Tsai (Ed.), *State capitalism, institutional adaptation, and the Chinese miracle*. Cambridge University.

People's Bank of China. (2020). Guanyu fafang zhuanxiang zaidaikuan zhichi fangkong xinxing guanzhuang bingdu ganran de feiyuan yiqing youguan shixiang de tongzhi [Notice concerning issuing earmarked relending to support the control and prevention of novel coronavirus]. https://cbgc.scol.com.cn/news/272949

Qin, A. (2020a, April 17). China raises coronavirus death toll by 50% in Wuhan. *The New York Times*, 2.

Qin, A. (2020b, March 10). China may be beating the coronavirus, at a painful cost. *The New York Times*, 2.

Qin, A. (2020c, March 3). "No way out": In China, coronavirus takes toll on other patients. *The New York Times*, 1–2.

Read, B. L. (2012). *Roots of the state: Neighborhood organization and social networks in Beijing and Taipei*. Stanford University Press.

Shih, V. (2008). *Factions and finance in China: Elite conflicts and inflation*. Cambridge University Press.

Shijianchou: Wuhan 'fengcheng' de 76tian [Timeline: 76 days of the Wuhan Lockdown]. (2020, April 8). BBC (Chinese). https://www.bbc.com/zhongwen/simp/chinese-news-52197004

Wallace, J. (2014). *Cities and stability: Urbanization, redistribution, and regime survival in China*. Oxford University Press.

Wang, V. (2020, February 21). They documented the coronavirus crisis in Wuhan; then they disappeared. *The New York Times*, 1–2.

Wen, J., Bao, Y., Zhou, L., & Deng, H. (2020, February 20). Yingshou jinshou jianjue daying Wuhan zhan "yi" [Take in all who should be taken in to triumph in the battle against Covid]. *Jingji Ribao [Economic Times]*, 2.

Xi, J. (2020). Zai zhongyang zhengzhiju changwei huiyi yanjiu yingdui xinxing guanzhuang bingdu feiyan Yiqing gongzuo shi de jianghua [Remarks at the Politburo Standing Committee meeting studying work to counter the novel corona virus pneumonia]. *Qiushi [Seek Truth]*, 4, 1–5.

Xia, K. (2020, March 13). *Beijing Xiaotangshan yiyuan qiyong sheqian zhang zhuangwei [Beijing Xiaotangshan Hospital goes into use, equipped with 1000 beds]*. Xinhua. http://www.xinhuanet.com/health/2020-03/16/c_1125721408.htm

Xianchangpian: Wuhan weicheng [Live: The closing of Wuhan]. (2020). *Caixin*, 2–19.

Xinhua. (2020, January 25). Zhonggong zhongyang zhengzhiju changweihui zhaokai huiyi yanjiu xinxing guanzhuang bingdu ganran de feiyan Yiqing fangkong gongzuo; zhonggong zhongyang zongshuji Xi Jinping zhuchi huiyi [The Politburo Standing Committee convenes a meeting to study the control and prevention of novel coronavirus pneumonia, chaired by secretary general Xi Jinping]. *Xinhua*. http://www.gov.cn/xinwen/2020-01/25/content_5472188.htm

Yisi bingren nanti: sheilaiguanxin "yidong de chuanranyuan" [The dilemma of symptomatic patients: Who will care about a "mobile source of infection"]. (2020). *Caixin*, 20–41. Retrieved from http://m.weekly.caixin.com/m/2020-02-01/101510146.html

Yiwan yi zaidaikuan zaitiexian shiyong mingque: meijimeiyiyuan zaidaikuan zhishao zhichi 200 hu [The usage of the 1 trillion yuan in re-lending became clear: every 100 million yuan in relending supports at least 200 enterprises per quarter]. (2020, February 26). *Securities Times*, 1.

Zhang, X., Ren, W., & Lan, Z. (2020, February 13). "Fengcheng" ershirili de Wuhan Baibuting [Wuhan's Baibuting neighborhood during 20 days of "sealed city"]. *Xinhua*. http://www.xinhuanet.com/politics/2020-02/13/c_1125566998.htm

5 PUBLIC POLICY AND LEARNING FROM SARS
Explaining COVID-19 in Hong Kong

John P. Burns

Health outcomes in Hong Kong, a city of 7.3 million, are among the best in the world (Goodman, 2009; Kong et al., 2015). Life expectancy for men (82.2) and women (87.6) makes them the longest lived in the world (Food and Health Bureau, 2019). Infant mortality rates (1.5 per 1000 registered live births) are fourth lowest globally (Food and Health Bureau, 2019). All of this is achieved by spending just 6.2 percent of gross domestic product (GDP) on health care (Food and Health Bureau, 2019), compared to an average of 8.8 percent in Organization for Economic Cooperation and Development (OECD) countries, and 17.1 percent in the United States (OECD, 2020). This makes Hong Kong's healthcare system one of the most efficient (Miller & Lu, 2018). Yet, despite its experience of SARS in 2003 and community solidarity to implement measures to fight the virus, Hong Kong experienced uncontrolled community outbreak of COVID-19. Beginning January 23, 2020, for five months Hong Kong recorded only six deaths from COVID-19. However, by August 26, 2020, Hong Kong had recorded 4,736 confirmed/probable cases and 78 deaths in three waves of COVID-19 infection, each more severe than the previous one (The Government of Hong Kong Special Administrative Region, 2020l). Hong Kong's third wave of contagion, beginning July 5, 2020, was so serious that for the first time since 1997, when China resumed sovereignty over Hong Kong, local authorities sought emergency help from the central government. What happened? Why was Hong Kong unable to cope?

Successive governments in Hong Kong established a dual-track public and private healthcare system. The public system, centered around the Hospital Authority (HA), provides about 90 percent of inpatient services, open to all residents of Hong Kong needing medical care at an "affordable" (nominal) price. The HA delivers these services through a network of forty-three hospitals, employing about 40 percent of local doctors (Hospital Authority, 2020). The private sector provides about 70 percent of all fee-for-service outpatient services (Our Hong Kong Foundation, 2018; Schoeb, 2016). The HA picks up the rest through its public outpatient clinics, again at a nominal charge. The HA system faces a chronic shortage of public health professionals, and patients face long delays for nonemergency services (Cheung & Tsang, 2019; Schoeb, 2016). The public system provides most services for Hong Kong's rapidly aging population. The government estimates that from 2020 to 2066, the percentage of Hong Kong's population sixty-five years or older will grow from 18 percent to 33 percent (Hong Kong Special Administrative Region Census and Statistics Department, 2017b).

The Hong Kong colonial government long ago established a business-friendly low tax system (15 percent salaries tax; 17 percent business tax; and neither value-added tax (VAT), inheritance, nor capital gains taxes). Authorities chose to keep the tax base narrow, relying instead on land and property sales (stamp duty), and property taxes to help balance the budget (Poon, 2010). Only 40 percent of employed people pay any salaries tax, and only 10 percent of businesses pay business tax ("Hong Kong's Narrow Tax Base Is Storing Up Trouble for the Future," 2016). Neither employers nor employees in Hong Kong contribute to a mandatory health insurance scheme. Business-funded think tanks argue that the public health system, funded from annual government appropriations, is financially unsustainable at current levels of service, affordability, and revenue (Bauhinia Foundation Research Center Health Care Study Group, 2007; Hsiao & Yip, 1999; Our Hong Kong Foundation, 2018).

In 2003 the public health system was severely tested by the less infectious but more deadly SARS-1. Then Hong Kong recorded 1,775 cases of SARS-1, of which 299 people died (Legislative Council, 2004; SARS Expert Committee, 2003). Public inquiries into Hong Kong's handling of SARS-1 resulted in reform of Hong Kong's institutions for handling epidemics. Government set up the Center for Health Protection; introduced preparedness and control plans; established a command and control structure for epidemics; and facilitated cross-border public health experts' networks (see The Government of Hong Kong Special Administrative Region, 2014). The most senior government official responsible for Hong Kong's response to SARS-1 resigned to take responsibility for the government's performance (Lee & Benitez, 2004). SARS-1, however, impressed on the people of Hong Kong the importance of following medical advice (wearing masks; hand washing; social distancing), and the community overwhelmingly complied when COVID-19 struck.

Hong Kong's battle with COVID-19 came during a bitter political struggle over the future relationship of Hong Kong to the mainland. Beginning in June 2019 almost daily mass street protests, sometimes involving hundreds of thousands of people, increasingly violent, paralyzed Hong Kong, sank the economy, especially tourism on which Hong Kong depends, and by November, closed the entire school system. Civil servants and white-collar workers spent days working from home (Purbrick, 2019; "The Revolt of Hong Kong," 2019). In 2019 the economy contracted by 2.8 percent and 2.9 percent in the third and fourth quarters "as the local social incidents involving violence [anti-government protests] dealt a heavy blow to economic sentiment and consumption- and tourism-related activities," deepening Hong Kong's recession (The Government of Hong Kong Special Administrative Region, 2020a). Authorities in Beijing and Hong Kong fought back, relying on the police to suppress protest. By December 2019 protests waned.

During the pandemic, authorities imposed a new centrally drafted and draconian national security regime, removed opposition politicians from office, arrested and jailed those who advocated independence for Hong Kong, and most recently postponed local elections to Hong Kong's legislature ("Hong Kong Postpones Legislative Election for a Year Citing COVID-19," 2020). Public trust in government fell from 30.6 percent in December 2018 before the protests to 17.8 percent by March 2020 after nearly a year of protest and two months of pandemic (Hong Kong Institute of Asia Pacific Studies, 2020).

In summary, the government has waged Hong Kong's battle with COVID-19 in an environment of low trust in government (Hartley & Jarvis, 2020). Yet, in the pandemic, the community pulled together (Wan et al., 2020). Public health has mostly not become a political issue.

Public Health Policy

Authorities recorded Hong Kong's first COVID-19 case on January 23, 2020. By that time the government, with more than three weeks' advance warning, was reasonably well prepared, within the limitations of its fragile public healthcare system and its experience of SARS-1. These limitations encouraged officials to take a high-risk, low-cost approach that by early July 2020 led to uncontrolled community spread. The government's strategy was to manage COVID-19 at a level that would not overwhelm Hong Kong's public healthcare system—not to suppress the virus to zero as was attempted on the mainland (Dharmangadan, 2020). By not sufficiently expanding testing, tracing, and isolation capacity, which saved resources in the short term, the government failed to prepare for the community spread that characterized the third wave. Hong Kong authorities relaxed suppression when they perceived that hospitals could cope, well above zero new cases.

At the time of this writing, Hong Kong had experienced three waves of infection. During the first two waves (January 23 to March 14, 2020, and March 15 to July 4, 2020) authorities succeeded in managing the virus, in cycles of "suppression and lift." As they lifted restrictions at the end of the second wave, however, the government implemented policies especially relaxing border control that allowed the infection to enter and spread in the community unchecked (third wave, July 5, 2020, to end of August 2020). Hong Kong found that, like water, the virus seeps through every crack. Local authorities, overwhelmed, requested central government help to ramp up Hong Kong's testing and isolation capacity to bring the virus under control.

Hong Kong acted swiftly to manage COVID-19 in early January, *not* waiting for official notification from the mainland government of the virus's infectiousness, which authorities there delayed (Associated Press, 2020; Da, 2020; Yang, 2020). On December 31, 2019, Hong Kong's infectious disease experts informed the Hong Kong government of what colleagues on the mainland told them had emerged in Wuhan (G. M. Leung, personal communication, June 12, 2020; K. Y. Yuen, personal communication, June 12, 2020). By January 15, 2020, Hong Kong authorities already knew that the virus could spread efficiently from person to person (Chan et al., 2020; K. Y. Yuen, personal communication, June 12, 2020). Hong Kong public health authorities' action in early and mid-January was based on locally sourced expert information and preparations planned in the wake of the 2003 SARS-1 epidemic.

The health minister called the first of scores of meetings on the issue on December 31, 2019. On January 4, 2020, the Hong Kong government raised its official alert level to "serious" on a three-tier scale and promulgated the Preparedness and Response Plan for Novel Infectious Disease of Public Health Significance prepared in advance (Food and Health Bureau, Department of Health, Hospital Authority, 2020; The Government of Hong Kong Special Administrative Region, 2020k). The plan identified in detail the actions required at each response level, assigned responsibilities for each action, and laid down a command and coordination infrastructure, its leadership, membership, and responsibilities (Food and Health Bureau, Department of Health, Center for Health Protection, 2020). By January 14, 2020, nine days before the first recorded case in Hong Kong, because of its stepped-up surveillance of inbound travelers, the Hong Kong government had isolated sixty-eight people in the hospital for observation and put under surveillance 763 close contacts of those hospitalized ("HK Experts to Make Public Wuhan Trip," 2020, January 14). On January 25, 2020, the government raised the alert level to "emergency," and the Chief Executive took over chairing the steering committee and established a four-person advisory experts' group (Lam, 2020a).

Suppression of COVID-19 in Hong Kong included travel-based, community-based, and case-based measures (Cowling et al., 2020; Wu et al., 2020). Travel-based measures targeted travel restrictions, port control, and inbound traveler screening. Community-based measures included physical distancing (e.g., working from home; closure of schools, bars, nightclubs, fitness centers, and theaters; restrictions on dining-in at restaurants) and behavioral changes (e.g., masks, hand hygiene, social distancing) among the general population. Case identification and isolation, and quarantine of close contacts of confirmed cases made up case-based measures (classification of measures is based on Wu et al., 2020). The government used various combinations of these measures to suppress each of the three waves. After bringing the virus to manageable levels, authorities gradually lifted restrictions, attempting to return to some kind of normalcy.

Travel controls. The epidemic hit Hong Kong during the peak Chinese Lunar New Year holiday (January 25 to 28, 2020) travel period. From early February 2020 authorities suspended eleven of thirteen land border control points. At the airport, the government stepped up controls, eventually banning most non-Hong Kong residents, with some exemptions, from entering the territory on March 25, 2020. These measures cut the total number of inbound travelers from 162,000 on January 24, 2020, to about 20,000 by mid-February 2020 and to 1,200 by mid-April 2020, most of whom were Hong Kong residents (Hong Kong Immigration Department, 2020). From February 8, 2020, the government required all inbound travelers to be tested and then either isolated in hospital (all those with positive test results) or quarantined for fourteen days. Wu et al. (2020, p. 4) estimate that the effective reproductive number from imported cases was mostly below one from mid-February[1] and that the fourteen-day mandatory quarantine for travelers was 95 percent effective up to early May.

With no new local infections reported from April 20, 2020, to May 12, 2020, authorities may have perceived that they had managed the second wave. Indeed, by June 25, 2020, the government reported that "people's lives have generally returned to normal" (Lam, 2020d). As part of its measures to lift suppression, in May the government widened the scope of exemptions granted from the mandatory fourteen-day quarantine imposed on all inbound travelers. These included thirty-three categories of inbound travelers, such as essential business travelers, cross-border students, and cross-border truck drivers on whom Hong Kong depended for food and other supplies. By July 5, 2020, the number of confirmed cases began to creep up and then increased rapidly, with a reproductive rate of four. The virus spread quickly through Hong Kong's high-density housing estates and elderly care homes, where visitors previously banned were once again allowed in (Lum et al., 2020). This time the virus infected taxi drivers, restaurant workers and customers, port workers, domestic helpers, hospital and clinic staff and patients, private medical practitioners, civil servants, and students and many other groups, their numerous close contacts mostly untraceable (Lam, 2020e).

It later emerged that authorities had exempted air and sea crews, and that Hong Kong had become a hub for crew changes for airlines, mostly cargo flights, and ships. According to one report, Hong Kong was the only place in southeast Asia that permitted unrestricted crew changes for shipping (Choy et al., 2020). Experts repeatedly pressed the government to close exempted traveler loopholes (J. Wong, 2020). Government resisted, arguing that Hong Kong depended on imports and should facilitate air and sea crew rotation for "humanitarian" reasons (The Government of Hong Kong Special Administrative Region, 2020f; "Up to 250 Crew Members a Day Arrive Without Quarantine," 2020). Authorities eventually tightened the loopholes effective on July 29, 2020 (Siu et al., 2020), but only after it became known that from February to July 2020, the government had exempted from quarantine 290,000 inbound travelers (The Government of Hong Kong Special Administrative Region, 2020e; "Zhèngfǔ Jìn Yuè Fā Yú 29 Wàn Fèn Yīxué Jiānchá Tōngzhī Shū Huòmiǎn Qiángzhì Jiǎnyì" ["The Government Issued More Than 290,000 Medical Surveillance Notices In Recent Months Exempted From Compulsory Quarantine"], 2020). Tests proved that many carried the virus ("Chén Zhàoshī: Dì Sān Bō Yìqíng Yuántóu Láizì Huòmiǎn Jiǎnyì Rénshì Yǒu Shízhèng Zhīchí Huì Yánsù Gēn Jìn," ["Sophia Chan Siu-chee: The Source of the Third Wave of the Epidemic Comes From People Who Are Exempt from Quarantine"], 2020; Ho, 2020a). Asymptomatic, they moved around Hong Kong freely, spreading the disease. The need to obtain central government approval and the government's reluctance to admit that it was wrong may account for the local authorities' delay in tightening the loopholes.

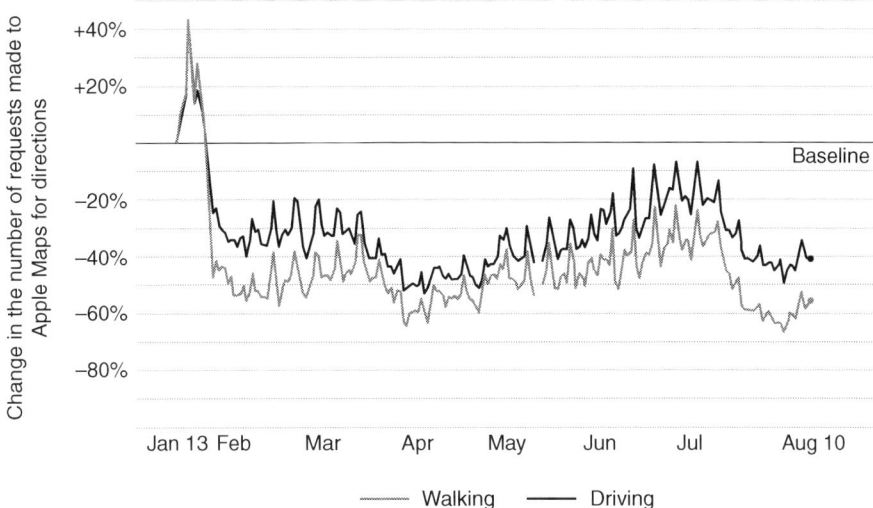

Figure 5.1. Apple mobility trends in Hong Kong, from January 13, 2020 to August 10, 2020.
Source: Apple Maps (2020).

Community measures. It is likely that before mandatory testing of all inbound travelers, asymptomatic carriers infected others in the community. As a result, local clusters of infection emerged in the community (in restaurants and bars and a place of prayer before the government-imposed controls). To suppress COVID-19, the government required civil servants to work from home in February 2020 to March 2, 2020; from March 21, 2020 to May 3, 2020; and from July 20, 2020 to August 24, 2020. About 40 percent of Hong Kong's more than 170,000 civil servants, because of the nature of their jobs, could manage this ("Forty Percent of Civil Servants to Work from Home Starting Tomorrow," 2020). Many businesses and non-government organizations followed. Authorities closed schools and universities from early February 2020 until late May, closing them again in July and August. These measures cut the mobility of the population dramatically (Figure 5.1; Apple Maps, 2020). Wu et al. (2020, pp. 4–5) estimate that working from home and reinstituting working from home reduced the transmissibility to one,[2] and that the effectiveness of civil servants working from home was 67 percent.

Surveys confirm behavioral changes among Hong Kong residents. Respondents reported greater personal hygiene and, by mid-February 2020, the use of face masks in public exceeded 98 percent (Wu et al., 2020, p. 5). After first banning masks in October 2019 to help police identify antigovernment protesters who mostly wore masks (K. Cheng, 2019; The Government of Hong Kong Special Administrative Region, 2019) and then receiving conflicting advice from experts about the efficacy of masks in the fight against COVID-19 (K. Y. Yuen, personal communication, June 12, 2020), the Hong Kong government reversed its position on wearing masks by late February 2020. On July 22, 2020, faced with a third wave of infection, authorities made wearing masks compulsory indoors in public places, and later, on public transport and in public areas (The Government of Hong Kong Special Administrative Region, 2020m).

At the end of each suppression cycle, authorities lifted restrictions, reopening closed businesses such as bars, karaoke lounges, entertainment venues, and theaters. In June 2020 they permitted groups of fifty to meet, up from four and then eight during suppression, for example, in restaurants. With the emergence of a third wave, authorities pointed to "pandemic fatigue": less cautious residents ventured out in large groups, letting their social distancing guard down (Lam, 2020e). Still, the government used the pandemic restrictions to ban all antigovernment protests: when protesters continued to demonstrate in numbers allowed by the regulations, riot police still arrested protesters for violating the regulations (Lau et al., 2020).

Case measures. The Hong Kong government's PCR (polymerase chain reaction) antigen test detects the sequence of the virus RNA (ribonucleic acid) and is generally considered the most accurate (Xia, 2020). Samples may be collected by nasal swab, deep throat saliva, or throat swab (Cheng, 2020). Authorities increased the number of tests from about six hundred per day in early February 2020 (first wave) to from two thousand to four thousand per day from late March 2020 until May (second wave) (Wu et al., 2020, p. 5). The government isolated all who tested positive in the hospital. The government reduced the time from symptom onset to isolation in hospital from ten days in late January 2020 to five days by late March 2020. Still 59 percent of the local cases in March 2020 took five days or longer to isolate (Wu et al., 2020, p. 5). The government published the street addresses of local residents who tested positive to encourage possible additional close contacts to come forward for testing and isolation or quarantine. Case-based quarantine arrangements varied from closed and guarded quarantine camps to less tightly managed quarantine housing estates and hotels, to self-supervised home quarantine for inbound travelers who tested negative, providing them with e-wrist bands that initially failed to allow effective monitoring. Government policy depended on the active cooperation of those quarantined. Authorities fined and jailed the relatively small number caught violating quarantine, five by mid-August (The Government of Hong Kong Special Administrative Region, 2020b, 2020i, 2020j).

By early May 2020 local authorities had tested 170,000 specimens, mostly from pneumonia inpatients and inbound travelers (Wu et al., 2020, p. 5). By July 2020, well into the third wave, demand for tests far exceeded local capacity of about 10,000 tests per day. Moreover, the close contacts of most local infected persons were untraceable, so widespread had the virus become. At the time of this writing, the central government had established temporary testing labs in Hong Kong with a reported target capacity of 500,000 tests per day, based on testing five samples at a time (V. Wong, 2020). The central government also planned to build two temporary emergency COVID-19 hospitals in Hong Kong, similar to those built in Wuhan, to supplement local public hospitals and locally established temporary isolation units (e.g., at Asia World Expo, Lei Yue Mun, and other repurposed facilities) (The Government of Hong Kong Special Administrative Region, 2020h). Government also acted in anticipation of further outbreaks of COVID-19 during the peak winter flu season in the autumn and winter.

Economic and Social Policy

Hong Kong is characterized by high rates of inequality, densely packed and unaffordable housing, and a miserly social welfare net. In 2016 the Gini coefficient[3] was 0.539, adjusted to 0.473 if benefits are included (Hong Kong Special Administrative Region Census and Statistics Department, 2017a). Thousands of poor families in Hong Kong who have yet to qualify for relatively scarce public housing live in subdivided flats, sharing bathrooms and kitchens, or, for elderly singles, in caged bunk spaces. Hong Kong's neoliberal economy provides neither a universal pension nor social security for the elderly (Poon & Wong, 2018). Social distancing measures have impacted the poor and elderly disproportionally. When government shut schools and demanded online learning, poor parents, many single, could hardly cope (Marques, 2020). These issues languished while the government fought COVID-19, trying to mitigate its impact on the economy.

In 2019 and 2020 Hong Kong's economy was hit by a triple whammy: the US-China trade war, six months of almost daily and increasingly violent antigovernment protests, and from late January 2020, COVID-19. As a result, Hong Kong's economy slipped into recession and months of economic contraction. From the second quarter of 2019 Hong Kong's economy contracted rapidly, so that by the first and second quarter 2020 real GDP fell by 9.1 percent and 9.0 percent, year-on-year, respectively ("2nd Tranche of Wage Subsidy Set," 2020; The Government of Hong Kong Special Administrative Region, 2020d). The government forecast a contraction of 6 to 8 percent for the year. Unemployment grew at seldom-seen rates of from about 2 to 3 percent in 2019 to 6.2 percent, the highest in more than fifteen years. Job losses rose by 10.7 percent in April to June 2020 in tourism-related retail, accommodation, and food and beverage, the biggest fall since SARS-1 in 2003. Among them restaurants recorded a 14.7 percent unemployment rate as government restrictions to fight COVID-19 kicked in (The Government of Hong Kong Special Administrative Region Census and Statistics Department, 2020).

A year earlier, months of antigovernment protest hammered these same sectors. In November 2019 alone, tourist arrivals fell by 56 percent, a steeper decline than even during SARS-1 when the WHO posted a travel advisory for Hong Kong and travelers stayed away (L. Cheng, 2019). Hong Kong provides no unemployment compensation, instead supporting the unemployed via a means-tested welfare benefit, set at near destitution levels (comprehensive social security assistance,

CSSA [Hong Kong Social Welfare Department, 2020]). In April and May 2020 the government reported a "sharp" increase in unemployment-related CSSA payments of 3,950 payments and 2,160 payments, respectively ("2nd Tranche of Wage Subsidy Set," 2020). Yet the government's own unemployment statistics indicate that at least 250,000 people lost their jobs during the pandemic ("Hong Kong Facts: Employment," 2019). The government did distribute a one-time payment of HK$10,000 (US$1,282) to each resident.

At the time of this writing, the Hong Kong government had introduced three relatively large-subsidy, tax concession, and stimulus packages to cushion the economy (The Government of Hong Kong Special Administrative Region, 2020d), totaling HK$280 billion (US$36 billion), or 10 percent of the city's GDP. The centerpiece was the Employment Support Scheme (ESS) designed to provide businesses with "time-limited subsidies" to reduce the need for employers to lay off their employees. The government's stated goal was to protect employees and "guarantee employment." On August 18, authorities announced that they had delivered HK$44 billion (US$5.7 billion) in the form of subsidies to 148,000 employers, mostly small and medium-sized enterprises employing fifty or fewer people ("2nd Tranche of Wage Subsidy Set," 2020).

The government intended that 1.9 million workers would benefit from this scheme. Labor groups pointed out, however, that some employers accepted the subsidies and then forced their employees to take pay cuts, unpaid leave, or layoffs. Union representatives complained that 'the scheme doesn't require employers to disclose if they have received the subsidy, and called on employees to file a report if their employer has applied for the subsidy but either failed to pay it out or forced employees to take a reduced wage or unpaid leave" ("Give Anti-Epidemic Funds Directly to Workers: Unions," 2020). Labor groups demanded that the subsidies be paid directly to workers.

Some sectors have prospered during COVID-19, including supermarkets. Under the scheme authorities provided HK$560 million (US$72 million) to the owners of Hong Kong's duopoly supermarket chains, run by two conglomerates, CK Hutchison Holdings (Li Kashing family, Hong Kong's wealthiest) and Dairy Farm (Jardines) ("Hong Kong Subsidies Must End Up in Hands of Those Who Need Them Most," 2020). Each engaged hundreds of thousands of employees. Anticipating criticism, on August 18, 2020, the government promised the conglomerates further subsidies only if they passed on benefits to their customers. How this would be monitored was unclear.

In addition to the ESS, the Hong Kong government subsidized job creation, job advancement, and specific sectors required to fully or partially close because of COVID-19. Authorities also announced a variety of other measures, such as government rent concessions, fee waivers, and deferral of loans. The Hong Kong Monetary Authority, the region's central bank, increased its support for banks (cut reserve requirements, deferred new regulations, and increased bank liquidity), approved payment extensions from corporate customers, and granted other relief in total valued at about HK$1.1 trillion (US$142 billion) (Hong Kong Monetary

Authority, 2020). With help from the Hong Kong government, the local Airport Authority provided a HK$2 trillion (US$258 billion) relief package to the aviation sector. The Hong Kong government also invested HK$30 billion (US$3.9 billion) in Cathay Pacific Airlines, mostly grounded during the pandemic, taking a six percent stake, and $5.4 billion (US$700,000) in a local theme park, Ocean Park (The Government of Hong Kong Special Administrative Region, 2020g; Schofield, 2020; T. K. Wong, 2020).

Explanation

By late August 2020 Hong Kong had managed three waves of COVID-19 relatively successfully. This interim outcome was the result of learning from Hong Kong's experience of SARS-1, support from the central government, a relatively meritocratic bureaucracy, sufficient healthcare investment to support a fragile public health care system, and cross-border networks of infectious disease experts that enabled early detection.

First, Hong Kong is a local government of China, an authoritarian country ruled by the Chinese Communist Party (CCP). Hong Kong's authoritarianism is characterized by centralized political leadership (the CCP), local government that focuses on policy implementation, and a politically dependent and corporatized civil society, which privileges big business (Glasius, 2018; Ma, 2015; Purcell, 1973). This system is implemented via colonial-era political, bureaucratic, economic, and educational institutions, which transitioned mostly unchanged from British to Chinese sovereignty in 1997. The CCP provides political leadership in Hong Kong, guiding, supervising, and directing Hong Kong's civil service-led government. The party rules Hong Kong with the active and enthusiastic support of the united front, of which the Hong Kong government is a core member. Since 2006 but accelerated in 2019, the CCP has shifted Hong Kong's hybrid system of accountability (mixed external political and internal bureaucratic accountability) to one that is predominantly bureaucratic (internal), similar to the rest of China (Romzek & Dubnick, 1987). As of this writing, the party still permits a somewhat greater degree of autonomy for the internet, media, education, and legal/judicial institutions in Hong Kong than exists on the mainland (Basic Law, 1990).

The early post-1997 hybrid system allowed local authorities in Hong Kong to carry out relatively thorough, critical, and transparent investigations into the local government's mismanagement of SARS-1 when it hit Hong Kong in 2003 (Abraham, 2004; Davis & Siu, 2007; Lee & Yun, 2006; Legislative Council, 2004; Thomson & Yow, 2004). Authorities learned from this experience, better preparing Hong Kong for the outbreak of COVID-19 (see the forty-six recommendations in SARS Expert Committee, 2003). Crucially, authorities set up the Center for Health Protection in 2004 with specific responsibility, authority, and accountability for the prevention and control of communicable diseases (Recommendation

No. 2). Authorities improved coordination between the Hospital Authority, which has taken key responsibility for suppression in COVID-19, and the Department of Health (Recommendation No. 3). The government set up a new command structure, the "Steering Committee cum Command Centre," chaired by the Hong Kong Special Administrative Region chief executive when the response level is "emergency," as officials set it on January 25, 2020. Authorities prepared a pandemic management plan for Hong Kong, which they rolled out swiftly on January 4, 2020. They established regular official channels of information sharing with cross-border organizations in the Pearl River Delta and with the National Health Commission in Beijing. The government planned for epidemic surges and all that entails with the HA as the core (Recommendation No. 16). Authorities improved communications with the public, resulting in daily briefings delivered by Center for Health Protection experts, and the informative COVID-19 thematic website and dashboard (Recommendation No. 23) (Hong Kong Center for Health Protection, 2020b). Government increased support for research on newly emerging infectious diseases and university medical schools redirected research to this topic (Recommendation Nos. 35–40) (K. Y. Yuen, personal communications, June 12 and 14, 2020, and August 4 and 11, 2020; also see Wong et al., 2017). Officials have had less success, however, at improving coordination between the public and private healthcare systems. Public doctors continue to be attracted to lucrative private practice, which the medical profession is unwilling to touch.

Hong Kong's experience of SARS prepared the people of Hong Kong for months of nearly universal mask wearing, stepped up personal hygiene, and social distancing that, although not completely locking down the territory, produced the economic dislocation discussed previously (Wan et al., 2020). Hong Kongers are pragmatic and seek to protect themselves and their families. They are also generally law abiding, and COVID-19 management rules were made law. Respect for experts and peer pressure also contributed to this result, largely unaffected by deep political divisions, months of antigovernment protest, and distrust of government.

Second, China is a unitary, not federal, system. Once the central government decided to suppress COVID-19, it did so very effectively, imposing tight border controls and complete lockdowns (see chapter 4). Hong Kong benefited from China's unitary system. The central government provided border control, access to masks and personal protective equipment, improved testing and isolation capacity, and a postponed legislative election. From late June 2020 new tools were provided to suppress antigovernment protests (the national security law and its infrastructure). Further, Hong Kong could close its border with the mainland because the central government agreed to this move.

Third, the technical competence, professionalism, and reputation of the Hong Kong public healthcare system are relatively high (Goodman, 2009; Kong et al., 2015). In 1991 the government centralized management of all public hospitals in a hybrid organization, the HA, headed by a medical doctor. A board of directors governs the system, now employing 67,000 people. Authorities organized public hospitals into seven regional clusters, each with a CEO to improve efficiency and service delivery. The system has allowed specialization across the territory. These moves better coordinated public health care and improved performance monitoring. The Secretary for Food and Health, traditionally a medical specialist, provides policy guidance to the HA (Gauld & Gould, 2002). Fourth, the government subsidizes the HA, amounting to about 14 percent of annual recurrent expenditure, third only to education (19 percent) and social welfare (14 percent) (Legislative Council, 2020). Substantial infrastructural and financial investments were made in pandemic preparations in the wake of SARS-1. Still, as we have seen, Hong Kong's public hospital-based healthcare system is fragile and financially unsustainable.

Finally, Hong Kong's infectious disease specialists have developed dense networks of professional collaboration with colleagues on the mainland and overseas. Hong Kong is a global hub for the study of coronaviruses and avian influenza, based on its location. Western specialists visit Hong Kong to study these diseases. Hong Kong epidemiologists and public health experts serve in senior positions in mainland hospitals (e.g., the University of Hong Kong-Shenzhen Hospital), giving them access to patients. The central government and the WHO invite Hong Kong's medical experts to join fact-finding missions to investigate novel coronaviruses. K. Y. Yuen, University of Hong Kong, joined the third National Health Commission mission to Wuhan in January 2020, which reported the infectiousness of COVID-19 at a Beijing press conference on 20 January. G. M. Leung, University of Hong Kong, joined the WHO mission to Wuhan in February 2020. Both Yuen and Leung, and undoubtedly others, received information on December 31, 2019, about the situation in Wuhan that the Hong Kong authorities acted on in early January 2020. As a result of these networks, Hong Kong could act early, and it did.

Conclusion

Hong Kong learned from its experience of SARS-1. Political leadership capable of learning is an asset. Still Hong Kong's preparations were incomplete. Prepared as they were by experts and bureaucrats, the plans assumed the continued existence of an unreformed colonial-era public finance system and a fragile, barely able to cope public health system. That was to be expected. Political leaders should consider the larger picture. Yet Hong Kong's political system has proven unable to produce political leaders up to the challenge.

Hong Kong's authoritarian political system, even though contested, has thus far prevented deep political divisions and distrust of government from fracturing the community's response to COVID-19. In Hong Kong, the community appears to have compartmentalized politics and its pandemic response. The lack of electoral politics during a pandemic and the relatively low stakes of elections in Hong Kong (voters do not elect the government) may account for this outcome.

Notes

1. This is the estimated number of people an infected person would infect. Authorities sought to reduce it to less than one.
2. This is the estimated number of people an infected person would infect. Authorities sought to reduce it to less than one.
3. The Gini coefficient is a measure of the distribution of income across a population used as a gauge of economic inequality. The coefficient ranges from 0 (or 0%) to 1 (or 100%), with 0 representing perfect equality and 1 representing perfect inequality.

References

2nd tranche of wage subsidy set. (2020, August 18). news.gov.hk. https://www.news.gov.hk/eng/2020/08/20200818/20200818_171926_948.html

Abraham, T. (2004). *Twenty-first century plague: The story of SARS.* University of Hong Kong Press.

Apple Maps. (2020). *Mobility trends reports*, Hong Kong. https://covid19.apple.com/mobility

Associated Press. (2020, April 15). *China didn't warn public of likely pandemic for 6 key days.* https://www.cnbc.com/2020/04/15/china-didnt-warn-public-of-likely-pandemic-for-6-key-days.html

Basic Law of the Hong Kong Special Administrative Region of the People's Republic of China (Basic Law) (1990). http://www.law.hku.hk/hrportal/wp-content/uploads/file/HK-Basic-Law.pdf

Bauhinia Foundation Research Center Health Care Study Group. (2007). *Development and financing of Hong Kong's future health care: Final report.* http://www.bauhinia.org/assets/pdf/research/20070824/BFRC-HC-FR-EN.pdf

Chan, J. F. W., Yuan, S. F., Kok, K. H., To, K. K., Chu, H., Yang, J., Xing, F., Liu, J., Yip, C. C., Poon, R. W., Tsoi, H. W., Lo, S. K., Chan, K. H., Poon, V. K., Chan, W. M., Ip, J. D., Cai, J. P., Cheng, V. C., Chen, H., . . . Yuen, K. Y. (2020, February 15). A familial cluster of pneumonia associated with the 2019 novel coronavirus indicating person-to-person transmission: a study of a family cluster. *Lancet, 395*(10223), 514–523.

Chén zhàoshǐ: Dì sān bō yìqíng yuántóu láizì huòmiǎn jiǎnyì rénshì yǒu shízhèng zhīchí huì yánsù gēn jìn [Sophia Chan Siu-chee (Secretary for Food and Health): The source of the third wave of the epidemic comes from people who are exempt from quarantine. There is empirical support and will follow up seriously]. (2020, July 28). Now News Channel. https://news.now.com/home/local/player?newsId=399580

Cheng, K. (2019, October 4). Hong Kong officially enacts emergency laws to ban masks at protests as NGOs criticize "draconian" measures. *Hong Kong Free Press.* https://hongkongfp.com/2019/10/04/breaking-hong-kong-officially-enacts-emergency-laws-ban-masks-protests-ngos-criticise-draconian-measure/

Cheng, L. (2019, December 31). Tourist arrivals take sharpest plunge in November since protests began in Hong Kong. *South China Morning Post.* https://www.scmp.com/news/hong-kong/hong-kong-economy/article/3044121/tourist-arrivals-take-sharpest-plunge-november

Cheng, L. (2020, August 10). Coronavirus: Hong Kong health experts urge authorities to use various testing methods for residents of different age groups. *South China*

Morning Post. https://www.scmp.com/news/hong-kong/health-environment/article/3096771/coronavirus-hong-kong-health-experts-urge

Cheung, E., & Tsang, E. (2019, February 26). Hong Kong's health care system is teetering on the brink. *South China Morning Post.* https://www.scmp.com/news/hong-kong/health-environment/article/2187630/hong-kongs-health-care-system-teetering-brink

Choy, G., Ting, V., & Cheng, L. (2020, July 23). Hong Kong third wave: Fresh record set with 118 Covid-19 as city confronts risk of infected crew aboard cargo ships. *South China Morning Post.* https://www.scmp.com/news/hong-kong/health-environment/article/3094340/hong-kong-third-wave-another-record-day-covid-19

Chung, R. Y. N, & Marmot, M. (2020, January 21). *People in Hong Kong have the longest life expectancy in the world: Some possible explanations.* National Academy of Medicine. https://nam.edu/people-in-hong-kong-have-the-longest-life-expectancy-in-the-world-some-possible-explanations/

Cowling, B. J., Ali, S. T., Ng, T. W. Y., Tsang, T. K., Li, J. C. M., Fong, M. W., Liao, Q. Y., Kwan, M. W. Y., Lee, S. L., Chiu, S. S., Wu, J. T., Wu, P., & Leung, G. M. (2020). Impact assessment of non-pharmaceutical interventions against coronavirus disease 2019 and influenza in Hong Kong: an observational study. *Lancet Public Health, 5*(5), e279–e288. https://www.sciencedirect.com/science/article/pii/S2468266720300906

Da, S. J. (2020, January 27). The truth about "dramatic action." https://chinamediaproject.org/2020/01/27/dramatic-actions/

Davis, D., & Siu, H. (Eds.). (2007). *SARS: Reception and interpretations in three Chinese cities* Routledge.

Dharmangadan, M. (2020, July 13). Hong Kong third wave: Public needs to step up and keep coronavirus at bay. *South China Morning Post.* https://www.scmp.com/comment/opinion/article/3092922/hong-kong-third-wave-public-needs-step-and-keep-coronavirus-bay

Food and Health Bureau. (2019). *Health facts of Hong Kong.* https://www.dh.gov.hk/english/statistics/statistics_hs/files/Health_Statistics_pamphlet_E.pdf

Food and Health Bureau, Department of Health, Center for Health Protection. (2020). *Preparedness and response plan for novel infectious disease of public health significance.* https://www.chp.gov.hk/files/pdf/govt_preparedness_and_response_plan_for_novel_infectious_disease_of_public_health_significance_eng.pdf

Food and Health Bureau, Department of Health, Hospital Authority. (2020, February 18). *Prevention and control of novel coronavirus in Hong Kong.* https://www.legco.gov.hk/yr19-20/english/counmtg/papers/cm20200219p-e.pdf

Forty percent of civil servants to work from home starting tomorrow. (2020, July 19). *The Standard.* https://www.thestandard.com.hk/breaking-news/section/4/151254/Forty-percent-of-civil-servants-to-work-from-home-starting-tomorrow:-CE

Gauld, R., & Gould, D. (2002). *The Hong Kong health sector: Development and change.* Chinese University Press.

Give anti-epidemic funds directly to workers: unions. (2020, August 18). Radio Television Hong Kong. https://news.rthk.hk/rthk/en/component/k2/1544394-20200818.htm

Glasius, M. (2018). What authoritarianism is . . . and is not: a practice perspective. *International Affairs, 94*(3), 515–533.

Goodman, J. (2009). *Hong Kong's health care system is number one.* http://healthblog.ncpathinktank.org/hong-kong-health-care-system-is-number-one/#sthash.SYELTDgT.dpbs

The Government of Hong Kong Special Administrative Region. (2014). *Preparedness plan for influenza pandemic.* https://www.chp.gov.hk/files/pdf/erib_preparedness_plan_for_influenza_pandemic_2014_eng.pdf

The Government of Hong Kong Special Administrative Region. (2019, October 4). *CE's opening remarks at press conference* [Press release]. https://www.info.gov.hk/gia/general/201910/04/P2019100400773.htm

The Government of Hong Kong Special Administrative Region. (2020a). *2019 economic background and 2020 economic prospects.* https://www.hkeconomy.gov.hk/en/pdf/er_19q4.pdf

The Government of Hong Kong Special Administrative Region. (2020b, March 30). *3 jailed for violating quarantine.* [Press release]. https://www.news.gov.hk/eng/2020/03/20200330/20200330_174317_389.html

The Government of Hong Kong Special Administrative Region. (2020c). *Anti-epidemic fund.* https://www.coronavirus.gov.hk/eng/anti-epidemic-fund.html

The Government of Hong Kong Special Administrative Region. (2020d, August 14). *Economic situation in second quarter of 2020 and latest GDP and price forecasts for 2020.* https://www.info.gov.hk/gia/general/202008/14/P2020081400405.htm

The Government of Hong Kong Special Administrative Region. (2020e, March 18). *Exemption arrangement under compulsory quarantine of persons arriving at Hong Kong from foreign places regulation.* https://www.info.gov.hk/gia/general/202003/18/P2020031800812.htm

The Government of Hong Kong Special Administrative Region. (2020f, July 19). *Government clarifies on necessity of quarantine exemption arrangement* [Press release]. https://www.info.gov.hk/gia/general/202007/19/P2020071900491.htm

The Government of Hong Kong Special Administrative Region. (2020g, June 9). *Government upholds Hong Kong's international aviation hub status through Land Fund investment* [Press release]. https://www.info.gov.hk/gia/general/202006/09/P2020060900753.htm

The Government of Hong Kong Special Administrative Region. (2020h, August 7). *HKSAR Government explains work plan of support team from central government* [Press release]. https://www.info.gov.hk/gia/general/202008/07/P2020080700861.htm

The Government of Hong Kong Special Administrative Region. (2020i, May 26). *Man fined for breaching compulsory quarantine order* [Press release]. https://www.info.gov.hk/gia/general/202005/26/P2020052600577.htm

The Government of Hong Kong Special Administrative Region. (2020j, August 10). *Man fined for breaching compulsory quarantine order* [Press release]. https://www.info.gov.hk/gia/general/202008/10/P2020081000628.htm

The Government of Hong Kong Special Administrative Region. (2020k, January 4). *Shíwù jí wèishēng jú júzhǎng huìjiàn chuánméi tánhuà nèiróng [Secretary for Food and Health Talks to the Media].* https://www.info.gov.hk/gia/general/202001/04/P2020010400407.htm?fontSize=1

The Government of Hong Kong Special Administrative Region. (2020l). *Together we fight the virus.* https://www.coronavirus.gov.hk/eng/index.html#Useful_Information

The Government of Hong Kong Special Administrative Region. (2020m). *Together we fight the virus. Wearing masks in public places*. https://www.coronavirus.gov.hk/eng/public-transport-faq.html

The Government of Hong Kong Special Administrative Region Census and Statistics Department. (2020, July 20). *Unemployment and underemployment statistics April-June 2020* [Press release]. https://www.censtatd.gov.hk/press_release/pressReleaseDetail.jsp?pressRID=4662&charsetID=1

Hartley, K., & Jarvis, D. S. L. (2020). Policymaking in a low-trust state: Legitimacy, state capacity, and responses to COVID-19 in Hong Kong. *Policy and Society*, 1–21.

Health Welfare and Food Bureau. (2003). *Checklist of measures to combat SARS*. https://www.chp.gov.hk/files/pdf/erib_checklist_of_measures_to_combat_sars_en.pdf

HK experts to make public Wuhan trip details. (2020, January 14). Radio Television Hong Kong. https://news.rthk.hk/rthk/en/component/k2/1502685-20200114.htm

Ho, K. (2020a, July 28). Covid-19 surge: Hong Kong admits quarantine exemptions may be to blame, as city sees 106 new infections. *Hong Kong Free Press*. https://hongkongfp.com/2020/07/28/covid-19-surge-hong-kong-admits-quarantine-exemptions-may-be-to-blame-as-city-sees-106-new-infections/

Ho, K. (2020b, August 7). Hong Kong government to offer city-wide Covid-19 testing amid third wave. *Hong Kong Free Press*. https://hongkongfp.com/2020/08/07/breaking-hong-kong-govt-to-offer-city-wide-covid-19-testing-amid-third-wave/

Hong Kong Center for Health Protection. (2020a, January 9). *Proper use of mask*. https://www.chp.gov.hk/en/healthtopics/content/460/19731.html

Hong Kong Center for Health Protection. (2020b). Covid-19 Dashboard. https://chp-dashboard.geodata.gov.hk/covid-19/en.html

Hong Kong facts: Employment. (2019). GovHK. https://www.gov.hk/en/about/abouthk/factsheets/docs/employment.pdf

Hong Kong Immigration Department. (2020). *Statistics on passenger traffic*. https://www.immd.gov.hk/eng/message_from_us/stat_menu.html

Hong Kong Institute of Asia Pacific Studies, Chinese University of Hong Kong. (2020). *Trust in government surveys*. https://www.cpr.cuhk.edu.hk/en/press_detail.php?id=3252&t=survey-findings-on-hksar-government-s-popularity-in-march-2020-released-by-hong-kong-institute-of-asia-pacific-studies-at-cuhk

Hong Kong Monetary Authority. (2020, April 22) *Riding through COVID 19 outbreaks and supporting Hong Kong economy*. https://www.hkma.gov.hk/media/eng/doc/relief-measures-one-pager.pdf

Hong Kong postpones legislative election for a year citing COVID-19. (2020, July 31). *Hong Kong Free Press*. https://hongkongfp.com/2020/07/31/breaking-hong-kong-postpones-legislative-election-citing-covid-19/

Hong Kong Social Welfare Department. (2020). *Comprehensive Social Security Assistance Scheme*. https://www.swd.gov.hk/en/index/site_pubsvc/page_socsecu/sub_comprehens/

Hong Kong Special Administrative Region Census and Statistics Department. (2017a, June 9). *Census and Statistics Department announces results of study on household income distribution in Hong Kong*. https://www.censtatd.gov.hk/press_release/pressReleaseDetail.jsp?charsetID=1&pressRID=4180

Hong Kong Special Administrative Region Census and Statistics Department. (2017b). *Hong Kong population projection, 2017–2066*. https://www.statistics.gov.hk/pub/B1120015072017XXXXB0100.pdf

Hong Kong's narrow tax base is storing up trouble for the future. [Editorial]. (2016, March 1). *South China Morning Post.* https://www.scmp.com/comment/insight-opinion/article/1919533/hong-kongs-narrow-tax-base-storing-trouble-future

Hong Kong subsidies must end up in hands of those who need them most. [Editorial]. (2020, August 19). *South China Morning Post.* https://www.scmp.com/comment/opinion/article/3097875/hong-kong-subsidies-must-end-hands-those-who-need-them-most

Hospital Authority. (2020). https://www.ha.org.hk/visitor/ha_visitor_index.asp?Content_ID=10008&Lang=ENG&Dimension=100&Parent_ID=10004

Hsiao, W., & Yip, W. (1999). Improving Hong Kong's health care system: Why and for whom? (Harvard University study). https://www.fhb.gov.hk/en/press_and_publications/consultation/HCS.HTM#MAIN%20REPORT

Kong, X. Y., Yang, Y., Gao, J., Guan, J., Liu, Y., Wang, R. Z., Xing, B., Li, Y. N., & Ma, W. B. (2015). Overview of the health care system in Hong Kong and its referential significance to mainland China. *Science Direct, 78,* 569–573. https://www.sciencedirect.com/science/article/pii/S1726490115001458

Lam, C. (HKSAR Chief Executive). (2020a, February 25). *Continue our fight, determined to win.* https://www.ceo.gov.hk/eng/pdf/article20200225.pdf

Lam, C. (2020b, April 25). *Three months into our fight, seeing the arrival of dawn.* https://www.ceo.gov.hk/eng/pdf/article20200425.pdf

Lam, C. (2020c, May 25). *Four months into our fight, striking the right balance.* https://www.ceo.gov.hk/eng/pdf/article20200525.pdf

Lam, C. (2020d, June 25). *Resuming activities after fight the virus for five months.* https://www.ceo.gov.hk/eng/pdf/article20200625.pdf

Lam, C. (2020e, July 25). *Fighting the virus for six months, battling another wave of the epidemic together.* https://www.ceo.gov.hk/eng/pdf/article20200725.pdf

Lau, C., Ng, K. C., & Siu, P. (2020, July 21). Hong Kong protests: activists holding banner arrested on suspicion of breaking new security law on anniversary of Yuen Long attack. *South China Morning Post.* https://www.scmp.com/news/hong-kong/politics/article/3094111/hong-kong-protests-activists-fined-breaking-social

Lee, D. T. S., & Yun, K. W. (2006). Psychological responses to SARS in Hong Kong—Report from the front line. In A. Kleinman & J. L. Watson (Eds.), *SARS in China: Prelude to pandemic?* (pp. 133–147). Stanford University Press.

Lee, K., & Benitez, M. (2004, July 8). Dedicated Yeoh quits over Sars. *South China Morning Post.* https://www.scmp.com/article/462297/dedicated-yeoh-quits-over-sars

Legislative Council of the Hong Kong Special Administrative Region of the People's Republic of China. (2004). *Report into the select committee to inquire into the handling of the severe acute respiratory syndrome (SARS) by the government and the hospital authority.* https://www.legco.gov.hk/yr03-04/english/sc/sc_sars/reports/sars_rpt.htm

Legislative Council of the Hong Kong Special Administrative Region of the People's Republic of China. (2020). *The 2020–2021 Budget. Research Brief,* 1, https://www.legco.gov.hk/research-publications/english/1920rb01-the-2020-2021-budget-20200403-e.pdf

Lum, T., Shi, C., Wong, G., & Wong, K. (2020, May 31). COVID-19 and long-term care policy for older people in Hong Kong. *Journal of Aging and Social Policy, 32,* 4–5, 373–379.

Ma, N. (2015). The making of a corporatist state in Hong Kong: The road to sectoral intervention. *Journal of Contemporary Asia, 46*(2), 1–20.

Marques, C. F. (2020, August 17). *Hong Kong's closed schools risk a lost generation. Bloomberg.* https://www.bloomberg.com/opinion/articles/2020-08-16/hong-kong-school-closures-risk-long-term-economic-damage

Miller, L. J., & Lu, W. (2018, September 19). These are the economies with the most (and least) efficient health care. *Bloomberg.* https://www.bloomberg.com/news/articles/2018-09-19/u-s-near-bottom-of-health-index-hong-kong-and-singapore-at-top

Organization for Economic Cooperation and Development. (2020). https://www.oecd.org/els/health-systems/health-expenditure.htm

Our Hong Kong Foundation. (2018). *Fit for purpose: A health care system for the 21st century research report.* https://www.ourhkfoundation.org.hk/sites/default/files/media/pdf/ohkf_research_report_digital_1201.pdf

Poon, A. W. H. (2010). *Land and the ruling class in Hong Kong.* (2nd ed.) Enrich Professional Publishing.

Poon, C. C., & Wong, F. K. J. (2018, July 1). Pension reform options in Hong Kong. *Journal of Financial Counseling and Planning, 29,* 2. https://www.questia.com/library/journal/1P4-2200124830/pension-reform-options-in-hong-kong

Purbrick, M. (2019). A report of the 2019 protests. *Journal of Asian Affairs, 50*(4), 465–487.

Purcell, S. K. (1973). Review: Authoritarianism. *Comparative Politics, 5*(2), 301–312.

The revolt of Hong Kong. (2019, August 16–December 20). *Reuters Investigates.* https://www.reuters.com/investigates/section/hongkong-protests/

Romzek, B. S., & Dubnick, M. J. (1987, May/June). Accountability in the public sector: Lessons from the Challenger tragedy. *Public Administration Review,* 227–238.

SARS Expert Committee. (2003). *SARS in Hong Kong: From experience to action.* https://www.sars-expertcom.gov.hk/english/reports/reports.html

Schoeb, V. (2016). Healthcare service in Hong Kong and its challenges: The role of health professionals within a social model of health. *China Perspectives, 4,* 51–58.

Schofield, A. (2020, April 9). *Cathay Pacific and other Hong Kong-based airlines will gain substantial financial benefits from a new COVID-19 aid package unveiled by the government.* https://www.routesonline.com/news/29/breaking-news/290728/cathay-hong-kong-airlines-to-get-more-covid-19-government-aid/

Siu, P., Choy, G., & Low, Z. (2020, July 26) Hong Kong third wave: health experts question "late" move to plug Covid-19 loopholes for seafarers and air crew as city records another 128 infections. *South China Morning Post.* https://www.scmp.com/news/hong-kong/health-environment/article/3094738/hong-kong-third-wave-sea-crew-changes-passenger

Thomson, E., & Yow, C. H. (2004). The Hong Kong SAR government, civil society and SARS. In J. Wong & Y. N. Zheng (Eds.), *The SARS epidemic: Challenges to China's crisis management* (pp. 199–220). World Scientific.

Up to 250 crew members a day arrive without quarantine. (2020, July 28). *The Standard.* https://www.thestandard.com.hk/section-news/section/4/221310/Up-to-250-crew-members-a-day-arrive-without-quarantine

Wan, K. M., Ho, L. K. K., Wong, N. W. M., & Chiu, A. (2020, October). Fighting COVID-19 in Hong Kong: The effects of community and social mobilization. *World Development, 134,* 105055.

Wong, A. T. Y., Chen, H., Liu, S. H., Hsu, E. K., Luk, K. S., Lai, C. K. C., Chan, R. F. Y., Tsang, O. T. Y, Choi, K. W., Kwan, Y. W., Tong, A. T. H., Cheng, V. C. C., Tsang, D. N. C., &

Central Committee on Infectious Diseases and Emergency Response, Hospital Authority. (2017, May 15). From SARS to avian influenza preparedness in Hong Kong. *Clinical Infectious Diseases, 64*(suppl 2), S98–S104.

Wong, J. (2020, July 20). *Hong Kong may need a virtual lockdown if surge continues.* Radio Television Hong Kong. https://news.rthk.hk/rthk/en/component/k2/1538790-20200720.htm

Wong, T. K. (2020, June 9). Hong Kong government announces HK$30 billion bailout for Cathay Pacific. *South China Morning Post.* https://www.scmp.com/yp/discover/news/hong-kong/article/3088216/hong-kong-government-announces-hk30-billion-bailout

Wong, V. (2020, August 13). *Sai Ying Pun Center can handle 500,000 tests: Expert.* Radio Television Hong Kong. https://news.rthk.hk/rthk/en/component/k2/1543486-20200813.htm

Wu, P., Tsang, T. K., Wong, J. Y., Ho, F., Gao, H. Z., Adam, D. C., Cheung, D. H., Lau, E. H. Y., Lim, W. W., Ali, S. T., Ip, D. K. M., Wu, J. T., Cowling, B. J., & Leung, G. M. (2020, June). Suppressing COVID-19 transmission in Hong Kong: an observational study of the first four months. *Lancet.* https://www.researchgate.net/publication/342057183_Suppressing_COVID-19_transmission_in_Hong_Kong_an_observational_study_of_the_first_four_months

Xia, S. (2020, April 5). Coronavirus testing: how it works and where to get tested for Covid-19. *South China Morning Post.* https://www.scmp.com/news/hong-kong/health-environment/article/3078508/coronavirus-testing-how-it-works-and-where-get

Yang, D. L. (2020, March 10). Wuhan officials tried to cover up COVID-19—and sent it careening outward. *The Washington Post.*

Yung, C. (2006, December 6). Sales tax sunk. *The Standard.* https://web.archive.org/web/20090916233902/http://www.thestandard.com.hk/news_detail.asp?pp_cat=2&art_id=33467&sid=11208287&con_type=3&d_str=20061206&sear_year=2006

Zhèngfǔ jìn yuè fā yú 29 wàn fèn yīxué jiānchá tōngzhī shū huòmiǎn qiángzhì jiǎnyì [The government issued more than 290,000 medical surveillance notices in recent months exempted from compulsory quarantine]. (2020, July 24). Radio Television Hong Kong. https://news.rthk.hk/rthk/ch/component/k2/1539729-20200724.htm

6 INSTITUTIONS MATTER IN FIGHTING COVID-19

Public Health, Social Policies, and the Control Tower in South Korea

June Park

South Korea's Response to the COVID-19 Pandemic

What role do institutions play in overcoming a public health crisis? The case of COVID-19 in South Korea suggests that, amid the country's whirlwind of populism and geopolitical struggles, the country's resilience in the pandemic relies heavily on technocratic measures that derive from the political necessity of the leadership and the demand by the public to end the pandemic, while simultaneously relying on the participation of the people and resisting public protests as a democracy.

Institutions have been critical to South Korea's response to COVID-19. South Korea's handling of COVID-19 has been based on its experience of the Middle East respiratory syndrome (MERS) in 2015—another coronavirus that rocked the country, albeit in a relatively short period compared to COVID-19. In 2015 South Korea recorded 38 deaths and 186 confirmed cases, higher than anywhere in the world outside the Middle East—an appalling figure for a country that is well equipped with a universal healthcare system and high quality public health infrastructure. The realization from MERS that full utilization of the country's extant facilities must be coupled with institutional change resonated through the public health bureaucracy. Many of the institutional measures that were transformed post-MERS were critical to the response to COVID-19, and additional institutional changes were made during the COVID-19 pandemic. Overall, institutional transformation of public health and social policies in South Korea is built on experience and responses from the public.

Specifically, what has become more salient during the COVID-19 pandemic is that public health authorities formulate policies from the technocratic perspective but at the same time are constantly met with demands to satisfy the public from their own perspectives. South Korea has evolved in the past three decades since the country's democratization in the 1980s, and the country can no longer tolerate a system whereby policies are dictated to its people. The policy think-through, therefore, must resonate with the public to bring about strong participation among them. A plethora of its citizens would participate rigorously in a government-driven initiative to combat the virus by choice—be it large-scale real-time polymerase chain reaction (RT-PCR) testing and QR code-check-ins for personal data sharing under the Infectious Disease Control and Prevention Act (IDCPA) and the Medical Service Act, or social distancing measures and quarantine under the Quarantine Act—in the hopes of getting back to normal life as law-abiding citizens.

This chapter broadly examines the role of institutions in South Korea in its response to the COVID-19 pandemic through public health and social policies, embodied by the three Ts: testing, tracing, and treatment, spearheaded by the Korea Disease Control and Prevention Agency (KDCA). On health policy and public health measures, the chapter centers on the implementation of the revised IDCPA and the Medical Service Act. These provided legal grounds for emergency-use authorization (EUA) of RT-PCR test kits by KCDC in public and private hospitals as well as drive-through test sites; the electronic contact-tracing "Smart Management System" (SMS) under the by the Ministry of Land, Infrastructure and Transport (MOLIT) based on personal data; and free testing and treatment under South Korea's universal healthcare system. The implementation of the revised Quarantine Act allowed for quarantining individuals with confirmed cases of COVID-19, while social distancing measures based on the COVID-19 reproduction rate (R-value: the number of people that one infected person will pass on a virus to, on average) were enacted by the Ministry of Health and Welfare (MOHW) in lieu of full-fledged lockdowns. The chapter also examines disinfection and public mask provision through controlled domestic production by the Ministry of Food and Drug Safety (MFDS) and mask-wearing guidelines by the MOHW and KDCA. The public responded to these measures with proactive participation, which proved to be crucial for controlling the virus amid several unexpected peaks in confirmed case numbers throughout the pandemic. The limitations of South Korea's COVID-19 pandemic governance are revealed in domestic vaccine development for COVID-19, despite showing some progress on development of treatment drugs.

On social policy, the chapter examines the South Korean government's financial support for the public, the vulnerable, small business owners, and medical facilities as regions throughout the country were hard hit continuously by the COVID-19 pandemic. The distribution of financial relief packages by the South Korean government to revitalize the economy sparked a heated public debate on basic income, while simultaneously raising criticisms on populist policies, in a country where capitalism has prevailed. Emergency care was provided to children and the elderly in need of care.

Among these policies, what stirred the most heated debate were the paychecks to the overall population given out by the government. Although the government is responsible for the well-being of the citizens under the Framework Act on Social Security, the concept of basic income is underwritten in this law, and the concept was rather new to the South Korean citizens. Therefore, the provision of economic stimulus packages provided by the Ministry of Economy and

Finance (MOEF) was met with divided responses from the public. At the local government level, the Local Public Enterprises Act served as the legal grounds for regional development bond issuance toward the livelihood of citizens. The Framework Act on the Management of Disasters and Safety as well as the Disaster Relief Act gave way to financial support of the public in different forms, such as prepaid cards, cash, or regional currency cards. The amounts per household or business by regional governments varied as well.

Overall, this chapter argues that functioning institutions matter in pandemic governance and determines the level of their effectiveness by scrutinizing the case of South Korea under COVID-19, focusing on public health bureaucracy and policy coordination supported by public participation, which are vital to effective policy response. It serves as a record of South Korea's institutional experience of COVID-19 and provides an overview of the health policies and social policies in South Korea under the COVID-19 pandemic. Although the crux of the chapter lies with the institutional measures and the public response, it highlights the technocracy at the core in public health and the significant role it has come to play as the "control tower."

Nonetheless, although South Korea may have been relatively successful in controlling the virus compared to other nations, especially those in Europe and the United States, as of this writing, the country remains in the process of handling the crisis and faces further challenges for economic recovery ahead.

Health Policies and Public Health in South Korea under COVID-19

Upon the discovery of Patient Zero from Wuhan, China, in the city of Incheon, South Korea, on January 20, 2020 (the same date as the discovery of Patient Zero in Seattle in the state of Washington in the United States), South Korea's immediate public health response to COVID-19 (Government of Korea, 2020; Ministry of Health and Welfare, 2020a, 2020b) has been best described as the three Ts: test, trace, and treatment. Alongside public health policies of social distancing, disinfection, and public mask provision, the prescriptions of the South Korean public health officials embodying the three Ts became the fundamental pillars in carrying out public health policy under COVID-19 (Cha & Kim, 2020). South Korea was not new to coronaviruses—before encountering SARS-CoV-2 (COVID-19), the country had experienced SARS-CoV under the severe acute respiratory syndrome (SARS) outbreak in 2002 and the rather distinct SARS-CoV-1 under the MERS outbreak in 2015 (Koh, 2020; Our World in Data, 2020).

The amendments to the IDCPA in addition to the Medical Service Act and the Quarantine Act on February 26, 2020—only one month into the outbreak of COVID-19 in South Korea (Table 6.1)—were instrumental to shaping South Korea's policy choices under COVID-19, as the first two laws served as the cornerstone of the three Ts in public health policies and the final law the crux of quarantine measures (Library of Congress, 2020). Without the legal foundations firmly in place, implementing new measures with public persuasion in an effective manner would not have been possible, regardless of the competency of public health officials (Park & Chung, 2021).

Testing: Large-Scale Testing at Drive-Through and Designated Test Sites by KDCA and MFDS

Most important, the IDCPA made possible large-scale testing nationwide through the EUA of RT-PCR test kits by KDCA and MFDS in public and private hospitals as well as drive-through test sites (Park & Chung, 2021). As of September 12, 2020, the Korea Center for Disease Control (KCDC) under the Ministry of Health and Welfare (MOHW) was elevated to the Korea Disease Control and Prevention Agency (KDCA), allowing for more independence in policy making. Nonetheless, it must still work in coordination with MOHW, as a new deputy minister position has been created to liaise with the KDCA. To ensure high levels of accuracy, only RT-PCR test kits (with accuracy levels of 95 percent) were given under EUA. A public-private partnership (PPP) mechanism between the KDCA and the MFDS ensured quality control and competition-based applications by leapfroggers of the South Korean In Vitro Diagnostics (IVD) industry. Notably, big data analysis conducted by supercomputers enabled by artificial intelligence relying only on the RNA information provided by the World Health Organization on COVID-19 at the time of outbreak in Wuhan gave impetus to RT-PCR kit development by a South Korean molecular diagnosis company, Seegene (Watson et al., 2020). Drive-through RT-PCR test sites (Kwon et al., 2020; D. Lee & Lee, 2020) and designated test sites at public and private hospitals nationwide enabled large-scale testing with results in an expedited six hours, which did not exist during MERS even with an EUA mechanism. Only the then-KCDC (now KDCA) processed tests at that time, prolonging wait times for test results. Under the IDCPA, the tests were provided free unless someone volunteered to be tested without being contacted and advised by KDCA's COVID-19 tracking team to be tested and tested negative.

Tracing: COVID-19 Smart Management System by MOLIT in Cooperation with KCDC

Electronic tracing was one of the crucial elements that prevented South Korea from lockdowns. The electronic contact tracing platform, SMS, under MOLIT, was launched based on the conditional use of personal data under public health emergency, based on Article 76–2(1) of the IDCPA, which was an existing clause written into law post-MERS.

Elaborate amendments to subsidiary clauses of the IDCPA have been made in accordance with the unfolding COVID-19 situation (Ministry of Health and Welfare, 2020h). The conditions that bolstered the use of such measures in South Korea were its reliance on extant technology on smart cities: (1) its heavily wired environment with 5G stations rolled out where 95 percent of South Koreans possess a cell phone (Koh, 2019) and (2) its credit card distribution rate at 64 percent (World Bank Indicators, 2017), where nine out of ten South Koreans possess a credit card, with an average of 1.88 cards per person (J. Choi, 2020a), albeit the caveats of financial technology usage and provision rate under expansion but still at relatively lower levels (Yoon, 2019). Although GPS location data (based stations of the mobile networks) and credit card payment records are the main sources of information used for the SMS, CCTV-surveillance footage (e-National Figures, 2019), the most disputed component of data collection (originally implemented in South Korea for criminal investigation purposes), is not uploaded onto the SMS but used on a separate track. It was publicly noted by a MOLIT official at the joint MOLIT and KCDC online briefing on April 9, 2020, that GPS data and credit card payment data are only uploaded to SMS for additional verification efforts that are deemed necessary, at the request of health officials for epidemiological survey. Further, CCTV footage is used for supplementary efforts to connect the logistics of an infection case and to verify the testimonies of an infected person, given the crucial need of identifying the exact date of infection (day 1) of COVID-19 in the contact tracing process to accurately conduct epidemiological investigations (KTV YouTube Channel, 2020a).

In March 2020 the COVID-19 SMS (KTV YouTube Channel, 2020b; Smart City Korea, 2020) using GPS cell phone data and credit card transaction data, was developed by MOLIT (Lee, 2020c). Otherwise dubbed the "COVID-19 Epidemic Investigation Support System" by the KDCA, the SMS enabled the expedition of epidemiological surveys and exhaustive search for new cases of infection, which had been conducted entirely manually until that point (KTV YouTube Channel, 2020a). According to the KDCA, the manual method would take at least a day for results to be obtained, whereas the SMS enabled the tracking in ten minutes. Testimony by a MOLIT official revealed that the ministry had already been working on a Smart City application (app) system, which covered all regions of South Korea, and that the SMS was launched based on a suggestion by an official that had been working on the Smart City data hub technology at MOLIT. In addition to the SMS, the Ministry of the Interior and Safety launched the Self-Quarantine app and the Self-Diagnosis app, available for Android mobile phones on Google Play (March 7, 2020) and iPhones through the Apple App Store (March 16, 2020) for public download and use. The apps were used to implement strict two-week quarantine measures for South Korean nationals and foreign entrants through the South Korean border (Van der Veere & Ha, 2020).

Other digital technologies involving artificial intelligence (Lin & Hou, 2020; Ting et al., 2020) or internet of things (IoT) were also deployed in South Korea. Hi-COVIDNet (M. Kim et al., 2020), by the Korea Advanced Institute of Technology (KAIST), used big data and deep learning methods to predict the two-week number of infectees from abroad (KAIST Public Relations, 2020; H. Lee,

2020b). Korea Telecom (KT) developed the COVID-19 risk measurement model and AI hotel and food server robots (J. Park, 2020b) for servicing customers to further enhance the effects of social distancing (M. Choi, 2020; M. Park, 2020).

Treatment: Free Treatment under the Healthcare System and Community Treatment Centers

Article 6 of the IDCPA as amended on March 3, 2020, stipulates that all citizens have a "right to receive the diagnosis and medical treatment of any infectious disease" and that "State and local governments shall bear expenses incurred within." Free testing and treatment were provided to the South Korean public through its high-quality universal healthcare system (Maizland & Felter, 2020). According to the Organisation for Economic Cooperation and Development (OECD) based on 2017 figures, South Korea's number of hospital beds per 1,000 population remains the highest among OECD countries: South Korea (12.27), Germany (8), France (5.98), Italy (3.18), Spain (2.97), United States (2.77), and United Kingdom (2.54) (Ministry of Health and Welfare, 2020c; OECD, 2020). Maintenance of capacity of hospitals was emphasized to prevent the breakdown of the medical system in South Korea. Patients were categorized by severity of symptoms to prioritize the acute patients in the intensive care units with pressurized beds in hospitals. Up to 303 hospitals applied to be designated COVID-19 protection hospitals operating outpatient clinics for respiratory patients and confirmed patients with minor symptoms were housed at community treatment centers (W. S. Choi et al., 2020; Kang et al., 2020; Y.-H. Lee et al., 2020; P. G. Park et al., 2020), which proved to be a cost-effective and resource-saving strategy in managing massive cases of COVID-19 (Ministry of Health and Welfare, 2020b). The amended Medical Service Act required hospitals and medical facilities to streamline their management of charts and patient documents even after repose or closure of facilities, defined the term "medical related infections" arising from hospitals and related care facilities, and required medical institutions to voluntarily report any signs of infections in preemptive measures to track cluster infections in nursing homes and hospitals (Medical Service Act, 2020).

With the continued influx of confirmed cases of COVID-19 in foreigners entering the South Korean border that remained open, the free treatment and care for foreign entrants to South Korea came under scrutiny and received criticism by the South Korean public for wasting tax money. The free treatment scheme for foreigners was then shifted to conditional free treatment based on reciprocity by nationality to ensure reciprocal treatment of overseas South Koreans by foreign countries (Ministry of Health and Welfare, 2020i).

Social Distancing Measures without Total Lockdowns and Medical System Maintenance

Social distancing measures and quarantine guidelines were based on reproduction rate by the MOHW in lieu of full-fledged lockdowns. Under the amended

Quarantine Act, the quarantine at the South Korean border was streamlined for efficiency and quality control, and the MOHW was granted the authority to quarantine individuals arriving or transiting through the South Korean border if affected by COVID-19, under a period of fourteen days if confirmed COVID-19 positive or epidemiologically presumed positive. Those who broke quarantine under Article 6 of the IDCPA were subject to a fine of KRW 1,000,000 or 1 year in prison. Social distancing campaigns throughout the country contributed to preventing the spread of COVID-19 (S. W. Lee et al., 2020; S. W. Park et al., 2020), of which the levels for implementation would range from 1 to 3 (level 1: small cluster infections, level 2: community-level infections, level 3: massive scale infections) after weekly assessments by public health authorities. Each time a big cluster infection was witnessed—in the Shincheonji religious sect infections in Daegu in February 2020, the Itaewon clubs in early June 2020, or the August 15 Gwanghwamun protests, as seen in Figure 6.1—the levels were elevated to keep the virus reproduction rate under control and to maintain hospital capacity.

The MOHW evaluated the effects of social distancing and public participation, evidenced by tracking cell phone mobility during the targeted time periods (and cell phone mobility data during observed time periods and public transportation ridership fluctuations) (Ministry of Health and Welfare, 2020e). However, gradual increase of ridership after high-level social distancing periods (J. Park, 2020a) indicated a societal inertia returning to normal patterns, whereas the economic downturn (i.e., losses in business revenue from infections that lead to disinfection and temporary closures, or abiding by social distancing measures) from COVID-19 continued to be exacerbated (Park & Maher, 2020). Public criticisms were based on the grounds of the need to resume economic activities, as there were dire economic ramifications from reinforced measures of social distancing. The details of the criticisms were toward public health officials of MOHW formulating policy centering on reproduction rates (S. Choi & Ki, 2020; Ministry of Health and Welfare, 2020e), medical system capacity, and its maintenance, rather than economic consequences from the measures.

Disinfection of Public Venues for Prevention of Virus Spread

As much as the South Korean response to COVID-19 did not entail complete lockdowns, it was vital for the public health authorities to maintain and restore public health by sanitation and disinfection efforts, particularly public spaces, on a regular basis throughout the country under Articles 50 to 60 of the IDCPA. For this social endeavor the KDCA laid out guidelines for disinfection via official documents, indicating the training, equipment, and methods of disinfection, as well as a case-by-case approach on the use of specific nonmedical chemicals for virus disinfection efforts (Ministry of Health and Welfare, 2020f). The guidelines were updated in August 2020 (Ministry of Health and Welfare, 2020g).

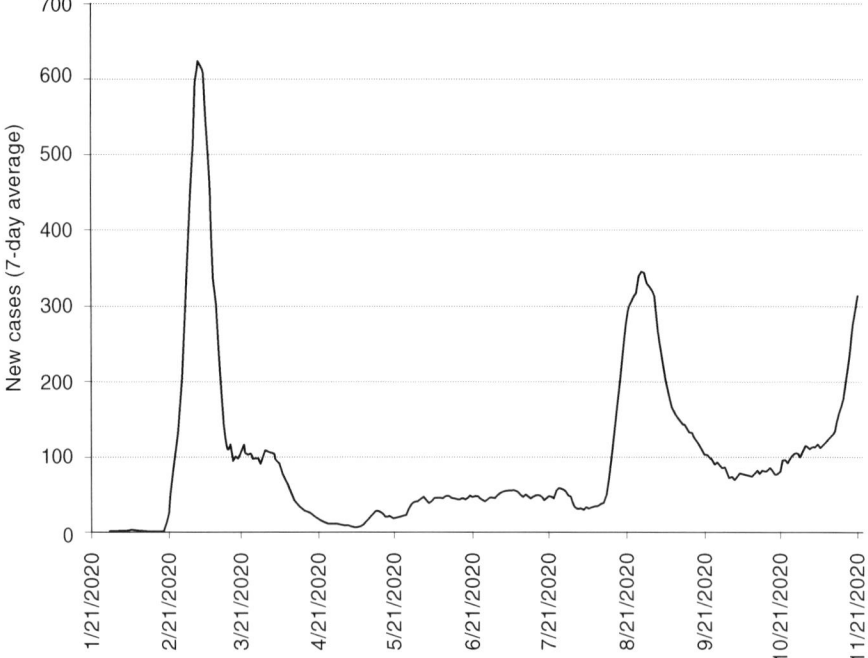

Figure 6.1. Daily new confirmed COVID-19 cases.
Source: "Our World in Data" based on data published by COVID-19 Data Repository by the Center for Systems Science and Engineering (CSSE) at Johns Hopkins University. https://ourworldindata.org/coronavirus-data-explorer?zoomToSelection=true&time =2020-01-03..latest&country=~KOR&region=World&casesMetric=true&interval =smoothed&hideControls=true&smoothing=7&pickerMetric=total_cases&pickerSort =desc.
Note: The three main slopes point to the first, second, and third major waves of COVID-19 in South Korea. The first wave was caused by major cluster infections in Daegu surrounding the religious group Shincheonji, the second by the August 15 demonstrations in Gwanghwamun, and the third wave in which small and big cluster infections at the community and grassroots level are the main causes of newly confirmed cases.

Public Mask Provision System under IDCPA and Mandatory Mask-Wearing Guidelines

Before the COVID-19 pandemic, the use of face masks was common among South Korean citizens because of the micro-fine dust and yellow dust from China and domestic air pollution impacting the country seasonally. Cultural or religious taboos on mask wearing were therefore difficult to find, and as soon as the COVID-19 outbreak in China made headlines, the South Korean public sought to secure face masks. In a country where online retail and grocery delivery based on supply-and-demand algorithms worked smoothly, peculiar panic buying on masks continued in February 2020. To prevent unequal distribution of face masks, under the amended IDCPA Article 6, public health officials were granted the legal authority to take "necessary means to make masks available to children and the elderly in a public health crisis involving any respiratory virus." The MFDS pursued a public mask provision program from March 2020 based on associating the final digit of birth year with day of the week, procuring masks sold at marts and pharmacies, whereby citizens would acquire masks with their ID cards. After controlled domestic production, the MFDS abolished the public mask provision system in July 2020 and lifted the export restriction on masks produced domestically in September 2020.

Mask-wearing guidelines by the MOHW and KDCA were not met with too much backlash as in the West, and the public responded with proactive participation to end the pandemic as soon as possible. Because there was a high level of policy reception on wearing masks by the public, mandatory mask-wearing guidelines were not in place until masks on public transport became compulsory on May 25, 2020, and in indoor and public spaces in thirteen out of seventeen metropolitan cities or provinces in South Korea, including Seoul Metropolitan City on August 24, 2020, by an administrative order, following the August 15 Gwanghwamun protests, which caused large cluster infections. From November 13, 2020, fines of up to KRW 100,000 on violations of mandatory mask-wearing guidelines in public were enforced in South Korea (Seoul Metropolitan City, 2020). Nonetheless, as in other Western countries, mandating mask-wearing guidelines resulted in public responses of noncompliance and refusal to cooperate in public health safety efforts. Such cases often resulted in escalated conflict and violence on public transport and other public venues in South Korea, to which the public health authorities responded by a fine and criminal prosecution by the Korean Police Agency (Ministry of the Interior and Safety, 2020). Overall, high public participation rate in wearing masks proved to be crucial for controlling the virus in the absence of vaccines, amid several unexpected peaks in confirmed case numbers throughout the pandemic.

Limitations in Treatment Drugs and Vaccine Development

Although South Korea made strides in the three Ts during the course of the COVID-19 pandemic, it still fell short of competency and speed in vaccine development, with a relatively shorter history of the industry compared to countries where Big Pharma—large pharmaceutical companies—has played a significant role in the development of vaccines. Although SK Bioscience demonstrated the potential for vaccine development with support from the Bill and Melinda Gates Foundation since 2016 (The Bill and Melinda Gates Foundation, 2016) coupled with an additional financial backing for research and development in May 2020 (Jung, 2020), it has gone nowhere near the global competition on COVID-19 vaccines. SK Bioscience is highly likely to produce vaccines on behalf of Big Pharma's vaccines when they are introduced, rather than announce its own (H. Lee, 2020a). Such lackluster performance reaffirms the difficulty, time, and effort required to excel in the vaccines industry. Similarly, reagents of South Korean RT-PCR test kits have relied on imported sources; for them to excel further, domestic development and production of the reagents will be required to ensure stable supply and competitiveness (J. Choi, 2020b; Han, 2020).

On treatment drug development, South Korean pharmaceutical company Celltrion yielded positive results in the development of CT-P59, an anti-COVID-19 monoclonal antibody treatment candidate as a preventative measure, under the approval of the Investigational New Drug (IND) application under MFDS on October 8, 2020. The treatment entered phase III clinical trials in twelve different countries, with the planned timeline of completion by end of 2020 (S. Cha, 2020; Ministry of Food and Drug Safety, 2020).

Social and Economic Policies in South Korea under COVID-19

Fiscal Response by the South Korean Government and Supplementary Budgets Approved

The early successful efforts to reduce the incidence of COVID-19 cases received positive responses domestically and from abroad, but as time passed, public complaints from various sectors of the economy pressured the government to provide economic stimulus packages. The initial support package prepared by the executive branch and the MOEF in late February 2020 did not suffice in responding to the economic damages to the South Korean government. Leading up to the April 15, 2020, legislative election, the government faced more pressures on financial support provision.

COVID-19 Relief Funds by the South Korean Government and the Debate on Basic Income

These events led to a major supplementary budget allocation and approval prior to the election and subsequent series of supplementary budgets in the aftermath of the election under the Framework Act on the Management of Disasters and Safety and the Disaster Relief Act. Notably, the government's emergency relief payment (Ministry of Economy and Finance, 2020c) from the first supplementary budget sparked a long-awaited, heated debate on basic income in South Korea (Kim, 2018). Under the Framework Act on Social Security, South Korea focused more on public assistance and social insurance in welfare policy, but had not dwelt upon the concepts of social service and income provision leading up to COVID-19, and the legal grounds for a basic income concept are not made explicit in the law.

In disseminating the emergency funds, using digital tools, South Korea introduced cash transfers for quarantined individuals, coupons for low-income households, and wage and rent support for small businesses, which were administered by the MOEF and the Ministry of Interior and Safety. The government's initial rollout via the MOEF of comprehensive stimulus packages catering to all citizens received mixed responses from the public (Kim & Lee, 2020; Ministry of Health and Welfare, 2020d). Although some expressed gratitude for the lump-sum cash in their bank accounts, there was also backlash by critics for populist economic strategy and demands on targeted support. The Ministry of Employment and Labor then provided stabilization funds for individuals engaged in specific industries and freelancers the second time around (Ministry of Employment and Labor, 2020). As of this writing, the third wave of COVID-19 continues in South Korea, and there are discussions of a plausible third round of emergency relief payment.

Table 6.1 is a breakdown of the fiscal responses and disaster relief packages that were proposed by the South Korean government with the MOEF (executive branch) and later passed by the South Korean National Assembly. These stimulus packages would not be able to account for the array of economic damages resulting from COVID-19, which were accumulated through a series of social distancing periods. Going forward, the biggest challenge for South Korea will be recovery of its economic potential at the household level.

Institutions and the Control Tower in South Korea's COVID-19 Pandemic Governance

State capacity in pandemic governance in South Korea has been a combination of public health and socioeconomic policies on top of existing public health infrastructure, coupled with transparency and information delivered in a timely manner by the public health authorities that served as the control tower and public participation. For South Korea, large-scale RT-PCR testing made it possible to slow down the rate of virus transmission, thereby lowering mortality rate from COVID-19 at an early stage of the outbreak.

The policy choices made by South Korea indicate the significance of prior coronavirus experiences that have impacted solutions written into law, as in the IDCPA. South Korea's legislative election on April 15, 2020, during the pandemic, also influenced the government's need to demonstrate positive results in pandemic governance performance. The incumbent Moon Jae-in government won the general election by a landslide victory, having flattened the curve with the MOHW and KDCA at the forefront, acting as the control tower. The concept of the control tower in the South Korean policy-making system has been coined as the "Government Administrative Control Tower (GACT) in a Crisis Management System" in the aftermath of MERS. In engineering technology, a control tower

TABLE 6.1. South Korea's Fiscal Response to the COVID-19 Pandemic (as of November 24, 2020)

Package proposal and amount	Implementation/date	Details of fiscal response
Support package for the COVID-19 outbreak (Ministry of Economy and Finance, 2020a): KRW 20 trillion	Executive branch and MOEF/February 28, 2020	- About KRW 4 trillion, including government reserve funds and policy financing to support disease prevention, local governments, imports of manufacturing supplies, and small merchants - About KRW 7 trillion to provide financial and tax support for families and businesses affected, including 50 percent income tax cuts given to landlords for rent reduction and individual consumption tax cuts for car purchases to boost consumption - About KRW 9 trillion of loans, guarantees, and investment through financial institutions and public institutions - Supplementary budget to support local economies, as well as disease control
First 2020 supplementary budget (Ministry of Economy and Finance, 2020b): KRW 50 trillion	National Assembly and MOEF/March 19, 2020	*Help maintain business* 1. Provide small businesses with liquidity: a total of KRW 12 trillion to be spent on emergency funding for business operation and low-interest-rate loans (1.5 percent, lower than ordinary rates by an average of 2.3 percent) 2. Provide special guarantees on small and medium-sized enterprises (SMEs) and small business loans: a total of KRW 5.5 trillion worth of guarantees to be provided through Korea Technology Finance Corporation, Korea Credit Guarantee Fund, and local credit guarantee foundations 3. Provide a 100 percent loan guarantee worth KRW 3 trillion for small merchants

Ease the burden on borrowers

4. Defer loan repayment for SMEs and small businesses: at least six months of deferment to be offered by banks and nonbanking financial institutions
5. Suspend loan interest payments for SMEs and small businesses for six months starting on April 1, 2020
6. Support debt workout programs: debt relief programs at Credit Counseling and Recovery Service, and outstanding debt purchases by Korea Asset Management Corporation

Avoid credit crunch

7. Use Bond Market Stabilization Funds to provide liquidity to corporations
8. Issue a total of 6.7 trillion won worth of Primary Collateralized Bond Obligation (P-CBOs from the Korea Credit Guarantee Fund) over the next three years
9. Create an equity market stabilization fund: a temporary fund jointly invested by the financial sector, designed to be invested in equity index products

Second 2020 supplementary budget (Ministry of Economy and Finance, 2020d): KRW 7.6 trillion

National Assembly and MOEF/April 30, 2020

Spending restructuring and public sector costs saved (KRW 3.6 trillion)
- Developing country aid programs suspended because of the lockdown (KRW 0.3 trillion)
- Public projects suspended (KRW 2.0 trillion)
- Public sector costs saved: labor costs (KRW 0.7 trillion) and government complex construction costs (KRW 0.1 trillion)
- Energy costs saved because of falling oil prices (KRW 0.2 trillion)
- Korea Treasury Bond (KTB) yield payments saved because of falling market interest rates (KRW 0.3 trillion)

(continued)

TABLE 6.1. continued

Package proposal and amount	Implementation/date	Details of fiscal response
		Borrowings from public funds (KRW 4.0 trillion)
		- Public funds saved because of the weak won (KRW 2.8 trillion)
		- Housing funds (KRW 1.2 trillion)
Third 2020 Supplementary Budget (Ministry of Economy and Finance, 2020e, 2020f): KRW 35.3 trillion	National Assembly and MOEF/July 3, 2020	*Budget* KRW 35.3 trillion = KRW 11.4 trillion (revenue adjustment) + KRW 23.9 trillion (new spending) - Revenue adjustment: KRW 11.4 trillion - Finance emergency support: KRW 5.0 trillion - Improve job security and expand social safety nets: KRW 9.4 trillion - Finance economic stimulus packages, including the Korean New Deal: KRW 11.3 trillion *Source of finance* - Spending restructuring: KRW 10.1 trillion - Borrowings from public fund reserves: KRW 1.4 trillion - Bond issuance: KRW 23.8 trillion
Fourth 2020 supplementary budget (Ministry of Economy and Finance, 2020g): KRW 7.8 trillion	National Assembly and MOEF/September 22, 2020	*COVID-19 reliefs* - Emergency support for small businesses and SMEs: KRW 3.9 trillion - Emergency unemployment reliefs: KRW 1.5 trillion - Emergency reliefs for low-income households: KRW 0.4 trillion - Emergency childcare support: KRW 1.8 trillion - Emergency disease prevention: KRW 0.2 trillion

Source: Based on press releases by the Ministry of Economy and Finance (2020a, 2020b, 2020c, 2020d, 2020e, 2020f, and 2020g) of the Republic of Korea.

refers to a central hub at the top of a tall building used in aviation, from which controllers with a high level of authority direct takeoff and landing. In supply chain management, a control tower refers to a process of decision making and execution by visualizing distribution flow with real-time data (Bentz, 2014).

The control tower concept, which is commonly found in engineering technology or supply chain management, is applied in domestic policy-making to refer to the chain of command, or in more narrowly defined terms, "a systematic method whereby a central organization controls a situation by directing certain individuals to act as planned, agilely adjusting its approach in the face of uncertainty and the ever-present possibility of expanding disaster" (Lee, 2015). The control tower is a system by which decisions are made through interorganizational efforts in the shape of a pyramid, in which every organization has its own role and task, akin to a chain of command. In spite of the existence of the KCDC in 2015, the absence of a clear and transparent control tower during MERS was considered one of the main elements of policy failure and gave a wake-up call to South Korea's lawmakers, which prompted them to make a series of institutional changes and legal amendments to make the MOHW the main and highest control tower for disaster prevention and control mechanisms.

Despite the economic downturn and low popularity because of the administration's constant maneuvers with North Korea, without delivering substantial results in foreign policy results, the early response to the pandemic led to victory for the incumbent party in the general election on April 15, 2020. The election results reveal that despite dissatisfaction with the incumbents, citizens hoped for ending the pandemic with a significant level of trust in the public health authorities, with further expectations of their role as control tower. Given public perception that South Korea has a relatively superb public health infrastructure among OECD countries but failed in pandemic governance in MERS, another pandemic governance failure in COVID-19, like that witnessed in MERS, would have been considered unforgivable by South Korean citizens.

South Korea's centralized power structure evolves around the presidency, and it extends to regional governments in a centrifugal manner. To secure nationwide support, the legislative efforts were crucial in pandemic governance, and fast-track processes were conducted to pass the amendments to the IDCPA. South Korea went through democratization in the 1980s; the impeachment process of former President Park Geun-hye in 2017 served as a litmus test to South Korean democracy while the remnants of authoritarianism remain embedded in the centralized power structure and the presidency. Responding to public opinion and pressures on the government for delivering on crisis management became central to leadership maintenance.

Conclusion: Crisis Recovery and the Road Ahead for South Korea

In the aftermath of the general election, having secured a majority in the National Assembly, bipartisanship is regrettably absent on multiple domestic and foreign policy fronts. The left-leaning incumbent government has been turning a blind eye not just on public opinion but policy suggestions from other political parties. Since democratization, South Korean presidencies are five-year terms without reelections. With the next election coming up in 2022, the Moon Jae-in government needs to continuously deliver on pandemic governance for the progressives to stay in power. Nonetheless, pandemic governance, however successful it may be, will not suffice in clearing the Moon Jae-in administration of the missteps taken in the failed détente with North Korea and lackluster results on the economy. The probability of a more deeply divided political arena into progressive and conservative parties remains high in South Korea.

Into the future, pandemics or other infectious diseases will come in shorter cycles, with new viruses emerging constantly. Maintaining the quality of the universal healthcare system is paramount to South Korea, because the country's population is aging rapidly. The pressure on the government to perform well in public health crises will keep the government in check and public health technocrats occupied and strengthen legal foundations and institutions as the country experiences any subsequent pandemics. In the prolonged pandemic, the policy solutions on economic recovery from COVID-19 remains the elephant in the room in South Korea just as elsewhere in the world, and despite South Korea's Personal Information Protection Act, the questions regarding data privacy will arise more frequently as the shift to the contactless economy under COVID-19 demands more use of personal data in cyberspace. Data governance in this regard will be crucial under the tech-oriented features of South Korea's economy, as the contactless economy is further bolstered by the deployment of artificial intelligence and seamless network infrastructure, in which the control and use of data would be key.

References

Al-Rousan, N., & Al-Najjar, H. (2020). Data analysis of coronavirus COVID-19 epidemic in South Korea based on recovered and death cases. *Journal of Medical Virology*, 92(9), 1603–1608. https://doi.org/10.1002/jmv.25850

Bentz, B. (2014). Supply chain control towers help organizations respond to new pressures. *Supply Chain Management Review*. https://www.scmr.com/article/supply_chain_control_towers_help_organizations_respond_to_new_pressures

The Bill and Melinda Gates Foundation. (2016, November). *How We Work: The Bill and Melinda Gates Foundation*. https://www.gatesfoundation.org/How-We-Work/Quick-Links/Grants-Database/Grants/2016/11/OPP1148601

Cha, S. (2020, October 11). *South Korea's Celltrion gets approval for Phase 3 trials of COVID-19 antibody drug*. Reuters. https://www.reuters.com/article/us-health-coronavirus-southkorea-celltri-idUSKBN26X0FG

Cha, V., & Kim, D. (2020, March 27). *A timeline of South Korea's response to COVID-19* [CSIS Korea Chair Newsletter]. https://www.csis.org/analysis/timeline-south-koreas-response-covid-19

Choi, J. (2020a, April 9). *South Korea's best method of tracking COVID-19 spread: Credit card transactions*. http://www.koreaherald.com/view.php?ud=20200408000918

Choi, J. (2020b, June 3). Interview with Cheon Jong-yoon, CEO of Seegene, a leading South Korean IVD company: RT-PCR Test-kit Reagent ingredients rely on imports—Materials, parts and equipment of bio industry should be domestically produced. *JoongAng Ilbo*. https://news.joins.com/article/23792090

Choi, M. (2020, August 6). *KT to measure COVID-19 infection risk through AI technology*. BusinessKorea. http://www.businesskorea.co.kr/news/articleView.html?idxno=50098

Choi, S., & Ki, M. (2020). Estimating the reproductive number and the outbreak size of COVID-19 in Korea. *Epidemiology and Health*, 42, e2020011. https://doi.org/10.4178/epih.e2020011

Choi, W. S., Kim, H. S., Kim, B., Nam, S., & Sohn, J. W. (2020). Community treatment centers for isolation of asymptomatic and mildly symptomatic patients with coronavirus disease, South Korea. *Emerging Infectious Diseases*, 26(10), 2338–2345. https://doi.org/10.3201/eid2610.201539

Cohen, J., & Kupferschmidt, K. (2020). Countries test tactics in "war" against COVID-19. *Science*, 367(6484), 1287–1288. https://doi.org/10.1126/science.367.6484.1287

e-National Figures. (2019). *Installation and operation of CCTVs in public agencies* (translated). http://www.index.go.kr/potal/main/EachDtlPageDetail.do?idx_cd=2855

Gallagher, J. (2020, October 1). *Coronavirus: What is the R number and how is it calculated?* https://www.bbc.com/news/health-52473523

Government of Korea. (2020). *How South Korea responded to a pandemic using ICT: Flattening the curve on COVID-19* [Press Release]. http://www.moef.go.kr/com/cmm/fms/FileDown.do?atchFileId=ATCH_000000000013739&fileSn=2

Han, E., Tan, M. M. J., Turk, E., Sridhar, D., Leung, G. M., Shibuya, K., Asgari, N., Oh, J., García-Basteiro, A. L., Hanefeld, J., Cook, A. R., Hsu, L. Y., Teo, Y. Y., Heymann, D., Clark, H., McKee, M., & Legido-Quigley, H. (2020). Lessons learnt from easing COVID-19 restrictions: An analysis of countries and regions in Asia Pacific and Europe. *The Lancet*, S0140673620320079. https://doi.org/10.1016/S0140-6736(20)32007-9

Han, M. (2020, September 7). Pharmicell to convene government project on the development of COVID-19 PCR test-kit agents reliant on imports (translated). *Korean Economy*. https://www.hankyung.com/finance/article/202009070992i

Her, M. (2020). How is COVID-19 affecting South Korea? What is our current strategy? *Disaster Medicine and Public Health Preparedness*, 1–3. https://doi.org/10.1017/dmp.2020.69

Jeon, J., Kim, H., & Yu, K.-S. (2020). The impact of COVID-19 on the conduct of clinical trials for medical products in Korea. *Journal of Korean Medical Science*, 35(36), e329. https://doi.org/10.3346/jkms.2020.35.e329

Jung, J. (2020, October 27). *SK Bioscience: Gates Foundation funds 4.4 billion won for vaccine R&D*. Korea Tech Today. https://www.koreatechtoday.com/sk-bioscience-gates-foundation-funds-4-4-bln-won-for-vaccine-rd/

Jung, S. J., & Jun, J. Y. (2020). Mental health and psychological intervention amid COVID-19 outbreak: Perspectives from South Korea. *Yonsei Medical Journal*, 61(4), 271. https://doi.org/10.3349/ymj.2020.61.4.271

KAIST Public Relations. (2020, August 23). Technology on predicting imported COVID-19 cases developed (translated). *KAIST News*. https://news.kaist.ac.kr/news/html/news/?mode=V&mng_no=9551&skey=keyword&sval=Hi-COVIDNet&list_s_date=&list_e_date=&GotoPage=1

Kang, E., Lee, S. Y., Jung, H., Kim, M. S., Cho, B., & Kim, Y. S. (2020). Operating protocols of a community treatment center for isolation of patients with coronavirus disease, South Korea. *Emerging Infectious Diseases, 26*(10), 2329–2337. https://doi.org/10.3201/eid2610.201460

Kim, C. (2016). Legal issues in quarantine and isolation for control of emerging infectious diseases. *Journal of Preventive Medicine and Public Health, 49*(1), 1–17. https://doi.org/10.3961/jpmph.16.009

Kim, J.-H., An, J. A.-R., Min, P., Bitton, A., & Gawande, A. A. (2020). How South Korea responded to the Covid-19 outbreak in Daegu. *NEJM Catalyst, 1*(4), CAT.20.0159. https://doi.org/10.1056/CAT.20.0159

Kim, K. (2018). *Kibon sodŭk i onda: Punbae e taehan saeroun sangsang* [Basic income is coming: New considerations about on redistribution] (Ch'op'an). Sahoe P'yŏngnon Ak'ademi.

Kim, M., Kang, J., Kim, D., Song, H., Min, H., Nam, Y., Park, D., & Lee, J.-G. (2020). Hi-COVIDNet: Deep learning approach to predict inbound COVID-19 patients and case study in South Korea. *Proceedings of the 26th ACM SIGKDD International Conference on Knowledge Discovery & Data Mining*, 3466–3473. https://doi.org/10.1145/3394486.3412864

Kim, M. J., & Lee, S. (2020). *Can stimulus checks boost an economy under COVID-19? Evidence from South Korea* (IZA Discussion Paper No. 13567). https://ssrn.com/abstract=3669496

Koh, D. (2020). Occupational risks for COVID-19 infection. *Occupational Medicine, 70*(1), 3–5. https://doi.org/10.1093/occmed/kqaa036

Koh, Y. (2019, February 11). 95% of the population uses a smartphone.... Which country ranks first in the world in smartphone usage? *KBS*. http://mn.kbs.co.kr/news/view.do?ncd=4135732

KTV YouTube Channel. (2020a, April 9). *MOLIT & KCDC online briefing on COVID-19 Smart Management System* (translated). https://www.youtube.com/watch?v=C9o_HGN6v8E

KTV YouTube Channel. (2020b, April 14). *KOREA COVID-19 Smart Management System*. https://www.youtube.com/watch?v=_sjUtzwDiYQ&t=1s

Kwon, K. T., Ko, J.-H., Shin, H., Sung, M., & Kim, J. Y. (2020). Drive-through screening center for COVID-19: A safe and efficient screening system against massive community outbreak. *Journal of Korean Medical Science, 35*(11), e123. https://doi.org/10.3346/jkms.2020.35.e123

Kye, B., & Hwang, S.-J. (2020). Social trust in the midst of pandemic crisis: Implications from COVID-19 of South Korea. *Research in Social Stratification and Mobility, 68*, 100523. https://doi.org/10.1016/j.rssm.2020.100523

Lee, D. (2015). Government administrative control tower in crisis management system: Definition, issues, and policy implications. *Korean Journal of Policy Studies, 30*(3), 125–145.

Lee, D., & Lee, J. (2020). Testing on the move: South Korea's rapid response to the COVID-19 pandemic. *Transportation Research Interdisciplinary Perspectives, 5*, 100111. https://doi.org/10.1016/j.trip.2020.100111

Lee, H. (2020a, July 22). AZ selects SK Bioscience as global supplier of Covid-19 vaccine. *Korea Biomedical Review*. https://www.koreabiomed.com/news/articleView.html?idxno=8810

Lee, H. (2020b, August 19). KAIST develops model predicting number of imported Covid-19 cases. *Korea Biomedical Review.* https://www.koreabiomed.com/news/articleView.html?idxno=8997

Lee, S. (2020c). *COVID-19 Smart Management System (SMS) in Korea*. Asia Development Bank. https://events.development.asia/system/files/materials/2020/04/202004-covid-19-smart-management-system-sms-republic-korea.pdf

Lee, S. W., Yuh, W. T., Yang, J. M., Cho, Y.-S., Yoo, I. K., Koh, H. Y., Marshall, D., Oh, D., Ha, E. K., Han, M. Y., & Yon, D. K. (2020). Nationwide results of COVID-19 contact tracing in South Korea: Individual participant data from an epidemiological survey. *JMIR Medical Informatics, 8*(8), e20992. https://doi.org/10.2196/20992

Lee, Y.-H., Hong, C. M., Kim, D. H., Lee, T. H., & Lee, J. (2020). Clinical course of asymptomatic and mildly symptomatic patients with coronavirus disease admitted to community treatment centers, South Korea. *Emerging Infectious Diseases, 26*(10), 2346–2352. https://doi.org/10.3201/eid2610.201620

Library of Congress. (2020). *South Korea: Legal responses to health emergencies.* https://www.loc.gov/law/help/health-emergencies/southkorea.php

Lin, L., & Hou, Z. (2020). Combat COVID-19 with artificial intelligence and big data. *Journal of Travel Medicine, 27*(5), taaa080. https://doi.org/10.1093/jtm/taaa080

Maizland, L., & Felter, C. (2020). *Comparing six health-care systems in a pandemic.* Council on Foreign Relations. https://www.cfr.org/backgrounder/comparing-six-health-care-systems-pandemic

Medical Service Act. (2020). https://elaw.klri.re.kr/kor_service/lawView.do?hseq=53532&lang=ENG

Ministry of Economy and Finance. (2020a). *2nd round of 2020 supplementary budget proposal.* https://english.moef.go.kr/pc/selectTbPressCenterDtl.do?boardCd=N0001&seq=4880

Ministry of Economy and Finance. (2020b). *3rd supplementary budget proposal of 2020*. https://english.moef.go.kr/pc/selectTbPressCenterDtl.do?boardCd=N0001&seq=4914

Ministry of Economy and Finance. (2020c). *3rd supplementary budget of 2020 Passed*. https://english.moef.go.kr/pc/selectTbPressCenterDtl.do?boardCd=N0001&seq=4932

Ministry of Economy and Finance. (2020d). *4th supplementary budget passed at the National Assembly.* https://english.moef.go.kr/pc/selectTbPressCenterDtl.do?boardCd=N0001&seq=4987

Ministry of Economy and Finance. (2020e). *50 Trillion won support package to combat COVID-19.* https://english.moef.go.kr/pc/selectTbPressCenterDtl.do?boardCd=N0001&seq=4862

Ministry of Economy and Finance. (2020f). *COVID-19 support package.* https://english.moef.go.kr/pc/selectTbPressCenterDtl.do?boardCd=N0001&seq=4849

Ministry of Economy and Finance. (2020g). *Government announces emergency relief payment.* https://english.moef.go.kr/pc/selectTbPressCenterDtl.do?boardCd=N0001&seq=4869

Ministry of Employment and Labor. (2020). *COVID-19 emergency relief fund for stabilizing employment* (translated). https://covid19.ei.go.kr/eisp/eih/es/cv/main.do

Ministry of Food and Drug Safety. (2020). *CellTrion—Clinical Trials Information Search Engine.* https://nedrug.mfds.go.kr/pbp/CCBBC01/nexacroPageOpen?approvalEnd=2020-08-25&approvalDtStart=2017-08-25&searchType=ST1&searchYn

=true&searchKeyword=%EC%85%80%ED%8A%B8%EB%A6%AC%EC%98%A8&lo
calList2=000&localList=000&approvalStart=2017-08-25&page=1&approvalDtEnd
=2020-08-25&&clinicExamSeq=202000708&clinicExamNo=33062&receiptNo
=20200184577&approvalDt=2020-08-25

Ministry of Health and Welfare. (2020a). *Briefing on the pan-governmental meeting for COVID-19*. http://www.mohw.go.kr/eng/nw/nw0101vw.jsp?PAR_MENU_ID=1007&MENU_ID=100701&page=3&CONT_SEQ=353124

Ministry of Health and Welfare. (2020b). *Government policy on supporting the public losses from COVID-19* (translated). http://ncov.mohw.go.kr/shBoardView.do?brdId=5&brdGubun=51&ncvContSeq=692

Ministry of Health and Welfare. (2020c). *Guidelines on disinfection of the novel Coronavirus in public facilities for group use, 1st–2nd edition* (translated). http://www.mohw.go.kr/react/jb/sjb0406vw.jsp?PAR_MENU_ID=03&MENU_ID=030406&CONT_SEQ=352806&page=1

Ministry of Health and Welfare. (2020d). *Guidelines on disinfection of the novel Coronavirus in public facilities for group use, 3rd–4th edition* (translated). http://ncov.mohw.go.kr/shBoardView.do?brdId=2&brdGubun=25&ncvContSeq=3411

Ministry of Health and Welfare. (2020e). *The Korean government takes all-out measures to prevent coronavirus infection within the community* [Press release]. http://www.mohw.go.kr/eng/nw/nw0101vw.jsp?PAR_MENU_ID=1007&MENU_ID=100701&page=4&CONT_SEQ=352623

Ministry of Health and Welfare. (2020f). *Legislative Notice to the Amendment of Subsidiary Clauses of the IDPCA* (translated). http://www.mohw.go.kr/react/al/sal0301vw.jsp?PAR_MENU_ID=04&MENU_ID=0403&CONT_SEQ=354182

Ministry of Health and Welfare. (2020g). *List of countries eligible for financial support for quarantine and treatment of COVID-19 based on the principles of reciprocity, based on the date of entry, from September 1 to 30, 2020* (translated). http://ncov.mohw.go.kr/upload/ncov/file/202009/1598935233763_20200901134033.pdf

Ministry of Health and Welfare. (2020h). *Regular briefing of Central Disaster and Safety Countermeasure Headquarters on COVID-19*. http://www.mohw.go.kr/eng/nw/nw0101vw.jsp?PAR_MENU_ID=1007&MENU_ID=100701&page=3&CONT_SEQ=353495

Ministry of Health and Welfare. (2020i). *Regular briefing of the Central Disaster Safety and Countermeasure Headquarters on COVID-19*. http://www.mohw.go.kr/react/al/sal0301vw.jsp?PAR_MENU_ID=04&MENU_ID=0403&page=1&CONT_SEQ=355454

Ministry of Health and Welfare. (2020j). *Regular briefing of the Central Disaster Safety and Countermeasure Headquarters on COVID-19*. http://ncov.mohw.go.kr/upload/140/202010/1602210903639_20201009113503.pdf

Ministry of Health and Welfare. (2020k). *Regular briefing of the Central Incidence Management System for Novel Coronavirus Infection* [Press Release]. http://www.mohw.go.kr/eng/nw/nw0101vw.jsp?PAR_MENU_ID=1007&MENU_ID=100701&page=4&CONT_SEQ=352672

Ministry of the Interior and Safety. (2020). *Korean Police Agency to strictly address violence associated with mask-wearing guidelines and interference with epidemiological survey efforts* (translated). https://www.gov.kr/portal/ntnadmNews/2246574

Organisation for Economic Cooperation and Development [OECD]. (2020). *Hospital beds (indicator)*. OECD. https://doi.org/10.1787/0191328e-en

Our World in Data. (2020). *Emerging COVID-19 success story: South Korea learned the lessons of MERS*. https://ourworldindata.org/covid-exemplar-south-korea

Palaniappan, A., Dave, U., & Gosine, B. (2020). Comparing South Korea and Italy's healthcare systems and initiatives to combat COVID-19. *Revista Panamericana de Salud Pública*, *44*, 1. https://doi.org/10.26633/RPSP.2020.53

Park, J. (2020a). Changes in subway ridership in response to COVID-19 in Seoul, South Korea: Implications for social distancing. *Cureus*. https://doi.org/10.7759/cureus.7668

Park, J. (2020b, September 1). *[The Era of AI Sapiens] KT responds rapidly to the contactless era by commercializing food serving robots and hotel robots* (translated). Electronics News. https://m.etnews.com/20200901000097

Park, J., & Chung, E. (2021). Learning from past pandemic governance: Early response and public–private partnerships in testing of COVID-19 in South Korea. *World Development*, *137*, 105198. https://doi.org/10.1016/j.worlddev.2020.105198

Park, M. (2017). Infectious disease-related laws: Prevention and control measures. *Epidemiology and Health*, *39*, e2017033. https://doi.org/10.4178/epih.e2017033

Park, M. (2020, September 15). *A.I. robot serves customers at Seoul restaurant*. Reuters. https://www.reuters.com/article/us-health-coronavirus-southkorea-serving-idUSKBN2661KB

Park, P. G., Kim, C. H., Heo, Y., Kim, T. S., Park, C. W., & Kim, C.-H. (2020). Out-of-hospital cohort treatment of coronavirus disease 2019 patients with mild symptoms in Korea: An experience from a single community treatment center. *Journal of Korean Medical Science*, *35*(13), e140. https://doi.org/10.3346/jkms.2020.35.e140

Park, S., Choi, G. J., & Ko, H. (2020). Information technology–based tracing strategy in response to COVID-19 in South Korea—Privacy controversies. *JAMA*, *323*(21), 2129. https://doi.org/10.1001/jama.2020.6602

Park, S., & Maher, C. S. (2020). Government financial management and the coronavirus pandemic: A comparative look at South Korea and the United States. *The American Review of Public Administration*, *50*(6–7), 590–597. https://doi.org/10.1177/0275074020941720

Park, S. W., Sun, K., Viboud, C., Grenfell, B. T., & Dushoff, J. (2020). Potential role of social distancing in mitigating spread of coronavirus disease, South Korea. *Emerging Infectious Diseases*, *26*(11), 2697–2700. https://doi.org/10.3201/eid2611.201099

Park, W. B., Kwon, N.-J., Choi, S.-J., Kang, C. K., Choe, P. G., Kim, J. Y., Yun, J., Lee, G. W., Seong, M.-W., Kim, N. J., Seo, J.-S., & Oh, M. (2020). Virus isolation from the first patient with SARS-CoV-2 in Korea. *Journal of Korean Medical Science*, *35*(7), e84. https://doi.org/10.3346/jkms.2020.35.e84

Park, Y. J., Choe, Y. J., Park, O., Park, S. Y., Kim, Y.-M., Kim, J., Kweon, S., Woo, Y., Gwack, J., Kim, S. S., Lee, J., Hyun, J., Ryu, B., Jang, Y. S., Kim, H., Shin, S. H., Yi, S., Lee, S., Kim, H. K., . . . on behalf of the COVID-19 National Emergency Response Center, Epidemiology and Case Management Team. (2020). Contact tracing during coronavirus disease outbreak, South Korea, 2020. *Emerging Infectious Diseases*, *26*(10), 2465–2468. https://doi.org/10.3201/eid2610.201315

Ring, S. (2020, October 27). *Astra-Oxford vaccine stays near front of line despite U.S. delay*. Bloomberg Business. https://www.bloomberg.com/news/articles/2020-10-27/astra-oxford-vaccine-stays-near-front-of-line-despite-u-s-delay

Seoul Metropolitan City. (2020). *Specific guidelines on mandatory mask-wearing* (translated). https://news.seoul.go.kr/html/27/522238/

Shim, E., Tariq, A., Choi, W., Lee, Y., & Chowell, G. (2020). Transmission potential and severity of COVID-19 in South Korea. *International Journal of Infectious Diseases*, 93, 339–344. https://doi.org/10.1016/j.ijid.2020.03.031

Smart City Korea. (2020). *South Korea's COVID-19 Smart Management System at a glance* (translated). https://smartcity.go.kr/2020/05/07/한-눈에-살펴보는-한국의-코로나19-역학조사-지원시/

Song, J.-Y., Yun, J.-G., Noh, J.-Y., Cheong, H.-J., & Kim, W.-J. (2020). Covid-19 in South Korea—Challenges of subclinical manifestations. *New England Journal of Medicine*, 382(19), 1858–1859. https://doi.org/10.1056/NEJMc2001801

Ting, D. S. W., Carin, L., Dzau, V., & Wong, T. Y. (2020). Digital technology and COVID-19. *Nature Medicine*, 26(4), 459–461. https://doi.org/10.1038/s41591-020-0824-5

Van der Veere, A. P., & Ha, S. (2020). *South Korea: Containing COVID-19 through big data (How Asia confronts COVID-19 through technology)*. Leiden Asia Centre. https://leidenasiacentre.nl/wp-content/uploads/2020/05/LeidenAsiaCentre-How-Asia-Confronts-COVID-19-through-Technology-3.pdf

Watson, I., Jeong, S., Hollingsworth, J., & Booth, T. (2020, March 13). *How this South Korean company created coronavirus test kits in three weeks*. CNN. https://edition.cnn.com/2020/03/12/asia/coronavirus-south-korea-testing-intl-hnk/index.html

World Bank Indicators. (2017). *Credit card ownership (% age 15+), Korea, Republic of (TCdata360, World Bank Indicators–Financial Inclusion Index [Findex])*. https://tcdata360.worldbank.org/indicators/h83ea0f24?country=KOR&indicator=3360&viz=line_chart&years=2011,2017

Yoon, Y. (2019, August 20). *S. Korean credit card firms losing customers to Fintech companies*. BusinessKorea. http://www.businesskorea.co.kr/news/articleView.html?idxno=35067

7 UNIFIED, PREVENTIVE, LOW-COST GOVERNMENT RESPONSE TO COVID-19 IN VIỆT NAM

Emma Willoughby

Việt Nam has become a poster child of the COVID-19 pandemic. It serves as a counterpoint to the other communist powerhouse country in Asia—China, which has, by many media accounts, been blamed for the emergence of COVID-19 and sequestering important data about the virus. In contrast, the Vietnamese government has been praised for its swift and early action to quell the spread of COVID-19 in the country by closing off the nearly 800-mile-long Chinese border, which is along the country's most mountainous territory. With approximately 96 million people, Việt Nam ranks first as the most populated country with the fewest number of coronavirus cases. It is also one of the few countries among those most populated with a government that is strongly committed to stopping the virus. Yet Việt Nam remains a relatively poor country, with an average gross domestic product (GDP) per capita of US$2,566. Like many countries, Việt Nam faces persistent challenges in improving population health and education opportunities for all. As major cities Hà Nội and Hồ Chí Minh City continue to see massive economic growth, urban poverty persists as more people relocate from the countryside. There are also significant regional inequalities between more urban and rural provinces, particularly among ethnic minority communities located in the country's mountain regions, which have seen poverty reduction at slower rates than the rest of the country (World Bank, 2014).

Nevertheless, the Vietnamese government took early, targeted action against COVID-19 to spare its population from a disastrous outbreak. In January 2020, when reports from Wuhan about the virus emerged, the Ministry of Health mobilized the Public Health Emergency Operation Center to meet and discuss pandemic preparation.[1] Similarly, as in China, citizens throughout Việt Nam were at this time celebrating the Lunar New Year holiday, *Tết*, a week-long public holiday during which time families travel to gather together. Schools remained closed for several weeks after the holiday (La et al., 2020). Early response focused on China as a source of viral transmission, but by March 2020, as case numbers continued to rise, the Vietnamese government turned attention to all foreigners entering the country as cases were increasingly linked to Europe and the United States. On March 12, 2020, the government mandated a fourteen-day quarantine for all incoming travelers, which they hosted at converted military bases. By March 22, all foreigners were barred entry into the country (La et al., 2020). Nonessential businesses were shut down for only two weeks' time in April 2020. Once cases of COVID-19 were identified, individuals were directed to quarantine and those in possible contact with the virus were identified, traced, and also sent to a state-run quarantine facility. As a result of the country's stringent, but also short-lived, efforts, Việt Nam had reported no deaths related to the COVID-19 virus for one hundred days, until July 24.

With only 417 total cases of COVID-19 at the end of July 2020, Việt Nam was reporting no more community transmission of the virus. However, on July 24, a new case was reported in the city of Đà Nẵng. By August 10, 2020, the country reported fourteen deaths from COVID-19 and linked 347 cases to the outbreak in Đà Nẵng and Quảng Nam province (Viet, 2020). As of late August, the country reported a total of thirty-five COVID-related deaths.

With fears of further community spread into the month of September 2020, the country faced the new challenge of quickly isolating cases from this new outbreak. Yet, at the time of revising this chapter, Việt Nam has demonstrated yet again, no community transmission for the past nineteen days. Viral resurgence will test the country's health care system and the government's effectiveness. At the time of the Đà Nẵng outbreak, citywide lockdowns were reintroduced, as bars and karaoke clubs in Hà Nội and Hồ Chí Minh City were closed and in Đà Nẵng, only pharmacies, hospitals, ATMs, and supermarkets remained open. Nonessential workers teleworked for two weeks. Approximately 80,000 tourists were evacuated from Đà Nẵng, and estimates report that approximately 180,000 people were quarantined at home or in facilities (including hotels) around the country (Viet, 2020).

In large part, the country's success is indebted to the surveillance capacity of the Vietnamese government, a one-party state led by the Vietnamese Communist Party (VCP). The country has maintained a hierarchical structure of communism with extensive party networks since its independence in 1945, providing it with valuable tools in rolling out a preventative, low-cost strategy to combat COVID-19 (London, 2014). The international community has heralded the government's response, which has relied on thorough contact tracing, enforced quarantine, mass temperature screenings, and widespread consistent public health messaging, often conducted by party-affiliated social groups and unions. The government was able to effectively deploy strict preventative measures during an event in which their general distrust of China aligned with preserving economic development and tourism (T. Vu, personal communication, July 8, 2020). The legitimacy of the VCP relies on its ability to deliver on economic development, especially for elites and the middle class (Vu, 2014). Government success in quelling COVID-19 would have major impact on the country's trade and tourism industries.

In sum, the Vietnamese government has used its available tools to deliver an impressively coordinated, seemingly ordered, preventative pandemic response effort. The unity and strength of the VCP were important factors in demonstrating such a response. It is not yet entirely clear the influence of factors that contributed to mass citizen compliance with such efforts. Yet it might be that most stringent pandemic response efforts in Việt Nam remained targeted and limited to select regions, rather than countrywide. Considering that most of the effort was done to prevent spread early in 2020, the government's response was impressive but perhaps not as herculean as presented in most media sources.

Health Policy

Importantly, the Vietnamese government quickly implemented extensive preventative measures to stop spread of COVID-19 within the country. Hospitals were put on high alert about the possibility of the virus on January 3, 2020, and guidelines on transmission prevention were distributed when China reported only twenty-seven confirmed cases (Nortajuddin, 2020). The first case of COVID-19 in Việt Nam was linked to a group of Vietnamese workers who had been to Wuhan on a business trip, returning January 17, 2020 (Le Van et al., 2020). This first case served as an important early warning signal for the government about the real possibility of outbreak. The United States and Việt Nam both reported their first case of COVID-19 in the same week in 2020, but by February 1, Việt Nam declared the threat of a pandemic. News that a novel virus possibly emerged from China fit within the very long history of general mistrust toward China in Việt Nam. Vietnamese and Chinese relations have always been fraught. More recently, continued dam projects in China on the Mê Kông River and proposed building of Việt Nam special economic zones, which would receive a significant amount of Chinese investment, have received a lot of backlash from Vietnamese citizens in recent years (ASEAN Post Team, 2018; Eyler, 2019).

Besides early information cues, Việt Nam had other advantages to preventing spread of COVID-19. First, the government quickly took a strong preventative approach. By locking down their borders early, the Vietnamese government deterred a mass outbreak from ever happening. It did not have to use the same institutional muscle that was required of China to undertake the large outbreak that emanated from Wuhan. Việt Nam simply does not have an extensive health care system that could have endured treating thousands of patients with COVID-19. Additionally, the role of masking has probably been underplayed in many reports coming from Việt Nam. Because the most common form of transportation in the country is the motorcycle, it is common on a daily basis for individuals to cover most of their faces and bodies to accommodate for the harsh air pollution. Masking for most Vietnamese is not a novel practice. Last, Việt Nam has only dealt with smaller outbreaks in its cities, not the countryside, meaning that disease hotspots have the advantage of access to proper sanitation and clean water (in addition to healthcare facilities). The cities most affected (Hà Nội and Đà Nẵng) lack vast urban slums, unlike other low- and middle-income countries in Asia that have been adversely affected by COVID-19 (including the Philippines, Indonesia, and India). Some have even suggested that the use of fresh ventilation in Việt

Nam, compared to air conditioning mainly used in urban China, may have also affected disease transmission ("Why Has the Pandemic Spared the Buddhist Parts of South-East Asia?," 2020).

The puzzle remains—mainland Southeast Asian countries seemed to avoid major COVID-19 crises. It might have something to do with masking, the role of the Buddhist greeting, called the *wai* (which is more distanced than a handshake), or perhaps we will later learn that a combination of environmental and population health factors played a large role in shielding Việt Nam, Thailand, Cambodia, Laos PDR, and Myanmar. Although there has been skepticism around Việt Nam's reporting of COVID-19 cases, a number of international research groups and non-governmental organizations in the country validate the government's published data ("As Investors Move from China, Vietnam Adds EU Trade Pact to Arsenal," 2020; Pollack et al., 2020). Additionally, there was not the same reporting on widespread outbreaks and health system surge as in Indonesia and the Philippines.

Việt Nam has made real strides toward achieving universal health coverage through its social health insurance program, which covers 87 percent of the country (Teo et al., 2019; Van Tien et al., 2011). Total health expenditure in is approximately 6 percent of GDP, which mainly consists of out-of-pocket payments and social health insurance subsidies for low-income populations (Teo et al., 2019). Although there is a growing and profitable private health sector, it caters to wealthier Vietnamese, citizens from neighboring countries, and tourists. In contrast to strong health financing, Việt Nam has weaker healthcare infrastructure, with estimated 0.8 physicians per 1,000 individuals and limited critical care capacity (Vu et al., 2017; World Bank, 2020).

Việt Nam has one of the highest life expectancies in the region, at 76 years, and is increasingly characterized by an aging population coping with chronic disease, notably heart disease and cancers (high smoking rates). With such a rapidly aging population, there is concern about future pressure on the health care system and financial solvency (Teo et al., 2019). At the same time, the country continues to experience infectious disease outbreaks. In 2019 Việt Nam dealt with a more widespread outbreak of dengue, but smaller outbreaks occur yearly. Rural areas in the Mê Kông River delta still combat malaria. Many have noted that Việt Nam's approach to COVID-19 was a consequence of pandemic preparedness implemented after previous experience with SARS-1 in 2003 (Le Thu, 2020). Importantly, the spread of SARS-1 began in China; perhaps this also cued the Vietnamese government to take early action when learning about the possibility of another novel virus.

Yet there are differences between the situation of SARS-1 and SARS-CoV-2. First, the SARS-1 outbreak occurred nearly twenty years ago. Việt Nam has grown much more in terms of economic, technological, and social development since then; this past disease experience alone is not the only factor informing the current government's approach to combatting the COVID-19 pandemic. There were only sixty-three cases of SARS-1 in Việt Nam, and that virus certainly did not disturb global supply chains as much as COVID-19 has (World Health Organization [WHO], 2003). Việt Nam has a lot more at stake this time. However, SARS-1 did contribute to increased infectious disease surveillance in the country. Indeed, since 2003, Việt Nam has dealt with avian flu outbreaks and, through these experiences, has developed rigorous animal health monitoring and vaccination programs (World Bank, 2015). When H5N1 avian flu emerged, the Vietnamese government took swift action to quell the spread by culling 44 million poultry, willing to sacrifice short-run economic gains in the interest of long-term public health and likely, reputation of the government on the world stage (Vu, 2009). Since then, Việt Nam has had repeated outbreaks of avian flu, resulting in mass vaccination efforts and culling poultry when necessary as the government increasingly monitors food supply chains and prioritizes food safety.

Việt Nam's fast response to COVID-19 centered on closing borders, contact tracing, and isolation of confirmed cases. Unlike other Asian countries responding early to COVID-19, such as South Korea and Taiwan, Việt Nam did not at first conduct an extensive number of tests (only 200,000) (Nortajuddin, 2020). Instead, the government relied heavily on contact tracing and isolation of suspected cases. On February 13, 2020, a town of ten thousand called Sơn Lôi, located 16 km outside Hà Nội, was placed under a military-enforced lockdown with checkpoints, along with health, police, and military officials after four cases of COVID-19 were confirmed there (Trevisan et al., 2020). When it was discovered that a woman in Hà Nội had returned from a trip to Europe, those living along her entire street were placed under strict quarantine, not allowed to leave their houses at all. At the beginning of the Đà Nẵng outbreak, approximately 12,000 people remained in mandatory quarantine in facilities or their homes throughout the country (Vu & Nguyen, 2020a).

At the beginning of March 2020, the Ministries of Information and Communications released NCOVI, or Bluezone, a contact tracing app on which residents should not only report their own COVID-19 status but also could track to see where in the cities other confirmed cases of the virus were located (Dang, 2020). As of this writing, nearly 8.5 million users are on the app, but the Ministry of Health insists that there will need more than 50 million users for the tracing to be most effective ("Vietnam PM Says Risk of COVID-19 Community Spread 'Very High,'" 2020). Because of the party structure of the VCP, citizens are encouraged to report about others' whereabouts and any suspected cases of COVID-19 (Fages, 2020). In general, citizens of Việt Nam are expected to participate in party-affiliated organizations, and many are paid small stipends to work for the party in various capacities down to the local level, including organizing, community service, and informing party officials of suspected dissenters (Vu, 2014). Since the founding of the communist-led government in the 1950s, the VCP has relied on community organizations as the government's primary link to civil society. These organizations, including peasants, labor, and women's unions, as well as cultural and religious associations, both delivered party doctrine and transmitted information back to higher-level officials (Vasavakul, 2019). Many of these same groups still operate today and have facilitated much of the sanitation, quarantine, and short-term aid efforts related to COVID-19. These existing VCP networks have provided an immense amount of human capacity needed for adequate surveillance and monitoring for COVID-19 prevention.

The government's public health messaging about the virus has also received significant attention (Wamsley, 2020). A song made the rounds on social media, called *"Ghen Cô Vy,"* or "Jealous Coronavirus." Adapted from a 2017 pop song and re-released by the original singers, the song advocates that individuals should avoid crowded areas, keep their homes sanitized, and wash their hands. Dancer Quang Đăng even started a TikTok dance challenge, which helped gain additional international attention for Việt Nam's efforts. In the video, the cartoons are wearing masks and standing beside public health officers. Towns and cities were adorned with PSA billboards of similar imagery. But these are usual, common sights in Việt Nam, as the VCP often promotes various messages to the public in many formats. Towns in Việt Nam are dotted with loudspeakers from which local party officials make regular announcements. The Vietnamese government and the VCP did not hesitate to use all its resources, networks, and communication channels as necessary to spread a clear, unified message regarding its response to COVID-19. The Ministry of Information has actively censored social media to dispel misinformation about the virus and has enforced penalty of fines (Đức, 2020; Nguyen & Pearson, 2020).

Social Policy

In addition to swift response to confirmed cases of COVID-19, Việt Nam took steps to enforce compliance with quarantine in those locations under lockdown (Vu & Tranh, 2020). Military personnel and workers (likely from VCP-affiliated unions) delivered food and supplies to all individuals on the street. Checkpoints were enforced in which individuals leaving and entering had to undergo to temperature checks. Around this time, all incoming foreign visitors were subjected to fourteen days of quarantine held at converted military bases. Additionally, as contact tracing continued, individuals who were known to have come in contact with a positive COVID-19 case were also required to stay in these quarantine facilities. During quarantine, individuals were supervised by military personnel and delivered supplies. Government intervened to stabilize prices for the public and seized supplies that were hoarded, as ways to curb panic stockpiling (Đức, 2020; Ngoc, 2020).

When Bạch Mai hospital in Hà Nội, the country's top medical facility, harbored a COVID-19 outbreak, the entire facility was placed under lockdown for fourteen days, reopening April 12 (Boudreau & Nguyen, 2020; Sở Y Tế Thành Phố Hồ Chí Minh, 2020). Forty-five cases were linked to the hospital, half of which were from food delivery and logistics workers (Vo, 2020). Staff were required to quarantine in the hospital and not return to their homes after workdays. Approximately forty thousand individuals with connections to the Bạch Mai outbreak were contacted and asked to self-isolate at home for fourteen days (La et al., 2020). The outbreak in Hồ Chí Minh City began at Buddha Bar, a popular hangout for expatriates and foreign travelers. By March 22, 2020, the country suspended all foreign entry and imposed a short two-week lockdown in major cities beginning April 1 (Vu & Tran, 2020).

At the end of April 2020, social distancing campaigns had been eased because of low case counts. Party organizations and businessmen in major cities across the country had constructed philanthropic "rice ATMs" to bolster food security during economic uncertainty, as well as providing free masks (X. Q. Nguyen, 2020; Quỳnh, 2020; Vietnam News Agency, 2020). By mid-July, *bia hơi*, the famed crossroads in Hà Nội where people flock to drink fresh cheap beer out on the streets, had returned. The country had resumed most business as usual, and perhaps it was under pressure to do so because of economic stagnation.

To accommodate for the loss of revenue from international tourism (as of this writing, the country remains barred from visitors with the exception of diplomatic officials[2]), the government issued campaigns to encourage local tourism and reopened domestic airlines by the end of June 2020 (Pearson, 2020). However, on July 25, 2020, the country reported a new case of COVID-19 from a fifty-seven-year-old man in Đà Nẵng, a popular resort city for many Vietnamese. A few days later, new cases were linked back to the hospital in Đà Nẵng where he was treated, as well as in Hà Nội and Hồ Chí Minh City, and the more remote Central Highlands region (Dinh, 2020a). With the August 2020 outbreak, the government closed all nonessential businesses and implemented mass serological testing efforts (Dinh, 2020b). The Vietnamese health minister reported that this outbreak might be linked a strain of the virus new to the country, and more contagious, as cases in Đà Nẵng had been noticeably more severe (Nhóm, 2020; Vu, 2020). As of this writing, the country planned to test the entire city of Đà Nẵng, over 1 million people, along with tens of thousands of those who had been visiting Đà Nẵng and now returned to Hà Nội and Hồ Chí Minh City; its previous strategy had only included 200,000 tests (Nguyen & Vu, 2020).

Certainly, the Vietnamese government has demonstrated concerted effort to provide stopgaps for essential needs to increase compliance for effective quarantine. However, the government has not yet demonstrated effective plans for long-term social policy that will sustain its citizens. Since Việt Nam's easing of their lockdown, the economy has not bounced back mainly because it largely relies on exports to the United States and other countries that are still struggling to manage their own outbreaks. Việt Nam has seen a massive decline in demand for their manufacturing, textiles, and tourism industries. According to government authorities, as of late June 2020, approximately 900,000 Vietnamese were unemployed, and another 18 million now work dramatically reduced hours ("COVID-19 Dampens Vietnam Employment Figures," 2020). The government passed a US$2.7 billion relief fund for which 20 million individuals would be eligible, but the overwhelming request for unemployment benefits has led to long delays for recipients ("For Vietnam's Poor, Access to Relief Aid Key To Joining Re-Opening Economy," 2020; D. Nguyen, 2020). However, the country just signed a significant trade deal with the European Union that may help secure its position as an alternative to China as a key trading partner for the West ("As Investors Move from China, Vietnam Adds EU Trade Pact to Arsenal," 2020). Still, Việt Nam is missing a strong social welfare system. The government has primarily relied on the private sector for economic security, heightening the precarity of citizen welfare as trade slows during the pandemic.

Explanation

One-Party Authoritarian State Capacity

Although Việt Nam is classified as a single-party authoritarian regime, these regimes are not uniform in character (Kerkvliet, 2019; London, 2014). Việt Nam originally modeled its government structure on the Chinese-Leninist system, but there are some key differences within their central-provincial relations that have implications for COVID-19 response and pathways to economic development in the country. Việt Nam has had a central, unified government solely under the leadership of the VCP but includes a lot of internal bargaining. The VCP is unique in that it has maintained a cohesive party elite for some time with limited purges of leadership: for example, nothing as devastating as China's Great Leap Forward (Vasavakul, 2019; Vu, 2010). In Việt Nam this unity is actually a result of negotiations between regional and provincial officials and the central state, rather than strictly top-down implementation of orders. These negotiations may actually buffer the party from fragmentation and protect unity, which as we have seen, has been a key component to Việt Nam's successful COVID-19 response. As the country transitioned from planned economy to market economy in the 1980s, state authority and regulation over business transactions became more fragmented and the VCP had to adapt. As Thomas Jandl writes, the *Đổi Mới* economic reforms were "the accumulation of lessons of continuous local experimentation" (2014, p. 69). Jandl and others argue that the economic development generated within a province "buys" its leaders political clout within the VCP. Edmund Malesky (2008) has demonstrated that provincial leaders who successfully garner and administer foreign direct investment have more autonomous governance in their regions. This has a few implications for Việt Nam's COVID-19 response. Regional leaders are under pressure to protect manufacturing, tourism, and investment opportunities, which means that preserving the health of workers (citizens) might be a high priority as well, particularly in major cities. Preventing spread of disease meant that Vietnamese firms were able to manufacture and export masks, equipment, and ventilators to the United States and others (USAID, 2020). Additionally, provincial leaders have more autonomy on the whole and may be less likely to cover up any threat of pandemic to central leadership, unlike China's case. At the same time, Việt Nam also has not experienced as a large an outbreak as China, so the degree of pressure on political leaders may have been less. So far, government response to the pandemic has been extraordinarily well managed and perhaps is a result of balanced relations between provincial and central leadership, and business leaders.

Việt Nam's government, although authoritarian, has been committed to stopping the spread of COVID-19 and has used the VCP's networks, including party-affiliated social groups and state surveillance (strengths of the regime) to mobilize a concerted public health campaign to protect the health of its citizens. In contrast, long-time authoritarian leader of neighboring Cambodia, Hun Sen, denied impact of the virus, continued to accept visitors from China, refused wearing a mask in public, and administered a low-effort campaign against COVID-19—except to incriminate those posting in social media about the virus (Human Rights Watch, 2020). As of this writing, Cambodia still reports very few cases of COVID-19 and also no deaths (Roser et al., 2020a).

Information Flow

Authoritarian regimes usually face challenges with information flowing primarily from the central government, which often shrouds transparency. In Việt Nam, the government along with state-run media[3] have consistently delivered a unified message about the virus and clear steps how to combat its spread. Actually, they have used transparency to manage contact tracing, by reporting all known cases of COVID-19 through an online tracker. Reporting known cases worked not only to demonstrate legitimacy of the VCP in handling the pandemic but also helped illustrate the severity of the problem of COVID-19 in Việt Nam. This has likely increased public trust in the VCP. At the same time, the Bluezone contact tracing app has received some backlash regarding privacy concerns (An Duong, 2020). Vietnamese citizens tacitly complying with government orders should not be taken as a given.

Ben Kerkvliet (2019, p. 6) has written about the public outspokenness of Vietnamese citizens and the government's increasing tolerance to dissent, calling the Vietnamese system "a responsive-repressive party-state." In the case of COVID-19, exactly how compliance to government orders played out in Việt Nam remains a puzzle. Accounts of citizen skepticism have been absent from Western media, but there was a lot of discussion about the legitimacy of early reports of the virus. Citizens are constantly bombarded with government messaging and orders—they work to parse out which orders are definitive, legitimate, or false. At the same time, mass compliance might not have been necessary in Việt Nam. The most stringent COVID-19 containment orders were for the most part isolated to a few cities within the country, and with the exception of Đà Nẵng, limited to only certain neighborhoods. There have only been approximately one thousand total cases of COVID-19 in Việt Nam. In effect, although there was impressive logistical coordination between the central government and provinces, and very clear messaging, perhaps the Vietnamese containment and compliance efforts were not as herculean as Western reports have described, especially since there was not a large disease outbreak to cope with.

Prime Minister Nguyễn Xuân Phúc and Minister of Health Nguyễn Thanh Long were the main spokespeople for the country's coronavirus strategy and updates. Fortunately for the people of Việt Nam, the government's stance on the virus aligns with protecting public health. The strong state surveillance capacity also made it easier to provide mass communication and contact trace. The Vietnamese government was able to send SMS messages to all mobile phones, rely on party groups to help enforce quarantine and masking behaviors, and promote public health education through state media. During the pandemic, government has censored social media to dispel misinformation about the virus, emphasizing the importance of a national unified public health effort.

Labor witnessed renewed bargaining power in Việt Nam in the beginning of the viral spread. Reports indicated that workers' unions were campaigning as early as February 2020 for necessary workplace sanitation protections, back-due overtime payments, and benefits contributions, contributing to the success of virus prevention efforts (Buckley, 2020a). At a garment factory, workers even went on strike when an employee, a Chinese national, returned from China and was suspected of having COVID-19. He was tested and quarantined (Minh, 2020). Although, with renewed viral spread and increased economic pressure, as of this writing, there have been higher demands on labor, and it seems like COVID-19 may have spread in factories (Buckley, 2020b).

Nationalism was another component to the government's COVID-19 strategy. State media continued to report that most of its cases of COVID-19 were imported into the country (Bộ Y Tế, 2020). As of this writing, news suggests, although does not confirm, that illegal-status Chinese migrants in Đà Nẵng might be linked to the new outbreak, invoking more anti-Chinese sentiment (Dac, 2020; Do, 2020).

Critically, there has been no indication that Vietnamese leaders lied about the spread of coronavirus. They were transparent in communicating to citizens how to prevent spread. There are a few possible reasons why they have done this. First is Việt Nam's positioning in contrast to China. Unlike China, provincial leaders were not reportedly misleading higher-up officials about case counts and deaths. If Việt Nam could successfully defeat coronavirus without lying, the world would notice the success of the communist state, and the leaders of Việt Nam would benefit economically and diplomatically. Additionally, in recent years, the Vietnamese government has invested effort in demonstrating improved transparency, illustrated by the Provincial Competitive Index (PCI) and Provincial Governance and Public Administration Performance Index (PAPI), projects developed in tandem with USAID and UNDP, respectively, to highlight improved regional governance for the purpose of attracting business to Việt Nam. As discussed, political leaders also can advance within the party if they encourage foreign investment in their provinces. These studies also show evidence of increased citizen trust in government, which may have aided compliance with social distancing and quarantine policies. Last, perhaps political transactional norms are changing in Việt Nam. Leaders must respond willingly to anti-corruption campaigns and transparency efforts if they wish to maintain friendly relations with foreign investment and, therefore, political power. Technocrats have demonstrated transparency in addressing COVID-19, but whether this diffuses to other spheres of politics remains to be seen. If the VCP can show that it governs effectively by generating income and saving lives, the party's current leadership might secure a very long future.

Congressional elections are scheduled for January 2021; the previous elections were held in 2016. As the VCP is the sole political party in Việt Nam, these elections will primarily be important for the VCP in reappointing or identifying new internal leadership. Party members will elect officials to the Central Committee, the two hundred-member body primarily directing national policy. At this time they will also elect members to the Politburo, the highest-ranking group of the VCP. Performance of Prime Minister Nguyễn Xuân Phúc during the COVID-19 outbreak may improve his chances of advancing to the position of party general secretary, the leader of the VCP.

Social Policy

The Vietnamese government has demonstrated that it can deploy a strong, consistent, effective response to preventing the spread of COVID-19. It successfully maintained quarantine by providing shelter and necessary supplies needed to isolate those suspected and confirmed to be infected. However, these have been short-term efforts. In the larger context, Việt Nam's economy remains primarily dependent on tourism, real estate, and manufacturing for the United States and Europe as it positions itself as a competitor with China for Western markets (Delteil et al., 2020). Millions of Vietnamese applied for unemployment benefits since the economic downturn from the pandemic, but overwhelmed administration has left many empty-handed.

Việt Nam remains a relatively poor country with low resources to provide long-term social policy for all people. Nevertheless, the country has witnessed unprecedented economic growth since 1986 with the implementation of major policy reforms colloquially known as *Đổi Mới*, literally "new change," or more properly "renovation," when the government moved the country from a closed economy to a market-oriented socialist economy. Earlier, the central government tightly managed all trade, even between provinces and districts. All markets were strictly local (Jandl, 2014). At the time of Reunification in 1975, and the end of the Vietnam-American War, Việt Nam's economy was devastated and was largely financed by the Soviet Union and foreign aid (Vu, 2010). But between 2001 and 2007, the country managed to double its average annual GDP largely because of foreign direct investment (Jandl, 2014; Vasavakul, 2019). Importantly, the VCP relies on economic development as a primary indicator demonstrating government effectiveness. In the context of COVID-19, the VCP will be concerned about sustaining economic growth for its primary constituents if it wants to maintain support and continued authority.

Since 1992 when social health insurance was introduced, Việt Nam now has a population that is 87 percent covered by insurance, and rates are even closer to 100 percent in the cities (WHO, 2020). Nevertheless, the quality and accessibility of health care for all Vietnamese is far from ideal. As Việt Nam's health is increasingly characterized by aging and chronic disease, the country's healthcare system will face more challenges in financing and capacity. Although reported corruption is declining, the Vietnamese health care system still faces the "envelope problem," as many doctors still rely on receiving a bribe, and out-of-pocket payments remain high (Nguyen, 2019). The best medical care is available only in cities, so many circumvent local communal clinics and seek treatment at urban hospitals instead, driving up medical costs and inefficiencies. Although authorities converted a sports arena in Đà Nẵng into a one thousand-bed field hospital, advanced medical care needed to treat severe cases of coronavirus might be difficult to secure (Vu & Nguyen, 2020b). As of this writing, if coronavirus continues to re-emerge, it will put a higher demand on the health care system than in previous months, when the government was able to implement primarily preventive strategies.

The re-emergence of COVID-19 in Đà Nẵng, and global persistence truly tested state capacity to protect citizens both economically and in terms of health in the long run. The puzzle remains, to what extent did the Vietnamese government have an interest in improving public health and social welfare for its citizens amid the coronavirus pandemic, and for what reasons?

Conclusion

At the beginning of this book project, Việt Nam had reported no community spread of COVID-19 since April 2020, no deaths, and was the most populous country in the world to achieve such a feat. As the country lifted restrictions and began encouraging domestic travel as a buffer from further economic downturn, the country experienced a second outbreak in August 2020 originating in Đà Nẵng, which is today a popular resort city. A country that had been devastated by war in the twentieth century now claims massive economic growth, improved life expectancy, and strong government support for health, despite the VCP's continued authoritarian rule. As of this writing, Việt Nam reports 1,068 cases of COVID-19 and 35 deaths from the Đà Nẵng outbreak (Roser et al., 2020b). The country's pandemic response and healthcare system will be tested as outbreaks continue. Additionally, Tropical Storm Noul recently made landfall in central Việt Nam, affecting Đà Nẵng and several surrounding provinces with structural damage, flooding, and leading to at least twenty-nine injuries and one death (Q. Nguyen, 2020). In August 2020, Hồ Chí Minh City sustained mass flooding with many residents living with standing water in their homes for weeks (Huu, 2020).

Việt Nam, like many other countries, will be facing compound threats alongside the COVID-19 outbreak. However, from early on in 2020, there was strong public support and government buy-in to manage and prevent the spread of COVID-19. The world has noticed these successes in Việt Nam. With the resurgence of COVID-19 in August 2020, Việt Nam demonstrated that government responses will have to constantly adapt to the virus before a vaccine is widely available. Importantly, the government may have to face a reckoning with delivering viable long-term social policy, which it currently lacks. The government may have been motivated to prevent the spread of COVID-19 in order to protect the country's economic growth and demonstrate its legitimacy, though the VCP maintains a strong grip on the country. By and large, as COVID-19 cases continued to climb, there was strong citizen compliance to public health orders. This may have something to do with strengthened government-citizen relations as transparency has improved in the past decade and has been key to the effective COVID-19 response (Nguyen & Malesky, 2020).

In the future, Vietnamese citizens may begin to demand more transparency in other sectors of government besides public health (Truong, 2020). Because of their early success with the virus, the government is under renewed pressure to demonstrate its effectiveness not only to protect public health but also to deliver economic prosperity for the country, which is now proving to be exceedingly difficult as international markets remain stagnant. Thus far, the single-party Vietnamese government has relied on coordinated and transparent surveillance to deliver targeted efforts preventing a large-scale COVID-19 outbreak.

Acknowledgments

I would like to thank the scholars who devoted additional time and energy to review this chapter, including Eddy Malesky, Dan Slater, and Tuong Vu, whose feedback greatly strengthened my analysis. I would also like to generously thank my Vietnamese language instructor, Cô Thúy Anh Nguyễn, and my friend and colleague, Tran Doan, along with her mother, Thuy Doan, for their assistance with sources written in Vietnamese. Thank you to my friends and mentors for your generosity.

Notes

1. Việt Nam's Public Health Emergency Operation Centers were initially developed in 2015 in coordination with the US Centers for Disease Control and Department of Health and Human Services and have been further expanded throughout the country in recent years (CDC, 2016; US Embassy and Consulate, 2017; Vietnam News Agency, 2019).

2. Although Việt Nam was soon to permit entry for visitors from China, Korea, and Taiwan, and had permitted flights from Japan in July, with the Đà Nẵng outbreak, these plans had been reversed (Dezan Shira & Associates, 2020).

3. All media in Việt Nam are subject to state censorship.

References

An Duong, D. N. (2020, August 24). Vietnam's coronavirus app Bluezone treads grey line between safety, privacy. *South China Morning Post.* https://www.scmp.com/week-asia/opinion/article/3098566/vietnams-coronavirus-app-bluezone-treads-grey-line-between-safety

As investors move from China, Vietnam adds EU trade pact to arsenal. (2020, June 25). VOA News. https://www.voanews.com/east-asia-pacific/investors-move-china-Vietnam-adds-eu-trade-pact-arsenal

ASEAN Post Team. 2018. *Special economic zones to spur Vietnam's growth.* The ASEAN Post. https://theaseanpost.com/article/special-economic-zones-spur-vietnams-growth-1

Bộ Y Tế [Việt Nam Ministry of Health]. (2020). Trang tin về dịch bệnh viêm đường hô hấp cấp COVID-19 [COVID-19 epidemic tracking webpage]. https://ncov.moh.gov.vn/trang-chu

Boudreau, J., & Nguyen, X. Q. (2020, March 28). *Hanoi's largest hospital locked down on virus outbreak fears.* Bloomberg Business. https://www.bloomberg.com/news/articles/2020-03-28/hanoi-s-largest-hospital-locked-down-on-virus-outbreak-fears

Buckley, J. (2020a, July 2). *The role of labour activism in Vietnam's success.* Equal Times. https://www.equaltimes.org/the-role-of-labour-activism-in?lang=en#.XyXdevhKhE6

Buckley, J. (2020b). *Vietnam labour update #71.* Tiny Letter. https://tinyletter.com/joebuckley/letters/vietnam-labour-update-71

Centers for Disease Control and Prevention (CDC). (2016). *Vietnam: Connecting for stronger emergency response.* CDC and the Global Health Security Agenda. https://www.cdc.gov/globalhealth/security/stories/vietnam_emergency_response.html

COVID-19 dampens Vietnam employment figures. (2020, July 15). VOA News. https://www.voanews.com/east-asia-pacific/covid-19-dampens-vietnam-employment-figures

Dac, T. (2020, July 19). *21 Chinese illegal immigrants isolated.* VN Express International. https://e.vnexpress.net/news/news/21-chinese-illegal-immigrants-isolated-4132756.html

Dang, K. (2020, March 16). *Health declaration app NCOVI surpasses Facebook as most downloaded in Vietnam.* VN Express International. https://e.vnexpress.net/news/news/health-declaration-app-ncovi-surpasses-facebook-as-most-downloaded-in-vietnam-4069215.html

Delteil, B., Francois, M., & Nguyen, N. (2020, July 1). *Emerging from the pandemic, Vietnam must position itself for recovery.* McKinsey & Company. https://www.mckinsey.com/featured-insights/asia-pacific/emerging-from-the-pandemic-vietnam-must-position-itself-for-recovery

Dezan Shira & Associates. (2020). *Vietnam business operations and the coronavirus: Updates.* Vietnam Briefing. https://www.vietnam-briefing.com/news/vietnam-business-operations-and-the-coronavirus-updates.html/

Dinh, H. (2020a, August 1). *Vietnam reports more than 3 dozen new cases, 3rd death.* Associated Press. https://apnews.com/b4c79f2ab82e9cf4ab625547ffa020fc

Dinh, H. (2020b, July 30). *After 99 days of success, virus returns to haunt Vietnam.* ABC News. https://abcnews.go.com/Health/wireStory/vietnam-imposes-virus-restrictions-outbreak-spreads-72068604

Do, B. (2020, July 31). *Gang busted for smuggling 40 Chinese into Vietnam.* VN Express International. https://e.vnexpress.net/news/news/gang-busted-for-smuggling-40-chinese-into-vietnam-4139260.html

Đức, T. (2020, March 9). Thủ tướng Nguyễn Xuân Phúc: Việt Nam sẽ chặn đứng dịch bệnh [Prime Minister Nguyễn Xuân Phúc: Việt Nam will stop the epidemic]. *Hà Nội Mới.* http://www.hanoimoi.com.vn/tin-tuc/Xa-hoi/960600/thu-tuong-nguyen-xuan-phuc-viet-nam-se-chan-dung-dich-benh

Eyler, B. (2019). *The last days of the mighty Mekong.* Zed Books.

Fages, V. M. (2020, May 29). *Here are 4 ways Viet Nam has managed to control COVID-19.* The World Economic Forum Covid Action Platform. https://www.weforum.org/agenda/2020/05/vietnam-control-covid-19

For Vietnam's poor, access to relief aid key to joining re-opening economy. (2020, June 23). VOA News. https://www.voanews.com/covid-19-pandemic/vietnams-poor-access-relief-aid-key-joining-re-opening-economy

How did Vietnam become biggest nation without coronavirus deaths? (2020, June 21). VOA News. https://www.voanews.com/covid-19-pandemic/how-did-vietnam-become-biggest-nation-without-coronavirus-deaths

Human Rights Watch. (2020). *Cambodia: End crackdown on opposition.* https://www.hrw.org/news/2020/06/17/cambodia-end-crackdown-opposition

Huu, K. (2020, August 9). *Saigon neighborhood still afloat days after heavy rains.* VN Express International. https://e.vnexpress.net/photo/news/saigon-neighborhood-still-afloat-days-after-heavy-rains-4143519.html

Jandl, T. (2014). State versus State: The principal-agent problem in Vietnam's decentralizing economic reforms. In J. D. London (Ed.), *Politics in contemporary Vietnam: Party, state, and authority relations.* Palgrave McMillan.

Kerkvliet, B. J. T. (2014). Government repression and toleration of dissidents in contemporary Vietnam. In J. D. London (Ed.), *Politics in Contemporary Vietnam: Party, State, and Authority Relations.* Palgrave McMillan.

Kerkvliet, B. J. T. (2019). *Speaking out in Vietnam: Public political criticism in a communist-party ruled nation.* Cornell University Press.

La, V. P., Pham, T. H., Ho, M. T., Nguyen, M. H., Nguyen, K. L. P., Vuong, T. T., Nguyen, H. K. T., Tran, T., Khuc, Q., Ho, M. T., & Vuong, Q. H. (2020). Policy response, social media and science journalism for the sustainability of the public health system amid the COVID-19 outbreak: The Vietnam lessons. *Sustainability, 12*(7). https://doi.org/10.3390/su12072931

Le Thu, H. (2020). Vietnam: a successful battle against the virus. *Council on Foreign Relations, Asian Unbound Blog.* https://www.cfr.org/blog/vietnam-successful-battle-against-virus

Le Van, C., Giang, H., Le, K. L., Shah, J., Le, V. S., Trinh, H. H., Reda, A., Luong, N. T., Do, X. T., & Nguyen, T. H. (2020). The first Vietnamese case of Covid-19 acquired from China. *The Lancet: Infectious Diseases, 20*(4), 408–409. https://doi.org/10.1016/S1473-3099(20)30111-0

London, J. D. (2014). Politics in contemporary Vietnam. In J. D. London (Ed.), *Politics in contemporary Vietnam: Party, state, and authority relations.* Palgrave McMillan.

Malesky, E. (2008). Straight ahead on red: How foreign direct investment empowers subnational leaders. *The Journal of Politics.* https://doi.org/10.1017/S0022381607080085

Minh, H. (2020, February 4). Nghi 1 người Trung Quốc nhiễm virus Corona, hàng trăm công nhân ở Quảng Nam ngừng việc [Suspecting 1 Chinese person infected with corona virus, hundreds of workers in Quảng Nam province stop working]. *Tuổi Trẻ, Pháp Luật*. http://phapluat.tuoitrethudo.com.vn/nghi-1-nguoi-trung-quoc-nhiem-virus-corona-hang-tram-cong-nhan-o-quang-nam-ngung-viec-40362.html

Minh Le, S. (2020, April 30). Containing the coronavirus (COVID-19): Lessons from Vietnam. *Investing in Health, World Bank Blogs*. https://blogs.worldbank.org/health/containing-coronavirus-covid-19-lessons-vietnam

Ngoc, M. (2020, February 3). 1,220 drug stores in Vietnam fined for making use of nCoV. *Hanoi Times*. http://hanoitimes.vn/vietnam-authority-fines-1221-drug-stores-for-raising-prices-of-medical-equipment-300938.html

Nguyen, D. (2020, June 30). *7.8 million Vietnamese workers' jobs affected by Covid-19.* VN Express International. https://e.vnexpress.net/news/business/economy/7-8-million-vietnamese-workers-jobs-affected-by-covid-19-4123111.html

Nguyen, H. (2019, April 23). *Is health care still a basic right as communist Vietnam privatizes?* VOA News. https://www.voanews.com/east-asia/health-care-still-basic-right-communist-vietnam-privatizes

Nguyen, Q. (2020, September 18). *One dead as Storm Noul hits Central Vietnam.* VN Express International. https://e.vnexpress.net/news/news/one-dead-as-storm-noul-hits-central-vietnam-4163885.html

Nguyen, X. Q. (2020, April 24). *"Rice ATMs" dispense free food to out-of-work Vietnamese.* Bloomberg. https://www.bloomberg.com/news/articles/2020-04-24/-rice-atms-dispense-free-food-to-out-of-work-vietnamese

Nguyen, P., & Pearson, J. (2020, April 15). *Vietnam introduces 'fake news' fines for coronavirus misinformation.* Reuters World News. https://www.reuters.com/article/us-health-coronavirus-vietnam-security/vietnam-introduces-fake-news-fines-for-coronavirus-misinformation-idUSKCN21X0EB

Nguyen, P., & Vu, K. (2020, July 31). *Vietnam's Danang to test entire population as outbreak spreads beyond city.* Reuters World News. https://www.reuters.com/article/us-health-coronavirus-vietnam-cases/vietnams-danang-to-test-entire-population-as-outbreak-spreads-beyond-city-idUSKCN24W39A

Nguyen, T. M., & Malesky, E. (2020). Reopening Vietnam: How the country's improving governance helped it weather the COVID-19 pandemic. *Order from Chaos, Brookings*. https://www.brookings.edu/blog/order-from-chaos/2020/05/20/reopening-vietnam-how-the-countrys-improving-governance-helped-it-weather-the-covid-19-pandemic/

Nhóm, P. V. (2020, August 1). 5 diếm khác biệt giữa 2 lần bùng phát dịch COVID-19 [5 differences between the 2 outbreaks of COVID-19]. *Tuổi Trẻ Pháp Luật*. https://phapluat.tuoitrethudo.com.vn/5-diem-khac-biet-giua-2-lan-bung-phat-dich-covid-19-49255.html

Nortajuddin, A. (2020). Vietnam's exemplary response To COVID-19. *The ASEAN Post*. https://theaseanpost.com/article/vietnams-exemplary-response-covid-19

Pearson, J. (2020, May 20). *Vietnam offers cut-price paradise to lure local travellers post coronavirus.* Reuters World News. https://www.reuters.com/article/uk-health-coronavirus-vietnam-tourism/vietnam-offers-cut-price-paradise-to-lure-local-travellers-post-coronavirus-idUKKBN22V15U

Pollack, T., Thwaites, G., Rabaa, M., Choisy, M., van Doorn, R., Duong, H. L., Dang, Q. T., Tran, D. Q., Phung, C. D., Ngu, D. N., Tran, A. T., La, N. Q., Nguyen, C. K., Dang, D. A., Tran, N. D., Sang, M. L., & Thai, P. Q. (2020, June 30). *Emerging Covid-19 success story:*

Vietnam's commitment to containment. *Our World in Data.* https://ourworldindata.org/covid-exemplar-vietnam

Quỳnh, T. (2020, April 9). Nhiều người tiếp sức cho cây 'ATM gạo' [Many people are donating to the "rice ATMs"]. VN Express International. https://vnexpress.net/nhieu-nguoi-tiep-suc-cho-cay-atm-gao-4082091.html

Roser, M., Ritchie, H., Ortiz-Ospina, E., & Hasell, J. (2020a). *Cambodia: Coronavirus pandemic country profile.* Our World in Data. https://ourworldindata.org/coronavirus/country/cambodia?country=~KHM

Roser, M., Ritchie, H., Ortiz-Ospina, E., & Hasell, J. (2020b). *Vietnam: Coronavirus pandemic country profile.* Our World in Data. https://ourworldindata.org/coronavirus/country/vietnam?country=~VNM

Sở Y Tế Thành Phố Hồ Chí Minh [Hồ Chí Minh City Department of Health]. (2020, April 16). Các y bác sĩ tại bệnh viện Bạch Mai vỡ oà niềm vui trong giây phút dỡ bỏ lệnh cách ly [Health workers in Bạch Mai hospital burst into joy when quarantine is lifted]. http://taimuihongtphcm.vn/cac-y-bac-si-tai-benh-vien-bach-mai-vo-oa-niem-vui-trong-giay-phut-do-bo-lenh-cach-ly/

Teo, H. S., Bales, S., Bredenkamp, C., & Cain, J. S. (2019). The future of health financing in Vietnam: Ensuring sufficiency, efficiency, and sustainability. *World Bank.* https://openknowledge.worldbank.org/handle/10986/32187

Thayer, C. A. (2014). The apparatus of authoritarian rule in Vietnam. In J. D. London (Ed.), *Politics in contemporary Vietnam: Party, state, and authority relations.* Palgrave McMillan.

Trevisan, M., Linh, L. C., & Le, A. V. (2020). The Covid-19 pandemic: A view from Vietnam. *American Journal of Public Health, 110*(8), 1152–1153. https://doi-org /10.2105/AJPH.2020.305751

Truong, M. (2020). Vietnam's COVID-19 success is a double-edged sword for the communist party. *The Diplomat.* https://thediplomat.com/2020/08/vietnams-covid-19-success-is-a-double-edged-sword-for-the-communist-party/

USAID. (2020, April). USAID identifies Vietnamese suppliers of personal protective equipment (PPE) and other medical supplies needed for the U.S. Domestic COVID-19 Response. *USAID News and Information.* https://www.usaid.gov/vietnam/program-updates/apr-2020-usaid-identifies-vietnamese-suppliers-personal-protective-equipment-ppe-covid-19

US Embassy and Consulate. (2017). Vietnam Ministry of Health and United States Department of Health and Human Services Inaugurate Emergency Operations Center, Advancing Health Security. *United States Department of State Press Releases.* https://vn.usembassy.gov/Vietnam-ministry-health-united-states-department-health-human-services-inaugurate-emergency-operations-center-advancing-health-security/

Van Tien, T., Phuong, H. T., Mathauer, I., & Phuong, N. T. K. (2011). A health financing review of Viet Nam with a focus on social health insurance." *World Health Organization.* https://www.who.int/health_financing/documents/cov-oasis_e_11-vietnam/en/

Vasavakul, T. (2019). *Vietnam: A pathway from state socialism.* Cambridge University Press.

Viet, T. (2020, August 9). *COVID-19 cases continue to climb in Da Nang.* Tuổi Trẻ News. https://tuoitrenews.vn/news/society/20200809/covid19-cases-continue-to-climb-in-da-nang/56046.html

Vietnam News Agency. (2019, March 16). *Public health emergency operation centre inaugurated in central region.* Vietnam Plus News. https://en.vietnamplus.vn/public-health-emergency-operation-centre-inaugurated-in-central-region/148373.vnp

Vietnam News Agency. (2020, April 13). *Hue, Da Nang cities set up free "rice ATMs."* Vietnam Plus News. https://en.vietnamplus.vn/hue-da-nang-cities-set-up-free-rice-atms/171643.vnp

Vietnam PM says risk of COVID-19 community spread "very high." (2020, August 8). Tuổi Trẻ News. https://tuoitrenews.vn/news/society/20200808/vietnam-pm-says-risk-of-covid19-community-spread-very-high/56019.htmls

Vo, H. (2020, April 9). *15,000 Associated with virus-hit Hanoi hospital test Covid-19 negative.* VN Express International. https://e.vnexpress.net/news/news/15-000-associated-with-virus-hit-hanoi-hospital-test-covid-19-negative-4081966.html

Vu, K. (2020, August 2). *Vietnam says origin of Danang outbreak hard to track as virus cases rise.* Reuters World News. https://www.reuters.com/article/us-health-coronavirus-Vietnam-idUSKBN24Y0CL

Vu, K., & Nguyen, P. (2020a, July 25). *Vietnam goes on coronavirus alert after first local infection in 100 days.* Reuters World News. https://www.reuters.com/article/us-health-coronavirus-vietnam/vietnam-goes-on-coronavirus-alert-after-first-local-infection-in-100-days-idUSKCN24Q05V

Vu, K., & Nguyen, P. (2020b, August 6). *Vietnam turns Danang stadium into field hospital amid virus outbreak.* Reuters World News. https://www.reuters.com/article/us-health-coronavirus-vietnam-fieldhospi/vietnam-turns-danang-stadium-into-field-hospital-amid-virus-outbreak-idUSKCN2521B0

Vu, M., & Tran, B. T. (2020, April). *The secret to Vietnam's COVID-19 response success.* The Diplomat. https://thediplomat.com/2020/04/the-secret-to-vietnams-covid-19-response-success/

Vu, Q. D., Nguyen, T. L., Giang, K. B., Diep, P. B., Giang, T. H., & Diaz, J. (2017). Healthcare infrastructure capacity to respond to severe acute respiratory infection (SARI) and sepsis in Vietnam: A low-middle income country. *Journal of Critical Care, 42,* 109–115. http://dx.doi.org/10.1016/j.jcrc.2017.07.020

Vu, T. (2009). *The political economy of avian influenza response and control in Vietnam,* STEPS Working Paper 19, Brighton: STEPS Centre.

Vu, T. (2010). *Paths to development in Asia.* Cambridge University Press.

Vu, T. (2014). Persistence amid decay: The communist party of Vietnam at 83. In J. D. London (Ed.), *Politics in Contemporary Vietnam: Party, State, and Authority Relations.* Palgrave McMillan.

Wamsley, L. (2020, March 4). *Coronavirus fears have led to a golden age of hand-washing PSAs.* NPR. https://www.npr.org/2020/03/04/811609241/coronavirus-fears-have-led-to-a-golden-age-of-hand-washing-psas

Why has the pandemic spared the Buddhist parts of South-East Asia? (2020, July 9). The Economist. https://www.economist.com/asia/2020/07/09/why-has-the-pandemic-spared-the-buddhist-parts-of-south-east-asia

World Bank. (2014). Inequality in Vietnam: A special focus of the taking stock report July 2014—Key findings. In *Taking stock: An update on Vietnam's recent economic developments (July 2014).* https://www.worldbank.org/en/news/feature/2014/07/08/inequality-in-vietnam-a-special-focus-of-the-taking-stock-report-july-2014

World Bank. (2015, May 12). *Vietnam avian and human influenza control and preparedness.* https://www.worldbank.org/en/results/2015/05/12/vietnam-avian-and-human-influenza-control-and-preparedness

World Bank. (2020). *World Bank DataBank.* https://data.worldbank.org/indicator/SH.MED.PHYS.ZS

World Health Organization. (2003). *Viet Nam SARS-free.* WHO Media Centre. https://www.who.int/mediacentre/news/releases/2003/pr_sars/en/

World Health Organization. (2020). *Health financing in Viet Nam.* https://www.who.int/Vietnam/health-topics/health-financing

8 FIGHTING COVID-19 IN JAPAN

A Success Story?

Takashi Nagata, Akihito Hagihara, Alan Kawarai Lefor, Ryozo Matsuda, and Monika Steffen

The outbreak of COVID-19, sometimes referred to as "Wuhan fever" in Japan, developed into a national epidemic by July 2020. After the first patient, who came directly from Wuhan and was formally identified on January 16, 2020, Japan experienced several waves of domestic outbreaks. Public authorities tried to control the situation by using existing institutional tools and adding new measures.

Before discussing the health and social policies adopted to fight the epidemic, we will highlight two background elements by which Japan differs from other countries with mature health systems.

Japan has a universal health care system in which equal access is guaranteed (Hatanaka et al., 2015). In recent years, health expenditures as a proportion of gross domestic product (GDP) increased considerably. In 2010 Japan ranked fifteenth in healthcare expenditure among the Organization for Economic Co-operation and Development (OECD) countries, just above its average. In 2018 it ranked fifth, spending 11.0 percent of its GDP on health care, just behind France (11.2 percent), Germany (11.7 percent), and Switzerland (12.1 percent) (OECD, 2020b). Although patient copayments are high compared with other universal healthcare systems (30 percent of billed charges), Japan enjoys the highest life expectancy worldwide at 84.2 years in 2017, more than half a year ahead of the runner-up, Switzerland (OECD, 2020c). This suggests that copayment does not necessarily indicate insufficient access to medical care, as commonly assumed, but may reflect a greater attention given to prevention and public health than in other nations with advanced healthcare systems.

Japan does not rely only on health policy in its classical sense for the management of a contagious epidemic. Japan also has considerable scientific and institutional resources, with highly professionalized intervention forces for "disaster preparedness" and for crisis management in response to events such as earthquakes, typhoons, tsunamis, and nuclear power plant incidents (Ishii & Nagata, 2013). The occurrence of serious natural disasters is increasing every year, and the Japanese people as well as municipalities, prefectures, and the central government understand the importance of disaster preparedness. Regular disaster drills are common. This preparedness capacity, together with public awareness and acceptance, also worked well in the response to COVID-19. The Japanese COVID-19 case demonstrates that such capabilities imported from other sectors can contribute to effectively fighting infectious disease outbreaks.

Policy Response to the Epidemic

Policy responses to the COVID-19 epidemic in Japan in 2020 were implemented in three phases, each responding to a specific stage of the epidemic and a set of related policy measures: (1) January and February (fighting the first wave of infections), (2) March to May (declaring a state of emergency), and (3) June and July (fighting the second wave of infections). The timeline of each stage is shown in Tables 8.1 through 8.3 (International Science Council 2020; "The Oxford COVID-19 Government Response Tracker," 2020).

After Japanese medical surveillance confirmed the first positive case of infection on January 16, 2020, in a Chinese resident of Kanagawa Prefecture who had returned to Japan from Wuhan, the initial government response to the COVID-19 outbreak was a policy of containment, focused on repatriation of Japanese citizens from Wuhan and the introduction of new regulations for border control. On January 24, 2020, the Japanese government announced that it would arrange repatriation services for all Japanese citizens in Hubei Province. On January 27, 2020, Japan's Prime Minister Abe designated the novel coronavirus as an "infectious disease" under the Infectious Diseases Control Law and designated the disease as a *"quarantinable infectious disease"* under the Quarantine Act. Because of its geographical proximity to China, Japan realized the significance of the public

TABLE 8.1. January and February (The first wave of the pandemic)

January 16	Kanagawa Prefecture confirmed its first positive case of COVID-19, a Chinese man in his thirties who had traveled to Wuhan.
January 27	Japan's Prime Minister Abe designated the novel coronavirus a "designated infectious disease" under the Infectious Diseases Control Law. In addition, he designated the disease as a "quarantinable infectious disease" under the Quarantine Act.
February 3	The Japanese government announced entry restrictions for all foreign citizens with a travel history to and from Hubei Province or anyone who held a Chinese passport issued from Hubei.
February 16	Prime Minister Abe convened the government's first Novel Coronavirus Expert Meeting at the Prime Minister's Office to draft national guidelines for COVID-19 testing and treatment.
February 25	The Ministry of Health, Labor, and Welfare established the Cluster Response Team in accordance with the Basic Policies for Novel Coronavirus Disease Control.
February 27	Prime Minister Abe requested closure of all elementary, junior high, and high schools from March 2 to the end of spring vacation (which concluded in early April).

TABLE 8.2. March through May (Declaring a state of emergency)

March 9	Medical experts reviewed the data from the Cluster Response Team and refined its definition of a high-risk environment as a place with overlapping "three Cs" (closed spaces, crowded places, close contact).
March 13	The amended Special Measures Act to Counter New Types of Influenza of 2012, which extended the law's emergency measures for influenza outbreaks to include COVID-19, was approved by the Diet (Japan's legislative branch).
April 7	Prime Minister Abe proclaimed a State of Emergency from April 8 to May 6 for Tokyo and Kanagawa, Saitama, Chiba, Osaka, Hyogo, and Fukuoka Prefectures. In addition, Prime Minister Abe stated that the pandemic created the nation's greatest economic crisis since the end of World War II.
April 16	The Japanese government expanded the state of emergency to include all forty-seven prefectures in Japan.
May 1	Distribution of the 100,000-yen stimulus payment to residents began (approximately US$960).
May 25	Prime Minister Abe announced lifting of the government's emergency declaration for five remaining prefectures (Saitama, Chiba, Tokyo, Kanagawa, and Hokkaido).

TABLE 8.3. June and July (The second wave of the pandemic)

June 19	Voluntary restraint of movement in five remaining prefectures (Saitama, Chiba, Tokyo, Kanagawa, and Hokkaido) lifted.
July 15	The "Go-to campaign," a tourism revitalization project actively pursued by the Abe government to promote domestic tourism demand, was launched in Tokyo.
July 18	The total number of COVID-19 fatalities in Japan exceeded 1,000. It rose to 1,519 by the time of writing (September 24, 2020).

health emergency and quickly took measures to counteract the emerging pandemic. Almost simultaneously, Japan faced an outbreak of COVID-19 on board a cruise ship, the *Diamond Princess,* registered in Britain and operated by Princess Cruises. Follow-up surveys, conducted later, showed that more than 712 out of 3,711 people on board became infected (567 of 2,666 passengers and 145 of 1,045 crew), and 14 people (passengers) died (Ahmad et al., 2020; Yamahata & Shibata, 2020).

On February 3, 2020, the cruise ship arrived at the Port of Yokohama and was not allowed to dock but remained anchored off the coast. In an unusual initiative, the Japanese government decided to re-quarantine the ship because there was concern that COVID-19–infected people may have remained on board. The quarantine officer of the Ministry of Health, Labor and Welfare (MHLW) boarded the ship to establish the quarantine. All passengers and crew members were then quarantined by the MHLW for fourteen days in the waters off Yokohama. The response was led by the MHLW and the government of Kanagawa Prefecture (where Yokohama is located).

At the same time, other government agencies, such as the Ministry of Defense and the Cabinet Office, closely collaborated. Healthcare professionals from the

Japan Self-Defense Forces (the Japanese military), Disaster Medical Assistant Teams, Japan Medical Association Teams, national institutions, and the Japanese Society for Infection Prevention and Control, were on the front lines of the public health and medical responses. During this response to the *Diamond Princess* infections, deployed medical professionals faced multiple challenges (Sawano et al., 2020). Command and control were not properly established, and many medical teams were deployed with little or no coordination. Standardized command structures, such as an incident management system, were not used on the ship (World Health Organization, 2018). Isolation of areas on the ship, such as strictly separating clean and infected areas, was not correctly implemented. Many medical teams lacked adequate training for the management of people with contagious and infectious diseases. There were inadequate supplies of appropriate personal protective equipment. Press conferences about daily activities were not conducted on a regular basis. Public information intended for foreign countries was insufficient.

The difficult experience with the *Diamond Princess*, however, taught many important lessons and yielded important scientific findings, particularly with respect to the specific clinical characteristics of COVID-19 infections. It was quickly confirmed that COVID-19 is transmitted by aerosolized droplets and appears to be more contagious than other viruses (Morawska et al., 2020). Droplets containing COVID-19 virus remained on surfaces aboard the ship much longer than expected. Respiratory failure in several patients who initially needed oxygen support suddenly developed into a critical illness (Tabata et al., 2020). Respiratory management and extracorporeal membrane oxygenation were introduced. Infection control on ships is difficult for structural reasons. The lesson learned from the case of the *Diamond Princess* was that greater availability of personal protective equipment would likely have reduced disease transmission and death.

In March 2020 the number of confirmed infection cases in Japan increased dramatically, and hospital beds were occupied by patients with COVID-19 infections. However, at that time, the capability of polymerase chain reaction (PCR) testing was not yet well established (Matsuda, 2020). This uncertainty caused social confusion and distrust, especially as the media severely criticized this situation. In March 2020 Chinese President Xi Jinping's state visit to Japan was canceled, and the 2020 Summer Olympics and Paralympics in Tokyo were postponed for one year (Gallego et al., 2020; Nakamura et al., 2018).

After the influenza pandemic in 2009, the Japanese government realized the importance of preparedness for a pandemic and then enacted the Special Measures Act to Counter New Types of Influenza of 2012. The Office for Pandemic Influenza and New Infectious Diseases Preparedness and Response (part of the Cabinet Secretariat) was established as the headquarters for governmental responses in collaboration with the MHLW. In April 2020 a state of emergency was declared according to an amendment to this law. The requirements to declare a state of emergency are (1) potential for serious health and life damage and (2) rapid transmission of infection, with a significant impact on daily life and on the economy. To prevent or mitigate the transmission of COVID-19, contact with people should be reduced. Yet, under this law, the Japanese government lacks authority to enforce citywide lockdowns. Apart from individual quarantine measures, officials cannot restrict the movement of people for the purpose of containing the virus. Consequently, compliance with government requests to restrict movements in Japan is *voluntary*.

In April 2020 healthcare workers sounded the alarm about the possibility of medical system collapse resulting from COVID-19 overcrowding. People in Japan realized and accepted the reality of the crisis and practiced self-restraint in order to prevent a collapse of the medical care system. On April 7, 2020, Prime Minister Abe proclaimed a one-month state of emergency, from April 8 to May 6, for Tokyo and the prefectures of Kanagawa, Saitama, Chiba, Osaka, Hyogo, and Fukuoka (Looi, 2020a, 2020b, 2020c). On April 16, 2020, the government expanded the state of emergency to include all forty-seven prefectures. The number of confirmed cases started decreasing in late April 2020, permitting hospitals to resolve the acute crisis. On May 25, 2020, Prime Minister Abe announced the lifting of the government's emergency declaration for all prefectures.

Staying at home and requesting store closures initiated by a seven-week state of emergency had an expectedly serious economic impact, with economic losses estimated at approximately US$50 billion (Ahmad et al., 2020; König & Winkler, 2020; Lenzen et al., 2020). After the state of emergency was lifted, society resumed activities, and people returned to towns to restart their businesses. As a result, the confirmed number of cases of COVID-19 began to gradually increase by June 2020. The highest number of confirmed cases during this second wave of infections surpassed the number in the first wave. The specific characteristics of patients with COVID-19 infections during the second wave changed compared to the first wave: most people infected were young, symptoms were milder, and consequently hospitals were not overwhelmed. The Survey of Critically Ill COVID-19 Patients, managed by the Japan ECMOnet for COVID-19 ("Nationwide System to Centralize Decisions Around ECMO Use for Severe COVID-19 Pneumonia in Japan," 2020; Shime, 2020; Takeda, 2020; Worku et al., 2020), covering more than 80 percent of the ICU beds in Japan, showed that the peak number of critically ill patients requiring extracorporeal membrane oxygenation (ECMO) during the second wave was half of that during the first wave (Figure 8.1). This second wave subsided gradually in July 2020, and the government and the people tried to balance restarting economic activity with controlling the infection.

Several clusters of COVID-19 outbreaks occurred at nursing homes. At a nursing home in Toyama Prefecture, forty-one of sixty-one residents were infected and fifteen died; eighteen staff members were also infected with COVID-19 ("Outbreak among Care-Workers and Elderly Deaths: How to Prepare for the Second Wave in the Nursing Home," 2020). The infection spread so rapidly that, when medical teams arrived, only five staff were available to provide basic care services for forty-one people, such as dietary and incontinence management. It took about six weeks to control the infection at this nursing home.

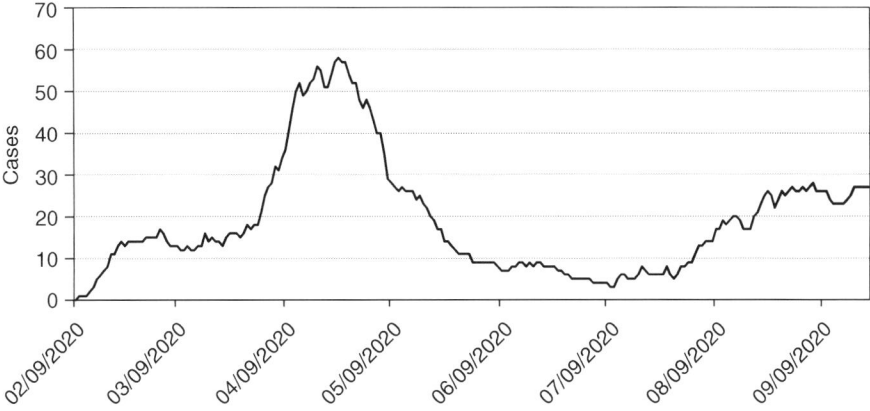

Figure 8.1. Number of patients in Japan treated with ECMO to treat COVID-19 infections.

Similar situations occurred in several areas, and the MHLW and prefectures deployed medical teams to provide medical support and distribute medical equipment. Nursing homes tried to take action to promote infection control, such as staff training, preventing the 3Cs (closed spaces, crowded places, close contact), and restricting visits. Although only sporadic COVID-19 clusters at nursing homes were reported; these were controlled with effort (Iritani et al., 2020). If nursing home residents became severely ill, they were transferred to an intensive care unit. Age is a significant factor associated with COVID-19 mortality. The MHLW showed that the case fatality rate is 18.1 percent among people in their eighties, 8.5 percent among those in their seventies, and 2.7 percent for those in their sixties.

Public Health Policy

Coordination

The MHLW organized the Cluster Response Team, or "cluster busters," on February 25, 2020, to identify and contain small-scale clusters of COVID-19 infections before they become community-wide mega-clusters (Furuse et al., 2020; Oshitani, 2020). The team included epidemiologists, infection control specialists from universities and the National Institute of Infectious Diseases, and a managerial staff. If a local government confirmed the existence of a new cluster, the MHLW deployed a surveillance team to the area to conduct an epidemiological survey and contact tracing in coordination with the staff of the local public health center.[1] After determining the source of an infection, the MHLW and local government officials put countermeasures in place to locate, test, and place people under medical surveillance who may have had close contact with an infected person. The Cluster Response Team also requested suspensions of affected businesses and restricted planned events. Based on the findings of contact tracing, the MHLW estimated that 80 percent of infected people did not transmit COVID-19 to another person. In contrast, those who did infect another person tended to spread it to multiple people and thus tended to form infection clusters in certain environments. On March 9, 2020, medical experts reviewed data from the Cluster Response Team and refined the definition of a high-risk environment as a place where the "3Cs" overlap, namely (1) closed spaces with poor ventilation; (2) crowded places with many people nearby; and (3) close-contact settings, such as close-range conversations. Consequently, gyms, music clubs, exhibition conferences, social gatherings, and other gathering places were considered high-risk locations for COVID-19 transmission.

On April 10, 2020, Dr. Mike Ryan, Executive Director of the WHO Health Emergencies Program, mentioned that Japan, with its teams of "cluster busters," had collected a lot of very useful information. The Cluster Response Team was divided into several new subcommittees for COVID-19 responses on June 24, 2020.

Medical Issues

Over the last several years, the Japanese government has been making efforts to prepare for emerging public health issues such as pandemics. In 2014 the MHLW approved the use of favipiravir, which is an anti-influenza medication developed by Fujifilm (Sissoko et al., 2016). Although its safety was demonstrated in more than two thousand patients and accelerated clearance of influenza viruses in phase III trials was demonstrated, favipiravir was initially not approved because of potential side effects in the young. In animal experiments, teratogenic and embryotoxic effects were shown in four animal species (Shiraki & Daikoku, 2020). With a strong request from the Japan Medical Association, favipiravir was finally approved as the second choice for treating influenza strains unresponsive to currently available antiviral agents (Nagata et al., 2015). At the time, favipiravir was considered as a candidate for the treatment of the Ebola virus. It is a promising candidate for the treatment of viral illnesses that may emerge in the future. Currently, favipiravir is considered as a candidate antiviral medication to treat patients with COVID-19 infections (Kaptein et al., 2020; Koba et al., 2020).

Japan and the United States have continued and strengthened their existing relationship regarding pandemic preparation. At the time of the Ebola outbreak in West Africa, both countries considered a collaboration plan. In 2018 the Centers for Disease Control and Prevention (USA) in Atlanta conducted a closed three-day command post exercise for pandemic simulation. Delegates from allied countries including Japan were invited. The Japanese government carefully investigated the process of invoking a state of emergency during pandemics, because no regulation currently exists regarding states of emergency in the Japanese Constitution. A state of emergency has never been declared after World War II in Japan. Based on its investigation, the government of Japan conducted tabletop exercises in 2018 and 2019 to prepare for a pandemic and to simulate situations that necessitate a state of emergency (Mitsubishi Research Institute, 2020).

However, Japan was spared from most recent pandemics before the COVID-19 outbreak. Consequently, it has lacked on-scene, clinical, and practical public health responses to the severe acute respiratory syndrome that originated in Guangdong, China, in 2003, to the H1N1 pandemic influenza in 2009, the Ebola virus disease from West African countries in 2014, and the Middle East Respiratory Syndrome from Middle Eastern countries and South Korea in 2015. Because these diseases did not occur in Japan, the urgent need for comprehensive public health preparedness for infectious pandemics, with practical training, equipment storages (personal protective equipment and PCR testing), surveillance systems, and scientific priority programs for the discovery of new vaccination and drugs, was underestimated. COVID-19 provided Japan with the necessary and fruitful experience for learning and training.

Social Policy and Economic Measures

As economic activity imploded during the pandemic, the Japanese government provided, in addition to existing measures, large-scale financial support plans from the national treasury to support companies and individuals. These plans were developed to prioritize promptness rather than consistency. Prefectural governments also developed additional financial support plans.

First, a variety of benefits were set up for people with economic difficulties. They were partly useful for those facing an abrupt decrease in income. Unemployment insurance, social assistance, leave compensation paid by statutory health insurance, long-term care leave system, and more were included in a package of social support for those affected by COVID-19. New applicants for social assistance in April 2020 amounted to 21,486 cases, which is an increase of 24.8 percent compared to the same period of the previous year (based on data from a press release of the Ministry of Health, Labour and Welfare on July 1, 2020).

Second, because it took time and complex procedures to use traditional benefits, such as social assistance, the government implemented additional measures, including (1) personal benefits in the form of immediate cash handouts of JPY100,000 (approximately US$960), and postponements and exemptions for social security contributions and fiscal payments and (2) individual financial support for those who needed social assistance. The government also introduced financial supports for small businesses and the self-employed. For example, companies whose revenues dropped to half what it was in 2019 could receive financial support to maintain their businesses. Additionally, low-interest loans, postponement and exemptions of taxes, and rent subsidies were made available. These socioeconomic measures aimed to stabilize employment for those who suffered severe income setbacks because of the COVID-19 pandemic.

Elements of Explanation

A media controversy existed in Japan, questioning whether its policy responses to the COVID-19 epidemic were timely and adequate. Contradictory arguments compared Japan either to other East Asian countries (e.g., South Korea, Taiwan, or China) and judged Japan's measures as late and inefficient, or alternatively to Western countries (e.g., the European Union, United Kingdom, or United States of America) against whom Japan's performance is cast in a positive light (Allen et al., 2020; Tabari et al., 2020; Watanabe, 2020). This highlights the relative nature of comparing policy outcomes and a possible dual perspective on what happened in Japan. The contrasting evaluations may be less contradictory than they seem.

The following pages present background elements that may contribute to understanding, and perhaps explaining, the ways the COVID-19 epidemic was managed in Japan, and the outcome. They may also indicate specific lessons that could be learned from the Japanese case.

Experienced observers refer to Japan as the most westernized country in Asia (Pilling, 2014), although it developed its own civilization over two thousand years. Japan was influenced by China, Europe, and the United States, but it also isolated itself for more than two hundred years to escape the risk of Western colonization, as experienced by China and much of the world. In sharp contrast to the preceding isolation, the second half of the nineteenth century saw Japan engaged in an extremely rapid process of modernization and industrialization. Japan was the first Asian country to be fully industrialized and to renew its political system from the feudal-like shogunate system to a modern state with a parliament and political parties. Democratization was finally achieved after World War II, when a liberal and antimilitary constitution was enacted under the influence of the Allied Powers.

Although largely westernized, Japan kept many homegrown social traditions, such as respect for the emperor, who symbolizes the nation; authority figures and the elderly; family responsibility; consensus-seeking; disciplined behavior; and strict attention to cleanliness and hygiene. For example, the widespread voluntary use of facial masks as protection against pollution, allergies, or infection and the respect of a certain physical distance between people, bowing in front of each other rather than handshaking, are common social norms in Japan. These behavioral patterns limit the spread of infection.

Geographical and demographic elements are of immediate importance in a contagious epidemic. Japan is an island country, which should facilitate control of an epidemic. However, shipping, harbors, and modern air travel provide open doors for pathogens. The Japanese islands are next to China, a short travel distance from the epicenter of the COVID-19 pandemic. Japan is connected worldwide, as a global economic player and a member of the G7. It has the United States as its largest business partner. Japan also keeps close political and economic connections with its neighbors, including China and South Korea. Similar to many countries throughout the world, Japan's supply chains are largely dependent on China. In contrast to a commonly held misconception, Japan is not a small, isolated country. It is the world's third largest economy with a population of 127 million in 2019, equal to that of the United Kingdom and Italy combined. Japan's GDP per capita amounts to US$43,279 (2019), which situates Japan between South Korea (US$42,925) and New Zealand (US$43,774) and the EU-28 average (US$46,776) (OECD, 2020a).

Further elements impacting epidemics in Japan are the extremely dense concentration of the population in megacities such as Tokyo, with 15,000 persons per square kilometer, and a large depopulated countryside where access to medical care can be a problem, especially for a rapidly aging population. Japan has the world's highest elderly dependency rate (47), a ratio of people aged sixty-five and older to those aged fifteen to sixty-four years. This places Japan far ahead of the second and third oldest countries, which are Italy (36.1) and Finland (35.8) (World Data Atlas, 2020). Geographical, territorial, and demographic factors should place Japan among the most COVID-19–affected countries, but it figures among the least affected.

The Japanese government is a constitutional monarchy, with democratic institutions and the separation of power into legislative, judicial, and executive branches. The emperor is the symbol of the nation and the state, independent from political affairs and without political power. The emperor's mission is symbolic and consists of standing for peace and the comfort of the people. Japan's political system is comparable to a parliamentary cabinet system, like that in the United Kingdom and Canada. Inside the country, there are three political layers, the national or central government, the prefectural governments, and the municipal governments. Japan is not a federal state, like Germany, the United States, or Brazil, although it is divided into forty-seven prefectures, each of which has a regional government with important autonomy and competency. Prefectures implement regulations for medical facilities, coordinate healthcare delivery, and lead crisis management in their jurisdictions, while the national government decides social security cash benefits and the regulatory framework. The national and local governments have complex top-down and bottom-up relationships that follow administrative law or common practice between politicians for consensus building (Council of Local Authorities for International Relations, 2019).

Like most industrialized countries, Japan has promoted decentralization of political power from the central government to the local level. Thus, policy decisions and operations such as infection control for COVID-19 or disaster responses are mainly conducted by local governments. Public health centers and public health institutes, which are at the core of infection control efforts, exist in all prefectures and municipalities. The capacity for public health responses is vital for the response to COVID-19. However, occasionally, for this unprecedented challenge, gaps or disagreements may occur between the national government and prefectural governments. For example, Hokkaido, the northernmost prefecture, declared its state of emergency on February 28, 2020, and the Tokyo metropolitan government did so on March 23, 2020, both without a precise legal basis, whereas the national government did not declare the state of emergency until April 7, 2020, according to the Special Measures Act to Counter New Types of Influenza of 2012. This discordance caused confusion in public understanding and public opinion.

In a similar way, the social security system seems rather unique compared to other countries, especially the organization of the statutory health insurance, which combines employer-linked private health insurance funds and local public health insurance funds. The social security system is described as "productivist welfare capitalism" (Holliday, 2000), placing priority on the economic stability of companies to provide employment, rather than subsidies and assistance to individuals as in European welfare states, although Japan's social security system also assists the unemployed to some extent.

Japan is a democratic country, where restriction of freedom without a legal basis is clearly a violation of the constitution. Therefore, the Japanese government amended the Act on Special Measures for Pandemic Influenza and New Infectious Diseases because there was controversy as to whether COVID-19 was to be regarded as a target disease of the act. Because this act has only limited power to restrict the freedom of individuals and companies, even after the declaration of a state of emergency, the action taken by the government to modify behavior was to ask people and companies alike to change their behavior voluntarily and conduct self-restraint, just by request and persuasion from the Japanese government.

Sociological literature suggests two general classifications of culture worldwide: individualist culture and groupist culture (Gudykunst et al., 1997; Kagawa-Singer, 1996). The characteristics of the individualist culture are respect for an individual's choices, emphasis of individual requests, and the importance of personal autonomy. The United States, Canada, and most European countries are categorized as individualist cultures. Characteristics of the groupist culture are the predominance of the group over the individuals that compose the group, and the emphasis on harmony and agreement as a fact of the group. Japan, Thailand, and most South American countries are categorized as groupist cultures. The Japanese government requested and persuaded people and businesses to restrain themselves and refrain from moving, such as business or personal trips by using public transportation or private vehicles, without a legal basis, and this approach was successful in controlling COVID-19 to a remarkable extent.

Groupist culture may be part of the explanation for this voluntary self-restraint. Most Japanese people seem to comply with apparently reasonable requests of the government: compliance is not 100 percent but is generally high. The predominant culture leads people to act on the recommendations of the government by wearing masks, respecting social distance, and limiting the 3Cs. Employers and their organizations made recommendations about what employees shall and shall not do in their spare time (such as not visiting Tokyo and not going to restaurants), and most employees appear to comply with these recommendations. This may not be the case in an individualist culture, where people may not comply with such voluntary recommendations, and it would be necessary to legislate limitations to enforce compliance.

The ability of the Japanese government to influence the actions of people has been studied extensively. The interrelationships between the state and society remain complex in Japan (Garon, 1997). Bouissou (2020) considered the respect of social norms in Japan as the essential active link in this relationship and termed it "making society" *(faire société)*. The ability of the government to affect the everyday lives of people so strongly may at least in part explain the voluntary cooperation of Japanese people with the recommendations made to control the COVID-19 pandemic.

However, the request and careful persuasion from the government have no legal force upon people who do not follow the request. Furthermore, voluntarily refraining from business activities might cause restriction of freedom for the sales activities of others, which is also against rights granted under the Constitution of Japan, Article 22. There was an ongoing discussion concerning the question of compensation for people who are the second-line victims of the voluntary restriction: should compensation be given to them, and would such compensation be in accordance with the constitution, or not? At the time of this writing, there are public demands that the government should be given legal power to enforce restrictions on freedom if an emergency makes it necessary and to assert such limitations with appropriate compensation.

Initially the MHLW planned that all patients with confirmed COVID-19 infections would be admitted to "designated hospitals." Consequently, hospital beds were quickly occupied by COVID-19 patients. The lack of alternatives and additional accommodation capacities became evident. The MHLW then called on the prefectures to revise the Plan for COVID-19 Public Health and Medical Responses, and rather strict and effective infection control interventions were initiated. For example, patients with confirmed infections but only mild symptoms were accommodated in hotels, available hospital beds were categorized, and their usage was triaged. Furthermore, the use of other limited resources, such as intensive care unit beds, advanced medical equipment (e.g., respiratory, extracorporeal membrane oxygenation, hemodialysis), personal protective equipment, medications, and so on, was prioritized. Distribution was controlled to ensure the optimal medical efficiency. If elderly people with COVID-19 infections became sick and a medical indication was validated, the elderly also were admitted to an intensive care unit. In March 2020, the MHLW almost failed to control the logistics; consequently a declaration of a state of emergency was considered and finally adopted in April.

A further major issue in Japan's public health response to the COVID-19 pandemic was PCR testing (Sawano et al., 2020). In the first wave, the MHLW was internationally and domestically criticized that the number of PCR tests was low compared with other countries. For example, South Korea rapidly established an effective PCR testing system, the so-called "drive-through PCR." Implementation and expansion of PCR testing capacity in Japan were controversial and slow between April and July 2020. There was international interest why the number of PCR tests in Japan was lower than that in other countries. A bureaucratic silo phenomenon in governmental organization and the agencies involved in managing the pandemic might have delayed the establishment of a similarly effective PCR testing system in Japan. However, the PCR capacity was gradually increased at local levels, with the collaboration of hospitals, public health centers, public health institutions, and laboratory companies.

Conclusion

By September 24, 2020, the cumulative number of patients with COVID-19 infections confirmed by PCR testing, death, and critically ill treated with ECMO were 79,621, 1,519, and 250, respectively. These numbers suggest that Japan was successful in responding to the COVID-19 epidemic, by applying existing public health preparedness measures, effective countermeasures such as the "cluster buster approach" for preventing the 3Cs, and requesting the nation to practice self-restraint. Social support policy was initiated, under existing policy measures, legislative temporal measures, and adopting a supplementary budget, complemented according to special needs resulting from the COVID-19 crisis. At the same time, however, there were some confusing and inappropriate public health and social policy interventions. At the time of this writing, a third COVID-19 wave has come in the fall/winter season 2020–2021, for which adequate preparedness must be ascertained well in advance.

It seems too early to draw final conclusions from the COVID-19 crisis, but the Japanese case already suggests three lessons. First, it illustrates how an Asian country, with a high level of group discipline, can operate in a democratic way and context and control an epidemic *without* legal constraints from a centralized authority. The basic condition for such successful combination of both individual freedom and public health seems to be a culture shared by all citizens of hygiene and of disciplined behavior by respect for the common good (Andrew, 2020). Second, the particular features of the Japanese welfare and healthcare systems together with a set of behavioral pattern are likely to facilitate the otherwise very difficult political compromise during a pandemic between the protection of health or the economy. Third, the subtle interplay of central, prefectural, and local governments in decision-making and policy implementation is based on multi-professional and multi-institutional expertise with large-scale disaster preparedness, rather than on narrow bureaucratic rules and exclusive medical advice.

Note

1. Prefectures and large cities organize public health centers, where physician and other specialists work in multi-professional teams responsible for protecting and maintaining the population health. According to the Japanese Association of Public Health Center Directors, 472 centers were in operation countrywide in 2019.

References

Ahmad, T., Haroon, H., Baig, M., & Hui, J. (2020). Coronavirus disease 2019 (COVID-19) pandemic and economic impact. *Pakistan Journal of Medical Sciences, 36*(Covid19-s4), S73–s78. https://doi.org/10.12669/pjms.36.COVID19-S4.2638

Allen, K., Buklijas, T., Chen, A., Simon-Kumar, N., Cowen, L., Wilsdon, J., & Gluckman, P. (2020). *Tracking global evidence-to-policy pathways in the coronavirus crisis: A preliminary report.* International Network for Government Science Advice. https://www.ingsa.org/wp-content/uploads/2020/09/INGSA-Evidence-to-Policy-Tracker_Report-1_FINAL_17Sept.pdf

Andrew, G. (2020). *Explaining Japan's soft approach to COVID-19.* Weatherhead Centre for International Affairs, Harvard University. https://epicenter.wcfia.harvard.edu/blog/explaining-japans-soft-approach-to-covid-19

Bouissou, J.-M. (2020). *Les leçons du Japon. Un pays très incorrect* [Lessons from Japan. A very incorrect country]. Editions Fayard.

Council of Local Authorities for International Relations (CLAIR). (2019). *Local government in Japan 2016* (2019 revised edition). Council of Local Authorities for International Relations.

Furuse, Y., Sando, E., Tsuchiya, N., Miyahara, R., Yasuda, I., Ko, Y. K., Saito, M., Morimoto, K., Imamura, T., Shobugawa, Y., Nagata, S., Jindai, K., Imamura, T., Sunagawa, T., Suzuki, M., Nishiura, H., & Oshitani, H. (2020). Clusters of Coronavirus disease in communities, Japan, January–April 2020. *Emerging Infectious Diseases, 26*(9), 2176–2179. https://doi.org/10.3201/eid2609.202272

Gallego, V., Nishiura, H., Sah, R., & Rodriguez-Morales, A. J. (2020). The COVID-19 outbreak and implications for the Tokyo 2020 Summer Olympic Games. *Travel Medicine and Infectious Disease, 34,* 101604. https://doi.org/10.1016/j.tmaid.2020.101604

Garon, S. (1997). *Molding Japanese minds.* Princeton University Press.

Gudykunst W. B., & Kim, Y. Y. (1997). *Communicating with strangers: An approach to intercultural communication* (3rd ed.). McGraw-Hill.

Hatanaka, T., Eguchi, N., Deguchi, M., Yazawa, M., & Ishii, M. (2015). Study of global health strategy based on international trends: Promoting universal health coverage globally and ensuring the sustainability of Japan's universal coverage of health insurance system: Problems and proposals. *Japan Medical Association Journal, 58*(3), 78–101.

Holliday, I. (2000). Productivist welfare capitalism: Social Policy in East Asia. *Political Studies, 48*(4), 706–723. https://doi.org/10.1111/1467-9248.00279

International Science Council. (2020). *Japan COVID-19 policy-making tracker.* https://www.ingsa.org/covid/policymaking-tracker/asia/japan/?_page=2

Iritani, O., Okuno, T., Hama, D., Kane, A., Kodera, K., Morigaki, K., Terai, T., Maeno, N., & Morimoto, S. (2020). Clusters of COVID-19 in long-term care hospitals and facilities in Japan from 16 January to 9 May 2020. *Geriatrics & Gerontology International, 20*(7), 715–719. https://doi.org/10.1111/ggi.13973

Ishii, M., & Nagata, T. (2013). The Japan Medical Association's disaster preparedness: Lessons from the Great East Japan Earthquake and Tsunami. *Disaster Medicine and Public Health Preparedness, 7*(5), 507–512. https://doi.org/10.1017/dmp.2013.97

Kagawa-Singer, M. (1996). Cultural systems. In R. McCorkle, M. Grant, M. Frank-Sromborg, & S. B. Baird (Eds.), *Cancer nursing: A comprehensive textbook* (2nd ed., pp. 38–52). Saunders.

Kaptein, S. J. F., Jacobs, S., Langendries, L., Seldeslachts, L., Ter Horst, S., Liesenborghs, L., Hens, B., Vergote, V., Heylen, E., Barthelemy, K., Maas, E., De Keyzer, C., Bervoets, L.,

Rymenants, J., Van Buyten, T., Zhang, X., Abdelnabi, R., Pang, J., Williams, R., ... Thibaut, H. J. (2020). Favipiravir at high doses has potent antiviral activity in SARS-CoV-2-infected hamsters, whereas hydroxychloroquine lacks activity. *Proceedings of the National Academy of Sciences of the United States of America.* https://doi.org/10.1073/pnas.2014441117

Koba, H., Yoneda, T., Kaneda, T., Ueda, T., Kimura, H., & Kasahara, K. (2020). Severe coronavirus disease 2019 (COVID-19) pneumonia patients treated successfully with a combination of lopinavir/ritonavir plus favipiravir: Case series. *Clinical Case Reports.* https://doi.org/10.1002/ccr3.3358

König, M., & Winkler, A. (2020). COVID-19 and economic growth: Does good government performance pay off? *Intereconomics, 55*(4), 224–231. https://doi.org/10.1007/s10272-020-0906-0

Lenzen, M., Li, M., Malik, A., Pomponi, F., Sun, Y. Y., Wiedmann, T., Faturay, F., Fry, J., Gallego, B., Geschke, A., Gómez-Paredes, J., Kanemoto, K., Kenway, S., Nansai, K., Prokopenko, M., Wakiyama, T., Wang, Y., &Yousefzadeh, M. (2020). Global socioeconomic losses and environmental gains from the Coronavirus pandemic. *PLoS One, 15*(7), e0235654. https://doi.org/10.1371/journal.pone.0235654

Looi, M. K. (2020a). Covid-19: Japan declares state of emergency as Tokyo cases soar. *BMJ, 369*, m1447. https://doi.org/10.1136/bmj.300.6737.1447

Looi, M. K. (2020b). Covid-19: Japan ends state of emergency but warns of "new normal." *BMJ, 369*, m2100. https://doi.org/10.1136/bmj.m2100

Looi, M. K. (2020c). Covid-19: Japan prepares to extend state of emergency nationwide as "untraceable" cases soar. *BMJ, 369*, m1543. https://doi.org/10.1136/bmj.m1543

Matsuda, R. (2020, May). Japan's response to the coronavirus pandemic: Update (May 2020). *Cambridge Core.* https://www.cambridge.org/core/blog/2020/04/11/japans-response-to-the-coronavirus-pandemic/

Mimura, S., Kodera, T., Kitagaki, M., Sato, M., Suzuki, S., Ito, T., Uwabe, Y., & Tamura, K. (2020). Clinical characteristics of COVID-19 in 104 people with SARS-CoV-2 infection on the Diamond Princess cruise ship: A retrospective analysis. *The Lancet Infectious Diseases, 20*(9), 1043–1050. https://doi.org/10.1016/S1473-3099(20)30482-5

Mitsubishi Research Institute. (2020). Case report series for risk communication in the case of pandemic. (in press).

Morawska, L., Tang, J. W., Bahnfleth, W., Bluyssen, P. M., Boerstra, A., Buonanno, G., Cao, J., Dancer, S., Floto, A., Franchimon, F., Haworth, C., Hogeling, J., Isaxon, C., Jimenez, J. L., Kurnitski, J., Li, Y., Loomans, M., Marks, G., Marr, L. C., ... Mazzarella, L. (2020). How can airborne transmission of COVID-19 indoors be minimised? *Environment International, 142*, 105832. https://doi.org/10.1016/j.envint.2020.105832

Nagata, T., Lefor, A. K., Hasegawa, M., & Ishii, M. (2015). Favipiravir: A new medication for the Ebola virus disease pandemic. *Disaster Medicine and Public Health Preparedness, 9*(1), 79–81. https://doi.org/10.1017/dmp.2014.151

Nakamura, S., Wada, K., Yanagisawa, N., & Smith, D. R. (2018). Health risks and precautions for visitors to the Tokyo 2020 Olympic and Paralympic Games. *Travel Medicine and Infectious Disease, 22*, 3–7. https://doi.org/10.1016/j.tmaid.2018.01.005

Nationwide system to centralize decisions around ECMO use for severe COVID-19 pneumonia in Japan (Special Correspondence). (2020). *Journal of Intensive Care, 8*, 29. https://doi.org/10.1186/s40560-020-00445-4

Organization for Economic Co-operation and Development. (2020a). *GDP per capita: OECD (2020), Gross domestic product (GDP) (indicator).* Retrieved September 20, 2020, from https://data.oecd.org/gdp/gross-domestic-product-gdp.htm

Organization for Economic Co-operation and Development. (2020b). *Health expenditure and financing.* Retrieved September 20, 2020, from https://stats.oecd.org/Index.aspx?ThemeTreeId=9

Organization for Economic Co-operation and Development. (2020c). *Health status: Life expectancy.* Retrieved September 20, 2020, from https://stats.oecd.org/Index.aspx?DatasetCode=HEALTH_STAT

Oshitani, H. (2020). Cluster-based approach to Coronavirus Disease 2019 (COVID-19) response in Japan-February-April 2020. *Japanese Journal of Infectious Diseases.* https://doi.org/10.7883/yoken.JJID.2020.363

Outbreak among care-workers and elderly deaths. How to prepare for the second wave in the nursing home. (2020, June 23). *Mainichi Shimbun.* https://mainichi.jp/articles/20200623/k00/00m/040/247000c

The Oxford COVID-19 Government Response Tracker. Retrieved September 20, 2020, from https://www.reopeningaftercovid.com

Pilling, D. (2014). *Bending adversity. Japan and the art of survival.* Penguin Books.

Sawano, T., Kotera, Y., Ozaki, A., Murayama, A., Tanimoto, T., Sah, R., & Wang, J. (2020). Underestimation of COVID-19 cases in Japan: An analysis of RT-PCR testing for COVID-19 among 47 prefectures in Japan. *QJM, 113*(8), 551–555. https://doi.org/10.1093/qjmed/hcaa209

Shime, N. (2020). Save the ICU and save lives during the COVID-19 pandemic. *Journal of Intensive Care, 8,* 40. https://doi.org/10.1186/s40560-020-00456-1

Shiraki, K., & Daikoku, T. (2020). Favipiravir, an anti-influenza drug against life-threatening RNA virus infections. *Pharmacology & Therapeutics, 209,* 107512. https://doi.org/10.1016/j.pharmthera.2020.107512

Sissoko, D., Laouenan, C., Folkesson, E., M'Lebing, A. B., Beavogui, A. H., Baize, S., Camara, A. M., Maes, P., Shepherd, S., Danel, C., Carazo, S., Conde, M. N., Gala, J. L., Colin, G., Savini, H., Bore, J. A., Le Marcis, F., Koundouno, F. R., Petitjean, F., . . . Diederich, S. (2016). Correction: Experimental treatment with favipiravir for ebola virus disease (the JIKI Trial): A historically controlled, single-arm proof-of-concept trial in Guinea. *PLoS Medicine, 13*(4), e1002009. https://doi.org/10.1371/journal.pmed.1002009

Tabari, P., Amini, M., Moghadami, M., & Moosavi, M. (2020). International public health responses to COVID-19 outbreak: A rapid review. *Iranian Journal of Medical Sciences, 45*(3), 157–169. https://doi.org.10.30476/ijms.2020.85810.1537

Tabata, S., Imai, K., Kawano, S., Ikeda, M., Kodama, T., Miyoshi, K., Obinata, H., Mimura, S., Kodera, T., Kitagaki, M., Sato, M.,Suzuki, S., Ito, T., Uwabe, Y., & Tamura, K. (2020). Clinical characteristics of COVID-19 in 104 people with SARS-CoV-2 infection on the Diamond Princess cruise ship: A retrospective analysis. *The Lancet Infectious Diseases, 20*(9), 1043–1050. https://doi.org/10.1016/S1473-3099(20)30482-5

Takeda, S. (2020). Nationwide system to centralize decisions around extracorporeal membranous oxygenation use for severe COVID-19 pneumonia in Japan. *Acute Medicine & Surgery, 7*(1), e510. https://doi.org/10.1002/ams2.510

Watanabe, M. (2020). The COVID-19 Pandemic in Japan. *Surgery Today, 50*(8), 787–793. https://doi.org/10.1007/s00595-020-02033-3

Worku, E., Gill, D., Brodie, D., Lorusso, R., Combes, A., & Shekar, K. (2020). Provision of ECPR during COVID-19: evidence, equity, and ethical dilemmas. *Critical Care, 24*(1), 462. https://doi.org/10.1186/s13054-020-03172-2

World Data Atlas (2020). *(Demographics, dependency ratios): Ratio of population aged 65+ per 100 population 15–64 years.* https://knoema.com/atlas/topics/Demographics/Dependency-Ratios/Old-age-dependency-ratio-65-per-15-64?baseRegion=JP

World Health Organization. (2018). *Joint external evaluation of IHR core capacities of Japan Mission report: 26 February–2 March 2018.* https://apps.who.int/iris/bitstream/handle/10665/274355/WHO-WHE-CPI-REP-2018.23-eng.pdf?ua=1

Yamahata, Y., & Shibata, A. (2020). Preparation for quarantine on the cruise ship Diamond Princess in Japan due to COVID-19. *JMIR Public Health and Surveillance, 6*(2), e18821. https://doi.org/10.2196/18821

9 SINGAPORE'S RESPONSE TO COVID-19

An Explosion of Cases despite Being a "Gold Standard"

Rebecca Wai

When COVID-19 first hit, Singapore was held up as the "gold standard of near-perfect detection" of cases (Niehus et al., 2020). Singapore is used to this kind of praise; it is internationally known as a prosperous, well-functioning country that has low corruption and impressively high scores on many social policy indexes, such as the United Nations Human Development Index and World Economic Forum's Social Mobility Index. According to the Global Health Security Index (GHSI), which measures countries' preparedness for handling public health crises, Singapore ranks third in southeast Asia and twenty-fourth overall (Global Health Security Index, 2019). It was unsurprising that Singapore would handle the COVID-19 pandemic well, especially after learning hard lessons from the SARS epidemic in 2003. However, a second wave of cases hit Singapore in March 2020. At first, the cause was easily identifiable and manageable. Thousands of Singaporean students and expatriates living in the west were coming back home to be somewhere more well managed and predictable. Even with this great influx of travelers, the government easily monitored them through mandatory fourteen-day quarantine orders in four- or five-star hotel rooms, which the government paid for.

However, there was a second source of cases that was largely ignored by the Singaporean government and society—migrant worker communities. Singapore relies on almost a million low-paid migrant workers to keep itself running (Ministry of Manpower, n.d.). These migrant workers, who usually come from China and south Asian countries, provide cheap labor for manual labor jobs that the highly educated Singaporean workforce would prefer to forgo (Phua & Chew, 2020). About 300,000 migrant workers live in government-commissioned dormitories that are commercially built and operated. They live in circumstances that are not conducive to COVID-19 prevention measures. They live twelve to twenty workers in one room, often cramped and poorly ventilated. Hygiene facilities are also often inadequate. In his surveys of migrant workers in Singapore, Mohan Dutta, a professor at Massey University in New Zealand, found that workers often lacked access to soap and cleaning supplies (Ratcliffe, 2020). In some cases, a hundred workers shared just five toilets and five showers.

When COVID-19 first appeared in Singapore, the government knew that migrant worker dormitories could be a potential hotspot, and they told the commercial operators to take precautions such as increasing cleaning and disinfecting efforts (Cheong, 2020a). Although it seems like the government anticipated that COVID-19 would spread quickly through these dormitories, they still dedicated the bulk of state resources to stemming the spread in Singaporean citizen and permanent resident (PR) communities, which makes up about 70 percent of Singapore's total population ("Singapore's Population Grows," 2019). They largely left efforts to monitor and contain the spread in migrant worker communities to nongovernment organizations and commercial operators. At the end of March 2020, Singapore had less than one thousand total cases of COVID-19. By mid-April 2020, Singapore was seeing close to one thousand new cases per day, the bulk of which came from migrant worker dormitories (Yong, 2020).

Inequalities in countries all around the world are being revealed during the pandemic, but Singapore gives us one of the starkest cases of how a country's response to a public health crisis is only as good as its response to its least privileged populations. In this chapter, we explore how Singapore's expansive state capacity and public services were able to contain the spread of COVID-19 within the general population at first but allowed the virus to spread as a result of the government's blind spot of the migrant worker community. This blind spot exists because of the tight control of civil society by the government and treatment of migrant workers as "second-class citizens" who do not have equal access to public services (Stilz, 2010). These shortcomings led to case counts rising from less than a few dozens a day to more than a one thousand a day, making Singapore the bearer of the highest number of cases per capita in southeast Asia.

Health Policies

Singapore was quick to institute travel restrictions and precautions because of the outbreak. Early in January 2020, Singapore was made aware of the novel coronavirus cases in Wuhan, China, and said they would start screening all incoming travelers from Wuhan. In late January 2020, when there was an increase in travelers from China because of the Chinese New Year holidays, Singapore expanded temperature screening to all travelers from China and announced a quarantine of fourteen days for anyone who had pneumonia and travel history to China (Ministry of Health, 2020).

The first case of COVID-19 in Singapore was confirmed on January 23, 2020, as a Chinese citizen traveling from Wuhan. Very quickly, Singapore moved to restrict travel from China, only allowing Singaporean citizens, PRs, and visa holders to land in Singapore from China. All travelers from China were placed on a fourteen-day quarantine. Those who breached their quarantine orders were prosecuted under Singapore's Infectious Disease Act, with fines of up to SGD$10,000 (US$7,500) and jail time of up to six months, or both (Lam, 2020). Non-citizens would be at risk of losing their visas or PR status. These punishments were meted out quickly and forcefully. In late February 2020, two Chinese citizens who broke their quarantine orders lost their PR status in Singapore and were barred from coming into the country in the future (Lam, 2020).

In March 2020, Singapore quickly increased travel restrictions and the criteria of who would be placed under quarantine. This culminated in all travelers except citizens, PRs and certain visa holders being barred from coming into the country. All travelers from any country were required to serve a fourteen-day quarantine order in dedicated facilities, which were mostly four and five-star hotels. The luxurious accommodations paid for by the government that returning travelers faced during their quarantine caught public attention; they were housed in five-star hotel rooms that would usually cost hundreds of dollars per night for their quarantine. More than 7,500 hotel rooms were booked by the government for returning travelers to serve out their quarantine orders (Mokhtar & Mookerjee, 2020). Around the same time, public facilities were quickly being shut down, and very soon Prime Minister Lee Hsien Loong announced the strict lockdown measures, termed "circuit breaker." This lockdown period was at first slated to run from April 7 to May 4, 2020, but it was later extended to June 1. During the "circuit breaker" period, only essential services, such as supermarkets, pharmacies, and restaurants (for takeout only) could be opened, and all schooling and other workplaces transitioned online.

On April 14, 2020, Singapore made it mandatory to wear masks and implemented a fine of SGD$300 (US$225) if those who flout the rules were caught in public for the first time without a mask, and SGD$1,000 (US$750) fine if they are caught subsequent times (Yong, 2020). To make it easier for residents of Singapore to adhere to mandatory mask rules, the government started distributing in February two free reusable masks that could be collected from vending machines at convenient locations such as bus interchanges, among other mask distribution efforts. In total, almost 10 million masks were distributed to residents in Singapore (Goh, 2020). However, mask distribution efforts notably did not include distribution to migrant workers in dormitories (Geddie & Aravindan, 2020).

To facilitate the enforcement of mandatory masks in public, about three thousand enforcement officers and safe distancing ambassadors were deployed to ensure that people were wearing masks in public and keep a safe distance from others (Ang & Phua, 2020). Another initiative that caught much public attention was a two-week pilot trial of a robot dog, named SPOT, that barked at people who were not adhering to social distancing measures. SPOT was fitted with cameras and sensors to estimate the number of people in the park and the distance between people (Tan, 2020). As of June 25, 2020, more than eleven hundred fines had been issued for those who flouted mask-wearing rules, and more than fifty-five hundred fines had been issued for breaches of safe distancing measures (Goh, 2020). Furthermore, one hundred forty people had their work visas revoked for breaching lockdown measures and quarantine orders (Goh, 2020). The government also set up a far-reaching digital contact tracing system, called SafeEntry. It required all residents to check in at any public venue visited through their phone or by giving their national identity card information ("COVID-19: SafeEntry," 2020). Singapore also developed a phone application called TraceTogether, which detected when people were near someone who had tested positive for COVID-19. The government also planned to distribute wearable tokens that were part of the TraceTogether system to increase the adoption of it. The government emphasized that it had no location-tracking capabilities and only detected proximity to positive test cases through Bluetooth (Ang, 2020).

Although the world was looking enviably at Singaporean citizens returning from overseas being put up in five-star hotels, Singapore's 300,000 migrant workers who lived in purpose-built dormitories were packed twelve to twenty people a room, while COVID-19 spread through their living spaces like wildfire starting in March 2020. Almost 95 percent of Singapore's COVID-19 cases were migrant workers living in purpose-built dormitories (Ministry of Health, 2020).

The disparity between the treatment of Singaporean citizens and migrant workers could already been seen in early February 2020, when a thirty-nine-year-old Bangladeshi national who lived in a migrant worker dormitory developed symptoms of COVID-19 and visited a clinic and hospital only to be sent back to the dormitory. It took a few days for him to be admitted to the hospital, and he eventually tested positive for COVID-19. This is in contrast to the experiences of Singaporean citizens who were brought to the hospital as soon as they were showing symptoms of COVID-19, even if the symptoms were not severe, and whose close contacts were quickly traced and quarantined. Despite the attempts of migrant worker advocacy groups, such as Transient Workers Count Too, to call attention to their cramped living conditions that would allow the virus to spread very quickly, the government's response was lukewarm (Chandran, 2020b). They only tested and quarantined those who were in contact with the worker and asked the dormitory operators to increase cleaning of premises and take residents' temperatures regularly.

However, this was not enough to prevent the spread of the virus; by early April 2020, cases in migrant worker dormitories were making up half of daily cases. Singapore did not report on the number of tests done in dormitories after the first reported case, but on April 14, it was reported that only fifteen hundred migrant workers were tested so far and there were plans to test only five thousand more (Mokhtar, 2020). In contrast, it was reported on April 6 that "2,800 to 2,900 tests [were] done each day in the last three to four weeks" (Wong, 2020). According to the Ministry of Health, as of August 10, 0.04 percent of the general population tested positive for COVID-19, whereas 16.2 percent of migrant workers living dormitories tested positive. As the cases in the migrant worker dormitories rose, the government started to divide the reporting of cases into those in the community and those in dormitories, further entrenching the division of the general and migrant communities in the minds of the Singaporean public. Furthermore, while Singaporeans were quarantined in hotels, migrant workers were either quarantined in their cramped dormitories or in unused carparks and construction sites that were hastily set up after the sudden increase in positive cases among migrant workers in early April 2020 (P. Ang, 2020).

Social Policies

Singapore has announced four budgets for COVID-19 support measures from February to May 2020, totaling SGD$93 billion (US$68 billion). SGD$52 billion (US$38 billion) comes from past reserves, which are estimated to be above SGD$500 billion (US$370 billion) (Ng & Jaipragas, 2019). Support measures mostly focused on preventing job loss. SGD$72 billion (US$53 billion) of the announced budgets was used for supporting businesses and ensuring job retention. Introduced in February 2020, the Jobs Support Scheme provided wage subsidies between 25 percent to 75 percent of the first SGD$4,600 (US$3,356) of gross month wages for each local employee (Inland Revenue Authority of Singapore, 2020). During the circuit breaker period, 75 percent of all wages were co-funded by the government. Businesses who were not allowed to resume operations even after restrictions eased continued to receive 75 percent wage support until August 2020. This was fairly successful in keeping businesses afloat as the number of businesses that closed down during the month of April were comparable to the number recorded in the same month from the past five years (Tang, 2020).

Although there were support schemes targeted toward individuals, compared to countries like the United States, there was less focus on support for individuals because of Singapore's circumstances. For example, there were no specific assistance schemes for residential renters as Singapore's home ownership rate is more than 90 percent of the citizen population, which in turn makes up about 60 percent of Singapore's total population (Tan, 2020). This is in large part due to its emphasis on building affordable public housing, of which 80 percent of Singaporeans live in (Housing Development Board, n.d.). The rate is one of the highest in the world and is much higher than the home ownership rates in many other developed countries (Majendie, 2020).

Singapore also does not have a universal unemployment benefit system. The government's approach to supporting the unemployed is focused on helping them find jobs through skills training and such. There is financial support for those who are unemployed, but usually only the old, ill, or disabled can apply. However, those who were retrenched because of the COVID-19 outbreak could apply for up to SGD$800 (US$584) for three months, but they must have a monthly household income of less than SGD$10,000 (US$7,295) or per capita household income of less than SGD$3,100 (US$2,261) a month before becoming unemployed (Government of Singapore, 2020). Although this might seem less robust than in many other developed countries, such as the United States, where unemployed workers could get USD$600 a week, Singapore's unemployment rate increased by just 0.1 percent in the first quarter of the year from 2.3 percent in the previous quarter to 2.4 percent (Phua, 2020). Although this was Singapore's highest unemployment rate in a decade, compared to many countries, such as the United States, which saw an unemployment rate of 14.7 percent in April 2020, Singapore managed to weather the effects of the economic downturn relatively well (Rosenberg & Long, 2020). Therefore, its focus on employer and job support rather than individual support was arguably an effective and suitable decision for Singapore's circumstances.

Individual support included SGD$600 (US$438) in cash as a "solidarity payment" for all Singaporean citizens, with some PRs and visa holders who hold white-collar jobs receiving SGD$300 (US$219) in April 2020. A second cash payment of SGD$600 (US$438) for Singaporeans earning less than SGD$28,000 (US$20,426) and SGD$300 (US$219) for those earning from SGD$28,000 to SGD$100,000 (US$20,426 to US$72,950), was disbursed in June 2020 (Ministry of Finance, 2020). All parents also received an additional SGD$300 (USD$219). In addition, those in need can apply for a one-off cash assistance of SGD$500 (USD$365) and low income households whose members contracted COVID get up to SGD$1000 (USD$730).

Explanation

Public Health Investment

A factor that played into Singapore's quick and effective initial response to the outbreak was from the protocols in place after its experience with the severe acute respiratory syndrome (SARS) outbreak in 2003 and the H1N1 outbreak in 2009. The government developed the National Influenza Pandemic Readiness and Response Plan (PRRP) in the aftermath of the SARS epidemic in 2003. Part of the PRRP was the establishment of a Homefront Crisis Management System (HCMS), which sought to address the inadequacy of Singapore's public health crisis management system during SARS (Woo, 2020). Another integral part to the PRRP plan was the Disease Outbreak Response System (DORS), which is a color-coded framework that served to guide the intensity of response measures. Its different levels corresponded with WHO's alert phases 1 through 6, and the levels were based on the transmissibility of the virus. However, it should be noted that SARS mainly spread through the citizen and PR population, which meant the PRRP focused on planning for the spread in those communities, not in the migrant worker community. This meant that despite creating a plan that included lessons learned from the SARS epidemic, Singapore was still blindsided by the rapid spread of COVID-19 in the migrant worker dormitories.

Singapore's ability to contain the spread of COVID-19 in the early days of the pandemic is also attributed to its high capacity for contact tracing, which undoubtedly stemmed from Singapore's experience with SARS. As Singapore's Prime Minister Lee Hsien Loong noted, "We [the Singapore government] have been preparing for this [COVID-19] since SARS, which was 17 years ago" (Lee,

2020). They were quickly able to form contact-tracing teams and easily mobilized other parts of the civil service, such as the military, which contributed greatly to their capacity to contact trace. Furthermore, Singapore ensured its citizens, PRs, and white-collar visa holders that COVID-19 testing would be free for everyone and their medical bills would be taken care of by the government if they were to be infected with COVID-19. This further contributed to Singapore's high COVID-19 detection rate because it ensured that people would not be hesitant to get tested or treated for COVID-19 because of prohibitive costs; those that tested positive were immediately sent to isolation in hospitals.

Serendipitously, Singapore completed the National Centre for Infectious Diseases (NCID) in May 2019, to take over Tan Tock Seng Hospital's Communicable Disease Centre (CDC), which was the facility used to contain and handle the 2003 SARS outbreak. The NCID is a 330-bed purpose-built medical facility that is "designed to manage an outbreak on the scale of SARS" (Kurohi, 2019). It is meant to be a form of excess medical capacity to be used in major outbreaks of infectious diseases. Outside of major outbreaks, it was used to detect and treat major food poisoning cases and conduct research on infectious diseases. However, because it was built in anticipation of a SARS-like virus, which was less infectious than COVID-19, the NCID's capacity was not enough to handle the spread of the highly contagious COVID-19 virus, and it had to be quickly ramped up to more than five hundred beds.

Authoritarian with High State Capacity and Tight Control of Civil Society

Singapore is a one-party state and has been ruled by the People's Action Party (PAP), the party of Singapore's famous founding father, Lee Kuan Yew, since Singapore's founding in 1965. PAP maintains a supermajority in Singapore's parliament to this day. Singapore has been termed an "electoral authoritarian regime," which refers to "regimes in which electoral institutions exist but yield no meaningful contestation for power" (Levitsky & Way, 2002). In 2019 Singapore scored a 3.45 out of 10 on Varieties of Democracy's (V-Dem) Liberal Democracy Index, which measures how strongly individual rights are protected against state interference (Coppedge et al., 2020). V-Dem is a research institute that measures how democratic countries are based on five dimensions. This low score indicates that individual rights in Singapore are not well protected and the state has a high level of control over the population. This can be seen in how much harsher Singapore's punishments for flouting COVID-19 rules were than other countries. As mentioned previously, more than 6,600 fines had been issued for breaking COVID-19 rules, and 140 work visa holders had their visa revoked. The Oxford COVID-19 Government Response Tracker (OxCGRT) shows that during the "circuit breaker" period, Singapore scored a high of 85 out of a 100 on their COVID-19 Government Response Stringency Index, which measures the strictness of policies that limit people's freedom of movement (e.g., restrictions on public gatherings, closure of restaurants and retail). For comparison, China's high is 82 out of a 100 and United States had a high of 73 out of a 100. Stringent rules are of no use if they are not complied with, but Singapore was able to ensure compliance with the rules because of high state capacity. Singapore was able to mobilize different parts of the civil service quickly to mete out fines for rule-breakers. They also made it easier on citizens to comply with mask-wearing rules by distributing millions of masks in a short amount of time. This was also because they were able to mobilize the civil service to pack and distribute masks, and the government had easy access to public venues to set up distribution stations.

However, despite their authoritarian setting, Singaporeans have a high level of trust in the government and willingness to give up their personal information, unlike citizens in many authoritarian countries. According to the Edelman Trust Barometer, 70 percent of Singapore trusts the government (Rekhi, 2020). This can be seen in how easily Singapore's far-reaching and robust digital contact-tracing system was rolled out. Singaporeans were even willing to use a phone app called TraceTogether that always records Bluetooth proximity information used for contact tracing in the background (Ang, 2020). Undoubtedly, there is a high level of compliance among the population because Singapore has a high state capacity to enforce its rules and there is a lack of privacy laws, which gives the government easy access to individual's data (Privacy International, 2015). However, trust in the government also plays a great part in increasing the information flow from the population to the government. According to an April 2020 poll, over 80 percent of Singaporeans comply with the rules, and about 70 percent said they were coping well with the rules (Kurohi, 2020). Singapore's authoritarian setting, high state capacity, and high level of citizen trust in the government contributed to the effectiveness of Singapore's response to COVID-19 and its containment of the virus. Singapore was able to set strict rules as the population was already used to having their individual rights curtailed by the government. They were able to enforce it because of the state capacity they have built up over the years, and Singaporeans were willing to comply with the rules and seek the government's help when they were infected.

Another consequence of Singapore's rule as a one-party state is that its civil society has been kept anemic. In 2019 Singapore scored a 3.29 out of 10 on V-Dem's Core Civil Society Index, which measures the robustness of a country's civil society, signaling that Singapore has a weak civil society (Coppedge et al., 2020). The government's approach to civil society has always been to enforce strict restrictions on civil society organizations to limit their influence and power. This is because PAP's government thinks of itself as a neutral party, which is only interested in pursuing the interests for the common. Therefore, the government does not see a need for "interest groups that pursue particularistic goals" as the PAP perceives that it is able to "absorb virtually all demands from society" (Ortmann, 2015). The government has been largely successful in creating a depoliticized civic space. As a result, activists—even if they are non-partisan—who challenge the system are framed as just trying to create trouble for Singaporean society.

Singapore's Societies Act requires civil society organizations to register with the government, if not they will be deemed illegal. Furthermore, organizations will not be registered if the government deems the purpose of the organization "contrary to national interest" or "prejudicial to public peace, welfare or good order in Singapore" ("Societies Act," n.d.). Unless an organization is registered as a political party, is it illegal for them to engage in political activities. Organizations that operate without approval from the government will be subjected to fines and imprisonment. This allows the government to control who is allowed in Singapore's civic space and greatly limits the scope of activities organizations are allowed to participate in, which limits their influence.

This is relevant because migrant workers have to work with advocacy groups and nongovernmental organizations to fight for their rights, because the workers have very few resources to make their plight known because of lack of access to stakeholders, language barriers, and other issues. Advocacy for migrant labor rights has been especially curtailed because of its controversial history. First, the general labor rights movement in Singapore has been suppressed and co-opted by the government after most independent unions were closed down or weakened in the 1960s. These unions were replaced by a state-sponsored National Trades Union Congress (NTUC), which acted as an "umbrella group for affiliated organizations that are largely supportive of the government's economic and labor policies" (Rodan, 1996, p. 100). Second, many NGOs are unwilling to advocate for migrant labor rights because there is an association of the issue with the "Marxist conspiracy," "a term used to describe the arrest and detention under Singapore's Internal Security Act of 22 people in May 1987 for threatening the state and national interests" (Lyons, 2005, p. 216). Social workers from the Geylang Catholic Centre for Foreign Workers, which advocated for better working conditions for migrant workers, were arrested. When the arrests happened, the government said that Catholic organizations were "a cover for political agitation" to "radicalize student and Christian activists" (Haas, 1989, p. 59).

Therefore, the migrant labor rights movement was not allowed to grow and has only recently, in the early 2000s, been revived. Furthermore, because of the rules curtailing the activities of civil society organizations, the work often focuses more on public education and volunteer work rather than advocacy in the political and legal sphere for improved migrant labor rights. These groups for many years have tried to bring the public and government's attention to the subpar living conditions of migrant workers and their resultant high susceptibility to infectious disease outbreaks (Chandran, 2020a). However, because the government has created a civic space where organizations who advocate for issues outside the scope of what they explicitly recognize are unwelcome, little attention has been paid to the living conditions of migrant workers. Although the government has worked hard to ensure that there are facilities to handle a public health crisis in the general population, they have largely forgone building up public health capacity with migrant workers in mind. This can be seen from the aforementioned reluctance to carry out the same level of testing for COVID-19 in the migrant worker community as in the general population.

Migrant Workers as Second-Class Citizens

Public health experts in Singapore have done research that shows migrant worker communities are at a higher risk of spreading and contracting infectious diseases because of their living conditions (Sadarangani et al., 2017). However, it did not seem to be a pressing issue for the government because there was little risk of them burdening the healthcare system because migrant workers lack access to it for many reasons. A survey of doctors found that the two main barriers to healthcare access were language/cultural problems and financial costs (Ang et al., 2019). There are few medical translation services for migrant workers, who often do not speak English or one of Singapore's other official languages. Employers of migrant workers are required to bear their healthcare costs if they fall ill or are injured, and migrant workers do not have access to subsidized healthcare as most other residents of Singapore do. However, many employers are unwilling to pay these costs, even when they are required by law to provide healthcare for their migrant worker employees (Ang et al., 2019). Employers are rarely held accountable for lapses in healthcare provision because of migrant workers' lack of knowledge about their right to healthcare and minimal oversight by the government; therefore, migrant workers often have inadequate medical care. About 40 percent of doctors saw migrant worker patients discharging themselves against medical advice or not receiving the treatment needed because of financial reasons (Ang et al., 2019). Many doctors said that migrant worker employers often sought to downplay the extent of their employees' illnesses and injuries and would even sometimes send them back to their home country to avoid paying for their treatment (Ang et al., 2019).

Furthermore, even though the government carried out almost every aspect of Singapore's COVID-19 response in the general population, they largely ceded responsibility of the handling of the outbreak to private contractors who operate the workers' dormitories. It had been known for years that the living conditions of these privately run dormitories were often cramped and unsanitary. The government's hands-off approach to migrant workers meant that nearly half of dormitories failed to meet requirements of appropriate living conditions that the government had initially laid out (Cheong, 2020b).

This disparity in oversight further illustrates migrant workers as second-class citizens and how the government did not think migrant workers' living conditions was a public health issue that would affect Singaporean citizens. The handling of the outbreak in the general population was efficient and effective because of the government's heavy involvement. However, because the government did not see migrant workers as a population integrated with the general Singaporean society and one they had the responsibility to protect, the ability to detect and contain the spread of the virus in the migrant worker community was lackluster.

Conclusion

Singapore excels at many indicators needed to address a public health crisis: extensive social policies, well-managed information flow, high citizen trust in the government, and great capacity for coercion. However, the stellar performance on many indicators does not apply to migrant workers. They do not have access to Singapore's public resources, are largely ignored by the government, and are often subject to exploitative employers. These employers, until very recently, were not subject to the strict regulations that Singapore is known for because of the lack of attention on the subpar working and living conditions of migrant workers. Many are surprised that Singapore went from the gold standard of pandemic response to one of the hardest hit countries in East Asia. But if we look closely at Singapore's political system and societal structure, early warning signs and generalizable lessons will be revealed.

An important lesson here is that a strong civil society is necessary to reveal the blind spots of the government. Often vulnerable populations such as minorities and migrant workers are not seen by the government because of their lack of political access and influence. Civil society organizations that work closely with vulnerable populations would be able to contribute to the robustness of a public health crisis response by providing means to monitor and provide care for these populations. A stronger civil society will also contribute to a strong response to public health crises by providing resources and educating people on the ground to reinforce outbreak mitigation measures. Although Singaporeans in general have a high trust in the government, their forceful punitive measures may dissuade certain populations who the government has not fostered as strong a relationship with, from adopting government-led measures such contact-tracing phone apps. Civil society organizations can fill that gap in monitoring because they are more likely to have built trust within these populations.

Furthermore, it is important to expand access to basic public services to all populations. Certainly, provision of basic healthcare and welfare services allowed Singaporeans to seek help if they were sick and adhere to lockdown measures because their basic needs were met. However, because these basic services were not expanded to the migrant worker community, they were less willing to come forward when they were sick, leading to a lower detection rate and a faster and wider spread of the virus. Civil society organizations in Singapore have for a long time warned that if we do not take care of the basic needs of migrant workers to the same extent as the government takes care of the general population, it will be detrimental for public health and the economy. Unfortunately, Singapore turned a blind eye to these warnings and even took active steps to silo migrant workers from the general population and restrict their access to basic public services to avoid having to pay for the provision of healthcare and other basic services to them. In the end, the decision to ignore migrant workers because it was economically and logistically easier led to even more economic and social problems.

As a result of Singapore's unwillingness to address migrant labor issues, the virus spread to the point where Singapore had to enforce its strictest lockdown measures to prevent the spread of the virus from the migrant worker community to the general population. Therefore, if Singapore wants to ensure that the next public health crisis is not mishandled in the same way, it needs to include more civil society organizations or loosen restrictions on existing ones in its policy and decision-making process and ensure that the basic needs of all populations—not just "legitimate" citizens—are met. Viruses are apolitical; even if the government wants to ignore certain populations, virus outbreaks will not.

References

Ang, J. W., Koh, C. J., Chua, B. W., Narayanaswamy, S., Wijaya, L., Chan, L. G., Soh, L. L., Goh, W. L., & Vasoo, S. (2019). Are migrant workers in Singapore receiving adequate healthcare? A survey of doctors working in public tertiary healthcare institutions. *Singapore Medical Journal.* https://doi.org/10.11622/smedj.2019101

Ang, P. (2020, April 11). Coronavirus: Healthy migrant workers to be housed at void decks and multi-storey carparks at HDB construction sites. *The Straits Times.* https://www.straitstimes.com/singapore/coronavirus-healthy-migrant-workers-to-be-housed-at-void-decks-and-multi-storey-carparks

Ang, W. M. (2020, June 8). COVID-19 contact tracing "absolutely essential"; wearable TraceTogether tokens to be rolled out in June. *Channel NewsAsia.* https://www.channelnewsasia.com/news/singapore/covid-19-contact-tracing-wearable-devices-trace-together-12815796

Ang, W. M., & Phua, R. (2020, April 14). COVID-19: Compulsory to wear mask when leaving the house, says Lawrence Wong. *Channel NewsAsia.* https://www.channelnewsasia.com/news/singapore/covid19-wearing-masks-compulsory-lawrence-wong-12640828

Chandran, R. (2020a, June 10). Singapore calls for 'mindset' change as migrant workers are rehoused. *Reuters.* https://www.reuters.com/article/us-health-coronavirus-singapore-trfn-idUSKBN23H1EO

Chandran, R. (2020b, April 21). "Packed like sardines": Coronavirus exposes cramped migrant housing. *Reuters.* https://www.reuters.com/article/us-health-coronavirus-migrantworker-trfn-idUSKBN22315Z

Cheong, D. (2020a, February 11). Coronavirus: Foreign workers at Kaki Bukit dormitory told to stay away from work on Monday morning. *The Straits Times.* https://www.straitstimes.com/singapore/health/coronavirus-foreign-workers-at-kaki-bukit-dormitory-told-to-stay-away-from-work-on

Cheong, D. (2020b, May 4). Parliament: About half of dorm operators flout licensing conditions each year, says Josephine Teo. *The Straits Times.* https://www.straitstimes.com/politics/majority-of-dorm-operators-flout-licensing-conditions-each-year-says-josephine-teo

Coppedge, M., Gerring, J., Knutsen, C. H., Lindberg, S. I., Teorell, J., Altman, D., Bernhard, M., Fish, M. S., Glynn, A., Hicken, A., Luhrmann, A., Marquardt, K. S., McMann, K., Paxton, P., Pemstein, D., Seim, B., Sigman, R., Skaaning, S., Staton, J., . . .

Ziblatt, D. (2020). V-Dem Dataset 2020. *Varieties of Democracy (V-Dem) Project.* https://doi.org/10.23696/VDEMDS20

COVID-19: SafeEntry digital check-in system deployed to more than 16,000 venues. (2020, May 9). *Channel NewsAsia.* https://www.channelnewsasia.com/news/singapore/covid-19-safe-entry-digital-checkin-deployed-16000-venues-12717392

Geddie, J., & Aravindan, A. (2020, April 15). In Singapore, migrant coronavirus cases highlight containment weak link. *Reuters.* https://www.reuters.com/article/us-health-coronavirus-singapore-migrants-idUSKCN21X19G

Global Health Security Index: Building collective action and accountability. (2019). Global Health Security Index. https://www.ghsindex.org/wp-content/uploads/2019/10/2019-Global-Health-Security-Index.pdf

Goh, T. (2020, July 5). Over 6,600 fines issued for flouting Covid-19 rules. *The Straits Times.* https://www.straitstimes.com/singapore/health/over-6600-fines-issued-for-flouting-covid-19-rules

Government of Singapore. (2020, May 1). *Financial support to help Singaporeans affected by COVID-19.* http://www.gov.sg/article/financial-support-to-help-singaporeans-affected-by-covid-19

Haas, M. (1989). The politics of Singapore in the 1980s. *Journal of Contemporary Asia, 19*(1), 48–77.

Housing Development Board. (n.d.). *Public housing—A Singapore icon.* Retrieved on August 8, 2020, from https://www.hdb.gov.sg/cs/infoweb/about-us/our-role/public-housing-a-singapore-icon

Inland Revenue Authority of Singapore. (2020, July 19). *Over $4 billion to be disbursed from 29 Jul under the jobs support scheme.* https://www.iras.gov.sg/irashome/News-and-Events/Newsroom/Media-Releases-and-Speeches/Media-Releases/2020/Over-$4-billion-to-be-disbursed-from-29-Jul-under-the-Jobs-Support-Scheme/

Kurohi, R. (2019, January 17). Centre to Boost Infectious Disease Management. *The Straits Times.* https://www.straitstimes.com/singapore/health/centre-to-boost-infectious-disease-management

Kurohi, R. (2020, April 20). Reach poll shows most Singaporeans complied with circuit breaker measures to stem spread of Covid-19. *The Straits Times.* https://www.straitstimes.com/singapore/reach-poll-shows-most-singaporeans-complied-with-circuit-breaker-measures-to-stem-spread

Lam, L. (2020, February 28). China couple charged under Infectious Diseases Act for obstructing COVID-19 containment work. *Channel NewsAsia.* https://www.channelnewsasia.com/news/singapore/covid19-coronavirus-china-couple-charged-infectious-diseases-act-12480170

Lee, H. L. (2020). PM Lee Hsien Loong's interview with CNN [online]. *Prime Minister's Office Singapore.* http://www.pmo.gov.sg/Newsroom/PM-interview-with-CNN

Levitsky, S., & Way, J. (2002). The rise of competitive authoritarianism. *Journal of Democracy, 13*(2), 51–65.

Lyons, L. (2005). Transient workers count too? The intersection of citizenship and gender in Singapore's Civil Society. *Sojourn: Journal of Social Issues in Southeast Asia, 20*(2), 208–248.

Majendie, A. (2020, July 8). *Why Singapore has one of the highest home ownership rates.* Bloomberg. https://www.bloomberg.com/news/articles/2020-07-08/behind-the-design-of-singapore-s-low-cost-housing

Ministry of Finance. (2020, June 4). *Budget 2020 Care and Support—Cash to be paid from 18 June 2020*. https://www.mof.gov.sg/newsroom/press-releases

Ministry of Health. (2020, January 31). *Ministry of Health News Highlights*. https://www.moh.gov.sg/news-highlights/details/extension-of-precautionary-measures-to-minimise-risk-of-community-spread-in-singapore

Ministry of Health. (n.d.). *COVID-19 situation report*. Retrieved on August 8, 2020, from https://covidsitrep.moh.gov.sg/

Ministry of Manpower. (n.d.). *Foreign workforce numbers*. Retrieved on August 14, 2020, from https://www.mom.gov.sg/documents-and-publications/foreign-workforce-numbers

Mokhtar, F. (2020, April 22). How Singapore flipped from virus hero to cautionary tale. *Bloomberg*. https://www.bloomberg.com/news/articles/2020-04-21/how-singapore-flipped-from-virus-hero-to-cautionary-tale

Mokhtar, F., & Mookerjee, I. (2020, March 28). In Singapore, quarantine comes with sea view, room service. *Bloomberg*. https://www.bloomberg.com/news/articles/2020-03-28/in-singapore-quarantine-comes-with-a-sea-view-and-room-service

Ng, J. Y., & Jaipragas, B. (2019, February 16). Singapore's giant reserves: A taxing question for Heng Swee Keat. *South China Morning Post*. https://www.scmp.com/week-asia/politics/article/2186409/singapores-giant-reserves-taxing-question-its-next-prime-minister

Niehus, R., De Salazar, P. M., Taylor, A. R., & Lipsitch, M. (2020). Quantifying bias of COVID-19 prevalence and severity estimates in Wuhan, China that depend on reported cases in international travelers. *medRxiv*. https://doi.org/10.1101/2020.02.13.20022707

Ortmann, S. (2015). Political change and civil society coalitions in Singapore. *Government and Opposition*, 50(1), 119–139.

Phua, R. (2020, June 15). Singapore's jobless rate highest in 10 years, total employment registers record decline in Q1. *Channel NewsAsia*. https://www.channelnewsasia.com/news/singapore/unemployment-jobless-highest-10-years-retrenchments-mom-12835166

Phua, R., & Chew, H. M. (2020, June 9). Can Singapore rely less on foreign workers? It's not just about dollars and cents, say observers. *Channel NewsAsia*. https://www.channelnewsasia.com/news/singapore/singapore-foreign-workers-reliance-challenges-12806970

Privacy International. (2015, June). *Universal Periodic Review Stakeholder Report: 24th Session, Singapore—The right to privacy in Singapore*. https://privacyinternational.org/advocacy-briefing/722/right-privacy-singapore

Ratcliffe, R. (2020, April 17). Singapore's cramped migrant worker dorms hide Covid-19 surge risk. *The Guardian*. https://www.theguardian.com/world/2020/apr/17/singapores-cramped-migrant-worker-dorms-hide-covid-19-surge-risk

Rekhi, S. (2020, June 22). Trust in Singapore government up: Edelman Poll. *The Straits Times*. https://www.straitstimes.com/asia/trust-in-singapore-government-up-edelman-poll

Rodan, G. (1996). State–society relations and political opposition in Singapore. In G. Rodan (Ed.), *Political oppositions in industrialising Asia*. (pp. 97–127). Routledge.

Rosenberg, E., & Long, H. (2020, June 6). Unemployment rate drops and 2.5 million jobs added, after states reopened. *Washington Post*. https://www.washingtonpost.com/business/2020/06/05/may-2020-jobs-report/

Sadarangani, S. P., Lim, P. L., & Vasoo, S. (2017). Infectious diseases and migrant worker health in Singapore: A receiving country's perspective. *Journal of Travel Medicine*, 24(4). https://doi.org/10.1093/jtm/tax014

Singapore's population grows to 5.7 million, boosted by increase in foreign workers. (2019, September 25). *Channel NewsAsia*. https://www.channelnewsasia.com/news/singapore/population-number-singapore-foreign-workers-new-citizens-11941034

Societies Act—Singapore Statutes Online. (n.d.) Attorney General's Chambers. Retrieved on August 11, 2020, from https://sso.agc.gov.sg/Act/SA1966

Stilz, A. (2010). Guestworkers and second-class citizenship. *Policy and Society, 29*(4), 295–307. https://doi.org/10.1016/j.polsoc.2010.09.005

Tan, C. (2020, May 9). Meet Spot, the safe distancing robot on trial in Bishan-AMK Park. *The Straits Times*. https://www.straitstimes.com/singapore/meet-spot-the-safe-distancing-robot-on-trial-in-bishan-amk-park

Tan, J. M. (2018, June 17). Commentary: An over-emphasis on home ownership can come at a cost to society. Time for a review of public housing policy. *Channel NewsAsia*. https://www.channelnewsasia.com/news/commentary/emphasis-home-ownership-hdb-lease-review-of-public-housing-10423116

Tang, S. K. (2020, June 5). About 3,800 companies closed down in April; Expect uptick in coming months: Chee Hong Tat. *Channel NewsAsia*. https://www.channelnewsasia.com/news/business/3800-business-closures-april-uptick-ahead-covid19-coronavirus-12802912

Wong, L. (2020, April 6). Covid-19 tests stepped up to around 2,900 every day. *The Straits Times*. https://www.straitstimes.com/singapore/covid-19-tests-stepped-up-to-around-2900-every-day

Woo, J. J. (2020). Policy capacity and Singapore's response to the COVID-19 pandemic. *Policy and Society, 39*(3), 345–362.

Yong, M. (2020, April 15). COVID-19: What the law says about having to wear a mask when outside your home. *Channel NewsAsia*. https://www.channelnewsasia.com/news/singapore/covid-19-singapore-masks-going-out-law-12643120

10 INDIA'S RESPONSE TO COVID-19

Minakshi Raj

India's first confirmed case of coronavirus was observed on January 30, 2020, in a patient in the southern, coastal state of Kerala (Reid, 2020). Because the patient was a student at Wuhan University in China, upon receiving permission, a plane was prepared immediately to send to China to bring Indian nationals back to India (Reid, 2020). Over the next several months, India would experience a strikingly low number of cases and deaths followed by a rapid spike in close tandem with a national lockdown and then a phased "unlock." In the country of 1.35 billion individuals, by July 31, 2020, there were 1.64 million confirmed cases with 35,747 deaths.

Understanding India's response to the virus requires first recognizing that India's modern identity has emerged from layer upon layer of external and internal monarchy regimes over time. With each successive empire that ruled the country—the most recent being imperial Britain until 1947—India's culture and character has evolved. Although each of these invading regimes enforced arbitrary divisions within the country for economic and political expediency, over time language, religion, and other aspects of culture have brought about diversity and, oddly amid that, a sense of unity.

Sunil Khilnani refers to modern India as an "experiment," wherein members of the Indian democracy must "entrust their destiny to a modern state" while maintaining their distinctive culture and the cultures within (Khilnani, 2017, p. 5). India's history is important for understanding its response to the virus. Under British rule remote management for purposes of extracting resources made salient a collective sense of loss of culture and subsequently catalyzed an ongoing effort to maintain the country's identity even after seventy years of independence. State boundaries drawn by the British were arbitrary and informed by trading posts established by the East India Company in the 1600s, with parallel colonization of much smaller regions by the French and Portuguese, and progressive military coercion (Dalrymple, 2019). The boundaries have since shifted across the country, established primarily on the basis of language and population density (Aula, 2014; Sur, 2015). Accordingly, cultural diversity is still observed in India (Riley, 2007). However, cultural memory and collective trauma underlie the broader unity that has persisted in India (Alexander, 2017; Yusin, 2009).

Various groups were underrepresented from formal legislative bodies during colonization and were neglected entirely even in local government bodies. The desire for representation in modern India is steadfast and has resulted in a multitude of political parties seeking to represent communities based on language, religion, caste, and other markers of identity. This, in addition to other forms of regional variation that other countries experience—such as population density, public health infrastructure, geographical characteristics, and border instability—shape the complexity and variation of policy decisions and implementation across India. Accordingly, COVID-19 represents striking unity in decision-making, and challenges in policy implementation reflect the diversity of political representation across the country.

In this chapter, we explore the public health response in India during the COVID-19 pandemic, the social policies initiated to enable the public to quarantine, and the political factors shaping India's policy decisions, implementation, and general response.

Public Health and Health Policy Response

In this section, we describe India's chronological public health response to the pandemic. We describe the response in three parts: the first constitutes the initial response from the state of Kerala, where the virus was first reported; the second focuses on the public health policy response led by the central government; and the third demonstrates decisions that were once again left to the states.

Although India's constitution deems health as a human right, the government's expenditure on health, roughly 1.28 percent of gross domestic product, remains lower than healthcare spending of other countries (Chetterjee, 2020). Despite persistent underinvestment in public health infrastructure for its population needs, many factors had the potential to prepare India to control spread and deliver care. The first is perhaps the fact that the first case of coronavirus was reported in a patient in Kerala, the southern coastal state that successfully handled a Nipah outbreak only two years ago, and intensive flooding a year before that (Arunkumar et al., 2019; Chetterjee, 2020). Further, Kerala has emerged as an outlier for successful health outcomes when compared to most states in India, which may be in part attributed to its historical leadership in health policy planning and its emphasis on preventive care in addition to its high literacy rate. For instance, the maternal mortality rate in Kerala is 66 per 100,000 live births as compared to 178 per 100,000 live births in the rest of the country (PHPCI, 2018). As another example, vaccines were made mandatory for public workers and students as early as 1879 (Kutty, 2000). The Kerala government has also invested in health information technology to support population health management with a focus on surveillance of communicable diseases (Mannathukkaren, 2013; PHCPI, 2018).

The first three cases in Kerala were managed swiftly and, by the third case on February 3, 2020, a health emergency had been declared in the state. Subsequent measures included surveillance and screening of incoming passengers from China and immediate collaboration between the Kerala State Disaster Management Authority and the health department. Kerala observed no cases for about one month; and about a month later three travelers returned to the state from Italy and from there on, cases began to rise (WHO, 2020b). In early March new cases were reported in New Delhi and Telangana. As travel continued, cases began to rise across the country as those returning to India from Italy, Germany, and the Middle East had begun spreading the virus to their contacts both through typical social gatherings as well as through various religious gatherings of entire communities ("Coronavirus: Search for Hundreds of People after Delhi Prayer Meeting," 2020). After a religious gathering on March 9, 2020, in Kerala despite rising numbers of cases, the state banned all mass gatherings and suspended classes for students up to seventh grade. Just a few days later, other states in India started reporting deaths from COVID-19. On March 14, 2020, the central government declared the virus a "notified disaster" as cases surpassed one hundred. Meanwhile, Kerala's government launched a "Break the Chain" campaign to ensure hand hygiene and on March 23, announced a lockdown until March 31, 2020, to contain the virus (WHO, 2020b).

By March 23, there were purportedly 468 reported cases and 9 deaths resulting from COVID-19 across India. Indeed, tracking cases is challenging in a country of more than 1.3 billion individuals, where migration between states and movement within cities is common. This denotes the transition to India's centralized response to COVID-19; however, it is important to note that India is considered a federalist country, meaning that power is divided between national and state governments (Greer et al., 2020). Health care, for instance, is considered a responsibility of states by the Indian constitution, although the central government shares in the funding of infrastructure and resources in states.

The largest lockdown in India's history evolved from the "Janata (People's) Curfew" of fourteen hours a day on March 22, 2020. Travelers were screened from select countries. On March 24 a complete national lockdown was announced, requiring all nonessential workers to stay at home with the exception of obtaining essential services, including groceries and banking. There was an international travel ban as well as a domestic travel ban, including suspension of travel by railway for the first time in 167 years (Press Trust of India, 2020). The decision was marked not only for the rarity of a centralized, authoritarian decision in the nation but also because of its fairly unified implementation across the states. Enforcement certainly varied—for example, one police offer in Rishikesh, a tourist spot in the northern state of Uttar Pradesh, demanded that foreign tourists violating the lockdown write five hundred times, "I did not follow the lockdown, I am very sorry"; yet lockdown was still an anticipated success (Frayer, 2020).

One of the clear complexities of India's response lies in its confidence in the health care system to manage compound threats. According to recent estimates,

India faces a shortage of roughly 600,000 doctors and 2 million nurses primarily in primary care ("India Facing Shortage of 600,000 Doctors and Two Million Nurses," 2019). The national lockdown likely initially prevented shocks to the healthcare system, which has been recognized globally for its developed capacity in emergency and intensive care (Haseltine, 2019). Indian hospitals face 300,000 emergencies per day, with a majority of emergency visits for infectious diseases, cardiac issues, and trauma (e.g., road traffic accidents) (Clark et al., 2016). Further, India's climate makes it susceptible to natural disasters ranging from torrential rains and landslides to tsunamis, making hospitals uniquely prepared for unpredictable care delivery needs. Patients may travel extensively in inappropriate medical transportation and/or through traffic congestion, resulting in hospitals' preparedness to manage urgent and severe needs associated with delays in care (Bajpai, 2014). India's intensive care structure is less well defined and, as such, providers across hospital units are versatile and equipped to triage and provide intensive care even in facilities lacking designated wards. There are ongoing efforts to address the general qualified workforce shortage in the country. However, persistent high patient volume, including those patients with the highly contagious coronavirus infection, presented a threat to capacity (Anand & Fan, 2016).

In response to anticipated challenges with healthcare infrastructure, at the end of March 2020, Prime Minister Modi called for the conversion of India's trains into mobile healthcare facilities. He responded positively to a proposal to convert 12,617 trains with twenty-three to thirty coaches into "mobile hospitals" with consultation rooms, medical stores, intensive care units, and pantries (Dhingra, 2020). But India—like many other countries—faced a shortage of testing kits. As a result, health and government workers set out to trace and quarantine individuals across the country, using a symptom-based surveillance approach to close the large testing gap, which can be attributed to a shortage of testing kits, lack of facilities for testing samples, and missing information linked to tests (e.g., missing information about date of onset and whether the patient was symptomatic) (Kadidal, 2020). By April 9, 2020, India had conducted 144,910 formal tests and a week later, it had conducted more than 274,000 tests; however, some states had not reported any testing at all at that point (Vaidyanathan, 2020). On April 8, the Supreme Court of India ordered private labs to offer free COVID-19 tests. However, after it was deemed an unsustainable option, a week later the Court clarified that those who could afford the test should pay and reserve free testing by the government for the poor. Meanwhile, private companies and government as well as research institutions had begun developing and producing their own testing kits (Raghunathan, 2020). India has faced a double burden of disease (i.e., communicable diseases such as typhoid and malaria in addition to noncommunicable diseases such as diabetes and cancer) and has a proclivity to manufacturing low-cost healthcare products, including medical devices, which likely prepared the country for rapid production of COVID-19 tests. Before the pandemic, India was producing no personal protective equipment (PPE) kits; by May 2020, it was reportedly producing an average of 150,000 PPE kits per day and became the second largest producer of PPE in the world (Bhowmick, 2020; Mandal, 2020; PTI, 2020). By August 2020 asymptomatic contacts of confirmed cases constituted the largest group to be tested and symptomatic contacts of confirmed COVID-19 cases accounted for more than 10 percent of positive tests (Kadidal, 2020).

Unlock 1.0 commenced in June 2020 with large gatherings still banned, but with the opening of other activities primarily for economic purposes, including hospitality services, places of religious worship, and interstate travel mainly for migrant workers ("Govt Releases Lockdown 5.0 Guidelines: Here's What's Allowed and What's Not," 2020). The initial Unlock phases did not apply to "containment zones," or "hotspots" of dense areas with positive cases. These zones would be determined at the district level and continue only essential activities, contact tracing, and surveillance, with states lifting restrictions as deemed appropriate ("Govt Releases Lockdown 5.0 Guidelines: Here's What's Allowed and What's Not," 2020). Trains and domestic flights resumed as well, and mask wearing and social distancing were mandated practices.

Early in June 2020, concurrent with Unlock, India began to see a spike in its death toll. It was unclear at the time, however, whether the increase in deaths was a reflection of deaths that had not been classified as being related to COVID-19 or had not necessarily been recognized and documented at all. The central government assured states in early June 2020 that spread was under control and that "timely tracing, treatment and reporting" were contributing to an increasing number of patients recovering from the virus (Perrigo, 2020). But June also brought about shifts that were anticipated yet unpredictable in their nature and intensity.

In April 2020, Indian scientists had begun expressing concerns about models predicting a surge of cases in July or August during the monsoon season. One of their major concerns included that monsoon months coincide with flu season in many places in India, which may require additional COVID-19 testing ("India May See Second Wave of Coronavirus Outbreak in Monsoon, Say Scientists," 2020; Kumar, 2020). Yet cyclones complicated the situation even earlier than monsoon season, presenting a glimpse of the effect of compound climate risks (Phillips et al., 2020). In mid-May 2020 Cyclone Amphan brought torrential rains and winds to the eastern coast of India, near the major city of Kolkata in West Bengal (Agarwal, 2020). Tragedy associated with the cyclone was perhaps mitigated as millions were evacuated ahead of time and more than twenty relief teams were deployed by both the Indian and Bangladesh governments. An estimated eighty people were killed in a region where more than 130 million reside. Thousands were left homeless with residents grappling with the decision to stay at home and risk lacking supplies or seek help from a crowded shelter and risk infection from cyclone shelters, some of which were partially converted into COVID-19 quarantine centers ("Amphan: India and Bangladesh Evacuate Millions Ahead of Super Cyclone," 2020). Subsequently, the West Bengal government converted schools, colleges, and village administration buildings into cyclone shelters (Dasgupta, 2020). The number of confirmed infections in these shelters is unclear as officials in these areas anticipated difficulties with maintaining social distancing as they prioritized the sheltering of evacuee victims (HT Correspondents, 2020).

It is important to note here that Unlock efforts were only initiating during Cyclone Amphan. But in early June 2020, Unlock was well underway as Cyclone Nisarga made its appearance in the western coast city of Mumbai, which is home to 20 million people and considered a hotspot (Masih, 2020). At least one coronavirus care center had been evacuated but was subsequently flooded, and other healthcare facilities were damaged or destroyed.

Although the central government had issued guidelines for opening services outside of containment zones at the end of July 2020 in response to economic pressures, at the end of June several states (Maharashtra, Tamil Nadu, Meghalaya, Mizoram, Nagaland, Assam, Jharkhand, Telangana, West Bengal, Delhi, and Karnataka) had extended their lockdowns until the middle or end of July. As of July 2020, states continued to extend or reimpose their lockdowns through the end of August. These states include Tamil Nadu (245,859 total cases as of July 31), Maharashtra (422,118 as of July 31), Nagaland, Jharkhand, Himachal Pradesh, Mizoram, and Bihar. Although most of the lockdown authority was up to states, at the end of June the central government re-suspended Indian Railways until mid-August (Athrady, 2020). By July 31, 2020, India had 1,638,870 cases, including recoveries, and 35,747 reported deaths from COVID-19. Popular media attributed this striking rise in cases during July to both the ease of restrictions and increased testing across the country.

Social Policies

The efficacy of the government's response in terms of health policies relied upon its social policies. In this section, we discuss social policies that were formally implemented by the government and also, community-driven social efforts to enable people to quarantine and sustain lockdown efforts through the pandemic, as well as the implications of these efforts.

As Prime Minister Modi announced the national lockdown in March 2020, Finance Minister Nirmala Sitharaman announced a Rs 20 lakh crore (US$307 billion) stimulus package. Of this, Rs 170,000 crore (US$24 billion) were allocated toward providing food security and cooking gas through direct cash transfers to avoid delays or corruption in money reaching individuals ("India's Rs 20 lakh crore Covid Relief Package One Among the Largest in the World," 2020). India's population is estimated at over 1.3 billion with people residing in different formal and informal housing environments, across rural and urban regions, and spanning a variety of topographies, including the mountainous Himalayas in the north, the Thar Desert in Rajasthan, and coastal states such as Kerala and Gujarat. Ensuring that every individual obtained access to the stimulus package was expected to be complicated ("India's Rs 20 lakh crore Covid Relief Package One Among the Largest in the World," 2020).

At the beginning of the pandemic, unemployment was at 23.5 percent in India, but by mid-June was down to 8.5 percent. In addition to cash transfers of 500 billion rupees (US$6.7 million) to women and farmers, and subsidized food grains, which supplied 800 million people, the Mahatma Gandhi National Rural Employment Guarantee Scheme (MGNREGA) was critical in mitigating unemployment issues. MGNREGA was passed in 2005 under Prime Minister Dr. Manmohan Singh and provides at least one hundred days of guaranteed wage employment in a year to household adults who agree to do unskilled manual labor (such as building roads) in rural areas. Forty million people sought work in June 2020 as compared to 23 million between years 2013 and 2019 (Kugler & Sinha, 2020).

Still, more than an estimated 100 million internal migrant workers were stranded in their state of work during the initial lockdown because of the suspension of Indian Railways (Athrady, 2020; Maji et al., 2020). Although the stimulus package was intended to support migrant workers by enabling them to access food through their One Nation One Ration Card either in their district of residence or of work, many did not use the card because of misinformation about eligibility in their place of work. Further, the system used to identify individuals requires biometric measurements that increase risk of infection (Jebaraj, 2020). Because the railways were closed, many migrant workers opted to walk or cycle hundreds of kilometers back to their home states, although some were able to take special Indian Railways trains established specifically for migrant workers ("DSGMC Launches 'Langar on Wheels' for Migrants," 2020).

On April 29, 2020, in response to the plight of stranded migrant workers, the Ministry of Home Affairs issued orders to state governments to facilitate interstate movement of stranded individuals including migrant workers. The central government resumed service for one train on May 1 to bring twelve hundred migrant workers from the southern state of Telangana back to the eastern state of Jharkhand with the plan of screening and institutionally quarantining them upon their arrival (Mitra, 2020). In early June 2020, the Supreme Court ordered the government to register migrant workers, ensure transportation, and provide them with shelter, food, and water during their journey home after reports of violence against these workers (WHO, 2020a). Yet on June 1, railway stations received huge crowds as individuals both with and without tickets arrived at train stations expecting to travel. Although social distancing and masks were observed when entering trains, public health measures were not followed at ticket counters ("India Coronavirus: Huge Crowds as Some Train Services Resume," 2020).

India is considered a highly collectivistic society, and community-level isolation and quarantine were anticipated challenges throughout the pandemic. Isolation and separation are challenging in this context, where family members are depended upon for proximal support (Chetterjee, 2020). India's aging population and multigenerational households typical to family and community dynamics shaped the expectation that many families would likely be quarantining within the same household. Nearly half of households comprise multiple generations, including even three or four generations. Indeed, it was presumed that the infection was initially fairly well contained. However, later, as Unlock efforts commenced, the risks increased with one Delhi family even describing their home as turning into a hospital overnight as eleven of seventeen family members living in the household tested positive (Pathi, 2020).

However, this same collectivism supports the notion that individuals—and families—saw their isolation efforts as being necessary—and perhaps even obligatory—to the well-being of their family members, community, and country. India showed this notion of collectivism in the initial Janata Curfew and national lockdown phases—both by staying at home and by ringing bells and clapping as encouraged by Prime Minister Modi as a demonstration of gratitude to essential workers ("What Is Janata Curfew: A Curfew of the People, by the People, for the People to Fight Coronavirus," 2020). Furthermore, communities developed ways to support other members. For example, the *langar* is a term used to describe a community kitchen in Sikhism, wherein a free meal is served to any visitor regardless of their religious background. Although the *langar* was initially serving forty thousand meals a day in Gurdwaras (Sikh religious sites) during the pandemic across India as is typical practice, by June 2020 the Sikh community in Delhi had served roughly fifteen thousand people living in informal housing using a "langar on wheels" (Agrawal, 2020; "Coronavirus Warriors: Amid Lockdown, Gurudwara Bangla Sahib Is Serving 40,000 Meals a Day," 2020). In fact, upon recognizing that migrant workers were not able to benefit from the national stimulus package because of restrictions in identification processes, the "langar on wheels" also started providing food to migrant workers.

Despite these efforts, quality of health care remained a significant issue because there is no mandatory system for monitoring and evaluating health indicators or health status. Because of a lack of oversight of whether public or private hospitals follow infection control guidelines as developed by health agencies such as the Indian Council of Medical Research and the Indian Public Health Standards, many hospitals do not have minimum standards for infection control, resulting in high rates of hospital-acquired infections (Pulla, 2020). Further, literacy presents a barrier in healthcare settings because patients and their families may not understand information related to their health and/or to safety protocols within hospitals (e.g., reading signs with information on infection control procedures) (D'Cruz & Aradhya, 2013). Professionals may also have limited language competency, especially, for instance, if they are working in another region of India where another language is predominant (Barker et al., 2017). Controlling community infection spread is also challenging in an environment with limited or insufficient health literacy because of reduced adoption of preventive or protective behaviors (Castro-Sanchez et al., 2016).

Further, because citizens can receive free care in public health facilities and government funding is limited, much health care in India is still delivered at private, expensive facilities; these out-of-pocket payments accounted for 65 percent of health expenditures in 2015 and 2016 (Tikkanen et al., 2020). During COVID-19, these issues came to light as public hospitals were disproportionately burdened with pandemic-related services and private hospitals avoided the limelight, concerned about having to deal with unpaid bills. Subsequently, state governments such as that of Maharashtra capped the fees hospitals can charge, took over 80 percent of private hospital beds, and asked private doctors to volunteer at public hospitals, even inviting personnel from Kerala to help ease staff shortages in Mumbai (Chandrashekhar, 2020).

The central government's sense of innovation—with two salient instances demonstrated through the conversion of railway coaches into healthcare facilities and its continued efforts to expand health insurance coverage over the past eighty years—reflects a broader sense of innovation that has been recognized in India (Krishnan, 2020). Frugal scientific and technological innovations particularly in the domains of healthcare delivery and community health, have been critical social efforts to enable individuals to quarantine and also survive (Krishnan, 2020; McNicoll, 2014). For example, mobile health vehicles, telemedicine, and training of community health workers have demonstrated success in facilitating healthcare access for rural communities and have been used during the pandemic (DeSouza et al., 2014; Lahariya, 2017; Mishra et al., 2012). After an earthquake in Gujarat in 2001 that left 400,000 residents without their homes, entrepreneur Mansukhbhai Prajapati designed a low-cost clay fridge that would function without electricity to be used in rural communities and in instances of natural disasters and other catastrophies (McNicoll, 2014). These innovations—in addition to formal social policies such as the stimulus package—may have instilled a particular sense of trust early on in the pandemic (Stevens & Reinhart, 2020). However, as has been the case in India for centuries, states faced different situations and compound threats whether natural disasters, stranded migrant workers, or border instabilities, that led to competing priorities and a search for decisions that could represent the welfare of all groups across the country.

Policy Choices

India has twenty-eight states and eight union territories and is a democratic republic that has a parliamentary system operating under the 1950 constitution (Heitzman & Worden, 1996; "India: Constitution and Politics," 2018). It has a president, who is the head of state, and a prime minister, who is the chief executive of the executive branch. Parliament, modeled after the United Kingdom, is divided into two houses, including the Council of States (Rajya Sabha) and the House of the People (Lok Sabha). The president appoints twelve members for field expertise in science, art, and literature for the Rajya Sabha, and legislative bodies at the state and territory levels of government elect the remaining members. The Lok Sabha has a limit of 552 members with about one-quarter reserved for representatives of Scheduled Castes and Scheduled Tribes, who comprise historically disadvantaged populations; the remainder of seats in the Lok Sabha are determined by the general election as well as by population size of individual states and territories ("India: Constitution and Politics," 2018).

The legislative branch of India is responsible for the development of laws and policies, and the executive branch is responsible for implementing these policies. The Parliament also has control over the executive branch in many ways, but in particular relevance to COVID-19, it has authority in preparing budgets and is the main source of information to the Houses. According to the Election Commission of India, the country has 8 national parties, 52 state parties, and 2,538 unrecognized parties. Indeed, as described in the introduction to this chapter, the desire and need for representation and inclusiveness across highly diverse states likely drives the multitude of political parties in the country (Sangita, 2017).

India supported the idea of health for all since its independence in 1947. The Bhore Committee Report of 1946 recommended a publicly financed health service plan, envisioning a country "where no individual would fail to secure adequate care because of the inability to pay" (Zodpey & Farooqui, 2018). Over time the Indian government developed various health insurance schemes that may be organized differentially by state, to improve coverage for specific populations. For example, the National Health Insurance Program (Rashtriya Swasthya Bima Yojana; RSBY) launched in 2008 to provide coverage for lower-income populations. As of 2016, 41 million families were enrolled in RSBY (Tikkanen et al., 2020). However, observing little reduction in out-of-pocket spending and other barriers to access to care, including long wait times and infrastructure issues, in 2018 the central government implemented the Ayushman Bharat Pradhan Mantri Jan Arogya Yojana (PM-JAY), considered the largest health insurance scheme in the world (Tikkanen et al., 2020). The tax-financed PM-JAY offers free hospital coverage for 40 percent of the country's impoverished residents, and further, transforms primary health facilities into comprehensive Health and Wellness Centers. Through PM-JAY, the central and state governments continue to share responsibility for governance, financing, and operations of the health system. Local government institutions are responsible for administration in rural villages, including establishment of health and wellness centers and education, agriculture, and transportation (Tikkanen et al., 2020; "WHO DG Praises PM Modi, Health Minister Nadda for Ayushman Bharat Scheme," 2019). During COVID-19, the federalist approach of dividing power between national and state governments was a hallmark of the public health and social policy efforts that were ultimately pushed by individual states (Greer et al., 2020).

State Capacity

India is considered a federal system wherein states have their own legislatures and union territories are directly controlled by the central government. State legislatures make laws regarding criminal justice, education, health taxation, public order, lands, and forests. However, once a state of emergency has been declared, the federal government has the authority to temporarily assume executive and financial control of a state, and the president may even impose President's rule ("India: Constitution and Politics," 2018). Although states seemingly have quite a bit of control and autonomy in India, because financial control is exerted by the federal government, states may not ultimately garner as much power in implementing laws. During COVID-19, however, states exercised their authority under the law that granted them authority to manage epidemics and disasters.

Although India intended to "Unlock" in mid-April 2020, some state governments (Odisha, Punjab, Maharashtra, Karnataka, West Bengal, and Telangana) individually extended their lockdowns until the end of the month ("Coronavirus India Live Updates: Telangana Follows Maha and West Bengal, Extends Lockdown till April 30," 2020; "Covid-19: Karnataka Extends Lockdown by 2 Weeks, Throws in Some Relaxations," 2020). Concurrently Prime Minister Modi also extended the national lockdown until early May with a "carrot and stick" approach of promising relaxed measures regionally in the last week of April, depending on spread and presence of hotspots. At the end of April, farming and agriculture—a large economic sector—resumed, and the Ministry of Home Affairs released guidelines for interstate movement of stranded persons through airlines. As states began to implement "Unlock" procedures differently, individuals began to mobilize prematurely as a product of misinformation about their respective state's procedures. In Maharashtra by early July 2020, when the lockdown was still in effect, police had collected over 10 crore rupees (over US$1 million) from lockdown violators (Yadav, 2020).

In fact, states such as Kerala, Karnataka, and Odisha implemented their own stay-at-home orders before the national government announced a national lockdown. Throughout the pandemic, states were also completing COVID-19 testing to varying degrees. Some states such as Odisha used infrastructure previously reserved for cyclones for attending to patients with coronavirus. Uttar Pradesh designated certain hospitals in the state as being specifically for COVID-19 treatment and provided its own financial support to workers. Tamil Nadu and Rajasthan implemented contact tracing efforts of their own while developing tests. For instance, in the southern Tamil Nadu city of Chennai, health workers were conducting door-to-door monitoring and testing of any individuals showing influenza-like symptoms; in Kerala, phone records were obtained to conduct contact tracing.

As demonstrated, states varied in their responses and also varied from the central government response. For example, Maharashtra monitored physical distancing during lockdown by using drones. Of course, law enforcement used a variety of punitive methods ranging from asking lockdown violators to write an apology five hundred times on papers, to monetary fines ("India under COVID-19 Lockdown," 2020; Pahwa, 2020). Still, studies showed that even before the pandemic trust and confidence in governments were high, particularly among individuals of lower socioeconomic status and those living in less developed states (Kumar et al.,

2020). This trust has likely been critical to population support of state-level public health measures.

Conclusion

During the pandemic, India observed the bluest skies in "living memory" (Biswas, 2020). India faces a high burden of chronic respiratory diseases such as asthma and chronic obstructive pulmonary disease in particular because of pollution and tobacco use (Salvi et al., 2018). The presence of these underlying respiratory conditions may exacerbate complications associated with COVID-19 and research conducted during the pandemic encouraged policymakers to consider pollution in their "Unlocking" plans to extend the positive effects of clean air (Mani & Yamada, 2020). But, unfortunately, as of this writing, pollution is the least of India's concerns as active cases continue to rise across India, hinting at state-driven lockdowns that may extend well beyond August 2020.

That India faces multiple challenges—natural disasters, border instability, pollution, and the double burden of disease to name a few—is important to recognize to understand India's response to the COVID-19 pandemic. India's national lockdown was the first of its kind in decades and was a decision that likely contributed to trust in the government. Although the sweeping lockdown early in the pandemic was critical to early mitigation of COVID-19 spread, that millions of migrant workers were left stranded undoubtedly has lasting consequences because of the government's overlooking of a key population. As has been a commitment throughout its history, in seeking to ensure responsiveness to the needs of underserved communities, a national lockdown was no longer feasible. As is protocol, further decisions were left to individual states, which could implement policies based on the individual needs and circumstances of their populations and geographies (Greer et al., 2020). Centralized "Unlocking" led to the spread of misinformation, which certainly may have contributed to the subsequent rise in cases across the country.

In India, time and again calamity carves the way for collectivism and creativity. Public trust in the government in general rose 6 percent during the pandemic and is higher than several other countries; so is trust in doctors and nurses (Edelman, 2020; Stevens & Reinhart, 2020). This trust has been, and is likely, key to the population's resilience and subsequently, its willingness to forego short-term freedoms for collective well-being (Hall et al., 2001; Mayer et al., 1995). As with any government, transparency is fundamental to trust; in India's case, despite the central government's lifting of the lockdown, state governments have continued to pick up the responsibility by extending lockdowns as needed, signaling to constituents that the pandemic is not yet over. As a collective, the country—both through government and community efforts—has come together to develop creative means of providing health care, COVID-19 testing, PPE, transportation, and food for its underserved. In a country that depends heavily on the well-being of the economy for its continued development, the impact of the pandemic will resonate long after its exit. However, we hope that India continues on her path of prioritizing the well-being of her people as she seeks to grow economically.

References

Agarwal, V. (2020, May 20). Powerful cyclone hits India, complicating coronavirus response. *The Wall Street Journal*. https://www.wsj.com/articles/powerful-cyclone-hits-india-complicating-coronavirus-response-11589979601

Agrawal, P. (2020, June). *Delhi: For poor who can't find nearest Gurudwara, Sikh Community launches "Langar on Wheels."* The Logical Indian. https://thelogicalindian.com/news/delhi-gurudwara-langar-on-wheels-feeds-needy-covid-19-21462

Alexander, C. (2017, August). *Colonialism in India was traumatic—including for some of the British officials who ruled the Raj.* The Conversation. https://theconversation.com/colonialism-in-india-was-traumatic-including-for-some-of-the-british-officials-who-ruled-the-raj-77068

Amphan: India and Bangladesh evacuate millions ahead of super cyclone. (2020, May 19). BBC News. https://www.bbc.com/news/world-asia-india-52718826#:~:text=India%20and%20Bangladesh%20are%20evacuating,two%20countries%20later%20on%20Wednesday

Anand, S., & Fan, V. (2016). *The health workforce in India*. World Health Organization, Switzerland.

Arunkumar, G., Chandni, R., Mourya, D. T., Singh, S. K., Sadanandan, R., Sudan, P., Bhargava, B., & Nipah Investigators People and Health Study Group. (2019). Outbreak investigation of Nipah virus disease in Kerala, India, 2018. *The Journal of Infectious Diseases*, 219(12).

Athrady, A. (2020, June 25). Coronavirus lockdown: Indian Railways suspends regular train services till August 12. *Deccan Herald*. https://www.deccanherald.com/national/coronavirus-lockdown-indian-railways-suspends-regular-train-services-till-august-12-853721.html

Aula, S. (2014, November). The problem with the English language in India. *Forbes*. https://www.forbes.com/sites/realspin/2014/11/06/the-problem-with-the-english-language-in-india/#54eeccfa403e

Bajpai, V. (2014, July 13). The challenges confronting public hospitals in India, their origins, and possible solutions. *Advances in Public Health*. https://www.hindawi.com/journals/aph/2014/898502/

Barker, A. K., Brown, K., Siraj, D., Ahsan, M., Sengupta, S., & Safdar, N. (2017). Barriers and facilitators to infection control at a hospital in northern India: A qualitative study. *Antimicrobial Resistance and Infection Control*, 6(35).

Bhowmick, S. (2020, June 19). Covid-19: Indian healthcare workers need adequate PPE. *The BMJ Opinion*. https://blogs.bmj.com/bmj/2020/06/19/covid-19-indian-healthcare-workers-need-adequate-ppe/

Biswas, S. (2020, April 21). *India coronavirus: Can the Covid-19 lockdown spark a clean air movement?* BBC News. https://www.bbc.com/news/world-asia-india-52313972

Castro-Sanchez, E., Chang, P. W. S., Vila-Candel, R., Escobedo, A. A., & Holmes, A. H. (2016). Health literacy and infectious diseases: Why does it matter? *International Journal of Infectious Diseases*, 43, 103–110.

Chandrashekhar, V. (2020, May). As India's lockdown ends, exodus from cities risks spreading COVID-19 far and wide. *Science*. https://www.sciencemag.org/news/2020/05/india-s-lockdown-ends-exodus-cities-risks-spreading-covid-19-far-and-wide

Chetterjee, P. (2020). Gaps in India's preparedness for COVID-19 control. *The Lancet Infectious Diseases*. https://doi.org/https://doi.org/10.1016/S1473-3099(20)30300-5

Clark, E. G., Watson, J., Leemann, A., Breaud, A. H., Feeley, F. G., Wolff, J., Kole, T., & Jacquet, G. A. (2016). Acute care needs in an Indian emergency department: A retrospective analysis. *World Journal of Emergency Medicine*, *7*(3), 191–195.

Coronavirus: Search for hundreds of people after Delhi prayer meeting. (2020, March 31). BBC News. https://www.bbc.com/news/world-asia-india-52104753

Coronavirus India live updates: Telangana follows Maha and West Bengal, extends lockdown till April 30. (2020b, April 12). *The Economic Times*. https://economictimes.indiatimes.com/news/politics-and-nation/coronavirus-cases-in-india-live-news-latest-updates-april11/liveblog/75089891.cms

Coronavirus warriors: Amid lockdown, Gurudwara Bangla Sahib is serving 40,000 meals a day. (2020, April 7). *The Economic Times*. https://economictimes.indiatimes.com/news/politics-and-nation/coronavirus-warriors-amid-lockdown-bangla-sahib-is-serving-40000-meals-a-day/feeding-40000-needy-a-day/slideshow/75022785.cms

Covid-19: Karnataka extends lockdown by 2 weeks, throws in some relaxations. (2020, April 11). *Hindustan Times*.

D'Cruz, A. M., & Aradhya, M. R. S. (2013). Health literacy among Indian adults seeking dental care. *Dental Research Journal*, *10*(1), 20–24.

Dalrymple, W. (2019). *The anarchy: The East India Company, corporate violence, and the pillage of an empire*. Bloomsbury Publishing.

Dasgupta, A. (2020). A cyclone-battered state struggles with COVID-19 compliance. *Nature India*. https://doi.org/10.1038/nindia.2020.90

DeSouza, S. I., Rashmi, M. R., Vasanthi, A. P., Joseph, S. M., & Rodrigues, R. (2014). Mobile phones: The next step towards healthcare delivery in rural India? *PLOS One*, *14*(9), 8. https://doi.org/https://doi.org/10.1371/journal.pone.0104895

Dhingra, S. (2020, March 25). Rail coach as ICU—how Modi govt plans to beat healthcare gaps in remote areas. *The Print*. https://theprint.in/india/governance/rail-coach-as-icu-how-modi-govt-plans-to-beat-healthcare-gaps-in-remote-areas/388043/

DSGMC launches "Langar on Wheels" for migrants. (2020, May 18). *The Tribune*. https://www.tribuneindia.com/news/punjab/dsgmc-launches-langar-on-wheels-for-migrants-86473

Edelman. (2020). *2020 Edelman Trust barometer spring update: Trust and the COVID-19 pandemic*. https://www.edelman.com/research/trust-2020-spring-update

Frayer, L. (2020, April 13). *Indian police force tourists violating lockdown to write "I Am Very Sorry" 500 Times*. NPR. https://www.npr.org/sections/coronavirus-live-updates/2020/04/13/833444624/indian-police-force-tourists-violating-lockdown-to-write-i-am-very-sorry-500-tim#:~:text=Live%20Sessions-,Indian%20Police%20Force%20Tourists%20Who%20Violate%20Lockdown%20To%20Apologize%20500,am%20very%20sorry%22%20500%20times

Govt releases lockdown 5.0 guidelines: Here's what's allowed and what's not. (2020, May 31). *The Economic Times*. https://economictimes.indiatimes.com/news/politics-and-nation/centre-extends-lockdown-in-containment-zones-till-june-30/articleshow/76109621.cms

Greer, S. L., King, E. J., da Fonseca, E. M., & Peralta-Santos, A. (2020). The comparative politics of COVID-19: The need to understand government responses. *Global Public Health*. https://doi.org/https://doi.org/10.1080/17441692.2020.1783340

Hall, M. A., Dugan, E., Zheng, B., & Mishra, A. K. (2001). Trust in physicians and medical institutions: What is it, can it be measured, and does it matter? *The Milbank Quarterly*, 79(4), 613–639.

Haseltine, W. A. (2019, January 23). What the U.S. can learn from India's Emergency Response System. *Forbes*.

Heitzman, J., & Worden, R. L. (1996). *India: A country study*. Library of Congress.

HT Correspondents. (2020, May 21). Cyclone Amphan: Rescue operations hampered because of Covid fears. *Hindustan Times*. https://www.hindustantimes.com/india-news/rescue-operations-hampered-because-of-covid-fears/story-SrZG2QVNrVKxjjp8eV6mMP.html

India: Constitution and politics. (2018). The Commonwealth. https://thecommonwealth.org/our-member-countries/india/constitution-politics

India coronavirus: Huge crowds as some train services resume. (2020, June 1). BBC News. https://www.bbc.com/news/world-asia-india-52874298

India facing shortage of 600,000 doctors and two million nurses: Study. (2019, April 14). *The Economic Times*. https://economictimes.indiatimes.com/industry/healthcare/biotech/healthcare/india-facing-shortage-of-600000-doctors-2-million-nurses-study/articleshow/68875822.cms?from=mdr

India may see second wave of coronavirus outbreak in monsoon, say scientists. (2020, April 24). *Times of India*. https://timesofindia.indiatimes.com/india/india-may-see-second-wave-of-coronavirus-outbreak-in-monsoon-say-scientists/articleshow/75345505.cms

India under COVID-19 lockdown. (2020). *The Lancet*, 395(10233). https://doi.org/https://doi.org/10.1016/S0140-6736(20)30938-7

India's Rs 20 lakh crore Covid relief package one among the largest in the world. (2020, May 15). *The Economic Times*. https://economictimes.indiatimes.com/news/economy/finance/latest-stimulus-package-among-largest-in-the-world/articleshow/75701976.cms

Jebaraj, P. (2020, May 8). Inter-State ration card portability usage very low: Food Minister. *The Hindu*. https://www.thehindu.com/news/national/inter-state-ration-card-portability-usage-very-low-food-minister/article31537575.ece

Kadidal, A. (2020, May 31). New study finds gaps in India's COVID-19 testing data collection. *Deccan Herald*. https://www.deccanherald.com/science-and-environment/new-study-finds-gaps-in-indias-covid-19-testing-data-collection-843859.html

Khilnani, S. (2017). *The idea of India* (4th ed.). Farrar, Straus, and Giroux.

Krishnan, R. T. (2020). The changing contours of innovation in India. *Forbes India*. https://www.forbesindia.com/article/isbinsight/the-changing-contours-of-innovation-in-india/57059/1

Kugler, M., & Sinha, S. (2020, July). The impact of COVID-19 and the policy response in India. *Brookings*. https://www.brookings.edu/blog/future-development/2020/07/13/the-impact-of-covid-19-and-the-policy-response-in-india/

Kumar, D., Pratap, B., & Aggarwal, A. (2020). Public trust in state governments in India: Who are more confident and what makes them confident about the government? *Asian Journal of Comparative Politics.* https://doi.org/https://doi.org/10.1177/2057891119898763

Kumar, S. (2020). Will COVID-19 pandemic diminish by summer-monsoon in India? Lesson from the first lockdown. *MedRxiv.* https://doi.org/10.1101/2020.04.22.20075499

Kutty, V. R. (2000). Historical analysis of the development of health care facilities in Kerala State, India. *Health Policy Plan, 15*(1), 103–109.

Lahariya, C. (2017). Mohalla Clinics of Delhi, India: Could these become platform to strengthen primary healthcare? *Journal of Family Medicine and Primary Care, 6*(1), 1–10.

Maji, A., Sushma, M. B., & Choudhari, T. (2020). *Implication of inter-state movement of migrant workers during COVID-19 lockdown using modified SEIR model.* Mumbai. https://arxiv.org/pdf/2005.04424.pdf

Mandal, S. (2020). *COVID-19: From zero, India now produces two Lakh PPE kits per day.* https://thelogicalindian.com/story-feed/awareness/toi-22548?infinitescroll=1

Mani, M., & Yamada, T. (2020). Is air pollution aggravating COVID-19 in South Asia? https://blogs.worldbank.org/endpovertyinsouthasia/air-pollution-aggravating-covid-19-south-asia

Mannathukkaren, N. (2013). The rise of the national-popular and its limits: Communism and the cultural in Kerala. *Inter-Asia Cultural Studies, 14,* 494–518.

Masih, N. (2020, June 3). Severe cyclone bears down on Mumbai, India's coronavirus hot spot. *Washington Post.*

Mayer, R. C., Davis, J. H., & Schoorman, F. D. (1995). An integrative model of organizational trust. *The Academy of Management Review, 20*(3), 709–732. https://doi.org/10.2307/258792

McNicoll, A. (2014, September 16). *Enter India's amazing world of frugal innovation.* CNN Business. https://www.cnn.com/2013/06/25/tech/innovation/frugal-innovation-india-inventors/index.html

Mishra, S. K., Singh, I. P., & Chand, R. D. (2012). Current status of telemedicine network in india and future perspective. *Proceedings of the Asia-Pacific Advanced Network, 32,* 151–163.

Mitra, E. (2020, May 1). *India sends first train to bring stranded migrant workers home, ahead of lifting lockdown.* CNN World. https://www.cnn.com/world/live-news/coronavirus-pandemic-05-01-20-intl/h_8bad1824b3bb714b0767a0b9bd57a493

Paliwa, N. (2020, May). *India's states are leading on COVID-19.* Slate. https://slate.com/news-and-politics/2020/05/india-states-covid-federalism-kerala.html

Pathi, K. (2020, June 10). *Coronavirus: "Our home turned into a hospital overnight."* BBC News. https://www.bbc.com/news/world-asia-india-52976190

Perrigo, B. (2020, June 18). India's coronavirus death toll is surging. Prime Minister Modi is easing lockdown anyway. *Time.* https://time.com/5855555/india-coronavirus/

PHCPI. (2018). *Kerala, India: Decentralized governance and community engagement strengthen primary care.* https://improvingphc.org/promising-practices/kerala

Phillips, C. A., Caldas, A., Cleetus, R., Dahl, K. A., Declet-Barreto, J., Licker, R., Merner, L. D., Ortiz-Partida, J. P., Phelan, A. L., Spanger-Siegfried, E., Talati, S., Trisos, C. H., & Carlson, C. J. (2020). Compound climate risks in the COVID-19 pandemic. *Nature Climate Change, 10,* 586–588.

Press Trust of India. (2020, April 17). *Coronavirus lockdown: First time in 167 years, railways didn't ferry passengers on its birthday.* India Today. https://www.indiatoday

.in/india/story/coronavirus-lockdown-first-time-in-167-years-railways-didn-t-ferry-passengers-on-its-birthday-1667778-2020-04-17

PTI. (2020, May 21). India becomes world's second largest manufacturer of PPE body coveralls, next to China: Government. *The Hindu.* https://www.thehindu.com/news/national/india-becomes-worlds-second-largest-manufacturer-of-ppe-body-coveralls-next-to-china-government/article31643400.ece

Pulla, P. (2020, December). India's hospitals have an infection problem. Could accreditation be the way to go? *Science: The Wire.* https://science.thewire.in/health/healthcare-acquired-infections-multi-drug-resistance-nabh-accreditation/

Raghunathan, A. (2020, April 16). India ramps up coronavirus testing, approves slew of local test kit makers. *Forbes.* https://www.forbes.com/sites/anuraghunathan/2020/04/16/india-ramps-up-coronavirus-testing-approves-slew-of-local-and-foreign-makers/?sh=4a7725a69a59

Reid, D. (2020, January 30). *India confirms its first coronavirus case.* CNBC. https://www.cnbc.com/2020/01/30/india-confirms-first-case-of-the-coronavirus.html

Riley, P. (2007). *Language, culture and identity: An ethnolinguistic perspective.* Bloomsbury Publishing.

Salvi, S., Kumar, G. A., Dhaliwal, R. S., Paulson, K., Agrawal, A., Koul, P. A., Mahesh, P. A., Nair, S., Singh, V., Aggarwal, A. N., Christopher, D. J., Guleria, R., Mohan, B.V.M., Tripathi, S. K., Ghoshal, A. G., Kumar, R. V., Mehrotra, R., Shukla, D. K., Dutta, E., . . . Furtado, M. (2018). The burden of chronic respiratory diseases and their heterogeneity across the states of India: The Global Burden of Disease Study 1990–2016. *The Lancet Global Health,* 6(12), E1363–E1374.

Sangita, S. N. (2017). Ethical leadership and inclusive governance in India: Role of political parties. *Indian Journal of Public Administration,* 59(3), 562–572.

Stevens, L., & Reinhart, R. J. (2020). *India's COVID-19 lockdown depends on trust in institutions.* Gallup. https://news.gallup.com/opinion/gallup/305816/india-covid-lockdown-depends-trust-institutions.aspx

Sur, M. (2015). Indelible lines: Revisiting borders and partitions in modern South Asia. *Mobility in History,* 6(1).

Tikkanen, R., Osborn, R., Mossialos, E., Djordjevic, A., & Wharton, G. A. (2020). *India.* https://www.commonwealthfund.org/international-health-policy-center/countries/india

Vaidyanathan, G. (2020). How India is attempting to slow the coronavirus. *Nature India.* https://doi.org/10.1038/nindia.2020.68

What is Janata Curfew: A curfew of the people, by the people, for the people to fight coronavirus. (2020, March 19). *India Today.* https://www.indiatoday.in/india/story/janata-curfew-to-fight-coronavirus-pm-modi-urges-citizens-to-stay-off-roads-from-7-am-to-9-pm-on-sunday-1657581-2020-03-19

WHO DG praises PM Modi, Health Minister Nadda for Ayushman Bharat scheme. (2019, January 3). *Times of India.* https://timesofindia.indiatimes.com/india/who-praises-pm-modi-health-minister-nadda-for-ayushman-bharat-scheme/articleshow/67370832.cms

World Health Organization. (2020a). India must follow Supreme Court orders to protect 100 million migrant workers: UN rights experts. https://news.un.org/en/story/2020/06/1065662

World Health Organization. (2020b). Responding to COVID-19—Learnings from Kerala. https://www.who.int/india/news/feature-stories/detail/responding-to-covid-19---learnings-from-kerala

Yadav, V. K. (2020, July 4). Maharashtra Police collects Rs 53,06,050 as one day fine from lockdown violators. *Hindustan Times*. https://www.hindustantimes.com/india-news/maharashtra-police-collects-rs-53-06-050-lakh-as-one-day-fine-from-covid-19-lockdown-violators/story-NEcO0TO5hvDXlrpM7z8PIP.html

Yusin, J. (2009). The silence of partition: Borders, trauma, and partition history. *Journal of Social Semiotics*, *19*(4), 453–468.

Zodpey, S., & Farooqui, H. H. (2018). Universal Health Coverage in India: Progress achieved & the way forward. *Indian Journal of Medical Research*, *147*(4), 327–329.

11 COVID-19 RESPONSE IN CENTRAL ASIA
A Cautionary Tale

Pauline Jones and Elizabeth J. King

The Central Asian region, comprising five countries that emerged after the end of the Soviet Union in 1991, continues to struggle economically and face developmental challenges. Three of these countries—Kazakhstan, Kyrgyzstan, and Uzbekistan—thus surprised many by taking some critical steps early on to combat the spread of SARS-CoV-2 to their respective populations. In terms of both their timing and comprehensiveness, these three countries developed a response that seemed much more promising than that of their counterparts in Tajikistan and Turkmenistan. Kazakhstan moved swiftly and decisively to close borders and impose strict social distancing measures before having any officially recorded cases. Kyrgyzstan and Uzbekistan adopted similarly aggressive measures but albeit were slower to implement them. In contrast, Tajikistan was initially very reluctant to even acknowledge the risk associated with COVID-19 and was late in advising its citizens not to travel to certain destinations and then closing its airports. Turkmenistan finally took some similar steps, such as canceling flights and closing borders, but continued to deny the risk of COVID-19. Yet, despite their relatively swift and decisive responses in March and April 2020, Kazakhstan, Kyrgyzstan, and Uzbekistan experienced a dramatic resurgence of COVID-19 cases in June and July 2020.[1] This chapter aims to offer insight into why the social distancing measures put in place at the start of the pandemic in these three countries were ultimately ineffective. In short, it argues that the crucial (but perhaps understandable) mistake was lifting these restrictions too soon.

Central Asia's struggle with COVID-19 suggests two valuable lessons for understanding both government response to the pandemic and its effectiveness. First, although many point to regime type and state capacity as the major determinants of government responses to crises, these do not seem to be the crucial factors explaining how swiftly or decisively governments acted to mitigate COVID-19 in Central Asia. Kazakhstan and Uzbekistan are both authoritarian countries with a high and medium degree of state capacity, respectively. Kyrgyzstan is a democratic country with a low degree of state capacity. Second, the experience of these three countries strongly suggests the need for continued vigilance. After less than two months, Kazakhstan, Kyrgyzstan, and Uzbekistan all relaxed the stringent measures they had put in place. The number of confirmed cases and deaths quickly began to increase, leading many to express concern that Central Asia was experiencing a "second wave" of COVID-19. This dramatic spike in new cases overburdened the chronically weak healthcare infrastructure that is common across the region.

In short, Central Asia is a cautionary tale in three key respects. First, it demonstrates what happens when restrictions are lifted too soon. The dramatic rise in COVID-19 cases and deaths in June and July 2020 was arguably not a so-called "second wave," but rather, the continuation of its first wave that had been interrupted or at least slowed down by the vigilance early on but was accelerated by the relaxation in these policies. Second, the experiences of Kazakhstan, Kyrgyzstan, and Uzbekistan seem to suggest that neither the stringency of policies nor compliance with these policies is primarily about regime type and state capacity. Despite different regime types and varying levels of state capacity, at the start of the pandemic, all three countries were willing to acknowledge its potential severity and take necessary but unpopular actions. Yet all three countries reversed course. Third, the effectiveness of these policies is nonetheless tied to health infrastructure. In other words, even though all three countries reinstated strict social distancing measures after it was clear that COVID-19 was continuing to spread, their ability to contain the virus was limited by their pre-existing weak healthcare systems.

Health Policy Measures

Despite their many similarities, the five states that make up Central Asia have exhibited varied responses to the threat of COVID-19 since the first cases were confirmed in early March 2020. These can best be distinguished along two key dimensions: timing and comprehensiveness. Three countries in particular—Kazakhstan, Kyrgyzstan, and Uzbekistan—introduced fairly swift and decisive health policy measures. In comparison to their counterparts in Tajikistan and Turkmenistan, by mid-March, the leaders of these three countries had closed borders and imposed strict social distancing measures, including canceling all public events and gatherings to celebrate the Nowruz holiday on March 21. However, by early June all three countries also began to relax these measures largely because of the economic implications of maintaining them. This led to a resurgence in confirmed cases in mid-June and July 2020. Subsequently, each government seemed to recognize the need to return to the initial stringency despite the economic, and possibly political, consequences.

Kazakhstan

Kazakhstan was quickest to both acknowledge the threat and develop a health policy response to COVID-19. After several of its citizens returned from China with what seemed like symptoms of the virus in late January 2020, the government organized an emergency meeting, at which it took additional measures to reduce exposure (for details, see Strategy 2050, 2020). Although the Chinese government had already proactively closed its land borders with Central Asia, the Kazakhstani government decided to close its side of the Khorgos border crossing[2] as well as to suspend a seventy-two-hour visa waiver for transit passengers from China. It was not until March 15, 2020, after the first case was confirmed, that President Kassym-Jomart Tokayev declared a state of emergency. Days before, the government had already decided to close all schools (Ministry of Education and Science, 2020) and cancel all major public events, which included the celebration of the popular holiday Nowruz. When the number of confirmed cases began to rise in the weeks that followed, concentrated in the country's two largest cities, Almaty and, the capital, Nur-Sultan, the government responded by imposing a quarantine on the cities' inhabitants and suspending the activities of all businesses that are not considered essential from March 30, 2020, until April 5, 2020 (Official Information Resource of the Prime Minister, 2020a). When COVID-19 appeared to have spread beyond these three cities, the government renewed the quarantine it had imposed on those two cities and extended it to six other cities, including Shymkent and Atyrau, and to one region (Akmola). It also renewed the nationwide state of emergency through the end of April (Vlast, 2020).

By early May 2020, however, Kazakhstan's government began lifting these restrictions. Flights between Almaty and Nur Sultan were allowed to resume on May 1, 2020, and some small businesses were allowed to reopen on May 4. Then on May 11, the Deputy Prime Minister announced the end of the state of emergency and that "[r]estrictive measures would be lifted in stages, depending on the epidemiological situation of each region" (Official Information Resource of the Prime Minister, 2020c). Focusing on the economy, the first to be lifted were restrictions on domestic flights between most cities and small businesses, including hotels and restaurants with outdoor seating. Churches and mosques were also allowed to reopen but not with full capacity (Official Information Resource of the Prime Minister, 2020c). The quarantine, however, remained in effect and citizens were instructed to continue wearing masks and gloves and to observe social distancing regulations ("Tokaev: Karantinnyi Rezhim Sokhranyaetsya" ["Tokayev Says That The Quarantine Measures Will Continue"], 2020). And, in some places, the quarantine regulations were tightened in response to COVID-related deaths. Yet, even as the government threatened renewing quarantine measures and adopting tighter restrictions, compliance among businesses and the general population seemed to be loosening.

Meanwhile, by early June, the spread of the pandemic showed no signs of abatement. The number of confirmed COVID-19 cases continued to rise as did the mortality rate, which continued to be underreported, partly because Kazakhstan was not including deaths from "strange pneumonia" in its calculation.[3] In mid-June, several cities and regions reported increases, including the capital city, Nur-Sultan, where hospitalizations were reportedly increasing by five hundred per day ("V bol'nitsy Nur-Sultana Postupaet Po 500 Chelovek v Den" ["500 People Are Admitted to the Hospital in Nur-Sultan Each Day"], 2020). Medical professionals were among those hardest hit with COVID-19 infections, which the Health Ministry blamed on their own negligence, yet the higher rate of infections among these frontline workers was already apparent in April (KazInform, 2020). Government officials, including the country's former president Nursultan Nazarbayev, were also among those diagnosed with and hospitalized for COVID-19.

The government once again responded swiftly, immediately moving to tighten restrictions. Although initially these were limited to weekend lockdowns in major cities and mandates to wear masks in public throughout the country, by the beginning of July 2020 a new lockdown was put in place and then extended through the end of the Month ("Tokaev Poruchil Prodlit' Karantin v Kazakhstane" [Tokayev Instructed the Quarantine to Be Extended in Kazakhstan"], 2020). The extended lockdown meant that the country's Muslim majority would have to celebrate the upcoming holiday, Kurban Ait (or Eid al-Adha), without gathering with family and friends and with sacrificing an animal only remotely. Perhaps more importantly, the government agreed to change the way it calculated deaths from COVID-19, beginning August 1, 2020, to provide a more accurate measure of the virus' impact on the country (Kumenov, 2020).

Kyrgyzstan

Kyrgyzstan's response was not quite as swift as Kazakhstan's, but it was decisive. President Sooronbay Jeenbekov officially declared "an emergency situation" on March 22, 2020—a week after Kazakhstan did—by which time it had already reported over a dozen cases of confirmed COVID-19 (Orlova, 2020).[4] Schools were closed and residents of the country's three major cities were placed under a strict curfew with the exception of essential personnel (Government of the Kyrgyz Republic, 2020b). Checkpoints were established around Bishkek to limit travel into and out of the capital city, where it was made illegal to gather in groups larger than three people. The government also canceled public events, including the celebration of Nowruz. On April 16, 2020, Mufti Maksat Azhy Toktomushev pleaded with the country's predominantly Muslim population to abide by the quarantine restrictions and to refrain from public worship and *iftar* meals during Ramadan (Masalieva, 2020).

Yet, like neighboring Kazakhstan, the government of Kyrgyzstan moved to lift restrictions in early May despite an increase in the number of confirmed COVID-19 cases and hospitalizations. It also focused on the economy and allowed the reopening of small businesses first beginning on May 1, 2020 (Government of the Kyrgyz Republic, April 28, 2020), followed by the lifting of curfews in the country's major cities on May 11 (Government of the Kyrgyz Republic, 2020d), and the reopening of public transportation on May 25, albeit with masks required. Unlike its neighbor, Kyrgyzstan kept the nationwide state of emergency in place. Nonetheless, more restrictions continued to be lifted through the beginning of June, including the resumption of domestic and international flights (June 5, 2020) and the re-opening of mosques and churches (June 8).

Kyrgyzstan was also much slower than Kazakhstan to react to the continued increase in COVID-19 cases in May and June. Yet, by mid-June, it seems that the government was forced to recognize that the pandemic was not under control. The capital city of Bishkek was hit particularly hard, as were medical care workers.[5] Nor were government officials spared.[6] The government of Kyrgyzstan responded by acknowledging that both the infection and morbidity rates were on the rise and warning that new restrictions could follow. Along with Kazakhstan, in an attempt to increase transparency, it decided to include deaths from pneumonia when calculating the number of deaths attributed to COVID-19. As a result, the number of COVID-related deaths essentially doubled (Human Rights Watch, 2020a). But it did not act decisively beyond requiring masks in public. Meanwhile, officials in Bishkek reinstated a weekend curfew, promised to ramp up punishments for those businesses that did not properly implement regulations (Irgebaeyeva, 2020a), and began removing anyone not wearing a mask from public transit. Despite these measures, the number of new cases continued to rise in July 2020, and the majority of them continued to be in Bishkek (Irgebaeyeva, 2020a).

Uzbekistan

Uzbekistan's response was later than Kazakhstan's but quicker than Kyrgyzstan's and was equally decisive as both of its neighbors. The government declared a state of emergency on March 16, 2020, just after its first case of COVID-19 was confirmed, closed its borders and all schools, and canceled all major public events, including those in celebration of Nowruz ("Uzbekistan Confirms COVID-19 Case, Closes Borders," 2020). In the weeks that followed, the government severely limited transportation to mitigate the spread of the virus: effective March 20, it suspended all car, bus, train, and air travel into and out of the country; effective March 22, it suspended all public transit within the capital city (Tashkent); effective March 27, it suspended all car, bus, train, and air travel within the country, except for trucks carrying freight; and effective March 30, it suspended car travel within cities. The government also adopted and began enforcing several other important health policy measures, such as requiring Tashkent residents to wear masks in public or pay a large fine, prohibiting gatherings of more than ten to fifteen people (including weddings and funerals), and calling upon the chief mufti to issue a fatwa recommending that Muslims stay home to perform their daily prayers ("Upravlenie Musul'man Uzbekistana i Sovet Ulemov Prizvali Musul'man Prinyat' vs Emery Dlya Predotvrashcheniya Rasrostraneniya Koronavirusa" ["The Board of Muslims of Uzbekistan and the Council of Ulemas Called on Muslims to Take All Precautions to Prevent the Spread of Coronavirus"], 2020).[7]

Similar to its counterparts in Kyrgyzstan and Kazakhstan, the government of Uzbekistan also began to lift restrictions before the virus was completely under control, although it proceeded more cautiously. At the end of April 2020, President Shavkat Mirziyoyev announced that the situation had stabilized and that the quarantine requirements could be gradually relaxed. He also emphasized the strain on the economy and the need to allow some forms of transportation between and within cities to resume to "prevent the loss of ripe agricultural products" and enable people to return to work ("Prishlo Vrenya Prinyat' Sleduiushchie Shagi k Poetapnomu Snyatiiu Karantina" ["It Is Time to Take the Next Steps to Phase Out Quarantine"], 2020).[8] By mid-May 2020, domestic travel by rail and air was allowed to resume with some restrictions ("Kompaniya Uzbekistan Airways Vozobnovila Prodazhi Biletov na Vnutrennie Reisy" ["Uzbekistan Airways Has Resumed Ticket Sales for Domestic Flights"], 2020). By the end of May, the government was encouraging domestic travel to revive the tourism industry ("Uzbekistan Gotovitsya Prinimat' Turistov" ["Uzbekistan Is Preparing to Welcome Tourists"], 2020). In mid-May, the government published a long list of "sanitary rules and norms" developed by the Ministry of Health that businesses would be required to follow in order to reopen (Agency for Sanitary and Epidemiological Welfare, 2020). Then in early June 2020, it announced that small businesses, including retail stores, restaurants, and kindergartens (but not nightclubs or public transportation) would be allowed to reopen on June 15 (Mamatkulov, 2020). Requirements for wearing masks in public and observing social distancing, however, were extended until August 1, 2020, and the zoning system also remained in place indefinitely ("Karantin v Uzbekistane Prodlili do Avgusta" ["Quarantine in Uzbekistan Was Extended until August"], 2020).

Uzbekistan was perhaps slowest to respond to the unrelenting spread of the virus. New reported cases of COVID-19 began to increase already by the end of May 2020 and continued to spike in June. They also began to appear in regions that had not previously been considered to be at high risk ("Novye Bol'nye s Koronavirusom Obnaruzheny v Vos'mi Regionakh. Vysokie Pokazateli v Khorezme, Surkhandar'e i Tashkente" ["New Patients with Coronavirus Have Been Found in Eight Regions. High Rates in Khorezm, Surkhandarya and Tashkent"], 2020). Nonetheless, the government did not respond until the number of cases per day hit a new record (318 on July 3, 2020) and then surpassed that record (342 on July 6, 2020) in less than one week ("Uzbekistan Obnovil Record Po Chislu Zabolevshikh COVID-19 Za Sutki" ["Uzbekistan Set a New Record for the Number of COVID-19 Cases Per Day"], 2020). On July 7, 2020, the government announced that the quarantine would be tightened and extended beginning July 10 ("S 10 Iiulya v Uzbekistane Zakroiut Rynki i Zapretyat Svad'by" ["Starting July 10, Markets Will Be Closed and Weddings Will Be Forbidden in Uzbekistan"], 2020). These new measures included stricter limitations on the travel between regions and the banning of most large gatherings (specifically, weddings). Over a week later, President Mirziyoyev officially acknowledged that the country was experiencing a so-called "second wave" and pleaded with its citizens not to panic (Yakubov, 2020). In late July 2020, the government extended the lockdown once again, this time through mid-August, citing the success of its decision earlier that month to tighten quarantine measures in combating the further spread of the virus (Radio Azzatyk, 2020b).[9]

Social Policy Measures

Social policy measures, which were necessary to address the social and economic costs of the stringent health policy measures, followed a similar pattern to the health policy measures described earlier. Kazakhstan acted the most swiftly and comprehensively. It was the first and only country in Central Asia to introduce a significant domestic anticrisis package. The primary reason for this is that Kazakhstan had greater financial capacity than its neighbors before the COVID-19 pandemic, fueled by its large oil and gas sector.[10] With more limited fiscal means before the pandemic and both the loss of remittances from migrant laborers in Russia and the expense of trying to bring them home once the crisis began to unfold, Kyrgyzstan and Uzbekistan faced greater constraints. As a result, both depended on receiving emergency aid from the international community. All three countries banned the export of basic foodstuff by the end of March to ensure a sufficient domestic supply. Despite the best intentions, none were able to fully address the economic consequences of the lockdown measures.

Kazakhstan

The day after President Tokayev declared an official state of emergency, he issued two additional decrees[11] outlining measures for steps that the government would take to provide social and economic support to its citizens and industry. The measures amounted to a significant "anti-crisis package"[12] that included cash payments to the unemployed and self-employed,[13] an increase in pension and welfare benefits, and support for small and medium enterprises (SMEs). The package for SMEs in particular includes tax breaks (payroll and value added tax, or VAT), subsidized lending and suspension of debt payments, as well as employment support. As the crisis continued in May and June and the impact on the economy became greater,[14] the government renewed its commitment to providing social and economic benefits, focusing on restoring growth. These social policy measures included subsidizing mortgages, tax breaks for the hardest hit sectors (e.g., agriculture), and continued subsidies to SMEs (World Bank, 2020b, pp. 6–9). By July, the country's economy had shrunk by almost 2 percent since the beginning of the year. Yet, confident in its ability to rely on its reserves, the government continued these measures ("Den'gi est'- Ministr Finansov o Bor'be s Korornavirusom" ["The Minister of Finance Says That There Is Money to Fight Coronavirus"], 2020). It also continued to promise cash payments to those who lost substantial income as a result of the quarantine, although it has been criticized for reducing the amount of these payments in August 2020 (Human Rights Watch, 2020b) and for its inability to process the increased volume of requests ("Kazakhstantsy 'Polozhili' Sait Dlya Podachi Zayavok na Karantinnye Posobiya" ["Kazakhstanis 'Shut Down' the Website for Submitting Applications for Quarantine Benefits"], 2020). Finally, the government announced that it would grant a special one-time payment to compensate medical workers ("Skol'ko Zarazivshikhsya Koronavirusom Medikov Poluchili po 2 Milliona Tenge" ["How Many Medical Workers Infected with Coronavirus Each Received 2 Million Tenge"], 2020).

Kyrgyzstan

The government of Kyrgyzstan also quickly acknowledged the economic impact concerning both the pandemic in general and the health policy measures it had enacted but could not provide much relief on its own. President Jeenbekov almost immediately reached out to various international institutions—including the Asian Development Bank (ADB), the European Union, and the International Monetary Fund (IMF)—for financial assistance to cover the anticipated gaps in the country's budget.[15] Meanwhile, the government could do little more than assert that it was working on measures to provide assistance to those most affected. In particular, the government announced that it was considering a package of loan payment deferrals and tax breaks for small Businesses ("Pravitel'stvo o Vesenne-Polevykh Rabotakh: S Segodnyashnego Dnya na «Kudaibergene» Budut Rabotat' Ryady s Zapchastyami" ["The Government on Spring Field Work: From Today on, Rows of Spare Parts Will Work at Kudaibergen"], 2020). Like its neighbors, Kyrgyzstan was concerned about food security and so had already banned the export of most basic foodstuffs by the end of March. It also allowed farmers to harvest their spring crops and bring them to market (Government of the Kyrgyz Republic, 2020a). However, this did not prevent the closing of the Dordoi Bazaar, located on the northeastern outskirts of Kyrgyzstan's capital, Bishkek, on March 23 "until further notice."[16] Dordoi is not only Central Asia's largest market and one of the main entry points for Chinese goods but also the main source of income for approximately 150,000 people.[17] This contributed to the already high level of unemployment in the country; by mid-April, it was estimated to be about 50 percent for the formal labor force and even higher for the informal one (OECD, 2020a).

Uzbekistan

Like its counterparts in Kazakhstan and Kyrgyzstan, the government of Uzbekistan was well aware of the potential social and economic impact of the pandemic and the health policies that were put in place to mitigate its spread. Although it moved faster than Kyrgyzstan, its package was not as extensive as Kazakhstan's. On March 19, 2020, the government announced that it would create an "Anti-Crisis Fund in the amount of 10 trillion soms," which would be directed primarily at the medial system to ensure adequate supplies of needed equipment and compensate medial workers but was also intended to offset the impact on SMEs.[18] High rates of unemployment were of particular concern, particularly given the large number of people employed outside the formal sector.[19] Those in the informal labor sector, however, account for the largest portion of the population that was employed before COVID-19 and were the most vulnerable to the consequent economic shutdown (OECD, 2020a, p. 45). Also unlike Kazakhstan, the government of Uzbekistan was ill equipped to fulfill these promises without foreign assistance. Thus, similar to Kyrgyzstan, it began to seek comprehensive international aid from various financial institutions early into the crisis, beginning with a request for US$1 billion in budget support from the ADB. By the end of April, it had reportedly received significant financing from the World Bank and IMF to support its anticrisis measures by funding social welfare programs and to stimulate its economy (IMF, 2020).

Explanation

Although many point to regime type and state capacity as the major determinants of government responses to crises, these do not seem to be the crucial factors explaining how swiftly or decisively governments acted to mitigate COVID-19 in Central Asia. In fact, one of the main reasons for comparing Kazakhstan, Kyrgyzstan, and Uzbekistan is that they differ in both of these key explanatory variables. Regarding regime type, across multiple indices, Kazakhstan and Uzbekistan have consistently been characterized as consolidated authoritarian regimes, whereas Kyrgyzstan has consistently been characterized as democratic (Haerpfer & Kizilova, 2020). When it comes to state capacity, which we conceptualize along two dimensions (administrative reach and fiscal resources), there is greater variation across these three countries. Kazakhstan has a high degree of state capacity, given its centralized structure of decision-making and access to oil revenue. Uzbekistan has a medium degree of state capacity; like Kazakhstan, it is centralized administratively and yet, as previously described, has limited fiscal resources. Kyrgyzstan has a low degree of state capacity; it is both administratively and fiscally decentralized in comparison to Kazakhstan and Uzbekistan.

Further, neither regime type nor state capacity can explain the early relaxation or lifting of strict health policy measures by governments in all three countries. Here, economic conditions seem to be the key factor influencing not only the extent to which each country could adopt social policies (as previously described) but also their willingness and ability to maintain lockdowns. Kyrgyzstan and Uzbekistan are lower-middle income countries. Kazakhstan is an upper-middle income country; nonetheless, the World Bank (2020b) expects that the country will suffer grave economic consequences from the pandemic. Kyrgyzstan and Uzbekistan are both highly dependent on revenue from labor migration of their citizens. As early as April 2020, the World Bank (2020a) projected that the global migration economy will suffer from the COVID-19 pandemic and that Europe and Central Asia will suffer the most. It estimated that the Central Asian countries dependent on these remittances would experience a 28 percent decrease in remittances this year (World Bank, 2020a). There is no doubt that the pandemic has had major economic consequences across the globe. However, COVID-19 has also shined light on which countries are economically unable to maintain stay-at-home measures for the length of time necessary to effectively contain the spread of coronavirus. In countries with weak healthcare infrastructure, moreover, maintaining longer lockdowns seems crucial to averting a full-blown crisis.

Indeed, although Kazakhstan, Kyrgyzstan, and Uzbekistan vary according to regime type and state capacity, what they do have in common is a weak healthcare system. As in many other parts of the former Soviet Union, long-neglected public healthcare systems meant that during the COVID-19 pandemic, citizens lacked access to diagnostic tests and high-quality medical care, and medical workers were particularly vulnerable to infection. COVID-19 has again exposed the fragility of the underdeveloped and neglected healthcare systems and demonstrated the need for further health systems strengthening across the region.

Although Central Asian countries have undergone decades of healthcare reforms since the Soviet Union's collapse, they have not been sufficient. Central Asia faces the double burden of both from noncommunicable diseases, namely cardiovascular and cancer, and from infectious diseases, namely tuberculosis, viral hepatitis, and HIV (Adambekov et al., 2016). The comorbidities that have been shown to be associated with complications and deaths from COVID-19 are highly prevalent in the region. The leading causes of death in all three countries are ischemic heart disease, stroke, and cirrhosis. Moreover, lower respiratory infections are in the top ten leading causes of death in all three countries (CDC, 2019). Central Asian countries inherited the Soviet model healthcare systems that are hierarchical but also fragmented in service provision. Since the end of the Soviet Union, the healthcare systems in Central Asia have further deteriorated because of the political and economic crises over the past three decades. For example, the availability of hospital beds in acute care has been in the decline since the 1990s (World Bank, 2020c). And human resource capacity has suffered as indicated by the decreasing number of physicians per capita, particularly in more rural areas (Rechel et al., 2012). Universal access to free government healthcare services remains; however, we know that informal payments and the increase in private healthcare services undermine efforts to achieve health equity and provide quality health care to all citizens. All of the countries in Central Asia have experienced challenges in healthcare reform and healthcare financing. Although Kazakhstan, the most economically well off, spends more per capita than the other countries in the region, health expenditure makes up a smaller percentage of its gross domestic product (GDP) than in the others (Rechel et al., 2012). The Kazakhstani government has introduced healthcare reform repeatedly; however, it seems that with each new policy introduced, the situation actually worsens (Koneev & Kaldybaev, 2019). Central Asian countries are also plagued by vast inequities in healthcare resources, problems with access to care exacerbated by poverty and inefficient and poor-quality healthcare services (Rechel et al., 2012).

Thus, even as the governments in all three countries publicly recognized their mistake and reinstituted necessary but unpopular policies, most importantly lockdowns, it was too little too late. In other words, their policy reversal was insufficient given these deficiencies in the healthcare infrastructure, which proved detrimental to their ability to combat COVID-19. For example, there were not enough hospital beds and medicines available in Kyrgyzstan, Kazakhstan, and Uzbekistan during the summer when the number of COVID-19 patients needing medical care was surging. Reports from Kyrgyzstan showed that this was not just lack of hospital beds, but also ventilators, intensive care unit spaces, and lack of healthcare workers (Eshaliyeva, 2020). The deputy health minister of Kyrgyzstan reportedly admitted on live television in April that just over half of the 649 ventilators in the country are in working condition. Healthcare workers in the region have been particularly negatively affected by the novel coronavirus, reflecting the high burden of patient numbers and lack of adequate personal protective equipment. Although healthcare workers who have been infected with COVID-19 have been promised financial compensation from the government, there have been complaints that no payments have been made (Radio Azzatyk, 2020a). Arguably, the weak healthcare infrastructure before the COVID-19 pandemic and the precarious economic situation contributed to the surge in cases over the summer in Kazakhstan, Kyrgyzstan, and Uzbekistan. Although they were able to all react quickly early on, the extended lockdowns were not sustainable, and the healthcare systems were not strong enough to adequately deal with the rapid increase in cases. In fact, this trend was observed across the countries irrespective of regime type.

Conclusion

Central Asia is a cautionary tale in three key respects. First, it demonstrates what happens when restrictions are lifted too soon. The dramatic rise in COVID-19 cases and deaths in June and July 2020 was arguably not a so-called "second wave," but rather, the continuation of its first wave that had been interrupted or at least slowed down by the vigilance early on but was accelerated by the relaxation in these policies. Second, the experiences of Kazakhstan, Kyrgyzstan, and Uzbekistan seem to suggest that neither the stringency of policies nor compliance with these policies is primarily about regime type and state capacity. Despite different regime types and varying levels of state capacity, at the start of the pandemic, all three countries were willing to acknowledge its potential severity and take necessary but unpopular actions. Yet, all three countries also reversed course. Third, the effectiveness of these policies is nonetheless tied to health infrastructure. In other words, even though all three countries reinstated strict social distancing measures after it was clear that COVID-19 was continuing to spread, their ability to contain the virus was limited by their pre-existing weak healthcare systems. As countries around the world will likely be facing a second wave of the COVID-19 pandemic in fall, Central Asia's experience demonstrates the importance of focusing on health systems and their capacity to address pandemic threats.

Notes

1. It is worth noting that both Tajikistan and Turkmenistan have also been criticized for limiting press coverage of COVID-19 in their countries and reporting very few (or any) cases of the novel coronavirus. Thus, we cannot compare the outcomes in these countries with the other three, only their policies (or lack thereof).

2. This is the gateway to the special trade zone between the two countries.

3. Kazakhstan was apparently using the same method as Russia, which did not include those who had underlying health issues in the count of COVID-19 deaths.

4. Just a week before, on March 16th, the government had ordered night clubs and movie theaters to close as a precaution.

5. Also like Kazakhstan, this disproportionate impact was apparent early on; medical care workers already accounted for roughly 25 percent of all cases in April.

6. The former speaker of parliament, Mukar Cholponbaev, died of COVID-19 in late May.

7. A similar fatwa was issued on April 14 prohibiting public gatherings related to Ramadan, which began on April 23, 2020.

8. The country was divided into zones, allowing private cars to travel freely in those "green" areas where the risk was deemed to be low and greater restrictions in those "red" areas where the risk was deemed to be high. (For details, see Kumenov & Imanaliyeva, 2020.)

9. The number of COVID-19 cases had reportedly begun to decrease.

10. Real GDP rose by 4.1 percent in 2019 and unemployment was low (4.9 percent). See OECD, 2020a for details.

11. Decree No. 286 "On measures for ensuring social and economic stability" and Decree No. 287 "On further stabilization efforts."

12. The OECD (2020b) estimated that, "excluding tax breaks and local support," the total package "[would] amount to KZT 4.4 trillion tenge (roughly USD 10bn or 6–7 percent of GDP)."

13. Within a month, over 4 million people had received these payments, but over half those who applied were denied ("4 Milliona Kazakhstantsev Poluchili 42 500 Tenge" ["4 Million Kazakhstanis Received 42,500 Tenge"], 2020).

14. By early April, Kazakhstan was forced to utilize its National Oil Fund to subsidize the economy while it faced a decline in both oil prices and production ("Kazakhstan Cuts Oil Output Forecast, Sees GDP Shrinking This Year," 2020).

15. Kyrgyzstan was the first country to receive emergency funding from the IMF because of the dire situation concerning its balance of payments. In April, President Jeenbekov asked China for debt relief.

16. It also did not prevent the huge increase in food prices, which had reportedly doubled by May.

17. The bazaar's closure meant unemployment and possibly starvation for approximately 50,000 people. For details, see Furlong, 2020.

18. As in Kazakhstan, the pledged relief for SMEs included interest-free loans and tax breaks and temporary debt forgiveness.

19. By some estimates, the number of officially unemployed had risen by 30 percent in June as a result of the quarantine ("Chislo Bezrabotnykh V Uzebkistane Dostiglo 2 Millionov" ["The Number of Unemployed in Uzbekistan Has Reached 2 Million"], 2020). This figure does not include the approximately 500,000 who could no longer work abroad.

References

4 milliona kazakhstantsev poluchili 42 500 tenge [4 million Kazakhstanis received 42,500 tenge]. (2020, April 23). Tengrinews. https://tengrinews.kz/kazakhstan_news/4-milliona-kazakhstantsev-poluchili-42-500-tenge-399890/

Adambekov, S., Kaiyrlykyzy, A., Igissinov, N., & Linkov, F. (2016). Health challenges in Kazakhstan and Central Asia. *Journal of Epidemiology and Community Health, 70,* 104–108.

Agency for Sanitary and Epidemiological Welfare (SEB Agency), Scientific Research Institute of Sanitation, Hygiene and Occupational Diseases under the Ministry of Health of the Republic of Uzbekistan. (2020). *Vremennye sanitarnye pravila i standardty dlya organizatsii deyteľ'nosti gosudarstvennykh organov i organizatsii, a takhzhe sub″ektov khozyaistvovaniya, podpadaiushchikh pod mery ogranicheniya pandemii COVID-19.* [Temporary sanitation rules and standards for organizing the activities of state bodies and organizations, as well as business entities subject to measures to stop the COVID-19 pandemic]. Ministry of Health of the Republic of Uzbekistan. Tashkent.

Center for Disease Control and Prevention (CDC). (2019). *Global health: Central Asia.* https://www.cdc.gov/globalhealth/countries/central-asia/index.html

Chislo bezrabotnykh v Uzebkistane dostiglo 2 millionov [The number of unemployed in Uzbekistan has reached 2 million]. (2020). CentralAsia.media. Retrieved from https://centralasia.media/news:1627701/

Den'gi est'- ministr finansov o bor'be s korornavirusom [The minister of finance says that there is money to fight coronavirus]. (2020, June 12). Tengrinews. https://tengrinews.kz/kazakhstan_news/dengi-est-ministr-finansov-o-borbe-s-koronavirusom-405215/

Eshaliyeva, K. (2020, July 13). *Is Kyrgyzstan losing the fight against coronavirus?* Open democracy.net. https://www.opendemocracy.net/en/odr/kyrgyzstan-losing-fight-against-coronavirus/

Furlong, R. (2020, May 12). Workers go hungry as Central Asia's largest bazaar stands empty. *Radio Free Liberty/Radio Europe.* https://www.rferl.org/a/workers-go-hungry-as-central-asia-s-largest-bazaar-stands-empty/30607483.html

Government of the Kyrgyz Republic. (2020a, March 23). *Vveden vremennyi zapret na vyvoz otdeľ'nykh vidov tovarov iz Kyrgyzstana* [A temporary ban has been introduced on the export of certain types of goods from Kyrgyzstan]. https://www.gov.kg/ru/post/s/kyrgyzstandan-ayrym-tovarlardyn-trlrn-tashyp-chyguuga-ubaktyluu-chekt-kirgizildi

Government of the Kyrgyz Republic. (2020b, March 25). *Kubatbek Boronov: Rezhim ChP dostavit neudobstva grazhdanam, no vse delaetsya radi ikh bezopasnosti* [Kubatbek Boronov: The state of emergency will cause inconvenience to citizens, but it is all done for their safety]. https://www.gov.kg/ru/post/s/kubatbek-boronov-rezhim-chp-dostavit-neudobstva-grazhdanam-no-vse-delaetsya-radi-ikh-bezopasnosti%C2%A0

Government of the Kyrgyz Republic. (2020c, April 28). *Razrabotan poetapnyi poryadok vozobnovleniya ekonomicheskoi deyateľ'nosti* [A step-by-step procedure for the resumption of economic activity was developed]. https://www.gov.kg/ru/post/s/razrabotan-poetapnyy-poryadok-vozobnovleniya-ekonomicheskoy-deyatelnosti%C2%A0.

Government of the Kyrgyz Republic. (2020d, May 10). *Prim'er-ministr Mukhammedkalyi Abylgaziev: Sobliudenie rezhima chrezvychainoi situatsii trebuet osoboi otvetstvennosti ot kazhdogo kyrgyzstantsa* [Prime Minister Mukhammedkaly Abylgaziev: Compliance with the emergency situation requires special responsibility from every Kyrgyz citizen]. https://www.gov.kg/ru/post/s/premer-ministr-mukhammedkalyy-abylgaziev-soblyudenie-rezhima-chrezvychaynoy-situatsii-trebuet-osoboy-otvetstvennosti-ot-kazhdogo-kyrgyzstantsa

Haerpfer, C. W., & Kizilova, K. (2020). Values and transformation in Central Asia. In Mihr A. (Ed.), *Transformation and development*. Springer.

Human Rights Watch. (2020a, July 21). *Kyrgyzstan/Kazakhstan: New rules for tallying Covid-19 data.* https://www.hrw.org/news/2020/07/21/kyrgyzstan/kazakhstan-new-rules-tallying-covid-19-data

Human Rights Watch. (2020b, August 17). *Kazakhstan: Extend, expand Covid-19 aid.* https://www.hrw.org/news/2020/08/17/kazakhstan-extend-expand-covid-19-aid

International Monetary Fund (IMF). (2020, May 18). *IMF executive board approves a US$375 million disbursement to the Republic of Uzbekistan to address the impact of the COVID-19 Crisis* [Press Release]. https://www.imf.org/en/News/Articles/2020/05/18/pr20220-uzbekistan-imf-executive-board-approves-us-375m-disbursement-address-impact-covid19

Irgebaeyeva, A. (2020a, June 12). *Vlasti budut zakryvat' biznes za narushenie sanitarnykh pravil* [Authorities will close businesses for violating sanitation laws]. https://kloop.kg/blog/2020/06/12/vlasti-budut-zakryvat-biznes-za-narushenie-sanitarnyh-pravil/

Irgebaeyeva, A. (2020b, July 12). *V Kyrgyzstane bol'she 10 tysyach sluchaev koronavirusa. Za sutki zafiksirovano 719 novykh zarazhennykh, 500 iz nikh v Bishkeke* [There are more than 10,000 cases of coronavirus in Kyrgyzstan. 719 new infections recorded in a day, 500 of them in Bishkek]. https://kloop.kg/blog/2020/07/12/za-sutki-zafiksirovano-719-novyh-zarazhennyh-koronavirusom-500-iz-nih-v-bishkeke/

Karantin v Uzbekistane prodlili do avgusta [Quarantine in Uzbekistan was extended until August]. (2020, June 14). Fergana.news. https://fergana.news/news/119109/

Kazakhstan cuts oil output forecast, sees GDP shrinking this year. (2020, April 1). Reuters News. https://www.reuters.com/article/kazakhstan-budget/kazakhstan-cuts-oil-output-forecast-sees-gdp-shrinking-this-year-idUSR4N28J017

Kazakhstantsy 'polozhili' sait dlya podachi zayavok na karantinnye posobiya [Kazakhstanis "shut down" the website for submitting applications for quarantine benefits]. (2020, July 17). Fergana.news. https://fergana.news/news/120228/

KazInform. (2020, April 6). *120 medikov zaboleli koronavirusom v Kazakhstane* [120 medical workers were infected with coronavirus in Kazakhsten]. https://www.inform.kz/ru/120-medikov-zaboleli-koronavirusom-v-kazahstane_a3634368

Kompaniya Uzbekistan Airways vozobnovila prodazhi biletov na vnutrennie reisy [Uzbekistan Airways has resumed ticket sales for domestic flights]. (2020, May 15). Kun.uz. https://kun.uz/ru/news/2020/05/15/kompaniya-uzbekistan-airways-vozobnovila-prodaji-biletov-na-vnutrenniye-reysy

Koneev, K., & Kaldybaev, A. (2019, January 14). *Chto ne daet razvyvat'sya zdravookhraneniiu Kazakhstana* [What prevents healthcare development in Kazakhstan]. Forbes Kazakhstan. https://forbes.kz/process/medicine/chto_ne_daet_razvivatsya_zdravoohraneniyu_kazahstana/

Kumenov, A. (2020, July 23). *Kazakhstan to merge pneumonia and coronavirus cases, but only from Aug. 1.* Eurasianet. https://eurasianet.org/kazakhstan-to-merge-pneumonia-and-coronavirus-cases-but-only-from-aug-1

Kumenov, A., & Imanaliyeva, A. (2020, May 18). *Kazakhs, Kyrgyz, Uzbeks cautiously, anxiously, eye return to familiar patterns.* Eurasianet. https://eurasianet.org/kazakhs-kyrgyz-uzbeks-cautiously-anxiously-eye-return-to-familiar-patterns

Mamatkulov, M. (2020, June 4). Uzbekistan announces further easing of coronavirus restrictions. *Real News Now*. https://whtc.com/2020/06/04/uzbekistan-announces-further-easing-of-coronavirus-restrictions/1025539/?refer-section=world

Masalieva, Z. (2020, April 16). *Muftii prizval musul'man Kyrgyzstana strogo priderzhivat'sya trebovanii karantina* [The mufti called on Muslims in Kyrgyzstan to strictly adhere to the quarantine requirements]. 24.kg. https://24.kg/obschestvo/150253_muftiy_prizval_musulman_kyirgyizstana_strogo_priderjivatsya_trebovaniy_karantina_/

Ministry of Education and Science, Republic of Kazakhstan. (2020, March 16). *Informatsiya dlya shkol'nikov, studentov, pedagogov i roditelei v period pandemii* [Information for schoolchildren, students, teachers, and parents during the pandemic]. https://www.gov.kz/memleket/entities/edu/press/news/details/informaciya-dlya-shkolnikov-studentov-pedagogov-i-roditeley-v-period-pandemii?lang=ru

Novye bol'nye s koronavirusom obnaruzheny v vos'mi regionakh. Vysokie pokazateli v Khorezme, Surkhandar'e i Tashkente [New patients with coronavirus have been found in eight regions. High rates in Khorezm, Surkhandarya and Tashkent]. (2020, June 24). Podrobnoo.uz. https://podrobno.uz/cat/obchestvo/novye-bolnye-s-koronavirusom-obnaruzheny-v-vosmi-regionakh-vysokie-pokazateli-v-khorezme-surkhandare/

Office of Economic Cooperation and Development (OECD). (2020a). *COVID-19 crisis response in Central Asia.* https://read.oecd-ilibrary.org/view/?ref=129_129634-ujyjsqu30i&title=COVID-19-crisis-response-in-central-asia

Office of Economic Cooperation and Development (OECD). (2020b). *The COVID-19 crisis in Kazakhstan.* https://www.oecd.org/eurasia/competitiveness-programme/central-asia/COVID-19-CRISIS-IN-KAZAKHSTAN.pdf

Official Information Resource of the Prime Minister, Republic of Kazakhstan. (2020a, March 27). *S 30 marta po 5 aprelya t.g. v Nur-Sultane i Almaty budet priostanovlena deyatel'nost' predpriyatii i organizatsii* [From March 30 to April 5 this year in Nur-Sultan and Almaty the activities of enterprises and organizations will be suspended]. https://primeminister.kz/ru/news/s-30-marta-po-5-aprelya-tg-v-nur-sultane-i-almaty-budet-priostanovlena-deyatelnost-predpriyatiy-i-organizaciy-2725915

Official Information Resource of the Prime Minister, Republic of Kazakhstan. (2020b, May 11). *Ogranichitel'nye mery budut snyaty poetapno* [The restrictive measures will be lifted in stages]. https://primeminister.kz/ru/news/press/ogranichitelnye-mery-budut-snyaty-poetapno-e-tugzhanov-114352

Official Information Resource of the Prime Minister, Republic of Kazakhstan. (2020c, May 13). *Novyi paket mer po voznobnovleniiu otraslei ekonomiki* [A new package of measures to revive sectors of the economy]. https://primeminister.kz/ru/news/novyy-paket-mer-po-vozobnovleniyu-otrasley-ekonomiki-1344056

Orlova, M. (2020, March 21). *V Kyrgyzstane vveli rezhim chrezvychainoi situatsii* [An emergency regime was introduced in Kyrgyzstan]. 24.kg. https://24.kg/obschestvo/147446_vkyirgyizstane_vveli_rejim_chrezvyichaynoy_situatsii/

Pravitel'stvo o vesenne-polevykh rabotakh: S segodnyashnego dnya na «Kudaibergene» budut rabotat' ryady s zapchastyami [The government on spring field work: From today on, rows of spare parts will work at Kudaibergen]. (2020, March 30). Tazabek. http://www.tazabek.kg/news:1606980/

Prishlo vrenya prinyat' sleduiushchie shagi k poetapnomu snyatiiu karantina [It is time to take the next steps to phase out quarantine]. (2020, April 29). Gazeta.uz. https://www.gazeta.uz/ru/2020/04/29/measures/

Radio Azzatyk. (2020a, July 21). *Eshche ni odin iz zarazivshikhsya koronavirusom medikov ne poluchil obeshchannyiu pravitel'stvom kompensatsiiu* [None of the doctors infected with the coronavirus have yet received compensation as promised by the government]. https://rus.azattyk.org/a/30738979.html

Radio Azzatyk. (2020b, July 27). *V Uzbekistane karantinnye ogranicheniya prodleny do 15 avgusta* [Quarantine restrictions in Uzbekistan are extended until August 15]. https://rus.azattyk.org/a/30748966.html

Rechel, B., Ahmedov, M., Akkazieva, B., Katsaga, A., Khodjamurodov, G., & McKee, M. (2012). Lessons from two decades of health reform in Central Asia. *Health Policy and Planning, 27*(4), 281–287.

S 10 iiulya v Uzbekistane zakroiut rynki i zapretyat svad'by [Starting July 10, markets will be closed and weddings will be forbidden in Uzbekistan]. (2020, July 8). Fergana.media. https://fergana.media/news/119915/

S 30 marta po 5 aprelya t.g.v Nur-Sultane i Almaty budet priostanovlena deyatel'nost' predpriyatiii organizatsii. [Activities of enterprises and organizations will be suspended in Nur-Sultan and Almaty from March 30 to April 5 of this year]. https://primeminister.kz/ru/news/s-30-marta-po-5-aprelya-tg-v-nur-sultane-i-almaty-budet-priostanovlena-deyatelnost-predpriyatiy-i-organizaciy-2725915

Skol'ko zarazivshikhsya koronavirusom medikov poluchili po 2 milliona tenge [How many medical workers infected with coronavirus each received 2 million tenge]. (2020, July 24). Tengrinews. https://tengrinews.kz/kazakhstan_news/skolko-zarazivshihsya-koronavirusom-medikov-poluchili-2-409409/

Strategy 2050. (2020, January 27). *Kakie mery prinimaiutsya v Kazakhstane po predyprezhdeniiu zavoza koronavirusnoi infektsii* [What measures are being taken in Kazakhstan to prevent the importation of coronavirus disease]. https://strategy2050.kz/ru/news/kakie-mery-prinyaty-v-kazakhstane-po-preduprezhdeniyu-zavoza-koronavirusnoy-infektsii/

Tokaev: Karantinnyi rezhim sokhranyaetsya [Tokayev says that the quarantine measures will continue]. (2020, May 18). Tengrinews. https://tengrinews.kz/kazakhstan_news/tokaev-karantinnyiy-rejim-sohranyaetsya-402643/

Tokaev poruchil prodlit' karantin v Kazakhstane [Tokayev instructed the quarantine to be extended in Kazakhstan]. (2020, July 29). Tengrinews. https://tengrinews.kz/kazakhstan_news/tokaev-poruchil-prodlit-karantin-v-kazahstane-409789/

Upravlenie musul'man Uzbekistana i Sovet ulemov prizvali musul'man prinyat' vs emery dlya predotvrashcheniya rasrostraneniya koronavirusa [The Board of Muslims of Uzbekistan and the Council of Ulemas called on Muslims to take all precautions to prevent the spread of coronavirus]. (2020, March 16). Podrobnoo.uz. https://podrobno.uz/cat/obchestvo/upravlenie-musulman-uzbekistana-i-sovet-ulemov-prizvali-musulman-prinyat-vse-mery-dlya-predotvrashch/

Uzbekistan confirms COVID-19 case, closes borders. (2020, March 16). Eurasianet. https://eurasianet.org/uzbekistan-confirms-covid-19-case-closes-borders

Uzbekistan gotovitsya prinimat' turistov [Uzbekistan is preparing to welcome tourists]. (2020, May 27). Gazeta.uz. https://www.gazeta.uz/ru/2020/05/27/tourism/

Uzbekistan obnovil record po chislu zabolevshikh COVID-19 za sutki [Uzbekistan set a new record for the number of COVID-19 cases per day]. (2020, July 7). Fergana.media. https://fergana.media/news/119858/

V bol'nitsy Nur-Sultana postupaet po 500 chelovek v den', kazhdyi vtoroi-c pnevmoniei [500 people are admitted to the hospital in Nur-Sultan each day, every second person has pneumonia]. (2020, June 17). Tengrinews. https://tengrinews.kz/kazakhstan_news/bolnitsyi-nur-sultana-postupaet-500-v-den-kajdyiy-vtoroy-405613

Vlast. (2020, April 10). *Rezhim chrezvychainogo polozheniya v Kazakhstane prodlen do kontsa aprelya* [The state of emergency in Kazakhstan has been extended to the end of April]. https://vlast.kz/novosti/38701-rezim-crezvycajnogo-polozenia-v-kazahstane-prodlen-do-konca-aprela.html

World Bank. (2020a, April 22). *World Bank predicts sharpest decline of remittances in recent history.* [Press Release]. https://www.worldbank.org/en/news/press-release/2020/04/22/world-bank-predicts-sharpest-decline-of-remittances-in-recent-history

World Bank. (2020b, Summer). Navigating the crisis. *Kazakhstan Economic Update.*

World Bank. (2020c). Hospital bed (per 1,000 people)—Europe & Central Asia. Retrieved on December 15, 2020, from https://data.worldbank.org/indicator/SH.MED.BEDS.ZS?end=2018&locations=Z7&start=1980&view=chart

Yakubov, A. (2020, July 21). *Po tu storonu dveri* [On the other side of the door]. Fergana.ru. https://fergana.ru/articles/120313/

PART III EUROPE

12 COVID-19 IN THE UNITED KINGDOM

How Austerity and a Loss of State Capacity Undermined the Crisis Response

*Gemma A. Williams, Selina Rajan, and Jonathan D. Cylus**

When the World Health Organization (WHO) declared COVID-19 a public health emergency of international concern in January 2020 (WHO, 2020a), there was much optimism that the United Kingdom was well prepared to deal with the outbreak. The threat of a pandemic had been taken seriously in the past, with a world-renowned plan to combat an influenza outbreak in place and nationwide stress tests of the country's preparedness for such an eventuality first being conducted in 2007 and most recently in 2016 (House of Lords, 2020). In the last decade, an independent review found that the country had responded effectively to the H1N1 influenza pandemic (Hine, 2010), and its actions in helping to combat the Zika and Ebola outbreaks received substantial international praise, seemingly cementing its place as a leader of global public health (Middleton & Williams, 2019). As recently as October 2019, the Global Health Security Index ranked the United Kingdom as the second-best prepared country in the world to cope with an epidemic or pandemic (GHS, 2019). What has since transpired, however, was far removed from what many predicted: a country that should have been one of the best placed to tackle the pandemic has, as of the time of writing, been among the worst affected in Europe.

By August 2020, the United Kingdom had recorded the highest number of excess deaths and among the highest number of infections per capita in Europe (European Centre for Disease Prevention and Control, 2020; Office for National Statistics [ONS], 2020a; Tallack, 2020). Over the eleven worst weeks of the crisis, from March 23, 2020, to June 7, 2020, the United Kingdom reported an estimated 64,451 excess deaths (Tallack, 2020). This translates to the second highest excess mortality rate in Europe after Spain, and the highest in the region when adjusted for age (Public Health England, 2020a; Tallack, 2020). England was the worst affected UK nation, with approximately 991 excess deaths per million population, followed by Scotland (880), Wales (701), and Northern Ireland (514) (FactCheckNI, 2020).

---

*Disclaimer: The views and opinions expressed in this chapter represent those of the authors only and do not necessarily reflect the views or position of their respective institutions.

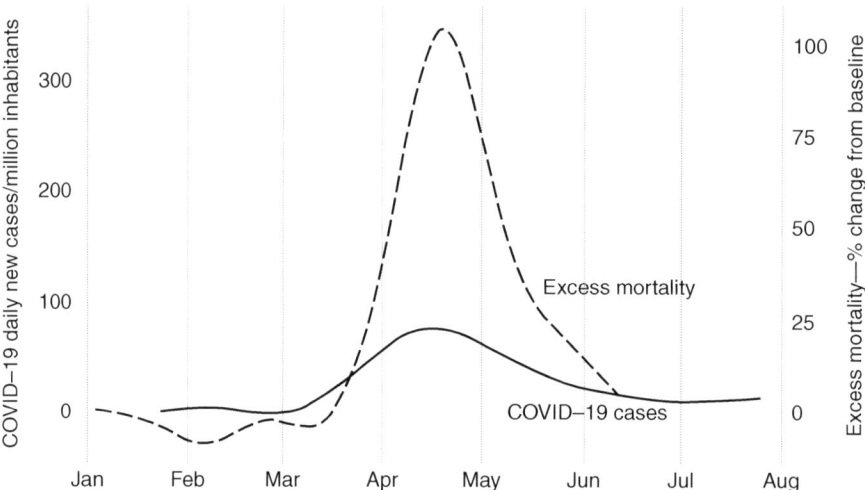

Figure 12.1. COVID-19 cases and all-cause excess mortality in the United Kingdom.
Source: "Excess Mortality during the COVID-19 Pandemic," 2020; Johns Hopkins University Center for Systems Science and Engineering (2020).

At the peak of the outbreak in April, the United Kingdom had an excess mortality rate of more than 100 percent above the five-year average (Figure 12.1), with only Spain faring worse (ONS, 2020a). England recorded the highest peak excess death rate in the United Kingdom at 107.8 percent, followed by Scotland (71.7 percent), Wales (68.7 percent), and Northern Ireland (48.2 percent) (ONS, 2020a). Yet, although England has been the worst affected nation of the United Kingdom, excess death rates in all of the devolved nations are among the highest in Europe (ONS, 2020a). Moreover, although outbreaks in France, Italy, and Spain were geographically concentrated, all of the UK regions reported higher excess mortality rates than the five-year average. It should nevertheless be emphasized that there was no excess mortality from mid-June to early August 2020. At the time of writing, the number of infections has generally been in decline since mid-April 2020, albeit with a recent uptick driven by localized outbreaks at the end of July.

The high incidence and mortality in the United Kingdom so far raises a key question and one we aim to answer in this chapter: Why did a country that should have been well prepared for a pandemic fare so poorly? This is inevitably a complex question, and many of the reasons are not yet fully clear. However, by analyzing the health and social policy measures put in place, we can already pinpoint some factors that have likely contributed to the United Kingdom's experience with COVID-19. We show that many of the right decisions were actually taken to tackle the pandemic, with a range of public health measures implemented to suppress the spread of the virus, health services quickly reconfigured, and the full apparatus of the state operationalized to protect livelihoods and the most vulnerable to try to ensure everyone could adhere to lockdown measures. Some key actions were nevertheless implemented too late, when the virus had already spread widely across the country. Notable impediments to a successful response appear to be structural reform to public health in England and a prolonged period of underinvestment in public services, particularly public health, during ten years of austerity that has eroded the country's ability to respond to emergencies. COVID-19 has also highlighted long-standing economic and ethnic inequalities that have caused some communities to be disproportionately affected by the virus. We consider some lessons that can be learned from the United Kingdom's response to help the country prepare for future waves and to meet the health and economic challenges of the future.

Health Policy Measures

Public Health Measures

Health is a devolved issue in the United Kingdom, with responsibility for organizing and commissioning health and social care services falling to devolved administrations in Northern Ireland, Scotland, and Wales, and the UK government in England. During the pandemic, emergency legislation, The Coronavirus Act 2020, was implemented, giving devolved administrations greater powers in the area of public health, such as the ability to restrict public gatherings or close down premises that represent a threat to public health (Paun, 2020). Public health actions until mid-May 2020 in all nations were nevertheless largely aligned.

Test and trace systems for COVID-19 were not scaled up until after the peak of the outbreak.

A key aim of the United Kingdom's pandemic response early on was to delay the spread of the virus to ensure the National Health Service (NHS) did not become overwhelmed. To achieve this, the response was divided into two phases: (1) contain, in which early cases were detected and close contacts followed up in an effort to delay the spread of the virus in the population for as long as possible and (2) delay, designed to slow the spread of the virus and delay the peak until summer (Department of Health and Social Care [DHSC], 2020a).

Early on in the contain phase, community testing and contact tracing were operational, with the number of tests per day initially second only to China. The process was controlled centrally and coordinated regionally by Public Health England (PHE) (an independent agency of the DHSC), Health Protection Scotland, Public Health Wales, Public Health Agency Northern Ireland, and the NHS. However, public health laboratories soon reached capacity. On March 12, 2020, with suspected widespread community transmission and numbers rising rapidly, the country moved into the delay phase, and a consequential decision was taken in line with the pandemic plan for influenza: community testing for suspected cases was scaled down, with testing capacity pivoted toward testing symptomatic people in hospitals, care homes, and prisons (Mahase, 2020b). Contact tracing was halted, except in specific locations such as prisons and care homes. Up until this point, testing per capita in the United Kingdom had been highest in Northern Ireland (503 per 100,000 population) and lowest in England (320 per 100,000 population) (Morris & Barnes, 2020).

The government did not commit to expanding testing eligibility criteria until early April, and no action was taken by the NHS to scale up testing capacity until this time. New regional drive-through and mobile testing units were introduced, along with home testing kits and "satellite" centers at places such as hospitals with significant demand, while steps were taken to increase laboratory capacity (DHSC, 2020b). Rather than focus on scaling up localized laboratory capacity in the public sector, the government elected to establish several new "lighthouse" mega-laboratories (with at least one in each country), with a number of private companies and public organizations partnering with the government to construct and run these new facilities. Unlike the NHS laboratory system, which has established local logistic planning and supply chains in place, the "lighthouse" labs created a highly centralized system, resulting in transport bottlenecks and delays in returning test results (Rajan et al., 2020).

On April 27, 2020, Northern Ireland became the first nation to launch a pilot contact tracing program, which was rolled out nationwide on May 19, 2020. Programs were launched at the end of May in England and Scotland and early June in Wales, with everyone over the age of five and with COVID-19 symptoms eligible for testing. The NHS, local health protection teams, and other public sector actors were tasked with contact tracing in the devolved nations and with tracing complex cases (e.g., in care homes, prisons, schools) in England. However, contracts to run certain other elements of test and trace services in England, including contact tracing for non-complex cases, were awarded to private companies with little experience in the area. The English test and trace system, for which £10 billion of funding has been set aside, has since faced a number of challenges, and questions have been raised over its value for money (Mahase, 2020a). A major criticism has been the low number of contacts traced for non-complex cases, which is currently around 49 percent, far below the estimated 80 percent of infections that must be traced to contain the spread of the virus and less than the numbers traced by smaller local health protection teams (DHSC, 2020c; Mahase, 2020a). There has also been no systematic effort to conduct retrospective tracing to find common infection sources (e.g., super-spreader events), which has proved successful in identifying clusters of infections in some countries (Crozier et al., 2020). The start of contact tracing programs in the United Kingdom were meant to be supported by the launch of new contact-tracing apps. Although Northern Ireland successfully launched a decentralized application (app) using Bluetooth technology in early August 2020 (which is interoperable with the app available in the Republic of Ireland), the rest of the United Kingdom has yet to follow suit.

Unprecedented physical distancing measures were implemented, but comparatively later than in some other countries.

A broad range of physical distancing measures were introduced to suppress the spread of the virus. At the start of the "delay" phase on March 12, 2020, people with COVID-19 symptoms were told to self-isolate for seven days, with vulnerable individuals (those over seventy years of age, people with chronic conditions, and pregnant women), advised to "shield" on March 16, 2020 (NHS England and Improvement, 2020a). On this date, the public was also asked to work at home if possible and avoid mass gatherings, public transport, and social venues. These measures nevertheless remained voluntary at a time when much of Europe was already locked down (March 10, 2020, in Italy, March 14 in Spain, and March 17 in France). Pubs, restaurants, social venues, and schools were not ordered to close until March 20, with a UK-wide mandatory lockdown announced on March 23 (in effect from March 26 in England, Scotland, and Wales and March 28 in Northern Ireland), when people were told to stay at home, except for one form of exercise per day, essential work that could not be done at home, and shopping for food or collecting medicines (Rajan & Curry, 2020). The police were granted powers to enforce lockdown measures through fines and dispersing gatherings in exceptional circumstances (Rajan & Curry, 2020). Adherence levels to physical distancing measures was generally high, with the number of visitors to retail and recreation venues, including restaurants, cafes, shopping centers, theme parks, museums, libraries, and cinemas and the use of public transportation both falling by more than 70 percent from mid-February to early April (Figure 12.2).

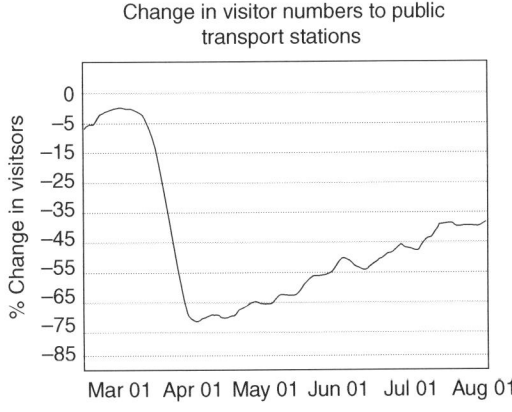

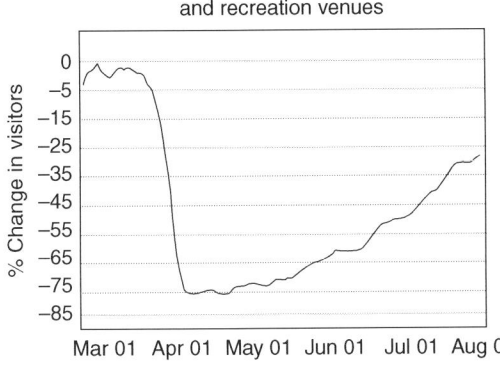

Figure 12.2. Google Community Mobility Trends: Visits to retail and recreation venues and public transport stations, February 17–July 31, 2020, United Kingdom. *Source:* Ritchie (2020).

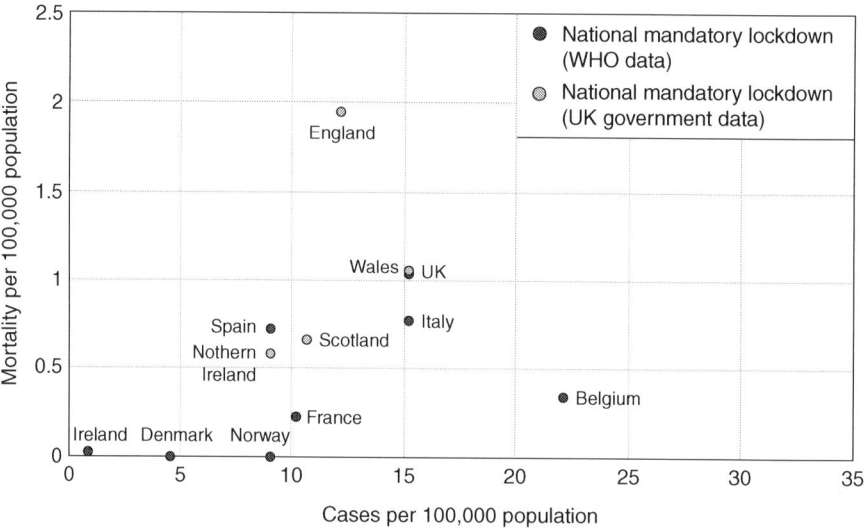

Figure 12.3. Mortality from COVID-19 and number of cases at the time of lockdown, Europe, selected countries.
Source: World Health Organization (2020b); data for individual UK nations are taken from the UK government (2020) website and include deaths within 28 days of a positive test. These figures are therefore not directly comparable with those from the WHO.

Data suggest that lockdown in the United Kingdom was implemented comparatively late and at a time when the virus had already spread throughout the country. As shown in Figure 12.3, the United Kingdom had a higher number of deaths and COVID-19 infections per 100,000 population at the time of lockdown than many neighboring countries in Europe. It should, however, be strongly emphasized that this analysis comes with the important caveat that comparing deaths and cases between countries is difficult because of the different ways countries classify COVID-19 deaths and the fact that case numbers partly reflect the extent of testing. A former government advisor has nevertheless suggested that the death toll in the United Kingdom could have been reduced "by at least half" had a mandatory lockdown been introduced a week earlier ("Coronavirus: 'Earlier Lockdown Would Have Halved Death Toll,'" 2020). The timing of lockdown came eighteen days after the first death in England, nine days after the first death in Scotland, and eight days after the first death in Wales (Centre on Constitutional Change, 2020). The number of COVID-19 deaths per 100,000 population at this time was almost twice as high in England compared to the other UK nations, although cases per 100,000 population were highest in Wales (see Figure 12.3). The comparatively later lockdown may partly have contributed to England having the worst excess death toll in the United Kingdom.

On May 10th, 2020, the United Kingdom government announced a roadmap for releasing lockdown restrictions in England in a phased manner. The public health messaging was changed from "Stay home, protect the NHS, save lives," to "Stay alert, control the virus, save lives," a slogan that received criticism from the public and the media, who felt it was confusing and lacked clarity. The new slogan was rejected by the devolved administrations, who also announced divergent plans to ease lockdown restrictions at a slower pace than England because of concerns that deaths and infection rates were still too high (Fancourt et al., 2020). These actions reduced public confidence in the UK government's ability to manage the pandemic, while trust in devolved administrations remained high (Fancourt et al., 2020). Public confidence fell further in late May 2020 after it was revealed a key government advisor had broken lockdown rules but would not be resigning (Fancourt et al., 2020). Fancourt et al. (2020) have posited that levels of trust in government will affect "people's willingness to follow rules and guidelines" in the event of future waves.

By the end of July 2020, most nonessential business in the United Kingdom were open, with some exceptions (e.g., cinemas and theatres), although schools had not fully reopened for all pupils to return. Local lockdowns had also been imposed in areas of England and Scotland reporting high infection rates, with less stringent measures taken in others (DHSC, 2020d). In England, criticisms have been raised that local measures (e.g., a local lockdown in the city of Leicester) were often dictated by central government with little consultation and coordination with local governments, creating "confusion" as to why measures had been taken and whether they were "desirable or practical" (Association of Directors of Public Health, 2020). Local public health experts have also voiced concerns that they have had insufficient early access to local-level data held on national databases that would have allowed them to pre-empt and respond to local outbreaks effectively (Stone, 2020).

Self-isolation and quarantine measures directed at travelers were also put in place in an effort to contain virus transmission. In January and February 2020 these targeted people returning from Wuhan and Hubei Provinces in China, followed by other high-risk areas in Asia and Italy. Returning travelers from other countries with known outbreaks were also asked to isolate if they developed symptoms as well as close contacts of confirmed cases. Whole genome sequencing subsequently confirmed that a very small proportion of cases in the United Kingdom originated from China, with most originating from France and Spain, which were not subject to quarantine restrictions (Pybus et al., 2020). UK borders were never officially closed. It was not until the start of the "delay" phase on March 12, 2020, that anyone with COVID-19 symptoms, regardless of whether they had recently been in a high-risk area, was told to self-isolate for seven days. COVID-19 symptoms were classified as a continuous cough or fever, a narrower range of symptoms than those included in WHO guidance (2020c), which likely reduced the number of people who felt they had to self-isolate and get a test. UK guidance was not updated until May 18, 2020, when they were amended to include loss of sense of smell or taste as symptoms.

Guidance on the public wearing cloth masks has evolved slowly during the pandemic, from being recommended in early May 2020, becoming mandatory on public transport in mid-June 2020 in England and Scotland (July in Wales), and finally compulsory in shops in July 2020 (August in Northern Ireland), with people subject to a £100 fine if they do not comply (Rajan & Curry, 2020). Conversely, those working in close contact settings such as hairdressers were advised by the government to wear a visor or a face shield rather than a cloth mask. Despite officially being mandatory in many indoor settings, approximately 70 percent of the population reported using cloth masks in indoor public spaces, as of this writing (Le Page et al., 2020).

Measures in the Health Sector

The United Kingdom entered the COVID-19 crisis with among the lowest number of acute care beds per population among comparable health systems in Europe, and shortages of health and social care workers in all four countries (European Commission, OECD, and European Observatory on Health Systems and Policies, 2019; Gershlick & Charlesworth, 2019; Rolewicz & Palmer, 2019). The devolved health systems took similar measures to create extra capacity in NHS hospitals by freeing up beds through the postponement of all nonurgent elective operations and discharging medically fit patients into the community (Hignett et al., 2020). The latter measure proved controversial as many patients were discharged into care homes without being tested or isolating as this was not required by government guidance at the time, potentially seeding the virus to the most vulnerable communities. Several temporary hospitals were also built in major cities to provide surge capacity (Day, 2020), while NHS England took over private sector hospitals and staff in England for the duration of the crisis (NHS England and Improvement, 2020b). Although hospital bed shortages were predicted during the crisis, this generally did not materialize everywhere; it is unclear to what extent this was because of the combined measures or the rate of epidemic growth in different regions. The availability of health workers was initially maintained by encouraging retired and inactive health workers to return to work, extending visas of foreign-trained professionals, and speeding up licensing procedures for newly qualified nursing and medical graduates (Rajan & Curry, 2020).

One area that has proved particularly challenging during the COVID-19 outbreak has been the procurement and supply of adequate personal protective equipment (PPE). Although some difficulties inevitably result from having to compete on a global market where supply has been limited, procurement inefficiencies have exacerbated these issues. Criticisms in particular have been raised over emergency contracts for the supply and distribution of PPE in England being awarded to private companies with little experience in the area, some of whom initially failed to deliver on targets (McKee, 2020). The United Kingdom also opted not to join an EU procurement scheme to bulk-buy PPE and other equipment, despite being invited

TABLE 12.1. The Office for Budget Responsibility estimates of the costs (billions £) of various COVID-19 policy interventions in the United Kingdom 2020–2021

	2020–2021
Total	192.3
Public services spending	18.8
Employment support	62.2
Business support: loans and guarantees	20.0
Business support: tax and spending	30.2
Welfare spending measures	9.3
Other tax measures	1.7
Summer Economic Update: Plan for Jobs measures	19.8
Summer Economic Update: Other measures	30.4

Source: Office for Budget Responsibility, 2020.

Note: The table shows costs to the Exchequer (i.e., how much a measure will raise public sector borrowing) for measures announced up until July 14, 2020.

to participate (Boffey & Booth, 2020). Inadequate supply of PPE early in the crisis potentially contributed to spreading the virus in hospitals and care homes, leading to deaths among staff, patients, and residents (McKee, 2020). It should nevertheless be noted that after spending an estimated £15 billion to procure PPE (Office for Budget Responsibility, 2020), as of this writing, supply is reported to be adequate, and stockpiles are in place ahead of an expected second wave.

Social Policy Measures

The UK government implemented an unprecedented array of social policy measures to support jobs, public services, and the most vulnerable through the COVID-19 pandemic. The Office for Budget Responsibility (OBR, 2020) estimates that COVID-19 health and social policy measures taken through July 14, 2020) will cost £192.3[1] billion in 2020 and 2021 (see Table 12.1), approximately 8.8 percent of national income. Some social policy decisions such as on education are devolved matters, and devolved administrations can determine how funding for these areas is spent (Paun, 2020).

A large focus of social policy measures has been on protecting incomes and supporting jobs. A coronavirus job retention scheme was implemented, which saw the government paying a proportion of the wages of workers furloughed as a result of lockdown from April to October 2020, with a separate Self-Employment Income Support Scheme (SEISS) launched in May 2020 for the self-employed. Up to July 5, 2020, 9.4 million jobs had been furloughed, costing an estimated £27.4 billion, with 2.7 million SEISS claims made, at a cost of £7.7 billion (OBR, 2020). A £1.25 billion coronavirus package to protect firms driving innovation in the United Kingdom was also launched. In recognition that young people often bear the brunt of recessions, the government launched a £2 billion "Kickstart" Scheme to fund six-month job placements for sixteen- to twenty-four-year-olds, with a further £1.6 billion invested in expanding job support schemes, training, and apprenticeships (HM Treasury, 2020a).

Schools in the United Kingdom closed to most pupils on March 23, 2020, although they remained open for children of key workers and vulnerable students (e.g., those eligible for free school meals). To ensure disadvantaged students do not fall behind in their learning, a "£1 billion COVID-19 "catch-up" package to directly tackle the impact of lost teaching time" was launched in England (Department for Education, 2020). Devolved governments and the UK government in England also agreed to provide free school meals to vulnerable children through the summer following a highly publicized campaign spearheaded by charities and celebrities.

To help adherence to shielding requirements, £900 million was allocated for local authorities to distribute a weekly food package to the most clinically vulnerable. An additional £63 million was allocated in June to help those struggling to afford food (Ministry of Housing, Communities and Local Government, 2020a). Changes have been made to welfare payments, with universal credit and working tax credits rising by £20 each per week on a temporary basis to strengthen the social safety net for vulnerable people. Overall, an estimated extra £6.5 billion has been provided through the welfare system to support those most in need through the crisis.

Local authorities have found temporary accommodation for more than 90 percent of homeless people sleeping without shelter to help reduce transmission of the virus (Ministry of Housing, Communities and Local Government, 2020b). An additional £85 million was later committed to help homeless people move into more secure, long-term accommodation and to access training and employment opportunities. To support low-income renters, the Local Housing Allowance (a government housing benefit) was increased to cover 30 percent of market rents in each area for twelve months, with the initiative costing an estimated £1 billion (HM Treasury, 2020b). Emergency legislation was also implemented to prevent landlords from evicting tenants for a 3-month period during lockdown and to provide mortgage holidays for those unable to make payments.

Even before lockdown, travel by rail decreased by 70 percent compared to the same time in 2019 as people adhered to physical distancing recommendations (Department for Transport, 2020a). To ensure railways could continue to operate to transport key workers and vital supplies, the government agreed to take on all revenue and cost risk for six months, at an estimated cost of over £3 billion. Emergency funds of £1.6 billion were also allocated to Transport for London, although conditions tied to the bailout such as removing free travel for those people over sixty and under eighteen years of age have been criticized for penalizing some of the most vulnerable groups. More than £2 billion of spending on cycling and walking infrastructure has also been brought forward, including £250 million for local authorities to fund "pop-up" infrastructure to facilitate physical distancing (Department for Transport, 2020b).

Why Did This Happen?

There are no simple answers as to why the United Kingdom fared so badly during the COVID-19 pandemic, and it will likely take years for the full picture to emerge. Nonetheless, we can already see that certain policy choices such as the late decisions to lock down and delays in scaling up test and trace capacity have likely proved consequential. Just as important, the virus has exposed long-standing systemic issues in the United Kingdom resulting from a weakening of public services and the welfare state in recent decades and failure to address persistent economic and ethnicity-related inequalities that have undermined the country's resilience and ability to respond to emergencies.

Some of these issues can be traced back to 2010, when the Conservative-led coalition government of the time announced a policy of austerity that would last for the next decade. During this period, the role of the state was diminished in favor of increased marketization, with public spending falling from 42 percent of GDP in 2009–2010 to 35 percent in 2018–2019 (Marmot, 2020). These cuts were regressive with the poorest individuals in the most deprived, working-class areas disproportionately affected (Gray & Barford, 2018). Reduced government spending was stated as being necessary to eliminate the government's budget deficit and reduce national debt in the aftermath of the 2008–2009 economic crisis but was also a political choice in support of neoliberalist policies favoring limited state intervention, free markets, and limited protection for workers (Bailey, 2013; Farnsworth & Irving, 2018). Indeed, the United Nations' Humans Rights Council (UN HRC) concluded that austerity in the United Kingdom is "a policy pursued more as an ideological than an economic agenda" and one that "has badly damaged" the country's social safety net (United Nations Human Rights Council, 2019). Austerity harkened back to the era of Thatcherism in the 1970s and 1980s, which began the process of privatizing state-run industries, deregulating financial markets, and diminishing the "cradle-to-grave" welfare state (of which the NHS was perhaps the crowning achievement) that had been created by the post-war Labour government.

Under austerity, public spending was cut by 3 percent in real terms in just the first five years; welfare, with real-term reductions in budgets of 30 percent, and local government, with cuts of more than 50 percent, were hardest hit (Gray & Barford, 2018). In England, these cuts came at the same time that the Health and Social Care Act 2012 transferred responsibility for the delivery of most public health services to local authorities (DHSC, 2012). Strategic Health Authorities, which were responsible for improving regional health services and played a key role in local planning for emergencies, were also abolished. Public Health England, which took over responsibilities previously coordinated by the NHS was also created, although its budget was ultimately cut by 40 percent in real terms from 2012 to 2019 (Marmot et al., 2020).

These reforms, in combination with significant underfunding, led to a substantial weakening of local public health structures, something preeminent public health experts warned at the time would curtail the country's ability to respond to a pandemic (Horti, 2020). Public health infrastructure has been lost with, for example, the number of public sector labs being reduced from thirty, two decades previously, to just eight pre-crisis (Rajan & Curry, 2020). The public health workforce was also reduced, leading to an institutional loss of knowledge on how to deal with pandemics at the national and local level. Ten years later, this loss of staff and infrastructure had significant repercussions for the United Kingdom's pandemic response, including contributing to difficulties in rapidly scaling up testing and contact-tracing capabilities. It is also possible that the weakening of local departments to some extent necessitated the centralization of certain programs (e.g., test and trace) during the pandemic.

Under austerity, NHS budgets grew at less than half the historical average (The King's Fund, 2019), contributing (albeit not solely) to a critical shortage of beds and staff before the crisis. This necessitated the implementation of unprecedented actions to rapidly scale-up surge capacity. Some of these actions, such as discharging people to care homes without testing, have likely contributed to the United Kingdom's high death toll. It should also be stressed that social care has been substantially underfunded over a number of decades and has no single representative or unifying body other than the Care Quality Commission that regulates it, leading to a lack of resilience to cope with the coronavirus crisis.

COVID-19 has also exposed and amplified existing economic and ethnic inequalities in the United Kingdom, with death rates disproportionately higher for those in deprived areas and for some ethnic minority groups (National Records of Scotland, 2020; Office for National Statistics, 2020b). These interrelated inequalities have placed these groups at greater risk of exposure to infection, partly because of a higher likelihood of working essential jobs that cannot be done at home, using public transport and living in overcrowded, multi-generational households (Bibby et al., 2020). Socioeconomic inequalities have also been linked to higher rates of pre-existing health conditions that raise the risk of COVID-19 complications (Marmot et al., 2020). Although a commitment to tackle health inequalities has been on the political agenda in the United Kingdom since the late 1990s, they have persisted and widened in recent years under austerity (Marmot et al., 2020). A recent report by PHE has also suggested that inequalities for ethnic minorities are linked to structural racism and discrimination, which have reduced life chances and access to public services for certain groups (Public Health England, 2020b).

The persistence of these inequalities in the United Kingdom is perhaps unsurprising given that wealth and power in Britain's majority white and highly class-based society has for centuries been concentrated in the hands of relatively few wealthy and largely upper-class individuals. These "elites" have shaped and continue to shape institutions, make laws, run the economy, and set the agenda for public debate and political discourse, thereby ensuring their wealth, power, and influence is maintained. Although economic inequalities were reduced during the post-war years, they widened substantially following economic reforms in the 1980s. Efforts to reduce the United Kingdom's inequalities and poverty levels, which are relatively high for a Western European country, have stalled under austerity because of wage stagnation and welfare cuts for the poorest at a time when wages for the top earners have increased (United Nations Human Rights Council, 2019). The precarious financial situation of many households amplified the need for multifaceted social policies during the crisis to protect a vulnerable population. In spite of these measures, however, those with the lowest incomes are reported to be three times less likely to self-isolate when required than higher earners, which has implications for reducing transmission, in particular in more deprived areas (Atchison et al., 2020).

Although many of the issues that have impeded delivery of an effective crisis stem from weakened systems and demographics, policy decisions made during the COVID-19 response also must be examined. Lockdown, for example, was implemented a week after the Scientific Advisory Group for Emergencies (SAGE) gave advice to do so and cloth masks only made mandatory a month after initially being recommended (Allegretti, 2020; SAGE, 2020). Although this may result from a natural lag in decision-making, hesitation in implementing mandatory physical distancing measures may also have been influenced by the liberalist-leanings of the Conservative cabinet, who have traditionally opposed the "nanny-state" and prefer to limit state interference in personal choices (Raynor, 2019). We should note that, although allegations have been made that lockdown delays were due to an initial strategy of developing "herd immunity," it has been strenuously denied this was ever official policy (Gallardo, 2020).

The top-down-approach to decision-making during the pandemic and lack of coordination between central and local government in England is another area of the United Kingdom's response that has been scrutinized. The Association of Directors of Public Health, for example, has called the top-down-approach to governing "costly," stating that local public health experts have been sidelined and suggesting that a lack of communication and data sharing between central and local government has created confusion over why and how local measures should be implemented (Association of Directors of Public Health, 2020). This top-down approach to governing risks undermining local adherence to public health measures if there is confusion as to which measures are in place where, and if some areas are viewed as being unfairly targeted with restrictions. This may in particular be the case if local areas are placed under lockdown without additional fiscal and social policy measures being put in place to support businesses and individual livelihoods.

Conclusion

Calls have already been made for a public inquiry into the United Kingdom's response to COVID-19 to identify mistakes that have been made and to learn lessons for the future (McKee et al., 2020). This will inevitably unearth more information on why certain decisions over the implementation of health and social policy responses were made (or not made) than we know at this time. Yet, even with some uncertainty around what has happened so far, it remains possible to untangle some key lessons that can help the country prepare for a possible second wave and to build a more resilient economy and national health systems in the longer-term.

First, it is fundamental that a functioning test and trace system is put in place ahead of a predicted second wave. At the time of writing, the government's NHS test and trace system in England, which will cost an estimated £10 billion, is failing to test, trace, and isolate a sufficient number of people at speed to suppress the spread of the virus. Strengthening partnerships with local authorities to enhance their capacity to deliver test and trace functions at the local level, will likely be needed to help manage future outbreaks. This will also enable systems to be designed with the specific needs of the local population in mind (e.g., delivering non-English language or culturally specific services) and will be better placed to support people to isolate, something which is essential to break the chain of transmission. Overall, greater coordination and communication between central and local government on all aspects of the public health response are needed to avoid policy missteps and to improve local implementation of and adherence to policy actions.

Perhaps one of the biggest lessons to learn from the United Kingdom is that stable and adequate investment in public health and wider health services is needed to help build health system resilience to ensure it can cope with catastrophic events. Cuts to public health under austerity and sustained underfunding of the NHS over decades have likely proved to be a "false economy" (Middleton & Williams, 2019), with injections of emergency funding now required to ensure the health system can respond to the challenges posed by COVID-19 and to help health services return to normal (or the new normal) in the longer term. It is important that the NHS learns quickly from the rapid measures put in place during the crisis to learn which approaches (e.g., an expansion of digital health services or different care pathways) may support delivery of more effective care. Improving health system resilience should be the goal moving forward to ensure the health services of all four nations can meet any future challenges (Thomas et al., 2020). Providing extra funding to the health sector (including public health) should not be seen as a cost, but as a strategic investment that will contribute to improving the health of the nation, something which is essential for a well-performing economy (Boyce & Brown, 2019). A significant overhaul of the organization and funding of social care and public health systems and their respective abilities to work with the NHS will also be needed to ensure that both are fit to meet future population care needs.

Finally, the pandemic has exposed entrenched economic and ethnic inequalities in the United Kingdom. Although the virus is still with us, it is important that local authorities in the most deprived areas are given additional funding to protect their communities. There is also now a risk that the economic recession that is likely forthcoming will exacerbate these inequalities in the future. Rather than a return to austerity as happened in the aftermath of the last financial crisis, sustained investment in strengthening public services and providing secure and good-quality housing would help make society and the economy more resilient in the longer term. The pandemic has shown the value of strong state intervention in terms of protecting the economy, jobs, and the most vulnerable. This should be harnessed in the future to help provide good quality education and better-quality jobs for all, as well as to implement a comprehensive social protection system that can help reduce poverty and vulnerability. Reducing inequalities will be fundamental to promote prosperity and health and well-being in the future.

Note

1. Money is distributed to devolved nations based on the "Barnett formula," which allocates money according to population and the comparability of services in each nation.

References

Allegretti, A. (2020, July 16). Coronavirus: SAGE urged government to lockdown a week earlier, UK's chief scientific adviser says. *Sky News.* https://news.sky.com/story/coronavirus-sage-urged-govt-to-lockdown-a-week-earlier-uks-chief-scientific-adviser-says-12029956

Association of Directors of Public Health. (2020). *House of Lords Public Services Committee Inquiry—Lessons from coronavirus.* https://committees.parliament.uk/writtenevidence/8105/pdf/

Atchison, C. J., Bowman, L., Vrinten, C., Redd, R., Pristera, P., Eaton, J. W., & Ward, H. (2020). Perceptions and behavioural responses of the general public during the COVID-19 pandemic: A cross-sectional survey of UK Adults. *medRxiv*, https://doi.org/10.1101/2020.04.01.20050039

Bailey, D. (2013). David Cameron's speech this week revealed the neoliberal undercurrents of state austerity. *British Politics and Policy, LSE.* https://blogs.lse.ac.uk/politicsandpolicy/david-cameron-and-the-neoliberal-undercurrents-of-state-austerity/

Bibby, J., Everest, G., & Abbs, I. (2020). *Will COVID 19 be a watershed moment for health inequalities?* The Health Foundation. https://www.health.org.uk/publications/long-reads/will-covid-19-be-a-watershed-moment-for-health-inequalities

Boffey, D., & Booth, D. (2020). *UK missed three chances to join EU scheme to bulk-buy PPE. Health Policy.* The Guardian. https://www.theguardian.com/world/2020/apr/13/uk-missed-three-chances-to-join-eu-scheme-to-bulk-buy-ppe

Boyce, T., & Brown, C. (2019). *Economic and social impacts and benefits of health systems.* WHO/Europe. https://www.euro.who.int/__data/assets/pdf_file/0006/395718/Economic-Social-Impact-Health-FINAL.pdf?ua=1

Centre on Constitutional Change. (2020). *Covid-19 excess deaths: A comparison between Scotland and England/Wales.* https://www.centreonconstitutionalchange.ac.uk/news-and-opinion/covid-19-excess-deaths-comparison

Coronavirus: 'Earlier lockdown would have halved death toll.' (2020, June 10). BBC News. https://www.bbc.co.uk/news/health-52995064

Crozier, A., Mckee, M., & Rajan, S. (2020, October 15). Fixing England's COVID-19 response: Learning from international experience. *Journal of the Royal Society of Medicine.*

Day, M. (2020). Covid-19: Nightingale hospitals set to shut down after seeing few patients. *BMJ*, 369, m1860. https://www.bmj.com/content/369/bmj.m1860

Department for Education, Prime Minister's Office. (2020, June 19). *Billion pound Covid catch-up plan to tackle impact of lost teaching time* [Press release]. https://www.gov.uk/government/news/billion-pound-covid-catch-up-plan-to-tackle-impact-of-lost-teaching-time

Department for Transport. (2020a). Rail emergency measures during the COVID-19 pandemic [Written statement to Parliament]. https://www.gov.uk/government/speeches/rail-emergency-measures-during-the-covid-19-pandemic

Department for Transport, Office for Low Emission Vehicles. (2020b). *£2 billion package to create new era for cycling and walking.* https://www.gov.uk/government/news/2-billion-package-to-create-new-era-for-cycling-and-walking

Department of Health and Social Care. (2012). Health and Social Care Act 2012. https://www.legislation.gov.uk/ukpga/2012/7/contents/enacted

Department of Health and Social Care. (2020a). *Coronavirus action plan: A guide to what you can expect across the UK. Policy Paper.* GOV.UK. https://www.gov.uk/government/publications/coronavirus-action-plan/coronavirus-action-plan-a-guide-to-what-you-can-expect-across-the-uk

Department of Health and Social Care. (2020b, April 4). *COVID-19: Scaling up our testing programmes.* GOV.UK. https://assets.publishing.service.gov.uk/government/uploads/system/uploads/attachment_data/file/878121/coronavirus-covid-19-testing-strategy.pdf

Department of Health and Social Care. (2020c). *NHS Test and Trace statistics (England): 16 July to 22 July 2020.* Transparency data. https://www.gov.uk/government/publications/nhs-test-and-trace-statistics-england-16-july-to-22-july-2020

Department of Health and Social Care. (2020d). *Plans for managing the coronavirus (COVID-19) outbreak in Leicester.* https://www.gov.uk/government/speeches/local-action-to-tackle-coronavirus

European Centre for Disease Prevention and Control. (2020). *Situation dashboard—COVID-19 cases in Europe and Worldwide.* Retrieved August 31, 2020, from https://qap.ecdc.europa.eu/public/extensions/COVID-19/COVID-19.html

European Commission, OECD, European Observatory on Health Systems and Policies. (2019). *State of health in the EU: United Kingdom.* https://ec.europa.eu/health/sites/health/files/state/docs/2019_chp_uk_english.pdf

Excess mortality during the COVID-19 pandemic. (2020). Financial Times. https://github.com/Financial-Times/coronavirus-excess-mortality-data

FactCheckNI. (2020). *How has COVID-19 contributed to excess deaths in Northern Ireland?* https://factcheckni.org/articles/how-has-covid-19-contributed-to-excess-deaths-in-northern-ireland/

Fancourt, D., Steptoe, A., & Wright, L. (2020). The Cummings effect: Politics, trust, and behaviours during the COVID-19 pandemic. *The Lancet.* https://doi.org/10.1016/S0140-6736(20)31690-1

Farnsworth, K., & Irving, Z. (2018). Austerity: Neoliberal dreams come true? *Critical Social Policy*, 38(3), 461–481.

Gallardo, C. (2020). *Herd immunity was never UK's corona strategy, chief scientific adviser says.* Politico.EU. https://www.politico.eu/article/herd-immunity-was-never-uk-coronavirus-strategy-chief-scientific-adviser-says/

Gershlick, B., & Charlesworth, A. (2019). *Health and social care workforce priorities for the new government.* Health Foundation. https://www.health.org.uk/publications/long-reads/health-and-social-care-workforce

Global Health Security Index. (2019). *Building collective action and accountability.* John Hopkins Bloomberg School of Public Health, NTI and The Economist. https://www.ghsindex.org/wp-content/uploads/2020/04/2019-Global-Health-Security-Index.pdf

Gray, M., & Barford, A. (2018). The depths of the cuts: The uneven geography of local government austerity. *Cambridge Journal of Regions, Economy and Society, 11*(3), 541–563.

HM Treasury. (2020a). *Chancellor provides over £14 billion for our NHS and vital public services.* https://www.gov.uk/government/news/chancellor-provides-over-14-billion-for-our-nhs-and-vital-public-services

HM Treasury. (2020b). *The Chancellor Rishi Sunak provides an updated statement on coronavirus* [Speech]. https://www.gov.uk/government/speeches/the-chancellor-rishi-sunak-provides-an-updated-statement-on-coronavirus

Hignett, K., Serle, J., & Moore, A. (2020). NHS to free up 30,000 beds for coronavirus. *Health Service Journal.* https://www.hsj.co.uk/free-for-non-subscribers/nhs-to-free-up-30000-beds-for-coronavirus/7027148.article

Hine, D. (2010). *The 2009 Influenza Pandemic An independent review of the UK response to the 2009 influenza pandemic.* Cabinet Office. https://www.gov.uk/government/publications/independent-review-into-the-response-to-the-2009-swine-flu-pandemic

Horti, S. (2020, May 29). *Experts warned Cameron's government the Lansley reforms would hobble Britain's epidemic response.* New Statesman. https://www.newstatesman.com/2020/05/cameron-government-pandemic-NHS-reforms-lansley-health-social-care-act

House of Lords. (2020). *UK preparedness for Covid-19: Lords scrutiny of the 2009 swine flu pandemic.* https://lordslibrary.parliament.uk/infocus/uk-preparedness-for-covid-19-lords-scrutiny-of-the-2009-swine-flu-pandemic/

Johns Hopkins University Center for Systems Science and Engineering. (2020). *COVID-19 data repository.* https://github.com/CSSEGISandData/COVID-19

The King's Fund. (2019). The Department for Health and Social Care's Budget. https://www.kingsfund.org.uk/projects/nhs-in-a-nutshell/nhs-budget

Le Page, M., Wilson, C., Hamzelou, J., Vaughan, A., Quilty-Harper, C., & Liverpool, L. (2020). Covid-19 news: Rising cases in England delay easing of restrictions. *New Scientist.* https://www.newscientist.com/article/2237475-covid-19-news-rising-cases-in-england-delay-easing-of-restrictions/#ixzz6TyrID8BQ

Mahase, E. (2020a). Covid-19: Local health teams trace eight times more contacts than national service, *BMJ, 369,* m2486.

Mahase, E. (2020b). Covid-19: UK holds off closing schools and restricts testing to people in hospital. *BMJ, 368,* m1060.

Marmot, M. (2020). *Why did England have Europe's worst Covid figures? The answer starts with austerity.* The Guardian. https://www.theguardian.com/commentisfree/2020/aug/10/england-worst-covid-figures-austerity-inequality

Marmot, M., Allen, J., Boyce, T., Goldblatt, P., & Morrison, J. (2020). *Health equity in England: The Marmot Review 10 years on.* Institute for Health Equity. https://www.health.org.uk/publications/reports/the-marmot-review-10-years-on

McKee, M. (2020). England's PPE procurement failures must never happen again. *BMJ, 370*, m2858.

McKee, M., Gill, M., & Wollaston, S. (2020). Public inquiry into UK's response to covid-19 [Editorial]. *BMJ, 369*, m2052.

Middleton, J., & Williams, G. A. (2019). *England in organization and financing of public health services in Europe country reports.* World Health Organization 2018. https://www.euro.who.int/__data/assets/pdf_file/0011/370946/public-health-services.pdf%3Fua%3D1

Ministry of Housing, Communities and Local Government, Department for Environment, Food & Rural Affairs, Department for Work and Pensions. (2020a). *£63 million for local authorities to assist those struggling to afford food and other essentials* [Press release]. https://www.gov.uk/government/news/63-million-for-local-authorities-to-assist-those-struggling-to-afford-food-and-other-essentials

Ministry of Housing, Communities and Local Government. (2020b). *6,000 new supported homes as part of landmark commitment to end rough sleeping* [Press release]. https://www.gov.uk/government/news/6-000-new-supported-homes-as-part-of-landmark-commitment-to-end-rough-sleeping

Morris, C., & Barnes, O. (2020). *Coronavirus: How England lags behind other UK nations on testing.* BBC News. https://www.bbc.co.uk/news/52149297

NHS England and Improvement. (2020a). Caring for people at highest risk during COVID-19 incident. [Letter to all NHS medical and nursing directors from the Chief Nursing Officer and National Medical Director, NHS England and Improvement]. https://www.england.nhs.uk/coronavirus/wp-content/uploads/sites/52/2020/03/2020-03-21-COVID-19-at-risk-Trust-letter_FINAL.pdf

NHS England and Improvement. (2020b). *NHS strikes major deal to expand hospital capacity to battle coronavirus.* https://www.england.nhs.uk/2020/03/nhs-strikes-major-deal-to-expand-hospital-capacity-to-battle-coronavirus/

National Records of Scotland. (2020, June). *Analysis of deaths involving coronavirus (COVID-19) in Scotland, by ethnic group.* Data to June 14, 2020. https://www.nrscotland.gov.uk/files//statistics/covid19/ethnicity-deceased-covid-19-june20.pdf

Office for Budget Responsibility. (2020). *Coronavirus analysis.* http://obr.uk/coronavirus-analysis/

Office for National Statistics. (2020a). Comparisons of all-cause mortality between European countries and regions: January to June 2020. https://www.ons.gov.uk/peoplepopulationandcommunity/birthsdeathsandmarriages/deaths/articles/comparisonsofallcausemortalitybetweeneuropeancountriesandregions/januarytojune2020

Office for National Statistics. (2020b). *Deaths involving COVID-19 by local area and socioeconomic deprivation: Deaths occurring between 1 March and 30 June 2020.* Statistical Bulletin. https://www.ons.gov.uk/peoplepopulationandcommunity/birthsdeathsandmarriages/deaths/bulletins/deathsinvolvingcovid19bylocalareasanddeprivation/deathsoccurringbetween1marchand30june2020#english-index-of-multiple-deprivation

Paun, A., Shuttleworth, K., Nice, A., & Sargeant, J. (2020). *Coronavirus and devolution.* Institute for Government. https://www.instituteforgovernment.org.uk/explainers/coronavirus-and-devolution

Public Health England. (2020a). *Excess Mortality in England, week ending 17 July 2020.* Experimental Statistics. https://fingertips.phe.org.uk/static-reports/mortality-surveillance/excess-mortality-in-england-latest.html

Public Health England. (2020b). *Beyond the data: Understanding the impact of COVID-19 on BAME groups.* https://assets.publishing.service.gov.uk/government/uploads/system/uploads/attachment_data/file/892376/COVID_stakeholder_engagement_synthesis_beyond_the_data.pdf

Pybus, O., Rambau, A., du Plessis, L., Zarebski, A. E., Kraemer M. U. G., Raghwani, J., Gutiérrez, B., Hill, V., McCrone, J., Colquhoun, R., Jackson, B., O'Toole, Á., & Ashworth, J., on behalf of the COG-UK consortium. (2020). Preliminary analysis of SARS-CoV-2 importation & establishment of UK transmission lineages. https://virological.org/t/preliminary-analysis-of-sars-cov-2-importation-establishment-of-uk-transmission-lineages/507

Rajan, S., & Curry, N. *United Kingdom. Health System and Response Monitor.* European Observatory on Healthy Systems and Policies, European Commission, WHO/Europe. https://www.covid19healthsystem.org/countries/unitedkingdom/countrypage.aspx

Rajan, S., Cylus, J., & Mckee, M. (2020). What do countries need to do to implement effective 'find, test, trace, isolate and support' systems? *Journal of the Royal Society of Medicine, 113*(7), 245–250.

Raynor, G. (2019). Boris Johnson aims to put end to the "nanny state" and its "sin taxes" on food. *The Telegraph.* https://www.telegraph.co.uk/politics/2019/07/02/boris-johnson-aims-put-end-nanny-state-sin-taxes-food/

Ritchie, H. (2020). Google Mobility Trends: How has the pandemic changed the movement of people around the world? *Our World In Data.* https://ourworldindata.org/covid-mobility-trends

Rolewicz, L., & Palmer, B. (2019). *The NHS workforce in numbers: Facts on staffing and staff shortages in England*. Explainer. Nuffield Trust. https://www.nuffieldtrust.org.uk/public/resource/the-nhs-workforce-in-numbers

Scientific Advisory Group for Emergencies. (2020). *SAGE 27 minutes: Coronavirus (COVID-19) response, 21 April 2020.* https://assets.publishing.service.gov.uk/government/uploads/system/uploads/attachment_data/file/888799/S0396_Twenty-seventh_SAGE_meeting_on_Covid-19.pdf

Stone, J. (2020). *Government hindering Covid response by ignoring councils and failing to share data, MPs told.* Independent. https://www.independent.co.uk/news/uk/politics/coronavirus-government-local-councils-data-leicester-peter-soulsby-a9689606.html

Tallack, C. (2020). *Understanding excess mortality: Comparing COVID-19's impact in the UK to other European countries.* The Health Foundation. https://www.health.org.uk/news-and-comment/charts-and-infographics/comparing-covid-19-impact-in-the-uk-to-european-countries

Thomas, S., Sagan, A., Larkin, J., Cylus, J., Figueras, J., & Karanikolos, M. (2020). *Strengthening health systems resilience: Key concepts and strategies.* Policy Brief 36. World Health Organization. https://apps.who.int/iris/bitstream/handle/10665/332441/Policy-brief%2036-1997-8073-eng.pdf

United Nations Human Rights Council. (2019). *Report of the Special Rapporteur on extreme poverty and human rights on his visit to the United Kingdom of Great Britain and Northern Ireland.* Agenda item 3, Forty-first session General Assembly. 24 June–12 July 2019. https://undocs.org/pdf?symbol=en/A/HRC/41/39/Add.1

World Health Organization. (2020a). *Statement on the second meeting of the International Health Regulations (2005) Emergency Committee regarding the outbreak of novel coronavirus (2019-nCoV).* https://www.who.int/news-room/detail/30-01-2020-statement

-on-the-second-meeting-of-the-international-health-regulations-(2005)-emergency-committee-regarding-the-outbreak-of-novel-coronavirus-(2019-ncov)

World Health Organization. (2020b). *WHO Coronavirus Disease (COVID-19) Dashboard.* Retrieved August 31, 2020, from https://covid19.who.int

World Health Organization. (2020c). *Coronavirus symptoms.* https://www.who.int/health-topics/coronavirus#tab=tab_3

13 THE EUROPEAN UNION CONFRONTS COVID-19

Another European Rescue of the Nation-State?

Eleanor Brooks, Anniek de Ruijter, and Scott L. Greer

The politics of European Union (EU) health policy are also the politics of European integration. Debate about EU policies always entails debate about the appropriate role and powers granted to the EU. We ask what policy a member state might make, but, in the case of the EU, many ask if the EU should have a policy at all. Should it respond, and, if so, how and to whose benefit?

From some angles, the EU looks more like a federation, comparable to the United States or Germany. The EU is deeply entrenched in its citizens' lives. It has a powerful shared culture among leaders and strong, entrepreneurial, and state-like political institutions. Its legal system is entwined with member state law to such an extent that member state courts have driven legal integration and change as much as EU institutions, both in general (Alter, 1998; Mattli & Slaughter, 1998) and in health (Brooks, 2012; Greer & Rauscher, 2011a; Greer & Rauscher, 2011b; Obermaier, 2008, 2009).

From another angle, it still looks like an international organization, comparable to the World Health Organization (WHO) or a regional trade block such as the Association of Southeast Asian Nations or Mercosur. Like international organizations or confederations, though, the EU responds primarily to and is shaped by the demands of its member states. They have actively maintained this dichotomous structure so as to prevent transfer of power and loss of sovereignty. Member states ultimately determine the direction of the EU, and they have supported EU expansion only when they require a "European rescue of the nation state"—an opportunity to use the EU to solve problems they share (Milward, 1999). The EU's weak public health and social policy responses to the crisis reflect this effort on the part of member states to limit its role over the decades, whereas the major expansion in its role over the summer of 2020 reflects the perceived interests of member states, which now seek another European rescue of the nation state.

The roots of the EU's split personality can be found in its evolution as a market-building, economic community. It was built, historically, around the development of its internal market and supporting legal system, maintaining only a small staff, nonexistent coercive capacity, and a minimal budget. It began as a set of small treaty-based organizations, with the first focused on the regulation of the production and labor markets for coal and steel. Over time a market for nuclear power was formed, and then a much broader, economic community. The latter was based on a common market, with a central Common Agricultural Policy, and the background idea, after World War II, that Europe would never be hungry again.

Although efforts at political and social union have consistently followed along, the EU has developed, first and foremost, as an economic union, and for most member states the monetary union is also an important add-on to this membership. By contrast to the Weberian concept of the state, whose key characteristics are territory and coercion, this makes the EU primarily a "law-state" (Kelemen, 2019; Pavone & Kelemen, 2019; Strayer, 1970). Its main tool is deregulation and reregulation: actions to eliminate member state rules that might be discriminatory, and to create new, European rules that establish a floor for the relevant provisions (Majone, 1996). In this, it has developed much stronger powers over its member governments' regulations than comparable federations possess. For example, EU regulation of the recognition of medical professional qualifications is much stronger than the equivalent regimes in Australia, Canada, or the United States (Matthijs et al., 2019). Once the regulation is established, national courts, for the purpose of enforcement of EU law, become "European courts." EU law can create direct rights and obligations for EU citizens (i.e., it has a direct effect), and EU law has supremacy over national rules. This is to ensure that EU law is applied similarly in all member states. Explicit defiance in one national court or by a member state would undercut the effectiveness of EU law, whether from the German constitutional court or Hungary's authoritarian regime, and thus poses a serious threat to the EU's existence.

This regulatory logic has expanded beyond the internal market to the EU's management of its unbalanced currency union. Rather than commit to serious redistribution between countries or citizens, as federations do, member states historically opted for harsher and harsher regulation of each other's fiscal policies, setting limits on debt and deficit, threatening sanctions where these are breached, and imposing conditions until a breach is remedied. This approach has created a structural north-south divergence because the Eurozone—the group of states that uses the euro as its currency—locks all of its member states into their trajectories and offers debtor states no way out, save for massive reductions in wages and investment (Hancké, 2013; Johnston, 2016). Many of the EU's internal tensions spring from this combination of weak redistribution, intense regulation, and an imbalanced currency union (Greer, 2020; Pérez, 2019). Those tensions appear likely to become more acute over time, creating more disparities, internal migration, and incentives for authoritarianism among peripheral governments that could not please their citizens.

European Union Public Health Policy Response

The EU policies in place on the eve of the COVID-19 crisis were governed by this basic, largely regulatory, structure (Greer & Kurzer, 2013; Greer et al., 2019).

Member states had limited the EU's public health policies and its disaster response role to, for the most part, that of an international organization (Treaty on the Functioning of the European Union, TFEU, Article 168). A small coordinating system, much of which was created in the aftermath of previous crises, included a health emergencies unit in the European Commission (although with no specific budget), a Health Security Committee of member state representatives, a joint purchasing scheme (de Ruijter, 2019), and a small European Centre for Disease Control and Prevention (Deruelle, 2016, 2020; Greer, 2012; Guigner, 2007). The elements of this public health system that were hosted by the EU enjoyed minimal resources, little recourse to coercion and limited scope, whereas the intergovernmental elements (namely the joint procurement mechanism) had greater potential but remained little more than a slow and voluntary buyer's club.

The civil protection system for disaster response, meanwhile, began to develop some effective mechanisms for addressing disasters within the EU. Built largely within the context of contributions to international disaster relief efforts, it had been more deeply institutionalized in 2019 with the addition of RescEU, a co-financed stockpile system holding resources such as firefighting equipment. However, this is primarily a matchmaking system. Rather than controlling resources, it maintains a list of member state resources that can be made available and would then pair these with requests for assistance from other states (e.g., deploying listed search-and-rescue teams to member states that had suffered earthquakes). It depends largely upon member state solidarity and does not function well where many states are suffering the same problems at the same time.

In sum, although the EU entered COVID-19 better prepared to coordinate than it had been when it faced the last pandemic, H1N1 influenza in 2009, its capabilities remained limited to below-the-surface activity and were secondary to national government responses. The EU's explicit health policies had, over the years, exercised an increasing normative influence on technical issues such as epidemiological case definition but the more important policies, and those where the EU exerted more state-like powers, were rooted in the law of the internal market. These exist in areas such as health workforce mobility, the integrated market in pharmaceuticals and medical devices, and cross-border consumption of health care, where health policy is made under the guise of facilitating the market's functioning. Although the EU's internal market law is less directly concerned with health, less immediately relevant to disaster relief, and has not positioned the EU to lead the public health response to COVID-19 (Hervey & McHale, 2015; Hervey et al., 2017), it was this set of powers that enabled the EU to step in and take a more forceful role as the coronavirus pandemic unfolded.

For the first few months of the COVID-19 crisis, March and April 2020 in particular, observers of the EU despaired, and most people justifiably paid the EU little attention. Member states had successfully ensured that it would not play a leadership role in a major health emergency, and it did not. The first responses of the member states showed that they, and their populations, expected national governments to play the leading role. This involved not only a failure to coordinate, or even to identify a shared agenda between member states, but also flamboyant exercises in national egotism. Border closures and bans on the export of key medical supplies to other EU member states were moves that attacked the core principles of European integration and the value of solidarity meant to underpin the project.

But although the EU as an international organization was forced to work below the radar, these market-distorting actions enabled the EU as a law-state to intervene. Under threat of infringement proceedings from the European Commission, border closures within the EU soon came to be accepted as pragmatic and temporary, and interference with trade in goods—the export bans—quickly began to be lifted. Member states could try to invoke the "public health" exception to EU law enumerated in Article 36 TFEU, but the Commission, in a stroke, redefined public health and transformed it from a member state justification for an exception, to an EU-level principle. To be permitted, export bans would have to show a contribution to EU-wide public health, and not just national public health, which they almost certainly would not be able to do. Thus, the result of the brief burst of national egotism was not decomposition but rather a redefinition of public health in EU law. If the Commission's redefinition sticks, public health will cease to be a member state-level exception and instead become a warrant for positive EU action (de Ruijter et al., 2020; Purnhagen et al., 2020).

The speed with which member states undid their export bans and started to coordinate their restrictions on travel suggested a realization of shared interest. In the same vein, and with the internal market defended, member state leaders soon turned to the EU to rescue them more broadly. They reactivated and reinforced RescEU, creating EU stockpiles of materials that could be shared with member states as needs arose—an achievement in itself given the global scarcity of resources relevant to handling COVID-19. RescEU is fully centralized (overseen by the Directorate General for Civil Protection) and can work with as few as one member state (to co-finance and house the given stockpile). The EU also began to activate its facilities for joint procurement. The Joint Procurement Agreement (JPA) was established in 2014 as part of the 2013 Health Threats Decision and provides for the collective purchasing of medicines, medical devices, and other goods or services, such as laboratory equipment or personal protective equipment, with sufficient financing to support high-volume purchases. Since COVID-19 struck, four calls for supplies have been launched and resources distributed to several member states.

However, whilst the revisions to RescEU increase its speed and flexibility, they do little to increase its budget. Although the existence of a joint procurement mechanisms is to be celebrated, the framework remains intergovernmental, voluntary, and rather too slow to respond to urgent needs (de Ruijter, 2019). What COVID-19 has made clear is that the EU's lack of distributive capacity, its position as "risk assessor" but not "risk manager," and its inability to act as much more than a platform for the supporting of national action hinders its ability to act in the collective interest. As the first wave of the virus has passed, the EU has capitalized on these obvious and salient shortcomings to propose a series of longer-term changes to its role in future health crises.

Chief among these is a new health program called EU4Health. It is a hasty redesign that reverses the pre-existing plans for EU health policy post-2020, which were to roll health into the much broader European Social Fund Plus and to earmark it just EUR 413 million (European Commission, 2018). EU4Health had a proposed budget for 2021 to 2027 of approximately EUR 10 billion and would prevail as a standalone instrument, with its own set of priorities. However, after several rounds of negotiation the budget was cut to EUR 5.1 billion, still a significant increase on the previous program, which was allocated just EUR 450 million. The priorities of EU4Health have been identified as protecting people from cross-border threats, improving the availability of medicines, and strengthening health systems. Cross-border health threats and health security have long been features of EU health programs—EU4Health being the fourth program since 2003—but are predictably highlighted and frontloaded in the new text. This focuses on building preparedness and response capacities, increasing surveillance and monitoring of threats, establishing EU level emergency expertise, and ensuring the availability of critical health supplies, among other related objectives. But the program also retains many of the "pre-crisis" agenda items that the steady expansion of the EU's health influence has been built upon. Tackling cancer and other noncommunicable diseases, reducing health inequalities, exchanging best practice on health promotion, and improving the accessibility and efficiency of health systems all remain, and these help to frame EU4Health as a well-rounded, holistic response to COVID-19. Although EU4Health is still a large expansion from the previous public health programs, it is clear that member states, even after a crisis, remain steadfast in their wish to not establish redistributive health programs to level access to health across EU member state borders.

The EU4Health program was published on May 28, 2020, and was followed less than three weeks later by an EU Vaccines Strategy. This again puts front and center the pressing need for a vaccine to fight COVID-19, establishing the possibility for EU-led Advance Purchase Agreements (APAs) with pharmaceutical companies that have a promising product in development. Beneath the surface, however, it also responds to weaknesses in the JPA and RescEU, giving the EU a more central role (in signing APAs on behalf of member states) and power to coordinate the supply and distribution of any resulting vaccine, and involving the European Medicines Agency more directly. Similar themes appear in the EU Pharmaceutical Strategy, published in November 2020. This will address the longer-term issues that COVID-19 has exposed, including the safeguarding and diversification of supply chains for active ingredients, incentivization of pharmaceutical production within the EU, and innovation within the sector. It will also pick up on some of the priorities identified in the EU4Health program, addressing availability and affordability of medicines, for instance, as a historically intractable issue made salient in the current crisis.

This is an impressive list of EU activities and developments. They reinforce and greatly expand the EU's existing public health policies, whether by legally redefining public health or increasing the health program budget by more than ten times. They even create a greater role for the EU in health systems strengthening. This reflects the fact that, in an integrated EU, the health status of any one country can affect those of the others, and the realization on the part of member states that a collective response by an empowered EU is thus desirable, even if that means some direct support to healthcare systems.

European Union's Social Policy Response

The EU was poorly placed to respond to the unprecedented social and economic policy challenges that its member states faced as the pandemic developed throughout early 2020. As a regulatory state, it lacked a centralized fiscal capacity. None of its tiny budget was geared to sustain health systems or stabilize economies in a crisis. If anything, a dominant coalition of member states, mostly northern "creditor" ones, had seized the opportunity of the 2010 debt crises to build an elaborate structure designed to contain the putatively profligate southern European member states (Greer & Jarman, 2016).

Although externally impressive, EU fiscal governance was already a rickety structure by 2020. Advocates of forceful and crude austerity policy had to defend it against advocates of greater spending, solidarity, and subtlety. These ranged from left parties to governments facing economic decline, to ministries seeking additional budgets, to politicians of any affiliation who wanted to spend more on social protection and investment. They used the tricks that any advocate or bureaucrat uses to undermine a governance structure such as austerity: expanding the goals, expanding participation, and questioning the indicators. This worked well enough to defeat the policy, if not the antidemocratic potential, of the overarching fiscal governance regime (Greer & Brooks, 2020).

The comprehensively undermined fiscal governance structure was, unsurprisingly, the first to change when the crisis hit. The EU activated the "general escape clause" in April, reflecting the impossibility of hitting deficit and debt targets in the middle of a major economic crisis, as well as the difficulty of blaming any government for the scale of the meltdown. Although there will undoubtedly be a push from the political right against the often-impressive public expenditures that got European governments through the early stages of the crisis, it is unlikely that partisans of austerity will find the existing fiscal governance system very useful.

A "general escape" from austerity was one thing, but that did not solve the economic problems created by lockdowns, reduced demand in sectors such as restaurants and live performance, or serious breakdowns in existing patterns of world trade. Even a 20 percent reduction in custom will often be enough to break a business, and a 20 percent reduction in tax revenue a powerful shock to any government. Member state governments were facing falls in GDP of anything up to 17 percent (Eurostat, 2020). Just as social and health needs ballooned, European states found themselves in dire need of money. The EU has no funds to directly address these problems or powers to redistribute; income replacement, basic income, business support, and other schemes had to come from member states. This meant that the collective European response seemed likely to further entrench the enormous economic inequalities that already exist between member states (Makszin, 2020).

In economic policy debates, March and April 2020 felt like 2010, with EU policy distorted by some governments' determined resistance to EU action even as all member states saw dramatic economic declines associated with their shutdowns and shocks to the world economy. The European Central Bank (ECB) jumped to the defense of the Eurozone, initiating a robust crisis response in which it dramatically increased its bond-buying program and cut its interest rates to deeply negative levels in an effort to provide cheap liquidity. It had taken on a similar role, some would argue beyond its mandate, in 2010 and was again forced to do so by the lack of a coordinated fiscal policy at the EU level. And although national governments have welcomed the ECB's actions, they have done little to address this policy gap. An instrument to provide loans for employment preservation measures—Support to mitigate Unemployment Risks in an Emergency (SURE)—was adopted but is temporary and does little to address medium- and longer-term economic stability. The broader, central fiscal policy needed continues to be opposed by mostly northern, "creditor" states, as they were in 2010. The stances of these governments were then and remain normatively indefensible. Self-styled "frugal" governments from countries such as Austria, the Netherlands, and Finland have been happy to vote through large subsidies to sustain corrupt authoritarian regimes in Hungary and Poland (Kelemen, 2017; Magyar & Vasarhelyi, 2017). Yet they were determined to impose punishing conditionality on support to democracies such as Spain, Portugal, Italy, and Greece during a crisis and seemed bent on maintaining this position through the COVID-19 pandemic.

However, just as the EU pulled out of the assault on the single market and began to develop a serious health policy with surprising rapidity, it left the arguments of 2010 behind quickly and with innovation. So much so that, by late summer 2020, scholars were debating whether the EU had experienced its "Hamiltonian moment," a reference to the US government's assumption of the states' war debts in 1790 and the moment the federal government developed its own independent fiscal capacity. The reason for their excitement was that the EU would now be granted its own debt issuance capacity, distributing funds as grants to member states to respond to the COVID-19 crisis. Reflecting an earlier proposal by Emmanuel Macron and Angela Merkel, the EU's recovery plan would see EUR 500 billion, raised by the EU using member states' future contributions as a guarantee, made available as grants to those countries hardest hit by the COVID-19 crisis. For the first time, the EU will issue its own debts to make grants to member states to solve their problems. What explains this turn toward more cooperation and solidarity?

Political Structure and Context

EU policy—including its health policies and its response to COVID-19—can be productively understood by comparing it to other federations (Fierlbeck & Palley, 2015; Greer, 2020; Greer & Elliott, 2019; Vollaard et al., 2016). It is a sprawling and complex system with enumerated powers that make its influence variable from issue to issue. It is filled with formal and informal veto points at which interested parties can block legislation. Its central institutions are divided, its member states powerful and inclined to defer to each other (Kleine, 2013), and its treaties written to constrain its activity. Legislative activity requires creativity and workarounds, but each creative workaround creates new complexity, special interests, and confoundingly intricate legal situations. This is typical in many federations, but a far cry from the often more decisive and coherent unified politics of many EU member states. No member state has to have a website explaining what each of its three presidents do and how they differ (European Union, 2020).

The EU, then, is something like a weakly resourced federation with an unusually complex legal system that operates through regulating and guiding the activities of other governments. This is the core of the EU system and the source of its greatest durable strengths. Where the issue at hand is one of market or economic regulation—such as trade in essential medical supplies or the validity of travel bans—this legal system snaps into action, making up for the weak center and enabling a state-like reaction. Where the issue is outside of this sphere, however—providing frontline response to emergencies, such as deployment of health professionals or comprehensive and comparable data on infection rates, being pertinent examples—the weakness of the EU's resourcing is more of a hindrance. In such areas, the EU performs as a coordination platform; it can be very effective, as was the case, generally speaking, with the provision of timely data and guidance from the ECDC, but only in areas where its member states have provided for this and cooperate with the relevant bodies.

In this sense, the EU's response to COVID-19 is explained by its democratic structure. The EU is an essentially democratic regime; most of its member states are well-consolidated democracies, and the EU is accountable to voters via elections to the European Parliaments, as well as the elections that send member state representatives to vote in the Council. EU democracy has its weaknesses, and a sprawling body of literature exists regarding the EU's democratic deficits. The most important is probably the extent to which it indulges the authoritarian enclaves Hungary and Poland, and indeed finances those governments, so as to reap the benefits of those countries' ruling parties' votes (Gibson, 2013; Kelemen, 2017). Nonetheless the EU's action generally reflects the will of the majority.

This basic democracy of the EU is nicely illustrated by the experience of health policy under the commission presidency of Jean-Claude Juncker. Juncker's appointment and seeming lack of enthusiasm for public health reflected a solid majority of member state governments of the right, who were more interested in an agenda of business-friendly economic growth than in solidarity, environmental regulation, or health. Juncker gave the health commissioner a weak mandate and even issued a paper proposing a scenario in which the EU cease to work for health altogether (Brooks & Guy, 2020; European Commission, 2017). By the end of his term there was only one open legislative dossier before the health council formation (a proposal on health technology assessment), and it was not advancing quickly. Although dispiriting and frustrating for health advocates, this lack of action reflected the perceived interests of the majority of national governments.

In the summer of 2020, these perceived interests began to shift. The shift reflects not only the unprecedented scale and impact of the COVID-19 crisis but also the new decision-making landscape created by Brexit. EU health policy, like many EU policy areas, has seen a long-standing division between larger states and smaller states. Smaller member states are generally more in favor of strong EU capacities and strong EU institutions because they see that they will fare better as a collective than on their own or in intergovernmental contexts. Bigger member states are more likely to see a potential draw on their resources and constraint on their freedom of action and may be suspicious of the European Commission and its propensity to develop its own political projects.

COVID-19 is changing this dynamic in a way that previous crises have not been able. Human immunodeficiency virus/acquired immunodeficiency syndrome and bovine spongiform encephalopathy (BSE) in the 1990s, SARS and H1N1 in the 2000s, and the various other public health crises that the EU has endured over the years were enough to expose the logic of a European agency for monitoring infectious diseases, or a common regulatory framework for food safety, but not to prompt a deeper shift. COVID-19 is different. It threatens to exceed the health and social policy capacities of all states, not just because of the scale of the problem but also because of their interconnection: endemic COVID-19 anywhere in the EU will be endemic COVID-19 everywhere in the EU. It is also likely to pose this threat for a considerably longer period of time than previous pandemics. As such, calls to strengthen the EU's role in crisis response, public health, and social policy reflect member state governments' perceived interest in responding collectively to a crisis that has affected their interlocking economies and societies.

The crisis is also the first time that we are getting a glimpse of the effects of Brexit on EU decision-making (Greer & Laible, 2020). Put simply, vote-counting in the EU meant that an effective coalition had to have a big country: France, Germany, or the United Kingdom. That big country's votes and leadership could stitch together coalitions. The question was not whether Finland, Ireland, and Sweden are the same, but whether they tended to agree with the British more than they agree with other countries. The United Kingdom had anchored a largely right-wing, pro-market arc of states stretching from Ireland to the Baltic states. This economically liberal bloc could easily frustrate more solidaristic proposals from countries led by France, and gave Germany and its allies a great deal of strategic flexibility. For most of the twenty-first century, France was effectively in opposition as Germany and its allies frequently shared preferences with the United Kingdom and its allies. Brexit, predictably enough, empowered France. In an EU without the United Kingdom, Germany and France have to work together. This new reality is beginning to emerge: a splintering of the northern liberal bloc, which does not have the votes to veto or drive policy, and a redefinition of the areas where the preferences of French and German governments overlap. A crucial early example was the Franco-German proposals for the European recovery, which included an agenda for "health sovereignty" and laid the foundations for the common debt mechanism now in operation.

The self-styled "frugals," an opportunistic coalition of Austria, Denmark, Finland, the Netherlands, and Sweden, fought for policy conditionality on EU grants as well as a smaller health policy budget in July 2020. Although they managed to cut the increase in the EU health budget, they were in an essentially defensive action once they had been abandoned by their usual ally Germany in favor of deals with France. This action took place at a European Council negotiation over the Multiannual Financial Framework, the EU's budget, where any member state can effectively veto progress. All that the frugals managed to achieve in that very favorable venue was to cut the health budget increase and the new EU grants. A European Union dominated by Franco-German relations might be a difficult place for them.

Conclusion: Failing Forward?

The EU's development is often presented in the form of debates between "intergovernmentalists" who think that member states largely control the EU, and "neofunctionalists" who posit that there are broader and self-sustaining trends toward integration. The EU response to COVID-19 and EU health law and policy analysis more generally has shown the drawbacks of such a stylized approach to European integration and public policy. Previous health emergencies all contributed to the development of EU capacity and a sense of shared fate among EU governments. Public health decision-makers shared a sense that they faced common problems and could work together, even if normal politics of public health in the EU were fissiparous and crises could just as easily lead to selfishness as collective action.

Perhaps Jean Monnet, one of the most important figures in the history of EU, put it better when he said that "L'Europe se fera dans les crises et elle sera la somme des solutions apportées à ces crises" [Europe will be forged in crises, and will be the sum of the solutions adopted for those crises] (1976). Put another way, the EU has a long history of "failing forward," in which:

> Intergovernmental bargaining leads to incompleteness because it forces states with diverse preferences to settle on lowest common denominator solutions. Incompleteness then unleashes forces that lead to crisis. Member states respond by again agreeing to lowest common denominator solutions, which address the crisis and lead to deeper integration. To date, this sequential cycle of piecemeal reform, followed by policy failure, followed by further reform, has managed to sustain both the European project and the common currency. However, this

approach entails clear risks. Economically, the policy failures engendered by this incremental approach to the construction of EMU have been catastrophic for the citizens of many crisis-plagued member states. Politically, the perception that the EU is constantly in crisis and in need of reforms to salvage the union is undermining popular support for European integration. (Jones et al., 2015)

EU public health has long been such a case, with various communicable disease crises putting public health on the EU agenda (de Ruijter, 2019; Greer et al., 2021). It was the sum of those crises that created the infrastructure, such as the Health Security Committee and RescEU, that the EU initially used to respond. This crisis of COVID-19 also promises to leave behind a different EU. Between the redefinition in salience, resource, and law of public health, shared European actions such as blocking travel from some of the EU's biggest trading partners (e.g., the United States), and the development of EU debt for member states, it is likely that future historians of the EU will see the pandemic as a moment when integration stepped forward, in health and beyond.

In a number of the federations that this book discusses, such as Brazil and the United States, federalism meant that an otiose central government shirked responsibility or acted erratically, leaving ill-prepared and variable states to compensate. Disasters ensued. In the case of the EU, responsibility for managing health emergencies clearly lay with the member states from the outset. The EU's immediate response was therefore constrained to that of an international organization, coordinating from the sidelines at the mercy of the resources and solidarity of its member states. An initial period of member state dominance—and even egotism—was therefore inevitable. But as this first phase passed, and the scale of their shared problems became apparent, member states' perceived interest shifted. Their response has been to begin to strengthen and expand the EU's more state-like powers. A common European debt mechanism, a central role for the EU in vaccine procurement and distribution, even a new agenda in health systems strengthening—these are sizeable steps forward, which acknowledge the integral role of Europe in post-COVID-19 recovery and the positive-sum nature of further integration. It is just a beginning. The process will be long, shaped by the EU's peculiar institutional structures and the new, post-Brexit reality of decision-making, but, faced with a public health crisis of a magnitude previously unseen, the response so far has been to seek another European rescue of the nation state (Greer et al., 2021).

References

Alter, K. J. (1998). Who are the "masters of the treaty"?: European governments and the European court of justice. *International Organization, 52,* 121–147.

Brooks, E. (2012). Crossing borders: A critical review of the role of the European court of justice in EU health policy. *Health Policy, 105,* 33–37.

Brooks, E., & Guy, M. (2020). EU health law and policy: Shaping a future research agenda. *Health Economics, Policy and Law,* 1–7, https://doi.org/10.1017/S1744133120000274

de Ruijter, A. (2019). *Eu health law & policy: The expansion of EU power in public health and health care*. Oxford University Press.

de Ruijter, A., Beetsma, R. M. J. W., Burgoon, B., Nicoli, F., & Vandenbroucke, F. (2020). EU solidarity and policy in fighting infectious diseases: State of play, obstacles, citizen preferences and ways forward. *Amsterdam Centre for European Studies Research Paper.* https://papers.ssrn.com/sol3/papers.cfm?abstract_id=3570550#

Deruelle, T. (2016). Bricolage or entrepreneurship? Lessons from the creation of the European Centre for Disease Prevention and Control. *European Policy Analysis, 2,* 43–67.

Deruelle, T. (2020). *Beyond health: Looking for Europe's strategy vis-à-vis the Covid-19 crisis*. Al Jazeera Centre for Studies.

European Commission. (2017). *White paper on the future of Europe: Five scenarios*. European Commission.

European Commission. (2018). *Proposal for a regulation on the European Social Fund Plus*. European Commission.

European Union. (2020). *EU presidents—Who does what?* European Union. https://europa.eu/european-union/about-eu/presidents_en

Eurostat. (2020, December 8). *GDP main aggregates and employment estimates for the third quarter of 2020.* https://ec.europa.eu/eurostat/documents/portlet_file_entry/2995521/2-08122020-AP-EN.pdf/1795cf84-4c30-9bae-33b0-b8a1755925c4

Fierlbeck, K., & Palley, H. A. (Eds.). (2015). *Comparative health care federalism*. Ashgate.

Gibson, E. L. (2013). *Boundary control: Subnational authoritarianism in federal democracies*. Cambridge University Press.

Greer, S. L. (2012). The European Centre for Disease Prevention and Control: Hub or hollow core? *Journal of Health Politics, Policy, and Law, 37,* 1001–1030.

Greer, S. L. (2020). Health, federalism and the European Union: Lessons from comparative federalism about the European Union. *Health Economics, Policy and Law,* 1–14. https://doi.org/10.1017/S1744133120000055

Greer, S. L., & Brooks, E. (2020). Termites of solidarity in the house of austerity: Undermining fiscal governance in the European Union. *Journal of Health Politics, Policy and Law.* https://doi.org/10.1215/03616878-8706615

Greer, S. L., de Ruijter, A., & Brooks, E. (2021). The Covid-19 pandemic: Failing forward in public health. In M. Riddervold, J. Trondal, & A. Newsome (Eds.), *Palgrave handbook of EU crises*. Palgrave.

Greer, S. L., & Elliott, H. (Eds.). (2019). *Federalism and social policy: Patterns of redistribution in eleven democracies*. University of Michigan Press.

Greer, S. L., Fahy, N., Rozenblum, S., Jarman, H., Palm, W., Elliott, H. A., & Wismar, M. (2019). *Everything you always wanted to know about European Union health policy but were afraid to ask.* (2nd ed.). European Observatory on Health Systems and Policies.

Greer, S. L., & Jarman, H. (2016). European citizenship rights and European fiscal politics after the crisis. *Government and Opposition,* 1–28.

Greer, S. L., & Kurzer, P. (Eds.). (2013). *European Union public health policies: Regional and global perspectives.* Routledge.

Greer, S. L., & Laible, J. (Eds.). (2020). *The European Union after Brexit.* Manchester University Press.

Greer, S. L., & Rauscher, S. (2011a). Destabilization rights and restabilization politics: Policy and political reactions to European Union health care services law. *Journal of European Public Policy, 18,* 220–240.

Greer, S. L., & Rauscher, S. (2011b). When does market-marking make markets? EU health services policy at work in the UK and Germany. *Journal of Common Market Studies, 49,* 797–822.

Guigner, S. (2007). L'Européanisation cognitive de la santé: Entre imposition et persuasion [The cognitive Europeanization of health: Between imposition and persuasion]. In O. Baisnee & Romain Pasquier (Eds.), *L'Europe telle qu'elle se fait* [Europe as it is]. CNRS Editions.

Hancké, B. (2013). *Unions, central banks, and Emu: Labour market institutions and monetary integration in Europe.* Oxford University Press.

Hervey, T. K., & McHale, J. V. (2015). *European Union health law: Themes and implications.* Cambridge University Press.

Hervey, T. K., Young, C. A., & Bishop, L. E. (Eds.) (2017). *Research handbook on EU health law and policy.* Edward Elgar.

Johnston, A. (2016). *From convergence to crisis: Labor markets and the instability of the euro.* Cornell University Press.

Jones, E., Kelemen, R. D., & Meunier, S. (2015). Failing forward? The Euro crisis and the incomplete nature of European integration. *Comparative Political Studies, 49,* 1010–1034.

Kelemen, R. D. (2017). Europe's other democratic deficit: National authoritarianism in Europe's democratic union. *Government and Opposition, 52,* 211–238.

Kelemen, R. D. (2019). Is differentiation possible in rule of law. *Comparative European Politics, 17,* 246–260.

Kleine, M. (2013). *Informal governance in the European Union: How governments make international organizations work.* Cornell University Press.

Magyar, B., & Vasarhelyi, J. (2017). *Twenty-five sides of a post-communist mafia state.* CEU Press.

Majone, G. (1996). *Regulating Europe.* Routledge.

Makszin, K. (2020). The East-West divide: Obstacles to further integration. In S. L. Greer & J. Liable (Eds.), *The European Union after Brexit.* Manchester University Press.

Matthijs, M., Parsons, C., & Toenshoff, C. (2019). Ever tighter union? Brexit, Grexit, and frustrated differentiation in the single market and Eurozone. *Comparative European Politics, 17,* 209–230.

Mattli, W., & Slaughter, A.-M. (1998). Revisiting the European Court of Justice. *International Organization, 52,* 177–209.

Milward, A. (1999). *The European rescue of the nation state.* Routledge.

Monnet, J. (1976). *Mémoires.* Fayard.

Obermaier, A. J. (2008). The National Judiciary-Sword of European Court of Justice rulings: The example of the Kohll/Decker jurisprudence. *European Law Journal, 14,* 735–752.

Obermaier, A. J. (2009). *The end of territoriality? The impact of ECJ rulings on British, German and French social policy.* Ashgate.

Pavone, T., & Kelemen, R. D. (2019). The evolving judicial politics of European integration: The European Court of Justice and national courts revisited. *European Law Journal, 25,* 352–373.

Pérez, S. A. (2019). A Europe of creditor and debtor states: Explaining the north/south divide in the Eurozone. *West European Politics, 42,* 989–1014.

Purnhagen, K. P., de Ruijter, A., Flear, M. L., Hervey, T. K., & Herwig, A. (2020). More competences than you knew? The web of health competence for European Union action in response to the Covid-19 outbreak. *European Journal of Risk Regulation.* 11(2), 297–306.

Strayer, J. R. (1970). *On the medieval origins of the modern state.* Princeton University Press.

Treaty on the Functioning of the European Union, TFEU. (2007). *Official Journal of the European Union* (OJ C 115/47).

Vollaard, H., van de Bovenkamp, H., & Sindbjerg Martinsen, D. (2016). The making of a European healthcare union: A federalist perspective. *Journal of European Public Policy*, 23(2), 157–176.

14 DENMARK'S RESPONSE TO COVID-19
A Participatory Approach to Policy Innovation
Darius Ornston

Denmark's first case of COVID-19 was detected at the end of February 2020. Like other West European countries, initial cases were concentrated among travelers returning from Italy, but they accelerated sharply with community spread by the second week of March 2020. By the end of the month, Denmark was averaging 200 cases a day. After peaking in early April 2020, cases slowly but steadily decreased to 38 a day in the last week of June 2020. By this point, Denmark had reported 12,994 cases and 609 deaths. On a per capita basis, this was comparable to Germany and lower than many other West European countries. Mortality figures reflect this pattern, increasing to 7 percent above expected levels in April 2020 before returning to historical norms in May 2020 ("Tracking Covid-19 excess deaths across countries," 2020).

There are multiple explanations for this satisfactory performance. This chapter instead investigates Denmark's *response* to the pandemic, focusing on the political variables that influenced these policy choices. Denmark is a small (six million inhabitants), wealthy democracy with a large and capacious public sector (Campbell & Hall, 2009). Its generous and encompassing postwar welfare state, which includes universal health insurance, has contributed to a low level of income inequality and a high degree of social capital (Esping-Andersen, 1990; Rothstein & Stolle, 2003). A minority Social Democratic government, a common consequence of proportional representation in Denmark, presided over the pandemic. The Ministry of Health, which at times ignored the recommendations of its own public health agency, was directly responsible for the policy choices described in this chapter. In practice, however, most decisions were subject to cabinet and parliamentary discussion and were supported by the entire government and all represented political parties. Consistent with Denmark's tradition of "neo-corporatist" governance (Katzenstein, 1985), the country's largest employer associations and trade unions were also deeply involved in the policy-making process.

We might expect this democratic and consensual approach to governance to inhibit action. After all, democracies are more commonly known for cumbersome decision-making processes and risk-averse politicians (Greer et al., 2020). To the extent that these countries embrace reform, they tend to import tried-and-tested policies from local neighbors rather than pioneering new ones (Weyland, 2009).

Denmark, however, was a regional pioneer, consistently experimenting with risky and untested strategies. For example, Denmark was one of the first European countries to lock down in its economy between March 10, 2020, and March 18, 2020. This early lockdown was paired with an ambitious and unprecedented economic assistance program, which would become a template for other countries. Although the lockdown enjoyed widespread social support, Denmark led the way in reopening its economy in mid-April. The loosening of restrictions coincided with a dramatic increase in testing levels to one of the highest in the world. In doing so, the Danish government did not rely on a powerful executive, a legislative majority, nor independent agencies to overpower opponents and special interests. Instead, it drew on an inclusive and participatory approach to policy-making, negotiating with opposition parties as well as industry and labor.

Drawing on literature on small states (Campbell & Hall, 2017; Katzenstein, 1985; Ornston, 2012b), this chapter explains how institutionalized cooperation between policy-makers and civil society, specifically large, encompassing producer associations, can accelerate policy reform and social change. First, the trust that stems from repeated interaction makes it easier for reform-oriented actors to persuade skeptics. Second, widely distributed networks enable policy-makers to design more effective interventions using local information. Third, this extends to social protection, which can reduce opposition by compensating adversely affected actors. Finally, consensus improves policy effectiveness by coordinating public and private sector action. Because this inclusive and participatory approach is so attractive, the chapter concludes on a cautionary note, identifying limitations and vulnerabilities. Although Denmark appears successful, a brief analysis of another Nordic country, Sweden, illustrates how cohesive and encompassing networks can go awry during periods of heightened uncertainty.

Health Policy: From Early Lockdown to Early Exit

Denmark was one of the first countries in Europe to begin locking down its economy in March 2020. Social distancing measures began with the recommendation on March 5 to stay at home and the cancellation of public events on March 6, when the country was averaging less than ten cases a day. As the number of detected cases spiked (767 between March 9 and March 13), the minority Social Democratic government announced more radical measures. Ignoring the guidance of its own health agency (Kjær et al., 2020), the government sent all nonessential public sector employees home with pay and closed high schools and universities by March 13 (Olsen & Hjorth, 2020). The country was an early leader in this respect, ranking ninth in the world and fifth in Europe (after Italy, San Marino, Kosovo, and Albania) on the Blavatnik Government Response Stringency Index (Roser et al., 2020). More restrictive policies would follow. Denmark was one of the first countries to close its borders to international travel on March 14, 2020 (Roser et al., 2020); elementary schools and day care facilities were closed on March 16 (Olsen & Hjorth, 2020). By March 18 the government banned assemblies of more than ten people and mandated the closure of restaurants, clubs, shopping centers, sports facilities, and other businesses involving close contact (Vrangbæk et al., 2020).

Although Denmark was one of the first countries to restrict economic and social activity, the lockdown itself was not particularly strict. By the end of March, Denmark's public health measures were in fact among the least stringent in Europe, exceeded in leniency only by Andorra, Belarus, Finland, Iceland, Latvia, and Sweden (Roser et al., 2020). Borders were closed and assemblies of greater than ten individuals were banned, but the government never required all businesses to close, did not issue mandatory stay-at-home orders, never restricted internal travel, and maintained public transit (Roser et al., 2020; Vrangbæk et al., 2020). Visits to public parks and other outdoor spaces, which were never forbidden, increased markedly in March (Roser et al., 2020).

Compliance with these public recommendations and mandatory measures, although imperfect (Vrangbæk et al., 2020), reduced mobility by roughly 40 percent by the end of March 2020. This was less dramatic than the shifts observed in the hardest-hit West European countries, such as France, Italy, Spain, and the United Kingdom, but it rivaled the changes observed in other (albeit significantly less affected) European states with mandatory stay-at-home orders, such as the Czech Republic, Poland, and Romania (Roser et al., 2020). Where Denmark truly stands out in comparative perspective is the breadth of social support. Unlike the United States, all political parties supported the lockdown, and there were no protests against social distancing measures in Denmark. Public approval of the government's COVID-19 response, which consistently exceeded 80 percent between March and June 2020, was among the highest in Europe ("COVID-19: Government Handling and Confidence in Health Authorities," 2020; Devlin & Connaughton, 2020).

Despite broad support, Denmark (with Austria) was one of the first countries to announce its intention to exit the lockdown on April 6, 2020. The loosening of social distancing measures, which began on April 15, extended to the reopening of primary schools, childcare facilities, and some private service providers on April 20. Shops, shopping malls, community organizations, and outdoor sports followed on May 11. Restaurants, libraries, and secondary schools were permitted to reopen on May 18. On June 8, the cap on assemblies was lifted from ten to fifty. Travel restrictions were also rolled back in June, with visitors and Danes from selected countries exempted from self-isolation requirements beginning on June 17 (Vrangbæk et al., 2020).

Denmark's timing in reopening its economy is striking and is discussed in more depth later. Unlike the early adoption of social distancing, which followed a sharp spike in COVID-19 cases between March 9 and 11, 2020, one cannot link Danish leadership in this area to a dramatic decline in cases. The initial plan to reopen schools was announced on April 6, the day before Denmark's highest daily case count (393). Unlike other communities, such as several US states, the Danish government was not pressured to reopen by protest activity, skepticism about the virus, or an ideological aversion to government intervention. Instead, the decision was based on Denmark's self-perceived shortcomings relative to South Korea and (post-lockdown) China, which were able to contain the virus with a less restrictive program of mass testing, contact tracing, and quarantining. Denmark was an early laggard in this respect. The country struggled to run a thousand tests a day in March 2020, trailing Australia, Austria, Germany, Iceland, Italy, and others on per-capita adjusted measures of testing. As a result, testing was restricted to individuals with severe symptoms (Ritchie et al., 2020; Vrangbæk et al., 2020).

Testing levels improved in April, particularly after the announcement of a partnership with Denmark's largest pharmaceutical firm, Novo Nordisk, on April 21, 2020. This deal enabled Denmark to extend eligibility to individuals with mild symptoms and close contacts of known cases as well as assemble testing facilities outside of its hospitals (Vrangbæk et al., 2020). By mid-May, testing was opened to the public, including asymptomatic individuals, and Denmark was preemptively testing key groups such as healthcare workers (Roser et al., 2020; Vrangbæk et al., 2020). By July, Denmark had become a global leader in per-capita adjusted measures of testing, trailing only a handful of countries such as Bahrain, the United Arab Emirates, and several European micro-states (Ritchie et al., 2020).

Although the shift in testing was more conspicuous, Denmark also expanded its contact tracing and quarantine facilities. Denmark developed the capacity to trace all COVID-19 cases beginning on April 23, 2020 (at the time, Luxembourg, Iceland, and Italy were the only other West European countries to do so). By June, the government was providing facilities for individuals who were unable to self-isolate after a positive COVID-19 test or exposure (Vrangbæk et al., 2020). Denmark was slower to develop a contact-tracing application because of concerns about cost-sharing and privacy, but a partnership with the private enterprise, Netcompany, was approved by parliament on May 15, 2020 and the Smitte|stop app was launched on June 18. As of this writing, it is too soon to speculate on its success. Although it was downloaded by approximately 10 percent of the population by the beginning of July, this was not high enough to replace conventional contact tracing efforts (OPSI, 2020; Vrangbæk et al., 2020).

The Danish response to the virus did not always involve rapid and radical reform. Because Denmark entered the crisis with a high-quality, comprehensive healthcare system and the pandemic was contained, it did not introduce measures adopted by some other countries. Because legal residents and foreign visitors were already entitled to health care, no efforts were made to extend access. A centralized hospital structure facilitated the redistribution of resources. There were no reports of equipment shortages or rationing care, except for the cancellation of noncritical, elective surgeries. Digital consultations became more common, but these were permitted before the crisis. The government mandated the disclosure of private stockpiles of protective equipment, machinery, and medicine and was prepared to requisition or mandate the production of these resources, but it never did so (Vrangbæk et al., 2020). In these areas, Denmark's public health response was a story about continuity, not change.

Economic Policy: Creative Compensation

Like health policy, aspects of Danish economic policy were also characterized by continuity. With one of the most comprehensive welfare states in the world, Denmark was already well equipped to manage disruptive economic shocks such as COVID-19. For example, there was no impulse to increase sickness or unemployment benefit levels, because these were already among the most generous in the Organisation for Economic Co-operation and Development (OECD, 2020). Denmark's robust system of automatic stabilizers, in the form of lower taxation and higher spending on countercyclical social benefits, was projected to contribute 5.1 percent of 2019 gross domestic product (GDP) without any government intervention (IMF, 2020). As a result, reforms to existing social policies involved only minor adjustments rather than extensive restructuring. For example, the government temporarily relaxed the tightening of eligibility requirements, which had been introduced in earlier decades to boost labor force participation (Madsen, 2003). Between March 17 and 19, 2020, the government eliminated waiting periods, increased benefit duration, extended access to quarantined groups, eased reporting requirements, and canceled job search requirements. The collective cost of these adjustments was marginal, representing less than 1 percent of Denmark's total economic response package (IMF, 2020; OECD, 2020).

Because of the unique threat associated with the pandemic and the lockdown of the economy, however, Denmark could not rely on existing social policies alone. Naturally, monetary policy played an important role, but it did not differ significantly from other developed economies (OECD, 2020) and is not discussed here. The most distinctive element of Denmark's response to COVID-19 was fiscal, specifically a job retention scheme, which was unrolled in mid-March. On March 12, 2020, the government made minor adjustments to an existing work-sharing scheme, in which furloughed employees could collect a supplementary unemployment benefit for thirteen weeks. This was superseded three days later by a more ambitious and unprecedented *midlertidig lønkompensation,* or temporary wage compensation program, in which the government covered 75 percent of the wages of furloughed salaried workers (90 percent for hourly workers) up to a maximum monthly salary of 26,000 DKK for firms facing a significant decrease in demand and the prospect of layoffs. In exchange, firms would cover the remainder of the salary and refrained from firing their employees, while workers contributed five days of annual leave. A separate program for self-employed workers, who were not covered by the initial scheme, was announced on March 19 (ILO, 2020; OECD, 2020).

To a German observer, this temporary wage compensation program does not look particularly innovative, resembling the *Kurzarbeit* program, or short-time work benefit that stabilized the German labor market in the wake of the 2008 financial crisis (Vail, 2018, pp. 140–141). For Denmark, however, this involved swimming against powerful historical and institutional forces. In contrast to Germany (Hall & Soskice, 2001), Denmark uses labor market policies to accelerate the redistribution of resources from declining sectors to new ones. For example, the country not only champions free trade and eschews defensive industrial policies, but also imposes few restrictions on firing workers and invests heavily in worker retraining (Campbell & Pedersen, 2007; Madsen, 2006; Mjøset, 1987; Ornston, 2012b). As a result, preexisting efforts to protect existing jobs were marginal, employing only 18,000 at the height of the 2008 financial crisis (Jørgensen, 2011). By protecting over 200,000 established jobs or 5 percent of the Danish labour force from redundancy between March and May 2020 (OECD, 2020), the temporary wage compensation program represented a sharp break with past practice.

This volte-face in Danish social policy was taken with surprising speed. Although this new "Danish" model would eventually influence policymakers in other countries such as Canada and the United States (Bouw, 2020; Thompson, 2020), it represented a novel response to an unprecedented crisis when unveiled on March 15, 2020. It was unclear whether German-style *Kurzarbeit* could be applied to a very different institutional context in Denmark or whether it would work on this unprecedented scale. Moreover, the Danes adapted the program in several ways. First, the wage benefit was more generous than the original *Kurzarbeit* program. Second, on March 19, 2020, the Danish government agreed to cover 25 percent to 100 percent of the fixed costs for businesses adversely affected by the crisis. This represented an even larger commitment to protect established enterprises, roughly six times more expensive (65 billion DKK) than the temporary wage compensation program (10 billion DKK) itself, and was at odds with Denmark's laissez-faire tradition in industrial policy (Mjøset, 1987; Ornston, 2012a). This was flanked by the deferral of VAT payments, labor market contributions, and withheld income tax payments providing roughly 200 billion DKK in additional liquidity. The government also used a suite of instruments to deliver emergency recapitalization, loan guarantees, export credits, and a sector-specific bailout of the travel industry representing approximately 100 billion DKK. The total cost of this discretionary fiscal response was roughly 5 percent of 2019 GDP. When tax deferrals, credit guarantees, liquidity measures, and automatic stabilizers are included, the figure is closer to 20 percent of GDP (IMF, 2020; OECD, 2020).

In the short term, this rapid economic response appears to have limited the fallout from the crisis. A June 2020 analysis by the Central Bank of Denmark projected a 4.1 percent decline in GDP in 2020 and unemployment was just 5.0 percent as of May, well below the OECD average of 8.4 percent (OECD, 2020). Firm-level analysis suggests that these programs, and the temporary wage compensation program in particular, were successful in reducing layoffs (Bennedsen et al., 2020). With the decline in COVID-19 cases, the Danish government has already started to transition from pandemic response to a conventional, economic recovery program. This began with a government announcement that it would frontload investments in public housing on May 19 and was followed on June 16 by plans to release frozen holiday money (part of a pension reform package) and issue a one-time check to pensioners, students, and others on social transfers (ILO, 2020; OECD, 2020).

Explaining Denmark's COVID-19 Response: Cooperation and Change

Denmark's response to the pandemic could be depicted as a story about either continuity or change. In some ways, Denmark did not need to reform to manage the virus. Its high-capacity public health system successfully absorbed a modest surge in COVID-19 cases, its egalitarian social structure reduced (but did not fully eliminate) vulnerable populations, and its traditional social policies served as an automatic stabilizer, blunting the economic impact of the crisis. Framed in this way, the Danish case underscores the value of state capacity (Besley & Persson, 2011) and universal social policies in particular (Esping-Andersen, 1990).

Even an egalitarian society with a high-capacity state, however, needed to make adjustments. Here, Denmark's capacity for rapid and bold reform stands out in comparative perspective. Instead of stalling, vacillating, or mimicking neighbors, Denmark was an early adopter of new and relatively untested strategies. It was one of the first countries to lock down its economy and also one of the first to reverse course in April, replacing the lockdown with a massive expansion of testing and contact tracing. Denmark also creatively adapted Germany's *Kurzarbeit* program to tackle the economic fallout of the pandemic, popularizing a model others would emulate. How can Denmark's capacity for change be explained?

First and foremost, the Danish case underscores the complementary relationship between social protection and change (Cameron, 1984; Levy, 1999; Polanyi, 1944). The Nordic countries have long used generous social policies to reduce opposition to political reform, technological innovation, and economic restructuring (Andersen et al., 2007; Katzenstein, 1985; Ornston, 2018). COVID-19 was no exception, and the second and third parts of this chapter are thus closely connected. Danish workers were insulated from the economic costs of the lockdown, and the pandemic itself, by generous social safety nets. The situation confronting employers was different, but policy innovations such as the temporary wage compensation program dramatically reduced their costs. In contrast to other countries such as the United States, adversely affected industries were well covered by Denmark's temporary wage compensation program (Bennedsen et al., 2020). As a result, it is hardly surprising that all major labor market actors and political parties endorsed the lockdown and protest activity was insignificant.

By contrast, authoritarianism and functional equivalents played a marginal role. Other democracies have fostered experimentation by insulating policymakers from popular pressure, either by building "electoral slack" with first-past-the-post voting systems (Pierson, 1996), delegating authority to independent agencies

(Fuchs, 2010; Johnson, 1982) or engaging in below-the-radar reform (Block, 2008; Breznitz & Ornston, 2013). None of these apply to Denmark's COVID-19 response. Prime Minister Mette Frederiksen's minority government ignored the recommendations of its public health agency and weakened its authority (Kjær et al., 2020). It also involved both opposition parties and leading producer associations in negotiations over the lockdown and related economic measures (Bouw, 2020). The mid-June release of worker holiday pay, which underpins Denmark's recovery package, was based on a proposal that was originally floated by Denmark's largest trade union and employer organization (ILO, 2020).

This participatory and inclusive approach is a common feature of postwar Danish policymaking and the Nordic region more generally (Katzenstein, 1985; Pekkarinen et al., 1992). It has been conceptualized in different ways. Scholars focusing on electoral institutions emphasize proportional representation and cross-partisan collaboration (Lijphart, 1977), whereas political economists privilege the integration of encompassing trade unions and employer associations (Pekkarinen et al., 1992). Other studies highlight the importance of informal relationships (Katzenstein, 1985) or a cohesive national identity (Campbell & Hall, 2017). These conceptual distinctions matter (Ornston & Schulze-Cleven, 2015), but in the case of Denmark (and the other Nordics), they generally coincide, integrated actors within widely distributed, high-trust networks which cut across religious, regional, sectoral, and political cleavages (Ornston, 2018).

Although often depicted as inhibiting change (Alesina & Giavazzi, 2006; Grabher, 1993; Hall & Soskice, 2001; Immergut, 1992), cohesive and encompassing networks can accelerate it in four ways. First, as noted previously, repeated interaction can build consensus by compensating adversely affected actors, either through formal social programs (Andersen et al., 2007) or alternative arrangements (Katzenstein, 1985). In the Danish case, however, the compensatory scheme *itself* was innovative. This illuminates several additional sources of dynamism.

By facilitating access to high-quality expertise from across society, cohesive and encompassing networks facilitate the design of new policies (Breznitz, 2007, p. 16). In the case of the temporary wage compensation program, Danish policymakers could negotiate with organized labor and industry to ensure that the initiative would reach adversely affected firms. By contrast, patchwork consultations in the United States resulted in the large but comparatively ineffective Paycheck Protection Program, which was limited in its scope and mired by bureaucratic obstacles (Bennedsen et al., 2020). Naturally, easy access to information also supported the design of other policies, from the construction of socially acceptable distancing measures in mid-March to the order in which they were reversed.

High-trust networks can also accelerate the diffusion of new ideas, making it easier for reform-oriented actors to convince skeptics by persuasive argumentation (Ornston, 2018, p. 17) or patriotic appeals (Campbell & Hall, 2009, p. 552). In the case of the temporary wage compensation program, Danish trade unions and employers embraced the proposal within 24 hours (Olsen, 2020). As other chapters discuss, the high regard for public authority extended beyond economic measures to public health. Stakeholders did not question the government's decisions but instead endorsed them (Thompson, 2020), and public support remained high from the initial crisis into the summer ("COVID-19: Government Handling and Confidence in Health Authorities," 2020).

Finally, whether achieved by persuasion, compensation, or a combination of the two, consensus made it easier to coordinate state and societal action. The temporary wage compensation program was based on the expectation that firms receiving public support would refrain from firing workers, even without significant administrative oversight. The social distancing measures it complemented also needed societal buy-in, as evidenced by the fact that compliance was correlated with trust in government (Olsen & Hjorth, 2020). When Denmark exited the lockdown, mass testing was predicated on a partnership with the private sector, specifically Novo Nordisk. The software developer Netcompany supported contact tracing with the release of COVIDmeter in April 2020 and, less swiftly, Smitte|stop in June 2020.

Viewed in this light, the Danish case represents a contrast to authoritarianism and a democratic pathway to rapid and bold reform. It succeeded not by replicating authoritarian advantages with a powerful executive, majoritarian electoral institutions, or independent agencies, but instead leveraging the distinct advantages of a participatory and inclusive approach to policymaking. This characteristically Nordic response supported early and risky policy action by gathering information, persuading skeptics, compensating adversely affected actors, and coordinating state and societal action.

Conclusion: Denmark in Comparative Perspective

This chapter contributes to a growing body of research about how dense, high-trust networks can accelerate change, encouraging experimentation and facilitating reform (Campbell & Hall, 2017; Katzenstein, 1985; Rhodes, 2001). This argument could be generalized by extending the analysis to other areas such as technological innovation (Ornston, 2012b) or financial markets (Ornston, 2018). Because it is tempting to copy this participatory and inclusive approach, however, the chapter instead concludes by identifying several weaknesses.

First and most obviously, the dense, cross-cutting, cohesive relationships that underpin the Danish model do not exist in large countries, particularly at the national level (Ornston, 2018). Although they can be constructed locally (Fung, 2009; Katz & Bradley, 2013; Putnam, 1993), these jurisdictions may lack the fiscal resources and regulatory authority to fully replicate the Nordic experience (Ornston, 2019). Moreover, the Danish model does not even generalize across the universe of small states. Although some small nations are characterized by cohesive and encompassing networks (Campbell & Hall, 2017; Katzenstein, 1985) many are more fragmented or polarized (Fioretos, 2013; Ornston, 2018). It is not clear that the intensely participatory process that facilitated reform in Denmark would deliver the same results elsewhere.

Second, participation is limited within Denmark. The government's commitment to including opposition parties and encompassing business and labor associations did not extend to all actors. As in other countries, cases were concentrated among ethnic minorities (Krause, 2020). Although legal residents and foreign visitors were entitled to health care, the Danish government made no effort to target undocumented or irregular immigrants (beyond mandating their confinement in an asylum center if they tested positive for the virus). In another example of its restrictive stance on immigration, the government was also quick to close its border on March 14, 2020, before the introduction of a general lockdown (Vrangbæk et al., 2020). Finally, the country's capacity for bold and innovative action in domestic policy did not extend to the European level, where its contributions to EU-level action were decidedly conservative (Kurz, 2020).

Finally, it is important to acknowledge the risks of swift and bold action in an uncertain environment. Finland and Norway, which adopted similar strategies, were broadly successful in containing the virus and the economic fallout associated with it, as was Iceland, which paired a looser lockdown with extensive testing. Sweden's approach has proven more controversial. Sweden maintained the least restrictive lockdown in Western Europe, relying on voluntary social distancing rather than mass testing or contact tracing to handle the pandemic. This was innovative and bold in the sense that it deviated from European practice and attracted significant international criticism after mid-March. It is too early to comment on the long-term consequences of this strategy, but the short-term results were discouraging. Excess mortality approached 40 percent in April and remained elevated for months ("Tracking Covid-19 Excess Deaths across Countries," 2020). Nor did the strategy yield immediate economic benefits. Swedish performance was comparable to Denmark, with unemployment increasing from 7.1 percent to 9 percent between March and May 2020 and the Central Bank projecting a 4.5 percent contraction in output (Ringstrom & Fulton, 2020).

Several lessons can be drawn from this brief comparison, besides the obvious point that the Nordic region is not a monolithic bloc. First, the proximate cause of Sweden's response to the pandemic is the country's distinctive constitutional structure and the resulting independence of the Swedish National Health Agency (Jonung, 2020; Karlson et al., 2020). Framed in this way, Sweden underscores the risks of delegating authority to experts in response to a pandemic or another highly uncertain event. Although public health authorities championed more robust social distancing in other countries, in Sweden (as well as Denmark) they recommended a more relaxed approach. By delegating authority to an independent agency, Swedish policymakers were left with few instruments to incorporate local information or correct course.

Second, to the extent that Sweden resembles Denmark, it illustrates how cohesive and encompassing networks can get countries into trouble. Just as overconfidence in financial regulators led to policy errors and banking crises in Finland, Sweden, and Iceland (Ornston, 2018), faith in the National Health Agency led the

Social Democrats and all other major political parties to embrace its recommendations. Satisfied with this response, they not only refrained from introducing a more stringent lockdown but also failed to introduce alternative measures such as Danish- or Icelandic-style mass testing (Roser et al., 2020). Cross-partisan support for the national health agency was mirrored by the public, where a majority (64 percent) approved of the government's response as recently as May 2020, despite intense international criticism. This was lower than Denmark, but considerably higher than other countries such as France and Spain ("COVID-19: Government Handling and Confidence in Health Authorities," 2020). Like Denmark, strong social safety nets neutralized dissent, but in this case by making it easier for individuals unhappy with Sweden's lax approach to self-isolate.

If history judges Sweden's COVID-19 response harshly, it will be tempting to dismiss it as an anomaly, an unusual error by an otherwise competent agency (Nygren & Olofsson, 2020) or a product of Sweden's distinctive constitutional structure (Jonung, 2020; Karlson et al., 2020). In fact, however, this is a recurring theme in the Nordic region (Ornston, 2018). The same high-trust networks that helped André Oscar Wallenberg industrialize Sweden in the late nineteenth century (Sjögren, 2008) enabled Ivar Kreuger to bankrupt it in the 1930s (Partnoy, 2010). The capacity for collective action, which dramatically increased technological research and development in Finland (Moen & Lilja, 2005), created a skewed innovation system (Ornston, 2012a) and increased Finland's vulnerability to disruptive shocks (Ornston, 2014). In short, the Swedish case is important because it shows that an inclusive and participatory approach to policy making does not guarantee optimal results, particularly during periods of heightened uncertainty when the best course of action is unclear.

In the long run, the benefits of flexibility have exceeded the costs in the Nordic region. In Sweden's case, declining government support and growing scientific dissent have already prompted a reassessment of the country's strategy and a (belated) increase in testing. Denmark and even Sweden thus illuminate an alternative pathway to rapid and radical reform. Adaptive capacity is based not on powerful executives, majoritarian electoral institutions, or independent agencies, but rather an inclusive process that excels at gathering local information, persuading skeptics, compensating adversely affected actors, and fostering coordination. It is not perfect, but it has enabled these countries to successfully adapt to a wide range of technological, economic, and social challenges.

References

Alesina, A., & Giavazzi, F. (2006). *The future of Europe*. The MIT Press.
Andersen, T. M., Holmström, B., Honkapohja, S., Korkman, S., Söderström, H. T., & Vartiainen, J. (2007). *The Nordic model: Embracing globalization and sharing risks*. Taloustieto Oy.
Bennedsen, M., Schmutte, I., Larsen, B., & Scur, D. (2020). *Preserving job matches during the COVID-19 Pandemic: Firm-level evidence on the role of government aid* [Unpublished manuscript].

Besley, T., & Persson, T. (2011). *Pillars of prosperity: The political economics of development clusters*. Princeton University Press.

Block, F. (2008). Swimming against the current: The rise of a hidden developmental state in the United States. *Politics and Society, 36*(2), 169–206.

Bouw, B. (2020, March 26). How Denmark got ahead of the COVID-19 economic crisis. *Maclean's*. https://www.macleans.ca/economy/economicanalysis/how-denmark-got-ahead-of-the-covid-19-economic-crisis/

Breznitz, D. (2007). *Innovation and the state: Political choice and strategies for growth in Israel, Taiwan, and Ireland*. Yale University Press.

Breznitz, D., & Ornston, D. (2013). The revolutionary power of peripheral agencies: Explaining radical policy innovation in Finland and Israel. *Comparative Political Studies, 46*(10), 1219–1245.

Cameron, D. (1984). Social democracy, corporatism, labour quiescence and the representation of economic interests in advanced capitalist society. In J. H. Goldthorpe (Ed.), *Order and conflict in contemporary capitalism* (pp. 143–178). Clarendon Press.

Campbell, J. L., & Hall, J. A. (2009). National identity and the political economy of small states. *Review of International Political Economy, 16*(4), 547–572.

Campbell, J. L., & Hall, P. A. (2017). *The paradox of vulnerability: States, nationalism and the financial crisis*. Princeton University Press.

Campbell, J. L., & Pedersen, O. K. (2007). The varieties of capitalism and hybrid success: Denmark in the global economy. *Comparative Political Studies, 40*(3), 307–332.

COVID-19: Government handling and confidence in health authorities. (2020). *YouGov*. https://yougov.co.uk/topics/international/articles-reports/2020/03/17/perception-government-handling-covid-19

Devlin, K., & Connaughton, A. (2020, August 27). COVID-19 response approved by most in 14 nations with advanced economies. *Pew Research Center: Global Attitudes Project*. https://www.pewresearch.org/global/2020/08/27/most-approve-of-national-response-to-covid-19-in-14-advanced-economies/

Esping-Andersen, G. (1990). *The three worlds of welfare capitalism*. Polity.

Fioretos, O. (2013). Origins of embedded orthodoxy: International cooperation and political unity in Greece. *European Political Studies, 12*, 305–319.

Fuchs, E. (2010). Rethinking the role of the state in technology development: DARPA and the case for embedded network governance. *Research Policy, 39*, 1133–1147.

Fung, A. (2009). *Empowered participation: Reinventing urban democracy*. Princeton University Press.

Grabher, G. (1993). The weakness of strong ties: The lock-in of regional development in the Ruhr area. In G. Grabher (Ed.), *The embedded firm* (pp. 255–277). Routledge.

Greer, S. L., King, E. J., Fonseca, E. M. da, & Peralta-Santos, A. (2020). The comparative politics of COVID-19: The need to understand government responses. *Global Public Health, 15*(9), 1413–1416. https://doi.org/10.1080/17441692.2020.1783340

Hall, P., & Soskice, D. (2001). An introduction to varieties of capitalism. In P. Hall & D. Soskice (Eds.), *Varieties of capitalism: The institutional foundations of comparative advantage* (pp. 1–70). Oxford University Press.

ILO. (2020). *COVID-19 and the world of work: Country policy responses*. International Labour Organization. https://www.ilo.org/global/topics/coronavirus/country-responses/lang—en/index.htm#DK

IMF. (2020). *Policy responses to COVID-19*. International Monetary Fund. https://www.imf.org/en/Topics/imf-and-covid19/Policy-Responses-to-COVID-19#D

Immergut, E. M. (1992). *Health politics: Interests and institutions in Western Europe*. Cambridge University Press.

Johnson, C. (1982). *MITI and the Japanese miracle*. Stanford University Press.

Jonung, L. (2020, June 18). Sweden's constitution decides its exceptional Covid-19 policy. *VoxEU.Org*. https://voxeu.org/article/sweden-s-constitution-decides-its-exceptional-covid-19-policy

Jørgensen, C. (2011, January 27). Work-sharing saves jobs. *Eurofound*. https://www.eurofound.europa.eu/publications/article/2011/work-sharing-saves-jobs

Karlson, N., Stern, C., & Klein, D. (2020, April 20). The underpinnings of Sweden's permissive COVID regime. *VoxEU*. https://voxeu.org/article/underpinnings-sweden-s-permissive-covid-regime

Katz, B., & Bradley, J. (2013). *The metropolitan revolution: How cities and metros are fixing our broken politics and fragile economy*. Brookings Institution Press.

Katzenstein, P. J. (1985). *Small states in world markets: Industrial policy in Europe*. Cornell University Press.

Kjær, J. S., Rasmussen, L. I., & Larsen, J. B. (2020, May 29). Mette Frederiksen var uenig med Søren Brostrøm og tog magten fra ham [Mette Frederiksen disagreed with Søren Brostrøm and took power from him]. *Politiken*. https://politiken.dk/forbrugogliv/sundhedogmotion/art7803218/Mette-Frederiksen-var-uenig-med-S%C3%B8ren-Brostr%C3%B8m-og-tog-magten-fra-ham

Krause, T. G. (2020). *Smittetallet steg yderligere i uge 32* [The number of infections increased further in week 32]. Statens Serum Institut. https://www.ssi.dk/aktuelt/nyheder/2020/smittetallet-steg-yderligere—i-uge-32

Kurz, S. (2020, February 16). The "frugal four" advocate a responsible EU Budget. *Financial Times*. https://www.ft.com/content/7faae690-4e65-11ea-95a0-43d18ec715f5

Levy, J. (1999). *Tocqueville's revenge: State, society, and economy in contemporary France*. Harvard University Press.

Lijphart, A. (1977). *Democracy in plural societies: A comparative exploration*. Yale University Press.

Madsen, P. K. (2003). Flexicurity through labour market policies and institutions in Denmark. In P. L. Auer & S. Cazes (Eds.), *Employment stability in an age of flexibility* (pp. 59–105). International Labour Organization.

Madsen, P. K. (2006). How can it possibly fly? The paradox of a dynamic labor market in a Scandinavian State. In J. L. Campbell, J. A. Hall, & O. K. Pedersen (Eds.), *National identity and the varieties of capitalism: The Danish experience* (pp. 323–355). McGill University Press.

Mjøset, L. (1987). Nordic economic policies in the 1970s and 1980s. *International Organization*, *41*(3), 403–456.

Moen, E., & Lilja, K. (2005). Change in coordinated market economies: The case of Nokia and Finland. In G. Morgan, R. Whitley, & E. Moen (Eds.), *Changing capitalisms: Internationalization, institutional change and systems of economic organization* (pp. 352–379). Oxford University Press.

Nygren, K. G., & Olofsson, A. (2020). Managing the COVID-19 pandemic through individual responsibility: The consequences of a world risk society and enhanced ethopolitics. *Journal of Risk Research*, 1–5. https://doi.org/10.1080/13669877.2020.1756382

OECD. (2020). *Country policy tracker: Denmark*. Organization for Economic Co-operation and Development. https://www.oecd.org/coronavirus/country-policy-tracker/

Olsen, A. L., & Hjorth, F. (2020). *Willingness to distance in the COVID-19 pandemic* [Unpublished manuscript]. https://osf.io/xpwg2/download

Olsen, M. (2020, March 23). Denmark: How a "high-tax" state responds to coronavirus. *EUobserver*. https://euobserver.com/coronavirus/147827

OPSI. (2020, July 6). Danish COVID-19 Infection Tracing App (Smitte|stop). *Observatory of Public Sector Innovation Blog*. https://www.oecd-opsi.org/covid-response/danish-covid-19-infection-tracing-app-smittestop/

Ornston, D. (2012a). Old ideas and new investments: Divergent pathways to a knowledge economy in Denmark and Finland. *Governance*, *25*(4), 687–710.

Ornston, D. (2012b). *When small states make big leaps: Institutional innovation and high-tech competition in Western Europe*. Cornell University Press.

Ornston, D. (2014). When the high road becomes the low road: The limits of high tech competition in Finland. *Review of Policy Research*, *31*(5), 454–477.

Ornston, D. (2018). *Good governance gone bad: How Nordic adaptability leads to excess*. Cornell University Press.

Ornston, D. (2019, September 1). *Ideas as an innovation policy instrument*. Annual Meeting of the American Political Science Association, Washington D.C.

Ornston, D., & Schulze-Cleven, T. (2015). Concertation and coordination: Two logics of collective action. *Comparative Political Studies*, *48*(5), 555–585.

Partnoy, F. (2010). *The match king: Ivar Kreuger, the financial genius behind a century of Wall Street scandals*. Public Affairs.

Pekkarinen, J., Pohjola, M., & Rowthorn, B. (1992). *Social corporatism: A superior economic system?* Clarendon.

Pierson, P. (1996). The new politics of the welfare state. *World Politics*, *48*(2), 143–179.

Polanyi, K. (1944). *The great transformation*. Beacon Press.

Putnam, R. D. (1993). *Making democracy work*. Princeton University Press.

Rhodes, M. (2001). The political economy of social pacts: Competitive corporatism and European welfare reform. In P. Pierson (Ed.), *The new politics of the welfare state* (pp. 165–194). Oxford University Press.

Ringstrom, A., & Fulton, C. (2020, July 1). Swedish Central Bank forecasts key rate at 0% for coming years. *Reuters*. https://www.reuters.com/article/sweden-cenbank-forecast/table-swedish-cbank-forecasts-key-rate-at-0-for-coming-years-idUSS3N2AC001

Ritchie, H., Ortiz-Ospina, E., Beltekian, D., Mathieu, E., Hassell, J., Macdonald, B., Giattino, C., & Roser, M. (2020, July 11). Coronavirus (COVID-19) Testing. *Our world in data*. https://ourworldindata.org/coronavirus-testing

Roser, M., Ritchie, H., Ortiz-Ospina, E., & Hasell, J. (2020). *Coronavirus pandemic (COVID-19)*. Blavatnik School of Government. https://ourworldindata.org/coronavirus

Rothstein, B., & Stolle, D. (2003). Introduction: Social capital in Scandinavia. *Scandinavian Political Studies*, *26*(1), 1–26.

Sjögren, H. (2008). Welfare capitalism: The Swedish economy, 1850–2005. In S. Fellman, M. J. Iversen, H. Sjögren, & L. Thue (Eds.), *Creating Nordic capitalism: The business history of a competitive periphery* (pp. 22–74). Palgrave MacMillan.

Thompson, D. (2020, March 21). Denmark's idea could help the world avoid a Great Depression. *The Atlantic.* https://www.theatlantic.com/ideas/archive/2020/03/denmark-freezing-its-economy-should-us/608533/

Tracking Covid-19 excess deaths across countries. (2020). *The Economist.* https://www.economist.com/graphic-detail/2020/07/15/tracking-covid-19-excess-deaths-across-countries

Vail, M. I. (2018). *Liberalism in illiberal states: Ideas and economic adjustment in contemporary Europe.* Oxford University Press.

Vrangbæk, K., Jervelund, S. S., Krasnik, A., & Birk, H. O. (2020). *Denmark: Policy responses* (COVID-19 Health System Response Monitor). World Health Organization Regional Office for Europe, European Commission, and European Observatory on Health Systems and Policies. https://www.covid19healthsystem.org/countries/denmark/countrypage.aspx

Weyland, K. (2009). *Bounded rationality and policy diffusion: Social sector reform in Latin America.* Princeton University Press.

15 FRANCE'S MULTIDIMENSIONAL COVID-19 RESPONSE

Ad Hoc Committees and the Sidelining of Public Health Agencies

Sarah D. Rozenblum

Introduction: The Surprising Weakness of the French Arsenal of Health Security and Public Health during the COVID-19 Crisis

France was severely affected by COVID-19, with 30,601 recorded deaths in late August 2020 (Assemblée Nationale, 2020). Between March and September2020, the French government took a series of comprehensive actions to protect its population from the consequences of the COVID-19 pandemic, ranging from health services measures to socioeconomic policies. This multidimensional response limited the social and health impacts of the crisis (Conseil d'Analyse Economique, 2020). Although unprecedented in their scale and binding nature, public health measures were taken rather late, using heterodox methods (Bergeron et al., 2020). Public health experts trained in emergency preparedness were sidelined, while the crisis management was centralized by the executive branch, whose members have minimal training in public health (Bergeron & Borraz, 2020). The progressive expansion that the public health sphere has undergone since the late 1990s was not enough to give public health experts a monopoly of advice and action in the eyes of generalist officials, who not only reached out to other professions but also treated public health professionals with no special regard (Rozenblum et al., 2020). Although these governance choices do not seem to have undermined France's response to COVID-19, they eroded public trust in the government (Nossiter, 2020; Odoxa, 2020) and raise several questions for researchers regarding the role and use of public health expertise in times of crisis. The French response combined protective social and economic policies with an ambivalent attitude toward public health institutions and tools, which were created precisely to respond to a pandemic of this magnitude. Their marginalization is all the more surprising given that France has created many public health institutions since the late 1990s, which could have been more extensively mobilized (Rozenblum et al., 2020).

The French public health arena became a privileged space for political action in the late 1990s, as a direct outcome of several health scandals (Tabuteau, 2002, 2007). These crises—including mad cow disease and scandals over tainted blood samples and growth hormones—revealed the shortcomings of the French public health approach. As a result, they raised the political profile of public health (Bergeron & Nathanson, 2012). Previously marginalized, public health was redefined in the late 1990s as a responsibility of the French state to protect its population against disease risks and to ensure equal access to the healthcare system (Rozenblum, in press). This dual responsibility was captured through the newly coined legal notions of *sécurité sanitaire* ("health security") and *démocratie sanitaire* ("health democracy"). Framing public health interventions in the language of "security" changed their place in the hierarchical structure of the state and increased their political salience (Bergeron & Nathanson, 2017). This framing reinforced public health as a legitimate field of intervention (viewed as an essential function of government, similar to defense) and presented the state as the legitimate protector of population health (Rozenblum et al., 2020).

As "health security" became the centerpiece of the renewed French public health arena, more than ten agencies were created or reorganized in its name, including the Institute for Disease Surveillance (acronym in French, InVS, 1998), the Agency for Medicines and Medical Devices Safety (acronym in French, ANSM, 2011), and Public Health France (acronym in French, SPF, 2016). Six laws devoted to health security were passed by the National Assembly in 1993, 1998, 2001, 2006, 2007, and 2011 (Rozenblum, in press).

France's public health arena became highly institutionalized over the last three decades. As French researchers observed, "the density of institutional expertise in public health in France . . . is among the most important in Europe" (Bergeron & Borraz, 2020). These institutions fall into four categories. First, within the Ministry of Health, the General Directorate of Health (acronym in French, DGS) and the General Directorate of Health Care Services (acronym in French, DGOS) are responsible for defining health policies and ensuring monitoring, forecasting, regulation, and health security missions. Public health experts joined the ranks of the Ministry of Health in the wake of the 1990s scandals (Tabuteau, 2016). Both directorates were mobilized throughout the COVID-19 crisis. Second, the Regional Health Agencies (acronym in French, ARS), created in 2009, carry out prevention and health planning missions at the regional level. They played a critical role during the COVID-19 crisis (Assemblée Nationale, 2020). Third, "health security" agencies, such as the National Drug Safety Agency, ensure medical devices and drug safety as well as health surveillance. Finally, "expert agencies" issue recommendations and conduct scientific studies on behalf of the executive (Tabuteau, 2016). This category includes—but is not limited to—the High Authority for Health (acronym in French, HAS), the High Council for Public Health (acronym in French, HCSP) and Public Health France (Santé Publique France, SPF). Despite their expertise and resources, these agencies were relegated to a logistical and technical role during the COVID-19 crisis. Public health agencies seemed to have been sidelined by governments in countries as different as France, Denmark, and the United States (Rozenblum et al., 2020). Their marginalization raises a series of questions addressed throughout this chapter. Finally, the backbone of the French emergency management system—the *sécurité civile* [civil protection]—relies on a specialized set of actors, including a secretariat supervised by the prime minister. The *sécurité civile* is responsible for emergency planning, and periodically organizes crisis management simulation exercises (Bergeron et al., 2020).

The COVID-19 pandemic broke out during a particularly tense moment for French hospitals. Demanding more resources for public hospitals, healthcare professionals had been on strike since November 2019 (Béguin, 2020). More than 1,200 hospital professionals resigned on January 14, 2020 (Béguin, 2020). As the COVID-19 pandemic spread in France, the government realized—without publicly acknowledging it—that essential resources, including protective equipment, hand sanitizers, and diagnostic tests were scarce nationwide (Gandre & Or, 2020). This is the result of ten years of disinvestment in public health that followed the mismanagement of the 2009 H1N1 epidemic (Davet & Lhomme, 2020). In 2009, the government had been accused of overpredicting the number of H1N1 casualties and purchasing too many masks and vaccines (Gandre & Or, 2020). One billion euros were spent on protective equipment, although the virus "only" killed 342 individuals (Davet & Lhomme, 2020). As a result, consecutive governments chose to reduce the national stockpile. They required hospitals and private companies to build up their own supply of masks. None of these stakeholders, however, were informed of this new requirement, and stockpiles were scarce both within hospitals and in the private sector (Gandre & Or, 2020). In February 2020, the government only had 100 million surgical masks (Rouquet, 2020).

Before January 2020, France's robust slate of public health institutions looked well prepared for a major health emergency, despite a somehow ambivalent attitude toward crisis preparedness that followed the mismanagement of 2009 H1N1 crisis. By January 2020, French officials could point to extensive institutionalization of public health infrastructure, despite having a relatively smaller public health workforce than in the United States (Rozenblum et al., 2020). In March 2020, however, the government set up two ad hoc scientific committees tasked with providing **strategic** public health expertise to the executive branch, while established agencies such as SPF and the High Council of Public Health did not lead the institutional response to the pandemic. Public health agencies appear to have been marginalized by the executive branch when they were needed most. Were they purposefully sidelined during the crisis? Was the French arsenal of public health created over the last three decades insufficient or inadequate to tackle a health crisis of this magnitude? Finally, what are the consequences of this fragmented scientific landscape for established public health institutions and the national responses to COVID-19? Several hypotheses can be examined to answer these questions, which will ultimately shed light on the politicization of French public health expertise during the COVID-19 pandemic.

Hypothesis 1: Public Health alongside French Presidentialism. "Public health" is legally conceived in France as the responsibility of the state to protect its population from health risks. In this sense, during the COVID-19 crisis, the protection of the population was framed as a mission that should be imposed from above by an executive that highly centralized the governance of the health crisis (Bergeron & Borraz, 2020; Pedrot, 2020). President Macron compared the pandemic to a war on several occasions (Elysée, 2020a). He posed as a military leader, who should defeat the virus and handle the crisis on his own (Elysée, 2020a) and played an influential role in controlling the crisis through France's institutions (Perera & Tarrow, 2020). The centralization of power under the *loi d'urgence sanitaire* (health emergency law) led to the creation of ad hoc institutions placed directly under presidential control. Such centralization of power was made possible by the institutions of the Fifth Republic, which gave the president significant powers in times of crisis and allowed him to deviate from preexisting plans and laws.

Hypothesis 2: Multidimensional Crisis Management. The executive branch took a series of social, economic, and health measures to contain a pandemic politically framed as a multidimensional event by the government. Economic, social, and public health tools were given equal importance. This polymorphic approach may have overshadowed health agencies whose expertise was deemed too technical and narrow. Consequently, public health professionals were not given exclusive authority to design the national COVID-19 strategy, nor exclusive control over the tools required to implement this multidimensional strategy on the ground (Rozenblum et al., 2020).

Hypothesis 3: Absence of a Culture of Health Security. France, as most European countries, has never experienced a public health crisis of this magnitude and lacked practice in mobilizing its public health arsenal, formidable as it may have been. Over the last ten years, there also has been a drift toward terrorism and natural disaster preparedness, and away from pandemic preparedness in France (Bergeron et al., 2020). Communication between scientific experts and public officials can be difficult, and the creation of ad hoc scientific committees allowed the executive branch to bridge to gap, while also handpicking members of its own choice.

Hypothesis 4: (Presumed) Slowness of Health Bureaucracy. France's top policymakers may have worried that the bureaucracy of public health institutions was incompatible with managing a rapidly evolving crisis that called for quick decision-making. Pre-existing plans for responding to pandemics were perhaps thought to be too slow to mobilize the relevant actors, or too complex to be put into action. Historically, the French Ministries of Health and the Interior have competed against one another to handle crisis management efforts (Bergeron et al., 2020). Interministerial rivalry may have been seen as hindering the response to COVID-19. As a result, ad hoc structures were needed to respond more nimbly.

Centralized, Multidimensional Crisis Response,
Which Eroded Trust in Government

The crisis led to a delayed but unprecedented centralization of health governance. The pandemic response was originally led by the Ministry of Health but was then shifted to the prime minister (Assemblée Nationale, 2020). The General Directorate of Health activated its Health Crisis Center on January 27, 2020, but failed to activate the 2011 Influenza Pandemic Preparedness Response plan. The prime minister did not activate the Interministerial Crisis Unit (placed under the supervision of the Ministry of Interior) until March 17, 2020 (Assemblée Nationale, 2020). Consequently, this delay confined the response to COVID-19 to a strictly medical dimension for two months. The virus was not framed as a public health and multidimensional problem until mid-March (Pedrot, 2020). In contrast, some countries decided to give their head of state full authority in defining the national COVID-19 strategy early on, including Canada, Estonia, Finland, Israel, Serbia, and Ukraine (Greer et al., 2020).

The government's communication strategy generated confusion among healthcare providers as well as the general population. Although the first cases of coronavirus were detected in France on January 24, 2020 (Assemblée Nationale, 2020), the first official recommendations on hand hygiene were issued "rather late" by the Ministry of Health, on March 20, 2020, according to researchers Gandre and Or (Gandre & Or, 2020; Ministère de la Santé, 2020). The government reversed its position regarding the use of face masks and testing kits on several occasions, resulting from the scarcity of these resources. Deemed "unnecessary" in February, face masks became mandatory in all public places in Paris, Marseille, Bordeaux, and other major cities on August 27, 2020, as the number of new COVID-19 cases increased significantly (Decree of July 17, 2020). Initial quarantine and isolation recommendations were also inconsistent. Travelers flying from Wuhan were quarantined in closed facilities in southern France for fourteen days. Individuals coming from Italy, however, were advised to self-quarantine and monitor their symptoms (Gandre & Or, 2020). Known cases were initially isolated in hospitals, regardless of the gravity of their symptoms. When they reached full capacity, COVID-19 patients were advised to stay at home. The executive branch's communication strategy—regarding the use of face masks, quarantine, and management of known cases—fluctuated over a short period of time, generating confusion among healthcare providers and the population. Finally, the state of emergency was not declared until March 23, 2020, much later than France's neighbors (Greer et al., 2020). France's health ministry approved hydroxychloroquine for emergency prescriptions on March 25, 2020, only to revoke this decree on May 27, 2020, on the grounds that there was no proof that it helps patients and citing data that showed it could pose health risks.

Physical distancing measures expanded gradually but also generated confusion. The government banned large gatherings of more than five thousand individuals (on March 4, 2020), then of more than one thousand people (on March 8), then of more than one hundred (on March 13) (Assemblée Nationale, 2020). Nursing homes were closed to the public on March 11, and schools and universities closed on March 13 (Assemblée Nationale, 2020). Surprisingly, even though all public places except grocery stores were closed, the government declined to reschedule municipal elections held on March 15. The elections do not seem to have intensified the spread of the disease at the national level according to a study, but the incongruity of this decision provoked widespread controversy (Zeitoun et al., 2020). Only three days later, the government unilaterally imposed a national lockdown. Instead of relying on previously tested policy solutions such as quarantine, contact tracing, and school closures, President Macron chose to declare a lockdown whose socioeconomic consequences had never been modeled before, and which had not been planned for by the 2011 Influenza Pandemic Preparedness Response plan (Bergeron et al., 2020; Gandre & Or, 2020). All employers were required to let their employees work remotely, except for essential workers. Individuals were allowed to leave their homes only to get food, seek medical assistance, or for short recreational activities near their place of residence (Gandre & Or, 2020). Those measures were enforced by police officers patrolling the streets and fining violators. Local authorities took additional measures at the regional level. The lockdown was supposed to come to an end on April 15 but was extended until May 11 (Assemblée Nationale, 2020).

In terms of systemic health measures, the government launched the *Plan blanc* on March 6, 2020, but disregarded the 2011 Influenza Pandemic Preparedness Response plan. The *Plan blanc* entailed postponing all nonurgent procedures in French hospitals, and creating new organizational measures to provide emergency care for the influx of patients (Gandre & Or, 2020). As a result, most hospitals reorganized their operations, expanded intensive care capacity, and created specialized COVID-19 units. Contrary to the 2011 plan, however, the *Plan blanc* was not designed to help healthcare professionals treat contagious patients for an extended period of time (Bergeron et al., 2020). Meanwhile, on March 14 the government enacted the ORSAN REB plan, which ended systematic COVID-19 testing for symptomatic patients, prioritizing antibody tests. Between March 1 and June 16, France recorded approximately 29,547 deaths, 19,090 of which occurred in the hospital. Of these, 10,457 occurred in assisted nursing homes (acronym in French, EHPAD) and other social medical establishments (Milon, 2020). The French government struggled to get data on the spread of coronavirus from nursing homes. These data were not included in the government's daily count until April 27.

Santé Publique France created a reporting tool as a result of strong pressure from public opinion. Shortly after this new reporting system was implemented, it became clear that nursing homes were major hotspots: around one-third of all deaths incurred by COVID-19 occurred in nursing homes. As of September 3, 2020, 43,000 COVID-19 cases had been reported in nursing homes (Santé Publique France, 2020b). A fourth of the residents (10,514) who contracted the disease in these facilities later died from it (Santé Publique France, 2020b). This presentation, however, overlooked the large number of infected nursing home residents who had been sent to the hospital and died there from COVID-19 complications. According to Santé Publique France, as of May 7, 3,428 out of the 12,958 individuals who died from COVID-19 in French hospitals initially contracted the disease in nursing homes and other medical centers (2020). Nursing homes were allowed to hire community-based physicians and nurses to increase their workforce capacity during these critical times (Gandre & Or, 2020).

France officially began transitioning out of the first lockdown on May 11, 2020 (Santé Publique France, 2020a). The government imposed targeted restrictions at the regional or local levels during the summer. In an interview with the newspaper *Le Monde* published on July 29, the head of the parliamentary inquiry commission, Eric Ciotti (a member of the right-wing opposition), stated that "public health measures have been cruelly deficient... Few measures were taken before the month of March, and the management of the crisis seemed particularly chaotic" (Hecketsweiler & de Royer, 2020). This statement is partially justified given France's inability to limit the extent of infection and subsequent high COVID-19 infections and mortality rates, especially among the elderly. The government, however, mobilized its safety net to protect its population from the financial, economic, and social consequences of the pandemic.

Health Response Accompanied by Unparalleled Social and Economic Measures

France's effort to provide financial relief to struggling individuals and businesses during the crisis was unequaled both in Europe and worldwide. First, most health expenses linked to COVID-19 were covered by the National Health Insurance Fund (NHIF, known as *Sécurité sociale* in France). Second, France's safety net played a critical role in protecting the population. Several EU governments have taken social and economic measures to mitigate the effects of the crisis on their population and economy. The Danish government defined COVID-19 as a work-related injury that qualifies for government compensation (Jarman et al., 2020). The German Education Ministry committed to providing loans for students experiencing financial difficulty because of the pandemic. Austria strengthened social benefits for individuals financially affected by the crisis (around 1 percent of the population fell into the "risk groups" entitled to public assistance). In France, the government has taken unprecedented measures to help workers, vulnerable populations, and business. The president acknowledged the "social" and "economic" dimensions of the crisis early on, on April 13, 2020 (Elysée, 2020b). In a subsequent address to the nation on June 14, President Macron committed to prevent layoffs and help young professionals remained employed (Elysée, 2020c).

The French NHIF covered most expenses incurred for COVID-19 testing, treatment, and hospital stay. Most hospital costs were reimbursed, although patients were required to pay a daily rate of EUR 15 to 20, which could be covered by complementary health insurances. COVID-19 diagnostic tests were charged EUR 54 (Gandre & Or, 2020). The NHIF covered 60 percent of the test if it was administered in a community-based setting and 100 percent of it was carried out in a hospital setting. As France transitioned out of the first lockdown in May 2020, COVID-19 tests became fully reimbursed, whether carried out in hospital or community-based settings (Gandre & Or, 2020). Teleconsultations were entirely covered by the NHIF until December 31, 2020 (Gandre & Or, 2020). Physicians, nurses, midwives, speech therapists, occupational therapists, and psychometricians were able to use teleconsultations without restrictions. The government also took a series of measures to improve access to care for vulnerable groups during the pandemic. They included mechanisms for migrants to receive state medical assistance (*Aide Médicale d'Etat*) and patients with chronic conditions who benefit from the long-term illness scheme (*Affection Longue Durée*). The NHIF also immediately covered expatriates who came back to France during the pandemic (Gandre & Or, 2020). Finally, the executive opened eighty-eight residential centers for homeless people infected with the virus and set up a free hotline to provide medical advice to homeless individuals with COVID-19 symptoms (Ministère de la Cohésion des Territoires, 2020).

The French government has also taken a series of proactive measures to support businesses and mitigate the impact of the crisis on the economy. The law n°2020–290 du 23 mars 2020 (*loi d'urgence pour faire face à l'épidémie de Covid-19* [Emergency law to deal with the Covid-19 pandemic]) and the law n°2020–289 du 23 mars 2020 (*loi de finances rectificative pour 2020* [Amending finance law for 2020]) both include large-scale measures to support businesses. These measures were gradually adapted as the situation evolved. The government created a "solidarity fund" on March 25, 2020, to provide financial assistance to small businesses. As of May 27, 2020, two months after its creation, the fund had granted more than EUR 3.4 billion in aid (Assemblée Nationale, 2020). The government loaned 66.46 billion euros to more than 400,000 struggling businesses by May 12 (Assemblée Nationale, 2020). According to the Economic Council, responsible for advising the government on economic policy, the loans "put in place to support business liquidity have been effective" (Conseil d'Analyse Economique [CAE], 2020). The volume of state-guaranteed loans disbursed (EUR 105 billion by June 26) is higher in proportion of gross domestic product (GDP) than in the other major EU countries, with the exception of Spain. The executive also postponed the payment dates for social security contributions and tax withholdings for March, April, and May for a total amount of EUR 42 billion. Finally, the government granted sectorial aids, targeting industries that had been deeply affected by the crisis, including tourism, culture, construction, and air travel. Were these measures sufficient to prevent an economic crisis? According to the Economic Council, the executive took a series of "reassuring" measures during the lockdown (CAE, 2020). The economic "shock" the country experienced, however, was "stronger than elsewhere." The GDP decreased by 5.3 percent during the first quarter of 2020. This trend was comparable to what was observed in Spain and Italy, but more than double the 2.2 percent drop in the German GDP (CAE, 2020). Early evidence suggests that the COVID-19 crisis will deepen inequalities in the long term, disproportionately affecting young adults under 30 (Observatoire des Inégalités, 2020).

The government's response targeting the workforce has been structured along three main objectives: maintaining employment, preserving workers' financial resources, and ensuring safety for all employees—especially health professionals and essential workers. First, the government ensured income replacement for those who could not work because of physical distancing requirements or business closure (Jarman et al., 2020). This system, known as the "partial activity scheme" or "partial unemployment scheme" (*dispositif d'activité partielle* or *dispositif de chômage partiel*), existed before 2020. The government significantly expanded it on March 25, 2020, allowing employees to temporarily stop working, while retaining their jobs and receiving an income until December 31, 2020 (Assemblée Nationale, 2020). Under this special job furlough scheme, employees on furlough received 84 percent of their net wage (100 percent for employees on the minimum wage). This allowance was paid by the employer but was entirely funded by the government and was exempt from social insurance contributions.

According to data collected by the Ministry of Labor, this scheme benefited 12.9 million employees and 1.04 million firms as of May 26. The equivalent of 5.6 million hours were paid for by the government (approximately twelve thirty-five-hour weeks) (Ministère du Travail, 2020). According to the Economic Council, this job furlough scheme effectively protected French households' income. Although the national income fell by more than a third during the eight-week lockdown, individual income fell by 5 percent (CAE, 2020). In addition to the *dispositif d'activité partielle*, the government exempted from taxation overtime earnings for workers mobilized during the crisis. Finally, financial bonuses were paid to health professionals, civil servants, and contractual workers employed by the state, local governments, and public hospitals who were mobilized during the state of emergency.

Despite these supplemental incomes, health professionals expressed their frustration over public hospitals' scarce resources and deteriorating working conditions. As France transitioned out of the first lockdown in May 2020, the government convened a health consultation called *Ségur de la Santé* (name after Avenue de Ségur, the Parisian street on which France's health ministry is located), which only partially met their demands (Stromboni, 2020). Self-employed physicians who experienced a significant loss of income because of reduced activity during the lockdown received a financial aid from the government (Gandre & Or, 2020). The executive branch also offered financial bonuses aid to public hospital workers—regardless of their activity during the pandemic—and to professionals working in private hospitals that treated COVID-19 patients. These bonuses ranged from EUR 500 to 1,500, depending on the number of patients their hospital treated (Gandre & Or, 2020).

Last, but not least, the government sought to protect vulnerable families through financial assistance and housing protection. Modest households received an "exceptional solidarity assistance" payment of EUR 150, to which EUR 100 were added per dependent child. This measure was funded by the state and represented EUR 900 million (Assemblée Nationale, 2020). The government also enacted rules to protect tenants and prevent evictions resulting from the pandemic. France's *trêve hivernale* ("winter truce")—during which landlords may not evict tenants for any reason—usually runs for five months from November 1 until March 31, but it was extended until July 10. The rules instituted by the government during the pandemic also prevented landlords and providers from cutting off gas, heat, and electricity to tenants during this period. Finally, students and young professionals under twenty-five who were laid off during the pandemic received EUR 200 from the government. Maintaining emergency public health actions such as a national lockdown required social and economic policies that ensured widespread compliance with governmental measures. France's safety net and emergency measures helped mitigate the social and economic consequences of the crisis on the population. The long-term consequences of the crisis, however, will require future studies to be fully understood. Evidence so far suggests that the crisis will have a dramatic and long-lasting socioeconomic impact on France's most vulnerable populations, including young adults (Observatoire des Inégalités, 2020).

Insufficiencies and Contradictions of French Public Health Agencies Revealed by the Crisis

Relegated to missions of epidemiological surveillance and logistical organization, Santé Publique France did not play a strategic role during the first months of the crisis. Under Article L.1413-1 of the Code of Public Health, SPF is charged with monitoring health conditions in France, and with alerting public authorities "in order to aide decision" (*optique d'aide à la décision*) (Che et al., 2016). But to the extent that SPF was mobilized during the COVID-19 crisis starting on January 10, 2020, it was in a strictly operational and nonstrategic capacity. The missions it was given by the executive branch, although within its capacities, did not exhaust them. For example, SPF was instructed to mobilize one thousand volunteer health professionals as part of a health reserve. Through a decree on March 30, 2020, it was given an emergency budget of EUR 4 billion to finance the acquisition of masks, ventilators, and medicines to replenish France's depleted supplies (Assemblée Nationale, 2020). In findings released in February 2020, the Institut Pasteur accurately modeled French hospitals' growing inability to treat COVID-19, but the government disregarded these findings (Bergeron et al., 2020). The Haut Conseil de la Santé Publique (HCSP)—whose mission is to provide counsel to elected authorities on emerging health problems—saw a similar fate (Pedrot, 2020). Although the HCSP did formulate a number of proposals on subjects including at-risk patient care or the use of hydroxychloroquine (Assemblée Nationale, 2020), it never became a privileged interlocutor of the government (Pedrot, 2020). SPF nonetheless oversaw numerous surveillance efforts, despite finding itself overwhelmed by the task at hand. SPF's Data Division was understaffed at the onset of the crisis, relying on only fifty data analysts. Between January and mid-March, SPF was unable to share information with Regional Health Agencies and public hospitals. Its indicators mapped out the spread of the virus at the national level only and were described as "shallow" by the prime minister himself (Hecketsweiler &

de Royer, 2020). Beginning on March 19, 2020, SPF created a mechanism of epidemiological surveillance for cases of severe infections of COVID-19 in intensive care. And on March 31, 2020, it designed a similar surveillance system for COVID-19 cases in nursing homes (Assemblée Nationale, 2020). Based on these surveillance efforts, SPF published weekly epidemiological bulletins on its website. Additionally, it established a weekly publication of scientific articles on the coronavirus (Pedrot, 2020).

According to its mandate under Article L.1413-1 of the code of public health, one of SPF's core missions is to "prepare and respond to health threats, alerts, and crises." It is therefore supposed to play a role beyond epidemiological surveillance and logistical organization. By law, SPF's role ought to include developing and implementing strategies to contain health crises. But this strategic function was largely delegated to two scientific committees created at the request of President Macron, which he relied on to provide expert legitimacy for his political decisions. Some of these decisions proved controversial among experts and the general public.

The response to COVID-19 was led by the French government, with the support of two scientific committees set up on March 12 and March 24, 2020 (Assemblée Nationale, 2020). The president also relied on a defense and national security council to handle the pandemic. This council existed before the crisis but was designed to manage issues pertaining to wars and domestic or international conflicts only. The council gained significance over the summer and became the main deciding body on questions related to physical distancing and other restrictive measures. The first scientific committee was composed of twelve scientists, including medical experts, a sociologist, and an anthropologist (Assemblée Nationale, 2020). It was initially created to provide guidance on questions related to treatment and testing, but it later saw its mandate expand to include recommendations on all questions related to the pandemic. A second scientific committee, known as the CARE (Committee for Analysis, Research, and Expertise) was set up to make recommendations on therapeutic options for COVID-19 patients (Assemblée Nationale, 2020). These committees were mostly made up of medical doctors, thus giving greater weight to clinical judgments than public health reasoning in the decision-making process. Public health officials and social scientists were sidelined by biomedical expertise, however much clinical medicine and life sciences research might be ill-adapted to population-level problems (Rozenblum et al., 2020). Between March 12 and May 18, 2020, the first council made thirteen recommendations. A number of these were adopted by the government in relation to politically sensitive actions. Notably, the committee recommended, in its first opinion on March 12, putting in place "barrier gestures" (*gestes barrière*) to ensure social distancing. Its second opinion on March 14 detailed particular measures to conduct the March municipal elections. The third opinion on March 16 outlined the terms of the nationwide lockdown, and its fourth opinion on April 2 specified the conditions under which the lockdown could be lifted. President Macron specifically invoked the committees' decisions to justify controversial decisions such as the holding of municipal elections. However, in other instances, such as the opening of schools or the end of the lockdown, the government did not follow the scientific committees' opinions. The first scientific council also proposed creating a liaison committee with the public and called for more systematic public engagement with the scientific community. These latter proposals were not adopted by the government.

The creation of two ad hoc scientific committees was surprising in several respects. The executive branch could have mobilized France's existing public health agencies to create a strategy to contain the virus. In its first report regarding the government's response to COVID-19, the parliamentary mission highlighted the "unprecedented" nature of the pandemic to justify the creation of two scientific committees (Assemblée Nationale, 2020). The novelty of the crisis does not, however, fully explain why "one of the densest public health networks in Europe" was underutilized by the government when it was needed the most. In a recent interview, the sociologist Daniel Benamouzig, one of the two social scientists on the first committee, explained that "the role of the scientific council was to guide public action by identifying the major aspects of a strategy against the epidemic. The scientific counsel had no operational responsibility" (Guénard & Naudet, 2020). Benamouzig continued, "The aim [of the scientific council] was less to set specific results than to evaluate the extent to which new findings—provided they were true and authenticated—could allow us to envision new instruments for effective public action to define strategies to reduce risk" (Guénard & Naudet, 2020). This approach is not unique to France. Several countries created ad hoc expert groups tasked with reviewing scientific evidence and communicating advice on appropriate health system measures to the government and the public. Examples include Belgium, Canada, Estonia, Ireland, Italy, Luxembourg, the Netherlands, and Spain, which established new expert advisory groups to bring scientific evidence into policy responses to COVID-19 (Williams et al., 2020).

The scientific councils were not subordinate to public powers (Benamouzig, 2020; Delfraissy, 2020). A number of their opinions were nonetheless published later by the government (Benamouzig, 2020; Delfraissy, 2020). It is worth noting that SPF and the HCSP were invited by the scientific council to attend meetings as "permanent observers," without actually participating (Delfraissy, 2020). As Benamouzig said, "As I see it, one of the strengths of the scientific council was the construction of broad orientations, what we might call 'pandemic thinking,' shared by all" (2020). The purpose of the scientific councils was to provide a strategic approach ordinarily reserved for the public health agencies, whose roles were reduced to logistical and operational matters.

Conclusion

The French response to the coronavirus crisis is instructive. Widely judged as "tardy" and "chaotic" by observers (Delfraissy, 2020; Pedrot, 2020), it was nonetheless distinct from that of neighboring countries. Despite the country's robust public health infrastructure, the government chose to create ad hoc bodies to define a public health strategy. If France reacted relatively late to the public health threat in mid-March—thereby losing time to acquire key protective equipment and tests—the government's socioeconomic strategy allowed it effectively to reduce the impact of the crisis on its population (CAE, 2020). But despite having a robust arsenal in the field of "health security" and numerous pre-existing public health agencies, the government found it necessary to create two ad hoc scientific committees to advise the executive and draft a strategy to confront the pandemic. No matter how consolidated, the French public health profession and institutions did not seem to enjoy a monopoly of advice or action—as in the United States with both the politicization and the marginalization of the Centers for Disease Control (CDC) and the Food and Drug Administration (FDA) (Rozenblum et al., in press).

The experience of these committees calls into question either the effectiveness of the pre-existing public health institutions or their place within the hierarchical structure of the state. As mentioned in the introduction, the sidelining of France's public health agencies might be attributable to the government's desire and inability to control these institutions. The executive branch may have also wanted to claim credit for its public health strategy, which it cannot do if it leaves control in the hands of external and independent public health actors. Another plausible explanation may be that the president wanted to create flexible scientific taskforces unconstrained by administrative rules (and therefore able to advise him quickly and proactively). Although these hypotheses deserve further investigation, our preliminary research suggests that the French government wanted to both control the production of public health norms and prompt their dissemination within the French population. This was made possible by the government's ability to concentrate powers during the state of emergency.

COVID-19 therefore shed light on the limits of the public health profession and institutions, which did not control its own key instruments, nor did it appear to be a legitimate and sufficient source of production of public health norms and recommendations (Rozenblum et al., 2020). In summary, the French case provides two key insights: a multidimensional health and socioeconomic response allowed the government to protect the population from the worst effects of the coronavirus in the short term; but at the same time, its public health agencies were revealed to be insufficient, if not inadequate, sources of strategic guidance in the face of a major public health crisis.

References

Assemblée Nationale. (2020, June 3). *Rapport d'information sur l'impact, la gestion et les conséquences dans toutes ses dimensions de l'épidémie de Coronavirus-Covid-19* [Information report on the impact, management and consequences in all its dimensions of the Coronavirus-Covid-19 pandemic].

Béguin, F. (2020, January 14). Crise de l'hôpital public: 1 200 médecins hospitaliers démissionnent de leur fonction d'encadrement [Public hospital crisis: 1,200 hospital healthcare professionals resign from their supervisory role]. *Le Monde*.

Bergeron, H., & Borraz, O. (2020, March 31). Covid-19: Impréparation et crise de l'Etat [Covid-19: Unpreparedness and state crisis]. *AOC*.

Bergeron, H., Borraz, O., Castel, P., & Dedieu F. (2020). *Covid-19: Une crise organisationnelle* [Covid-19: An organizational crisis]. Presses de Sciences Po.

Bergeron, H., & Nathanson, C. (2012, February). Construction of a policy arena: The case of public health in France. *Journal of Health Politics, Policy and Law, 37*, 1.

Bergeron, H., & Nathanson, C. (2017). Crise and changes: The making of the French FDA. *The Milbrank Quarterly, 95*(3), 634–675.

Bernard Stoecklin, S., Rolland, P., Silue, Y., Mailles, A., Campese, C., Simondon, A., Mechain, M., Meurice, L., Nguyen, M., Bassi, C., Yamani, E., Behili, S., Ismael, S., Nguyen, D., Malvy, D., Lescure, F-X., Georges, S., Lazarus, C., Tabaï, A., . . . Stempfelet, M. (2020). First cases of coronavirus disease 2019 (COVID-19) in France: surveillance, investigations and control measures, January 2020. *Euro Surveillance, 25*(6).

Che, D., Barret, A-S., & Desenclos, J-C. (2016). Maladies infectieuses émergentes [Emerging infectious diseases]. In *Traité de Santé publique* (3rd ed.). Lavoisier Médecine Sciences.

Conseil d'Analyse Economique (CAE), Martin, P., Pisani-Ferry, J., and Ragot, X. (2020, July). Note du CAE n°57. "Une stratégie économique face à la crise" [An economic strategy against the crisis].

Conseil Scientifique COVID-19 [COVID-19 scientific council]. (2020, March 12). Avis du Conseil scientifique COVID-19–12 mars 2020 [Recommendation of the scientific council of March 12, 2020].

Conseil Scientifique COVID-19 [COVID-19 scientific council]. (2020, March 14). Avis du Conseil scientifique COVID-19–14 mars 2020 [Recommendation of the scientific council of March 14, 2020].

Conseil Scientifique COVID-19 [COVID-19 scientific council]. (2020, March 16). Avis du Conseil scientifique COVID-19–16 mars 2020 [Recommendation of the scientific council of March 16, 2020].

Conseil Scientifique COVID-19 [COVID-19 scientific council]. (2020, April 2). Avis du Conseil scientifique COVID-29–2 avril 2020 [Recommendation of the scientific council of April 2, 2020].

Davet, G., & Lhomme, F. (2020, May 5). La France et les épidémies: 2010–2011, le changement de doctrine. [France and epidemics: 2010–2011, the change in doctrine]. *Le Monde*.

Décret n°2020–884 du 17 juillet 2020 modifiant le décret n°2020–860 du 10 juillet 2020 prescrivant les mesures générales nécessaires pour faire face à l'épidémie de covid-19 dans les territoires sortis de l'état d'urgence sanitaire et dans ceux où il a été prorogé [Decree n° 2020–884 of July 17, 2020 modifying decree n° 2020–860 of July 10, 2020 prescribing the general measures necessary to deal with the epidemic of covid-19 in the territories emerging from the state of health emergency and in those where it has been extended].

Delfraissy, J-F. (2020, June 18). Président du Conseil scientifique Covid-19. Audition devant la Mission d'information parlementaire [Chairman of the Covid-19 scientific council. Hearing before the parliamentary information Mission]. Assemblée Nationale.

Elysée. (2020a, March 16). Adresse aux Français du Président de la République Emmanuel Macron [Address to the French nation].

Elysée. (2020b, June 13). Adresse aux Français du Président de la République Emmanuel Macron [Address to the French nation].

Elysée. (2020c, June 14). Adresse au Français du Président de la République Emmanuel Macron [Address to the French nation].

Gandre, C., & Or, Z. (2020). France. *COVID-19 Health System Response Monitor.* European Observatory for Health Systems and Policies.

Greer, S., Jarman, H., Rozenblum, S., & Wismar, M. (2020). Who is in charge and why? Centralization within and between governments. *Eurohealth*, 26(2).

Guénard, F., & Naudet, J. (2020, July 1). Covid-19 et expertise sanitaire—Entretien avec Daniel Benamouzig [Covid-19 and health expertise—Interview with Daniel Benamouzig]. *La Vie des Idées.*

Hecketsweiler, C., & de Royer, e-S. (2020, July 29). Eric Ciotti: "Notre système de santé a bel et bien été débordé' par le coronavirus" [Eric Ciotti: "Our healthcare system has indeed been overwhelmed" by the coronavirus]. *Le Monde.*

Jarman, H., & Rozenblum, S., & Greer, S. (2020, May 11). What US states can learn from Covid-19 transition planning in Europe. *The Conversation.*

Jarman, H., Rozenblum, S., Greer, S., & Wismar, M. (2020, May 7). *What do governments need to consider as they implement transition plans?* European Observatory on Health Systems and Policies. Covid-19 Health System Response Monitor. https://analysis.covid19healthsystem.org/index.php/2020/05/07/what-do-governments-need-to-consider-as-they-implement-transition-plans/

Milon, A. (2020, June 24). *Rapport fait au nom de la commission des affaires sociales sur la proposition de résolution tendant à créer une commission d'enquête pour l'évaluation des politiques publiques face aux grandes pandémies à la lumière de la crise sanitaire de la covid-19 et de sa gestion.* [Report written on behalf of the Social Affairs Committee on the motion for a resolution to create a committee of inquiry to assess public policies in the face of major pandemics in the light of the Covid-19 crisis and its management]. Social Affairs Committee, Sénat.

Ministère de la Cohésion des Territoires et des Relations avec les Collectivités Territoriales [Territory Ministry]. (2020, April 23). *COVID-19: Hébergement d'urgence* [COVID-19: Emergency Accommodation] [Press release].

Ministère de la Santé [Health Ministry]. (2020, May 20). *COVID-19: Comment faire un lavage de mains efficace?* [Covid-19: How to wash your hands effectively?], Vidéo.

Ministère du Travail [Ministry of Labor]. (2020, May 27). DARES. Situation sur le marché du travail au 26 mai 2020 [Situation of the labor market as of May 26, 2020].

Nossiter, A. (2020, June 5). Macron beat back the coronavirus. France is not impressed. *The New York Times.* https://www.nytimes.com/2020/06/05/world/europe/coronavirus-france-macron-reopening.html

Observatoire des Inégalités [Observatory for Inequalities]. (2020). *Rapport sur la pauvreté en France* [Report on poverty in France].

Odoxa. (2020, April). Baromètre politique pour CGI, la presse régionale, France Inter et l'Express [Political barometer for CGI, regional press, France Inter and Express].

Pedrot, F. (2020, July 20). Covid-19: Les alertes ignorées de la veille sanitaire [Covid-19: Alerts ignored by the health surveillance system]. *AOC.*

Perera, I., & Tarrow, S. (2020, August 26). What America got wrong about COVID-19 and what we can learn from France and Italy. *Public Seminar.*

Rouquet, A. (2020, May 5). La tragédie industrielle et logistique des masques: Récit en cinq actes [The industrial and logistical tragedy of masks: A story in five acts]. *The Conversation.*

Rozenblum, S. (in press). The French public health system. In S. Greer & M. Mäzke (Eds.), *Comparative Public Health Politics*.

Rozenblum, S., Greer, S., & Jarman, H. (2020, May 20). Coronavirus: "Les stratégies de déconfinement sont pour l'essentiel graduelles, reversible et régionalisées, comme en France ou en Espagne" [Coronavirus: "The transition strategies are for the most part gradual, reversible and regionalized, as in France or Spain"]. *Le Monde*.

Rozenblum, S., Greer, S., & Jarman, H. (2020). *Quo Vadis? Under-performance of public health in France and the United States during the COVID-19 pandemic*. Manuscript submitted for publication.

Santé Publique France. (2020a, June 30). Recensement national des cas de COVID-19 chez les professionnels en établissements de santé [National census of COVID-19 cases among professionals in healthcare settings]. Études et enquêtes.

Santé Publique France. (2020b, July 30). Covid-19: point épidémiologique du 30 juillet 2020. [Covid-19 : Briefing on Covid-19 statistics].

Stromboni, C. (2020, July 14). L'hôpital va continuer à se casser la figure: Après les accords du Ségur, des soignants de nouveau dans la rue [The hospital will continue to fall apart: After the Ségur agreements, caregivers are back in the street]. *Le Monde*.

Tabuteau, D. (2002). *La sécurité sanitaire* [Health security]. (2nd ed.). Berger, Levrault.

Tabuteau, D. (2007, Autumn). La sécurité sanitaire, réforme institutionnelle ou résurgence des politiques de santé? [Health security, institutional reform or resurgence of health policies?]. *Les Tribunes de la Santé, SEVE*, 16.

Tabuteau, D. (2016). Principes et organisation de la sécurité sanitaire [Principles and organization of health security]. In *Traité de Santé publique* (3rd ed.). Lavoisier Médecine Sciences.

Williams, G., Ulla Diaz S., Figueras J., & Lessof, S. (2020). Translating evidence into policy during the Covid-19 pandemic: Bridging science and policy (and politics), *Eurohealth*, 26(2).

Zeitoun, J-D., Faron, M., Manternach, S., Fourquet, J., Lavielle, M., & Lefèvre, J. (2020, May 19). Reciprocal association between participation to a national election and the epidemic spread of COVID-19 in France: Nationwide observational and dynamic modeling study. *MedRxiv*.

16 POLITICAL RESONANCE IN AUSTRIA'S CORONAVIRUS CRISIS MANAGEMENT

Margitta Mätzke

Political Feasibility and Compliance in Austria's COVID-19 Response

Austria shares some of the disintegration tendencies in electoral alignments and party systems that trouble many representative democracies and put political institutions under strain. The country has seen both grand coalitions, with enormous need for interest mediation, producing sluggish decision procedures, and political constellations prone to reform gridlock and hardly qualified for swift action and resolute crisis management (Bröchler, 2014). Every so often, though, the country's electorate and political system are capable of empowering uncommon government coalitions, allowing for right-wing populist participation in central government, a political leadership team of extremely young people, or most recently an entirely novel partisan alliance in government. Such was the situation when the coronavirus reached Europe in February 2020. The national government had been in office for less than fifty days. It was a new government coalition of Christian Democrats and the Green party, keen on proving itself capable of governing after a period of great political turmoil. A lot of damage previously had been done to Austria's political institutions by its right-wing government predecessors.

Against this backdrop it came as a surprise to many observers of Austrian coronavirus policies that the country's initial crisis response was so swift and effective (Czypionka, 2020; Hofmarcher-Holzhacker, 2020). Austrian authorities had gotten off to a bad start handling COVID-19, when they did not even attempt to contain the spread of the disease in an early cluster in one of the country's ski resorts in late February 2020 (Fleischhacker, 2020; Lehermayr & Reinhart, 2020, p. 33). Subsequently, though, and possibly under a lot of international pressure from the many European countries where COVID-19 was brought home from Tyrolean vacations, a strategy for fighting COVID-19 was devised promptly and available resources coordinated effectively. The Austrian federal government also put great effort into a political communication campaign, presenting the containment measures as good common sense and the generally agreed-upon course of action, with little by way of visible public controversy or discord among expert advisors and participants in decision-making.

The strategy succeeded in that compliance was generally high, even in the face of severe infringements on civil liberties and private property rights, and the spread of the disease could be controlled effectively. "One week after the introduction of strict measures, the number of daily new cases began to decline, while the reproduction number had already dropped immediately after the measures were implemented" (Heger & Moshammer, 2020). The number of coronavirus deaths remained very low and did not start to rise again until late June 2020, and at no time was the health system even close to being overwhelmed by the number of coronavirus patients in need of hospital care or intensive care.

As undisputed as entering the lockdown was, decisions on when and how to start exiting it and cushioning its economic and social repercussions were much more controversial, as was the right course of action in the second wave of the disease in the fall of 2020. It was at these subsequent stages that the Austrian federal government has been subject to increasing criticism. The timing of the exit from lockdown, distortions in the sequence of loosening the contact limitations (Sprenger, 2020; Wetz, 2020), and inequalities in the coronavirus aid measures were the center of critical commentary. Some of the decisions on what kind of business may reopen and what other stores have to remain closed were even declared unconstitutional by the constitutional court. Furthermore, increasing numbers of observers and parliamentarians found the following inappropriate, if not indicating illegitimate amounts of executive dominance: the federal government's inclination to make unilateral decisions with not much explanation nor opportunity to discuss the course of action taken and a somewhat overprofessional public relations strategy, with which the federal government sought to uphold compliance and bolster its image as heroic crisis managers (Ehs, 2020).

As this chapter demonstrates, Austria's success at imposing contact restrictions swiftly and effectively and some of the controversial aspects of the decisions about exit strategies and coronavirus aid programs are two sides of the same coin. The inequalities in the burdens of crisis that different groups in society have to bear are in no way unexpected; they are all-too- familiar in the context of the conservatism of Austria's social protection system and political culture. At the same time, the relative ease with which the Austrian government could decide and implement the early lockdown likewise hinged on Austria's well-oiled political and administrative machinery. No country was fully prepared for the pandemic, and Austria was no exception. As in many other countries, political and administrative elites scrambled for a viable strategy to fight the disease, learn about its epidemiology, collect information on their healthcare capacities, boost their testing facilities, and get hold of protective gear and distribute it among healthcare providers. But they scrambled more successfully than elsewhere and got a grip on the disease's first wave.

This chapter argues that this success—the relative ease of finding a viable mode of operation for early crisis management—has been greatly helped along by initial cooperative and power-sharing institutions and behaviors, key procedural traits of *consensus democracy* (Crepaz & Lijphart, 1995; Lijphart, 1999). The multilateralism typical of that form of political organization makes political and administrative actors, even potential veto players, bent on collaboration, and it makes them skilled at it. Moreover, consensus democracy's structured inclusiveness produces the social capital (Bartscher et al., 2020) on which broad and reliable acquiescence in the broader society hinges.

Two aspects of policy are of great help if a political response to an epidemic is to be successful. One is *political feasibility:* Governments must be able to enact policies in the first place, and they must also be able to get policies implemented in public health bureaucracies that are decentralized in almost every country. The other important property of containment strategies is *compliance.* Compliance depends on many factors: a developed system of social protection, trust in government, and some basic accord about crisis management among political elites. In situations of great uncertainty, though, feasibility and compliance do not hinge merely on actors' motivation. There is also a cognitive element to political feasibility and compliance, which benefits from decision-making procedures and substantive policies that are not completely arbitrary and alien. Political feasibility and compliance are a great deal more likely where policies and procedures are predictable to some extent and *politically resonant* in important respects.

Political resonance is critical; both the advantages and the flaws of Austrian political institutions reproduce themselves in a crisis. Although of course highly exceptional in the extent and type of state intervention, the Austrian COVID-19 policies enacted in the second quarter of 2020 are not unfamiliar. In part precisely because of the unequal burdens they impose, they relate to established ways of organizing politics and society in Austria. For example, an important institution of Austrian consensus democracy, social partnership, made a significant contribution to overcoming the previous (economic) crisis of 2008 and 2009 (Eichhorst & Weißhaupt, 2013). Social partners were habitually consulted when it came to implementing the same type of labor market policy measures in 2020. Therefore, to some extent, crisis management is politically resonant to the extent that it draws on *old ideas* about policy measures and modes of political decision-making (Mätzke & Ostner, 2010). Substantively the old ideas ingrained in some of the coronavirus policies drew on core norms of Austria's conservative welfare state. Procedurally they partially took advantage of central traits of the country's famed consensus democracy, but they also assumed tendencies in the development of political institutions and behaviors—some of them problematic ones—that had been underway before the crisis.

Fighting the Spread of COVID-19: Largely Effective "Reasons Remain Opaque"[1]

The most salient aspect of Austria's public health measures is the relative ease with which the Austrian federal government could make and implement a U-turn from its passive stance in February 2020 toward a resolute and invasive course of action in the second week of March 2020. This was unexpected from a brand-new government coalition of two parties that had never formed a federal government together.

This new government had taken over bureaucracies that were still busy processing a lot of organizational dislocation caused by the preceding government's attempts at consolidating its power in the country's public administration. Observers of Austrian politics in the country and abroad would not have trusted the country to pull that off and manage the emergency situation so effectively, because they usually complain about fragmentation of the country's healthcare system (Aiginger, 2011; Mätzke & Stöger, 2015; Meggeneder, 2004), poorly developed public health capacity (Sprenger, 2020), and a political system not set up for quick and effective decision-making (Bröchler, 2014). Relative to the country-specific course of the disease, the Austrian response came very early. Austria was among the first European countries to impose a lockdown and among the first who could start lifting contact restrictions again.

The Austrian COVID-19 response started with recommendations concerning hand hygiene and physical distancing, the latter of which quickly turned into mandatory measures (Neubauer & Schnidt, 2020). [2] From the beginning the federal government assumed the leading role, with regional and district governments in charge of implementation. Parliament enacted a comprehensive package of lockdown measures on March 15, 2020, which took effect March 16. This first COVID-19 act empowered the federal health ministry to decree emergency measures. Apart from select regions, there was no complete curfew in Austria, and everyone was allowed to leave their homes for working, buying essential food supplies, and helping others. Also permitted was going out to get some fresh air or walking the dog, as long as physical contact with other people was avoided and distancing rules were followed. Less invasive than in some of the European neighbors, the Austrian lockdown remained in place for a long time, roughly seven weeks (Hofer et al., 2020). Stores began to reopen in mid-April 2020 and schools in mid-May 2020, but it all happened very slowly with setbacks and a timing and sequencing that many, including the constitutional court, did not fully understand. As of April 6, 2020, wearing face masks in public (indoor) places became mandatory. The lockdown was accompanied by an extensive health education campaign, with many televised spots, which the relevant federal ministry had developed in collaboration with the Red Cross Austria.

Social distancing became easier to implement as summer progressed and many activities could take place outside. As vacation times arrived, the challenges of home schooling and home office faded from the center of attention to some extent. It was then, in late June and July 2020, that new infections started to spread again, and a number of new hotspots of the disease emerged across the country. To prevent a second lockdown from becoming necessary, much effort was put into better fine-tuning of distancing measures and only imposing local or district-level contact restrictions. For this purpose, a system of district-level traffic-light coding, based on the number of positive tested cases per 10,000 inhabitants, was implemented (Complexity Science Hub Vienna, 2020).

Capacities and procedures were developed for monitoring the spread of the disease, tracing individual infection chains, and monitoring home quarantine.

Test capacities were expanded from just a few hundred toward a target of 15,000 tests per day, to be carried out in a decentralized structure of forty laboratories across the country. Likewise, a system for taking stock of the country's extensive hospital sector and overall medical and nursing workforce was devised, to get a sense of the resources available. As a result, it became clear as early as in the end of March 2020 that there was no danger at any time that the number of COVID-19 cases would overwhelm the capacity of the Austrian healthcare system.

By and large the Austrian range of interventions is consistent with the activities of many other countries, with the one qualification that Austria can draw on one of the most extensive welfare states and healthcare systems worldwide, with per capita healthcare resources (especially hospital care) among the strongest in the world. This made crisis handling easier. Some felt the crisis policies and their implementation were less than perfectly organized, but it would be an exaggeration to call crisis management chaotic (Tóth, 2020). There is no evidence that it was dramatically less competent than elsewhere; the opposite is true. However, it is admittedly somewhat odd that, in a moment of national emergency, a non-governmental organization (NGO), the Red Cross Austria, played such a central role in organizing the procurement and distribution of protective gear, developing the federal government's information campaign, and programming the country's coronavirus warning application.

In principle, though, it is not alien to Austrian policy implementation that a social welfare association such as the Red Cross is involved in the implementation and logistics of public policies. Cooperative policy implementation is the established mode of problem-solving in Austria. It is politically resonant and allows for effective political responses even where administrative capacity is not particularly strong. Although Austria has an extensive healthcare system, the country does not have much by way of public health capacity. There are few universities that offer public health training, few people who would describe themselves as public health experts (as opposed to medical professionals), and organizations in charge of public health that range far below institutions such as the German Robert Koch Institute or the American Centers for Disease Control when it comes to public visibility and presence in the mass media. Public health tasks are folded into the organizations of the healthcare system: there are few organizations exclusively in charge of public health. This is a long-standing condition of health care in Austria and has extensively been bemoaned by observers and academics keen on having an American-style, autonomous, and highly visible public health agency, surrounded by prestigious research universities specialized on public health. This does not exist, and not much specialized public health nor epidemiological expertise is available in Austria (Sprenger, 2020, p. pos. 1682), which has consequences for the kind of expert advice that a government can obtain in Austria (Redl, 2020). Indeed, it is primarily medical or mathematical model-building expertise that the Austrian federal government draws on as sources of information about the spread of the disease. This may be less than optimal conceptually, but when it came to the *practice* of public health intervention, this practice in fact did not hinder the adequate response to COVID-19. In the very beginning even the federal health ministry found itself in a vulnerable position (Fleischhacker, 2020, pp. 46–49), because it had recently undergone major reorganization: the minister had been in office for no more than ten weeks when the public health crisis started. The ministry's council of expert advisors, "the National Sanitary Council, whose term had expired on 31 December 2019, had not been re-established. The position of the National General Director for Public Health had been removed by a previous government and never been reinstalled and the country's pandemic plan dated back to the emergence of H5N1 and H1N1 and focused on influenza" (Müller, 2020, p. 353).

But this highlights precisely the point: there is an important role for political institutions and political culture. In a polarized political system with intense political competition, this organizational weakness of public health might have been the recipe for failure, but not so in the political environment of consensus democracy. That environment is nonconfrontational, and its power-sharing arrangements allowed the federal government to (re-)organize and consolidate state capacity as the situation evolved. Public health capacity is scattered across Austria's large health system, welfare state, and public administration. Folded into primary care, forming part of regional bureaucracies or local public administration, there is little room for maneuver for defining an explicit population perspective and a distinctive public health agenda, but it is certainly suitable for implementing the federal government's emergency measures.

So it was the classical setup of consensus democracy that ensured the effective crisis response: the social partners were consulted habitually. They were involved in the implementation of some of the policies, and they advised employers and employees about the labor-law and labor market policy aspects of crisis management. Most important, they contributed to unfussy policy implementation, because their consent helped secure their members' acquiescence, one of the classical roles of corporatist social partner participation in policy-making (Cameron, 1984). A second key veto player of consensus democracy, the constitutional court, is also intact; it began its task of quality-monitoring legislation some time after it was enacted. As a result of time pressure and high workloads of the ministerial bureaucracy, decrees and legislation had a number of loose ends. On July 14, 2020, the Austrian constitutional court declared unconstitutional some of the restrictions concerning citizens' entering public space and concerning the selectivity in the regulations on what retail businesses were allowed to reopen first (Verfassungsgerichtshof Österreich, 2020). As of this writing, both policies are no longer in effect, though, and the question of what to do with penalties for violating these restrictions is still subject to discussion (e.g., Should there be a general amnesty?).

Finally, Austrian federalism and administrative decentralization play an important role in public health policy, in that the regional governments, districts, and municipalities are in charge of implementing most of what is decided in Vienna (e.g., providing hospital facilities, enforcing contact restrictions and quarantine, or actually performing large parts of the testing). This indirect federal administration has produced some variation in policy implementation. Some districts in Tyrol, where the spread of the disease was most dramatic, imposed strict curfews, whereas in the rest of the country people were allowed to leave their homes. A greater source of annoyance was uneven enforcement of the federal social distancing decrees or incomprehensible decisions about closures of public places. The Viennese could visit their city parks at all times, but they could not go to Schönbrunn or Augarten, because those were federal parks. Small-scale bickering occurred, which sparked some criticism, but it would be an exaggeration to call this organizational dysfunction. Regional variation is a feature of coronavirus policies in many countries, and by and large decentralized implementation of the federal degrees worked, so that overall Austria's "cooperative federalism has passed its test in the face of the COVID-19 pandemic" (Bußjäger, 2020).

Even though the coronavirus epidemic is an emergency situation, in which the main political responsibility rests with the federal government, the policy challenges were addressed in power-sharing arrangements, in which cooperation was possible across various organizational and territorial boundaries. Collaboration did not even require great effort. It was not mentioned in the media; most actors involved in it hardly considered it consciously: it was simply the most plausible course of action. This is political resonance, and this made the stark measures in the beginning of crisis management politically feasible. It allowed a young government, less than a quarter-year in office, to deliver their journeyman's piece with a set of public health policies enacted at the right moment, effectively, and more or less efficiently.

Collateral Damage of Lockdown and the Social Policies of the Conservative Welfare State

It could have been their masterpiece, but for this, easing the lockdown measures should have been just as timely, and the economic and social fallout of lockdown would have to be distributed more equitably. This was not the case. Although many of those who lost their jobs or income during the time of the lockdown were compensated for their losses through state aid programs, which quickly swelled to an overall amount of more than EUR 50 billion, one-tenth of Austria's gross domestic product (GDP), some groups in society were overlooked. Aid for these groups came late and reluctantly and fell short of both their needs and the amounts that other groups received.

Is this surprising? No, it is not, and this lack of surprise, too, is political resonance, the tendency to favor familiar policies over novel ones. Resonance is an aspect of policies geared toward political feasibility and compliance; it is not a safeguard of their quality, legitimacy, or desirability.

The very first COVID-19 law began making resources available for aiding people who lost their income or business as a result of the lockdown measures. One of the core instruments was short-time work, the option to reduce employees' working hours up to 90 percent and pay them a subsidized income of 80 to 90 percent of their previous net income. The benefit can be received for three months, with an option of extending it for another three months. This stabilizes employment and businesses' liquidity and protects the connection between employees and their firms and thus their job-related knowledge. It is an old measure of active labor market policy, hugely popular (Schnetzer et al., 2020), with more than 1.3 million people receiving benefits in June 2020. But it is politically resonant and popular precisely *because* it is so seamlessly in sync with the way in which Austria's conservative, social insurance-based welfare state organizes social protection: negotiated and implemented with the social partners, closely tied to the employment relationship, focused on people who have regular jobs, and planned with income-related benefits careful not to disturb the wage distribution. This is also the character of the way in which many of Austria's extensive regular social protection systems operate in the labor market crisis caused by the COVID-19 response. Benefits for the unemployed, for instance, echo this story: they can be generous, but they are also unequal, and they are not for everyone.

There is also a range of aid programs more specifically designed to compensate for income losses resulting from the lockdown. Several coronavirus aid programs allow private enterprises to maintain liquidity. Some of them, the earliest programs of state aid, are targeted toward small business, others are for larger firms. Of course, there are also spectacular bailout deals, such as the one for the Lufthansa subsidiary, Austrian Airlines. Public aid programs for enterprises grew into a broad range of tools, including subsidies, credits, and tax policy measures (Bundesministerium Finanzen, 2020). Likewise, support measures for families and individuals were developed, mostly in the form of targeted measures for people in need and—as part of an aid package devised quite late, in June 2020—also as a one-time bonus for families with children (Bundesministerium Arbeit, Familie, Jugend, 2020). Support measures have been mushrooming into complex schemes of different benefits, in which over time assistance was made available for most groups in need.

Two aspects stand out as characteristic traits of coronavirus aid in Austria, and both aspects are familiar to the point of tedium. They demonstrate the extent to which resonance—for good or for bad—is shaping policy designs and their political feasibility. One is the strenuous and lengthy process it took until people precariously employed could receive support. "Precariously employed" refers, for example, to people working in the arts and entertainment industry, many of whom are self-employed or earn their living with contracts for services or non-standard combinations of several smaller work contracts. They were the first to get hit by the contact limitations, the last to be allowed to work again, and among the people hardest hit. Yet support programs for artists were slow to develop, and it also took a long time until they reached a magnitude and generosity that would allow cultural workers to secure their existence in 2020 (Kulturrat Österreich, 2020). As much as this treatment of the artists and many Third Sector organizations stands out as an unresolved problem of Austria's COVID-19 response, it is still unsurprising, because it merely reflects how many artists work and live:

precariously. It also reminds us that "precariousness" is a political construction, and that there is no divine verdict that it has to be reproduced and amplified in the coronavirus crisis. Since political resonance is at work driving feasibility and likelihood of policies, though, it comes as no surprise that the situation of cultural workers persists, maybe becomes worse, under the conditions of COVID-19, the great accelerator of existing inequalities.

The second outstanding characteristic of the social policy side of Austria's coronavirus response is the role of the family in the crisis. Here it is not only the design of public financial assistance but also, more important, the timing and sequencing of lockdown measures and exit strategies that amounts to burdens that no other group in society has to bear. The long duration of the lockdown was criticized especially in this context, because the combination of home office and home schooling was embraced as a solution with very little energy spent on trying to find alternative organizational solutions. Educational institutions were the first to be closed, and when it came to opening public places again, it was shops, garden centers, and hardware stores that opened first, while schools remained closed. Little attention was paid to the families who may have neither a garden nor a porch and spend spring days in their apartments, with public parks and playgrounds closed, trying to support their kids with home schooling and reconcile that with home office. In political discussions about the lockdown, the social challenges of the long school closures were noticed, early, but nothing was done. Shops and restaurants had priority when it came to lifting the contact restrictions. Aid for families affected by the COVID-19 crisis for the longest time remained within the domain of targeted benefits: need-based, individualized support for "hardship cases" and extraordinary crises. Decisions about a more universalistic policy design of across-the-board benefits were not made until mid-June 2020. It was not until after the summer that extended periods of home-schooling were recognized as a highly problematic approach to containing the spread of the disease.

Is this surprising? No. On the contrary; it resonates: progress toward family policy modernization has been slow in Austria (Morgan, 2013). The designers of social protection are inclined to seek the solution to some of the greatest challenges of social care, organizing childcare and care for the elderly, in the privacy of the family. Often families receive financial support from the state; sometimes, if their way of life is not in line with social norms, they do not (Strell & Duncan, 2001). Gender analyses of social policy have called an organization of social care with no alternatives to family-based care *familialism* (Leitner, 2003), and analyzed countries, policy fields, or developments over time with regard to the question of whether alternatives to family-based care are available, or are becoming available. This would allow individuals and potential family caretakers to opt for institutionalized settings, if they choose. Whatever progress has been made toward recognition of the right to choose care arrangements, this has been undone in the COVID-19 crisis, and with it much of what has been gained in terms of a more equitable distribution of care obligations at home.

In that respect COVID-19 has acted as a conservative force. No question, opening the schools and childcare facilities has indeed been a hard question, because the risks associated with school opening are hard to assess. However, the collateral damage of keeping the children at home for the better part of March 2020 through August 2020 is a certainty, not a risk. It is faithfully mentioned in discussions about lockdowns. Beyond that it has not informed policy.

The same resonance that allowed politics to act quickly and effectively favors conservative solutions when it comes to policy content. If the familiar and plausible COVID-19 measures are the ones most seamlessly in sync with existing Austrian social protection institutions, then their primary aim is not to compensate for inequalities resulting from the uneven effects of illness and lockdown. Explicitly redistributive policies are the exception than the rule in some areas of Austria's conservative welfare state. One of them is social care. The unpaid (or poorly paid) care work hidden in families is often used as a quick fix when education and childcare require solutions that are organizationally and financially more demanding than deemed appropriate. Therefore, the plausible solution, the politically resonant one, is a conservative solution here too.

Old Policies for New Challenges: Explaining the Lure of Resonance

To be politically feasible and command compliance, COVID-19 measures had better be *politically resonant* and not stray too far off the beaten path of how social policy is "normally" organized in Austria. For one thing, it is often the regular social protection schemes that people turn to in times of COVID-19-induced need. These may be generous, but not necessarily so, and not for all. Second, COVID-19 responses are politically resonant when they draw on policies that are tried and tested, such as short-time work. Third, resonance can also take the form of prioritizing policy designs that match the traditional principles underlying social protection in Austria: conceptualizing coronavirus aid programs as targeted support for hardship cases, treating different groups of people unequally when it comes to the timeliness and generosity of aid, and relying on unpaid work in the family for important functions of care and education.

Because of the important role of political resonance, COVID-19 policies emphasize the conformist element that is always an aspect of consensus and cooperation. As the lure of political resonance may refer us back to the familiar policy solutions, it may even become an impulse that *undermines* social and political progress in some areas: reversing headway made toward a more gender-egalitarian distribution of care obligations and defeating steps of improvements toward greater tolerance vis-á-vis diverse ways of life, demeanors, dress codes. COVID-19, in other words, may not only induce a surge of digital innovation and, for better or worse, transform the way we work, it may unfold a strong conservative bias.

Political resonance does not pertain only to substantive policy content, though; it also has a political process dimension, in which policy-making is better organized, policy implementation more effective, and administration more competent when it is in sync with established procedural and behavioral norms in a polity. In Austria this procedural template is tied to the institutions of consensus democracy. One key political process and counterpart of consensus democracy is democratic corporatism, as superbly described by Peter Katzenstein in *Small States in World Markets* (1985). Here the connection between the characteristics of political process and a policy outcome—capacity to adjust to industrial change—is explicitly established. In the case of the small European countries adjustment capacity is a function of cooperation across various organizational and political boundaries, multilateral clearing of different interests in a structured and fairly centralized system of interest representation, and a spirit of social partnership that allows for consensual decisions. It is "low-voltage politics" as Katzenstein (1985, p. 32) characterizes this mode of unexcited cooperation, in which political competition is sidelined in favor of an orientation toward the task at hand, and even the big heroic leadership gestures depend, for their implementation, on the collaboration of others with large degrees of discretion. As procedural template for COVID-19 policy-making this set of institutions and behavioral norms was politically resonant and presented the most plausible course of action. As it turns out, it explains adjustment capacity not only in the slow-moving process of industrial change that Katzenstein has described but also the relatively successful response to the COVID-19 crisis in Austria: low-voltage politics, facilitating high-voltage policies.

There are two causal mechanisms that explain why political resonance is so significant. The first focuses on the cognitive aspects of policy processes. In this perspective political resonance provides *focal points*, which can coordinate activities in multiactor settings. The coronavirus crisis is not an emergency that can be managed single-handedly. In the large areas of parliamentary politics, healthcare provision, epidemiological research, and implementation of non-pharmaceutical intervention by public administration and police departments, separate agendas and activities must be coordinated by guiding ideas. It pays off if these ideas are old, because then they are mature: they are tried and tested, at times even evidence-based, and they are familiar (Mätzke & Ostner, 2010, pp. 132–135). As such they can be the lubricant of collaboration in complex political and administrative systems.

The question of whether actors can *perceive* a course of action is only part of the story, though. The second part concerns *willingness*, the motivational aspect of policy processes. Why should actors in the broad decision-making and implementation system comply with decisions that are not their own? Administrative decree alone is often not sufficient for securing compliance, and systems of sanctions and punishment are neither efficient nor desirable. In that situation, political resonance provides the glue that makes policy decisions stick, and again it is old ideas that are better suited as resonant points of reference. In an adaption of Schumpeter (1975 [1942]), who observed that "restrictive practices" of precapitalist organization made entrepreneurship and innovation possible in the first place, we can think of political resonance, with its attachment to the familiar procedures and solutions, as providing guarantees and *promises of protection*, where protection pertains not only to well-being and material livelihood, but importantly also to status and position in an established structure of inequality. Such promises have always been instrumental in sustaining a politico-administrative system or, in Schumpeter's terms, they provided "the flying buttresses that prevented its collapse" (p. 139) in the face of great uncertainty

Political Resonance and State Capacity

This account of the COVID-19 response in Austria emphasizes the importance of political resonance, that is, of old ideas for handling new policy challenges successfully. Procedurally this means that rather than inventing a completely new, extraordinary set of procedures for the state of emergency, it may pay off to draw on, rather than suspend, established modes of decision-making and implementation. In Austria that established mode of operation is multilateralism. Multilateralism and collaboration make an effective crisis-response possible, despite the fact that institutionally the country is in many respects less than optimally prepared for handling a public health crisis of that magnitude. Where specialized public health capacity similar to Robert Koch Institute is lacking, competence for handling the crisis can very effectively be created out of problem-solving capacity in the broader polity.

There are two general lessons from Austria's handling of the coronavirus pandemic. One is that we should probably think about the ability to manage the pandemic not in terms of resources, institutions, and workforce already in place, but in terms of a more dynamic and open-ended process of resource acquisition and capacity building over the course of the response to the crisis. The other lesson may be an Austria-specific one: adjustment capacity and the ability to appropriate those public health resources were a collective accomplishment. It resulted not only from compliance on the part of the broader society, but importantly also from cooperation of actors within the political system across a multitude of organizational and spatial boundaries. To the extent that there is a success story to be told—and this chapter has argued that this is warranted only partially and only preliminarily—then this is not first and foremost one about executive leadership, but one about cooperative followership and collaboration.

This is what the federal government's increasingly professionalized public relations management misses. Strict message control and daily press conferences[3] trying to tell the media what to think mark a tendency toward a more personalized politics, focused on key figures of the federal executive (Ehs, 2020). Presenting crisis management as unilateral executive decision-making not only misses an important part of the story, though. Federal Chancellor Sebastian Kurz was even biting the hand that was feeding him when he presented himself as the pivotal crisis manager, for as this chapter has shown, crisis response capacity is a systemic, collective capability, not a quality of solitary heroic leadership.

Notes

1. This is actually a commentary by one observer regarding the resilience of the Austrian health system during the crisis. See Hofmarcher-Holzhacker (2020), but it is also an apt portrayal of crisis management at large.

2. Sonja Neubauer and Andreas Schmidt (2020) compiled all information about Austrian response to COVID-19 in the country report in the COVID-19 Health System Response Monitor, compiled by the European Observatory of Health Systems and Policies. This section draws on their compilation as principal source of information.

3. Ninety-nine COVID19-related press conferences were held between Feb. 27 and May 31, 2020.

References

Aiginger, K. (2011). *Herausforderungen einer alternden Gesellschaft: Schwerpunkt Reformbedarf im österreichischen Gesundheitssystem* [Challenges of an aging society. Focus reform requirements in the health system]. Vorträge des Österreichischen Instituts für Wirtschaftsforschung (WIFO) No. 111.

Bartscher, A. K., Seitz, S., Siegloch, S., Slotwinski, M., & Wehrhöfer, N. (2020). *Social capital and the spread of Covid-19: Insights from European Countries.* (CESifo Working Papers [Nr. 8346]). Munich.

Bröchler, S. (2014). Informales Regieren auf Österreichisch. Formales und informales Regieren als wechselseitiger Prozess [Austrian style informal government: Formal and informal governance as interactive process]. In S. Bröchler & T. Grunden (Eds.), *Informelle Politik. Konzepte, Akteure und Prozesse* [Informal politics: Concepts, actors and processes] (pp. 129–154). Springer VS.

Bundesministerium Arbeit, Familie, Jugend. (2020). Coronavirus (COVID-19). Das Bundesministerium für Arbeit, Familie und Jugend informiert nachfolgend über die derzeit geltenden Maßnahmen [Coronavirus (COVID-19) The Federal Ministry of Labor, Family and Youth provides the following information about the currently applicable measures]. https://www.bmafj.gv.at/Services/News/Coronavirus.html

Bundesministerium Finanzen. (2020). *Coronavirus: Info, relief and simplifications.* Retrieved on December 15, 2020, from https://www.bmf.gv.at/en/current-issues/Corona/information/information-coronavirus.html

Bußjäger, P. (2020). Federalism and the COVID-19 crisis: COVID-19 crisis challenging Austria's cooperative federalism. *Forum of Federations. The Global Network o Federalism and Devolved Governance.* Retrieved December 15, 2020, from http://www.forumfed.org/publications/federalism-and-the-covid-19-crisis-covid-19-crisis-challenging-austrias-cooperative-federalism/

Cameron, D. (1984). Social democracy, corporatism, labour quiescence, and the representation of economic interest in advanced capitalist society. In J. H. Goldthorpe (Ed.), *Order and conflict in contemporary capitalism. Studies in the political economy of Western European Nations* (pp. 143–179). Clarendon Press.

Complexity Science Hub Vienna (2020). *CSH Corona Traffic Light—Austria.* Retrieved December 15, 2020, from https://vis.csh.ac.at/corona-ampel/index.html?lang=en

Crepaz, M. L., & Lijphart, A. (1995). Linking and integrating corporatism and consensus democracy: Theory, concepts and evidence. *British Journal of Political Science, 25*(2), 281–288.

Czypionka, T. (2020). Austria's response to the coronavirus pandemic—A second perspective. *Cambridge Core.* https://www.cambridge.org/core/blog/2020/04/12/austrias-response-to-the-coronavirus-pandemic-a-second-perspective/

Ehs, T. (2020). *Krisen-Demokratie. Sieben Lektionen aus der Coronakrise* [Crisis-democracy: Seven lessons of the coronavirus-crisis]. Mandelbaum Verlag.

Eichhorst, W., & Weißhaupt, T. (2013). *Mit Neo-Korporatismus durch die Krise? Die Rolle des Sozialen Dialogs in Deutschland, Österreich und der Schweiz* [With neo-corporatism through the crisis? The role of social dialogue in Germany, Austria, and Switzerland]. (IZA Discussion Paper [No. 7498]). Bonn.

Fleischhacker, M. (2020). Das Ministerium braucht zwei Bypässe [The ministry needs two bypasses]. In M. Fleischhacker (Ed.), *Corona. Chronologie einer Entgleisung* [Corona. Chronology of a derailment] (pp. 37–55). Edition QVV.

Heger, F., & Moshammer, H. (2020). COVID-19: The Austrian Experience. *Asian Pacific Journal of Environment and Cancer, 2*(S1), 3–4. https://doi.org/10.31557/APJEC.2020.3.S1.3-4

Hofer, E., Hammerl, M., Grasl, R., Schrettl, L., Kada, K., Hoepke, S., Gaul, B., & Böhmer, C. (2020, May 3). 50 Tage Corona: Der lockdown und seine Folgen [Fifty days of coronavirus: The lockdown and its consequences]. *Kurier.*

Hofmarcher-Holzhacker, M. M. (2020). Austria's response to the coronavirus pandemic. *Cambridge Core.* https://www.cambridge.org/core/blog/2020/04/10/austrias-response-to-the-coronavirus-pandemic/

Katzenstein, P. J. (1985). *Small states in world markets. Industrial policy in Europe.* Cornell University Press.

Kulturrat Österreich (Producer). (2020). 100 Tage Corona-Krise in Österreich [One hundred days of coronavirus crisis in Austria]. Retrieved December 15, 2020, from https://igkultur.at/artikel/100-tage-corona-krise-oesterreich

Lehermayr, C., & Reinhart, S. (2020). Wie das Coronavirus nach Europa kam [How the coronavirus came to Europe]. In M. Fleischhacker (Ed.), *Corona. Chronologie einer Entgleisung* [Corona. Chronology of a derailment] (pp. 11–36). Edition QVV.

Leitner, S. (2003). Varieties of familiarism: The caring function of the family in comparative perspective. *European Societies, 5*(4), 353–375.

Lijphart, A. (1999). *Patterns of democracy: Government forms and performance in thirty-six countries.* Yale University Press.

Mätzke, M., & Ostner, I. (2010). The role of old ideas in the new German family policy agenda. *German Policy Studies, 6*(3), 119–163.

Mätzke, M., & Stöger, H. (2015). Health care federalism in Austria. In K. Fierlback & H. Palley (Eds.), *Comparative health care federalism: Competition and collaboration in multistate systems* (pp. 15–28). Ashgate Press.

Meggeneder, O. (2004). *Reformbedarf und Reformwirklichkeit des österreichischen Gesundheitswesens: Was sagt die Wissenschaft dazu?* [Reform requirements and the reality of reform in the Austrian health system: What is the perspective of scientific research?]. Mabuse Verlag.

Morgan, K. (2013). Path shifting of the welfare state: Electoral competition and the expansion of work family policies in western Europe. *World Politics, 65*(1), 73–115.

Müller, M. (2020). The start of the Austrian response to the COVID-19 crisis: A personal account. *Wiener Klinische Wochenschrift,* 132, 353–355. https://doi.org/10.1007/s00508-020-01693-y

Neubauer, S., & Schmidt, A. (2020). *Austria. COVID-19 Health Systems Response Monitor.* Retrieved December 15, 2020, from https://www.covid19healthsystem.org/countries/austria/countrypage.aspx

Redl, B. (2020, April 30). Gesundheitsexpertin: "Es ist eine angstbesetzte Politik der Kontrolle. Interview mit Claudia Wild" [Health expert: It is a fearful policy of control. Interview with Claudia Wild]. *Der Standard.*

Schnetzer, M., Tamesberger, D., & Theurl, S. (2020). Mitigating mass layoffs in the COVID-19 crisis: Austrian short-time work as international role model. *VOX, CEPR Policy Portal.* https://voxeu.org/article/mitigating-mass-layoffs-covid-19-crisis-austrian-short-time-model

Schumpeter, J. A. (1975 [1942]). *Capitalism, socialism and democracy.* Harper and Row.

Sprenger, M. (2020). *Das Corona-Rätsel. Tagebuch einer Pandemie* [The riddle of the coronavirus. Diary of a pandemic]. Seifert Verlag.

Strell, M., & Duncan, S. (2001). Lone motherhood, ideal type care regimes and the case of Austria. *Journal of European Social Policy, 11*(2), 149–164.

Tóth, B. (2020, May 12). Was passiert, wenn es eng wird? [What if it gets tight?]. *Falter,* 20.

Verfassungsgerichtshof Österreich. (2020, July 22). *COVID-19-Gesetz ist verfassungskonform, Verordnungen über Betretungsverbote waren teilweise gesetzwidrig* [COVID-19 law is constitutional, regulations on bans on public space were partly illegal]. https://www.vfgh.gv.at/medien/Covid_Entschaedigungen_Betretungsverbot.de.php

Wetz, A. (2020). Die große Entgleisung: Angst statt Entspannung [The great derailment: Fear instead of relaxation]. In M. Fleischhacker (Ed.), *Corona. Chronologie einer Entgleisung* [Corona. Chronology of a derailment] (pp. 83–122). Edition QVV.

17 THREE APPROACHES TO HANDLING THE COVID-19 CRISIS IN FEDERAL COUNTRIES

Germany, Austria, and Switzerland

Thomas Czypionka and Miriam Reiss

Despite their geographical and cultural proximity, Germany, Austria, and Switzerland can teach very different lessons on how to handle the COVID-19 pandemic. Timing and severity of outbreaks were fairly similar in Germany and Austria (see Figures 17.1 through 17.3), whereas Switzerland faced a higher infection rate at the peak of the crisis (although far from rates in France or Italy). Response measures eventually taken by the three countries were not too different, either, but how decisions were made and subsequently communicated to the public varied considerably.

In all three countries, containment measures were met by a high level of adherence within the population, as mobility indices illustrate (see Figures 17.1 through 17.3). As a result, the three countries fared well in reducing transmission rates and never came close to reaching capacity limits in their health systems. This chapter aims to examine the outbreak responses of the three countries and give insight into the dynamics and rationales behind these responses.

Health Policy Measures

Although **Germany** had its first case of SARS-CoV-2 confirmed as early as January 27, 2020, in Bavaria (a man who contracted the virus from a Chinese colleague), official case numbers increased at a rather slow pace in the subsequent weeks and were still below one hundred by the end of February. Hence, public health measures at that time were essentially limited to testing, contact tracing, and isolation of confirmed and potential cases, as well as communication of recommendations regarding hygiene and physical distancing. In early March, however, the identification of multiple clusters across the country (Robert Koch Institute, 2020b) led to growing public awareness and triggered the gradual introduction of containment measures.

Although some recommendations were issued by the federal government ("Spahn Empfiehlt Absage" ["Spahn Recommends Cancellation"], 2020), early

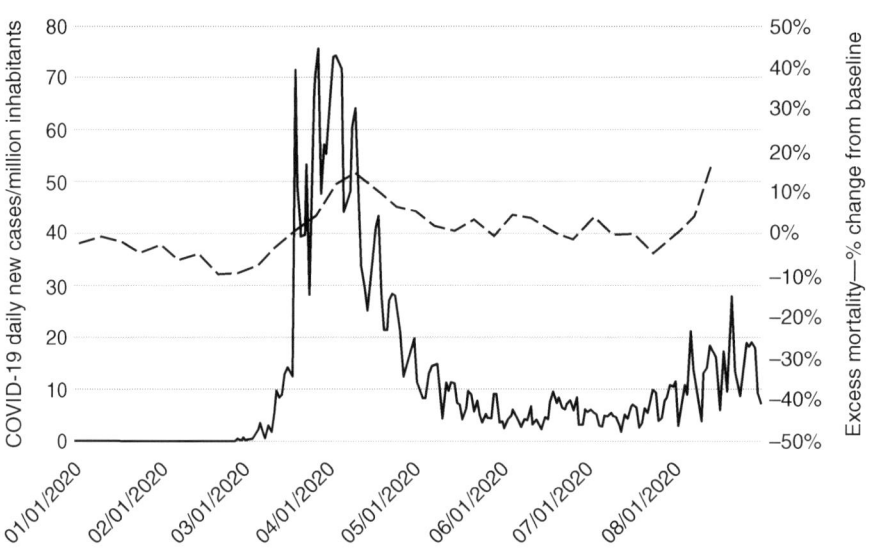

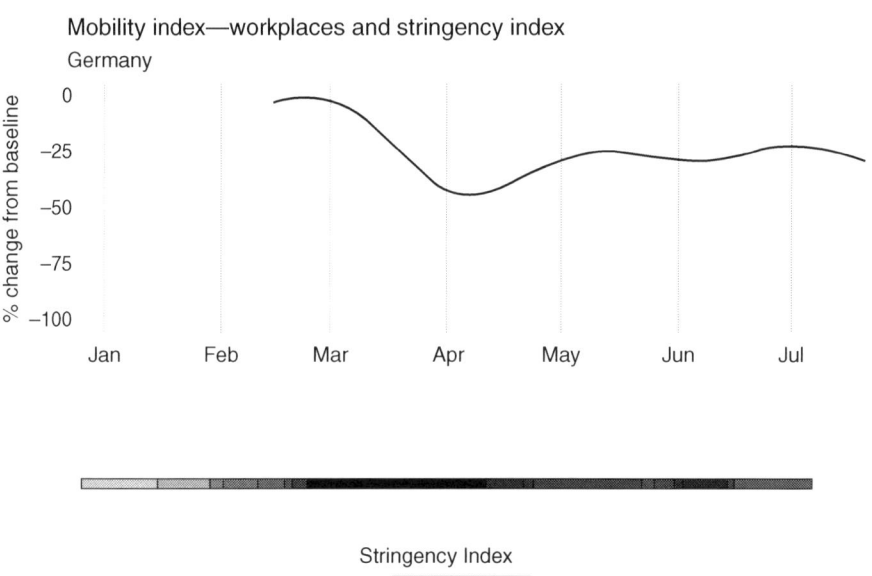

Figure 17.1. Daily confirmed cases of COVID-19, all-cause excess mortality, and change of mobility in Germany.

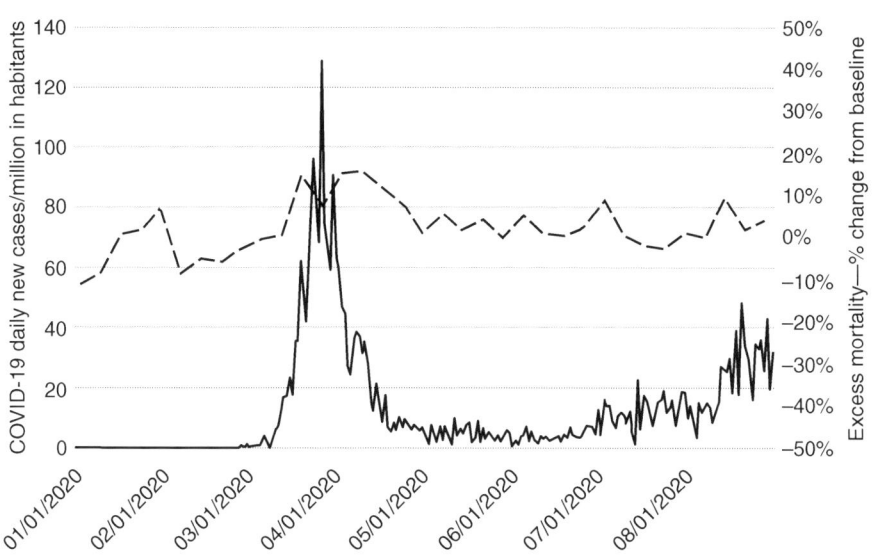

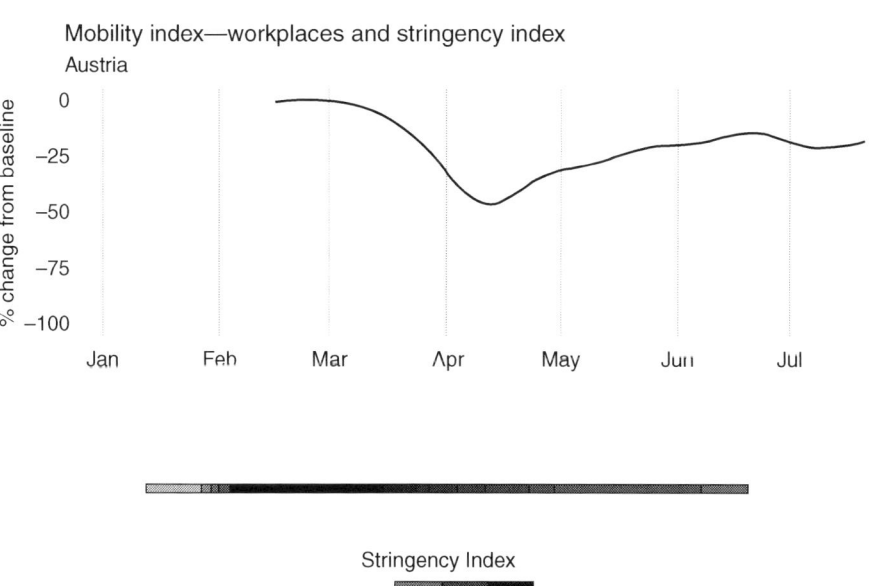

Figure 17.2. Daily confirmed cases of COVID-19, all-cause excess mortality, and change of mobility in Austria.

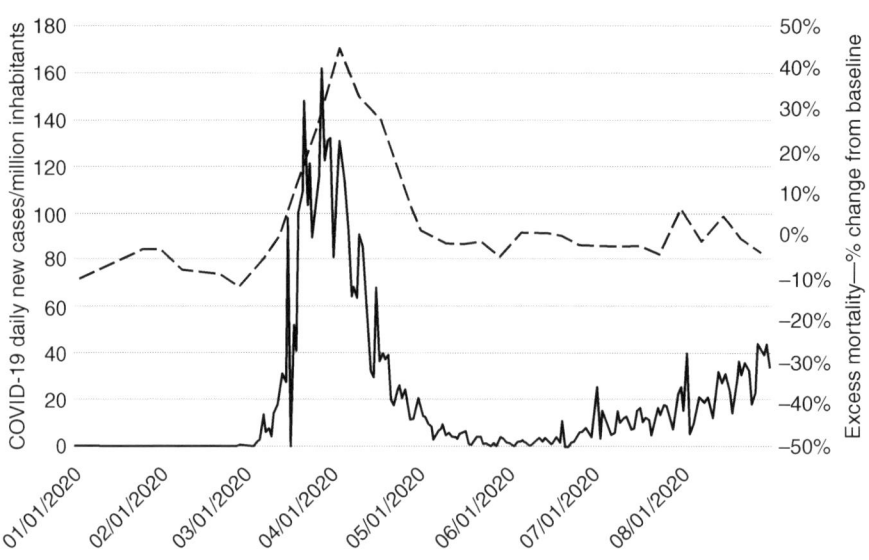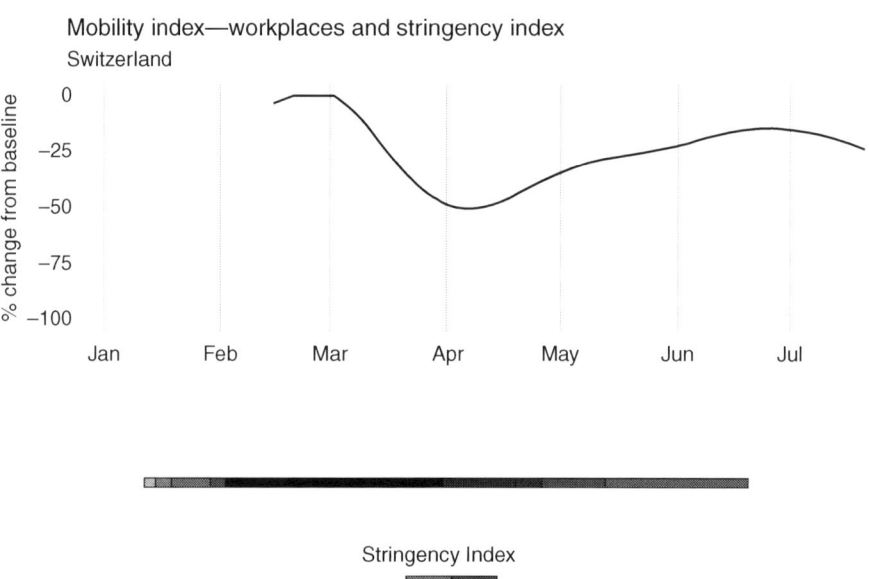

Figure 17.3. Daily confirmed cases of COVID-19, all-cause excess mortality, and change of mobility in Switzerland.

policy responses were mostly on the state level as they hold the legislative and executive competences in case of a pandemic (Robert Koch Institute, 2020c). Bavaria and North Rhine-Westphalia, where some of the first clusters emerged, were the first states to ban events with more than one thousand participants on March 10, 2020 ("Bayern Untersagt Wegen Corona Großveranstaltungen" ["Bavaria Bans Major Events Because of Coronavirus"], 2020; State Government of North Rhine-Westphalia, 2020). In the following days, the majority of states decided to close schools and nurseries ("Nachbarn Schliessen Grenzen" ["Neighbors Close Borders"], 2020). Increasingly, regional differences in essential restrictions of daily life and businesses led to considerable public dissatisfaction and calls for more centrally aligned interventions (Welty, 2020). Bavaria in particular pressed ahead with restrictive measures such as stay-at-home orders ("Katastrophenfall" [Emergencies], 2020).

Coordinated action on the federal level was eventually taken on March 16, 2020, when Chancellor Angela Merkel announced containment measures for the entire country agreed upon by the federal and state governments. These measures included closure of nonessential shops and sports facilities, school closures, and restrictions for restaurants (Winkelmann & Reichebner, 2020). Furthermore, borders with Austria, Denmark, France, Luxembourg, and Switzerland were shut down ("Kampf Gegen Coronavirus" ["Fight against the Coronavirus"], 2020). Considering the exponential growth path of case numbers, RKI—Germany's federal scientific institution in the field of biomedicine—raised the epidemic risk level to "high" on March 17, 2020 (Robert Koch Institute, 2020b). As European Union (EU) leaders decided on a thirty-day entry ban for non-EU citizens, Germany also widened its travel restrictions to EU citizens from countries classified as high-risk areas ("Deutschland," 2020).

A further notable tightening of lockdown measures followed on March 22, 2020, when the federal government and the sixteen state governments agreed to ban gatherings of more than two people and to mandate a minimum distance of 1.5 meters in public with the exception of families, partners, and persons living in the same household. Residents were only allowed to leave their homes for work, basic errands, helping others, and exercising. The agreement also included the closure of all restaurants and personal service facilities, allowing individual states to impose further restrictions (Federal Government of Germany, 2020a).

Within the health system, service provision was reorganized to safeguard sufficient capacities for management of the pandemic. From mid-March, hospitals were ordered to postpone elective surgeries and nonurgent treatments, while specialized treatment centers for COVID-19 patients as well as an intensive care registry were set up ("Corona: Krankenhaeuser" ["Corona: Hospitals"], 2020; Robert Koch Institute, 2020a). In parallel, restrictions on video consultations and telemedicine in outpatient practice were relaxed, and physicians were granted a temporary provision to issue or renew prescriptions, referrals, and sick notes digitally or via telephone ("COVID-19," 2020). As in many other countries, there were shortages of personal protective equipment (PPE) in the early phase of the pandemic. These were particularly severe in general practitioners' (GP) offices, but supplies were also insufficient in hospitals and long-term care facilities; this led to reusing disposable masks. In response, the procurement of PPE was transferred from the states to the central level and handled by the Ministry of Health from early March onward. In addition, Germany prohibited exports of PPE, which led to tensions with other European countries (see later in this chapter) and was later partially revoked (Winkelmann & Reichebner, 2020). What is more, production capacities (e.g., in the textile industry) were soon repurposed to producing masks and respirators.

Testing volumes have been comparatively high in Germany from the beginning of the crisis and were continuously increased (Winkelmann & Reichebner, 2020). Access to testing kits was facilitated by the fact that the first polymerase chain reaction (PCR) test for SARS-CoV-2 was developed by the German Center for Infection Research at Charité Berlin (Charité—Universitaetsmedizin Berlin, 2020). Public and private laboratories were quickly mobilized to increase testing capacities. Because testing is rather decentralized and performed at various types of health facilities, data on test numbers are merged only once a week at RKI.

In the face of a sharp decline in daily new infections, lockdown measures were gradually relaxed beginning April 20, 2020. From April 17, 2020, onward, the majority of states introduced some form of mandatory use of face masks with regulation relaxations, but specific regulations varied by state (Winkelmann & Reichebner, 2020).

Although the introduction of restrictions had to some extent been coordinated on the federal level, exit from lockdown was again mostly guided by the individual states. This can be considered a re-shift to common prepandemic policy, in which federal states were considered to hold the decision mandate (Schlette et al., 2020). In light of the debate on constitutionality, legality, and proportionality of the restrictions that had been imposed, discussions about measure appropriateness and noncoordinated action continued throughout May and June 2020. From the standpoint of democratic politics, it was clear that with the acute phase of the crisis abating, imposing new restrictions or extending restrictions had to be justified more rigorously, whereas relaxation had to be the norm ("Merkel zur Corona-Krise" ["Merkel about Coronacrisis"], 2020; Papier, 2020).

Austria had its first two cases of SARS-CoV-2 confirmed on February 25, 2020 (a young couple that had recently been to Lombardy), four weeks later than Germany's first case. In early March 2020, however, it became apparent that a major infection cluster had been active in the Tyrolean ski resort town of Ischgl from late February onward. Because of the late detection of the hotspot and delayed action from regional authorities, the virus was then carried to other countries (mostly Germany and Nordic countries) and regions by returning tourists who had contracted it in Ischgl.

On March 10, 2020, the Austrian federal government announced that events with more than five hundred participants would be banned and that universities and upper secondary schools would have to switch to distance learning ("Coronavirus: Starke Einschraenkungen Beschlossen" ["Coronavirus: Severe Restrictions Adopted"], 2020; Tritschler, 2020). The latter was then extended to all schools; primary and lower secondary schools, however, stayed open for supervision where children could not be looked after privately (Peitler-Hasewend & Jungwirth, 2020).

Continuously increasing case numbers and alarming footage from neighboring northern Italy led the government to announce far stricter lockdown measures only few days later, on March 13, 2020. The Austrian regulations, which later served as a model for the German measures, included shelter-in-place orders with few exceptions, a mandatory 1-meter distance to nonhousehold members and closures of restaurants and nonessential retail. On the same day, in addition to travel warnings and flight bans for several high-risk countries, Austria closed its borders to Italy almost entirely. Furthermore, some severely affected municipalities (including Ischgl) were put under curfew ("Ausgangsbeschraenkungen" ["Curfew"], 2020; "Austria's Tyrol Province Orders Lockdown," 2020).

On March 30, 2020, additional restrictions were announced, most notably the requirement to wear face masks in stores (and later also in public transport) (Habimana et al., 2020). Austria was among the first countries in Europe to introduce the mandatory use of face masks. Furthermore, companies were obligated to enable employees belonging to risk groups to work from home. Accompanying this regulation, a salary replacement scheme for reimbursement of employers' costs was introduced ("Maskenpflicht" ["Mandatory Face Masks"], 2020; Parliament of the Republic of Austria, 2020).

As in Germany, hospitals in Austria were called upon to postpone all nonurgent surgeries and examinations ("Operationen Verschieben Statt Risiken Eingehen" ["Postpone Operations Instead of Taking Risks"], 2020). Specific hospitals or hospital units across the country were designated for treatment of COVID-19 patients ("59 Spitaeler" ["59 Hospitals"], 2020). Physicians were enabled to issue prescriptions electronically, sick notes via telephone, and teleconsultations in psychotherapy were made reimbursable by health insurance funds ("OEGK," 2020). Procurement and distribution of PPE were coordinated by the Ministry of Health from early March 2020 onward. Controversy arose when shipments of PPE destined for Austria were held back at the German border because of the export ban while the health and long-term care sectors began to run short of supplies ("Lkw Mit Schutzmasken" ["Trucks with Face Masks"], 2020). The issue was resolved in mid-March at the EU level when a joint procurement by the EU Commission and export restrictions to non-EU member states was agreed upon (Representation of the European Commission in Germany, 2020).

Testing of suspected cases was initiated either by a call to the helpline 1450 or by a GP (Federal Ministry of Social Affairs, Health, Care and Consumer Protection, 2020b). Testing volumes were ramped up after increasing criticism that the available capacities were not being used optimally. The target of fifteen thousand tests per day as communicated by the government has, however, not been reached as of this writing ("Coronavirus: Das 'Nadeloehr' bei den Testungen" ["Coronavirus: The 'Eye of the Needle' in Testing"], 2020). When daily new cases began to decline, freed-up capacities were partly used for targeted testing of healthcare professionals, residents of nursing homes, and persons working in critical infrastructure ("Coronavirus: Gezielte Tests," 2020). Although there is a uniform definition of testing criteria, actual practice varies by state (Federal Ministry of Social Affairs, Health, Care and Consumer Protection, 2020b).

The favorable development of infection rates allowed Austria to begin lifting some lockdown measures as early as mid-April 2020 ("Coronavirus: Fahrplan," 2020). Starting with opening shops and restaurants and followed by resumption of classroom teaching in schools, measures were relaxed mostly at two-week intervals to allow for monitoring effects on the epidemiological development and to potentially reassess the strategy ("Coronavirus: Ausgangsbeschraenkungen Laufen Aus" ["Coronavirus: Curfew Expires"], 2020). In late July, the health minister announced the introduction of a traffic-light system that would determine the requirement for a regional reintroduction of containment measures based on a set of indicators. These indicators include epidemiological measures as well as regionally available resources (Gaigg & Mueller, 2020).

In **Switzerland**, the first case of SARS-CoV-2 (a seventy-year-old man who had recently visited Milan) was confirmed on the same day as in Austria (i.e., February 25, 2020). Only three days later, Switzerland was among the first countries in Europe to impose containment measures as the Federal Council banned events with more than one thousand participants (Federal Council, 2020c).

Case numbers continued to rise fast in early March—significantly faster than in Germany or Austria at that time—especially in urban areas (Trein & Rodwin Wagner, 2020). The ban of events was extended to events with more than one hundred people on March 13, 2020, and classroom teaching was suspended in schools and universities, while childcare facilities had to remain open for children where parental supervision was not possible (Federal Council, 2020a).

In the face of continuously increasing case numbers, the Federal Council declared the "extraordinary situation" on March 16, 2020, which allowed them to uniformly impose containment measures across all cantons. Like in the other countries, restaurants and nonessential shops had to close. In addition, border checks were introduced and entry bans imposed. Besides transit and goods traffic, only Swiss citizens, persons holding a residence permit, and persons working in Switzerland were allowed to enter the country (Federal Council, 2020d; Mantwill et al., 2020).

Further physical distancing regulations were announced by the Federal Council on March 20, 2020, after the number of daily new cases had risen to more than fourteen hundred (S. Buehler et al., 2020). Gatherings of more than five persons were banned and a distance of 2 meters between persons not living in the same household was mandated. Although the industry and construction sectors were allowed to continue operating, they were required to follow strict regulations regarding hygiene and physical distancing. In case they did not comply, cantons were allowed to close down individual companies (Federal Council, 2020b). This was later extended by the possibility to shut down whole sectors on canton level if deemed necessary (Federal Office of Public Health, 2020d).

A notable measure related to the health system was the authorization of cantons to oblige private hospitals to free capacities for the treatment of COVID-19 patients (Federal Office of Public Health, 2020f). All hospitals were prohibited from performing nonurgent procedures and examinations. Furthermore, the declaration of the extraordinary situation allowed to mobilize up to eight thousand armed forces to assist with healthcare logistics and security (Federal Council, 2020d). Switzerland also faced a shortage of PPE at the outbreak of the crisis, which led to criticism of the authorities for taking action too late (see later in this chapter). As Switzerland, unlike Germany, does not produce much protective gear, it had been heavily reliant on imports. As a result, tensions arose between Switzerland and Germany when shipments of PPE headed to Switzerland were temporarily detained at the German border, as it was later also the case with Austria ("Mask Hysteria," 2020). In April, Switzerland began to produce protective masks ("Coronavirus: Switzerland," 2020).

Testing volumes had been relatively high in Switzerland, albeit not as high as in Germany. Criteria for testing were defined on the national level and had been evolving in the course of the crisis. The actual administration and procedure of testing fell, however, within the responsibility of the individual cantons. They determined whether tests were to be performed in designated hospitals, at GP practices, or by mobile teams (Mantwill et al., 2020). By June 2020, the federal government agreed to assume the total costs for all PCR and antibody tests performed. Before that, the costs were split between health insurers and cantons (Federal Office of Public Health, 2020c).

Switzerland began easing restrictions on April 27, 2020, when hardware stores, hairdressers, and other personal service providers were allowed to reopen and elective medical treatments could be performed again. From mid-May, restaurants and shops were opened and classroom teaching in schools gradually resumed (Federal Office of Public Health, 2020b).

The rather coordinated manner of economic reopening throughout May was later met with challenges, because the Federal Council withdrew from the extraordinary situation and dissolved its crisis unit on June 19, 2020 (Federal Office of Public Health, 2020e). From that point onward, the Federal Council publicly stressed its withdrawal from extraordinary exertion of power and the prime responsibility of cantons to manage a renewed increase in infections (Federal Office of Public Health, 2020e). In the light of slightly increasing case numbers and the occurrence of super-spreader events, this coordinated action proved challenging on questions such as mask regulations in cross-canton public transports or coordinated contact-tracing strategies (U. Buehler, Mueller, & Fritzsche, 2020).

Because Germany, Austria, and Switzerland are so closely interconnected in both economic and cultural terms, cross-country travel and transit has been a highly relevant aspect during the crisis. The three countries belong to the Schengen area and therefore normally do not apply any border controls. However, all three countries closed their borders in March 2020, and entry was only granted to foreign citizens under certain exceptions. These exceptions included (essential) work, transit, and goods traffic. In mid-May 2020, the first easing of entry restrictions between Austria, Germany, and Switzerland was announced. Exceptions to the entry ban were extended to also include visits of partners or relatives, important family occasions, care for animals, or maintenance of property (Federal Ministry of the Interior, Building and Community, 2020). As of June 15, 2020, there were no more border controls between the three countries.

Social Policy Measures

As of this writing, the **German** federal government issued two major economic relief packages: the first of EUR 156 billion (approximately 4.9 percent of the gross domestic product, GDP) from mid-March and the second of EUR 130 billion (approximately 4.0 percent of GDP) in late June (International Monetary Fund, 2020). The packages comprise a broad range of measures aimed at stimulating the economy, supporting businesses, protecting jobs, and mitigating the effects of the crisis on socially deprived groups.

Short-time work (*Kurzarbeit*) benefits, which Germany already heavily relied on during and after the financial crisis of 2008, were introduced as part of the first package. Benefits have since been increased and extended multiple times and access has been eased. The plan allows for benefits of up to 80 percent of former net income, with even higher benefits for workers with children (International Labour Organization, 2020b).

Access to basic income support for the unemployed was eased, and unemployment benefits were partially extended. To support families, they received a one-time "family bonus" of EUR 300 per child and increased parental-leave benefits, while access to childcare benefits for low-income families was eased (International Labour Organization, 2020b). Single parents were granted additional tax allowances (Federal Ministry of Finance, 2020). In the field of housing, a rental protection act was enacted that temporarily prevented lessors from terminating rental agreements because of outstanding rent payments ("What's in Germany's Emergency Coronavirus Budget?," 2020).

Self-employed workers and small businesses could apply for a one-time emergency aid if they were heavily affected by the crisis (Arbeitsagentur, 2020). Credit guarantees were granted, and companies expecting losses for 2020 may clear these with tax prepayments they have already paid for 2019. Furthermore, several tax reliefs were granted, including moratoriums on tax debts, adjusted prepayments, and suspensions of sequestrations (International Labour Organization, 2020b). VAT rates were temporarily reduced from 19 percent to 16 percent and from 7 percent to 5 percent, respectively (Federal Ministry of Finance, 2020). Support packages specifically for start-ups and artists also were set up. In addition to these federal-level measures, many states individually passed further relief packages (Federal Government of Germany, 2020b).

In **Austria**, a crisis management fund amounting to EUR 4 billion was issued on March 15, 2020, but the fiscal package has since been extended to a total of EUR 50 billion (approximately 9.5 percent of GDP) (International Monetary Fund, 2020). The budgeted measures are similar to the ones taken in Germany.

The central measure taken in the field of the labor market was the short-time working scheme specifically developed for the COVID-19 crisis. As in Germany, the scheme was extended several times. It allowed working hours to be reduced to a minimum of 10 percent at 80 percent to 90 percent of regular pay (International Labour Organization, 2020a). An adapted short-time working scheme in force from October onward involved training opportunities for workers with reduced hours (Reisner, 2020).

The unemployed received a one-time additional benefit of EUR 450, and access to several other social benefits was eased ("Arbeitslosengeld" ["Unemployment Benefit"], 2020; "Austria Plans Coronavirus Help," 2020). Families in need could apply for a benefit of up to EUR 1,200 per month for a maximum of three months from the so-called Corona Family Hardship Fund (Federal Ministry of Labour, Family and Youth, 2020a). Furthermore, workers with care responsibilities can get additional paid leave of up to three weeks (Federal Ministry of Labour, Family and Youth, 2020b).

Support for businesses includes a so-called "hardship fund" that grants one-time cash payments to individual entrepreneurs and small businesses affected by the crisis (International Labour Organization, 2020a). Another fund covers guarantees for loans and subsidies for up to 75 percent of fixed operating costs of businesses that accrued during the lockdown. Special guarantee schemes were established for exporting companies and small and medium enterprises (SMEs) in the tourism sector (Reisner, 2020). Furthermore, the obligation to file for insolvency in case of overindebtedness was temporarily suspended (Scherbaum Seebacher, 2020). Relaxed tax regulations included the temporary deferral of personal and corporate income taxes and social security contributions as well as of value-added tax payments. Employers could apply for reimbursement of social security contributions by the government if operations had to be suspended during the lockdown (Reisner, 2020).

Beginning on March 13, 2020, the Federal Council in **Switzerland** announced several relief packages that amount to a total of CHF 73 billion (approximately 10.4 percent of GDP; International Monetary Fund, 2020) as of this writing.

As in Germany and Austria, firms in Switzerland could claim benefits from a short-time working scheme. The scheme was extended several times. It was adapted to also cover on-call workers and some self-employed, and the application process has been simplified (International Monetary Fund, 2020).

Furthermore, the Swiss support packages involved partial unemployment compensation and compensation for loss of earnings for the self-employed and for some employees affected by the lockdown. In particular, parents with caring responsibilities resulting from school closures were eligible for income support (Federal Department of Economic Affairs, Education and Research, 2020a; Federal Office of Public Health, 2020a).

Measures aimed at businesses included direct financial aid for severely affected firms (e.g., in the tourism sector), a loan guarantee program, and bridging loans for SMEs and start-ups and temporary interest-free deferral of social-security contribution payments (International Monetary Fund, 2020). The government also granted specific compensations for the railway and aviation-related businesses, as well as for cancelled events (Federal Department of Economic Affairs, Education and Research, 2020b, 2020c).

Explanation

Germany, Austria, and Switzerland are textbook examples of federal countries, in particular when it comes to the organization of health and social care. However, in the specific context of the pandemic, federal structures came into play in very different ways across the three countries.

In Germany, responsibility for epidemic management fell largely to the sixteen states as well as local public health authorities. Similarly, other policy areas that became relevant in the context of crisis management (e.g., education, regulations for businesses) were largely within state responsibility. Hence, especially in the early phase of the outbreak, Germany's response was mostly characterized by heterogeneity across the individual states. The spread of the virus was rather uneven across the states, which led some state governors to press ahead in imposing measures, whereas others remained hesitant (Schlette et al., 2020). State-by-state management was also foreseen by the German National Pandemic Plan, which was published in 2005. Considering the lack of historical precedent for the current situation, however, it quickly became clear that more coordinated action would be required at least in some policy areas.

As the crisis evolved and case numbers began to increase all over Germany, the federal government began to weigh in. The power of the Ministry of Health was temporarily expanded on the basis of the "Act for protecting the public health in an epidemic situation of national importance," which granted it competences in the provision of pharmaceutical and medical devices, as well as in the planning of the medical workforce (Greer et al., 2020). Furthermore, the so-called Small Corona Cabinet, consisting of the ministers of defense, finance, interior, foreign affairs, health, and the head of the Federal Chancellery, began to play a more central role during this phase (Winkelmann & Reichebner, 2020). However, major decisions on measures such as contact restrictions and border closures still had to be taken in coordination with the states. In extensive and reportedly conflictual telephone conferences, Chancellor Angela Merkel and the members of the Corona Cabinet discussed with state governors until a certain degree of consensus was reached (Fried & Herrmann, 2020). When first reopening steps were considered, state interests regained weight, and the level of disagreement between state governors and the federal government increased. As a result, state governors again took the lead in lifting restrictions from early May onward.

In general, regional interests appeared to outweigh party interests in Germany, as state governors heavily criticized measures taken by other governors from the same party, resulting in polyphony about correct behavioral measures in the pandemic. However, this controversy also was fueled by the current discussion around Merkel's succession, both as the leader of the Christian Democratic Union (CDU) and as candidate for chancellorship in the next elections. The party congress scheduled to agree on the new party leader had to be postponed because of the outbreak. The crisis gave some conservative state governors the chance to strengthen their profiles and increase their stakes in the succession race. Before the outbreak, three men were officially in the race for party leadership of the CDU and expected to later on run for chancellor. Among them was Armin Laschet, state governor of North Rhine-Westphalia, whose candidacy was eventually supported by Health Minister Jens Spahn (Karnitschnig, 2020). Because his state was among the first with large infection clusters, Laschet attempted to use the resulting media attention to his advantage, but seemed to have failed to convince the public during his public appearances. Instead, Markus Söder, state governor of Bavaria and leader of CDU's sister party, Christian Social Union (CSU), received wide praise for his handling of the crisis and has since gained popularity all across Germany. Because the two sister parties, CDU and CSU, traditionally appoint a joint candidate for chancellorship, he has increasingly been discussed as the most promising candidate in that race (Rossmann, 2020).

In Austria, although competences on health matters are distributed between the federation and the states, the field of public health—including the management of epidemics and pandemics, according to the Epidemics Act—largely falls within the responsibility of the federation (Bussjaeger, 2020). From the beginning of the crisis, the chancellor and vice-chancellor as well as the ministers of health and the interior were the central figures in the fight against the epidemic. The new government had just been sworn in in early January 2020 after several months of political turmoil and lack of political leadership on the national level. This made the conservative-green coalition particularly eager to show resolve and unity in their crisis response (Czypionka et al., 2020).

The states were clearly in a subordinate role. The system of indirect federal administration required them (and consequently the district authorities) to execute regulations passed at the federal level. In addition, it remained the task of the states to provide sufficient capacity in hospitals or with regard to testing and contact tracing (Bussjaeger, 2020). Furthermore, the states had the power to apply stricter measures in some areas, which allowed the states of Tyrol and Salzburg to impose curfew regulations on some municipalities that were more heavily affected by the outbreak (Gamper, 2020).

Switzerland lies somewhere between Germany and Austria when it comes to the role of federalism in the COVID-19 crisis. The twenty-six cantons usually hold a large share of competences in various policy fields, including health policy. Hence, in the early phase of the crisis, some cantons took action independently and imposed first containment measures. However, declaration of the extraordinary situation activated the Epidemics Act, which authorized the Federal Council to impose public health measures on a national level; this in turn shifted the weight of decision-making to the federal level (Belser et al., 2020; Mantwill et al., 2020).

As in Austria, the cantons were responsible for the implementation and detailed configuration of measures while also organizing and maintaining their cantonal health systems (Mantwill et al., 2020). Any restrictions imposed by cantons that went beyond the ones decided upon on at the federal level were at first regarded unlawful by the Federal Council. In particular, this became relevant when the canton of Ticino required all nonessential manufacturing to close despite the federal decision to allow firms to continue production. However, continuous protest from several cantons led the Federal Council to change their stance in late March and allow cantons to make exceptions from the federal decree (Belser et al., 2020; Trein & Rodwin Wagner, 2020). In the transition phase toward exit from lockdown, an east-west rift arose, as the German-speaking cantons called for an end to the lockdown, whereas the more severely affected Italian- and French-speaking cantons preferred to keep restrictions in place (Trein & Rodwin Wagner, 2020). This controversy was among the reasons why the Federal Council decided to leave the potential reintroduction of lockdown measures to the cantons in case of a surge in infection rates.

Whether a federalist or centralist organization of the pandemic response yields better results is a controversial question. Leaving the responsibility with regional authorities allows for testing different policy approaches and subsequently adopting the ones that prove to work best in other regions as well. Because the virus spread unevenly and public health capacities varied by region, a regional response also gave states/cantons the chance to tailor measures to their individual situation (Schlette et al., 2020). Furthermore, regional governments could eventually be held accountable for their decisions (Sturm, 2020). In Germany, for example, policy makers and media stressed federalism as conditional for successfully providing targeted responses and tailored prevention approaches (Esslinger, 2020; Hipp, 2020; Pergande, 2020; von Marschall, 2020). However, a federalist organization of the response also has substantial downsides. A lack of coordination and the resulting regional differences in regulations can create undesired incentives (e.g., "tourism" to regions with stricter or less strict regulations) (Belser et al., 2020). It may also result in confusion and a lack of acceptance in the population, as it may be difficult to justify different responses in regions facing similar situations. Moreover, a centralist approach allows for fast responses because it does not require extensive negotiations and coordination efforts. In addition, knowledge resources on how to fight a pandemic may also have considerable economies of scale. Accordingly, evaluations of the three countries' outbreak responses with respect to the role of federalism vary considerably (Belser et al., 2020; Bussjaeger, 2020; Gamper, 2020; Sturm, 2020).

Another aspect that was handled very differently across the three countries was communication. This refers to *how* the public was informed about the virus, the epidemiological situation and the measures taken, but also *who* the central figures in crisis management and communication were. Hence, this aspect was interconnected with the role played by experts during the crisis.

In Germany, the role of information provision with respect to the virus and the epidemiological situation—in part resulting from the polyphony from the political players in the beginning of the crisis—was to a great part taken on by the RKI, which can be regarded Germany's national public health institute, and Christian Drosten, director of the Institute for Virology at Charité Berlin. During the peak of the crisis, the RKI and its team of scientists created a steady flow of information by giving daily press conferences and publishing numerous risk assessments, strategy documents, response plans, surveillance reports, and technical guidelines (Wieler et al., 2020). Its recommendations and guidelines were also adopted by authorities in other countries (e.g., the Austrian Ministry of Health; Federal Ministry of Social Affairs, Health, Care and Consumer Protection, 2020a). In her press appearances related to COVID-19, Chancellor Merkel was usually flanked by Lothar Wieler, the head of the RKI. Christian Drosten, an expert on the SARS-CoV-1 virus, became one of the central figures in German media coverage on the virus. He had also been part of the team that developed the PCR diagnostic test and later started a daily half-hour podcast with the broadcaster NDR. The charismatic scientist was dubbed by German media "the nation's corona-explainer-in-chief" (Oltermann, 2020a). Especially in the early phase of the pandemic, the RKI and Drosten were the main advisors to the federal government and the populace in Germany. As the crisis evolved and impacts on other spheres than just health became apparent, the government extended its advisory group to include other disciplines (Schlette et al., 2020).

In comparison, the federal government of Germany played a less prominent role in crisis communication. Although some media viewed her as a leading figure in Europe's fight against the pandemic, Chancellor Merkel, a scientist herself, in fact left the floor mainly to the medical experts. Her communication mainly consisted in calm explanations of the rationales behind strict lockdown measures and appeals for solidarity, stressing the importance to uphold basic human rights (Miller, 2020; Oltermann, 2020b). Especially during Merkel's self-quarantine after having been in contact with a doctor who tested positive, Health Minister Jens Spahn took on a bigger role in the government's communication, which increased his popularity ratings. As a result, although he had previously announced not to run, he re-entered discussions around Merkel's succession as party leader and chancellor candidate (Rossmann, 2020).

In Austria, the characteristics of crisis communication were entirely different from Germany. The federal government was the central entity in decision-making and took the lead in nearly all aspects of communication. Chancellor Sebastian Kurz, Vice-Chancellor Werner Kogler, Health Minister Rudolf Anschober, and Interior Minister Karl Nehammer became the faces of crisis management, as they gave press conferences under great media fanfare almost on a daily basis at the peak of the crisis.

The Austrian government did to some extent rely on expert advice. The scientific advisory board of the "Taskforce Corona" at the Ministry of Health included experts in various medical fields. Furthermore, decisions were aided by an agent-based simulation model of epidemic spread developed by a group of researchers at the Vienna University of Technology (Czypionka et al., 2020). However, there was a lack of transparency regarding on which evidence decisions were eventually based, and members of the advisory board began to publicly voice criticism. For example, experts had warned officials to take care of the procurement of sufficient protective equipment and test kits already in February, which would have prevented shortages that occurred at the peak of the crisis. Moreover, several of the advisors in the "Taskforce Corona" had argued for a less strict and more targeted lockdown to contain social and economic impacts. However, in both instances, the government preferred not to follow the expert advice (Tóth, 2020).

Instead, leaked protocols revealed that Chancellor Kurz had, at the peak of the crisis, aimed for a strategy driven by fear ("Regierungsprotokoll" ["Government Protocol"], 2020). His rhetoric was shaped accordingly, very much in contrast to Merkel's calming and unemotional demeanor. He repeatedly drew lines to the disturbing footage from Italian hospitals and famously said in an interview on March 30, 2020, that "soon, everyone will know someone who has died of the coronavirus," although at that time daily new infections had already been decreasing ("Regierungskommunikation" ["Government Communication"], 2020). This strategy was heavily criticized by the opposition. Furthermore, at multiple occasions, it was implied in press conferences that certain activities were prohibited, whereas this was in fact not in line with the actual legislation ("Corona-Verbote," 2020). A lot of controversy also arose around the constitutionality of the measures taken. In the meantime, the Constitutional Court ruled that the legislation, in particular a ban on entering public spaces, was partly unlawful, which provoked even more criticism from the opposition ("VfGH" ["Constitutional Court"], 2020). Nevertheless, the government enjoyed high approval ratings throughout the crisis (Seidl, 2020).

In Switzerland, official crisis communication was also centered around the federal government, but not as exclusively as in Austria, because the principle of collegiality is firmly rooted in its Swiss government. The government's press conferences featured all seven ministers of the Federal Council, most prominently Interior Minister Alain Berset, who is also responsible for health matters. As the measures taken were not particularly harsh considering the country's fast increase in infections, the government's communication strategy was characterized by a measured tone appealing to the public's rationality and solidarity (Wong Sak Hoi, 2020). Berset's promise from April 16, 2020, to act "as quickly as possible and as slowly as necessary" became the mantra of the Swiss crisis management and was even printed on t-shirts to raise money for charity ("Minister's Quote," 2020).

Besides the federal government, the central figure in COVID-19–related communication was Daniel Koch, who at the time was the head of the infectious diseases unit at the Federal Office of Public Health (FOPH) and was named the government's COVID-19 delegate. Especially early on in the crisis, the civil servant with a medical background was praised by the press for his calm explanations of the epidemiological situation (Romy, 2020).

However, both the government and Koch also had to face some criticism, especially from epidemiological experts. In late January, Swiss epidemiologists published a study on the transmission of SARS-CoV-2 (Riou & Althaus, 2020) and contacted the FOPH to offer their help in preparing for a potential spread of the virus to Switzerland. Officials reportedly were not interested in cooperation, and Koch instead made several statements about the virus not being more dangerous than the common flu. In late February, renowned scientists Marcel Salathé and Christian Althaus publicly criticized Koch and Berset for ignoring their advice and taking action too late, resulting in a severe shortage of masks at the outbreak of the crisis (S. Buehler et al., 2020). The Federal Council eventually decided to set up the "Swiss National COVID-19 Science Task Force," an expert advisory board that also includes Salathé and Althaus. The task force was, however, established as late as March 31 when national lockdown measures had already been in place for almost two weeks (S. Buehler et al., 2020; Mantwill et al., 2020).

The Swiss political system is famous for its tradition of debate and compromise because it constantly needs to coordinate the interests of its twenty-six cantons. With some exceptions—most notably the divide between eastern and western cantons about the lifting of lockdown measures—this spirit was also upheld during the COVID-19 crisis and the government's response was mostly based on a broad political and regional consensus (Trein & Rodwin Wagner, 2020).

Conclusion

Although the three countries studied in this chapter are all prime examples of federalism, Austria and Switzerland showed a decisive, uniform public health response resulting from epidemic laws granting the central level precedence under such circumstances. By contrast, a lot of confusion arose when states in Germany engaged in a wide variety of interventions introduced at different times including even differing social distancing rules. After a phase of more coordinated policy action brought about by Chancellor Merkel, the question of how and when to lift lockdown became fuzzy again. At least in the beginning of the crisis and in the absence of unity in the political leadership, guidance primarily came from prominent scientists. The crisis also found the country in the midst of a struggle for Angela Merkel's succession and its protagonists as competitors in the fight against the virus. Politicians and the public strongly relied on the advice of the Robert Koch Institute and Christian Drosten, a world-leading expert on coronaviruses. By contrast, the Swiss federal government, with its strong tradition of collegiality, steered the country calmly despite a comparably higher death toll. A rift in the unanimous response arose only on the question when to lift the lockdown measures, with Italian- and French-speaking cantons more cautious than the German-speaking ones. The main media attention in Switzerland, often dubbed the "land of direct democracy," centered around Daniel Koch, an expert civil servant, at least until he became heavily criticized by prominent Swiss epidemiologists. In Austria, the newly formed and novel (Conservative-Green) government was bound to show strength and unity and implemented comparably harsh lockdown measures at an early stage. Probably reflective of this hegemony of politics over science, the main protagonist on the media during the crisis was not a scientist, but rather Chancellor Kurz. Close ties to Italy and disturbing footage from Italian intensive care units helped to garner support in the population, but were likely also used strategically in government communication to instill a sense of fear.

Although all three countries managed to get through the crisis—or at least the first wave—relatively well, it remains to be seen what effects the different policy approaches will have in the long run. As more and more background information on the dynamics and motivations behind decisions made during the crisis comes to light, policy-makers will be held accountable for their actions. No doubt the comparably good outcome has increased approval ratings for the ruling parties in all three countries. It remains to be seen, however, whether this is a lasting effect or whether some questionable actions (e.g., the disorderly lockdown and transition phases in Germany or the fear-based communication strategy in Austria) will catch up with the ones in charge at the time. This and the question of constitutionality of some of the measures have likely also contributed to the growing number of "corona-deniers." But even the majority of the population may eventually grow tired of mask-wearing and physical distancing. Together with other aspects like prevention in schools or concurrence of COVID-19 and influenza-like illnesses, these challenges will continue to put health systems and political leadership to the test in the face of resurging infection waves.

References

59 Spitaeler für Coronavirus geruestet—Oesterreich [59 hospitals equipped for coronavirus—Austria]. (2020, February 25). orf.at. https://oesterreich.orf.at/stories/3036229/
Arbeitsagentur. (2020, April 24). *Übersicht Soforthilfen zur Abfederung der finanziellen Auswirkungen während der Corona-Pandemie* [Overview of emergency aids to alleviate financial impacts of the coronavirus pandemic]. https://www.arbeitsagentur.de/datei/uebersicht-soforthilfeprogramme-corona_ba146398.pdf
Arbeitslosengeld: 450 Euro Einmalzahlung, keine Erhoehung [Unemployment benefit: 450 Euro single payment, no increase]. (2020, June 13). orf.at. https://orf.at/stories/3169409/
Ausgangsbeschraenkungen: Was nun erlaubt ist und was nicht [Curfew: What is now allowed and what is not]. (2020, March 16). orf.at. https://orf.at/stories/3158055/
Austria plans coronavirus help for jobless, families. (2020, June 13). Reuters Business News. https://uk.reuters.com/article/uk-health-coronavirus-austria/austria-plans-coronavirus-help-for-jobless-families-idUKKBN23K0D6
Austria's Tyrol province orders lockdown. (2020, March 15). *The Boston Globe.* https://www.bostonglobe.com/2020/03/15/business/austria-shuts-restaurants-bans-some-flights

Bayern untersagt wegen Corona Großveranstaltungen [Bavaria bans major events because of Corona]. (2020, March 10). *Sueddeutsche Zeitung.* https://www.sueddeutsche.de/bayern/bayern-coronavirus-grossveranstaltungen-verbot-1.4839247

Belser, E. M., Stoeckli, A., & Waldmann, B. (2020, April 9). Der schweizerische Foederalismus funktioniert auch im Krisenmodus [Swiss federalism also works in crisis mode]. *Institut fuer Foederalismus.* https://www.foederalismus.at/blog/der-schweizerische-foederalismus-funktioniert-auch-im-krisenmodus_233.php

Buehler, S., Burri, A., Furger, M., Haeuptli, L., Hossli, P., Luethi, T., Pfister, F., Roth, R., & Eisenring, R. (2020, June 6). Der Koch, sein Chef und das Virus: Hat der Bundesrat in der Krise auf die richtigen Experten gehoert? [The cook, his boss and the virus: Did the Federal Council listen to the right experts during the crisis?]. *NZZ Am Sonntag.* https://nzzas.nzz.ch/hintergrund/corona-in-der-schweiz-wie-der-bundesrat-die-krise-bewaeltigte-ld.1560010?reduced=true

Buehler, U., Mueller, A., & Fritzsche, D. (2020, June 29). Nach dem ersten moeglichen Superspreader-Fall im Kanton warnt die Zuercher Gesundheitsdirektorin Natalie Rickli: "Dieses Virus ist kein Spass, auch nicht für die Spassgesellschaft am Wochenende" [After the first possible superspreader case in the canton, Zurich Health Director Natalie Rickli warns: "This virus is no joke, not even for the weekend fun society"]. *NZZ.* https://www.nzz.ch/zuerich/coronavirus-in-zuerich-superspreader-steckt-in-club-6-leute-an-ld.1563558

Bussjaeger, P. (2020, April 28). COVID-19 crisis challenging Austria's cooperative federalism. *Institut fuer Foederalismus Blog.* https://www.foederalismus.at/blog/covid-19-crisis-challenging-austria%E2%80%99s-cooperative-federalism_235.php

Charité—Universitaetsmedizin Berlin. (2020, January 16). *Researchers develop first diagnostic test for novel coronavirus in China.* https://www.charite.de/en/service/press_reports/artikel/detail/researchers_develop_first_diagnostic_test_for_novel_coronavirus_in_china/

Corona: Krankenhaeuser sollen ab Montag alle planbaren Eingriffe verschieben [Corona: Hospitals should postpone all plannable procedures from Monday]. (2020, March 13). *Aerzteblatt.de.* https://www.aerzteblatt.de/nachrichten/111034/Corona-Krankenhaeuser-sollen-ab-Montag-alle-planbaren-Eingriffe-verschieben

Corona-Verbote: Es ist mehr erlaubt, als wir glauben [Corona bans: More is allowed than we think]. (2020, July 22). *Addendum.* https://www.addendum.org/coronavirus/was-ist-erlaubt/

Coronavirus: Ausgangsbeschraenkungen laufen aus [Coronavirus: Curfew expires]. (2020, April 28). orf.at. https://orf.at/stories/3163548/

Coronavirus: Das "Nadeloehr" bei den Testungen [Coronavirus: The "eye of the needle" in testing]. (2020, March 29). orf.at. https://orf.at/stories/3159619/

Coronavirus: Fahrplan bis Ende April steht [Coronavirus: Timetable until end of April]. (2020, April 6). orf.at. https://orf.at/stories/3160816/

Coronavirus: Gezielte Tests sollen Licht ins Dunkel bringen [Coronavirus: Targeted tests to shed light on the situation]. (2020, March 31). orf.at. https://orf.at/stories/3159951/

Coronavirus: Starke Einschraenkungen beschlossen [Coronavirus: Severe restrictions adopted]. (2020, March 10). orf.at. https://orf.at/stories/3157262/

Coronavirus: Switzerland begins production of protective masks amid international shortage. (2020, April 14). *The Local Switzerland.* https://www.thelocal.ch/20200414/switzerland-begins-production-of-protective-masks-amid-international-shortage

COVID-19: Krankschreibung bis zu sieben Tage nach telefonischer Ruecksprache bei leichten Atemwegserkrankungen [COVID-19: Sick leave up to seven days after telephone consultation for mild respiratory diseases]. (2020, March 9). *Gemeinsame Pressemitteilung der Kassenärztlichen Bundesvereinigung und des GKV-Spitzenverbandes.* https://www.gkv-spitzenverband.de/gkv_spitzenverband/presse/pressemitteilungen_und_statements/pressemitteilung_995776.jsp

Czypionka, T., Reiss, M., & Pham, I. (2020, April 12). Austria's response to the coronavirus—A second perspective. *Cambridge Core.* https://www.cambridge.org/core/blog/2020/04/12/austrias-response-to-the-coronavirus-pandemic-a-second-perspective/

Deutschland weitet Einreisebeschraenkungen für EU-Buerger aus [Germany extends entry restrictions for EU citizens]. (2020, March 18). *Sueddeutsche Zeitung.* https://www.sueddeutsche.de/gesundheit/gesundheit-deutschland-weitet-einreisebeschraenkungen-fuer-eu-buerger-aus-dpa.urn-newsml-dpa-com-20090101-200318-99-384431

Esslinger, D. (2020, November 3). Der Foederalismus kann eine Waffe sein [Federalism can be a weapon]. *Sueddeutsche Zeitung.* https://www.sueddeutsche.de/politik/corona-foederalismus-1.4840253

Federal Council. (2020a, March 13). *Bundesrat verschaerft Massnahmen gegen das Coronavirus zum Schutz der Gesundheit und unterstuetzt betroffene Branchen* [Federal Council strengthens measures against coronavirus to protect health and supports affected industries]. https://www.admin.ch/gov/de/start/dokumentation/medienmitteilungen/bundesrat.msg-id-78437.html

Federal Council. (2020b, March 20). *Federal Council bans gatherings of more than five people.* https://www.bag.admin.ch/bag/en/home/das-bag/aktuell/medienmitteilungen.msg-id-78513.html

Federal Council. (2020c, February 28). *Federal Council bans large-scale events.* https://www.admin.ch/opc/en/classified-compilation/20201774/index.html

Federal Council. (2020d, March 16). *Federal Council declares 'extraordinary situation' and introduces more stringent measures.* https://www.admin.ch/gov/en/start/documentation/media-releases.msg-id-78454.html

Federal Department of Economic Affairs, Education and Research. (2020a, May 27). *Coronavirus: Dringliche Aenderung des Arbeitslosenversicherungsgesetzes* [Coronavirus: Urgent amendment to unemployment insurance law]. https://www.wbf.admin.ch/wbf/de/home/dokumentation/nsb-news_list.msg-id-79256.html

Federal Department of Economic Affairs, Education and Research. (2020b, March 20). *Coronavirus: Massnahmenpaket zur Abfederung der wirtschaftlichen Folgen* [Coronavirus: Package of measures to mitigate the economic consequences]. https://www.wbf.admin.ch/wbf/de/home/dokumentation/nsb-news_list.msg-id-78515.html

Federal Department of Economic Affairs, Education and Research. (2020c, April 5). *COVID19: Liquidity support for startups up and running.* https://www.wbf.admin.ch/wbf/en/home/dokumentation/nsb-news_list.msg-id-79006.html

Federal Government of Germany. (2020a, March 22). *Besprechung der Bundeskanzlerin mit den Regierungschefinnen und Regierungschefs der Laender* [Discussion between the Chancellor and the Heads of Government of the Federal States]. https://www.bundesregierung.de/breg-de/themen/coronavirus/besprechung-der-bundeskanzlerin-mit-den-regierungschefinnen-und-regierungschefs-der-laender-1733248

Federal Government of Germany. (2020b, June 17). *Eine Milliarde Euro für die Kultur* [One billion euros for the cultural sector]. https://www.bundesregierung.de/breg-de/themen/coronavirus/neustart-kultur-1761060

Federal Ministry of Finance. (2020, June 4). *Emerging from the crisis with full strength.* https://www.bundesfinanzministerium.de/Content/EN/Standardartikel/Topics/Public-Finances/Articles/2020-06-04-fiscal-package.html

Federal Ministry of Labour, Family and Youth. (2020a, July 21). *Corona Familienhaertefonds* [Corona Family Hardship Fund]. https://www.bmafj.gv.at/en/Services/News/Coronavirus.html

Federal Ministry of Labour, Family and Youth. (2020b, August 11). *FAQ: Sommer-Sonderbetreuungszeit* [FAQ: Summer special care time]. https://www.bmafj.gv.at/Services/News/Coronavirus/FAQ—Sonderbetreuungszeit.html

Federal Ministry of Social Affairs, Health, Care and Consumer Protection. (2020a, August 11). *Coronavirus—fachinformationen und handlungsempfehlungen* [Coronavirus—specialist information and recommendations for action]. https://www.sozialministerium.at/Informationen-zum-Coronavirus/Coronavirus—Fachinformationen.html

Federal Ministry of Social Affairs, Health, Care and Consumer Protection. (2020b, August 7). *FAQ: Testungen und quarantaene* [FAQ: Tests and quarantines]. https://www.sozialministerium.at/Informationen-zum-Coronavirus/Coronavirus—Haeufig-gestellte-Fragen/FAQ—Testungen-und-Quarantaene.html

Federal Ministry of the Interior, Building and Community. (2020, May 15). *Lockerungen im grenzueberschreitenden Verkehr zwischen Deutschland, Oesterreich und der Schweiz* [Relaxation in cross-border traffic between Germany, Austria and Switzerland]. http://www.bmi.bund.de/SharedDocs/pressemitteilungen/DE/2020/05/absichtserklaerung-lockerungen-grenzueberschreitender-verkehr.html?nn=9390260

Federal Office of Public Health. (2020a, June 19). *Klare fristen fuer anspruch auf Corona-erwerbsersatz* [Clear deadlines for entitlement to Corona compensation]. https://www.bag.admin.ch/bag/en/home/das-bag/aktuell/medienmitteilungen.msg-id-79505.html

Federal Office of Public Health. (2020b, April 16). *Federal Council to gradually ease measures against the new coronavirus.* https://www.bag.admin.ch/bag/en/home/das-bag/aktuell/medienmitteilungen.msg-id-78818.html

Federal Office of Public Health. (2020c, June 24). *Federal government to assume test costs, SwissCovid app to start on 25 June.* https://www.bag.admin.ch/bag/en/home/das-bag/aktuell/medienmitteilungen.msg-id-79584.html

Federal Office of Public Health. (2020d, March 27). *Kantone koennen in ausnahmefaellen kurzzeitig zusaetzliche massnahmen beantragen* [Cantons may in exceptional cases request additional measures in the short term]. https://www.bag.admin.ch/bag/de/home/das-bag/aktuell/medienmitteilungen.msg-id-78606.html

Federal Office of Public Health. (2020e, June 19). *Move towards normalisation and simplified basic rules to protect the population.* https://www.bag.admin.ch/bag/en/home/das-bag/aktuell/medienmitteilungen.msg-id-79522.html

Federal Office of Public Health. (2020f, August 6). *New coronavirus: Measures and ordinances.* https://www.bag.admin.ch/bag/en/home/krankheiten/ausbrueche-epidemien-pandemien/aktuelle-ausbrueche-epidemien/novel-cov/massnahmen-des-bundes.html

Fried, N., & Herrmann, B. (2020, March 22). Coronavirus: Streit zwischen Soeder und Laschet [Coronavirus: Dispute between Soeder and Laschet]. *Sueddeutsche.de*.

https://www.sueddeutsche.de/politik/coronavirus-telefonkonferenz-merkel-soeder-laschet-1.4853990

Gaigg, V., & Mueller, W. (2020, August 7). Risikoabwaegung im sommer und herbst durch Corona-ampel und reisewarnungen [Risk assessment in summer and autumn through Corona traffic lights and travel warnings]. *DER STANDARD*. https://www.derstandard.at/story/2000119222309/risikoabwaegung-im-sommer-und-im-herbst-durch-corona-ampel-und

Gamper, A. (2020, June 5). Austrian federalism and the corona pandemic. *Institut fuer Foederalismus*. https://www.foederalismus.at/blog/austrian-federalism-and-the-corona-pandemic_237.php

Greer, S. L., Rozenblum, S., Wismar, M., & Jarman, H. (2020, July 16). How have federal countries organized their COVID-19 response?. *COVID-19 Health System Response Monitor*. https://analysis.covid19healthsystem.org/index.php/2020/07/16/how-have-federal-countries-organized-their-covid-19-response/

Habimana, K., Neubauer, S., Schmidt, A., Haindl, A., & Bachner, F. (2020, July 19). COVID-19 health system response monitor: Austria. *WHO Europe/European Commission/European Observatory on Health Systems and Policies*. https://www.covid19healthsystem.org/countries/austria/countrypage.aspx

Hipp, D. (2020, April 27). Die staerke liegt im unterschied [The strength lies in the difference]. *Spiegel*. https://www.spiegel.de/politik/deutschland/foederalismus-in-zeiten-von-corona-die-staerke-liegt-im-unterschied-a-b5afb929-4905-4349-992c-cdab3ca54105

International Labour Organization. (2020a, July 13). *Country policy responses (COVID-19 and the world of work): Austria*. https://www.ilo.org/global/topics/coronavirus/country-responses/lang—en/index.htm#AT

International Labour Organization. (2020b, July 13). *Country policy responses (COVID-19 and the world of work): Germany*. https://www.ilo.org/global/topics/coronavirus/country-responses/lang—en/index.htm#DE

International Monetary Fund. (2020, July 17). *Policy Responses to COVID19*. https://www.imf.org/en/Topics/imf-and-covid19/Policy-Responses-to-COVID-19

Kampf gegen Coronavirus: Freie Fahrt nur für Pendler und Waren [Fight against the coronavirus: Free passage for commuters and goods]. (2020, March 16). Tagesschau.de. https://www.tagesschau.de/inland/corona-grenzschliessung-deutschland-101.html

Karnitschnig, M. (2020, April 29). Germany's would-be chancellors struggle in Merkel's shadow. *Politico*. https://www.politico.com/news/2020/04/29/germany-angela-merkel-chancellor-225029

Katastrophenfall: Diese regeln gelten in Bayern [Emergencies: These rules apply in Bavaria]. (2020, March 16). *Bayerischer Rundfunk*. https://www.br.de/nachrichten/bayern/katastrophenfall-in-bayern-diese-regeln-gelten-ab-sofort,RtNxMZq

Lkw mit Schutzmasken steckt an Grenze zu Oberoesterreich fest [Truck with face masks stuck at the border to Upper Austria]. (2020, March 7). *Kurier*. https://kurier.at/chronik/oberoesterreich/lkw-mit-schutzmasken-steckt-an-grenze-zu-oberoesterreich-fest/400774679

Mantwill, S., Kasper Wicki, T., & Boes, S. (2020, August 9). COVID-19 Health System Response Monitor: Switzerland. *WHO Europe/European Commission/European Observatory on Health Systems and Policies*. https://www.covid19healthsystem.org/countries/switzerland/countrypage.aspx

Mask hysteria: Germany denies export ban despite blocking Swiss-bound medical supplies. (2020, March 12). *The Local Switzerland.* https://www.thelocal.com/20200312/mask-hysteria

Maskenpflicht: Regierung verschaerft massnahmen [Mandatory face masks: Government tightens measures]. (2020, March 30). orf.at. https://orf.at/stories/3159909/

Merkel zur Corona-Krise: "Beschraenkungen waren notwendig" [Merkel about Corona-crisis: "Restrictions were necessary"]. (2020, May 23). *Tagesschau.de.* https://www.tagesschau.de/inland/coronavirus-merkel-103.html

Miller, S. (2020, April 20). The secret to Germany's COVID-19 success: Angela Merkel is a scientist. *The Atlantic.* https://www.theatlantic.com/international/archive/2020/04/angela-merkel-germany-coronavirus-pandemic/610225/

Minister's quote on a T-shirt raises money for coronavirus poor. (2020, April 24). *Swissinfo.* https://www.swissinfo.ch/eng/coronavirus-solidarity_minister-s-quote-on-a-t-shirt-raises-money-for-coronavirus-poor/45715242

Nachbarn schliessen Grenzen: Coronavirus: Fast alle Bundeslaender schliessen die Schulen [Neighbours close borders: Coronavirus: Almost all German states close their schools]. (2020, March 13). *Zeit Online.* https://www.zeit.de/news/2020-03/13/bayern-schliesst-alle-schulen-wegen-coronavirus-krise

OEGK: Leichtere Arzt-Patient-Kommunikation [Austrian Labor Union: Easier doctor-patient communication]. (2020, March 13). orf.at. https://oesterreich.orf.at/stories/3038944/

Oltermann, P. (2020a, March 22). Coronavirus: Meet the scientists who are now household names—Germany. *The Guardian.* https://www.theguardian.com/world/2020/mar/22/coronavirus-meet-the-scientists-who-are-now-household-names

Oltermann, P. (2020b, April 16). Angela Merkel draws on science background in Covid-19 explainer. *The Guardian.* https://www.theguardian.com/world/2020/apr/16/angela-merkel-draws-on-science-background-in-covid-19-explainer-lockdown-exit

Operationen verschieben, statt Risiken eingehen [Postpone operations instead of taking risks]. (2020, March 24). orf.at. https://science.orf.at/stories/3200396/

Papier, H.-J. (2020, April 1). Selbst in Kriegszeiten werden die Grundrechte nicht angetastet [Even in times of war, fundamental rights remain unaffected]. *SZ.de.* https://www.sueddeutsche.de/politik/coronavirus-grundrechte-freiheit-verfassungsgericht-hans-juergen-papier-1.4864792?reduced=true

Parliament of the Republic of Austria. (2020, April 3). *Nationalrat beschliesst drei weitere COVID-19-Gesetzespakete [PK-Nr. 310]* [National Council approves three further COVID-19 legislative packages {PK-Nr. 310}]. https://www.parlament.gv.at/PAKT/PR/JAHR_2020/PK0310/index.shtml

Peitler-Hasewend, S., & Jungwirth, M. (2020, March 11). Coronavirus: Stufenweise ab Montag: Oesterreich schließt schulen [Coronavirus: Gradually from Monday: Austria closes schools]. *Kleine Zeitung.* https://www.kleinezeitung.at/politik/5783037/Coronavirus_Stufenweise-ab-Montag_Oesterreich-schliesst-Schulen

Pergande, F. (2020, April 19). Foederalismus hilft in der krise [Federalism helps in the crisis]. *Frankfurter Allgemeine.* https://www.faz.net/aktuell/politik/inland/kommentar-der-foederalismus-hilft-die-corona-krise-zu-bewaeltigen-16731184.html

Regierungskommunikation: Aufregung ueber kolportierte Angststrategie [Government communication: Irritations about rumors that spreading fear is used as strategy]. (2020, April 27). orf.at. https://orf.at/stories/3163480/

Regierungsprotokoll: Angst vor Infektion offenbar erwuenscht [Government protocol: Fear of infection apparently desired]. (2020, April 27). orf.at. https://orf.at/stories/3163435/

Reisner, C. (2020, June 17). Support measures for companies affected by COVID-19. *Invest in Austria.* https://investinaustria.at/en/blog/2020/03/covid-19-support-measures-companies.php

Representation of the European Commission in Germany. (2020, March 16). *Schutzausruestung: Lieferungen ueberall in die EU sind moeglich, exporte ausserhalb der EU genehmigungspflichtig* [Protective equipment: Deliveries anywhere in the EU are possible, exports outside the EU are subject to authorization]. https://ec.europa.eu/germany/news/20200316-schutzausruestung-lieferungen_de

Riou, J., & Althaus, C. L. (2020). Pattern of early human-to-human transmission of Wuhan 2019 novel coronavirus (2019-nCoV), December 2019 to January 2020. *Eurosurveillance, 25*(4), 2000058. https://doi.org/10.2807/1560-7917.ES.2020.25.4.2000058

Robert Koch Institute. (2020a, March 17). *Corona-Pandemie: Website zur deutschlandweiten abfrage freier beatmungsplaetze startet heute* [Corona pandemic: Website for nationwide search for free ventilation places starts today]. https://www.rki.de/DE/Content/InfAZ/N/Neuartiges_Coronavirus/PM_Intensivregister.html

Robert Koch Institute. (2020b, July 3). *Coronavirus disease 2019. (COVID-19). Daily situation report of the Robert Koch Institute.* https://www.rki.de/DE/Content/InfAZ/N/Neuartiges_Coronavirus/Situationsberichte/2020-03-07-en.pdf?__blob=publicationFile

Robert Koch Institute. (2020c, November 8). *Pandemieplaene der Bundeslaender* [Pandemic plans of the federal states]. https://www.rki.de/DE/Content/InfAZ/I/Influenza/Pandemieplanung/Pandemieplaene_Bundeslaender.html

Romy, K. (2020, March 26). Who is Switzerland's "Mr Coronavirus"? *Swissinfo.* https://www.swissinfo.ch/eng/covid-19_who-is-switzerland-s—mr-coronavirus—/45643236

Rossmann, R. (2020, July 17). CDU: Das Laschet-Soeder-Spahn-Szenario [CDU: The Laschet-Soeder-Spahn scenario]. *Sueddeutsche.de.* https://www.sueddeutsche.de/politik/cdu-laschet-spahn-soeder-szenario-1.4970196

Scherbaum Seebacher. (2020, July 30). Obligation to file for insolvency in case of over-indebtedness. *Scherbaum Seebacher Rechtsanwaelte.* https://scherbaum-seebacher.at/2020/07/30/obligation-to-file-for-insolvency-in-case-of-over-indebtedness/?lang=en

Schlette, S., Henke, K.-D., Klenk, T., Cacace, M., Ettelt, S., & Siegel, M. (2020, May 15). Germany's response to the coronavirus pandemic—Now updated. *Cambridge Core.* https://www.cambridge.org/core/blog/2020/04/08/germanys-response-to-the-coronavirus-pandemic/

Seidl, C. (2020, May 7). Umfrage zeigt Vertrauen in Stabilitaet der Regierung [Survey shows confidence in government stability]. *DER STANDARD.* https://www.derstandard.at/story/2000117347093/umfrage-zeigt-vertrauen-in-stabilitaet-der-regierung

Spahn empfiehlt Absage von Veranstaltungen mit mehr als 1000 Teilnehmern [Spahn recommends cancellation of events with more than 1000 participants.]. (2020, March 8). *Sueddeutsche Zeitung.* https://www.sueddeutsche.de/politik/coronavirus-spahn-grossveranstaltungen-1.4836673

State Government of North Rhine-Westphalia. (2020, March 10). *Corona-Infektionen: Umgang mit Grossveranstaltungen* [Corona infections: Dealing with major events]. https://www.land.nrw/de/pressemitteilung/corona-infektionen-neuer-erlass-regelt-umgang-mit-grossveranstaltungen

Sturm, R. (2020, May 18). Der deutsche Foederalismus in Corona-Zeiten [German federalism in times of Corona]. http://www.foederalismus.at/blog/der-deutsche-foederalismus-in-corona-zeiten_236.php

Tóth, B. (2020, May 12). Was passiert, wenn es eng wird? [What happens when things get tight?]. *Falter.at*. https://www.falter.at/zeitung/20200512/was-passiert-wenn-es-eng-wird

Trein, P., & Rodwin Wagner, V. G. (2020, May 15). Switzerland's response to the coronavirus pandemic—Now updated. *Cambridge Core*. https://www.cambridge.org/core/blog/2020/04/08/switzerlands-response-to-the-coronavirus-pandemic/

Tritschler, L. (2020, March 10). *Austria to close border to arrivals from Italy over coronavirus*. Politico. https://www.politico.eu/article/austria-to-close-border-to-arrivals-from-italy-over-coronavirus/

VfGH: Betretungsverbote teilweise rechtswidrig [Constitutional Court: Bans on entry partially illegal]. (2020, July 22). orf.at. https://orf.at/stories/3174524/

von Marschall, C. (2020, April 15). Foederalismus hilft in der Krise [Federalism helps in the crisis]. *Der Tagesspiegel*. https://www.tagesspiegel.de/politik/bund-laender-beschluss-zu-corona-der-foederalismus-hilft-in-der-krise/25743574.html

Welty, U. (2020, March 12). Forderung nach mehr Kompetenzen für den Bund [Call for an extension of federal competences]. *Deutschlandfunk Kultur*. https://www.deutschlandfunkkultur.de/corona-pandemie-forderung-nach-mehr-kompetenzen-fuer-den.1008.de.html?dram:article_id=472312

What's in Germany's emergency coronavirus budget? (2020, March 25). *DW*. https://www.dw.com/en/whats-in-germanys-emergency-coronavirus-budget/a-52917360

Wieler, L., Rexroth, U., & Gottschalk, R. (2020). Emerging COVID-19 success story: Germany's strong enabling environment. *Exemplars in Global Health*. https://www.exemplars.health/emerging-topics/epidemic-preparedness-and-response/covid-19/germany

Winkelmann, J., & Reichebner, C. (2020, July 19). COVID-19 health system response monitor: Germany. *WHO Europe/European Commission/European Observatory on Health Systems and Policies*. https://www.covid19healthsystem.org/countries/germany/countrypage.aspx

Wong Sak Hoi, G. (2020, May 24). How the Swiss have navigated crisis (mis)communication during Covid-19. *Swissinfo*. https://www.swissinfo.ch/eng/government-response-_how-the-swiss-have-navigated-crisis—mis-communication-during-covid-19—/45773636

18 ITALY'S RESPONSE TO COVID-19

Michelle Falkenbach and Manuela Caiani

With close to 250,000 confirmed cases and more than 35,000 deaths, as of this writing (World Health Organization [WHO], 2020b), Italy was the first country on the European continent crippled by the coronavirus. Although a state of emergency was declared at the end of January 2020, just a few days after the first case was discovered, country leaders as well as medical professionals underestimated the outbreak. Authoritarian public health measures were not promptly implemented; instead regions were initially left to deal with the virus as they saw fit, thereby creating a fragmented approach to containment. Luca Zaia, governor of the Veneto region, stated at the beginning of March 2020 that he remained convinced that a standardized approach "from north to south" should be persued, "given that the virus knows no boundaries" ("Coronavirus, le Regioni Contro il Governo" ["Coronavirus, the Regions against the Government"], 2020). There was no immediate country lockdown; this came about two weeks after the third confirmed death (Hirsch, 2020). Alternatively, the country took a gradual approach quarantining hard-hit municipalities first, then locking down certain northern regions and culminating in a complete country lockdown by March 9, 2020. Precious time was wasted with miscommunication and a general miscalculation of the severity of the disease, ultimately resulting in a strict and lengthy countrywide lockdown that led to drastic socioeconomic effects.

Although the citizens' trust in Prime Minister Conte was high, there was noticeable disagreement among the parties, resulting in the politicization of the pandemic (Capano, 2020). Populist radical right (PRR) parties such as the Brothers of Italy led by Giorgia Meloni or Matteo Salvini's Lega party regularly criticized the government for its weak leadership and the European Union (EU) for its lack of solidarity. Naturally, this decreased the level of trust in the Italian government for some citizens, often making it difficult to understand the drastic measures that were eventually set. The other pole of citizens showed much solidarity with governmental messaging, launching the initiative *"andrà tutto bene"* [everything will be fine], where banners could be seen from the windows of almost every Italian household from the north to the south. In addition, the musical "flash mobs" on balconies garnered much attention as did the commitment of many popular TV show actors and singers in the organization of "educational" entertainment for Italian citizens at home.

In sum, the country's unpreparedness and inexperience coupled with a weak administrative and political capacity cost the country much time and allowed the virus to spread, practically unhindered. Not until Conte's "stay at home" decree was implemented on March 10, 2020, did the government begin to move in a quicker and more efficient way. This democratic regime had a difficult time with communication, coordination, and implementation strategies as some political parties opted to use the pandemic for political gains, leading to the government's decision to take more forceful action (high fines for violations of the strict curfew and drone surveillance to keep people inside and safe) against noncompliant citizens.

This chapter begins by laying out the public health and health systems measures that the country adopted to protect the public and contain the virus. After which, the social policy measures implemented to counterbalance the hard-hit country are discussed, followed by potential explanations as to why Italy was so hard hit. The chapter closes with an analysis regarding what was learned from the Italian case and where further research may be necessary in gaining a more holistic understanding of the Italian government's response to the pandemic and its consequences.

Health Policy Measures: Public Health, Health Systems, and Borders

The Italian government played a big role in the implementation of public health and containment measures throughout the coronavirus outbreak. The lockdown of the entire country helped stop the spread of the virus into the far less financially and medically equipped southern Italy, but the initial nonuniform approach allowed some municipalities in the north, such as Brescia, Bergamo, and Piacenza, to opt out of more restrictive lockdown measures, resulting in staggering death rates and legal hassles.

The Italian Healthcare System

In 1978 the Italian National Health Service (*Servizio Sanitario Nazionale,* or *SSN*) was created and subsequently ranked as one of the best in the world (WHO, 2000). The SSN is organized on a regional level and controlled by all three levels of government: national, regional, and local. Article 32 of the Italian constitution ensures that all residents, in any region, have access to services either completely free of cost (even for surgeries) or at a cost that is much lower than the market price (Presidenza della Repubblica, n.d.); while Article 117 clarifies the distribution of legal power between the federal government and the regions. The regions are then responsible for organizing and distributing healthcare resources through local healthcare units (Armocida et al., 2020). In addition, the national government, through the Ministry of Health, is also responsible for defining the essential levels of care and constructing policy and planning frameworks. This role, however, is shifting more and more to the Government Regions Committee (De Belvis et al., 2012). Public health is also interwoven throughout the SNN structure. On the federal level, the Ministry of Health works with various national public health agencies to determine appropriate policies, and the regions are then in charge of implementing them through their health departments (Poscia et al., 2018). Basically, the national government's role is one of guidance and strategy in terms of health policy while also guaranteeing the financial resources to maintain the system. The regions deliver the essential levels of care and are held responsible for any deficit incurred while doing so (see Ferré et al., 2014 for more information on the Italian healthcare system). The implication here is that each region can determine its own healthcare system structure, resulting in essentially twenty different health systems within the same country.

The problem with this type of system in a healthcare crisis is that the Italian government is left with a weak strategic leadership role, which was reflected in the inconsistency of data between different administrative levels during the pandemic (see Berardi et al., 2020). Additional problematic elements in Italy's health system include years of fragmentation (Adinolfi, 2014), decades of financial cuts (De Belvis et al., 2012; Prante et al., 2020), privatization (Quercioli et al., 2013), and deprivation of human and technical resources (Armocida et al., 2020; Rocco & Stievano, 2013). These considerations help explain how a healthcare crisis of such magnitude was possible in Italy.

Coronavirus Pandemic and Public Health Responses

On January 23, 2020, Italy reported its first two coronavirus cases carried into the country by Chinese tourists. By January 25 health checkpoints were erected at all Italian airports for passengers coming from China; five days later, Health Minister Roberto Speranza suspended all flights to and from China ("Misure Profilattiche Contro Il Nuovo Coronavirus" ["Prophylactic Measures against the New Coronavirus"], 2020). On January 31, 2020, shortly after the World Health Organization declared the coronavirus a pandemic, the government and the Council of Ministers declared a six-month state of emergency and appointed Angelo Borrelli, head of the Civil Protection, as special commissioner for the coronavirus emergency (Ministerio della Salute, 2020) whose job it would be to coordinate the interventions necessary to deal with emergency.

By the beginning of February 2020, three cases of the virus had been discovered; all were individuals who had recently returned from China. Not until February 20 was the first case diagnosed, in Lombardy, without possible exposure from abroad (Torri et al., 2020). By February 2020, outbreaks were counted in eleven municipalities (Vo' Euganeo, Codogno, Castiglione d'Adda, Casalpusterlengo, Fombio, Maleo, Somaglia, Bertonico, Terranova dei Passerini, Castelgerundo, and San Fiorano) across the province of Lodi (Lombardy) and the region of Veneto. As a result of these outbreaks, the Ministry of Health ordered a mandatory supervised quarantine for anyone that had come into contact with individuals confirmed positive for the virus (Ministero della Salute, 2020). Furthermore, it became mandatory to notify the Department of Prevention, the section of the Local Health Authority in charge of public health, if an individual entered the country from a high risk area (Signorelli et al., 2020); this was followed by mandatory quarantine and surveillance.

Following the municipal outbreaks in the regions of Lombardy and Veneto, the prime minister, with the approval of the Council of Ministers, issued the decree-law 6/2020 (Presidenza della Repubblica, 2020) on February 23, 2020, introducing urgent containment measures and management of the epidemiological emergency. This decree, requiring authorities in the impacted municipalities to take all containment measures necessary to manage the spread of the disease adequately and proportionately, led to the creation of "red zones" in the eleven aforementioned municipalities. On March 2, 2020, there was a proposal to expand the "red zones" to include the heavily impacted municipalities of Brescia, Piacenza, and Bergamo, but this was not adopted. (For an overview of the epidemiological trends see Berardi et al., 2020, Figure 1.)

It was not until March 9, 2020, however, that Prime Minister Conte signed the prime ministerial decree extending the reinforced measures to contain the virus to the entire country and forbidding individuals to gather in public places (Governo Italiano, 2020b), essentially placing the entire country on lockdown. After the decree went into effect on March 10, further ordinances and decrees were passed, prohibiting the access to public parks, play areas, or gardens (March 20), prohibiting individuals from leaving the municipality in which they were located (March 22), and suspending all production (March 25); see Table 18.1. Masses and religious services were forbidden, a difficult decision considering the countries primarily Catholic population, but parishes found alternatives. Pope Francis set the creative tone by livestreaming prayers, and priests created a WhatsApp group for parishioners (Roberts & Stamouli, 2020). The country remained in this state until May 4, 2020, after which a slow reopening of the country, beginning with factories, ensued.

There was an almost two-week gap between the creation of the first red zones and the lockdown of the entire country, allowing the virus to spread throughout the entire region of Lombardy down into the region of Emilia Romagna and west into the regions of Piedmont and Liguria. The daily deaths per 100,000 inhabitants in these four regions were the highest in the country at 5.7, 3.2, 2.3, and 1.9, respectively (Ciminelli & Garcia-Mandicó, 2020). This suggests that the initial step-by-step public health containment measures adapted in Italy were unsuccessful in stopping the spread of the virus in most regions[1] and that the northern regions would have benefited from a general lockdown much sooner.

Health System Responses

From a health systems point of view, measures to combat the pandemic were also characterized by an uneven approach among the Italian regions. Three dominant

TABLE 18.1. Health protection and containment measures

Date	Measure implemented	Place	Authority
January 25	Health checkpoints for passengers coming from China	All Italian airports	Minister of Health
January 30	Air traffic from China banned	All Italian airports	Government
January 31	State of emergency and appointment of Special Commissioner for the coronavirus emergency	All of Italy	Government
February 21	Mandatory notification to health department for those coming from high-risk areas followed by mandatory 14-day quarantine and surveillance	Public Health department	Ministry of Health
February 23	Red zones—containment areas	11 municipalities in the regions of Lombardy and Veneto	Government
March 2	Proposal to expand red zones to include municipalities in Brescia, Piacenza, and Bergamo	3 municipalities in Brescia, Piacenza, and Bergamo	Not adopted
March 10	National lockdown	All of Italy	Government
March 22	Suspension of all commercial activities non-indispensable for production	All of Italy	Government
March 23	Extension of limitations on individual freedom and other business activities not previously mentioned	All of Italy	Government

Sources: Adapted from Signorelli et al. (2020) and Ministerio della Salute (2020).

organizational models crystalized throughout the country: (1) hospital-centered approach, (2) community care approach, and (3) an integrated approach (Ciccetti, 2020). These three approaches and their relation to testing, hospital use, primary and community care involvement, intensive care units, and digital solutions can been seen in Table 18.2. Each of the twenty Italian regions can be placed in one of these organizational models based on the characterization of their health system (Ciccetti, 2020). The Veneto model, with a strong community network, tested both symptomatic and asymptomatic individuals, was characterized by a very limited use of hospitals (less than 20 percent hospitalizations), vigorously traced contacts, and focused on at-home care provisions, proved to be the most successful in combating the virus. The integrated approach minimized collateral damage with its focus on mental health aspects, chronic diseases, as well as testing and collaborative mobile strategies. The regions with a heavily hospital-centered approach (over 40 percent hospital utilization), most notably Lombardy, that tested only symptomatic individuals had a more difficult time managing the virus from a health systems point of view.

TABLE 18.2. Overview of health systems approach for Italy

Dimensions	Hospital-centered approach	Integrated approach	Community-home approach
Regions	Lombardy, Liguria, Lazio, Piemonte, Basilicata, Sicilia and Umbria	Emilia-Romagna, Marche, Toscana, Valle D'Aosta, Calabria, Campania	Veneto, Friuli-Venezia-Giulia, Puglia, Molise, Abruzzo, Sardegna, PA Trento, PA Bolzano
Testing	Used for hospitalized or symptomatic patients only	Diffused in specific territories (symptomatic and asymptomatic patients)	Diffused in the whole region (Symptomatic and asymptomatic patients)
Hospital use	Intensive use > 40%	Intermediate use 20–30%	Limited use < 20%
Primary and community care involvement	General Practitioners active on an individual basis	General Practitioners active in structured mobile teams in collaboration with nurses	General Practitioners active in structured mobile teams in collaboration with nurses
Intensive Care Units	Intensively used and rapidly saturated < 15%	Used to support specific contagion outbreaks 10%	Used to support specific contagion outbreaks > 20%
Digital solutions	Use limited for contract traces	Regional platforms to support COVID-19 patients at home	Local platforms to support COVID-19 patients at home

Source: Adapted from Ciccetti (2020).

Most of the ordinances and decrees passed during the initial phase of the coronavirus pandemic concerned public health and containment measures; two, however, addressed the health system. On March 6, 2020, the Council of Ministers approved a decree law set to reinforce the National Health Service. The aim of the decree was to strengthen the territorial assistance network and the functions of the Ministry of Health by increasing human and instrumental resources. This would include recruiting specialist doctors, bringing retired doctors out of retirement, and increasing the hours of outpatient specialists (Governo Italiano, 2020a). Shortly after the national lockdown, on March 11, 2020, the Council of Ministers approved an additional amendment to further strengthen the support provided for the health system by increasing the financial resources available for civil protection and security (Governo Italiano, 2020a).

National efforts to strengthen the Italian health system as a whole through increased resources (financial, human, and instrumental) proved essential during the crisis; the fact that they were even necessary highlighted the country's years of health budget cuts. The differences in regional health systems, made apparent through varying regional characteristics, left some regions better off than others. The bottom line was this: public health and health system response in Italy was good, but not fast and good enough for every region.

Boarders

In contrast to many other European countries who closed their borders (i.e., implemented strict controls) to specific countries (i.e., those whose infection rates were high: Italy, France, United Kingdom, Spain), Italy never officially closed its Schengen borders. Initially, Prime Minister Conte stated that he was opposed to suspending the Schengen agreement, claiming that the suspension "is a draconian measure that does not meet the needs of Italian citizens in the field of containment of infection" ("Italy Refuses to Suspend Schengen Agreement Amid Coronavirus Outbreak," 2020). There are two reasons the government never had to close the borders: (1) all the neighboring countries had already done so and (2) in Italy after March 10, 2020, you needed to fill out an autodeclaration form to leave your home. In fact, leaving ones home and the municipality in which a person lived was absolutely banned without proof that a person was going to work (medical professionals), had health issues in which case a certificate would be necessary, or could prove that leaving the house was a necessity. Thus, getting across a border was the least of citizens' worries.

Social Policy Measures

Socioeconomic Response to the Crisis

The lockdown implemented by the Italian government to counteract the spread of the coronavirus, (later adjusted together with the help of the ad hoc appointed Scientific Task Force[2]), drastically impacted the Italian economy, making evident the need for stronger (than the ordinary ones) social protection measures. To mitigate the socioeconomic effects of the pandemic the Italian government issued three decree laws in March, April, and May, distributing approximately EUR 80 billion to those sectors of the population most in need. The first, Cura Italia, was published on the March 17, 2020, as a collection of measures foreseeing the distribution of EUR 10 billion. This money would not only further empower the national healthcare service but would also guarantee the economic sustainability of families, workers, and enterprises impacted by the pandemic.

The most important measures foreseen by the decree, including social safety nets, can be summarized as follows:

- Workers from both the private and the public sector would be guaranteed pay if laid off.
- Each worker from both private and public sectors with children (max twelve years old) could ask for fifteen days of paid parental leave. No age threshold was given for parents with children who have a severe disability.
- Babysitting vouchers amounting to a maximum of EUR 600 per month were foreseen as an alternative measure to the parental leave.

- The parental leave was extended for those families that had a relative with a severe disability.
- EUR 3 billion were allocated to autonomous workers and professionals. Approximately 4,854,000 people received EUR 600 for the month of March.
- An additional EUR 300 million were allocated and specifically dedicated to all people in need who did not qualify for aid in the above-listed categories.

On April 8, 2020, the "liquidity decree" was announced, granting credit and deferring tax obligations for companies as well as extending administrative and procedural terms in the health fields (Liquidity Decree, 2020).

On April 24, 2020, the Italian Parliament passed the decree No. 18 of 2020 ("Cura Italia" decree). The so-called "Cura Italia" law (Cura Italia Law, 2020) was published in the official journal on April 29, 2020, and implemented on April 30, 2020. During the process of converting the decree into law, some of the provisions introduced to address the economic impact of the pandemic (e.g., employment measures, financial measures, taxes, and public law provisions) were amended by Parliament (see "COVID-19: Cura Italia Decree Converted into Law," 2020 for more information).

Reinforcing the Socioeconomic Response

These first measures of government support were not adequate enough to counteract the effects of the crisis and its social repercussions. After a brief period of time, the so-called *Reddito di emergenza* ("Relaunch Decree") was established with the decree n. 34 of May 19, 2020, (Decreto-Legge, 2020). On July 19, 2020, the Relaunch Decree went into effect, thereby leading to the amendment of several provisions introduced to address the economic impact of the pandemic. The law granted a generous two-month income replacement between EUR 400 and 800 to those families mostly heavily exposed to the economic fallouts produced by the crisis (Brocardi, 2020). Moreover, it increased the available resources for the realization of volunteers' association and social promotion association dedicated to face the social and welfare emergencies deriving from the COVID-19 crisis. Similarly, and with the same intention, the government also adopted the prohibition to lay off workers.

Finally, to sustain the supply of adequate nutrition, the government, in close connection with Civil Protection, passed a solidarity-nutrition-measure (Borrelli, 2020), wherein EUR 400 million were collected and distributed among the most impacted municipalities. These three measures had two core objectives: maintaining the country's purchasing power and supporting the country's stability.

What is striking about these measures is that Italy, already heavily in debt and struggling to keep its expenditures under control, wanted to guarantee a large credit program for companies (32.1 percent of 2019 GDP), while the Italian fiscal stimulus tended to be normal in relation to other EU countries at 3.4 percent of 2019 GDP (Anderson et al., 2020).

Explanation

Limited Public Health Investment

Since the 1990s Italy has implemented reforms attempting to contain costs associated with the healthcare needs of an aging population. The goal was to cut down on the country's debt and public deficits to meet the Maastricht criteria and the requirements of the Stability and Growth Pact (Erber, 2011). Further cuts to the already strained system followed with the global financial crisis (2007–2008) and the euro crisis (2009), resulting in even more restrictions to healthcare spending (Pavolini & Vicarelli, 2013; Figure 18.1). The result of these thirty yearlong cuts to the public health system led to two very important developments discussed in detail by (Prante et al., 2020): (1) The number of acute care hospitals (inpatient hospitals as opposed to outpatient hospitals) were drastically reduced from 2.5 per 100,000 in the 1990s to no more than 1.6 by 2014, falling below the EU average. (2) The number of acute care beds, central in combating the coronavirus, in Italy were reduced by a staggering amount. In 1990 the country still had seven beds per 1,000 inhabitants. This number was cut to 2.6 per 1,000 by 2017. Because of these reductions, it is not surprising that the number of ICU beds, also fundamental in the treatment of the coronavirus, decreased by 19 percent over a ten-year time period (Prante et al., 2020).

Two concerns presented themselves during the pandemic as direct consequences of these consistent and substantial cuts to the public health system: (1) a lack of medical equipment (e.g. medical masks, protective suits, respirators) and (2) not enough medical staff. The lack of medical equipment must first and foremost be attributed to a poor disaster preparedness strategy, which affected every country (WHO, 2020a). Unfortunately for Italy, it had less time to prepare

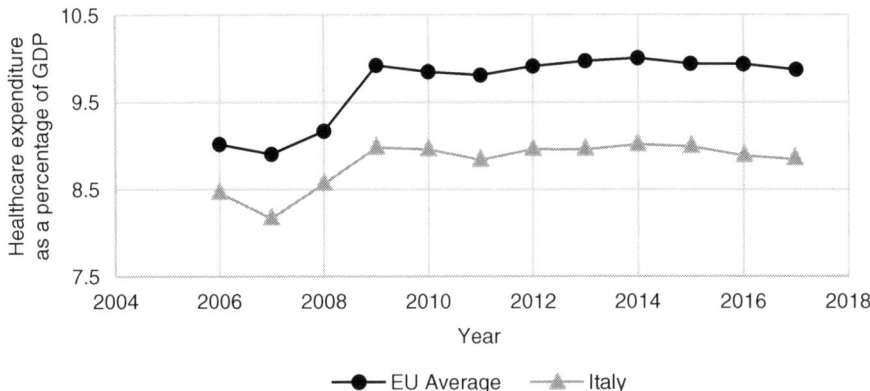

Figure 18.1. Healthcare expenditure as a percentage of gross domestic product (GDP).
Source: World Bank (2020).

than other countries, and authorities failed to update the preparedness plan in case of a pandemic (Graziani, 2020). Second, a lack of solidarity among EU countries delayed and downright prevented the transfer of medical supplies to Italy during the initial phases of the pandemic (Sardone, 2020). Finally, because of the fact that Italy had much less medical equipment to begin with, it was especially difficult to make these purchases amid a pandemic in which everyone needed the same supplies. The chief executive, Robert Hamilton, of the world's largest ventilator producer, Hamilton Medical, mentioned that "Italy may have less than a quarter of the breathing machines necessary to help patients" (Miller, 2020).

The Italian problem with doctors is and has been that, although the country has a proportionally high amount of doctors compared to the EU average (European Observatory on Health Systems, 2019), more than 50 percent of these are above the age of fifty, and 15.5 percent are over the age of sixty-five (Figure 18.2). For this reason and because many medical professionals were contracting the disease as a direct result of insufficient protective gear, medical retirees were asked to come back to work and medical students in their last year of education were employed by hospitals.

The long history of financial cuts to the healthcare sector in Italy directly impacted the country's death toll. Without adequate and sufficient medical supplies, the disproportionately older medical staff was contracting the virus, thereby causing a shortage of doctors within the system. This, in turn, reduced the number of human resources the country had to combat the spread of the virus, resulting in a death spiral.

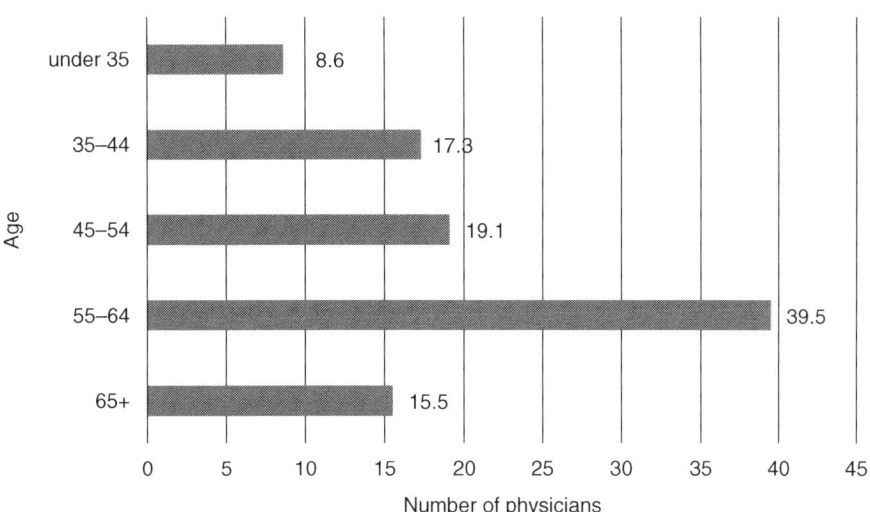

Figure 18.2. Italian physicians by age in 2017.
Source: Adapted from Eurostat (2019).

Political and Administrative Capacity Combined with Inexperience

Three intertwined problems made it difficult for the Italian government to respond efficiently and effectively to the virus and the ensuing social crisis that resulted from the lengthy lockdown period. The first focuses on Italy's fundamental unpreparedness and inexperience. Although a national pandemic plan was present (Italian Ministry of Health, 2002), it was outdated and practically never used, and thus all the procedures had to be reinvented in the midst of the pandemic. The result was, among other things, that overfilled hospitals began transferring infected patients to retirement homes, leading to mass deaths among the elderly (Priviteria, 2020). In addition, because there had been no similarly severe outbreaks in recent years, the Italian government was slow to move from a period of "denial" (denying the severity and potential repercussion of the virus) to trying to normalize the threat, to actually beginning to recognize that the threat was a real problem that required a solution. What resulted was complete disarray among institutional actors (national and regional governments). The government began creating red zones in certain municipalities, and the opposition leaders requested that these be revoked, only to then request that the entire country be closed off (Capano, 2020).

The second problem highlights the country's weak administrative capacity (also problematic in other Western countries). This could most clearly be seen in efforts to supply aid packages to citizens and businesses. At the beginning of May, President Conte apologized on behalf of the government because thousands of Italian workers had not yet received state aid (Good, 2020). Many measures meant to help families, businesses, and individuals were hampered by long administrative delays typical of the inefficient Italian bureaucracy (Bouckaert & Jann, 2020), ultimately resulting in increased inequalities (Brunori et al., 2020; Pavolini, 2020). Simply put, people were not receiving the promised financial support.

The final and biggest problem points to limited political capacity. Recent political developments in the country, including the PRR Lega entering into a governmental coalition with the equally instable 5 Star Movement in 2018 and then leaving the coalition after a failed takeover (see Poli, 2020 for more information), resulted in a "ruling government that was composed of many ministers with a substantial lack of experience and very short political careers" (Capano, 2020, p. 340). This fact produced not only conflictual policy agendas, thereby decreasing the government's consensual ability to design coherent policies, but also a government that did not want to make drastic decisions for which they would then be held accountable. The result was twofold: on the one hand, the political discourse taking place in the country during the pandemic became increasingly unproductive, and on the other, experts and technocrats were called upon to help the government out of its political stalemate as well as share the responsibility and eventual blame that accompanies decision-making (Capano, 2020).

Although the involvement of experts[3] helped convince the public that the government recognized the relevance and importance of the problem and was taking concrete steps to counteract it, the immense number of experts presented two new problems. It showcased the fundamental uncertainty of Italian officials in making decisions, and it risked weakening the democratic accountability of the entire political system. In other words, involving such a high number of experts in the decision-making process impacted the transparency of the process itself. This resulted in questions such as, Who is in charge of making decisions? Are these the best decisions only because experts suggested them? Although it is surely fundamental to establish a technical committee during a pandemic, why were so many experts actually involved, and why were they involved in issues not strictly related to healthcare?

The Pandemic and the Italian Party Politics

What is perhaps most interesting in terms of the pandemic in Italy is not so much how party politics impacted the management of the pandemic, but rather how the pandemic impacted party politics. The pandemic resulted in an increased electoral appeal for certain parties, specifically PRR parties; however, the nature of this effect is still ambiguous and in progress. At the beginning of the pandemic, some commentators argued that the coronavirus would represent the end of populism in Italy ("Italy's Young Doctors Protest Lack of Training Pushing Them to Go Abroad," 2020; Kendall-Taylor & Nietsche, 2020; Rossi & Parodi, 2020); as if the biological virus could counteract the "populist virus." However, the reality turned out to be different.

Both the Populist Radical Right leader, Salvini, and the representative of the radical right party Fratelli d'Italia, Meloni, initially negated the evidence of the pandemic. Salvini's Facebook posts encouraged followers to continue with their normal lives, while Meloni told her Facebook followers not to believe anything that was being said on TV (Nardelli & D'Urso, 2020a). After the lockdown, they both adapted their rhetoric to the normalization and consequent awareness of the emergency, wherein Salvini argued that the lockdowns were not going far enough and that everything needed to be shut down. Both PRR leaders started attacking the EU's response to the crisis, and they released a video stating that the virus was bioengineered in China (Nardelli & D'Urso, 2020b). At that point, the slowness in the implementation of the above-mentioned measures to counteract the socioeconomic crisis became the substance of the PRRs political discourse and the parties capitalized on the crisis to reinforce their anti-EU stances. In parallel to the evolution of their rhetoric, the consensus for their leadership also changed throughout the course of the pandemic. The PRR flank (represented by Salvini's Lega and Meloni's Brothers of Italy) blamed the government for not being able to make substantive decisions and implementing them. During times of crisis, Italians, like any other citizens, appeared to look for solemn and stable leaders. Despite still being the strongest party in terms of consensus, Salvini's Lega lost 4 percentage points of support since the end of February and ten points since last summer's peak

(Roberts, 2020), putting it at 27 percent as of July 2020. At first glance, this might confirm the notion that the coronavirus is killing the PRR; however, the decrease in consensus for the Lega made room for the even more right-wing Brothers of Italy under Giorgia Meloni. This party saw a rise in support from approximately 7 to 14 percentage points, the highest level ever reached by the party (Roberts, 2020). To be sure, the (slight) increase of Meloni's success looks like a consequence of the loss of appeal by Salvini.

In addition, as Salvini's favorability decreased, Luca Zaia, the governor of Veneto and more moderate figure within the Lega party, experienced a political boost. Zaia's handling of the crisis in Veneto, one of the regions most affected by the pandemic, garnered him much support, leading to his third term as governor (Pianigiani, 2020) and making him the second most loved politician in Italy (51 percent of the consensus) behind Prime Minister Conte (Roberts, 2020). Although Salvini's light might be fading, there is no shortage of PRR politicians waiting for their chance at center stage.

Furthermore, right-wing forces capitalized on the crisis scapegoating on their traditional targets (i.e., immigrants and minorities). The coronavirus pandemic coupled with the increased support for the PRR shed a new light on the problems associated with the managing of refugees and migrants in the country. To begin with, refugees, asylum seekers, and migrants were among the most severely impacted by the crisis ("Life in Italy Under COVID-19," 2020). Second, the issue of how to provide the basic voluntary and welfare services while also guaranteeing the safety of their personnel and volunteers had been amplified. As the coronavirus makes its reappearance in Italy during the writing of this conclusion (September 2020), migrants are being made into a recurring target for PRR politicians who (continue to) claim, despite official data proving the contrary, that they are transporting the virus into Italy.

Finally, it should be noted that, while the visibility and success of the right-wing forces increased during the first wave of the pandemic, the two political parties in government (i.e., the 5SM and the Democratic Party) did not seem to be able to increase their support. In fact, only support for Prime Minister Conte increased.

However, on a more positive note, the pandemic also gave way to a strong and collective civil society led by activists that created new forms of expressing their grievances (della Porta, 2020). In Italy, for example, "100,000 doctors signed a petition calling for the territorially decentralized organization of healthcare provision," and in Milan "the health care personnel of private hospitals staged 'stay-ins' (keeping social distance) to protest the deterioration of their working conditions" (della Porta, 2020). In this sense, civil society actors were not only suggesting alternative approaches to the management of the crisis, as well as many other economic categories, but also indicating that the path to achieving favorable results would not be through the centralization of political decision-making and even less through technocratic actions, but rather by increasing the participation of the citizens (della Porta, 2020).

Conclusion

The corona pandemic engulfed Italy while it was still trying to recover from decades of strict cost-containment measures, particularly impacting hospital capacity, the healthcare workforce, public expenditure for pharmaceuticals, and out-of-pocket payments for patients. This fact combined with an outdated disaster preparedness plan and an inexperienced government resulted in 35,724 deaths (as of September 2020), second only to the United Kingdom in Europe.

The Italian government's coronavirus approach went from a period of denial to a federal patchwork strategy of containment, to a very rigid and strict lockdown. During the initial containment strategies, certain federal, regional, and municipal officials took the virus more serious than others, leading to confusion and disagreement among some of the Italian public. Statements such as the ones made by Prime Minister Conte and other officials blaming Italy's high number of infections on the aggressive testing of people without symptoms in the north, which they argued only created hysteria and tarnished the country's image abroad (Horowitz, 2020), not only slowed the drive for increased testing in many northern regions but also signaled to the public that the virus was not that dangerous. Similarly, Italy's Foreign Minister Luigi di Maio and Health Minister Roberto Speranza told international journalists at the end of February that Italy had gone from an "epidemic risk to an 'info-demic' of confirmed disinformation, which at this moment is hitting our flow of tourists, our business and our whole economic system" (D'Emilio & Winfield, 2020) certainly did not help the credibility of proposed lockdowns a few weeks later.

The Italian case is one that has and will undoubtedly continue to be studied not only because it was the first country drastically impacted by the virus but also because the virus claimed a disproportionately high number of lives, for which the reasons are still highly debated. Furthermore, the impact of the pandemic on Italy was strong not only from a health standpoint but also from an economic one. Italy entered the pandemic in a less stable economic state than its neighboring countries with a government debt of 132 percent of GDP in 2018 (Gramlich, 2020), never really having recovered from the 2008 economic crisis. The European Commission's projections for the Italian postpandemic economy are a decrease of 11.2 percent of GDP for 2020 and an increase of 6.1 percent of GDP for 2021 (European Commission, 2020). What makes the economic situation in Italy particularly bad is that overdue reforms were held up because of the complex and old-fashioned Italian bureaucracy, the slow judicial system, and outdated infrastructure. Within such a context the social assistance and aid for citizens and business heavily impacted by the crisis was undeniably slow and filled with administrative hurdles.

Subsequent research could investigate the most efficient and effective ways the country could use the EUR 209 billion, a combination of grants and loans from the EU, to stabilize the economy, reinvest in health care and public health, and perhaps, most importantly, take initial steps in simplifying the overly complicated Italian bureaucracy and reforming the slow judicial system. In addition, eyes should be directed to the PRR leaders as they continue to polarize society and capitalize on the pandemic. By accusing migrants and minorities as virus spreaders (della Porta, 2020), blaming the EU for their lack of solidarity, and the denouncing EU loans as weakening Italian sovereignty, these parties are refueling heated *Italexit* debates (see Di Quirico, 2020 for more information). The needs of the Italian citizens and the Italian economy must be addressed, and one might be left wondering whether the substantial weaknesses displayed by the political parties in government vis-à-vis the increased visibility of the radical Right could have negative effects on the Italian political system after the pandemic.

Acknowledgment

Thank you to Giliberto Capano for his valuable insights.

Notes

1. The region of Veneto is an exception as mass testing, at-home care provision, and contact tracing significantly helped curb the death rate in this region, which was the lowest out of all the Northern regions with 1.1 daily deaths per 100,000 inhabitants (Ciminelli & Garcia-Mandicó, 2020).

2. The term *scientific task force* refers to a group of scientific experts appointed by the Italian government to limit and counteract the effects of the COVID-19 crisis on the population. Lead by Walter Ricciardi, Paolo De Rosa, and Fidelia Cascini, the core objective was to provide regions with guidelines on hospital reorganization, community care networks, and related facilities.

3. Fifteen different taskforces were established at the national level, some of them with curious and interesting roles (see Capano [2020] for more details).

References

Adinolfi, P. (2014). Barriers to reforming healthcare: The Italian case. *Health Care Analysis*, 22(1), 36–58. https://doi.org/10.1007/s10728-012-0209-0

ANALYSIS: How Italy's far right was stalled by the coronavirus crisis. (2020). AFP/The Local. https://www.thelocal.it/20200609/analysis-how-italys-far-right-was-stalled-by-the-coronavirus-crisis

Anderson, J., Bergamini, E., Brekelmans, S., Cameron, A., Dravas, Z., Jíménez, M., & Midões, C. (2020). *The fiscal response to the economic fallout from the coronavirus.* Bruegel. https://www.bruegel.org/publications/datasets/covid-national-dataset/#italy

Armocida, B., Formenti, B., Ussai, S., Palestra, F., & Missoni, E. (2020). The Italian health system and the COVID-19 challenge. *The Lancet. Public Health*, 5(5), e253–e253. https://doi.org/10.1016/S2468-2667(20)30074-8

Berardi, C., Antonini, M., Genie, M. G., Cotugno, G., Lanteri, A., Melia, A., & Paolucci, F. (2020). The COVID-19 pandemic in Italy: Policy and technology impact on health and non-health outcomes. *Health Policy and Technology*. https://doi.org/10.1016/j.hlpt.2020.08.019

Borrelli, A. (2020). *Ordinanza sulla protezione civile n. 38 del 28 marzo 2020* [Civil Protection Ordinance number 38 from the 28th of March 2020]. Protezione Civile. http://www.protezionecivile.gov.it/amministrazione-trasparente/provvedimenti/dettaglio/-/asset_publisher/default/content/ocdpc-n-657-del-28-marzo-2020-disposizioni-urgenti-di-protezione-civile-nel-territorio-dei-comuni-di-lipari-e-santa-marina-salina-e-ma

Bouckaert, G., & Jann, W. (2020). *European perspectives for public administration: The way forward*. Leuven University Press.

Brocardi. (2020). *Articolo 82 Decreto "Rilancio"* [Article 82 "Relaunch" Decree]. Brocardi.It. https://www.brocardi.it/decreto-rilancio/titolo-iii/capo-ii/art82.html

Brunori, P., Maitino, M. L., Ravagli, L., & Sciclone, N. (2020). *Distant and unequal. Lockdown and inequalities in Italy*. http://www.unicaldine.it/research/BMRS_2020.pdf

Capano, G. (2020). Policy design and state capacity in the COVID-19 emergency in Italy: If you are not prepared for the (un)expected, you can be only what you already are. *Policy and Society, 39*(3), 326–344. https://doi.org/10.1080/14494035.2020.1783790

Ciccetti, A. (2020). *Facing COVID 19 Emergency: Comparing organizational models for response in Italian Regions*. https://ehma.org/covid-19-webinar-series/webinar-managing-covid-19-an-italian-perspective/

Ciminelli, G., & Garcia-Mandicó, S. (2020, August). *COVID-19 in Italy: An analysis of death registry data*. https://www.researchgate.net/publication/340649273

Coronavirus, le Regioni contro il governo [Coronavirus, the regions against the government]. (2020). *Italia Oggi*. https://www.italiaoggi.it/news/coronavirus-le-regioni-contro-il-governo-202003090934303372

Cura Italia Law. (2020, April). G.U. n. 110 del 29 aprile 2020, S.O. n. 16. Retrieved July 20, 2020, from https://www.gazzettaufficiale.it/showNewsDetail?id=2632&provenienza=home

D'Emilio, F., & Winfield, N. (2020). *Italy blasts virus panic as it eyes new testing criteria*. https://apnews.com/article/6c7e40fbec09858a3b4dbd65fe0f14f5

De Belvis, A. G., Ferrè, F., Specchia, M. L., Valerio, L., Fattore, G., & Ricciardi, W. (2012). The financial crisis in Italy: Implications for the healthcare sector. *Health Policy, 106*(1), 10–16. https://doi.org/10.1016/j.healthpol.2012.04.003

Decreto-Legge. (2020 May 19). Misure urgenti in materia di salute, sostegno al lavoro e all'economia, nonché di politiche sociali connesse all'emergenza epidemiologica da COVID-19 [Urgent health measures, support for work and the economy, as well as social policies related to the epidemiological emergency from COVID-19]. https://www.lavoro.gov.it/documenti-e-norme/normative/Documents/2020/D-L-19-maggio-2020.pdf

della Porta, D. (2020). *How progressive social movements can save democracy in pandemic times*. https://www.interfacejournal.net/wp-content/uploads/2020/05/Della-Porta.pdf

Di Quirico, R. (2020). Challenging the Euro: The politics of anti-Euro parties in Italy during the first Conte government. *Contemporary Italian Politics*, 1–17. https://doi.org/10.1080/23248823.2020.1793073

Erber, G. (2011). Italy's fiscal crisis. *Intereconomics: Review of European Economic Policy, 46*, 332–339. https://doi.org/10.1007/s10272-011-0397-0

European Commission. (2020). *Economic forecast for Italy*. Retrieved July 30, 2020, from https://ec.europa.eu/info/business-economy-euro/economic-performance-and-forecasts/economic-performance-country/italy/economic-forecast-italy_en

European Observatory on Health Systems. (2019). *State of health in the EU Italy: Country health profile 2019.* OECD Publishing.

Eurostat. (2019). *Healthcare personnel statistics—physicians.* Retrieved July 30, 2020, from https://ec.europa.eu/info/business-economy-euro/economic-performance-and-forecasts/economic-performance-country/italy/economic-forecast-italy_en

Ferré, F., de Belvis, A. G., Valerio, L., Longhi, S., Lazzari, A., Fattore, G., Ricciardi, W., & Maresso, A. (2014). Italy: Health system review. In *Health Systems in Transition 16*(4).

Good, R. (2020). Italian workers still waiting for their wages two months into lockdown. *Euronews.* https://www.euronews.com/2020/05/01/italian-workers-still-waiting-for-their-wages-two-months-into-lockdown

Governo Italiano. (2020a). *Comunicato stampa del Consiglio dei Ministri n. 35* [Press release of the Council of Ministers n. 35]. Retrieved July 8, 2020, from http://www.governo.it/node/14263

Governo Italiano. (2020b). *Coronavirus, le misure adottate dal Governo* [Coronavirus, the measures taken by the government]. Retrieved July 8, 2020, from http://www.governo.it/it/coronavirus-misure-del-governo

Gramlich, J. (2020). *Coronavirus downturn likely to add to high government debt in some countries.* Pew Research Center. https://www.pewresearch.org/fact-tank/2020/04/29/coronavirus-downturn-likely-to-add-to-high-government-debt-in-some-countries/

Graziani, M. R. (2020). L'Oms critica la gestione italiana dell'emergenza Covid, ma censura il documento: l'inchiesta di Report [WHO criticizes the Italian management of the Covid emergency, but censors the document: The report investigation]. https://www.dire.it/02-11-2020/523710-inchiesta-report-oms-italia-coronavirus/

Hirsch, C. (2020, March 31). *Europe's coronavirus lockdown measures compared.* Politico. https://www.politico.eu/article/europes-coronavirus-lockdown-measures-compared/

Horowitz, J. (2020, February 7). Italy, mired in politics over virus, asks how much testing is too much. *The New York Times.* https://www.nytimes.com/2020/02/27/world/europe/italy-coronavirus.html

Italian Ministry of Health. (2002). *National plan for preparedness and response to an influenza pandemic.* Salute.Gov.It. http://www.salute.gov.it/imgs/C_17_pubblicazioni_511_allegato.pdf

Italy refuses to suspend Schengen agreement amid coronavirus outbreak. (2020, February 24). Schengen Visa Info News. https://www.schengenvisainfo.com/news/italy-refuses-to-suspend-schengen-agreement-amid-coronavirus-outbreak/

Italy's young doctors protest lack of training pushing them to go abroad. (2020, May 29). AFP/The Local. https://www.thelocal.it/20200529/italys-young-doctors-protest-lack-of-training-pushing-them-to-go-abroad

Kendall-Taylor, A., & Nietsche, C. (2020). *The coronavirus is exposing populists' hollow politics.* Foreign Policy. https://www.cnas.org/publications/commentary/the-coronavirus-is-exposing-populists-hollow-politics

Life in Italy under COVID-19: Caritas keeps its doors open to refugees, asylum seekers and migrants in need. (2020). Caritas.Eu. https://www.caritas.eu/life-in-italy-under-covid-19/

Linklaters. (2020). COVID-19: Cura Italia Decree converted into law. https://lpscdn.linklaters.com/-/media/files/document-store/pdf/milan/2020/may/client_alert_cura_italia_law_may_2020.ashx?rev=c72b5a40-f248-44dc-b931-9b40597504c0&extension=pdf

Liquidity Decree. (2020, April). Decree-Law No. 23 of 8 April 2020. https://www.assarmatori.eu/wp-content/uploads/2020/04/DecreeLaw_23_08042020_ENG.pdf

Miller, J. (2020). *Germany, Italy rush to buy life-saving ventilators as manufacturers warn of shortages.* Reuters. https://www.reuters.com/article/us-health-coronavirus-draegerwerk-ventil/germany-italy-rush-to-buy-life-saving-ventilators-as-manufacturers-warn-of-shortages-idUSKBN210362

Ministerio della Salute. (2020). *Covid-19 - Situazione in Italia.* Salute.Gov.It. http://www.salute.gov.it/portale/nuovocoronavirus/dettaglioContenutiNuovoCoronavirus.jsp?area=nuovoCoronavirus&id=5351&lingua=italiano&menu=vuoto

Misure profilattiche contro il nuovo Coronavirus [Prophylactic measures against the new Coronavirus] (2019 - nCoV). (2020). (20A00618) (GU Serie Generale n.21 del 27-01-2020). https://www.gazzettaufficiale.it/eli/id/2020/01/27/20A00618/sg

Nardelli, A., & D'Urso, J. (2020a). *Italy's far-right and nationalist leaders are pushing debunked conspiracy theories about the coronavirus to millions of followers.* BuzzFeed News. https://www.buzzfeed.com/albertonardelli/coronavirus-matteo-salvini-giorgia-meloni-conspiracy

Nardelli, A., & D'Urso, J. (2020b, March 26). *Italy's far-right and nationalist leaders are pushing debunked conspiracy theories about the coronavirus to millions of followers.* BuzzFeed News. https://www.buzzfeed.com/albertonardelli/coronavirus-matteo-salvini-giorgia-meloni-conspiracy

Pavolini, E. (2020). *Criticità latenti e nuove sfide: la sanità italiana alla prova del Covid.* https://osservatoriocoesionesociale.eu/wp-content/uploads/2020/07/Quaderno-collettivo-COVID.pdf

Pavolini, E., & Vicarelli, G. (2013). Italy: A strange NHS with its paradoxes. In *Health Care Systems in Europe under Austerity* (pp. 81–101). Palgrave Macmillan.

Pianigiani, G. (2020, September 21). In Italy elections, Salvini coalition fails to take Tuscan prize. *The New York Times.* https://www.nytimes.com/2020/09/21/world/europe/italy-salvini-league-regional-elections.html

Poli, E. (2020). Italy: Has Salvini saved the country from himself? Not yet. In Kaeding, M., Pollak, J., & Schmidt, P. (Ed.), *Euroscepticism and the future of Europe.* Palgrave Macmillan. https://doi.org/https://doi.org/10.1007/978-3-030-41272-2_18

Poscia, A., Silenzi, A., & Ricciardi, W. (2018). Italy. In *Organization and financing of public health services in Europe: Country reports.* European Observatory on Health Systems and Policies. https://www.ncbi.nlm.nih.gov/books/NBK507328/

Prante, F. J., Bramucci, A., & Truger, A. (2020). Decades of tight fiscal policy have left the health care system in Italy ill-prepared to fight the COVID-19 outbreak. *Intereconomics, 55*(3), 147–152. https://doi.org/10.1007/s10272-020-0886-0

Presidenza della Repubblica. (n.d.). *La Costituzione della Repubblica italiana.* Quirinale.It. https://www.quirinale.it/page/costituzione

Presidenza della Repubblica. (2020). Misure per il contenimento e gestione dell'emergenza epidemiologica [Measures for the containment and management of the epidemiological emergency]. Retrieved July 20, 2020, from http://www.governo.it/it/iorestoacasa-misure-governo

Priviteria, G. (2020). *The "silent massacre" in Italy's nursing homes.* Politico. https://www.politico.eu/article/the-silent-coronavirus-covid19-massacre-in-italy-milan-lombardy-nursing-care-homes-elderly/

Quercioli, C., Messina, G., Basu, S., McKee, M., Nante, N., & Stuckler, D. (2013). The effect of healthcare delivery privatisation on avoidable mortality: Longitudinal cross-regional results from Italy, 1993–2003. *Journal of Epidemiology and Community Health, 67*(2), 132 LP—138. https://doi.org/10.1136/jech-2011-200640

Ren, X. (2020). Pandemic and lockdown: a territorial approach to COVID-19 in China, Italy and the United States. *Eurasian Geography and Economics*, 1–12. https://doi.org/10.1080/15387216.2020.1762103

Roberts, H. (2020, June 2). *Matteo Salvini's coronavirus slump.* Politico. https://www.politico.eu/article/italy-matteo-salvinis-league-coronavirus-slump/

Roberts, H., & Stamouli, N. (2020, March 17). *In Italy and beyond, churches grapple with coronavirus.* Politico. https://www.politico.eu/article/coronavirus-church-online-live-stream-congregation/

Rocco, G., & Stievano, A. (2013). The presence of foreign nurses in Italy: Towards the ethical recruitment of health workers. *SALUTE E SOCIETÀ*, *XII*(3En), 19–33. http://www.francoangeli.it/Riviste/Scheda_rivista.aspx?idArticolo=50216

Rossi, S., & Parodi, E. (2020, April 26). *Italy's far-right League hurt by response to coronavirus in heartland.* Reuters. https://www.reuters.com/article/us-health-coronavirus-italy-lombardy-idUSKCN2280GX

Sardone, S. (2020). *Parliamentary questions.* European Parliament. Retrieved September 20, 2020, from https://www.europarl.europa.eu/meps/en/197578/SILVIA_SARDONE/other-activities/written-questions-other

Signorelli, C., Scognamiglio, T., & Odone, A. (2020). COVID-19 in Italy: Impact of containment measures and prevalence estimates of infection in the general population. *Acta Biomedica*, *91*(1), 175–179. https://doi.org/10.23750/abm.v91i3-S.9511

Torri, E., Sbrogiò, L. G., Di Rosa, E., Cinquetti, S., Francia, F., & Ferro, A. (2020). Italian public health response to the COVID-19 pandemic: Case report from the field, insights and challenges for the department of prevention. *International Journal of Environmental Research and Public Health*, *17*(10), 1–12. https://doi.org/10.3390/ijerph17103666

World Bank. (2020). *Current health expenditure (% of GDP)—European Union, Italy.* Data.Worldbank.Org.

World Health Organization. (2000). *The World Health report 2000: Health systems: Improving performance.* Retrieved July 20, 2020, from https://www.who.int/whr/2000/en/

World Health Organization. (2020a). *Shortage of personal protective equipment endangering health workers worldwide.* https://www.who.int/news-room/detail/03-03-2020-shortage-of-personal-protective-equipment-endangering-health-workers-worldwide

World Health Organization. (2020b). *WHO Dashboard Latest Health Statistics.* Covid19.Who.Int. https://covid19.who.int/region/euro/country/IT

19 SPAIN'S RESPONSE TO COVID-19

Kenneth A. Dubin

A World-Class Health System?

> Spain has been hit hard by COVID-19, with more than 300,000 cases, 28,498 confirmed deaths, and around 44,000 excess deaths, as of Aug 4, 2020. More than 50,000 health workers have been infected, and nearly 20,000 deaths were in nursing homes. With a population of 47 million, these data place Spain among the worst affected countries. Spain is also reported to have one of the best performing health systems in the world and ranks 15th in the Global Health Security index. So how is it possible that Spain now finds itself in this position? (García-Basteiro et al., 2020)

So begins an open letter in *The Lancet* by twenty public health experts calling for an independent evaluation of Spain's COVID-19 response. They demand that the evaluation consider "governance and decision-making, scientific and technical advice, and operational capacity," along with rising economic inequality. This chapter provides an early look at these very questions.

The Spanish government was slower to respond to rising infection rates than most of its closest peers, leading to some of the world's highest infection rates and mortality rates, particularly in its two largest metropolitan areas, Madrid and Barcelona. The central government then proceeded to institute one of the strictest lockdowns in Europe, with mobility data suggesting some of the highest rates of compliance (Otero-Iglesias et al., 2020) anywhere. Given these high compliance rates and the long lockdown (five fifteen-day extensions of the initial two-week state of alarm), one might have expected authorities to be prepared to manage the subsequent relaxation of controls on movement. Unfortunately, Spain experienced one of the most rapid increases in infection rates anywhere, with authorities woefully unprepared to manage isolated outbreaks as infection rates threaten to spiral out of control.[1]

Public Health and Health System Response in Spain

Spain is a quasi-federalist system (Dubin, 2019). All seventeen regional governments (autonomous communities, or ACs) have been responsible for the delivery of health care since 2002 and, beyond basic standards set by the central government, enjoy substantial discretionary authority over the structuring of health delivery. Health policy is in principle coordinated through a variety of intergovernmental working groups; however, these mechanisms have long been characterized by the reluctance of some regions, such as Catalonia and the Basque Country, to participate.

Pandemic response in Spain has been managed through a National System of Early Alert and Rapid Response (acronym in Spanish, SIAPR) led by a subdirectorate of the Ministry of Health, the Center for the Coordination of Warnings and Health Emergencies (acronym in Spanish, CCAES). The CCAES is the lead node of a network composed of representatives from the AC health services, with support from various agencies of the Ministry of Health, the Ministry of Defense, the Agency for Food Security and Nutrition (acronym in Spanish, AESAN), the Agency for Medicines and Health Products (acronym in Spanish, AEMPS) and the national health research center, the Instituto de Salud Carlos III (Ministerio de Sanidad, 2013).

The 2019 Global Health Security Index evaluated Spain's system highly in terms of its ability to detect epidemics (ranked eleventh out of 195 countries) but called into question its ability to respond. There is an Interterritorial Council within the SIAPR to facilitate technical coordination with the regions but no formal mechanism for policy coordination and no role whatsoever for the private sector. More critically, the SIAPR lacks a dedicated budget, a fact that led the Global Health Security Index to rank Spain in position 131 with respect to financing. Indeed, the entire budget for public health only represented approximately 1 percent of the country's total health budget (Otero-Iglesias et al., 2020). There is also no provision for external evaluation (whether public or private) of the SIAPR's planning, as evaluation was delegated to a working group formed by technical personnel participating in the SIAPR, the Ponencia de Alertas y Planes de Preparación y Respuesta (Arteaga, 2020).

Chronology of Crisis

Community transmission in Spain began in mid-February 2020. On March, 5, 2020, the Ministry of Health issued its first protection protocol for healthcare workers, leaving each AC health service to decide if cases met the definition of "high-risk exposure," warranting a fourteen-day withdrawal from active service. However, testing was only recommended for those exhibiting symptoms and quarantine was not addressed (Ministerio de Sanidad, 2020). The circular was updated on March 14, 2020, classifying staff interactions according to intensity of contact and whether PPE (personal protective equipment) was in use. The government now recommended home quarantine in cases of high-risk exposure with a polymerase chain reaction (PCR) diagnostic test after seven days.

On March 7, 2020, lockdown was ordered in several neighborhoods of the town of Haro in the region of La Rioja after the failure by a group of thirty-nine residents infected with the virus at a funeral to follow self-confinement. The Civil

Guard was ordered to ensure the peace and the regional president threatened fines of up to EUR 60,000 for those failing to observe quarantine.

The following day 120,000 people in Madrid attended the International Women's Day march and some 9,000 people attended an indoor rally by the far-right VOX party to protest against demands for greater gender equality. Two days later the VOX general secretary tested positive, leading to the suspension of the national parliament for two weeks and self-quarantine for all fifty-two VOX deputies. On March 9, 2020, the Madrid regional government closed all schools, ushering in an exodus of madrileños from their urban apartments to second homes around the country in anticipation of a national lockdown announcement, carrying the virus out across the nation (Minder, 2020).

On March 10, 2020, all direct flights to Italy were suspended until March 25, and on March 12 all traffic was suspended with Morocco. By March 12, all ACs had ordered the closure of schools and the Ministry of the Interior had imposed a nationwide prison lockdown. On that same day, the Catalan regional government ordered confinement for four towns covering some 70,000 people after an outbreak affecting mostly hospital personnel (EFE, 2020).

The following day the prime minister declared a constitutional state of alarm for fifteen days beginning on March 14.[2] A full thirty days had passed since the first confirmed COVID-19 death in Spain (and forty-three days since the first confirmed case) and the banning of nonessential movement, the closing of nonessential shops, and the closing of schools (Pappas, 2020). The central government took control of the regional health systems and all regional and local policing bodies, although operational management structures remained unchanged. It also reserved for itself the right to direct the actions of private health providers.[3] On March 16, 2020, Spain closed its land borders, interrupting the Schengen Agreement, with the exception of returning citizens and residents, diplomatic personnel, and workers involved in supply chains of essential goods.[4] A more restrictive state of alarm was imposed for fifteen days on March 28, 2020, with all nonessential workers now required to remain in their homes and firms prohibited from laying off workers for quarantine-related causes.

Confinement would be extended five more times, lasting until midnight on June 20, 2020, with some nonessential workers able to return to work on April 12. In the April 24 meeting of the Inter-territorial Health Council (Consejo Interterritorial de Salud), the health system directors of each AC presented their proposals for relaxing confinement to the Minister of Health. Some regions favored unified criteria managed by the central government (Valencia, Andalucía, Castile-La Mancha, and Castile-León), whereas others preferred an asymmetric and self-managed approach ("Asimétrica y Dirigida por el Gobierno" ["Asymmetric and Led by the Government"], 2020). The Ministry's request for more detailed information provoked widespread criticism, particularly from the Catalans and Basques. The renewal of the state of alarm on April 26 permitted children under fourteen to leave their homes for one hour a day in the company of an adult member of their household.[5]

Each renewal of the state of alarm required ratification by a simple majority in the Congress. By the time the fifth state of alarm was declared on May 6, 2020, support for the measure was beginning to slip. Pablo Casado, leader of the largest opposition party, the conservative Popular party (PP), denounced the government for imposing a "constitutional dictatorship" and abstained rather than voting in favor as it had done four times previously. The government was thus forced to make further concessions to gain the support of the conservative Basque Nationalist party (PNV) and the liberal Citizens party (Ciudadanos). The Basques achieved "joint" decision-making between the central government and the ACs in the relaxation of confinement and greater regional discretion in "interpreting" ministerial orders. They also obtained government approval to celebrate regional elections in July 2020 (Castro & Riveiro, 2020).

The final state of alarm was declared on May 20, 2020. The government had initially sought to extend this final alarm a full month, but to gain the support of the Citizens party, it was, like the previous ones, limited to fifteen days. For the first time, the PP voted against the measure, demanding the end of quarantine for international tourists.

The government's asymmetrical plan for relaxing confinement established four phases, allowing regions to proceed at different rates. In principle, each Wednesday the ACs would present their phase proposals for the following week, and on Friday the government would announce which regions could move from phase to phase and with which measures. Some ACs defined their entire territory as a single zone, whereas others distinguished between more or less populated areas; however, the primary region for relaxation criteria was the province (of which there are fifty), as these most closely correspond to the country's main metropolitan areas (Otero-Iglesias, 2020). From phase 3, the ACs took over management of the crisis.

The Ministry of Health would make its decision based on regional transmission rates and regional health system capacities—early alerts and epidemiological tracking, rapid identification and control of contagion, capacity for isolating confirmed and potential cases, primary health capacity, hospital capacity (1.5 to 2 2 UCI beds/10,000 inhabitants; 37–40 beds/10,000 inhabitants), and prompt and high-quality reporting of the information requested from ACs on March 15 (Boletín Oficial del Estado. 15 de marzo, Orden SND/234/2020; Boletín Oficial del Estado, 3 de mayo 2020; Boletín Oficial del Estado; SND/387/2020, de 3 de mayo [Orders of the National Dependent Care System]).

Exiting Lockdown

On June 9, 2020, the government published its decree law outlining measures to keep the pandemic under control after a phased exit from the state of alarm.[6] Masks were required for all persons age six and older on all public transportation and any public or private space, indoor or outdoor where a distance of 1.5 meters could not be maintained, with fines of up to EUR 100. Specific limits on gatherings were left to the ACs. Firms were required to promote remote work where possible, maintain distances of 1.5 meters where possible, and provide special protections when impossible. There were no additional special measures for schools.

Residences and day centers for the elderly were required to coordinate measures with the AC health services to identify cases quickly among residents and workers and to ensure safe visits and outings. The ACs were asked to "guarantee" PCR or equivalent tests for any suspected cases "as soon as possible," particularly in primary care, and to report all cases and outbreaks as established by protocols to be approved in the Inter-territorial Council of the National Health System. The protocol objectives were defined as homogeneity in control, information, data flows, and timely analysis.

The government also created a contact-tracing smartphone application (app) called "Radar COVID." After a pilot program on La Gomera in the Canary Islands, the app was released on August 10, 2020. However, each AC had to connect the app to its own contact-tracing system to activate it, and they were not required to do so until September 15, 2020 ("Radar COVID," 2020).

On June 11, 2020, the government approved a pilot project for tourists from other Schengen countries, as long as both the country and the Balearic Islands had COVID-19 infection rates below 9 per 100,000 inhabitants for at least seven consecutive days. Visitors were required to provide proof of a minimum five-night stay with a return ticket to the same airport.[7]

Social and Economic Policy Measures to Ease the Crisis

On March 12, 2020, the government approved a decree law to advance EUR 2.87 billion to the fifteen ACs in the common financing system[8], half on March 23 and the remainder in mid-April. The decree included monetary or in-kind assistance for families with school-aged children who qualified for assistance with school meals as long as schools remained closed.[9]

On March 17, 2020, the government published a battery of extraordinary measures to combat the effects of the social and economic crisis. Working time reductions and temporary layoffs were incentivized by eliminating or reducing firms' social security obligations for the affected workers during the crisis, eliminating minimum working periods for access to benefits and excluding payments received from workers' overall eligibility. Workers could receive a maximum of 70 percent of their salary, up to EUR 1,412/month. The self-employed gained easier access to unemployment benefits, and workers with new, crisis-related dependent care responsibilities were provided with exceptional facilities to adapt working hours and conditions.[10]

A mortgage payment moratorium was approved for qualified debtors, and utility providers were prohibited from cutting off water, electricity, and gas to the vulnerable; providers were also prohibited from cutting off basic telephone and internet service to existing subscribers. EUR 300 million was provided to the ACs (which they could transfer as needed to provincial and local governmental entities) for COVID-19 social services delivery costs such as meals for the elderly, home care and telemedicine, PPE purchases, and additional staff for retirement homes.

The government also set aside EUR 100 billion for funding and financing programs for businesses. The Ministry of Economy and Digital Transformation was able to provide loan guarantees of up to EUR 100 million through December 31, 2020. The ceiling for total outstanding credits issuable by the Official Credit Institute (ICO) was increased by EUR 10 billion, with special emphasis on expanding credit access for small and medium enterprises (SMEs) and the self-employed. Up to EUR 2 billion was set aside for export lines of credit, again with special emphasis for SMEs and the self-employed. Meanwhile, a battery of extensions were set out for individual and corporate tax payments.

Finally, funds were mobilized for COVID-19-related research. The Carlos III Health Institute, an entity within the Ministry of Health, was granted EUR 24 million to subsidize third-party research projects and EUR 1.2 million for increased internal costs such as overtime. The country's main public research institute, the CSIC, was granted EUR 4 million for virus-related projects.

On May 29, 2020, the coalition government introduced by decree law a nationwide minimum income for impoverished households.[11] Spain had been the only EU member state without such a program at the national level. Although several of the ACs offered some kind of basic income support, only the Basque Country's program had been significant enough to have a measurable impact on poverty (Ayala et al., 2020). This conditional basic minimum income was a cornerstone of the Socialist-Podemos coalition government formed on January 7, 2020, rather than a direct product of the crisis. Notably, in a moment of intense partisan conflict, the measure was supported by all parties except the extreme-right VOX. The maximum benefit was set at EUR 461 for individuals and EUR 1,015 for families of five or more. The government allocated EUR 3 billion/year for the program and estimated that it would benefit 2.3 million citizens and legal residents (of which 1.6 million were living in extreme poverty) aged 23 to 65 with at least one year registered with the Spanish social security and incomes of less than EUR 451/month (individuals) or EUR 993 (families with 5 or more members), excluding benefits from AC and other basic income programs. More than 1.3 million children were expected to benefit from the measure. Beneficiaries had to register with the public employment service and participate in schemes to improve social inclusion.[12]

Explanations

Proximate Causes of Spain's COVID-19 Disaster

The immediate causes of high infection and mortality rates during March and April 2020 and the rapid increase in infection rates after the relaxation of lockdown are relatively clear: a failure to stockpile sufficient PPE and test kits as the threat of the pandemic grew, a failure to isolate facilities for the elderly, limited data about the evolution of cases, and a failure to put in place a robust system of testing and contact tracing before relaxing lockdown. All of these factors can be traced back to problems in the structure and dynamics of the Spanish national health system and its political institutions more generally.

Severe Material Shortages

The Spanish pandemic preparedness system was woefully underfunded, had few strategic reserves, and was largely unprepared to take over purchasing from the regions or even to coordinate AC purchases. Despite warnings from the World Health Organization (WHO) on February 2, 2020, and again on February 11 and from the European Commission (EC) two days later to ensure adequate supplies of medical equipment, Spain only began to purchase additional materials on global markets after lockdown was declared, paying enormously inflated prices for goods that were defective or simply never arrived (Lamet, 2020).

The abject failure of central and regional governments to ensure an adequate supply of PPE at the beginning of the crisis can be seen in the rate of infection of healthcare personnel. By late April, according the European Centre for Disease Protection and Control, healthcare personnel represented 20 percent of COVID-19 cases in Spain, double the rate in Italy, and much higher than anywhere else. This figure excluded rates of infection among those caring for the elderly in retirement homes and day centers, but a review of AC data on infections in this latter group suggests that they represent roughly 7 to 8 percent of all cases in Spain (Güell, 2020).

There does appear to be some belated learning on this issue. On August 6, 2020, the government reached an agreement with the ACs for a new public tender to purchase EUR 2.5 billion in strategic supplies (gowns, gloves, masks, PCR test kits) for COVID-19. The tender was delayed for two weeks while the government negotiated with four regions who initially did not ask to be included. In the end all but Valencia (which claimed that local SMEs could not meet provider solvency conditions) agreed to participate (Sevillano, 2020).

Faulty Data Collection and Reporting

Data collection and reporting problems have hampered Spain's coronavirus response throughout the crisis and raised serious doubts about the reliability of reported data. Until February 25, 2020, the Ministry of Health limited testing to people who had been in Wuhan, leaving authorities blind to local contagion. Not until April 3 did the government issue an order requesting epidemiological information on nursing homes from the regions (Boletín Oficial del Estado, 4 April SND/322/2020 [Order of the National Dependent Care System]), even though they were the epicenter of the epidemic.

Once data were requested, the ACs failed to upload much of the requested individual data to SiVies, the National Epidemiological Center's platform. On March 16, 2020, some ten thousand cases were reported in Spain; the platform only reported some seven hundred. At the end of March 2020, Catalonia, the Basque Country, and Galicia (the first two particularly hard hit) had only uploaded some 20 percent of their known cases to SiVies, and Castile-La Mancha none. Only on May 12, 2020, did the government formalize its request for individualized data. However, the process was managed so badly that from May 21 to June 10, 2020, the Ministry's panel data for the "Covid-19 Situation" was not updated (Llaneras, 2020).

Why has reporting been so difficult? Central and regional government information systems are often obsolete, operations are understaffed, and reporting processes and systems differ across regions, sometimes even from health unit to health unit. These problems predated the crisis but were compounded by repeated changes in the information requested (Andrino et al., 2020). The crisis management team was improvising because no previous central government had legislated an obligatory harmonization of epidemiological information or provided the regions with the resources to put such a solution into place.

Insufficient Contact Tracing

According to a member of the interdisciplinary committee charged with plotting the lockdown relaxation strategy, the first and most important pillar of their strategy was "the capacity to test, trace and isolate (potential) cases and to have the strategic healthcare infrastructure to deal with a possible new outbreak" (Otero-Iglesias, 2020).

However, in both Catalonia and Madrid, the two hardest-hit ACs during the first phase of the crisis, governments proved themselves unwilling or unable to recruit even remotely enough contact tracers to meet international best practices. Instead, both governments have sought volunteers and outsourced efforts to contractors already providing operators for standard emergency services. Contract tracers receive insufficient training and coordination with primary care centers—identified by the ministry as the key actor to ensure prompt testing and tracking—is tenuous at best (Galaup, 2020; Rodríguez & Puente, 2020). Why? Press reports suggest a reliance on volunteers that never appeared, a reluctance to increase staffing and a belief that cases would not increase until the fall left many regions unprepared for the rapid increase in cases (e.g., Pérez Mendoza & Caballero, 2020).

The Tragedy of Elder Care

From 2005 to 2015, Spain increased the number of dedicated spaces in nursing homes from twenty to almost forty-five per one thousand inhabitants over the age of sixty-five. The rapid demand for such beds took place against a backdrop of increasing austerity, encouraging the ACs responsible for these homes to invite private sector participation as a cheap way to satisfy a growing political demand. Large firms entered the sector, taking advantage of abundant low-skilled labor and lax inspection regimes (Palomera Zaidel, 2020).

The Ministry of Health estimates that from April 6 to June 20, 27,359 people died in nursing homes, some 69 percent of all COVID-19 deaths. Many died unnecessarily, and many died alone with inadequate palliative care. The Spanish chapter of Doctors Without Borders provided support to almost five hundred homes, mostly in Barcelona and Madrid, and has recently published a scathing report (Médicos sin Fronteras, 2020). Almost uniformly, the homes were under-resourced and lacked contingency plans. Little testing was available, and no clear protocol existed for patients and staff testing positive. Many homes lacked the space to isolate patients. Personnel were forced to provide quasi-medical support without adequate training; when staff fell sick, remaining colleagues were totally overwhelmed. There was scarce collaboration between AC departments of health and human services, provincial authorities, municipal authorities, and nongovernmental providers (nonprofit foundations and for-profit corporations). Requests to admit the sick to hospitals were often denied, even though there were beds available (Médicos sin Fronteras, 2020).

Not until early August 2020 did the Ministry of Social Rights reach an agreement with the ACs and the Federation of Municipalities and Provinces with recommendations for nursing homes in case of new outbreaks (Borraz & Zas Marcos, 2020). Yet diverse criteria continue to be applied, with, for example, some regions requiring PCR tests for visitors and personnel, others only for personnel, and still others not requiring them at all. As of late August 2020, numerous COVID-19 cases were again being reported in nursing homes.

Structural Explanations

Few countries have seen COVID-19 infection and mortality rates as high as Spain, and no European country has seen its infection rates rise as quickly after lockdown was lifted. This is, at its surface, surprising given the strong international reputation of Spain's national health system. Yet, in many ways, an airborne virus has brought to the surface every weakness of the Spanish public health system and its political institutions. Before analyzing these institutional problems, however, we need to take note of the structural challenges that exacerbated the institutional challenges faced by the country's political leaders.

Spain has one of the oldest populations in the world. Because the virus is particularly lethal for older people, it makes sense that Spain's mortality rate would be relatively high. This demographic challenge has been compounded by urban development and long-standing cultural patterns that favor virus transmission. The territory of Spain is sparsely populated; however, if we consider only the areas where people live, then Spanish population density is second only to Malta in the European Union (Rae, 2020). Spaniards are also quite social, and socializing in Spain traditionally involves close physical contact, with frequent hugging and kissing; physical distancing is not a part of the Spanish social repertoire. Spaniards are also familial in comparison to northern Europeans. Although multigenerational homes are less common then they once were, extended family meetings are frequent, and visits to the elderly are common (Otero-Iglesias et al., 2020).

Spain's economy also relies heavily on sectors that facilitate the spread of airborne viruses. Almost 15 percent of the economy is based on tourism, and much of that tourist infrastructure is devoted to delivering intensely social experiences for foreigners on beaches and in city and town centers. Spain is also one of Europe's leading producers of fruits and vegetables. The harvesting season extends across much of the year, and migrant laborers move from region-to-region following seasonal harvests. Labor laws are poorly enforced and living conditions often abysmal. About 18 percent of outbreaks since the relaxation of confinement have been concentrated among seasonal agricultural workers, particularly in Catalonia and Aragón. However, the government failed to provide the ACs with specific instructions for tracking this population until July 27, 2020 (Estévez Torreblanca & Oliveres, 2020; Estévez Torreblanca & Sánchez, 2020).

Finally, Spain is one of the most unequal societies in Europe, with the EU's second-highest rate of students who fail to complete high school. Tourism, hospitality, construction, and other personal services mean low-wage jobs that cannot be done remotely. Low-wage work also means low incomes, which force a significant segment of the population into crowded, often substandard housing. For almost all of the Spanish population, social distancing is culturally foreign; for much of the population, it is also logistically complex.

Institutional Explanations

Spain's quasi-federalist constitutional system is characterized by what I have elsewhere labeled "the politics of who not what" (Dubin, 2019). The 1978 Spanish Constitution balanced the demands of regional nationalists, especially the Basques and the Catalans, with those of fervent Spanish nationalists close to the previous Francoist regime by creating a "State of the Autonomies." The entire country was divided into these political units, limiting the asymmetrical powers demanded by the regional nationalists. Although certain powers were devolved to the historic regions more rapidly, all ACs enjoyed full competencies over health and education by the early 2000s. Decision-making is coordinated vertically and horizontally through sectoral interregional councils. However, nationalist politicians in the historical regions seek a more bilateral relationship with the central government—or simply go their own way—whenever they can.

As a result, intergovernmental cooperation is often politically charged, even when the issues at stake are largely technical (Aja & Colino, 2014). For example, when the director of the Catalan health service attended meetings of the Inter-

Territorial Health Council in the weeks before the March state of the alarm declaration, it was the first time in years that the Catalan regional government had sent a representative to this forum. Similarly, the Conference of AC Presidents convened by the prime minister on March 22, 2020, was its first meeting in four years. By July 30, 2020, the leaders of both Catalonia and the Basque Country were refusing to attend the President's Conference convened for July 31 (Ormazabal, 2020).

Contested federalism discourages data sharing and learning and stymies the emergence of a culture of evaluation (López-Valcarcel & Barber, 2017). The structure and culture of national institutions suffer similar problems. The Spanish public administration is dominated by a corporatist bureaucracy with a change-resistant culture that discourages information flows. Inattention to policy evaluation is reinforced by a performance evaluation system focused on outputs rather than outcomes, not surprising in a civil service dominated by legal backgrounds and where data specialists are in short supply (Lapuente et al., 2018; Longo et al., 2020). At the same time, Spanish political appointments reach down to the secretary general level (two levels below ministers or their AC equivalents). The result is a highly politicized policy-making process that prizes loyalty over competence and policy-making autonomy over policy-making effectiveness ("who not what").

These dynamics have long forestalled efforts to coordinate and develop policy areas such as public health, which are not politically salient in normal times (Artells et al., 2014). Consider one paradigmatic example. Drafts of the 2011 General Framework Law for Public Health proposed the creation of an independent agency to develop, coordinate, and evaluate national and regional health policy rather than leaving such measures to internal units within the Ministry of Health and the respective AC health departments. However, the idea was resisted by an Economy Ministry concerned about the budget implications and a Health Ministry loath to cede territory. The final law called for the creation of a much more limited State Center for Public Health, which is only now, in the wake of the pandemic, moving beyond the proposal stage (Aguado, 2018).

All of these institutional problems were compounded by the increasingly parlous state of the country's health system. When Spain was forced to pursue deep cutbacks in public spending in the wake of the European financial crisis in 2011, the government of Mariano Rajoy pushed much of the burden of adjustment on to the regions, as had, to a lesser degree, the previous socialist government of José Luis Rodríguez Zapatero. Cut off from sovereign debt markets, the ACs had no choice but to impose deep cuts in health spending. Where total public spending fell 6 percent from 2009 to 2013, public health spending fell by 14 percent (López-Valcarcel & Barber, 2017). Many regions responded by privatizing the development and management of public care as a way of reducing capital expenditures. They also introduced sharp cuts in primary care and public health spending. However, there was little in the way of systematic efforts to rethink health priorities

(Padilla, 2020). These changes would prove enormously problematic during the pandemic.

Conjunctural Political Factors

Spain's ability to address the pandemic was further hampered by conjunctural political circumstances. Pedro Sánchez took charge of the country's first coalitional government in January 2020. The Socialists' agreement with Podemos included the division of the Ministry of Health, Consumption and Welfare (Sanidad, Consumo y Bienestar Social) into three separate ministries. Health would remain with the socialists, although María Luisa Carcedo, a healthcare specialist and previous minister, was replaced by Salvador Illa, a veteran of the socialist organization with no healthcare management experience. Social Services and Agenda 2030 were entrusted to the new vice-president of the government from Podemos, Pablo Iglesias, and Consumption to another Podemos minister. Multiple reports suggest that the restructuring and reassignment of civil servants in January and February hindered the already limited coordinating capacities of the central government (León, 2020).

The epidemic also took place at a moment of enormous partisan conflict in Spain. First, the pro-independence position of the coalition government in Catalonia and, to a lesser extent, the Basque Country, has, as noted, complicated cooperation with the national government. The Euro crisis and the Catalan independence drive created a space for the far-left Podemos the quasi-liberal, Spanish nationalist Citizens party, and now the emergence of VOX, the first far-right party to gain a significant presence (15 percent of seats) in parliament since the return to democracy. This transformation of the party system has unsettled electoral dynamics, leading to four general elections since 2015, including two in 2019, and contributed to a polarization of public discourse. Where COVID-19 has muted oppositional discourse in most European countries, it has generated furious opposition from the right and regional nationalists against Spain's new government.

However, polarization and contestation does not seem to be a good explanation for Spain's catastrophic pandemic response. On the one hand, coordination failures have affected all of the regions; partisan affiliation does not appear to have affected responses positively or negatively. On the other hand, public support for the measures taken by the government has been overwhelmingly positive: 97.3 percent of the Spanish population believed the measures were "necessary" or "very necessary" (Centro de Investigaciones Sociológicas, 2020), and self-reported mask-wearing rates were among the very highest in Europe (Otero-Iglesias et al., 2020). In other words, the many failures of the Spanish authorities documented in this chapter are largely attributable to long-standing problems in the country's institutional structure, its political culture ("who not what"), and the problems generated by disinvestment since the financial crisis rather than the partisan challenges of the current moment.

Conclusion: Late-Summer Winds of Change?

As of this writing, new cases of COVID-19 have increased more rapidly in Spain than any other EU nation since early August 2020. Given the failures of the ACs to prepare adequately for the test and trace regime stipulated by the government during the phased relaxation of confinement and the many structural factors favoring transmission, this is not wholly surprising. Nevertheless, one can detect small signs of positive change. The central government appears disinclined—and perhaps lacks the parliamentary support—to reimpose another state of alarm and so deprive the ACs of control within their regions. It is now the ACs who will be making critical and highly visible policy decisions about testing and tracing, protecting elder care facilities, and school openings. Citizens will be more likely to hold their AC political leaders responsible for regional outcomes over the coming weeks and months, raising the stakes for regional decision-makers.

This emerging political reality and a sharp uptick in new cases is beginning to concentrate the minds of AC and national-level political leaders alike. First, after much hesitation, the hardest-affected regions are finally beginning to roll out large-scale testing programs. Although the effectiveness of these efforts remains to be seen, their rapidly increasing, if unequal, intensity is undeniable (Caballero, 2020; Puente, 2020). Second, many ACs are now asserting their authority to manage the crisis. Some of their more recent efforts to restrict movement in specific localities, impose mask requirements, and limit leisure establishments have been met by judicial resistance. However, regions such as Catalonia have used decree laws to strengthen their authority, and as such measures grow more frequent, judicial doctrine may increasingly accept the ACs' assertion of constitutional authority to take the measures they see fit to control pandemics within their territories (Boix Palop, 2020; Herrera, 2020).

Finally, for the first time since the crisis started—indeed, for the first time since the transition to democracy—the ACs and the central government reached a unanimous agreement on August 14, 2020, in the Interterritorial Health Council to impose measures to track and limit contagion. Many of the measures were inspired in initiatives of some ACs; in any event, their implementation will depend on their transposition to each AC's regulations (González, 2020; Ministerio de Sanidad, 2020d). The agreement is a potential landmark marking a new approach to the crisis.

The first serious response to COVID-19 in Spain began with an unparalleled degree of recentralization of health policy (Viciosa, 2020). Given the profound problems with intergovernmental coordination in a country where political leaders often view competencies more as trophies than mandates, this initial response by the central government was perhaps understandable. Nevertheless, the consequences for Spaniards of a poorly coordinated central government response have been devastating. Going forward, coordinated action facilitated by the central government but led by the regional governments who enjoy the legal mandate to develop and executive health policy may be the only way to avoid a repeat of Spain's disastrous initial response to the virus.

Notes

1. Over the two weeks preceding August 18, 2020, Spain was reported to have the EU's highest per capita infection rate, with an accumulated incidence over the previous 14 days of 131.1 cases per 100,000 residents. Romania was a distant second at 77.1 (Centro de Coordinación de Alertas y Emergencias Sanitarias, 2020, Table 4).

2. Article 116 of the Spanish Constitution defines three levels of crisis response: alarm, emergency, and siege, in ascending order.

3. Real Decreto 463/2020, de 14 de marzo, por el que se declara el estado de alarma para la gestión de la situación de crisis sanitaria ocasionada por el COVID-19 [Royal Decree 463/2020, 14 March, declaring a state of alarm for the management of the health crisis situation created by COVID-19].

4. Orden INT/239/2020, de 16 de marzo, por la que se restablecen los controles en las fronteras interiores terrestres con motivo de la situación de crisis sanitaria ocasionada por el COVID-19 [Interministerial order 239/2020, 16 March, which reestablishes controls in internal ground borders given the health crisis created by COVID-19].

5. Children had previously been allowed out only to accompany one parent to make necessary purchases. Most children had not left their homes for more than six weeks.

6. Real Decreto-ley 21/2020, de 9 de junio, de medidas urgentes de prevención, contención y coordinación para hacer frente a la crisis sanitaria ocasionada por el COVID-19 [Royal Decree-law 21/2020, 9 June, urgent measures of prevention, containment and coordination in response to the health crisis created by COVID-19].

7. Orden SND/518/2020, de 11 de junio, por la que se regula la autorización de un programa piloto de apertura de corredores turísticos seguros en la Comunidad Autónoma de Illes Balears mediante el levantamiento parcial de los controles temporales en las fronteras interiores establecidos con motivo de la situación de crisis sanitaria ocasionada por el COVID-19 [National Dependent Care System Order 518/2020, 11 June, regulation of the authorization of a pilot program to open safe tourism corridors in the Autonomous Community of the Balearic Islands through the partial lifting of the temporary controls on internal borders established in response to the health crisis situation created by COVID-19].

8. The 15 ACs in the Common Regime receive obtain most of their funding from taxes collected by the state and then transferred; the Basque Country and Navarre collect most taxes in their regions and transfer a portion to the State for state-delivered services. In practice, the latter system provides these two regions with far more resources per capita than their Common Regime counterparts. See Dubin, 2019 for additional details.

9. Real Decreto-ley 7/2020, de 12 de marzo, por el que se adoptan medidas urgentes para responder al impacto económico del COVID-19.

10. Real Decreto-ley 8/2020, de 17 de marzo, de medidas urgentes extraordinarias para hacer frente al impacto económico y social del COVID-19 [Royal Decree-law 8/2020, 17 March, urgent extraordinary measures in response to the social and economic impact of COVID-19].

11. Real Decreto-Ley 20/2020, de 29 de mayo, por el que se establece el ingreso mínimo vital [Royal Decree-Law 20/2020, 29 May, for the establishment of a minimal basic income].

12. Early reports suggest bureaucratic red tape is limiting the arrival of aid. As of August 7, 2020, it appeared that less than 1 percent of applications had been approved since the program opened on June 15, even though the relevant minister expected some 50 percent of applications to ultimately quality (Zuil, 2020).

References

La AEMPS impide la exportación de mascarillas desde España [The AEMPS blocks the exportation of masks outside of Spain]. (2020, April 9). redacción médica. https://www.redaccionmedica.com/secciones/ministerio-sanidad/coronavirus-la-aemps-impide-la-exportacion-de-mascarillas-desde-espana-6603

Aguado, I. H. (2018). Diseño institucional y buen gobierno: avances y reformas pendientes [Institutional design and good governance: Advances and pending reforms]. *Cuadernos Económicos de ICE, 96*, 145–164.

Aja, E., & Colino, C. (2014). Multilevel structures, coordination and partisan politics in Spanish intergovernmental relations. *Comparative European Politics, 12*, 444–467. https://doi.org/10.1057/cep.2014.9

Andrino, S., Grasso, D., & Llaneras, K. (2020, May 27). Asteriscos, incoherencias y opacidad: 15 problemas de Sanidad con la gestión de datos del coronavirus [Asterisks, incoherencies and opacity: 15 National Health System problems with the management of coronavirus data]. *El País*. https://elpais.com/sociedad/2020-05-26/asteriscos-incoherencias-y-opacidad-15-problemas-del-ministerio-con-la-gestion-de-datos-del-coronavirus.html

Arteaga, F. (2020, April 13). *La gestión de pandemias como el COVID-19 en España: ¿enfoque de salud o de seguridad?* [The management of pandemics like COVID-19 in Spain: A health or security focus?]. Real Instituto Elcano. http://www.realinstitutoelcano.org/wps/portal/rielcano_es/contenido?WCM_GLOBAL_CONTEXT=/elcano/elcano_es/zonas_es/ari42-2020-arteaga-gestion-de-pandemias-covid-19-en-espana-enfoque-de-salud-o-de-seguridad

Artells, J. J., Peiró, S., & Meneu, R. (2014). Barreras a la introducción de una agencia evaluadora para informar la financiación o la desinversión de prestaciones sanitarias del Sistema Nacional de Salud [Barriers to the introduction of an evaluation agency to inform decisions regarding the inclusion or exclusion of medical services in the National Health System]. *Revista Española de Salud Pública, 88*, 217–231.

Asenjo, I. & Lastra, R. G. (2020, March 7). La Guardia Civil se despliega en Haro para controlar el aislamiento de los afectados por el COVID-19 [The Civil Guard deploys in Haro to control the isolation of those affected by COVID-19]. *El Comercio*. https://www.elcomercio.es/sociedad/salud/muertos-espana-balance-fernando-simon-sabado-coronavirus-20200307101510-ntrc.html

Asimétrica y dirigida por el Gobierno: así será la desescalada del confinamiento de las comunidades [Asymmetric and led by the government: This is how the relaxing of confinement in the Autonomous Communities will be]. (2020, April 24). https://www.rtve.es/noticias/20200424/gobierno-prepara-comunidades-autonomas-fase-desescalada/2012712.shtml

Ayala, L., Arranz, J. M., García-Serrano, C., & Martínez-Virto, L. (2020). The effectiveness of minimum income benefits in poverty reduction in Spain. *International Journal of Social Welfare*. https://doi.org/10.1111/ijsw.12447

Benach, J. (2020, July 22). Confinamientos 2.0. ¿Dónde está la Salud Pública? [Confinement 2.0. Where is public health?]. *Ctxt.es*. https://ctxt.es/es/20200701/Firmas/32899/Joan-Benach-salud-publica-sanidad-tratamientos-prevencion-covid-pandemia.htm

Bernardo, A., Del Vayo, M. A., & Torrecillas, C. (2020, June 23). La falta de personal de enfermería, el talón de Aquiles que el coronavirus dejó al descubierto [The lack of nursing personnel, the Achilles' Heel that coronavirus has made evident]. *Civio*. https://civio.es/medicamentalia/2020/06/23/coronavirus-covid-19-espana-italia-enfermeria/

Boix Palop, A. (2020, August 13). El baile "agarrao" entre Estado, Comunidades Autónomas y jueces para una mejor gestión de la pandemia de Covid-19 [The slow dance between the State, the Autonomous Communities and judges for a better management of the COVID-19 pandemic]. *Iustel*. https://www.iustel.com/diario_del_derecho/noticia.asp?ref_iustel=1201691

Boletín Oficial del Estado. Real Decreto-ley 7/2020, de 12 de marzo, por el que se adoptan medidas urgentes para responder al impacto económico del COVID-19 [Royal Decree law 7/2020, 12 March, for the adoption of urgent measures in order to respond to the economic impact of COVD-19].

Boletín Oficial del Estado. Real Decreto 463/2020, de 14 de marzo, por el que se declara el estado de alarma para la gestión de la situación de crisis sanitaria ocasionada por el COVID-19 [Royal Decree law 463/2020, 12 March, for the declaration of a state of alarm for the management of the situation of the health crisis created by COVID-19].

Boletín Oficial del Estado. Orden SND/234/2020, de 15 de marzo, sobre adopción de disposiciones y medidas de contención y remisión de información al Ministerio de Sanidad ante la situación de crisis sanitaria ocasionada por el COVID-19 [Order of the National Dependent Care System (SND), 15 March, on the adoption of dispositions and measures of contention and remission of information to the Ministry of Health in the context of the health crisis created by COVID-19].

Boletín Oficial del Estado. Orden SND/322/2020, de 3 de abril, por la que se modifican la Orden SND/ 275/2020, de 23 de marzo y la Orden SND/295/2020, de 26 de marzo, y se establecen nuevas medidas para atender necesidades urgentes de carácter social o sanitario en el ámbito de la situación de la crisis sanitaria ocasionada por el COVID-19 [Order of the National Dependent Care System (SND), 3 April, modifying Order SND/275/2020, 23 March and Order SND/295/2020, 26 March, and establishing new measures to attend urgent social or health needs in the context of the health crisis created by COVD-19].

Boletín Oficial del Estado. Orden SND/387/2020, de 3 de mayo, por la que se regula el proceso de cogobernanza con las comunidades autónomas y ciudades de Ceuta y Melilla para la transición a una nueva normalidad [Order of the National Dependent Care System (SND) 387/2020, 3 May, for the regulation of a process of cogovernance with the autonomous communities and the cities of Ceuta and Melilla for the transition toward a new normality].

Boletín Oficial del Estado. Real Decreto-Ley 20/2020, de 29 de mayo, por el que se establece el ingreso mínimo vital [Royal Decree Law 20/2020, 29 May, for the establishment of a minimal basic income].

Boletín Oficial del Estado. Real Decreto-ley 21/2020, de 9 de junio, de medidas urgentes de prevención, contención y coordinación para hacer frente a la crisis sanitaria ocasionada por el COVID-19 [Royal Decree Law 21/2020, 9 June, urgent measures for prevention, containment and coordination to address the health crisis created by COVID-19].

Borraz, M., & Zas Marcos, M. (2020, August 10). La falta de anticipación en las residencias de mayores hace que la COVID-19 vuelva a golpear al colectivo más débil [The lack of preparation in elder care facilities allows COVID-19 to attack again the weakest social group]. *El Diario.* https://www.eldiario.es/sociedad/falta-anticipacion-residencias-mayores-covid-19-vuelva-golpear-colectivo-debil_1_6156734.html

Caballero, F. (2020, August 18). Los test masivos de la Comunidad de Madrid chocan con el discurso de Ayuso sobre Barajas [The Community of Madrid's mass testing program conflicts with Ayuso's discourse regarding Barajas airport]. *El Diario.* https://www.eldiario.es/madrid/test-masivos-comunidad-madrid-chocan-discurso-ayuso-barajas_1_6168080.html

Castro, I. & Riveiro, A. (2020, May 6). Sánchez logra la cuarta prórroga del estado de alarma con menos apoyos y la petición unánime de que el Gobierno dialogue más [Sánchez obtains the fourth extension of the state of alarm with less support and a unanimous petition for the government to engage in more dialogue]. *El Diario.* https://www.eldiario.es/politica/sanchez-compromete-protagonismo-autonomias-pnv_1_5958914.html

Centro de Coordinación de Alertas y Emergencias Sanitarias. (2020, August). *Actualización no 187. Enfermedad por el coronavirus (COVID-19). 18.08.2020.* [Update number 187, Coronavirus cases (COVID-19). 18.08.2020]. https://www.mscbs.gob.es/profesionales/saludPublica/ccayes/alertasActual/nCov/documentos/Actualizacion_187_COVID-19.pdf

Centro de Investigaciones Sociológicas (CIS). (2020, April). *Barómetro especial de abril 2020. Avance de resultados* [Special April 2020 Barometer. Advanced Results]. *Study 3279* http://datos.cis.es/pdf/Es3279mar_A.pdf

Dombey, D., & Burn-Murdoch, J. (2020, June 4). Flawed data casts cloud over Spain's lockdown strategy. *The Financial Times.* https://www.ft.com/content/77eb7a13-cd26-41dd-9642-616708b43673

Dubin, K. (2019). Spain: The politics of who not what. In S. L. Greer & H. Elliott (Eds.), *Federalism and social policy: Patterns of redistribution in 11 democracies* (pp. 57–90). University of Michigan Press.

EFE. (2020, March 12). El Govern ordena el confinamiento de la población de Igualada y otros tres municipios por el coronavirus [The Government orders the confinement of the populace in Igualada and three other municipalities due to coronavirus]. *Público.* https://www.publico.es/politica/govern-ordena-confinamiento-poblacion-igualada-coronavirus.html.

España tuvo que comprar respiradores chinos pagando el doblé [Spain had to buy Chinese ventilators paying double]. (2020, March 24). redacción médica. https://www.redaccionmedica.com/secciones/ministerio-sanidad/coronavirus-espana-tuvo-que-comprar-respiradores-chinos-pagando-el-doble-3322

Estévez Torreblanca, M. (2020, August 12). Trabajo investiga 1.600 posibles irregularidades laborales y sanitarias en explotaciones agrarias, uno de los focos de rebrotes de COVID-19 [The Ministry of Labor investigates 1,600 possible employment and health irregularities in agricultural facilities, one of the foci of new outbreaks of COVD-19]. *El Diario.* https://www.eldiario.es/sociedad/trabajo-investiga-1-600-posibles

-irregularidades-laborales-sanitarias-explotaciones-agrarias-focos-rebrotes-covid-19_1_6160109.html

Estévez Torreblanca, M., & Oliveres, V. (2020, August 2). Las próximas campañas agrícolas masivas ponen en guardia al Gobierno y las CCAA para evitar brotes de COVID entre temporeros [The massive upcoming agricultural harvests have put the government and the Autonomous Communities in alert to avoid outbreaks of COVID-19 among temporary workers]. *El Diario.* https://www.eldiario.es/sociedad/proximas-campanas-agricolas-masivas-ponen-guardia-gobierno-ccaa-evitar-brotes-covid-temporeros_1_6140998.html

Estévez Torreblanca, M., & Sánchez, G. (2020, August 13). Las irregularidades en la contratación de temporeros mediante intermediarios dificultan el control de la COVID-19 [Irregular contracting of temporary workers through intermediaries is making it difficult to control COVID-19]. *El Diario.* https://www.eldiario.es/sociedad/irregularidades-contratacion-temporeros-mediante-intermediarios-dificultan-control-covid-19_1_6161655.html

Galaup, L. (2020, August 12). Madrid sigue a la caza de rastreadores en 'entidades externas' y sin lograr la plantilla recomendada por los expertos [Madrid continues to hunt for contact tracers in "outside entities" and without reaching the staffing levels recommended by experts]. *El Diario.* https://www.eldiario.es/madrid/madrid-sigue-caza-rastreadores-entidades-externas-lograr-plantilla-recomendada-expertos_1_6160906.html

García, L. (2020, June 14). Lecciones políticas de una epidemia [Political lessons of an epidemic]. *La Vanguardia.* https://www.lavanguardia.com/politica/20200614/481764735369/gestion-crisis-sanitaria-pandemia-gobierno-govern-espana-sanchez-cataluna.html

García-Basteiro, A., Alvarez-Dardet, C., Arenas, A., Bengoa, R., Borrell, C., Del Val, M., Franco, M., Gea-Sánchez, M., Gestal Otero, J. J., González López Valcárcel, B., Hernández, I., March, J. C., Martin-Moreno, J. M., Menéndez, C., Minué, S., Muntaner, C., Porta, M., Prieto-Alhambra, D., Vives-Cases, C., & Legido-Quigley, H. (2020). The need for an independent evaluation of the COVID-19 response in Spain. *The Lancet, 396* (10250), 529–530. https://doi.org/10.1016/S0140-6736(20)31713-X

González, Y. (2020, August 14). Ayuso, año I en la Puerta del Sol [Ayuso, year I in the Puerta del Sol]. *Infolibre.* https://www.infolibre.es/noticias/politica/2020/08/12/avalmadrid_crisis_con_drama_las_residencias_choque_frontal_con_sanchez_primer_ano_ayuso_como_presidenta_109913_1012.html

González, Y. (2020, August 15). Sanidad toma las riendas sin oposición ante el miedo al colapso en septiembre y la disparidad de medidas autonómicas [The Health Ministry takes the reins without opposition in the face of fears of a collapse in September and disparities in the measures taken by the autonomous communities]. *Infolibre.* https://www.infolibre.es/noticias/politica/2020/08/15/sanidad_toma_las_riendas_unifica_medidas_urgentes_para_las_comunidades_por_miedo_colapso_septiembre_110006_1012.html

Government and institutional measures in response to COVID-19. (2020, June 24). KPMG. https://home.kpmg/xx/en/home/insights/2020/04/spain-government-and-institution-measures-in-response-to-covid.html

Güell, O. (2020, April 25). España es el país con más contagios entre el personal sanitario [Spain is the country with the most cases of contagion among health personnel]. *El

País. https://elpais.com/sociedad/2020-04-24/espana-es-el-pais-con-mas-contagios-entre-el-personal-sanitario.html

Herrera, E. (2020, August 16). Los intentos de las autonomías de limitar la expansión del virus derivan en una cascada de decisiones judiciales contradictorias [The efforts of the autonomous communities to limit the expansion of the virus generate a cascade of contradictory judicial decisions]. *El Diario.* https://www.eldiario.es/politica/intentos-autonomias-limitar-expansion-virus-derivan-cascada-decisiones-judiciales-contradictorias_1_6160534.html

Instituto de Salud Carlos III. (2020). Estrategia de detección precoz, vigilancia y control de COVID-19 [Strategy for the early detection, monitoring and control of COVID-19]. https://www.mscbs.gob.es/profesionales/saludPublica/ccayes/alertasActual/nCov-China/documentos/COVID19_Estrategia_vigilancia_y_control_e_indicadores.pdf

Lamet, J. (2020, April 3). España desoyó las llamadas de la OMS y de la UE a hacer acopio de material sanitario frente al coronavirus [Spain ignored the calls of the WHO and the EU to obtain health equipment in the face of the coronavirus]. *El Mundo.* https://www.elmundo.es/espana/2020/04/02/5e84fb84fc6c8384018b467f.html

Lapuente, V., Fernández-Albertos, J., Ahumada, M., González Alonso, A., Llobet, G., Parrado, S., Villoria, M., & Gortázar, V. (2018). *La calidad de las instituciones en España* [The quality of institutions in Spain]. Círculo de Empresarios.

León, S. (2020, June 12). *De gestión centralizada a gestión autonómica de la pandemia: desafíos y oportunidades* [From centralized management to regional management of the pandemic: Challenges and opportunities]. EsadeEcPol Insight #14. https://dobetter.esade.edu/es/gestion-autonomica-coronavirus

Llaneras, K. (2020, June 21). Los problemas de usar datos del siglo pasado para una pandemia del siglo XXI [The challenges of using data from the last century for a pandemic of the XXI century]. *El País.* https://elpais.com/sociedad/crisis-del-coronavirus/2020-06-20/los-problemas-de-usar-datos-del-siglo-pasado-para-una-pandemia-del-siglo-xxi.html

Longo, F., del Pino Matute, E., & Lapuente, V. (2020, June 2). Por un sector público capaz de liderar la recuperación [For public sector capable of leading the recovery]. *Agenda Pública.* http://agendapublica.elpais.com/por-un-sector-publico-capaz-de-liderar-la-recuperacion/

López-Valcarcel, B., & Barber, P. (2017). Economic crisis, austerity policies, health and fairness: Lessons learned in Spain. *Applied Health Economics and Health Policy, 15,* 13–21.

Médicos Sin Fronteras. (2020, August). *Poco, tarde y mal. El inaceptable desamparo de los mayores en las residencias durante la COVID-19 en España* [Little, late and badly: The unacceptable defenselessness of the elderly in nursing homes during COVID-19 in Spain]. http://static.msf.es/web/archivos/cov-19/AAFF-MSF-Informe-COVID19-Residencias-BAJA.pdf

Melle Hernández, M. (2020, April 20). Lecciones del "COVID-19" para la sanidad pública madrileña [Lessons of "COVID-19" for the Madrid public health system]. *Agenda Pública.* http://agendapublica.elpais.com/lecciones-del-covid-19-para-la-sanidad-publica-madrilena/

Minder, R. (2020, July 23). Spain's coronavirus crisis accelerated as warnings went unheeded. *The New York Times.* https://www.nytimes.com/2020/04/07/world/europe/spain-coronavirus.html

Ministerio de Hacienda. (2020, March 18). Hacienda comunica el primer pago de la actualización de las entregas a cuenta a las CCAA [The Revenue Service communicates the first payment of the update of the payments on account to the Autonomous Communities]. https://www.lamoncloa.gob.es/serviciosdeprensa/notasprensa/hacienda/Paginas/2020/180320-hacienda.aspx

Ministerio de Sanidad. (2013, March 21). Sistema de Alerta Precoz y Respuesta Rápida [System of early alerts and rapid response]. https://www.mscbs.gob.es/profesionales/saludPublica/ccayes/SIARP/Msssi_SIAPR_21032013.pdf

Ministerio de Sanidad. (2020a, March 5). Guía de actuación con los profesionales sanitarios en el caso de exposiciones de riesgo en el ámbito sanitario [Guide for health professionals in cases of risk exposure in the healthcare environment]. *Centro de Coordinación de Alertas y Emergencias Sanitarias.*

Ministerio de Sanidad. (2020b, March 14). Guía de actuación con los profesionales sanitarios en el caso de exposiciones de riesgo en el ámbito sanitario [Guide for health professionals in cases of risk exposure in the healthcare environment]. *Centro de Coordinación de Alertas y Emergencias Sanitarias.*

Ministerio de Sanidad. (2020c, July 16). Plan de respuesta temprana en un escenario de control de la pandemia por COVID-19 acordado en Consejo Interterritorial del Sistema Nacional de Salud [Plan for early response in a control scenario for the COVID-19 pandemic as agreed in the Interterritorial Council of the National Health System]. https://www.mscbs.gob.es/profesionales/saludPublica/ccayes/alertasActual/nCov-China/documentos/COVID19_Plan_de_respuesta_temprana_escenario_control.pdf

Ministerio de Sanidad. (2020d, August 14). El Ministerio de Sanidad y las CCAA acuerdan por unanimidad actuaciones coordinadas para controlar la transmisión de la COVID-19 [The Ministry of Health and the Autonomous Communities agree unanimously coordinated actions to control the transmission of COVD-19]. https://www.mscbs.gob.es/gabinete/notasPrensa.do?id=5025

Ormazabal, M. (2020, July 30). Torra y Urkullu no asistirán este viernes a la conferencia de presidentes autonómicos [Torra and Urkullu won't attend the conference of autonomic presidents this coming Friday]. *El País.* https://elpais.com/espana/catalunya/2020-07-30/torra-y-urkullu-no-asistiran-este-viernes-a-la-conferencia-de-presidentes-autonomicos.html

Otero-Iglesias, M. (2020, June 2). Living with COVID-19: the thinking behind Spain's lockdown exit plan. *Real Instituto Elcano*, Expert Comment 21/2020.

Otero-Iglesias, M., Molina, I., & Martínez, J. P. (2020, July 17). ¿Ha sido un fracaso la gestión española del COVID-19? Errores, lecciones y recomendaciones [Has the Spanish management of COVID-19 been a failure? Errors, lessons, and recommendations]. *Real Instituto Elcano.*

Padilla, J. (2020, July 30). COVID-19 y el futuro: La necesidad de hacer lo que funciona [COVID-19 and the future: The need to do what works]. *Agenda Pública.* http://agendapublica.elpais.com/covid-19-y-el-futuro-la-necesidad-de-hacer-lo-que-funciona/

Palomera Zaidel, D. (2020, April 1). Los problemas de las residencias [The problems of the nursing homes]. *Agenda Pública.* http://agendapublica.elpais.com/los-problemas-de-las-residencias/

Pappas, T. (2020, April 5). The politics of pandemic prevention in Spain and Greece. https://pappaspopulism.com/coronavirus-spain-and-greece/

Pazos-Vidal, S. (2020, April 14). Federalismo sanitario en tiempos de Coronavirus [Health federalism in times of Coronavirus]. *Agenda Pública.* http://agendapublica.elpais.com/federalismo-sanitario-en-tiempos-de-coronavirus/

Pérez-Durán, I. (2020, May 26). Efectos de la opacidad en las residencias de mayores antes de la COVID-19 [Effects of opacity in nursing homes in the face of COVID-19]. *Agenda Pública.* http://agendapublica.elpais.com/efectos-de-la-opacidad-en-las-residencias-de-mayores-antes-de-la-covid-19/

Pérez Mendoza, S., & Caballero, F. (2020, August 19). La Comunidad de Madrid vuelve a pedir rastreadores voluntarios al Ayuntamiento rebajando las exigencias de los perfiles [The Community of Madrid once again requests voluntary contact-tracers from City Hall and lowers the level of profile required]. *El Diario.* https://www.eldiario.es/madrid/comunidad-madrid-vuelve-pedir-rastreadores-voluntarios-ayuntamiento-rebajando-exigencias-perfiles_1_6171622.html

Puente, A. (2020, August 16). Josep Maria Argimon, un veterano de la gestión sanitaria que ha dado un vuelco en la estrategia catalana contra la COVID [Josep Maria Argimon, a health management veteran has transformed the Catalan strategy against COVID]. *El Diario.* https://www.eldiario.es/catalunya/politica/josep-maria-argimon-veterano-gestion-sanitaria-dado-vuelco-estrategia-catalana-covid_1_6162775.html

Radar COVID: Toda España usará la app de rastreo desde el 15 de septiembre [Radar COVID: All of Spain will use the contact-tracing app from 15 September]. (2020, August 4). https://www.newtral.es/radar-covid-app-espana-septiembre/20200804/

Rae, A. (2020, January 23). Think your country is crowded? These maps reveal the truth about population density across Europe. *The Conversation.* https://theconversation.com/think-your-country-is-crowded-these-maps-reveal-the-truth-about-population-density-across-europe-90345

Rodríguez, P., & Puente, A. (2020, July 7). El brote de Lleida evidencia las carencias y descoordinación en el sistema de rastreo en Catalunya [The outbreak in Lerida reveals the weaknesses and lack of coordination in the Catalan contact-tracing system]. *El Diario.* https://www.eldiario.es/catalunya/brote-lleida-evidencia-carencias-descoordinacion-sistema-rastreo-catalunya_1_6085986.html

Romero, J. M., & Güell, O. (2020, June 14). El agujero negro por el que se coló el virus [The black hole where the virus got in]. *El País.* https://elpais.com/sociedad/2020-06-13/el-agujero-negro-por-el-que-se-colo-el-virus.html

Sevillano, E. (2020, August 6). Cataluña y País Vasco se suman por primera vez a una compra centralizada para crear la reserva de material contra el coronavirus [Catalonia and the Basque Country participate for the first time in a centralized purchase to create a reserve of equipment against the coronavirus]. *El País.* https://elpais.com/sociedad/2020-08-06/cataluna-y-pais-vasco-se-suman-por-primera-vez-a-una-compra-centralizada-para-crear-la-reserva-de-material-contra-el-coronavirus.html

Sevillano, E. (2020, August 7). Los respiradores que nunca llegaron y el gel que no servía: los fiascos de las compras del Gobierno [The ventilators that never arrived and the sanitizers that were useless: The fiascos of the government's purchases]. *El País.* https://elpais.com/sociedad/2020-08-07/los-respiradores-que-nunca-llegaron-y-el-gel-que-no-servia-los-fiascos-de-las-compras-del-gobierno.html

Viciosa, M. (2020, August 8). España ante la segunda ola [Spain in the face of the second wave]. Interview with Dr. Helena Legido-Quigley. *Newtral.* https://www.newtral.es/espana-segunda-ola-legido-quigley-comportamiento-poblacion/20200808/

Zalakain, J. (2020, April 7). La urgencia de cambiar el modelo de residencias para mayores [The urgency of changing the model of nursing homes]. *Agenda Pública.* http://agendapublica.elpais.com/la-urgencia-de-cambiar-el-modelo-de-residencias-para-mayores/

Zuil, M. (2020. August 19). El IMV llega a menos del 1% de los hogares que lo piden [The minimal basic income reaches less than 1% of the households that have applied for it]. *El Confidencial.* https://www.elconfidencial.com/espana/2020-08-19/imv-hogares-espana-pobreza-ingreso-minimo-vital_2718159/

20 A TALE OF TWO PANDEMICS IN THREE COUNTRIES

Portugal, Spain, and Italy

André Peralta-Santos, Luis Saboga-Nunes, and Pedro C. Magalhães

On February 20, 2020, a young man admitted to the hospital in Italy with COVID-19 marked the start of uncontrolled COVID-19 transmission in Europe (Livingston & Bucher, 2020). Like other times in the past, Italy played the central role in the history of European epidemics: from the Antonine plague, described by Galen during the Roman Empire, to Genoa and the Black Death in the fourteenth century.

Over the next two weeks, in late February and early March 2020, the epidemic kept expanding in the Lombardian region in Italy. On March 8, 2020, the Italian government implemented a localized lockdown in the region, restricting movement to minimize social contact (Remuzzi & Remuzzi, 2020). The lockdown was expanded to the entire country on March 9, 2020.

In Spain, transmission had been underway, mainly undetected, since mid-February (Fuertes et al., 2020). On February 28, the Basque Country reported the first case, and by March 13, 2020, its regional government declared a health emergency. By then, all the provinces already had cases, motivating the national government to issue a royal decree (463/2020), declaring the state of emergency and a curfew.

In Portugal, the first cases were detected on March 2, 2020, in the northern regions, with links to Italian cases. The government rapidly convened the National Public Health Council, a committee composed of national experts (Peixoto et al., 2020), to gather advice about the necessary measures to control the pandemic. This council suggested on March 12 (Gomes, 2020) that no action be taken, but the prime minister ignored this advice, and between March 13 and March 16, 2020, a total lockdown of the country was implemented, even before the first death from COVID-19 was registered.

The synchronicity of physical distancing policies between these south European countries hides different epidemic dynamics, as well as diverse speeds in responding to the events. It is also noteworthy that different structural challenges existed when it came to responding to the most challenging health crisis in over a century. The COVID-19 pandemic is remarkable in many ways: first, never before in the history of modern health systems in Europe have we witnessed the spectacular collapse of two of the most regarded national health systems (Arango, 2020; Horowitz, 2020; Remuzzi & Remuzzi, 2020), the Italian and the Spanish; second, the resilience of the Portuguese health system in the early stages of the pandemic was, in many ways, surprising, given decades of underfunding reinforced by more recent austerity policies.

After the great lockdown that took place during the months of March and April of 2020, the epidemic took another twist in the subsequent months. Spain and Italy managed to suppress the transmission to levels of less than 20 cases per 100,000 inhabitants. Instead, the pandemic resurged in Portugal, in the deprived areas on capital suburbs, with reports of outbreaks in factories and among the immigrant population. Combined with inefficient contact tracing, this led to a prolonged plateau of the epidemic curve. Although the health system managed to avoid collapse at the time, the inability to suppress the transmission led to Portugal's exclusion from the safe travel bubbles and to consequent damage in the tourism industry.

This chapter explores the structural similarities and differences between these three countries: on the one hand, in their respective health sectors' capacities and reorganization; and on the other hand, in the different degrees of state capacity to respond to the pressing needs of their populations. In the last great epidemic, the 1918 flu, there was a transparent north-south gradient in the extent to which European countries were hit by the pandemic, with Portugal, Spain, and Italy among those that were hit the hardest (Ansart et al., 2009). How was it this time? To what extent does the impact of COVID-19 reflect resilient societal and institutional vulnerabilities in these countries? And to what extent have national specificities interacted with those shared vulnerabilities, leading to different outcomes?

Public Health

Public Health Strengths and Vulnerabilities

Italy, Spain, and Portugal's health systems are financed through general taxation, are generally free at the point of care, and provide universal health coverage (de Almeida Simões et al., 2017; García-Armesto et al., 2010; Lo Scalzo et al., 2009). The three national health systems emerged in the late 1970s, in Italy as the result of the collapse of the previous social health insurance system and in Spain and Portugal as part of their democratization. They share some standard organizational and performance features that constitute potential strengths and vulnerabilities when facing a pandemic event.

One of the most salient of these features is the impact of a decade of fiscal austerity. During the Great Recession and the Eurozone crisis, the governments of Italy, Spain, and Portugal decreased the budget available for health care (Stuckler et al., 2017), leading to cuts in long-term infrastructure investments and making it even more difficult to deal with the problem of an aging workforce (Karanikolos et al., 2013; Legido-Quigley et al., 2016). Nevertheless, compared with northern European countries, these countries have very efficient healthcare systems (Cylus et al., 2017; Perleth et al., 2001). In other words, the return in terms of population health is very good for every Euro invested. However, in what is only apparently a paradox, efficiency is not an advantage during a pandemic. If all the resources are fully optimized, any significant surges in demand, such as those experienced during early March 2020 in Italy and Spain, this favors a collapse of the health system. Portugal seemed especially vulnerable, as it had the lowest number of intensive care unit beds per inhabitant in Europe and one of the lowest levels of investment in public health services in Europe (Rhodes et al., 2012). In 2015, on average, the countries of the Organization for Economic Co-operation and Development (OECD) allocated 2.8 percent of their total healthcare budget to health promotion and disease prevention. Portugal and Spain devoted below 2 percent to prevention, whereas Italy (2.9 percent) was above the OECD figure (OECD, 2017).

Another feature important to consider is the governance structure of the national health system. Italy and Spain have a rationalized governance model in which regions play a more decisive role in the definition of delivery, managing human resources and budget allocation (García-Armesto et al., 2010; Giovannini & Vampa, 2019; Lo Scalzo et al., 2009). In contrast, Portugal has a highly centralized health system, with a national agency responsible for budget, and regional health administrations play only a minor role in health system organization, serving mainly as links in the transmission chain under the command of the national level. In theory, Spain and Italy's regional organization has many advantages, such as greater flexibility in adjusting delivery to local needs and preferences and an increased room for innovative experiences in delivery models. However, during a pandemic that requires an unprecedented level of coordination and speed, this regionalization can be a disadvantage. A centralized governance model such as the one in Portugal will tend to be faster in implementing the dramatic reorganization that is needed. In sum, efficiency level and governance model are the salient features that directly determine the capacity of the health system to respond to the pandemic.

Public Health Response to the Pandemic

Why did the Italian and the Spanish health systems collapse in the early stages of the pandemic, and not the Portuguese? A quote attributed to Franklin D. Roosevelt illustrates one of the reasons for this difference: *"I think we consider too much the luck of the early bird and not enough the bad luck of the early worm."*[1] Italy and Spain were the first countries experiencing uncontrolled transmission in Europe, when a lot was still unknown about the virus, from clinical management to the appropriate non-pharmacological interventions. As late as February 2020, the ability of this virus to lead to a health system collapse in high-income countries was not yet evident. The influential paper by Neil Ferguson, the British mathematician and epidemiologist, stating that only suppression (lockdowns) measures would prevent health system collapse was published March 16, 2020 (Flaxman et al., 2020; Walker et al., 2020). The knowledge transferred by Italian doctors to the European medical community was an important factor in changing clinical practices and helped health systems elsewhere (Grasselli et al., 2020). In sum, the bad luck of being an early worm should not be understated, as countries that were hit later had the opportunity to benefit from the knowledge transfer from Italy and—partially—Spain. Portugal was one of these countries.

Furthermore, when Italy and Spain had accumulated one hundred cases, their levels of mobility were still close to normal. In contrast, by the time Portugal reached the same number of cases, mobility was already more than 30 percent below average. The first death attributed to the virus in Italy was reported on February 22, 2020. The Italian press was caught by surprise by the quick spreading of the pandemic and did not act in sync with government decisions regarding the best ways to prevent the virus to spread. On March 8, 2020, the day before the northern region of Lombardy, Italy's COVID-19 epicenter, went into lockdown, *Corriere della Sera,* Italy's most widely read newspaper, published an early draft of the government decree ordering inhabitants to stay indoors. This leak provoked a general upheaval, and more than 41,000 people anticipated their traveling plans and moved around the country without any barriers or control. Prime Minister Giuseppe Conte was forced (amidst an outcry from some political parties, echoed by the press) to close the country the next day. Similarly, in Spain, wealthy and middle-class madrileños flight to their second homes—spreading the virus over the weekend before the first state of alarm was declared—had a huge impact in the countryside levels of contagion. In contrast, a social self-lockdown was already happening in Portugal even before governmental actions, as the media were saturated with catastrophic news about Spain and Italy.

The differences in the virulence of the COVID-19 epidemic among Italy, Spain, and Portugal are best shown comparing excess mortality from all causes (Kontis et al., 2020). How many more people are dying than usual for a specific time of the year? Italy and Spain have staggering numbers of 44 percent and 56 percent, respectively, and these numbers hide significant variations between regions (e.g., in Madrid the excess mortality is 157 percent higher than usual). In Portugal, the excess mortality increased by only 11 percent. This put Portugal close to Germany, Austria, and Denmark, countries with some of the best performances on this indicator. Hence, differences between Portugal, on the one hand, and Italy/Spain, on the other, are a tale of two pandemics in three countries. At the earlier stage of the pandemic, Portugal managed to protect the population more efficiently and avoid the detrimental effects of the collapse of the health system in the COVID-19 hotspots.

However, in the months right after the end of the lockdowns, June and July 2020, Spain and Italy achieved a level of suppression of transmission never achieved by Portugal. On the one hand, Italy and Spain had decreases in mobility that were more severe than in Portugal, whereas "deconfinement"—the return to a new baseline close to normal—happened faster in Portugal. On the other hand, Portugal's inability to "crush" the epidemic curve in the same way as Italy or Spain can also be explained by a public health workforce that was not sufficiently large to deal with the pandemic, and by difficulties implementing an effective test-trace-isolate-support system. The epidemic in Portugal maintained a "slow burn" level in the deprived areas in the outskirts of the Lisbon metropolitan region, in a population that was dependent on crowded public transportation, living in substandard housing conditions, and suffering low literacy levels (Instituto Nacional de Estatística, 2020). Although the health system was never in danger of collapsing in Portugal, the "slow burn" and the inability to "crush the curve" damaged the country's image of having excelled in pandemic management.

Finally, all three countries faced common governance problems. Several studies have suggested that national variations in the quality of response to the COVID-19 pandemic across the world seem to be linked to countries' differential *state capacity* (Bosancianu et al., 2020; Liang et al., 2020; Serikbayeva et al., 2020). Whether these broad cross-sectional snapshots will find confirmation as more evidence emerges and the full consequences of the pandemic unfold is yet to be determined. However, a priori, none of these three countries seemed particularly well positioned from this point of view. Although commonly used cross-national and cross-regional indicators have shown signs of improvement in the quality of governance in Portugal and northern Spain (Charron & Lapuente, 2018), government effectiveness in all three countries—particularly Italy—is below the average of the high-income OECD countries (Kaufmann et al., 2010).

How this played out in the ability to mount an effective public health policy response in the three countries can be illustrated in different ways. In Portugal, as concerns about the spread of infection in nursing homes mounted, it was soon "discovered" that there were more illegal such establishments in the country than legal ones, hosting close to 35,000 older or disabled adults and raising enormous challenges for testing, isolation and contact tracing (Penela, 2020). In Italy, although approved in mid-April 2020, the "test, trace, and treat" strategy was still not entirely on the ground by mid-June (Capano, 2020), whereas in Spain, data collection and contact tracing suffered from lack of expert personnel and minimally appropriate information systems (Llaneras, 2020). Although the supply of medical material was problematic in many European countries, such problems were particularly egregious in Spain, as defective equipment continued to be deployed by the Ministry of Health and used by professionals for several weeks despite early suspicions (Ramos, 2020). Characteristically, although the Portuguese government approved a plethora of highly detailed rules about "physical distancing" as the country abandoned confinement in May 2020, the government was ultimately forced to admit that it was "impossible" to enforce some of those rules, particularly those related to safety in public transportation (Santos, 2020). As stated by Saboga-Nunes et al., the decrease of preventive disease measures and proactive health promotion strategies is detrimental to the pandemic control (Saboga-Nunes, 2020).

In sum, deficits in these countries' "state capacity," understood as "their ability to exert control over their populations and territories, and their ability to formulate and implement policy," (Bosancianu et al., 2020) encumbered their public health response to the crisis.

Social Policy

Socioeconomic and Political Vulnerabilities

Portugal, Spain, and Italy also share several features that made their societies and economies particularly vulnerable to the pandemic. The first is a very strong economic dependence from the tourism sector. In 2019 the total contribution of travel and tourism to the gross domestic product (GDP) of Italy, Spain, and Portugal was, respectively, 13 percent, 14 percent, and 17 percent, far above the median of high-income countries and, in all cases, only behind the contribution of financial services and—another hard-hit sector—retail (WTTC, 2020). Second, a comparatively high proportion of the workforce in these countries is composed of low-skilled manual and service sector workers (Afonso & Bulfone, 2019) as well as by temporary employees (22 percent in Spain, 17 percent in Portugal, and 13 percent in Italy, against an EU average of 11 percent) (Eurostat, 2020b). That results in large shares of jobs at risk of destruction by the pandemic and that cannot be performed remotely (OECD, 2020), and, on the other hand, in comparatively high numbers of employees that enjoy limited social protection and job security (Sabat et al., 2020). Finally, the three countries have been fiscally constrained for a considerable time. The consequences of the austerity policies adopted to address the 2010–2013 financial crisis left a resilient mark in the material and human resources available to their public sectors (Petmesidou et al., 2014). Although the worst depths of the crisis had been overcome by the end of 2019, Italy, Portugal, and Spain still had the second, third, and sixth largest public debts in the European Union.

The lockdowns that followed the epidemic combined with these vulnerabilities to generate profoundly negative economic consequences and limit the scope and depth of the possible policy responses. On the one hand, during the second quarter of 2020, our three countries, along with France, experienced the most significant economic contractions among all Eurozone countries (Eurostat, 2020a). On the other hand, although their governments provided cash-based transfers, wage subsidies, and increased benefits to a variety of vulnerable sectors of the population (Gentilini et al., 2020), these measures represented a significantly lower share of each country's GDP than similar policies in less constrained economies. Instead, the lion's share of the fiscal effort in southern Europe was devoted to deferrals of tax and social security contributions (in Italy and Portugal) and credit lines/liquidity guarantees (again in Italy, and to a lesser extent, in Spain)

(Anderson et al., 2020), "a textbook example of what limited fiscal elbow room allows when the rainy days come" (Nicola Rossi, 2020).

Finally, in the same way deficits in state capacity encumbered the health policy response, they also encumbered the social policy response. In all three countries, social and economic support strategies were affected by inefficiencies and delays. In Italy, redundancy funds for employees of small firms and credit guarantees for enterprises suffered from extremely cumbersome procedures, with the result that, by July 2020, such measures had only reached a small number of the potential beneficiaries (Mascio et al., 2020). In Portugal, the implementation of credit lines for enterprises and financial support for self-employed workers was also protracted (Andrada, 2020). Meanwhile, unemployment benefits for temporarily redundant workers failed to reach many thousands of beneficiaries in Spain (Rodriguez, 2020).

Explanation

The Challenges of Multilevel Governance

There is, however, one aspect in which our countries differ significantly. As argued by Dergiades and others, "the greater the strength of government interventions at an early stage, the more effective these are in slowing down or reversing the growth rate of deaths" (Dergiades et al., 2020; see also Petherick et al., 2020). And in this respect, Portugal benefited not only from avoiding being "the early worm" but also from its centralized chain of command, allowing a faster and broader implementation of the lockdown measures.

Portugal is a unitary state, and one of the most centralized in Europe. Although the country is divided into regional health authorities, responsible for implementing national health goals, they respond directly to the Ministry of Health, which concentrates planning, regulation, and management of the national health service. In other words, "[i]n Portugal, most of the health system steering happens at a central level" (OECD, 2015). Centralization facilitated a unified and coordinated emergency response, and it has also helped deliver one of the Portuguese system's significant strengths, a well-developed, coherent, and rich information infrastructure (OECD, 2015).

In contrast, in the other two southern European countries, regions (Italy) and autonomous communities (Spain) enjoy vast competencies in health care, elder care, and economic assistance policies. That has the potential to create coordination problems. In Italy, the regional governments started by completely failing to implement their regional pandemic plans as requested by the Ministry of Health in January. In Lombardy, for example, the regional government leader started by downplaying the threat posed by COVID-19 and criticized lockdown decisions based on their potential economic consequences. That led the national government to dispense consulting with regions when issuing lockdown decisions (Capano, 2020). Still, despite the explicit advice from experts to declare two municipalities in the province of Bergamo as "red zones," both the central and the regional government failed to do so, an omission now is seen as having had catastrophic consequences but that both the central and regional governments, in typical blame-shifting mode, have assigned to each other's inaction. A fundamental misalignment between the central government and regional authorities seems to have contributed to "severely undermine the management of the crisis, increase confusion, and create an image of chaos outside" (Ruiu, 2020).

In Spain, the initial coordination problems between the seventeen autonomous communities and the central government around the closing of schools appeared to be solved with the state of emergency decree's approval on March 14, 2020 (Jiménez, 2020). However, such problems were soon to make their comeback. By late March 2020, at the height of the rise in new cases, the much-needed reallocation of resources and personnel between regions struck very differently by the pandemic was "a bureaucratic tangle in which, for the moment, no community wants to get bogged down" (Sevillano & Linde, 2020). Different protocols and resources for contact tracing, isolation of infected medical professionals, and collection and sharing of data about new cases and fatalities contributed to a high asymmetry of information and performance between communities (Fresno, 2020). None of this is particularly new: the lack of coordination between health services of the different communities has long been signaled as a pending issue in Spain's healthcare reforms (Sánchez Fierro, 2016), which the pandemic only served to bring to fore with particular intensity (Molina et al., 2020).

Facets of Public Response

How did the publics of these countries respond to the pandemic crisis and the measures adopted to face it? A look at survey data allows us to trace a few similarities and differences among Italy, Portugal, and Spain.

Approval of the government's management of the pandemic seems to show different patterns in the three countries. In Portugal, a government whose popularity had changed little since the October 2019 elections experienced a small decisive burst after the pandemic. Studies conducted in both March and May 2020 showed that more than 70 percent of respondents trusted the government's and national health authority's response to the pandemic, an attitude only weakly related to partisanship or ideology (Magalhães et al., 2020). The governing party experienced a five-point increase in voting intention from February until May 2020, which remained stable until early August ("Europe Elects: Portugal," 2020). In Italy, the government started facing the crisis in a more disadvantaged position, with an approval rate below 40 percent and a significant gap in evaluations by partisans of the M5S and Partito Democratico in government and by those of the opposition parties. Since then, however, the government appears to have benefitted from a "rally 'round the flag" effect (Segatti, 2020) that has dramatically neutralized partisan differences in government evaluations. The primary victim seems to be Lega Nord, which experienced a significant drop in the polls in one of hardest hit regions by the crisis in Italy. Finally, in Spain, no "rally 'round the flag" effect seems to have existed. The approval level of the government's response to the crisis always stayed below Portuguese and Italian levels ("COVID-29: Government Handling and Confidence in Health Authorities," 2020), and voting intentions for the Spanish Socialist Party (PSOE) and for United We Can (Unidas Podemos), the main parties in government, have remained mostly stable. The perception of government competence in dealing with the pandemic and how that translates to government approval seem to be very heterogeneous in these three countries. However, the unfolding public health and economic situation in all three countries could change this picture quickly. For example, in a similar poll conducted in September 2020, confidence in the Portuguese government's public response to the pandemic had already dropped almost twenty points in relation to May.

A second important dimension concerns the adoption of personal measures to avoid contagion. Italians and Spaniards led European countries (on which we have data) in the use of masks. By late March 2020, 70 percent in Italy, 42 percent in Spain, and 27 percent in Portugal reported the use masks in public places, above countries such as France, Germany, and, especially, the United Kingdom and Scandinavian countries. By May 2020, these percentages had increased to much higher levels, around 80 percent, and have remained mostly stable ever since. Similar patterns can be found in the self-reported avoidance of crowded public spaces, increased personal hygiene, and avoidance of physical proximity ("COVID-29: Government Handling and Confidence in Health Authorities," 2020). In other words, with a lag that approximately fits the staggered severity of the pandemic in each country, the self-reported adoption of personal protective measures seems generalized in the south by July 2020 to a majority of citizens. However, a false sense of safety, economic necessity, and deeply ingrained patterns of sociability seem to have conspired, at least for a minority of citizens, to reverse some of previous behaviors. In Spain, for example, the resurgence of cases in August was attributed to a return to close interpersonal contacts, partying, and social gatherings (Güell, 2020).

A third relevant dimension concerns citizens' support for the government's measures to contain the pandemic. By April 2020, when the epidemic situation remained most challenging, and all three countries had their most stringent measures in place, one distinguishing feature of Southern European countries was more robust support of their populations for such restrictive measures than that found among Northern European countries ("COVID-29: Government Handling and Confidence in Health Authorities," 2020). That could correspond to a worse situation on the ground: by mid-April, Spain and Italy were experiencing, respectively, twelve and eight new COVID-19-related daily casualties per million inhabitants. However, Portugal's situation was much less dramatic, with about three new daily casualties per million, numbers that were not very different from those in countries that had less stringent policies at the time, such as Germany or Denmark. This suggests—and will need to be more systematically tested—that cross-national differences in popular support for stringent measures seem to be more directly related to what government policies happen to be at the moment than with the epidemiological situation on the ground. Congruently with this notion, as both Spain and Italy started adopting measures reversing some aspects of deconfinement in July 2020, support for enforced quarantines, which had been dwindling since April 2020, increased again ("COVID-29: Government Handling and Confidence in Health Authorities," 2020).

Another (and potentially darker) aspect of this endorsement of government policies is visible in the public support for measures that might impinge more grievously on privacy and personal freedoms. For example, by April 2020, a study had already found that the most polarizing issue in Europe was the use of mobile data for tracking cases and their contacts, with important shares of the population in Denmark, Netherlands, and Germany opposing such measures. Such use, however, found greater acceptance in Italy or Portugal (Sabat et al., 2020). Similarly, a panel study showed that, after the outbreak, Spaniards became more willing to support "strong leaders," give up individual freedoms, and endorse technocratic governance (Amat et al., 2020). However, as we have discussed previously in the case of Spain, although elements of political culture—such as the comparatively lower value placed on individual freedom and autonomy in southern than in northern Europe (Welzel, 2013)—may contribute to produce a more passive acceptance of government-dictated restrictions, that may not be enough to curtail deeply ingrained patterns of sociability.

Political Polarization

The problems faced by Italy and Spain have been compounded by the more intense political rivalry and polarization that can be observed in those two countries when compared to Portugal. In the former, Matteo Salvini, the leader of the populist Lega Nord, the party controlling two of the most affected regions—Lombardy and Veneto—but out of the coalition supporting the national government since September 2019, was intensely critical of the government's response from the start, beginning by downplaying the importance of the pandemic, then criticizing the slow response, and later the delay in ending the lockdown. One study suggests that this overt public dissent affected compliance with lockdown orders: reductions in mobility—as captured through geolocation data—in response to physical distancing orders were less sharp in areas with higher vote shares for Lega Nord, whereas they were sharper in areas with higher shares of votes for the largest party in government, MS5 (Barbieri & Bonini, 2020). The same effect was seen in the United States (Adolph et al., 2020).

In Spain, a background of rising political acrimony, affective polarization, and distance between the political parties on the country's crucial ideological issue—the territorial cleavage (Alfonso, 2020)—has also played out in the management of the COVID-19 crisis. Following a brief period of respite at the height of the pandemic, disputes about the extension of lockdowns, struggles between the government and nationalist parties around the centralization of health policy, blame-shifting between the government and opposition-controlled municipalities, and even the refusal of one the major parties—the far-right Vox—to discuss future COVID-19-related measures with the government (Gallardo, 2020) have been observed. Sánchez, Spain's prime minister, ultimately evoked Portugal's case and the leader of its opposition party, the PSD, as an example of cooperation that was missing in Spain. However, the absence of a territorial cleavage in Portugal, the much smaller political weight of the populist far-right, and a horizon of likely governmental stability and distant elections were background conditions favoring a more robust political consensus that Spain could not replicate.

Tourism and the "Race to the Bottom"

One of the pandemic's impressive political dimensions is the impact of the measures imposed to travelers to and from different European countries, whereby some nations imposed quarantines—not fully endorsed by the scientific community—to their own citizens if they had traveled from nations deemed of high risk. The central political aspect that emerges is southern European countries' willingness to take more risks of admitting citizens from other countries with worse incidence indicators. That aspect was very salient for Italy, Spain, and Portugal, where no travel restrictions were imposed for countries such as the United Kingdom. That shows that the economic relevance of keeping the tourism economy afloat was more important than the risk of importation of COVID-19 cases. Spain was in the first UK safe-travel list published on July 3, 2020; it was later removed on July 25, 2020, at the time with a lower incidence of COVID-19 than the United Kingdom. Portugal was only added to the list on August 22. The exclusion from the UK safe-travel list prompted a ferocious political response at the highest level, labeling this exclusion unfair and arbitrary. The "Race to the bottom" term was used to describe the competition between countries for lower taxes to attack foreign capital (Plümper et al., 2009). A similar effect seems to be happening in the competition for tourism in southern European countries.

Conclusions

This chapter explores the similarities and differences between Portugal, Spain, and Italy, and how they played out in the response to public health and social policy responses to the pandemic. Italy, Spain, and Portugal shared similar vulnerabilities before the pandemic started: a decade of austerity, limited fiscal room to implement new social policies, and an employment sector poorly prepared for working from home and vulnerable to unemployment resulting from lockdowns. However, Italy and Spain faced an additional challenge: a multilevel government structure, where taking and implementing political decisions takes more time and is more complicated. The inability to coordinate a fast response in the early days of the pandemic seems to have played a role in the initial collapse of the health system in Italy and Spain and in the higher levels of excess all-cause mortality. Higher levels of political polarization in Spain and Italy and the weight of the populist far-right were also factors that have surely not contributed to a more effective political response.

In contrast, Portugal benefited not only from the early warning from Spain and Italy, but also from a faster, more coordinated, and politically consensual response. The Portuguese health system avoided collapse, and mortality was kept at comparatively lower levels in the early stages of the pandemic. However, after the first lockdown, and as restrictions eased, this relative advantage of Portugal began to dissipate. Deficits in state capacity and economic pressures created conditions that prevented the country from maintaining the previous levels of suppression of the transmission, leading to a prolonged plateau of the epidemic curve. As the "second wave" unfolded in the last quarter of 2020, the structural similarities between the three countries exerted their influence, leading to much less dissimilar outcomes than those that could be observed at the earliest stages of the pandemic.

Note

1. Letter from FDR to Judge Henry M. Heymann, December 2, 1919.

References

Adolph, C., Amano, K., Bang-Jensen, B., Fullman, N., & Wilkerson, J. (2020). Pandemic politics: Timing state-level social distancing responses to COVID-19. *Journal of Health Politics, Policy and Law*. https://doi.org/10.1215/03616878-8802162

Afonso, A., & Bulfone, F. (2019). Electoral coalitions and policy reversals in Portugal and Italy in the aftermath of the eurozone crisis. *South European Society and Politics*, 24(2), 233–257.

Alfonso, S. L. (2020). La brecha ideológica. *Diario.es-Piedras de Papel*. https://www.eldiario.es/piedrasdepapel/brecha-ideologica_132_1003509.html

Amat, F., Arenas, A., Falcó-Gimeno. A., & Muñoz, J. (2020). Pandemics meet democracy. Experimental evidence from the COVID-19 crisis in Spain. *SocArXiv*. https://doi.org/10.31235/osf.io/dkusw

Anderson, J., Bergamini, E., Brekelmans, S., Cameron, A., Zsolt, D., & Jiménez, M. D. (2020, April 25). *The fiscal response to the economic fallout from the coronavirus*. Bruegel Datasets. https://www.bruegel.org/publications/datasets/covid-national-dataset

Andrada, V. (2020, May 11). *Forum para a Competitividade considera atrasos nos apoios às empresas "inaceitáveis."* Expresso. https://expresso.pt/economia/2020-05-11-Forum-para-a-Competitividade-considera-atrasos-nos-apoios-as-empresas-inaceitaveis

Ansart, S., Pelat, C., Boelle, P. Y., Carrat, F., Flahault, A., & Valleron, A. J. (2009). Mortality burden of the 1918–1919 influenza pandemic in Europe. *Influenza and Other Respiratory Viruses*, 3(3), 99–106.

Arango, C. (2020). Lessons learned from the coronavirus health crisis in Madrid, Spain: How COVID-19 has changed our lives in the last 2 weeks. *Biological Psychiatry*, 88(7), e33–e34.

Barbieri, P., & Bonini, B. (2020). *Populism and political (mis-) belief effect on individual adherence to lockdown during the COVID-19 pandemic in Italy.* https://ssrn.com/abstract=3640324 or http://dx.doi.org/10.2139/ssrn.3640324

Bosancianu, C. M., Dionne, K. Y., Hilbig, H., Humphreys, M., Sampada, K., Lieber, K. Y., & Scacco, A. (2020). Political and social correlates of Covid-19 mortality. *SocArXiv.* https://doi.org/10.31235/osf.io/ub3zd

Capano, G. (2020). Policy design and state capacity in the COVID-19 emergency in Italy: If you are not prepared for the (un) expected, you can be only what you already are. *Policy and Society, 39*(3), 326–344.

Charron, N., & Lapuente, V. (2018). Quality of government in EU regions: Spatial and temporal patterns. *QoG Working Paper Series, 1*(1).

COVID-19: Government handling and confidence in health authorities. (2020). https://today.yougov.com/topics/international/articles-reports/2020/03/17/perception-government-handling-covid-19

Cylus, J., Papanicolas, I., & Smith, P. C. (2017). *How to make sense of health system efficiency comparisons?,* World Health Organization, Regional Office for Europe Copenhagen. https://www.euro.who.int/__data/assets/pdf_file/0005/362912/policy-brief-27-eng.pdf

de Almeida Simões, J., Augusto, G. F., Fronteira, I., & Hernández-Quevedo, C. (2017). Portugal. *Health Systems in Transition, 19*(2), 1–184.

Dergiades, T., Milas, C., & Panagiotidis, T. (2020). *Effectiveness of government policies in response to the COVID-19 outbreak.* https://ssrn.com/abstract=3602004

Europe elects: Portugal. (2020). https://europeelects.eu/portugal/

Eurostat. (2020a). *Preliminary flash estimate for the second quarter of 2020.* Retrieved August 24, 2020, from https://ec.europa.eu/eurostat/en/web/products-press-releases/-/2-31072020-BP

Eurostat. (2020b). *Temporary employees as percentage of the total number of employees.* Retrieved August 24, 2020, from https://ec.europa.eu/eurostat/web/products-datasets/-/tesem110

Flaxman, S., Mishra, S., Gandy, A., Unwin, H. J. T., Mellan, T. A., Coupland, H., Whittaker, C., Zhu, H., Berah, T., & Eaton, J. W. (2020). Estimating the effects of non-pharmaceutical interventions on COVID-19 in Europe. *Nature, 584*, 257–261.

Fresno, D. (2020, March 13). La descoordinación entre comunidades autónomas agrava la crisis del coronavirus. *VozPopuli.* https://www.vozpopuli.com/sanidad/descoordinacion-comunidades-autonomas-agrava-coronavirus_0_1336367804.html

Fuertes, F. D., Caballero, M. I., Monzón, S., Jiménez, P., Varona, S., Cuesta, I., Zaballos, Á., Thomson, M. M., Jiménez, M., & Pérez, J. G. (2020). Phylodynamics of SARS-CoV-2 transmission in Spain. *bioRxiv.* https://doi.org/10.1101/2020.04.20.050039

Gallardo, C. (2020, April 9). *Spain's coronavirus truce is over.* Politico EU. https://www.politico.eu/article/spain-coronavirus-truce-is-over/

García-Armesto, S., Abadía-Taira, M., Durán, A., Hernández-Quevedo, C., & Bernal-Delgado, E. (2010). Spain: Health system review. *Health Systems in Transition,* 12(4):1–295.

Gentilini, U. et al. (2020). *Social protection and jobs responses to COVID-19. A real-time review of country measures.* Washington, DC: World Bank. https://documents.worldbank.org/en/publication/documents-reports/documentdetail/295321600473897712/social-protection-and-jobs-responses-to-covid-19-a-real-time-review-of-country-measures-september-18-2020

Giovannini, A. & Vampa, D. (2019). Towards a new era of regionalism in Italy? A comparative perspective on autonomy referendums. *Territory, Politics, Governance, 8*(4), 579–597.

Gomes, M. (2020, March 12). *Coronavírus: Decisão de rejeitar fecho das escolas foi consensual e votada por unanimidade* [Decision to reject school closing was consensual and voted by unanimity]. Público. https://www.publico.pt/2020/03/12/politica/noticia/coronavirus-decisao-rejeitar-fecho-escolas-consensual-votada-unanimidade-1907428

Grasselli, G., Pesenti, A., & Cecconi, M. (2020). Critical care utilization for the COVID-19 outbreak in Lombardy, Italy: Early experience and forecast during an emergency response. *Journal of the American Medical Association, 323*(16), 1545–1546.

Güell, O. (2020, August 23). El virus golpea a España por segunda vez [The virus strikes Spain for the second time]. *El País.* https://elpais.com/sociedad/2020-08-22/expertos-coronavirus.html

Horowitz, J. (2020, March 17). Italy's health care system groans under coronavirus—a warning to the world. *The New York Times.* https://www.nytimes.com/2020/03/12/world/europe/12italy-coronavirus-health-care.html

Instituto Nacional de Estatística. (2020). *COVID-19 na Area Metropolitana de Lisboa* [COVID-19 in the Metropolitan Area of Lisbon]. https://www.ine.pt/xportal/xmain?xpid=INE&xpgid=ine_destaques&DESTAQUESdest_boui=450739771&DESTAQUEStema=00&DESTAQUESmodo=2

Jiménez, F. (2020, April). *Informe crisis covid19 España para Fondation Robert Schuman* [Report about the COVID-10 crisis in Spain for the Robery Schuman Foundation]. https://www.researchgate.net/publication/340719968_Informe_crisis_covid19_Espana_para_Fondation_Robert_Schuman_12_abril_20

Karanikolos, M., Mladovsky, P., Cylus, J., Thomson, S., Basu, S., Stuckler, D., Mackenbach, J. P., & McKee, M. (2013). Financial crisis, austerity, and health in Europe. *The Lancet, 381*(9874), 1323–1331.

Kaufmann, D., Kraay, A., & Mastruzzi, M. (2010). *The worldwide governance indicators: Methodology and analytical issues.* World Bank Policy Research Working Paper No. 5430. The World Bank.

Kontis, V., Bennett, J. E., Rashid, T. Parks, R. M., Pearson-Stuttard, J., Guillot, M., Asaria, P., Zhou, B., Battaglini, M., Corsetti, G., McKee, M., Di Cesare, M., Mathers, C. D., & Ezzati, M. (2020). Magnitude, demographics and dynamics of the impact of the first phase of the Covid-19 pandemic on all-cause mortality in 17 industrialised countries. *Nature Medicine, 26,* 1919–1928.

Legido-Quigley, H., Karanikolos, M., Hernandez-Plaza, S., de Freitas, C., Bernardo, L., Padilla, B., Machado, R. S., Diaz-Ordaz, K. Stuckler, D., & McKee, M. (2016). Effects of the financial crisis and Troika austerity measures on health and health care access in Portugal. *Health Policy, 120*(7), 833–839.

Liang, L.-L., Tseng, C.-H., Ho, H. H., & Wu, C.-Y. (2020). Covid-19 mortality is negatively associated with test number and government effectiveness. *Scientific Reports, 10*(1), 1–7.

Livingston, E., & Bucher, K. (2020). Coronavirus disease 2019 (COVID-19) in Italy. *Journal of the American Medical Association, 323*(14), 1335.

Llaneras, K. (2020, June 21). Los problemas de usar datos del siglo pasado para una pandemia del siglo XXI. *El País.* https://elpais.com/sociedad/crisis-del-coronavirus/2020

-06-20/los-problemas-de-usar-datos-del-siglo-pasado-para-una-pandemia-del-siglo-xxi.html
Lo Scalzo, A., Donatini, A., Orzella, L., Cicchetti, A., Profili, S., & Maresso, A. (2009). Italy: Health system review. *Health Systems in Transition, 11*(6), 1–216.
Magalhães, P. C., Lobo, M. C., Pereira, J. S., Ramos, A., Silva, P. A, & Vicente, P. (2020). *Sondagem Maio 2020 Covid-19* [COVID-19 Poll, May 2020]. Retrieved June 1, 2020, from https://sondagens-ics-ul.iscte-iul.pt/2020/05/13/sondagem-maio-2020-para-sic-expresso-especial-covid-19/
Mascio, F. D., Natalini, A., & Cacciatore, F. (2020). Public administration and creeping crises: Insights from COVID-19 pandemic in Italy. *The American Review of Public Administration, 50* (6–7), 621–627.
Molina, I., Otero-Iglesias, M., & Martínez, J. P. (2020). *Has Spain's management of COVID19 been a failure? Errors, lessons and recommendations.* (Real Instituto Elcano Working Paper 16/2020). http://www.realinstitutoelcano.org/wps/wcm/connect/a632f4bb-00aa-480a-82fd-d2aee4b44cca/WP-16-2020-Otero-Molina-Martinez-Has-Spains-management-of-COVID-19-been-a-failure.pdf?MOD=AJPERES&CACHEID=a632f4bb-00aa-480a-82fd-d2aee4b44cca
Nicola Rossi, A. M. (2020). Italy and COVID-19: Winning the war, losing the peace? *Economic Affairs, 40*(2), 148–154.
OECD. (2015). *OECD Reviews of health care quality: Portugal 2015-raising standards.* OECD Publishing. http://dx.doi.org/10.1787/9789264225985-en
OECD. (2017). *A system of health accounts 2011: Revised Edition.* OECD Publishing. https://dx.doi.org/10.1787/9789264270985-en
OECD. (2020). *The territorial impact of COVID-19: Managing the crisis across levels of government.* OECD Publishing. http://www.oecd.org/coronavirus/policy-responses/the-territorial-impact-of-covid-19-managing-the-crisis-across-levels-of-government-d3e314e1/
Peixoto, V. R., Mexia, R., de Sousa Santos, N., Carvalho, C., & Abrantes, A. (2020). Da tuberculose ao COVID-19: Legitimidade jurídico—constitucional do isolamento/tratamento compulsivo for doenças contagiosas [Portugal from tuberculosis to COVID-19: Legal and constitutional framework regarding compulsory isolation/treatment]. *Acta Médica Portuguesa, 33*(4), 225–228.
Pcnela, R. (2020, April 22). Milhares de lares ilegais colocam 35 mil idosos em risco, diz estudo de associação [Thousands of illegal homes place 35 thousand elderly people at risk, association study says]. *Observador.* https://observador.pt/2020/04/22/milhares-de-lares-ilegais-colocam-35-mil-idosos-em-risco-diz-estudo-de-associacao/
Perleth, M., Jakubowski, E., & Busse, R. (2001). What is "best practice" in health care? State of the art and perspectives in improving the effectiveness and efficiency of the European health care systems. *Health Policy, 56*(3), 235–50.
Petherick, A., Kira, B., Hale, T., Phillips, T., Webster, S., Cameron-Blake, E., Hallas, L., Majumdar, S., Tatlow, H., Boby, T., & Angrist, N. (2020). *Variation in government responses to COVID-19.* (Blavatnik School of Government Working Paper 31). https://www.bsg.ox.ac.uk/research/publications/variation-government-responses-covid-19
Petmesidou, M., Pavolini, E., & Guillén, A. M. (2014). South European healthcare systems under harsh austerity: a progress–regression mix? *South European Society and Politics, 19*(3), 331–352.

Plümper, T., Troeger, V. E., & Winner, H. (2009). Why is there no race to the bottom in capital taxation? *International Studies Quarterly, 53*(3), 761–786.

Ramos, F. (2020, May 5). Sanidad, obligada a retirar 1 millón de mascarillas defectuosas que se utilizaban desde hace un mês [Health ministry forced to withdraw 1 million deffective masks that have been used already for a month]. *Diario de Castilla y Leon.* https://diariodecastillayleon.elmundo.es/articulo/castilla-y-leon/sanidad-obligada-retirar-1-millon-mascarillas-defectuosas-utilizaban-hace-mes/20200509203643009115.html

Remuzzi, A., & Remuzzi, G. (2020). COVID-19 and Italy: what next? *Lancet, 395*(10231): 1225–1228.

Rhodes, A., Ferdinande, P., Flaatten, H., Guidet, B., Metnitz, P. G., & Moreno, R. P. (2012). The variability of critical care bed numbers in Europe. *Intensive Care Medicine 38*(10), 1647–1653.

Rodriguez, D. (2020, July 27). Retrasos e impagos: los "olvidados" de los ERTE [Delays and non-payments: the "forgotten" of the ERTE]. *Público.es.* https://www.publico.es/sociedad/coronavirus-retrasos-e-impagos-olvidados-erte.html

Ruiu, M. L. (2020). Mismanagement of Covid-19: Lessons learned from Italy. *Journal of Risk Research, 23*(7-8), 1007–1020.

Sabat, I., Neuman-Böhme, S., Varghese, N. E., Barros, P. P., Brouwer, W., van Exel, J., Schreyögg, J., & Stargardt, T. (2020). United but divided: Policy responses and people's perceptions in the EU during the COVID-19 outbreak. *Health Policy, 124*(9), 909–918.

Saboga-Nunes, L., Levin-Zamir, D., Bittlingmayer, U., Contu, P., Pinheiro, P., & Ivassenko, V. (2020). A health promotion focus on COVID-19: Keep the Trojan horse out of our health systems. *EUPHA-HP, IUHPE, UNESCO Chair Global Health & Education.* https://eupha.org/repository/sections/hp/A_Health_Promotion_Focus_on_COVID-19_with_S.pdf

Sánchez Fierro, J., & Isaías Rodríguez, J. (2016). Health care in Europe and Spain: Unresolved issues. *Special Report, Llorente & Cuenca.* https://ideas.llorenteycuenca.com/wp-content/uploads/sites/5/2016/04/160419_DI_report_health_ENG.pdf

Santos, N. F. (2020, July 17). *Governo admite transporte público sem limites de lotação* [Goverment admits public transportation without capacity limits]. Público. https://www.publico.pt/2020/07/17/economia/noticia/governo-admite-transporte-publico-limites-lotacao-1924806

Segatti, P. (2020, June 9). La popolarità del governo Conte [The popularity of the Conte cabinet]. *La Rivista Il Mulino.* https://www.rivistailmulino.it/news/newsitem/index/Item/News:NEWS_ITEM:5262

Serikbayeva, B., Abdulla, K., & Oskenbayev, Y. (2020). *State capacity in responding to COVID-19.* (MPRA Paper No. 101511). https://mpra.ub.uni-muenchen.de/101511/1/MPRA_paper_101511.pdf

Sevillano, E. G., & Linde, P. (2020, March 30). España libra 17 batallas dispares contra el coronavirus [Spain fights 17 different battels against the coronavírus]. *El País.* https://elpais.com/sociedad/2020-03-30/espana-libra-17-batallas-dispares-contra-el-coronavirus.html

Stuckler, D., Reeves, A., Loopstra, R., Karanikolos, M. & McKee, M. (2017). Austerity and health: The impact in the UK and Europe. *European Journal of Public Health, 27*(suppl_4), 18–21.

Walker, P., Whittaker, C., Watson, O., Baguelin, M., Ainslie, K., Bhatia, S., Bhatt, S., Boonyasiri, A., Boyd, O., & Cattarino, L. (2020). *Report 12: The global impact of COVID-19 and strategies for mitigation and suppression.* Imperial College London. https://www.imperial.ac.uk/mrc-global-infectious-disease-analysis/covid-19/report-12-global-impact-covid-19/

Welzel, C. (2013). *Freedom rising. Human empowerment and the quest for emancipation.* Cambridge: Cambridge University Press.

World Travel Tourism Council. (2020). *Economic impact reports.* https://wttc.org/Research/Economic-Impact.

21 GREECE AT THE TIME OF COVID-19

Caught between Scylla and Charybdis

Elena Petelos, Dimitra Lingri, and Christos Lionis

> For on one side lay Scylla and on the other divine Charybdis terribly sucked down the salt water of the sea. Verily whenever she belched it forth, like a cauldron on a great fire she would seethe and bubble in utter turmoil, and high over head the spray would fall on the tops of both the cliffs.
>
> —ODYSSEY 12.235–240

On February 26, 2020, two weeks before the World Health Organization (WHO) declared the severe acute respiratory coronavirus-2 (SARS-CoV-2) pandemic, the Ministry of Health announced the first confirmed case of COVID-19 in Greece, a woman who had just arrived from neighboring Italy. Italy and many other European countries had already had their first cases three to four weeks earlier. In Greece, not having similar levels of winter tourism, nor business travel, a simple temperature screening only for passengers arriving from China had been deemed an adequate measure. Within hours of the announcement, all leave of absence was revoked for administrative personnel at the Ministry of Health and for medical and scientific personnel across the country (Ministry of Health, 2020).

The range of containment and mitigation policies adopted in Greece ought to be examined within the broader context in which these policies were shaped and implemented. The preceding financial crisis brought about a series of specific consecutive Memoranda of Understanding (MoUs) (including the "Supplemental Memorandum of Understanding: Greece," 2019). The MoUs were agreed upon by the Greek government and the European Troika (i.e., the International Monetary Fund, European Central Bank, and European Commission) and set out conditions and prescribed reform measures. Financial assistance depended on their implementation, according to the principle of conditionality (Kivotidis, 2018). Although the aim was reform, the significant budgetary restrictions compromised implementation and resulted in reduced capacity across all levels of care (Economou et al., 2017).

The case of Greece carries high relevance for Balkan and Southern European countries and beyond. Disconnectedness between public health bodies and institutions, as well as the organization of care delivery across the levels of health and social care are issues affecting many settings. The first months of the pandemic, given the level of uncertainty, there were no clear guidelines in terms of referral protocols, risk communication, and mechanisms for tackling misinformation, a situation prompting fear and apprehension among patients and citizens across Europe and, indeed, the world.

In Greece, the previous decade had been one of depleted resources, restricted capacity, and inefficient resource allocation. Despite the fragmented efforts of different governments, there is still no comprehensive primary health care (PHC) system. The rise in life expectancy and the low fertility rates have resulted in a population with more than 22 percent of the people being aged 65 years or over. In 2017 life expectancy at the age of 65 was 20.1 years (i.e., slightly higher than that of other European Union [EU] countries). However, Greek people could expect to live only 40 percent (vs. 50 percent in the EU) of these years without disability (Cassini et al., 2019; "State of Health in the EU: The Country Health Profile Series," 2019). Furthermore, underlying social disparities remain largely unresolved, both from a legal and a social standpoint.

Greece has a low score on the Global Health Security Index (Global Health Security Index, 2019), the first comprehensive assessment benchmarking health security across 196 countries, that is, the States Parties to the International Health Regulations (IHR) (WHO, 2014). It has one of the lowest scores in the national planning for zoonotic diseases/pathogens, which is critical for prevention and preparedness. Additionally, it does not have a public workforce strategy with mechanisms or indicators to identify gaps. Results from a previously conducted, rudimentary from a global health perspective, gap analysis were incorporated into the National Strategy on Health 2014–2020, but without any quantifiable elements.

The relevance of the EU is high in terms of the overall pandemic impact. Reinforcing joint procurement and cooperation beyond disease management and control have been considered, including monetary, budgetary, and macroeconomic measures, including the tourism and aviation industries. The Greek government proposed various EU-level actions, including two specific measures, an initiative on intellectual property rights, including diagnostics and therapeutics, and vaccines, in an effort to ensure accessibility and affordability, and, jointly with several other EU countries, the "Coronabond" to offset the damage to the economy. The exchanges ensuing highlight this crisis was rather different to the 2012 crisis when Greece and Germany were at opposing ends of which policies ought to be followed. With some of the biggest economies, now, requesting help, the European institutions were much more willing to extend support, including a different kind of response from the European Central Bank (ECB) (Johnson, 2020).

EU-wide cross-sectoral collaboration for certain infectious diseases (zoonotic diseases) has been integrated through EU policies (e.g., One Health approach) and implemented through the European Centre for Disease Control (ECDC). However, EU public health competences are limited. Instruments such as the Decision on Serious Cross-border Healthcare, Early Warning and Response System (EWRS) ("Decision No 1082/2013/EU of the European Parliament and of the Council," 2013; Moore & Furberg, 2014) allow for recommendations regarding cross-border measures by the Health Security Committee (HSC), and even joint procurement (European Union, 2013; Greer & de Ruijter, 2020). Key recommendations, such as those issued by the ECDC on testing and tracing (ECDC, 2020), are not binding for Member-States, thus leading to highly divergent responses in border control. Health information from heterogeneous sources prompts ambiguity, leaving at worst a margin to political rather than expert interpretations. Health information has been of inconsistent quality and detail level, for example, not all countries shared data on the number of cases by age and sex (Renda & Castro, 2020). Furthermore, the EU's Global Health Strategy (GHS) lacks a coherent frame beyond the IHR to align responsibility and accountability among the WHO, the EU, and Member-States. Efforts for an up-to-date GHS (Steurs et al., 2017) and urgent calls for a robust and cohesive strategy remained largely unaddressed (Speakman et al., 2017). The importance of such measures and a cohesive strategy is magnified when it comes to countries with limited preparedness expertise, capacity, and resourcing. This becomes even more critical when these countries are at the borders of Europe and have high geopolitical importance, with potentially conflicting state, EU, and global priorities, and the strong emergence of strong biogeopolitical dynamics at the Southeastern EU borderland of Greece and Turkey (Jauhiainen, 2020).

In Greece, measures were mainly introduced through legislative acts handled as emergency procedures. The Emergency Act instrument is used in cases of threats to national sovereignty and security from external or internal enemies of the state. According to the Constitution of the Hellenic Republic (Art. 44 par. 1) emergency acts can be introduced as an Act of Legislative Content (ALC) or by declaration of a state of siege (Art. 48 par. 1 and 5, The Constitution of Greece, 2008). ALCs are issued in case of unpredictable need by the President of the Republic, upon proposal by the Cabinet, but without prior suspension of human rights, contrary to the acts issued following the declaration of a state of siege. Critically, ALCs are administrative acts issued only for a limited period of time, unless submitted to and ratified by the Parliament within a specific period of time. According to the jurisprudence of the Council of the State, the exceptional nature of the particular circumstances that led to the publication of an ALC is not subject to judicial review (Symvoulion Epikrateias, 1987, 1989, 2002, 2003, 2015b), contrary to its content, which is, theoretically, subject to judicial control (Gerapetritis, 2012); such was recently the case of the Austrian COVID-19 legislation, which was considered to be partially illegal according to the jurisprudence (Verfassungsgerichtshof, 2020).

COVID-19 ALCs introduced structural dispositions but also substantial human rights' limitations to safeguard public health, which is considered an element of public interest. According to the Hellenic Constitution, but also to the European Convention on Human Rights (ECHR), human rights limitations should be prescribed by law, be of legitimate aim and proportionate, a necessary condition in a democratic society according to the ECHR (Renucci, 2005). Seven ALCs were introduced into national legal order, ratified in due course by the Parliament, thus, acquiring timeless retrospective force. By acquiring a rather permanent character, the totality of the measures introduced through delegated acts (ministerial decisions) rendered them susceptible to common judicial review.

Health Policy Response

Since 2008, Greece has been severely affected by the financial crisis and the ensuing austerity measures. This protracted effect had direct impact on the state-funded National Healthcare System (NHS). Despite the focus on reform and PHC provision with two legislative bills, implementation was hindered by contextual factors and political agendas. The reform was protracted, with multiple governments involved in its negotiation and implementation. One government negotiated its initial funding (New Democracy, the liberal-conservative party), and another decided on how it was to be executed in terms of the creation of the PHC network (SYRIZA, the left-wing party ruling from 2015 to 2019). A third government, previously being the opposition, which had strongly opposed most of the steps taken between 2015 and 2019, came to power less than a year before the pandemic (New Democracy came into power in June 2019). It was this government that was called to continue a reform implementation. A direct country-specific recommendation regarding PHC, with explicit mention of the need to establish an adequate number of functional PHC units (the new institution of PHC unit called Topiki Monada Ygias [TOMY] in Greek, which was a key aspect of the introduced reform), and the need for investment to enhance access to these newly created TOMYs, as well as inclusive, affordable and high-quality social services, was included in the European Semester of June 2019 (European Commission, 2019a). The Enhanced Surveillance Report (ESR) of June 2019 (Commission Economic & Affairs European Economy Institutional Papers, 2019) coincided with the time of the national election and the change of government to the New Democracy party. The ESR, also, noted the reform was proceeding at a slow pace and with marked disparities (i.e., less than one-fifth of the population was registered in the new PHC system) with unresolved issues regarding recruiting practitioners. In view of the flawed efforts, besmirched by inconsistency and lack of sustainable financing, and with the Eurogroup commitment to open 240 TOMYs by mid-2020, one wonders how, pandemic excluded, this milestone would have ever been reached.

Given this backdrop, the government moved with exceptional speed. Procedures for staff recruitment were initiated on the very day of the first confirmed case. All scheduled leaves of absence were canceled across all levels of care, from the National Center for Emergency Care, to urban tertiary care institutions, and across regional and local settings. At the beginning of March 2020, approximately 5000 temporary vacancies (medical, nursing, and supporting personnel) were created. Within a month, almost 50 percent of these vacancies were filled. In terms of incentives, both health and civil protection workers received a special bonus, extensively reported in the press. This, however, generated mixed reactions, as the workers eligible to receive it were only those in COVID-19 clinics and reference hospitals caring for patients suffering severe symptoms.

The first measure affecting the wider population focused on massive social distancing, that is, the cancellation of carnival celebrations on March 1, 2020, a longstanding tradition in Greece. The measure was considered to be excessive, resulting in heated debate, in view of the fact similar celebrations took place in several other countries as usual. At the time, less than one hundred cases of COVID-19 were confirmed, whereas no death had been reported. Within a month of the first case, the number of cases had risen to almost seven hundred; in anticipation of the March 25 National Day celebration, a nationwide lockdown was enforced.

On the day of the lockdown enforcement, more than eight thousand volunteers registered in the digital platform of the Ministry of Health. According to the European Observatory's COVID-19 Health System Response, ten thousand volunteers registered to offer their services in a program aiming to use the services of available qualified physicians, nursing personnel, paramedics, medical students, and retired practitioners (European Observatory, 2020). Criticism came from various quarters in terms of the permanence and the effectiveness of the public safety measures. Nevertheless, a feeling of solidarity was generated given the strong response to the call for volunteers. Notably, the public health reform bill that was enacted a few weeks before the pandemic was declared, and which was drafted before COVID-19 emerged, was strongly criticized by professional associations, the opposition, and even members of the ruling party in that the success of the measures and actions proposed in it largely relied on voluntary actions and donations. Although the spirit of the bill and the encouragement of voluntary action were positively received, concerns were raised on the expertise, skill set, permanence, coordination, and effectiveness such an approach can yield for a sustainable health system, particularly when funding mechanisms are not in place to ensure coordination and training even on a voluntary basis, let alone overall sustainability.

All COVID-19 measures were emergency actions. They were relevant for a limited period and were questionable in terms of offering an efficient and effective longer-term solution, particularly in terms of potential trend of rapidly rising cases, which up to the point of this writing (July 2020), Greece managed to avoid. Characteristically, legislation pertaining to employment of private physicians in public hospitals to deal with emergencies referenced two months, with the possibility of extending contracts for an additional two months. This approach was not complemented by any long-term planning or the parallel development of contractual provisions for public-private partnerships with permanence, and certainly with no development in terms of enhancing capacity in PHC and social care. This was noted by researchers and practitioners, including the implications for potential exclusion of specific social groups (Giannopoulou & Tsobanoglou, 2020).

Overall, measures were focused on ICU beds and hospitals, in other words, on tertiary care. Despite the limited number of cases in Greece, capacity was seriously challenged, with clinics and wards being redesignated as COVID-19 facilities and cancellation of scheduled surgeries and outpatient appointments for weeks to months. Although political rhetoric brought PHC services to the fore in April 2020, with the designation of health centers in major urban areas, these were not integrated centers to provide outpatient care and to meet the needs of patients with chronic needs or those particularly vulnerable, but rather, simply centers to solely screen patients with respiratory infections. Mobile units for testing, used to ensure primary care services were provided independently of care provision to acute cases, remained a debate issue in the spring and early summer of 2020.

Health policy measures introduced by ALCs were either structural/organizational measures for the healthcare system or pertained to limiting freedoms on the grounds of the need to protect public health. According to Article 21 par. 3 of the Constitution (The Constitution of Greece, 2008), public health constitutes not only a fundamental right but also an element of public interest (Symvoulion Epikrateias, 2015a, 2017), justifying legitimate limitations of individual rights and freedoms. Interestingly, during the period of the financial crisis, this represented the grounds for justifying the limitation of financial rights and freedoms to protect the provision of public healthcare services, and public health.

ALCs led to broader limitations, which this time touched upon the core of the fundamental rights, such as the freedom of movement and education. The ALC of February 25, 2020, prescribed compulsory clinical and laboratory medical examination, health monitoring, vaccination, medication, and hospitalization of all persons for whom there was reasonable suspicion that they could transmit the disease directly or indirectly. Additionally, it provided for the need to impose any necessary clinical and laboratory medical examinations, as well as measures of preventive health monitoring, vaccination, medication, and preventive treatment of persons coming from areas where the spread of the disease has been observed. Further restrictive measures of the freedom of movement included confinement of persons susceptible to transmit the disease and limitation of transport within the country. Moreover, staying-at-home restrictions could be imposed on a person or persons to prevent actions that could be considered to cause the disease to spread.

ALCs also prescribed that interested (affected) persons could submit objections against the measures taken against them before the President of the Administrative Court of First Instance, who decides irrevocably on the specific case. Furthermore, it was stipulated (FairTrials, 2020) that persons failing to comply could be subjected to punishment by imprisonment of up to ten years according to the stipulations of the Greek Criminal Code. Indeed, two circulars were issued by the Office of the Public Prosecutor of the Supreme Court (Areios Pagos, Eisaggelia, 2020a, 2020b), informing the Prosecutors' Offices at the First Instance Court and the Courts of Appeal about the immediate need for vigilance and constant intervention to prosecute crimes relating to COVID-19, including violations of implemented or forthcoming measures for its suppression, as well as relevant crimes of the Greek Criminal Code, incl., the violation of measures for prevention of disease (Poinikos Kodikas, 2020).

The need to move forward with substantial reform in chronic care ensuring integrated care provision was previously highlighted by public health experts and primary care researchers within and outside Greece (Lionis et al., 2018; Tsiachristas et al., 2015). It was also noted that the system was under significant risk of collapse with all that this would imply for those directly affected, as well as for the well-being of all citizens. The lack of integration between public health and PHC, as well as social care, remains a challenging issue with severe implications in terms of COVID-19 collateral damage, with a concrete risk of magnifying adverse impacts, particularly for the chronically ill, their carers, their families, and their friends (Lionis & Petelos, 2020).

Social Policy Response

Greece is characterized by high income inequality. It is also the country with the lowest impact of social transfers (social benefits in cash or in kind) in the EU (15.83 percent in 2017 vs. an EU average of 33.98 percent). These transfers to persons or families are intended to lighten the financial burden or to protect from various risks. In the Council recommendation of June 2019, an explicit recommendation was for targeted investment to enhance access to inclusive, affordable, and high-quality social services, as well as on the development of day care centers (European Commission, 2019b). Emphasis was given on providing support to the most deprived and promoting the social integration for children at risk of poverty, persons with disabilities, and migrants and refugees, while highlighting the opportunity to improve social inclusion by paying attention to geographical disparities. With an interval of a few months between this recommendation and the pandemic and the lockdown, there had been no focused investment for these population groups, thus leaving the most vulnerable at higher risk of collateral damage from containment measures, as well as from the pandemic.

Part of the recommendation on mitigating the impact of the crisis was to ensure adequate income replacement to all affected workers and the self-employed, duly considering gaps in access to social protection. Vulnerability, unemployment, and illegal work were highlighted as needing prompt attention to strengthen social safety nets, particularly through ensuring a minimum income support and comprehensive access to social services, including for people with disabilities, refugees, and asylum seekers. It was further noted that long-term care was ill developed, with the need to establish schemes for vulnerable homeowners particularly for households at risk of poverty through state-subsidized mortgages. In Greece, thousands of refugees and migrants reside in settlements run beyond capacity where distancing is impossible. Early calls to decongest these centers remain unanswered until now (July 2020) (Hargreaves et al., 2020; Subbaraman, 2020) with reasons for concern well beyond the COVID-19 pandemic

Many mitigating measures were taken cross-sectorally to combat the effects of the pandemic, and at these early stages, additionally to containment measures. According to the National Reform Program for 2020 (Hellenic Republic, 2020) submitted to the Council of the EU in April 2020, key measures related to COVID-19, mostly enacted through ALCs and often with applicability of limited time periods, include the following:

- Special allowance of EUR 800 to company employees affected by the COVID-19 crisis in case of their employment contract being suspended, as well as for freelancers, the self-employed, and the sole proprietors of small businesses
- Suspension of payment of value-added tax (VAT) and other tax liabilities and insurance contributions for companies, freelancers, and sole proprietors
- Insurance contributions of company employees affected by the COVID-19 crisis whose employment contract has been suspended, as well as the contributions of the self-employed who are treated as employees for tax reasons will be covered through public funds
- Financial scheme in the form of a repayable advance with a five-year repayment period and a grace period of one year to companies affected by the crisis and having serviced loans, based on the reduction of turnover or other factors
- Supporting business loans by providing additional liquidity from the European Investment Bank (EIB) to banks for granting new business loans, creating a guarantee mechanism that will provide support for loans related to investment projects and interest rate subsidy for loans to small- and medium-sized enterprises (SMEs) with payment coverage interest on performing loans of companies affected for a period of three months, if these companies retain jobs
- Possibility for employees to provide distance work, as well as flexible working hours and special purpose leave, partially financed by the state
- Extraordinary financial aid of EUR 400 to the long-term unemployed and extension of the payment of unemployment benefit

The Council Opinion on the basis of the 2020 National Reform Programme (NRP) of Greece placed strong emphasis on certain key aspects to be considered (European Commission, 2019a). More specifically, socioeconomic consequences were likely to be unevenly distributed, given different specialization patterns for regions relying on tourism and on face-to-face business to consumers. The Council went further to highlight the widening disparities of insular and mountainous regions, already intensified during the financial crisis. As of this writing, specific measures have yet to be taken for these regions. The recommendation highlighted risks regarding the overall convergence between Member-States, taking into consideration both the 2020 Stability Programme, essentially, rules designed to ensure EU countries are pursuing sound measures in terms of public finances and regarding the coordination of their fiscal policies and the 2020 NRP.

Considering COVID-19 measures proportionate and relevant to tackle it, the Council warned of the economic impact of such measures. The critical aspect of tourism was named as the most important service export. It stated that confinement measures would result in lower disposable incomes and increased unemployment, the expectation being demand would significantly contract. In response to this, additional efforts were made to boost tourism, including domestic tourism. The criteria for eligibility for the Social Tourism Program were expanded, whereas a global advertising campaign was mounted. For many Greeks, particularly those for whom tourism is not a source of income, the decision to open the borders was made on the basis of financial interests rather than public health considerations. Also, whereas social distancing measures were discussed (e.g., more routes for fewer people to travel with ships, planes, buses, and trains), the necessary changes never fully materialized.

Explanation

According to WHO, a challenge to sustained action on preparedness is inconsistent financing (WHO, 2017). Also, sound preparedness is compromised without a process to include evidence in public health decision-making and for evidence-informed policy, in preparation, and during public health emergencies (ECDC, 2018). Greece has had limited financial resources, including sustainable financing and contingency funding for the COVID-19 response. Greece also lacks developed health technology assessment (HTA) or procurement linked to evidence-based assessment and appraisal. For sustainable financing, detailed long-term national strategic plans with budget allocations should be developed in partnership between government, national stakeholders, and non-state actors. Sustainable funding must be defined and adjusted to develop and maintain outbreak preparedness core capacities such as surveillance, laboratory diagnostic capability, training, designated treatment facilities, equipment and supplies, risk communication, human and logistics resources, and so on. The lack of a solid, proactive (rather than reactive) comprehensive communication strategy and policy to facilitate understanding of measures became apparent over time, compromising risk perception over the summer months and representing a critical risk for the ensuing season.

The plethora of information resulted in an excessive amount of information, which was often unreliable, the infodemia witnessed across the world. Infodemic management and tackling misinformation were not addressed systematically. Citizens and healthcare professionals, alike, often relied on information coming from the press, diaspora scientists taking initiatives through social media, and TV broadcasts. This was the case across a broad spectrum of topics, such as tests, medicines, vaccines, and even protective measures. In the case of healthcare professionals, multiple closed groups were created in social media, where the difficulty in interpreting guidance was diffuse and consistently rising.

The COVID-19 pandemic highlights once again the need to implement coordinated evidence-informed actions to be able to respond to public health emergencies when time is of the essence, scientific uncertainties and political pressures tend to be high, and irrefutable evidence may be lacking. To strengthen the impact of scientific evidence, while eliminating uncertainty, such mechanisms ought to encompass interdisciplinary evidence generation and the uptake thereof through sound decision-making processes. Decision-making must be proactive and transparent.

Efforts should be made to foster cooperation and generate incentives, for example, in local contexts, to avoid conflict stemming from partisan politics. In Greece, the lack of participation and engagement of the local authorities to support local and regional planning, spread the right messages, and ensure timely behavioral change raises serious concerns on what the autumn and winter months of the first year of the pandemic will bring, particularly as people return to urban centers, and academic centers and schools re-open.

The key to community engagement is consistent and coordinated risk communication. This aspect has simply not been adequately addressed. The beginning of summer and the opening of the borders brought tourists to Greece. Naturally, cases were imported. Intense political debate ensued, with panic in some communities and indifference in others. What became apparent was the confusion of the people as a contributing factor to the nonadherence to the basic protective measures. Furthermore, there was a lack of understanding as to what personal accountability and responsibility practically meant as opposed to an intentional disregard for one's own safety and the safety of others. As of this writing, there is intense debate as to whether schools should reopen. Initial response by the Ministry of Education was prompt, with the launch of digital tools enabling distance learning. Although access was theoretically universal, implementation was compromised, with many not having access to the Internet or home computers, or even a quiet place to study at home (Markus, 2020). An integral part of smooth implementation also necessitates appropriate resources to provide psychosocial support (UNESCO, 2020).

The political and legal narratives of Greece remain tightly intertwined. It is worth examining legislative proposals of the past first six months of 2020 in a broader context; that is, examining the rights and rights-based approach to the provision of care. The financial crisis and the period of austerity that preceded saw both social and individual rights being compromised. The impact on the health of individuals, community resilience, and societal cohesion was never systematically evaluated and assessed nor was it incorporated in the planning of services over the past decade.

Greece was already scoring low in terms of resilience, with privacy and gender issues, exacerbated inequalities, and a rift between what constitutes public versus private interest, with polarized rhetoric in partisan politics. The COVID-19 pandemic reached Greece at a time of depleted resources, amid an incomplete primary care reform, at the exact moment where the role of the state in public health was being discussed. Legislation on public health had just gone through the parliament, placing emphasis on voluntary efforts and promotional actions, without due consideration to the integration of public health and primary care. The legislation did not include a coherent preparedness plan in terms of how centralized and local decision-making would ensure alignment, sound communication, and implementation of decisions in local settings. Most important, sound governance structures and allocated resources in terms of investment, prioritization, and assessment of interventions are still desperately needed.

Conclusion

The initial response in Greece demonstrated timely measures and sound choice of communication channels (i.e., TV broadcasts every afternoon), which seemed to perfectly match the needs of the population. The low number of cases and fatalities, contrasted to the alarming rates of other EU countries, largely contributed to the wide acceptance of the measures and approval of the government's response as far as the management of the pandemic in the first stage was concerned. People demonstrated unprecedented trust toward the government and the state, accepting the strict measures with sound compliance and excellent results in the spring months. At the same time, this success generated a false sense of safety, rather unwarranted considering the degree of spread prior to the lockdown.

Nevertheless, the time gained through the initial timely response was not used to re-orient healthcare services toward an integrated care policy. The main means of increasing preparedness targeted an increase in personnel and an effort to double the capacity of ICUs. Primary care remained neglected as means to ensure elimination of disparities, detection of vulnerability, and establishment of syndromic surveillance in key nodes to ensure timely monitoring of future disease waves.

Most important, at a time of the parallel infodemic, an opportunity to have an active link to citizens and communities through PHC, thus reinforcing preparedness, was missed. This would have allowed the Greek government to combat misinformation regarding vaccines, to eliminate hesitancy, and to prepare the groundwork for acceptance of measures and enactment of sound public health strategies. In well-integrated care systems, primary care can inform public health strategies and policymaking priorities through local data and by harvesting data from electronic health records. In the Council of the European Union, the recommendation initially assessed the current state, highlighting the fact early indications suggested boosting primary care capacity is proving to be key to protect citizens and limit the spread of the virus and ensuring the full capacity of the system can be employed to treat patients according to their needs. With no progress on sustainable financing and adequate structural measures to ensure a strong health system, a protracted COVID-19 pandemic may be the straw to break the camel's back, so to speak. The lack of HTA further contributes to the notably weak centralized procurement mechanism, while the Greek healthcare budget still remains well below the EU average.

Political decision-making has had to proceed on the basis of trade-offs between safeguarding the public health of Greek people and ensuring the minimum possible impact on the economy, navigating through dangerous waters, and in search of authentic leadership, much like Odysseus navigating the Messina Strait. Rather than moving forward to economic growth and sustainable development, Greece may have to face the worst financial impact among EU countries. Particularly in cases of protracted lockdowns and inadequate social protection and mitigation measures, COVID-19 may bring yet another cycle of financial and political instability. The newly elected government found itself in the position of tackling a borderless threat at a time of intense debate on migrants and refugees.

Still, the pandemic introduced an opportunity to develop an integrated health and social care system, with emphasis on health promotion and on the basis of democratic dialogue and participatory decision-making, with engaged communities and empowered stakeholders. As of this writing, it remains to be seen whether this challenge will be successfully met, moving the country to more resilient and safe communities or whether it will remain unaddressed, sending the country down yet another spiral of increasing disparities and irreversible damage to the societal cohesion.

References

Areios Pagos, Eisaggelia [Office of the Public Prosecutor of the Supreme Court]. (2020a, April). Circular 4/2020 (Greece).

Areios Pagos, Eisaggelia [Office of the Public Prosecutor of the Supreme Court]. (2020b, July). Circular 7/2020 (Greece).

Cassini, A., Högberg, L. D., Plachouras, D., Quattrocchi, A., Hoxha, A., Simonsen, G. S., Colomb-Cotinat, M., Kretzschmar, M. E., Devleesschauwer, B., Cecchini, M., Ouakrim, D. A., Oliveira, T. C., Struelens, M. J., Suetens, C., Monnet, D. L., Burden of AMR Collaborative Group, R., Mertens, K., Struyf, T., Catry, B., . . . Hopkins, S. (2019). Attributable deaths and disability-adjusted life-years caused by infections with antibiotic-resistant bacteria in the EU and the European Economic Area in 2015: A population-level modelling analysis. *The Lancet. Infectious Diseases*, 19(1), 56–66. https://doi.org/10.1016/S1473-3099(18)30605-4

Commission Economic & Affairs European Economy Institutional Papers. (2018). *Enhanced Surveillance Report Economic and Financial Affairs EUROPEAN ECONOMY*. https://doi.org/10.2765/93517

The Constitution of Greece. (2008). https://www.hellenicparliament.gr/UserFiles/f3c70a23-7696-49db-9148-f24dce6a27c8/001-156 aggliko.pdf

Decision No 1082/2013/EU of the European Parliament and of the Council. (2013, October 2013). Retrieved August 24, 2020, from https://ec.europa.eu/health/sites/health/files/preparedness_response/docs/decision_serious_crossborder_threats_22102013_en.pdf

Economou, C., Kaitelidou, D., Karanikolos, M., & Maresso, A. (2017). *Greece: Health system review*. http://www.euro.who.int/en/what-we-publish/publication-

European Centre for Disease Control. (2018). *The use of evidence in decision-making during public health emergencies*. https://doi.org/10.2900/63594

European Centre for Disease Control. (2020, March 31). *Public health management of persons having had contact with novel coronavirus cases in the EU - first update 31 March 2020*. https://www.ecdc.europa.eu/sites/default/files/documents/Public-health-management-persons-contact-novel-coronavirus-cases-2020-03-31.pdf

European Commission. (2019a). *Recommendation for a council recommendation on the 2019 National Reform Programme of Greece and delivering a council opinion on the 2019 Stability Programme of Greece*. EUR-Lex. https://eur-lex.europa.eu/legal-content/en/TXT/?uri=CELEX%3A52019DC0508

European Commission. (2019b). *Recommendation for a COUNCIL RECOMMENDATION on the 2019 National Reform Programme of Greece and delivering a Council opinion on the 2019 Stability Programme of Greece*. https://ec.europa.eu/info/sites/info/files/file_import/2019-european-semester-country-specific-recommendation-commission-recommendation-greece_en.pdf

European Observatory. (2020). *COVID-19 Health Systems Response Monitor: Greece*. https://www.covid19healthsystem.org/countries/greece/countrypage.aspx

European Union. (2013). *I/EU of the European Parliament and of the council of 22 October 2013 on serious cross-border threats to health and repealing decision No 2119/98/EC*. EUR-Lex. https://eur-lex.europa.eu/legal-content/EN/TXT/?uri=celex%3A32013D1082

FairTrials Admin. (2020). *Short update: Greek public prosecutors receive circular order for the prosecution of crimes relating to COVID-19 pandemic*. https://www.fairtrials.org/news/short-update-greek-public-prosecutors-receive-circular-order-prosecution-crimes-relating-covid

Gerapetritis, Y., (2012). *Syntagma kai Koinovoulio—Aftonomia kai Anelegkto ton Esoterikon tou Somatos* [Constitution and parliament—Autonomy and uncontrolled of the Internal Affairs of the Body] (pp. 216–217). Nomiki Vivliothiki.

Giannopoulou, I., & Tsobanoglou, G. O. (2020). COVID-19 pandemic: Challenges and opportunities for the Greek health care system. *Irish Journal of Psychological Medicine*, 1–5. https://doi.org/10.1017/ipm.2020.35

Global Health Security Index. (2019). *Greece—GHS Index*. Retrieved August 23, 2020, from https://www.ghsindex.org/country/greece/

Greer, S., & de Ruijter, A. (2020). EU health law and policy in and after the COVID-19 crisis. *European Journal of Public Health*, 30(4), 623–624. https://doi.org/10.1093/eurpub/ckaa088

Hargreaves, S., Kumar, B. N., McKee, M., Jones, L., & Veizis, A. (2020). Europe's migrant containment policies threaten the response to covid-19. *BMJ (Clinical Research Ed.)*, 368, m1213. https://doi.org/10.1136/bmj.m1213

Hellenic Republic. (2020). *National Reform Programme of the Hellenic Republic*. https://ec.europa.eu/info/sites/info/files/2020-european-semester-national-reform-programme-greece_el.pdf

Jauhiainen, J. S. (2020). Biogeopolitics of COVID-19: Asylum-related migrants at the European Union Borderlands. *Tijdschrift Voor Economische En Sociale Geografie*, 111(3), 260–274. https://doi.org/10.1111/tesg.12448

Johnson, K. (2020). *Europe is torn between north and south over coronavirus response*. https://foreignpolicy.com/2020/03/30/coronavirus-pandemic-europe-north-south-eurobond/

Kivotidis, D. (2018). The form and content of the Greek crisis legislation. *Law and Critique*, 29(1), 57–81. https://doi.org/10.1007/s10978-017-9217-4

Lionis, C., & Petelos, E. (2020). Challenges, priorities and tasks for the generalists at the time of the COVID-19 pandemic. *European Journal of General Practice*, 26(1), 104–105. https://doi.org/10.1080/13814788.2020.1791073

Lionis, C., Petelos, E., Mechili, E.-A., Sifaki-Pistolla, D., Chatzea, V.-E., Angelaki, A., Rurik, I., Pavlic, D. R., Dowrick, C., Dückers, M., Ajdukovic, D., Bakic, H., Jirovsky, E., Mayrhuber, E. S., Van Den Muijsenbergh, M., & Hoffmann, K. (2018). Assessing refugee healthcare needs in Europe and implementing educational interventions in primary care: A focus on methods. *BMC International Health and Human Rights*, 18(1). https://doi.org/10.1186/s12914-018-0150-x

Markus, S. (2020). *School education during COVID-19: Were teachers and students ready?* OECD. http://www.oecd.org/education/Greece-coronavirus-education-country-note.pdf

Ministry of Health. (2020). *Ministerial Decision 13338/26-02-2020, on Suspension of regular leave of the staff of the Ministry of Health, hospitals and healthcare provision entities*. https://www.moh.gov.gr/articles/ministry/grafeio-typoy/press-releases/6719-anastolh-kanonikwn-adeiwn-toy-proswpikoy-toy-ypoyrgeioy-ygeias-twn-nosokomeiwn-kai-olwn-twn-ygeionomikwn-sxhmatismwn-ths-xwras

Moore, T. J., & Furberg, C. D. (2014). Development times, clinical testing, postmarket follow-up, and safety risks for the new drugs approved by the US Food and Drug Administration. *JAMA Internal Medicine*, 174(1), 90. https://doi.org/10.1001/jamainternmed.2013.11813

Poinikos Kodikas [Criminal Code], 13:285 (Greece). (2020).

Renda, A., & Castro, R. (2020). Towards stronger EU governance of health threats after the COVID-19 pandemic. *European Journal of Risk Regulation*, 11(2), 273–282. https://doi.org/10.1017/err.2020.34

Renucci, J.-F. (2005). *Introduction to the European Convention on Human Rights: The rights guaranteed and the protection mechanism*. https://www.echr.coe.int/LibraryDocs/DG2/HRFILES/DG2-EN-HRFILES-01(2005).pdf

Speakman, E. M., McKee, M., & Coker, R. (2017). If not now, when? Time for the European Union to define a global health strategy. *The Lancet. Global Health*, 5(4), e392–e393. https://doi.org/10.1016/S2214-109X(17)30085-2

State of health in the EU: The Country Health Profile series. (n.d.). Retrieved October 21, 2020, from http://www.who.int/bulletin/disclaimer/en/

Steurs, L., Van de Pas, R., Delputte, S., & Orbie, J. (2017). The global health policies of the EU and its member states: A common vision? *International Journal of Health Policy and Management*, 7(5), 433–442. https://doi.org/10.15171/ijhpm.2017.112

Subbaraman, N. (2020). "Distancing is impossible": Refugee camps race to avert coronavirus catastrophe. *Nature*, 581, 7806.

Supplemental memorandum of understanding: Greece. (2019). https://ec.europa.eu/info/sites/info/files/economy-finance/third_smou_-_final.pdf

Symvoulion Epikrateias [Hellenic Council of the State, Supreme Administrative Court] 2289/1987 (Greece). (1987).

Symvoulion Epikrateias [Hellenic Council of the State, Supreme Administrative Court] 3636/1989 (Greece). (1989).

Symvoulion Epikrateias [Hellenic Council of the State, Supreme Administrative Court]1250/2003 (Greece). (2003).

Symvoulion Epikrateias [Hellenic Council of the State, Supreme Administrative Court] 3612/2002 (Greece). (2002).

Symvoulion Epikrateias [Hellenic Council of the State, Supreme Administrative Court] 2439/2015, (Greece). (2015a).

Symvoulion Epikrateias [Hellenic Council of the State, Supreme Administrative Court] 2567/2015 (Greece). (2015b).

Symvoulion Epikrateias [Hellenic Council of the State, Supreme Administrative Court] 3047/2017, (Greece). (2017).

Tsiachristas, A., Lionis, C., & Yfantopoulos, J. (2015). Bridging knowledge to develop an action plan for integrated care for chronic diseases in Greece. *International Journal of Integrated Care*, *15*, e040. https://doi.org/10.5334/ijic.2228

UNESCO. (2020). *School closures caused by coronavirus (Covid-19)*. https://en.unesco.org/covid19/educationresponse/

Verfassungsgerichtshof [VfGH] [Constitutional Court], Jul. 14, 2020, No. 202/2020, (Austria). (2020).

World Health Organization. (2014). International Health Regulations (2005). *Summary of states parties 2012 report on IHR core capacity implementation: Report for national IHR focal points*. World Health Organization. https://apps.who.int/iris/handle/10665/112788.

World Health Organization. (2017). *A strategic framework for emergency preparedness*. http://apps.who.int/bookorders

22 COVID-19 IN TURKEY
Public Health Centralism

Saime Özçürümez

The COVID-19 pandemic threatened people's health, social lives, and economies around the world. In this challenging era, national governments stood out as the prominent actors to manage all coordination and communication efforts in response to existing and future pandemics (World Health Organization [WHO], 2009). As the pandemic ran its course, the variation among states' institutional capacities and political strategies while coping with the consequences of the pandemic became more obvious. The deficiencies in national pandemic preparedness, such as in Italy where there was a shortage of incentive care units (ICUs) from the early weeks of the pandemic, resulted in public health disasters (Torri et al., 2020; Van Beusekom, 2020). The initial approaches of political leaders while addressing the severity of the pandemic had devastating consequences for the countries in question and also globally. Among these were the leaders of Brazil ("Coronavirus," 2020) and the United States (Brooks, 2020), who underestimated the effects of the pandemic in all spheres of life, and did not implement timely and comprehensive precautions, risking the health of their own populations and the whole world. In the COVID-19 pandemic context, many states could not implement public health measures swiftly. They could not assess healthcare system preparedness and improve institutional capacity to facilitate healthcare service delivery while protecting healthcare workers. They could not enhance national and international communication and collaboration strategies to fight against the pandemic together. Although states insisted on continuing to respond to the COVID-19 pandemic with their own resources and measures, the cross-border, multisector, and global negative impact of the pandemic became more severe, and the need for global cooperation became more evident than ever.

Turkey entered the COVID-19 pandemic context with a well-functioning and inclusive healthcare system and adopted a serious health crisis and risk management approach, which could be characterized as public health centralism. Reforms in Turkey's healthcare system improved access for the whole population: for example, the total number of infant and newborn intensive care beds increased by 82 percent from 2011 to 2018 ("Türkiye'de Hangi Bölgede Kişi Başına Kaç Yoğun Bakım Yatağı Düşüyor?" ["How Many Intensive Care Hospital Beds..."], 2020), and overall, hospital bed capacity had increased by 60 percent from 1997 to 2018 ("Türkiye'nin Hastane Yatağı Kapasitesi Kaç?" ["What Is the Hospital Bed Capacity in Turkey?"], 2020). Until August 2020, the capacity of hospitals and the healthcare system as a whole seemed adequately resourced to meet the pandemic challenge.[1] All public actors in Turkey displayed a very serious approach toward the COVID-19 pandemic since its beginnings in Wuhan On January 10, 2020, the Ministry of Health, for example, established a Coronavirus Scientific Advisory Board (CSAB), consisting mainly of specialists in pulmonology, infectious diseases, clinical microbiology, virology, internal medicine, and intensive care ("Bilim Kurulu Üyeleri Kimler?" ["Who Are the Members of the Science Council?"], 2020). The CSAB began working on the necessary measures quickly and professionally to devise and implement a COVID-19 pandemic response strategy.

The Ministry of Health announced its COVID-19 response strategy as implementing the restrictive public health measures. The Presidential System in Turkey ensured the compulsory and country-wide implementation of all the measures resulting from the centralized political system, state-centric governance, and the strong executive role of the presidential office. As the social, economic, and health effects of the pandemic began to reveal themselves in several months, the setbacks in the design and implementation of the COVID-19 response by public actors and the public themselves became apparent. Among the challenges in Turkey's response strategy were (1) implementing public health measures effectively and continuously; (2) establishing trust among the public and securing ownership of the measures to ensure sustainability of carrying out of public health precautions by all sections of the society; (3) compensating adequately for the devastating effects of the pandemic ridden economic downturn for all sectors; (4) devising a proper pandemic-specific data collection, public information dissemination, and communication strategy covering COVID-19 cases data as well as the emerging impact of the pandemic in social and economic life in the country; (5) administering a gradual "normalization" process; (6) introducing pandemic-specific reforms to ameliorate national-local level governance collaboration and knowledge and know-how exchange among different national and local agencies; (7) involving all pertinent stakeholders such as the Turkish Medical Association consistently throughout the process of combating COVID-19 pandemic.

Timeline Analysis: An Introductory Overview of Turkey's Response to COVID-19

Dr. Fahrettin Koca, Minister of Health, officially announced the first case of coronavirus on March 11, 2020, a Turkish citizen arriving from Europe ("Turkey Announces Its First Case of Coronavirus," 2020). Since then the CSAB and the Minister of Health were the most visible public actors in Turkey's response to COVID-19 pandemic (Kodaz, 2020). From the outset, the public agencies in Turkey introduced public health measures of social distancing and self-isolation within the country, travel restrictions (intercity and international), border closures, and bans on international destinations as well as repatriation of citizens. There are strong indicators that the public agencies adopted a gradual, not-so-transparent, and not-so-public strategy to mitigate the effects of the spread of the virus even before the public announcement of the first case. The timeline of the policy initiatives before March 11, 2020, is as follows.

On January 22, 2020, the Ministry of Health introduced thermal cameras at airports and began to increase healthcare personnel presence at ports and airports. On January 24, thermal cameras began to scan all passengers from China. On February 1, 2020, the Ministry of Foreign Affairs evacuated Turkish citizens from Wuhan, and on February 3, all flights from China stopped with the recommendation of the CSAB. Beginning February 6, all passengers arriving from abroad were subject to thermal screening. On February 23, Turkey stopped cross-border mobility between Iran and Turkey. On February 27, the Ministry of Health established field hospitals in Ağrı, Dilucu, Van, and Hakkâri, near its eastern borders. On February 29, all incoming flights from China, Iran, South Korea, and Italy were discontinued. On March 8, in some provinces, disinfection activities were initiated in public places, public transportation, vehicles, and schools.

After the first case was announced, the measures to fight the coronavirus expanded, diversified, and intensified. On March 12, 2020, primary, secondary, and high school level education was interrupted, initially for a week, and higher education for three weeks. Sports competitions were expected to be held without audiences, and public officials were restricted from traveling abroad. On March 13, flights to Azerbaijan, Georgia, Germany, France, Spain, Norway, Denmark, Belgium, Austria, Sweden, and the Netherlands were suspended and day care centers were closed with no reopening date specified. On March 14, the COVID-19 hotline was established (Hotline ALO 184; https://sabim.gov.tr). On March 15, flights stopped from Germany, Spain, France, Austria, Norway, Denmark, Sweden, Belgium, and the Netherlands, and bars and nightclubs were closed. On March 16, mosque attendance, especially for Friday prayers, was interrupted, and cinemas, concert halls, wedding halls, cafes, massage parlors, and gyms were temporarily closed. On March 17, the first loss of life resulting from coronavirus was publicly announced by the Minister of Health. On the same day, the Ministry of National Education announced that all schools would start distance education as of March 23, and institutions of higher education also began their preparation to transition to distance learning. On March 19, the Ministry of Youth and Sports announced the postponement of spectator sports. On March 20, the Ministry of Health announced that all private and foundation hospitals were re-designated as pandemic hospitals and that all types of scientific and cultural activities, including concerts and performances, had to be canceled or postponed until the end of April. From March 21, comprehensive quarantine measures began to be implemented, including those aged sixty-five and over being required to stay indoors at all times, imposing restrictions on urban and intercity transportation from March 24, and announcing distance education for all levels for the entire spring semester.

On April 3, 2020, a curfew was imposed for those born on January 1, 2000, and later throughout the country until further notice; wearing masks in supermarkets became obligatory, and entrance and exit to thirty metropolitan cities and Zonguldak was halted for fifteen days (except for those with special permits), or until further notice. On April 10 at 10 a.m., the Ministry of the Interior announced a curfew for the weekend starting on April 11 at midnight. After the announcement, many people rushed to the supermarkets, which violated all kinds of social distancing and self-isolation measures essential to controlling the spread of the infection. This led the minister of the interior to publicly apologize for the communication strategy mishap and its possible health ramifications; he announced his resignation from office, which was rejected by the president. From April 11 on, there were curfews every weekend starting from midnight on Friday until Monday morning.

Given the projected socioeconomic impact of these initial public health measures, on April 16, 2020, Turkey's parliament ratified a government bill including measures to temporarily relieve financial pressure on the population, municipalities, and private enterprises by postponing or waiving certain rent payments, layoffs and redundancies, loans, fees, taxes, dividends, and other obligations, while the government postponed some activities of its sovereign wealth fund and some local elections. The Bill also included strict controls on price increases and mandated a supervisory committee to monitor and fine (from 10,000 to 500,000 liras) stockpiling or price-gouging activities.

On May 4, 2020, President Erdoğan announced a schedule for easing of the pandemic response restrictions: from May 7, those aged sixty-five and over and under twenty were allowed to go outside for a number of hours on designated days, and shopping malls and hairdressers were allowed to open for a limited number of hours conditional to their following virus control regulations (Borzou, 2020). The weekend of May 16, 2020, was announced as a four-day curfew, including the Monday before the May 19 Youth and Sports Day. As of May 21, citizens living in twenty-five provinces with the most coronavirus cases were obliged to wear masks in public spaces. As of June 1, 2020, travel restrictions had been lifted. Restaurant, cafe, pastry shops, swimming pools, and spa-type businesses were open until 10 p.m. within the determined regulations. Restrictions on the use of beaches and parks were removed. On June 9, it was announced that citizens over sixty-five can go out between 10 a.m. and 8 p.m. every day of the week (Deutsch-Türkische Industrie-und Handelskammer, 2020). Countrywide high school entrance examinations and university entrance examinations were held on June 20, 27, and 28 with the administration of various COVID-19 measures (Gemici, 2020). More than 3.8 million students took these exams in closed spaces. During the exams, the air conditioners were not operated, the students were placed in the classes observing social distancing rules, and free masks were distributed to the students who would take the exams. A curfew was additionally imposed during exam hours so that students who took the exam were protected and could travel safely to their exam venues (Gemici, 2020). On July 29, it was

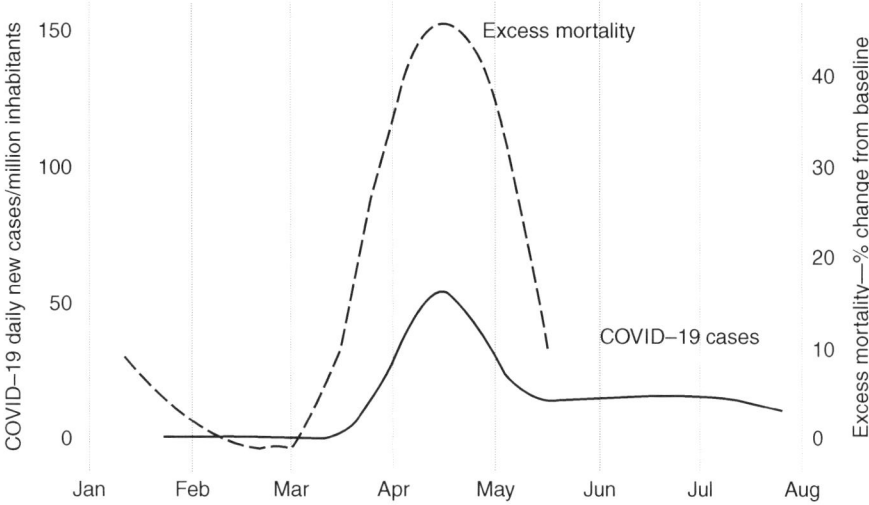

Figure 22.1. Coronavirus cases and mortality trend in Turkey.

announced that no restrictions would be imposed under the COVID-19 measures during the Eid al-Adha ("Koca," 2020). All these initiatives were announced against a backdrop of a steady decrease in coronavirus-related mortality in Turkey (Figure 22.1), but warnings of a second wave of infections globally.

The pandemic response policies in Turkey can be characterized as constituting a centralized governance model around public health centralism. The model is challenged by controversy over the accuracy of the data collection and public dissemination and the effectiveness and sustainability of the measures implemented by the authorities. Physicians who work in the Ministry of Health and the CSAB participated in the consultative processes for managing the pandemic before the shaping of strategies based on emerging data and finalization of executive decisions. Several questions have been raised publicly in terms of the extent to which the CSAB's input was incorporated into the final policy decisions concerning the COVID-19 response; however, the body continued to operate in the governance model made up of reputable medical doctors. Through open collaboration with public health specialists in an advisory role and the Ministry of Health steering the implementation of all public health measures and treatment protocols, the governance model aimed to accomplish two tasks: to legitimize the public health restrictions with medical justification and to ensure control over the hospital bed capacity (Cakir, 2020). The centralized, executive actor and health specialist–centered governance model seemed dependable in the initial stages of the COVID-19 response in Turkey with significant accomplishments in controlling the spread of the virus. However, over time, as cases and those in need of treatment increased, the firm institutional foundations of the governance model have proven to be less adaptive than expected to the diversifying and rapidly changing conditions over time.

Health Policies

Health care system reforms dating back to the period between 2003 and 2013 resulted in a transformation process aimed at improving and reshaping the primary care structure. The Family Medicine (FM) model was at the core of the transformation process for effective primary care service provision and for enabling easy public access to these services. Universal health coverage has also been established to improve the healthcare services at all stages in Turkey (Sumer et al., 2019). In terms of healthcare resources, just before the outbreak began, Turkey was performing close to the Organization for Economic Cooperation and Development (OECD) average on health indicators such as population in poor health, risk factors for health, and quality of access to care, but below average on health resources such as health spending per capita, health spending share as a percentage of gross domestic product (GDP), the number of practicing physicians and nurses per 1000 inhabitants, and physician density across localities (OECD, 2019).

During the initial months of the COVID-19 pandemic, hospital bed capacity was considered sufficient; however, concern arose over sustaining this capacity to meet patient needs, which depend on the spread of the pandemic and the acuteness of the cases. At the end of March 2020, the Ministry of Health announced that it would recruit an additional 32,000 healthcare professionals to fight the pandemic (Milliyet, 2020). At the beginning of April, plans for the construction of two new hospitals were announced (Kurukız, Aktürk, & Aktürk, 2020), and two additional city hospitals became operational, increasing available beds in Istanbul ("Başakşehir Şehir Hastanesi'nin Ilk Etabı Açıldı" ["First Phase of Başakşehir City Hospital Has Been Opened"], 2020). The Ministry of Health (2019) implemented the National Pandemic Preparedness Plan and started preparatory measures in early January, at the time when the initial reports of COVID-19 appeared. The National COVID-19 Treatment Protocol was drawn up at an early stage and was regularly updated by the CSAB (Güner et al., 2020). In August 2020, the data on the number of cases across cities indicated that the demand for care and treatment must be addressed differently in Istanbul, Ankara, and other cities and provinces. The contact tracing method of screening the chain of contact remained critical in predicting the likelihood of the changes in demand in different cities (Demirtaş & Tekiner, 2020).

Public health centralism characterizes Turkey's healthcare policies and measures in the COVID-19 pandemic response strategy. The Ministry of Health established an operation center within the General Directorate of Public Health in Ankara. CSAB began to play a pivotal role in this operation center to manage the process and monitor all data flow at the local, national, and international levels. Public health centralism aimed to accomplish nationwide standardization of all health-related agenda items, policy decisions, and procedures for implementation across all provinces. All testing, examination and treatment procedures, and protocols regarding the COVID-19 pandemic were applied uniformly. However, recognizing a need for local-level responses, on March 28, 2020, Provincial Pandemic Committees (PPCs), chaired by governorships in each province, were established. Provincial-level actors began to cooperate to identify their own needs and implement targeted measures for their own provinces (Erdoğan, 2020). PPCs continued to be responsible for identifying province-specific precautions and implementing measures based on epidemiological data on the COVID-19 pandemic available at the provincial level. PPCs work with the Ministry of Health and the Ministry of Interior closely during carrying out their responsibilities.

The public health centralism governance model operates through collaboration among many public actors. These actors include the General Directorate of Border and Coastal Health, the General Directorate of Public Hospitals, and Turkish Airlines to manage the process through the steering of the central institutions by taking into account the multifaceted nature of the pandemic and emphasizing effective policy implementation (Kılıç et al., 2020). The scope of effective collaboration and coordination among public and private actors at the local, national, and international levels shapes any country's performance in coping with the pandemic. The Ministry of Health and Ministry of Interior have engaged in wide-ranging and inclusive multiactor cooperation and coordination networks, enhancing their institutional capacity to identify new strategies to mitigate the negative impacts of the pandemic. The collaborative governance involves (1) supranational and international organizations, particularly the WHO, EU, World Bank, and UNICEF (Worldbank, 2020a), (2) civil society organizations (TUSEV, 2020), (3) municipalities and local governing bodies ("Municipalities, Support Groups Help Foreigners Living in Turkey," 2020), (4) professional organizations including the Turkish Psychiatry Association (2020), (5) universities and innovation centers such as Erciyes University Vaccine Research and Development Center and Ankara University Biotechnology Institute ("Turkish Researchers Take Initial Step for Development of Covid-19 Vaccine," 2020, April 9), as well as Bilkent University's UNAM (UNAM, 2020) and Middle East Technical University's TEKNOKENT, and (6) the private sector ("Sağlıkta Üretim Atağı" ["Production Leap in Health"], 2020).

These actors exchange knowledge around measures to prevent the spread of the virus and work together on supplying medicine; producing masks, ventilators, and medical supplies as well as PPE for healthcare workers; addressing the economic challenges caused by pandemic response measures; and ensuring continuous food supply and distribution. The Ministry of Health's public information campaigns have been supported by NGOs, public institutions at all levels, and international organizations. Spontaneous collaborative networks also formed, bringing together research institutions, private sector, and individual entrepreneurs. One such entrepreneur was the Turkey COVID-19 Shared Intelligence Platform, a mainly voluntary effort to fund innovative ideas and projects to address the pandemic-related challenges, including production of test kits and other diagnostic tools, new medicine for treatment and cure, and projects with social impact geared toward alleviating the economic and social shock that shook the structure of social relations in the country (TR-Covid-19, 2020).

The centralized pandemic governance with an extensive cooperation network and well-established critical care system enabled public agencies to implement nationwide standardized procedures such as free testing, contact tracing, and quarantine practices (Cakir, 2020). All COVID-19 related treatments in Turkey are accessible free of charge regardless of individuals' insurance schemes. The Ministry of Health announced COVID-19 treatment algorithms and updated them regularly (Ministry of Health, 2020a). Turkey (2) treated each patient with hydroxychloroquine and azithromycin initially, (2) treated ICU patients with favipiravir, (3) provided a tocilizumab treatment option in the ICU for patients with severe COVID-19–related cytokine release syndrome, and (4) added anticoagulant drugs to the treatment algorithm (Kodaz, 2020). The filiation system is a significant part of the Ministry of Health's strategy to fight the COVID-19 pandemic. The system established by the Ministry of Health to disrupt the chain of transmission to pursue a process of tracing patients systematically to isolate susceptible individuals. The system was implemented by the nationwide medical teams administered by the Ministry of Health all over Turkey. Turkish Public Health Management System's tracing module enabled medical filiation teams to monitor patients and susceptible individuals closely to prevent the transmission of COVID-19 within the country (Demirtaş & Tekiner, 2020). The system of "HayatEveSığar" (HES, Lifefitsinthehome) operated through an application that can be downloaded to mobile phones to receive data on the situation in the immediate surroundings of the subscriber. Moreover, citizens were expected to acquire HES codes before they traveled across cities (Ministry of Health, 2020b). Healthcare services were continuously provided during the COVID-19 pandemic period with no reported discernible disruption to the healthcare ecosystem. The number of ICUs, ventilators, and health personnel were reported as sufficient (Ersoy, 2020) through August 2020.

Although the multisector, multiactor, and multilevel collaboration functioned well in the first months of the pandemic response, the consequences of the easing of measures from the first week of June onward revealed the troubles of public health centralism model. Public compliance with social distancing and social isolation decreased significantly, resulting in an increase in the number of infected individuals, a jump in the number of patients in need of hospital treatment, and a peak of the spread of the virus among healthcare workers. However, the publicly announced data concerning the number of cases after the end of July did not seem to reflect the observations of the public in their immediate environment, which led to a drop in confidence in the publicly available epidemiological data, results of polymerase chain reaction tests, and the effectiveness of measures. Moreover, critical non-state actors such as the Turkish Medical Association raised concerns about the inclusiveness of the governance model. The Turkish Medical Association was the most active professional association informing the public through publication of updated, evidence-based reports on the progress against the pandemic; knowledge dissemination on the public health precautions through broadcasts, newspapers, and social media; and on the needs of healthcare professionals for protective equipment. In early September 2020, representatives met exclusively with the Minister of Health to represent the concerns of the Turkish Medical Association concerning the progress in the pandemic response (Ministry of Health, 2020c).

Social Policies

Turkey's annual growth rate has been unstable since 2012, and there was a sharp decline from 7.5 percent in 2017 to 0.9 percent in 2019 (Worldbank, 2020a). Unemployment rate came to the forefront as the main challenge for the Turkish economy, particularly since 2015. Between 2012 and 2019, the unemployment rate in Turkey increased from 8.15 percent to 13.49 percent (Worldbank, 2020b). Labor force participation rate in Turkey has also been declining since May 2019. Labor force participation rate decreased from 51.8 percent to 47.5 percent in Turkey from April 2020 onward ("Turkey Labor Force Participation Rate," 2020).

The Turkish economy had not been performing well even before the pandemic had started. The main challenges of the economy were increasing inflation, higher unemployment rates, and the exchange rate crisis, which have become more severe with the impact of the COVID-19 pandemic. The restrictions and curfews imposed under the COVID-19 pandemic posed a great threat to trade, education, and tourism. On March 18, President Erdoğan announced the Economic Stability Shield and Social Protection Shield packages. These policy packages were prepared in a collaboration with the Ministry of Treasury and Finance (MoTF) and the Ministry of Family, Labor and Social Services (MoFLSS). Economic Stability Shield and Social Protection Shield packages mainly included providing short-term employment allowance, providing 4.4 million families in need with 1,000 Turkish liras, postponement of payment of student loans and rental payments for three months on several types of state-owned immovable properties, providing support of 39.24 Turkish liras per day to workers forced to take unpaid leave because of the coronavirus outbreak for three months, enabling municipalities to be able to postpone water bills for three months for private homes and companies, and providing financial support to natural and legal persons, and prohibiting termination of workers' contracts for three months except in unconscionable situations, and encouraging the introduction of social credit packages for citizens.

Economic Stability Shield and Social Protection Shield programs aimed at protecting the economy and Turkish citizens from the devastating economic and social effects of the COVID-19 pandemic. With the normalization process that was announced on the May 4, 2020, the economy was expected to recover even if slowly. The state support aimed to encourage citizens to spend holidays to support the tourism sector, cover wedding expenses, and shop through social and personal credit packages (Invest, 2020, April).The main rationale for such promotion of credit availability was to jump-start the economy, which had become stagnant to an unprecedented degree because of the COVID-19 pandemic, and to mildly compensate for the financial loss in various sectors.

The president's office pursued a communication strategy emphasizing national unity and solidarity in the fight against the pandemic and promoted fundraising campaigns calling for all citizens to donate to public funds ("Bizbize Yeteriz Türkiyem Kampanyası Başladı" ["We Are Enough for Each Other Campaign Has Begun," 2020). The main campaign, "Together we are enough for each other, my Turkey" aims to secure and expand the financial resources available to low-income groups. These campaigns initially caused some controversy over why the state needed to appeal to a public already suffering from the socioeconomic impact of the pandemic and raised anxiety over whether the state had sufficient resources to properly respond to the pandemic ("'Biz Bize Yeteriz' Kampanyasına Tepki Yağıyor" ["Protests Against the 'We Are Enough For Each Other' Campaign Are Increasing"], 2020). Moreover, tensions around party politics and national-local level responsibilities concerning which actor may legitimately engage in fund raising and distribution of social assistance became apparent in social media. When metropolitan municipalities controlled by the main opposition party, Istanbul and Ankara in particular, launched their own donation campaigns to support local households in need (Turetken, 2020), the Ministry of the Interior questioned the validity of these municipal campaigns and attempted to stall the activities involved, such as paying an anonymous gas bill through the internet, which resulted in tension among the population throughout the country reflected in the social media ("'Biz Bize Yeteriz' Kampanyasına Tepki Yağıyor" ["Protests Against the 'We Are Enough For Each Other' Campaign Are Increasing"], 2020).

Vulnerable Populations: The Case of Forcibly Displaced People

Turkey hosts around 4 million forcibly displaced individuals, mainly from Syria but also from Afghanistan, Iran, Iraq, and Somalia, and migrants. At over 4.8 percent of its total population, they constitute a very significant vulnerable group within the country. Around 98 percent of registered Syrians under temporary protection (SuTP) live in urban settings across the country (UNHCR, 2020), and they are mostly concentrated in ten cities near Turkey's southeastern border (Özçürümez & İçduygu, 2020). SuTP can access healthcare services. Turkey had recently introduced Migrant Health Centres before the pandemic began as part of a comprehensive effort to advance health care access to this population. The Fourth Annual Report on the European Union Funded Coordination Strategy, the Facility for Refugees in Turkey (FRiT), published on April 30, 2020, highlights Turkey's "magnificent efforts in hosting and addressing the needs of almost four million refugees," including in the healthcare sector (WHO, 2020). The COVID-19 pandemic context, however, exposed striking challenges concerning the needs of the forcibly displaced as well.

At the end of February 2020, as the COVID-19 pandemic was picking up pace, Turkey declared that refugees aiming to cross to Europe would not be stopped as of February 29, 2020. As a consequence of the EU-Turkey Statement of March 2016, Turkey had agreed to stop irregular migration toward Europe, which had peaked in fall 2015, and received humanitarian assistance in return. However, growing discontent among the local population toward having to host the forcibly displaced since 2011 and neighboring a protracted conflict in Syria, the Turkish state had conducted military operations to build a "safe zone" as well as extend humanitarian assistance inside Syria in collaboration with many international organizations such as UN OCHA.

As violence escalated in the Idlib province over the summer of 2019, Turkey began to voice objections to receiving another mass influx of hundreds of thousands of refugees. In the same period, the EU continued to support humanitarian assistance programs inside Syria while remaining vague about the EU's "strategic position" toward solving the Syrian conflict (European Commission, 2020a; Stanicek, 2020). In an uneasy context about both the Syrian conflict and the presence of Syrians in Turkey, news of the deaths of thirty-three Turkish soldiers killed in an attack in Idlib on February 28, 2020, constituted a justification for the state to deliver a long-overdue message to the international community and the EU. This message, from Turkey's perspective, was about the multilayered political calculus of prolonged refugee protection for a middle-income country with a fragile economy, and the approaching financial, social, and health-related turmoil of the global pandemic. It raised the possibility of yet more uncertainty about sharing responsibilities around international protection in a context where a protracted conflict continued to displace populations with no end in sight. As tens of thousands of refugees arrived at Greece's borders, the Prime Minister of Greece openly declared that "Greece does not bear any responsibility for the tragic events in Syria and will not suffer the consequences of decisions taken by others" (Van Hagen, 2020). No matter how controversial the Turkish state's strategy was of announcing that it would stop controlling irregular migration toward Europe from a humanitarian, human rights, and international protection regime perspective, Turkey accomplished its objective of focusing the EU's attention on the situation in Northwest Syria, and as a cause of, refugee flows (European Commission, 2020b).

Turkey and the EU immediately started negotiating policy preferences, aligning interests, and sifting through alternatives for governing irregular migration flows. However, the Turkish Medical Association's report examining the situation of refugees at the Turkey-Greece border during that time pointed out serious health risks resulting from the COVID-19 pandemic and bullet wounds caused by weapons fire by the Greek border guards (Turkish Medical Association, 2020). At the end of March 2020, the Ministry of the Interior announced the transfer of all the refugees to temporary settlements in nine different cities to observe the fourteen-day quarantine measures ("Refugees Waiting at Greek Border Settled in Repatriation Centers in Turkey," 2020). In the meantime, Turkey prepared and announced a circular on COVID-19–related health services, which communicated that COVID-19–related health services would be provided free regardless of the registration status of the migrants and refugees, facilitating access to around 500,000 undocumented migrants (Official Gazette, 2020, April 9). In August 2020, data on the severity with which migrants and the forcibly displaced had been affected during the pandemic indicated that many lost their jobs and continued to struggle in need of cash support, psychosocial assistance, and basic health and hygiene supplies (International Organization for Migration, 2020, August 6). In times of crisis, even if the host state may be pursuing an effective pandemic response strategy, the forcibly displaced individuals and migrants remain the most vulnerable group susceptible to suffer the devastating health and socioeconomic effects of the pandemic.

Explanations

The pandemic response in Turkey had, as of this writing, so far maintained a steady course. However, as with all response strategies, the inherent contradictions of the political system may challenge its structure, performance, and sustainability. In this section, we discuss and explain the impact of the two most prominent challenges: the political system (presidentialism) and party politics as well as national-local responsibility sharing in pandemic response strategies.

Presidentialism as Enabler and Inhibitor of Sustained Pandemic Response Effectiveness

Turkey shifted from a parliamentary system to a new political system that is close to super-presidentialism (Cinar, 2015; Özbudun, 2015). During the COVID-19 pandemic, Turkey took quick and firm steps to implement public health measures. The results of these initiatives can be observed as high capacity of public agencies to implement authoritative policy tools such as curfews, travel restrictions, and keeping citizens at home with accompanying compliance measures such as high fines for violations. However, although the presidential system in Turkey enables authorities to act and implement public health measures swiftly in the form of decisive policy responses, some scholars cast doubts on whether the presidential system is inherently prone to cause some setbacks in policy design and implementation because of authoritative tendencies in the system (Bakir, 2020). Some examples of the drawbacks of pursuing a centralized strategy implemented with executive dominance surfaced in the early days of the response: for example, during the minister of the interior's resignation because of the panic resulting in crowd contact, risking further infection in the hours before the start of the of first curfew implementation in April; the public's total disregard of the COVID-19 measures during the ceremony for opening Hagia Sophia to worship in late July; and later gathering in large groups in weddings, celebrations, and funerals.

The public communication strategy for the fight against the COVID-19 pandemic includes framing the coronavirus as constituting a "serious danger" to and an "enemy" of humanity. Public authorities and the media reminded people of the need to observe public health measures, especially social distancing, wearing masks, and hygiene practices. In the summer months, the communication strategy focused on emphasizing the likelihood of repeated peak periods and why continuous solidarity for observing the measures is necessary because the public began to discard compliance with the measures, especially at seaside resorts. Medical specialists from the CSAB stress the significance of strict compliance with restrictive measures such as wearing masks in open public spaces and all communal closed spaces as critical for controlling the spread of the pandemic. Public authorities work to ensure compliance with restrictive measures through increased surveillance and issuing of fines to those who violate the regulations, such as not wearing their masks in designated areas. Against a backdrop of increased medical warnings and public authorities' stringent policy implementation efforts, the regular epidemiological data from the Ministry of Health reported little increase in the number of new cases or deaths (Ministry of Health, 2020d). This discrepancy undermined the public's trust in the announced data and legitimacy of the measures related to the COVID-19 pandemic. The presidential system and the centralized governance model accelerated the decision-making speed and policy implementation capacity; however, the heavy-handedness of implementation swayed public opinion toward concerns over whether the pandemic is another excuse for increasing political control. The major setback in this setting is that the public becomes less convinced and less willing to sustain the public health measures. This is a huge obstacle for success in the fight against COVID-19 because all measures rely on taking individual responsibility for one's own health to ensure the well-being of the community as a whole.

Party Politics and National-Local Responsibility Nexus

In the fight against COVID-19, Turkey's governance model constitutes public health centralism steered by the Ministry of Health and complemented by an extensive cooperation network in all sectors at both central and local levels. The organization of the policy process reflected Turkey's presidential system, established with a referendum held on the April, 16, 2017, and began with June 2018 parliamentary and presidential elections, in which the Justice and Development Party (JDP) became the majority, and Recep Tayyip Erdoğan was elected as the president with popular vote. Between 2017 and 2019, a majority of metropolitan municipality mayors and the president were from the ruling party (JDP), which reinforced unwavering cooperation between the central and local administration. However, in March 2019 elections, Turkey's major metropolitan centers (Istanbul,

Ankara, Izmir, Antalya, Adana, and Mersin) elected mayors from the main opposition party, Republican People's Party (RPP). The strain between the president's office and the metropolitan mayors of the opposition party was reflected also in the COVID-19 pandemic response.

Local governments in Turkey had been playing a key role in the fight against the COVID-19 pandemic to reduce the negative economic and social effects of COVID-19 among local populations. They pursued activities such as (1) awareness-raising campaigns, (2) fundraising, (3) providing humanitarian assistance for vulnerable groups and people who are affected negatively from the COVID-19 pandemic because of job losses, (4) pursuing solidarity strategies to enhance cooperation among citizens, and (5) disinfection of streets, public transportation vehicles, and other public places. As key local actors, metropolitan mayors from RPP seized the opportunity to increase their effectiveness at the local level through their practices against the pandemic. The central government became uneasy about the opposition party's potential for political gain from establishing a close relationship with the people through the municipalities. Based on this observation, the central government took several steps, such as the cancellation of fundraising campaigns and blocking the donation accounts of municipalities to restrict mayors' from the opposition party to increase their sphere of influence (Zaman, 2020). Although party politics and controversy over national-local level actors' dominance over policy implementation strategies may interfere with the success of the COVID-19 response, especially because of visible economic hardship, in an environment of heightened anxiety among the public about being infected, such structural tensions may be sidelined. This, however, seems to depend upon the public health centralism model of governance resuming its initial accomplishments of relatively low infection rates, effective access to treatment, data transparency, and collaboration with multiple actors to circumvent the possible detrimental effects of the inherent contradictions in the political system.

Conclusion

The COVID-19 pandemic response performance of Turkey through public health centralism, as of this writing, depended on several factors: (1) the effectiveness of screening for infection using filiation methods; (2) the level of public compliance to stringent social distancing and hygiene practices during "normalization" processes; (3) the impact of efforts to mitigate the effect of the economic crisis on the socioeconomic determinants of health; (4) the comprehensiveness of the legislation on workplace health and safety for healthcare workers, including availability of high-quality personal protective equipment for healthcare personnel and the resources to be allocated to implement the legislation (Turkish Medical Association, 2020e); (5) the effectiveness and range of psychosocial support available to healthcare professionals under severe stress as well as the general public (Turkish Medical Association, 2020b); (6) the support for and progress of research on the epidemiology and transmission of coronavirus in Turkey, which was reportedly experiencing delays in the process of the Ministry of Health approval for data collection; (7) the policy design with which epidemiological evidence and public policy responses were constructed and maintained, including the management of the "normalization" process; (8) the regional and city-level differences in the challenges induced by the pandemic as well as the success of the responses to those challenges; (9) the countrywide capability to meet the intensifying and emerging needs of vulnerable populations in a context of increasing inequalities, (10) political tension among main political parties and between central government and municipalities, and (11) building social and institutional trust in society related to the data released and measures taken against the COVID-19 to secure nationwide compliance.

All countries seemed to monitor the success of their pandemic response strategy by examining the extent to which their policy preferences, choices, practices, and capacity resulted in a reduction of national and local rates of the COVID-19-related mortality and viral spread. However, the globally diffuse and long-term characteristics of the coronavirus pandemic complicate any attempt to identify sufficiently reliable local indicators of success. Battling a global pandemic requires global response strategies, and it is imperative that humanity act in solidarity and cooperate toward a common comprehensive solution. The success of any country's response to the pandemic is, in the last instance, constrained or enabled by the success of each country's contribution to the global ensemble.

Note

1. As of this writing, the COVID-19 pandemic is still an ongoing process. The argument mentioned in this section is based on the period until August 2020. Some estimates are made that problems related to hospital capacity may occur in the upcoming period, depending on the spread of the virus.

References

Bakir, C. (2020). The Turkish state's responses to existential COVID-19 crisis. *Policy and Society, 39*(3), 424–441. https://doi:10.1080/14494035.2020.1783786

Başakşehir Şehir Hastanesi'nin ilk etabı açıldı [First phase of Başakşehir City Hospital has been opened]. (2020, April 20). NTV. https://www.ntv.com.tr/galeri/saglik/basaksehir-sehir-hastanesinin-ilk-etabi-acildi,dkGc4eFEbUOj5rzPjJqYtQ/JOWgUBrFsECGrKzvwXuxtA

Bilim Kurulu Üyeleri Kimler? Koronavirüs Bilim Kurulu nedir, kaç doctor var? [Who are the members of the Science Council? What is the Coronavirus Science Council, how many doctors are there in the Council?]. (2020, April 3). *Hurriyet.* https://www.hurriyet.com.tr/gundem/koronavirusu-bilim-kurulu-nedir-bilim-kurulu-uyeleri-kimler-41485816

"Biz bize yeteriz" kampanyasına tepki yağıyor [Protests against the "We are enough for each other" campaign are increasing]. (2020, March 31). *DW News.* https://www

.dw.com/tr/biz-bize-yeteriz-kampanyas%C4%B1na-tepki-ya%C4%9F%C4%B1yor/a-52972379

Bizbize yeteriz Türkiyem kampanyası başladı [We are enough for each other campaign has begun]. (2020, April 4). TRTHaber. https://www.trthaber.com/haber/guncel/biz-bize-yeteriz-turkiyem-kampanyasi-basladi-iste-milli-dayanisma-kampanyasinin-hesap-numaralari-473102.html

Borzou, D. (2020). *Youth and elderly to leave homes at different times as Turkey eases lockdown.* Independent. https://www.independent.co.uk/news/world/europe/turkey-coronavirus-lockdown-elderly-age-cases-social-distancing-a9498676.html

Brooks, B. (2020, April 13). *Like the flu? Trump's coronavirus messaging confuses public, pandemic researchers say.* Reuters. https://www.reuters.com/article/us-health-coronavirus-mixed-messages/like-the-flu-trumps-coronavirus-messaging-confuses-public-pandemic-researchers-say-idUSKBN2102GY

Cakir, B. (2020). COVID-19 in Turkey: Lessons learned. *Journal of Epidemiology and Global Health.* https://doi:10.2991/jegh.k.200520.001

Cinar, M. U. (2015). Letter from Ankara. *The Political Quarterly,* 86(3), 359–363. https://doi:10.1111/1467-923x.12174

Coronavirus: Brazil's President Bolsonaro removes mask despite positive Covid-19 test. (2020, July 7). BBC News. https://www.bbc.com/news/av/world-latin-america-53328739

Demirtaş, T., & Tekiner, H. (2020). Filiation: A historical term the COVID-19 outbreak recalled in Turkey. *Erciyes Med J,* 42, 3, 354–358. https://doi: 10.14744/etd.2020.54782

Deutsch-Türkische Industrie-und Handelskammer (dtr-ihk). (2020) Önlemler [Precautions]. https://www.dtr-ihk.de/tr/koronavirus/oenlemler

Erdoğan, M. N. (2020). Valiliklerde il idare kurulları ve pandemi kurulları toplanacak [Provincial Administrative Councils and Pandemic Councils will convene at governorates]. https://www.aa.com.tr/tr/koronavirus/valiliklerde-il-idare-kurullari-ve-pandemi-kurullari-toplanacak/1782778

Ergöçün, G. (2020). Turkey passes bill to tackle pandemic's impact. https://www.aa.com.tr/en/latest-on-coronavirus-outbreak/turkey-passes-bill-to-tackle-pandemics-impact/1806673

Ersoy, A. (2020). The frontline of the COVID-19 pandemic: Healthcare workers. *Turk J Int Med,* 2, 2, 31–32. https://doi:10.46310/tjim.726917

European Commission. (2020a, April 30). Communication from the Commission to the European Parliament and the Council. https://ec.europa.eu/neighbourhood-enlargement/sites/near/files/fourth_annual_report_on_the_facility_for_refugees_in_turkey.pdf

European Commission. (2020b). *Turkey: Common interest to end conflict in Syria and cooperate on the refugee crisis.* https://ec.europa.eu/commission/presscorner/detail/en/IP_20_387

Gemici, O. O. (2020). *LGS ve YKS'nin yapılacağı günlerde 81 ilde sokağa çıkma kısıtlaması uygulanacak* [Curfews will be implemented in 81 provinces where LGS and YKS will take place]. https://www.aa.com.tr/tr/turkiye/lgs-ve-yksnin-yapilacagi-gunlerde-81-ilde-sokaga-cikma-kisitlamasi-uygulanacak/1881795

Güner, A. E., Surmeli, A., Kural, K., Yılmaz, H., Kocayiğit, E., Şahin, E., & Maral, I. (2020). ICU admission rates in Istanbul following the addition of favipiravir to the national COVID-19 treatment protocol. *SSRN Electronic Journal*. https://doi:10.2139/ssrn.3622357

International Organization for Migration. (2020, August 6). *IOM Turkey calls for greater assistance for migrants and refugees as COVID-19 restrictions ease.* https://turkey.iom.int/news/iom-turkey-calls-greater-assistance-migrants-and-refugees-covid-19-restrictions-ease

Invest. (2020, April). *President Erdoğan unveils economic stability shield program.* https://www.invest.gov.tr/tr/news/newsletters/lists/investnewsletter/yat%C4%B1r%C4%B1m-ofisi-nis-2020-b%C3%BClten.pdf

Kılıç, A. U., Kara, F., Alp, E., & Doganay, M. (2020). New threat: 2019 novel coronavirus infection and infection control perspective in Turkey. *Northern Clinics of Istanbul*. https://www.ncbi.nlm.nih.gov/pmc/articles/PMC7117643/

Koca: Kurban Bayramında kısıtlama yok, 65 yaş üstü vatandaşlar lütfen bayram namazına gitmesin [Koca: No restriction in Eid Al-Adha, 65 plus citizens please do not go to Eid Al-Adha prayers]. (2020, July 29). Sputniknews. https://tr.sputniknews.com/turkiye/202007291042553306-koca-kurban-bayraminda-kisitlama-yok-65-yas-ustu-vatandaslar-lutfen-bayram-namazina-gitmesin/

Kodaz, H. (2020). Editorial: Successful treatment strategy of turkey against Covid-19 outbreak. *Eurasian Journal of Medicine and Oncology*. https://doi:10.14744/ejmo.2020.12345

Kurukız, H. Ş., Aktürk A. C., & Aktürk, İ. H. (2020). *İstanbul'a kazandırılacak iki yeni hastanenin çalışmalarına başlandı* [Construction of two new İstanbul hospitals has begun]. https://www.aa.com.tr/tr/turkiye/istanbula-kazandirilacak-iki-yeni-hastanenin-calismalarina-baslandi/1795450

Milliyet. (2020, March 25). *Sağlık Bakanlığı 32 personel alımı başvuru tarihleri ve kadro dağılımı belli oldu! 32 binf personel alımı başvuru kılavuzu yayımlandı mı?* [Ministry of Health 32 personnel recruitment application dates and distribution of posts are identified. Is the guidebook for personnel application published?]. https://www.milliyet.com.tr/gundem/saglik-bakanligi-32-personel-alimi-basvuru-tarihleri-ve-kadro-dagilimi-belli-oldu-32-bin-personel-alimi-basvuru-kilavuzu-yayimlandi-mi-6173820

Ministry of Health. (2019). *Pandemic influenza national preparedness plan 2019.* https://grip.gov.tr/depo/saglik-calisanlari/ulusal_pandemi_plani.pdf

Ministry of Health. (2020a). *T.C. Sağlık Bakanlığı COVID 19 Bilgilendirme Sayfası* [Turkısh Republic Ministry of Health COVID-19 Information Page]. https://covid19.saglik.gov.tr/

Ministry of Health. (2020b). *Hayatevesığar* [Life fits in the home]. https://hayatevesigar.saglik.gov.tr/

Ministry of Health. (2020c). *Sağlık Bakanı Fahrettin Koca TTB Başkanı Sinan Adıyaman'I Kabul Etti* [Minister of Health Fahrettin Koca received TTB (Turkish Medical Association) President Sinan Adıyaman]. https://www.saglik.gov.tr/TR,68754/saglik-bakani-fahrettin-koca-ttb-baskani-sinan-adiyamani-kabul-etti.html,%20ttb.org.tr

Ministry of Health. (2020d). *Covid-19 situation report Turkey.* https://sbsgm.saglik.gov.tr/TR,66424/covid-19-turkiye-durum-raporu-covid-19-situation-report-turkey.html

Municipalities, support groups help foreigners living in Turkey. (2020, April 27). *Daily Sabah.* https://www.dailysabah.com/turkey/municipalities-support-groups-help-foreigners-living-in-turkey-amid-covid-19-outbreak/news

Official Gazette of the Republic of Turkey. (2020, April 9). *Sosyal Güvenlik Kurumu Sağlık Uygulama Tebliğinde Değişiklik Yapılmasına Dair Tebliğ* [Declaration on the Amendment to the Social Security Institution Health Practice Declaration]. https://www.resmigazete.gov.tr/eskiler/2020/04/20200409-7.htm

Organization for Economic Cooperation and Development. (2019). *Health at a glance 2019: OECD indicators.* OECD Publishing. https://doi.org/10.1787/4dd50c09-en

Özbudun, E. (2015). Turkey's judiciary and the drift toward competitive authoritarianism. *The International Spectator, 50*(2), 42–55. https://doi:10.1080/03932729.2015.1020651

Özçürümez, S., & İçduygu, A. (2020). *Zorunlu göç deneyimi ve toplumsal bütünleşme: Kavramlar, modeller ve uygulamalar ile Türkiye* [Forced migration experience and social cohesion: Concepts, models, practices in Turkey]. Istanbul Bilgi Üniversitesi Yayınları.

Refugees waiting at Greek Border settled in repatriation center in Turkey, Interior Minister says. (2020, April 30). *Daily Sabah.* https://www.dailysabah.com/politics/eu-affairs/refugees-waiting-at-greek-border-settled-in-repatriation-centers-in-turkey-interior-minister-says

Sağlıkta üretim atağı [Production leap in health]. (2020, March 25). Dunya. https://www.dunya.com/ekonomi/saglikta-uretim-atagi-haberi-465823

South Korea braces for second wave of COVID-19 pandemic. (2020, May 10). *DW News.* https://www.dw.com/en/south-korea-braces-for-second-wave-of-covid-19-pandemic/av-53384919

Stanicek, B. (2020). EU-Turkey relations in light of the Syrian conflict and refugee crisis. *European Parliamentary Research Service.* https://www.europarl.europa.eu/RegData/etudes/BRIE/2020/649327/EPRS_BRI(2020)649327_EN.pdf

Sumer, S., Shear, J., & Yener, A. L. (2019). *Building an improved primary health care system in Turkey through care integration.* The World Bank Group. http://documents1.worldbank.org/curated/en/895321576170471609/pdf/Building-an-Improved-Primary-Health-Care-System-in-Turkey-through-Care-Integration.pdf

Torri, E., Sbrogiò, L. G., Rosa, E. D., Cinquetti, S., Francia, F., & Ferro, A. (2020). Italian public health response to the COVID-19 pandemic: Case report from the field, insights and challenges for the Department of Prevention. *International Journal of Environmental Research and Public Health, 17*(10), 3666. https://doi:10.3390/ijerph17103666

Turkey announces its first case of coronavirus. (2020, March 11). *The Guardian.* https://www.theguardian.com/world/2020/mar/11/turkey-announces-its-first-case-of-coronavirus

Turkey labor force participation rate. (2020). Tradingeconomics. https://tradingeconomics.com/turkey/labor-force-participation-rate

Turkish Psychiatry Association (TPD). (2020). *Covid-19.* http://tpdegitim.psikiyatri.org.tr/Covid19.aspx

Turkish researchers take initial step for development of Covid-19 vaccine. (2020, April 9). TRTWorld. https://www.trtworld.com/turkey/turkish-researchers-take-initial-step-for-development-of-covid-19-vaccine-35252

Türkiye'de hangi bölgede kişi başına kaç yoğun bakım yatağı düşüyor? [How many intensive care hospital beds per person are there in Turkey?]. (2020, April 5). Euronews. https://tr.euronews.com/2020/04/05/koronavirus-turkiye-de-hangi-bolgede-kisi-basina-kac-yogun-bakim-yatagi-dusuyor

Türkiye'nin hastane yatağı kapasitesi kaçç? Kişi başına kaç yatak düşüyor? [What is the hospital bed capacity in Turkey? How many beds per patient?]. (2020, March 16).

Euronews. https://tr.euronews.com/2020/03/16/turkiye-nin-hastane-yatag-kapasitesi-kac-kisi-bas-na-kac-yatak-dusuyor

Turetken, M. (2020). *Istanbul launches aid campaign amid the virus outbreak.* https://www.aa.com.tr/en/latest-on-coronavirus-outbreak/istanbul-launches-aid-campaign-amid-virus-outbreak/1785034

Turkish Medical Association. (2020a). *Situation analysis report for migrants in Edirne.* https://www.ttb.org.tr/haber_goster.php?Guid=b3a85e86-5faa-11ea-ba01-377ed3a5c4e3

Turkish Medical Association. (2020b, May 13). *TTB ve TPD Salgın döneminde sağlık çalışanlarının ruh sağlığı anketi* [Mental health of health care workers in the pandemic context conducted by TTB and TPD]. https://www.ttb.org.tr/haber_goster.php?Guid=0d3165fa-954e-11ea-baf3-777c09b98775

Turkish Medical Association. (2020c, May 14). *TTB'den COVID-19 Pandemisi İkinci Ay Raporu: Süreç şeffaf yönetilmiyor* [Second Month Report by TTB on COVID-19 Pandemic: The Process is not governed transparently]. https://www.ttb.org.tr/kollar/COVID19/haber_goster.php?Guid=aed6e5a4-95e1-11ea-baf3-777c09b98775

Turkish Medical Association. (2020d, May 15). *Bilimsel Araştırmalar geleceğie ışıktır; kısıtlanamaz* [Scientific Research is light for the future; [they] cannot be restrained]. https://www.ttb.org.tr/kollar/COVID19/haber_goster.php?Guid=ad162464-96a9-11ea-baf3-777c09b98775

Turkish Medical Association. (2020e, May 15). *Sağlık çalışanında COVID-19 tanısı işe bağlı hastalıktır; ilgili düzenlemeler buna göre yapılmalıdır* [COVID-19 Diagnosis for a healthcare worker is a work-related disease; the regulations need to be formulated as such]. https://www.ttb.org.tr/haber_goster.php?Guid=76bde838-96b9-11ea-baf3-777c09b98775

TUSEV-Third Sector Foundation of Turkey. (2020, April 7). *The State of civil society organizations in turkey amid the precautions against COVID-19.* https://www.tusev.org.tr/en/announcement/the-state-of-civil-society-organizations-in-turkey-amid-the-precautions-against-covid-19#.X8LBNhMzaHE

UNAM National Nanotechnology Research Center. (2020). *Covid-19 research at UNAM.* Bilkent University. http://unam.bilkent.edu.tr/covid-19-projects/

UNHCR. (2020). *Türkiye İstatistikleri* [Turkey statistics]. https://www.unhcr.org/tr/unhcr-turkiye-istatistikleri

Van Beusekom, M. (2020, April 13). *Doctors: COVID-19 pushing Italian ICUs toward collapse.* University of Minnesota Center for Infectious Disease Research and Policy. https://www.cidrap.umn.edu/news-perspective/2020/03/doctors-covid-19-pushing-italian-icus-toward-collapse

Van Hagen, I. (2020). *Turkey opens borders with Europe as tensions rise with Syria and Russia.* EuroNews. https://www.euronews.com/2020/02/29/turkey-opens-borders-europe-tensions-rise-syria-russia-n1145811

Worldbank. (2020a, April 24). *Dünya Bankası desteği Türkiye'nin COVID-19 pandemisine daha iyi müdahale etmesine yardımcı olacak* [Worldbank support will help Turkey fight the Covid-19 pandemic better]. https://www.worldbank.org/tr/news/press-release/2020/04/24/world-bank-support-will-help-turkeys-health-system-better-respond-to-covid-19-pandemic

Worldbank. (2020b). *GDP Growth (annual %)-Turkey.* https://data.worldbank.org/indicator/NY.GDP.MKTP.KD.ZG?locations=TR

Worldbank. (2020c). *Unemployment, total (% of total labor force (modeled ILO estimate)—Turkey*. https://data.worldbank.org/indicator/SL.UEM.TOTL.ZS?locations=TR

World Health Organization. (2009). *Pandemic influenza preparedness and response: A WHO guidance document*. https://www.ncbi.nlm.nih.gov/books/NBK143062/

World Health Organization. (2020, February 4). *Ensuring equitable access to healthcare for refugees and migrants in Turkey*. http://www.euro.who.int/en/countries/turkey/news/news/2020/2/ensuring-equitable-access-to-health-care-for-refugees-and-migrants-in-turkey

Zaman, A. (2020). *Turkey investigates opposition mayors over coronavirus campaign*. AL-Monitor. https://www.al-monitor.com/pulse/originals/2020/04/turkey-mayor-probe-coronavirus-istanbul-imamoglu-ankara.html

23 COVID-19 IN CENTRAL AND EASTERN EUROPE

Focus on Czechia, Hungary, and Bulgaria

Olga Löblová, Julia Rone, and Endre Borbáth

Countries of central and eastern Europe (CEE) are rarely accustomed to praise when compared to their western European neighbors. During the early months of the COVID-19 pandemic, however, as core European countries such as Italy, Spain, or the United Kingdom reported hundreds of confirmed cases and even deaths per day, all CEE countries managed to contain the disease with considerably lower rates of infection and deaths. This changed with the second wave in late summer and fall of 2020, when many CEE countries overtook western Europe in the number of new COVID-19 cases, as well as deaths, per population, but for a few months the region could enjoy its unusual accomplishment.

A number of hypotheses have been suggested to explain the surprising containment success in the spring, including the widespread prevalence of the bacille Calmette-Guérin tuberculosis vaccine, lower population density and exposure to tourism, lack of trust in the healthcare system and government in general (leading the population, in theory, to fear the health threat more than in wealthy countries), low testing numbers (which may have led to underreporting of cases), and an autocratic advantage leaders of imperfect democracies, such as in CEE, enjoy when imposing lockdowns and other restrictive policies (Cepaluni et al., 2020; Gotev, 2020; Shotter & Jones, 2020; Toshkov et al., 2020; Walker & Smith, 2020). One thing is certain: in the spring, CEE governments implemented strict measures to protect public health at a time when their countries had few COVID-19 cases and deaths at most in the single digits.

This chapter focuses on three CEE countries: Czechia, Hungary, and Bulgaria. These three countries are not necessarily representative of all CEE countries, but they share several important structural characteristics with the rest of the region. Before COVID-19, the three countries were hardly obvious candidates for successful health threat management. All three are often categorized as backsliding democracies (Cianetti et al., 2018; Dimitrova, 2018; Hanley & Vachudova, 2018). Compared to western Europe, they score lower on indexes of government effectiveness and regulatory quality (Kaufmann & Kraay, 2020) and, despite a common legacy of strong public health governance (Apostolova, 2020; Szabó & Wirth, 2020), their investment in health care has been lower than in countries of the European core ("Healthcare Expenditure Statistics," 2020). The Global Health Security Index (2019) ranked Hungary, Czechia, and Bulgaria thirty-five, forty-two, and sixty-one, respectively, in terms of pandemic preparedness, well behind projected frontrunners such as the United States, United Kingdom, or Sweden.

Even when focusing on agency instead of structural factors, as emphasized by recent re-examinations of the public health preparedness literature (Kavanagh & Singh, 2020), the three countries hardly had an advantageous starting position: their political leaders (prime ministers in all three cases) are frequently qualified as populist, either of the radical right, authoritarian variety as in Hungary (Mudde, 2019; Scheiring & Szombati, 2020), the anticivic kind in Bulgaria (Kabakchieva, 2020), or the technocratic sort in Czechia (Buštíková & Guasti, 2019). In this they resemble the trend of democratic backsliding under populist/illiberal leadership, observed in other postcommunist EU member states, such as Poland, Romania, Slovakia, or Slovenia (Cianetti et al., 2018). Populist leaders' policies are often understood to be of questionable rationality, driven by clientelism or the whims of public opinion, and, crucially for a health threat, antiscientific and anti-elitist (Scheiring, 2020). Their actions are rarely seen as responsible policymaking in the public interest—this hypothesis was to a large extent confirmed during the early months of the COVID-19 pandemic by the populist leaders of the United States, United Kingdom, or Brazil (see chapters 12, 26, and 27), as well as by the Czech, Bulgarian, and to some extent Hungarian, governments later in 2020. In health policy, an emerging literature has tentatively associated populist leaders and parties with negative consequences for public health (Falkenbach & Greer, 2018; Rinaldi & Bekker, 2020). The initial strong emphasis on public health protection in Czechia, Hungary, and Bulgaria is therefore puzzling from theoretical and comparative empirical perspectives.

Notwithstanding these commonalities, there are important differences among the three countries. Despite comparable population sizes, Czechia's gross domestic product (GDP) per capita is 3.8 times as much as Bulgaria's and 1.6 times as Hungary's. Czechia is also a country with net immigration, unlike Hungary and Bulgaria, which have known significant emigration since joining the European Union. This trend is especially noticeable among healthcare workers, with Czechia importing nurses and doctors notably from Slovakia, Ukraine, and Russia, and Bulgaria and Hungary exporting health workforce to western Europe (Hervey, 2017). Quality of democracy in the three countries differs, too, as shown by a combination of institutional indicators and expert assessment, collected, aggregated, and published in the form of the electoral or liberal democracy indices of V-Dem (Coppedge et al., 2020). Hungary and Bulgaria are comparable, whereas Czechia has better functioning democratic institutions, even if democratic consolidation has declined in all three since 2010. In terms of social policy, Czechia and Hungary combine elements of the Bismarckian welfare state with neoliberal policies (although neoliberal elements have been somewhat attenuated in Czechia by two center-left coalitions in power since 2014); Bulgaria attests to a more clear-cut neoliberal type as a result of policy preferences and low state capacity (Bohle &

Greskovits, 2012). As expected by Greer et al. (2020), these differences in regime type, existing welfare state, and state capacity proved significant for the divergence in the three countries' response to COVID-19, which accentuated, rather than modified, existing trends (see also Guasti, 2020).

The swift and decisive adoption of public health measures initially revealed eastern European populist leaders as "responsible" regarding health. It is of course possible that the responsible impulse to protect public health came from a place of responsiveness: in March 2020, populations in CEE were significantly concerned about the new disease (certainly more than later in the year) (National Pandemic Alarm, 2020). Nevertheless, instead of minimizing or denying the threat, in the manner of Donald Trump or Jair Bolsonaro, the Czech, Hungarian, and Bulgarian populists made a distinct choice to prioritize public health over concerns about the economy or even, initially, particularistic sectoral interests. Their authoritarian tendencies found an outlet elsewhere throughout the COVID-19 crisis: in power grabs and attacks on the rule of law and, to a degree less obvious in the immediate term, in redistributive issues. In Hungary the pandemic provided a key opportunity for even deeper concentration of power; in Bulgaria it acted as background for ongoing oligarchic rearrangements and mass protests; and in the Czech Republic the parliamentary opposition and civil society successfully checked governmental power. In all three countries the governments redistributed resources in line with their interests, including bonuses to retirees who traditionally constitute their core constituencies (cf. Bohle & Greskovits, 2012). In Hungary the government cut budgets of political parties and local governments, especially of opposition-led Budapest. At the same time, the level of politicization and polarization of COVID-19 as well as economic measures along party political lines remained remarkably low during the first wave, especially compared to, for example, Brazil or the United States. The seriousness of the health threat, as well as the need for strict measures and mandatory face coverings, did not become objects of political competition or divide the public in the first months of the pandemic. In late summer 2020, face masks and restrictions became controversial in Czechia, although not along clearly articulated political lines. Throughout the spring and summer, the three countries witnessed only small, episodic protests. Bulgaria was the only country that experienced mass protests in the summer, but protesters' demands were not related to the COVID-19 pandemic.

The responsibility of the three governments could be questioned in the summer. Czechia and Bulgaria relaxed containment measures rapidly in April and May 2020 but saw new peaks in cases in July and August 2020, with a major rise in cases in September and October 2020. In October 2020 Czechia had the highest number of new cases per population in Europe, with infections regularly surpassing five thousand a day. The governments found it difficult to reimpose even relatively minor public health measures, although Hungary had maintained some containment measures throughout the summer and only saw increased infection rates in late August 2020. Testing and tracing systems in all three countries were overwhelmed, suggesting the time the three "responsible populists" gained by swift action in March 2020 had been misspent. It is nevertheless difficult to assess how not ramping up testing, tracing, and supporting capacities during the summer had been an adequate response to still relatively low infection rates and how far it constitutes a failure of crisis management or structural capacity limits; none of the three governments communicated openly or provided detailed rationales and scientific evidence for its choices. Indeed, although the populist leaders acted responsibly during the first months of the pandemic, they behaved throughout the whole COVID-19 crisis in a highly unaccountable way.

This chapter provides details of the public health as well as social policy and economic measures in Czechia, Hungary, and Bulgaria, before discussing issues of rule of law and broader governance linked to COVID-19 in the three countries and broader lessons for political science and health policy. The focus is predominantly on the first months of the pandemic until August 2020.

Public Health Measures

Early responses of the Czech, Hungarian, and Bulgarian governments followed similar patterns. One of the first measures adopted by all three governments involved border closures and extensive travel bans in early March 2020. Czechia banned, already in early February, all incoming flights from China, followed on March 1, 2020 (when the first positive tests were confirmed), by flights from northern Italy, and later mandated self-quarantine upon arrival from Italy and a list of other EU and Asian countries. In one of the most controversial measures, Czech citizens and residents were banned from leaving the country from March 16, 2020, (a first since 1989), and no foreigners without a residence permit were allowed entry (notable exceptions included cross-border workers, especially with Germany and Austria). When there were fewer than twenty infections in the country, Hungary canceled flights to and from Iran and Italy, and by the time the number of confirmed cases rose to thirty-nine, only Hungarian citizens were allowed to enter Hungary via air or land border crossings. A focus on border control was clear in Hungary throughout the spring and summer of 2020, as the country continued to impose quarantines on travelers from numerous European countries (including, notably, the United Kingdom). In late August 2020, Prime Minister Viktor Orbán announced borders would again close to foreigners beginning September 1, and Hungarian nationals coming from abroad would be subject to quarantine, although foreign football fans were granted an exemption (Kaszás, 2020c). In Bulgaria, freedom of movement into and out of the country was not suspended, but quarantines were introduced. On March 17, the Ministry of Health imposed quarantine for all Bulgarian citizens arriving from several EU and Asian countries. During the height of the lockdown, many Bulgarian seasonal agricultural and care workers were flown to western Europe, despite the acute labor force shortage within Bulgaria (Weisskircher, et al., 2020). Numerous cases of returning *gastarbeiters* (guest workers) importing the virus to Bulgaria were documented ("Gurbetchiite, natupkani v busove i leki koli" ["Returning Guest Workers, Packed in Buses and Cars"], 2020).

The three governments also introduced lockdowns with relatively few confirmed COVID-19 cases: on March 13, 2020, in Bulgaria (24 cases total), and March 16 in Czechia (383 cases) and Hungary (19 cases). Schools and universities closed, as did most retail shops, restaurants, and theaters, with exemptions for essential businesses in all three countries. In Bulgaria, the use of parks, city gardens, sports, and playgrounds, even for health walks, was forbidden, thus making the lockdown one of the strictest in Europe despite the low numbers of infections. Breaking the quarantine rules in Bulgaria became subject to a prison sentence of up to three years and a fine between EUR 5 and 25,000 ("Do 10 godini zatvor" ["Up to 10 Years in Prison"], 2020). In Czechia and Hungary, apart from isolated incidents ("Městská policie" ["Municipal Police"], 2020), there were no reports of exaggerated police enforcement of the lockdown rules.

The Czech government mandated the use of "respiratory protective devices" everywhere outside of one's home on March 18, 2020. Given the shortage of surgical face masks and respirators, the decree clarified that scarves and other cloths were acceptable, and within hours the Czech population responded by sewing do-it-yourself cloth masks (Tait, 2020). Homemade cloth masks quickly became a symbol of national pride, with Czech civil society and politicians promoting their use as good practice internationally (ČTK, 2020a). Paradoxically, masks became a point of contention in late summer. From July 2020, the health minister lifted the obligation to face masks indoors and in public transport (authorities argued that masks are less effective in hot weather, without presenting scientific evidence to support the claim). In August 2020, the health minister announced a renewed obligation to wear masks indoors, but Prime Minister Andrej Babiš softened the rules two days later after unfavorable public opinion feedback (Brodcová, 2020). In Hungary, face mask use was made obligatory in shops and public transport in late April 2020 in Budapest and on May 4, 2020, throughout the country ("Budapest Makes Masks Mandatory for Shoppers and Commuters," 2020; "Itthon" ["At Home"], 2020). Bulgaria had seen several volte-faces on face masks: initially made mandatory indoors and outdoors on March 30, 2020, and subject to fines up to 2,500 EUR, the Minister of Health made masks "recommended" but not obligatory on March 31 after public anger at the low availability and high prices of masks. Face masks later became mandatory in public spaces from April 12, 2020, to be canceled on May 1 and reintroduced in closed spaces (with notable exceptions of cafes and bars) from June 23, 2020.

Testing and tracing systems shared similarities across the three countries. Testing relied on a mixture of private and public laboratory provision and test financing. In Czechia and Bulgaria, contact tracing relied on regional public health bodies, while in Hungary the national-level public health body cooperated with local government authorities. The Czech Republic's early efforts at ramping up its testing and tracing system seemed promising. In May 2020, the Czech government launched a test-and-trace system called "Smart Quarantine," which included a Bluetooth-based application developed by volunteers, a collaboration with banks and mobile phone operators to share location data to aid contact tracers, and an update of contact-tracing processes. Maximum testing capacities, including in private, public, and academic laboratories, were reported at around twelve thousand tests a day ("Chytrou karanténou si kupujeme pojištění, tvrdí Jurajda " ["We're Buying Insurance with Smart Quarantine, Says Jurajda"], 2020); the actual testing rate was about six to seven thousand tests per day (about 0.60 per 1000 population, similar to Austria in May), but by the time infection rates began to rise again in mid-June, testing numbers were down to about four thousand a day, which the government explained by low COVID-19 incidence. By August, despite re-upped testing rates, positive test ratios were often over 5 percent (Ministry of Health of the Czech Republic, 2020a). Regional public health offices, tasked with contact tracing, were overwhelmed and did not make use of data from banks and phone operators or the app, whose uptake remained limited (Pokorná, 2020). This was similar in Bulgaria, where understaffed regional public health authorities were reportedly failing to trace and notify people on time in July ("RZI ne uvedomilo" ["The Regional Health Inspectorate Did Not Inform"], 2020), and a contact-tracing app developed by a private company and donated to the Bulgarian government for a symbolic price never reached widespread use because of concerns about privacy. Testing levels in Bulgaria grew consistently since March 2020, to about 0.58 per 1000 population. PCR tests for people with COVID-19 symptoms were mandatory but not free—they were covered by public health insurance only upon referral to an infectious disease specialist by the patient's general practitioner—a process that included physically visiting all three providers ("PCR testovete" ["PCR Tests"], 2020). Thus, most patients ended up paying for their own tests, which typically cost between 60 to 130 BGN (EUR 30 to 75), with discounts for group tests. Hungary's official testing numbers were systematically lower than elsewhere in the region, with about two to three thousand tests a day throughout July and early August 2020, although privately purchased negative tests had not been tallied in official statistics. This changed in late August when Hungary ramped up testing numbers up to a maximum of six thousand tests on some days (0.43 per 1,000 population) ("Daily COVID-19 Tests per 1,000 People," 2020). Accessing testing was difficult, even according to government-friendly media (Schőnviszky, 2020). Overall, the three countries tested noticeably less than western European countries.

Measures within the healthcare sector differed across the three countries. Czechia restricted the provision of non-COVID-19 care in March 2020 and required hospitals to allocate bed capacity to potential COVID-19 patients, but reopened routine care provision mid-April (Ministry of Health of the Czech Republic, 2020b). In contrast, Hungary implemented an unsophisticated, controversial measure to increase COVID-19-specific care capacity: in April 2020, the minister of human capacities, in charge of the healthcare portfolio, ordered hospitals to vacate 60 percent of hospital beds within eight days to make space for COVID-19 patients (Pintér, 2020). The order was implemented hastily and chaotically, resulting in many cases in discharging patients without ensuring adequate home care. Given the low rate of COVID-19 transmission in Hungary, the decision was criticized by opposition parties as unwarranted. Some observers have put it in context of the government's plans for hospital privatization (Scheiring, 2020). The government also spent EUR 1.5 billion on COVID-19-related equipment (Urfi, 2020). More than half of the budget (0.86 billion) was spent on approximately sixteen thousand ventilators—a figure that manifestly well exceeded the medical need, even as anticipated by Prime Minister Orbán himself ("300 milliárd forintért" ["The Government Spent 300 Billion Forints"], 2020; Haász, 2020).

In Bulgaria, the health minister declared that hospitals in the country have 7,391 beds to treat COVID-19 patients, with 1,324 beds reserved in anesthesiology departments, for a population of seven million. Yet the problem in Bulgaria was not the number of beds, which is in fact one of the highest in the EU—756.9 per 100,000 inhabitants ("Hospital Beds," 2020) but rather staffing levels (similar to Hungary and to some extent Czechia). Because of significant emigration of doctors and nurses to western Europe since 2004, Bulgaria has been facing a dramatic shortage of health professionals, especially in areas outside the capital, and an aging health workforce ("Bez aparatura is lekari v pensionna vuzrast" ["Without Adequate Machine and with Doctors in the Age of Retirement"], 2020). Combined with the lack of personal protective equipment, this led to entire hospital departments resigning, citing a lack of safety measures and adequate COVID-19 planning ("Masovi ostavki vuv Vtora Gradska Bolnitza sled prevrushtaneto i v infekciozna" ["Mass Resignations in the Second City Hospital after It Was Transformed into an Infectious Diseases Hospital"], (2020). In July 2020, some hospitals, including in Bulgaria's second biggest city, Plovdiv, and in the historical capital, Veliko Turnovo, called for paid and unpaid volunteers to supplant medical personnel (Maslyankova, 2020).

Lockdown relaxation was initially gradual in all three countries, starting in April 2020 in Czechia and early May 2020 in Bulgaria and Hungary, but accelerating as immediate rises in COVID-19 cases did not immediately materialize. However, all three countries lacked clear guidance on reintroducing public health measures, which made responses to dramatic surges in cases in July and August 2020 politically difficult. The Czech government's first plan of the lockdown relaxation timeline respected a fourteen-day distance between easing stages (Government of the Czech Republic, 2020) but had been repeatedly accelerated, and many areas of social and economic activity opened simultaneously. By May 25, much of daily life was back to normal, including a reopening of schools and indoor pubs. Similarly, in Bulgaria, the government, led by Prime Minister Boyko Borissov, quickly relaxed most public health measures beginning May 13, 2020, opening shopping malls, trade centers, and fitness and sports halls. The Bulgarian government opened indoor restaurants, bars, and night clubs on June 1, 2020.

Czechia and Bulgaria had low levels of infection in April and May 2020, which hardly justified a continuous strict lockdown, but economic concerns may have played an additional role. In Czechia, a court ruling in late April 2020 potentially exposed the state to damages liabilities. Within hours, the minister of health announced a precipitated opening of shops and lifted the ban on freedom of movement, including on travel abroad. In Bulgaria, it was considered that Bulgarian tourism, which represents 12 percent of the country's GDP, would not be able to survive continuing public health measures. Another force, potentially important for electoral politics in Bulgaria, were football fans: beginning June 5, 2020, stadiums were officially allowed to operate at maximum 30 percent capacity. In practice, thousands of football fans celebrated the 2020 Bulgarian cup final in close proximity.

In Hungary, a major controversy concerned school reopening. On April 19, 2020, Prime Minister Orbán announced on Facebook that infections were expected to peak on May 3, one day before the start of the centralized high school final examinations. Despite protests from teachers, parents, and students, as well as the opposition, the examinations (mandatory for eighty-four thousand students and supervised by sixty-five hundred teachers) took place. Indoor restaurants and pubs, as well as cultural and tourist establishments, reopened in late May 2020, but the ban on gatherings of over five hundred people remained in place, with a tangible impact throughout the summer on the music festival industry (Kaszás, 2020a).

Reintroduction of public health measures proved difficult in Czechia and Bulgaria over the summer, despite infection rates higher than during March and April 2020 (both countries regularly saw two to three hundred daily new cases in the summer), but smooth in Hungary, which had consistently low infection rates in July and August 2020 (below one hundred daily). In Czechia, an infection outbreak in a coal mine in the northeast in May and June 2020 initially seemed controlled by the regional public health body, but by July, the public health office noted widespread community transmission and immediately banned events over one hundred people, including an ongoing music festival. This provoked a two-thousand-strong demonstration (ČTK, 2020b). By early September 2020, the chief public health officer of Prague publicly apologized for no longer being able to trace new infections (ČTK, 2020c). Despite skyrocketing infection rates, few public health measures were introduced throughout September 2020, which many commentators put in the context of local and Senate elections in early October.

In Bulgaria the government attempted to close down night clubs and discotheques in July 2020, only to give in to public pressure and reopen them a few days later ("Praven Svyat" ["Legal World"], 2020). Hungary maintained public health measures, notably mandatory face masks indoors, bans on large events, and mandatory quarantine for visitors and returning residents from numerous EU and non-EU countries, throughout the summer, without significant pressure for further easing from the affected sector or the public. No major protests followed Prime Minister Orbán's announcement of Hungary's tightened travel restrictions from September 2020 (Bayer, 2020), suggesting an autocratic advantage may well be at play.

In summary, all three countries implemented similar, swift, and far-reaching measures to protect public health in March 2020, including travel bans and lockdowns. Where they diverged was in the extent to which these measures were relaxed in the summer. Hungary maintained some restrictions, such as face masks and large event bans, whereas Czechia and Bulgaria lifted virtually all measures in May 2020, and their governments hesitated to reimpose even partial restrictions. They also diverged in their adaptation of health systems, with Czechia coping with the shock of COVID-19 relatively well (at least until the severe second wave in the fall of 2020), Hungary overreacting by crudely restricting routine care, and Bulgaria having to deal with a health system with a high number of hospital beds but low number of doctors and nurses.

Social Policy Measures

All three countries adopted social policy measures supporting businesses and individuals. Support for businesses relied chiefly on guaranteed loans and public funding of furloughs and other short work week schemes. In all three countries, measures targeted at individuals through lockdowns and mitigating the effects of economic downturn in Czechia, Hungary, and Bulgaria have been characterized by a relatively heavy administrative burden. Beyond that, however, the responses of the three governments differ significantly.

In Czechia, the government's furlough scheme contributed 60, 80, or in some cases 100 percent of wages and social security contributions (capped at average gross wage) to employers for employees in quarantine, on caretaker leave, or if the business had been reduced or closed as a result of the pandemic or government measures (Eurofound, 2020). The government further waived the part of social security contributions paid by employers for small businesses in June through August 2020. In April the government implemented a lump-sum of 500 CZK (EUR 20) per day since March 12 for the self-employed. The program initially excluded workers on zero-hour contracts but was retroactively extended, at 350 CZK (14 EUR) per day, in July, following criticism by the opposition and the public. In August, it proposed (and later adopted) a lump-sum of 5,000 CZK (190 EUR) for all retirees. The government introduced interest-free guaranteed loans for businesses across several consecutive financing schemes. Advance payments on personal and corporate income tax were suspended for the second quarter 2020 and penalties waived for failing to pay property tax and file income tax returns on time, rents for businesses were subsidized and repayments of business and household loans and mortgages became subject to a three- to six-month moratorium. According to an independent group of economists, the eventual amount of direct and indirect state support to businesses and individuals amounted to about 300 billion CZK (EUR 11.4 billion) or about 5.4 percent of GDP; however, only about 100 billion CZK (1.7 percent of GDP) had been disbursed by mid-August (KoroNERV-20, 2020). Businesses notably complained about excessive bureaucratic burden and slow processing of the initial loan programs (Hospodářská Komora ČR, 2020). The government approved grants for tourism, notably a voucher system for spa tourism (International Monetary Fund, 2020). It further proposed to finance a large advertising campaign for domestic tourism, the revenues of which were to benefit progovernment media—it later retracted the plan following opposition criticism ("Návrh kampaně na dovolenou v Česku ministerstvo stáhlo" ["Ministry Retracts Proposal for PR Campaign for Holidays in Czechia"], 2020).

Compared to countries in the region, the Hungarian government acted relatively late and did little to decrease the impact of the crisis on the national economy. The government provided tax exemptions for the most hard-hit sectors of tourism, catering, entertainment, sport, culture, and transport. It introduced a furlough scheme available from May 1, but only businesses who lost 30 to 50 percent of employee working time could prove that their orders have not fallen by more than 50 percent and are working toward the "interests of the national economy" were eligible, if employees worked at least four hours daily (later reduced to two hours) and remained in training for another 30 percent of their time. The measure was later made more flexible but has been criticized as restrictive and belated (Krokovay, 2020). The government did not provide direct transfers to employers or employees, except for a one-time payment of about 1,500 EUR (500 000 HUF) to all healthcare workers, and did not prolong the three-month limit on unemployment benefits (after which health insurance contributions were no longer covered by the state), one of the shortest in Europe. In response to criticism from the opposition and civil society, the government pointed to its heavily criticized workfare program (see, e.g., Szikra, 2014), and Prime Minister Orbán suggested that those who remained without a source of income join the military. Pensioners, however, were promised an extra week of pension benefit in the coming three years (International Monetary Fund, 2020). Take-up of the furlough scheme was less than expected: about 200,000 employees benefited from the scheme by July 2020, as opposed to some 500,000 expected beneficiaries. Given the late introduction of the policy, Hungarian trade unions complained that little had been done for workers who had already been laid off by May (Krokovay, 2020). The size of the April economic package is hard to estimate because of the lack of transparency and creative accounting. However, the pledge includes an immediate 630 billion HUF (EUR 1.76 billion) to cover the immediate costs of the pandemic and an additional 8,370 billion HUF (EUR 23.32 billion) the government claims to invest to temper the economic effects of the crisis, although it announced an intention to keep the budget deficit below 2.7 percent, effectively amounting to an austerity policy (Csiki, 2020; Scheiring, 2020). One study puts the immediate fiscal impulse, as adopted, at 0.4 percent of Hungary's 2019 GDP (Anderson et al., 2020).

Bulgaria implemented a "60:40" furlough scheme, expected to cost beyond EUR 500 million: 60 percent of employee salaries were to be covered by the state and 40 percent by employers (Government of Bulgaria, 2020). Yet only EUR

26.3 million were spent on the 60:40 scheme by end of May 2020; at the same time, expenses for unemployment benefits rose sharply and reached 30.5 million EUR (Grigorova, 2020). Many companies applied for support from the 60:40 measure only for some of their workers, usually the top management, while laying off other workers. In March, the Bulgarian government pledged to provide 4.5 billion BGN (approximately EUR 2.25 billion) in guaranteed loans ("Pravitelstvoto s ikonomicheski merki za 4.5mlrd. lv. za borba s coronavirusa" ["The Government Offers Economic Measures for 4.5 Billion for Fighting the Coronavirus"], 2020). Further EUR 250 million were allocated for covering the increased expenses of the Ministry of Health, Ministry of Defense, and the Interior Ministry, and EUR 100 million were pledged to guarantee zero-interest consumer credits up to EUR 750 for individuals on unpaid leave.

As in Czechia, most of the money allocated for tackling the crisis and reviving the economy remained unused. The Bulgarian government further adopted several new social policy measures targeting individuals (Government of Bulgaria, 2020), which were nevertheless often subject to excessively complex means-testing. For example, parents could apply for a one-time sum of approximately EUR 190 but only provided that they could prove satisfying a total of nine conditions. Thus, a large part of the population was practically excluded from benefiting from the support. Less cumbersome new measures included the possibility for parents to receive help in hiring a carer for children, including their own unemployed relatives. EUR 25 million were distributed among retired people with low pensions: pensioners were to receive EUR 25 extra for August, September, and October 2020. Meanwhile, the government of Bulgaria pledged to provide EUR 500 extra per month for frontline health workers fighting the virus. Unemployment benefits were slightly increased (by EUR 1.50 per day), and the term for which they could be paid was increased by three months. The salaries of social workers as well as standards for financing delegated social services were increased. In the fall, the government introduced a new series of social measures and direct transfers. Yet, rather than addressing the impact of COVID-19, these late and partial measures aimed to decrease social pressure and buy support for the Bulgarian government in the context of mass protests and approaching elections.

Overall, the social policy response demonstrates diversity, rather than commonalities, among these three countries. Czechia's social policy measures followed, in principle, broad lines of responses of western European governments by offering unconditional direct transfers to the self-employed and loans to businesses, as well as furlough schemes for employees, although their effects are still up for debate. Bulgaria, in comparison, implemented few measures to alleviate the economic impact of the COVID-19 for the population, offering support subject to excessively complex means-testing and a furlough scheme with limited impact. Finally, the Hungarian government refused to abandon its "workfare society" social policy, declining to adjust its restrictive unemployment benefit rules, and implemented a narrow furlough scheme. Notably, however, all three governments implemented bonus transfers to pensioners, traditionally their core electorates.

Discussion

If the initial successes of the Czech, Hungarian, and Bulgarian governments in containing the spread of COVID-19 stand out in the European context, so do two other kinds of actions common to the three countries: the use of the public health and economic crises to effectuate power grabs and the opaque, top-down, and arbitrary decision-making style of governments and their crisis teams. The approach of these three CEE countries to the COVID-19 crisis can be summarized as responsible initially, unaccountable throughout. Here again, these governance issues affected the three countries to varying degrees.

In Hungary, the government treated the pandemic as an opportunity for further executive power grabs. Perhaps unsurprisingly, given Prime Minister Orbán's long-established craftsmanship in using technical pretexts to centralize power, Hungary's government implemented an ostentatious power grab in March 2020. Orbán seized the opportunity and relied on his two-thirds parliamentary majority to introduce special provisions, allowing the government to indefinitely rule by decree, despite criticism from domestic opposition parties, EU leaders, national, and international observers (Borbáth, 2020). In addition, the legislation allowed the government to postpone elections and prosecute those who deliberately "spread misinformation" regarding the pandemic. The latter provision was heavily criticized and led to high-profile arrests of a political activist and a farmer (charges were later dropped) (Kaszás, 2020b). The law was rescinded in June 2020, as new regulations were introduced to allow the government the continued exercise of some of its special powers. The government further appropriated some of the funding initially allocated for party financing and for local governments, arguing with the need to finance the economic recovery package. The move was widely seen as a power grab for two reasons: one, opposition parties had ascended to power in Budapest and other urban centers in 2019, and two, party financing made up a minor part of the state budget. As an immediate consequence, local governments were left without funds to mitigate the economic and public health effects of COVID-19 despite being designated as first responders. In an even clearer power grab move, the 2021 budget, adopted in July 2020, appropriated further funds from opposition-run Budapest, leading to a political clash with the mayor. As in pre-coronavirus times, decision-making and government communication in Hungary remained highly centralized around Prime Minister Orbán, with little transparency and public involvement of experts. The main channel of information provided by the government was regular press briefings by the surgeon general, mainly picking up questions from government-friendly media outlets. New measures, including, for instance, the economic package or organization of high school exams, were frequently announced by Orbán on his

Facebook page. Data on testing have been seen as unreliable: in July 2020, Norway excluded Hungary from its list of COVID-19 safe countries on the basis of incomplete reporting on testing to the European Centre for Disease Prevention and Control (Flachner, 2020).

In Bulgaria, abuses of rule of law were more limited than in Hungary, but the pandemic served as a backdrop to existing cleavages. Decision-making during the pandemic was highly centralized in the hands of Prime Minister Borissov. Dealing with the pandemic was presented as a matter for experts. In practice, however, Borissov's government created two expert advisory teams: one supported strict lockdown measures, whereas some members of the other downplayed the threat of the virus and argued in favor of herd immunity. Borissov frequently played the two teams against each other as "opposing experts" to avoid taking the blame for decision regarding the virus. Mainstream media invited experts from both teams, thriving on the conflict and doing little to address the widespread confusion caused by the spread of fake news online. All in all, however, COVID-19 seemed to have little importance in Bulgaria's political life, which developed in parallel. Although the nationalist party Vuzrazhdane organized in mid-May 2020 small protests against the lack of economic support, strict lockdown measures, and 5G (seen in some conspiracy theories as responsible for the spread of COVID-19), the massive protests in July were primarily targeted at the capture of the state by oligarchic players. Rather than the government's handling of the pandemic, the protests reflected the population's frustration with state capture, which had transpired in a series of scandals before as well as during lockdown ("Anti-corruption Protests Enter Thirtieth Consecutive Day in Bulgaria," 2020). Only in August 2020 did nurses join the antigovernment protests demanding better salaries and working conditions. Connections between the protests and COVID-19 were thus mainly indirect—reflected in Borissov's reluctance to reintroduce strict measures to avoid popular anger and in the social measures meant above all to appease key groups in the electorate in a complex political situation.

Finally, Czechia withstood attempts at executive overreach relatively well. Government measures were met with scrutiny by the parliamentary opposition, civil society watchdogs, and the judiciary, which proved to be an effective source of checks and balances. In May, the Parliament refused to approve a second extension of the state of emergency, and opposition politicians criticized numerous parameters of individual measures: for instance, the restrictive rules for cross-border workers. When the government proposed a bill that would make due diligence unnecessary for selected public procurement contracts, the parliamentary debate was eventually postponed until after the end of the state of emergency following pressure from nongovernmental organizations and the opposition ("Korupční zákon i legalizace zlodějin" ["Corrupt Law and Legalization of Theft"], 2020). Private individuals as well as senators also contested the constitutionality of key government measures (notably the travel and shopping bans) via the judiciary, including the Constitutional Court. In April 2020 a Prague court ruled that the limits to fundamental rights imposed by the lockdown and shop closure measures were too great for the measures to be issued single-handedly by the minister of health as decrees based on the Public Health Protection Act ("Soud zrušil opatření omezující obchod a volný pohyb" ["Court Cancels Measures Limiting Retail and Free Movement"], 2020). Instead, the court insisted they be reissued by the government based on the Crisis Act, subject to parliamentary scrutiny. In fact, the measures were initially, in mid-March 2020, issued under the Crisis Act but canceled only days later and replaced with identical measures under the Public Health Protection Act—possibly because the state was potentially liable for damages under the Crisis Act (Zíta, 2020). The ruling led to an immediate easing of the lockdown. Despite numerous expert advisory teams, the government rarely provided detailed scientific rationale for its policies, which at times seemed to follow public opinion and had been criticized for a lack of transparency by experts as well as politicians (Bidrmanová, 2020).

Several conclusions can be drawn from the responses of the Czech, Hungarian, and Bulgarian governments to the COVID-19 pandemic. First, structural factors typically assessed in health threat preparedness indexes, such as state capacity or health system resilience, may not be sufficient to explain eventual outcomes. Observing the failures to prevent deaths of several typically high-capacity countries such as the United Kingdom and United States led to calls for reintegration of agency, specifically the role of political leadership, to future thinking about preparedness (e.g., Kavanagh & Singh, 2020). Eastern Europe's experience with COVID-19, however, suggests that what is perhaps needed is a nuance of the kind of capacity necessary for particular threats: in the case of COVID-19, the appropriate first response to the threat involved crude measures such as stay-at-home orders, which hardly correlate with measures of government effectiveness or regulatory capacity, for example. Building effective testing and tracing systems and designing and implementing more nuanced public health measures, however, requires more sophisticated capacity. The dramatic rise in new infections and deaths in the region since August 2020 (Shotter & Hopkins, 2020) show that CEE countries have not been, and likely will not be, as successful in the long run as in the first months of the pandemic.

Second, leadership matters, but even leaders traditionally associated with suboptimal policies such as populists can adopt responsible policies in a crisis. In contrast to other populist leaders, the three prime ministers of Czechia, Hungary, and Bulgaria placed surprising emphasis on the protection of public health, contrary to assumptions of some of the literature on the impact of populism on public health (Rinaldi & Bekker, 2020). This emphasis surely contributed to halting the exponential growth of new infections (although other confounding variables are likely to have played a role, notably the presumably low COVID-19 incidence in CEE in January and February 2020). Given the low transparency of government decision-making in the three countries, it is difficult to determine what prompted the adoption of the "responsible" option (i.e., in what aspects was leadership of central and eastern European populists different from, for example, Brazil's Bolsonaro or the United States' Trump).

There are few indications suggesting the three governments engaged in complex reviews of scientific evidence; it is more likely the initial policies, such as lockdowns and border closures, were the result of learning or emulation of other countries. After the initial swift reaction, however, experience with face masks in Czechia or nightclub closures in Bulgaria suggest leaders may become less responsible in terms of infection prevention and more responsive in terms of catering to public opinion, which had shifted from scared to unconcerned by June 2020 (National Pandemic Alarm, 2020).

Third, there were some indications in favor of the authoritarian advantage hypothesis in the three countries (Cepaluni et al., 2020; Toshkov et al., 2020). In Hungary, Prime Minister Orbán, who rules the country virtually unchecked, was able to maintain restrictive public health measures longer and introduce new restrictions easier than Czechia's Prime Minister Babiš, constrained by effective parliamentary opposition, independent judiciary, and active civil society, or than Bulgaria's Prime Minister Borissov, weakened by oligarchic infighting and mass protests. However, in the case of early COVID-19 pandemic (Cepaluni et al., 2020), the authoritarian advantage should lead to fewer deaths: Hungary, despite its low overall case numbers, had a remarkably high mortality rate from COVID-19 during the first wave, which the authorities explained by an unusually high proportion of transmissions occurring in hospitals. In autumn 2020, though, COVID-19 deaths per population seemed to rise slower in Hungary than in the other two countries. Furthermore, this advantage is, by definition, accompanied by abuses of power and disrespect of rule of law and limited pluralism in decision-making, which may have nefarious consequences on policies, including on health (Rinaldi & Bekker, 2020), as day-to-day policy-making retakes precedence over the initial period of high uncertainty.

Fourth, unlike, for example, in Brazil or the United States, responses to the pandemic need not become a politicized topic in all polarized societies, or at least not immediately. The three CEE countries are polarized along partisan identities (Reiljan, 2020; Vegetti, 2018), but the broad directions of government measures as well as the severity of the health threat itself were subject to general cross-party consensus. Similarly to other European countries, opposition parties found it difficult to contest the incumbent party's policies, as executive power became more important vis-à-vis parliaments (Merkel, 2020). In Bulgaria, notably, anti-government protests were effectively decoupled from COVID-19, and there was little criticism of anti-COVID-19 measures along party lines. Face masks became a polarizing topic in Czechia in late summer, but no major political party overtly claimed an anti-face-mask line. Similarly, in Hungary and in Bulgaria, political opposition did not oppose public health measures introduced by the government. One potential explanation for this relates to populists' monopolization of anti-establishment sentiments: when populists adopt a responsible policy, competitor parties may not be able, or willing, to credibly exploit antisystem, antiscience moods in the population, for fear of alienating their core electorate and failing to reach supporters of the populists in power.

Conclusions

Czechia, Hungary, and Bulgaria, and much of the rest of central and eastern Europe, provide a counter-example to some pre-COVID-19, as well as post-COVID-19, received wisdom on the role of structure and agency in crises. Among the old ideas, the region's successful initial containment of the virus questions the assumption that higher state capacity leads to better outcomes. Among the new ones, it qualifies some of the emerging hypotheses about ineffective leadership of populist leaders, as well as about politicization of the pandemic in polarized societies. To be sure, the region is certainly not the only case puzzling for theories of COVID-19 politics induced from a handful of prominent policy failures (the United States) and textbook successes (South Korea); similar unexpected successes have been noted, for example, in Vietnam and on the African continent (Dabla-Norris et al., 2020; Pilling, 2020). It is nevertheless interesting because of its particular combination of successful initial leadership followed by the "responsible" populists' rule of law abuses, which were mediated by democratic institutions in some countries (e.g., Czechia, Bulgaria) or left unchecked in others (e.g., Hungary), and in all cases opaque and unaccountable.

The subsequent rise in COVID-19 cases in CEE in the summer and fall put to test the limits of individual leaders' agency as a replacement for institutions prepared to tackle the health and societal risks of a pandemic without plying to the partisan interests of those in power. As governments hesitated to impose renewed restrictions, new cases overwhelmed test and trace systems, as well as hospitals, and COVID-19 deaths rose to levels on par with the worst-hit western European countries during the first wave. It is therefore tempting to conclude that the CEE populists' responsibility in spring 2020 was likely a case of a broken clock. The clock shows the correct time twice a day; from time to time, populists act responsibly. In the longer run, however, initial responsibility may not be enough to compensate for subsequent responsiveness to irresponsible public opinion or economic interests. Judging from the experience of a deadly second wave, central and eastern European countries are likely to join the ranks of other countries led by populist leaders—and end up with poor public health, as well as economic, outcomes regardless of their initial successes (Greer et al., 2020).

Acknowledgment

The authors would like to thank Dorothee Bohle and Lili Török for comments on an early version of this chapter.

References

300 milliárd forintért vett duplaannyi lélegeztetőgépet a kormány, mint amennyire a lehető legrosszabb esetben szükség lett volna [The government spent 300 billion

Forints to buy twice as many ventilators than would be needed in the worst-case scenario]. (2020, June 25). *444.hu.* https://444.hu/2020/06/25/300-milliard-forintert-vett-duplaannyi-lelegeztetogepet-a-kormany-mint-amennyire-a-leheto-legrosszabb-esetben-szukseg-lett-volna

Anderson, J., Bergamini, E., Brekelmans, S., Cameron, A., Darvas, Z., Domínguez Jíménez, M., Lenaerts, K., & Midões, C. (2020). *The fiscal response to the economic fallout from the coronavirus.* Bruegel. https://www.bruegel.org/publications/datasets/covid-national-dataset/#hungary

Anti-corruption protests enter thirtieth consecutive day in Bulgaria. (2020, August 8). Euronews. https://www.euronews.com/2020/08/08/anti-corruption-protests-enter-thirtieth-consecutive-day-in-bulgaria

Apostolova, R. (2020, May 20). *Epidemiology must be a mass movement.* Dversia.net. https://dversia.net/5883/epidemiology-mass-movement/?fbclid=IwAR3SJ_HNMVDXVZLGqbADjR1pW0zRvw7Y5oc-gkotbSvzP6oKgOSl_pEc9sY

Bayer, L. (2020, August 28). *Hungary to close borders starting September 1.* Politico.eu. https://www.politico.eu/article/coronavirus-hungary-to-close-borders-starting-september-1/

Bez aparatura is lekari v pensionna vuzrast: Kak shte se spravyat s koronavirusa v Provadia [Without adequate machines and with doctors in the age of retirement: How will they deal with the coronavirus in Provadia]. (2020, August 31). Nova.bg. https://nova.bg/news/view/2020/04/18/285419/без-апаратура-и-с-лекари-в-пенсионна-възр

Bidrmanová, M. (2020). *Vláda řídí epidemii podle intuice. Stylem brzda plyn, říká Münich* [Government manages epidemic according to intuition, stop-start-style, says Münich]. SeznamZpravy.cz. https://www.seznamzpravy.cz/clanek/munich-vlada-ridi-epidemii-podle-intuice-s-koronavirem-bojuje-ode-zdi-ke-zdi-102900#

Bohle, D., & Greskovits, B. (2012). *Capitalist diversity on Europe's periphery.* Cornell University Press.

Borbáth, E. (2020, April 15). *How does the corona virus strengthen authoritarianism in Hungary?* WZB. https://www.wzb.eu/en/research/corona-und-die-folgen/how-does-the-corona-virus-strengthen-authoritarianism-in-hungary

Brodcová, D. (2020). Prudký obrat v rouškách přehledně. Co bude platit . . . prozatím Definitivně [U-Turn in face masks with clarity. What measures will be valid . . . for the moment definitively]. *SeznamZpravy.cz.* https://www.seznamzpravy.cz/clanek/prudky-obrat-v-rouskach-prehledne-co-bude-platit-prozatim-definitivne-116819

Budapest makes masks mandatory for shoppers and commuters. (2020). TheMayor.eu. https://www.themayor.eu/en/budapest-makes-masks-mandatory-for-shoppers-and-commuters

Buštíková, L., & Guasti, P. (2019). The State as a firm: Understanding the autocratic roots of technocratic populism. *East European Politics and Societies, 33*(2), 302–30.

Cepaluni, G., Dorsch, M., & Branyiczki, R. (2020). Political regimes and deaths in the early stages of the COVID-19 pandemic. *SSRN Electronic Journal.* https://papers.ssrn.com/sol3/papers.cfm?abstract_id=3586767

Chytrou karanténou si kupujeme pojištění, tvrdí Jurajda [We're buying insurance with Smart Quarantine, says Jurajda]. (2020, May 5). CNN Prima News. https://cnn.iprima.cz/k-veci-chytrou-karantenou-si-kupujeme-pojisteni-tvrdi-clen-nervu-jurajda-2643

Cianetti, L., Dawson, J., & Hanley, S. (2018). Rethinking "democratic backsliding" in central and eastern Europe–Looking beyond Hungary and Poland. *East European Politics, 34*(3), 243–256.

Coppedge, M., Gerring, J., Knutsen, C. H., Lindberg, S. I., Teorell, J., Altman, D., Bernhard, M., Fish, M. S., Glynn, A., Hicken, A., Luhrmann, A., Marquardt, K. L., McMann, K., Paxton, P., Pemstein, D., Seim, B., Sigman, R., Skaaning, S-E, Staton, J., … Daniel Ziblatt, D. (2020). *V-Dem [Country–Year/Country–Date] Dataset v10.* Varieties of Democracy (V-Dem) Project. https://doi.org/10.23696/vdemds20

Csiki, G. (2020). Szerintünk így néz ki eddig a koronavírus elleni Orbán-csomag [This is how the anti-COVID19 Orbán packet looks according to us]. *Portfolio.hu*. https://www.portfolio.hu/gazdasag/20200406/szerintunk-igy-nez-ki-eddig-a-koronavirus-elleni-orban-csomag-424514#

ČTK. (2020a, March 29). Czech PM Andrej Babiš calls on Donald Trump to make face masks obligatory—Prague, Czech Republic. *Expats.cz*. https://news.expats.cz/weekly-czech-news/czech-pm-andrej-babis-calls-on-donlad-trump-to-make-face-masks-obligatory/

ČTK. (2020b, July 21). Thousands of people protest against tightened lockdown measures in Ostrava. *Expats.cz*. https://news.expats.cz/weekly-czech-news/rally-protesting-against-lockdown-measures-in-ostrava/

ČTK. (2020c, September 4). Situace je tristní, přiznala Jágrová. Pražská hygiena stíhá trasovat kontakty nakažených jen obtížně [The situation is terrible, admitted Jágrová. Prague public health office manages to trace contacts only with difficulty]. *Lidovky.cz*. https://www.lidovky.cz/domov/prazska-hygiena-stiha-trasovat-jen-obtizne-pozitivne-testovane-zada-o-shovivavost.A200904_153419_ln_domov_ele

Dabla-Norris, E., Gulde-Wolf, A.-M., & Painchaud, F. (2020, June 29). Vietnam's success in containing COVID-19 offers roadmap for other developing countries. *IMF News*. https://www.imf.org/en/News/Articles/2020/06/29/na062920-vietnams-success-in-containing-covid19-offers-roadmap-for-other-developing-countries

Daily COVID-19 tests per 1,000 people. (2020, September 1). Our World in Data. https://ourworldindata.org/coronavirus-data-explorer?zoomToSelection=true&time=earliest..2020-12-01&country=CZE~HUN~BGR&region=Europe&testsMetric=true&interval=daily&perCapita=true&smoothing=0&pickerMetric=location&pickerSort=asc

Dimitrova, A. L. (2018). The uncertain road to sustainable democracy: Elite coalitions, citizen protests and the prospects of democracy in central and eastern Europe. *East European Politics, 34*(3), 257–275.

Do 10 godini zatvor i do 50 000 leva globa pri nespazvane na karantina [Up to 10 years in prison and up to 50,000 leva for breaking the quarantine]. (2020, March 13). *Nova.bg*. https://nova.bg/news/view/2020/03/13/281201/

Eurofound. (2020, September 1). Czechia - Eurofound COVID-19 EU PolicyWatch. *COVID-19 EU PolicyWatch Database of national-level responses*. https://static.eurofound.europa.eu/covid19db/countries/CZ.html

Falkenbach, M., & Greer, S. L. (2018). Political parties matter: The impact of the populist radical right on health. *European Journal of Public Health, 28*, 15–18.

Flachner, B. (2020, July 11). A Norvégok szerint Magyarország nem jelenti az EU-nak a koronavírussal kapcsolatos adatokat [According to the Norwegians Hungary does not report data related to COVID-19 to the EU]. *Index.hu*. https://index.hu/kulfold/2020/07/11/norvegia-magyarorszag-koronavirus-beutazas-karanten/

Global Health Security Index. (2019). *Global Health Security Index: Building collective action and accountability.* https://www.ghsindex.org/wp-content/uploads/2020/04/2019-Global-Health-Security-Index.pdf

Gotev, G. (2020). The Brief—Is Eastern Europe more resilient to COVID-19? *Euractiv.com.* https://www.euractiv.com/section/coronavirus/news/the-brief-is-eastern-europe-more-resilient-to-covid-19/

Government of Bulgaria. (2020). *Ikonomicheski merki | Coronavirus.Bg. Edinen Informacionen portal* [Economic measures /Coronavirus.Bg. Information Portal]. Retrieved September 1, 2020, from https://coronavirus.bg/bg/merki/ikonomicheski

Government of the Czech Republic. (2020). Harmonogram uvolnění podnikatelských a dalších činností 14/04/2020 [Timetable of re-opening of business and other activities]. https://web.archive.org/web/20200427005201/https://www.vlada.cz/assets/epidemie-koronaviru/dulezite-informace/uvolneni_schema_podnikatele_zivnostnici_14042020.pdf

Greer, S. L., King, E. J., Massard da Fonseca, E., & Peralta-Santos, A. (2020). The comparative politics of COVID-19: The need to understand government responses. *Global Public Health, 15*(9), 1413–1416. https://doi.org/10.1080/17441692.2020.1783340

Grigorova, V. (2020). 60-40 - Propaganda i fakti [60-40—Propaganda and facts]. *Barikada.* https://baricada.org/2020/05/29/60-40-propaganda-fakti/

Guasti, P. (2020). The impact of the COVID-19 pandemic in central and eastern Europe. *Democratic Theory, 7*(2), 47–60.

Gurbetchiite, natupkani v busove i leki koli, nosyat COVID-10 v Kurdzhaliysko [Returning guest workers, packed in buses and cars, bring Covid-19 in Kurzhali region]. (2020). *Konkurent.bg.* https://www.konkurent.bg/news/15844564091756/gurbetchiite-natapkani-v-busove-i-leki-koli-nosyat-covid-19-v-kardzhaliysko

Haász, J. (2020, April 10). Orbán: 7500–8000 Lélegeztetőgép Kellhet Majd [Orbán: There might be a need for 7500-8000 ventilators]. *Index.hu.* https://index.hu/belfold/2020/04/10/orban_7500-8000_lelegeztetogep_kell_majd/

Hanley, S., & Vachudova, M. A. (2018). Understanding the illiberal turn: Democratic backsliding in the Czech Republic. *East European Politics, 34*(3), 276–296.

Healthcare expenditure statistics—statistics explained. (2020, April). Eurostat. https://ec.europa.eu/eurostat/statistics-explained/index.php/Healthcare_expenditure_statistics

Hervcy, G. (2017, September 27). *The EU Exodus: When doctors and nurses follow the money.* Politico.eu. https://www.politico.eu/article/doctors-nurses-migration-health-care-crisis-workers-follow-the-money-european-commission-data/

Hospital beds. (2020). Eurostat. https://ec.europa.eu/eurostat/databrowser/view/tps00046/default/table?lang=en

Hospodářská komora ČR [Czech Chamber of Commerce]. (2020). Podnikatelé při podávání žádostí o pomoc státu musí překonávat zmatečnost a nesmyslnost požadavků úřadů, nedostatečné informace a zbytečnou byrokracii [When asking for help from the state, businesses need to fight confusion and senselessness of authorities' demands, insufficient information, and pointless bureaucracy]. *komora.cz.* https://www.komora.cz/press_release/podnikatele-pri-podavani-zadosti-o-pomoc-statu-musi-prekonavat-zmatecnost-a-nesmyslnost-pozadavku-uradu-nedostatecne-informace-a-zbytecnou-byrokracii/

International Monetary Fund. (2020). Policy responses to COVID19. *imf.org.* https://www.imf.org/en/Topics/imf-and-covid19/Policy-Responses-to-COVID-19#C

Itthon: A kötelező maszkviselést is felülvizsgálhatja a kormány [At home: The government will re-examine mandatory face masks]. (2020, June). *HVG.hu*. https://hvg.hu/itthon/20200616_kotelezo_maszkviseles_felulvizsgalat

Kabakchieva, P. (2020). From representative to anti-civic populist democracy?: Development and forms of civil society in contemporary Bulgaria. *Southeastern Europe, 44*(2), 208–232.

Kaszás, F. (2020a, August 6). Gov't to help pop musicians, festivals, clubs hit by the coronavirus with billions. *Hungary Today*. https://hungarytoday.hu/coronavirus-hungary-musicians-garage-concerts-festivals-clubs/

Kaszás, F. (2020b, May 13). Police investigating Facebook users for "spreading fake news" causes uproar in Hungary. *Hungary Today*. https://hungarytoday.hu/coronavirus-fake-news-hungary-police/

Kaszás, F. (2020c, August 31). UEFA super cup still a go but gov't may rethink final scenario. *Hungary Today*. https://hungarytoday.hu/uefa-super-cup-finalk-hungary-budapest-fans-covid/

Kaufmann, D., & Kraay, A. (2020). Worldwide governance indicators. *Worldwide Governance Indicators*. https://info.worldbank.org/governance/wgi/Home/Reports

Kavanagh, M. M., & Singh, R. (2020). Democracy, capacity, and coercion in pandemic response—COVID 19 in comparative political perspective. *Journal of Health Politics, Policy and Law*, 1–19.

KoroNERV-20. (2020). Protikovidový balíček státu [The State anti-COVID package]. *KoroNERV20.cz*. Retrieved on September 1, 2020, from http://www.koronerv-20.cz/2020/05/protikovidovy-balicek-statu-dosud/

Korupční zákon i legalizace zlodějin. Opozice kritizuje vládní změnu pravidel pro zakázky bez soutěže [Corrupt law and legalization of theft. Opposition criticizes government changes to procurement rules]. (2020, May 13). *iRozhlas.cz*. https://www.irozhlas.cz/zpravy-domov/koronavirus-nakup-ochrannych-pomucek-verejne-zakazky-zmena-pravidel-vlada_2005131615_kno?fbclid=IwAR15xyQtooOyPCb2FNmGrjSYgeHI9EDIV7p1OLWK_hDoKhqw3PZX_Zre1ZE

Krokovay, N. (2020). Hungary—wage support programme for job retention—Kurzarbeit with training obligation—Eurofound COVID-19 EU PolicyWatch. *COVID-19 EU PolicyWatch Database of National-Level Responses*. https://static.eurofound.europa.eu/covid19db/cases/HU-2020-18_640.html

Maslyankova, Z. (2020, July 15). Oblastnata Bolnitza vuv Veliko Turnovo tursi dobrovoltzi za Covid otdelenieto [The regional hospital in Veliko Turnovo searches for volunteers to work in its Covid department]. *BNR.bg*. https://bnr.bg/post/101310801/oblastnata-bolnica-vav-veliko-tarnovo-tarsi-dobrovolci-za-kovid-otdelenieto

Masovi ostavki vuv Vtora Gradska Bolnitza sled Prevrushtaneto i v infekciozna [Mass resignations in the Second City Hospital after it was transformed into an infectious diseases hospital]. (2020, March 7). *BNT News*. https://bntnews.bg/news/masovi-ostavki-vav-vtora-gradska-bolnica-sled-prevrashtaneto-y-v-infekciozna-1043965news.html

Merkel, W. (2020, September 4). Europe: Who is the sovereign during the corona crisis? *IPS Journal*. https://www.ips-journal.eu/regions/europe/article/show/who-is-the-sovereign-during-the-corona-crisis-4248/

Městská policie propustila strážníka, který v Praze udeřil a srazil ženu [Municipal police fires policeman who hit and shoved woman in Prague]. (2020). *idnes.cz*. https://www

.idnes.cz/zpravy/domaci/koronavirus-rouska-facka-mestska-policie-straznik-praha-repy-agrese-napadeni.A200405_193101_domaci_kane

Ministry of Health of the Czech Republic. (2020a, August 31). *COVID-19: Přehled aktuální situace v ČR* [COVID-19: Overview of current situation in Czechia]. https://onemocneni-aktualne.mzcr.cz/covid-19

Ministry of Health of the Czech Republic. (2020b). Výzva Ministerstva zdravotnictví k postupnému restartu zdravotní péče—aktuální informace o COVID-19 [Minister of Health calls for staggered restart of care—up-to-date information on COVID-19]. *koronavirus.mzcr.cz*. https://koronavirus.mzcr.cz/vyzva-ministerstva-zdravotnictvi-k-postupnemu-restartu-zdravotni-pece/

Mudde, C. (2019). *The far right today*. John Wiley & Sons.

National Pandemic Alarm. (2020). *Representative survey monitoring public opinion, emotions and experience with novelty Corona virus spread in five Central European countries.* Retrieved on December 13, 2020, from https://www.nationalpandemicalarm.eu/en/

Návrh kampaně na dovolenou v Česku ministerstvo stáhlo. Dvěma miliardami měla podpořit i média [Ministry retracts proposal for PR campaign for holidays in Czechia. It should have supported also the media with two billion]. (2020). *ceskatelevize.cz*. https://ct24.ceskatelevize.cz/domaci/3149418-navrh-kampane-na-dovolenou-v-cesku-ministerstvo-stahlo-dvema-miliardami-mela-podporit

PCR testovete—zadulzhitelni, no ne bezplatni [PCR tests—obligatory but not for free]. (2020). *BNR.bg* https://bnr.bg/sofia/post/101314577/pcr-testovete-zadaljitelni-no-ne-bezplatni

Pilling, D. (2020, April 30). *Africa's Covid-19 response is a glimpse of how things could be different.* FT.com. https://www.ft.com/content/124dd4f4-8a0b-11ea-9dcb-fe6871f4145a

Pintér, L. (2020). Nyolc nap alatt kellett felszabadítaniuk a kórházaknak az ágyakat [Hospitals needed to liberate beds in eight days]. *Index.hu.* https://index.hu/belfold/2020/04/30/kasler_miklos_korhazak_nyilatkozat_titltas_szel_bernadett_kikerte/

Pokorná, Z. (2020). Nejdůležitější ochrana před šířením viru v Česku nefunguje [The most important safety measure to protect from virus spread not working in Czechia]. *SeznamZpravy.cz*. https://www.seznamzpravy.cz/clanek/nejdulezitejsi-ochrana-pred-sirenim-viru-v-cesku-dosud-nefunguje-111954

Praven svyat—noshtnite klubove i barovete otnovo otvaryat vrati [Legal World—night clubs and bars open their doors again]. (2020). *LegalWorld.bg.* https://legalworld.bg/noshtnite-klubove-i-barovete-otnovo-otvariat-vrati

Pravitelstvoto s ikonomicheski merki za 4.5mlrd. lv. za borba s koronavirusa [The government offers economic measures for 4.5 billion for fighting the coronavirus]. (2020). *BNR.bg.* https://bnr.bg/post/101246163/pravitelstvoto-s-ikonomicheski-merki-za-45-mlrd-lv-za-borba-s-koronavirusa.

Reiljan, A. (2020). Fear and loathing across party lines (also) in Europe: Affective polarisation in European party systems. *European Journal of Political Research, 59*(2), 376–396.

Rinaldi, C., & Bekker, M. (2020). A scoping review of populist radical right parties' influence on welfare policy and its implications for population health in Europe. *International Journal of Health Policy and Management, 0*(0), 1–11. https://doi.org/10.34172/ijhpm.2020.48

RZI ne uvedomilo 28 chasa sled polozhitelen test zarazeniya Milen Keremidchiev [The Regional Health Inspectorate did not inform 28 hours after a positive test infected Milen Keremidchiev]. (2020, August 7). *actualno.com*. https://www.actualno.com/healthy/rzi-ne-uvedomilo-28-chasa-sled-polojitelen-test-zarazenija-milen-keremedchiev-news_1479455.html

Scheiring, G. (2020, July 1). The political consequences of populist health crisis management: The political economy of coronavirus responses in Hungary: Transregional Center for Democratic Studies. *The New School blog*. https://blogs.newschool.edu/tcds/2020/07/01/the-political-consequences-of-populist-health-crisis-management-the-political-economy-of-coronavirus-responses-in-hungary

Scheiring, G., & Szombati, K. (2020). From neoliberal disembedding to authoritarian re-embedding: The making of illiberal hegemony in Hungary. *International Sociology*. https://doi.org/10.1177/0268580920930591

Schőnviszky, C. (2020, July 30). No more free coronavirus testing for inbound travelers as of Saturday. *Hungary Today*. https://hungarytoday.hu/coronavirus-testing-hungary

Shotter, J., & Hopkins, V. (2020). *Central Europe struggles in second Covid Surge after earlier success*. FT.com. https://www.ft.com/content/86820127-3bf5-4c3a-83b6-d25eafac96df

Shotter, J., & Jones. S. (2020). How central and eastern Europe contained coronavirus. FT.com. https://www.ft.com/content/f9850a8d-7323-4de5-93ed-9ecda7f6de1c

Soud zrušil opatření omezující obchod a volný pohyb [Court cancels measures limiting retail and free movement]. (2020, April 23). *Novinky.cz*. https://www.novinky.cz/koronavirus/clanek/soud-zrusil-ministerstvu-zdravotnictvi-opatreni-omezujici-obchod-a-volny-pohyb-40321565

Szabó, A., & Wirth, Z. (2020). *After 15 years of constant reorganization, Hungarian epidemiology was hit hard by coronavirus*. Direkt36. https://www.direkt36.hu/en/gyurcsany-es-orban-is-felforgatta-a-jarvanyugyet-igy-meggyengult-allapotban-talalta-telibe-a-koronavirus

Szikra, D. (2014). Democracy and welfare in hard times: The social policy of the Orbán government in Hungary between 2010 and 2014. *Journal of European Social Policy*, 24(5), 486–500.

Tait, R. (2020). Czechs get to work making masks after government decree. *The Guardian*. https://www.theguardian.com/world/2020/mar/30/czechs-get-to-work-making-masks-after-government-decree-coronavirus

Toshkov, D., Yesilkagit, K., & Carroll, B. (2020). *Government capacity, societal trust or party preferences? What accounts for the variety of national policy responses to the COVID-19 pandemic in Europe?*, 1–32. https://osf.io/7chpu/

Urfi, P. (2020). *520 milliárdot költött a kormány a járványhoz kapcsolódó eszközbeszerzésekre* [The Government spent 520 billion on equipment connected to the pandemic]. 444.hu. https://444.hu/2020/07/08/520-milliardot-koltott-a-kormany-a-jarvanyhoz-kapcsolodo-eszkozbeszerzesekre

Vegetti, F. (2018). The political nature of ideological polarization: The case of Hungary. *The ANNALS of the American Academy of Political and Social Science, 681*(1), 78–96. https://doi.org/10.1177/0002716218813895

Walker, S., & Smith, H. (2020). Why has Eastern Europe suffered less from coronavirus than the West? *The Guardian*. https://www.theguardian.com/world/2020/may/05/why-has-eastern-europe-suffered-less-from-coronavirus-than-the-west

Weisskircher, M., Rone, J., & Mendes, M. S. (2020). *The only frequent flyers left: Migrant workers in the EU in times of Covid-19.* OpenDemocracy. https://www.opendemocracy.net/en/can-europe-make-it/only-frequent-flyers-left-migrant-workers-eu-times-covid-19/

Zíta, M. (2020, April 23). Jedna podmínka pro náhradu škody je splněná, říká o zrušení opatření soudem ústavní právník Wintr [One condition for damages is fulfilled, says Llawyer Wintr about court's cancellation of measures]. *iRozhlas.cz*. https://www.irozhlas.cz/zpravy-domov/koronavirus-nahrada-skody-volny-pohyb-maloobchod-jan-wintr_2004231429_zit

24 COVID-19 IN THE RUSSIAN FEDERATION
Government Control during the Epidemic

Elizabeth J. King and Victoria I. Dudina

By the end of August 2020, there were more than one million diagnosed COVID-19 cases in the Russian Federation (Russian Federal Government, 2020a), making it one of the countries most affected by the pandemic. However, unlike other countries with large case counts, such as United States and Brazil, the official statistics indicate that there were just over seventeen thousand deaths attributed to COVID-19 in Russia in the first seven months of its epidemic (Russian Federal Government, 2020a). The first case of COVID-19 in Russia was documented on January 30, 2020. At the time, the government response was highly focused on stopping movement from China and containing the isolated cases found among Chinese citizens entering Russia and Russian citizens returning from China. Then, as the virus spread across Europe, Russia soon after began to see the number of new cases increase starting in March 2020. In particular, cases were on the rise after the return of tourists who traveled internationally for the March 8 holiday weekend. Moscow, the capital city, has been hit the hardest by the epidemic with more than 270,000 cases (Russian Federal Government, 2020a). Although some regions wanted to try to keep Muscovites from coming to their cities and towns, the virus continued to spread across the country, and by the next month cases were confirmed in all of the eighty-five federal subjects in the country. The Altai Republic in Siberia was the last to document its first confirmed COVID-19 case. The epidemic in Russia reached its peak in May 2020 and then began to decrease. However, in the first half of September the country was still averaging more than five thousand new cases a day with a very slow but steady increase in the number of new cases. These official statistics beg the questions of how and why Russia has done what is has to "flatten the curve" in the country and what lessons can we learn for the rest of the pandemic's trajectory.

It has been difficult to track Russia's COVID-19 epidemic. The data for Moscow are more complete, but we know less about how the epidemic has developed in many regions in the vast country with stark geographical disparities, including economic, social, and accessibility of quality health care. Only at the beginning of August 2020 did Russia release official information on excess mortality in the country; reporting that there were 3.1 percent more deaths (or 28,036 excess deaths) in the first six months of 2020 compared to the first half of 2019 (Federal

State Statistic Service, 2020a). International organizations have criticized Russia for hiding the true scope of the epidemic. More importantly, there has been criticism within the country (Verkhovskii, 2020; Zhvik, 2020): for example, from Doctors' Alliance and some independent journalists, calling Russia's coronavirus epidemic a "virus of silence" (Shikhman, 2020).

A constant theme in the Russian government's response to COVID-19 has been that the situation is under complete control in the country. President Putin made several speeches addressed to Russian citizens and regional leaders to provide information about what the federal government was doing to address COVID-19, visited a specialized coronavirus hospital outside of Moscow in March, and hosted several world leaders for a delayed Victory Day parade in June. These public appearances (usually via video conference calls) stressed the fact that the Russian government had everything under control and the country had successfully responded to the virus. At the same time, reports surfaced of the risks of hospital staff needing to quarantine with patients at the hospitals where there was a COVID-19 diagnosis and ambulances having to wait for hours to check in patients with symptoms of COVID-19. Subsequently, much of the COVID-19–related discussion centered around the vaccine development and promoting the idea that Russia had developed the first vaccine against the novel coronavirus and would make it available en masse by late 2020. This reflected the desire to demonstrate ability to control the epidemic in Russia and Russia's desire to be seen as a strong influence in global health governance. Arguably, for many Russians, coronavirus in the spring and summer was overshadowed by constitutional reform granting Putin the opportunity to remain in power until 2036, political protests in the Far East, the arrests of journalists, and environmental disasters in the arctic and Siberian regions.

In this chapter, we describe and reflect on the public health and the social policy responses to COVID-19, highlighting what was standard but also unique in the Russian approach. We then reflect on possible explanations for how and why Russia responded to the pandemic. We draw on government documents and websites, the limited published scientific literature, international sources, and Russian-language online newspaper, independent journalism, and social media sources.

Public Health Response

> *"Бережёного Бог бережёт"* ["Better safe than sorry"; lit. God protects those who protect themselves].
>
> —President Putin's call for regional political representatives to prepare for COVID-19 during a public videoconference on Coronavirus. March 30, 2020

Russia has a centralized, federally coordinated response to COVID-19, primarily led by the president, prime minister, and Rospotrebnadzor (The Federal Service for Surveillance on Consumer Rights Protection and Human Wellbeing). Russia launched a centralized website (https://стопкоронавирус.рф), which includes official statistics, health information for the general population, health education materials, and official documents. The "Stop Coronavirus" information campaign also included a wide social media reach on several different platforms. However, numerous additional policy measures were for governors and mayors to decide and/or enforce at the local level. In general, the public health response moved from one of strict measures to contain the virus in the winter and early spring to larger-scale mitigation efforts through lockdowns and travel restrictions in the spring, to relaxation of mandated restrictions by summer for most of the country.

Russia shares a 4,209-kilometer border with China, and therefore some awareness of and concern over the novel coronavirus was evident early on in the pandemic. By the end of January 2020, Russia closed its border with China and banned Chinese citizens from entering the country. Russia then watched as COVID-19 started to spread in Europe in February and March and finally made the decision to close all international borders on April 4, 2020. Only at the beginning of August 2020 did the federal government start allowing some international flights.

The decision to close international borders was not without concern, both for Russian citizens trapped abroad and for foreign nationals unable to leave Russia. During the peak of the pandemic in spring 2020, when countries were closing their borders and flights were extremely limited, there were an estimated thirty thousand Russian citizens unable to return home from abroad (TASS Russian News Agency, 2020a). Russia is host to one of the largest populations of labor migrants in the world, and last year there were nearly five million temporary migrants from Central Asia in the country (McAuliffe & Khadria, 2020). There were thousands of labor migrants from Kyrgyzstan, Uzbekistan, and Tajikistan attempting to return home from Russia but not able to get out ("Rodina ne mozhet pomoch'" ["The Motherland Cannot Help"], 2020). The COVID-19 pandemic appeared to exacerbate the vulnerabilities that temporary labor migrants are subjected to in Russia, including poor access to healthcare services, lack of adequate medical insurance coverage, fear of discrimination, low-paying jobs in the service sectors (which were cut during the lockdown period), and overcrowded and unsanitary living conditions (Nechepurenko, 2020). No data were made available on the number of COVID-19 cases among noncitizens residing in Russia. The Russian government added COVID-19 to the list of "dangerous diseases" for which a foreigner can be deported (Russian Federal Government, 2020b), which may have had strong implications for migrants seeking testing and care for coronavirus.

Another strategy was to limit movement inside the country. Moscow implemented a system that allowed for travel into the city using digital passes. There were no federal orders that restricted internal travel; however, some regions did so, and most regional-level recommendations were for residents to not travel. Both air and train travel were very limited because of low demand. In late summer, with lockdown restrictions easing up, some Russians were vacationing in resort towns that were seeing new COVID cases on the rise (Chernyi, 2020; Dremliugin, 2020).

Russia promptly implemented strict public health control measures earlier in the year. These included measures such as locked quarantine rooms in infectious disease hospitals for people who tested positive for the virus, obligatory isolation stays at designated sanatoriums for those exposed to COVID-19 or who broke home isolation orders, and an intensive tracking system for home-quarantined individuals in Moscow. These policies could easily be implemented in a country with a long-standing infectious disease control approach that favors the public good over worries of infringement on individual rights. In February and March 2020, individuals presenting with upper respiratory infection symptoms and having traveled to China (and later Italy was added to the list) were quarantined in isolation wards in infectious disease hospitals. Patients were forced to stay in the locked isolation rooms until they had two negative results from COVID-19 tests. One example that received media attention was a woman with symptoms but no official diagnosis who escaped from lockdown in Botkin Infectious Disease Hospital in St. Petersburg. The woman was subsequently taken to court by Rospotrebnadzor and returned by ambulance to the hospital to complete her mandatory quarantine. The Moscow Mayor implemented a "social monitoring" system to track COVID-19 patients who were in home quarantine (Suntsova, 2020). They installed an app to their phones, which sent requests for the user to confirm their location several times during the day and monitored their location via GPS. If the patient did not send a prompt confirmation, then they would be subject to a fine (Vasil'chuk, 2020).

By late March 2020, lockdown measures began to take effect throughout the country. Higher education institutions and schools switched to distance learning. State-run day cares and kindergartens closed. People sixty-five and older were instructed to remain at home across most regions in Russia and were paid if they followed the policy of self-isolation in Moscow (4,000 rubles) and St. Petersburg (2,000 rubles). President Putin first declared March 28, 2020, to April 5, 2020, as a "non-working week" and then extended this to April 30. Starting March 30, 2020, residents of Moscow were mandated to self-isolate and only leave home for essential trips. At that time, Prime Minister Mishustin instructed all regions to follow Moscow's lead in mandating stay-at-home measures. All eighty-five federal subjects implemented some form of "self-isolation" measures (TASS Russian News Agency, 2020b). These included only leaving home to seek emergency medical care, if there was life-threatening reason, to go to the nearest grocery store or pharmacy, to work (if not allowed to work from home), to throw away trash, or to walk a pet within one hundred meters from home. At the federal level, the State Duma made it an administrative offense to violate the stay-at-home orders. Some cities, such as Moscow and St. Petersburg, implemented additional policies that included fines for residents who visited parks or playgrounds, were walking further than their closest grocery store, or not wearing a mask and gloves.

Many large-scale events and celebrations were canceled or reorganized. The most notable was the seventy-fifth anniversary of Victory Day. The federal government left the decision up to local leaders to cancel the parades and other commemorative events. For the most part the regions followed this recommendation by canceling the parades or switching to televised events. President Putin then hosted a grandiose Victory Day parade on June 24, 2020, after the lockdown period ended, which included fifteen thousand troops marching in Moscow and the attendance of some foreign heads of state. The next week, the delayed (because of coronavirus) constitutional referendum took place across the country. Moscow relaxed most of its lockdown restrictions starting in late June 2020, as had been the case in most other regions as restaurants, museums, theaters, and shopping centers gradually began to open with mask wearing and social distancing measures. By early September, nearly all of the regions were in the third or fourth stage of reopening, which meant that most lockdown restrictions had been lifted.

The federal government emphasized its commitment to strengthening the healthcare system to address the novel coronavirus. The federal government committed 33.4 billion rubles to seventy-seven regions to get enough hospital beds ready and to buy necessary equipment to treat COVID-19 patients (Russian Federal Government, 2020c). Another 5 billion rubles were allocated from the federal budget reserves to buy more ambulances ("Pravitel'stvo vydelilo den'gi" ["The Government Allocated Money"], 2020). Testing has been an important policy in the Russian response. More than 32 million tests were completed by early August 2020 (Rospotrebnadzor, 2020), and the average daily positivity rate was 2.51 percent.

Healthcare reform has been a persistent issue in post-Soviet Russia. There are regional disparities reflected in rural populations and poorer populations having less access to quality health care (Popovich et al., 2011). The Audit Chamber of the Russian government reported that most children's hospitals across the country are in "unsatisfactory sanitary and technical condition," including half without hot water, 30 percent without any running water, a third without proper sewage, and 40 percent without central heating (Izotova, 2020). Perhaps unique to the Russian and post-socialist context, doctors are a socially vulnerable population in part because they work in an "overregulated and centralized" healthcare system that offers them little room for professional autonomy (Litvina et al., 2020). Attempts to decentralize the healthcare system left it fragmented, making it difficult to understand the vast channels of financing, decision-making, and management of healthcare provision across the many regions in Russia (Danishevski et al., 2006). More recent healthcare reform in the country, especially of primary health care, makes it centralized at the regional level (Sheiman et al., 2018).

Ultimately, the responsibility fell on regional governments and health departments to ensure they were prepared for COVID-19. Many hospitals, not just infectious disease hospitals, had to reorganize to prepare for COVID-19 patients. Kommunarka, a general hospital that specialized in cancer, opened at the beginning of 2020 as the main COVID-19 hospital, where President Putin made a visit in a hazmat suit in March to show support for healthcare workers. An additional COVID-19–specific, eight hundred-bed hospital was built in about one month just outside Moscow and opened in late April 2020 as cases in the city began to surge. St. Petersburg turned one of its largest exposition centers into a makeshift hospital for overflow of COVID-19 patients. However, not all regions in Russia have healthcare systems able to deal with the number of COVID patients. Dagestan, one of the regions hit earliest by the epidemic in Russia and with one of the highest fatality rates in the country (4.68 percent), did not have the capacity. Doctors from Moscow traveled to Dagestan to treat patients. As Moscow and other regions were claiming that they succeeded in "flattening the curve" in early summer, other more remote regions were reporting insufficient number of hospital beds and overflowing morgues (e.g., in Murmansk [Britskaya, 2020]).

The federal government allocated "presidential" bonus payments to Russian healthcare workers treating patients with COVID-19. However, numerous healthcare workers across Russia have reported that they have not received this compensation (Yakoreva et al., 2020). There were also many reports of healthcare workers becoming infected with COVID-19, the overall harsh conditions of working in "red zones" of a hospital, and deaths of healthcare workers. Civil society activists organized a memorial wall in St. Petersburg, and a virtual memorial site indicates that more than six hundred healthcare workers have died during the epidemic in Russia ("Spisok Pamyati" ["Memorial List"], 2020).

President Putin announced the symbolically named *Sputnik V*, the first registered vaccine against COVID-19 in the world, on August 11, 2020 ("Rossiya opyat' zapustila pervyi v mire 'Sputnik'" ["Russia Has Again Launched the World's First Sputnik"], 2020). The president proclaimed the effectiveness of the vaccine; however, the adenoviral-based vaccine against SARS-CoV-2, developed by Gamaleya Research Institute of Epidemiology and Microbiology, had not yet gone through Phase III trials. Moreover, the vaccine was registered before any peer-reviewed published results from the first phases. The results on the safety and efficacy of the vaccine were published in September in *The Lancet* (Logunov et al., 2020); however, scientists from other countries replied with "notes of concern" about inconsistencies, reproducibility, and insufficient details in the data (Bucci, 2020). The Russian government has supported and publicly praised its vaccine development capacity from the start of the novel coronavirus.

As of this writing, there are twenty-six COVID-19 vaccines under development in the Russian Federation; however, they are in the early stages and no scientific papers or data have been produced. This does not mean that the vaccines will not be successful, but it does call into question the ethics and health concerns around rushing through clinical trials. Gamaleya Research Institute announced that Phase III trials are set to take place among volunteers. Nonetheless, the Russian Ministry of Health has already registered the vaccine. Mass production was to begin in October 2020, and medical care workers and teachers were the expected target priority populations in the country to receive the vaccine. However, many raise concerns about the ethics of carrying out these plans. Moreover, there is a great deal of fear among both doctors and teachers about being forced to get a vaccine that has not been adequately tested (Gubernatorov & Filipenok, 2020; "Net nedostatochno izuchennoi vaktsine" ["No to the Insufficiently Studied Vaccine"], 2020).

Social Policy Response

> *#МыМожем* [#WeCan]
>
> —One of the hashtags among the social media campaigns for the government's plan to address the social and economic consequences of the pandemic

The periods of lockdown and the "nonworking days," of course, came with great financial risk. Like most countries, the Russian government implemented a series of social policies intended to offset some of the economic and social consequences, at least in the short term, of the pandemic (Russian Federal Government, 2020d). Russia's social policy measures during the COVID-19 pandemic can be grouped into the following areas: support of vulnerable populations, including families with children, unemployed, labor migrants, Russian citizens stuck abroad; financial compensation for social services and healthcare workers treating COVID patients; support for nongovernmental organizations; help to businesses; loan restructuring programs; and tourism promotion.

The Russian government primarily focused on social support for families with children, while only minimally subsidizing lost wages during the lockdown period. The focus on families is understandable both in the context of President Putin's demographic policies and the fact that young families with children most often take on mortgages and thus were at heightened financial risk during the pandemic. Financial payments were established at the federal level, including a monthly 5,000 rubles per child under the age of three from April to June 2020 (President of the Russian Federation, 2020a) and a one-time 10,000 rubles per child aged three to fifteen years in June (Russian Federal Government, 2020e). The payment amount is similar to the official minimum cost of a raising a child in Russia, which is currently 10,721 rubles per month (Russian Federal Government, 2020f). This financial support was intended for all families, independent of income level and whether two-parent or single-parent household, under the conditions that the child is a Russian citizen. Unemployed parents received an additional 3,000 rubles per child under the age of eighteen for those three months. There were complaints that this universal approach was unfair given that the cost of living is different across the eighty-five regions (Ivushkina, 2020). Thus, additional support measures were implemented at the regional level. These measures ranged from providing additional cash transfers to providing food packages to the most vulnerable groups (large and low-income families, single parents, children with disabilities, and low-income pregnant women) (Pishnyak et al., 2020).

A second important social policy implemented at the federal level was support to those who lost their job during the pandemic. In April 2020, the number of unemployed in the country was 4.3 million, a 23 percent increase compared to March (Federal State Statistic Service, 2020b). In May 2020, the number of unemployed grew to 4.5 million (Federal State Statistic Service, 2020b). The main support measures to address unemployment during the pandemic focused on those who lost their jobs *after* March 1, by providing them 12,130 rubles per month (minimal cost of living in Russia) in April to June (Russian Federal Government, 2020g). The rest of the unemployed received only a slight increase in the minimum monthly unemployment benefits (from 1,500 to 4,500 rubles) (TASS Russian News Agency, 2020c). Although these measures provided some relief for those who lost their jobs during the lockdown period, it was viewed as unfair to those who were already without work and was a hot topic in social media discussions.

State-sponsored foundations launched the volunteer movement #МыВместе (#UsTogether, similar to the "we are all in this together" global campaigns) to help the elderly and people with limited mobility and medical workers (https://мывместе2020.рф). Nearly 120,000 volunteers across all regions in Russia helped to deliver medicines and food, and psychologists and lawyers provided consultation to those in need. Both Russian and international companies sponsored the movement as well.

Two forms of social policy helped to address the pandemic-induced international travel restrictions. The Russian government allocated one billion rubles in funds to the Ministry of Foreign Affairs to help Russians stranded abroad, through evacuation flights and per-diem payments to those stranded abroad (Russian Federal Government, 2020h; Russian Federal Government, 2020i). Despite the Ministry of Foreign Affairs' optimistic claims and the government's social media campaign of #СвоихНеБросаем ("we don't abandon our own"), people who were unable to return home complained of lack of assistance, confusion, and hidden mechanisms in the selection of candidates for evacuation flights (Barysheva, 2020). Given the difficult situation that many labor migrants faced during the pandemic because of border closings and job losses, the Russian government implemented some minimal social policies to make it easier for foreigners to keep their legal residence documents and work permits. Under the presidential order, the Ministry of Internal Affairs ceased deportations, expulsions, and illegal resident status for foreigners; and, no existing documentation, such as visas or residence permits, would expire until September 15, 2020 (President of the Russian Federation, 2020b; President of the Russian Federation, 2020c). Employers received the right to hire foreigners without work permits during the period from March 15 to June 15, 2020 (TASS Russian News Agency, 2020d). Despite the easing of regulations to obtain all the necessary documents to live and work legally in the country, the situation was still very dire for many labor migrants. Labor migrants were not entitled to the same unemployment benefits or childcare payments that Russian citizens received. It was difficult for many of the most vulnerable people from poorer Central Asian countries to have the means to provide safe housing, food, and medical care for themselves and their families.

Furthermore, the lockdown measures needed to prevent the spread of COVID-19 resulted in difficult situations for businesses and employees. The negative consequences were especially noticeable for small businesses. More than 81.1 billion rubles were allocated to help small and medium-sized businesses to retain at least 90 percent of their workforce (Russian Federal Government, 2020j).

Businesses were provided with subsidies corresponding to the minimum cost of living (12,130 rubles) to pay employee salaries during the months of April and May 2020 (Federal Tax Service of Russia, 2020). This is still significantly less than the average monthly wage of 43,400 rubles in 2020. Interest-free payroll loans were also introduced. Large, medium, and small businesses, as well as individual entrepreneurs from the most affected industries could take out an interest-free loan from the bank for six months (until October 1, 2020) to pay salaries to employees (Russian Federal Government, 2020k). Despite the limited nature of such measures, the recipients of loans and subsidies assessed these measures as necessary support that helped them through the most difficult period (Satanovskii, 2020). An additional measure of social policy was to support civil society and nonprofit organizations through the provision of subsidized loans and the deferral of payment of taxes and insurance premiums. The federal government allocated three billion rubles (President of the Russian Federation, 2020d) to provide additional support to socially oriented nonprofit organizations that are registered and eligible for federal funding, such as through the Presidential Grants mechanism ("Obshchestvennikov podderzhat kak biznesmenov" ["The Social Activists Will Be Supported Like Businessmen"], 2020).

The Russian government implemented a law on the provision of "credit holidays" (loan payment deferrals) to citizens, individual entrepreneurs, and small and medium-sized businesses that have been affected by COVID-19 (Russian Federal Government, 2020l). Individuals were eligible for the loan payment deferrals on consumer loans if they experienced an income reduction of more than 30 percent (Russian Federal Government, 2020m). According to the Central Bank, Russians have submitted about 1.4 million applications for loan restructuring and the largest number of approved applications were for mortgage loans ("Rossiyane Podali 1,4 Mln Zayavok" ["Russians Filed 1.4 Million Applications"], 2020). Although these measures will help people to survive short-term financial difficulties, "credit holidays" are not free, and banks will continue to charge interest on loans. This will increase the amount of debt and could have lasting negative consequences for people, especially if the economic consequences of the COVID-19 epidemic end up being long lasting.

As restrictions were being lifted and as part of the government's planning for post-covid initiatives, the internal tourist season officially started on July 1, 2020, in the majority of the regions across Russia. The Russian government used this opportunity to promote tourism. In fact, the COVID-19 social media campaign switched from stories about a patient's life inside a COVID-19 ward and encouragement for maintaining self-isolation to promotions of the picturesque tourist sites, multinational cuisine, and natural wonders across Russia. Prime Minister Mishustin signed an order allocating 15 million rubles from the Federal Reserve to support Rostourism, the federal tourism agency. Russian tourists were eligible to received cashback savings of 5,000–15,000 rubles for booking domestic vacations (https://мирпутешествий.рф).

Explanation

Russia's potential success in responding to the pandemic was an opportunity for President Putin to demonstrate his effective leadership and show that the country was doing well. Ensuring that COVID-19 was under control in Russia arguably came at an important time given the nationwide voting on constitutional reform in early July that granted Putin the possibility to remain president for another two terms. This was especially important at a time when Putin's rating among Russians was falling (Levada Center, 2020a). Thus, a major explanation for how Russia responded to COVID-19 response was the need to **show that the epidemic was under control**. Control, or creating the illusion of control, is a demonstration of strong leadership that has characterized the entire period of Putin's presidency (Chotnier, 2020; Stanovaya, 2018). The federal government showed its strength and leadership (and thus benefited from any successes of the response), but regional leaders needed to implement and enforce the policies and recommendations (and thus were subject to any blame if things go badly).

Allowing regional authorities to implement the "self-isolation" policies was also characteristic of the "appearance of democratic legitimacy" in Russia (Chotnier, 2020). There was almost no push-back from regional authorities on any of the federal recommendations; this is in line with how authoritarian-like tendencies play out in Russia. Unlike what we saw with numerous governors and mayors in the United States, regional leaders in Russia do not criticize the federal leadership but instead show that they are following the recommendations that the president and his government have made. Putin's political representatives in the regions received their marching orders and were reminded that "better safe than sorry," implying that quick preparation was necessary to keep citizens "self-isolated" and hospital capacity to be enhanced. Lower-level government authorities are the ones who have something to lose from a failed COVID-19 response. Local authorities would hold responsibility for outbreaks, lack of hospital beds, and high death counts in their regions. Putin and Mishustin both threatened serious consequences, albeit with vague details, for ineffective local responses. Thus, this created a situation in which it was better for local authorities to report only data that show the situation to be under control rather than publicize any problems in their towns or hospitals.

President Putin allocated federal funding to increase the number of hospital beds and ambulances. He also declared that although regional authorities would be responsible for organizing the response, there would be a centralized platform for reporting COVID-19 data in the country. The federal government would control the information flow. The official objective is for the government to ensure precise and factual information and to attempt to stop the "infodemic" or spread of disinformation about COVID-19.

The social policy response to COVID-19 in Russia is also characteristic of President Putin's past approaches. The focus on financial support for families with children is reflective of the "maternal capital" policies implemented in 2007 to incentivize young families to have more children to address the demographic crisis in the country. The Russian government used the halt of international travel during the summer of 2020 to promote domestic tourism, including through financial incentive to travelers and a social media campaign.

Russia has also tried to use the opportunity to **strengthen its global image** and exercise its soft power in the field of global health. Russia has emerged a significant donor in the sphere of development assistance, pivoting from its position as a recipient of global financial aid in the 1990s (Berenson et al., 2014). Russia's role in global health governance is complicated: the country has contributed to the global response on tuberculosis and noncommunicable disease; however, it is also known for spreading misinformation and turning away from evidenced-based policies (Morrison & Twigg, 2019). Earlier in the pandemic Russia sent humanitarian aid to Italy and the United States, which aside from a demonstration of goodwill, can also be viewed as seizing the opportunity to demonstrate that Russia is not only capable of controlling its own epidemic but also doing better than Western countries. During the surge of COVID-19 cases in summer 2020 in Kazakhstan, Russia sent medical aid to the country. Russia has a vested interest in maintaining ties with Kazakhstan and competes with China and the United States for exercising its soft power through development aid to the country.

Being the first to develop an effective vaccine against COVID-19 would no doubt be a major accomplishment, with important public health benefits for Russians and the world. However, the lack of data and scientific rigor of the vaccine trials resulted in major skepticism both outside (Zimmer, 2020) and inside (Vasileva, 2020) the country. The Director of Rospotrebnadzor, Dr. Anna Popova, publicly supported the safety and effectiveness of the vaccine, and the Minister of Health, Dr. Mikhail Murashko, declared that mass vaccination can take place as early as the end of 2020. However, the lack of scientific publications and transparent data challenged their credibility. Scientists across the globe were racing at unprecedented speed to discover an effective vaccine. Considering that there were few signs of global solidarity fostering collaboration among countries, the world perhaps needed to rely on competition to foster research and development. Although the scientists who developed the vaccine admitted that there was still much more research to be done (Reiter & Ershov, 2020), President Putin arguably launched a global "vaccine race" by announcing that Russia has the first registered vaccine, *Sputnik V.* Moreover, Russia used the opportunity for global reach with plans to conduct Phase III trials in several countries (e.g., Saudi Arabia, Philippines, and United Arab Emirates) and negotiations with several countries to purchase the vaccine if scientifically determined to be effective. During their meeting in early September, President Putin promised Alexander Lukashenko that Belarus would be the first foreign country to receive the vaccine. In his address to the 75th United Nations General Assembly, President Putin commented that in response to COVID-19, "We are ready to share experience and continue cooperating with all states and international entities, including in supplying the Russian vaccine" (Ministry of Foreign Affairs, 2020) and offered voluntary vaccination of the UN staff.

Unfortunately, the major factor impeding the Russian coronavirus response is the **lack of trust** in the official statistics and information provided by the government about the epidemic. Building an image of a strong state that solves all problems and never fails requires controlling information. This control includes not allowing information about any problems or mistakes into the media or outright concealing information that could damage the image of a strong government (Kevere, 2020). This "culture of silence" is typical of the disaster response approach that existed in the Soviet Union, such as we saw with the infamous Chernobyl catastrophe (Abbott et al., 2006). Therefore, inside the country, official information is often perceived with skepticism and generates distrust of the authorities and what the authorities say (Veselov et al., 2016).

With COVID-19, the federal government has created a centralized website for keeping people informed. They even include this in the list of frequently asked questions: "Is the government hiding something about the coronavirus situation?" to which the answer is, "No. All reliable and confirmed information about the situation with coronavirus infection in Russia is promptly published on the websites of the Ministry of Health and Rospotrebnadzor, and also on the Stop Coronavirus website" (Russian Federal Government, 2020a). However, many Russians do not trust the official data and information about coronavirus in Russia; 39 percent of Russians only believe part of the information and 27 percent do not believe any of the information (Levada Center, 2020b). This is true among doctors as well. Nearly 60 percent of doctors surveyed reported that they do not trust the official statistics on COVID-19, and about half said that they believe the numbers of reported of cases and deaths to be underestimated (Levada Center, 2020c). Some regions have decided to switch how they report mortality data from monthly to quarterly (Chernyi & Zhilova, 2020). When data are neither transparent nor readily available, it is difficult to assess the true extent of the COVID-19 epidemic in Russia. This is reflected in the data that Russians are split on how worried they are about the virus, and 70 percent have said that they have not changed their work practices (Levada Center, 2020b). The "virus of silence" is most apparent in the extent to which healthcare workers are afraid to speak out about hospital conditions, lack of PPE, deaths from COVID-19, and the extent to which the virus has affected medical care workers themselves. There is pressure then for regional hospitals to revamp their specializations and become prepared for COVID-19 patients and to have enough PPE to protect their staff and patients (Amnesty International, 2020; Borozdina et al., 2020; Semenova, 2020). This type of pressure led to reports of suicides among healthcare workers (Bakin, 2020; Tsikulina, 2020), hospitals afraid to report that healthcare workers have died from COVID-19, and life insurance policies not paid to family members of deceased healthcare workers (Petlyanova, 2020).

Conclusion

The Russian approach to addressing COVID-19 reflects the messiness of classifying "regime type." Some of the responses used were more authoritarian in their approach, such as quarantining people against their will who were suspected of having the novel coronavirus, placing face recognition cameras, and tracking individuals through their cellphones. However, these were mostly at the beginning of the epidemic when the approach was on containing the virus as opposed to mitigating the spread. These later responses, such as recommended "self-isolation" measures and promotion of mask wearing, were more reflective of a democratic regime.

The relationship between presidentialism and federalism as played out in Russia's response to COVID-19 is also difficult to categorize as completely democratic or strictly authoritarian. The president and prime minister have made recommendations, but regional leaders were the ones to implement the health policies to stop the virus, indicating more of a democratic policy approach. However, this relationship between the federal government and regional officials is reflective of an authoritarian structure. Although Russia is a multiparty system, the country is controlled by Putin's "United Russia" party. Thus, there is little space for debate or discourse about the politics of the COVID-19 response. In fact, we see little evidence of regional authorities criticizing or questioning the federal government's actions, but rather they show that they are following the recommendations of the federal government. This system discourages criticism from local officials (e.g., heads of administrations, governors and other local officials, chief doctors in government clinics), and this lack of critical voice on the ground prevents the system from effectively responding to local problems. Local problems are not addressed until grassroots organizations or individuals who have little or nothing to lose raise concerns (e.g., ordinary healthcare workers and patients). The idea of one-time payments to select populations, especially right before any type of election, but with less concern for longer-term impact is also characteristic of Putin's social policy politics (Sokhey, 2020). Also, the lack of discussion and transparency around the official statistics and information has also been referred to as authoritarian (Martynov, 2020).

If it is true that Russia managed to be #postcovid and #выходизэпидемии (exit from the epidemic), then what lessons can other countries learn? A greater flow of information and more transparency in the data would allow a more complete assessment of Russia's response to COVID-19. Creating a "virus of silence," short-cutting global standards for vaccine clinical trials, and not providing disaggregated and timely data make it difficult to evaluate the reasons for Russia's relatively low case count and low fatality rate. These also place healthcare workers and the population's health at risk. As of this writing, there is much discussion about a "second wave" of COVID-19 hitting Russia in the winter of 2020. Having more information about the scope of the epidemic and how it was controlled from the first six months could provide a valuable foundation for what is to come, both in Russia and globally.

References

Abbott, P., Claire, W., & Matthias, B. (2006). Chernobyl: Living with risk and uncertainty. *Health Risk & Society, 8*(2), 105–121.

Amnesty International. (2020, August 5). *Potrebuite prekratit' presledovnie meditsinskikh rabotnikov v Rossii* [Demand an end to the harassment of medical workers in Russia]. https://eurasia.amnesty.org/2020/08/05/potrebujte-prekratit-presledovanie-mediczinskih-rabotnikov-v-rossii/

Bakin, I. (2020, May 4). V Rossii neskol'ko vrachei vypali is okon vo vremya epidemii koronavirusa [In Russia, several doctors fell from windows during the coronavirus epidemic]. *Znak.* https://www.znak.com/2020-05-04/v_rossii_vrachi_vypadayut_iz_okon_vo_vremya_epidemii_koronavirusa_podrobnosti_chp

Barysheva, E. (2020, April 11). "Derzhites' i obzhivaites'": Rasskazy zastryavshikh za granitsei turistov iz RF ["Hold on and settle in": Stories from Russian tourists stranded abroad]. (2020, April 11). *Deutsche Welle.* https://p.dw.com/p/3akrY

Berenson, M. P., Larionova, M., & Rakhmangulov, M. (2014). *Promoting greater cooperation between Russia and OECD donors*, IDS Policy Briefing, 53, Brighton, IDS.

Borozdina, E. Vyatchina, M., Litvina, D., Nizamova, A. Novokunskaya, A., Temkina, A., & Ugarova, A. Kogda vse zakonchitsya, pridet sledstvennyi komitet [When it's all over, the investigative committee will come]. *Novaya Gazeta.* https://novayagazeta.ru/articles/2020/07/11/86243-kogda-vse-zakonchitsya-pridet-sledstvennyy-komitet

Britskaya, T. (2020, June 15). Liudei meryaiut kilogrammami [People are measured by the kilograms]. *Novaya Gazeta.* https://novayagazeta.ru/articles/2020/07/15/86284-lyudey-meryayut-kilogrammami

Bucci, E. (2020, September 7). Note of concern. *Cattivi Scienziati: fighting bad and pseudo-science.* https://cattiviscienziati.com/2020/09/07/note-of-concern/

Chernyi, G., & Zhilova, A. (2020, August 7). Sverdlovskii ZAGS zasekretil statistiku smertnostis iiule [Sverdlovsk registry office classified mortality statistics in July]. *E1.RU Yekaterinburg Online.* https://www.e1.ru/news/spool/news_id-69409591.html

Chernyi, K. (2020, August 8). Liderami po zabolevaemosti koronavirusom za sutki stali Krasnodar i Sochi [Krasnodar and Sochi became the leaders in the daily incidence of coronavirus cases]. *Bloknot Krasnodar.* https://bloknot-krasnodar.ru/news/liderami-po-zabolevaemosti-koronavirusom-za-stuki—1252095

Chotner, I. (2020, January 23). How Putin controls Russia. *The New Yorker.* https://www.newyorker.com/news/q-and-a/how-putin-controls-russia

Danishevski, K., Balabanova, D., McKee, M., & Atkinson, S. (2006). The fragmentary federation: Experiences with the decentralized health system in Russia. *Health Policy and Planning, 21*(3), 183–194.

Dremliugin, A. (2020, August 6). Krym b'et antirekord po koronavirusu [Crimea beats antirecord for coronavirus]. *Kommersant.* https://www.kommersant.ru/doc/4443624

Federal State Statistic Service (Rosstat). (2020a, August 7). *Rosstat predstavil dannye o estestvennom dvizhenii naseleniya v iiune 2020 goda* [Rosstat provided data on the population trends in June 2020], (2020, August 7). https://rosstat.gov.ru/folder/313/document/94975

Federal State Statistic Service (Rosstat). (2020b). *Informatsiya o sotsial'no-ekonomicheskom polozhenii Rossii, yanvar'-aprel' 2020 goda* [Information about the social-economic status of Russia, January-April, 2020]. https://rosstat.gov.ru/storage/mediabank/oper-04-2020.pdf

Federal Tax Service of Russia. (2020, August 15). *Subsidii dlya malogo biznesa* [Subsidies for small businesses]. https://www.nalog.ru/rn77/business-support-2020/subsidy/

Gubernatorov, E., & Filipenok, A. (2020, August 14). Opros prodemonstriroval nedoverie vrachei k vaktsine ot koronavirusa [Poll shows that doctors do not trust the coronavirus vaccine]. *RBK*. https://www.rbc.ru/society/14/08/2020/5f35d9579a79471d249e8374

Ivushkina, A. (2020, June 1). Zatratnoe neravenstvo: posobiya na detei okazalis' neodinakovo polezny [Costly inequality: Child benefits turned out to be unequally beneficial]. *Izvestiya*. https://iz.ru/1017376/anna-ivushkina/zatratnoe-neravenstvo-posobiia-na-detei-okazalis-neodinakovo-polezny

Izotova, G. (2020). Biulleten' schetnoi palaty RF [Bulletin of the Accounts Chamber of the Russian Federation]. *Zdravookhranenie*, 2 (267). https://ach.gov.ru/upload/iblock/84e/84ed13237c0fe2b0dae052063e371cfe.pdf

Kevere, O. (2020, May 13). The illusion of control. Russia's media ecosystem and COVID-19 propaganda narratives. *Visegrad Insight*. https://visegradinsight.eu/the-illusion-of-control-russian-propaganda-covid19/

Levada Center. (2020a, July 29). *Odobrenie organov vlasti i doverie politikam* [Government approval and trust in politicians]. https://www.levada.ru/2020/07/29/odobrenie-organov-vlasti-i-doverie-politikam/

Levada Center. (2020b, July 31). *Koronavirus: Strakh i zanyatost'* [Coronavirus: Fear and employment]. https://www.levada.ru/2020/07/31/koronavirus-strah-i-zanyatost/

Levada Center. (2020c, July 7). *Bol'shinstvo rossiiskikh vrachei ne doveryaiut ofitsial'noi statistike po koronavirusu* [Most Russian doctors do not trust the official statistics on coronavirus]. https://www.levada.ru/2020/07/07/bolshinstvo-rossijskih-vrachej-ne-doveryayut-ofitsialnoj-statistike-po-koronavirusu/

Litvina, D., Novkunskaya, A., & Temkina, A. (2020). Multiple vulnerabilities in medical settings: invisible suffering of doctors. *Societies, 10*(5), 1–17. https://doi.org/10.3390/soc10010005

Logunov, D. Y., Dolzhikova, I. V., Zubkova, O. V., Tukhvatullin, A. I., Shcheblyakov, D. V., Dzharullaeva, A. S., Grousova, D. M., Erokhova, A. S., Kovryrshina, A. V., Botikov, A. G., Izhaeva, F. M., Popova, O., Ozharovskaya, T. A., Esmagambetov, I. B., Favorskaya, I. A., Zrelkin, D. I., Voronina, D. V., Shcherbinin, D. N., Semikhin, A. S., . . . Gintsburg A. L. (2020). Safety and immunogenicity of an rAd26 and rAd5 vector-based heterologous prime-boost COVID-19 vaccine in two formulations: Two open, non-randomised phase 1/2 studies from Russia. *The Lancet, 396*, 887–897. https://doi.org.10.1016/S0140-6736(20)31866-3

Martynov, K. (2020, June 6). Suverennaya epidemiologiya [Sovereign epidemiology]. *Novaya Gazeta*. https://novayagazeta.ru/articles/2020/06/06/85725-suverennaya-epidemiologi

McAuliffe, M. & Khadria, B. (Eds.) (2020). *World Migration Report 2020*. Geneva: International Organization for Migration.

Ministry of Economic Development. (2020, July 21). *Obnovlen reestr SONKO dlya okazaniya mer podderzhki v period rasprostraneniya koronavirusa* [The SONKO registry has been updated to provide support measures during the spread of coronavirus]. https://economy.gov.ru/material/news/ekonomika_bez_virusa/obnovlyon_reestr_sonko_dlya_okazaniya_mer_podderzhki_v_period_rasprostraneniya_koronavirusa_.html

Ministry of Foreign Affairs [@mfa_russia]. (2020, September 22). President #Putin: We are ready to share experience and continue cooperating with all States and international entities, including in supplying [Tweet]. *Twitter.* https://twitter.com/mfa_russia/status/1308451562130468864

Morrison, J. S., & Twigg, J. (2019, September 6). *Putin and global health: Friend or foe.* Center for Strategic and International Studies. https://www.csis.org/analysis/putin-and-global-health-friend-or-foe

Nechepurenko, I. (2020, June 15). For migrants in Russia, virus means no money to live and no way to leave. *The New York Times.* https://www.nytimes.com/2020/06/15/world/europe/russia-coronavirus-migrant-workers.html

"Net nedostatochno izuchennoi vaktsine." Uchitelya opasaiutsia, chto ikh zastavyat stavit' privivki ot COVID-19 ["No to the insufficiently studied vaccine." Teachers fear that they will be forced to get vaccinated against COVID-19]. (2020, August 14). *Takie dela.* https://takiedela.ru/news/2020/08/15/uchitelya-za-dobrovolnuyu-vakcinaciyu/

Obshchestvennikov podderzhat kak biznesmenov [The social activists will be supported like businessmen]. (2020, May 18). *Kommersant.* https://www.kommersant.ru/doc/4348440

Petlyanova, N. (2020, August 12). Eto ne nash virus, on uvolilsya dve nedeli nazad [This is not our virus. It quit two weeks ago]. *Novaya Gazeta.* https://novayagazeta.ru/articles/2020/08/12/86625-eto-ne-nash-virus-on-uvolilsya-dve-nedeli-nazad

Pishnyak, A., Korchagina, I., Gorina, E., & Ter-Akopov, S. (2020). Discussion paper #4. *Podderzhka semei s det'mi v usloviyakh pandemii COVID-19* [Support for families with children during the COVID-19 pandemic]. Institute for Social Policy. National Research University: Higher School of Economics. https://www.hse.ru/data/2020/06/29/1610612279/ISP%20HSE_COVID-19%20and%20Families%20with%20Child..ussion%20Paper%204_June%2025%202020_RUS.pdf

Popovich, L., Potapchik, E., Shishkin, S., Richardson, E., Vacroux A., & Mathivet, B. (2011). Russian Federation. Health system review. *Health Systems in Transition, 13*(7), 1-xiv.

Pravitel'stvo vydelilo den'gi na pokupku 1200 mashin skoroi pomoshchi [The government allocated money to purchase 1200 ambulances]. (2020, March 30). *Izvestiya.* https://iz.ru/993148/2020-03-30/pravitelstvo-vydelilo-dengi-na-pokupku-1200-mashin-skoroi-pomoshchi

President of the Russian Federation. (2020a, April 7). Uzak № 249 "O dopolnitel'nykh merakh sotsial'noi podderzhki semei, imeiushchikh detei" [Decree No. 249 "On additional measures of social support for families with children"]. http://publication.pravo.gov.ru/Document/View/0001202004070063

President of the Russian Federation. (2020b, April 18). Ukaz № 274 "O vremennykh merakh po uregulirovaniiu pravovogo polozheniya inostrannykh grazhdan i lits bez grazhdanstva v Rossiiskoi Federatsii v svyazi s ugrozoi dal'neishego rasprostraneniya novoi koronavirusnoi infektsii (COVID-19)" [Decree No 274 "On temporary measures to regulate the legal status of foreign citizens and stateless persons in the Russian Federation in connection with the threat of the further spread of a novel coronavirus infection"]. http://www.garant.ru/hotlaw/federal/1380010/

President of the Russian Federation. (2020c, June 15). Ukaz № 392 "O vnesenii izmenenii v Ukaz Prezidenta Rossiiskoi Federatsii ot 18 aprelya 2020 g. № 274 "O vremennykh merakh po uregulirovaniiu pravovogo polozheniya inostrannykh grazhdan i lits bez grazhdanstva v Rossiiskoi Federatisii v svyazi s ugrozoi dal'neishego rasprostraneniya novoi koronavirusnoi infektsii (COVID-19)" [Decree No. 392 "On amendments to the Decree of the President of the Russian Federation of April 18, 2020 Decree No 274

"On temporary measures to regulate the legal status of foreign citizens and stateless persons in the Russian Federation in connection with the threat of the further spread of a novel coronavirus infection""]. http://publication.pravo.gov.ru/Document/View/0001202006150016

President of the Russian Federation. (2020d, May 6). Rasporyazhenie № 120-rp [Order No. 120-rp.] http://www.kremlin.ru/acts/bank/45510

Reiter, C., & Ershov, A. (2020, July 23). Pervoe bol'shoe interv'iu sozdatel' rossiiskoi vaktsiny ot koronavirusa Denis Logunov dal "Meduze" [Denis Logunov, the creator of the Russian coronavirus vaccine, gave his first big interview to Meduza]. *Meduza*. https://meduza.io/feature/2020/07/23/sozdatel-rossiyskoy-vaktsiny-ot-koronavirusa-denis-logunov-dal-meduze-pervoe-bolshoe-intervyu-on-rasskazal-stoit-li-zhdat-privivok-k-sentyabryu-2020-goda

Rodina ne mozhet pomoch'. Tysiachi vykhodtsev iz stran TsA iz-za koronavirusa zastraili za rubezhom [The motherland cannot help. Thousands of immigrants from Central Asian countries are stuck abroad due to coronavirus]. (2020, April 10). Central Asian Bureau for Analytical Reporting. https://cabar.asia/ru/rodina-ne-mozhet-pomoch-tysyachi-vyhodtsev-iz-stran-tsa-iz-za-koronavirusa-zastryali-za-rubezhom/

Rospotrebnadzor. (2020). *Federal'naya sluzhba po nadzory v sfere zashchity prav potrebitelei i blagopoluchiya cheloveka* [The Federal Service for Surveillance on Consumer Rights Protection and Human Well-Being]. https://www.rospotrebnadzor.ru/about/info/news_time/news_details.php?ELEMENT_ID=13566

Rossiya opyat' zapustila pervyi v mire "Sputnik" [Russia again launched the world's first "Sputnik"]. (2020, August 11). *Vesti*. https://www.vesti.ru/article/2439570

Rossiyane podali 1,4 mln zayavok na restrukturizatsiiu kreditov vo vremya pandemii [Russians filed 1.4 million applications for loan restructuring during the pandemic]. (2020, May 8). *Vedomosti*. https://www.vedomosti.ru/finance/news/2020/05/08/829838-rossiyane-podali-14-mln

Russian Federal Government. (2020a). Operativnye dannye po sostoyaniiu na 15 sentyabyra 2020 [Latest data from September 15, 2020]. https://стопкоронавирус.рф

Russian Federal Government. (2020b, January 31). Postanovlenie № 66 "O vnesenii izmenenii v perechen' zabolevanii, predstavlyaiushchikh opasnost' dlya okruzhaiushchikh" [Resolution No 66. "On amendments to the list of diseases that pose a danger to others"]. https://base.garant.ru/73492109/

Russian Federal Government. (2020c, March 27). Rasporyazhenie № 748-r [Order No. 748-r]. http://publication.pravo.gov.ru/Document/View/0001202003300026

Russian Federal Government. (2020d, August 14). Mery pravitel'stva RF po borbe s koronavirusnoi infektsiei i podderzhke ekonomiki [Measures of the Russian government to combat coronavirus infection and support the economy]. http://government.ru/support_measures/

Russian Federal Government. (2020e, May 11). Postanovlenie № 652 "O vnesenii izmenenii v postanovlenie Pravitel'stva Rossiiskoi Federatsii ot 9 aprelya 2020 g. № 474" [Resolution No 652 "On amendments to Resolution No. 474 of the Russian government on April 9, 2020"]. http://gov.garant.ru/SESSION/PILOT/main.htm

Russian Federal Government. (2020f, August 14). Spravka o velichine prozhitochnogo minimuma [Certificate on the amount of cost of living]. http://base.garant.ru/3921257/

Russian Federal Government. (2020g, June 10). Postanovlenie Pravitel'stva RF ot 10 iiunya 2020 g. № 844 "O vnesenii v nekotorye akty Pravitel'stva Rossiiskoi Federatsiya"

[Resolution of the Russian government dated June 10, 2020 No. 844 "On amendments to some acts of the government of the Russian Federation"]. https://www.garant.ru/products/ipo/prime/doc/74150108/

Russian Federal Government. (2020h, April 3). Postanovlenie № 433 "Ob utverzhdenii Polozheniya ob okazanii sotsial'noi podderzhki (pomoshchi) rossiiskim grazhdanam, nakhodyashchimsya na territorii inostrannogo gosudarstva i ne imeiushchim vozmozhnosti vernut'sya v Rossiiskuiu Federatsiiu v svyazi s rasprostraneniem novoi koronavirusnoi infektsii" [Resolution No. 433 "On approval of the Regulation on the provision of social support (assistance) to Russian citizens who are on the territory of a foreign state and who cannot return to the Russian Federation due to the spread of a novel coronavirus infection"]. https://www.garant.ru/products/ipo/prime/doc/73743068/

Russian Federal Government. (2020i, April 30). Postanovlenie № 621 "O vnesenii izmenenii v postanovlenie Pravitel'stva Rossiiskoi Federatsii ot 3 aprelya 2020 g. № 433" [Resolution No. 621 "On Amendments to the Resolution of the Government of the Russian Federation No. 433 dated April 3, 2020 "]. https://www.garant.ru/products/ipo/prime/doc/73879143/

Russian Federal Government. (2020j, May 8). Razporyazhenie № 1229-r [Order No. 1229]. https://стопкоронавирус.рф/ai/doc/216/attach/rasporyaxhenie_ot_8_maya_2020_goda_1229-r.pdf

Russian Federal Government. (2020k, August 13). *Besprotsentnye kredity na zarplatu* [Interest-free loans for salaries]. https://стопкоронавирус.рф/what-to-do/business/besprotsentnye-kredity.html

Russian Federal Government. (2020l, April 2). Federal'nyi zakon № 106-FZ "O vnesenii izmenenii v Federal'nyi zakon "O Tsentral'nom banke Rossiiskoi Federatsii (Banke Rossii)" i otdel'nye zakonodatel'nye akty Rossiiskoi Federatsii v chasti osobennostei izmeneniya uslovii kreditnogo dogovora, dogovora zaima" [Federal law No. 106-FZ "On amendments to the Federal law "On the Central Bank of the Russian Federation (Bank of Russia)" and on certain legislative acts of the Russian Federation in terms of the specifics of changing the terms of the credit agreement, loan agreement""]. http://publication.pravo.gov.ru/File/GetFile/0001202004030061?type=pdf

Russian Federal Government. (2020m, April 3). Postanovlenie № 436 "Ob utverzhdenii metodiki rascheta srednemesyachnogo dokhoda zaemshchika (sovokupnogo srednemesyachnogo dokhoda zaemshchikov) v tselyakh ustanovleniya l'gotnogo perioda, predusmatrivaushchego priostanovlenie ispoleniya zaemshchikom svoikh obyazatel'stev po kreditnomu dogovoru (dogovoru zaima)" [Resolution No. 436 "Resolution No. 436 "On approval of the methodology for calculating the average monthly income of the borrower (aggregate average monthly income of borrowers) in order to establish a grace period providing for the suspension of the borrower's performance of its obligations under the credit agreement (loan agreement)""]. https://www.garant.ru/products/ipo/prime/doc/73746658/

Satanovskii, S. (2020, June 17). Kak gosudarstvo pomogaet biznesu iz-za COVID-19? Rasskazy rossiyan [How does the government help businesses because of COVID-19? Russians' stories]. *Deutsche Welle.* https://p.dw.com/p/3dqg5

Semenova, A. (2020, July 2). My ne mozhem eto ostanovit' [We cannot stop this]. *Novaya Gazeta*. https://novayagazeta.ru/articles/2020/07/02/86116-my-ne-mozhem-eto-ostanovit

Sheiman, I., Shishkin, S., & Shevksy, V. (2018). The evolving Semashko model of primary health care: The case of the Russian Federation. *Risk Management and Health Policy*, *11*, 209–220. https://doi.org/10.2147/RMHP.S168399

Shikhman I. [A pogovorit'?]. (2020, May 8). *Virus molchaniya: O chem kategoricheski zapreshcheno govorit' vracham?* [Virus of silence: What are healthcare workers not allowed to talk about?]. [Video]. YouTube. https://www.youtube.com/watch?v=eJPeMeN5tpA&t=9s

Sokhey, S. W. (2020). What does Putin promise Russians? Russia's authoritarian social policy. *Orbis*, *64*(3), 390–402. https://doi.org/10.1016/j.orbis.2020.05.003

Spisok pamyati [Memorial list]. Retrieved September 15, 2020, from https://sites.google.com/view/covid-memory/home

Stanovaya, T. (2018, November 13). The illusion of control: The Kremlin prepares for falling ratings. *Carnegie Moscow Center*. https://carnegie.ru/commentary/77702

Suntsova, Iu. (2020, May 14). "Sotsial'nyi monitoring": kak Moskva izdevaetsya nad zapertymi v karantin bol'nymi ["Social monitoring": How Moscow mocks the patients locked in quarantine]. *Novye izvestiya*. https://newizv.ru/news/city/14-05-2020/sotsialnyy-monitoring-kak-moskva-izdevaetsya-nad-zapertymi-v-karantin-bolnymi

TASS Russian News Agency. (2020a, April 22). *Zakharova zayavila, chto chislo zhelaiushchikh vernut'sya v Rossiu iz-za rubezha postoyanno rastet* [Zakharova said that the number of people wishing to return to Russia from abroad is constantly increasing]. https://tass.ru/obschestvo/8309977

TASS Russian News Agency. (2020b, April 18). *Vse regioni Rossii prodlili rezhim samoizolyatsii eshche na nedeliu ili do kontsa mesyatsa* [All regions of Russia extended the self-isolation regime for another week or until the end of the month]. https://tass.ru/obschestvo/8279513

TASS Russian News Agency. (2020c, July 7). *Minimal'noe posobie po bezrabotitse v 4 500 rublei sokhranitsya do avgusta* [The minimum unemployment benefit of 4,500 rubles will remain until August]. https://tass.ru/ekonomika/8901965

TASS Russian News Agency. (2020d, April 23). *MVD v usloviyakh pandemii koronavirusa ne budet deportirovat' inostrantsev* [The Ministry of Internal Affairs will not deport foreigners during the coronavirus pandemic]. https://tass.ru/obschestvo/8313729

Tsikulina, S. (2020, April 27). Eksperty rasskazali, kak koronavirus tolkaet medikov na samoubiistvo [Experts described how the coronavirus is pushing doctors to commit suicide]. *MK.RU*. https://www.mk.ru/social/2020/04/27/eksperty-rasskazali-kak-koronavirus-tolkaet-medikov-na-samoubiystvo.html

Vasil'chuk, T. (2020, May 31). Antisotsial'nyi monitoring [Antisocial monitoring]. *Novaya Gazeta*. https://novayagazeta.ru/articles/2020/05/31/85630-antisotsialnyy-monitoring

Vasileva, A. (2020, August 13). Politicheskaya piar-vaktsinatsiya: opasna i nepredskazuema [Political PR vaccination: Dangerous and unpredictable]. [Video]. YouTube. https://www.youtube.com/watch?v=nSoOk23P7rM&feature=youtu.be

Verkhovskii, A. (2020, May 29). Unizitel'nyi monitoring: chto ne tak so stolichnoi sistemoi slezheniya za bol'nymi COVID-19 [Humiliating monitoring: What's wrong with the metropolitan tracking system for COVID-19 patients]. *Forbes*. https://www.forbes.ru/obshchestvo/401629-unizitelnyy-monitoring-chto-ne-tak-so-stolichnoy-sistemoy-slezheniya-za-bolnymi

Veselov, Y., Sinyutin, M., & Kapustkina, E. (2016). *Trust, morality, and markets. Rethinking economy and society via the Russian case.* Peter Lang Gmbh.

Yakoreva, A., Safonova, K., & Merzlikin, P. (2020, May 18). Vrachi massovo ne poluchaiut obeschannykh Putinym vyplat za rabotu s koronavirusom [Doctors en masse do not receive the payments promised by Putin for work with coronavirus]. *Meduza.* https://meduza.io/feature/2020/05/18/vrachi-massovo-ne-poluchayut-obeschannyh-putinym-vyplat-za-rabotu-s-koronavirusom-a-mnogim-medikam-zarplatu-voobsche-urezali

Zhvik, A. (May 20, 2020). V regionakh neskol'ko dnei podryad publikuiut odno i to zhe kolichestvo novykh sluchaev COVID-19. Eto normal'no? [In the regions, they are publishing the same number of new cases of COVID-19 for several days in row. Is this normal?]. *Takie Dela.* https://takiedela.ru/news/2020/05/20/odinakovaya_statistika/

Zimmer, C. (2020, August 11). "This is all beyond stupid." Experts worry about Russia's rushed vaccine. *The New York Times.* https://www.nytimes.com/2020/08/11/health/russia-covid-19-vaccine-safety.html

PART IV AMERICAS

25 THE POLITICS AND POLICY OF CANADA'S COVID-19 RESPONSE

Patrick Fafard, Adèle Cassola, Margaret MacAulay, and Michèle Palkovits

On January 25, 2020, Canada announced its first case of COVID-19 (Ontario Ministry of Health, 2020). By mid-July 2020, the case count had surpassed 100,000 and the country ranked fifty-seventh globally in cases per capita (World Health Organization [WHO], 2020). By the beginning of July, which marked the end of the first wave of the pandemic in Canada, Quebec and Ontario had been the most affected provinces, reporting the highest number of cases both as a proportion of total Canadian cases and per capita (Public Health Agency of Canada [PHAC], 2020b). At that time, these two provinces accounted for 87 percent of cases and 95 percent of deaths (PHAC, 2020b).[1]

Despite its decentralized federal structure and a welfare state that is modest compared to many Organisation for Economic Co-operation and Development (OECD) countries, Canada's governments quickly formulated a pandemic policy response that was generally well received across partisan lines, within different orders of government, and among the public. A single-payer healthcare system, moderately generous social benefits policies, and a political culture that values scientific expertise enabled the government to request that the public stay home, get tested, and receive treatment when necessary—and to trust that residents could and would do so with minimal enforcement. With a centrist party in power that was historically committed to social programs, the federal government was also well placed to incrementally expand the existing social benefits architecture. Intergovernmental mechanisms, some of which were expressly introduced after coordination failures during the 2003 SARS epidemic, also helped to ensure a relatively coherent response across the federation. Nonetheless, the pandemic revealed gaps in Canada's welfare state in the form of policy delays in the long-term care (LTC) sector and laid bare long-standing conceptual disagreements regarding federal authority over health services delivery and public health.

Canada's Health Policy Response to COVID-19

The early response to the pandemic in Canada aimed to limit the import of new cases from abroad (Allin et al., 2020b). Throughout February 2020, the federal government introduced increasingly stringent screening, self-isolation, and quarantine measures for arriving travelers (Department of Justice, 2020; Staples, 2020), culminating in an advisory against all international travel on March 13, 2020 (Global Affairs Canada, 2020) and a near-total border closure five days later (Trudeau, 2020). A negotiated border closure with the United States took effect March 21 (Public Safety Canada, 2020). Days later, using the authority of the federal *Quarantine Act,* the Government of Canada ordered self-isolation for fourteen days for all persons entering the country, irrespective of symptoms. Although enforcement was not as strict as in some other countries, violations of these orders could result in substantial fines or imprisonment (PHAC, 2020a).

As described in more detail later, although the federal government plays a role, provincial and territorial (PT) governments are responsible for most public health measures and the delivery of health services. Over a two-week period leading up to March 22, 2020, as national case numbers began to escalate, all PT governments declared a state of emergency (Allin et al., 2020b). Other measures included the closure of schools and most community settings, restrictions on mass gatherings, and encouragement and enforcement of physical distancing (Boire-Schwab et al., 2020). Data from the Oxford COVID-19 Government Response Tracker indicate that the strictness of Canada's containment and closure response was broadly similar to that of the average OECD country (Hale et al., 2020b).

Faced with a strain on hospital capacity that predated the pandemic (Canadian Institute for Health Information [CIHI], 2016; OECD, 2020b), PTs also worked to improve surge capacity by transferring hospital patients to ad hoc or LTC facilities (Allin et al., 2020b; Tang et al., 2020). Elective surgeries were canceled, and where possible, primary care transitioned to virtual settings (Allin et al., 2020b). To support PTs, in March 2020 the federal government agreed to a transfer of CAD 500 million for health services (PHAC, 2020c). In July 2020 a "Safe Restart" agreement was announced that would see an additional CAD 19 billion in federal transfers to PTs in seven priority areas, including testing and contact tracing, and long-term and palliative care (Prime Minister of Canada, 2020b). Federal and PT governments also collaborated to support healthcare workers by increasing essential worker wages and purchasing additional personal protective equipment (PPE) (Allin et al., 2020a; Prime Minister of Canada, 2020b).

Supply constraints also impacted Canada's testing regime. Because of a limited supply of diagnostics tests, some provinces introduced narrow testing criteria, prioritizing or restricting testing for vulnerable or symptomatic persons (Weeks, 2020). The response varied across jurisdictions, with governments in Ontario and Quebec in particular struggling initially to implement a comprehensive system of testing and contact tracing (Marchildon et al., 2020a, 2020b; Owen, 2020). A federal order in mid-March to expedite test availability allowed PTs to increase their daily tests and overcome severe backlogs (Health Canada, 2020). Other supply and equipment shortages, including PPE and ventilators, were also felt throughout the country. In response, the federal government announced a "Plan to Mobilize Industry" to expand availability (Prime Minister of Canada, 2020a).

Canada's Social Policy Response to COVID-19

The economic impact of the societal lockdown was also addressed by multiple orders of government, with the expansion of existing programs and the introduction of new ones. The scale of Canada's economic response was in line with that of the average OECD country (Hale et al., 2020b). The most widely available support introduced for individuals was the Canada Emergency Relief Benefit (CERB), a monthly benefit for those whose income was affected by COVID-19 that aimed to "allow workers to reduce their supply to protect public health" (Government of Canada, 2020b; Robson, 2020, p. S7). Additional federal supports for individuals included the Canada Emergency Student Benefit, the Emergency Care Benefit for workers ineligible for Employment Insurance (EI) sickness benefits, increased Canada Child Benefit payments, a goods and service tax credit payment for low- and moderate-income households, and targeted programs for specific vulnerable groups (Canada Revenue Agency, 2020; Department of Finance, 2020b). Federal support for businesses included the Canada Emergency Wage Subsidy, interest-free loans, tax deferrals, and rent assistance, among others (Department of Finance, 2020a).

PTs also introduced or expanded programs to provide economic support to residents and businesses. Most included income support, rent supplements, child care support, deferred tax payments, and targeted support for vulnerable populations (Nathans et al., 2020). Many also passed measures to protect workers and tenants from job losses and evictions, respectively (Executive Council, 2020; Government of Prince Edward Island, 2020; Office of the Premier, 2020a). Finally, economic stimulus plans for the reopening of the economy later became central to PTs' economic response (Marchildon et al., 2020a).

PTs initiated the first phase of reopening as early as April 24 (Office of the Premier, 2020b), and as late as June 1, 2020 (Government of Nunavut, 2020). Variation in the start date of reopening did not reflect case count nor risk. Nunavut was the latest to initiate reopening but had no confirmed cases (PHAC, 2020b). In contrast, Ontario and Quebec were among the earliest to ease restrictions, despite having recorded hundreds of new cases the day reopening was initiated (PHAC, 2020b). Quebec in particular drew criticism for its perceived premature easing of restrictions (Marchildon et al., 2020b). According to the Oxford Lockdown Rollback Checklist, as of June 1, 2020, Canada did not meet any of the six WHO requirements for easing lockdowns (Hale et al., 2020a). However, phased reopening enabled a 10.6 percent recovery of COVID-19-related job and productivity losses in May (Statistics Canada, 2020).

Explaining Canada's Policy Response to COVID-19

Policy Choices and Underlying State Capacity

Canada's welfare state architecture facilitated the rapid expansion of income supports and buttressed policy choices on infection control by increasing the public's ability to comply with self-isolation, testing, and treatment protocols. At the same time, long-standing gaps in regulation and coordination in the LTC sector delayed policy action during the pandemic, with catastrophic results.

Canada's welfare state is modest compared to many other high-income countries (Esping-Andersen, 2013; OECD, 2018). In 2017 public social spending amounted to 17.3 percent of the country's GDP, below the OECD average of 20.2 percent (OECD, 2018). The redistributive impact of Canada's social spending has declined since the 1990s, amid growing market inequality and a failure to adjust policies to new economic risks (Banting & Myles, 2013a). The scale and form of redistributive programs also differs among PTs (Banting & Myles, 2013a). Within Canada's uneven social protection landscape, its publicly financed healthcare system—which more closely resembles a social democratic welfare regime than other aspects of its redistributive state—has stood relatively firm over time (Banting & Myles, 2013b; Tuohy, 2013). In 2019 Canada devoted a projected 10.8 percent of GDP to health-related expenditures, exceeding the projected OECD average of 8.8 percent (CIHI, 2019; OECD, 2020a). Notwithstanding pre-existing capacity constraints, the universal accessibility of most (but not all) of Canada's healthcare system influenced what governments could reasonably expect citizens to do when it came to compliance with containment measures during the pandemic. In particular, the government-funded system meant that individuals did not have to pay out-of-pocket for the cost of testing and treatment.

Paid sick leave policies are also essential to ensure that individuals can afford to comply with self-isolation requirements, absent themselves from work when sick, and take time off to get tested and receive treatment—both during lockdown and reopening phases of a pandemic (Heymann et al., 2020; Piper et al., 2017; Zhai et al., 2018). Federal and PT governments share jurisdiction over income assistance programs, with income support for long-term, illness-related absences administered federally through the broader EI system. For eligible claimants who have accumulated 600 insured hours of employment in the previous year, EI benefits normally provide a maximum of fifteen weeks of support at 55 percent of their average earnings (up to a capped amount) (Employment and Social Development Canada, 2020).

Canada's pre-existing social assistance policies provided a safety net for some workers, but like most high-income countries, the system also had gaps when it came to enabling employees to obey self-isolation policies without losing income (Heymann et al., 2020; Heymann & Daku, 2014; World Policy Analysis Center, 2019). A consensus across party lines and among different orders of government regarding the serious nature of COVID-19 enabled Prime Minister Trudeau's minority government to move quickly to address these gaps (Loewen et al., 2020; Merkley et al., 2020; Robson, 2020). The pre-existing social support architecture provided a basis for policy shifts that were initially incremental, using and building on what was already in place, and only later saw the introduction of novel tools (Robson, 2020). For example, the initial tweaking of EI sick-leave rules in early March 2020 was followed a week later by one-time increases in other income benefits and deferrals of certain financial payments, in recognition of the pandemic's broadening impact on employment and income (Robson, 2020). As the inadequacy of the existing EI system to cope with the economic fallout of the pandemic and lockdown became clear, the federal government introduced the CERB in early April, using aspects of the existing EI administrative system for implementation (Robson, 2020). As part of the "Safe Restart" program announced in July 2020, the Government of Canada then allocated CAD 1.1 billion to enable PTs to establish or enhance job-protected sick leave, granting workers up to ten days of leave related to COVID-19 (Prime Minister of Canada, 2020c).

Although Canada's governments were able to rely on the country's healthcare system and build on its social architecture to facilitate compliance with pandemic policy measures, they failed to take sufficient action to contain the virus in the LTC sector. Canada's single-payer healthcare system extends only to physician and hospital expenses, with other services residually funded through financing regimes that vary across the country. This includes LTC for seniors. By the end of May 2020, the proportion of COVID-19 deaths connected to the LTC sector in Canada stood at 81 percent—the highest among seventeen OECD countries with available data, and far exceeding the average among them (38 percent) (CIHI, 2020). Although some provinces reported no LTC-related COVID-19 deaths, Quebec, Ontario, Alberta, and Nova Scotia had proportions exceeding 70 percent (CIHI, 2020).

Responsibility for regulating LTC facilities lies with PT governments, reflecting the broader allocation of authority over social policy and programs (Estabrooks et al., 2020). There is considerable variation in the balance of public and for-profit/non-profit private provision, the level of integration with other health services, and the regulations governing the system (Béland & Marier, 2020; Estabrooks et al., 2020; National Institute on Ageing, 2019). Budgetary constraints in the LTC sector have led to long wait lists, understaffing, precarious working conditions, and growing private sector ownership (Béland & Marier, 2020; National Institute on Ageing, 2019). Government spending and staffing per capita in this sector fall below the OECD average (OECD, 2017, 2019). Understaffing weakens facilities' ability to meet regulatory standards, and low wages in the sector compel many employees to work in more than one facility—which has been identified as contributing to COVID-19 transmission (Fisman et al., 2020; Holroyd-Leduc & Laupacis, 2020; Jansen, 2011; National Institute on Ageing, 2019; Wherry, 2020).

Within this patchwork and under-resourced system, policy action to contain the pandemic was uneven and delayed. Early analyses show that countries that instituted mandatory measures in areas such as testing, training, PPE, staff support, and isolation in the LTC sector contemporaneously with the broader societal introduction of physical distancing measures experienced lower LTC-related cases and deaths (CIHI, 2020). For example, Australia's early national action to coordinate PPE, staffing, and virus control in LTC facilities has been credited with their relatively low rates of cases and deaths in this sector (Low, 2020; McKenna, 2020). The province of British Columbia's rapid action in March 2020 to introduce containment measures in LTC facilities, including the decision on March 26, 2020, to prevent care workers from working at multiple sites, has similarly been identified as reducing LTC facility-related deaths (Harris & Burke, 2020; Hsu et al., 2020; National Institute on Ageing, 2020). Other provinces were slow to introduce limitations on staff migrating among facilities and adequate testing protocols for sector residents and workers (Holroyd-Leduc & Laupacis, 2020; McKenna, 2020; Wherry, 2020). For example, the governments of Alberta, Ontario, Newfoundland and Labrador, and Saskatchewan waited until well into April 2020 to implement directives limiting staff from working at multiple sites, and other provinces relied on voluntary actions to reduce multi-site employment (Harris & Burke, 2020; National Institute on Ageing, 2020; Stone et al., 2020).

The lack of integration between the LTC and acute care sectors has been identified as contributing to the inadequacy of PPE and testing in LTC facilities as well as the readmission to nursing homes from hospitals of individuals who tested positive for COVID-19 (Estabrooks et al., 2020; Holroyd-Leduc & Laupacis, 2020). The situation became so dire that the governments of Ontario and Quebec were compelled to ask for help from the Canadian military amid employee shortages. By mid-April 2020, when statistics began showing the large proportion of COVID-19 deaths related to LTC, the federal government stepped in with new guidance (developed with the PT governments) for preventing and controlling infection in this sector (Aiello, 2020a). The coordination and preparedness gaps that were laid bare by the delayed policy measures led to calls for the federal government to ensure core national standards tied to funding in this sector (Estabrooks et al., 2020; Holroyd-Leduc & Laupacis, 2020).

Policy Coordination and the Role of Federalism

As the previous sections suggest, Canada's federal structure played an important role in the country's pandemic policy response. Like other federations, Canada faced a coordination challenge to organize a more or less uniform response to the pandemic. Although other federations have curtailed or limited the policy and program autonomy of subnational governments, this has not been the case in Canada; compared to other federations, the pandemic has not been used by the national government to centralize the federation (Greer et al., 2020). Rather, Canada relied on enhanced and intensified intergovernmental coordination mechanisms to manage the pandemic response.

Canada is a relatively decentralized federation made up of ten provinces and three northern territories (Inwood, 2013). Although hospitals are expressly the responsibility of provincial governments, in practice health (both public health and health services delivery) is an area of shared jurisdiction. PTs fund and organize most health services, including hospitals and primary care. They are also responsible for organizing and delivering public health services at the local and PT levels. The federal government is responsible for regulating health products, funding health research, setting the price of pharmaceutical drugs, and providing conditional funding to PTs for health service delivery and some areas of public health. Federal authority also extends to several aspects of public health, including quarantine (Marchildon, 2013).

To coordinate their activity in general and with respect to health in particular, governments in Canada have developed an array of weakly institutionalized intergovernmental arrangements. At the apex, the prime minister and his or her PT counterparts meet regularly but informally (Schertzer, 2020). Provincial premiers and territorial leaders also meet regularly (without the federal government) under the auspices of the Council of the Federation (Wallner, 2017). The overall pattern moves from conflict to collaboration to just ignoring one another and is contingent on a host of factors (Schertzer, 2020). With some exceptions, and unlike in other federations, intergovernmental relations in Canada are not particularly shaped by partisan conflict, reflecting the nature of the Canadian party system and the modest degree of polarization in Canadian politics. Ministers of Health also meet regularly to coordinate health services and public health.

Following public health coordination challenges during the 2003 SARS epidemic, the Government of Canada created the Public Health Agency of Canada (PHAC), which worked with PT governments to establish the Pan-Canadian Public Health Network, described as the "beating heart" of PHAC (Fierlbeck & Hardcastle, 2020, p. 30). The Network brings together representatives of all PT governments. The Council of Chief Medical Officers of Health (CCMOH), which is chaired by Canada's chief public health officer (CPHO) and brings together PT medical officers of health, provides another tool to coordinate public health policy in Canada. Before the current pandemic, Canada thus had established mechanisms to manage intergovernmental relations and the particular challenges associated with public health emergencies (Fierlbeck & Hardcastle, 2020).

Did it work? Faced with a major pandemic, did the division of responsibility for public health and healthcare, along with the intergovernmental machinery, enable governments in Canada to effectively respond to the crisis despite the coordination challenges characteristic of federations? Would a stronger role for the federal government have made a significant difference? On this question, opinion is divided and a major driver of disagreement turns on what should be expected in a federation faced with a public health emergency.

There are two overarching views about the policy and program impact of Canadian federalism—a "federal Canada" view and a "national" or "one Canada" view. The "federal" view holds that in policy areas that are under PT or shared jurisdiction, it is normal and desirable for provinces to vary in their policy approaches (Hubbard & Paquet, 2010). These differences are normal because PT governments more or less independently decide how to address policy and program challenges. They are also desirable because they reflect the underlying diversity of the country, allowing jurisdictions to fashion distinct responses and learn from one another over time. In contrast, the "national" view emphasizes the fact that Canada remains a single country and that Canadians nationwide should be able to expect to be governed in a broadly similar fashion (Digiacomo & Flumian, 2010). This view has gained strength in the last few decades as a result of several long-term trends, including increasing urbanization and rural depopulation, and the advent of the Charter of Rights and Freedoms, which emphasizes Canadians' shared rights as opposed to the regional and linguistic differences that federalism is designed to express and protect (Cairns, 1992). This "national" conception of federalism is also supported by the fact that Canadians have a weak grasp of what it means to live in a federation (Fafard et al., 2010).

These normative views yield different perspectives of the impact of federalism on the Canadian response to COVID-19. From a more "federal" view, the response to the pandemic has been generally positive. PT governments, acting on their own authority and aided by a significant increase in federal transfers, responded relatively quickly and adapted a broadly similar set of public health responses to local and regional conditions (Schertzer & Paquet, 2020). PT efforts were also broadly similar because of the intergovernmental mechanisms that allow for pan-Canadian policy coordination. As the pandemic became a major area of concern for the whole of government, the prime minister and his PT counterparts became deeply and directly involved in the response management and, to ensure a degree of coordination, began to meet regularly by teleconference. There was very limited explicitly partisan disagreement, in marked contrast to other federations such as the United States or Australia. These high-level meetings were supplemented by regular meetings of health ministers and the CCMOH (Council of Chief Medical Officers of Health, 2020; Lecours et al., 2020). These efforts at coordination resulted in a relatively "coherent response across our federal, provincial-territorial and municipal borders" (Schertzer & Paquet, 2020). In marked contrast, those who take a more "national" view of the federation focus on the differences between provinces, the inconsistency in the overall response to the pandemic, and the failures of some provincial governments to address the LTC sector, quickly ramp up testing, and share epidemiological information with the federal government in a timely and effective manner (e.g., Attaran & Houston, 2020; Flood & Thomas, 2020).

One illustration of the contrast between these "federal" and "national" viewpoints concerns the debate regarding the fact that although all provinces declared a state of emergency early in the pandemic, the Government of Canada did not make extensive use of the federal Emergencies Act. Flood and Thomas (2020,

p. 107) claim, for example, that Canada, "stands alone among federated developed countries in not declaring an emergency or issuing a national lockdown," with proponents of a "national view" perplexed that the federal government had not declared a national emergency to date. However, there are several reasons for this, including the self-limiting nature of what can be done under the Emergencies Act (e.g., implementation requires cooperation by PT governments; declarations must be renewed every ninety days) (Kirkey, 2020). Most important, the federal government is unlikely to be able to make the political and policy case that the response by PT governments is so inadequate that drastic federal action is required. Not surprisingly, provincial premiers explicitly rejected use of the federal Emergencies Act (Bell, 2020). As a result, any of the perceived benefits of declaring a national emergency would be offset if not overwhelmed by the associated intergovernmental conflict. As Fierlbeck and Hardcastle put it, any "intemperate" exercise of federal emergency powers would be seen as "intrusive, pernicious, illegitimate, and fundamentally destructive" of Canadian intergovernmental relations (2020, p. 46).

Another area of contention on federal coordination during the pandemic involves data sharing. Canadians are particularly attuned to this issue because during SARS, the WHO recommended postponing nonessential travel to Toronto following the inability of the Government of Ontario to provide accurate data on the spread of the virus (National Advisory Committee on SARS and Public Health, 2003). In principle, the creation of PHAC was meant to address this problem. In practice, data sharing has to respect provincial legislation ensuring the privacy of health information (Fafard, 2011). The resulting compromise gives PT governments the right to be consulted before PHAC releases reports that use their data (Wolfson, 2020). Although PT governments have released varying amounts of data about COVID-19, data sharing with the federal government is uneven. Consequently, as of this writing, the federal government has been slow to release a pan-Canadian account of the pandemic that includes microdata on the specific characteristics of those affected (Attaran & Houston, 2020).

Attaran and Houston argue that this "makes accurate epidemiological modelling and forecasting ... entirely impossible" and recommend amending federal legislation to compel PTs to share the relevant data by making "emergency federal relief" conditional on it (2020, p. 100). However, there are two objections to this proposal. First, individual PT governments are responsible for coordinating the pandemic response. The benefits of faster and better data for the federal capacity to conduct modeling and forecasting must be spelled out in greater detail to evaluate whether the problem is commensurate with the response. Second, the proposed reforms are very likely to be deemed an unconstitutional encroachment on PT jurisdiction (Robitaille, 2020). As Robitaille (2020, p. 85) further argues, the ineffectiveness of Canadian federalism to respond to the pandemic has been alleged but not yet demonstrated, and the argument for a major expansion of federal authority is based less on careful empirical observation and more on a particular (and in effect, "national") conception of Canada.

Policy Compliance and the Role of Public Trust

In addition to the country's underlying welfare state capacity and mechanisms for federal coordination, the character of the state response to the pandemic is shaped by the broader political culture and, particularly, the level of public trust in scientific expertise. Trust plays a central role in public health governance, as it "can increase citizens' tolerance of otherwise intrusive government interventions" (Blair et al., 2017, p. 91). Trust facilitates cooperation and compliance by reducing the anxiety surrounding ambiguous or uncertain situations while also helping individuals and institutions assimilate novel, provisional, and complex information they may not immediately or innately understand (Holmes, 2008; Luhmann, 1989; Siegrist & Zingg, 2014).

Securing compliance through public trust is particularly important in liberal democracies such as Canada's, in which authorities typically rely on citizens to cooperate with public health efforts by emphasizing collective responsibility over punishment. This was evident in the public communication efforts of Canada's provincial medical officers of health, in which collective responsibility emerged as an important theme, particularly as cases began to escalate in mid-March 2020 (Fafard et al., 2020). Even before the COVID-19 pandemic, Canada was relatively well positioned to secure citizen compliance with public health efforts because of a political culture that trusts and values scientific and medical expertise. In the 2018 Wellcome Global Trust survey (Wellcome Trust, 2019), 88 percent of Canadians reported trusting science "a lot" or "some," on par with the average among OECD countries; however, Canadians were much more likely than the OECD average to report trusting science "a lot" (54 percent compared to 42 percent). Respondents from Canada were also more likely than those from the average OECD country to respond "some" or "a lot" when asked about their level of trust in health advice from medical workers (94 percent compared to 91 percent) and health advice from their government (78 percent compared to 73 percent), with much larger differences in those reporting the highest level of trust in advice from medical workers (63 percent among Canadians compared to 50 percent in OECD countries) and from their government (36 percent compared to 26 percent).

Our survey data from the first few months of the pandemic suggest similar levels of trust in scientific, medical, and public health expertise among Canadians (Kennedy et al., 2020). The majority of Canadians ranked provincial medical officers of health as figures who could "be trusted" or "trusted a lot" (72 percent), followed by the federal CPHO (70 percent), and the World Health Organization (69 percent). Canadians were slightly less likely to indicate these levels of trust in their provincial and federal health ministers (65 percent and 61 percent, respectively) as well as their provincial and federal governments (54 percent and 48 percent, respectively). Additional (and at the time of writing, unpublished) analysis of this data reveals that the majority of Canadians viewed nurses (86 percent), medical doctors (84 percent), and scientists (80 percent) as figures who "can be trusted" or "can be trusted a lot," ranked only behind people's family members (90 percent). Canadians' trust in these figures surpassed the perceived trustworthiness of peers/colleagues (61 percent), neighbors (51 percent), journalists (33 percent), and politicians (19 percent).

The survey also found high levels of support for and compliance with public health efforts (Kennedy et al., 2020). The majority of Canadians reported being "very" or "mainly" supportive of measures such as encouraging people to stay home, canceling public events, and making home self-isolation of COVID-19 exposure cases mandatory (94 percent, respectively), as well as closing schools and places of worship (91 percent, respectively). Our survey data also saw high reported levels of compliance with public health advice. Respondents reported practicing hygienic efforts such as washing their hands more frequently (98 percent), coughing into their elbows or a tissue (85 percent), and touching their faces less often (81 percent). They also reported avoiding social gatherings (96 percent), shopping for groceries less frequently (81 percent), avoiding public transit (76 percent), and staying home from work (70 percent). Although these are self-reported data, they suggest that in the first several weeks of the pandemic, Canadians accepted public health actions as credible. These findings are also consistent with the results of thousands of home visits by law enforcement officials, which indicated high levels of compliance (Aiello, 2020b; Tunney, 2020), and with findings that there were not substantial differences among members of the Canadian public of varying partisan stripes in their views about the seriousness of and response to the virus (Merkley et al., 2020).

Conclusion

As the other chapters in this book demonstrate, unlike some other high-income countries, Canada has been unable to prevent relatively high numbers of COVID-19 cases and a high number of related deaths in LTC. At the same time, again by comparison, Canada has done reasonably well in implementing policies to mitigate the impact of the pandemic and the resulting economic downturn. Canadian governments responded to the pandemic by doing more of what they already did: they expanded social benefits, increased funding for strained aspects of the single-payer healthcare system, and met more frequently to try and offer a coordinated response. The pandemic made clear the importance of the country's underlying social policy architecture in supporting public health measures, mitigating economic distress, and enabling the expansion of benefits; the significance of intergovernmental coordination mechanisms in creating a relatively coherent policy response; and the contribution of a political culture that values science in fostering public acceptance of far-reaching public health measures. Some PTs struggled to quickly ramp up testing and to contain the virus in the LTC sector, and regional variation has raised questions about whether the federal government should exercise more authority in some areas. In general, the overall impact of the first six months of the pandemic did not irretrievably stress Canada's institutional arrangements or public trust in the way that some other countries have experienced. In the context of an unprecedented global crisis, this might be considered a remarkable achievement. However, it remains to be seen whether the early consensus will survive the more fraught questions about lifting and reimposing public health restrictions as the pandemic wears on. More importantly, by the fall of 2020, well over 9000 people had died directly as a result of the COVID-19 virus in Canada, and this figure is certainly an underestimate (Government of Canada, 2020a). Eventually, we will also learn how many more died as a result of the lack of timely access to medical care and other services during the crisis. The families and friends of each of these people grieve their loss. For them, the Canadian experience with COVID-19 has been nothing less than tragic.

Note

1. The material in this chapter primarily covers events from the beginning of the COVID-19 outbreak in Canada in January 2020 to August 2020.

References

Aiello, R. (2020a, April 13*). Nearly half of known COVID-19 deaths in Canada linked to long-term care homes: Tam.* CTV News. https://www.ctvnews.ca/canada/nearly-half-of-known-covid-19-deaths-in-canada-linked-to-long-term-care-homes-tam-1.4893419

Aiello, R. (2020b, May 21). *Police have checked in on nearly 2,200 quarantining travellers at home.* CTV News. https://www.ctvnews.ca/health/coronavirus/police-have-checked-in-on-nearly-2-200-quarantining-travellers-at-home-1.4949021

Allin, S., Grignon, M., Karsentis, N., King, M., Kurdina, A., & Marchildon, G. (2020a). *Covid-19 Health System Response Monitor: Canada*. World Health Organization.

Allin, S., Marchildon, G., & Born, K. (2020b, May 15). Canada's response to the coronavirus. *Cambridge Core Blog.* https://www.cambridge.org/core/blog/2020/04/09/canadas-response-to-the-coronavirus-pandemic/

Attaran, A., & Houston, A. R. (2020). Pandemic data sharing: How the Canadian constitution has turned into a suicide pact. In C. M. Flood, V. MacDonnell, S. Thériault, S. Venkatapuram, & J. Philpott (Eds.), *Vulnerable: The law, policy & ethics of COVID-19* (pp. 91–104). University of Ottawa Press.

Banting, K., & Myles, J. (Eds.). (2013a). *Inequality and the fading of redistributive politics*. UBC Press.

Banting, K., & Myles, J. (2013b). Introduction: Inequality and the fading of redistributive politics. In K. Banting & J. Myles (Eds.), *Inequality and the fading of redistributive politics* (p. 1). UBC Press.

Béland, D., & Marier, P. (2020). COVID-19 and long-term care policy for older people in Canada. *Journal of Aging & Social Policy, 32*(4–5), 358–364. https://doi.org/10.1080/08959420.2020.1764319

Bell, M. (2020, April 15). Premiers don't want Emergencies Act used during COVID-19 pandemic—The Globe and Mail. *Globe and Mail.* https://www.theglobeandmail.com/canada/article-premiers-dont-want-emergencies-act-used-during-covid-19-pandemic-2/

Blair, R. A., Morse, B. S., & Tsai, L. L. (2017). Public health and public trust: Survey evidence from the Ebola Virus Disease epidemic in Liberia. *Social Science & Medicine*, 172, 89–97. https://doi.org/10.1016/j.socscimed.2016.11.016

Boire-Schwab, D., Goldenberg, A., Castonguay, J.-S., Hillstrom, M., & Landry-Plouffe, L. (2020, July 7). *COVID-19: Emergency Measures Tracker*. McCarthy Tétrault. https://www.mccarthy.ca/en/insights/articles/covid-19-emergency-measures-tracker

Cairns, A. (1992). *Charter versus federalism: The dilemmas of constitutional reform*. McGill-Queen's University Press.

Canada Revenue Agency. (2020, May 29). *Canada Emergency Student Benefit (CESB)*. Government of Canada. https://www.canada.ca/en/revenue-agency/services/benefits/emergency-student-benefit.html

Canadian Institute for Health Information. (2016). *Care in Canadian ICUs*. Canadian Institute for Health Information. https://secure.cihi.ca/free_products/ICU_Report_EN.pdf

Canadian Institute for Health Information. (2019). *How does Canada's health spending compare?* https://www.cihi.ca/en/how-does-canadas-health-spending-compare

Canadian Institute for Health Information. (2020). *Pandemic experience in the long-term care sector: How does Canada compare with other countries?* https://www.cihi.ca/sites/default/files/document/covid-19-rapid-response-long-term-care-snapshot-en.pdf?emktg_lang=en&emktg_order=1

Council of Chief Medical Officers of Health. (2020). *Council of Chief Medical Officers of Health communication: Use of non-medical masks (or facial coverings) by the public*. Public Health Agency of Canada. https://www.canada.ca/en/public-health/news/2020/04/ccmoh-communication-use-of-non-medical-masks-or-facial-coverings-by-the-public.html

Department of Finance, Government of Canada. (2020a, March 18). *Canada's COVID-19 economic response plan: Support for Canadians and businesses*. https://www.canada.ca/en/department-finance/news/2020/03/canadas-covid-19-economic-response-plan-support-for-canadians-and-businesses.html

Department of Finance, Government of Canada. (2020b, July 14). *Canada's COVID-19 Economic Response Plan*. https://www.canada.ca/en/department-finance/economic-response-plan.html#insure_mortgage_purchase_program

Department of Justice, Government of Canada. (2020). *Government of Canada's response to COVID-19*. https://www.justice.gc.ca/eng/csj-sjc/covid.html

Digiacomo, G., & Flumian, M. (2010). *The case for centralized federalism*. University of Ottawa Press.

Employment and Social Development Canada, Government of Canada. (2020). *EI sickness benefits: What these benefits offer*. https://www.canada.ca/en/services/benefits/ei/ei-sickness.html

Esping-Andersen, G. (2013). *The three worlds of welfare capitalism*. Polity.

Estabrooks, C., Straus, S., Flood, C., Keefe, J., Armstrong, P., Donner, G., Boscart, V., Ducharme, F., Silvius, J., & Wolfson, M. (2020). *Restoring trust: COVID-19 and the future of long-term care*. Royal Society of Canada. https://rsc-src.ca/sites/default/files/LTC%20PB%20%2B%20ES_EN.pdf

Executive Council, Government of Newfoundland and Labrador. (2020, March 26). *Urgent legislative sitting supports social and economic well-being of Newfoundlanders and Labradorians*. https://www.gov.nl.ca/releases/2020/exec/0326n03/

Fafard, P. (2011). Public health and collaborative federalism: Or why an allegedly weak system to prevent pandemics is not the result of intergovernmental relations, collaborative or otherwise. Paper presented at a Meeting of the Canadian Political Science Association, Waterloo. *Canadian Political Science Association*, 18. https://ruor.uottawa.ca/handle/10393/40457?mode=full

Fafard, P., Rocher, F., & Cote, C. (2010). The presence (or lack thereof) of a federal culture in Canada: The views of Canadians. *Regional & Federal Studies*, *20*(1), 19–43. https://doi.org/10.1080/13597560903174873

Fafard, P., Wilson, L. A., Cassola, A., & Hoffman, S. J. (2020). Communication about COVID-19 from Canadian provincial chief medical officers of health: A qualitative study. *CMAJ Open*, *8*(3), E560–E567. http://cmajopen.ca/content/8/3/E560.full

Fierlbeck, K., & Hardcastle, L. (2020). Have the post-SARS reforms prepared us for COVID-19? Mapping the institutional landscape. In C. M. Flood, V. MacDonnell, S. Thériault, S. Venkatapuram, & J. Philpott (Eds.), *Vulnerable: The law, policy & ethics of COVID-19* (pp. 31–48). University of Ottawa Press.

Fisman, D. N., Bogoch, I., Lapointe-Shaw, L., McCready, J., & Tuite, A. R. (2020). Risk factors associated with mortality among residents with coronavirus disease 2019 (COVID-19) in long-term care facilities in Ontario, Canada. *JAMA Network Open*, *3*(7), e2015957–e2015957. https://doi.org/10.1001/jamanetworkopen.2020.15957

Flood, C., & Thomas, B. (2020). The Federal Emergencies Act: A hollow promise in the face of COVID-19? In C. M. Flood, V. MacDonnell, S. Thériault, S. Venkatapuram, & J. Philpott (Eds.), *Vulnerable: The law, policy & ethics of COVID-19* (pp. 105–114). University of Ottawa Press.

Global Affairs Canada, Government of Canada. (2020, March 13). *Government of Canada advises Canadians to avoid non-essential travel abroad*. https://www.canada.ca/en/global-affairs/news/2020/03/government-of-canada-advises-canadians-to-avoid-non-essential-travel-abroad.html

Government of Canada. (2020a). *Coronavirus disease (COVID-19): Outbreak update*. https://www.canada.ca/en/public-health/services/diseases/2019-novel-coronavirus-infection.html

Government of Canada. (2020b, June 23). *Canada Emergency Response Benefit (CERB)*. https://www.canada.ca/en/services/benefits/ei/cerb-application.html

Government of Nunavut. (2020, June 1). *COVID-19 Department of Health Services update*. https://gov.nu.ca/health/news/covid-19-department-health-services-update

Government of Prince Edward Island. (2020, April 2). *Province announces moratorium on evictions*. https://www.princeedwardisland.ca/en/news/province-announces-moratorium-evictions

Greer, S., Rozenblum, S., Wismar, M., & Jarman, H. (2020, July 16). *How have federal countries organized their COVID-19 response?* COVID-19 Health System Response Monitor. https://analysis.covid19healthsystem.org/index.php/2020/07/16/how-have-federal-countries-organized-their-covid-19-response/

Hale, T., Philips, T., Petherick, A., Kira, B., Angrist, N., Aymar, K., & Webster, S. (2020a). *Lockdown rollback checklist: Do countries meet WHO recommendations for rolling back lockdown?* University of Oxford. https://www.bsg.ox.ac.uk/sites/default/files/2020-06/Lockdown%20Rollback%20Checklist%20v4.pdf

Hale, T., Webster, S., Petherick, A., Philips, T., & Kira, B. (2020b). *Oxford COVID-19 government response tracker, Blavatnik School of Government*. University of Oxford.

https://www.bsg.ox.ac.uk/research/research-projects/coronavirus-government-response-tracker

Harris, K., & Burke, A. (2020, May 28). *The long-term care crisis: How B.C. controlled COVID-19 while Ontario, Quebec face disaster*. CBC News. https://www.cbc.ca/news/politics/long-term-care-crisis-covid19-pandemic-1.5589097

Health Canada, Government of Canada. (2020, March 18). *Health Canada expedites access to COVID-19 diagnostic laboratory test kits and other medical devices*. https://www.canada.ca/en/health-canada/news/2020/03/health-canada-expedites-access-to-covid-19-diagnostic-laboratory-test-kits-and-other-medical-devices.html

Heymann, J., & Daku, M. (2014). Ensuring equitable access to sick leave. *Canadian Medical Association Journal*, 186(13), 975–976.

Heymann, J., Raub, A., Waisath, W., McCormack, M., Weistroffer, R., Moreno, G., Wong, E., & Earle, A. (2020). Protecting health during COVID-19 and beyond: A global examination of paid sick leave design in 193 countries. *Global Public Health*, 15(7), 925–934. https://doi.org/10.1080/17441692.2020.1764076

Holmes, B. J. (2008). Communicating about emerging infectious disease: The importance of research. *Health, Risk & Society*, 10(4), 349–360. https://doi.org/10.1080/13698570802166431

Holroyd-Leduc, J. M., & Laupacis, A. (2020). Continuing care and COVID-19: A Canadian tragedy that must not be allowed to happen again. *Canadian Medical Association Journal*, 192(23), E632–E633. https://doi.org/10.1503/cmaj.201017

Hsu, A. T., Lane, N., Sinha, S. K., Dunning, J., Dhuper, M., Kahiel, Z., & Sveistrup, H. (2020). *Understanding the impact of COVID-19 on residents of Canada's long-term care homes—ongoing challenges and policy responses*. International Long-Term Care Policy Network. https://ltccovid.org/wp-content/uploads/2020/06/LTCcovid-country-reports_Canada_June-4-2020.pdf

Hubbard, R., & Paquet, G. (2010). *The case for decentralized federalism*. University of Ottawa Press.

Inwood, G. J. (2013). *Understanding Canadian federalism: An introduction to theory and practice*. Pearson Canada.

Jansen, I. (2011). Residential long-term care: Public solutions to access and quality problems. *HealthcarePapers*, 10(4), 8–22. https://doi.org/10.12927/hcpap.2011.22186

Kennedy, E. B., Vikse, J., Chaufan, C., O'Doherty, K., Wu, C., Qian, Y., & Fafard, P. (2020). *Canadian COVID-19 social impacts survey rapid summary of results #1: Risk perceptions, trust, impacts, and responses*. York University. https://figshare.com/articles/Canadian_COVID-19_Social_Impacts_Survey_-_Summary_of_Results_1_Risk_Perceptions_Trust_Impacts_and_Responses/12121905

Kirkey, S. (2020, March 23). Is it time to invoke the Emergencies Act to thwart COVID-19? *National Post*. https://nationalpost.com/news/is-it-time-to-invoke-the-emergencies-act-to-thwart-covid-19

Lecours, A., Béland, D., Brassard-Dion, N., Tombe, T., & Wallner, J. (2020). *The COVID-19 crisis and Canadian federalism*. Forum of Federations and Centre on Governance Occasional Paper Series Number 48. http://www.forumfed.org/wp-content/uploads/2020/10/OPS48.pdf

Loewen, P., Owen, T., & Ruths, D. (2020, April 9). COVID-19 is helping to unite Canadians like nothing has in years—And we'll need unity for what's to come. *CBC*

News Opinion. https://www.cbc.ca/news/canada/opinion-partisanship-covid-19-government-response-1.5525186

Low, L.-F. (2020). *The long-term care COVID-19 situation in Australia*. International Long Term Care Policy Network. https://ltccovid.org/wp-content/uploads/2020/04/Australia-LTC-COVID19-situation-24-April-2020.pdf

Luhmann, N. (1989). *Trust and power* (English edition). Polity.

Marchildon, G. (2013). *Health systems in transition: Canada* (2nd ed.). University of Toronto Press.

Marchildon, G., Allin, S., & Born, K. (2020a, May 7). Ontario's response to the coronavirus. *Cambridge Core Blog*. https://www.cambridge.org/core/blog/2020/05/07/ontarios-response-to-the-coronavirus-pandemic/

Marchildon, G., Quesnel-Vallée, A., King, M., & Maltsec, A. (2020b, May 21). Quebec's response to the coronavirus. *Cambridge Core Blog*. https://www.cambridge.org/core/blog/2020/05/21/quebecs-response-to-the-coronavirus-pandemic/

McKenna, T. (2020, June 13). *Australia's COVID-19 successes shine a light on Canada's troubled long-term care sector*. CBC News. https://www.cbc.ca/news/world/australia-covid-19-long-term-care-1.5591912

Merkley, E., Bridgman, A., Loewen, P. J., Owen, T., Ruths, D., & Zhilin, O. (2020). A rare moment of cross-partisan consensus: Elite and public response to the COVID-19 pandemic in Canada. *Canadian Journal of Political Science*, *53*(2), 311–318. https://doi.org/10.1017/S0008423920000311

Nathans, L., Lawson, T., Block, E. S., Feder, M., & Smyth, K. L. (2020, July 13). *COVID-19: economic relief measures announced to date*. McCarthy Tétrault. https://www.mccarthy.ca/en/insights/articles/covid-19-economic-relief-measures-announced-date

National Advisory Committee on SARS and Public Health. (2003). *Learning from SARS: Renewal of public health in Canada—Report of the National Advisory Committee on SARS and Public Health*. Health Canada. https://www.canada.ca/content/dam/phac-aspc/migration/phac-aspc/publicat/sars-sras/pdf/sars-e.pdf

National Institute on Ageing. (2019). *Enabling the Future Provision of Long-Term Care in Canada* [National Institute on Ageing White Paper]. https://static1.squarespace.com/static/5c2fa7b03917eed9b5a436d8/t/5d9de15a38dca21e46009548/1570627931078/Enabling+the+Future+Provision+of+Long-Term+Care+in+Canada.pdf

National Institute on Ageing. (2020). *The NIA's recommended 'iron ring' for protecting older Canadians in long-term care and congregate living settings*. Ryerson University. https://static1.squarespace.com/static/5c2fa7b03917eed9b5a436d8/t/5ea744343bd3d336cd0685fe/1588020278276/Iron+Ring+Document+-+2020-04-27+-+FINAL.pdf

Office of the Premier, Government of Ontario. (2020a, March 19). *Employment Standards Amendment Act (Infectious Disease Emergencies), 2020*. https://news.ontario.ca/opo/en/2020/03/employment-standards-amendment-act-infectious-disease-emergencies-2020.html

Office of the Premier, Government of New Brunswick. (2020b, April 24). *Some COVID-19 public health restrictions being lessened; no new cases*. https://www2.gnb.ca/content/gnb/en/news/news_release.2020.04.0226.html

Ontario Ministry of Health, Government of Ontario. (2020, January 25). *Ontario confirms first case of Wuhan novel coronavirus*. https://news.ontario.ca/mohltc/en/2020/01/ontario-confirms-first-case-of-wuhan-novel-coronavirus.html

Organisation for Economic Co-operation and Development. (2017). *Health at a glance 2017: OECD indicators*. https://doi.org/10.1787/health_glance-2017-en

Organisation for Economic Co-operation and Development. (2018). *Expenditure for social purposes*. https://www1.compareyourcountry.org/social-expenditure/en/0/547/datatable/

Organisation for Economic Co-operation and Development. (2019). *Health at a glance 2019: OECD indicators*. https://doi.org/10.1787/4dd50c09-en

Organisation for Economic Co-operation and Development. (2020a). *Health expenditure and financing*. OECD Stat. https://stats.oecd.org/Index.aspx?DataSetCode=SHA

Organisation for Economic Co-operation and Development. (2020b). *Hospital beds (Indicator)*. http://data.oecd.org/healtheqt/hospital-beds.htm

Owen, B. (2020, May 11). *New coronavirus testing, contact tracing key to fending off second wave, experts say*. CTV News. ctvnews.ca/canada/new-coronavirus-testing-contact-tracing-key-to-fending-off-second-wave-experts-say-1.4933552

Piper, K., Youk, A., James, A. E., & Kumar, S. (2017). Paid sick days and stay-at-home behavior for influenza. *PLOS ONE, 12*(2), e0170698. https://doi.org/10.1371/journal.pone.0170698

Prime Minister of Canada. (2020a, March 20). *Prime Minister announces Canada's plan to mobilize industry to fight COVID-19*. https://pm.gc.ca/en/news/news-releases/2020/03/20/prime-minister-announces-canadas-plan-mobilize-industry-fight-covid

Prime Minister of Canada. (2020b, July 16). *More support for Canadians through the Safe Restart Agreement*. https://pm.gc.ca/en/news/news-releases/2020/07/16/more-support-canadians-through-safe-restart-agreement

Prime Minister of Canada. (2020c, July 16). *Priorities to safely restart Canada's economy*. https://pm.gc.ca/en/news/backgrounders/2020/07/16/priorities-safely-restart-canadas-economy

Public Health Agency of Canada, Government of Canada. (2020a, March 25). *New order makes self-isolation mandatory for individuals entering Canada*. https://www.canada.ca/en/public-health/news/2020/03/new-order-makes-self-isolation-mandatory-for-individuals-entering-canada.html

Public Health Agency of Canada, Government of Canada. (2020b, April 19). *Epidemiological summary of COVID-19 cases in Canada*. https://health-infobase.canada.ca/covid-19/epidemiological-summary-covid-19-cases.html

Public Health Agency of Canada, Government of Canada. (2020c, June 11). *Government of Canada takes action on COVID-19*. https://www.canada.ca/en/public-health/services/diseases/2019-novel-coronavirus-infection/canadas-reponse/government-canada-takes-action-covid-19.html

Public Safety Canada, Government of Canada. (2020, March 20). *U.S.-Canada Joint Initiative: Temporary Restriction of Travelers Crossing the U.S.-Canada Border for Non-Essential Purposes*. https://www.canada.ca/en/public-safety-canada/news/2020/03/us-canada-joint-initiative-temporary-restriction-of-travelers-crossing-the-us-canada-border-for-non-essential-purposes.html

Robitaille, D. (2020). La COVID-19 au Canada: Le fédéralisme coopératif à pied d'oeuvre. In C. M. Flood, V. MacDonnell, S. Thériault, S. Venkatapuram, & J. Philpott (Eds.), *Vulnerable: The law, policy & ethics of COVID-19* (pp. 79–90). University of Ottawa Press.

Robson, J. (2020). Radical incrementalism and trust in the citizen: Income security in Canada in the time of COVID-19. *Canadian Public Policy*, e2020080. https://doi.org/10.3138/cpp.2020-080

Schertzer, R. (2020). Intergovernmental relations in a complex federation. In H. Bakvis & G. Skogstad (Eds.), *Canadian federalism: Performance, effectiveness, and legitimacy* (pp. 165–190). University of Toronto Press.

Schertzer, R., & Paquet, M. (2020, April 8). How well is Canada's intergovernmental system handling the crisis? *Policy Options.* https://policyoptions.irpp.org/magazines/april-2020/how-well-is-canadas-intergovernmental-system-handling-the-crisis/

Siegrist, M., & Zingg, A. (2014). The role of public trust during pandemics: Implications for crisis communication. *European Psychologist, 19*(1), 23–32. https://doi.org/10.1027/1016-9040/a000169

Staples, D. (2020, April 2). The road to Canada's COVID-19 outbreak, Pt. 2: Timeline of federal government failure at border to slow the virus. *Edmonton Journal.* https://edmontonjournal.com/news/politics/the-road-to-canadas-covid-19-outbreak-pt-2-timeline-of-federal-government-failure-at-border-to-slow-the-virus-2

Statistics Canada. (2020). Labour force survey, May 2020. *The Daily, 11,* 50. https://www150.statcan.gc.ca/n1/daily-quotidien/200605/dq200605a-eng.htm

Stone, L., Howlett, K., & Ha, T. T. (2020, April 15). Ontario long-term care plan raises concerns about loopholes, staff wages amid COVID-19 pandemic. *Globe and Mail.* https://www.theglobeandmail.com/canada/article-ontario-long-term-care-plan-raises-concerns-about-loopholes-staff/

Tang, B., Allin, S., & Marchildon, G. (2020, April 25). British Columbia's response to the coronavirus. *Cambridge Core Blog.* https://www.cambridge.org/core/blog/2020/04/25/british-columbias-response-to-the-coronavirus-pandemic/

Trudeau, J. (2020, March 16). *Prime Minister's remarks on Canada's evolving response to COVID-19.* https://pm.gc.ca/en/news/speeches/2020/03/16/prime-ministers-remarks-canadas-evolving-response-covid-19

Tunney, C. (2020, July 15). *No arrests, few fines under Canada's federal quarantine laws, says public health agency.* CBC News. https://www.cbc.ca/news/politics/quarantine-act-police-1.5644838

Tuohy, C. H. (2013). Health care policy after universality: Canada in comparative perspective. In K. Banting & J. Myles (Eds.), *Inequality and the fading of redistributive politics* (p. 285). UBC Press.

Wallner, J. (2017). Ideas and intergovernmental relations in Canada. *PS: Political Science & Politics, 50*(3), 717–722. Cambridge Core. https://doi.org/10.1017/S1049096517000488

Weeks, C. (2020, March 22). Ottawa to intervene in lagging regions amid COVID-19 test backlog. *Globe and Mail.* https://www.theglobeandmail.com/canada/article-shortage-of-covid-19-tests-puts-canadians-at-risk-experts-say/

Wellcome Trust. (2019). *Wellcome global monitor 2018.* https://wellcome.org/reports/wellcome-global-monitor/2018#main

Wherry, A. (2020, April 25). *Can this pandemic be the crisis that finally forces us to fix long-term care?* CBC News. https://www.cbc.ca/news/politics/covid-pandemic-coronavirus-long-term-care-1.5544722

Wolfson, M. (2020, April 13). During the pandemic, why has Canada's data collection lagged so far behind? *Globe and Mail.* https://www.theglobeandmail.com/opinion/article-during-the-pandemic-why-has-canadas-data-collection-lagged-so-far/

World Health Organization. (2020). *EIOS COVID-19 Case Count Dashboard.* https://portal.who.int/report/eios-covid19-counts/#display=Countries_and

_Territories&nrow=2&ncol=3&arr=row&pg=7&labels=attack_rate,population&sort =attack_rate;desc&filter=&sidebar=4&fv=

World Policy Analysis Center. (2019). *Is short-term paid sick leave available that supports reducing infectious disease spread?* https://www.worldpolicycenter.org/policies/is-short-term-paid-sick-leave-available-that-supports-reducing-infectious-disease-spread

Zhai, Y., Santibanez, T. A., Kahn, K. E., Black, C. L., & de Perio, M. A. (2018). Paid sick leave benefits, influenza vaccination, and taking sick days due to influenza-like illness among U.S. workers. *Vaccine*, 36(48), 7316–7323. https://doi.org/10.1016/j.vaccine.2018.10.039

26 ANATOMY OF A FAILURE

COVID-19 in the United States

*Phillip M. Singer, Charley E. Willison,
N'dea Moore-Petinak, and Scott L. Greer*

In 2019 a consortium of experts led by the Johns Hopkins University ranked the pandemic preparedness of countries around the globe. Although the experts found fault with all countries, they rated the United States as the best prepared country (Global Health Security, 2019). This optimism was shared by US President Donald Trump, who, while endorsing the Johns Hopkins' color-coded map in February 2020, reassured the public that he had made "very good decisions" and that the public's risk from SARS-CoV-2, or the virus that causes coronavirus disease (COVID-19), "remains very low" (The White House, 2020b).

At the time of Trump's comment, the United States had fifteen cases and five deaths. Five months later, the United States had the most deaths attributed to COVID-19 of any country in the world. As of August 2020, with around 4 percent of the world population, the United States was responsible for 23 percent of the deaths (Johns Hopkins University & Medicine, 2020), and 122,300 excess deaths, the difference between the expected number of deaths in a given year and the actual observed number of deaths (Weinberger et al., 2020). The world's richest country, and supposedly its best-prepared one, turned in a worse performance than any other rich country and many lower- and middle-income nations.

So, what happened? Understanding the disastrous response to COVID-19 requires understanding the political, healthcare systems which provide direct care to individuals, and public health systems that prevent disease in the United States (Greer & Singer, 2017a). The United States healthcare sector is infamous for its waste, inequality, and focus on profit. As a result the United States spent more on health care than any other country, while also having nearly 30 million uninsured (Berchick et al., 2019). Often, this high spending on health care has come at the expense of preventative *public health* action at the population level, where the United States has traditionally underfunded capacity. Spending for the public health infrastructure at the federal and local levels has been cut by nearly 20 percent over the past three years, which follows a trend of continuous reductions over the past ten years (Centers for Disease Control and Prevention [CDC], 2017, 2019; Krisberg, 2020).

Political institutions in the United States are highly fragmented and decentralized, shaped by federalism. Health care in the United States sits at the nexus of federal and state control, with states overseeing many policy choices and implementation (Greer & Singer, 2017b). Under normal circumstances federalism can be a virtue for policy making, allowing states to experiment. Yet, in times of crisis, the United States public health system depends on the federal government to coordinate policy and distribute resources and expertise to the states (Willison et al., 2019). Federal action to respond to these crises depends on the White House, but President Donald Trump failed to lead the federal government's response, instead leveraging political polarization and partisanship, while attempting to deny or distract from the pandemic through misinformation. Federalism with an ineffective executive is a vulnerability, which has become more salient as Congress has become more polarized and the executive has accrued more power.

The United States traditionally had a strong federal role in disaster relief (Singer et al., 2020). A disaster relief bill was one of the first pieces of federal legislation passed in the United States (Dauber, 2013). Yet, in an increasingly partisan and gridlocked political system, the ability of the federal government to respond capably to disasters has eroded and become increasingly dependent on the effectiveness of the executive. A weak and decaying social welfare system and an increasingly polarized, unequal, and executive-dominated political system was unable to contain the virus. When the federal government eventually began to respond to COVID-19, the burden of responsibility to contain and mitigate the virus was placed on states, which lack the financial and technical expertise to manage a global pandemic absent federal resources and guidance. This has resulted in widely heterogenous responses across the United States, exacerbated by polarization and misinformation.

In this chapter, we analyze the health and social policies that emerged in the first six months of the pandemic to combat COVID-19 in the United States. These policies have a complicated record. The United States largely failed in its efforts to combat COVID-19 through its public health policies. In the weeks after the pandemic was declared, the United States appropriated trillions of dollars in an attempt to strengthen its social safety net. But, as will be shown, these efforts were hampered by the policies themselves and the politics that shaped them. We conclude by highlighting the factors that combined to pattern the failures of the US response to COVID-19.

Health Policy

The United States federal government took weeks to act in response to the December 2019 reports of a SARS-like virus in China. The primary public health agency in the United States, the Centers for Disease Control and Prevention (CDC), implemented public health entry screenings at airports in major cities across the United States in February 2020. Just days later, the first case was confirmed in the United States, when a Washington state resident who had recently returned from travel in Wuhan, China, tested positive. Without a rapid test, the sample was sent 2700 miles (4345 km) across the country to the CDC for testing (CDC, 2020). In response to the positive test, Jay Inslee, the governor of the state of Washington remarked, "Based on what we know now, risk to the general public is low. Our local and state health departments were prepared for this contingency. They have practiced and drilled for this situation, and they were ready. The quick response also shows the importance of a strong public health system, which we have in Washington state" (Inslee, 2020). The governor's remarks proved eerily prescient to the looming challenge of responding to COVID-19: states appeared to act independently, overly confident in local health departments to handle an unknown virus.

At the federal level, the US Department of Health and Human Services (HHS) took the lead on responding to the virus. HHS had been monitoring the disease since December 2019 but failed to develop a containment and mitigation policy. Instead of using executive power to defer to public health expertise and leverage that capacity, the White House named an elected politician, Vice President Mike Pence, as "coronavirus coordinator," eroding disaster response protocol and creating confusion over responsibility and coordination between HHS, the CDC, and the White House (Cancryn et al., 2020). Although HHS Secretary Alex Azar claimed to be in daily contact with Trump (Azar, 2020), there was a clear disconnect with how Trump spoke about COVID-19, stating, "We have it totally under control. It's one person coming in from China, and we have it under control. It's going to be just fine" (Owermohle, 2020). Yet, less than two weeks later Trump declared COVID-19 a national public health emergency (US Department of Health and Human Services, 2020).

February 2020 was the most consequential month for the US response to COVID-19. The total official case count only increased by seventeen during the month, and the first official death did not occur until the end of the month (CDC, 2020). Yet, during this period, the virus was spreading unchecked throughout communities across the country. Two individuals in California died in early February, but it was more than two months before their deaths were attributed to COVID-19 (Santa Clara County Public Health, 2020) because they did not meet the criteria for testing, which was still required to be completed at the CDC in Atlanta. Even as the federal government began decentralizing testing to the states, it was mired in a faulty rollout that did not standardize testing procedures or access to testing supplies. Thus, testing kits were not distributed equally, regardless of population size, and localities encountered many delays as a result of contaminated testing materials (Silverman & Kelly, 2020).

The challenges of federalism and addressing a pandemic turned February into a "lost month" responding to COVID-19 (Shear et al., 2020). The White House continued its message of low risk (i.e., those who fit the criteria should seek the limited testing that existed) and promoted misinformation about the virus. Without clear federal leadership and no deference to federal public health experts, no directives were given to governors to use their emergency powers to reduce mass gatherings or adopt other social distance policy that could contain the spread of the disease. The Trump administration made little attempt to ready the United States for spread until requesting $2.5 billion for PPE, vaccine development, and testing resources in late February 2020. On the same day, the president tweeted, "The Coronavirus is very much under control in the USA. We are in contact with everyone and all relevant countries. CDC & World Health have been working hard and very smart. Stock Market starting to look very good to me!" (Trump, 2020). The efforts to ensure that the necessary equipment was available was too late to be effective, particularly as the global pandemic shut down supply chains across the world and the national stockpile of critical medical supplies lapsed during the Trump administration (Dale, 2020).

By March 2020, the failures of the Trump administration to respond to the virus became apparent, with schools and universities, professional sports leagues, and many other organizations shutting down of their own accord or in response to subnational regulations. Unnecessary travel was discouraged but not forbidden, as was evidenced by the flocks of college students who gathered for spring break (Mangrum & Niekamp, 2020). States, not the federal government, have the "police powers" needed to take actions such as issuing stay-at-home orders. However, governors' choices to close their states did not arise solely from a delineation of constitutional powers; state closures happened because the federal government provided neither direction nor coordination. Central to all of these policy decisions made by states was partisanship. Republican governors were slower to adopt social distancing policies and moved more quickly, as in the cases of Florida and Texas, to reopen their economies, with disastrous results (Adolph et al., 2020). It was not until the end of March that the Trump administration unveiled their "30 Days to Slow the Spread" (The White House, 2020a), by which point more than half of the states had already instituted their own stay-at-home orders.

Over the coming months, with little federal guidance, the US efforts to contain the pandemic were fragmentary. Southern states, which are largely politically conservative, maintained minimal social distancing policies. New York, an early epicenter of the disease in the United States had to deposit bodies in refrigerator trucks behind overrun hospitals (Davies, 2020).

Fatigue over following social distancing policies led several states, many governed by Republicans, to ease restrictions, even as health officials warned that it was too soon (Fadel, 2020). President Trump, rather than support states that had extended stay-at-home orders, taunted figures such as Michigan's Governor Gretchen Whitmer for adopting social distancing policy (Burke, 2020). The administration trumpeted their achievements, declaring victory over the disease and highlighting the success of federal policies over COVID-19 (Pence, 2020), even as the virus became entrenched in new communities and the epicenter shifted.

Yet the virus was not affecting everyone equally. Rather, severe health disparities were emerging in the disease outbreak. For the first time in its history, Doctors Without Borders deployed medical personnel to the Navajo Nation in the American Southwest, which was experiencing the worst per capita outbreak of COVID-19 in the country (Capatides, 2020), even as mortality data collection efforts undertaken by the federal government largely ignored Native Americans (Nagle, 2020). Clinically, Black Americans had a rate of hospitalizations approximately five times higher than White Americans (with Latinx Americans not far behind at four times higher) (CDC, 2020a) and twice as likely to die from the disease (Oppel et al., 2020). COVID-19 exacerbates existing disparities, which disproportionately affect Black Americans, while also exposing those groups to more risk by working in more "essential" jobs, which do not allow them to work from home. Risks to Black Americans were further compounded by increased racial violence in multiple police killings of Black Americans during the peak of the spring outbreak. Black Americans subsequently faced weighing enduring, ongoing racial violence, or increased COVID-19 exposure to protest police killings.[1] If February 2020 had been the "lost month" and March 2020 the beginning of nationwide panic, April and May 2020 were the months in which the glaring cracks in the socioeconomic-sociopolitical foundation of the United States, and their impact on health, came sharply into view.

Social Policy

The social safety net in the United States is weaker than any of its peer countries, placing American lives in jeopardy during a pandemic. Although the United States appropriated more than $3 trillion to combat COVID-19, with portions of those appropriations earmarked for strengthening the safety net, spending on social policy before the pandemic was less robust and less efficiently used than many other countries. For example, France spends 31 percent of their GDP on social spending, whereas the United States spends 18 percent (Organisation for Economic Co-operation and Development, 2020). In addition to a less robust social safety net, social policy in the United States is also less efficient, with less investment in social policy than other wealthy countries. During times of crisis, the United States is not as prepared to quickly adjust social policy to meet new demands. Rather it must enact and adopt new programs to fill existing gaps further exposed during tumultuous times.

In the first six months of the pandemic, Congress passed four pieces of legislation to respond to COVID-19. The most substantial piece of social policy has been the Coronavirus Aid, Relief, and Economic Security (CARES) Act, which was signed into law on March 27, 2020, and was the largest economic relief package in American history (The White House, 2020c). There are several components of the CARES Act that impact social policy for individuals. First, the act appropriated $300 billion in direct cash payments, with adults with incomes below $75,000 ($150,000 for married couples) given a one-time $1,200 payment and $500 for each dependent, with 159 million checks sent to households (Internal Revenue Service, 2020).

Second, the CARES Act appropriated $250 billion by expanding eligibility and benefits for unemployment insurance. In the wake of COVID-19, the unemployment rate in the United States more than tripled over the first two months of the pandemic, cresting at 14.7 percent in April 2020 (Internal Revenue Service, 2020). The Federal Pandemic Unemployment Compensation adds an extra $600 per week to every unemployment check sent out, a sizable increase to unemployment benefits. Before COVID-19, the average unemployment check was $333, although it varied substantially across states (Center on Budget and Policy Priorities, 2020). With enhanced benefits, the majority of the unemployed received benefits that exceeded their lost earnings (Ganong et al., 2020). The combination of the onetime stimulus checks, as well as enhanced unemployment benefits, lifted personal income in the United States, with April 2020 seeing the highest increase in sixty years (Bureau of Economic Analysis, 2020).

Third, in addition to direct payments and unemployment benefits, the CARES Act included a temporary moratorium on eviction filings and other tenant protections (Goodman & Magder, 2020). With 44 million renter households in the country, the economic disruption from COVID-19 could have detrimental effects on the housing market and evictions (Goodman & Magder, 2020). However, the moratorium only applied to properties with federally backed mortgages and did nothing to stop rent payments from accumulating. So, even with these actions, a housing crisis loomed as federal and state moratoriums began to expire in the summer of 2020.

In addition to these components of the CARES Act focused on individuals, the Act also appropriated billions to prop up the economy and businesses. The Paycheck Protection Program was funded with $350 billion in appropriations as a loan program to help businesses endure the economic downturn from COVID-19. These forgivable loans were created to provide support for small businesses, requiring that the majority of funds received by businesses be spent on funding payroll and employee benefits, in an effort to keep unemployment down.

Although these portions of the CARES Act strengthened an already frayed social safety net, there are clear limitations of the legislation on social policy resulting from decades of failing to address underinvestment in social programs. In this way, the initial social policy response to COVID-19 was far more successful than the public health response. Additionally, instead of being constrained by an absent executive, social policy was inhibited by decades of underinvestment and fragmentation. Yet the absent federal action required to successfully drive COVID-19 public health policies largely positioned the social policy response for failure by promoting a state of socioeconomic distress as a result of wildly unrestricted disease spread.

Underscoring the severity of the economic collapse in the United States, appropriations to the Paycheck Protection Program were insufficient for demand and were exhausted within weeks of the passage of the CARES Act (Warmbrodt, 2020). Ultimately, funding for the program required an additional $310 billion in April 2020, with more than four million loans approved by the Small Business Administration. The distribution of funds was also marred by the haphazard and confusing administration of the program, with many large and publicly traded companies receiving payments that were earmarked for small businesses (Dunklin et al., 2020). Although the CARES Act underfunded support for small businesses, it also included $500 billion for the Exchange Stabilization Fund, which gave Treasury Secretary Steven Mnuchin broad authority to provide financial support to banks and other large financial institutions (Congressional Research Services, 2020), labeled by Congressional Democrats as a "slush fund" for corporations.

Other constraints notably reduced the success of the social programs for many individuals. The unemployment benefits under the CARES Act were time limited, expiring at the end of July 2020, even as the unemployment rate hovered above 11 percent. Congressional Republicans were loath to extend enhanced benefits, citing the costs associated with keeping the program going, as well as expressing concerns that the benefits would de-incentivize job-seeking behavior (Epstein, 2020). Because of the spike in numbers of uninsured, states' unemployment administration systems were overwhelmed, with nearly half of all unemployment applications through the first six months of the pandemic being denied or delayed (Desilver, 2020; Hess, 2020).

Additionally, addressing social policy in the pandemic response largely overlooked the need for financial support for state and local governments. As the federal government handed off authority to states to combat COVID-19, the financial burden was also taken up by subnational governments. The CARES Act included $150 billion in a new Coronavirus Relief Fund that state and local governments could use to reduce COVID-19-related costs (US Department of the Treasury, 2020). Yet this funding quickly proved to be insufficient to address the needs of subnational government. Senate Majority Leader Mitch McConnell signaled that he would oppose any more funds for states or local governments, suggesting that they could go down "the bankruptcy route" instead, even though states are not allowed to declare bankruptcy (Desiderio, 2020) and local governments often rely on federal bailouts in the face of extreme financial distress (Anderson, 2013). Further, the funds made available from the CARES Act can only be accessed by municipalities larger than 500,000 persons, putting smaller municipalities with fewer resources and a smaller tax base in jeopardy (Parrott et al., 2020). Without sufficient federal dollars in the CARES Act, state and local governments have now incurred massive debts. As of July 2020, these debts have required nearly half the states to enact supplemental appropriations to account for the budget hit from COVID-19, while thirteen states have had to draw from their financial reserves (National Conference of State Legislatures, 2020).

The CARES Act as social policy also overlooked marginalized populations who are at high risk of the disease, while also placing the administrative burden on the individual. Receiving financial support through direct payments is predicated on an individual having income tax filings *and* a social security number. Although the CARES Act does not place an income floor on eligibility for direct payments, relying on income tax filing to deliver direct payments inherently excludes large proportions of the population that are simultaneously at high risk of COVID-19 as well as face economic hardship from the pandemic-related economic downturn (Cajner et al., 2020). Populations that are excluded from receiving direct payments because they lack the proper documentation include immigrants that lack social security numbers and families in which a child is a citizen but other family members are not. This also includes individuals experiencing homelessness, who often lack any form of identification, do not file taxes, and often do not have any address. Certain groups, including those with very low income, or who receive their income from untaxed sources, such as Supplemental Security Income or Supplemental Security Disability Insurance, do not pay taxes, excluding them from receiving direct payments. Although non-tax-filers are eligible for receiving payments, the onus is placed on their shoulders.

Yet the limitations of the CARES Act as social policy would be blunted if the Trump administration had leveraged the time that the money bought to build up the public health infrastructure, contract tracing, and testing. Without building up those capacities, pressure built on budgets and businesses to reopen too quickly. Once the funding ran out, by design, in the summer of 2020, the limits of COVID-19's social policy became evident.

Explanation

COVID-19 wove many of America's best-known problems—health disparities, the uninsured, and a fraying social safety net—into a single, horrible, tapestry. The failure to contain and mitigate the COVID-19 pandemic has many explanations. The interacting inequalities of race and class have shaped the politics and policy of the nation, influencing voters' motivations and creating and sustaining highly undemocratic political institutions. As with other societies that were founded on slavery and other forms of racial hierarchy, class appeals or mobilization are constantly undermined by appeals to racial solidarity (Marx, 1998). Indeed, the fragmented and decentralized social safety net system was created to impede policy benefits given to minorities. This means that politics and policy in the United States are shaped by White people that receive psychological and economic benefits from white supremacy, even if cross-racial voting and mobilization might produce better social outcomes (Maxwell & Shields, 2019; Metzl, 2019).

The development of the US welfare state, anemic compared to other countries, is influenced by race and class. The welfare state was developed haphazardly and lacks generous benefits and programmatic coherence. US political institutions ensure that this is the case, with multiple veto points, which slow or block policy action (Stepan & Linz, 2011) but make it easy to add opportunities for rent-seeking or regulatory manipulation (Drutman, 2015). While in a racially hierarchical and low-trust society, it is easy to oppose social policies on the grounds that they will go to some undeserving group. Even White people who show little racial animus will often view Whites as a discrete category with shared interests and vote accordingly (Jardina, 2019). The result is that appeals for egalitarian policy are difficult to make, while also encountering the political systems that work very well to impede egalitarian social policy, such as competent public health.

The United States has a high level of elite and popular polarization (Carothers & O'Donohue 2019), which has been exploited by racial cleavages and class inequality, media (Benkler et al., 2018), increased partisanship (Azari, 2016), and political institutions. US political institutions have never been fully majoritarian but have become more undemocratic as urbanization occurs. The combination of increasingly undemocratic political institutions that reward Whites and the wealthy, with a demographically changing electorate, is dangerous for the functionality and legitimacy of the entire political system. The failure to respond to COVID-19 is, in this sense, to be expected: the Trump presidency is built around the exploitation of racial animus and undemocratic features of the political system, not its performance in the eyes of a majority of voters.

One institutional dimension linking the United States with some other notable failures of COVID-19 response such as Brazil and Russia are its combination of presidentialism and federalism. The United States is a *presidentialist* system, in which a directly elected president heads the executive branch and is constitutionally co-equal with the legislature. These systems create conflicts between different branches of government with equivalent mandates, while diffusing accountability. Legislators are incentivized to acquiesce to the empowerment of the executive because their prudent route to re-election is to avoid blameworthy votes. In the United States, legislatures and legislation had come to matter less and less, with the executive branch constrained mostly by a very partisan federal judicial system (Drezner, 2020).

This presidentialist model was weaponized by Trump, in a way reminiscent of how authoritarian regimes control information. Trump created problems of information flow that are seen in authoritarian regimes: lying and poor information flowed within the government, where politicians and officials censored themselves to avoid the anger of the leader, and poor information was given to the public. For example, Trump saying the virus would just go away and suggesting that drinking bleach might cure COVID-19. The CDC, which is a highly credible entity of the federal government, was largely invisible after being sidelined by the White House after comments that contradicted Trump and Vice President Pence (Milman, 2020).

To the extent that there was a bright spot for US political institutions, it was in *federalism:* the ability of the federal system to compensate for federal failure. Many governors acquitted themselves well during the crisis. States' abilities to fix problems created by the federal government was nonetheless limited (Kettl, 2020; Rocco et al., 2020). Yet state power was handcuffed because of the tightly integrated economies that span state boundaries. This led to economic competition between the states, which were already weakened by limited tax bases and stringent balanced budget rules. When faced with the deleterious economic consequences of a pandemic, states had to cut their budgets rather than expanding them to meet the crisis, pressuring them to delay closing economies to secure tax revenue. The price of a nationally integrated economy with competition between states and local governments is that we should not expect them to invest much in disaster preparedness or public health. The federal government traditionally enabled that system by spending money to maintain public health as a public good for the nation, albeit an unequal one. As the Republican party lost interest in that agenda, the erosion of federal public health capability left a gap no one else could fill. When Trump took charge during the pandemic and opted for denial and distraction rather than public health policies, there was no way governors could fill in the gaps.

Conclusion

There were many reasons why the United States should have been optimistic about their chances at responding to a global pandemic. Although the Trump administration had not dealt with an infectious disease epidemic before, experts in the federal government had responded successfully to H1N1, Ebola, SARS, MERS, and other disease outbreaks across the globe, although COVID-19 eclipses those earlier outbreaks in size and scope. Additionally, the United States has a vast health and public health system and clinical and epidemiological expertise.

Yet a postmortem on the failures of the United States to contain and mitigate the damage from COVID-19 highlights how the Trump administration did not do itself any favors. Although the political institutions that diffuse power across multiple levels of government in the United States were always going to be a challenge in a pandemic, Trump exacerbated those challenges through his policy decisions. One example is the Global Health Security and Biodefense unit, which was created in 2015 to provide expertise and advice to the National Security Council and the president. In 2018, as part of an effort to "streamline" the bureaucracy of the federal government, the unit was disbanded and reorganized; the top official in the National Security Council for pandemics left. Although some members of the unit did remain in the National Security Council, the timing of the action left the federal government without the expertise and organizational structure to help respond to COVID-19.

The Trump administration's failure to lead during the pandemic had debilitating effects on the United States' response to the disease. Prior policy responses to disease outbreaks have centered on federal leadership and funds. Although the federal government has appropriated billions in funding, those efforts have been limited by policy and political decisions. The leadership failure has proven to be the biggest barrier in the US response to COVID-19. There are more than ninety thousand individual governments in the United States, with stark variations in their expertise and capacity (United States Census Bureau, 2020). The political institutions are not set up to maximize the provision of public health services nor the production of public goods. Public goods, in the United States even more than in other federal countries, are best and most sustainably produced by the federal government (Greer, 2019). Yet Trump actively sought to hinder the response to COVID-19. Early in the pandemic, Trump made it clear that he opposed testing because it increased the numbers of reported cases (The White House, 2020a). In June 2020 he told a rally that "I said to my people, 'Slow the testing down'" (Lozano, 2020), and when his communications staff said he was joking, he reaffirmed it: "I don't kid . . . By having more tests we find more cases" (Forgey, 2020).

Trump's failure to lead and his disputing of science behind COVID-19 created an environment in which polarization and partisanship shaped views and behaviors of the disease. The most consistent factor that drives how individuals view COVID-19 and the adoption of social distancing behaviors is partisanship, with Republicans viewing the disease as safe and less likely to engage in behaviors that can minimize its spread (Kushner Gadarian, et al., 2020). Partisanship during COVID-19 also informed trust, with Republicans reporting that they most trust facts coming from Trump and his administration, while expressing disbelief at media coverage, and were more likely to believe conspiracy theories about the outbreak (Mitchell et al., 2020).

Taken together, there is no quick fix for the United States to improve its response to COVID-19, which by August 2020 caused more than 200,000 deaths. But these failures will reverberate into the future. Some of the challenges to respond to the next pandemic are structural and systemic, difficult, and unlikely to change. But much of the failures in the United States rest within the executive branch and the presidency itself. When the next pandemic occurs, and it will occur, hopefully the president will have learned from the failures of Donald Trump.

Note

1. The protests did not result in increased COVID-19 cases as a result of high rates of mask-compliance among protestors (Dave et al., 2020).

References

Adolph, C., Amano, K., Jensen-Bang, B., Fullman, N., & Wilkerson, J. (2020). *Pandemic politics: Timing state-level social distancing responses to COVID-19.* University of Washington.

Anderson, M. W. (2013). The new minimal cities. *Yale Law Journal, 123*, 1118.

Azar, A. M. (2020, January 28). Remarks at Coronavirus Press Briefing. https://www.hhs.gov/about/leadership/secretary/speeches/2020-speeches/remarks-at-coronavirus-press-briefing.html

Azari, J. (2016, November 3). Weak parties and strong partisanship are a bad combination. *Mischiefs of Faction.* https://www.vox.com/mischiefs-of-faction/2016/11/3/13512362/weak-parties-strong-partisanship-bad-combination

Benkler, Y., Faris, R., & Roberts, H. (2018). *Network propaganda: Manipulation, disinformation, and radicalization in American politics.* Oxford University Press.

Berchick, E. R., Barnett, J. C., & Upton, R. D. (2019). *Health insurance coverage in the United States: 2018.* US Government Printing Office.

Bureau of Economic Analysis. (2020, May 29). *Personal income and outlays: April 2020.* https://www.bea.gov/index.php/news/2020/personal-income-and-outlays-april-2020.

Burke, M. N. (2020, March 26). Trump rips Whitmer, who says state isn't getting virus supplies. *The Detroit News.* https://www.detroitnews.com/story/news/politics/2020/03/26/trump-digs-into-whitmer-after-she-criticizes-feds-covid-19-response/2923726001/

Cajner, T., Crane, L. D., Decker, R. A., Grigsby, J., Hamins-Puertolas, A., Hurst, E., Kurz, C., & Yildirmaz, A. (2020). *The US labor market during the beginning of the pandemic recession.* National Bureau of Economic Research. https://www.nber.org/papers/w27159

Cancryn, A., Forgey, Q., & Diamond, D. (2020, February 27). *After fumbled messaging, Trump gets a coronavirus czar by another name.* Politico. https://www.politico.com/news/2020/02/27/white-house-coronavirus-response-debbie-birx-117893

Capatides, C. (2020, May 11). *Doctors Without Borders dispatches team to the Navajo Nation.* CBS News. https://www.cbsnews.com/news/doctors-without-borders-navajo-nation-coronavirus/

Carothers, T., & O'Donohue, A. (2019). *Democracies divided: The global challenge of political polarization.* Brookings Institution Press.

Center on Budget and Policy Priorities. (2020, June 25). *Policy basics: Unemployment insurance.* https://www.cbpp.org/research/economy/policy-basics-unemployment-insurance

Centers for Disease Control and Prevention. (2017). *Overview of the CDC FY 2018 Budget Request.* https://www.cdc.gov/budget/documents/fy2018/fy-2018-cdc-budget-overview.pdf

Centers for Disease Control and Prevention. (2019). *Budget request overview.* https://www.cdc.gov/budget/documents/fy2019/cdc-overview-factsheet.pdf

Centers for Disease Control and Prevention. (2020a, July 24). *Health equity considerations and racial and ethnic minority groups.* https://www.cdc.gov/coronavirus/2019-ncov/community/health-equity/race-ethnicity.html

Centers for Disease Control and Prevention. (2020b, January 21). *First travel-related case of 2019 novel coronavirus detected in United States.* https://www.cdc.gov/media/releases/2020/p0121-novel-coronavirus-travel-case.html

Centers for Disease Control and Prevention. (2020c, February 29). *Washington state report first COVID-19 death.* https://www.cdc.gov/media/releases/2020/s0229-COVID-19-first-death.html

Congressional Research Services (2020, April 10). *Treasury's exchange stabilization fund and COVID-19.* https://crsreports.congress.gov/product/pdf/IF/IF11474

Dale, D. (2020, June 24). *Fact check: Trump claimed he was left "no ventilators." His administration just confirmed he had more than 16,000.* CNN. https://www.cnn.com/2020/06/24/politics/fact-check-trump-16000-ventilators-stockpile-obama/index.html

Dauber, M. L. (2013). *The sympathetic state: Disaster relief and the origins of the American welfare state.* University of Chicago Press.

Dave, D. M., Friedson, A. I., Matsuzawa, K., Sabia, J. J., & Safford, S. (2020). *Black lives matter protests, social distancing, and COVID-19.* National Bureau of Economic Research. https://www.nber.org/papers/w27408

Davies, D. (2020, May 28). *Reckoning with the dead: Journalist goes inside an NYC COVID-19 Disaster Morgue.* NPR. https://www.npr.org/sections/health-shots/2020

/05/28/863710050/reckoning-with-the-dead-journalist-goes-inside-an-nyc-covid-19-disaster-morgue

Desiderio, A. (2020, April 22). *McConnell pushes "bankruptcy route" as local governments struggle.* Politico. https://www.politico.com/news/2020/04/22/mitch-mcconnell-bankruptcy-route-201008

Desilver, D. (2020, April 24). *Not all unemployed people get unemployment benefits; in some states, very few do.* Pew Research Center. https://www.pewresearch.org/fact-tank/2020/04/24/not-all-unemployed-people-get-unemployment-benefits-in-some-states-very-few-do/

Drezner, D. W. (2020). *The toddler in chief: What Donald Trump teaches us about the modern presidency.* University of Chicago Press.

Drutman, L. (2015). *The business of America is lobbying: How corporations became politicized and politics became more corporate.* Oxford University Press.

Dunklin, R., Pritchard, J., Myers, J., & Fauria, K. (2020, April 21). *AP: Publicly traded firms get $365M in small-business loans.* AP News. https://apnews.com/article/6c5942eec36cc43b25ad5df5afebcfbd

Epstein, K. (2020, April 30). "Over our dead bodies": Lindsey Graham vows Congress won't extend additional $600 coronavirus-related unemployment benefits, as US death toll crosses the 60,000 mark. *Business Insider.* https://www.businessinsider.com/lindsey-graham-congress-coronavirus-unemployment-benefit-over-our-dead-bodies-2020-4

Fadel, L. (2020, May 9). *Public health experts say many states are opening too soon to do so safely.* NPR. https://www.npr.org/2020/05/09/853052174/public-health-experts-say-many-states-are-opening-too-soon-to-do-so-safely

Forgey, Q. (2020, June 23). *"I don't kid": Trump says he wasn't joking about slowing coronavirus testing.* Politico. https://www.politico.com/news/2020/06/23/trump-joking-slowing-coronavirus-testing-335459

Ganong, P., Noel, P. J., & Vavra, J. S. (2020). *US unemployment insurance replacement rates during the pandemic.* National Bureau of Economic Research.

Global Health Security. (2019, October). GHS Index Building Collective Action and Accountability. https://www.ghsindex.org/wp-content/uploads/2019/10/GHS-Index-Report_FINAL_Oct2019.pdf

Goodman, L., & Magder, D. (2020, April 13). *Avoiding a COVID-19 disaster for renters and the housing market.* Urban Institute. https://www.urban.org/research/publication/avoiding-covid-19-disaster-renters-and-housing-market

Greer, S. L. (2019). Comparative federalism: As if policy mattered. In Greer, S.L. & Elliott, H. (Eds.), *Federalism and Social Policy: Patterns of Redistribution in 11 Democracies,* University of Michigan Press.

Greer, S. L., & Singer, P. M. (2017a). Addressing Zika in the United States: Why so slow? *American Journal of Public Health, 107*(6), 861–862.

Greer, S. L., & Singer, P. M. (2017b). The United States confronts Ebola: suasion, executive action and fragmentation. *Journal of Health Economics, Policy and Law, 12*(1), 81–104.

Hess, A. (2020, May 15). *Study finds 44% of U.S. unemployment applicants have been denied or are still waiting.* CNBC. https://www.cnbc.com/2020/05/15/44percent-of-us-unemployment-applicants-have-been-denied-or-are-waiting.html

Inslee, J. (2020, January 21). Inslee statement on novel coronavirus case confirmed in Washington. https://www.governor.wa.gov/news-media/inslee-statement-novel-coronavirus-case-confirmed-washington

Internal Revenue Service. (2020, March 30). *Economic impact payments: What you need to know.* https://www.irs.gov/newsroom/economic-impact-payments-what-you-need-to-know.

Jardina, A. (2019). *White identity politics.* Cambridge University Press.

Johns Hopkins University & Medicine. (2020). *COVID-19 dashboard by the Center for Systems Science and Engineering (CSSE) at Johns Hopkins University (JHU).* Coronavirus Resource Center. Retrieved August 5, 2020, from https://coronavirus.jhu.edu/map.html

Kettl, D. F. (2020). States divided: The implications of American federalism for Covid-19. *Public Administration Review, 80*(4), 595–602.

Krisberg, K. (2020). Trump budget proposal a disinvestment in US health: Cuts to CDC, HRSA. *The Nation's Health, 50*(2), 1–10.

Kushner Gadarian, S., Goodman, S. W., & Pepinsky, T. B. (2020). *Partisanship, health behavior, and policy attitudes in the early stages of the COVID-19 Pandemic.* SSRN. https://papers.ssrn.com/sol3/papers.cfm?abstract_id=3562796

Lopez, G. (2020, September 2). *Just 4 states meet these basic criteria to reopen and stay safe.* Vox. https://www.vox.com/2020/5/28/21270515/coronavirus-covid-reopen-economy-social-distancing-states-map-data

Lozano, A. V. (2020, June 20). *Trump tells Tulsa crowd he wanted to "slow down" COVID-19 testing; White House says he was joking.* NBC News. https://www.nbcnews.com/politics/2020-election/trump-tells-tulsa-crowd-he-wanted-slow-down-covid-19-n1231658

Mangrum, D., & Niekamp, P. (2020, May 21). *College student contribution to local COVID-19 Spread: Evidence from university spring break timing.* SSRN. https://papers.ssrn.com/sol3/papers.cfm?abstract_id=3606811

Marx, A. W. (1998). *Making race and nation: A comparison of the United States, South Africa, and Brazil.* Cambridge University Press.

Maxwell, A., & Shields, T. (2019). *The long southern strategy: How chasing white voters in the south changed American politics.* Oxford University Press.

Metzl, J. M. (2019). *Dying of whiteness: How the politics of racial resentment is killing America's heartland.* Hachette UK.

Milman, O. (2020, May 14). Where is the CDC? How Trump sidelined the public health agency in a pandemic. *The Guardian.* https://www.theguardian.com/world/2020/may/14/where-is-the-cdc-trump-covid-19-pandemic

Mitchell, A., Jurkowitz, M., Oliphant, J., & Shearer, E. (2020, June 29). *Three months in, many Americans see exaggeration, conspiracy theories, and partisanship in COVID-19 news.* Pew Research Center. https://www.journalism.org/2020/06/29/three-months-in-many-americans-see-exaggeration-conspiracy-theories-and-partisanship-in-covid-19-news/

Nagle, R. (2020, April 24). Native Americans being left out of US coronavirus data and labelled as "other." *The Guardian.* https://www.theguardian.com/us-news/2020/apr/24/us-native-americans-left-out-coronavirus-data

National Conference of State Legislatures. (2020, June 30). *State fiscal responses to coronavirus (COVID-19).* https://www.ncsl.org/research/fiscal-policy/state-fiscal-responses-to-covid-19.aspx

Organisation for Economic Co-operation and Development. (2020). *Social Expenditure Database.* Retrieved August 5, 2020, from https://www.oecd.org/social/expenditure.htm

Oppel, R. A., Gebeloff, K. K., Lai, R., Wright, W., & Smith, M. (2020, July 5). The fullest look yet at the racial inequity of coronavirus. *The New York Times.* https://www.nytimes.com/interactive/2020/07/05/us/coronavirus-latinos-african-americans-cdc-data.html

Owermohle, S. (2020, January 22). *Trump: Chinese coronavirus "totally under control."* Politico. https://www.politico.com/news/2020/01/22/trump-chinese-coronavirus-totally-under-control-102054

Parrott, S., Stone, C., Huang G.-C., Leachman, M., Bailey, P., Aron-Dine, A., Dean, S., & Pavetti, L. (2020, March 27). CARES Act includes essential measures to respond to public health, economic crises, but more will be needed. *Center on Budget and Policy Priorities.* https://www.cbpp.org/research/economy/cares-act-includes-essential-measures-to-respond-to-public-health-economic-crises

Pence, M. R. (2020, June 16). There isn't a coronavirus "second wave." *The Wall Street Journal.* https://www.wsj.com/articles/there-isnt-a-coronavirus-second-wave-11592327890

Rocco, P., Béland, D., & Waddan, A. (2020). Stuck in neutral? Federalism, policy instruments, and counter-cyclical responses to COVID-19 in the United States." *Policy and Society, 39*(3), 1–20.

Santa Clara County Public Health (2020, April 21). *County of Santa Clara identifies three additional early COVID-19 deaths.* https://www.sccgov.org/sites/covid19/Pages/press-release-04-21-20-early.aspx

Selden, T. M., & Berdahl, T. A. (2020). COVID-19 and racial/ethnic disparities in health risk, employment, and household composition: Study examines potential explanations for racial-ethnic disparities in COVID-19 hospitalizations and mortality. *Health Affairs, 39*(9), 1624–1632.

Shear, M. D., Goodnough, A., Kaplan, S., Fink, S., Thomas, K., & Weiland, N. (2020, April 1). The lost month: how a failure to test blinded the U.S. to Covid-19. *The New York Times.* https://www.nytimes.com/2020/03/28/us/testing-coronavirus-pandemic.html

Silverman, H., & Kelly, C. (2020, June 25). *Early CDC test kits were delayed because of contamination issues, HHS report affirms.* CNN. https://www.cnn.com/2020/06/20/politics/cdc-test-kits-contamination/index.html

Singer, P. M., Willison, C. E., & Greer, S. L. (2020). Infectious disease, public health, and politics: United States response to Ebola and Zika. *Journal of Public Health Policy, 41*(4), 399–409.

Stepan, A., & Linz, J. J. (2011). Comparative perspectives on inequality and the quality of democracy in the United States. *Perspectives on Politics, 9*(4), 841–856.

Trump, D. [@realDonaldTrump]. (2020, February 24). The Coronavirus is very much under control in the USA. We are in contact with everyone and all relevant countries [Tweet]. *Twitter.* https://twitter.com/realdonaldtrump/status/1232058127740174339?lang=en

United States Census Bureau. (2020). *Census of governments.* https://www.census.gov/programs-surveys/cog.html

US Department of Health and Human Services. (2020, January 31). *Secretary Azar declares public health emergency for United States for 2019 novel coronavirus.* https://www.hhs.gov/about/news/2020/01/31/secretary-azar-declares-public-health-emergency-us-2019-novel-coronavirus.html

US Department of the Treasury. (2020). *The CARES Act provides assistance for state, local, and tribal governments.* https://home.treasury.gov/policy-issues/cares/state-and-local-governments

Warmbrodt, Z. (2020, April 20). *Banks warn that new small-business funding could evaporate in 2 days.* Politico. https://www.politico.com/news/2020/04/20/bank-small-business-funding-coronavirus-197372

Weinberger, D. M., Chen, J., Cohen, T., Crawford, F. W., Mostashari, F., Olson, D., Pitzer, V. E., Reich, N. G., Russi, M., & Simonsen, L. (2020). Estimation of excess deaths associated with the COVID-19 pandemic in the United States, March to May 2020. *JAMA Internal Medicine, 180*(10): 1336–1344.

The White House. (2020a, May 14). Remarks by President Trump at Owens & Minor, Inc. Distribution Center, Allentown, PA. https://www.whitehouse.gov/briefings-statements/remarks-president-trump-owens-minor-inc-distribution-center-allentown-pa/

The White House. (2020b, February 26). Remarks by President Trump, Vice President Pence, and Members of the Coronavirus Task Force in Press Conference. https://www.whitehouse.gov/briefings-statements/remarks-president-trump-vice-president-pence-members-coronavirus-task-force-press-conference/

Willison, C. E., Singer, P. M., Creary, M. S., & Greer, S. L. (2019). Quantifying inequities in US federal response to hurricane disaster in Texas and Florida compared with Puerto Rico. *BMJ Global Health, 4*, 1.

27 COVID-19 IN BRAZIL

Presidential Denialism and the Subnational Government's Response

*Elize Massard da Fonseca, Nicoli Nattrass,
Luísa Bolaffi Arantes, and Francisco Inácio Bastos*

Brazil has one of the largest public health systems in the world (Paim et al., 2011). It has successfully responded to epidemics such as human immunodeficiency virus and acquired immunodeficiency syndrome (HIV/AIDS), hepatitis C, and H1N1 influenza (Fonseca et al., 2019; Nunn, 2008). Brazil has a well-developed health surveillance system encompassing legal frameworks and infrastructure. It complies with the World Health Organization's (WHO) International Health Regulation, which establishes parameters for public health emergencies (Franco Netto et al., 2017) and provides guidelines for countries' rights and obligations in responding to potentially border-crossing epidemics.

The capacity of the health system to react during public health crises, however, may differ from its functioning ability during normal times (Medici, 2020). However, it was expected that Brazil would perform well during the COVID-19 pandemic. According to the Global Health Security Index, a system of measurement that classifies countries' preparedness to deal with public health emergencies across six dimensions and thirty-four indicators, Brazil ranked with the best score in Latin America (59.7 out of 100) (Nuclear Threat Initiative & Johns Hopkins Bloomberg School of Public Health, 2019). Why, then, was a country that was relatively well prepared for public health crises, that had performed in an exemplary manner in previous epidemics, and that has one of the largest public health infrastructures in the world not able to respond promptly and effectively to the COVID-19 pandemic? What went wrong?

In this chapter, we explore the evolution of public health initiatives during the COVID-19 pandemic in Brazil, the social policies adopted to allow people to quarantine, and the political and institutional factors shaping Brazil's response. We analyze the negative role played by President Bolsonaro's denialism and misinformation while emphasizing that a group of subnational governments led Brazil's response, at times aligned with the Ministry of Health (MoH) but against the president's perspective. We highlight the surprisingly proactive response by state governments given that this level of government has had little involvement in public health policy. Brazil is a federal system, with a federal government, 27 states, and more than 5,500 elected municipal governments. Response to the COVID-19 pandemic is a tale of intergovernmental competition, with several instances of blame avoidance and credit claiming. Public opinion vacillated, but it appears that Bolsonaro was able to reap credit for the cash transfer programs put in place during the epidemic, despite his initial opposition to increasing social spending.

COVID-19 Pandemic in Brazil

The first case of COVID-19 in Brazil was officially diagnosed on February 26, 2020, in a man returning from a trip to Italy. Later studies showed that the virus had been circulating since at least early January 2020 (Delatorre et al., 2020). In early March 2020, the MoH announced the first cases of community transmission (i.e., infections that did not stem from interactions with individuals in foreign countries). As of August 14, 2020, the pandemic had resulted in 3,224,876 confirmed cases and 105,463 deaths in Brazil (Dong et al., 2020).

At that point, the epidemic was far from being curbed—similar to that in the United States and Mexico. As of mid-August, Brazil was still facing a substantial epidemic. The curve had flattened somewhat but was plateauing at high levels in places such as São Paulo. Infections were rising rapidly in the southernmost states and in most regions of the center-west. In a large country like Brazil, a pandemic curve is likely to present different peaks at different places and different times (Bastos, 2020), which makes a coordinated response a formidable challenge.

Health Policy

Brazil has a public health system, the Unified Health System (acronym in Portuguese, SUS) that cares for 75 percent of the population, with most of the remaining 25 percent covered by private health insurance companies.[1] The country's health policies regarding international pandemics are in alignment with the WHO, and there is a national plan for curbing influenza epidemics (Y. Lima & Costa, 2015; Ministério da Saúde, 2010). In late February, thirty-four Brazilian citizens living in Wuhan, China (the epicenter of the epidemic at that time) were repatriated, but there was no quarantine regulation in the country. The Minister of Health, Luiz Henrique Mandetta, reacted quickly to get legislation passed on not only preparing to receive these citizens but also preparing for the impending epidemic (Law 13.979/2020; Coletta, 2020). Although none of the Brazilian citizens were infected, they were required to quarantine for fifteen days in a military facility in Brazil before returning to their homes ("Brasileiros que Vieram da China Deixam Quarentena em Anápolis" ["Brazilians Who Came from China Leave Quarantine in Anápolis"], 2020).

The MoH and the state of São Paulo, the most populous region in the country, created committees to manage the potential crisis. Several hospitals established protocols to deal with suspected cases. The MoH, in anticipation of the winter influenza season, was already embarking on its annual influenza vaccination campaign. Additionally, most states and municipalities acted promptly. On March 13, 2020, Rio de Janeiro became one of the first states in Brazil to close schools and shops and cancel large social events. São Paulo—the epicenter of the country's outbreak—did so ten days later (Rodrigues, 2020).

In contrast with the subnational governments, President Bolsonaro decided not to follow WHO guidelines or evidence-based health policy, apparently believing that this would have negative economic consequences for the country. The president and his supporters (the governors of four states, part of the military forces, and some government officials such as the minister of international relations and some extreme-right wing groups) advocated for health policies that reflected pseudoscience at best, and denialism at worst. They suggested that COVID-19 was a "small flu" and a "fantasy," while drawing on discredited or incomplete "science" in support of their light-touch approach to combatting COVID-19 ("Relembre Frases de Bolsonaro Sobre a COVID-19" ["Remember Bolsonaro Phrases About COVID-19"], 2020). For instance, they relied on non–peer-reviewed papers and statements to give a patina of scientific respectability to their construction of a moral economy[2] narrative framed around the right to earn a living. Conventional scientific advice, especially where this undermined the ability of business to earn a profit, was undermined or ignored.

March 2020 was a critical time with regard to both the bourgeoning epidemic and the dispute brewing between federal and most subnational governments. As the epidemic spread through the country and to the more vulnerable populations, the state governors began an aggressive campaign to promote social distancing initiatives, which were aligned with the MoH administration at that moment. Both Minister Mandetta and the state governors gained popularity for their scientifically informed guidance on COVID-19. This appears to have enraged President Bolsonaro and his supporters, who were against measures such as closing shops and schools and paralyzing commerce. Several protests against social distancing were scheduled during a critical period of the pandemic, some of which were led by the president himself.

A crystallizing moment was a virtual meeting on March 25, 2020, between the president and state governors. The previous day, President Bolsonaro addressed the nation, declaring, "Our lives have to go on. Jobs must be kept . . . We must, yes, get back to normal" (Phillips, 2020). During this virtual meeting, Bolsonaro accused the governor of São Paulo (a member of the Brazilian Social Democratic Party, PSDB, acronym in Portuguese) of using the health emergency as a political strategy for the 2022 presidential election. Bolsonaro is currently not affiliated with any political party but was elected under a minor, far-right political party, the Social Liberal Party.

In a presidential, federal system, the decisions to act during a pandemic are divided among different institutions. For instance, the president has the authority to close Brazil's borders. It was only on March 19, 2020, however, that the Ministry of Justice closed land borders and on March 27, 2020, that it completely shut airports to incoming international flights from all over the world (Fernandes, 2020; Schreiber, 2020). Although the MoH was active in producing mass campaigns to educate the population on how to prevent the spread of the virus, the Ministry of Economy delayed financial support (e.g., cash transfers) that would allow citizens and firms to adhere to social distancing measures.

In April and May of 2020, the lack of coordination became even more evident. On April 8, the Supreme Court ruled that state governments could implement measures to respond to the epidemic within their jurisdictions and municipal governments could complement decisions taken at federal and state levels. This decision was crucial in allowing states to adopt and maintain restrictive measures. President Bolsonaro responded with several presidential decrees listing essential activities that should continue and businesses that should remain open, including religious services, gyms, construction sites, and industrial activities, among others. In April 2020 the president began an aggressive campaign in support of the use of chloroquine and hydroxychloroquine to treat COVID-19 patients. Such strong advocacy was against the advice of Minister Mandetta, who was subsequently fired and replaced by a respected physician, Nelson Teich (Mazui, 2020). Because of his vehement disagreement with President Bolsonaro's plans to adjust the clinical protocols for COVID-19 treatment, Teich resigned less than a month after taking the position (Verdélio, 2020). Bolsonaro expressed his interest in including chloroquine and hydroxychloroquine as part of the MoH's clinical protocol for COVID-19, but Teich preferred to wait for adequate scientific evidence. Such disputes not only spread contradictory recommendations on how to deal with the COVID-19 but also have had apparent political effects, notably strengthening support for state governors.

The president replaced Teich with a military officer, General Eduardo Pazuello, as interim minister. Pazuello had no experience in the health sector, but his background in logistics was presented as a core competency for responding to the epidemic (Savarese & Biller, 2020). The temporary health minister not only yielded to the adjustment of the clinical protocols for COVID-19 but also replaced key managerial posts in the MoH with fellow military officers (B. Lima & Cardim, 2020). This decision was highly criticized by the public health community, such as the Brazilian Association of Collective Health (Abrasco), a strong organization in Brazil since the 1988 reform that introduced the public health service (Abrasco, 2020). Pazuello later took the controversial decision to reformulate the disclosure of epidemiological data, announcing only information about death and confirmed cases in the previous twenty-four hours rather than accumulated deaths and infections (Machado & Fernandes, 2020). As a response, a consortium between Health State Secretariats and a pool of media organizations established an online e-panel that was updated every day to monitor and compare the official data provided by the MoH ("Brasil Tem Média de 1.069 Mortes por Dia na Última Semana" ["Brazil Has an Average of 1,069 Deaths per Day in the Last Week"], 2020). Pazuello's decision was subsequently repealed by the Supreme Court (Xavier, 2020).

Social Policies

Since 2015 economic crises and austerity policies in Brazil severely constrained public expenditure and increased inequality (Deweck et al., 2018). In March 2020 a "state of calamity" decreed by the Brazilian National Congress allowed the federal government to increase public expenditure, which otherwise would have been frozen in line with the country's strict laws regulating public spending. In addition, in April, Congress approved a bill named "War Budget," which entailed a constitutional amendment to separate COVID-19–related spending from the government's main budget. The COVID-19 emergency resulted in the federal government investing more than US$2 billion in health and social policies (Agencia Saude, 2020). This would allow Brazilians to quarantine for longer periods but also posed challenges for Bolsanaro's anti-statist, free-market policies.

Paulo Guedes, an investment banker and minister of economy since 2019, was important politically for Bolsonaro. "Guedes may be a naively ambitious advocate of free-market policies serving the financial elite, but he provided [President] Bolsonaro with the necessary economic 'seal of approval' and removed the stain of a possible affinity for 'statism' created by Bolsonaro's career in the military" (Evans, 2018, p. 50). Economic policy is a crucial aspect of Brazil's politics. The Ministry of Economy is powerful in Brazil (and Bolsonaro defers to the minister of economy over decisions on public expenditure) because no one wants to experience again the debilitating effects of hyperinflation. Yet there are aspects of government spending that remain strongly entrenched and have helped people cope with the epidemic. Chief among these are cash transfer programs.

Brazil has one of the most successful conditional cash transfer programs in the world, the Family Allowance program (*Bolsa Familia*), with clear benefits for the health of impoverished people (Rasella et al., 2013). Brazil also created a new social program to provide salary relief to vulnerable populations: the Salary Relief program.[3] The creation of this program was a shared decision between Congress and the executive government; therefore, there were substantial controversies and disagreements between these governmental entities over the contents of these policies. We first explore the existing policies in place, then investigate the new Salary Relief Program.

The Continuous Cash Benefit (CCB) program, implemented in 1996, is an unconditional cash transfer to the elderly or extremely poor individuals with disabilities. During the pandemic, the Law 13982/2020 revised the criteria for inclusion in the program from those who earned a quarter of the minimum wage as household income per capita to those who earned half of the minimum wage. For those waiting to enter the program, the government provided a cash advance of R$600 (US$110). This advance was because legislative reforms in the entitlement criteria of the CCB program require regulation by the Social Security Institute, which might take several months and not be ready before the end of the pandemic (Bartholo et al., 2020). Although Congress intended to assist the elderly or extremely poor individuals with disabilities through CCB, as of mid-August 2020 this had not yet been implemented because it required further regulatory changes on the part of the federal government.

One of the most important social policies in Brazil, the Family Allowance program, was created in 2003. It targets poor families with a per capita income below US$40 per month and registered with the Unified Record (*Cadastro Único*). It is the responsibility of the local government to register and implement the program, which is then verified at the federal level. The Ministry of Citizenship suspended the penalties of those families that had not been able to fulfill the conditions of the program during the epidemic (such as school or basic healthcare attendance) or those with insufficient record information. As schools were closed and health services overwhelmed by COVID-19 cases, it proved impossible for families to fulfill these conditions (Bartholo et al., 2020). The Ministry of Citizenship suspended the monthly evaluation of municipalities' performance index, which assessed the municipality's local-level compliance with the rules of the program. In addition to the Family Allowance program some states distributed vouchers and food stipends to families registered with the Unified Record. For instance, the government of Santa Catarina waved the electricity bill and the government of Mato Grosso provided food parcels (*cesta basica*) for poor families. One of the consequences of this mix of national, state, and local regulations was that people living in different states were entitled to different social benefits.

Changes to the Family Allowance program meant that for the first time after more than a year (since Bolsonaro came to power) the waiting list of people wanting to enter the program was reduced from 1.7 million families to 500,000. This was thanks to a presidential provisional decree that allocated more than R$3 billion (US$578 million) to the program (because of the lack of funding, the Ministry of Citizenship could not expand the number of families in the program without this provisional decree). There was an enormous difference between new Family Allowance concessions to the south and southeast (75 percent), which are the wealthiest regions, compared to the northeast, which received only 3 percent of new concessions; therefore the governors of these states filed a lawsuit at the Supreme Court against the federal government (Mello, 2020).

In addition to calibrating existing social programs, the federal government created a new support, the Salary Relief Program. This was the most important social policy initiative during the epidemic because it covered both recipients of the Family Allowance and unemployed individuals with a household income below half the minimum wage. The program was announced mid-March 2020 after strong pressure from congressmen on the Ministry of Economy. Initially, the executive government announced a R$200 allowance (US$37) per month, which, after a debate in Congress, was increased to R$600 (US$110) (Piovesan & Siqueira, 2020). In May the government came under further pressure to extend the allowance for additional months. Again there was a dispute between the Minister of Economy and Congress. The former suggested an increase of the allowance by R$200 (US$38) per month for an additional two months. Congress, however, kept the value the same but allowed the additional two months (Presidential Decree 10.412/2020). As of July 2020, the program had cost R$113 billion (US$22 billion) and aided almost 109 million individuals (more than double the initial estimation) (Maximo, 2020). This meant that one in every three adults had received governmental support. Because of the economic recession, such expenditure was possible only because of the state of calamity and the war budget issued by Congress, which allowed an increase in the executive government's expenditure.

The implementation of the Salary Relief program encountered some obstacles, however. For example, Brazil adopted a fully online strategy to enroll new individuals and not all vulnerable people had access to the internet or a cell phone. Additionally, problems with incomplete applications or documentation had to be solved in person, which led to long waiting lines in Social Security offices throughout the country (Veloso, 2020). Despite such issues, the outcomes of the program were impressive: more than 5 percent of residences in Brazil (3.5 million) survived this period by relying only on the Salary Relief program. The average household incomes of beneficiaries were 95 percent of what they would have been earning in the absence of the epidemic, and for the poorest parts of the population, it was 103 percent (Bartholo et al., 2020).

These cash transfers provided a political boost for President Bolsonaro, who, as of mid-August 2020, was considering replacing the Family Allowance with a new program, Brazil Income (*Renda Brasil*). This program could be a valuable asset for Bolsonaro's re-election campaign in 2022 (Beck & Gamarski, 2020). This is ironic given Bolsonaro's initial reluctance to increase public expenditure and his opposition to measures that could require closing the economy. However, as social policies were implemented, the popularity of the president increased considerably (37 percent good/excellent, a record during his term) ("Datafolha: Aprovação de Bolsonaro Sobe para 37%" ["Datafolha: Bolsonaro's Approval Rises to 37"], 2020). Such policies also helped counterbalance the negative health policy decisions taken by the president. The polling data suggest that Bolsonaro was able to pass the blame onto state governors for unpopular initiatives while claiming credit for the social policies (particularly cash transfers) during the epidemic. Whether this was serendipitous or a shrewd political strategy is unclear.

Explanation

Presidentialism Effect

Brazil has a complex presidential regime, which lies between the model of the US presidential system (ceding significant decision-making control to the president) and European parliamentarianism, where political parties dominate government. It is important to note, however, that Brazil is not a semipresidential system (such as France or Peru), in which cabinet formation requires formal approval from Congress. Therefore, the bargaining space between coalition members and the executives in cabinet formation (including the MoH) and bureaucratic appointments is the result of the particular shape of the party-system.

Brazilian presidents are endowed with strong constitutional powers (Amorim Neto, 2002). Besides the allocating of positions in the vast federal administrative empire, presidents can issue presidential decrees and exercise substantial control over budgetary matter. As in other countries, the president is able to use his or her position to speak directly to voters via national radio and televised speeches. These are powerful instruments that allow the president to push forward his agenda, whether for the public good or for particular interests.

Bolsonaro is a far-right populist president who came into power in 2018 through an alliance between the economic liberals and social conservatives. Bolsonaro, a low-rank congressman who never had great political aspirations, was seen as an alternative to the Workers' Party's candidate. After corruption allegations that resulted in the impeachment of President Dilma Rousseff and the "lawfare" (the use of legal system against a political enemy) against President Luiz Inácio Lula da Silva, Bolsonaro was able to take advantage of this opportunity to push his campaign forward (Evans, 2018). With a moral discourse against corruption, during the initial months of his term in the presidency, he refused to form alliances with political parties in Congress. Nevertheless, he appointed Mandetta as Minister of Health, which was both a political decision (Mandetta is a member of the PSDB political party, an important political ally) and a technical one (Mandetta is a physician).

As discussed previously, Mandetta threatened Bolsonaro's political dominance, his pseudo-scientific rhetoric, and his stance on social distancing and plans to open up the economy. After the second health minister, Teich, resigned and was replaced by active-duty Army General Eduardo Pazuello, political analysts in Brazil suggested that Bolsonaro was ensuring that if any negative public health consequences or possible judicial decisions against the president arose, the blame would be shared with the Army (Barros, 2020).

President Bolsonaro's strong skepticism toward the science of COVID-19 (if not outright denial of it) seems to have been reinforced after returning from a visit to the United States, where he met with American populist president Donald Trump to discuss military cooperation. Bolsonaro's discourse became radicalized toward ignoring and minimizing the pandemic (Teófilo, 2020). Like Trump,

Bolsonaro was not keen to "stop" the national economy and gained notoriety for supporting protests against government lockdowns, for touting unproven medicines (notably hydroxychloroquine), and for downplaying the seriousness of the virus, even so far as vocally opposing state governors' decisions to impose social distancing measures. Many of Bolsonaro's statements contradicting the governors were typically framed in terms of his goal of reopening nonessential businesses. Bolsonaro often highlighted the economic consequences and costs of social distancing. For instance, he stated, "Brazil has to work. The best medicine for any disease is work. We have got to work" (Carvalho & Colletta, 2020). As noted previously, economic stability is valuable to politicians given Brazil's history of economically disruptive hyperinflation. Yet, as the consequence of lockdown and social distancing globally has been economic recession rather than hyperinflation, the political advantage he may have been seeking was to avoid the blame for the recession and to pass it on to regional governors (Ricard & Medeiros, 2020).

Denying, or marginalizing, scientific advice works politically to undermine the influence and power of institutions and local or regional governments basing their strategies on scientific information and practice. In South Africa, under ex-President Thabo Mbeki—who was infamous for denying the science of HIV pathogenesis and treatment—such "AIDS denialism" was linked to particular economic interests centered around the provision of "alternative" therapies (Nattrass, 2012). In Bolsonaro's Brazil, touting hydroxychloroquine as a "cure," despite scientific evidence that it was ineffective and could even harm patients (Mehra et al., 2020), appeared not to be linked directly to economic interests but rather functioned to support his desired rapid return to economic growth as well as his tried-and-tested use of misinformation as a political strategy. Ricard and Medeiros (2020) argue that Bolsonaro's use of antisystem rhetoric accompanied by "massive and orchestrated misinformation" functioned as a political weapon during his 2019 election campaign. They note a consequence was that "during this period, antiscientific theories that had no relevance in Brazil (for example, flat earth theories or negation of climate change) acquired strong advocates on the national level and paved the way for the dangerous equivalence between opinion and science" (Ricard & Medeiros, 2020, p. 5). Politically, this encouraged Bolsonaro's followers to understand his disregard of science as a courageous break with "the system" rather than "simple populist pyrotechnics" (Ricard & Medeiros, 2020, p. 6). This, however, placed him in a tense and contradictory position within the "system" over which he presided, especially during the COVID-19 epidemic.

Federalism and the Subnational Government Entrepreneurship

Several studies that have catalogued and analyzed Brazil's response to COVID-19 have been unanimous in describing the lack of coordination between federal government departments and the subnational governments (Cimini et al., 2020). An analysis using the Oxford COVID-19 Government Response Tracker coding system applied to federal, state, and selected state-capital governments suggested a large disparity between the severity of social distancing measures supported by federal and subnational governments, with the latter contributing a great deal more to Brazil's country-level stringency scores (Petherick et al., 2020).

There are two important aspects to explore regarding the effects of federalism in the response to the pandemic: the authority of state governments over health policy and their dependence on the federal government for debt relief.

First, the COVID-19 epidemic transformed the politics and authority pertaining to state governance of health. Whereas for almost three decades, state governments have had limited influence on Brazilian national politics given the institutional powers of the executive and the way that tax resources are distributed, disputes with President Bolsonaro over how to respond to the epidemic appeared to have unified the regional leaders in a subversion of the "rally-round-the-flag effect"[4] (Melo, 2020). State governors strongly disagreed with the president on the need to enforce social distancing measures and to postpone the reopening of commerce and other activities. For instance, in April, after the president's televised speech that underplayed the threat posed by COVID-19, the governor of Goiás, Ronaldo Caiado, a powerful leader of the agricultural caucus as well as a well-known orthopedic surgeon and one-time strong supporter of the president, declared, "There is no more dialogue with this man . . . Bolsonaro's decisions to limit social distancing measures to high-risk populations won't reach the state of Goiás." (Berti, 2020). He went on to call on the president to follow scientific advice on COVID-19 (Berti, 2020).

The Mandetta health administration strongly supported the subnational governments' decisions to favor social distancing measures and to follow WHO protocols and scientific guidelines. Despite the president's preferences, most state governments remained firm in their support of social distancing, business closures, and warnings against drugs and therapies that had yet to be tested. This helped inform the population and encouraged compliance with the initiatives taken in response to COVID-19.

Bolsonaro took advantage of the division of authority over the COVID 19 epidemic to adopt a blame-avoidance strategy. Bolsonaro declared that governors and mayors would have to pay a fine to businessmen for losses resulting from quarantine. Additionally, on many occasions, Bolsonaro stated that governors and mayors were responsible for the consequences of quarantine measures, claiming that regional leaders' decisions to shut down nonessential activities would have catastrophic consequences "far worse than the coronavirus" and that such individuals would be held accountable, along with the Supreme Court (Coletta et al., 2020). These statements and their language took the stance of an attempt to evade blame when epidemiological models and specialists, in reality, emphasized the disastrous consequences of lifting quarantine too soon (Brett & Rohani, 2020).

Second, because of the ongoing economic crisis that had affected Brazil since 2015, many states were in severe fiscal debt, particularly with difficulties in paying salaries and pensions, and were negotiating a relief plan with the federal government. The need to immediately respond to the COVID-19 pandemic further exacerbated the problem. In April 2020, state governors were able to secure a law in Congress that would force the executive government to provide them financial support without any conditionality.[5] The president of the Senate negotiated new legislation between state governors and the Minister of Economy in which states would receive R$120 billion (US$23 billion), including instituting bailout initiatives to honor foreign debts, suspending debts with the federal government, and transferring resources to the states (Act 173/2020). The only condition was that states would not provide the annual salary increase that civil servants were entitled to and resources would be transferred according to the number of COVID-19 cases in each state, regardless of the capacity of the state to levy taxes. Therefore, although states gained important authority to decide on the measures to fight COVID-19, they remained entrapped by the fiscal transfers and debt alleviation initiatives of the federal government.

Nevertheless, the financial support and autonomy gained by governors to decide on COVID-19 measures allowed the implementation of locally tailored initiatives. These proved particularly important as the spread of the COVID-19 occurred at different rates in different geographical regions.

Conclusion

We have argued that President Bolsonaro undermined efforts to base Brazil's response on scientific guidelines for both the prevention and treatment of COVID-19. Yet our analysis has also emphasized the importance of resistance to his policies both within the Health Ministry and among regional governors, some of whom supported Bolsonaro in the past. Paradoxically, the president who had obstructed an effective health policy response because of its economic consequences ended up reaping the benefits of additional social spending to assist the poor cope with the epidemic. In a federal system, with a decentralized health service, it proved strategic for the president to avoid the blame for unpopular health policies (at the cost of important health communication initiative that is crucial during pandemics), while claiming credit for the provision of social policies that benefited vulnerable populations.

As of mid-2020, Brazil was the second most affected country by the COVID-19 pandemic in terms of diagnosed cases and number of fatalities. The most likely scenario is a protracted epidemic, with transient ups and downs in different regions of the country and/or populations, with no definitive control in the short and medium term.

Underneath the circumstantial politics, there was a strong, path-dependent health infrastructure able to assist Brazil avoid the most catastrophic scenario. The country has a well-developed health surveillance infrastructure in place to deal with pandemics such as COVID-19. Several state governments were able to build field hospitals that were essential in treating severe cases of COVID-19 in

São Paulo, Manaus, and Recife—all large metropolitan areas. Additionally, Brazil has an extensive primary healthcare network, with, as of mid-2020, more than 43,000 family health teams and 260,000 community health agents. Because 80 percent of COVID-19 cases do not develop severe syndromes, primary health care is essential in caring for these patients (Collucci, 2020). Much research remains to be done, and future studies will hopefully shed more light on these successful aspects of Brazil's response as well as on recent efforts to purchase and produce a COVID-19 vaccine locally.

Case studies of particular states will also be useful. For example, Santa Catarina was the first state to fully resume all activities, as indicated by graphic broadcasts of crowded shopping centers with few masks in sight. Unsurprisingly, the state soon experienced a rebound in the number of cases and deaths, with an increase of more than 100 percent in the interval of a few days (Holland, 2020). Maranhão, by contrast, has been relatively successful at containing the epidemic. This has been attributed to the political decisions to implement the first, timely, lockdown in the whole country and to buy critical equipment directly from foreign firms, bypassing the slow paperwork associated with purchases from local branches and the much bigger purchase power of the United States and the European Union (Carneiro & Seto, 2020) and to strong cooperation with international partners, from the US state agencies to private funders, such as the Open Society Foundations (US Embassy Press Office, 2020).

As the WHO has advised, there are other pandemics to come. One of the key lessons we can learn from COVID-19 in Brazil and from the AIDS epidemic, paraphrasing Buse, Dickinson, and Sidibé (2008), is to know your epidemic, act on its politics (p. 572).

Acknowledgments

FMF receives a research grant from the Sao Paulo Research Foundation (FAPESP) (2015/18604–5 and 2020/05230–8), LBA receives a scholarship from FAPESP (2019/25141–2). We thank Beatriz Portella, Lucas Rosin, Carolina Coutinho, and Joseph Harris.

Notes

1. Private insurers use SUS when in need of expensive treatments not covered by the private sector.

2. See discussion of moral economy in Nattrass (2004) and its application to AIDS denialism in South Africa under Mbeki.

3. The government also created the Emergency Labor program, designed to allow the reduction of labor hours for ninety days or temporary suspension of labor contracts for sixty days. During that time the government would either complement the salary or, in the case of contract suspension, it would cover the full unemployment insurance.

4. This concept explains the "surge of public approval for the president when the nation is involved in an international crisis" (Murray, 2018).

5. The dispute around this bill was less a contention among political parties than among different Houses. The bill received seventy-nine votes in favor among eighty-one senators (only one left-wing senator was against and the president of session was not allowed to vote) (Tito, 2020).

References

Abrasco. (2020, July 3). Nota pela valorização dos profissionais do Ministério da Saúde [A note to support the Ministry of Health Professionals]. *Associacao Brasileira de Saude Coletiva [Brazilian Association of Post-Graduation in Collective Health] (Abrasco).*

Agencia Saude. (2020, April 3). *Governo do Brasil libera R$9,4 bilhões para combate ao coronavírus.* https://www.saude.gov.br/noticias/agencia-saude/46651-governo-do-brasil-libera-r-9-4-bilhoes-para-combate-ao-coronavirus

Alston, L., Melo, M., Mueller, B., & Pereira, C. (2006). *Political institutions, policymaking processes and policy outcomes in Brazil.* (Inter-American Development Bank Working Paper No. 204). https://dx.doi.org/10.2139/ssrn.1814758

Amorim Neto, O. (2002). Presidential cabinets, electoral cycles, and coalition discipline in Brazil. In S. Morgenstern & B. Nacif (Eds.),. *Legislative politics in Latin America.* Cambridge University Press.

Barros, C. (2020, July 19). Bolsonaro finalmente realizou seu projeto de juventude: Colocou uma bomba nos quartéis [Bolsonaro's youth dream come true: Put a bomb in military headquarters]. *Folha de Sao Paulo.*

Bartholo, L., Paiva, A., Natalino, M., Licio, E., & Pinheiro, M. (2020). *As transferências monetárias federais de caráter assistencial em resposta à COVID-19: Mudanças e desafios de implementação* [Federal cash transfers of assistance in response to Covid-19: Changes and implementation challenges]. http://repositorio.ipea.gov.br/handle/11058/10042

Bastos, L. (2020). *Cuidados com analises de dados da Covid-19* [Careful attention to COVID-19 data]. Retrieved on January 22, 2021, http://www.statpop.com.br/2020/05/cuidados-com-analises-de-dados-da.html?fbclid=IwAR29Nq8ezWEzU8rbLotaygR_zK3ty6FzYKeGLVm_5HDHhQ1l8nbSq-g9_js

Beck, M., & Gamarski, R. (2020, Jun 23). *Bolsonaro plans signature social program replacing Lula's legacy.* Bloomberg. https://www.bloomberg.com/news/articles/2020-06-23/bolsonaro-plans-signature-social-program-replacing-lula-s-legacy

Berti, L. (2020, March 25). Crisis unfolding: Bolsonaro loses support from powerful ally. *The Brazilian Report.*

Brasileiros que vieram da China deixam quarentena em Anápolis [Brazilians who came from China leave quarantine in Anápolis]. (2020, February 23). *Revista Veja.*

Brasil tem média de 1.069 mortes por dia na última semana; 10 estados e o DF têm alta de mortes [Brazil has an average of 1,069 deaths per day in the last week; 10 states and the DF have high deaths]. (2020, July 27). G1. https://g1.globo.com/bemestar/coronavirus/noticia/2020/07/27/casos-e-mortes-por-coronavirus-no-brasil-em-27-de-julho-segundo-consorcio-de-veiculos-de-imprensa.ghtml

Brett, T., & Rohani, P. (2020). *COVID-19 herd immunity strategies: Walking an elusive and dangerous tightrope.* https://www.medRxiv 2020.04.29.20082065

Buse, K., Dickinson, C., & Sidibé, M. (2008). HIV: Know your epidemic, act on its politics. *Journal of the Royal Society of Medicine, 101*, 572–573.

Carneiro, M., & Seto, G. (2020, April 16). Maranhão comprou da China, mandou para Etiópia e driblou governo federal para ter respiradores [Maranhão bought from China, sent to Ethiopia and circumvented the federal government to have respirators]. *Folha de São Paulo.*

Carvalho, D., & Colletta, R. (2020, March 27). Sem apresentar provas, Bolsonaro diz desconfiar do número de vítimas do coronavírus em SP [Without presenting evidence, Bolsonaro says he suspects the number of coronavirus victims in SP]. *Folha de São Paulo.*

Cimini, F., Juliao, N., Souza, A., Ferreira, J., Figueiredo, G., Garcia, L., Hargreaves, R., & Bagggia, F. (2020). *Análise das primeiras respostas políticas do Governo Brasileiro para o enfrentamento da COVID-19 disponíveis no Repositório Global Polimap* [Analysis of the first political responses from the Brazilian Government to confront COVID-19 available in the Global Polimap Repository]. Belo Horiizonte. https://geesc.cedeplar.ufmg.br/en/analise-das-primeiras-respostas-politicas-do-governo-brasileiro-para-o-enfrentamento-da-covid-19-disponiveis-no-repositorio-global-polimap/

Coletta, R. (2020, February 6). Bolsonaro sanciona lei que estabelece regras da quarentena do coronavírus [Bolsonaro sanctions law that establishes coronavirus quarantine rules]. *Folha de São Paulo.*

Coletta, R., Fabrini, F., & Onofre, R. (2020, April 18). Bolsonaro aponta ao STF e, de novo, pede o relaxamento de regras de isolamento [Bolsonaro points to STF and, again, calls for relaxation of isolation rules]. *Folha de São Paulo.*

Collucci, C. (2020, August 12). Municípios com atenção primária forte fazem a diferença na pandemia [Municipalities with strong primary care make a difference in the pandemic]. *Folha de Sao Paulo.*

Datafolha: Aprovação de Bolsonaro sobe para 37%, a melhor do mandato, e reprovação cai para 34% [Datafolha: Bolsonaro's approval rises to 37%, the best of the term, and disapproval falls to 34%]. (2020, August 13). G1. https://g1.globo.com/politica/noticia/2020/08/13/bolsonaro-tem-aprovacao-de-37percent-e-reprovacao-de-34percent-diz-datafolha.ghtml

Delatorre, E., Mir, D., Gräf, T., & Bello, G. (2020). Tracking the onset date of the community spread of SARS CoV 2 in Western countries. *Memórias do Instituto Oswaldo Cruz,* Pre-print.

Deweck, E., Oliveira, A., & Rossi, P. (2018). *Austeridade e retrocesso: Impactos sociais da política fiscal no Brasil* [Austerity and setback: Social impacts of fiscal policy in Brazil]. São Paulo: Brasil Debate e Fundação Friedrich Ebert.

Dong, E., Du, H., & Gardner, L. (2020). An interactive web-based dashboard to track COVID-19 in real time. *The Lancet Infectious Diseases, 20*(5), 533–534.

Evans, P. (2018, Fall). An unfolding tragedy. *Berkeley Review of Latin American Studies,* 9–13, 49–53.

Fernandes, T. (2020, March 27). Governo brasileiro fecha fronteiras aéreas a estrangeiros de todas as nacionalidades [Brazilian government closes air borders to foreigners of all nationalities]. *Folha de São Paulo.*

Fonseca, E. M., Shadlen, K., & Bastos, F. I. (2019). Brazil's fight against hepatitis C—universalism, local production, and patents. *New England Journal of Medicine, 380*(7), 605–607.

Franco Netto, G., Villardi, J., Machado, J., Souza, J., Brito, I., Santorum, J., & Fenner, A. (2017). Brazilian health surveillance: Reflections and contribution to the debate of the First National Conference on Health Surveillance. *Ciência & Saúde Coletiva* 22(10), 3137–3148.

General Pazuello likely stay atop health ministry. (2020, July 15). *Valor Economico.*

Holland, C. (2020, May 6). Após reabertura do comércio, casos de coronavírus triplicam em SC [After the reopening of trade, coronavirus cases triple in SC]. *G1.*

Lima, B., & Cardim, M. (2020, May 5). Ministério da Saúde chega a 25 militares nomeados [Ministry of Health reaches 25 military personnel appointed]. *Correio Brasiliense.*

Lima, Y., & Costa, E. (2015). Implementação do Regulamento Sanitário Internacional [Implementation of the International Health Regulations]. *Ciência & Saúde Coletiva, 20*(6), 1773–1783.

Machado, R., & Fernandes, T. (2020, June 10). Brazilian ministry of health backs down and resumes full disclosure of Covid-19 data after Supreme Court decision. *Folha de São Paulo.*

Maximo, W. (2020, July 2). No último dia de prazo, 1,9 mi têm auxílio emergencial em análise [On the last day of the term, 1.9 million have emergency aid under analysis]. *Agencia Brasil.*

Mazui, G. (2020, April 16). Mandetta anuncia em rede social que foi demitido por Bolsonaro do Ministério da Saúde [Mandetta announces on social network that he was fired by Bolsonaro from the Ministry of Health]. *G1.*

Medici, A. (2020). Informações preliminares sobre o estado de preparação para o Covid-19 e outras eventuais pandemias na América Latina e Caribe [Preliminary information on the state of preparedness for Covid-19 and other possible pandemics in Latin America and the Caribbean]. https://monitordesaude.blogspot.com

Mello, M. (2020). *Medida cautelar na ação cível originária 3.359 Distrito Federal* [Precautionary measure in the civil lawsuit originating 3,359 Distrito Federal]. Retrieved on January 12, 2021, from https://stf.jusbrasil.com.br/jurisprudencia/919526556/referendo-na-medida-cautelar-na-acao-civel-originaria-aco-3359-df-0088023-3220201000000/inteiro-teor-919526620?ref=juris-tabs

Melo, M. (2020, April 13). A sobrevida dos governadores [The survival of the governos]. *Folha de São Paulo.*

Mehra, M., Desai, S., Ruschitzka, F., & Patel, A. (2020). Hydroxychloroquine or chloroquine with or without a macrolide for treatment of COVID-19: A multinational registry analysis. *The Lancet*, Online First.

Ministério da Saúde. (2010). *Plano Brasileiro de Preparação para Enfrentamento de uma Pandemia de Influenza* [Brazilian Plan of Preparation for Confronting an Influenza Pandemic]. https://bvsms.saude.gov.br/bvs/publicacoes/plano_brasileiro_pandemia_influenza_IV.pdf

Murray, S. (2018). The "rally-'round-the-flag" phenomenon and the diversionary use of force. In W. Thompson (Ed.), *The Oxford Encyclopedia of Empirical International Relations Theory.* Oxford University Press.

Nattrass, N. (2004). *The moral economy of AIDS in South Africa.* Cambridge University Press.

Nattrass, N. (2012). *The AIDS conspiracy: Science fights back.* Columbia University Press.

Nuclear Threat Initiative, & Johns Hopkins Bloomberg School of Public Health. (2019). *Global Health Security Index: Building collective action and accountability.* https://www.ghsindex.org/wp-content/uploads/2019/10/2019-Global-Health-Security-Index.pdf

Nunn, A. (2008). *The politics and history of AIDS treatment in Brazil.* Springer.

Paim, J., Travassos, C., Almeida, C., Bahia, L., & Macinko, J. (2011). The Brazilian health system: History, advances, and challenges. *The Lancet, 377*(9779), 1778–1797.

Party fragmentation reaches a record high in Brazil and becomes a world abnormality. (2018, October 10). *Folha de São Paulo.*

Petherick, A., Goldszmidt, R., Kira, B., & Barberia, L. (2020). *Do Brazil's COVID-19 government response measures meet the WHO's criteria for policy easing?* https://www.bsg.ox.ac.uk/research/publications/do-brazils-covid-19-government-response-measures-meet-whos-criteria-policy

Phillips, T. (2020, March 25). Bolsonaro says he "wouldn't feel anything" if infected with Covid-19 and attacks state lockdowns. *The Guardian.*

Piovesan, E., & Siqueira, C. (2020, March 23). Relator anuncia acordo para auxílio emergencial de R$600 [Rapporteur announces R$ 600 emergency aid agreement]. *Agência Câmara de Notícias.*

Rasella, D., Aquino, R., Santos, C. A. T., Paes-Sousa, R., & Barreto, M. L. (2013). Effect of a conditional cash transfer programme on childhood mortality: A nationwide analysis of Brazilian municipalities. *The Lancet, 382*(9886), 57–64.

Relembre frases de Bolsonaro sobre a COVID-19 [Remember Bolsonaro phrases about COVID-19]. (2020, July 7). BBC News. https://www.bbc.com/portuguese/brasil-53327880

Ricard, J., & Medeiros, J. (2020). Using misinformation as a political weapon: COVID-19 and Bolsonaro in Brazil. *The Harvard Kennedy School (HKS) Misinformation Review, 1*(2), 1–6.

Rodrigues, A. (2020, March 18). Doria anuncia fechamento de shoppings e academias na Grande SP [Doria announces closure of shopping centers and gyms in Greater SP]. *Folha de São Paulo.*

Savarese, M., & Biller, D. (2020, September 16). Brazil general named health minister after months as interim. *ABC News.* https://abcnews.go.com/Health/wireStory/brazil-general-named-health-minister-months-interim-73061275

Schreiber, M. (2020, March 19). Coronavírus: Brasil fecha quase toda a fronteira terrestre, mas mantém entrada por aeroportos [Coronavirus: Brazil closes almost the entire land border, but maintains entry through airports]. *BBC Brasil.*

Teófilo, S. (2020, April 1). Bolsonaro diz que ligou para Trump e tratou sobre o novo coronavírus [Bolsonaro says he called Trump and dealt with the new coronavirus]. *Correio Brasiliense.*

Tito, B. (2020, May 3). PLP 39/2020: Um ataque aos trabalhadores do setor público e favorecimento do sistema financeiro disfarçado de ajuda fiscal aos Estados e Municípios [An attack on public sector workers and favoring the financial system disguised as fiscal aid to States and Municipalities]. *Esquerda Online.*

US Embassy Press Office. (2020, July 23). *U.S. to fund field hospital in Maranhão.* https://br.usembassy.gov/u-s-to-fund-field-hospital-in-maranhao/

Veloso, A. (2020, April 28). Agências da Caixa voltam a ter longas filas [Caixa branches have long lines again]. *Extra.*

Verdélio, A. (2020, May 15). Nelson Teich pede demissão do Ministério da Saúde [Nelson Teich resigns from the Ministry of Health]. *Agencia Brasil.*

Xavier, L. (2020, June 8). Maia elogia consórcio de comunicação que vai divulgar dados omitidos sobre mortes de Covid-19 [Maia praises communication consortium that will release missing data on Covid-19 deaths]. *Agência Câmara de Notícias.*

28 COLOMBIA'S RESPONSE TO COVID-19

Pragmatic Command, Social Contention, and Political Challenges

Claudia Acosta, Mónica Uribe-Gómez, and Durfari Velandia-Naranjo

Colombia is a centralized, presidential, democratic (although with a strong heritage of authoritarianism and war) middle-income country with high levels of poverty and inequality among people and territories.

According to the Global Health Security Index, by 2019 Colombia was among the broad group of countries "more prepared" for epidemics or pandemics, with a medium response capacity in prevention and mitigation of epidemics but a significant lag in the availability of hospital beds in intensive care units (Ministry of Health and Social Protection, 2020a, b). The forecasts to face the pandemic were cautious. Seven months after the beginning of the pandemic, the data reported acceptable performance by Colombia in managing the pandemic, with lower lethality than several of its neighbors and even some higher-income countries. The time that has elapsed since the beginning of the pandemic, however short, has been long enough to show that the response capacity relies not just on objective conditions such as health systems; politics weighs as much or more than policy.

On March 6, 2020, when the first case of COVID-19 in Colombia was reported, the national context included (1) a health system with almost universal coverage but persistent problems of access to services and reduced hospital capacity because of funding; (2) a national data collection system for the vulnerable population served by its conditional cash transfer programs, although with some shortcomings; and (3) the president's falling popularity with no upcoming electoral contests and mild political polarization. Given this situation, the forecast for the country dealing with COVID-19 was not optimistic.

Colombia had the advantage of the pandemic beginning a few weeks later than European countries and the United States. By March 2020, the government, citizens, and health workers were already on high alert. In less than two weeks, with some tension between local leaders and the national government, the country entered a strict and lengthy lockdown. After several months, this measure started to loosen not because the epidemic was under control, but because of economic and social pressure.

By September 2020, Colombia reported acceptable performance in the region, and the health system presented only isolated breakdowns (mainly in remote places). The hospital capacity was expanded and the country showed efficient epidemiological management. However, the pandemic brought out pre-existing regional disparities in health capacity and funding, which required issuing social relief aids. How can these results be explained? The constitutional provision of "economic, social, and ecological emergency" allowed the president to make quick and autonomous decisions. The key measures taken by the president included national-regional coordinated actions in public health, rapid realignment of public resources to expand hospital capacity, testing system decentralization, highly restrictive and lengthy lockdown, and other socioeconomic measures (including unconditional cash transfers).

President Duque won popularity and media attention. Apparently, the crisis brought out his greatest strength: technocratic capacity. Political opposition seemed to follow a cooperative response: the opposition criticized the president and some measures, but none questioned the seriousness of the problem, used massive disinformation strategies, nor suggested noncompliance with the lockdown. Nevertheless, the political arena is changing fast, and polarization in the debate has returned to the forefront.

As of this writing, there are still important challenges for national and local authorities in the management of the "COVID-19 cases curve" and the containment of outbreaks in specific territories. The economic crisis, insufficient social aid, and corruption will undoubtedly remain the most pressing challenges in a country where measures to reduce inequality have not been on the political agenda.

This chapter reports on the conditions of the healthcare system in the country at the time the pandemic started, details the main responses in health and social support by the government, and analyzes the political behavior and public debate in a deeply unequal middle-income country.

Health Policy Measures and the COVID-19 Response

The current healthcare system in Colombia, in operation since 1993, is centrally regulated, administratively decentralized, and publicly financed. The backbone of the system is the general social security health system (SGSSS, Spanish acronym), which provides a market-oriented compulsory universal healthcare insurance for individual risks. Collective health risks are territorially managed, with a disconnection between public health and healthcare insurance (Ministry of Health and Social Protection, 2016a). The Ministry of Health and Social Protection (MSPS, Spanish acronym) and its associated agencies are tasked with central command and coordination, setting policy agenda, regulation, inspection, surveillance, and control of the system.

Functions, resources, and actions related to public health are concentrated at district and municipality levels. Local health authorities follow national guidelines to monitor public health, evaluate local health situations, and prioritize needs to allocate resources in their respective jurisdictions. For instance, surveillance, prevention, and control of vector-transmitted diseases such as dengue fever, malaria, or chikungunya fever are mainly the responsibility of local authorities. Resources for public health come to municipalities mainly from earmarked intergovernmental transfers and other local taxes compulsorily assigned to finance health expenditures (Ministry of Health and Social Protection, 2016a).

In Colombia, in theory, no person is deprived of access to healthcare service. The enrollment in the healthcare insurance system is mandatory. Workers (and their relatives) are affiliated with the *contributory* regime and contribute with a specific healthcare payroll tax. People without payment capacity are assigned to the *subsidized* regime. Each person in any regime enjoys the same basic health coverage plan (PAB, Spanish acronym) that is regulated and annually updated by the MSPS. PABs are handled through public or private healthcare agencies known as EPS (from their Spanish acronym), which deliver healthcare services to citizens.

In practice, the system presents substantial problems of corruption, bureaucratization, lack of resources, and disconnection between the structure of the system, preventive and promotional health measures, and service provision. Since 2016, by virtue of new national regulations, the health system has tried to reduce those gaps through integral routes for comprehensive delivery of services (including promotion and disease prevention), better distribution of resources, transparency of epidemiological data, and other measures (Ministry of Health and Social Protection, 2016a). The following issues are of special importance in confronting the pandemic: (1) lack of effective access to services for the population; (2) reduced hospital capacity; and (3) the enormous inter- and intraregional inequality in hospital capacity and the financial conditions of public and private hospitals.

Colombia has extensive experience with infectious diseases, such as the outbreaks of measles in 2019, the Zika virus in 2015, the chikungunya fever in 2014, and influenza A-H1N1 in 2009. The health minister, Fernando Ruiz Gómez, is a competent technocrat, with a solid professional background as well as extensive knowledge about public health, the Colombian health system, and the country, in addition to experience with infectious diseases. He was appointed in February 2020 to strengthen the ministry's technical capacity to deal with the pandemic. He has coordinated and directed the healthcare sector, adopting important measures aimed at improving the health system's capacity to handle the increased demand.

The national government of Colombia has injected direct resources for the adaptation and renovation of hospitals, increased and decentralization of testing, health workers' training, and improvement of hospitals' capacity to respond to the virus. Supported by extraordinary powers for the executive level, owing to the declaration of a "state of sanitary emergency," the minister has the mandate, for example, to order private hospitals to better allocate hospital beds.

The country went from 5,346 intensive care unit (ICU) beds in February 2020 to 10,606 ICU beds at the end of September 2020 (official microdata is available at the Minister of Health webpage). Five months after the beginning of the pandemic, the majority of ICUs in the country were capable of managing the emergency. Hospital breakdowns happened in poor and/or peripheral regions of the country (highlighting the old underlying problem of regional inequity in the system).

Another relevant strategy to deal with COVID-19 is data availability: transparent, integrated, and timely, allowing quick and sectorized decisions by local authorities, such as the containment of specific neighborhoods or areas and targeted quarantines. From March to May 2020, data reveal a slight increase in the number of confirmed cases and deaths. By mid-June 2020, we observed a spike in both curves, with a peak in mid-August. Since then, both curves decreased and eventually flattened in mid-September but at a high level. As of the end of September 2020, the country recorded around 800,000 confirmed cases of COVID-19 and more than 25,000 deaths. Indicators developed along with the PAHO (Pan American Health Organization) report lower numbers in Colombia than in some OECD countries and other Latin American middle-income peers. With 15,105 infections per million, Colombia recorded 478 deaths per million while the United Kingdom reported 615, France 477, Italy 590, Chile 643, Mexico 570, Panama 525, and Ecuador 627 (World Health Organization, 2020). The transmissibility indicator (Rt, effective reproduction number) used to forecast impact, evaluate, and adjust public health response is, as of this writing, 1.06 in Colombia. (The goal is to reach an Rt below 1.) By September of 2020, the lethality rate in the country was 3.2 percent; 93.6 percent of infected people had recovered at home, 2.7 percent were admitted to a hospital, and 0.27 percent (2,165) needed an ICU (National Institute of Health, 2020).

Finally, the health surveillance system is centralized and coordinated by the national level headed by the National Institute of Health (acronym in Spanish, INS). This institute generates COVID-19 data daily that are published by national, regional, and local authorities without political debate. Even so, limited access to testing and delays in notification of results reduce the citizens' trust in COVID-19 data (Ministry of Health and Social Protection, 2020a, b).

Socioeconomic Measures

Economic inequality perhaps best describes the social condition of Colombians. The 2018 census reported that approximately 40 percent of the country's population is economically vulnerable, whereas another 20 percent suffer some condition of multidimensional poverty (e.g., lack of adequate access to health, education, public services such as water or energy). Since the year 2000, the leading social welfare program *Familias en Acción* attends part of the vulnerable population through conditional cash transfers, which require the fulfillment of certain health and educational obligations. In addition, smaller programs called *Jóvenes en Acción* and *Colombia Mayor* offer additional conditional cash-transfer programs. As of February 2020, *Familias en Acción* benefited approximately 2.6 million families (close to 10 million people). Nevertheless, an important but undetermined group of Colombians require public support but are not included in the programs. Also, this social support structure presents problems of uneven distribution among the poor who claim for revision.

Decree 417, enacted as early as March 27, 2020, provided additional resources for the group of recipients already included in any of the three social programs. It also established unconditional cash-transfers called *Ingreso Solidario* of approximately US$45 per month up until December 2020 for the remaining 3 million families not targeted by the existing programs (Uribe-Gómez, 2020). Most of the people in this group are informal workers (workers without affiliation to social security or welfare benefits; in Colombia, these workers represent more than half of the economically active population).

The pandemic has shown that poverty is one of the greatest risk factors to contracting COVID-19 in Colombia. In a country where more than half of the population suffers from a state of vulnerability, the contagious, lethal pandemic has especially affected those who cannot stay at home because they must leave their homes to make a living. Quarantine, social distancing, and even constant hand-washing are luxury practices for specific groups and regions. States such as Chocó or Amazonas have been hit hard by this virus; in addition to high poverty rates, there is a lack of potable water in many of their territories. Similarly, in the cities, the most affected areas are precarious settlements.

Also, since the beginning of the pandemic, the Colombian government has announced that it will undertake economic measures to alleviate the situation. In presidential broadcasts, President Duque has linked the discussion on social aid with the need to find adequate resources for this purpose. Two main sources have been employed by the government to fund the emergency, the first being the government's income from the revenue-sharing system (SGP, acronym in Spanish), the system of royalties from nonrenewable natural resources, mainly petroleum and mining (SGR, acronym in Spanish), and the national general budget (PGN, acronym in Spanish). The second source is the central government debt, funded by government bonds and loans. In 2020 Colombia will have the largest public debt in its history.

According to the Economic Commission for Latin America and the Caribbean (Economic Commission for Latin America and the Caribbean, 2020), by July 2020, the fiscal effort in the country to face the pandemic represented just 2.5 percent of the GDP when compared with other countries such as Chile (5.7 percent), Brazil (7.5 percent), or El Salvador (11 percent). As opposed to the centralized, transparent, and available data about the COVID-19 cases and deaths, there is neither centralization nor detailed information about funding sources, destination, and attention of specific groups. Unfortunately, corruption has been notoriously associated with health and social expenditures (Fiscal Observatory of Javeriana University, 2020).

Both the pandemic and the extension of compulsory confinement have produced a significant increase in poverty levels. The future is alarming: "Projections estimate that the country's poverty rate will reach 18% to 32%, and extreme poverty will reach between 4.5 to 16.7%, as a result of the loss of income in the informal sector, meaning that one-sixth of the country's population will earn income that is insufficient to afford staple foods" (Sánchez & Chaparro, 2020, p. 1).

A new political movement of fifty-four parliamentarians (supported by academics and social organizations) has proposed the national government approve an emergency basic income equal to one minimum wage for five months that would benefit 9.5 million families. Under the argument of stimulating consumption and providing relief to those who have been most affected by the lockdown decrees, this group is leading a call for solidarity ("Editorial," 2020).

Political Analysis (Explanations)

The aforementioned statistics about the pandemic put the national government in an acceptable position. As in many other places, COVID-19 has put not only the health and social systems but also the governmental authorities and political regimes to the test. Three components can partially explain the political response and its importance in containing the pandemic's lethality: the technocratic approach of the pandemic, the electoral calendar and cooperative behavior from the political opposition, and the strong enforcement of the extended lockdown.

President Duque demonstrated one of his professional strengths, his technocratic side, and found in the pandemic a space to regain popularity and increase communication with the population. From the beginning, he acknowledged the pandemic as a real problem that required technical decisions, without denial, irreverent attitudes, or blame-avoidance. He appointed as health minister a highly-skilled professional, well recognized in the public health sector, to spearhead the urgent measures in the health system. Mr. Duque started a daily television program providing information on the pandemic's evolution and the measures taken by the government to address it. To face the growing public spending, he opted to expand the public debt and extended the environmental and health emergency status to maintain tight restrictions on the mobility of the population and social distancing with the support of the police force.

The pandemic even brought a temporary improvement in President Duque's popularity, who had suffered from high levels of rejection almost since the beginning of his tenure. By February 2020, his approval rate was 23 percent ("Iván Duque," 2020), and by May 2020, it was 53 percent ("Aumenta el Optimismo en el País" ["Optimism Increases in the Country"], 2020). For the first time in office, the president experienced more approval than disapproval. By June 2020, his approval rate was 38 percent ("Aumenta el Optimismo en el País" ["Optimism Increases in the Country"], 2020b). This renewed decline of the president's popularity has been attributed to overexposure, lack of closeness to citizens, lack of transparency with public resources, and poor leadership (Lombo, 2020). Duque has used more central power than consensus with local authorities and showed more concern about economic factors than the heartfelt demands of citizens under lockdown.

Unlike other countries, the political and electoral calendar has been in favor of containing the pandemic: in 2020, President Duque was in his second year of a four-year term, and mayors began their terms in January 2020, which can reduce political aggression.

The country has also been free from organized media strategies of disinformation and fake news about the pandemic. Fake news networks cost time and money to be implemented. A possible explanation for the absence of those strategies could be the lack of a structured fake news network already working by the time the pandemic began. From the incumbent's point of view, there were no clear benefits from implementing fake news, and the challengers did not deny or minimize the risk of COVID-19 or reject scientific evidence.

Nonetheless, the country is experiencing strong political antagonism, represented by two political ideologies: Uribismo (Duque's political roots) and Petrismo (the main challenger), both of which receive electoral support largely defined by the voter's income. Uribismo, a mixture of conservative and neoliberal ideology, is associated with the high-income population, whereas Petrismo, a social-democratic populist ideology, receives support mainly among middle- and low-income groups (Kajsiu, 2020). The most aggressive attack against Duque happened in early July 2020, when Senator Gustavo Petro defied the president's legitimacy and encouraged people to engage in civil disobedience. As the pandemic advanced, political cooperation lost momentum, and the most affected social groups sought political voices to represent them. Because Petro aligned himself with the extreme left of the political spectrum, it was advantageous for Duque to move to the center and avoid extreme aggressive positions. Duque shaped the debate in technical language, without populist rhetoric or denial; his goal was to create the image of a trustworthy leader who performed well in dealing with the pandemic.

With its history of internal armed conflict for over half a century and the violent and disruptive presence of drug trafficking, Colombia demanded a high level of cooperation among the different levels of government to maintain public order. Duque centralized the public order decisions in the whole territory and decreed a national lockdown without consensus with local authorities, which is legal even though politically questionable. The rigid, across-the-board lockdown began on March 22, 2020, and was still in force at the end of July 2020 with the support of the police force and militarization of specific areas and neighborhoods. Individual freedom was considerably restricted for a period of more than a hundred days from March to July. Such level of lockdown (in duration and enforcement) would be unthinkable in many countries, including those in Latin America, where there is a greater tradition of respect for civil rights.

Last but not least, how did President Duque manage to take so many and extensive measures in a short time? The answer lies in the Colombian presidential system, characterized by the centrality and disproportionate importance of the executive at the expense of the legislative and even the judiciary (Gómez Mendez, 2019).

In this case, the president, together with all the ministers, enacted on March 17, 2020, the "State of Economic and Social Emergency" (a constitutional provision) to confront the pandemic. Invested with ample powers, Duque made numerous decisions without the need for consultation, debate, or approval by Congress. These decisions included mobility restrictions, social and economic measures, direct interventions in the health system to increase hospital capacity, increase in public debt, and presumption of the president's hierarchy in the matters of public order overruling those at the departmental and municipal levels.

As of this writing, the country has been governed "by decree," but the pandemic is still raging, and the political map is changing rapidly. The debate on the approval of an emergency universal basic income was initiated in Congress on July 20, 2020, the first day of the new legislature's sessions, along with proposals to reduce the presidential power during the pandemic.

Conclusions

As has been observed in cases such as Brazil or the United States, having a favorable history in managing health crises, a robust health system, or resources to tackle them does not guarantee that the response to challenges of COVID-19 will be adequate and lives preserved. The COVID-19 emergency has shown that political strategy and government decisions weigh as much or more than such conditions on the outcome. Colombia had medium preparedness in its health system to attend to and mitigate the pandemic and significant weaknesses in the supply of hospital beds and intensive care facilities.

The government has taken remarkable coordinated measures. There is a clear improvement in the supply of hospital beds and the financial standing of hospitals. Transparency and prompt delivery of COVID-19 information are great Colombian strengths. The government has requested a huge social effort from the population by way of a highly restrictive quarantine for more than a hundred consecutive days supported by the use of public force, instituting mandatory use of masks and sanitary guidelines. In parallel, unconditional cash transfers were created for beneficiaries of existing programs and for a large population group that subsists on informal activities, such as street vendors, house cleaners etc., that are highly affected by the pandemic. Such provisions have been funded from a variety of sources, the main one being international public debt. Some of President Duque's decisions are not popular with the Colombian people. Although political control is a necessity in dire situations, opposing political forces are already calling for the end of the "State of Economic and Social Emergency" that allows Mr. Duque to make decisions without Congress' agreement.

Colombia's healthcare system has survived the pandemic, but it is also experiencing financial problems that seriously affect hospitals and other healthcare suppliers. In addition, the pandemic has highlighted regional imbalances in service provision and funding. In many cases, poor, peripheral, or inaccessible areas present the highest infection rates and the main sites of healthcare breakdowns in the country. Poverty constitutes a significant risk factor for the pandemic in Colombia.

Public compliance with the restrictive measures was supported by unconditional cash transfer and other aids and strongly enforced by the lockdown. Nevertheless, as of this writing, Colombian citizens are growing weary of the lockdown not for ideological reasons but because of fatigue and economic pressure. The long duration and rigidity of the lockdown are only possible in a country with a history of war and restrictions on citizen liberties. In a country where profound inequality is perhaps the most stable feature of society, the pandemic has opened up a rare opportunity: the political debate about universal basic income.

Polarization of the political debate already existed before the pandemic. The pandemic's political wear and tear and the impoverishment of an important group of the population require new leadership and innovative proposals to avoid negative political ramifications.

References

Aumenta el optimismo en el país; Duque sigue a la baja [Optimism increases in the country; Duque continues down]. (2020, September 2). *Revista Semana.* https://www.semana.com/nacion/articulo/desaprobacion-del-gobierno-de-ivan-duque-aumento-al-55---noticias-hoy/699413/

Catorce asociaciones médicas le piden al gobierno cuarentena inmediata en toda Bogotá [Fourteen medical associations ask government for immediate lockdown in the whole city of Bogotá]. (2020, July 13). *El Espectador.* https://www.elespectador.com/noticias/salud/asociaciones-de-medicos-piden-cuarentena-inmediata-en-todo-bogota/

Colombia. Law No. 100, December 23 of 1993. Crea el sistema de seguridad social integral y se dictan otras disposiciones [This law creates the comprehensive social security system and other provisions]. (1993). Retrieved on October 15, 2020, from http://www.secretariasenado.gov.co/senado/basedoc/ley_0100_1993.html

Colombian Office of the Ombudsman. (2019). *La tutela y los derechos a la salud y la seguridad social.* [The right of amparo, health rights, and social security]. Bogotá, Defensoría del Pueblo de Colombia. Retrieved on from https://www.defensoria.gov.co/public/pdf/Tutela-los-derechos-de-la-salud-2018.pdf

Economic Commission for Latin America and the Caribbean, ECLAC. (2020, July 15). Special Report number 5 COVID-19. https://repositorio.cepal.org/bitstream/handle/11362/45782/4/S2000471_es.pdf

Editorial: Momento de impulsar la renta básica de emergencia [Editorial: It is time to boost the emergency basic income]. (2020, July 20). *El Espectador.* https://www.elespectador.com/opinion/editorial/momento-de-impulsar-la-renta-basica-de-emergencia/

Fiscal Observatory of Javeriana University. (2020). Informe #11 La transparencia en el uso de los recursos para atender la emergencia: análisis sobre la transparencia en disposición y destinación de los recursos públicos destinados a atender la emergencia sanitaria por la pandemia de la Covid-19 [Report #11 Transparency in the use of resources to attend the emergency: Analysis of the transparency in the disposition and allocation of public resources committed to attend the health emergency due to the Covid-19 pandemic]. https://imgcdn.larepublica.co/cms/2020/06/23170047/Transparencia-fiscal-COVID-19.pdf

Gómez Mendez, A. (2019). *El presidencialismo y el sistema presidencial en Colombia* [Presidentialism and the presidential system in Colombia]. Externado de Colombia University Press.

Iván Duque: La aprobación a su gestión sube 29 puntos [Iván Duque: Approval of his term rises 29 points]. (2020, April 29). *Revista Semana.* https://www.semana.com/nacion/articulo/duque-aumenta-la-aprobacion-a-su-gestion/666979/

Kajsiu, B. (2020). Las ideologías y movilizaciones políticas del Uribismo y Petrismo: Dos Colombias distintas [The ideologisms and political mobilizations of Uribismo and Petrismo: Two different Colombias]. *Análisis Político, 33*(98), 191–209. https://revistas.unal.edu.co/index.php/anpol/article/view/89417/75744

Lombo, J. S. (2020, July 3). ¿Por qué el bajonazo de Iván Duque en las últimas encuestas? [Why was Iván Duque downfall in the latest polls?]. *El Espectador.* https://www.elespectador.com/noticias/politica/las-razones-para-el-descenso-ivan-duque-en-las-encuestas/

Medellín, P. (2020, March 17). Tiene nuestro modelo de salud pública capacidad para enfrentar una pandemia como el Coronavirus? [Does our public health model have capacity the capacity to face a pandemic like the Coronavirus?]. *Boletín Instituto de Estudios Urbanos.* http://ieu.unal.edu.co/medios/noticias-del-ieu/item/tiene-nuestro-modelo-de-salud-publica-capacidad-para-enfrentar-una-pandemia-como-el-coronavirus

Ministry of Health and Social Protection. (2016a). Fuentes de financiación y usos de los recursos del Sistema General de Seguridad Social en Salud—SGSSS. Bogotá [Sources of financing and uses of resources from the Social Security General System in Health—SGSSS]. https://www.minsalud.gov.co/sites/rid/Lists/BibliotecaDigital/RIDE/VP/FS/fuentes-y-usos-de-recursos-del-sgsss.pdf

Ministry of Health and Social Protection. (2016b). Política de atención integral en salud. [Policy of integral attention in health]. https://www.minsalud.gov.co/sites/rid/Lists/BibliotecaDigital/RIDE/DE/modelo-pais-2016.pdf

Ministry of Health and Social Protection. (2020a, September 3). Microdata. Official source about hospital beds capacity and its increment. *Bulletin.* https://www.minsalud.gov.co/Paginas/Colombia-amplio-89-su-capacidad-de-UCI.aspx

Ministry of Health and Social Protection. (2020b). *Official microdata by region and locality.* Retrieved on October 1, 2020, from https://minsalud.maps.arcgis.com/apps/opsdashboard/index.html#/1de89936b24449edb77e162d485ed5d9

National Institute of Health, Colombia. (2020). *Report on Coronavirus. Data updated to September 25, 2020 except for European countries (September 20).* Retrieved on September 30, 2020, from https://www.ins.gov.co/Noticias/Paginas/Coronavirus-rt.aspx and https://www.ins.gov.co/Noticias/Paginas/coronavirus-casos.aspx

Rodríguez Pinzón, E. (2020, April 30). *Colombia. Impacto económico, social y político de la Covid19* [Colombia: Economic, social and political impact of Covid-19]. Document of analysis, Fundación Carolina. https://www.fundacioncarolina.es/wp-content/uploads/2020/04/AC-24.-2020.pdf

Sánchez, R., & Chaparro, S. (2020). *A social protection floor to preserve life: Informality, poverty and vulnerability in times of Covid19. Centro de Investigaciones para el Desarrollo CID, document FCE-CID No. 35.* http://www.fce.unal.edu.co/media/files/CentroEditorial/documentos/investigacionesCID/documentos-CID-35.pdf

Transparency of Colombia. (2020). Tercer reporte Ciudadanía Activa: Seguimiento al manejo de recursos para la atención de la emergencia del Covid-19 [Third active citizenship report: Follow-up on the management of resources for the attention of the Covid-19 emergency]. https://transparenciacolombia.org.co/Documentos/Publicaciones/gestion-publica/3-rep-Ciudadania-Activa-21-08-20.pdf

Uribe-Gómez, M. (2020, April 20). Subsidios para los más pobres ¿qué esta pasando en Colombia? [Subsidies for the poorest, what is happening in Colombia?]. *Razón Pública*. https://razonpublica.com/author/muribe/

World Health Organization. (2020). *Weekly epidemiological update, September 20*. Retrieved on October 20, 2020, from https://www.who.int/docs/default-source/coronaviruse/situation-reports/20200921-weekly-epi-update-6.pdf?sfvrsn=d9cf9496_6

29 THE POLITICS OF THE COVID-19 PANDEMIC RESPONSE IN CHILE

Claudio A. Méndez

Compared with other Latin American countries, Chile has been seen worldwide as an example of political transition, economic growth, fiscal responsibility, and incremental social policies. The 2019 political and social crisis, however, unveiled flaws in the "Chilean miracle." Social policies once considered successful were contested by social movements, and the structural reforms for the provision of welfare failed in pensions, education, and health systems (Taylor, 2003).

Since March 3, 2020, with the first confirmed case of COVID-19 in Chile, political institutions have been under public scrutiny. According to the Johns Hopkins University Coronavirus Resource Center, one month later, the country saw more than three hundred cases and eight deaths (Johns Hopkins University, 2020). In July 2020 the country registered more than one thousand cases in a day, and after that exhibited a steady decline in cases, with twenty-seven deaths in a day by September 29, 2020 (Johns Hopkins University, 2020).

Even with a favorable scenario, separating the 2019 political and social crisis from COVID-19 pandemic preparedness and response was far from being resolved through technical decisions. It was the same government incapable of making political and policy changes to alleviate the social unrest, that was responsible for designing and implementing health and social policy measures to cope with the COVID-19 pandemic.

This chapter explores Chile's preparedness and response to the pandemic from the first confirmed case of COVID-19. In addition, this chapter describes how President Piñera's government, within a scenario of profound distrust and disbelief, conducted incorrect early health policies and delayed implementation of social policies to address the social crisis due to the pandemic. Finally, how the National Congress and municipalities played a major role in counterbalancing executive power is also discussed.

Distrust and Disbelief in Institutions and Health Policy: What Can Go Wrong?

The Chilean health system is one of the older national health systems in Latin America. Through the last eighty years, the national health system has been convoluted by political and social clashes that shaped its current structure. However, these forces did not affect the health system's roots related to social segmentation and inequalities. Despite social segmentation, the country has been exhibiting lower infant and maternal mortality rates that are similar to those in developed countries (Jiménez & Romero, 2007; Koch et al., 2014). Nevertheless, there are still major inequalities regarding access to health services that are currently leading the technical and political debate.

Two major changes shaped the current Chilean health system. The first was the creation of the *Servicio Nacional de Salud*, acronym in Spanish (National Health Service) in 1952, which was a centralized health system with integrated health service goals across the country that expanded health services coverage and the number of health professionals (de la Jara & Bossert, 1995; Mardones-Restat & De Azevedo, 2006). The second major structural change was under the military dictatorship in 1979. After Pinochet took power, reforms were related to contracting public health services as an incentive for expanding private health services, creating private health insurance, and conducting a decentralization process (Manuel, 2002).

With democratization in the 1990s, the center left-wing coalition led by Patricio Aylwin embraced comprehensive public sector engagement on health policies (Bustamante & Méndez, 2014). Mandatory health insurance was strengthened by increasing public health financing (Mesa-Lago, 2008). The design and implementation of the explicit health guarantees in the next decade (best known as the *Plan de Acceso Universal con Garantías Explícitas en Salud*)—led by President Ricardo Lagos—allowed for the expansion of financial coverage for selected health problems. The Chilean health system has been able to improve universal health coverage and equity in access to health care with some restrictions (Frenz et al., 2013; Paraje & Vásquez, 2012).

In January 2020 Health Minister Jaime Mañalich announced the *Plan de Acción Coronavirus COVID-19* (Coronavirus Action Plan COVID-19). This plan was based on an early preparation enacted in the *Decreto de Alerta Sanitaria* (Sanitary Emergency Decree; Ministerio de Salud, 2020b) as a result of the "Public Health Emergency of International Concern" declared by the World Health Organization (WHO). The decree allowed for implementation of special measures within the health system, such as increasing staff and supplies (Ministerio de Salud, 2020b). Unfortunately for a government questioned by international human rights organizations for a lack of credibility, in March 2020 Minister Mañalich declared that a referendum for a new political constitution scheduled for April 26, 2020, could be in jeopardy in the event of a negative scenario related to a major SARS-CoV-2 virus transmission among the population (Infobae, 2020). This announcement did not alleviate the wider political and social distrust of political institutions.

The plan also considered four phases, following the pandemic stages described by the WHO. Phase 1: The country does not have positive cases, and public health institutions are taking preventive measures for readiness once the first case arrives. Phase 2: Imported cases have arrived from the countries with the virus; therefore, actions should be focused on isolation and a fourteen-day quarantine for travelers from countries with community transmission. Phase 3: A sustained increase in cases resulting from local transmission from imported cases. Phase 4: A wider spread across the country with difficulties identifying the transmission chain.

The protocols were adapted according to Phase 1 of the Coronavirus Action Plan. In this phase, borders were not closed, and there were only a few hospitals with real-time polymerase chain reaction (rtPCR) tests. Instead, a *Declaración Jurada para Viajeros* (Affidavit for Travelers) from countries with sustainable transmission of COVID-19 was implemented (Ministerio de Salud, 2020k). Thus, imported cases emerged from countries that did not show sustainable transmission, generating local transmission in travelers' regions of origin or destiny. Phase 1 could be seen as an early preparation to respond to the first confirmed cases of COVID-19 in Chile, but instead it is an example of ineffective health policy measures for the two months of preparation.

Phase 2 was enacted based on the first confirmed case of COVID-19 in Chile on March 3, 2020. Moreover, this new phase included a modified "Sanitary Alert Decree" (Ministerio de Salud, 2020f) and a new case definition published on March 6, three days after the first confirmed case. Borders continued to be open to travelers, while protocols were adopted for identifying and tracking travelers from countries with local transmission and detecting positive travelers from airports, harbors, and border crossings (Ministerio de Salud, 2020c, 2020d, 2020e). Medical leave for confirmed cases and closer contacts was established, as well as a house-based isolation protocol.

Using his constitutional prerogatives, President Piñera decreed on March 18, 2020, the *Decreto 104 Declara Estado de Excepción Constitucional de Catástrofe, por Calamidad Pública, en el Territorio de Chile* (Constitutional Exception for a State of Catastrophe for Public Calamity). The decree was to extend ninety days from its publication date and appointed army forces generals as *Jefes de la Defensa Nacional* (national defense chiefs) with executive powers for leading army and public security forces in the territory under their command. Furthermore, direct instructions for public servants were established, including communication of decisions using social media channels. However, the national defense chiefs were to consider the policy measures from the Ministry of Health (Ministerio del Interior y Seguridad Pública, 2020). The sixteen Chilean regions were forced to respond according to the guidelines from the Ministry of Health and the executive branch regarding quarantines, reactivation of the local economy, and security enforcement.

On March 25, 2020, the Ministry of Health ordered isolation or quarantine for the general population. Measures included prohibiting public circulation from 10 p.m. to 5 a.m. and restricting people over eighty years old to their homes. Sanitary cordons were implemented for some localities and regions as well as isolation or quarantines for certain persons, sanitary customs, and measures to protect vulnerable populations such as the elderly, children, and inmates (Ministerio de Salud, 2020l). Regarding health conditions with explicit health guarantees, on March 30, 2020, the Ministry of Health suspended healthcare guarantees for eighty-five health conditions as outlined in law and the sanitary code in the case of an outbreak in any part of the Chilean territory. Drugs for treatment stages and diagnosis and treatment for some cancers, noncommunicable diseases, and traumas were excluded from the suspension (Ministerio de Salud, 2020a). The suspension could be requested for one month, with extensions of time if necessary (Ministerio de Salud, 2020a).

Criticism for these policy measures came from the *Colegio Médico de Chile* (Chilean Physicians Union) and the *Asociación Chilena de Municipalidades* (Chilean Municipalities Association). The Colegio Médico's position on the health policy measures was based on a lack of inclusion of unions and other actors at the beginning of the COVID-19 outbreak in Chile (Bartlett, 2020a). Although Minister of Education Raul Figueroa and President Piñera avoided announcing any measures regarding schools, majors from the Asociación started to close schools without any coordination. This situation prompted the Asociación to meet with Health Minister Mañalich and Education Minister Figueroa regarding school closures; they initiated online schooling and ensuring the provision of food for the most vulnerable students (Garrido, 2020).

The Asociación was also able to overcome the lack of coordination because the media promoted the Asociación's leadership nationwide. This scenario allowed the Asociación to suggest the application of regulations to the central government such as fines for the nonuse of masks in public spaces as well as recognizing the importance of municipalities for the implementation of national policies in the COVID-19 response (Ramírez de la Cruz et al., 2020).

As a response to critics, the Ministry of Health gathered nonpartisan experts for a *Consejo Asesor para COVID-19* (Advisory Council for COVID-19). The Consejo was integrated by Ximena Aguilera, MD; Catterina Ferreccio, MD; María Teresa Valenzuela, MD; Gonzalo Valdivia, MD; Pablo Vial, MD; Fernando Otaiza, MD, head of the Infection Control Associate to Health Care Delivery; and Yohanna Acevedo, RN, head of the Department of Epidemiology at the Ministry of Health (Ministerio de Salud, 2020i). The Consejo's recommendations were not binding on the Ministry of Health nor President Piñera's decisions on COVID-19 health policy measures.

In a second move, in late March 2020, President Piñera promoted a *Mesa Social COVID-19* (Social Roundtable COVID-19) as a measure for improving coordination and collaboration, headed by the Minister of Interior Gonzalo Blumel and integrated by the Minister of Health Mañalich. Other participants included Andrés Couve, PhD, minister of science, technology, knowledge, and innovation; Izkia Sishes, MD, president of *Colegio Médico*; Carmen Castillo, MD, former minister of health (from former president Michelle Bachelet's second government); Ennio Vivaldi, MD, president of the *Universidad de Chile*; Ignacio Sánchez, MD, president of the *Pontificia Universidad Católica de Chile*; Fernando Leanes, MD, PhD, the Pan-American Health Organization/World Health Organization representation head in Chile; and German Codina, president of the *Asociación Chilena de Municipalidades* (Ministerio de Salud, 2020o). The initiative was replicated in Chile's sixteen regions; however, the regional programs were not in the spotlight like the Mesa Social COVID-19 roundtable implemented by central government.

Despite these measures, Brazil, Chile, and Ecuador showed a higher Basic Reproduction Number (R_0) and Effective Reproduction Number (R_e) in the earliest phase of the COVID-19 pandemic, also sharing the measure of fourteen days of isolation (Valcarce et al., 2020). Furthermore, one of the most controversial policy measures was the "dynamic quarantines," which were small lockdown areas within cities in the *región* Metropolitana, the main region of the country (Canals et al., 2020). The Colegio Médico and experts raised concerns about these measures because of the difficulty in stopping mobility in a region without clear boundaries between cities and a high urban landscape density (Contesse, 2020). Indeed, scientific evidence has shown that dynamic quarantines partially worked as the Ministry of Health expected (Grebe et al., 2020).

Despite Phase 1 and Phase 2 policy measures, from March 14, 2020, daily cases started to increase across the country. To cope with this new scenario, the Ministry of Health moved to Phase 3. Two days later, the level was raised to Phase 4, closing borders, implementing sanitary customs, sanitary cordons, and a protocol for contact tracing including primary health care (Ministerio de Salud, 2020k, 2020g). In April 2020 the use of masks was mandated (Ministerio de Salud, 2020m) and health measures were updated, including the Sanitary Alert Decree, which included financing for contact tracing in primary health care (Ministerio de Salud, 2020g).

In April 2020 the *Residencias Sanitarias* (Sanitary Residences) were announced as a measure of isolation for people unable to fulfill quarantine at home. Implemented in the sixteen regions, the *Residencias* strategy was managed by health professionals and technicians focusing on people who tested positive for COVID-19 with mild symptoms or who were asymptomatic (Ministerio de Salud, 2020h). Daily reports covered beds occupied but did not address people's satisfaction nor sanitary measures to avoid contagion in people without COVID-19 who started to use the *Residencias* to protect their families.

The health policy measures implemented did not include primary healthcare centers managed by municipalities; therefore, the pandemic response was centralized by the Ministry of Health at the national and regional level. The *Secretarías Regionales Ministeriales de Salud* (Regional Health Authorities) were responsible for epidemiological surveillance in the sixteen regions, and the twenty-nine *Servicios de Salud* (Health Services) managed the healthcare network under their responsibility. In was not until Phase 4 that primary health care was integrated by the Ministry of Health for testing, contact tracing, and isolation strategy (Ministerio de Salud, 2020j).

Minister of Health Mañalich received criticism not only for health policy measures but also for his erratic media response. One of his first communication controversies was his concern over the questioned legitimacy of the referendum results for a new constitution because of the coronavirus (Andrews, 2020). The statement was a day after the first case was confirmed on Chilean soil. The second controversy was in an interview in the same month, when Mañalich justified not moving to a national lockdown to stop the virus based on the notion that the virus could yet mutate into a "better person" (Palmer, 2020).

Regarding public opinion, pools exhibited a negative perception of the government measures at managing the COVID-19 pandemic. In March 2020, 58 percent of respondents to a CADEM survey perceived that Chile was less than prepared or unprepared for its COVID-19 response (CADEM, 2020a). By May 2020, 62 percent disapproved of how the government was managing the crisis (CADEM, 2020b).

In a decision shared by President Piñera and Education Minister Figueroa, an attempt was made to reopen schools in May 2020. Teachers, students, and parents had not allowed Minister Mañalich's measures to prevail (Saavedra, 2020). Nonetheless, the controversy that pushed Minister Mañalich to resign was his own unofficial criteria for counting new cases, disregarding the official information from the *Departamento de Estadística e Información de Salud* (Department of Statistic and Health Information), that excluded 30,000 cases from the official numbers reported to public (Medrano, 2020). Moreover, by June 2020, Mañalich's erratic health measures placed Chile as one of the countries with the highest numbers of daily coronavirus cases relative to population size (Bartlett, 2020b).

To fill the vacant health minister position, President Piñera appointed former *Colegio Médico* president Enrique Paris, MD, who was a member of his campaign's inner circle regarding health proposals. However, Chile was still focused on strengthening intensive care units (ICU) by importing ventilators rather than testing, contact tracing, and isolating patients as public health measures (Benítez et al., 2020). Moreover, communication was still focused on the population's responsibility for preventing contagion (Garcia et al., 2020).

In mid-July 2020, President Piñera and the new minister of health announced the *Plan Paso a Paso* (Step-by-Step Plan) for reopening cities and regions. The plan coincided with five confinement and deconfinement phases, according to epidemiological criteria such as active cases, R_e, and ICU bed availability. The phases included quarantine (Phase 1), transition (Phase 2), preparation (Phase 3), initial opening (Phase 4), and advance opening (Phase 5) ("Presidente Piñera Presenta Plan Paso a Paso" ["President Piñera Announces Step-by-Step Plan"], 2020).

From a Health to a Social Crisis: When Health Measures Do Not Include Comprehensive Social Policies

From the first democratic government after Pinochet's dictatorship, the agenda for public policy has strived to strengthen the social protection system in Chile. Unfortunately, the main policy and political debate is far from a policy option: the personal retirement accounts implemented in Pinochet's dictatorship, which privatized the Chilean pension system for most of the population, excluding army forces and the police institutions.

The pandemic has demonstrated the importance of comprehensive and integrated social protection systems to support health policy measures. In the same way, the crisis has shown how neglecting social policy measures can undermine the response from the health sector. The political opposition complained about social measures that were mostly undertaken toward rescuing business rather than protecting vulnerable populations. Moreover, unions and opposition leaders denounced a resolution from *Dirección del Trabajo* (Labor Department) that allowed employers to not pay salaries if work cannot be done because of quarantine or curfew (Castiglioni, 2020).

Thus, President Piñera's government was forced to unfold a first social measure—almost a month after the first confirmed case of COVID-19—known as *Ley de Protección del Empleo* (Employment Protection Law). The new law temporarily suspended the contract between employees and private sector companies for the enforcement of authority, suspension by mutual agreement, and reduction of work hours by mutual agreement (Ministerio del Trabajo y Previsión social, 2020b). This measure was mainly centered on private sector financial constraints rather than worker stability. In fact, the *Seguro de Cesantía* (unemployment insurance), which is the basis for the measure, was highly debated and resisted by employers and right-wing parties of the National Congress (Sehnbruch et al., 2019).

Because the government did not manage the pandemic as a complex social phenomenon, the *Ollas Comunes* (common pots) started to spread along the country, as a reminder that Chile still has poverty and underserved populations. The hunger in families already in poverty was neglected until the government decided upon a measure known as the *Plan Alimentos para Chile* (Food for Chile Plan), based on delivery boxes with first-necessity elements distributed throughout municipalities. The initiative was a disaster, mainly because of the logistic complexity of carrying out such a distribution and differences among municipalities about the timing of delivery of the boxes to families in need. Moreover, negative outcomes were also related to families who did not receive the aid and conflicts of interest in the box providers' contracts.

A second measure was the *Ley N° 21.230 Concede un Ingreso Familiar de Emergencia* (Law N° 21.230 Grant an Emergency Family Income Law), enacted on May 16, 2020. The Emergency Family Income Law sought to provide 4 emergency incomes per family with informal earnings from the fiscal budget: families within 90 percent of the most-vulnerable population according to the Social Households Registry and families within 80 percent of the vulnerable population according to the Emergency Socioeconomic Index (measuring social vulnerability in the short term using the latest data provided by the Social Households Registry, and supporting records provided by the beneficiary). Moreover, families were eligible whose eldest family members did not receive any income from pensions, work, salary due, or public benefits related to unemployment insurance or subsidies for work disability (Ministerio de Desarrollo Social y Familia, 2020). Under the Emergency Family Income Law, the first three incomes were adjusted by the number of family members; thus, a family with one member received a first US$88 and a third US$135 income in contrast with a family with ten members or more with a first US$670 and a third US$1,030 income (Ministerio de Desarrollo Social y Familia, 2020).

Because of complete inaction by the executive power, the political opposition in the National Congress started to play a major role in response to the social crisis. One of the measures promoted was to extend the maternity and parenthood leave because of COVID-19. In Chile, maternity and parenthood leave postpartum confers the right to twelve weeks of childcare, and the mother can return to work part-time in agreement with her employer (Ministerio del Trabajo y Previsión social, 2003a). Moreover, from week 7, parents can use the leave upon the mother's request (Ministerio del Trabajo y Previsión social, 2003a).

The *Ley N° 27.247 Establece Beneficios para Padres, Madres y Cuidadores de Niños o Niñas, en las Condiciones que se Indica* (Law N° 27.247 Establishing Benefits for Parents, Mothers, and Keepers of Children, in Some Conditions) (Ministerio del Trabajo y Previsión Social, 2020d) was enacted in July 2020, retroactively. Thus, parents were able to access the thirty days of extended leave from March 18, 2020, renewable for two periods (Ministerio del Trabajo y Previsión Social, 2020d).

The National Congress's milestone was the constitutional amendment, which with the support of some legislators from the governing coalition reached the necessary three-fifths votes in the bicameral system (Ministerio Secretaría General de la Presidencia, 2005). The amendment allowed Chileans to withdraw up to 10 percent of their money in their personal retirement accounts in order to mitigate hardships caused by the pandemic.

One of the social and political crises demands was the end of Pinochet's dictatorship pension systems based on personal retirement accounts, which even democratic governments have not been able to change yet. Nonetheless, the social crisis due to COVID-19 conducted to a constitutional reform by National Congress initiative. Thus, the *Ley N° 21.248 Reforma Constitucional que Permite el Retiro Excepcional de los Fondos Acumulados de Capitalización Individual en las Condiciones que se Indica* (Law N° 21.248 Constitutional Reform that Allow the Exceptional Retirement of Accumulated Funds of Individual Capitalization in Some Conditions), enacted on July 30, 2020, justified as exceptional, sought to mitigate social effects resulting from the *Estado de Excepcional Constitucional de Catástrofe por Calamidad Pública* decree related to COVID-19. In the private pension system regulated by the decree *Ley N° 3.500* of 1980, affiliates are authorized voluntarily, and for one time only, to request up to 10 percent of the total accumulated in their mandatory accounts (Ministerio del Trabajo y Previsión Social, 2020c). Affiliates can request the 10 percent until one year after the date when the law was enacted because the law established a maximum of US$5,934 and a US$1,384 minimum amount. In the case in which 10 percent of the accumulated funds are less than US$1,383, the affiliate can request up to this amount. In the same way, affiliates with less than US$1,384 could request all the funds accumulated in their accounts (Ministerio del Trabajo y Previsión Social, 2020c).

Why Did Chile Fail in a Comprehensive Response to COVID-19?

October 17, 2019, changed the political landscape when primary and high school students jumped turnstiles in the Santiago subway system to protest a US$4 fare increase during peak hours (Méndez et al., 2020). Protests soon escalated nationwide, with crowds gathering in rallies to demand major changes to social protection policies, including pensions, education, and health. Violence erupted and the police were unable to control the situation, despite deploying considerable violence themselves and engaging in human rights violations (Méndez et al., 2020). President Piñera declared a state of emergency on October 19, 2019, giving the armed forces responsibility for restoring order in the Chilean capital and other cities and enacting a curfew (Méndez et al., 2020).

On November 15, 2019, members of almost all Chile's political parties represented in the bicameral Congress signed the *Agreement for Peace and a New Political Constitution* (Hernandez & Gigova, 2019). The agreement includes a national referendum for a new political constitution replacing that enacted during Pinochet's dictatorship. The agreement was first scheduled for April 26, 2020, then postponed to October 25, 2020, because of the COVID-19 pandemic. Thus, the Chilean government faced its preparedness and response plan without a solution for the ongoing social and political crisis that presidentialism was unable to solve.

Presidentialism can be tracked in most Latin American political systems. The concentration of a considerable constitutional power, cabinet conformation and administration, only modified by several impeachments or popular elections has also paradoxically resulted in a strong executive power (Linz, 1990). According to Linz (1990), one of the main paradoxes is the dual legitimacy: legitimated presidents need to bargain and overcome conflicts with the also legitimated legislative branch controlled by the political opposition—or even its own coalition—in short periods of government in countries with no immediate reelection in their constitutions (Mainwaring, 1990). Thus, dual legitimacy contributes to a strong executive power.

In Chile the 1980 constitution represents the consolidation of a historical trend to expand presidential powers (Siavelis, 2000). This can explain why Chile failed in a comprehensive response to COVID-19 pandemic. President Piñera made decisions on the pandemic response without opposition and public disagreement from his cabinet for the economy, social protection, or health measures. He governed by decrees rather than taking advantage of his constitutional prerogatives regarding sending laws and constitutional amendments to the National Congress (Ministerio Secretaría General de la Presidencia, 2005). For the COVID-19 response, social measures were delayed because of the pandemic, opening a window of opportunity for the National Congress and municipalities as main stakeholders for the population's well-being. The only constitutional prerogative used by President Piñera was the Exception State of Catastrophe for Public Calamity.

Indeed, presidentialism is also exacerbated by centralism. Latin American countries have a long-standing tradition of centralism. According to Véliz (1968), this centralism tradition was political, economic, and religious because of the dominant Hispanic tradition in Latin American countries. In the last decades, decentralization has been posed as a political quest for many Latin American countries, mainly understood as a state reform process in administrative, fiscal, and political spheres (Falleti, 2005). In Chile the decentralization process does not share comprehensive state reform. Chilean decentralization was part of neoliberalism-based reforms under Pinochet's dictatorship, which sought privatization and financial liberalization (Baton, 2006). In particular, health and education were transferred to municipalities but not control over revenues (Eaton, 2006).

In the first democratic governments after Pinochet's dictatorship, political decentralization was a path for disputing right-wing political overrepresentation in National Congress as a result of the binominal system, maintaining a centralized revenue system (Eaton, 2004b). The status quo was challenged with the *Asociación Chilena de Municipalidades* (Chilean Municipalities Association). The *Asociación* arose in 1994 as a nonpartisan instrument for institutional change regarding decentralization (Eaton, 2004a). Still, centralism is a major barrier for the Chilean state, hampering territorial decision-making. Nevertheless, the *Asociación Chilena de Municipalidades* played a key role in the first weeks of COVID-19 pandemic.

The executive powers did not suspend attendance in schools, despite the inherent risk of faster COVID-19 spreading. Thus, President Piñera's government was challenged by the *Asociación* to suspend primary and secondary education schools' activities managed by municipalities. The *Pontificia Universidad Católica de Chile* and the *Universidad de Chile*, both from the *región Metropolitana*, which contains almost a third of the national population, announced the suspension of graduate and undergraduate attendance. Days later, Chilean universities from different regions did the same.

Conclusion

The Chilean presidentialist system tackled yet exacerbated a comprehensive response to the COVID-19 outbreak in Chile. A fragmented and delayed social response resulted from President Piñera's government. The Chilean experience has also shown how a political crisis not only in Latin America but also in some European countries has undermined strong health systems, social policies, and democratic legitimacy.

Chile's long-standing centralization revealed its weaknesses at a time when the decision-making for the allocation of territorial-based resources should have been delegated to regional governments. Although centralization can be useful in the early response to an outbreak, the Chilean case suggests that in later stages, the outcomes are inequality in access to health care and an irrelevant role for regional governments in the response. Moreover, an authoritarian centralization with a lack of coordination among the executive branch, regional governments, and municipalities does not allow for a comprehensive response because of territorial differences nationwide.

Nonetheless, the COVID-19 outbreak response in Chile can serve as an example for other countries regarding the use of municipalities as first responders. As political incumbents, municipalities have an advantage: they have superior knowledge of their communities, including primary and secondary education controls and the necessary primary health care for testing, contact tracing, and isolation strategies. Therefore, majors were well positioned to contest the political centralism of decision-making policies adopted by President Piñera because of their perceived legitimacy in public opinion as positive leaders for pandemic response.

References

Andrews, J. (2020). *Mañalich dice que le preocupa el nivel de convocatoria que tenga el plebiscito debido al coronavirus* [Mañalich worried on participation in the referendum due coronavirus]. La Tercera. https://www.latercera.com/politica/noticia/manalich-dice-que-le-preocupa-el-nivel-de-convocatoria-que-tenga-el-plebiscito-debido-al-coronavirus/TACBFXH3QRBV3F7UITGGMWH24M/

Bartlett, J. (2020a, April 2). *The 34-year-old doctor shaping Chile's pandemic response.* Americas Quarterly. https://www.americasquarterly.org/article/the-34-year-old-doctor-shaping-chiles-pandemic-response/

Bartlett, J. (2020b, June 14). *Chile's health minister quits over government response to Covid-19.* https://www.theguardian.com/global-development/2020/jun/14/chiles-health-minister-quits-over-government-response-to-covid-19

Baton, K. (2006). Decentralization's nondemocratic roots: Authoritarianism and subnational reform in Latin America. *Latin American Politics and Society*, *48*, 1–26. https://doi.org/https://doi.org/10.1111/j.1548-2456.2006.tb00336.x PDFPDF

Benítez, M. A., Velasco, C., Sequeira, A. R., Henríquez, J., Menezes, F. M., & Paolucci, F. (2020). Responses to COVID-19 in five Latin American countries. *Health Policy and Technology*, *9*, 525–559. https://doi.org/10.1016/j.hlpt.2020.08.014

Bustamante, A. V., & Méndez, C. A. (2014). Health care privatization in Latin America: Comparing divergent privatization approaches in Chile, Colombia, and Mexico. *Journal of Health Politics, Policy and Law*. https://doi.org/10.1215/03616878-2743063

Cabieses, B., Cookson, R. E. M., & Santorelli, G. D. I. (2015). Did socioeconomic inequality in self-reported health in Chile fall after the equity-based healthcare reform of 2005? A Concentration Index decomposition analysis. *PLoS ONE*, *10*(9). https://doi.org/10.1371/journal.pone.0138227

CADEM. (2020a). *Encuesta Plaza Pública-Primera semana de marzo-Estudio N° 321*. Primera Semana de Marzo-Estudio N° 321 [Public Plaza Survey—First week of March-Study No 321. First Week of March-Study No 321]. https://plazapublica.cl/wp-content/uploads/2020/03/Track-PP-321-Marzo-S1-VF_Baja.pdf

CADEM. (2020b). *Encuesta Plaza Pública-Primera semana de mayo-Estudio N° 330*. Encuesta Plaza Pública-Primera Semana de Mayo-Estudio N° 330 [Public Plaza Survey—First week of March-Study No 330. First Week of March-Study No 330].

https://plazapublica.cl/wp-content/uploads/2020/05/Track-PP-330-Mayo-S1_Baja.pdf

Canals M, C. C., Canals A, Yohannessen K, Lefio, L. A., Bertoglia, M. P., Eguiguren, P., Siches, I., Iglesias, V., & Arteaga, O. (2020). Epidemic trends, public health response and health system capacity: The Chilean experience in four months of the COVID-19 pandemic. *Rev Panam Salud Publica/Pan Am J Public Health Rev Panam Salud Publica*, *44*. https://doi.org/10.26633/RPSP.2020.99

Castiglioni, R. (2020). *Chile's new (fragile) social truce*. Americas Quarterly. https://www.americasquarterly.org/article/chiles-new-fragile-social-truce/

Contesse, J. (2020). *Responding to COVID-19 without public trust*. The Regulatory Review. https://www.theregreview.org/2020/06/02/contesse-responding-COVID-19-without-public-trust/

de la Jara, J. J., & Bossert, T. (1995). Chile's health sector reform: Lessons from four reform periods. *Health Policy*. https://doi.org/10.1016/0168-8510(95)00733-9

Eaton, K. (2004a). Designing subnational institutions: Regional and municipal reforms in postauthoritarian Chile. *Comparative Political Studies*, *37*(2), 218–244. https://doi.org/10.1177/0010414003260979

Eaton, K. (2004b). Risky business: Decentralization from above in Chile and Uruguay. *Comparative Politics*, *37*(1), 1–22. https://doi.org/10.2307/4150121

Eaton, K. (2006). Decentralization's nondemocratic roots: Authoritarianism and subnational reform in Latin America. *Latin American Politics and Society*, *48*, 1–26. https://doi.org/10.1111/j.1548-2456.2006.tb00336.x

Falleti, T. (2005). A sequential theory of decentralization: Latin American cases in comparative perspective. *The American Political Science Review*, *99*(327–346).

Frenz, P., Delgado, I., Kaufman, J. S., & Harper, S. (2013). Achieving effective universal health coverage with equity: Evidence from Chile. *Health Policy and Planning*. https://doi.org/10.1093/heapol/czt054

Garcia, P. J., Alarcón, A., Bayer, A., Buss, P., Guerra, G., Ribeiro, H., Rojas, K., Saenz, R., Salgado de Snyder, N., Solimano, G., Torres, R., Tobar, S., Tuesca, R., Vargas, G., & Atun, R. (2020). COVID-19 response in Latin America. *The American Journal of Tropical Medicine and Hygiene*, *103*(5), 1765–1772. https://doi.org/ 10.4269/ajtmh.20-0765

Garrido, M. (2020). *Asociación Chilena de Municipalidades y suspensión de clases: "Medidas no tienen sentido si se realizan de manera desarticulada"* [Chilean Municipalities Association and discontinued schooling: "Measures has not any sense if they are doing in a disarticulated way"]. La Tercera. https://www.latercera.com/nacional/noticia/asociacion-chilena-de-municipalidades-y-suspension-de-clases-medidas-no-tienen-sentido-si-se-realizan-de-manera-desarticulada/F4OTIBHO2BDFVNLHQTX5BCWVGU/

Grebe, G., Vélez, J., Tiutiunnyk, A., Aragón-Caqueo, D., Fernández-Salinas, J., & Navarrete M. L. D. (2020). Dynamic quarantine: A comparative analysis of the Chilean public health response to COVID-19. *Epidemiology and Infection*, *148*(e270), 1–9. https://doi.org/10.1017/S0950268820002678

Hernandez, D., & Gigova, R. (2019). *Chile pins hopes on "100% democratic" new constitution to end deadly protests*. CNN. https://edition.cnn.com/2019/11/15/americas/chile-congress-constitution-protests-intl-hnk/index.html

Infobae. (2020). *Analizan en Chile postergar el referéndum constitucional por el coronavirus* [Chile postpones constitutional referendum due to coronavirus]. https://

www.infobae.com/america/agencias/2020/03/17/analizan-en-chile-postergar-el-referendum-constitucional-por-el-coronavirus/

Jiménez, J., & Romero, M. I. (2007). Reducing infant mortality in Chile: Success in two phases. *Health Affairs*. https://doi.org/10.1377/hlthaff.26.2.458

Johns Hopkins University. (2020). *Johns Hopkins Coronavirus Resource Center*. https://coronavirus.jhu.edu/map.html

Koch, E., Calhoun, B., Aracena, P., Gatica, S., & Bravo, M. (2014). Women's education level, contraceptive use and maternal mortality estimates. *Public Health*. https://doi.org/10.1016/j.puhe.2014.01.008

Linz, J. (1990). The perils of presidentialism. *Journal of Democracy*, *1*(1), 51–59.

Mainwaring, S. (1990). Presidentialism in Latin America. *Latin American Research Review*, 25(1), 157–179.

Manuel, A. (2002). The Chilean health system: 20 years of reforms. In *Salud Publica de Mexico*. https://doi.org/10.1590/S0036-36342002000100009

Mardones-Restat, F., & De Azevedo, A. C. (2006). The essential health reform in Chile; a reflection on the 1952 process. In *Salud Publica de Mexico*. https://doi.org/10.1590/S0036-36342006000600009

Medrano, C. (2020). *Contraloría detecta errores en la cifra de contagiados e instruye sumario al Minsal* [Comptroller's office detects errors in the number of infected and instructs Minsal to investigate]. DiarioUChile. https://radio.uchile.cl/2020/07/14/contraloria-detecta-errores-en-las-cifras-de-contagiados-e-instruye-sumario-al-minsal/

Méndez, C. A., Greer, S. L., & McKee, M. (2020). The 2019 crisis in Chile: Fundamental change needed, not just technical fixes to the health system. *Journal of Public Health Policy*. https://doi.org/10.1057/s41271-020-00241-2

Mesa-Lago, C. (2008). Social protection in Chile: Reforms to improve equity. *International Labour Review*. https://doi.org/10.1111/j.1564-913X.2008.00041.x

Ministerio de Desarrollo Social y Familia. (2020). *Ley N° 21.230 Concede un Ingreso Familiar de Emergencia* [Law N° 21.230 Grant an Emergency Family Income Law]. http://bcn.cl/2f762

Ministerio de Salud. (2020a). *Decreto N° 11 suspende garantía de oportunidad de las garantías explícitas en salud en los problemas de salud que indica* [Decree No. 11 suspends the guaranteed opportunity of the explicit health guarantees in the health problems indicated]. http://bcn.cl/2kk3v

Ministerio de Salud. (2020b). *Decreto N° 4 decreta alerta sanitaria por el período que se señala y otorga facultades extraordinarias que indica por emergencia de salud pública de importancia internacional (ESPII) por brote del nuevo coronavirus (2019-NCOV)* [Decree No. 4 decrees sanitary emergency for the period indicated and grants extraordinary powers indicated by public health emergency of international concern (PHEIC) due to the outbreak of the new coronavirus (2019-NCOV)]. http://bcn.cl/2floo

Ministerio de Salud. (2020c). *Fase 2 del plan de preparación y respuesta COVID-19. protocolo de detección de viajeros en aeropuertos* [Phase 2 of the COVID-19 Preparedness and Response Plan. Airport Traveler Detection Protocol]. https://www.minsal.cl/wp-content/uploads/2020/03/2020.03.10_PROTOCOLO-DETECCION-VIAJEROS_AEROPUERTOS.pdf

Ministerio de Salud. (2020d). *Fase 2 del Plan de preparación y respuesta COVID-19. Protocolo de detección de viajeros en pasos fronterizos terrestres* [Phase 2 of the

COVID-19 Preparedness and response plan. Protocol for detection of travelers at land border crossings]. https://www.minsal.cl/wp-content/uploads/2020/03/2020.03.10_PROTOCOLO-DETECCION-VIAJEROS_PASOS-FRONTERIZOS.pdf

Ministerio de Salud. (2020e). *Fase 2 del plan de preparación y respuesta COVID-19. Protocolo de detección de viajeros en puertos* [Phase 2 of the COVID-19 preparedness and response plan. Traveler detection protocol in ports]. https://www.minsal.cl/wp-content/uploads/2020/03/2020.03.10_PROTOCOLO-DETECCION-VIAJEROS_PUERTOS.pdf

Ministerio de Salud. (2020f). *Modifica Decreto N° 4, de 2020, del Ministerio de Salud, que decreta alerta sanitaria por el período que se señala y otorga facultades extraordinarias que indica por emergencia de salud pública de importancia internacional (ESPII) por brote del nuevo coronavirus (2019-NCOV)* [Modifies Decree No. 4, of 2020, of the Ministry of Health, which decrees sanitary emergency for the period indicated and grants extraordinary powers indicated by public health emergency of international concern (PHEIC) due to the outbreak of the new coronavirus (2019-NCOV)]. https://www.minsal.cl/wp-content/uploads/2020/03/1737786.pdf

Ministerio de Salud. (2020g). *Modifica Decreto N° 4, de 2020, del Ministerio de Salud, que decreta alerta sanitaria por el período que se señala y otorga facultades extraordinarias que indica por emergencia de salud pública de importancia internacional (ESPII) por brote del nuevo coronavirus (2019-NCOV))* [Modifies Decree No. 4, of 2020, of the Ministry of Health, which decrees sanitary emergency for the period indicated and grants extraordinary powers indicated by public health emergency of international concern (PHEIC) due to the outbreak of the new coronavirus (2019-NCOV)]. http://bcn.cl/2l98s

Ministerio de Salud. (2020h). *Orientación técnica de las Residencias Sanitarias Plan COVID19* [Technical orientation of the Health Residences Plan COVID19]. http://bibliodigital.saludpublica.uchile.cl:8080/dspace/bitstream/handle/123456789/664/Orientación técnica de las Residencias Sanitarias. Plan COVID19.PDF?sequence=1&isAllowed=y

Ministerio de Salud. (2020i). *Presidente Piñera se reúne con Consejo Asesor del Minsal por COVID-19* [President Piñera meets with the Minsal Advisory Council for COVID-19]. Ministerio de Salud. https://www.minsal.cl/presidente-pinera-se-reune-con-consejo-asesor-del-minsal-por-COVID-19/

Ministerio de Salud. (2020j). *Protocolo de coordinación para acciones de vigilancia epidemiológica durante la pandemia COVID-19 en Chile: Estraegia nacional de testeo, trazabilidad y aislamiento* [Coordination protocol for epidemiological surveillance actions during the COVID-19 pandemic in Chile: National strategy for testing, contact tracing, and isolation]. https://www.minsal.cl/wp-content/uploads/2020/07/Estrategia-Testeo-Trazabilidad-y-Aislamiento.pdf

Ministerio de Salud. (2020k). *Resolución Exenta N⁰ 108 establece declaración jurada de estado de salud como medida de control sanitario obligatorio para viajeros que ingresan a Chile y aprueba formulario para realizar la declaración* [Exempt Resolution No. 108 establishes an affidavit of health status as a mandatory sanitary control measure for travelers entering Chile and approves the form to make the declaration]. https://www.minsal.cl/wp-content/uploads/2020/02/1734494-COVID-Declaracion.pdf

Ministerio de Salud. (2020l). *Resolución Exenta N⁰ 208 dispone medidas sanitarias que indica por brote de COVID-19* [Exempt Resolution No. 208 provides sanitary measures that indicate an outbreak of COVID-19]. https://www.minsal.cl/wp-content/uploads/2020/03/1745861_web.pdf

Ministerio de Salud. (2020m). *Resolución Exenta Nº 282 dispone uso obligatorio de mascarillas en lugares y circunstancias que indica* [Exempt Resolution No. 282 provides mandatory use of masks in places and circumstances indicated]. https://www.minsal.cl/wp-content/uploads/2020/04/1752570.pdf

Ministerio de Salud. (2020n). *Resolución Exenta Nº 409. Dispone Medidas Sanitarias que indica por brote de COVID-19.* http://bcn.cl/2n395

Ministerio de Salud. (2020o). *Se inaugura mesa social por COVID-19 y acuerdan sesionar dos veces por semana* [Social roundtable for COVID-19 is inaugurated and they agree to meet twice a week]. Ministerio de Salud. https://www.minsal.cl/se-inaugura-mesa-social-por-COVID-19-y-acuerdan-sesionar-dos-veces-por-semana/

Ministerio del Interior y Seguridad Pública. (2020). *Decreto 104 declara estado de excepción constitucional de catásrtrofe, por calamidad pública, en el territorio de Chile* [Decree 104 constitutional exception for a state of catastrophe for a public calamity]. http://bcn.cl/2ga7v

Ministerio del Trabajo y Previsión social. (2003a). *DFL 1 fija el texto refundido, coordinado y sistematizado del Código del Trabajo* [DFL 1 sets the consolidated, coordinated and systematized text of the Labor Code]. http://bcn.cl/2f6o9

Ministerio del Trabajo y Previsión social. (2020b). *Ley Nº 21.227 faculta el acceso a prestaciones del seguro de desempleo de la Ley Nº 19.728, en circunstancias excepcionales* [Law Nº 21.227 authorizes access to unemployment insurance benefits of Law No. 19,728, in exceptional circumstances]. http://bcn.cl/2f9m5

Ministerio del Trabajo y Previsión social. (2020c). *Ley Nº 21.248 Reforma Constitucional que permite el retiro excepcional de los fondos acumulados de capitalización individual en las condicones que se indica* [Law Nº 21.248 Constitutional reform that allows the exceptional retirement of accumulated funds of individual capitalization in some conditions]. http://bcn.cl/2f8ms

Ministerio del Trabajo y Previsión Social. (2020d). *Ley Nº 21.247 Establece beneficios para padres, madres y cuidadores de niños o niñas, en las condiciones que indica* [Law Nº 27.247 Establishing benefits for parents, mothers, and keepers of children, in some conditions]. http://bcn.cl/2f897

Ministerio Secretaría General de la Presidencia. (2005). *Decreto 100 fija el texto refundido, coordinado y sistematizado de la constitución política de la República de Chile* [Decree 100 sets the consolidated, coordinated, and systematized text of the political constitution of the Republic of Chile]. http://bcn.cl/2f6sk

Palmer, E. (2020). Chile's health minister says coronavirus could still mutate into a "better person" amid lockdown calls. *Newsweek.* https://www.newsweek.com/coronavirus-chile-lockdown-health-minister-1493708

Paraje, G., & Vásquez, F. (2012). Health equity in an unequal country: The use of medical services in Chile. *International Journal for Equity in Health.* https://doi.org/10.1186/1475-9276-11-81

Parro, F., & Reyes, L. (2017). The rise and fall of income inequality in Chile. *Latin American Economic Review*, 26(3), 4–31. https://doi.org/10.1007/s40503-017-0040-y

Presidente Piñera presenta Plan Paso a Paso: "Se aplicará en forma gradual, escuchando a la comunidad y recogiendo la realidad de cada comuna y región." [President Piñera announces Step-by-Step Plan: "It will be applied gradually, listening to the community and collecting the reality of each commune and region"]. (2020). Prensa Presidencia. https://prensa.presidencia.cl/comunicado.aspx?id=153176

Ramírez de la Cruz, E. E., Grin, E. J., Sanabria-Pulido, P., Cravacuore, D., & Orellana, A. (2020). The transaction costs of government responses to the COVID-19 emergency in Latin America. *Public Administration Review*, *80*(4), 683–695. https://doi.org/10.1111/puar.13259

Saavedra, M. (2020). *Teachers, parents and students defy order to reopen schools in Chile*. World Socialist Web Site. https://www.wsws.org/en/articles/2020/05/06/chil-m06.html

Sehnbruch, K., Carranza, R., & Prieto, J. (2019). The political economy of unemployment insurance based on individual savings accounts: Lessons from Chile. *Development and Change*, *50*(4), 948–975. https://doi.org/10.1111/dech.12457

Siavelis, P. M. (2000). *President and Congress in postauthoritarian Chile: Institutional constraints to democratic consolidation*. The Pennsylvania State University Press.

Taylor, M. (2003). The reformulation of social policy in Chile, 1973–2001. *Global Social Policy: An Interdisciplinary Journal of Public Policy and Social Development*, *3*(1), 21–44. https://doi.org/10.1177/14680181030030010101

Valcarce, B., Avilez, J. L., Torres-Roman, J. S., Poterico, J. A., Bazalar-Palacios, J., & La Vecchia, C. (2020). The effect of early-stage public health policies in the transmission of COVID-19 for South American countries. *Rev Panam Salud Publica/Pan Am J Public Health Rev Panam Salud Publica*, *44*. https://doi.org/10.26633/RPSP.2020.148

Véliz, C. (1968). Centralism and nationalism in Latin America. *Foreign Affairs*, *47*(1), 68–83. https://doi.org/10.2307/20039354

PART V AFRICA

30 PANDEMIC AMID POLITICAL CRISIS
Malawi's Experience with and Response to COVID-19

Kim Yi Dionne, Boniface Dulani, and Sara E. Fischer

> Due to the threat of coronavirus and the urgent need to seriously manage it, I have decided to declare a "State of Disaster" in the country.
>
> —MALAWI PRESIDENT PETER MUTHARIKA, MARCH 20, 2020[1]

With these words from President Peter Mutharika in a national address on March 20, 2020, Malawi joined the global trend of invoking special governmental powers to introduce measures for fighting the COVID-19 pandemic. A landlocked country in southern Africa with a largely youthful population, Malawi has a heavy preventable disease burden, inadequate public health infrastructure, and limited human resources for health. These characteristics concerned analysts, who questioned Malawi's ability to weather a significant outbreak of the deadly coronavirus, which has no vaccine nor known cure at the time of writing.[2] Following the introduction of basic prevention measures in March, Malawi recorded its first confirmed COVID-19 cases on April 2, 2020. By April 7, 2020, the country recorded its first COVID-19 death. The official number of COVID-19 cases increased to 4,078 by the end of July 2020, with a total of 114 deaths. This chapter outlines the Malawian government's early response to the COVID-19 pandemic, citizens' reactions to proposed measures, and how these interacted within a context of significant political change.

COVID-19 emerged in the midst of a national political crisis in Malawi (Evans, 2020; Munthali & Wu, 2020; Pensulo, 2020a). Two months before the first COVID-19 cases were diagnosed, Malawi's Constitutional Court nullified the previous year's presidential election results and called for fresh elections to be held within five months. In the months following the disputed 2019 polls, thousands of Malawians protested Mutharika's victory and called for the resignation of the Malawi Electoral Commission chairperson for her role in presiding over what many Malawians considered to be mismanaged elections (Africa Center for Strategic Studies, 2020; Dionne & Dulani, 2020). Meanwhile, the top two losing presidential candidates in the 2019 polls, Lazarus Chakwera of the Malawi Congress Party (MCP) and Saulos Chilima of the UTM party, challenged the results in the Constitutional Court, culminating in the nullification of the results in the February 2020 ruling and an order for fresh elections (Dionne & Dulani, 2020).

A historic pre-electoral coalition among opposition parties and a galvanized civil society may have served to delay an effective public health response. Mutharika lost his re-election bid in the new elections held on June 23, 2020, generating a major change in government as the number of COVID-19 cases climbed.

To what extent did the political upheaval in Malawi early in the COVID-19 pandemic shape the politics of response in the country? In this chapter, we describe and analyze available data to connect national political events, government response to COVID-19, Malawians' adherence to protective measures, and trends in COVID-19 infection. More specifically, our analysis draws on news accounts published by Malawi's two leading newspapers, public addresses by the president and minister of health, official reports and public health communications from Malawi's Ministry of Health and Public Health Institute, and survey data collected prior to and during the COVID-19 pandemic. Although our primary goal is to offer a rich description of the Malawian experience during the COVID-19 crisis, our chapter also aims to contribute to the broader scholarship on how citizens navigate both epidemics and state response to those epidemics. The Malawi case offers a window into how states and citizens in a low- or middle-income country (LMIC) navigate a pandemic. Furthermore, the Malawian case offers insights on how citizens and the state navigate a pandemic during a political crisis.

Malawi's COVID-19 Epidemic

The first COVID-19 case in the African region was confirmed in Egypt on February 14, 2020. Malawi registered its first three cases on April 2, 2020, among the last group of African countries to do so (Anna, 2020). The index case was a sixty-one-year-old woman who had returned from visiting family members in India. Two individuals who had close contact with her also tested positive that day.

By late July 2020, COVID-19 cases had been reported in all of Malawi's twenty-eight districts. The highest number of cases was confirmed in the two districts with the two largest cities, Blantyre and Lilongwe, which between them accounted for half of all confirmed cases by July's end.[3] Many cases were also recorded at the Mwanza border, which is the main entry point for Malawian returnees from South Africa traveling by road.[4] Because South Africa was a recognized "hotspot" for the virus (Nebehay, 2020), this had been the largest factor in Malawi's early jump in COVID-19 case numbers. Prior to this repatriation, Malawi had 101 positive cases over two months, spiking to 273 in a single day on May 29, 2020, as returnees' test results were confirmed (Masina, 2020b). In July 2020 alone, cases doubled and community spread surpassed imported cases for the first time.

Of 4,078 confirmed cases recorded by July 31, almost half had recovered, while 114 had died. Most fatalities were from Lilongwe and Blantyre, with twenty-four and fifty-one deaths, respectively (Ministry of Health, 2020). Most (83 percent) of the deaths were of men (Public Health Institute of Malawi, 2020). The average age

TABLE 30.1. COVID-19 case, fatality, and recovery numbers by region as of July 31, 2020

Region	Confirmed cases	Deaths	Recoveries
North	884	21	394
Center	1,177	32	536
South	1,815	61	772
Mwanza border	202	0	173
TOTAL MALAWI	4,078	114	1875

Source: Ministry of Health (2020).

among recorded COVID-19 cases was thirty-six years, whereas those who died of COVID-19 were on average older, at 56.7 years (Public Health Institute of Malawi, 2020).

As in other countries, Malawi's official COVID-19 figures are likely undercounts (Bariyo & Parkinson, 2020; Baskar, 2020). However, at the time of this writing, we have no reason to doubt that these figures track with the trends in infection and death (Table 30.1).

Malawi's Response to COVID-19

The WHO declared COVID-19 a public health emergency of international concern on January 30, 2020, and officially characterized it as a pandemic on March 11, 2020. President Peter Mutharika established a nine-member Special Cabinet Committee[5] on Coronavirus on March 7, 2020, and declared a national state of disaster on March 20. The government developed an initial National COVID-19 Preparedness and Response Plan (Malawi Government, 2020a), budgeted at US$20 million, and announced several interventions, often during speeches by the president or health minister. The membership of the cabinet committee was challenged for its lack of inclusivity, both in terms of ignoring the political opposition and public health experts (Kao et al., 2021). Members of the cabinet committee were further accused of seeking to profit from the pandemic by awarding themselves large allowances (Matonga, 2020). Following the public criticisms, Mutharika disbanded and replaced the cabinet committee with a presidential task force on COVID-19, co-chaired by John Phuka, the Minister of Health, and a public health professor from the Malawi College of Medicine ("Presidential Task Force on COVID-19," 2020). The Chakwera administration kept the task force, and official COVID-19 announcements continued to be made by Phuka (Table 30.2).

Although the initial response in Malawi came from the highest levels of government and focused in particular on public health interventions, we describe in this section the broader response to COVID-19, documenting both national government response and community and citizen response, including both public health interventions and social protection measures.

TABLE 30.2. COVID-19 and political crisis timeline in Malawi

Date	Event
January 30, 2020	WHO declares a Public Health Emergency of International Concern (PHEIC)
February 3, 2020	Constitutional Court nullifies May 2019 presidential elections
February 14,-2020	First COVID-19 case in Africa (Egypt)
March 20, 2020	Mutharika declares *State of National Disaster* in his first public COVID-19 address
April 1, 2020	Borders and airports close
April 2, 2020	First COVID-19 cases confirmed in Malawi
April 7, 2020	First COVID-19 death confirmed in Malawi
April 14, 2020	Attempted lockdown announced
April 17, 2020	High Court orders stay of lockdown
June 23, 2020	Fresh presidential elections
June 28, 2020	Inauguration of new president, Lazarus Chakwera
July 10, 2020	New social distancing measures announced

Public Health Interventions against COVID-19 in Malawi

Malawi's public health interventions against COVID-19 primarily included travel and border restrictions, health system preparedness, health communications, and policies promoting social distancing, and later, face covering.

The rapid spread of infection in Asia, Europe, and the United States in early 2020 put the Malawian government on high alert for entering travelers. Following the disaster declaration, Malawi introduced a compulsory screening protocol at borders, requiring that people entering from high-risk countries self-isolate for fourteen days. The government banned public gatherings of more than one hundred people, but this was not enforced, as evidenced by large political rallies held in the months before the June election (Pensulo, 2020d). On April 1, 2020, Malawi closed borders and airports, prohibiting travelers from entering, with exceptions for repatriating Malawians. The process of screening and quarantining returning Malawians was ineffective (Masina, 2020a), and airport worker strikes related to the outbreak disrupted COVID-19 equipment supply chains (Twea, 2020).

Malawi's health system lacks essential equipment and personnel to respond effectively to emerging disease threats (Manda-Taylor et al., 2017). The original national preparedness plan allocated resources to training frontline workers and procuring necessary supplies and equipment. Donors attempted to fill gaps to alleviate the resource shortage, but fell short. There were critical stockouts of COVID-19 testing kits following a sharp increase in infections in July 2020, requiring health officials to ration tests so that only people with symptoms could be tested (Pasungwi, 2020; Twea, 2020).

Health officials developed and disseminated health communications materials on basic COVID-19 information and widely encouraged basic hygiene practices

Figure 30.1. Front-page advertisement promoting face covering to stop the spread of COVID-19. *Source:* Photo from *The Nation,* July 31, 2020.

such as handwashing with soap; avoiding handshakes; not touching eyes, nose, and mouths; practicing cough and sneeze hygiene; maintaining social distance; and staying home when sick. Individuals who exhibited symptoms of COVID-19 were encouraged to seek medical care, although there was little capacity to isolate cases even within hospitals (Sonenthal et al., 2020). These messages were broadcast in various formats, including print, video, radio, and via social media. Malawi's major newspapers featured health promotion messages on their front pages (Figure 30.1). Malawians could also get daily updates on case counts on the Ministry of Health's Twitter or Facebook feeds (Figure 30.2) or by sending a message to the Ministry of Health using WhatsApp (Figure 30.3).

Following the confirmation of the first COVID-19 cases, the government introduced additional measures to contain the spread of COVID-19. The new proposals included a ban on religious gatherings, closure of markets and shops, and an abortive proposal to impose a twenty-one-day national lockdown to commence April 18, 2020. The lockdown sought to confine all individuals to their homes except for designated essential service providers. As we discuss later, the courts intervened, preventing the lockdown from being instituted.

Although large crowds continued to gather for election campaign rallies, there was no mention of masking in early health promotion campaign documents. The government had not mandated the use of face masks, but several organizations began to require their use as local transmission increased. Among these were commercial banks, the Road Traffic Directorate, the Office of the Ombudsman, supermarkets, and the High and Supreme Courts (Lunda, 2020). On July 9, 2020, the Malawi government issued a circular requiring the use of face masks in all government offices (Mkweu, 2020).

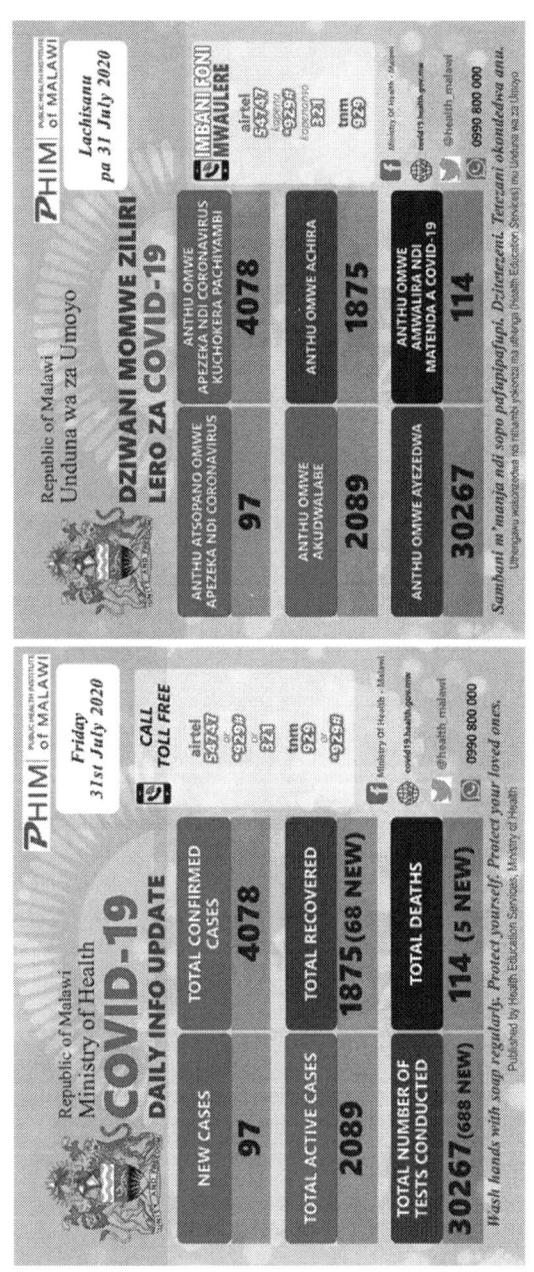

Figure 30.2. Social media graphics issued daily via Twitter and Facebook to communicate COVID-19 statistics in English and Chichewa.

Source: Malawi Ministry of Health (2020).

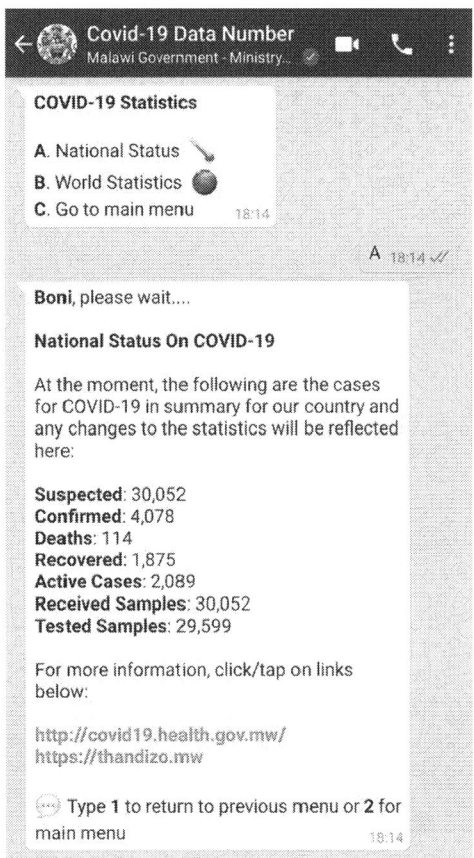

Figure 30.3. Messages to communicate COVID-19 statistics via WhatsApp.
Source: Malawi Ministry of Health, personal communication via WhatsApp, July 31, 2020.

Social Policy Interventions in the Wake of Malawi's COVID-19 Pandemic

The initial COVID-19 response focused on public health measures to prevent the spread of infection, and only later did government efforts include social protection measures. However, even these were not broadly applicable to all, or even most, Malawians. In a speech on April 4, 2020, when Malawi had only four confirmed COVID-19 cases, President Mutharika announced multiple social protection measures that included reduction of fuel prices, instituting a grace period for paying taxes, extending a cash loan scheme targeted at urban youth, and directing Malawi's Reserve Bank to have a three-month moratorium on repayment of loans for small and medium enterprises. Ten days later, with sixteen COVID-19 cases and two reported deaths ("Malawi Announces Coronavirus Lockdown," 2020), the Minister of Health announced plans to impose a nationwide, twenty-one-day lockdown; notably absent in that public address were any interventions aimed at social protection of the majority of Malawians, who depend on daily access to labor and markets to sustain their households' needs.[6]

Since Lazarus Chakwera took power as Malawi's sixth president in late June 2020, his administration introduced several social protection measures aimed at assisting Malawi's poor. These included a large increase in the number of households to benefit from the agriculture input subsidy program from 1 million households under the Mutharika administration to 3.5 million; doubling of the tax-free monthly income threshold from MWK45,000 (about US$60) to MWK100,000 (about US$135); and an increase from MWK15 billion to MWK40 billion in appropriations for the Malawi Enterprise Development Fund (MEDF) to target youth loans.[7] The new administration has further announced plans to increase the minimum wage from MWK35,000 per month (about US$50) to MWK50,000 (about US$68) (Malawi Government, 2020b).

Response of Average Citizens

Most Malawians had heard of the coronavirus, even when the overall case count was relatively low compared to other countries. In a nationally representative survey conducted between May 23 and June 5, 2020, of 1,346 adults, only one respondent reported having never heard of the coronavirus.[8] When asked how serious the COVID-19 pandemic is for Malawi, 68 percent of respondents said "very serious." Respondents varied in how much they worried about whether they would become infected, with 19 percent not worried at all, 17 percent not worried, 29 percent worried, and 35 percent very worried (Institute for Public Opinion Research [IPOR], 2020).

Compared to the high percentage concerned about the health risk, even more Malawians were concerned about the economic impacts of the COVID-19 pandemic. When asked if they worried that their household's economic situation would be negatively affected by COVID-19, 80 percent of Malawians said they were either worried or very worried. Even more (87 percent of) Malawians reported being worried or very worried about the COVID-19 pandemic's effect on Malawi's economy more generally (IPOR, 2020).

That same survey offers insights into Malawians' willingness to comply with health-promoting behaviors such as social distancing, hand washing, and face masking. Malawians reported that despite the COVID-19 crisis, they were likely to continue engaging in social activities (IPOR, 2020). Banda et al. (2020) found few Malawians were avoiding markets or staying at home, although half of their survey participants reported avoiding crowds. There did seem to be universal uptake on increased handwashing, however (Banda et al., 2020).

Communities and community-based organizations have come together to coordinate efforts to respond to the COVID-19 pandemic. For example, in May 2020, community members in the northern region's capital city Mzuzu fundraised to support a public-access COVID-19 quarantine center on the premises of a private clinic (Jali, 2020). A month later a local Lions Club donated reusable face masks to the Mzuzu Prison to help stop spread among inmates (Chirwa, 2020). The Dzuka Chilomoni Community Organization in Blantyre also distributed various goods, such as face masks and food, to elderly people in the community ("Malawi Youths Engage in Helping Elderly amid COVID-19," 2020). Malawi's daily newspapers reported on similar mutual aid efforts across the country throughout the early epidemic.

Explanations for Malawi's Epidemic and Response

Having described the initial epidemic and response in Malawi, we turn now to describing the health and sociopolitical contexts in which COVID-19 emerged.

Malawi's Health and Social Context

The most recent census estimates Malawi's population at 17,563,749, with a relatively high population density, especially in the southern region (National Statistical Office [NSO], 2019). The high population density as well as the burden of disease in Malawi—still predominated by infectious and preventable diseases such as HIV/AIDS, respiratory infections, and malaria (Institute for Health Metrics and Evaluation, 2015)—may contribute to an increase in or complications from COVID-19, particularly in certain populations with underlying medical conditions, such as HIV/AIDS and tuberculosis. The age distribution in Malawi is characterized by a majority (51 percent) of the population under age eighteen. In the context of COVID-19, the youthful population may have been protective because older people tend to be more at risk for serious complications and death from the virus (Diop et al., 2020).

Education in Malawi is lacking, with most people reporting having attended at least some school, but only 5 percent of females and 9 percent of males reporting having completed secondary education (National Statistical Office [NSO] & ICF, 2017). This has direct implications for health-seeking behavior and knowledge around COVID-19 health promotion efforts, as well as employment opportunities. Additionally, many people have limited media exposure, including radio, newspaper, and television (NSO & ICF, 2017). Together, these factors suggest citizens lack the means to access reliable information to protect their social welfare.

Consistent with the overall impact of COVID-19 elsewhere, the pandemic is worsening Malawi's fragile economic situation. Malawi's gross domestic product (GDP) per capita was estimated at around US$390 in 2018 (World Bank, n.d.), though monthly earnings are reported to be much lower, at a median of $37 (Ministry of Health, 2017). The World Bank (n.d.) estimated that in 2016, 71 percent of Malawians lived on less than US$2 a day. Malawi is dependent on commodity exports, and the COVID-19 pandemic has contributed to reduced demand in the global market for Malawi's main agricultural exports, such as tobacco, tea, cotton, and coffee (Chilundu, 2020). This reduced demand has resulted in an overall contraction of the economy, with a negative growth projection in 2020 of −3.5 percent against the 5.5 percent growth projection before COVID-19 (Chilundu, 2020). Meanwhile, the Malawi Ministry of Finance estimated that COVID-19 will result in a decline in GDP of approximately US$6 billion (Mangazi, 2020).

As an agriculture-based economy, the labor force is heavily skewed, with 59 percent of women and 44 percent of men employed in agriculture, contributing to nearly 30 percent of the country's GDP (NSO & ICF, 2017). Additionally, the International Labor Organization estimates that about 83 percent of total employment in the country is from the informal economy (International Labor Organization, 2019). In response to the most recent Afrobarometer survey in 2017, 68 percent of Malawians said they had no job and were not looking for one, and another 19 percent said they had no job but were looking for one. The high unemployment and underemployment levels make livelihood a high priority for most Malawians. This has been exacerbated during the pandemic, creating strong resistance to the possibility of a lockdown. Opposition to the proposed lockdown is consistent with Malawians' continued prioritization of accessing basic needs over health risks (Dionne, 2018). There were even stampedes when the Ministry of Health held recruitment interviews for COVID-19 response jobs (Masina, 2020b).

Apart from domestic labor, remittances also make up a large portion of the economy because of Malawi's significant emigrant labor force. Because of the youthful population mentioned previously, coupled with the lack of domestic livelihood opportunities, many young people continue to seek employment outside of the country. Most emigration from Malawi remains within the SADC region, with the largest percentage heading to South Africa (Ndegwa, 2015). As described earlier, the repatriation of workers from South Africa and other SADC countries contributed to the initial spike in COVID-19 cases in the country and likely, subsequent community spread.

Malawi's Public Health Infrastructure

Health care in Malawi is delivered in a three-tiered referral system, from primary care at local and district levels to the central hospitals (Ministry of Health, 2017). However, crowding at larger hospitals and a critical shortage of health workers mean the health system is overburdened. In terms of critical care capacity, Malawi had only twenty-five ICU beds spread across the four central hospitals and only sixteen ventilators (Manda-Taylor et al., 2017; Sonenthal et al., 2020). In the context of COVID-19, it was clear that a large outbreak would be impossible to manage within the existing healthcare delivery system, and healthcare workers were concerned about the consequences of a possible outbreak (Vidal, 2020).

Malawi's health sector has experience preparing for and managing prior epidemics. For example, Malawi introduced a comprehensive Ebola prevention and control plan, although they have yet to register a case of Ebola (Kalimira, 2019; Ziba, 2019). Malawi could leverage lessons from the HIV/AIDS response effort over the past twenty years, for example, with boosting testing capacity as they did with HIV and viral load testing, and tracing potential contacts as they did with partner HIV testing. Kavanagh et al. (2020) suggest that African countries—including Malawi—should have the capacity to manage adequate COVID-19 testing based on their HIV testing capacity.

COVID-19 prevention proved challenging in rural, income-poor areas, where the water, sanitation, and hygiene (WASH) capacity of many Malawians is inadequate. Nearly 60 percent of reported handwashing facilities did not have water or soap, making it difficult to exercise basic precautions such as hand washing (NSO & ICF, 2017). Even worse, many health workers contracted COVID-19, further depleting essential healthcare providers from an already shallow pool (Phiri, 2020). Despite these challenges, Malawi has a relatively successful community health system staffed by community health workers (CHWs) known locally as health surveillance assistants (HSAs), who conduct mainly health promotion and disease control activities, making them key human resources for health during a pandemic.[9] This cadre has been educating communities around proper procedures for preventing the spread of COVID-19.

Health spending in Malawi has been unpredictable over the past ten years, largely because of the 2013 "Cashgate" scandal, which led to donor distrust in government and a sharp decline in aid (Adhikari et al., 2019). The government has slowly increased domestic health spending since then but only spends about US$35 per capita (WHO, 2019). Malawi depends significantly on external financing of health, with contributions rising again after the initial shock of Cashgate; about 60 percent of total expenditure comes from donors. Since the outbreak, most of Malawi's donor partners have committed extra funds (or loans, in the case of the IMF) for COVID-19 prevention and control (Cornish, 2020).

Malawi's government faced challenges from within the health system that raised concern about the country's ability to safely handle a large outbreak of the disease. Health workers have gone on strike in Lilongwe and Blantyre because of the lack of personal protective equipment or risk allowance ("Malawi Coronavirus," 2020; Mhango, 2020; Pensulo, 2020b), and they have been stigmatized because of their profession, as fears of the virus spread (Pensulo, 2020c). This makes it more difficult for all cadres of health workers—from clinicians to CHWs—to do their jobs. It has also shed light on the popular perception that leaders are politicizing the pandemic. For example, a medical doctor at Queen Elizabeth Central Hospital in Blantyre, in an interview with *The Telegraph*, stated, "I feel like government is politicising the pandemic and I'm worried that donor funding for responding to COVID-19 might end in politicians' pockets" (Mhango, 2020).

Malawi's Embattled Government during the Early Epidemic

Malawi is a relatively young democracy, having won its independence from British rule in 1964, and reintroducing multiparty electoral competition in 1994. Personalist dictator and president-for-life Hastings Kamuzu Banda ruled Malawi in the intervening three decades. Despite alternations in executive power and increased civil liberties since his departure from office, Banda's dictatorial legacy lives on (Dionne, 2018). Power in Malawi is concentrated in the executive branch, with intermittent checks on overzealous presidents by the judiciary, the legislature, and civil society (Dulani & van Donge, 2005; Posner, 1995; VonDoepp, 2006). The concentration of power in the presidency raises the stakes for presidential elections in Malawi.

Two presidents have led Malawi's response to the COVID-19 pandemic: Mutharika and Chakwera. Mutharika was declared the winner of Malawi's 2019 presidential election on May 27, 2019. Demonstrations from the opposition, alleging foul play and fraud, began within days and continued into 2020 (Dionne & Dulani, 2020; Tostensen, 2019). The Constitutional Court nullified the results in February 2020, calling for a fresh election within 150 days.

The election annulment severely weakened Mutharika's administration and eroded his administration's capacity to mount an effective COVID-19 response. Several decisions made by the Mutharika-appointed Cabinet Committee to lead the anti-COVID-19 efforts were openly ignored by the public (Pensulo, 2020c).[10] With fresh presidential elections looming, political parties embarked on extensive campaigns, complete with rallies that ignored restrictions on public gatherings. Ordinary Malawians and opposition political elites ignored the government's advice on the pandemic, and some openly questioned the existence of COVID-19 cases in the country, casting doubt on the veracity of official figures. For example, former president Joyce Banda alleged that the government was inflating COVID-19 figures to delay elections and attract donor support ("JB Says Malawi Bloating Covid-19 Figures," 2020). Other critics contended that the number of cases was being underreported because of limited testing—only 4,590 COVID-19 tests had been performed by the end of May 2020 (Africa Press Office, 2020).

Although Mutharika made performative efforts to garner support for his government's COVID-19 response plan, the thwarted national lockdown described previously proved a decisive blow to his ability to manage the pandemic. In the absence of clear plans to provide a safety net to support vulnerable households and mitigate the effects of a lockdown, the announcement was met with sporadic outbursts of protests and demonstrations across the country (Pensulo, 2020a). The Human Rights Defenders Coalition (HRDC), a grouping of governance civil society organizations, went to the High Court and sought an injunction against the imposition of a lockdown, which they described as unconstitutional because it curtailed individual freedoms. Further, HRDC argued that in the absence of a social safety net provision to cushion against the effects of a lockdown, the plan would cause severe harm to marginalized and poor citizens. The High Court ruled in favor of HRDC and granted an injunction stopping government from implementing the lockdown (Kasanda, 2020). The politicization of Mutharika's lockdown attempt illustrates how political tensions in Malawi significantly affected the government's early COVID-19 response.

Chakwera's short tenure at the time of this writing offers little opportunity to analyze in depth his administration's COVID-19 response. The Presidential Taskforce on COVID-19 continued its work under the same leadership after Chakwera defeated Mutharika in the fresh elections and took office in June 2020. Cognizant of the risks of exposure, President Chakwera canceled independence day celebrations on July 6, 2020, when he was also to be inaugurated. Instead, a smaller ceremony was held at a military barracks in the capital city of Lilongwe. When infections rose steeply in July 2020, the Presidential Task Force on COVID-19 attempted to institute more restrictive measures. These measures included closing all open markets and pubs and halting religious gatherings. However, the government withdrew those guidelines because of concerns of their legality given the earlier court ruling on restrictive measures proposed by the Mutharika administration (Pasungwi, 2020).

Conclusion

COVID-19 emerged as a threat in Malawi relatively late compared to many other countries studied in this volume. Malawi's tense political context at the time when the pandemic hit the country stifled government response. Despite efforts by the embattled Mutharika administration to enact strict, even draconian, public health policies, low trust in government led to citizen rebellion and ultimately failure to mount an effective response against COVID-19.

Although Malawians celebrated the election of new leadership, infections and deaths rose sharply as the new president, Chakwera, took office. Hamstrung by court orders issued against the previous administration and continued political polarization, Chakwera's new administration struggled to overcome previously failed policies and enforce effective measures against COVID-19. However, Chakwera enjoyed relatively higher levels of public trust compared to Mutharika. In the IPOR survey mentioned previously, 39 percent of Malawians said they found Mutharika trustworthy, ten percentage points lower than the 49 percent who said Chakwera was trustworthy (IPOR, 2020). Chakwera's greater levels of public trust may translate into better observance of COVID-19 regulations introduced by his administration.

Absent the myriad political challenges, Malawi's disease burden and under-resourced health system together still posed serious obstacles to effective COVID-19 response. More important, the overwhelming majority of Malawians relying on daily earnings to cover their families' basic needs required pandemic interventions aimed not just at public health but also social protection. Even as their government struggled, many Malawians demonstrated resilience and offered mutual aid, as they have in previous pandemics and likely will continue to do in the face of ongoing and future crises.

Notes

1. Declaration of State of Disaster by Malawi President Peter Mutharika, March 20, 2020, https://malawi.un.org/en/46778-declaration-state-disaster-malawi-president-peter-mutharika

2. Coronaviruses are a type of virus known to cause respiratory disease. This particular strand of coronavirus has come to be known as COVID-19, or the novel COronaVIrus Disease of 2019. The official name for the virus that causes the disease is SARS-CoV-2.

3. On July 31, the Ministry of Health (2020) reported 875 cases in Lilongwe (Central Region) and 1,227 cases in Blantyre (Southern Region), which together account for 51 percent of Malawi's 4,078 total infections recorded to date.

4. On July 31, the Ministry of Health (2020) reported 202 cases at the Mwanza port of entry.

5. The Cabinet Committee was led by the Minister of Health, Jappie Mhango, and was tasked with overseeing the government's COVID-19 response.

6. Lockdowns are universally difficult to implement, but such difficulties are amplified in low-resource settings, where governments struggle to provide the necessary social safety net (Coetzee & Kagee, 2020).

7. On July 31, 2020, US$1 was equal to MWK742.

8. Likewise, in a phone-based survey that drew disproportionately on Malawians who lived in the northern region, only one respondent in the sample of 630 research participants reported not having heard of COVID-19 before (Banda et al., 2020).

9. HSAs have been integral in earlier pandemic response in Malawi, for example, in undertaking critical roles for the HIV/AIDS crisis (Bemelmans et al., 2010; Smith et al., 2014). Similar CHW cadres have also been critical in pandemic response in other countries (see, e.g., Bhaumik et al., 2020; Boyce & Katz, 2019).

10. Two prominent examples include failing to set up proper quarantine facilities for returned nationals, and attempting a national lockdown without any assurances for social protection.

References

Adhikari, R., Sharma, J. R., Smith, P., & Malata, A. (2019). Foreign aid, Cashgate and trusting relationships amongst stakeholders: Key factors contributing to (mal) functioning of the Malawian health system. *Health Policy and Planning, 34*(3), 197–206.

Africa Center for Strategic Studies. (2020, May 27). *Malawi's year-long election.* Africa Center for Strategic Studies. https://africacenter.org/spotlight/malawi-year-long-election/

Africa Press Office. (2020, May 31). *Coronavirus—Malawi: COVID-19 daily information update.* CNBC Africa. https://www.cnbcafrica.com/africa-press-office/2020/06/01/coronavirus-malawi-covid-19-daily-information-update-31-may-2020/

Anna, C. (2020, April 2). *Africa faces an "existential threat" as virus cases spread.* AP News. https://apnews.com/article/cc93493a99a3128519bd826fc3915f33

Arriola, L., & Namias Grossman, A. (in press). Ethnic marginalization and (non)compliance in public health emergencies. *Journal of Politics.*

Banda, J., Dube, A., Brumfield, S., Amoah, A., Crampin, A., Reniers, G., & Helleringer, S. (in press). Knowledge and behaviors related to the COVID-19 pandemic in Malawi. *medRxiv.*

Bariyo, N., & Parkinson, J. (2020, August 20). In the world's coronavirus blind spot, fears of a silent epidemic. *Wall Street Journal.* https://www.wsj.com/articles/in-the-worlds-coronavirus-blind-spot-fears-of-a-silent-epidemic-11598806800

Baskar, P. (2020, September 25). *Why the pandemic could change the way we record deaths.* NPR. https://www.npr.org/sections/goatsandsoda/2020/09/25/914073217/why-the-pandemic-could-change-the-way-we-record-deaths

Bemelmans, M., van den Akker, T., Ford, N., Philips, M., Zachariah, R., Harries, A., Schouten, E., Hermann, K., Mwangomba, B., & Massaquoi, M. (2010). Providing universal access to antiretroviral therapy in Thyolo, Malawi through task shifting and decentralization of HIV/AIDS care. *Tropical Medicine and International Health, 15*(12), 1413–1420.

Bhaumik, S., Moola, S., Tyagi, J., Nambiar, D., & Kakoti, M. (2020). Community health workers for pandemic response: a rapid evidence synthesis. *BMJ Global Health,* 5:e002769.

Blair, R. A., Morse, B. S., & Tsai, L. L. (2017). Public health and public trust: Survey evidence from the Ebola virus disease epidemic in Liberia. *Social Science & Medicine, 172,* 89–97.

Boyce, M. R., & Katz, R. Community health workers and pandemic preparedness: Current and prospective roles. *Frontiers in Public Health, 7*(62).

Chilundu, S. (2020, July 22). Covid-19 dampens Cash crops' prospects. *The Nation.* https://www.mwnation.com/covid-19-dampens-cash-crops-prospects/

Chirwa, J. (2020, June 15). Mzuzu Prison inmates get reusable face masks. *The Nation.* https://www.mwnation.com/mzuzu-prison-inmates-get-reusable-face-masks/

Coetzee, B. J., & Kagee, A. (2020). Structural barriers to adhering to health behaviours in the context of the COVID-19 crisis: Considerations for low- and middle-income countries, *Global Public Health, 15*(8), 1093–1102.

Cornish, L. (2020). *Who's funding the COVID-19 response and what are the priorities?* Devex Interactive. https://www.devex.com/news/sponsored/interactive-who-s-funding-the-covid-19-response-and-what-are-the-priorities-96833

Dionne, K. Y. (2018). *Doomed interventions: The failure of global responses to AIDS in Africa.* Cambridge University Press.

Dionne, K. Y., & Dulani, B. (2020, February 4). A Malawi court just ordered a do-over presidential election. Here's what you need to know. *The Washington Post.* https://www.washingtonpost.com/politics/2020/02/04/malawi-court-just-ordered-do-over-presidential-election-heres-what-you-need-know/

Dionne, K. Y., & Poulin, M. (2013). Ethnic identity, region and attitudes towards male circumcision in a high HIV-prevalence country. *Global Public Health, 8*(5), 607–618.

Diop, B. Z., Ngom, M., Pougué Biyong, C., & Pougué Biyong, J. N. (2020). The relatively young and rural population may limit the spread and severity of COVID-19 in Africa: a modelling study. *BMJ Global Health, 5,* e002699.

Dulani, B., & van Donge, J. K. (2005). A decade of legislature-executive squabble in Malawi, 1994–2004. In M. Salih (Ed.), *African parliaments: Between governance and government* (pp. 201–224). Palgrave Macmillan.

Evans, R. (2020, May). *With Malawi against COVID-19: The challenges.* Healthy Developments. http://health.bmz.de/events/In_focus/with-malawi-against-covid19/index.html

Gondwe, G. (2019, June 6). *Tear gas as US ambassador meets Malawi opposition leader.* AP News. https://apnews.com/31eefb33055a4c639e830490af6b4616

Institute for Health Metrics and Evaluation. (2015). *Health data: Malawi.* Institute for Health Metrics and Evaluation. Retrieved May 28, 2020, from http://www.healthdata.org/malawi

Institute for Public Opinion Research. (2020). *Malawi 2020 COVID-19 Survey: Final Report.* Institute for Public Opinion Research.

International Labor Organization. (2019). Interactions between Workers' Organizations and workers in the informal economy: A compendium of practice. International Labor Organization. https://www.ilo.org/wcmsp5/groups/public/—ed_protect/—protrav/—travail/documents/publication/wcms_735630.pdf

Jali, P. (2020, May 18). Communities raise K10m for COVID-19 quarantine. *The Nation.* https://www.mwnation.com/communities-raise-k10m-for-covid-19-quarantine/

JB says Malawi govt bloating Covid-19 figures. (2020, May 26). Zodiak Online. https://www.zodiakmalawi.com/nw/national-news/66-news-in-southern-region/1866-jb-says-malawi-govt-bloating-covid-19-figures

Kalimira, S. (2019, November 7). Government develops Ebola prevention strategy. *Daily Times* [Malawi]. https://times.mw/government-develops-ebola-prevention-strategy/

Kanyuka, M., et al. (2016). Malawi and Millennium Development Goal 4: A countdown to 2015 country case study. *The Lancet Global Health, 4*(3), e201–214.

Kao, K., Lust, E., Dulani, B., Ferree, K., Harris, A., & Metheney, E. (2021). The ABCs of Covid-19 prevention in Malawi: Authority, benefits, and costs of compliance, *World Development,* 137. https://doi.org/10.1016/j.worlddev.2020.105167

Kasanda, M. (2020, April 18). No lockdown: Day of protests as High Court grants 7-day injunction. *Daily Times.* https://times.mw/no-lockdown/

Kavanagh, M. M., Frondu, N. A., Tomori, O., Dzau, V. J., Okiro, E. A., Maleche, A., Aniebo, I. C., Rugege, U., Holmes, C. B., & Gostin, L. O. (2020). Access to lifesaving medical resources for African Countries: COVID-19 testing and response, ethics, and politics. *The Lancet, 395,* 1735–1738. https://www.thelancet.com/journals/lancet/article/PIIS0140-6736(20)31093-X/abstract

Lieberman, E. (2006). *Boundaries of contagion.* Princeton University Press.

Lunda, P. (2020, July 14). Government entities, others toughen Covid-19 measures. *Daily Times.* https://times.mw/government-entities-others-toughen-covid-19-measures/

Makwero, M. T. (2018). Delivery of primary health care in Malawi. *African Journal of Primary Health Care & Family Medicine, 10*(1). https://www.ncbi.nlm.nih.gov/pmc/articles/PMC6018651/

Malawi announces coronavirus lockdown. (2020, April 15). Al Jazeera. https://www.aljazeera.com/news/2020/04/malawi-announces-coronavirus-lockdown-200415160641669.html

Malawi coronavirus: Health workers protest over risk allowance. (2020, April 21). Africanews. https://www.africanews.com/2020/04/21/malawi-coronavirus-health-workers-protest-over-risk-allowance/

Malawi Government. (2020a). *National COVID-19 preparedness and response plan: March-June 2020.* https://reliefweb.int/report/malawi/national-covid-19-preparedness-and-response-plan-march-june-2020

Malawi Government. (2020b). *Provisional budget statement 2020-2021 financial year.* Zomba. Government Printer.

Malawi Ministers Mhango, Botomani caught lying on Covid-19 allowances. (2020, April 28). *Maravi Post.* https://www.maravipost.com/malawi-ministers-mhango-botomani-caught-lying-on-covid-19-allowances/

Malawi Ministry of Health. (2020, July 31). *COVID-19 statistics.* [Infographic]. Facebook. https://www.facebook.com/malawimoh/

Malawi youths engage in helping elderly amid COVID-19. (2020, July 20). XinhuaNet. http://www.xinhuanet.com/english/2020-07/20/c_139227074.htm

Manda-Taylor, L., Mndolo, S., & Baker, T. (2017). Critical care in Malawi: The ethics of beneficence and justice. *Malawi Medical Journal, 29*(3), 268–271.

Mangazi, C. (2020, July 24). Economy to lose K5 trillion to Covid-19. *Daily Times.* https://times.mw/economy-to-lose-k5-trillion-to-covid-19/

Masina, L. (2020a, May 28). 400 Migrant workers escape from COVID-19 screening camp in Malawi. *Voice of America.* https://www.voanews.com/covid-19-pandemic/400-migrant-workers-escape-covid-19-screening-camp-malawi

Masina, L. (2020b, June 10). Malawi job seekers injured in stampede for interviews. *Voice of America.* https://www.voanews.com/africa/malawi-job-seekers-injured-stampede-interviews

Matonga, G. (2020, April 28). Ministers, MPs, get COVID-19 allowances. *The Nation.* https://www.mwnation.com/ministers-mps-get-covid-19-allowances/

Mhango, H. (2020, April 24). Malawi's public hospitals close as medics strike over lack of funding for COVID-19. *The Telegraph.* https://www.telegraph.co.uk/global-health/science-and-disease/malawis-public-hospitals-close-medics-strike-lack-funding-covid/

Ministry of Health [Malawi]. (2017). *Health Sector Strategic Plan II (2017-2022).* Ministry of Health, Government of the Republic of Malawi.

Ministry of Health [Malawi]. (2020). *COVID-19 national information dashboard.* https://covid19.health.gov.mw

Mkweu, J. (2020). Government for mandatory use of face masks. *Daily Times.* https://times.mw/government-for-mandatory-use-of-face-masks/

Munthali, G., & Wu, X. (2020). Covid-19 outbreak on Malawi perspective. *Electronic Journal of General Medicine, 17*(4). https://doi.org/10.29333/ejgm/7871

National Statistical Office (NSO) [Malawi], & ICF. (2017). *Malawi Demographic and Health Survey 2015-16.* Zomba, Malawi, and Rockville, Maryland, USA.

National Statistical Office (NSO) [Malawi]. (2019). *2018 Malawi Population and Housing Census Main Report.* http://www.nsomalawi.mw/index.php%3Foption%3Dcom_content%26view%3Darticle%26id%3D226:2018-malawi-population-and-housing-census%26catid%E2%80%89%3D%E2%80%898·reports%26Itemid%E2%80%89%3D%E2%80%896

Ndegwa, D. (2015). *Migration in Malawi: A country profile 2014.* International Organization for Migration (IOM). https://publications.iom.int/system/files/pdf/mp_malawi.pdf

Nebehay, S. (2020). *Africa's Coronavirus 'hotspots' in South Africa, Algeria, Cameroon: WHO.* Reuters. https://www.reuters.com/article/us-health-coronavirus-africa-hotspots-idUSKBN23I1H9

Pasungwi, J. (2020, July 21). Covid test kits arrive today. *The Nation* [Malawi]. https://www.mwnation.com/covid-test-kits-arrive-today/

Pensulo, C. (2020a, April 21). *Of protests and polls: Malawi's very political pandemic.* African Arguments. https://africanarguments.org/2020/04/21/malawi-political-pandemic-protests-coronavirus-lockdown/

Pensulo, C. (2020b, April 14). *Malawi health workers protest against lack of protective gear.* Al Jazeera. https://www.aljazeera.com/news/2020/04/malawi-health-workers-protest-lack-protective-gear-200414165616071.html

Pensulo, C. (2020c, May 13). Coronavirus leaves Malawi's health workers facing threats and social stigma. *The Guardian*. http://www.theguardian.com/world/2020/may/13/coronavirus-leaves-malawis-health-workers-facing-threats-and-social-stigma

Pensulo, C. (2020d). Why are Malawian leaders holding mass rallies amid COVID-19? *Ubuntu Times*. https://www.ubuntutimes.com/why-are-malawian-leaders-holding-mass-rallies-amid-covid-19/

Phiri, F. (2020, July 24). 17 HSAs test positive for Covid-19 in Mchinji. *The Nation* [Malawi]. https://www.mwnation.com/17-hsas-test-positive-for-covid-19-in-mchinji/

Posner, D. N. (1995). Malawi's new dawn. *Journal of Democracy, 6*(1), 131–144.

Posner, D. N. (2004). The political salience of cultural difference: Why Chewas and Tumbukas are allies in Zambia and adversaries in Malawi. *American Political Science Review, 98*(4), 529–545.

Presidential Task Force on COVID-19: Mutharika hires 21 member team. (2020, May 7). MBC Online. https://www.mbc.mw/news/entertainment/item/9387-presidential-task-force-on-covid-19-mutharika-hires-21-member-team

Protect yourself, protect others. Wear a mask. Covid-19 is real. (2020, July 31). *The Nation*.

Public Health Institute of Malawi. (2020). *Malawi COVID-19 Daily Situation Report*. Lilongwe, Malawi.

Reuters. (2020, June 12). Malawi 2020 GDP to shrink if coronavirus persists, Finance Minister says. *The New York Times*. https://www.nytimes.com/reuters/2020/06/12/world/africa/12reuters-health-coronavirus-malawi-budget.html

Smith, S., Deveridge, A., Berman, J., Negin, J., Mwambene, N., Chingaipe, E., Puchalski Ritchie, L. M., & Martiniuk, A. (2014). Task-shifting and prioritization: A situational analysis examining the role and experiences of community health workers in Malawi, *Human Resources for Health, 12*(1), 24.

Sonenthal, P. D., Masiye, J., Kasomekera, N., Marsh, R. H., Wroe, E. B., Scott, K. W., Li, R., Murray, M. B., Bukhman, A., Connolly, E., Minyaliwa, T., Katete, M., Banda, G., Nyirenda, M., & Rouhani, S. A. (2020). COVID-19 preparedness in Malawi: A national facility-based critical care assessment. *The Lancet Global Health, 8*(7), E890–E892.

Tostensen, A. (2019). The Tipp-Ex election: Widespread unrest after the 2019 elections in Malawi. *CMI Blogpost*. https://www.cmi.no/publications/7252-the-tipp-ex-election-widespread-unrest-after-the-2019-elections-in-malawi

Twea, B. (2020, July 24). Malawi Gets 38 000 Covid-19 test kits. *The Nation* [Malawi]. https://www.mwnation.com/malawi-gets-38-000-covid-19-test-kits/

Vidal, J. (2020). "If it comes, it will overwhelm us": Malawi braces for coronavirus. *The Guardian*. https://www.theguardian.com/global-development/2020/apr/03/if-it-comes-it-will-overwhelm-us-malawi-braces-for-coronavirus

Vinck, P., Pham, P. N., Bindu, K. K., Bedford, J., & Nilles, E. J. (2019). Institutional trust and misinformation in the response to the 2018–19 Ebola outbreak in North Kivu, DR Congo: A population-based survey. *The Lancet Infectious Diseases, 19*(5), 529–536.

VonDoepp, P. (2006). Politics and judicial assertiveness in emerging democracies: High Court behavior in Malawi and Zambia. *Political Research Quarterly, 59*(3), 389–399.

World Bank. (n.d). *Malawi data*. Retrieved June 18, 2020, from https://data.worldbank.org/country/malawi?view=chart

World Health Organization. (2019). *Global health expenditure database.* World Health Organization Global Health Observatory Data Repository. Retrieved June 2, 2020, from https://apps.who.int/nha/database/ViewData/Indicators/en

Ziba, T. (2019, November 11). Minister highlights need for Malawi to stay prepared for Ebola Disease. *Malawi News Agency (MANA).* https://www.manaonline.gov.mw/index.php/component/k2/item/13530-minister-highlights-need-for-malawi-to-stay-prepared-for-ebola-disease

31 ADAPTING COVID-19 CONTAINMENT IN AFRICA

Lessons from Tanzania

Thespina (Nina) Yamanis, Ruth Carlitz, and Henry A. Mollel

Africa's first case of COVID-19 was recorded in Egypt on February 14, 2020. After that, the virus spread rapidly throughout the continent, with all fifty-four African states reporting confirmed cases just three months later (Cocks, 2020). However, the responses of African country governments were far from uniform. Figure 31.1 depicts the average stringency of government responses across all countries during the first seven months of the pandemic. This is a composite measure tracking policies such school closures, workplace closures, and travel bans, rescaled to a value from 0 to 100 (100 = strictest). We see the range from full-scale lockdowns (e.g., Angola, Rwanda, South Africa) to much more limited intervention (e.g., Zambia and Tanzania).

Furthermore, there is considerable variation *within* countries in terms of how local authorities interpreted guidelines from their governments and international organizations and adapted them to the local context. This chapter explores local efforts to control and mitigate the pandemic to provide a comprehensive picture of Tanzania's response.

Tanzania confirmed its first COVID-19 case on March 16, 2020: a Tanzanian woman who traveled to Belgium. The government responded quickly as additional cases were reported, closing schools and universities and developing a contact-tracing and testing system, designed based on previous experiences with Ebola (Taylor, 2020). Nevertheless, cases continued to rise, as shown in Figure 31.2.

The figure suggests a remarkable turnaround in controlling the spread of disease, and indeed Tanzania's President John Pombe Magufuli declared victory against coronavirus at the end of May (Sguazzin, 2020). However, such a claim is difficult to assess given that, as of this writing, Tanzania has not published nationwide surveillance data since May 8, 2020, when the country recorded 509 cases and 21 deaths. On May 13, 2020, the US Embassy warned its citizens to stay home except for essential activities because the risk of contracting COVID-19 in Dar es Salaam, Tanzania's commercial capital, was very high (US Embassy in Tanzania, 2020). However, the Tanzanian government did not issue a national stay-at-

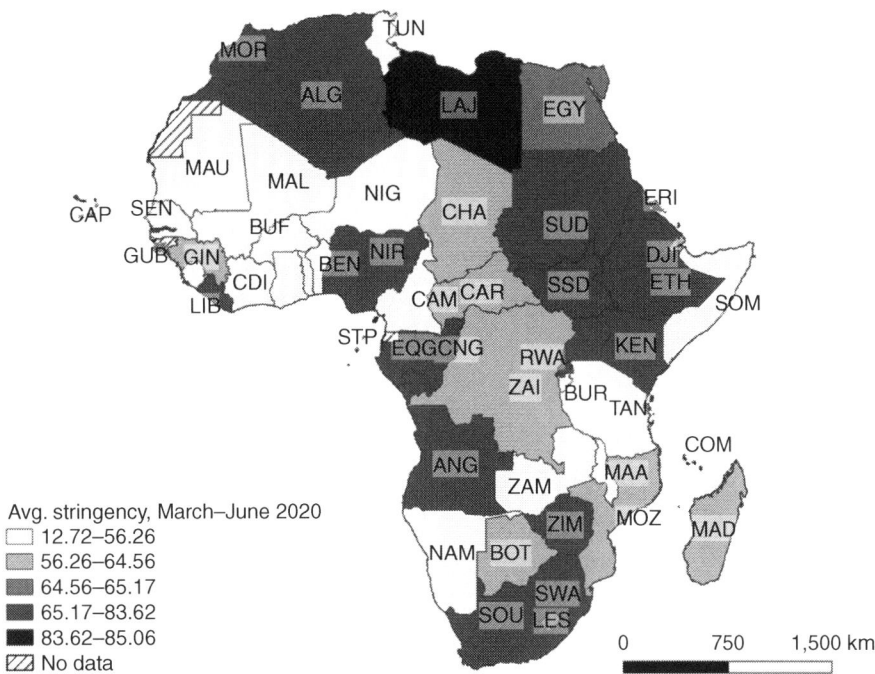

Figure 31.1. Stringency of African government responses (March to June 2020).
Source: Data from Oxford COVID-19 Government Response Tracker (Hale et al., 2020).

home policy, and Tanzanian citizens largely went about their daily lives. Indeed, Figure 31.3 suggests that patterns of mobility to workplaces had not changed considerably.[1]

Tanzania's response to COVID-19 can be understood in part as reflecting the governance challenges facing many African countries. The 58 million residents of East Africa's largest and most populous country are spread over a range of climatic zones and inhabit a variety of settlements. Tanzania has a healthcare worker shortage, and those living in urban areas have better access to health care than those in rural areas (West-Slevin et al., 2015). About one-third of the population lives in urban areas—with denser settlements along the coast and Northern regions (Figure 31.4). According to recent estimates, over half of these urban dwellers reside in informal settlements (Ministry of Lands, Housing and Human Settlements Development, 2016), where widespread community physical distancing measures may be impractical (Africa Centres for Disease Control and Prevention, 2020). The country has sustained relatively high economic growth in recent years and as of July 1, 2020, the World Bank reclassified Tanzania as a lower-middle income economy based on its Gross National Income per capita of US$1,080 (Serajuddin & Hamadeh, 2020). However, nearly half of the country's population lives on less than $1.90 per day.

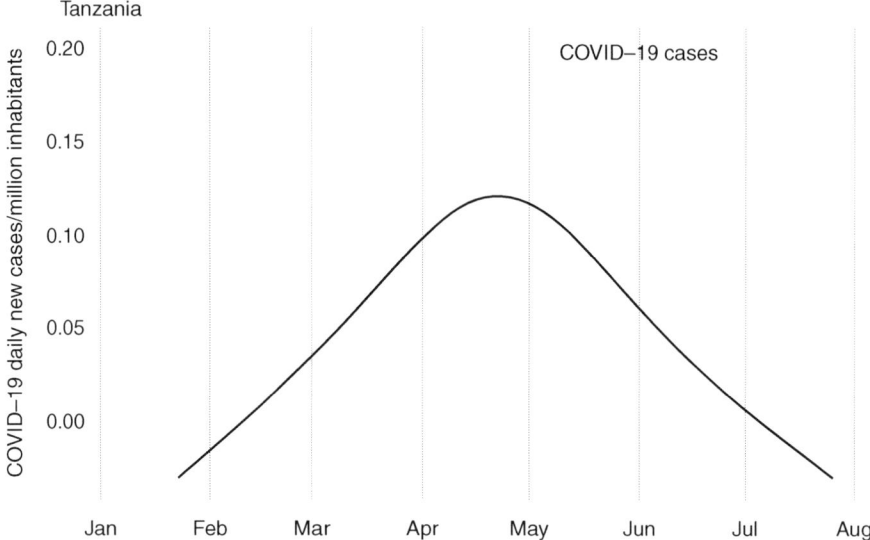

Figure 31.2. COVID-19 cases.
Source: Data on COVID-19 cases has been compiled by the Johns Hopkins University Center for Systems Science and Engineering (Dong et al., 2020).

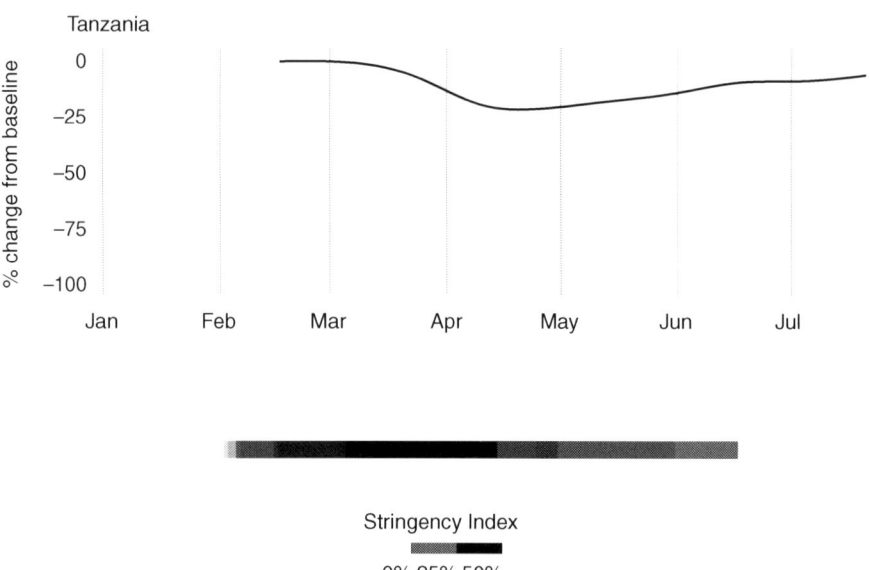

Figure 31.3. Mobility changes (workplaces) and stringency index.
Source: Mobility data from Google Mobility Reports (Google LLC, 2020); Stringency Index from Oxford COVID-19 Government Response Tracker (Hale et al., 2020).

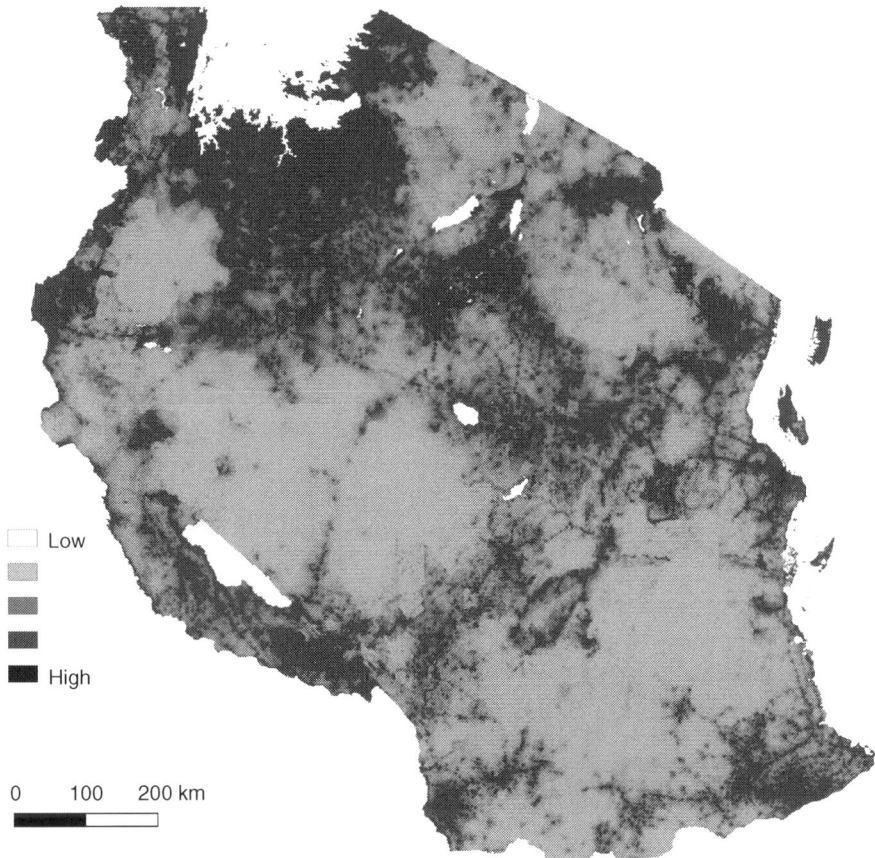

Figure 31.4. Tanzania population density.
Source: WorldPop (2020).

Tanzania's response to COVID-19 also reflects the country's political settlement. Although multi-party politics were legalized in 1992, the ruling Chama cha Mapinduzi (CCM) party has maintained a firm grip on power, and there is little separation between party and state (Morse, 2014, 2018). In 2015 the current president, John Pombe Magufuli, was elected with 58 percent of the vote. Although Magufuli has been praised for clamping down on corruption, improving public administration, and more efficiently managing public resources (World Bank, 2019), others point to backsliding with respect to various aspects of democracy (Carlitz & Manda, 2016; Manda, 2017; Paget, 2017).

In considering Tanzania's response to COVID-19, it is also important to understand the nature of decentralized governance in the country. Despite the adoption of a decentralization policy in 1998 (United Republic of Tanzania [URT], 1998) aimed at creating autonomous local government institutions, the reliance of local governments on the central government remains high (Mollel, 2010). Thus, although local governments deliver health services and employ health workers at the district level and below, all staff must be selected and approved centrally (Hutchinson, 2002). Nevertheless, local governments have the authority to interpret and implement national policies. Regional health management teams supervise and mentor district councils, who directly implement national guidelines (Kapologwe et al., 2019). Thus, the response to COVID-19 is heavily influenced by central government ministries. However, the adaptation of national guidelines can still vary based on local context.

We explore the nature and extent of local adaptation through a series of interviews with local officials in July 2020 in four purposefully selected regions[2]: Dar es Salaam, Dodoma, Morogoro, and Arusha. We selected these four regions because they vary with respect to population density and, thus, potential to spread COVID-19. Dodoma is the nation's capital, but, because it consists of mostly government buildings, it is not very dense in terms of population. Dar es Salaam is the commercial capital and is thus very dense. Morogoro is an area with substantial agricultural production and is not very dense. Arusha is a tourist region with mountains and national parks, and, as such, is not very dense.

We selected three different types of local officials to interview: (1) regional level officers, such as members of regional health management and referral hospitals who were involved in the implementation of response to COVID-19; (2) district level officers, including social welfare and medical officers; and (3) local officials at ward (urban)/village (rural), or *mtaa* ("street," i.e., urban) levels who were involved in the implementation of response to COVID-19. We interviewed a total of forty officials. We asked each respondent about the guidelines they received to respond to COVID-19, what activities they implemented, challenges to implementation, adaptations they made, and lessons learned. Our protocol was approved by the President's Office Regional Administration and Local Government as well as the Office of the Vice Chancellor at Mzumbe University.

This chapter proceeds as follows. We first present an overview of Tanzania's health and social policy measures in response to COVID-19 (the next two sections). We then present our explanation for the policies, including Tanzania's limited fiscal space, the president's attempts to minimize fear and obstruct public access to information, and, finally, the responsibility taken up by local officials to protect their communities (the final section). We conclude with a call for more research exploring local adaptations to COVID-19 policy measures, particularly under decentralized and authoritarian regimes.

Health Policy Measures

Federal Response (2020)

On March 17, 2020, the Tanzanian government banned all forms of public gatherings, including sports activities, and closed all schools ("Tanzania Bans All Public Gatherings, Closes Schools, Suspends the Premier League over Coronavirus," 2020). Beginning March 23, 2020, international travelers arriving in Tanzania from

COVID-19-affected countries were required to undergo and pay for fourteen days of quarantine in designated hotels (Taylor, 2020). Unlike its neighbors Kenya and Malawi, Tanzania did not close its borders. Nevertheless, on April 11, 2020, the Tanzanian Civil Aviation Authority suspended all international passenger, chartered, and private aircraft inbound flights (US Department of State OSAC, 2020).

In March 2020 the Ministry of Health, Community Development, Gender, Elderly and Children (MoHCDGEC) issued a series of standard operating procedures (SOPs) to respond to COVID-19 (MoHCDGEC, 2020). The SOPs detailed how health facilities should screen and isolate patients with suspected COVID-19, including setting up a treatment unit. The SOPs recommended that all patients entering health facilities be screened for COVID-19. If the case definition of COVID-19 was met, the patient should be given a mask and sent to an isolation area. Staff were to use PPE to check on isolated patients. Based on guidance from the WHO, the SOPs included instructions on how to properly don PPE and decontaminate isolation rooms. They also included instructions for quarantining confirmed cases at home or in hotels and minimizing exposure for household members or hotel workers. There was an SOP for providing psychosocial support to individuals affected by COVID-19 by reducing stress and addressing stigma and discrimination. Moreover, an SOP described how to provide a safe and dignified burial, including using PPE to transport the deceased person to a body bag and burial site (Figure 31.5).

The SOPs detailed protocols for community-based prevention efforts, including hand hygiene. Within communities, individuals were instructed to "maintain distance of at least 1 meter from any individual with respiratory symptoms (e.g., coughing, sneezing); perform hand hygiene frequently; and cover nose and mouth with flexed elbow or paper tissue when coughing or sneezing" (MoHCDGEC, 2020, p. 68). Masks were not required for non-sick persons. Within the MoHCDGEC SOPs, physical distancing was mentioned in the context of health care, isolation, and burials. This is in contrast to the Africa Centre for Disease Control and Prevention (CDC), which recommended that, to reduce transmission, communities should engage in physical distancing of one meter between people as soon as community transmission is evident (Africa CDC, 2020).

Many of the aforementioned public health guidelines were compromised by President Magufuli's actions. On May 3, 2020, President Magufuli suspended the head of the national laboratory and called for an investigation into faulty COVID-19 tests ("Tanzania Suspends Laboratory Head after President Questions Coronavirus Tests," 2020). On May 19, 2020, the Tanzania Civil Aviation Authority opened up its air space and allowed international flights. President Magufuli declared Tanzania COVID-19-free on May 22, 2020, and ordered students to return to schools in June.

Local Adaptation of Health Policy Measures

Our interviews revealed how these actions played out at the local level. Interview respondents stated that they received the MoHCDGEC SOPs through leaflets,

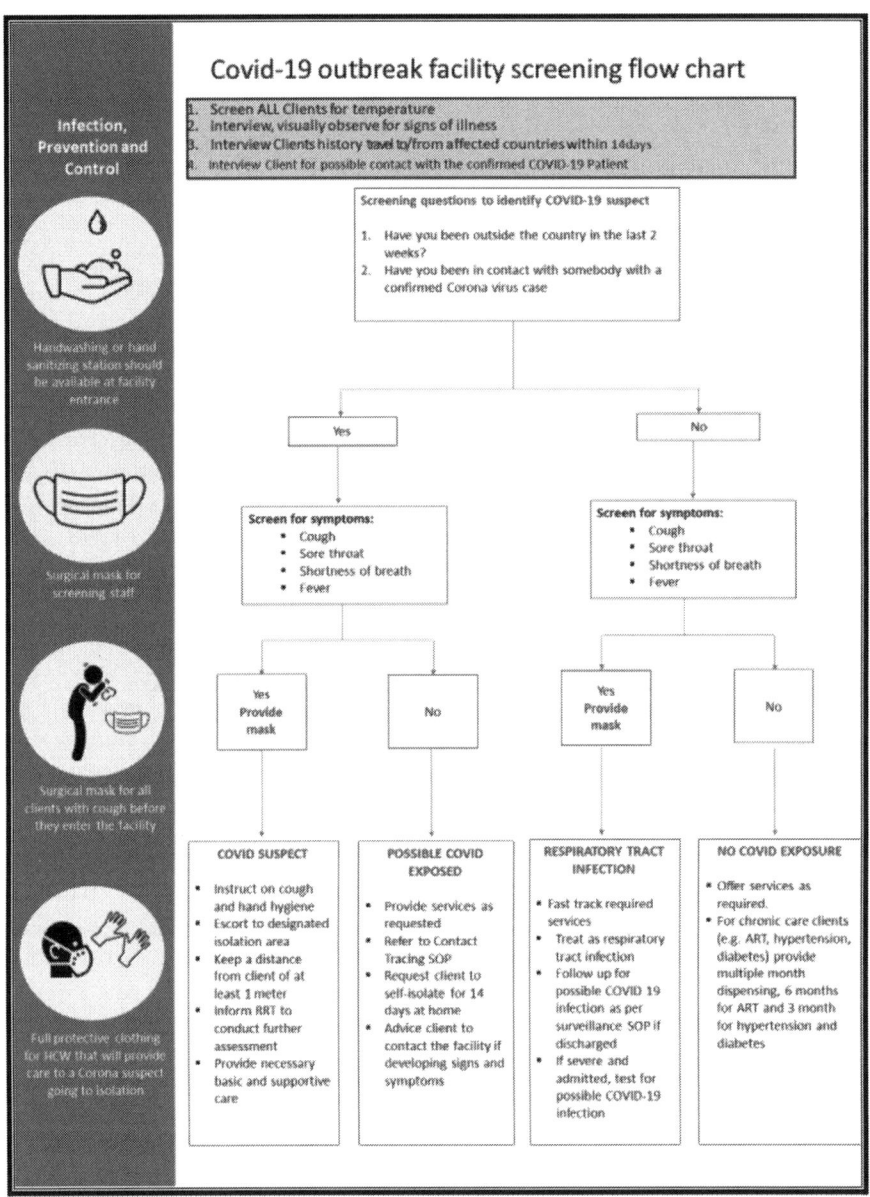

Figure 31.5. Image from Tanzania's MoHCDGEC *Standard Operating Procedures (SOPs) for case management and infection, prevention and control*, March, 2020, page 4. *Source:* Ministry of Health, Community Development, Gender, Elderly and Children (2020).

Figure 31.6. Tweet discussing President Magufuli's refusal to lockdown Dar es Salaam, April 22, 2020. (This tweet shows a statement made by President Magufuli. The statement translates as: "There are those giving their opinion to lockdown DSM [Dar es Salaam]. That is totally impossible. DSM is a center where a large percent of the national income is obtained. It has a population of six million. We cannot lock them down. Then, tomorrow, they will ask that we lock down Mwanza. No. We cannot lockdown Dar es Salaam.")
Source: Ayo (2020).

email, and WhatsApp. The district executive officer passed information to the ward and street officers, who then disseminated information to the community though public meetings. Respondents reported receiving guidance on the following: (1) surveillance; (2) case management; (3) health promotion/public education; (4) handwashing; (5) testing; (6) emergency preparedness; (7) handling of travelers; and (8) laboratory.

Nearly all respondents engaged in public education about the virus. One regional health official (respondent 22) indicated they reached the public through different platforms such as radio and TV. A community social welfare officer (24) conducted community education at bars, churches, mosques, and food vending places. Several respondents across levels (13, 14, 18, 21, 29) mentioned using microphones or public address (PA) systems to reach communities in the wards. They encouraged the public to engage in prevention behaviors, including hand washing, physical distancing, and mask wearing, and to help lower stigma of coronavirus patients. One respondent (14) mentioned involving other stakeholders, who provided PA systems, leaflets, and brochures. These stakeholders included the Red Cross and the Mkapa Foundation, who provided trained community health workers to conduct contact tracing.

Respondents reported conducting contact tracing, surveillance, case management, sample collection, and testing (10, 16, 38, 41, 43). They coordinated with different teams within and outside the regional hospital and mobilized necessary supplies. In conducting this work, respondents indicated that they drew on their prior experience managing epidemics such as cholera and tuberculosis.

Several respondents played a role in coordinating logistics for isolated or suspected COVID-19 patients (21, 24, 25, 33, 44, 46). For these people, respondents provided food delivery, transport to the health center, and follow-up with family members to check on children. District health officers in collaboration with community social welfare workers provided counseling and support to lower fear and stress during the fourteen days of mandatory isolation. These officials also organized visitations by faith leaders to help with spiritual counseling. They worked together with faith leaders to encourage coronavirus patients to have faith in recovery and not to fear to death.

Local Challenges to Adhering to Public Health Guidelines

Respondents mentioned several challenges they faced adhering to the guidelines. They stated that community members had difficulty maintaining physical distancing of one meter as recommended by the Africa CDC (Africa CDC, 2020). This was especially difficult in public transportation facilities (21), as well as congested places such as general markets and livestock markets (22). Some respondents claimed that citizens were deliberately ignoring the guidelines. One respondent stated that community members had difficulty "avoiding social gatherings in refreshment areas like bars. They shared local drinks in the clubs which is dangerous for spreading the coronavirus" (20). Respondents also mentioned the challenge in preventing gatherings during burials. As one respondent stated, "Based on traditional values, many people were still turning out in large numbers for burial services" (26).

Isolating coronavirus patients was also a significant challenge. Several respondents mentioned that there was insufficient space to isolate them (12, 21) and that the facilities were not designed to admit patients (13, 18, 11, 15). Some of the facilities lacked a self-contained room and toilet, leaving patients to share public toilets (13). There were poor waste management and food insecurity in the isolation centers (15). Respondents stated that there had been poor planning for food (12, 15). Given these miserable conditions, some people tried to escape isolation (18). Isolation centers were operational from April 5 until June 23, 2020, when all the isolation centers were closed (Taylor, 2020).

Nearly all respondents mentioned that community members expressed fear of the coronavirus. As one respondent stated, "(COVID-19) is a new experience to deal with, and requires building courage" (23). Another respondent (14) mentioned that a common challenge was that many people were afraid that if they tested positive they would not recover. Similarly, people were fearful to quarantine because of the low quality of the isolation centers and the need to leave their businesses and family.

Many respondents mentioned they would have liked more time to raise community awareness and combat fear of the virus. One respondent mentioned they were only given few minutes while visiting patients to explain their roles and what families should do (24). A few respondents mentioned would have liked to tailor their education strategies for different groups (children, disabled, and elderly) to take into account cultural values and practices.

A concern related to fear was stigma. Respondents reported that those who were diagnosed with coronavirus, or those who traveled from highly affected areas such as Dar es Salaam (25), suffered stigma from family and community members. Social welfare officers reported that the requirement for them to keep a distance from a patient or wear PPE made the patients feel stigmatized. Stigma resulted in some people who were diagnosed with the coronavirus to not want to disclose their diagnosis. As one respondent stated, "Stigmatization has huge impacts and can result into big fear to patients with so much psychological suffering that can trigger other health problems such as increasing in level of blood pressure and diabetes" (24). Respondents expressed that they also faced stigma because they worked on coronavirus issues, causing "family social challenges" (15).

COVID-19 surveillance was also a major challenge. Respondents complained that testing results were delayed or never processed by the national laboratory (13, 41, 44). They said that the laboratory took one to two weeks to deliver results. Another respondent mentioned that sometimes the laboratory results were confusing in that "a patient tested negative while he/she had critical signs" (11). One respondent mentioned that "delayed or not returned results affected the patients psychologically and created verbal fights with health personnel" (25). Another mentioned that surveillance officers were not appropriately persuasive when speaking with communities, resulting in little cooperation among community members (33).

A related challenge was dealing with travelers with suspected diagnoses of COVID-19. A respondent acknowledged that some citizens were hosting travelers from different locations, making it easier for the coronavirus to spread. One respondent (22) mentioned that "this was challenging because there was no guidance on what should be done in case a traveler is found with high temperature. Similarly, stopping travelers for body temperature testing also delayed their schedules."

Respondents also described the public not taking the coronavirus seriously as a challenge (11, 25, 34, 35, 37, 38, 44, 47, 49). One respondent described "community negligence thinking the disease.. only attacks . . . mostly white skinned and rich people" (25). Several described citizens ignoring advice about hand washing and wearing masks (25, 34, 47). Citizens complained that masks were uncomfortable and too expensive.

Twenty-five respondents mentioned the lack of supplies and resources as a major challenge to practically implementing the health guidelines: "We have few human and financial resources which constrain our ability to execute the tasks specified in the health guidance" (21). Respondents mentioned not having enough PPE for health workers who were treating COVID-19 patients. They stated that they had trouble procuring supplies. As one respondent stated, "We depend on a single government system of purchasing all facilities from Medical Store Department (MSD). We have few licensed private supplies which results in inconveniences and delay in delivery of supplies" (21).

Respondents mentioned the lack of resources for prevention activities, including lack of water, masks, gloves, and hand sanitizers. They also cited lacking personnel, transportation, and communication funds to contact trace. In terms of how to respond to such an enormous challenge, several respondents suggested that local officials should have been given the mandate or authority to develop their own guidelines "since we know our environment and people better. It wasn't proper for the ministry to develop generic guidelines" (10).

Social Policy Measures

In keeping with the limited federal response to COVID-19, Tanzania has not implemented any major social policies such as income support or debt/contract relief, and the government has not announced any economic stimulus spending (Hale et al., 2020). Rather, there has been more of an emphasis on overall health and well-being to build immunity. For instance, the MoHCDGEC SOP included nutrition advice for patients with COVID-19, noting, "People who eat a well-balanced diet tend to be healthier with stronger immune systems and lower risk of chronic illnesses and infectious diseases" (2020). However, some respondents noted challenges in ensuring food security for quarantined individuals. In some localities, voluntary food assistance was organized by local officials and stakeholders.

In addition, many respondents mentioned the use of traditional remedies as a strength in their fight against coronavirus. This is consistent with past approaches to emerging and endemic infectious diseases in Tanzania (Gessler et al., 1995; Kayombo et al., 2007). As one stated, "We can be independent when dealing with pandemics like Corona by using traditional ways, prayers and alternative treatments such as *kujifukiza* (breathing herb-infused steam), the use of lemons and drinking of *tangawizi* (ginger)" (29).

Respondents also discussed the importance of providing psychosocial support, which appears to have been the focus of trainings for health officials (URT, 2020). Several respondents mentioned the importance of psychosocial support to deal with stigma and fear for people diagnosed with coronavirus. As one stated "psychosocial support was effective since people were provided with sufficient knowledge (counseling) to lower fear that being in quarantine is not mean to punish them but to protect them and other people from getting Corona" (25). Although many respondents mentioned activities they engaged in to provide such support, large numbers also praised President Magufuli for taking bold action to reduce fear and stigma related to COVID-19. The president's actions and influence are discussed in greater detail in the following section.

Tanzania's Response in Context

To some extent, Tanzania's relatively limited national policy response can be explained as a result of weak state capacity and limited fiscal space. About half (twenty-three out of fifty) of the African countries included in the Oxford COVID-19 Government Response Tracker database also did not provide income support in response to the pandemic (Hale et al., 2020). However, nearly three-quarters (thirty-seven of fifty) did provide some form of debt relief (e.g., stopping loan repayments, preventing services such as water from being cut off, or banning evictions), and the majority (86 percent) announced some degree of economic stimulus spending.[3] In general, countries providing income support and debt relief were wealthier,[4] and there is a positive and significant correlation between gross domestic product (GDP) per capita and the amount of economic stimulus spending provided. Similarly, Tanzania is one of only four African countries (out of fifty in the database) that did not close workplaces, issue stay-at-home requirements, nor place restrictions on internal movement (Hale et al., 2020). However, there is no correlation between country income and the extent of containment and health policy measures.

Rather than see the relatively limited high-level response as a weakness, many of our interviewees (fourteen) interpreted the lack of action as a deliberate attempt to minimize the threat of COVID-19 to reduce fear and stigma. In particular, they cited the positive messages of the president and other top officials. As one respondent stated, "Top government official leaders' statements like the president help to lower fears and challenges in managing Corona. These was for example, the president's statement that Corona is just like any other disease we are living with and we should simply take all prevention measures and use traditional remedies" (18).

Another noted, "We learned from our top leaders like President Magufuli that fear can bring greater impacts than the disease itself" (17). Another stated, "Our president decided not to close borders with other countries, allowing all economic activities to take place and reopening of universities and schools. This helped citizens to see corona disease as normal, like other diseases."

The influence of the president and other high-level authorities on the actions and statements of local officials is in keeping with the hierarchical nature of governance in Tanzania. As noted previously, transfers from the central government fund the majority of local government activities (Carlitz, 2017). In addition, centrally appointed officials serve beside their locally elected counterparts at almost every level of government and have considerable decision-making power (Venugopal & Yilmaz, 2010).

Praise for Magufuli was not uniform among our respondents, however. Some respondents acknowledged that the president's statements "had very big impacts both positively and negatively given the trust members of the public accord to them" (24). Among the negative effects, a respondent explained, "The government's move to reassure its people that the disease (COVID-19) does not exist in Tanzania has made people to live carelessly without taking any precautions. This could lead to new infections and have serious impacts on people in our country" (45). Still another acknowledged that "traditional remedies without proper guidelines might threaten human life. In our ward there was one death caused by traditional remedies where the person's skin and internal organs burned. We request the government to issue safety control measures for traditional remedies" (36).

Moreover, several respondents noted experiencing more difficulties in educating communities after the president's statements that COVID-19 was not a threat. One respondent noted the difficulty of educating the public after "high official leaders' statements about reported positive cases of animals and fruits and discouraging the use of masks" (25). This respondent is likely referring to a speech the president made in early May 2020 (Ikulu Tanzania, 2020), in which he suggested the country's caseload was overstated as a result of "compromised" test kits resulting in false positives. He described having samples taken from animals (a goat, a sheep, and a bird) and a papaya and having them labeled with human names and sent to Tanzania's National Laboratory. He claimed the non-human samples tested positive and presented this as evidence that labs were falsifying positive test results. Opposition politicians have suggested this statement was part of a broader campaign to minimize the scope of the pandemic in light of the fact that Magufuli was gearing up to stand for re-election in October 2020 (Peralta, 2020).

The desire to suppress potentially politically damaging information can also explain the government's hesitancy to release official statistics on the number of confirmed COVID-19 cases and deaths.[5] Such obfuscation is in keeping with the Magufuli administration's broader efforts to obstruct access to public information (Carlitz & McLellan, 2020). According to Freedom House (2020), the Tanzanian government has increasingly "sought to obstruct access to public information in recent years." An Access to Information Act adopted in 2016 imposed prison terms on officials who "improperly" released state data. Journalists and civil society groups who attempt to expose official wrongdoing frequently face punitive action by authorities (Dahir, 2020). Under new legislation from August 3, 2020, the public is banned from sharing information about an infectious disease outbreak without government permission (Ross, 2020).

In sum, although political pressures likely shaped the responses of the president and other top officials, their actions clearly had a mixed effect on local officials. Diminishing fear boosted their morale and helped them to address fear and stigma. However, some found it more difficult to persuade the public to comply with prevention measures. With few national protection measures in place, many respondents took matters into their own hands by continuing to educate the public and adapting national guidelines to their local context.

Local Adaptations

Several respondents mentioned developing their own procedures or guidelines that were separate from the national guidelines. One respondent described this process: "We decided to have our own district council guidelines. For example, the general guideline for health service providers required to be full protected with PPE when providing medical services to a person confirmed to have the coronavirus. However, because of the lack of PPE we decided to use masks and maintain social distancing as a means of protection in order to save people's lives" (26).

Moreover, to address fear, stigma, and awareness, respondents engaged in several activities. They involved local government officials to reduce community resistance, as Figure 31.7 illustrates. A respondent gave another example from their community: "Community members had the perception that by making their health center an isolation station, it will be a source of bringing COVID-19 to their place. Two [district officers] intervened. Later on, the community agreed and the center was made" (23).

Respondents also engaged in direct community outreach. They conducted public education in churches, mosques, bars and food service provision areas, even sometimes going "door-to-door for individual households" (26). They involved religious leaders to help enforce social distancing (see Figure 31.8), including during burial services and mourning days. Several respondents also mentioned delivering public education through loudspeakers and public address systems while moving around the wards. They mobilized local resources to purchase the loudspeakers. In one ward, a respondent reported that they enforced fines on people who disregarded the health guidelines (20).

Figure 31.7. Facebook post from Plus TV describes Dar es Salaam Regional Commissioner Paul Makonda encouraging mask wearing in public after WHO announces that COVID-19 may be airborne, April 18, 2020. (Translation: "It is mandatory to wear mask"-RC [Regional Commissioner] DSM [Dar es Salaam].)
Source: Plus TV (2020).

Figure 31.8. Tweet from AzamTVTZ announcing the fourteen-day closure of Mtoro Mosque in Dar es Salaam to control the effects of the novel coronavirus, May 2, 2020. (Translation: "Mtoro Mosque in Dar es Salaam city is closed. Mtoro Mosque located in Dar es Salaam city is closed for two weeks to control the effect of spread of Corona.")
Source: Azam TV (2020).

Respondents involved non-state actors to address the challenge of low resources and supplies. To obtain transportation needed for in-person contact tracing, one respondent mentioned obtaining cars from local nongovernmental organizations (23). Seven respondents mentioned manufacturing their own supplies for local use, including PPE and affordable hand sanitizer. Another respondent mentioned collaborating with the Dar es Salaam Institute of Technology to manufacture face shields (18). State actors, such as district level leaders, also provided tangible support in procuring cars and fuel (25).

In sum, in the absence of a clear and coordinated national response, local officials in Tanzania adapted to the coronavirus situation by creating their own guidelines and manufacturing their own resources. This suggests that local officials in Tanzania have room to maneuver even in the absence of truly devolved power. Many of our respondents mentioned that they would like even more authority to create locally responsive policies for controlling disease spread. They suggested that the government invest more financial and human resources toward preparing local officials to respond to pandemics.

Conclusion

Relying solely on media reports available in English or international data sources may lead to the conclusion that Tanzania did not take the coronavirus pandemic seriously (e.g., Dahir, 2020). President Magufuli minimized the pandemic and encouraged Tanzanian citizens to go about their daily lives. For its level of state capacity, Tanzania underperformed on COVID-19 response and containment measures, relative to other countries in eastern and southern Africa. Citizens have mostly accepted the government's relatively limited measures.

Despite the lack of a strong federal response, our case study reveals that local officials, working in regions of varying density, took the outbreak seriously and responded to the coronavirus pandemic by adapting the national guidelines to suit their local contexts. Building on their prior experience with other pandemics, local officials made a concerted effort to respond to the pandemic, despite limited resources and a lack of strong national measures. They isolated patients who tested positive. Following the president's lead, they worked in their communities to abate fear. Our results revealed that this leadership was key to the country's success in keeping stress levels down and encouraging people not to panic. Local officials also worked with patients, families, and religious leaders to lower stigma. They used local resources to address the need for more PPE, including hand sanitizers and face shields. Nevertheless, given the lack of data on case counts since early May 2020, we cannot even speculate as to what, if any effect these efforts had on local transmission.

In decentralized systems such as Tanzania, local officials are often more trusted than federal officials and have better knowledge of what is happening on the ground. However, as our respondents stated, during a pandemic, local public health officials need the authority and resources to be able to adapt national guidance to their specific context. As of this writing, research is underway to examine whether giving local public health officials more control over local budgets improves overall healthcare quality in Tanzania (Kapologwe et al., 2019). Nevertheless, the overall lack of resources to fight COVID-19 was systematic across African countries and cannot be solved by authority alone. One respondent affirmed this message: "The global response plan on managing COVID-19 was difficult to be executed in Africa given the insufficient supply of necessary and recommended resources" (21). More research is needed to explore how other countries adapted at the local level in such circumstances, rather than solely presenting country responses in terms of national policies or surveillance statistics.

Our study is limited by the fact that we interviewed only public employees. To gain a more comprehensive picture of the local response to a pandemic, researchers should also interview non-state actors working in communities, as was done during the Ebola epidemic in west Africa (Abramowitz et al., 2015). Moreover, data on community members' perceptions of the response system would be helpful to reveal challenges to citizen cooperation and trust that, if overcome, could help to reduce disease spread (Yamanis et al., 2016).

Finally, another limitation is that we cannot link local response efforts to COVID-19 morbidity or mortality data given that Tanzania halted COVID-19 testing and surveillance. It is unclear to what extent people affected by COVID-19 were staying home because they were worried that the health facilities were inadequate. Lack of attendance at health facilities could limit the ability to collect accurate mortality data, or to infer COVID-19 deaths from overall mortality.

Despite these limitations and the evolving situation, our findings reveal that many local health officials in Tanzania were taking the pandemic seriously and creatively using resources to prevent disease spread in their communities. More research is necessary to understand how national policies play out in local contexts, especially in decentralized systems, and under authoritarian regimes.

Acknowledgments

We would like to acknowledge the data collectors for working quickly and diligently to collect these interviews and news sources over the course of three months. We would also like to thank the respondents for their generosity and willingness to participate in the interviews. We gratefully acknowledge funding from the School of Liberal Arts at Tulane University.

Notes

1. The Mobility Reports are based on aggregated, anonymized data from users of Google Maps and show how visits and length of stay at different places change compared to a baseline (https://www.google.com/covid19/mobility/). As such, the measure reflects the activities of smartphone users only. As of 2018, mobile internet penetration was estimated to be 18.5 percent (Okeleke, 2019). Data from the round 7 of the nationally representative Afrobarometer survey shows that urban dwellers were significantly more likely to have internet access on their phones than were rural residents (42 percent vs. 17 percent of respondents). This suggests that smartphone users predominate in urban areas, and thus these trends may not be reflective of mobility trends for all Tanzanians.

2. Tanzania is currently divided into thirty-one regions. Each region is administered by a commissioner appointed by the central government. Regions are further subdivided into districts, wards, and villages, which are governed by popularly elected councils with appointed executive officers.

3. Other than Tanzania, only six countries (Burkina Faso, Burundi, Cameroon, Libya, Madagascar, and South Sudan) did not announce stimulus spending.

4. The average GDP per capita (PPP, current US$) for countries that have not provided income relief was $9,968 compared to $26,905 that did provide such relief. Countries that did not provide some form of debt relief had average per capita income of $13,748 compared to $24,799 among those that did. These differences are statistically significant at conventional levels.

5. Tanzania had not published nationwide figures since May 8, when it recorded 509 cases and 21 deaths.

References

Abramowitz, S. A., McLean, K. E., McKune, S. L., Bardosh, K. L., Fallah, M., Monger, J., Tehoungue, K., & Omidian, P.A. (2015). Community-centered responses to Ebola in urban Liberia: The view from below. *PLoS Neglected Tropical Diseases, 9*(4), e0003706. https://doi.org/10.1371/journal.pntd.0003706

Africa Centres for Disease Control and Prevention (Africa CDC) (2020, May 12). *Guidance on community physical distancing during COVID-19 pandemic.* Africa CDC, Africa Union Commission. https://africacdc.org/download/guidance-on-community-social-distancing-during-covid-19-outbreak/

Afrobarometer Data, Tanzania, Round 7. (2018). http://www.afrobarometer.org

Ayo, Millard. [@millardayo]. (2020, April 22). *"Wapo wanaotoa mawazo"* [There are those who offer ideas]. [Tweet]. Twitter. https://twitter.com/millardayo/status/1252970761633042433

Azam TV [@azamtvtz]. (2002, May 2). #BreakingNews: MSIKITI [Tweet]. Twitter. https://twitter.com/azamtvtz/status/1256543708465500161

Carlitz, R. D. (2017). Money flows, water trickles: Understanding patterns of decentralized water provision in Tanzania. *World Development, 93*, 16–30.

Carlitz, R. D., & Manda, C. (2016, January 25). Tanzania loves its new anti-corruption president. Why is he shutting down media outlets? *The Washington Post.* https://www.washingtonpost.com/news/monkey-cage/wp/2016/01/25/tanzania-loves-its-new-anti-corruption-president-why-is-he-shutting-down-media-outlets/

Carlitz, R. D., & McLellan, R. (2020). Open data from authoritarian regimes: New opportunities, new challenges. *Perspectives on Politics*, 1–11.

Cocks, T. (2020, May 13). *Remote Lesotho becomes last country in Africa to record COVID-19 case.* Reuters. https://www.reuters.com/article/us-health-coronavirus-lesotho-idUSKBN22P1R4

Dahir, A. L. (2020, August 4). Tanzania's president says country is virus free. Others warn of disaster. *The New York Times.* https://nyti.ms/2Du2EeR

Devermont, J., & Harris, M. (2020, May 26). *Implications of Tanzania's bungled response to COVID-19.* CSIS Critical Questions. https://www.csis.org/analysis/implications-tanzanias-bungled-response-covid-19

Dong, E., Du, H., & Gardner, L. (2020). An interactive web-based dashboard to track COVID-19 in real time. *Lancet Infectious Diseases, 20*(5), 533–534. https://doi.org/10.1016/S1473-3099(20)30120-1

Freedom House. (2020). Tanzania. *Freedom in the World 2020.*

Gessler, M. C., Msuya, D. E., Nkunya, M. H., Mwasumbi, L. B., Schär, A., Heinrich, M., & Tanner, M. (1995). Traditional healers in Tanzania: the treatment of malaria with plant remedies. *Journal of Ethnopharmacology, 48*(3), 131–144.

Google LLC. (2020). *Google COVID-19 community mobility reports.* Retrieved August 3, 2020, from https://www.google.com/covid19/mobility/

Hale, T., Webster, S., Petherick, A., Phillips, T., & Kira, B. (2020). *Oxford COVID-19 Government Response Tracker (OxCGRT).* University of Oxford, Blavatnik School of Government. https://github.com/OxCGRT/covid-policy-tracker/blob/master/documentation/codebook.md#economic-policies

Hutchinson, P. (2002). *Decentralization in Tanzania: The view of district health management teams.* MEASURE Evaluation Project, WP-02-48. https://www.measureevaluation.org/resources/publications/wp-02-48

Ikulu (The White House) Tanzania. (2020, May 3). Rais Dkt. Magufuli Akimuapisha Dkt. Mwigulu Nchemba Kuwa Waziri Wa Katiba Na Sheria [President Dr. Magufuli sworn in. Dr. Mwigulu Nchemba to be Minister for Constitution and Law]. [Video].YouTube. https://www.youtube.com/watch?v=DbSZd8oyaGE

Kabwe, Z. (2020, February 3). *If the elections aren't free and fair, Tanzania will be a one-party state.* African Arguments. https://africanarguments.org/2020/02/03/if-the-elections-arent-free-and-fair-tanzania-will-be-a-one-party-state/

Kapologwe, N. A., Kalolo, A., Kibusi, S. M., Chaula, Z., Nswilla, A., Teuscher, T., Aung, K., & Borghi, J. (2019). Understanding the implementation of Direct Health Facility Financing and its effect on health system performance in Tanzania: A non-controlled before and after mixed method study protocol. *Health Research Policy and Systems, 17*, 11. https://doi.org/10.1186/s12961-018-0400-3

Kayombo, E. J., Uiso, F. C., Mbwambo, Z. H., Mahunnah, R. L., Moshi, M. J., & Mgonda, Y. H. (2007). Experience of initiating collaboration of traditional healers in managing HIV and AIDS in Tanzania. *Journal of Ethnobiology and Ethnomedicine*, *3*(1), 6.

Manda, C. (2017, March 29). It's not just a rapper's arrest that should raise alarms about authoritarianism in Tanzania. *The Washington Post.* https://www.washingtonpost.com/news/monkey-cage/wp/2017/03/29/its-not-just-a-rappers-arrest-that-should-raise-alarms-about-authoritarianism-in-tanzania/

Ministry of Health, Community Development, Gender, Elderly and Children (MoHCDGEC) (2020, March). *Standard Operating Procedures (SOPs) for case management and infection, prevention and control.* Case Management and Infection Prevention and Control Subcommittee. https://cquin.icap.columbia.edu/wp-content/uploads/2020/04/Tanzania_SOPs-for-Case-Management-and-Infection-Prevention-and-Control.pdf

Ministry of Lands, Housing and Human Settlements Development (MoLHHSD). (2016). *Habitat III National Report.* United Republic of Tanzania.

Mollel, H. A. (2010). *Participation for local development: The reality of decentralization in Tanzania.* Leiden, Netherlands: African Studies Centre.

Morse, Y. L. (2014). Party matters: The institutional origins of competitive hegemony in Tanzania. *Democratization*, *21*(4), 655–677.

Morse, Y. L. (2018). *How autocrats compete: Parties, patrons, and unfair elections in Africa.* Cambridge University Press.

Mwakideu, C. (2020, June 6). *Tanzania: Opposition cries foul over attacks on leaders as election looms.* DW. https://www.dw.com/en/tanzania-opposition-cries-foul-over-attacks-on-leaders-as-election-looms/a-53764518

Okeleke, K. (2019). *Digital transformation in Tanzania: The role of mobile technology and impact on development goals.* GSM Association.

Paget, D. (2017). Tanzania: shrinking space and opposition protest. *Journal of Democracy*, *28*(3), 153–167.

Penrose, K., de Castro, M. C., Werema, J., & Ryan, E. T. (2010). Informal urban settlements and cholera risk in Dar es Salaam, Tanzania. *PLoS Neglected Tropical Diseases*, *4*(3), e631.

Peralta, E. (2020, May 11). *Tanzania's President blames fake positive tests in the spike in coronavirus cases.* National Public Radio (NPR). https://www.npr.org/2020/05/11/854115407/tanzanias-president-blames-fake-positive-tests-in-the-spike-in-coronavirus-cases

Plus TV. (2020, April 18). "Whoever goes to all shopping zone must be wearing masks" [Status update]. Facebook. https://www.facebook.com/611750682346940/posts/anayekwenda-eneo-la-manunuzi-yotote-lazima-awe-amevaa-barakoa-mask-ununueukate-l/1328551647333503/

Ross, W. (2020, August 3). *Tanzania bans organising protests online.* BBC World Service. https://www.bbc.com/news/topics/cjnwl8q4qdrt/tanzania

Serajuddin, U., & Hamadeh, N. (2020, July 1). New World Bank country classifications by income level: 2020-2021. *World Bank Blogs.* https://blogs.worldbank.org/opendata/new-world-bank-country-classifications-income-level-2020-2021

Sguazzin, A. (2020, May 22). *Next Africa: As virus spreads, Tanzania declares victory.* Bloomberg. https://www.bloomberg.com/news/newsletters/2020-05-22/next-africa-as-virus-spreads-tanzania-declares-victory

Tanzania bans all public gatherings, closes schools, suspends the premier league over coronavirus. (2020, March 17). *The Citizen.* https://allafrica.com/stories/202003171108.html

Tanzania suspends laboratory head after president questions coronavirus tests. (2020, May 4). Reuters. https://www.reuters.com/article/us-health-coronavirus-tanzania/tanzania-suspends-laboratory-head-after-president-questions-coronavirus-tests-idUSKBN22G295

Taylor, B. (2020, May 21). COVID-19 hits Tanzania. *Tanzanian Affairs.* https://www.tzaffairs.org/2020/05/covid-19-hits-tanzania/

United Republic of Tanzania. (2020). *A brief teaching guide: Distance learning programme for SWOs on mental health and psychosocial support in response to COVID-19 outbreak.* Ministry of Health Community Development, Gender, Elderly and Children, Dodoma.

United Republic of Tanzania. (1998). *Local Government Reform Programme: Policy paper on local government reform.* Dar es Salaam: Prime Minister's Office Regional Administration and Local Government.

United Republic of Tanzania Ministry of Health and Social Welfare (2015, August). *Tanzania Health Sector Strategic Plan 2015–2020 (HSSP IV).* United Republic of Tanzania. http://www.tzdpg.or.tz/fileadmin/documents/dpg_internal/dpg_working_groups_clusters/cluster_2/health/Key_Sector_Documents/Induction_Pack/Final_HSSP_IV_Vs1.0_260815.pdf.

United States (U.S.) Department of State, Overseas Security Advisory Council (OSAC). (2020, April 12). *Health alert: Tanzania, COVID-19 update, international flights no longer available.* U.S. Department of State, OSAC. https://www.osac.gov/Content/Report/9f0d1e96-5c9a-4f33-91c0-186e56320dea

United States Embassy in Tanzania. (2020, May 13). *Health Alert: U.S. Embassy, Dar es Salaam.* https://tz.usembassy.gov/health-alert-u-s-embassy-dar-es-salaam-may-13-2020/

Venugopal, V., & Yilmaz, S. (2010). Decentralization in Tanzania: An assessment of local government discretion and accountability. *Public Administration and Development, 30*(3), 215–231.

West-Slevin, K., Barker, C., & Hickmann, M. (2015, February). *Snapshot: Tanzania's health system.* The Health Policy Project, Futures Group. https://www.healthpolicyproject.com/pubs/803_TanzaniaHealthsystembriefFINAL.pdf

World Bank. (2019). *The World Bank in Tanzania.* https://www.worldbank.org/en/country/tanzania/overview

World Bank. (2020). *World Development Indicators.* DataBank. The World Bank. https://databank.worldbank.org/source/world-development-indicators#

WorldPop. (2020). *Population density: Tanzania.* https://www.worldpop.org/geodata/summary?id=44519

Yamanis, T., Nolan, E., & Shepler, S. (2016). Fears and misperceptions of the Ebola response system during the 2014-2015 outbreak in Sierra Leone. *PLoS Neglected Tropical Diseases, 10*(10), e0005077.

32 CONFRONTING LEGACIES AND CHARTING A NEW COURSE?

The Politics of Coronavirus Response in South Africa

Joseph Harris

Under President Cyril Ramaphosa, democratic South Africa took an aggressive response to COVID-19 that stood in marked contrast to the Mbeki administration's denialist response to HIV/AIDS. The administration was initially praised for an aggressive nationwide lockdown that was informed by scientific advice. The lockdown provided the country's healthcare system time to prepare and, according to some estimates, may have saved as many as twenty thousand lives. However, as pressure grew to reopen and address the hunger and economic devastation the novel coronavirus and resulting lockdown had wrought, the administration increasingly found itself on the receiving end of criticism by scientists, opposition political parties, business, and citizens. Against the advice of the World Health Organization (WHO), the government reopened before the epidemic was at its peak. As infections surged and the death toll mounted, the novel coronavirus revealed long-standing weaknesses in health system capacity as well as deficiencies in the government's approach to addressing the economic, health, and food needs of its people. As of this writing, the country stands mired in the largest coronavirus outbreak on the continent and one of the largest in the world, with many of its people hungry and out of work. The looming effect of the pandemic on the country's large population positive for human immunodeficiency virus (HIV) and tuberculosis (TB) is likely to be dire. Although increased political competition helps explain the African National Congress's (ANC's) greater receptivity to scientific and medical professionals initially, the party's openness to expert advice deteriorated as the crisis intensified and additional pressures, including a major corruption scandal, led the ANC to come under fire.

Cyril Ramaphosa's election as president of South Africa in 2019 represented a sharp break from the prior two presidential administrations. Insulated from political competition with few serious challengers, the ANC under Thabo Mbeki had resisted the advice and counsel of seasoned medical and legal professionals and instead entertained dissident science, becoming infamous for denying that

HIV causes AIDS; promoting unproven therapies for AIDS, including garlic, beetroot, olive oil, and lemon juice; and delaying access to proven antiretroviral therapy (Harris, 2017)—decisions that ultimately cost the country more than 330,000 lives (Chigwedere et al., 2008). Jacob Zuma's presidency was marred by corruption, scandals, and an inability to address growing protests over provision of basic government services. Although a candidate of the ANC, like Mbeki and Zuma before him, Ramaphosa's experience as a former union leader and business tycoon offered South Africans the promise of someone who might be able to deliver needed reform.

Ramaphosa's election win marked the first time that the ANC—which has governed South Africa since 1994—won less than 60 percent of the vote, with the party earning just 57.5 percent of the vote nationally, as opposition parties, such as the Democratic Alliance and Economic Freedom Fighters, appealed to citizen concerns. Ramaphosa's win came on the heels of the ANC's poorest showing ever in the 2016 municipal elections, in which it lost the capital of Pretoria and Johannesburg for the first time since apartheid ended. Although opposition parties still trailed the ANC by large margins, the era of one-party dominance was closing, and an era of more intense political competition was beginning, one that signaled the possibility of an ANC that was less insulated from social pressure and more responsive to citizen demands.

As one observer noted, "Ramaphosa is the right man for the moment. He is a modern thinker who is sensitive to all the constituencies: business, labor and government" (quoted in Winning, 2019). However, although tackling corruption and reforming struggling utilities was on the ANC's agenda under Ramaphosa, neither Ramaphosa nor the ANC knew they would have to navigate the challenges or the wide-ranging health and economic consequences that a deadly new disease presented. The government's initial response was guided by science at first and bought the country's health system time to prepare for a surge of infections. However, an inability to address citizens' basic economic, health, and nutritional needs allowed the government's efforts to curb spread of the virus to fall victim to competing political and social pressures.

Public Health and Health System Responses

Arrival of the Virus

South Africa's first novel coronavirus (COVID-19) infection was diagnosed on March 5, 2020, with early cases appearing to follow a trajectory of exponential increase seen in many other countries. The infection took place in the context of a nation still grappling with the deep legacies wrought by apartheid and regarded as one of the most unequal societies in the world. In South Africa, the top 10 percent hold 86 percent of the country's wealth, with a significant portion of this inequality running along racial lines (Chatterjee et al., 2020). The country's stark income inequality, in the words of leading analysts, made it "a global outlier" (Seekings & Nattrass, 2015).

From the beginning, the government's response to the virus relied heavily on science and scientists—a departure from the Mbeki government's approach to AIDS. Government policy was initially guided by epidemiological predictions by the Stellanbosch University's South African Centre for Epidemiological Modelling and Analysis (SACEMA), in cooperation with the National Institute for Communicable Diseases (NICD), a national public health agency that monitors and researches outbreaks. These early projections suggested that "a slow and inadequate response by government to the outbreak could result in anywhere between 87,000 and 351,000 deaths" over the course of the pandemic (Cowan, 2020). The Ramaphosa administration then took decisive action in declaring a national emergency on March 15, 2020, which shuttered schools, prohibited large gatherings, closed the majority of the country's borders, and banned visitors from countries deemed high-risk (Nordling, 2020a). Schools were initially closed from March 19, 2020 to June 9, 2020 (Debut, 2020). According to the models, even under an optimistic scenario, the country could expect eight million infections by mid-August 2020 and 40,000 deaths in total (Muller, 2020). The Actuarial Society of South Africa predicted an even higher number of deaths, ranging from 48,300 to 88,000 (Child, 2020b). Dr. Harry Moultrie, a senior medical epidemiologist at NICD, then put together an expert team, called the South Africa COVID-19 Modelling Consortium, to do more rigorous modelling to try to understand what the country was up against. The team included professors, doctors, and statisticians from University of Cape Town, Stellenbosch University, and Boston University, many of whom had been involved in epidemiological forecasting of the country's AIDS epidemic (Child, 2020b).

The gravity of the impending calamity led the government to deepen its lockdown measures on March 27, 2020. These measures closed the nation's borders and required everyone but essential workers to stay at home, except to obtain medicine, groceries, or welfare payments (Nordling, 2020a), as well as an alcohol and tobacco ban. This policy, originally put in place for three weeks but extended to five, was aimed at slowing the spread of the virus. To help cushion the blow of the lockdown on workers, the government put in place a program called the Temporary Employer and Employee Relief Scheme in late March that was intended to help employers pay workers (Cabe, 2020).

As part of the lockdown, the government developed a five-tier alert system, with level one representing life as normal and level five involving the most serious restrictions to movement. The lockdown on March 27, 2020, put the country at level five (Wild, 2020). By May 2020 the country sat at level four, which allowed for limited operation of industries, the purchase of winter clothes and fast food delivery (Wild, 2020). Even at that level of restriction, however, large COVID-19 outbreaks still took place, some at sites that had notably been places where TB and HIV had spread in the 1980s and 1990s: 164 cases at the Mponeng gold mine near Johannesburg, which had been working at half capacity, were reported on May 24, 2020 ("Coronavirus in South Africa: Outbreak," 2020).

Effects of the Lockdown

Called by some the strictest lockdown on the continent, the government's lockdown was overseen by a "militaristic" Minister of Police, who likened the public health crisis to war (Seekings, 2020d, p. 4). The lockdown was enforced by a combination of military, police, and private security. As unrest began to flare around the globe related to police violence against Black people in the United States, the lockdown brought South Africans into greater contact and conflict with the police. Overall, two hundred and thirty thousand people were arrested during the lockdown (Reuter, 2020). More than a dozen people were killed by security forces enforcing the lockdown, including Sbusiso Amos, who was shot on March 29, 2020, in front of his four children, his cousin, and aunt (Bornman, 2020). Police used tear gas and rubber bullets to disperse crowds of people not wearing masks waiting in line for food (Nyoka, 2020).

Although the national government put a moratorium on evictions during the crisis, in practice electricity shutoffs and evictions still occurred (Harrisberg, 2020). The city of Cape Town used force to remove squatters from city land, in one high-profile case dragging one naked man out of his shack, tearing down makeshift dwellings, firing rubber bullets, and burning tents and belongings—this despite the fact that the municipality was legally required to provide him an alternative accommodation under the constitution (Flans et al., 2020). Police used stun grenades and riot shields to force community health workers who came for a meeting at the Eastern Cape Department of Health to leave after the manager did not show, and they lacked money to go home (Nortier, 2020a). This experience highlights both shortsighted human resource policies and community health workers' ill treatment by the police, which began before the lockdown (van de Ruit and Breckenridge, 2019).

The lockdown was instituted on March 27, 2020, on the day that the country reported its first death and 243 new cases had been reported in a single day. After that, new COVID-19 case numbers dropped rapidly and remained steady at between 50 to 70 new cases a day (Harding, 2020; Nordling, 2020a). Even though epidemiologists had predicted South Africa's caseload to grow to 4,000 by April 2 (Nordling, 2020a), by that date it had recorded just 1,380 cases. By the end of April 2020, South Africa had reported 5,647 cases and 103 deaths from COVID-19 (Ritchie et al., 2020). Many credited the country's aggressive lockdown measures for initially helping to "flatten the curve." As Minister of Health Zweli Mkhize reported, the lockdown created "a physical barrier that prevents the virus from moving" (quoted in Toyana, 2020). And by some estimates, the lockdown may have reduced the infection rate by as much as 60% (Toyana, 2020), saving more than 20,000 lives (Evans, 2020). Murders and road accidents were also down as a result of the lockdown (Mbalula, 2020; Singh, 2020).

Aside from the effect of the lockdown, a number of theories for why the pandemic did not play out the way experts expected initially included the fact that nearly all citizens had been given an anti-TB Bacille Calmette-Guérin (BCG) vaccine at birth, the effect of AIDS medication on the virus, and enzymes present in certain population groups (Harding, 2020). Other theories suggested that the lower epidemiological trajectory could be a product of missing cases because of inadequate testing (Karim, 2020a). However, the lion's share of praise for the country's having avoided a worse crisis, at least initially, was reserved for the government lockdown that slowed the spread of the virus. The Academy of Science of South Africa stated that the "strong, science-based governmental leadership has saved many lives for which South Africa can be thankful" (Academy of Science, 2020). John Nkengasong, the director of the Africa Centres for Disease Control and Prevention, stated, "What South Africa has done is impressive, absolutely" (quoted in Mogotsi & Bearak, 2020).

Using the Time to Prepare

Dr. Salim Abdool Karim, the chair of South Africa's COVID-19 advisory group and a veteran AIDS scientist, likened South Africa's response—unfolding as the virus spread across the country—to "sailing a ship while building it" (Karim, 2020b). The lockdown was the first and most important piece of the response, as it "bought us some time to become more proactive" (Nordling, 2020a). South Africa used that time to build field hospitals and overflow beds. As infections later began to surge, the Nasrec Expo Centre, originally slated to be a quarantine facility, was turned into a treatment center with more than one thousand beds, staffed by volunteers, with one hundred oxygen concentrators donated by the private sector (Smillie, 2020). However, in a country as unequal as South Africa in a crisis so large, donations would not be the only way in which the private sector would come to play a role in the coronavirus response.

South Africa has shortage of more than twelve thousand healthcare workers (Ramaphosa, 2020). Around 70 percent of the country's intensive care unit beds and doctors and half the nation's health expenditure were concentrated in the private sector, even though it served between 15 percent and 16 percent of the population (Benatar, 2020; Caincross et al., 2020). Although more than 80 percent of South Africans lack health insurance (or medical schemes) (Karim, 2020b), South Africa's National Health Insurance program envisioned that the country's citizens would one day be able to use the resources of the country's private health facilities (Harris, 2017). COVID-19 accelerated some negotiations between the government and the private sector around, for example, the cost of a critical care bed in a private facility, at rates that were reduced for the crisis; however, in the context of a crisis that involved immediate needs, the outcome of these negotiations were not always beneficial to the longer-term project of health equity envisioned by national health insurance (Cleary, 2020).

Even though significant questions remained about where the money would come from and what happened when the money ran out, the Western Cape became the first province to purchase three hundred beds from the private sector (Cleary, 2020), offering a "template for other provinces" (South Africa Private Practioners Forum quoted in Caincross et al., 2020). Critics, however, called the process flawed, and argued that it "adds to, rather than eases, existing challenges to equitable healthcare in our fragile society" (Benatar, 2020). With some private practices seeing declines in doctor visits by as much as 80 percent from COVID-19, some private providers also sought greater security by proposing a plan to medical schemes (the country's private health insurers) that would guarantee at least 70 percent of their 2019 income through 2021 (Gonzales, 2020a).

In addition to its work with the private sector, the government found an important role for more than twenty-eight thousand community health workers in the country's coronavirus response, going door to door in communities, screening more than eleven million people, approximately 20 percent of the country's population, and referring more than seventy thousand for testing (Karim, 2020b; Wild, 2020). According to Salim Abdool Karim, "Only South Africa has done [community testing on such a wide scale]" (quoted in Mogotsi & Bearak, 2020). The government has also integrated technology into its response, redesigning an antipoaching tool to collect data on coronavirus and alert authorities with the address of an infected person so that they can begin contact tracing (Wild, 2020).

The government also planned for randomized screening in schools and hospitals and trained a small army of community healthcare workers to screen and refer patients for testing in the country's villages and towns in a bid to "stop small flare-ups from turning into large wildfires of infection" (Nordling, 2020a). It acquired personal protective equipment (PPE) and ventilators (Muller, 2020) and received assistance from more than two hundred Cuban doctors, some of whom had experience fighting Ebola in other parts of Africa and cholera in Haiti (Magome & Meldrum, 2020).

A consequence of having the largest HIV epidemic in the world (at close to eight million) and one of the world's largest TB burdens (with TB the country's leading cause of death), South Africa's laboratories were accustomed to performing more than fifty thousand HIV viral load tests per day (Karim & Karim, 2020). When the novel coronavirus arrived, polymerase chain reaction (PCR) testing, originally developed for HIV and TB, became an integral part of COVID-19 testing (Karim & Karim, 2020). A testing system for coronavirus was developed using one the country had been using for TB, called GeneXpert (Mogotsi & Bearak, 2020). The government relied on the laboratory infrastructure that it used to monitor HIV and TB for coronavirus testing and hosted more than 180 testing sites (Wild, 2020). Contract tracing teams that had originally been formed for controlling TB and community health workers working on HIV were redeployed for the coronavirus response (Karim, 2020b).

Challenges in the Response

When the country's first case was reported, the National Health Laboratory Services (NHLS) took over responsibility for testing from the NICD (Mail and Guardian Data Desk, 2020). Although 40,000 tests were performed in March, allegations of a testing backlog of around 6,000 were met with blanket denials by NHLS (Mail and Guardian Data Desk, 2020). Targeted testing in Cape Town began on April 7 (Wroughton & Bearak 2020). More than 170,000 South Africans had been tested by April 27 (Magome & Meldrum, 2020) and 340,000 by May 12 with 16,000 tests administered daily (Wild, 2020), although this amount represented only about half the goal of 30,000 people per day set by the NHLS to achieve by the end of April (Mogotsi & Bearak, 2020). Because of a global shortage of test kits, substantial testing backlogs developed of around 15,000 in Johannesburg and 11,000 in the Western Cape by mid- to late May (Wroughton & Bearak, 2020). After maintaining there were no backlogs for weeks, the NHLS admitted that the national backlog was more than 80,000 tests (Mail and Guardian Data Desk, 2020). The backlog in testing meant that results were taking from six to ten days, which crippled the country's ability to do contact tracing effectively (Wroughton & Bearak, 2020).

Just as significant a problem as the lack of testing was the fact that, even with the extra time that the lockdown provided to prepare, because of the global shortage, some provinces still lacked necessary PPE and remained woefully unprepared for the surge in infections. Even after spending R 78 million (US$4.7 million) on PPE, the Eastern Cape still faced a shortage (Mail and Guardian Data Desk et al., 2020). Nationally, a spokesman for the Democratic Nursing Organisation of South Africa called PPE availability "extremely poor and disappointing" (Gilili, 2020). The effect of this lack of PPE on healthcare workers was substantial: by July 24, more than thirteen thousand healthcare workers were infected, and one hundred had died (Agence France-Presse, 2020).

A report by Eastern Cape's COVID-19 Command Council read, "It would appear from the data that the lockdown did not produce the required increase in capacity" (quoted in Mail and Guardian Data Desk et al., 2020). Amid a surge of infections, overwhelmed government clinics in the Eastern Cape's Mandela Bay area closed, with staff not reporting for work at a hospital in Zwide, leading to further strain on the health system (Majavu, 2020a). An emergency room doctor at Zwide's Dora Nginza Hospital remarked, "The Eastern Cape Department of Health is in crisis. The ship has long sunk. There are corpses inside the hospital—it is smelling, there is no human dignity. It is overcrowded . . . Our people are lying like dogs here inside" (quoted in Majavu, 2020a). More than one thousand critical care beds were still projected to be needed to manage the surge in August and September 2020 in the Eastern Cape alone (Nortier, 2020b). One opposition member of parliament remarked, "Mkhize told the country the health sector was ready for Covid when it wasn't" (quoted in Merten, 2020).

In addition, allegations of corruption and mismanagement dogged some money intended for coronavirus relief. The Eastern Cape Health Department intended to use R 10 million to purchase motorcycles with sidecars for sick patients, a move that was immediately criticized for its appropriateness in bumpy, rainy terrain. The provincial government then suggested the motorcycles were for tracing teams before awarding a tender for one hundred mobile clinics but then never paid for the clinics (Majavu, 2020b).

Backlash from the Lockdown

Although the National Academy of Science had publicly stated its approval for the science-based decision-making of the government, by mid-April 2020 concern, and later criticism, over the science that guided the government's approach began to surface. Even though some projections from the original model that guided government policy had been leaked to press in mid-March 2020, the chair of the Minister of Health's Advisory Committee, Salim Abdool Karim, offered no information on projected numbers of infections, admissions, or deaths at a briefing in mid-April, with the numbers kept from the public "to avoid panic" (quoted in Muller, 2020). However, the presentation recognized that the "population will be at high risk again after the lockdown" (Karim, 2020a). As of mid-May 2020, some outside analysts were contending that the government's coronavirus numbers were "'implausibly' low" and calling the government out on its lack of transparency (Wild, 2020). Alex van den Heever, an economist from the University of Witwatersrand, remarked, "That is not how you manage an epidemic. You manage an epidemic by being more open, more democratic and allowing for critical review and comment" (quoted in Wild, 2020). It was not until the end of May 2020 that the government began releasing details on its models (Muller, 2020).

Shabhir Madhi, a past head of NICD and a former head of the Medical Research Council, argued that "the [initial SACEMA] modelling of how many people would contract Covid-19 and die was 'flawed and illogical and made wild assumptions,'" issues he had apparently raised with the modelers at the beginning (quoted in Child, 2020a). The frightening initial figures forecast more than 350,000 deaths, which was ten times the number of people who die of TB in South Africa annually (28,678 in 2017) (Child, 2020a). Madhi himself projected 25,000 deaths this year and 43,000 over two (Child, 2020a). Another updated model in mid-May 2020 predicted that the country could see as many as 50,000 deaths and 3 million infections by year's end (Toyana, 2020).

Social Policy Responses

Debates raged among scientists over the epidemiological projections that informed the government's response in a country where the poor make up half the population and which had historically experienced unemployment rates between 25 and 50 percent. Meanwhile, lockdown of the continent's most industrialized economy also began to provoke strong reaction from society more broadly. Initially, some experts projected economic contraction of as much as 6 percent with more than a million jobs lost, with other projections half that (Child, 2020a; Zane, 2020). Of even greater concern was the lack of indication that the government had formulated a plan for critical emergency relief when the lockdown began; school feeding programs, which had provided meals for nine million children on a daily basis, simply shut down without any plan to fill the gap that was created (Seekings, 2020d, p. 12).

To address the economic devastation, in late April, President Ramaphosa announced a R 500 billion (US$26.64 billion) stimulus package, with approximately 10 percent of the package earmarked for the poor and unemployed (Cocks, 2020; Zane, 2020). These new programs stood on top of the country's social grant system, known to be one of the largest in the world and included increases to the country's existing Child Support Grants, Older Persons' Grants, and Disability Grants, in addition to the introduction of a new COVID-19 emergency grant and food parcel distribution (Seekings, 2020a). However, the programs' slow rollout (a budget was not tabled until June 24, 2020) and the smaller amount earmarked for the program (R 40 billion for social grants, rather than the R 50 billion originally promised by Ramaphosa) disappointed many (Webster, 2020a). Rapid rollout of a new COVID emergency grant fell prey to implementation problems, with just 120,000 paid out by the end of May 2020 and the scope of the program reduced to 3.5 million from 8 million originally (Seekings, 2020d, p. 41). For many of the country's poor, this meant emergency relief hinged entirely on the delivery of food parcels, whose total number (including those financed and distributed by civil society groups, which were the lion's share) is estimated to have been between 105,000 and 1 million, well below the 6 million that were needed over three months (Seekings, 2020c, pp. 18–19, 21; Seekings, 2020d, p. 42).

In mid-June 2020 President Ramaphosa announced a new six-month, means-tested coronavirus unemployment grant of R 350 (US$21) through October along with the distribution of 250,000 food packages ("Coronavirus South Africa: How to apply for unemployment grant," 2020). Together, the temporary unemployment insurance program and the new and enhanced social assistance measures aimed to expand financial support to between one-half to two-thirds of the population (Seekings, 2020d). Beset by new funding needs, South Africa applied for a R 73 billion (US$4.2 billion) loan from the International Monetary Fund (IMF)—its first in twenty-six years; the loan, equivalent to 1.4 percent of the gross domestic product would finance under 10 percent of the year's budget, the need for a much larger stimulus notwithstanding (Gqubule, 2020).

Economists such as Seán Muller of the University of Johannesburg argued, "The most glaring failure of the government in its Covid-19 response was that it did not conceive that greater social protection spending would be needed when it implemented the lockdown" (quoted in Webster, 2020a). The impact on the country's poor and vulnerable also made for particularly pitched battles among political parties competing for constituents. Julius Malema, head of the populist Economic Freedom Fighters, criticized the governing ANC for focusing the aid too much on Whites and the wealthy: "Our government ... loves to keep white people happy and safe, even at the expense of Africans ... Even when they want to be in self-isolation, our people do not have spacious houses to isolate into because they stay in shacks. Even when they want to keep maximum hygiene ... they do not have access to clean water" (quoted in Cocks, 2020).

The most robust estimates of the impact of COVID-19 on employment and job loss were released two and a half months later in mid-July as part of the National

Income Dynamics Study—Coronavirus Rapid Mobile Survey (NIDS-CRAM). The study found that the impacts were even more catastrophic than earlier predictions, with three million jobs lost as a result of COVID-19, 20 percent of them permanently (Webster, 2020b). The crisis had pushed nearly a third of those now out of work into poverty, which translated into three million people when their dependents were included, with Blacks, women, and the poor hardest hit (Webster, 2020b). Moreover, the study found that the COVID-19 Temporary Employee/Employer Relief Scheme set up to benefit the unemployed benefited just 20 percent of its target population, with domestic workers and farm workers among the excluded (Cabe, 2020; Webster, 2020b). Had grants such as these been put in place from the start of the crisis, rather than at April's end, poverty could have been reduced by as much as 40 percent (Webster, 2020b).

Many were also unhappy with the country's ban on cigarettes and alcohol as part of the lockdown. However, the problem of hunger loomed even larger: even before the pandemic, up to 14 million people faced food shortages in South Africa (Seekings, 2020b). Hunger is ultimately what led more than 500 people without masks to stand in line to receive food parcels in the community of Makause in eastern Gauteng (Nyoka, 2020). The lockdown forced food sellers in the informal sector, who provided food to many, to close, at the same time that food prices rose (Bassier et al., 2020). As activist General Alfred Moyo reported, "People no longer cared about sanitisers, toilet paper or water and soap, they were now worried about stomach and food" (quoted in Nyoka, 2020). Even the chair of the South African Medical Research Council, Glenda Gray, lambasted the administration over the effect of the lockdown on malnutrition, and Groote Schuur Hospital's head of infectious diseases and HIV medicine argued that the lockdown was "doing more harm than good" (quoted in Karrim & Evans, 2020). The Health Minister's response to Gray was to issue a detailed point-by-point statement saying that it was "devoid of the truth" (Mkhize, 2020).

By late May, the president conceded that "the current lockdown could not be sustained indefinitely" and announced an easing of restrictions to level three, even as the "numbers will rise even further and even faster," which they did (quoted in "Coronavirus in South Africa: President," 2020) (Figure 32.1).

At level three, the country's economy would begin to reopen. However, restaurants, hair salons, and bars would remain closed along with restrictions to air travel and public gatherings ("Ramaphosa: South Africa Coronavirus Lockdown to Ease from June 1," 2020). Further amendments allowed theatres, galleries, cinemas, libraries, and casinos to open with space and capacity restrictions (Mafolo, 2020). At level three, more than 500,000 people would be allowed to return to work (Ellis, 2020). However, some businesses that were to remain closed, including restaurants and cafes, organized protests by opening, supported by the Democratic Alliance, in opposition to the closure orders by the ANC; the police fired water cannons into the businesses to close them (Williams, 2020).

The decision to open the economy before the epidemic peaked went against the counsel of the WHO (Smith & Coleman, 2020), and the potential for different

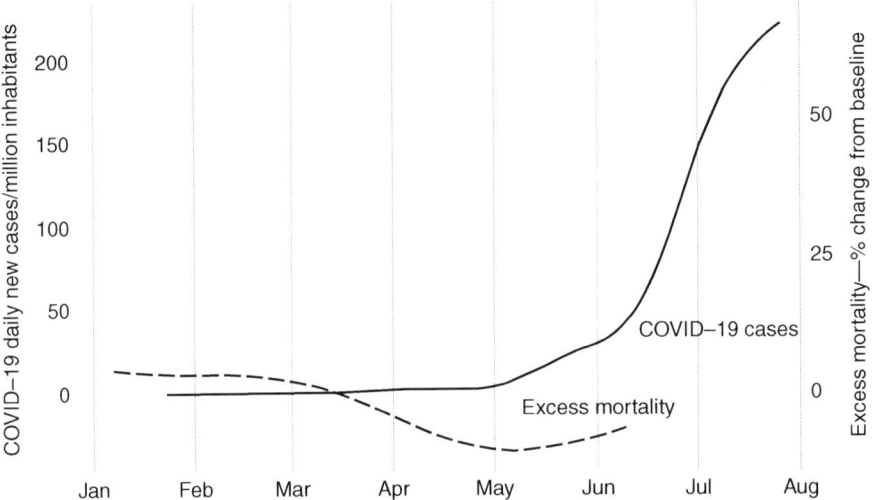

Figure 32.1. COVID-19 Cases and All-Cause Excess Mortality in South Africa.
Source: Johns Hopkins University Center for Systems Science and Engineering COVID-19 Data and the Financial Times, 2020.

regions of the country returning to level four or five restrictions remained ("Ramaphosa: South Africa Coronavirus Lockdown to Ease from June 1," 2020). But so committed to reopening was the government that it successfully fought a legal challenge that sought to prevent schools from reopening on the grounds of the danger posed to students and teachers (Magome, 2020). When the initial phase of school reopening began in June 2020 for grades 7 and 12, only students from those grades received meals, despite the school feeding schemes having been fully budgeted and planned for ("There Is No School Feeding," 2020). This led to a lawsuit by Section 27 and the Equal Education Law Centre, supported by an affidavit from the Director of University of Capetown's Centre for Social Science Research, on behalf of students and other concerned parties that aimed to force the government to reopen food programs to all students, because access to food and water was a constitutional right ("We Do Not Have Enough Food," 2020). The High Court of Gauteng recognized this right and required the government to bring back the National School Nutrition Program, which provided schoolchildren a meal each day (Nortier, 2020a). By mid-July, in spite of the sharply rising number of cases and against the advice of the Colleges of Medicine of South Africa, new regulations issued by President Ramaphosa and the cabinet allowed taxi bus operators to take passengers at 100 percent capacity for short distances with ventilation and 70 percent for long distances (Simelane, 2020). Notably, at this time, scientists stood less frequently alongside Ramaphosa at press conferences.

In spite of the administration's growing disagreements with scientists over reopening plans, the country's main opposition party, the Democratic Alliance argued that the move to level three came "six weeks too late" ("Ramaphosa: South Africa Coronavirus Lockdown to Ease from June 1," 2020). And a High Court decision in early June declared the third and fourth levels of South Africa's five-part COVID-19 restrictions unconstitutional and gave the government fourteen days to comply (Mayberry et al., 2020). While the courts were dissembling the government's ability to impose restrictions and lockdown restrictions were being eased, viral transmission was ramping up, with the country experiencing its largest case numbers to date the first week of June (Scott, 2020). The government filed an appeal of the judgment immediately (Rabkin, 2020). The cabinet once again closed schools for four weeks, July 27, 2020, to August 24, 2020, because of a rising surge of infections (Macupe & Kiewit, 2020). However, the closure went against the recommendations of the chair of the country's COVID-19 Advisory Committee on the grounds that it posed little risk to them ("Karim Explains Why Schools Should Remain Open," 2020).

Direct and Indirect Health Effects

Like the UK's original Imperial Model, South Africa's model originally projected far more death and devastation than initially played out. Toward the end of May, the country had the largest number of cases on the continent at 21,343 but had fewer deaths than Algeria or Egypt at 407 ("Coronavirus in South Africa: Outbreak," 2020). Early on, the majority of cases were centered in Durban and Johannesburg, but over time that began to change (Wroughton & Bearak, 2020). As of mid to late May, approximately 60 percent of the country's cases at that time were in Cape Town, largely a function of exposure to tourists from coronavirus hotspots in other parts of the world and superspreading events that had occurred at a pharmaceutical factory and two grocery stores; the working class, predominantly mixed race community of Tygerberg and majority black Khayelitsha were the hardest hit parts of the city (Wroughton & Bearak, 2020). By the end of July 2020, Gauteng province had the largest number of cases, with Western Cape, Eastern Cape, KwaZulu-Natal following; case numbers in the country's other provinces remained at or below 22,000 (Department of Health and National Institute for Communicable Diseases, 2020). However, KwaZulu-Natal was quickly becoming the country's new epicenter of the disease, with regular new infections of 3,000 or more daily; despite there being a regulation against them, large funerals—some larger than 1,000 people—were a driver of spread (Harper, 2020; Smit & Kiewit, 2020).

The inability to stem the spread of infection and the lack of effective testing and tracing was eventually reflected in the country's death toll. A report by the South African Medical Research Council found there to be 17,000 more deaths than normal ("excess deaths") between early May and mid-July 2020, suggesting that official statistics that had found approximately 6,800 COVID-19 deaths at that time might be dramatically underreporting the true total (Nortier, 2020b). By mid-September 2020, the number of excess deaths reported between May 6 and September 8 stood at 44,467, whereas the officially reported number of deaths attributed to COVID stood at just under 16,000, suggesting that the true total of devastation was much higher than officially reported (Bradshaw et al., 2020).

With a full fifth of the world's HIV and TB cases (Mogotsi & Bearak, 2020), a significant concern for South Africans was the role that compromised immune systems might play in facilitating the spread of infection and death (Toyana, 2020). The NIDS-CRAM study found that fear of contracting COVID-19 had led to dramatic increases in the number of patients needing acute healthcare who decided to forego it and the number of patients who were unable to access medication and contraceptives, as well as a sharp decrease in the number of women and mothers who visited healthcare facilities (Mmotla, 2020). A separate survey by the Human Sciences Research Council found access to medicine to be a particular problem in informal settlements; HIV viral load and TB testing were also both down, some by as much as 50 percent (Gonzales, 2020b; Bekker, 2020). In May 2020 alone, in Gauteng province, twelve thousand TB and HIV patients did not collect their medication (Mmotla, 2020), a development that could not only impact individual patients' health but also contribute to drug resistance and the country's ability to finance more expensive second- and third-line treatments.

The disruption of HIV treatment in sub-Saharan Africa more generally was projected to lead to a half a million AIDS deaths between 2020 and 2021 (Gonzales, 2020b). In addition, there was a growing possibility that the country would face additional threats from other diseases. Fewer vaccinations for diseases such as measles were also taking place during the lockdown (Child, 2020a). People locked down in crowded conditions also meant the potential for easy spread of TB (Blumberg et al., 2020).

Explanation of Policy Choices

The insulation that allowed the ANC to ignore social pressure and promote denialist policies at odds with mainstream science to devastating effect under the Mbeki administration is no longer. In the context of heightened political competition, the Ramaphosa administration heeded the advice of scientists and medical professionals and took aggressive measures to curb spread of the virus initially. Although the assumptions behind the epidemiological models that guided the government response ultimately proved to be flawed, the lockdown still bought the government time to shore up its health system to respond to the novel threat posed by the coronavirus. Some of the shortages in beds, PPE, and workers that did become evident are less ascribable to weaknesses in the administration's response, rather than to historical underinvestment in public health infrastructure and workforce. However, the administration's lack of plan to address hunger, access to medicine, and economic devastation and slow implementation allowed pressure for reopening to build. Over time, as more and more pressure built, a larger and larger schism developed between the administration and the scientists advising it. The decision to reopen before the epidemic had peaked—against the advice of the WHO—led to a surge of infections that has mired the country in an outbreak whose epicenter has moved from the country's largest cities to the periphery and, in the future, likely back again.

Although the party's increased exposure to political competition made it more receptive to science initially, as of this writing, these external pressures have not yet been strong enough to sustain that receptivity, nor have they been sufficient to resolve the party's susceptibility to corruption, even under a new leadership that had envisioned a decisive break from the Jacob Zuma and Thabo Mbeki eras. The country's coronavirus response itself became marred by major corruption scandals that have included the president's own spokeswoman, with desperately needed food parcels and unemployment insurance money being siphoned off to political cronies while citizens go hungry (Chutel, 2020). A lack of state capacity and a decentralized federalist system have complicated the response further, making a response that has been far from perfect more uneven.

Conclusion

The case of South Africa lays bare the complexities and pressures that leaders face who are governing countries in which a significant proportion of the population is vulnerable because of poverty. The additional vulnerability posed by the country's sizable TB and HIV epidemics made the South African population susceptible to more fatal cases of coronavirus. Officials had to balance the need for lockdown to stem spread of a virus with the need to ensure that the population has access to food and lifesaving medicine in the broader context of resource constraints. A great failure of the Ramaphosa government's response was an inability to plan for and then implement rapidly and effectively programs to serve these predictable needs. In fact, there is some strong evidence that the government's policymaking in these important areas actually represented steps backward. With the closure of school nutrition programs when schools shuttered, the "total volume of food distributed to the poor under three months of lockdown was small *compared to the total volume distributed ordinarily*" (Seekings, 2020d, p. 42, italics added). This lack of planning amounted to a "comprehensive failure to ensure that poor South Africans could access food during the lockdown," leaving civil society to scramble to address citizen needs in the wake of government failure (Seekings, 2020c, p. 1).

In this, the Ramaphosa and Mbeki administrations may have more in common than at first seems apparent. Both leaders recognized the need to address issues related to poverty when the country was grappling with the crisis posed by a pandemic. Although Thabo Mbeki is rightly criticized for the death and devastation his AIDS denialism wrought, he is also known for having been concerned with the relationship between poverty and health and was an advocate of the country's system of social grants, which are among the most sweeping in the world. Yet some of the measures that would have paid the largest dividends during

COVID-19, such as the basic income grant, failed to materialize. Whereas the unconscionable delays under Mbeki related to rollout of AIDS treatment and prophylaxis, under Ramaphosa the unconscionable delays were in relation to making sure food and income replacement were provided to people in desperate need, a problem that itself hurt the country's ability to maintain the lockdown. A universal basic income grant—which had been promoted by the Concerned Africans Forum and Black Sash—eventually came to be part of national policy discussions but came later and did so at a difficult moment (Seekings, 2020c, p. 9; "South Africa Is Getting a New Universal Income Grant," 2020). As other work has suggested (van de Ruit & Breckenridge, 2019), contentious public interest litigation in the courts can be a critical tool for advancing public health in both eras. However, the major lesson from these epidemics is the need to address basic human needs and public health concerns effectively at the same time.

Acknowledgments

I would like to thank Sara Compion, Nicoli Nattrass, and Catherine van de Ruit for their comments on this chapter, which helped improve it immensely.

References

Academy of Science of South Africa. (2020, May 18). *Public statement on COVID-19.* ASSAf.

Agence France-Presse. (2020, July 23). Over 13,000 S. African health workers contract coronavirus. *The Jakarta Post.* https://www.thejakartapost.com/news/2020/07/24/over-13000-s-african-health-workers-contract--coronavirus.html

Bassier, I., Joala, R, & Vilakazi, T. (2020, July 31). South Africa needs better food price controls to shield poor people from COVID-19 fallout. *The Conversation.* https://theconversation.com/south-africa-needs-better-food-price-controls-to-shield-poor-people-from-covid-19-fallout-143288

Bekker, L. [@LindaGailBekker]. (2020, July 23). Speaking of #collateraldamage. *Twitter.* https://twitter.com/LindaGailBekker?ref_src=twsrc%5Egoogle%7Ctwcamp%5Eserp%7Ctwgr%5Eauthor

Benatar, S. (2020, June 9). *The complex juggling act of healthcare resource allocation during the Covid-19 pandemic.* Daily Maverick. https://www.dailymaverick.co.za/article/2020-06-09-the-complex-juggling-act-of-healthcare-resource-allocation-during-the-covid-19-pandemic/

Blumberg, L., Jassat, W., Mendelson, M., & Cohen, C. (2020, July 8). *The COVID-19 crisis in South Africa: Protecting the vulnerable.* SAMJ Editorial.

Bornman, J. (2020, July 26). Police killings started early in SA's lockdown. *New Frame.* https://www.newframe.com/police-killings-started-early-in-sas-lockdown/

Bradshaw, D., Laubscher, R., Dorrington, R., Groenewald, P., & Moultrie, T. (2020, September 15). *Report on Weekly Deaths in South Africa 1 January –8 September 2020*

(Week 36). South African Medical Research Council. https://www.samrc.ac.za/sites/default/files/files/2020-09-16/weekly8September2020.pdf

Cabe, M. (2020, July 7). *Workers still can't access Covid-19 relief.* New Frame. https://www.newframe.com/workers-still-cant-access-covid-19-relief/

Caincross, L., Reynolds, L., & Benjamin, P. (2020, June 21). *A fundamental shift is required to pool health resources to ensure public sector patients aren't left behind.* Daily Maverick. https://www.dailymaverick.co.za/article/2020-06-21-a-fundamental-shift-is-required-to-pool-health-resources-to-ensure-public-sector-patients-arent-left-behind/

Chatterjee, A., Czajka, L, & Gethin, A. (2020, April). *Estimating the distribution of household wealth in South Africa*. WIDER Working Paper 2020/45. Helsinki: UNU-WIDER.

Chigwedere, P., Seage III, G., Gruskin, S., Lee, T., & Essex, M. (2008). Estimating the lost benefits of antiretroviral drug use in South Africa. *JAIDS, 49*(4), 410–15.

Child, K. (2020a, April 24). *SA's Covid-19 models were 'flawed,' says former NICD expert.* Financial Mail. https://www.businesslive.co.za/fm/features/2020-04-24-sas-covid-19-models-were-flawed-says-former-nicd-expert/

Child, K. (2020b, May 20). *More than 40,000 deaths predicted: Behind SA's Covid-19 models.* Financial Mail. https://www.businesslive.co.za/fm/features/2020-05-20-more-than-40000-deaths-predicted-behind-sas-covid-19-models/

Chutel, L. (2020, August 19). South Africa's big coronavirus aid effort tainted by corruption. *The New York Times.* https://www.nytimes.com/2020/08/19/world/africa/coronavirus-south-africa-aid-corruption.html

Cleary, K. (2020, June 23). *In depth: The deals that will see public sector patients in private hospitals.* Daily Maverick. https://www.dailymaverick.co.za/article/2020-06-23-in-depth-the-deals-that-will-see-public-sector-patients-in-private-hospitals/

Cocks, T. (2020, April 27). *Coronavirus stirs rancor in South Africa on democracy anniversary.* Reuters. https://www.reuters.com/article/us-health-coronavirus-safrica/coronavirus-stirs-rancour-in-south-africa-on-democracy-anniversary-idUSKCN229237

Coronavirus in South Africa: Outbreak closes Mponeng gold mine. (2020, May 24). BBC. https://www.bbc.com/news/world-africa-52791780

Coronavirus in South Africa: President Ramaphosa says outbreak will get worse. (2020, May 25). BBC. https://www.bbc.com/news/world-africa-52793349

Coronavirus South Africa: How to apply for unemployment grant. (2020, June 18). AS. https://en.as.com/en/2020/04/25/other_sports/1587843624_718597.html

Cowan, K. (2020, March 19). *The terrifying coronavirus projections that pushed government into lockdown.* News24. https://www.news24.com/news24/SouthAfrica/News/exclusive-the-terrifying-coronavirus-projections-that-pushed-government-into-lockdown-action-20200319

Debut, B. (2020, June 9). South African schools reopen after March lockdown eased. *The Jakarta Post.* https://www.thejakartapost.com/news/2020/06/09/south-african-schools-reopen-after-march-lockdown-eased-.html

Department of Health and National Institute for Communicable Diseases. (2020, July 31). National COVID-19 daily report. https://www.nicd.ac.za/wp-content/uploads/2020/07/COVID-19-Daily-Report-National-Internal-31July2020.pdf

Ellis, E. (2020, June 18). *Gender-based violence is South Africa's second pandemic, says Ramaphosa.* Daily Maverick. https://www.dailymaverick.co.za/article/2020-06-18-gender-based-violence-is-south-africas-second-pandemic-says-ramaphosa/

Evans, S. (2020, May 13). *Lockdown and other interventions potentially saved 20 000 lives—top scientist.* News24. https://www.news24.com/news24/SouthAfrica/News/lockdown-and-other-interventions-potentially-saved-20-000-lives-top-scientist-20200513

Flans, S., Fiphaza, A., & Njamela, A. (2020, July 16). *COVID EVICTIONS: "We're humans, not pigs."* Bhekisisa. https://bhekisisa.org/multimedia/videos/2020-07-16-covid-evictions-were-humans-not-pigs/

Gilili, C. (2020, June 19). *"We spread the virus knowingly at this hospital"—healthcare workers at Thelle Mogoerane.* Mail and Guardian. https://mg.co.za/coronavirus-essentials/2020-06-19-spread-the-virus-knowingly-at-this-hospital-thelle-mogoerane/

Gonzales, L. L. (2020a, July 10). *COVID-19 casualties: Why medical aids are keen on saving South Africa's failing medical practices.* Bhekisisa. https://www.newsbreak.com/news/1598203158637/covid-19-casualties-why-medical-aids-are-keen-on-saving-south-africas-failing-medical-practices

Gonzales, L. L. (2020b, July 24). *A tale of two pandemics: Covid-19 and lessons learnt from HIV.* Bhekisisa. https://bhekisisa.org/article/2020-07-24-hiv-and-covid19-south-africa-community-engagement/

Gqubule, D. (2020, July 2). *Is SA's IMF loan about economics or politics?* New Frame. https://www.newframe.com/is-sas-imf-loan-about-economics-or-politics/

Harding, A. (2020, April 10). *Coronavirus in South Africa: The lull before the surge?* BBC. https://www.bbc.com/news/world-africa-52228932

Harper, P. (2020, July 28). *KwaZulu-Natal is emerging as a new Covid-19 epicentre.* Mail and Guardian. https://mg.co.za/coronavirus-essentials/2020-07-28-kwazulu-natal-is-emerging-as-a-new-covid-19-epicentre/

Harris, J. (2017). *Achieving access: Professional movements and the politics of health universalism.* Cornell University Press.

Harrisberg, K. (2020, April 24). *Evictions, power cuts heighten S. Africa housing crisis amid lockdown.* Reuters. https://www.reuters.com/article/us-health-coronavirus-safrica-homes-feat/evictions-power-cuts-heighten-south-africa-housing-crisis-amid-lockdown-idUSKCN22615J

Karim explains why schools should remain open. (2020, July 22). eNCA. https://www.enca.com/news/watch-karim-explains-why-schools-should-remain-open

Karim, S. A. (2020a, April 13). *SA's COVID-19 epidemic: Trends & next steps.* Department of Health.

Karim, S. A. (2020b, May 29). The South African Response to the Pandemic. *New England Journal of Medicine, 382*, e95(1–3).

Karim, Q. A., & Karim, S. A. (2020, July 24). COVID-19 affects HIV and tuberculosis care. *Science.*

Karrim, A. & Evans, S. (2020, May 16). *Unscientific and nonsensical: Top scientist slams government's lockdown strategy.* News24. https://www.news24.com/news24/SouthAfrica/News/unscientific-and-nonsensical-top-scientific-adviser-slams-governments-lockdown-strategy-20200516

Macupe, B. & Kiewit, L. (2020, July 23). *Schools to close for a month due to Covid infection surge—Ramaphosa.* Mail and Guardian. https://mg.co.za/coronavirus-essentials/2020-07-23-schools-to-close-for-a-month-due-to-covid-infection-surge-ramaphosa/

Mafolo, K. (2020, June 26). *Theatres, cinemas, galleries and casinos to open under Level 3.* Daily Maverick. https://www.dailymaverick.co.za/article/2020-06-26-theatres-cinemas-galleries-and-casinos-to-open-under-level-3/

Magome, M. (2020, July 6). *South Africa begins second phase of reopening of schools.* Medical Xpress. https://medicalxpress.com/news/2020-07-south-africa-phase-reopening-schools.html

Magome, M., & Meldrum, A. (2020, April 27). South Africa's inequalities exposed by virus, says leader. *U.S. News and World Report.* https://www.usnews.com/news/world/articles/2020-04-27/cuban-doctors-arrive-to-help-south-africa-fight-coronavirus

Mail and Guardian Data Desk. (2020, June 3). *The backlogs, denials and future of testing Covid-19.* Mail and Guardian. https://mg.co.za/coronavirus-essentials/2020-06-03-the-backlogs-denials-and-future-of-testing-covid-19/

Mail and Guardian Data Desk, Smit, S., & Gilili, C. (2020, June 18). *SA accelerating towards virus peak without capacity, experts warn.* Mail and Guardian. https://mg.co.za/coronavirus-essentials/2020-06-18-sa-accelerating-towards-virus-peak-without-capacity-experts-warn/

Majavu, A. (2020a, July 1). *Port Elizabeth hospitals flooded as clinics close.* New Frame. https://www.newframe.com/port-elizabeth-hospitals-flooded-as-clinics-close/

Majavu, A. (2020b, July 16). *Mobile clinics on hold in Eastern Cape.* New Frame. https://www.newframe.com/mobile-clinics-on-hold-in-eastern-cape/

Mayberry, K., Melimopoulos, E., & Najjar, F. (2020, June 2). *S Africa Court Rules Some Coronavirus Curbs Invalid: Live Updates.* Al Jazeera. https://www.aljazeera.com/news/2020/6/2/s-africa-court-rules-some-coronavirus-curbs-invalid-live-updates

Mbalula, F. (2020, April 17). *Statement issued by the minister of transport, Fikile Mbalula, on the occasion of the release of Easter fatalities statistics on 17 April 2020.* Department of Transport, RSA.

Merten, M. (2020, July 24). *Zweli Mkhize plays down discrepancy in reported deaths.* Daily Maverick. https://www.dailymaverick.co.za/article/2020-07-24-zweli-mkhize-plays-down-discrepancy-in-reported-deaths/

Mkhize, Z. (2020, May 20). *Health Minister's statement on Professor Glenda Gray's public attack of government based on inaccurate information.* Department of Health.

Mitchley, A. (2020, July 2). *Gauteng health facilities have reached maximum bed capacity.* News24. https://www.news24.com/news24/southafrica/news/gauteng-health-facilities-have-reached-maximum-bed-capacity-department-20200702

Mmotla, T. (2020, July 15). *Counting Covid-19's cost on other health issues.* New Frame. https://www.newframe.com/counting-covid-19s-cost-on-other-health-issues/

Mogotsi, B., & Bearak, Max. (2020, April 21). *South Africa is hunting down coronavirus with thousands of health workers.* BBC. https://www.washingtonpost.com/world/africa/south-africa-is-hunting-down-coronavirus-with-tens-of-thousands-of-health-workers/2020/04/21/6511307a-8306-11ea-81a3-9690c9881111_story.html

Muller, S. M. (2020, June 9). *South Africa's modeling for Covid-19 has been deeply flawed with major consequences.* Quartz Africa. https://qz.com/africa/1866381/south-africas-covid-19-modeling-is-deeply-flawed/

Nordling, L. (2020a, April 15). South Africa flattens its coronavirus curve—and considers how to ease restrictions. *Science.*

Nordling, L. (2020b, July 24). "Our epidemic could exceed a million cases" South Africa's top coronavirus adviser. *Nature.*

Nortier, C. (2020a, July 17). *Court orders government to provide all schoolchildren with a daily meal.* Daily Maverick. https://www.dailymaverick.co.za/article/2020-07-17-court-orders-government-to-provide-all-schoolchildren-with-a-daily-meal/

Nortier, C. (2020b, July 24). *Ramaphosa takes tough stance on corruption, schools reclose for a month, and pandemic's official death toll is cast into doubt.* Daily Maverick. https://www.dailymaverick.co.za/article/2020-07-24-ramaphosa-takes-tough-stance-on-corruption-schools-reclose-for-a-month-and-pandemics-official-death-toll-is-cast-into-doubt/

Nyoka, N. (2020, July 14). *Starvation will kill faster than the virus.* New Frame. https://www.newframe.com/starvation-will-kill-faster-than-the-virus/

Rabkin, F. (2020, June 9). *Dlamini-Zuma seeks to appeal the judgment that set aside lockdown regulations.* Mail and Guardian. https://mg.co.za/politics/2020-06-09-dlamini-zuma-seeks-to-appeal-the-judgment-that-set-aside-lockdown-regulations/

Ramaphosa, C. (2020, July 12). *Statement by President Cyril Ramaphosa on progress in the national effort to contain the COVID-19 pandemic.* Office of the President, RSA.

Ramaphosa: South Africa coronavirus lockdown to ease from June 1. (2020, May 25), Al Jazeera. https://www.aljazeera.com/economy/2020/5/25/ramaphosa-south-africa-coronavirus-lockdown-to-ease-from-june-1

Reuter, L. (2020, July 12). The response by African states cannot be generalized. *Gerda Henkel Foundation Science Portal.* https://lisa.gerda-henkel-stiftung.de/corona_south_africa?language=en

Ritchie, H., Ortis-Ospina, E., Beltekian, D., Mathieu, E., Hasell, J., Macdonald, B., Giattino, C., & Roser, M. (2020, December 4). South Africa: Coronavirus Pandemic Country Profile. *Our World in Data.* https://ourworldindata.org/coronavirus/country/south-africa?country=~ZAF

Scott, D. (2020, June 8). *These 7 countries have the most worrying Covid-19 outbreaks.* Vox. https://www.vox.com/2020/6/8/21284315/coronavirus-cases-update-us-india-brazil-south-africa

Seekings, J. (2020a, April 23). *Covid-19: Ramaphosa's plan is good, but the budget is insufficient.* Daily Maverick. https://www.dailymaverick.co.za/article/2020-04-23-covid-19-ramaphosas-plan-is-good-but-the-budget-is-insufficient/

Seekings, J. (2020b, June 2). *Feeding poor people: The national government has failed.* Daily Maverick. https://www.dailymaverick.co.za/article/2020-06-02-feeding-poor-people-the-national-government-has-failed/

Seekings, J. (2020c, July). *Failure to feed: State, civil society and feeding schemes in South Africa in the first three months of Covid-19 lockdown, March to June 2020.* (CSSR Working Paper No. 455). Cape Town: Centre for Social Science Research.

Seekings, J. (2020d, July). *Bold promises, constrained capacity, stumbling delivery: The expansion of social protection in response to the Covid-19 lockdown in South Africa.* CSSR Working Paper No. 456. Cape Town: Centre for Social Science Research.

Seekings, J., & Nattrass, N. (2015). *Policy, politics and poverty in South Africa.* Springer.

Simelane, B. (2020, July 15). *"Review 100% taxi capacity"—Public health specialists plead with Ramaphosa.* Daily Maverick. https://www.dailymaverick.co.za/article/2020-07-15-review-100-taxi-capacity-public-health-specialists-plead-with-ramaphosa/

Singh, K. (2020, April 22). *Murder cases down by 72%.* News24. https://www.news24.com/news24/SouthAfrica/News/murder-down-by-1-110-cases-cele-attributes-drop-to-alcohol-ban-increased-patrols-and-lockdown-20200422

Smillie, S. (2020, July 21). *All systems go at Nasrec field hospital, thanks to public's generosity.* Daily Maverick. https://www.dailymaverick.co.za/article/2020-07-21-all-systems-go-at-nasrec-field-hospital-thanks-to-publics-generosity/

Smit, S., & Kiewit, L. (2020, July 12). *Ramaphosa asks all South Africans to help to avoid 50 000 Covid-19 deaths this year.* Mail and Guardian. https://mg.co.za/coronavirus-essentials/2020-07-12-ramaphosa-asks-all-south-africans-to-help-to-avoid-50-000-covid-19-deaths-this-year/

Smith, M., & Coleman, N. (2020, July 24). *Covid-19: Towards a safer more cautious and more equitable opening of the economy in SA.* Daily Maverick. https://www.dailymaverick.co.za/article/2020-07-24-covid-19-towards-a-safer-more-cautious-and-more-equitable-opening-of-the-economy-in-sa/

South Africa is getting a new universal income grant: Report. (2020, July 14). BusinessTech. https://businesstech.co.za/news/finance/415935/south-africa-is-getting-a-new-universal-income-grant-report/

There is no school feeding. (2020, June 12). Daily Maverick. https://www.dailymaverick.co.za/article/2020-06-12-there-is-no-school-feeding/

Toyana, M. (2020, May 21). *South Africa scientists say up to 50,000 COVID-19 deaths possible.* Reuters. https://www.reuters.com/article/us-health-coronavirus-safrica-models/south-africa-scientists-say-up-to-50000-covid-19-deaths-possible-idUSKBN22X180

van de Ruit, C., & Breckenridge, A. (2019, August 9). *A 2019 Community health workers' pursuit of workplace recognition in the South African health system.* American Sociological Association 2019 Global Health and HIV Preconference Workshop.

Webster, D. (2020a, June 26). *Slow rollout undermines Covid-19 social grant.* New Frame. https://www.newframe.com/slow-rollout-undermines-covid-19-social-grant/

Webster, D. (2020b, July 15). *Counting Covid-19's economic cost.* New Frame. https://www.newframe.com/counting-covid-19s-economic-cost/

"We do not have enough food." (2020, June 12). Daily Maverick. https://www.dailymaverick.co.za/article/2020-06-12-we-do-not-have-enough-food/

Wild, S. (2020, May 12). Antipoaching tech tracks COVID-19 flare-ups in South Africa. *Scientific American.* https://www.scientificamerican.com/article/antipoaching-tech-tracks-covid-19-flare-ups-in-south-africa/

Williams, M. (2020, July 24). *"You've been warned, disperse!"—Cape Town police get tough on tourism protesters.* News24. https://www.news24.com/news24/southafrica/news/watch-youve-been-warned-disperse-cape-town-police-get-tough-on-tourism-protesters-20200724

Winning, A. (2019, May 11). *South Africa's Ramaphosa targets reforms after election win.* Reuters. https://www.reuters.com/article/us-safrica-election-ramaphosa/south-africas-ramaphosa-targets-reforms-after-election-win-idUSKCN1SH0BL

World Food Programme. (2020, May 18). *COVID-19 response situation report.* WFP Southern Africa.

Wroughton, L., & Bearak, M. (2020, May 19). Cape Town has 10 percent of Africa's confirmed coronavirus cases. *Washington Post.* https://www.washingtonpost.com/world/africa/south-africa-coronavirus-cape-town-superspreader/2020/05/18/4d332248-9566-11ea-87a3-22d324235636_story.html

York, G. (2020, July 5). *COVID-19 exposes the fault lines of inequality in South Africa.* The Globe and Mail. https://www.theglobeandmail.com/world/article-covid-19-exposes-the-fault-lines-of-inequality-in-south-africa/

Zane, D. (2020, April 28). *Coronavirus: What African countries are doing to help people to eat amid the lockdowns.* BBC. https://www.bbc.com/news/world-africa-52426040

33 COMPARATIVE ANALYSIS OF COVID-19 TRANSMISSION AND MORTALITY IN SELECT AFRICAN COUNTRIES

Kanayo K. Ogujiuba and Uviwe Binase

COVID-19 cases spread inevitably in countries, ever since the initial confirmed cases in November 2019 at China. Although the number of COVID-19 cases and fatalities may still appear comparatively lower in Africa than in other world regions, as of this writing, the looming health shock of COVID-19 has adversely affected the continent's already stressed health systems and could quickly turn into a social and economic emergency. Beyond health jeopardies, the COVID-19 shock to African economies occurred in three waves: (1) lower trade and investment from China in the immediate term; (2) a demand slump associated with the lockdowns in the European Union and Organization for Economic Cooperation and Development (OECD) countries; and (3) a continental supply shock affecting domestic and intra-African trade.

In this chapter, the authors selected case studies by estimating the risk of African countries importing a COVID-19 case from China using data on the volume of air travel from infected Chinese provinces to Africa and the proportion of COVID-19 cases in the Chinese provinces as of February 11, 2020. Evidence suggests that Egypt, Algeria, and South Africa were at the highest risk of importing a COVID-19 case from China but had moderate to high preparedness and low vulnerability (Gilbert et al., 2020).

There were several countries in Africa with slightly lower risk of importing a case from China, and their levels of readiness and susceptibility varied. For example, Nigeria and Ethiopia had moderate preparedness but high vulnerability, and their countries had substantially larger populations that could be potentially exposed. However, Morocco, Sudan, Angola, Tanzania, Ghana, and Kenya had similar importation risk and population sizes but variable levels of preparedness and high vulnerability (except Morocco, which had low vulnerability). All other African countries had low to moderate importation risk with low to moderate vulnerability and mostly low preparedness, except for Tunisia and Rwanda.

In this chapter, analysis focuses on Nigeria, South Africa, and Egypt. South Africa and Egypt had moderate to high preparedness and low vulnerability, whereas Nigeria had moderate preparedness but high vulnerability. Furthermore, these countries are the three biggest economies in Africa. They are dissimilar

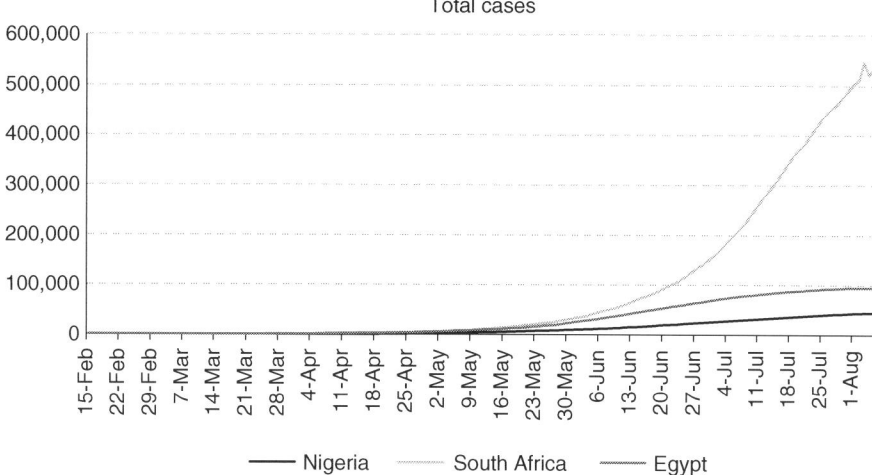

Figure 33.1. 2020 (February—August) Total COVID-19 cases in Nigeria, South Africa, and Egypt.
Source: Worldometer (2020).

regarding the governmental regime types but similar in terms of state capacity to handle emergencies and pandemics.

The spike in the total COVID-19 cases became evident beginning in June 2020 in Nigeria, South Africa, and Egypt (Figure 33.1). These countries had taken steps to build systems that would ensure prevention and early detection. To comprehend the effect of the COVID-19 pandemic, the public health policies and responses, social policies, and an evaluation of strategies used to combat COVID-19 are examined.

In comparison of COVID-19 confirmed cases in Nigeria, South Africa, and Egypt, Nigeria had the least reported cases and had reached only 1,000 reported cases by April 24, 2020 (WHO, 2020a). However, by May 31, 2020, Nigeria had 10,000 cases, and by June 17, they had 35,454 total cases. Among the three countries, South Africa was the first country to reach 1,000 cases (on March 27, 2020); Egypt reached this mark on April 3, 2020. On August 5, 2020, Nigeria had 94,875 confirmed cases. From February 15 to March 4, 2020, South Africa had no confirmed COVID-19 cases. The first case was reported on March 5, 2020, whereas Nigeria had its first case on February 28, 2020. Total cases increased dramatically in South Africa: by May 10, 2020, they had already reached more than 10,000 total cases and had more than 100,000 cases by June 22, 2020. South Africa reached an all-time high of 546,862 reported cases on August 3. This country saw a decline in COVID-19 reported cases days after, dropping to 529,877 on August 5. This was not the case for Egypt; they had their first case on February 15 and their second reported case on March 1, as evident from the Worldometer data. However, the International Monetary Fund (2020) reported Egypt's first case on February 14. Egypt had cases from February 15 until March 22, there was a

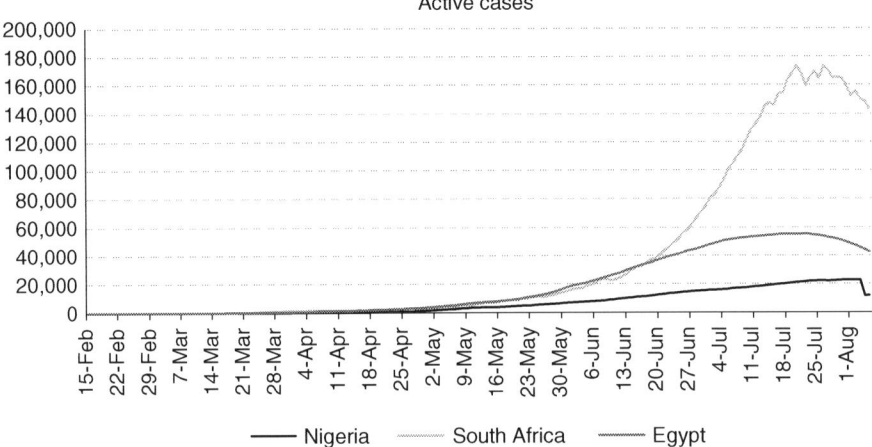

Figure 33.2. COVID-19 active cases in Nigeria, South Africa, and Egypt (February to August 2020).
Source: Worldometer (2020).

slight stability in reported cases days after whereas an increase was prominent in South African reported cases. However, by April 15, 2020, South Africa and Egypt both had approximately 2,505 total cases (Nordling, 2020). Nonetheless, subsequently Egypt had more cases than South Africa. South Africa had the highest confirmed total cases for COVID-19, active cases as well as death cases by July 17, 2020 (Wikipedia, 2020). However, South Africa and Egypt had overlapping cases in some instances, with Egypt having the highest reported cases.

Other countries in Africa have reported lower cases than South Africa, Nigeria, and Egypt. As of this writing, ten countries account for close to 80 percent of the total tests conducted: South Africa, Morocco, Ethiopia, Egypt, Ghana, Kenya, Nigeria, Rwanda, Uganda, and Mauritius. There are wide variations in testing rates, with South Africa doing the most and Nigeria doing relatively few per capita, according to World in Data, a UK-based project that collates COVID-19 information (Figure 33.2) (Our World in Data, 2020).

By October 11, 2020, South Africa had performed just over 74 tests per 1,000 people, as compared with more than 349 in the United Kingdom and 381 in the United States. Nigeria carried out just 2.7 tests per 1,000 people by October 13, 2020. About half of the countries on the continent had a ratio lower than the benchmark of doing at least ten tests for every positive case, as recommended by the Africa Centres for Disease Control and Prevention (CDC). Moreover, in some countries, there are insufficient data available on testing to know how much was done (WHO, 2020c). According to Our World in Data (2020), it is evident that Egypt had more active cases on March 21, whereas South Africa had more active cases after that date. There was a decrease in active cases in South Africa after May 9, 2020. The number of active cases in Egypt and South Africa were, at times,

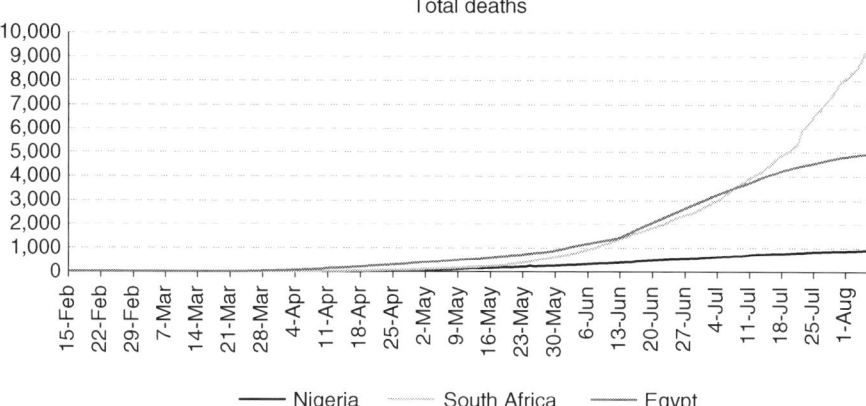

Figure 33.3. COVID-19 related deaths in Nigeria, South Africa, and Egypt (February to August 2020).
Source: Worldometer (2020).

similar, whereas active cases in Nigeria were low. In South Africa, there were no noticeable recoveries from the first reported case until March 21, when there were 240 total cases and 238 active cases with no reported deaths (WHO, 2020b). It took South Africa approximately sixteen days after the first confirmed COVID-19 cases to report a recovered infected individual. Nigeria had its first case on February 28, 2020, as indicated in the above Figure 33.1; the second case was reported on March 9, 2020. On March 15, 2020, one infected patient recovered in Nigeria. The number of active cases fluctuated, and the predominance of death from the virus was evident.

Statistics suggest that the three countries had a decrease in active cases. The highest number of active cases in South Africa was 173,590, by June 20, 2020 (National Institute for Communicable Diseases [NICD], 2020a); these cases declined to 159,833 on July 22, 2020, but increased slightly to 170,537 on July 27. Thereafter, a decline in active cases was evident, dropping to 143,313 active cases by August 5, 2020. In Egypt, active cases decreased from the July 24 to 54,584 and decreased further to 42,763 active cases on August 5, 2020. Active cases decreased to 11,672 on August 4, although a slight increase was evident August 5 with 11,798 active cases.

Egypt had more death cases when compared to Nigeria and South Africa from February 15, 2020, until July 7, 2020, as South Africa had more death cases. Nigeria had its first death case on March 23, 2020, South Africa on March 27, and Egypt on March 8. Nigeria reached 100 deaths on May 6, 2020, South Africa on April 29, and Egypt on March 8. By July 17, 2020, South Africa reported 4,804 deaths, Egypt 4,188, and Nigeria had 772. Reported COVID-19 related deaths continued to increase: three weeks later, on August 5, South Africa had 9,298 total deaths, Egypt had 4,930, and Nigeria had 927 ("Global Humanitarian Response Plan for COVID-19," 2020).

Public Health Policies and Responses (COVID-19) in Nigeria, South Africa, and Egypt

Nigeria

To curb the COVID-19 cases, South Africa and Egypt had a similar approach to that of Nigeria. The Nigerian Minister of Health, Dr. Osagie Ehanire, said the ministry had taken urgent steps to build a stronger system that would ensure prevention, early detection, and prompt response to COVID-19 (Federal Ministry of Health, 2020). An isolation center at the University of Abuja with a teaching hospital was equipped with a rapid response team and laboratory equipment for emergency control. In Nigeria, Lagos had the highest reported number of cases (13,097) by July 17, 2020, followed by Federal Capital Territory with 2,761 reported cases (Nigeria Centre for Disease Control, 2020b). As cases started to increase in Nigeria, it was evident that very sick persons were being rejected and abandoned by hospitals (Federal Ministry of Health, 2020); as a result many died because they received no attention or were told that there were no beds. One of the indicated cases of deaths was that of the waiting period of three to six days for results to be released that led to some deaths. A side Lab for GeneXpert COVID-19 diagnostic machine, which delivers results within an hour, was to be deployed and activated at the National Hospital Abuja and the University of Abuja Teaching Hospitals to cut down the waiting time (Federal Ministry of Health, 2020). Health workers were sent for special training for curbing COVID-19 so that they could all be prepared and equipped to protect themselves and scale up testing. Furthermore, community health workers were trained to provide health education to the population. They were positioned to explain and help implement and monitor preventative measures such as social distancing, hand hygiene, and cough etiquette compliance. Community health workers were trained to identify signs and symptoms among community members to minimize the magnitude of the outbreak (Bhaumik et al., 2020).

The national guideline encouraged a safe and dignified burial for people who died from COVID-19 (Nigeria Centre for Disease Control, 2020a), and family members were not permitted to perform the final burial rites, such as bathing, touching, or kissing the dead goodbye (Ajisegiri et al., 2020). The general guidelines for the use of personal protective equipment (PPE) in management of suspected cases of COVID-19 included wearing of masks by suspected or confirmed COVID-19 patients during triage and when being evaluated; all doctors, nurses, and health workers who worked with the suspected cases had to be scrupulous in donning and doffing PPE (National Primary Health Care Development Agency, 2020). Emphasis was made on the use of PPE even during physical examinations. In cases in which there were no PPE, a spatial distance of at least 1 meter had to be maintained. Nonetheless, the use of gloves did not replace the need for hand hygiene, and gloves were removed after touching or caring for a patient (National Primary Health Care Development Agency, 2020).

South Africa

South African strategies are evaluated using the risk adjusted strategy (RAS), which has five levels. Under level 5, drastic measures are required to contain the spread of the virus to save lives. Under level 4, some of the activities were allowed to resume subject to extreme precautions required to limit community transmissions and outbreak. With level 3, restrictions were eased, including on work and social activities to address a high risk of transmission. The SARS-CoV-2 was transmitted from one person to another through droplet and airborne transmission (National Institute for Communicable Diseases [NICD], 2020a). However, the exact contribution of each transmission was not fully understood. The NICD (2020a) stated that the viral shedding was greatest during the early phase of the illness, and some transmissions may have occurred from persons who were asymptomatic or presymptomatic. For this reason, infection prevention and control measures were recommended.

The South African National Department of Health, the NICD, and provincial health departments have structures for responding to outbreaks of communicable diseases; these were activated to respond to COVID-19 (NICD, 2020a). The patient meeting the definition of a suspected case of COVID-19 was sampled and isolated. The contact information as well as the SA National ID number was recorded on the specimen submission form. People who were in contact with the patient were then contacted immediately. Close contacts were required to self-quarantine and self-monitor themselves for at least fourteen days since the last exposure, using a symptom-monitoring tool. In some cases, the district outbreak team chose to telephonically monitor the close contacts. If the patient was unreachable by cell phone, a home visit was done. If the self-quarantined contact started developing symptoms, they were advised to be tested for COVID-19. Those infected but not needing hospitalization for medical reasons were advised to isolate in their homes.

Egypt

In Egypt, the Health Ministry published a three-stage plan for coronavirus management that contained required procedures in preparation for the gradual return of normal life in the country. From June 1, 2020, the nighttime curfew was an hour less, from 8:00 p.m. to 5:00 a.m. instead of 6:00 a.m. Delivering lifesaving assistance to those in need, decreasing public fear related to COVID-19 through knowledge and awareness, as well as preventing the spread of the virus by supporting good hygiene formed part of the public health measures in Egypt (Plan International, 2020). Further, the rigidity in governance was visible in the intervention modes deployed in Egypt, which infringed on some human rights, unlike South Africa and Nigeria (Plan International, 2020). In addition, Renu and Scott (2020) also indicated that to prove that Egypt had a deeply authoritarian government, the government proclaimed its intent to prosecute anyone spreading fake news about the pandemic on social media, which raised questions of whether the authorities had things to hide. The lack of transparency would possibly reduce Egyptians' willingness to comply with social distancing.

Social Policy and Responses to COVID-19 in Nigeria, South Africa, and Egypt

Nigeria

Nigeria was the first African country to report a COVID-19 case late February 2020; however, as of this writing, it has the third highest number of confirmed cases of any country. The outbreak led to travel restrictions, which led to full closure of all international airports and land borders (Nsisong, 2020). To curb the virus, in February the Nigerian government set up the Coronavirus Preparedness Group. This group represented the Federal Ministry of Health (FMoH), the Office of the National Security Adviser (ONSA), World Health Organization (WHO), US Centers for Disease Control and Prevention (US-CDC), Pro-Health International (PHI), Public Health England (PHE), and the staff of the Nigeria Centre for Disease Control (NCDC). This group assessed and managed the risk of importation of the disease to Nigeria while also preparing for early detection and response. Some of the measures to curb the virus in Nigeria included encouraging staying at home and travel bans to and from high-risk countries with COVID-19. In addition, border controls, deployment of rapid response teams to all affected states, state-level training, and capacity building of health personnel on infection, prevention, and disease control were introduced. Other efforts included case management, intensified risk communication, community engagement, heightened surveillance, field epidemiological investigations, rapid identification of suspected cases, isolation, diagnosis, contact tracing, monitoring, and follow-up of persons of interest ("Global Humanitarian Repose Plan for COVID-19," 2020; NCDC, 2020b; Tijjani & Ma, 2020; UK Government, 2020). Further, Nigeria also banned social and religious gatherings, schools and businesses were shut down, and there were restrictions in movement for nonessential activities.

South Africa

South Africa had the highest reported cases as well as the total COVID-19-related deaths when compared to Nigeria and Egypt. Keeping a distance of at least 1.5 to 2 meters, more especially in clustered areas, was a key part of the social policy in South Africa. The use of alcohol-based hand rubs or sanitizer were advised, as well as frequently washing hands (NICD, 2020b). People were advised to follow proper coughing etiquette to avoid respiratory droplets falling on high-touch surfaces. The use of PPE was encouraged, especially masks. In hospitals, ideally visitors were not allowed; exceptions were made only for caregivers of admitted children and close family members of patients who were extremely ill. Visitors were advised to wear surgical masks and were instructed on hand and cough hygiene as well as social distancing (NICD, 2020b). As of July 12, 2020, the Department of Co-Operative Governance and Traditional Affairs' amended regulation stated the importance of wearing a "a) cloth mask, b) a homemade item or c) another appropriate item that covers the nose and mouth as a mandatory measure whenever in a public place" (SACoronavirus, 2020a). People were confined to their places of residence from 9:00 p.m. until 4:00 a.m. daily except where a person had been granted a permit to perform a service under alert level 3 or was attending to a security or medical emergency. Social visits and gathering were prohibited as well as interprovincial traveling. Exceptions in social gatherings were made for places of worship with fifty people or less, depending on the size of the venue. Funerals were conducted with specific restrictions, which included social distancing and limiting to fifty people or less (SA Coronavirus, 2020a). Furthermore, South Africa implemented structures for rapid responses to COVID-19 outbreaks (separation of asymptomatic individuals potentially exposed to a disease from non-exposed).

Egypt

In Egypt, a three-stage plan for coronavirus management was initiated to curb the spread of the virus. The Egyptian government declared a state of emergency for three months on April 28, 2020, with ongoing extension. Egypt introduced a curfew varying from 5:00 p.m. to 08:00 a.m. for all individuals and businesses, including commercial shops, public and private transportation, banks, and grocery stores. Pharmacies, complete closure of entertainment and amusement facilities, including sports and youth centers, parks, beaches, hotels, bars, coffee shops, restaurants, nurseries, schools, universities, and air traffic were also included in the curfew. However, hospitals, medical centers, media outlets, and the transportation of medical supplies, petroleum, and food were exempted from the partial lockdown (Salem, 2020). In Egypt between June 14 and 30, 2020, the curfew was relaxed from 8:00 p.m. to 4:00 a.m. for the above-mentioned businesses as well as transportation of individuals. In July 2020, a gradual reopening of the economy occurred. Air travel resumed, as well as restaurants and cafes at 25 percent capacity. Stores were open until 9: 00 p.m., whereas restaurants closed at 10:00 p.m. Public places of worship were also open for daily prayers (International Monetary Fund, 2020).

Explanation of the Policy Choices

There are few indications suggesting the three governments engaged in complex reviews of scientific evidence. It is more likely the initial policies, such as lockdowns and border closures, were the result of learning from or emulation of Europe and the United States. Accordingly, Odubanjo (2020) stated what was missing in Nigeria's current narrative around COVID-19 was a coordinated response across the federation. The Federal Ministry of Health and the NCDC were supposed to be the national coordinators, but the states seemed to be making individual decisions. Adepoju (2020) further argued that the absence of accurate data in Nigeria limited the country's ability to tackle the coronavirus. In addition, the country's politicization of the pandemic and lack of interinstitutional and public collaboration were emerging key challenges.

By contrast, in the beginning of 2020, South African President Cyril Ramaphosa put forward the idea of "social compact" as a method to consult and build consensus for reviving the country's ailing economy (Kotze, 2020). The South African president used the same principle when building the broad consensus around the national state of disaster to fight COVID-19. Ramaphosa also emphasized the inclusive decision-making that was informed by scientific evidence. The inclusive decision-making was a method to depoliticize and rationalize decision-making to create more national coherence and allow for post-democratic decision-making. This approach received a lot of support from the public during the first weeks of COVID-19 crisis, although when the restrictions were scaled down, the consensus no longer existed (Kotze, 2020). Kotze (2020) argued that, at first glance, decision-making was simple and was dominated by government, although it gradually became more complex as the implications of disaster management became clearer. The long-term consensus is said to require a continuous consultation and sharing of information to sustain enough support for decision-making. "Democratic openness makes it difficult to achieve long-term consensus positions" (Kotze, 2020).

Nonetheless, the scenario in Egypt was different from South Africa and Nigeria. Renu and Scott (2020) argued that the Egyptians were unlikely to challenge their government over COVID-19 disruptions at that moment. In Egypt, flights to and from China were suspended even before the first COVID-19 case. By March 24, 2020, authorities in Egypt had already imposed restrictions.

Despite the measures in place to combat the disease, the government faced numerous obstacles in trying to mitigate the impact of the pandemic: the political institutions of Egypt are mostly designed to protect the interest of the narrow military elite and are poorly positioned to respond to a massive public health crisis effectively. As the negative economic impact begun to unfold, there were signs of dissatisfaction with government policies (Renu & Scott, 2020). Some Egyptians criticized the government's response in mitigating the burden of the poor, while others argued that the authorities had not done enough to contain the virus. However, it was also evident from the public's opinion data in Egypt that a majority of Egyptians trusted the state institutions' response to the virus (Renu & Scott, 2020). However, the Egyptians' trust in government may not be deserved: there were indications that the authorities had downplayed the severity of the outbreak.

Unlike in the United States, policy responses in South Africa, Nigeria, and Egypt to the virus did not become a partisan issue. Albeit the three countries differ along partisan identities, but the general directions of government measures as well as the severity of the health risk itself were subject to general cross-party consensus. In South Africa and Nigeria, political opposition was not directed toward public health measures introduced by the government, but there were visible different voices in Egypt because of the unpredictable political nature of the country.

Although many argue that regime type and state health capacity are the major causes of government responses to crises, these did not appear to be the vital factors affecting how decisively most governments acted to diminish COVID-19 effects in sub-Saharan Africa. In fact, one of the foremost reasons for comparing South Africa, Nigeria, and Egypt is that they differ in terms of governance structure and health capacity of the state. Regarding regime type, Egypt has consistently been characterized as an authoritarian regime, whereas South Africa and Nigeria are categorized as democratic. When it comes to state capacity for health, which we hypothesize along two scopes (administration and fiscal resources), there is a great disparity across these three countries. South Africa has a high degree of state health capacity, given its level of development and national structure of decision-making as well access to resources. Egypt and Nigeria have a medium degree of state health capacity, somewhat centralized government with inadequate fiscal resources. Regime type and state capacity do not explain the early relaxation health policy measures by governments in all three countries. Economic conditions seem to be the key factor influencing the extent to which each country could adopt social policies but also their willingness and ability to maintain lockdowns.

Although South Africa, Nigeria, and Egypt vary according to regime type and state capacity, what they do have in common is a weak healthcare system. As in many other parts of sub-Saharan Africa, weak public healthcare systems meant that during the COVID-19 pandemic, citizens lacked access to diagnostic tests and quality medical care, and medical workers were particularly vulnerable to infection. COVID-19 exposed the fragility of the underdeveloped and neglected healthcare systems and established the need for further health systems strengthening across the African region. Largely, weak health infrastructure was detrimental to their ability to combat COVID-19. Arguably, the weak healthcare infrastructure prior to the COVID-19 pandemic and the already precarious economic situation contributed to the surge in cases in South Africa, Nigeria, and Egypt. Although these countries were able to all react speedily early on, the extended lockdowns were not sustainable, and the healthcare systems were not strong enough to effectively deal with the swift upsurge in infections. South Africa had a more decisive leadership that stood on sound and contextual scientific, economic, and social advice, not political expediency, which was key to accelerate containment and recovery. This scenario played a role in the different results among the three countries. Further, full lockdowns were not enforced in Egypt and Nigeria, as was the case in South Africa. The lockdowns were not sustained in Egypt and Nigeria for more than a couple of weeks, even with some social protection. Strong willingness to adopt and deploy new technologies played to South Africa's advantage. South Africa established early response mechanisms supported by an innovation-friendly regulatory framework, sound infrastructure, and adequate funding to operationalize such plans. This dimension was not so visible in Egypt and Nigeria.

Conclusion

Some countries within the region implemented measures to keep economies buoyant because of COVID-19. For example, apart from slightly reducing the supply of oil, Nigeria instituted several stimulus packages to abate the effect of COVID-19 on the most susceptible sectors of their economy. Similar actions were taken by other countries, including Egypt, Ghana, Kenya, Senegal, and South Africa. The net fall in GDP among these countries is marginal; however, being among the continent's biggest economies, a small decrease in their GDP had a higher domestic influence overall than a larger loss in GDP in smaller economies. Of the six African countries (South Africa, Nigeria, Egypt, Kenya, Ghana, and Senegal) with the greatest number of registered COVID-19 cases, a significant drop in revenue was observed only for Egypt (−10.6%), which is hypothetically an effect of the plunge in oil prices.

The three countries had divergent approaches in containing the spread of the virus. Nonetheless, COVID-19 cases increased as well in many other countries in sub-Saharan Africa, showing the inadequacies inherent in health infrastructures in the region. Albeit, because of intervention modes, the curve gradually flattened in Nigeria, South Africa, and Egypt more so than in other African countries. Nonetheless, South Africa had early responses that built strategic stocks for healthcare emergencies better than Egypt and Nigeria, which made it stand out in terms of performance. In all the studied countries the strategies for combating COVID-19 are reviewed to ensure that a single integrated view exists that eliminates unnecessary fragmentations and overlapping. These strategies are evaluated based on the effect they have on the economy as well as the number of recoveries and deaths. Moving from one level or stage is one of the methods used in the studied countries to slightly move to normal. It has been evident in the reported statistics that South Africa (NICD, 2020a) had the highest reported cases. As they lifted their lockdown restrictions, the cases of COVID-19 increased.

South Africa moved from level 2 to level 1 in their lockdown procedures. Under level 1, most activities resumed with precautions and health guidelines followed at all times (SA Coronavirus, 2020b). Egypt, South Africa, and Nigeria further eased restrictions with maintenance of physical distancing and restrictions on some leisure and social activities to prevent a resurgence of the virus. The procedures for curbing the COVID-19 pandemic varied in each of the studied countries, and the level of infections in each country differed as well as the number of death cases.

Easing of restrictions in some other African countries saw an increase in confirmed cases. The results from the three case studies of Egypt, Nigeria, and South Africa indicate that the level of infections in each country and the number of deaths was vastly different, in part because of the dissimilar procedures for curbing COVID-19. This difference is a consequence of enforcement of health and safety measures and healthcare capacity of the countries. Thus, the need to reinforce national public health capabilities and infrastructure became imperative. These factors remain at the core of global health security, because they are the first line of defense in infectious disease emergencies.

Summarily, COVID-19 cases tested the capacity of healthcare systems in the three countries. COVID-19 meant that all healthcare centers had to adjust to the new norm without alienating those patients that had other underlying sicknesses besides COVID-19. The increase in COVID-19 cases as well as deaths brought too much pressure to healthcare centers. Healthcare workers had to treat patients and follow the necessary precautions for their safety in light of the shortage of PPE across South Africa, Nigeria, and Egypt. Educating people thoroughly about the important measures to curb the virus played a key role in effectively dealing with the virus, especially with those living with existing health conditions and those residing in disadvantaged areas. Greater capacities to test, protect, treat, and cure were essential to success.

On the socioeconomic front, policy measures were needed to cushion income and job losses, as well as tackling specific challenges for the weak economy. Beyond the immediate response, recovery strategies should include a strong structural component to reduce dependence on external financial flows and global markets and develop more value-adding, knowledge-intensive, and industrialized economies, underpinned by a more competitive and efficient services sector.

Specific steps are needed to deal with a pandemic. After reviewing the cases of Egypt, Nigeria, and South Africa, the authors of this chapter recommend the following for pandemic management:

1. Flexibility (regime type) in governance is encouraged to produce better results in pandemics. Countries need to share ideas of procedures followed to fight the pandemic.
2. Unity of purpose by all agents of State is the most important factor during times of crisis.
3. Mass education helps curb the incidence of COVID-19 cases.
4. Increasing health capacity and continuing with practicing the healthy precautions should be mandatory to avoid resurgence. It is evident that South Africa had more focus on these than Egypt and Nigeria. However, all three countries did see a decrease in COVID-19 confirmed cases.
5. Crisis management plans should be ready in each African country, and involvement of the international community should catalyze such preparedness. Further, promoting multiple helix partnerships to unlock innovative capacity across sectors and exploring the use of emerging technologies have become imperative.
6. In the longer term, Africa will need to build productive capacities to address fundamental economic susceptibilities and boost continental competencies to manage crises.

References

Adepoju, P. (2020). Tuberculosis and HIV responses threatened by COVID-19. *Lancet HIV*, 7(5), e319–e20.

Ajisegiri, W. S., Odusanya, O. O., & Joshi, R. (2020). COVID-19 outbreak situation in Nigeria and the need for effective engagement of community health workers for epidemic response. *Global Biosecurity, 1*(4), https://www.doi.org/10.31646/gbio.69

Bhaumik, S., Moola, S., Tyagi, J., Nambiar, D., & Kakoti, M. (2020). Community health workers for pandemic response: A rapid evidence synthesis. *BMJ Global Health, 5*(6), e002769. https://doi.org/10.1136/bmjgh-2020-002769

Department of Co-Operative Governance and Traditional Affairs. (2020). Disaster Management Act, 2002: Amendment of Regulations issued in terms of section 27(2).

Federal Ministry of Health. (2020). *Nigeria CoronaVirus report.* Retrieved on December 20, 2020, from https://health.gov.ng/index.php?option=com_k2&view=item&id=608:covid-19-latest-news-updates/

Gilbert, M., Pullano, G., Pinotti, F., Valdano, E., Poletto, C., Boelle, P., Ortenzio, E., Yazdanpana, Y., Etholie, S., Altmann, M., Guiterrez, B., Kraemer, M., & Colizza, V. (2020, February). Preparedness and vulnerability of African countries against importations of COVID-19: A modelling study. *The Lancet, 395*(10227), 871-877, https://doi.org/10.1016/SO140-6736 (20)30411-6

Global humanitarian response plan for COVID-19. (2020). https://www.humanitarianresponse.info/sites/www.humanitarianresponse.info/files/documents/files/global_humanitarian_response_plan_covid-19_.pdf

Hassanin, A. (2020). *Coronavirus origins: Genome analysis suggests two viruses may have combined.* World Economic Forum. https://www.weforum.org/agenda/2020/03/coronavirus-origins-genome-analysis-covid19-data-science-bats-pangolins/

International Monetary Fund. (2020). *Policy responses to COVID-19.* Policy Tracker. https://www.imf.org/en/Topics/imf-and-covid19/Policy-Responses-to-COVID-19#E

Kotze, D. (2020, June 16). What Ramaphosa's COVID-19 decisions say about South Africa's democracy. *The Conversation Daily Newsletter.* https://theconversation.com/what-ramaphosas-covid-19-decisions-say-about-south-africas-democracy-140186

Lempinen, E. (2020). Africa faces grave risks as COVID-19 emerges, says Berkeley economist. *Berkeley News.* https://news.berkeley.edu/2020/03/31/africa-faces-grave-risks-as-covid-19-emerges-says-berkeley-economist/

Marbot, O. (2020, March 9). Africa and coronavirus: Three charts to better understand the epidemic. *The Africareport.* https://www.theafricareport.com/24395/africa-and-coronavirus-three-infographics-to-better-understand-the-epidemic/

National Department of Health. (2020). *National Practical Manual for the implementation of the National IPC Strategic Framework*, p23. http://www.health.gov.za/index.php/antimicrobial-resistance/category/629-infection-prevention-and-control-documents

National Institute for Communicable Diseases (NICD). (2020a). *Coronavirus disease 2019 (COVID-19) caused by a Novel Coronavirus (SARS-CoV-2). Guidelines for case-finding, diagnosis, and public health response in South Africa.* Version 3.0. https://www.nicd.ac.za/wp-content/uploads/2020/07/NICD_DoH-COVID-19-Guidelines_Final_3-Jul-2020.pdf

National Institute for Communicable Diseases (NICD). (2020b, May 21). *COVID-19 DISEASE: Infection prevention and control guidelines.* Version 2. https://www.nicd.ac.za/wp-content/uploads/2020/05/ipc-guidelines-covid-19-version-2-21-may-2020.pdf

National Primary Health Care Development Agency. (2020). *Preparedness and response to Coronavirus Disease 2019 (COVID-19) at primary healthcare and community level.* https://reliefweb.int/sites/reliefweb.int/files/resources/guide_on_phc_preparedness_and_response-covid-19.pdf

Nigeria Centre for Disease Control. (2020a). *Guidelines for the safe management of a dead body in the context of COVID-19.* https://covid19.ncdc.gov.ng/media/files/MgtOfDeadBodies_elVIwls.pdf

Nordling, Linda. (2020, April 15). South Africa flattens its coronavirus curve—and considers how to ease restrictions. *Science.* https://www.sciencemag.org/news/2020/04/south-africa-flattens-its-coronavirus-curve-and-considers-how-ease-restrictions

Nigeria Centre for Disease Control. (2020b). *NCDC initiates new measures for pandemic control as COVID-19 spreads to 12 states in Nigeria.* https://ncdc.gov.ng/reports/weekly

Nsisong, A. (2020). *Opportunities amidst adversity in Nigeria's COVID-19 response.* IHP. https://www.internationalhealthpolicies.org/featured-article/opportunities-amidst-adversity-in-nigerias-covid-19-response/

Odubanjo. D. (2020, March 26). The biggest threats to Nigeria managing COVID-19: Panic, politics and indecision. *The Conversation Daily Newsletter.* https://theconversation.com/the-biggest-threats-to-nigeria-managing-covid-19-panic-politics-and-indecision-134756

Our World in Data. (2020). *Coronavirus (COVID-19) Cases.* Retrieved on November 15, 2020, from https://ourworldindata.org/covid-cases

Plan International. (2020). *COVID-19 response in Egypt.* Retrieved on December 10, 2020, from https://plan-international.org/egypt/covid-19-response-egypt

Renu, S., & Scott, W. (2020, April). Coronavirus and prospects for instability in Egypt. *Carnegie Endowment for International Peace.* https://carnegieendowment.org/sada/81615

SACoronavirus. (2020a). *Summary of Level 3 regulations.* https://sacoronavirus.co.za/2020/05/28/summary-of-level-3-regulations/

SACoronavirus. (2020b). *Schedule of services: Framework for sectors.* https://www.tralac.org/documents/resources/covid-19/countries/3602-south-africa-risk-adjusted-strategy-schedule-of-services-draft-framework-25-april-2020/file.html

Salem, N. (2020). *Too much too soon?—A snapshot of Egypt's COVID-19 response.* Opinio Juris. https://opiniojuris.org/2020/07/10/too-much-too-soon-a-snapshot-of-egypts-covid-19-response/

Tijjani, S. J., & Ma, L. (2020). Is Nigeria prepared and ready to respond to the COVID-19 pandemic in its Conflict-affected north-eastern states? *International Journal for Equity in Health 19,* 77. https://doi.org/10.1186/s12939-020-01192-6

UK Government. (2020). *Coronavirus—Nigeria travel advice.* Retrieved on November 28, 2020, from https://www.gov.uk/foreign-travel-advice/nigeria/coronavirus

Wikipedia. (2020). *COVID-19 pandemic in South Africa.* https://en.wikipedia.org/wiki/COVID-19_pandemic_in_South_Africa

World Health Organization. (2020a). *COVID-19 response in the World Health Organization African Region, February to July 15, 2020.* https://www.afro.who.int/health-topics/coronavirus-covid-19

World Health Organization. (2020b, March 19). *Rational use of personal protective equipment (PPE) for coronavirus disease (COVID-19), interim guidance.* https://apps.who.int/iris/bitstream/handle/10665/331498/WHO-2019-nCoV-IPCPPE_use-2020.2-eng.pdf

World Health Organization. (2020c, October 22). *COVID-19 new COVID-19 rapid tests a game changer for Africa.* https://www.afro.who.int/news/new-covid-19-rapid-tests-game-changer-africa

Worldometer (2020). *COVID-19 coronavirus pandemic—Worldometer. Coronavirus cases.* Retrieved on December 10, 2020, from https://www.worldometers.info/coronavirus/

34 CONCLUSION

Scott L. Greer, Elize Massard da Fonseca, and Elizabeth J. King

All happy countries are alike in their response to COVID-19; each unhappy country is unhappy in its own way. The famous opening line of Leo Tolstoy's *Anna Karenina* about unhappy families[1] seems to apply to what we have seen in government responses to COVID-19 around the world. A happy country, in late 2020, was one that had used non-pharmaceutical interventions (NPIs) such as masking or business closures to tamp down the initial wave of the epidemic and then successfully built test-trace-isolate-support (TTIS) systems that allowed them to return to normal life with few or no NPIs. There was really, it became clear, no other path to controlling or eliminating COVID-19 before vaccines became available. Unfortunately, that path was narrow and hard to follow.

This should not have been too surprising, given that NPIs and TTIS systems had been standard advice from public health researchers for decades, if not longer (some NPIs such as quarantines date back centuries). Unlike with other epidemics such as cholera, smallpox, and HIV/AIDS, scientists quickly identified the genetic sequence of SARS-CoV-2, its mechanisms of transmission, and strategies to prevent the virus spread. Therefore, there was relative agreement on what health systems should do to stop the disease from spreading. Not only were NPIs and TTIS crucial, as decades of research and experience had shown, but the precise NPIs, such as masking and restaurant closures, had been identified within months. The long periods of uncertainty and exploration that had marked previous pandemic responses were not found in this pandemic.

Happy countries were ones that reacted swiftly and with robust health and social policies. The unhappy countries responded with a wide variety of approaches, some expected and others unexpected, that have left many of them with surging COVID-19 case numbers and astonishing excess deaths in 2020.

There was fascinating international variation, leading to many different tragic outcomes in countries from the United States to Brazil and from Spain to India. Meanwhile, an intriguingly mismatched range of countries such as Vietnam, Mongolia, Germany, New Zealand, South Korea, Taiwan, and Norway, became happy cases. By the year's end, China and Vietnam, with negligible or no COVID-19, were happier than Germany or Canada, where normal life was marred by constant reassertion of NPIs and efforts to shore up TTIS systems in the face of persistent community spread of the virus. But relative to the diversity of problems and outcomes in the unhappy countries, the differences are small. Countries that built TTIS systems and used NPIs well limited the impact of COVID-19 on lives and deaths. Many more failed to do so. Some cases started out well and then became unhappy—for example, using NPIs initially but failing, or finding themselves unwilling to develop adequate TTIS systems or social policies. Each failure is interesting in its own way, and they contribute to a wide range of cases for the study of public health and politics.

Reflecting on Our Hypotheses

We opened this book with a set of hypotheses about what explains policy responses to COVID-19 in the first nine months of 2020, when its management depended on NPIs and TTIS systems. The introduction in chapter 1 presented the hypotheses' theoretical justification and reviewed the evidence in the book. Our authors covered the World Health Organisation (WHO), comparative analysis, and country case studies from Asia, Europe, the Americas, and Africa. However, we could not cover every country in the world, and we undoubtedly left out countries for which these hypotheses warrant further exploration. Higher-income countries were affected by COVID-19 earlier than lower-income countries and thus make up the majority of case studies in this book. For example, future research should include a focus on more countries in Africa and Latin America.

Social Policy

Perhaps our most important finding for public health, policy research, and political science is *the dependence of health policies on social policies*. Social policy is not just about managing consequences; it is part of the explanation of any emergency intervention. The Cask of Amontillado problem that we discussed in chapter 1 is real. It is just not feasible to close people into their houses if that means leaving them to die. If people need to leave their houses or open their businesses or work in order to eat, they will. It takes an extremely authoritarian state with very impressive coercive power to keep people at home without corresponding large-scale social policy compensations.

Many of the most impressive, or heartbreaking, case studies involved the interactions of social and health policies. In some countries, they were aligned. Thus Germany and Denmark were able to use social policies to cushion the blows of NPIs and pandemic-related demand shocks. They effectively put their economies into medically induced comas, using short-time work, unemployment benefits, and other income replacement schemes to pay people to stay at home. These comas meant that people were able to stay home from work and reduce mobility to good effect. They also reduced political pressure to reopen because they ensured that businesses could close, ensuring their own safety, without suffering.

In other countries, it did not go so well. India's experience was perhaps particularly tragic. Its federal government reacted early with a national lockdown unaccompanied by social policy measures (what the plausible social policy measures might have been is an unexplored question). It turned out that the weak point in such a lockdown was poor migrant laborers from rural districts who inhabited cities with high COVID-19 infection rates and needed to work every day to survive. The Indian government opted to return them to their villages, seeding infections across the country as six million people returned to rural areas in special trains. The result was a massive nationwide outbreak. By August 2020 it was clear that India bore the burden of the NPIs without the benefits.

South Africa had a similar experience, with an initially successful national lockdown in a country marked historically by high levels of labor mobility. Lacking the money, policy tools, and perhaps intent to solve the problem, the South African government simply ended many of its NPIs for want of social policy support without building a suitable public health response.

Institutions shaped the interaction between social policy and public health outcomes. Social policy interacted with federalism in unexpected ways because of the different allocations of health and social policy authority to governments on different levels. In Brazil and the United States, both the federal and state governments had public health powers to enact NPIs. State governments had some resources to enable NPIs and built TTIS systems, but in both countries the federal government had the resources necessary for real social policy responses. The results were strange. In both countries, federal social policy over the spring and summer was very supportive of NPIs; the federal government did not enact NPIs, leaving them to the states. Once the social policies ended, the result was a social and public health disaster, in which US local governments in particular were faced with a choice as stark as any restaurant or bar between reducing NPIs and insolvency. In the United States, as autumn wore on, it emerged that state revenues largely depended on taxes from wealthier people. NPIs consequently did not damage state tax revenue anywhere near as much as initially expected. State revenues remained relatively intact, while local experiences varied widely and politics decided whether states opened businesses that contributed relatively little tax revenue but were politically important. It turned out that, although local governments were mostly trapped, different state governments were not forced to enact or lift NPIs by their revenue sources; they chose to do so.

Naturally, the ability of states to pay their citizens to stay home and their businesses to stay closed varies with their fiscal and administrative capacity. Not all countries had Denmark's or the United Kingdom's fiscal autonomy and capacity. We could say that our study shows clearly that rich countries should have paid their people to stay home and businesses to stay closed until there were adequate TTIS systems, but the problems are obvious. In some higher-income countries, such as those of Southern Europe, states have limited fiscal space as a result of Eurozone membership, and their economies depend on tourism. It is hard to imagine the economies of Spain, Italy, or Greece without mass travel. In the summer of

2020 those countries' governments, many of which had successfully overcome or avoided disaster in the first wave, invited tourism because that is a core part of their economies. The contours of the second wave, in those tourist economies and in the home countries of the tourists, were predictable.

In lower-income countries, of course, the problem was more significant. Although dependence on donors means that some resource-limited countries are relatively shielded from the performance of their own economies, it is nonetheless obvious that paying people to stay home while a TTIS system was built was a challenge for lower- and middle-income countries. In many of the lower- and middle-income countries in our book, fiscal pressures were obvious problems. If expensive social policy measures were necessary to maintain NPIs, then NPIs were clearly going to happen for a short time at best. Furthermore, economic structures meant that lower- and middle-income countries had a smaller proportion of white collar workers or others who were able to socially distance and infrastructure suitable for physical distancing. The result was a tendency in many lower- and middle-income countries to one-time lockdowns, with drastic impositions of NPIs that did not require sophisticated public administration and enforcement, followed by reduction of NPIs and resurgent infections (in our book, cases include South Africa, India, and Central Asian republics).

It is important to note that international income inequality means that the impact of these issues is hard to analyze at the moment. Testing and even mortality statistics are endogenous to international politics because they are a function of state capacity. A country with widespread and effective testing and well-developed death recording is also probably a high-income country. In a number of countries in the world, even life expectancy data are based on random sampling and interviews. As a result, at the time of writing we just cannot say how bad the pandemic was in many lower-income countries in 2020. In very poor and failed states, such as Venezuela, Yemen, or South Sudan, we may never know how much mortality changed in 2020 and why.

Authoritarianism, Information, and Effectiveness

Authoritarian governments have limited contestation or participation. If we imagine regimes as existing in a two-dimensional space of contestation (scope to argue for views opposed to the government) and participation (scope to participate in decisions, notably voting), then the problem with generalizing about authoritarian regimes becomes clear. A two-dimensional space with democracies clustered, by definition, at the highest levels of observed contestation and participation, will produce two analytical problems. One is that the border is unclear because both contestation and participation are continuous variables: Hungary is less authoritarian than Russia, which is less authoritarian than China. One category that includes them all is likely to be very abstract. The other is that the diversity of regimes that are not high in both contestation and participation is wide-ranging, from absolute monarchies such as Saudi Arabia to personalistic autocracies such as Turkmenistan to hybrid, competitive authoritarian states such as Russia or Hungary to complex authoritarian regimes such as Egypt to totalitarian regimes such North Korea to failing states such as Venezuela. To make the problem more complex, big federations such as the United States, Brazil, Nigeria, India, or South Africa often have "authoritarian enclaves" that shape national politics while defending local autocracies.

We framed two hypotheses around authoritarianism. One stems from the diversity of authoritarian states and societies, which vary in authoritarianism itself as well as state capacity, institutions, wealth, and interactions between states and society. The hypothesis is that only some authoritarian states will have the capacity to effectively make and implement policy in response to an event such as the pandemic. Authoritarianism itself does not automatically produce decisive or effective government, and some forms of authoritarianism will reduce both decisiveness and effectiveness. The perceived success of China, in particular, has prompted apologetics for authoritarianism that claim it produces better pandemic responses. There is no reason to believe that China, nor Vietnam, is the norm for authoritarian states' public health responses. Tanzanian or Russian responses are at least as likely.

The other hypothesis tried to identify a commonality in authoritarian regimes going beyond their definitional characteristics of limited participation or inclusion. The hypothesis was that they would have problems of information flow. Internally, people in regimes without the discipline of public accountability and engagement would have incentive to misrepresent or limit the circulation of even useful information. Externally, authoritarian regimes, without the discipline of electoral politics, would have incentive to misrepresent the situation to their publics, and their publics might well expect that. Because participation and inclusion are continuous variables, this has to be expressed carefully: insofar as a regime is authoritarian, we predicted information flow problems.

The hypothesis that authoritarianism does not lead to better, more decisive, or more effective responses seems well supported. For every Vietnam or China, authoritarian regimes that stamped out COVID-19 with NPIs, there is a South Korea or New Zealand, democracies that did the same, and a Russia or Tanzania, which failed as badly as any democracy. Even within democracies, leaders with something of an authoritarian approach—populist radical right politicians such as Jair Bolsonaro, Boris Johnson, or Donald Trump—seem to have handled the pandemic particularly erratically.

The more adventurous hypothesis that authoritarianism breeds internal and information flow problems is harder to test, because it is hard to know if data are particularly untrustworthy in those regimes. Nonetheless there is at most suggestive evidence for it—that regime underlings in a diverse set of authoritarian states hid information that reflected poorly on them and sacrificed effective emergency response to clientelistic or purely corrupt goals under the cover of secrecy. Populist radical right leaders in democracies also seem to have suffered internal communications problems (they were told what they wanted to hear) and external ones (they discredited their public pronouncements).

We suspect that diversity within authoritarian regimes is more important than contrasts of authoritarian and democratic regimes. Exploring shared patterns of behavior across regime types is the productive research direction. For an example discussed later in this chapter, comparative federalism and presidentialism scholarship shed interesting light on Russia, even if Russia, being undemocratic, is not part of the set of cases that these theories are usually supposed to explain. The president of the Russian Federation, it turns out, can be studied as a president of a federation, as well as an autocrat. Democracy and authoritarianism are made up of two continuums, participation and contestation, and there are real limitations when we translate it into an authoritarian-democratic binary distinction.

Presidentialism, Federalism, and the Politics of Agency

Political institutions did not lead to any clear good or bad outcomes, but they clearly shaped the politics of pandemic response and the way choices were made. We framed the impact of political institutions in terms of the politics of agency. Political institutions structure who has agency in politics as well as their accountability. Presidentialist systems divide authority between an elected president and the legislature, with the president usually the more energetic and disruptive force. Some political systems have majoritarian features with the same results, in which a party with a strong majority can reside in power even without strong popular support because of winner-take-all electoral systems. The case for such kinds of governments is often made in terms of decisiveness: the advantages of a clear and powerful leader outweigh the loss of representativeness and consensus negotiations. In Colombia, that worked: the president coordinated a national response and regained popularity because of his approach to the pandemic. In France, the outcome is less clearly desirable. President Macron was decisive, but some of his decisions, especially regarding NPIs, were erratic. In both countries, the key point is that it was up to the president to decide how to wield such power.

In the COVID-19 pandemic, in short, it is far from clear that the strong democratic leaders performed well. According to this book, there seems to be little evidence that strong presidents in Brazil and the United States (and perhaps Russia and Chile) did well. Parliamentary leaders in the relatively majoritarian systems of India, Spain, South Africa, and the United Kingdom also were heavily criticized for their leadership.

Federalism fragments agency. In federalism, substantial authority is in the hands of federal states, with different levels of government competing or coordinating, depending on the details of politics, programs, and institutions. Many claims have been made about federalism: it promotes competition and efficiency, it promotes gridlock and vetoes, it makes excessive demands for coordination, it enables experimentation and learning, and it creates resilience by diversifying governments. In general, all of these things can be true, but that depends on intergovernmental finance, programmatic designs and legacies, and underlying economic geography.

In the COVID-19 pandemic, several of these dynamics were clearly visible. In Brazil, India, and the United States, decentralization did seem to lead to resilience insofar as state leaders could to some extent compensate for the health policy failures of the federal government (policy failures enabled by systems that concentrated agency in politicians who happened to be of the populist radical right). But equally the resilience was limited by fiscal and programmatic constraints on state governments, although neither politics nor epidemiology made it easy for states to diverge for long in NPIs. It also seems that in some cases federalism's competitive dimensions reduced preparedness. In the United States, for example, economically competitive states invested as little as possible in public health, so the system came to depend on the competence and leadership of the federal government. In 2020 that federal government was in the hands of Republican President Donald Trump, and so states were left to deal with a crisis they were not prepared to manage.

One of the interesting phenomena, for political science in general, was the interaction between hybrid authoritarian regimes and political institutions and dynamics usually associated with democracy. In many ways the Russian regime, for example, exhibited a politics of agency reminiscent of other big majoritarian federations such as Brazil, India, or the United States, with President Vladimir Putin using his agency to alternately centralize and decentralize action, credit, and blame. The politics of agency in the Russian Federation looked strangely like those of the United States, which supports the case for looking at institutional dynamics across authoritarian, hybrid, and democratic systems despite their obvious, definitional, differences.

"Successful responses hinge on decisive leadership" was the conclusion of one interim analysis of pandemic response (Forman et al., 2020). But what, other than the luck of who is leader, shapes the likelihood of decisive leadership that makes good decisions—and for whom? That is the political question. We found that the politics of agency was a promising way to think about the multiple, interacting variables that affected the COVID-19 response, and therefore a way to think about politics in the harsh light of this crisis. Much of the political science research focuses on the independent variable—on the impact of presidentialism or federalism, or the ways in which introducing another variable such as party systems affects the influence of institutions. We have argued that institutions matter in relationship to each other and to broader political forces, and so a configurational analysis might make sense for understanding how they matter. Who gets agency, institutionally?

Public Health Infrastructure

Finally, the professional and political institutionalization of public health had a surprisingly limited effect on policy. Many, if not most, public health establishments made broad claims to reducing avoidable mortality but had pandemic response at their center. This was true regardless of how much of their time and workforce were engaged in monitoring water quality, restaurant hygiene, or obesity. In the greatest pandemic of most peoples' lives, though, public health agencies and the public health profession were substantially sidelined by political leaders, relegated to technical functions in many cases, and sidelined altogether in a few. Heads of government in country after country turned to expert groups in which public health expertise was limited.

A look back at the AIDS pandemic, the last novel infectious disease to have anything like such global health impact, suggests that this might not be so surprising. In the AIDS pandemic, science has been constantly contested, some governments opted for denialist strategies, and public health agencies often are left absorbing criticism for decisions they had not influenced. In both pandemics there is a tone of frustration in public health scholarship, frustration that extensive research and practical experience on changing behavior (condoms and masks) or identifying and acting on risky activities has not been used. The frustration of public health scholars and policymakers extends beyond communicable diseases; much public health literature also laments the lack of public health influence on areas such as noncommunicable diseases.

We might frame the problem as being about generalist government and specialist government, as Dan Fox does (Fox, 2017). Generalist government is about allocating across broad competing priorities: guns and butter, health and the economy, taxes and spending, war and peace. It is the realm of professional politicians who are served by a few generalist officials, typically the officials around the executive and the finance department. Specialist government is everything else, from transportation to space exploration to the army to public health. Generalist government's very job is to allocate resources and therefore listen with appropriate skepticism to specialist government claims. Even if public health agencies and professionals had uniquely valuable expertise in a communicable disease pandemic with no vaccine or effective medical treatment, that does not mean that we should expect generalist government to simply cede a monopoly to them.

It has long been easy to poke fun at public health and its claims. The juxtaposition of big structural critiques of society from its leaders and scholarship with very small-scale interventions mostly focused on marginalized groups was always awkward. The resulting preoccupation with self-definition, lamentations about the limited role of public health considerations in policy, and arguments about the scope of the field were just facts of life in public health circles. It seemed in recent decades that a model of public health professionalism built on US-style Schools of Public Health and "CDCs" modeled on the Centers for Disease Control and Prevention might have cracked the problem, creating a model for an effective, elite profession, but it merits reflection that exactly that model turned out to lack political strength at a crucial moment.

New Directions

We structured chapter templates and the book around the hypotheses that we developed. Like any good research program, let alone one conducted on and in a rapidly changing global crisis, we found other issues arose that merit further study and for which the chapters provide suggestive evidence.

State Capacity and Its Use

Although investment in public health agencies, infrastructure, and professionalism seemed to have remarkably little effect on the way countries made policy in 2020, overall state capacity did seem to be a factor whose importance merits pursuit—a finding other comparative studies of the pandemic seem to support (Capano et al., 2020; Colfer, 2020; Kavanagh & Singh, 2020). Obviously, some very high-capacity states saw serious failures. France, unusually, built a competent TTIS system but failed to match it with effective NPIs in other areas. The United Kingdom spent a remarkable amount of money on TTIS systems and failed to get anything like an effective system for it, while pursuing a wildly erratic strategy on NPIs. But for some of the happy countries of the pandemic, such as Vietnam, it seems like strong state capacity explained the country's ability to largely avoid the pandemic through powerful NPIs.

There are two issues here, which we could frame in terms of necessary and sufficient conditions. Unlike in other epidemics such as cholera, smallpox, and HIV/AIDS, scientists quickly identified the genetic sequence of SARS-CoV-2, its mechanisms of transmission, and strategies to prevent the virus spread. Therefore, there was a relative agreement on what health systems should do to stop the disease from spreading. The problem lay in deciding to do it, and doing it. It is in these issues that state capacity starts to matter.

State capacity, it seems, might be a necessary condition for powerful NPIs. Weak states must depend on the thin reed of a persuadable, persuaded, and very conscientious public. That is a lot to ask, especially since persuasion is more easily achieved with a competent state. Some forms of state capacity might be specialist and particularly adapted to public health issues, as in some of the African cases, but it can also be generalist, taking the shape of a powerful bureaucracy that can operate across multiple areas, whether in Austria, Japan, China, Hong Kong, Singapore, or Vietnam.

The sufficient condition for response is *use* of state capacity. As Davies (2012) puts it, technical capacity to carry out public health tasks is not the same thing as political capacity. There is a virtual industry of capacity analysis and building, but the use made of capacity is clearly an important public health issue that requires political analysis. This book records government after government that might have been able to do better but instead found its own particular path to unhappiness. Powerful and well-developed states with extensive public health expertise, in case after case, left their state capacity unused or misused. State capacity matters—if it is used. It might well be a necessary condition, and it seems it is very fungible, but it is not a sufficient condition.

Inequality and Inequity

It is neither surprising nor controversial to find that COVID-19 preyed upon and exacerbated existing inequity in societies (Bambra et al., 2020; Lynch, 2020a; Pollack, 2020). Crises and health emergencies often do that, for they harm those with the least and prompt a competition for public action that the most powerful are likeliest to win. The specific ways in which the pandemic interacted with inequalities and politics in society varied with the society, but COVID-19, like most pandemics, proved that we aren't all in it together. In many societies, particularly the most unequal, the health, economic, and social effects are likely to durably increase inequality. Research in health inequalities is highly developed, particularly in Europe and the United States, and uses sophisticated theories and methods. It is already showing the ways in which the pandemic and responses affected inequalities.

Our goal is to explain policy choices. For our purposes, one of the most important issues is how inequalities, and awareness of inequalities, drove policies and politics. The methodological problem is that inequalities affect politics via other mechanisms such as partisanship, interest groups, sexism, racism, gender identity discrimination, caste, and all manner of ethnic, territorial, and economic stratification. Making inequity visible does not make it a political problem that will be solved. Discussion of health inequalities per se does not trouble people who are not bothered about inequality and therefore is not a dispositive argument in politics (Lynch, 2020b). For example, we would expect governments more responsive to wealthy voters or business owners both to create a trade-off between public health and the economy by failing to establish TTIS systems and then to come down on the side of the economy. As Mätzke notes (chapter 16, this volume), we would expect governments with no commitment to gender equality, such as Austria, to choose public health policies that are particularly harmful to working women and not compensate in social policy. We would expect blind spots, as in Singapore, where policy-makers disregarded migrant workers; the United States, where racial politics clearly shaped responses; or India, where journalists noted that Narendra Modi's "government and especially his COVID-19 task force, dominated by upper-caste Hindus, never adequately contemplated how shutting down the economy and quarantining 1.3 billion people would introduce desperation, then panic and then chaos for millions of migrant workers at the heart of Indian industry" (Gettleman et al., 2020).

None of these mechanisms are simple. Political scientists still argue about whether parties matter to public policy, let alone when and how. Parties and interest groups are mechanisms of interest aggregation and coalition management, which means that they are unlikely to be ideologically, scientifically, or otherwise coherent. In more authoritarian regimes, there are complex and opaque politics within the regime and its key supporters, as the regime's leaders work out whom to co-opt, whom to ignore, and whom to suppress.

COVID-19 has, in most countries, been a powerful engine of inequality. In most cases it seems that the interaction of the pandemic and social policy has been to exacerbate inequity, comforting the comfortable and afflicting the afflicted. Why policies have worked that way in so many different countries, and what it says about politics today, will be a crucial topic of study, one that our case studies can inform.

The Politics of Credit and Blame

One recurrent theme throughout the book's chapters that merits further exploration is the politics of credit and blame (see also Hassenteufel, 2020; Royo, 2020). It is close to axiomatic that politicians in any system seek credit and try to avoid blame (Weaver, 1986). Sometimes this means taking actions that will gain credit and avoiding blameworthy ones. Sometimes it means claiming credit for somebody else's achievement and shifting blame for your own mistakes. These are common political tactics in every walk of life. In the absence of traceability—in the situations in which there is no good way to attract credit or cast blame—politicians will often opt for "position-taking" tactics in which they draw attention to their views on some polarizing big issue outside their responsibilities (Arnold, 1992). That could mean blaming the WHO or China or migrants for the pandemic, or directing attention to various cultural conflicts.

Different political systems structure the tactics that allocate credit and blame, and different events shape their ability to do so. In general, most politicians pay more attention to some groups than others—for example, it is common for democratic politicians to pay less attention to the interests of groups who will never vote for them. In more authoritarian regimes, the politics of credit and blame are performed for a still narrower and less clear set of groups who in some way wield power that the regime must acknowledge.

We can see the politics of credit and blame at work in most of Europe over the spring and summer of 2020, for example (Greer et al., 2020). In almost every country represented, with the possible exception of Sweden, heads of government pushed to the fore of the initial response. They commonly centralized authority in their offices at the expense of other ministers, departments, and agencies (including public health agencies). In federations, central governments often took on new powers at the expense of regional governments. In some cases, such as Czechia, heads of government made decisions almost entirely unilaterally, and in most they processed advice and action through ad hoc committees rather than established government mechanisms. It was time to be a hero, so to speak, and heads of government raced to take the credit for beating the pandemic (or, raced to avoid the blame for letting it out of control).

Over the summer of 2020, as cases and mortality across most of Europe dropped toward zero, credit for containing the pandemic became less impressive than blame for continued NPIs. Closed schools, shuttered restaurants, limitations on gatherings, spoiled holidays, and no tourism in the world's tourist hub all had serious negative consequences. Heads of government became suddenly much more reticent, handing responsibility for the pandemic back to others, such as regional governments and health ministers. A constant diet of crisis and briefings from heads of government in most countries gave way to limited reopenings and the relatively unfamiliar faces of health ministers, regional leaders, or heads of public health agencies. Some countries, such as Russia, started campaigns to promote internal tourism, while the United Kingdom government, astoundingly, set up a scheme to subsidize restaurant dining in England ("Eat out to help out" was the slogan).

When the entirely predictable second wave hit Europe—and hit countries that had escaped it, such as those of Central Europe, especially hard—politicians at every level had a problem. When would blame for reinstating NPIs exceed blame for letting the second wave hit? What would be the most effective way to gain credit from reimposing NPIs after the virus was already doing huge damage to a tired and increasingly cynical population? Who would bear the blame for the policies—notably TTIS system failures—that meant the NPIs had to come back? And how would these tactics interact with business and other interests that were often lobbies for avoiding NPIs? Blaming the voters for eating subsidized restaurant meals, visiting their grandparents, or enjoying a Spanish beach holiday was unlikely to work, and so politicians in most of Europe found themselves allocating blame to each other in a souring environment where there was less and less credit to be had.

The European story had echoes around the world. In Brazil, Bolsonaro claimed credit for social policies that were proposed by Congress and shifted the blame for unpopular social distance measures to the states and municipalities. Trump did much the same in the United States. A variety of populists around the world blamed China and sought credit for responding to the pandemic with xenophobic rhetoric and politics. The politics of credit and blame shape much of what we saw, and they merit further investigation.

Populism and Science

One recurrent discussion in the pandemic focused on the interaction of populism, science, and pandemic response (Falkenbach & Greer, 2021; Pevehouse, 2020). Debates about the place of science, politics, and populism in the pandemic were remarkably ahistorical, with no sense of how much more or less "scientific" decisions had been in previous public health crises, or what it meant to be scientific. Epidemiological research finding that masking and social distancing reduce transmission is one kind of finding, but political and sociological research on issues that affect compliance with masking and social distance can produce different kinds of findings. Epidemiology might lead one to suggest that the police should enforce NPIs such as masking mandates, but other social sciences may suggest that would be counterproductive. Epidemiological surveillance technologies may seem heaven-sent to those who want to return to normality, but the politics of surveillance involved are extremely important and very complex (in general, scholarship pays far too little attention to the high-stakes politics of surveillance) (Greer, 2017; Greitens, 2020; Marx, 2015). To follow the science, as anybody who reads any kind of science knows, is to choose the science.

Framing the question of science, politics, and policy this way has two effects. On one hand, it focuses our attention on the question of when and how science is used by politicians. Science, like law or medicine, is highly political, but it still constrains most of its practitioners. We can imagine that scientists' political preferences (partisan, careerist, a mixture, or other) interact with the clarity of the findings. When findings are unclear, then we would expect that individual scientists' politics would matter more to their findings, but science is generally good at weeding out people who make political claims in opposition to well-supported findings. The vast range of questions about COVID-19, from the efficacy of masks to the efficacy of particular vaccines, gave us all great scope to watch the speed with which scientists worldwide evaluated findings and cast out those who seemed to be disagreeing with emerging consensus for political reasons. But that still does not mean that there is "a science" to be followed, which is what created scope for disagreement about, for example, Swedish strategy. Heads of government also proved, as noted, very reluctant to rely on expert public health agencies for "science," strongly preferring interdisciplinary ad hoc committees for advice.

The other effect of framing in such a way is that it isolates a set of politicians who seemed to have a genuine problem with science in principle. In most cases these were populists, some of them of the populist radical right (Falkenbach et al., 2018). The definition of populism includes opposition to elites, such as scientists. It is perhaps no surprise that populist leaders might say and do particularly extraordinary things in a public health crisis in which scientific findings are crucial to policy agendas and decisions. Furthermore, xenophobia is a core part of the populist radical right politics, and xenophobia in pandemics is as old as history (Dionne & Turkmen, 2020). But we should proceed with caution. Following science can mean many things; leaders who seem unscientific, such as Bolsonaro, Johnson, or Trump, can lead governments full of people committed to science, and science changed rapidly over the course of the pandemic. The topic merits further inquiry, because it is not clear how we would test the hypothesis that some political currents are more opposed to "science" than others.

Also substantially unexplored in literature on COVID-19 politics to date is the interaction of science, religion, and public health. Religion surely already shaped pandemic response, whether through the personal beliefs of leaders with agency or through popular responses to policy. It is likely that religious worldviews shaped receptiveness to different kind of scientific messages (e.g., Whitehead & Perry, 2020); that religious practices and denominational decisions shaped the course of the pandemic (e.g., Were some religious persuasions more fatalistic?); and that the shock of the pandemic will, in many countries, change the course of religious history. These effects should reverberate through politics.

Exploring the different ways in which, for example, Catholics and Pentecostal Christians dealt with the pandemic at the elite and mass level should be a priority for understanding not just policy-making but also the further effects of the pandemic on society.

Tired and Grumpy: The Politics of Second and Third Waves

The authors of the chapters in this book were commissioned to end their coverage at the start of September 2020. This was a deliberate editorial decision to use the dramatic first wave as the basis for the book's findings, in full awareness of the likelihood of a second wave in the northern hemisphere in autumn 2020. The second wave, which was well underway globally by the time this book went into production in December 2020, showed many of the patterns we would expect from reading past histories of epidemics and disasters. Governments and people relaxed NPIs too early in most countries; TTIS systems were very hard to set up in most countries, and some never really tried; the search for new balances between economy and public health too often turned out to just mean too few NPIs; and people became tired. It is unsurprising, in historical perspective, to see a pattern in which a first wave produces excitement, novelty, and social solidarity such as applauding health workers, and a second wave, which is actually worse, and which is marked by recrimination, distrust, and noncompliance with NPIs. There is often a third wave, concentrated in relatively untouched rural areas, which happens just as urban areas are putting the pandemic behind them. This third wave can easily contribute to rural anger, triggering new problems.

The politics and policy of the second wave in the last three months of 2020 are outside the scope of the book, but what is noticeable, in Tolstoy's terms, is the number of happy families that became unhappy in a new and distinctive way. The government of Czechia, which had been led to a relatively strong and effective set of NPIs by a private businessman with a model, started listening to a dentist with a reopening plan and was rewarded with a terrible wave of infections and deaths. Some countries, such as Kazakhstan, Kyrgyzstan, and Uzbekistan, served as cautionary tales of what can go wrong when public health policies to curb the epidemic are scaled back too early, especially when the healthcare capacity is too weak for a surge in cases. A number of governments seem to have just given up, even if they had levied impressive NPIs in the first wave. Others, such as Spain, Italy, Britain, and France, recreated their previous decisions in uncanny detail as if they had learned nothing. Unsurprisingly, popular cynicism and political disunity surged in the autumn of 2020 in these countries.

The politics of the second wave, broadly, are the politics of disenchantment and recrimination. We made the first wave the focus of our book because it was a time of emergency, political crisis, and political possibility when the United States briefly had a social policy reminiscent of Denmark, and Sweden was the darling of the world's libertarians. It was the equivalent of an adrenalin high for the world. We expected that the second wave in the northern hemisphere winter of 2020–2021 would be less interesting—an uneven, ill-tempered reversion to the mean that would be hard to interpret. The effectiveness of vaccines created hope in this time, but that hope was fighting against both popular impatience with lockdowns and, in country after country, political and interest group efforts to create an impression of impatience that could be used to their political ends. The political economy of vaccines became the site of the key decisions, discussed later in this chapter.

Bringing History Back In

We are not historians, and this is not a work of historical scholarship. But history was inescapable and should be at the center of inquiry into the pandemic and its lessons. In country after country, history mattered. For example, it could be that relatively high compliance with public health measures in East Asian countries was due to popular and policy-makers' memories of other respiratory diseases such as the first SARS or MERS, and what worked then (a dynamic visible in our chapters and in Lee et al., 2020). Masking was far from novel behavior in East Asia, and political elites might have had a better sense of what actions to take and how to communicate them than elites in other countries with limited recent pandemic exposure.

Likewise, history may be a guide to broader patterns of expectation. For example, the difficulty of maintaining political unity and popular compliance with NPIs in a second wave was obvious to anybody familiar with the histories of other outbreaks and even similar kinds of emergencies. So was the likelihood that some countries' leaderships would focus too much on vaccines as a solution. Peter Baldwin has gone further and made the simple, forceful argument that history drives responses: that countries reach back into their traditional repertoires when facing a disease, so that response to cholera in the nineteenth century prefigures response to AIDS in the late twentieth (Baldwin, 2005a, 2005b). Not all social scientists agree (Taylor, 2013), but figuring out what changes from pandemic to pandemic and country to country would be very valuable. There is a systematic gap between the historiography of medicine and public health, which is extremely rich, and the fields of public health and political science. Anthropology and sociology often also have contributions that span historiography and current events. They are frequently critical of public health reasoning (Dingwall et al., 2013). Developing frameworks for understanding COVID-19's lessons in relation to history as well as comparative politics and epidemiology may be an especially valuable interdisciplinary endeavor.

After the Pandemic

Our chapters have the least to say about the long-lasting consequences of the pandemic, and a focus on policy alone will not be able to capture the many ways in which class, gender, race, territory, ethnicity, religion, employment, and other inequalities shape and are shaped by the pandemic. But we want to underline that decisions taken in the pandemic—the crisis phase of which lasted throughout 2020 and well into 2021—started to become the policy baseline for the future. And so did the social effects. Mätzke, for example, highlights the extent to which Austria's health and social policy responses were not just effective public health; they were also effective ways to re-establish gender and economic inequalities that had been eroding. In many countries, if not all, the "high-touch" service sector most exposed to NPIs, physical distancing, and economic harm was also the dominant employer of women, migrant, and other vulnerable populations and ethnic, religious, racial, or other minorities. The pandemic, in many cases, dealt them a terrible, if temporary, blow.

One of the trickiest problems in policy is to understand which temporary decisions leave lasting effects. Will the short American holiday in Scandinavia leave a lasting impression on American voters and elites, and what will that be? Will the women and minorities of all kinds who lost out significantly in service-sector shutdowns be able to return to their previous place, and will that return, or their loss of ground, be politically sustainable? The previous global crisis, the financial crisis of 2008–2012, showed that many countries are easily able to sustain increasing inequality without backlash sufficient to worry their elites. Will this crisis have the same result?

Part of the problem of identifying temporary effects is that the meaning of "temporary" or "crisis" is somewhat elastic. COVID-19 and the associated NPIs will, by the time vaccines permit herd immunity, have influenced life in most countries of the world for years. There is a long tradition of "lessons learned" papers and "after-action reports" in public health and emergency management, with experts and policy-makers trying to learn from responses to events such as Ebola outbreaks. Journalists' and politicians' natural instinct is to hold inquiries. But policy decisions made in March or July 2020 had a long time to become part of life and change the way systems worked. This is an important point to remember as we enter a likely period of long crises, in particular those associated with climate change but also, for example, antimicrobial resistance. Political scientists have spent decades trying to develop a theoretical language for understanding institutional change. Understanding and explaining the scale and direction of institutional change in 2020–2021 will be a challenge and opportunity to test those ideas. And in future crises, including amorphous ones such as recurrent large-scale wildfires, storms, or floods, it will be a practical challenge to make policy without a sense of what is truly temporary and exception and what will become normal.

Likewise, political agendas and actions after the pandemic will re-allocate many serious burdens in a way that will shape life chances and political coalitions. For example, what will happen to proprietors of small business, or women, or minorities? What will happen to people living in areas that have been tipped into long-term decline as a result of economic changes? How will policy allocate burdens among, for example, renters, landlords, and the landlords' banks? There has been a slow repoliticization of the welfare state after decades in which the conventional wisdom was that welfare states were essentially stable. Policy changes, or failures to adapt policies to problems made clear by the pandemic, will be crucial in shaping societies. They will be highly political, but whether they are equally visible will be a different question.

Vaccines: Power and Political Economy

In December 2020 the image of a ninety-year-old woman receiving the first COVID-19 vaccine as part of the United Kingdom's nationwide immunization campaign made the news worldwide. The speed of vaccine development and production has been one of the most dramatic parts of the COVID-19 pandemic response. As of this writing, as research toward discovering vaccines for COVID-19 continues to progress, attention is increasingly turning to the challenges of ensuring affordable access to these products on a global scale. Crucial challenges include unequal vaccine allocation, the issue of vaccine production on a worldwide scale, and differences in regulatory capacity around the world.

Given the uncertainty in spring 2020 around the likely effectiveness of different COVID-19 vaccines, countries adopted different strategies to secure access to these products. Wealthy nations and supranational organizations such as the United States, United Kingdom, Canada, Japan, and the EU have engaged in unilateral negotiation with vaccine developers to secure a variety of products, some of which were in production and distribution at the end of 2020 and others which were still in clinical trials. Most notable is the US Operation Warp Speed, a public-private partnership to accelerate access to multiple vaccines with different technologies. These unilateral decisions have led to a concept known as *vaccine nationalism* (Bollyky & Bown, 2020; Fidler, 2020), in which countries seek to protect their own citizens ahead of anyone else, limiting the already scarce supply of vaccines as a result (to the unhappy countries).

Learning from what happened during the H1N1 pandemic, in which rich nations purchased the initial supplies of the vaccines, the WHO has promoted the COVAX initiative to coordinate more equitable access to COVID-19 vaccines. The COVAX facility is a pooled procurement mechanism that aims to deliver at least two billion doses of vaccines by the end of 2021. It includes a diverse portfolio of products, and countries have different purchasing options to complement their national strategies. The COVAX Advance Market Commitment uses donor funds to provide vaccines at close to zero cost to ninety-two low-income countries. As pointed out by Kavanagh et al. in this book, the WHO strategy has been challenging given the unilateral decisions taken by wealthy countries, the duplicative pooling strategies promoted by regional blocs such as the EU and the African Union, and the fact that this coordinated initiative received different levels of support from world leaders (with the United States and Russia being notably absent). Therefore, how countries make sense and adhere to these global initiatives requires future investigation.

Another crucial challenge for supplying COVID-19 vaccines on a global scale is production. Although in previous epidemics (such as HIV/AIDS) intellectual property protection acted as a limitation to access to innovative therapeutics because of the high cost of patented drugs (Sell, 2007), at this moment, the critical bottleneck for ensuring access to COVID-19 vaccines is mass production and distribution. Vaccine developers willing to establish global production networks have searched for partners with local production capabilities, which are based mainly in middle-income countries (Fonseca et al., 2020). For example, AstraZeneca has established technology transfer agreements in Brazil, Argentina, and Thailand, whereas Sinovac and Russia's Gamaleya Research Institute have agreements in Brazil and India.

For novel technologies, companies may need to transfer the manufacturing capacity as well as the knowledge about how to make these products in the first place, including information that is not contained in patents or other public documents (Price et al., 2020). Technology transfer has enormous political and legal challenges (O'Sullivan et al., 2020), including agreements on the knowledge transfer content, the product's price, whether intellectual property is shared, and other issues. Given these challenges, governments will have an essential role in providing incentives for sharing needed technologies or alternative paths to them. What do these agreements look like? To what extent are they coordinated with uptake?

Finally, an essential area for future investigation is how national regulatory agencies perceive and respond to risks in the context of scientific uncertainty. Market approval as well as patent registration are highly contested activities and contingent on national institutional arrangements (Shadlen, 2017; Vogel, 1995, 2012). Vaccines must be authorized for use in each country where the industry intends to commercialize its product. Because governments have different pathways for approving and licensing pharmaceuticals (Simpson et al., 2020), we should expect products to enter the market at different speeds. In the case of COVID-19 vaccines, a particularly important regulatory concept is the measurement of efficacy. It has been established by the WHO that the minimum acceptable efficacy is approximately 50% point estimate (Krause et al., 2020). However, political and economic pressures for rapid approval of a COVID-19 vaccine could result in distributing a product that is only weakly effective. The consequences may be devastating and may worsen the pandemic. Widespread distribution of a weakly effective vaccine could interfere with the evaluation of other vaccines (the control group in clinical trials would include individuals previously vaccinated rather than those who only received a placebo), for example, or people could relax their compliance with NPIs (Krause et al., 2020).

In regulation of COVID-19 vaccines, the different levels of regulatory capacity among countries could create very different political economies of product regulation. A small group of countries—including the United States, Canada, the countries of the EU, and Japan—are classified as stringent regulatory authorities, that is, founders of the International Council for Harmonization of Technical Requirements for Pharmaceuticals for Human Use (ICH), a network of regulatory agencies and drug producers that discusses regulatory convergence in the pharmaceutical sector. There are also countries with some regulatory capacity that are not a part of the ICH (or only recently joined), such as Brazil, China, Chile, and Argentina. Finally, low-income countries have little to no regulatory capacity.

Although the US Food and Drug Administration is known for its high regulatory capacity, the agency has been subjected to public pressure from the president to quickly approve a vaccine so that he could reap political gains at a particular point of the electoral cycle (LeBlanc, 2020). In the United Kingdom, many have expressed concerns about the speed with which the British regulator granted approval to the Pfizer/BioNTech vaccine (Manskar, 2020). Notably, Britain has recently exited the European Union, and therefore it does not need to wait for the decisions of the powerful European Medicines Agency for vaccine approval. On the other hand, Russia, China, and United Arab Emirates began administering vaccines even before the conclusion of clinical trials ("Eyes of the World Are on Medicines Regulators," 2020). Countries such as Chile, Brazil, and Argentina did not have accelerated pathways for vaccine and drug regulation such as emergency use or rapid assessment; therefore, they have mimicked what other agencies are doing or relied on the guidelines of international harmonization networks such as the ICH. Yet how international guidelines are implemented and thus become local rules depends on domestic politics (Shadlen, 2017; Weyland, 2007). Therefore, we must take into account agents, their interests, and institutions to be able to understand how countries approach risk assessment of COVID-19 vaccines. Low-income countries who have nascent or under-resourced regulatory agencies can use the WHO Emergency Use Listing Procedure as guidance for vaccine approval (World Health Organization, 2020). However, the extent to which they do so and how they do so warrant further investigation.

These are some of the political economy aspects that should be investigated in future analyses. Other issues may include the capacity of health systems to deliver vaccines and the uptake of these products in the context of increasing vaccine hesitancy. This will be a challenge for all of the fields involved, for an interdisciplinary inquiry into the political economy of vaccines will have to combine research in politics, economics, and health policy that runs on very different tracks.

Conclusion

We do not yet have a complete and subtle understanding of "what worked" in response to COVID-19. The excess mortality and longer-term consequences of the social, economic upheaval will take years and likely decades to fully comprehend. However, it was not too early to test hypotheses and draw conclusions about coronavirus *politics* in 2020. This book aims to draw conclusions about how and why governments responded the way that they did. This collaborative research endeavor also aims to break down disciplinary silos and demonstrates the significant contribution to global health of a group of international scholars thinking about politics, public health, and the social sciences as we grapple with understanding the COVID-19 pandemic.

We did find a strong policy case for better coordination between social and health policies, such that no health policies are made without consideration of social policy supports and effects. Social policy is not just a way to manage the effects of the pandemic; it is also necessary if NPIs are to work outside the most coercive settings.

In scholarly and policy terms, we also still need to "bring state back in" (Skocpol, 1985). Public health in most countries was born as an arm of the state rather than as an autonomous academic enterprise, and perhaps the determinedly apolitical way in which public health scholarship describes the state and political issues is a legacy of that history. Political institutions matter, and we need more political analysis to better understand and prepare countries for future health crises. Clearly, general state capacity is a necessary, not a sufficient condition (it is unclear whether specific public health investment is even a necessary condition, judging by the sidelining of public health agencies in so many countries). It was the decisions of politicians, decisions that can be modeled in the ways we discussed in this book, that made key differences.

Third, we need to understand regime types. Too much of the conversation about regimes has focused on their interaction with democratization and democratic breakdown, rather than asking how different regimes and institutions shape policy. Too much of the focus on the comparative politics of health has only asked whether democracy is good for health. Moving forward, scholarship in politics and public health should address the context and diversity of authoritarian and democratic regimes and their allocations of agency.

Fourth and finally, as Kavanagh et al. and Brooks et al. make clear (chapters 2 and 13 this volume), and the political economy of vaccines will make more clear, there are serious coordination problems in global health governance. We are already starting to sort through and evaluate the performance of different organizations such as WHO and the public-private coalitions that flank it, but we also need to be clear about the realistic ambitions and standards for such organizations.

As we send this book into production at the end of 2020, the pandemic continues and the number of "unhappy countries" increases with the second and third waves of the virus at the end of 2020 and beginning of 2021. The comparative aspects of their unhappiness should be of great interest to a wide range of scholars of public health and politics, in regard to COVID-19 as well as any future pandemics. Yet as 2020 came to an end, there was also great hope that many countries will be able to change their trajectory in the COVID-19 pandemic. Vaccines showed promise that surprised most informed observers. They created hope amid the disarray seen in many countries. But even if vaccines solve humanity's COVID-19 problem, neither the challenges of new infectious diseases nor politics will go away. As the scientific community builds the evidence on effective interventions, including non-pharmaceutical and pharmaceutical, the politics of coronavirus will persist in how governments choose to implement health and social policies.

Note

1. "Happy families are all alike; every unhappy family is unhappy in its own way." Leo Tolstoy, *Anna Karenina* (1887).

References

Arnold, R. D. (1992). *The logic of congressional action*. Yale University Press.
Baldwin, P. (2005a). *Contagion and the state in Europe, 1830–1930*. Cambridge University Press.
Baldwin, P. (2005b). *Disease and democracy: The industrialized world faces AIDS*. University of California Press.
Bambra, C., Riordan, R., Ford, J., & Matthews, F. (2020). The COVID-19 pandemic and health inequalities. *Journal of Epidemiology and Community Health*, 74(11). http://dx.doi.org/10.1136/jech-2020-214401
Bollyky, T., & Bown, C. (2020). The tragedy of vaccine nationalism: Only cooperation can end the pandemic. *Foreign Affairs*, 96.
Capano, G., Howlett, M., Jarvis, D. S. L., Ramesh, M., & Goyal, N. (2020). Mobilizing policy (in)capacity to fight COVID-19: Understanding variations in state responses. *Policy and Society* 39(3), 285–308.
Colfer, B. (2020). Public policy responses to COVID-19 in Europe. *European Policy Analysis*, 6(2), 126–137.
Davies, S. E. (2012). The challenge to know and control: Disease outbreak surveillance and alerts in China and India. *Global Public Health*, 7(7), 695–716.
Dingwall, R., Hoffman, L. M., & Staniland, K. (2013). Introduction: Why a sociology of pandemics? *Sociology of Health & Illness*, 35(2), 167–173.
Dionne, K. Y., & Turkmen, F. (2020). The politics of pandemic othering: Putting COVID-19 in global and historical context. *International Organization*. https://doi.org/10.1017/S0020818320000405
Eyes of the world are on medicines regulators. (2020). *Nature*, 588, 195.
Falkenbach, M., Bekker, M., & Greer, S. L. (2018). Political parties matter: The impact of the populist radical right on health. *European Journal of Public Health*, 28(supp 3), 15–18.
Falkenbach, M., & Greer, S. L. (Eds.). (2021). *The populist radical right and health: National policies and global trends*. Springer.
Fidler, D. (2020, August 14). Vaccine nationalism's politics. *Science, 369*, 749.
Fonseca, E., Shadlen, K., & Bastos, F. (2020). *The politics of ensuring access to Covid-19 vaccines in middle-income countries: Lessons from Brazil* (working paper Fundação Getulio Vargas).
Forman, R., Atun, R., McKee, M., & Mossialos, E. (2020). 12 lessons learned from the management of the coronavirus pandemic. *Health Policy*, 124(6), 577–580.
Fox, D. M. (2017). Toward a public health politics of consequence: An autobiographical reflection. *American Journal of Public Health*, 107(10), 1604.
Gettleman, J., Raj, S., Yasir, S., & Singh, K. D. (2020, December 15). The virus trains: How lockdown chaos spread COVID-19 across India. *The New York Times*. https://www.nytimes.com/2020/12/15/world/asia/india-coronavirus-shramik-specials.html
Greer, S. L. (2017). Constituting public health surveillance in twenty-first century Europe. In M. Weimer & A. de Ruijter (Eds.), *Regulating risks in the European Union: The co-production of expert and executive power* (pp. 121–141). Bloomsbury.

Greer, S. L., Jarman, H., Rozenblum, S., & Wismar, M. (2020). Centralisation within and between governments. *Eurohealth, 26*(2).

Greitens, S. C. (2020). Surveillance, security, and liberal democracy in the post-COVID world. *International Organization*, 1–22.

Hassenteufel, P. (2020). Handling the COVID-19 crisis in France: Paradoxes of a centralized state-led health system. *European Policy Analysis, 6*(2), 170–179.

Kavanagh, M. M., & Singh, R. (2020). Democracy, capacity, and coercion in pandemic response—COVID 19 in comparative political perspective. *Journal of Health Politics, Policy and Law, 45*(6), 997–1012.

Krause, P., Fleming, T. R., Longini, I., Henao-Restrepo, A. M., Peto, R., for the World Health Organization Solidarity Vaccines Trial Expert Group. (2020). COVID-19 vaccine trials should seek worthwhile efficacy. *The Lancet, 396*(10253), 741–743.

LeBlanc, P. (2020, Sept 24). *Trump claims White House can overrule FDA's attempt to toughen guidelines for coronavirus vaccine.* CNN. https://edition.cnn.com/2020/09/23/politics/trump-fda-coronavirus-vaccine/index.html

Lee, S., Hwang, C., & Moon, M. J. (2020). Policy learning and crisis policy-making: Quadruple-loop learning and COVID-19 responses in South Korea. *Policy and Society, 39*(3), 363–381.

Lynch, J. (2020a). Health equity, social policy, and promoting recovery from COVID-19. *Journal of Health Politics, Policy and Law, Journal of Health Politics, Policy and Law 45*(6), 983–995.

Lynch, J. (2020b). *Regimes of inequality: The political economy of health and wealth.* Cambridge University Press.

Manskar, N. (2020, Dec 2). European officials say UK rushed approval of Pfizer COVID-19 vaccine. *New York Post.*

Marx, G. T. (2015). *Windows into the soul: Surveillance and society in the age of high technology.* University of Chicago Press.

O'Sullivan, C., Rutten, P., & Schatz, C. (2020). *Why tech transfer may be critical to beating COVID-19.* McKinsey London. https://www.mckinsey.com/industries/pharmaceuticals-and-medical-products/our-insights/why-tech-transfer-may-be-critical-to-beating-covid-19

Pevehouse, J. C. W. (2020). The COVID-19 pandemic, international cooperation, and populism. *International Organization*, 1–22.

Pollack, H. A. (2020). Disaster preparedness and social justice in a public health emergency. *Journal of Health Politics, Policy and Law, 45*(6), 907–920.

Price, W., Rai, A., & Minssen, T. (2020). Knowledge transfer for large-scale vaccine manufacturing. *Science*, eabc9588.

Royo, S. (2020). Responding to COVID-19: The case of Spain. *European Policy Analysis, 6*(2), 180–190.

Sell, S. (2007). International institutions, intellectual property and the HIV/AIDS pandemic. In R. Ostergaard & J. Whitman (Eds.), *HIV/AIDS and the threat to national security.* Palgrave MacMillan.

Shadlen, K. (2017). *Coalitions and compliance: The political economy of pharmaceutical patents in Latin America.* Oxford University Press.

Simpson, S., Chakrabarti, A., Robinson, D., Chirgwin, K., & Lumpkin, M. (2020). Navigating facilitated regulatory pathways during a disease X pandemic. *npj Vaccines, 5*(1), 101.

Skocpol, T. (1985). Bringing the state back. In P. B. Evans, D. Rueschemeyer, & T. Skocpol (Eds.), *Strategies of analysis in current research* (pp. 3–32). Cambridge University Press.

Taylor, R. C. R. (2013). The politics of securing borders and the identities of disease. *Sociology of Health and Illness*, 35(2), 241–254.

Vogel, D. (1995). *Trading up—Consumer & environmental regulation in a global economy.* Harvard University Press.

Vogel, D. (2012). *The politics of precaution: Regulating health, safety, and environmental risks in Europe and the United States.* Princeton University Press.

Weaver, R. K. (1986). The politics of blame avoidance. *Journal of Public Policy*, 6, 371–398.

Weyland, K. (2007). *Bounded rationality and policy diffusion: Social sector reform in Latin America.* Princeton University Press.

Whitehead, A. L., & Perry, S. L. (2020). How culture wars delay herd immunity: Christian Nationalism and anti-vaccine attitudes. *Socius.* https://doi.org/10.1177/2378023120977727

World Health Organization. (2020). *Emergency Use Listing Procedure.* Retrieved on December 23, 2020, from https://www.who.int/diagnostics_laboratory/eual/procedure/en/

Contributors

Claudia Acosta is a PhD candidate in Public Administration and Government at Fundação Getulio Vargas (Brazil) and was a visiting student in the Political Science Department at MIT (United States). She teaches at Universidad del Rosario (Colombia) and at the Lincoln Institute of Land Policy. Her background includes Urban Studies and Law. Her research focuses on urban policies in Latin America, the political economy behind federal social policies locally implemented, and its territorial impacts.

Luisa Bolaffi Arantes is a master's degree student in Public Administration at the São Paulo School of Business Administration, Getulio Vargas Foundation, Brazil. She is interested in comparative public policies, federalism, and health policy. She was a visiting research student in the Universitat Autonoma de Barcelona in 2019 and a visiting research student at Universitat Pompeu Fabra in 2021.

Francisco Inácio Bastos, MD, PhD, is a Senior Researcher, physician, and former Chair of Graduate Studies in the Department of Epidemiology and Biostatistics at the Oswaldo Cruz Foundation (FIOCRUZ). He has substantial experience in the research of substance misuse, particularly its association with human immunodeficiency virus (HIV), viral hepatitis, and other sexually transmitted infections (STIs) and blood-borne diseases. Dr. Bastos has been the principal investigator on a number of large, multi-city studies on HIV and other blood-borne infections and STIs.

Uviwe Binase, MA, is a second-year PhD student at the University of the Western Cape, South Africa. Her research focuses on Health Economics (Economics of Tobacco Control in South Africa). She holds a bachelor's degree in Geography/Sociology and a master's degree in Population Studies from the University of the Western Cape, South Africa. Her master's dissertation investigated the socioeconomic determinants of life expectancy in post-apartheid South Africa.

Endre Borbáth, PhD, is a Postdoctoral Researcher working at the Institute of Sociology at the Freie Universität Berlin, and at the Center for Civil Society Research at the WZB Berlin Social Science Center. His research focuses on the interaction between party competition and protest politics in a comparative, European perspective. He holds a PhD in Political and Social Sciences from the European University Institute.

Eleanor Brooks, PhD, is a Lecturer in health policy in the Global Health Policy Unit at the University of Edinburgh and a Scientific Advisor to the European Public Health Alliance, Brussels. She holds a UKRI Future Leaders Fellowship, studying the impact of the Better Regulation Agenda on European Union health policy. Her broader research explores the changing governance of health within the EU.

John P. Burns, PhD, is Emeritus Professor and Honorary Professor of Politics and Public Administration at the University of Hong Kong and author of *Government Capacity and the Hong Kong Civil Service* (Oxford University Press, 2004 and 2010). He does research on the politics and public administration of China, including Hong Kong.

Manuela Caiani, PhD, is Associate Professor of Political Science at the Scuola Normale Superiore (SNS) in Florence, Italy. Her research interests focus on populism, extreme right political parties and movements, social movements, and Europeanization. She has been involved in several international comparative research projects on populism, radical right, and social movements. She currently conducts a project on the cultural side of populism (VolkswagenStiftung).

Ruth Carlitz, PhD, is an Assistant Professor of Political Science at Tulane University, where she teaches courses on international development and African Politics. Her research focuses primarily on the politics of public goods provision in low-income countries, from the perspectives of both governments and citizens. In addition to her academic research, she has worked on evaluations commissioned by USAID, the International Budget Partnership, DFID, and the World Bank.

Adèle Cassola, PhD, MSc, is an Investigator and Research Director–Public Health Institutions at the Global Strategy Lab, where she leads research that investigates the relationships among public health policy, institutional design, and the use of scientific evidence. Dr. Cassola has previously led comparative policy research on topics including equity in legal rights protections, educational inclusion, and affordable housing policy.

Jonathan D. Cylus, PhD, is Senior Research Fellow at LSE Health and Honorary Research Fellow, London School of Hygiene and Tropical Medicine. His main research is on health systems, focusing primarily on health financing policy, health economics, and health system performance. He is also interested in the impact of social policies and other social determinants on health.

Thomas Czypionka, MD, MSc, is Head of the Department of Health Economics and Health Policy at the Institute for Advanced Studies in Vienna and Visiting Senior Research Fellow at London School of Economics and Political Science. His main interests lie in health services research, comparative health systems analysis, and the political economy of health systems.

Anniek de Ruijter, PhD, is Associate Professor of Health Law and Policy at the University of Amsterdam (UvA). She is Co-Director of the Law Center for Health and Life at the Faculty of Law of the UvA and Research Fellow of the Amsterdam Center for European Law and Governance. She is a board member of the Amsterdam Centre for Global Health and Development.

Kim Yi Dionne, PhD, is an Associate Professor of Political Science at the University of California Riverside and the author of *Doomed Interventions: The Failure of Global Responses to AIDS in Africa* (Cambridge University Press, 2018). She collected much of the data for her book in Malawi, where she was a Fulbright Fellow from 2008 to 2009, and where she served as a credentialed election observer in 2014 and 2019.

Kenneth A. Dubin, PhD, is Managing Director at Medius Capital, an investment firm focused on Southern European technology companies pursuing Environmental, Social, and Governance (ESG) objectives. He is also Adjunct Professor of Strategy and Human Resources at IE Business School (Madrid). He has previously held full-time academic positions in labor law and human resource management at the Universidad Carlos III and Anglia Ruskin University, Cambridge (UK). He holds a PhD in political science from the University of California, Berkeley.

Victoria I. Dudina, PhD, is an Associate Professor and Chair of the Department of Applied Sociology at St. Petersburg State University in St. Petersburg, Russia. Dr. Dudina has extensive academic and research experience in the field of sociology of health and digital sociology. Her current research projects are devoted to vulnerable populations' access to health care services and peer support in online health communities.

Boniface Dulani, PhD, is a Senior Lecturer in Political Science at the University of Malawi and visiting Research Fellow at the Center for Social Science Research, University of Cape Town. Dr. Dulani is a senior member of the Afrobarometer, where he doubles as the Director of Surveys. He researches and publishes on presidential term limits, democracy, presidentialism, tolerance, elections, and public health.

Patrick Fafard, PhD, is a Professor of Public and International Affairs at the University of Ottawa and serves as the Associate Director of the Global Strategy Lab (York University and University of Ottawa). Patrick has had a lengthy career spanning both government and academe. His current research includes the governance of organ donation and transplantation and a comparative study of public health leadership and communication in the context of COVID-19.

Michelle Falkenbach, MA, is a PhD candidate within the Department of Health Management and Policy at the University of Michigan School of Public Health.

Her research interests include populist radical right politicians and their impact on health politics and policies, comparative health politics, and European health systems.

Sara E. Fischer, MPH, is a PhD candidate in the Department of Government at Georgetown University. She was a Fulbright-Hays Fellow in Malawi from 2019 to 2020, where she conducted ethnographic field research for her dissertation on the politics of the community health system. She previously completed a dual Master of Public Health degree from the Universities of Sheffield, UK, and Copenhagen, Denmark, where she studied the health policy agenda-setting process in Tanzania.

Scott L. Greer, PhD, is Professor of Health Management and Policy, Global Public Health, and Political Science at the University of Michigan. His most recent books include *Federalism and Social Policy* (2019), *Everything You Always Wanted to Know about European Union Health Policy but Were Afraid to Ask* (2019*)*, and *The European Union after Brexit* (2020).

Akihito Hagihara, PhD, MPH, is Professor Emeritus at Kyushu University in Fukuoka, Japan, and Visiting Director of the National Cerebral and Cardiovascular Center in Osaka, Japan. His research interest includes clinical epidemiology and health policy. He has authored about 300 publications and 10 textbooks in English and Japanese. He received an MPH from University of Michigan and a PhD in medical sciences from Osaka University.

Joseph Harris, PhD, is an Assistant Professor of Sociology at Boston University. He conducts comparative historical research that lies at the intersection of sociology, political science, and global health. He is author of *Achieving Access: Professional Movements and the Politics of Health Universalism* (Cornell University Press, 2017) and co-founder of the Global Health and Development Interest Group within the American Sociological Association's (ASA) Section on Development. He has received two Fulbright scholarships for his research on health politics.

Holly Jarman, PhD, is the John G. Searle Assistant Professor in the Department of Health Management and Policy at the University of Michigan. As a political scientist, she researches the relationship between economic regulation and health policy. Her publications appear in journals including *The Lancet*, *Milbank Quarterly*, and the *Journal of Health Politics, Policy and Law.* Her monograph, *The Politics of Trade and Tobacco Control*, explores the consequences of trade law for tobacco control policies.

Pauline Jones, PhD, is Professor of Political Science at the University of Michigan. Her scholarly work contributes to the study of institutions and identity-based mobilization. She focuses primarily on Central Asia. She has published four books and dozens of articles in both academic and policy journals. She founded and directs the Digital Islamic Studies Curriculum, a collaborative program of instruction that provides a global perspective on Islam and the Muslim world.

Matthew M. Kavanagh, PhD, is Assistant Professor of Global Health at Georgetown University and Director of the Global Health Policy & Politics Initiative at the O'Neill Institute for National & Global Health Law. A political scientist by training, with a long history of work on global health policy in the non-governmental organization (NGO) sphere, his research focuses on the political economy of health policy in low- and middle-income countries and the political impact of human and constitutional rights on population health.

Elizabeth J. King, PhD, MPH, is Associate Professor of Health Behavior and Health Education in the School of Public Health at the University of Michigan. She specializes in the structural and social inequities influencing access to human immunodeficiency virus (HIV) services, women's health and gender-equitable access to health care services, promotion of a rights-based approach to HIV testing and treatment policies, and the influence of global policies and funding on public health in Eastern Europe and Central Asia.

Alan Kawarai Lefor, PhD, is Professor of Surgery at Jichi Medical University in Japan, specializing in surgical education. He has authored almost seven hundred publications as well as twelve textbooks in English and Japanese. Dr. Lefor received a PhD in Theoretical Astrophysics from Tohoku University in Sendai, Japan. He is currently a PhD student in the Department of Bioengineering, School of Engineering, University of Tokyo studying robotic surgery education and simulation.

Dimitra Lingri, LLB, LLM, is a lawyer specializing in Public Law. She is the Head of the Legal Department of the Hellenic National Organization of Healthcare Provision (EOPYY, Greece). She is a member of multiple European Commission committees on safe and timely access to medicines, and member of the WHO's Fair Pricing Group. She is a Researcher (Faculty of Law, Aristotle University, Thessaloniki, Greece) and Visiting Fellow (Faculty of Medicine, National Kapodistrian, University of Athens).

Christos Lionis, MD, PhD, is Professor of General Practice and Primary Health Care, and Head of the Clinic of Social and Family Medicine (Faculty of Medicine, University of Crete, Greece). He is also Visiting Professor at the School of Medicine and Health (University of Linkoping, Sweden). He has published over 365 papers in international journals. Dr. Lionis is a member of the European Commission's Expert Panel on Effective Ways of Investing in Health.

Olga Löblová, PhD, is a Postdoctoral Research Associate at the Department of Sociology, University of Cambridge. Her research focuses on the political economy of resource allocation in health care and on the role of experts and evidence in health policy-making. She publishes on the politics of health technology assessment at the EU level, as well as in Central and Eastern Europe. She holds a PhD in public policy.

Margaret MacAulay, PhD, is an Investigator at the Global Strategy Lab, where she leads a comparative study examining senior public health leadership and communication in the context of COVID-19. Margaret has previously led qualitative studies investigating the role of media and its relationship to sexual health issues, including HIV prevention and sexual violence.

Pedro C. Magalhães, PhD, is a Research Fellow at the Institute of Social Sciences of the University of Lisbon. He studies elections, public opinion, and judicial behavior. Dr. Magalhães received his PhD in Political Science from the Ohio State University.

Elize Massard da Fonseca, PhD, is Assistant Professor of Public Administration at the São Paulo School of Business Administration, Getulio Vargas Foundation, Brazil. She is also a visiting scholar at the Latin America and Caribbean Center at the London School of Economics (LACC/LSE). She specializes in pharmaceutical regulation in Latin America, health industry policy, and the politics of infectious diseases (HIV/AIDS, hepatitis C). Her research on COVID-19 is funded by the São Paulo Research Foundation (grant #2020/05230-8).

Ryozo Matsuda, PhD, is Professor at the College of Social Sciences, Ritsumeikan University. His main research fields are comparative health policy and systems research and comparative welfare state studies. He has also been involved in policy research relevant to equity in health, inclusive health care, prison health, and the right to health. He has served as the president of the Japanese Society for Health and Welfare Policy since 2017.

Margitta Mätzke, PhD, is Professor of Politics and Social Policy at the Johannes Kepler University of Linz, Austria. She has a PhD from Northwestern University (2005) and the *venia docendi* from the University of Göttingen (2012), both in Political Science. Her research focuses on governance, decision-making, and institutional dynamics in the development of Western welfare states. In this field she is especially interested in family policy, health policy, and public health.

Claudio A. Méndez, MPH, holds the position of Associate Professor of health policy, and Director at the Instituto de Salud Pública, Facultad de Medicina, Universidad Austral de Chile. He served as Health Authority (April 2016 to March 2018) for the región de Los Ríos, appointed during President Michelle Bachelet's second term in office. His main teaching and research interests are health policies, global health, health systems, and the politics of health policies.

Henry A. Mollel, PhD, MSc, is Associate Professor of Health Systems Management and Local Governance at Mzumbe University in the Department of Health Systems Management. He is the Principal Investigator and Coordinator in the Centre of Excellence in Health Monitoring and Evaluation at Mzumbe University. He has published extensively in the areas of health systems management, human resources for health, data systems and data use in the health sector, and local governance.

N'dea Moore-Petinak, MSc, is a doctoral candidate in Health Services Organization & Policy and Rackham Merit Fellow at the University of Michigan. Her research examines the impact of federalism on health disparities in the United States. Her dissertation focuses on children's health and state policy flexibility. She received her bachelor's degrees from Santa Clara University and her master's degree from Trinity College Dublin.

Takashi Nagata, MD, PhD, is Assistant Professor in the Section of Disaster and Emergency Medicine, Department of Advanced Medical Initiatives, Faculty of Medical Sciences, Kyushu University. He is a front-line physician of emergency medicine and a researcher of public health and emergency management.

Nicoli Nattrass, PhD, is Professor of Economics at the University of Cape Town, South Africa. She has published widely on macroeconomic policy, inequality, AIDS, and the struggle for antiretroviral treatment, including AIDS denialist and AIDS conspiracy beliefs. Her most recent book (with Jeremy Seekings) is *Inclusive Dualism: Labour-Intensive Development, Decent Work and Surplus Labour in Southern Africa* (Oxford University Press, Oxford, 2019).

Kanayo K. Ogujiuba, PhD (Econs), PhD (Stats), is a Development Economist by training with interests in Behavioural Research/Population Health, Economics, and Public Policy. He has a long history of work with multilateral institutions, with a focus on development policy. Over the course of his career, Dr. Ogujiuba has played significant roles in cross-institutional collaboration, research development, and innovation activities. He is currently with the School of Development Studies, University of Mpumalanga (UMP) South Africa.

Darius Ornston, PhD, is an Associate Professor at the Munk School of Global Affairs and Public Policy at the University of Toronto, where he specializes in innovation policy and the political economy of small states. His latest book, *Good Governance Gone Bad* (Cornell University Press, 2018), illustrates how the same tight-knit networks that facilitate collective action in the Nordic region also contribute to policy overshooting and economic crises.

Saime Özçürümez, PhD, is an Associate Professor at the Department of Political Science and Public Administration at Bilkent University. She conducts comparative public policy research on migration governance, social cohesion, gender-based violence in forced migration contexts, social trauma, and forced migration. She is the co-editor of *Forced Migration and Social Trauma: Interdisciplinary Perspectives from Psychoanalysis, Psychology, Sociology and Politics* (Routledge, 2018). She was a Visiting Researcher at the Department of Global Health and Social Medicine at Harvard University.

Michèle Palkovits, MPP/MGA, joined the Global Strategy Lab (GSL) as a Research Fellow during the COVID-19 pandemic, where she primarily contributes to research conducted by the Public Health Institutions stream. Her research at GSL investigates different dimensions of decision-making for public health policy, including political factors, the use of scientific evidence, as well as leadership and governance structures.

June Park, PhD, is a political economist and East Asia Voices Initiative Fellow of the East Asia National Resources Center at George Washington University Elliott School of International Affairs. She is also a Next Generation Researcher at the National Research Foundation of Korea for her first book manuscript, "Trade Wars, Currency Conflict: China, South Korea and Japan's Responses to U.S. Pressures since the Global Financial Crisis." She has published in *World Development* and *Asian Perspective*.

André Peralta-Santos, MD, MPH, is a medical doctor, public health specialist, and Director of Health Information of the Directorate-General for Health in Portugal. He has worked for international organizations such as the World Health Organization and the European Commission, as well as national governments and local health organizations.

Elena Petelos, PhD, MPH, is Senior Research Fellow in Public Health and Lecturer for Evidence-Based Medicine (University of Crete), and Research & Teaching Fellow (Maastricht University). She is a member of the Steering Group of WHO's European Health Information Initiative (Chair of EU-OECD-WHO Mapping Indicators Subgroup and Vice-Chair of Evidence-Informed Policy Subgroup). Dr. Petelos is an expert with the European Commission.

Mara Pillinger, PhD, MPH, is an Associate in the Global Health Policy & Politics Initiative at the O'Neill Institute for National and Global Health Law at Georgetown University. Her research focuses on political dynamics and organizational reform at the World Health Organization and the major multisectoral global health partnerships.

Minakshi Raj, PhD, MPH, is an Assistant Professor in the Department of Kinesiology and Community Health at the University of Illinois at Urbana Champaign. She completed her PhD in Health Services Organization and Policy at the University of Michigan School of Public Health. Her research interests include health care decision making among older adults and caregivers, use and implications of health information technologies, and the role of cultural context in organizational approaches to quality improvement.

Selina Rajan, MSc, is a Specialist Public Health Registrar in London, Kent, Surrey, and Sussex and an Honorary Research Fellow at the London School of Hygiene and Tropical Medicine. She has experience working in local authority public health departments in the UK, and her research interests are in health systems, with a particular focus on mental health.

Miriam Reiss, MSc, is a Researcher at the Department of Health Economics and Health Policy at the Institute for Advanced Studies in Vienna. She has a background in economics and sociology and has mainly worked on projects in the fields of health economics, health policy analysis, and comparative studies in health care systems.

Julia Rone, PhD, is a Wiener-Anspach Postdoctoral Researcher at the Université libre de Bruxelles and the Department of Politics and International Studies (POLIS), Cambridge. She has a PhD from the European University Institute in Florence with a thesis on mobilizations against free trade agreements. Dr. Rone's current research explores contestations over sovereignty in Europe. She has written on hacktivism, digital disobedience, and more recently, the rise of far right media in Europe.

Sarah D. Rozenblum, MS, is a PhD candidate in Public Health and Political Science at the University of Michigan and a WHO Consultant. Her research interests include the comparative politics of public health, policy responses to the spread of communicable disease, and the political economy of medical devices, pharmaceuticals, and vaccines regulation.

Luis Saboga-Nunes, Lic Soc, MPH, PhD, EuHP, a health sociologist, is Associated Professor at the Institute of Sociology, University of Education Freiburg, Germany, and Professeur Affilié UNESCO Chair/WHO Collaborating Center in Global Health & Education. A certified European Health Promotion Practitioner (EuHP) (IUHPE), he is president of the Health Promotion Section at the European Public Health Association (EUPHA). His research interest has focused on theoretical and evidence-based good practice in public health and health literacy.

Victor C. Shih, PhD, is the Ho Miu Lam Chair Associate Professor at the School of Global Policy and Strategy at University of California San Diego. He is author of *Factions and Finance in China: Elite Conflict and Inflation* and the editor of *Economic Shocks and Authoritarian Stability: Duration, Institutions and Financial Conditions*. He is also the author of numerous articles appearing in academic and business journals, including *The American Political Science Review, Comparative Political Studies,* and the *Journal of Politics.*

Phillip M. Singer, PhD, is an Assistant Professor in the Department of Political Science and Adjunct Assistant Professor in the Department of Population Health Sciences at the University of Utah. He researches comparative health policy within the United States, the politics of health policy, health policies for vulnerable populations, and the politics of infectious diseases and public health disasters. He has published extensively in medical, public health, and health services journals.

Renu Singh, PhD, is a Research Assistant Professor in the Division of Public Policy and a Junior Fellow at the Jockey Club Institute for Advanced Study at the Hong Kong University of Science and Technology. She was formerly a Postdoctoral Fellow at the O'Neill Institute for National and Global Health Law at Georgetown Law. Her research focuses on comparative social policy, global health security, and the political economy of health.

Monika Steffen, PhD, is an Affiliated Researcher at the PACTE Social Science Research Center, Grenoble-Alps University (France) and former CNRS Research Professor. Her work focuses on comparative social and health policies. She has published extensively on AIDS policies and on health governance in Europe. She founded and directed the Health Policy master's program at Sciences-Po Grenoble and held visiting research and professor positions at Japanese universities (Ritsumeikan, Akita International, Keio, and Kyoto).

Mónica Uribe-Gómez, PhD, is Professor at the Political Science Department at the Facultad de Ciencias Humanas y Económicas of the Universidad Nacional de Colombia (Medellín, Colombia). She holds a PhD in Social Science from El Colegio de México (México). She has publications in social policy and political cycles in Latin America and health policy in comparative studies with a focus in Colombia and México.

Durfari Velandia-Naranjo, PhD, MSc, is Assistant Professor of Economics at the Facultad de Ciencias Humanas y Económicas of the Universidad Nacional de Colombia and coordinates the Laboratory of Applied Economics. Dr. Velandia-Naranjo holds degrees in Economics from El Colegio de México (México). She has worked in applied micro-econometric methods on health economics and other topics. In health, she has conducted economic evaluations and researched demand and use of care services, childcare, labor force participation decisions, and health measures.

Rebecca Wai is a PhD student in the Political Science Department and a Lieberthal-Rogel Center for China Studies Doctoral Fellow at the University of

Michigan. Her research focuses on environmental politics, specifically how citizens and bureaucrats solve collective action problems regarding water distribution in South and East Asia.

Gemma A. Williams, MSc, is PhD candidate in the Department of Social Policy, London School of Economics and Political Science. She conducts comparative research on health systems and policies in Europe, with a focus on the health workforce, health financing, health inequalities, digital health, and migration and health.

Charley E. Willison, PhD, MPH, MA, is a National Institutes of Mental Health Postdoctoral Fellow at the Harvard University Department of Health Care Policy and a Visiting Assistant Professor at Cornell University. Dr. Willison studies the effects of urban politics and intergovernmental relations on public health political decision-making and policy outcomes. Substantively, her work focuses on health policies that are designed and/or delivered at the local level. This includes housing, homelessness, behavioral health policies, and disaster responses.

Emma Willoughby, MSc, is a joint PhD student in the Departments of Health Management and Policy, and Political Science at the University of Michigan. She is affiliated with the Center for Southeast Asian Studies at the University of Michigan as a FLAS fellow studying Vietnamese language. Her research interests focus on health and development in the global south, with special interest in the political economy of food in Southeast Asia.

Thespina (Nina) Yamanis, PhD, is Associate Professor in the School of International Service at American University, where she teaches courses on program planning and global health. Her research focuses on social networks and HIV prevention in Tanzania and on immigrant health. A public health scholar, Dr. Yamanis uses mixed methods and community engagement in her research. She has been the principal investigator on grants from the U.S. National Institute of Mental Health and the Robert Wood Johnson Foundation.

Index

Australia, 17, 18, 464, 466
Austria, 14, 19, 22, 241, 244, 270, 280–294, 295–315, 416, 623–624, 630
authoritarian enclaves, 14, 242, 619
authoritarianism, 9–14, 27, 575, 616–621, 625, 634; in China, 38, 67, 79, 95; in Hong Kong, 97; in South Korea, 119; in Vietnam, 134–135, 138; in Singapore, 169–172; Denmark as alternative, 257; in Central and Eastern Europe, 414, 427; in Russia, 445, 448; behavior in the United States, 486; legacies in Colombia, 511, 532; in Tanzania, 575; in Egypt, 605, 609

Belarus, 54, 251, 446
Belgium, 6, 275, 560
blame-avoidance, 22, 368, 371, 503, 516, 625–626
Brazil, 7, 8, 16, 17–21, 23, 486, 494–510, 617, 620–621, 626, 632–633; and WHO, 42, 44
Bulgaria, 413–421, 423, 425–429, 431, 432

Cambodia, 130, 135, 141, 143
Canada, 17–18, 24, 26–27, 459–477, 631, 640
Central Asia, 9, 13, 196–212, 438, 443, 618
Chile, 18, 64, 514, 515, 522–539, 620, 633, 644
China (People's Republic of China), 8, 11–12, 14, 16, 67–85, 112, 619, 623, 633; and WHO, 35, 38–39, 41–44, 46; and Hong Kong, 86, 93, 95–96; and Vietnam, 127–129, 133–136; and Singapore, 163–164
civil society, 15, 30, 41, 57, 60, 62–63; in Hong Kong, 95, 103; in Singapore, 131, 164, 169–171, 173–176; in India, 185; in Denmark, 250; in Italy, 332; in Turkey, 399, 411; in Central and Eastern Europe, 415, 417, 422, 425, 427, 432; in Russia, 441, 444; in Malawi, 542, 552; in Tanzania, 572; in South Africa, 588, 593, 598
clientelism, 414; clientelistic, 19, 619
coercion, 57–58
collectivism, 184–185, 189
Colombia, 18–19, 26, 511–521, 620
consensus democracy, 281–282, 285, 290. *See also* neo-corporatism

contact tracing, 48, 51, 56; in China, 68, 74; in South Korea, 108; in Vietnam, 128, 131, 135; in Japan, 151–152; in Singapore, 165–166, 168; in India, 188; in the United Kingdom, 217–218, 225; in Denmark, 252, 255, 257–258; in France, 269; in Austria, 307; in Italy, 334; in Spain, 345–346, 365, 368; in Portugal, 362, 365; in Turkey, 398, 400; in Bulgaria, 417–418; in Czechia, 417–418; in Hungary, 417–418; in Canada, 460–461; in Chile, 527, 532; in Tanzania, 568, 574; in South Africa, 585–586; in Nigeria, 606. *See also* testing; test-trace-isolate-support (TTIS)
corruption, 14, 137–138, 163, 183, 501, 512–513, 563, 581, 586, 593. *See also* clientelism
credit-claiming, 22, 495, 500, 504, 625–626
Czechia, 14, 26, 421–435, 625, 628

democracy, 9–10, 13–14, 17–18, 20–21, 61, 255–256, 468, 618–620, 634; in South Korea, 119–120; in Japan, 158; in the European Union, 241–242; in Denmark, 249–251; in Austria, 281–282, 285, 290; in Italy, 331; in Central and Eastern Europe, 413–414, 428; in Russia, 448, 621; in Canada, 468; in the United States, 485–486; in South Africa, 608
democratic corporatism. *See* neo-corporatist governance
denial (denialism) of COVID-19, 12, 14, 19, 53, 135, 196, 330, 333, 479, 487, 494–496, 501–502, 622
Denmark, 25, 244, 249–263, 265, 370, 616–617

Egypt, 12, 600–613, 619
elections (during pandemic), 54–55; in Hong Kong, 86; in South Korea, 114–115, 119; in Vietnam, 137; in France, 268, 274; in Spain, 342; in Turkey, 396; in Czechia, 420; in Bulgaria, 423; in Hungary, 424; in Russia, 440; in Chile, 523, 526, 530; in Malawi, 541–542, 544–545, 552–553; in Tanzania, 572

England. *See* United Kingdom
European Union, 9, 23, 134, 203, 235–248, 299, 320, 374, 380, 388, 402, 414, 633
excess mortality, 7, 18, 633; in the United Kingdom, 216; in Sweden, 258; in Germany, 296; in Austria, 297; in Switzerland, 298; in Southern Europe, 364; in Turkey, 397; in Russia, 436; in South Africa, 590

federalism, 19–24, 27, 54; in India, 180, 187–188, 617, 621; and the European Union, 241, 245; in Austria, 281–286, 295–315; in Germany, 295–315; in Switzerland, 295–315; in Italy, 321–322, 333; in Spain, 339, 348–349; in Russia, 437, 439–447, 620; in Canada, 459–469; in the United States, 478–484, 486–487, 617, 621; in Brazil, 495–497, 499, 501–504, 617, 621; in Tanzania, 564, 570, 574–575; in South Africa, 593, 608, 617; in Nigeria, 607–608
France, 17–18, 25, 60, 220, 243–244, 264–279, 501, 620, 623, 628

Germany, 21–24, 26–27, 243–244, 255, 295–319, 370, 379, 416, 615–616
Global Health Security Index, 24, 55, 153, 251, 339–340, 379, 414, 478, 494, 511
Gogol, Nikolai (*Dead Souls*), 7
governance, 44–45; and WHO, 53–55; in South Korea, 106–107, 119–120; in Vietnam, 134–136; in the European Union, 240, 249; in France, 267; in Spain, 339, 363, 365; in Italy, 363, 365; in Portugal, 365; in Greece, 388; in Turkey, 394, 397, 399–400, 405–406; global, 446, 634; in Russia, 446; in Canada, 468; in Brazil, 503; in Tanzania, 561–563; in Egypt, 606, 609, 611; in South Africa, 606, 609, 611; in Nigeria, 609, 611
Greece, 8, 241, 378–392, 403, 617

Hong Kong, 11–12, 14, 16, 86–104, 631
Hungary, 14, 236, 241–242, 413–435, 619

India, 15–21, 23, 178–195, 617–621, 624, 632
individualism, 156
inequalities, 58–59, 60–61, 618, 624–625, 630; in China, 76; in Hong Kong, 93; in Vietnam, 127; in Singapore, 164; in the United Kingdom, 217, 225–229; in the European Union, 239, 241; in Denmark, 249; in France, 271; in Austria, 281, 288–289, 291; in Italy, 330; in Greece, 384, 387; in Turkey, 407; in Canada, 462; in the United States, 478, 485–486; in Brazil, 498; in Colombia, 511–514, 519; in Chile, 523, 531; in South Africa, 581–582
Israel, 54–55, 268

Kazakhstan, 196–212, 446, 628
Kurzarbeit. See short-time work
Kyrgyzstan, 196–212, 438, 628

majoritarianism, 17–19, 27, 257, 259, 486, 620, 621
Malawi, 19, 26, 54, 541–560
migrant laborers. *See* migrants
migrants, 60–61, 630; in Singapore, 12, 17, 163–167, 173–174, 624; in India, 16, 180, 182, 184–186, 189, 617; in China, 68, 71, 75–77, 80, 82; in Vietnam, 136; remittances to Central Asia, 202, 204; in the European Union, 236; in Denmark, 258; in France, 271; scapegoating in Italy, 332, 334; in Spain, 348; in Portugal, 362; in Greece, 384, 389; in Turkey, 402–404; in Czechia, 414; from Bulgaria, 419; in Russia, 438, 442–443; in the United States, 485; from Malawi, 542, 550

neo-corporatist governance, 249, 290
New Zealand, 5, 14, 615, 619
non-pharmaceutical interventions (NPIs), 5, 7–8, 12, 15–17, 23, 25, 51, 59, 615–621, 623, 626–629, 632, 634
Norway, 14, 258, 615

Poe, Edgar Allen (*The Cask of Amontillado*), 15, 616
police, 56–58, 626; in China, 68–69, 80; in Hong Kong, 87, 91–92; in South Korea, 113; in Vietnam, 131; in India, 180, 188; in the United Kingdom, 219; in France, 269; in Central and Eastern Europe, 417; in the United States, 482; in South Africa, 583, 591
police powers (US), 481
populism, 19, 45, 619, 626–627; in South Korea, 106, 115; in Austria, 280; in Italy, 320, 331; in Portugal, 365; Southern

Europe, 370–372; in Central and Eastern Europe, 414–416, 426–428; in Brazil, 501–502; in Colombia, 517; in South Africa, 588
populist radical right (PRR), 18–19, 320, 331–332, 415, 619, 621, 627. *See also* populism
Portugal, 241, 361–377
presidentialism, 17–19, 27, 620–621; in Turkey, 12, 402, 404–405; in France, 266–267; in Russia, 441, 448; in the United States, 486, 497, 499, 501–502; in Colombia, 511, 518; in Chile, 530–531; in Malawi, 541, 552–553
public health capacity, 24–26, 56; in South Korea, 108, 119; in Japan, 155; in Singapore, 168–169; in the United Kingdom, 216–217, 226–228; in Spain, 240; in the European Union, 242; in Denmark, 255; in France, 273–276; in Austria, 283–285; in Italy, 328–330; in the United States, 478–480, 486–487

refugees, 332, 384, 397, 404. *See also* migrants
regimes, 4, 9–21, 27, 618–621, 625, 634
Russia (Russian Federation), 8, 12, 14, 41, 202, 436–455, 486, 619–621, 631–633

Science, 19, 25, 61, 622, 626–628; and WHO, 44–46; in France, 274; in Austria, 312; in Canada, 468–469; in the United States, 488; in Brazil, 496, 501; in South Africa, 581–582, 593
short-time work, 15, 167, 253, 286–289, 304, 313, 422, 483, 616
Singapore, 11–12, 14, 16–17, 163–177, 624
social policy, 27, 58–61; definition, 15; and public health policy, 15–17
South Africa, 15–16, 18, 502, 580–599, 600–614, 617–620
South Korea (Republic of Korea), 14, 26, 54, 105–126, 154, 157, 252, 615
Spain, 18, 22–23, 60, 339–360, 361–377, 617, 620, 628
state capacity, 8, 53–59, 204–206, 426, 609, 617–619, 623–624, 634; in Tanzania, 12, 14, 560–579, 619; in China, 78; in Hong Kong, 115; in Vietnam, 128, 132, 134–136; in Japan, 146–147; in Singapore, 164, 169–171, 173; in India, 187, 189; in Central Asia, 196–197, 204–206; in the United Kingdom, 228; in the European Union, 235, 238, 240–241, 244; in Denmark, 249, 255; in Austria, 285, 291; in Italy, 321, 330; in Southern Europe, 362, 366–367; in Central and Eastern Europe, 426, 428; in Canada, 468
statistics, 6–8, 13; in Turkey, 399, 404–405; in Bulgaria, 414; in Russia, 436–438, 447–448; in South Africa, 593, 601; in Egypt, 601; in Nigeria, 601
Stringency Index (Oxford Blavatnik School), 169–170, 250, 296–298, 460, 503, 560–562
Sturgis (motorcycle rally), 23
surveillance, 55–57, 626–627; in China, 68, 69, 74; in Hong Kong, 89–90; in South Korea, 108–110; in Vietnam, 128, 131, 135–136, 139; in Japan, 151, 153; in Singapore, 166; in India, 179–182; in the European Union, 239; in France, 265, 273–274; in Germany, 309; in Italy, 321, 323; in Greece, 386, 388; in Turkey, 405; in Brazil, 494, 504; in Colombia, 512–514; in Chile, 526; in Tanzania, 560, 567–569, 575; in Nigeria, 606. *See also* testing
Sweden, 18, 26, 60, 243–244, 251, 258–259
Switzerland, 19, 295–319

Taiwan, 14, 38, 42, 154, 615
Tajikistan, 196–197, 438
Tanzania, 12, 14, 560–579, 619
testing, 5, 6, 55–57, 611; in Hong Kong, 92; in South Korea, 106–108, 114; in Vietnam, 131, 133; in Japan, 151; in India, 181; in the United Kingdom, 217–218, 225–226; in Denmark, 252, 255; in France, 269–271; in Austria, 284, 310; in Germany, 300, 309; in Spain, 340, 345–346, 351; in Portugal, 365; in Central Europe, 417–418; in Canada, 461; in the United States, 479–480; in Tanzania, 572; in South Africa, 585–586, 615–616, 623–624
test-trace-isolate-support (TTIS), 5, 11, 107, 615–618, 623–624, 626, 628. *See also* surveillance; testing
Thailand, 55, 130, 156, 632

Tolstoy, Leo (*Anna Karenina*), 615, 628
travel restrictions (international), 5, 39–40, 57; in Hong Kong, 89–90; in Vietnam, 128, 133; in Singapore, 164–165; in India, 180; in Central Asia, 196, 199–200; in the United Kingdom, 221; in the European Union, 238, 242, 245; in Denmark, 250–251; in Germany, 299, 303; in Austria, 301, 303; in Switzerland, 303; in Italy, 326; impact in Southern Europe, 366, 371; in Turkey, 394–396, 404; in Central and Eastern Europe, 416, 420, 421, 425; in Russia, 438, 443, 446; in Canada, 460; in the United States, 479, 481; in Chile, 523–524; in Malawi, 544; in Tanzania, 546, 567; in South Africa, 589, 607; in Nigeria, 606; in Egypt, 607
"Trench's Law," 7
Turkey, 12, 380, 393–412
Turkmenistan, 39, 196–197, 619

United Kingdom, 8, 17–18, 60, 215–234, 243–244, 426, 620, 623, 626, 631–633
United States, 8, 16, 17–19, 21–23, 55, 58, 156, 256, 265, 370, 460, 478–493, 583, 617–626, 631, 632; and WHO, 34, 37, 40–44, 46; and Vietnam, 134, 137; and Japan, 152
Uzbekistan, 196–214, 438, 628

vaccination (administration of vaccines), 25, 131, 179, 592
vaccines, 5, 631–633; and WHO, 41–42, 44–45, 61; in South Korea, 113; in the European Union, 39, 345; in Central and Eastern Europe, 413; in Russia, 437, 441, 446–449; in the United States, 481; in Brazil, 505
Vietnam, 5, 12, 14, 16, 127–145, 428, 615, 619, 623

World Health Organisation (WHO), 34–50, 55

Made in the USA
Middletown, DE
02 August 2021